2-4-03

SCRIBNER LIBRARY OF DAILY LIFE

ENCYCLOPEDIA OF FOOD AND CULTURE

EDITORIAL BOARD

Caribbean Called *The Coastal Dweller,* this nineteenth-century portrait by José Agustin Arrieta depicts a Latin American fruit vendor of African descent. Many blacks from the Caribbean settled along the east coast of Mexico and Central America, where they have left a lasting imprint on the food culture of the region. Private Collection, Mexico. © Archivo Iconografico, S. A./CORBIS.

SCRIBNER LIBRARY OF DAILY LIFE

ENCYCLOPEDIA OF FOOD AND CULTURE

VOLUME 1:
Acceptance to Food Politics

Solomon H. Katz, Editor in Chief

William Woys Weaver, Associate Editor

CHARLES SCRIBNER'S SONS®

New York • Detroit • San Diego • San Francisco • Cleveland • New Haven, Conn. • Waterville, Maine • London • Munich

Encyclopedia of Food and Culture

Solomon H. Katz, Editor in Chief

William Woys Weaver, Associate Editor

For permission to use material from this product, submit your request via Web at http://www.gale-edit.com/permissions, or you may download our Permissions Request form and submit your request by fax or mail to:

Permissions Department
The Gale Group, Inc.
27500 Drake Rd.
Farmington Hills, MI 48331-3535
Permissions Hotline:
248-699-8006 or 800-877-4253, ext. 8006
Fax: 248-699-8074 or 800-762-4058

LIBRARY OF CONGRESS CATALOGING-IN-PUBLICATION DATA

Encyclopedia of food and culture / Solomon H. Katz, editor in chief ; William Woys Weaver, associate editor.
    p. cm.
Includes bibliographical references and index.
    ISBN 0-684-80568-5 (set : alk. paper) — ISBN 0-684-80565-0 (v. 1) — ISBN 0-684-80566-9 (v. 2) — ISBN 0-684-80567-7 (v. 3)
    1. Food habits—Encyclopedias. 2. Food—Encyclopedias. I. Katz, Solomon H., 1939- II. Weaver, William Woys, 1947-   III. Title.
GT2850 .E53 2003
394.1'2'097303—dc21   2002014607

EDITORIAL AND PRODUCTION STAFF

Project Editor
Mark LaFlaur

Art Editor
William Woys Weaver

Production Editor
Georgia S. Maas

Editorial Assistants
Kelly Baiseley   Felix Beltran   Charles Scribner IV

Manuscript Collection and Database Management
Christopher Verdesi

Associate Editors
Anthony Aiello
Sarah Feehan   Amanda Materne

Manuscript Editors
Jonathan G. Aretakis   Carol Braham   Patti Brecht   Paul S. Cohen   Susan Derecskey
Archibald Hobson   Elizabeth J. Jewell   Jean Fortune Kaplan   Irene Cumming Kleeberg
Christine A. Lindberg   Anita Mondello   Katherine M. Moreau   Michael G. Parker   Julia Penelope
Robin L. Perlow   Joseph Pomerance   Neil Romanosky   Martha Schütz

Proofreaders
Dorothy Bauhoff   Donald Homolka

Cartography
XNR Productions
Madison, Wisconsin

Caption Writer
William Woys Weaver

Indexer
Katharyn Dunham, ParaGraphs
Sherri Dietrich

Design
Pamela A. E. Galbreath

Imaging
Barbara J. Yarrow
Dean Dauphinais
Randy Bassett   Leitha Etheridge-Sims   Mary K. Grimes   Lezlie Light   Dan Newell
David G. Oblender   Kelly A. Quin   Robyn Young

(*Staff continued on next page*)

Permissions
Margaret A. Chamberlain

Compositor
GGS Information Services
York, Pennsylvania

Manufacturing
Wendy Blurton

Senior Editor
John Fitzpatrick

Publisher
Frank Menchaca

CONTENTS

LIST OF MAPS

PREFACE

The *Encyclopedia of Food and Culture* is all about food: a single authoritative source about the most essential element of daily life. Here you will find articles by food historians, anthropologists, chefs and bakers, nutritionists and dieticians, farmers, agronomists and horticulturists, food stylists, and specialists in the culinary arts. In developing the *Encyclopedia*, the editors took special care to make the content interesting and the organization useful for those who want to learn about a particular topic, to make the text enjoyable for those who simply want to explore the wide and wonderful world of food, and to provide sufficient authority and depth for researchers. If this *Encyclopedia* does not tell you everything you need to know about food, it will show you where to find it.

The articles are arranged in alphabetical order, but the overall work was conceived thematically to ensure treatment of all essential aspects of food (see the Systematic Outline at the back of Volume 3). For example, the *Encyclopedia* covers staple foods, such as fruit, fish, meat, and vegetables; cooked and processed foods; food production, storage, distribution, preparation, and processing; and nutrition and constituents of food, such as fats, minerals, starch, and sugar. You will also find articles on festivals and feasts and on major countries and regions of the world, on world religions and their food customs, and on people who have been influential in food history. If a topic does not appear in the table of contents, look in the index; there will likely be several mentions of the subject in different articles. In the *Encyclopedia* you will find the topics you would normally expect in a book about food—such as bread and cheese, cooking, and vitamins—but you will also find some surprises, as in the articles on "Cannibalism," "Pet Pigs of New Guinea," "Seabirds and Their Eggs," "Disgust," and "Poisoning," as well as "Spam" and "How to Read an Old (Handwritten) Recipe." The *Encyclopedia* covers human history from Stone Age nutrition to the future of food, and it reaches all around the world—geographically and culturally—from Australian Aborigines and the Inuit peoples to Pacific Ocean societies and the Inca empire; from the Japanese tea ceremony to food as a weapon of war. Each article concludes with a bibliography and cross-references pointing readers to topics of related interest. The articles are generously illustrated with many rarely seen photographs, line drawings, and old advertisements, and are supplemented by maps, tables, and informative sidebars. Each volume contains a beautiful eight-page color insert of images selected by Associate Editor William Woys Weaver.

Entries explore what constitutes food, how it is procured, where it originates, and what is in the foods we eat. You will find detailed accounts of the production of food, including fishing, hunting and gathering, and types of agriculture as they relate to ecological and environmental considerations, and you will be introduced to some of the unusual foods that are consumed around the world. You can also read about what is done to food once it is procured, including preparation and processing, distribution, storage (such as ancient and modern preservatives), food preparatory rituals (religious and secular), and the science and technology underlying food processing (including the chemistry and physics of food preparation and processing).

In a larger context, the *Encyclopedia* enables readers to trace the ways in which food affects our lives both nutritionally and socially, across the boundaries of time and place, throughout many cultures and their traditions. The articles cover the nutrition and biochemistry of food, food science, various conditions and health disorders associated with food, dietetics, constituents of food, the pharmacological effects of foods, and the physiology of eating, digestion, and nutrition.

The editors are aware, however, that people eat food and not nutrition. For most of us, food customs and preferences are influenced by social determinants that are deeply rooted in cultural values and historic traditions. The next time you eat, ask yourself, Why this food and not some other? What does this food reveal about me socially, culturally, and physiologically? Where did its ingredients come from? Why were these ingredients and not others included in the food? Does it contain any additives I should know about? As even a casual reader will note, the food we eat does not begin and end on our plates: how and when we eat, what we eat, and where and with whom we eat—all these choices display a range of behaviors about food that define and symbolize who we are. Hence, the *Encyclopedia* documents the act of eating from the perspectives of cultural history, nutrition, ethnicity, religion, psychology, anthropology, geography, economics, and aesthetics. Further, food-related behaviors are considered for their symbolic and cultural meanings, as in the entries about religion, holidays, table manners, social class, gender, sexuality, taboos, the arts, magic, and mythology.

In order to cover important cultural dimensions of food, the editors looked for experts who could discuss ethnic and national traditions across multiple disciplines and regions of the world and, where possible, provide an integrative approach to the dietary traditions of a people, nation, or region. Entries on countries with great food traditions that have had worldwide influence, such as France, Italy, and China, give attention to the foods and typical diets of the various regions of these countries, both historically and culturally, and consider important social, religious, political, economic, migration, and environmental factors.

The editors sought the contributions of authorities in a variety of fields in order to consider food from many perspectives. For instance, a chef might look at the artful arrangement of food on the plate or how it sears in a hot pan or grill. But a nutritionist is more interested in how the nutrients in a food may be affected by what the chef did to the food during preparation, what kinds of fats were added to the searing pan, or what nutrients may have been lost or altered during cooking. A food scientist may focus on the degree to which the food was safer to eat after it was heated to such a high temperature in the pan.

Authors were urged to try, within the limits of the allotted space, to write as comprehensively about their topic as possible. For example, the entry for chocolate covers the botany, history, and archaeology of cacao (chocolate bean), the principal ingredient of chocolate, and gives detailed consideration to how chocolate is produced and procured, stored, transported, and processed into various forms to be used in foods like candy and confections. The author also covers chocolate's cultural aspects, from its Mayan origin to its diffusion to the royal courts of Europe, and explains the technical discoveries that led to its commercialization and widespread availability.

The contributors give attention to the geographic origins of many foods and include their diffusion around the world and through time. Food history entries span the human evolutionary time scale, through prehistoric, ancient, and more recent periods for well-known societies and civilizations. Contemporary topics include food politics, genetic engineering, water as a resource, food supply and food shortages, advertising and marketing, the restaurant industry (including fast foods), and the commodification of various food traditions.

We believe that the *Encyclopedia* addresses a serious need for an integrated information source that encourages a greater appreciation of food, its history, and its ethnic diversity, while also explaining its nutritional significance. It is by combining a wide range of perspectives—a collaborative effort of hundreds of specialists—that this source can provide answers to many questions about health, food policy, hunger, food studies, and the food industry, while at the same time enhancing appreciation for the wonderful variety and history of the foods we eat.

We hope that by providing an integrative approach to food, nutrition, and culture over time and throughout the many regions of the world, this *Encyclopedia* will stimulate new insights about human evolution, adaptation, and creativity, and a richer appreciation of the many meanings of food and culture in our everyday lives.

*

I want to acknowledge the enormous support and patience of my wife, Pauline, the steadfast help of Jim Coleman, and the great inspiration provided by Jacob, Rachael, Micah, Noah, and Megan. I also want to acknowledge the invaluable assistance of William Woys Weaver and the editorial board; the steady support of Scribner Publisher Frank Menchaca and John Fitzpatrick; and the outstanding efforts of Mark LaFlaur and the Scribner editorial staff, including Kelly Baiseley and Georgia Maas, who got the job done. I am grateful to Stephen Wagley and Karen Day, formerly of Scribners, for their help and advice in initiating the *Encyclopedia*.

Solomon H. Katz
Philadelphia, October 2002

SCRIBNER LIBRARY OF DAILY LIFE

ENCYCLOPEDIA OF
FOOD
AND CULTURE

ACCEPTANCE AND REJECTION.

Foods vary along a hedonic dimension, that is, in their ability to evoke pleasure. A food's hedonic value can differ significantly between individuals and among cultures. In developed countries at least, pleasure is probably the strongest determinant of diet. For most of us, most of the time, a global emotional response to the taste of a food determines whether it is consumed. Underlying this seemingly simple decision is a remarkable range of emotions—from blissful appreciation of haute cuisine to a profound rejection elicited by feelings of disgust. As with many other complex human behaviors, the development of food likes and dislikes reflects the operation of multiple influences—genetic inheritance, maternal diet, child raising practices, learning, cognition, and culture. In fact, the development of food preferences may be an ideal model of the interplay of these influences during our life span.

Foods may be selected or rejected for a variety of reasons, including their anticipated effects on health, their perceived ethical or environmental appropriateness, or practical considerations as price, availability, and convenience. However, it is our responses to the sensory properties of a food—its odor, taste, flavor, and texture—that provide the underlying basis of food acceptance. This article will focus on some of the influences that shape hedonic responses to foods, their flavors, and other sensory qualities.

Tastes

Despite evidence of innate hedonic responses to basic tastes, the vast majority of specific food likes and dislikes are not predetermined—no one is born liking blue cheese, for example. This is not to suggest that basic sensory qualities are unimportant. On the contrary, relatively fixed hedonic responses to sweet, salty, bitter, and umami (glutamate taste) tastes, and almost certainly fat, are present at or shortly after birth, and continue to exert an influence on food preferences. The strong affinity that children show for very sweet foods, and the persistence of the early development of liking for the taste of salt and salty foods throughout life appear to be universal. A majority in many Western societies also choose a diet that is high in fat.

However, innate responses do not account for the broad range of food likes and dislikes that develop beyond infancy. For instance, humans and many other mammals can detect bitterness at low levels and find it unpalatable because it is a potential sign of toxicity. Yet, while coffee and beer are typically rejected on first tasting, they are ultimately the strongest contenders for being the global beverages. The pungency of spicy foods is also initially rejected. Worldwide, though, chili is second only to salt as a food spice. Thus, although innate influences are clearly important in food selection, these are modified by our experience with foods (although both physiological makeup and culture will partly determine the extent to which experience is allowed to operate). What is more important than our innate preferences is the fact that we are predisposed to learn to like (and sometimes, dislike) foods. Some other preferences do appear to be common across cultures whose diets are very different. However, examples such as the widespread liking for vanilla and chocolate flavor are likely to reflect some degree of common experience.

Texture

Texture is a crucial criterion for sensory acceptance and rejection. Certain textures do seem to be universally liked, crispness, for example—perhaps through its association with freshness. Of course, to some extent, we will always prefer textures that are compatible with our dentition, and thus we would not expect infants to like hard foods. Foods that are difficult to manipulate in the mouth—such as soggy foods—are commonly disliked, as are foods that require excessive saliva and effort to swallow, such as dry, tough meat. While food texture is often cited as a reason for rejecting food, for example raw oysters, it is likely that such preferences are also a function of our prior expectations for specific foods.

Color

Food color is also undoubtedly a strong influence on acceptability, but again this is likely to reflect prior expectations. Whether we prefer white (U.S.) or yellow (U.K.) butter depends on what we have eaten in the past. Some colors have been thought to be inappropriate for food. The color blue, for instance, has been suggested as a candidate for a universally inappropriate food color—after all, very few foods are naturally blue. But recent marketing of brightly and "inappropriately" colored foods for children tends to undermine this notion, since the children appear receptive to unusual colors. Removing color from common foods does reliably reduce liking for those foods, perhaps by undermining our ability to identify their flavor, thus making them seem less familiar.

Fear of the New

The fact that humans are omnivores creates a paradox. On the one hand, we have access to a large range of potential nutrients; conversely (in nature at least), we are much more likely to be exposed to toxic substances. In the first two to three years of our lives, we exist in a highly protected environment, first in the context of breast or bottle feeding, and then through parental food selection and supervision. It is therefore adaptive for young infants to accept a wide variety of foods as the risk of exposure to potentially toxic nonfoods is low.

In later infancy, greater independence is typical, both in terms of the wider variety of other people encountered and also of the potential to come into contact with edible substances, which may be unsuitable for health or other reasons, outside direct parental influence. At this point, food neophobia often becomes apparent. Reluctance to consume novel foods at this age is most obviously reflected in statements of "I don't like it" to foods that have never been tried. The rejection of unfamiliar foods can now be seen as adaptive, given the wider risk of ingestion of potentially toxic substances. Food neophobia is found not just in humans, but also in a variety of non-human species, including rats, dogs, birds, and fish. Hence, it may be a universal safeguard against potential toxics.

The trait of food neophobia has been investigated in different age groups, as has the nature of the "fear" and how it can be modified. Even in adults, there often remain strong vestiges of childhood neophobia. While many welcome the chance to sample exotic foods or novel flavors, others remain unable to even consider consumption of foods beyond their usual repertoire.

Such reluctance is especially strong for foods of animal origin (unfamiliar meats, dairy products, or eggs), the same foods that elicit reactions of disgust, also thought to be a protective mechanism. Why this food-related personality trait varies so much among adults is unclear, but it might reflect the breadth of experience with different foods in childhood.

Interestingly, in both children and adults, food neophobia appears to be mediated less by any conscious awareness of the potential for danger, than by the much more immediate fear that foods will taste unpleasant. Consistent with this, willingness to try a novel food can be increased by strategies that reduce this anxiety, including providing information about the food's flavor or indicating that others have enjoyed it since. Highly neophobic individuals are more likely to choose an unfamiliar food after they have seen others select it. Specific nutritional information (such as the fact that a food is low in fat) also encourages selection of novel foods, but only for those for whom nutrition is important. In each case, the net effect is to assure the taster that the food is acceptable in terms of flavor and perhaps safety. Neophobia is a major issue for many parents concerned about the narrow range of foods that their children are willing to consume. A common strategy is to use one food as a reward for eating another food—one that the adult wants the child to eat. Unfortunately, these attempts frequently fail because the relative value of the foods is quite apparent. Rewarding the consumption of spinach by giving ice cream presents a message simple enough for any young child: ice cream is a good food (at least in terms of taste), otherwise why use it as a reward; spinach is bad, else why do I need to be rewarded for eating it? The unfortunate, if predictable, consequences of such strategies are increased liking for the reward and a decrease in liking for the target food.

Learning to Like

What does reduce neophobia and encourage consumption? In both children and adults, repeated exposure has been found to lead to increased acceptability of novel foods, with greater exposure producing greater liking. For example, three- and four-year-old children have been found to accept initially rejected cheese and fruits following ten exposures. It is possible that individuals who receive repeated exposure to a wide variety of foods as infants and children are least likely to be highly neophobic as adults, although this has yet to be established. That is, the more we experience different foods, the more we are willing to experience different foods.

Exposure appears to be the one mechanism that is necessary for liking to increase. With novel foods or flavors, repeated consumption might lead to increased liking via a reduction in neophobia—effectively a relief from the anxiety associated with novelty. It certainly produces an increase in familiarity, an important aspect of children's likes and dislikes, and it has been recognized for some time that sensations of recognition are in themselves positive. However, changes in liking for food ingredients or ingredient levels in already familiar foods strongly suggest that exposure per se produces liking, and that a food or flavor does not need to be completely novel. There are many commonplace examples of this, including the gradual increase in liking that accompanies changing from regular to low-fat milk or low-salt soup, or reducing sugar in tea or coffee.

Although it is a necessary precondition, by itself, exposure is insufficient to explain why we end up liking some foods more than others. There appears to be a variety of other processes that operate during repeated food experiences, producing preferences for the diverse range of food odors and flavors that we encounter. Whether sniffed as aromas, or as characteristic flavor qualities in the mouth, food odors reliably inform us whether we have previously experienced a food. Odors are thus most likely to be the source of neophobic responses. However, there is nothing intrinsic to the odor or flavor of any food that means we will develop a strong like or dislike for it. During our early infancy (up to about three years old), we appear to be neutral to most if not all odors, except for those that also produce nasal irritation, such as ammonia. In contrast to those for tastes, odor preferences are almost certainly all learned, and rely upon our ability to form associations with other liked qualities. Pairing a novel flavor with a sweet taste, for example, reliably increases subsequent liking for that flavor, even when the sweetness is not present. This process, known as classical conditioning or associative learning, was first described scientifically by Ivan Pavlov. He famously demonstrated that the sound of a bell, previously associated with the presentation of food, would elicit gastric secretions in his dogs. While the principles of Pavlovian conditioning were developed using animal (especially rat) models, they appear equally applicable to explaining aspects of human food likes and dislikes.

The universal high palatability of sweetness and fat is a reflection of the ability of substances associated with these qualities to provide energy to the body. Our bodies find the provision of energy inherently rewarding. Consequently, repeatedly pairing flavors with ingested carbohydrates or fats produces increases in liking for associated flavors. Other postingestional consequences have also been described, including enhanced liking for flavors paired with the alerting effects of caffeine—a plausible mechanism, together with the energy provided by the sugar and milk fat sometimes added, for the enormous popularity of coffee.

The effects of conditioning by positive association and the absorption of energy-rich foods are broad enough mechanisms to account for very many food likes. One implication of this process and the body's response to energy is that we end up showing a liking for foods that are high in sugar and fat. Clearly, this has implications for health. We may know that high-fat foods present us with a risk in the long term, but what drives our behavior primarily is the fact that we like the fat—it gives the food a pleasant mouthfeel, it carries flavor well, and its provides the body with energy. The body's response is to promote liking for flavor associated with the fat. Eventually, it is not just the fat or sugar content that we find palatable, but the specific flavor of the food as well.

Food dislikes may also result from Pavlovian conditioning. Associating a characteristic food flavor with nausea, as sometimes occurs with food poisoning or a coincidental illness, will promote a rapid, often irreversible, "taste" aversion that actually seems to make the flavor become unpleasant. The development of aversions can be seen as highly adaptive—it makes sense to avoid foods previously associated with gastric illness. Consequently, the conditioned association tends to be very

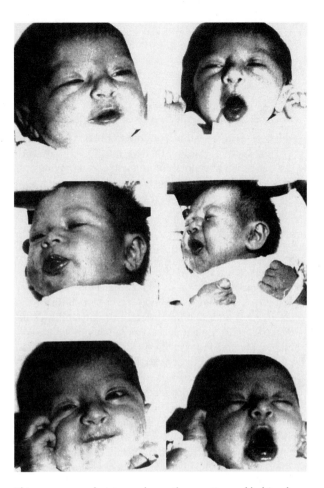

This sequence of pictures shows the reactions of babies from four to ten hours old prior to experiencing food of any sort. The left column shows their natural response to the sweetness of sucrose placed on the tongue, while the right column shows their response to the bitterness of quinine. Their facial expressions resemble those of adults tested for the same responses. PHOTO COURTESY OF DR. JACOB STEINER.

strong. In humans, taste aversions are typically both long lasting and robust enough to persist even if it is known that the food was not the source of the illness. As with neophobic responses, meat seems to be a common target when aversions do occur. An unfortunate consequence of the nausea associated with cancer chemotherapy is the development of taste aversions. Close to three-quarters of children aged two to fifteen years old undergoing treatment are reported to have at least one aversion. Taste aversions are not common enough to account for the majority of our food dislikes, since they appear to occur in only about 30 percent of people. However, they are a powerful indicator of the role that consequences of food ingestion can play in shaping our responses to a food's sensory qualities.

Odors are not the only sensory qualities in foods for which preferences are shaped by learning. Our most primitive sense is the detection of pain—unsurprisingly,

CRAVINGS FOR FOOD

At some time, most of us have experienced a craving for a specific food—something that we must have now, and which we will go out of our way to obtain. It is almost as if the body is insisting that we must have that food. There is much anecdotal information about craving and physiological needs, but less hard evidence for such specific appetites. It is clear that we get hungry and thirsty, but does the body really crave particular nutrients?

The one incontrovertible specific hunger that humans possess is for sodium chloride, common salt. Salt is metabolically essential and most of the time this need is both met and exceeded through diet. Clinical studies have demonstrated that in cases where the body is depleted of salt, humans develop strong appetites for the taste of salt, and its normal degree of palatability is increased. The same is true in experiments in which volunteers are fed low-salt diets—salty foods increase in palatability. Hence, it appears that a change in the hedonic value of the taste of salt is the mediator for increased intake when depleted.

Beyond salt appetite, however, there is little strong evidence that other specific appetites exist. There are reports suggesting an association between pica (the consumption of earth) and mineral (especially iron) deficiency. This practice appears to be most prevalent among pregnant women in poor rural communities. Pregnancy is well known to be associated with craving for foods, but it is not clear whether such "normal" cravings are related to metabolic needs.

The single most commonly craved food in Western societies is chocolate. Although chocolate contains phamacologically active compounds, there is no evidence these compounds are what is craved. Instead, the craving for chocolate is related to craving sweet foods generally and to chocolate's palatability, based on an optimal combination of sugar and fat. Chocolate craving is more common among women, and hormonal influences have been suggested as being important. The craving shows a peak around the time of menstruation and is also more common during pregnancy. While chocolate and sweet food cravings do occur among males, cravings for savory foods are more common.

A less extreme version of craving is the phenomenon of "moreishness." Again, wanting "just one more bite" appears to reflect the high palatability of certain foods, rather than a desire for any specific nutrient. Foods described as moreish also tend to be consumed in small amounts. Often their consumption is subject to a voluntary restraint determined by social mores; you may want another slice of cake, another piece of chocolate, or another potato chip, but will often hold back to avoid seem-ing intemperate. Because of the typically small portion sizes associated with moreish food, this may be an example of the appetizer effect, which occurs when the initial consumption of palatable foods increases appetite for further eating.

Explanations for craving, moreishness, and appetizer effects have recently focused on the brain's biochemistry, in particular those functions mediated by opioid (morphinelike) peptides. Interfering with the functioning of this biochemical system using opioid blocking drugs leads to reduced food consumption overall and also to attenuation of appetizer effects, apparently because the foods become less palatable. Conversely, it is possible that increased opioid levels may induce cravings by making foods more palatable. Such changes may occur in a variety of circumstances—dieting, stress, exercise, alcohol consumption—all of which are known to influence the brain's opioid systems.

Cravings thus tell us little about the body's nutritional needs, beyond the fact that highly palatable foods tend to be high in energy. Other evidence also points to strategies to maximize energy intake. At least in Western countries, given ample availability, we tend to consume a diet that contains 35 to 40 percent fat, well in excess of what we need to survive. Moreover, from early infancy onwards, we will attempt to compensate for reductions in calories at one meal with an increase at the next.

In addition to energy intake, we seem predisposed, as omnivores, to seek variety in our diet. As noted in the section on sensory-specific satiety, this may be one way of optimizing survival through ensuring adequate nutrient intake. Classic studies on dietary self-selection were carried out by Clara Davis in the 1920s and 1930s. She allowed recently weaned infants access to a varied selection of foods and found that they first tasted widely and then developed preferences for a selection of these foods. This research has been often misinterpreted to suggest that the body has an innate wisdom, in that the foods the infants selected represented a balanced nutrient intake. This was inevitable, however, given the range of foods available.

This is not to say that mechanisms responsive to our needs are not in operation. On the contrary, the palatability of energy and sodium sources, the avoidance of toxins through dislike of bitterness, the rapid formation of aversions to foods associated with gastric illness, and the maintenance of nutrient variety via sensory-specific satiety, are all innate predispositions that modulate the hedonic value of sensory properties of foods to help ensure survival.

since pain avoidance is the simplest key to survival. How then to explain the fact that at least a quarter of the world's population each day consume (and presumably enjoy) a meal containing an extremely potent irritant, capsaicin, which is present in chilies? Whatever the source of our increasing preference for pungency in foods, it must be a potent mechanism. Apart from the warning signals for pain, our bodies possess a built-in response to high levels of irritation. This defensive reflex, as it is known, consists of increased blood flow to the head, profuse sweating, tearing, and nasal discharge—physiological changes that are thought to have evolved as a means of rapidly eliminating toxins. Although frequent consumers of spicy foods experience somewhat less intense physiological responses and burn than infrequent users, there is no doubt that the burning sensations are actually part of the reason these foods are consumed, not something to be tolerated for other reasons.

Both regular exposure, commencing during breast-feeding, and postingestional energy conditioning are likely to play a part in the development of liking for hot foods, particularly in countries whose staple diet includes high levels of spiciness. To explain the recent increase in liking for hot foods in Western countries, though, a number of other interesting mechanisms have also been proposed. These include the hypothesis that the painful experience may activate the brain's natural opioid (morphinelike) biochemical systems, dampening pain and producing a chili eater's "high." Alternatively, it has been suggested that we derive pleasure from the "thrill" of the benign but highly stimulating experience of consuming hot foods.

Where Do Differences in Food Likes Come From?

If exposure, together with resultant learning processes, can substantially explain food preference development, what accounts for the differences in which foods we come to like? Exposure to flavors is now known to begin even prior to birth. Amniotic fluid, which comes into contact with the taste and odor receptors in the mouth and nose of the fetus, carries both taste and odor qualities. There is good evidence that the maternal diet during pregnancy can influence food preferences of the child following birth. Thus, it has been shown that infants whose mothers consumed carrot juice during pregnancy showed a greater liking for carrot-flavored cereal at six months of age than did a control group of children whose mothers consumed only water. Following birth, a wide range of flavors derived from the maternal diet is carried in breast milk, and this also influences an infant's later food preferences, including greater acceptance of novel flavors. In other words, the variety of a mother's diet can promote a varied set of food preferences in the infant. As a result, breast-fed babies are more likely to develop preferences following exposure to novel foods as infants. Whether this reflects early exposure to particular flavors, or a general effect of previous maternal dietary variety, is uncertain.

Social Influences

From childhood on, social interactions, whether within the family or with other groups, provide the context within which the majority of food experiences occur, and hence by which learning of food likes is facilitated. The pleasure associated with such interactions—the conviviality of a meal shared with friends, for example—may represent just as positive a conditioning stimulus for a new food flavor as sweetness. Thus, it may be that our estimation of the food at a restaurant has as much to do with the social environment as it does with the chef's skills. In children, pairing foods with the presence of friends, a liked celebrity, or attention by adults all increase liking for those foods, no doubt reflecting the positive hedonic value of each of these groups to the child.

This process is strongly evident in the relative impact of different social interactions on the food preferences of children. Surprisingly, despite the enormous opportunities in a family for exposing children to the foods eaten by the parents, parental preferences are poor predictors of child food preferences; in fact, they are no better predictors than the preferences of other adults. This suggests that the extent to which these sets of preferences are related has more to do with the wider culture than with any specific food habits within the family. A child's food likes and dislikes are much more likely to be associated with those of peers, especially specific friends, than those of its parents. Peers may also be as effective as families at helping to overcome neophobia, since the food choices of both friends or well-known adults strongly influence a child's food choices. The ultimate impact of social facilitation of food choice is that the liking eventually becomes internalized. That is, foods chosen because others do so become liked for their own sensory properties.

The Cultural Context

Dietary differences between cultures are almost always more pronounced than individual differences within a culture. The relatively limited amount of research that has been conducted on cross-cultural perceptions of sensory qualities finds fewer differences than are needed to explain the often markedly different preferences for foods. More plausibly, it is likely that differences in preferences reflect experiences with different foods. In addition to facilitating liking through exposure and the action of social influences, cultures act to define what substances are considered foods.

Foods that are unfamiliar to a culture may initially be seen as entirely unsuitable for consumption, while certain flavors may be regarded as inappropriate for specific foods. For example, bean paste is often used as a sweet filling in Japanese cakes, whereas in many Western countries, beans are expected to inhabit savory, not sweet, products. Again, porridge is either sweet or savory, depending on your heritage. In other cases, because of different histories of exposure, a preferred flavor in one culture may be perceived as unpleasant in another. The odor and flavor of lamb and mutton are highly liked in the West but rejected in the many parts of Asia that do not have the history of consuming sheep meat. Foods may of course be the subject of religious or cultural taboos, or even not be defined as food at all. In Western countries, we are unlikely to ever develop a taste for dog meat or snake blood.

The notion of culturally specific flavor principles has been proposed as a way of categorizing cultural differences in cuisines. Flavor principles are unique combinations of specific ingredients used in a variety of foods within a culture. This combination provides a characteristic flavor that foods within the culture share, and identifies them as originating from that culture. For example, a characteristic combination of ingredients in Japanese cooking is soy sauce, mirin (sweet rice wine) and dashi (a stock made from flakes of the bonito fish, which is high in umami taste). While Korea is geographically close to Japan, its flavor principle could not be less similar, with the intense flavors of garlic, chili, sesame, and soy dominating many dishes. Flavor principles not only define the national cuisine, they also perform a social role by acting as an expression of the individuality of the culture.

Flavor principles may help to provide a solution to the "omnivore's paradox" and the consequent neophobic response that novelty can elicit, thus limiting the foods available for consumption within a culture. A familiar flavor can provide a safe context for new foods, thus maximizing the breadth of the diet. On the individual level, recent findings suggest that a familiar sauce could increase the willingness of children to consume a novel food. A characteristic combination of flavorings may also provide variety and interest in diets dominated by bland staples such as corn or rice. Although a flavor principle might contain only a small set of characteristic seasonings, these can be combined in different ways. Moreover, what may appear to be a single ingredient or spice to an outsider may in fact have many subtle variations. Different chili varieties, for instance, vary considerably in the flavor and degree of heat that they impart to foods.

Increasingly, the food industry operates in a global setting. This is likely to mean that those foods that are purchased in your local supermarket are, or soon will be, also available on the other side of the world, perhaps within a culture whose cuisine is vastly different from your own. Whether this means that national flavor principles will ultimately be diluted or replaced is uncertain. Some evidence suggests they will not. Japanese urban populations have, for many years, enjoyed wide access to foods from other parts of the world, particularly Europe and the United States. Yet, while rice consumption has fallen and red meat and dairy food consumption has increased in recent years, there is little evidence that more traditional foods are disappearing. Moreover, Western food companies wishing to export to those cultures whose cuisines are substantially different are learning that in-

corporating aspects of the flavor principles of those cultures is essential for producing acceptable foods.

Food Choice: The Broader Context

Although a food's sensory properties may substantially determine what we like, they are only part of why we choose a particular food on a particular occasion. The determinants of our diet include factors that are both internal and external to the individual. Food choices are influenced by appetite, which in turn reflects when and what we last ate, and our overall state of physical and psychological health. In some extreme cases, these internal influences can render eating itself a pathological process, as in disorders such as anorexia and bulimia nervosa. Even in nonpathological circumstances, though, choosing a high-fat or -carbohydrate food may have more to do with our mood than anything else.

Liking is also heavily dependent on context. At its simplest level, cultural practices will determine whether or not we eat cooked meat or toast for breakfast. The extent to which either of these foods is acceptable will depend considerably on time of day. The same food can also vary in acceptability depending on where we experience it. Due to the influence of prior expectations, the same meal served in a restaurant is likely to be judged as more acceptable than if it is served in a student cafeteria.

Clearly, also, the reason why we first choose a food must be based on factors other than direct experience of, and therefore liking for, the sensory properties of the food. Food manufacturers and marketers rely on advertising and labeling to create a positive image for products, and attempt to create high (but not unrealistic) expectations for the product's sensory properties. If the food meets those expectations following purchase, then the consumer is likely to try the product again. Repeat consumption and the consequent associative and postingestive processes will then act to promote increased liking for the product.

See also **Anorexia, Bulimia; Appetite; Aversion to Food; Disgust; Sensation and the Senses; Taboos.**

BIBLIOGRAPHY

Bernstein, Ilene L. "Development of Taste Preferences." In *The Hedonics of Taste*, edited by Robert C. Bolles, pp. 143–157. Hillsdale, N.J.: Erlbaum, 1991.

Birch, Leann L., and D. W. Marlin. "I Don't Like It; I Never Tried It: Effects of Exposure on Two-Year-Old Children's Food Preferences." *Appetite* 3 (1982): 353–360.

Birch, Leann L., Jennifer O. Fisher, and Karen Grimm-Thomas. "The Development of Children's Eating Habits." In *Food Choice, Acceptance and Consumption*, edited by Herbert L. Meiselman and Hal J. H. MacFie, pp. 161–206. London: Blackie, 1996.

Cabanac, Michel. "Physiological Role of Pleasure." *Science* 173 (1971): 1103–1107.

Cardello, Armand V. "The Role of the Human Senses in Food Acceptance." In *Food Choice, Acceptance and Consumption*, edited by Herbert L. Meiselman and Hal J. H. MacFie, pp. 1–82. London: Blackie, 1996.

Davis, Clara M. "Self-Selection of Diet by Newly Weaned Infants." *American Journal of Diseases of Children* 36 (1928): 651–679.

Meiselman, Herbert L. "The Contextual Basis for Food Acceptance, Food Choice and Food Intake: The Food, The Situation and The Individual." In *Food Choice, Acceptance and Consumption*, edited by Herbert L. Meiselman and Hal J. H. MacFie, pp. 239–263. London: Blackie, 1996.

Mennella, Julie A., and Gary K. Beauchamp "The Ontogeny of Human Flavor Perception." In *Handbook of Perception and Cognition: Tasting and Smelling*, edited by Gary K. Beauchamp and Linda M. Bartoshuk. San Diego, Calif.: Academic Press, 1997.

Pliner, Patricia. "The Effects of Mere Exposure on Liking for Edible Substances." *Appetite* 3 (1982): 283–290.

Pliner, Patricia, Marcie Pelchat, and M. Grabski "Reduction of Neophobia in Humans by Exposure to Novel Foods." *Appetite* 20 (1993): 111–123.

Pliner, Patricia, and Marcia L. Pelchat. "Neophobia in Humans and The Special Status of Foods of Animal Origin." *Appetite* 16 (1991): 205–218.

Pliner, Patricia and Catherine Stallberg-White "'Pass the ketchup, please': Familiar Flavors Increase Children's Willingness to Taste Novel Foods." *Appetite* 34 (2000): 95–103.

Pliner, Patricia, Paul Rozin, Myra Cooper, and George Woody. "Role of Specific Postingestional Effects and Medicinal Context in the Acquisition of Liking for Tastes." *Appetite* 6 (1985): 243–252.

Prescott, John, and Graham A. Bell. "Cross-Cultural Determinants of Food Acceptability: Recent Research on Sensory Perceptions and Preferences." *Trends in Food Science and Technology* 6 (1995): 201–205.

Rolls, Barbara J. "Sensory-Specific Satiety." *Nutrition Reviews* 44 (1986): 93–101.

Rozin, Elisabeth. *Ethnic Cuisine: The Flavor-Principle Cookbook.* Brattleboro, Vt.: The Stephen Greene Press, 1983.

Rozin, Elisabeth, and Paul Rozin. "Culinary Themes and Variations." *Natural History* 90 (1981): 6–14.

Rozin, Paul, and April E. Fallon. "A Perspective on Disgust." *Psychological Review* 94 (1987): 23–41.

Rozin, Paul. "Human Food Selection: The Interaction of Biology, Culture and Individual Experience." In *The Psychobiology of Human Food Selection*, edited by L. M. Barker, pp. 225–254. Westport, Conn.: AVI Publishing, 1982.

Rozin, Paul, and Theresa A. Vollmecke. "Food Likes and Dislikes." *Annual Review of Nutrition* 6 (1986): 433–456.

Rozin, Paul, and Debra Zellner. "The Role of Pavlovian Conditioning in the Acquisition of Food Likes and Dislikes." *Annals of the New York Academy of Sciences* 443 (1985): 189–202.

Sullivan, Susan A., and Leanne L. Birch. "Pass the sugar, pass the salt: Experience Dictates Preference." *Developmental Psychology* 26 (1990): 546–551.

John Prescott

ADDITIVES. Food additives are regulated substances and therefore defined in law. Unfortunately, definitions vary among jurisdictions. A typical definition of a food additive may be: a substance the use of which in a food causes it to become a part of that food or to alter the characteristics of that food. A list of exceptions (Table 1) often follows because such a definition is vague and can include many substances not normally regarded as additives. Regulations are then required that control which additives can be added to which foods, and at what levels they can be added to those foods in which they are permitted.

In the U.S. Code of Federal Regulations, Title 21—Food and Drugs (21CFR170.3), the following definition appears: "Food additives includes all substances not exempted by section 201(s) of the act, the intended use of which results or may reasonably be expected to result, directly or indirectly, either in their becoming a component of food or otherwise affecting the characteristics of food."

The European Union (1994) defined a food additive as "any substance not normally consumed as a food in itself and not normally used as a characteristic ingredient of food whether or not it has nutritive value, the intentional addition of which to food for a technological purpose in the manufacture, processing, preparation, treatment, packaging, transport or storage of such food results, or may be reasonably expected to result, in it or its by-products becoming directly or indirectly a component of such foods."

The Codex Alimentarius Commission (a joint Food and Agriculture Organization of the United Nations [FAO] and World Health Organization [WHO] organization established to develop uniformity of food standards for international trade) has defined a food additive as "any substance not normally consumed as a food by itself and not normally used as a typical ingredient of the food, whether or not it has nutritive value, the intentional addition of which to food for a technological (including organoleptic) purpose in the manufacture, processing, preparation, treatment, packing, packaging, transport or holding of such food results, or may be reasonably expected to result, (directly or indirectly) in it or its by-products becoming a component of or otherwise affecting the characteristics of such foods. The term does not include contaminants or substances added to food for maintaining or improving nutritional qualities" (Codex Alimentarius Commission, 1999).

In the Canadian Regulations, Part B, Food, Division 1, General, B.01.001, p. 16, of the Canadian Food and Drugs Act (Amendments 1999), "food additive" is defined as "any substance the use of which results, or may reasonably be expected to result, in it or its by-products becoming a part of or affecting the characteristics of a food, but does not include (a) any nutritive material that is used, recognized, or commonly sold as an article or ingredient of food, (b) vitamins, mineral nutrients and amino acids,

EXCEPTIONS OFTEN DECLARED BY GOVERNMENTS TO THE DEFINITION OF A "FOOD ADDITIVE"

Exceptions to Definition of Food Additive

- Flavoring preparations such as spices, natural extractives, oleoresins, essential oils, and seasonings
- Nutrients such as amino acids, vitamins, and mineral supplements, some of which may be regulated as to levels permitted in foods
- Any nutritive substance (that is, food ingredient) sold as an article of food or as an ingredient
- Certain permitted agricultural chemicals (used in growing plants) and drugs (administered to animals)
- Packaging materials and their components

other than thosse listed in the tables to Division 16, (c) spices, seasonings, flavouring preparations, essential oils, oleoresins and natural extractives, (d) agricultural chemicals, other than those listed in the tables to Division 16, (e) food packaging materials and components thereof, and (f) drugs recommended for administration to animals that may be consumed as food."

These definitions differ in their specificity, and exceptions to the definitions vary from country to country and trading bloc to trading bloc. These differences can be a source of confusion in the mind of the public regarding what food additives are, as well as a source of nontariff trade barriers between countries.

In the United States, there are two categories of exemptions to the definition (Food Additives Amendment 1958): prior-sanctioned items and GRAS (generally recognized as safe) items [21CFR170.3 (k, l, n, and o)]. The former category was sanctioned by existing legislation (prior to September 6, 1958) as outlined in the Federal Food, Drug, and Cosmetic Act, the Poultry Products Inspection Act, and the Meat Inspection Act. GRAS substances, so declared based on opinions of experts and an extensive history of use, are listed in forty-two categories and include salt, alcoholic beverages, cheeses, baked goods (mixes, flours, ready-to-bake products), condiments, fats and oils, and so forth. They can very loosely be described as the "ingredients" usually found in recipes. Also exempted are thirty-two categories of GRAS food chemicals, which can broadly be classed as processing aids.

In the Directive of the European Communities the exceptions to the definition are: processing aids (which are further defined); agricultural chemicals used in conformity to European Community rules; flavorings as defined by Council Directive; and substances added to foods as nutrients.

Indirect (Unintentional) and Direct Additives and "Carry-Over"

In addition to the definition of "additive" itself, there are also definitions of direct and indirect (unintentional) additives, and the principle of carry-over. Direct additives are added directly to foods for a specific aesthetic or technological purpose. They are usually declared on labels. Indirect additives become part of the food usually in trace amounts that are harmless to consumers and are present because of packaging, storage, processing, or handling. These are also referred to as unintentional additives. Their presence in foods results from the principle of "carry-over," that is, they are permitted agricultural chemicals used on farm products or accepted drugs and nutrients fed to animals. Such agricultural chemicals, even when used according to good husbandry practices, may end up in the food supply, or additives used as a component in ingredients may turn up in trace amounts in finished food products. Such substances are permitted only if the substance was permitted in the raw material or ingredient initially; the amount in the raw material does not exceed the maximum amount so permitted in the raw material or ingredient; and the amount carried over into the food does not exceed that expected by good manufacturing practice [see, for example, Codex Stan 192-1995 (Rev.2-1999) p. 3, Section 4].

History of Food Additives

Substances have been added to foods to achieve some desirable characteristic in a finished food product for many hundreds, if not thousands, of years. For example, salt has been used to preserve hams as well as some hard sausages and salted cod; to flavor foods; and to control the fermentation of a variety of vegetables such as sauerkraut and *sauerrüben* (fermented rutabagas), and fish products (for example, *rollmops*, Bismarck herring, fish sauce, Malaysian *nuoc-mam*, shrimp paste, *belacan*, and anchovies). Historically bakers used fats to "shorten," that is, lubricate, dough for certain baking products. In these two examples, salt and certain fats have been used as processing aids.

Spices, herbs, and some vegetables were added to foods to develop unique and pleasing flavors, and in some cases to enhance or preserve foods. For example, Hartley, in *Food in England* (1985, p. 563), describes claims made by cider processors that straw mats (processing aids) used to separate layers of apples in presses for cider making produced the best cider because of the minerals drawn up by the straw from the soil. There are many kinds of leavening agents used in baking: yeast, sourdough starter cultures, baking soda and an acid (for example, soured milk) for soda breads, or commercially prepared baking powder which contains the previous two agents (plus others) together in one mix. Salts of sulfurous acid (sulfites) are used to control the fermentation of grape musts and were also used by fraudulent butchers to give a fresher, brighter appearance to ground meats.

Prior to the development of food science and before the establishment of a rigorous system of food inspections, food manufacturers and food retailers often took advantage of this lack of good analytical methods for food products by mixing adulterants into foods to deceive the consumers. Elisa Maria Rundell in her book, *A New System of Domestic Cookery*, describes a procedure (1828, p. 336) to determine whether bread has been adulterated with whiting or chalk, commenting that this type of adulteration was common practice.

A. H. Hassall (1817–1894), an early food analyst, determined (ca.1850) that much of the coffee sold in England had, as "additives," chicory, roasted wheat, burnt sugar for coloring matter, beans, and potato flour. An earlier chemist, Fredrick Accum (1769–1838), started one of the first training centers in practical (analytical) chemistry in England and reported such fraudulent practices as mustard adulterated with radish seed; vinegar sophisticated with sulfuric acid; cream enhanced with rice powder and arrowroot; cayenne pepper adulterated with red lead; and confectionery colored with vermilion (mercuric sulfide) (see also Skuse, c. 1900). The work of Accum, but primarily that of Hassall, led directly to the passing of food legislation preventing the adulteration of foods and drink in the U.K. (Farrer, 1996, 1997).

Traditionally, innocent additives have been added to foods. Cooking skills passed on from mothers to daughters and often to be found in some of today's older cookbooks taught the use of unripe apples (or apple skins) to assist the gelling of fruit jams; lemon juice added for acidification of foods; and Hart's horn (deer antler) shavings used for gelation. Today, the active components of these natural ingredients, pectin in the apples, citric acid in the lemons, and gelatin in the antlers are well-recognized food additives.

In many people's minds, however, food additives are considered to be a suspicious, comparatively modern invention created in large part by food manufacturers to cheapen products and hoodwink the public.

In earlier times, there was some truth to this suspicion. Today, this is far from the truth. There was, and is, an absolute need for improved processing aids to satisfy the demands by consumers for attractive, tasty, safe food products of uniformly high quality as well as for new products.

In the United States, individual states were the first to develop food legislation and a system of food inspection. In terms of federal legislation, the Federal Food and Drugs Act of 1906, popularly known as the Pure Food Law, for prevention of adulteration of foodstuffs, was

In Skuse's *Complete Confectioner* (10th ed.), published ca. 1900, the author found it necessary to list poisonous colors that confectioners should avoid. Among those he listed are chrome yellow (lead chromate), sulfate of arsenic, red lead, and copper sulfate. Skuse noted that he "knows sugar boilers who are very partial to use a little chrome yellow for stripes."

* * *

Marketing people and retailers often defend adding color and flavor to processed foods. Only safe, attractive, nutritious, and flavorful food can be marketed successfully and therefore only such foods will be purchased by consumers. It is only these foods that are ultimately consumed. Good nutrition can be maintained within the population only if attractive, wholesome foods are presented.

* * *

Chicory, considered an adulterant in ground coffee, is also used as a coffee-substitute beverage in its own right and is often added to some coffees to give a richer, stronger, roasted flavor to the final beverage.

passed, and came into force on January 1, 1907. It dealt largely with adulteration and misbranding of foods.

The Need for Additives

Using such natural products as apple skins or lemon juice as food processing aids causes problems in large-scale manufacturing situations. First, the desired active ingredients in natural products are not consistent in quality, properties, versatility, or concentration in their natural state. Furthermore, they may bring both undesirable flavor attributes, associated with their source, to the finished product, as well as microbiological contamination. For example, using orange or lemon juice to acidify a food inevitably brings the flavor of oranges or lemons, which may not be desired in the finished product. It would be the rare householder who would want to make her own red color by crushing the dried insect used to make an extract of cochineal for baking or candy making.

Consumers who shop for groceries only once a week or even only once every two weeks still want their food purchases to remain as fresh, wholesome, and safe as the day they were purchased. The consumer's demand for manufactured, prepared foods that have a high uniform quality with good shelf life characteristics and are as close to the natural state as possible has been the major determinant for an increase in the use of additives. Additives preserve color and flavor as well as maintaining safety and nutritive value throughout both processing and the product's shelf life.

NEED FOR FOOD ADDITIVES IN MANUFACTURING

Quality Characteristics in Processed Foods Demanded by Consumers that Require Use of Additives in Manufacturing

- Uniformity of products sold by count, size, shape, volume, or weight
- Desire for fresh, semiprepared foods "as fresh and natural appearing as possible" with a safe, long shelf life
- Replacement of nutrients lost or reduced in processing as well as the addition of other health-giving properties equivalent to the unprocessed product
- Additions of special nutrients or other substances for foods for consumers with special nutritional needs
- Dietetic foods with same eating characteristics (flavor, taste, color, texture, and mouth feel) as the regular product
- Flavor, color, and texture (crispness, eye appeal, or moistness) of unprocessed, natural product
- Unique characteristics such a spreadability at room temperature, adherence, flow properties
- Enhancement of keeping qualities and organoleptic characteristics of processed foods for eating enjoyment

The box above lists some quality characteristics consumers prefer that require food additives to be added to foods. For example, in dietetic foods (low-salt, low-fat, low-sugar, or lactose-free foods), there must be some alternative substance (an additive) to replace the taste impact that salt provides, or to provide the mouth feel found in full-fat foods, to replace the sweetness provided by sugar, or to remove (along with the enzyme lactase) the lactose inherent in milk products. Hence there was a need for new additives that were either synthesized de novo, extracted and purified from natural sources (these additives are termed "nature identical"), or modified chemically to provide unique properties not found with nature-identical substances, for example, modified starches. Some of these properties are resistance to heat and acetic acid, constant viscosity in sauces during prolonged heating or without prolonged storage, special textures such as creaminess or pulpy granularity, or pregelatinization for "instant" rices. Thus, along with consumers' desire for a decreased use of additives there is also a need for newer and more effective additives (Smith, 1993).

Classification and Functions of Additives

Additives perform a specific and necessary aesthetic or functional role in foods. If they did not have a purpose, no government would have considered allowing them. Many additives have several different functions depending on the foods they are added to. In addition to their flavoring and nutritive properties, some herbs, spices, vegetables, and vitamins added to foods have other functional properties as processing aids. For example, vitamin C (ascorbic acid) and vitamin E (tocopherols) are both excellent antioxidants and are used to remove oxygen and prevent oxidation, thus extending the shelf life of many food products. Garlic has long been used for its antimicrobial properties. Thyme and oregano contain thymol, which has a wide spectrum of antimicrobial effectiveness (Beuchat and Golden, 1989).

The only practical way to classify additives is by the purpose for which they are added to foods. The table presents one classification of additives with some typical examples within each classification and examples of foods in which they may be found.

Colors. Colors are either water soluble or oil soluble (see Carriers, extractants, and solvents) and are designed for specific application in aqueous or oily foods. There are three categories of colors: natural or nature-identical, synthetic, and inorganic. Natural or nature-identical colors (colors extracted from natural products or synthesized to resemble their natural counterpart) have two disadvantages. They are frequently mixtures and are, in general, not as stable in foods as are the synthetic colorants. Many change color with the acidity or alkalinity of the food they are added to; many are susceptible to breakdown by oxidation and heat. Synthetic colors are preferred colorants in foods, but questions of their safety have arisen in the past and hence there is widely differing acceptance of their use in many foods by different countries. Inorganic colorants are very stable but have a limited use in foods such as sugars, jams, and confectionery.

In most instances, colorants are permitted according to "good manufacturing practices," that is, governments, working closely with food manufacturers and with the advice of experts, have established minimal, acceptable levels of usage in practice.

Enzymes. Enzymes are biological catalysts that can break down specific materials (substrates) into simpler components or cause changes in the substrate's structure. Carbohydrases break down complex sugars (for example, starches, cellulose, lactose, maltose, and so on) into simpler sugars (saccharification). Lipases break down fats into glycerol and fatty acids. Proteases break down proteins into their constituent amino acids. Other enzymes act as preservatives and scavenge oxygen that may be dissolved in plant tissues or in headspaces in packages and remove it.

TABLE 1

Classification of additives according to functions with examples and products they might be used in[a]

Function or category of additive	Typical examples of additive[b]	Products benefited by addition[c]
Coloring agents		
Natural or nature-identical	Annatto, carotenes, chlorophyll, cochineal, paprika, turmeric, anthocyanins	Fruit jams, jellies, and marmalades; ice cream and ice cream mixes, cheeses; pickles and relishes; butter; liqueurs and cordials
Synthetic	Tartrazine, amaranth, allura red, sunset yellow	Similar to above
Inorganic	Titanium dioxide, iron oxide, silver metal, aluminum metal	Certain sugar products, jams; surface colorants of confectionery products
Enzymes		
Carbohydrases	Amylase, cellulase, invertase, lactase, pullulanase, pentosanase, glucose isomerase	Ale, beer, malt liquor, cider wine, bread, flour; mash, coffee and tea extracts, fruit juice; liquid and soft-centered confectionery; reduced-lactose products; bread, flour, production of dextrins, maltose; ale, beer, bread, fructose syrups
Lipases	Lipase	Dairy-based flavorings, cheeses, modified fats for dietetic foods, bread, flour
Proteinase	Bromelain, ficin, papain, pancreatin, pepsin, protease, rennin	Beer, malt liquor, bread, flour, cheeses, meat-tenderizing preparations, precooked cereals, milk, animal and vegetable hydrolysates, meat pickles
Preservation	Catalase, glucose oxidase	Oxygen scavengers used in egg products and dairy products
Carriers or extractants	Acetone, benzyl alcohol, carbon dioxide, ethyl acetate, tributryrin, mono- and diglycerides, hexane	Spice extracts; flavoring preparations; added to coffee and tea for decaffeination; hops extraction, fats and oils seed meals
Sweeteners	Aspartame, mannitol, sorbitol, xylitol, isomalt, sucralose, thaumatin	Dietetic foods (low calorie), soft drinks, bakery products, confectionery
Preservatives	Acetic acid, ascorbic acid and salts, sodium and potassium nitrates, sodium and potassium nitrites, wood smoke, benzoic acid and salts, sulfurous acid and salts, propionic acid and salts, sorbic acid and salts, ascorbyl palmitate and stearate, BHA, BHT, citric acid and salts, propyl gallate, tartaric acid	Meat and meat products, cured meat and fish products, fish and fish products, ale, beer, cider, malt liquor, cheeses and cheese spreads, canned or frozen fruit and vegetable products, fruit beverages, seafood products, bread and baked goods, fats, oils, and so forth
Bleaching, maturing, and dough conditioning agents	Ammonium persulfate, ascorbic acid, benzoyl peroxide, chlorine and chlorine dioxide, sodium sulfite, potassium iodate	Flour, whole wheat flour, bread, cake mixes, some dough mixes
Anticaking agents	Silicon dioxide, magnesium stearate, cellulose, various calcium salts	Salt, baking powder, and other dry mixes and powders
Emulsifying, gelling, stabilizing, and thickening agents	Various plant and microbial gums and polysaccharides and salts thereof, gelatin, pectin, acetylated monoglycerides, lecithin, methyl cellulose, various calcium and magnesium salts	Used in a wide range of food products from alcoholic beverages to milk and dairy products, fruit and vegetable products, to meat and meat products and oils and margarines
Firming agents	Aluminum, calcium, and sodium salts of various acids, for example, aluminum sulfate of calcium lactate	Canned fish and fish products, canned fruit and vegetable products, pickles and relishes
Glazing and polishing agents	Various gums and waxes, for example, beeswax, gum arabic, mineral oil, acetylated monoglycerides	Primarily confectionery products
Buffering agents, pH adjusting agents, acid reacting materials, and water correcting agents	Acetic acid and various salts, ammonium aluminum sulfate, ammonium or calcium hydroxide, citric acid and various salts, salts of phosphoric acid, cream of tartar	Baking powder, cocoa products, cheeses, ice cream mixes, alcoholic beverages, fruit and vegetable products
Sequestering agents	EDTA and salts thereof, citric acid and its salts, phosphoric acid and its salts	Pumping pickles, alcoholic beverages, canned seafood (lobster, clams, sea snails, and so forth), dairy products, meat and poultry products
Starch modifying agents	Hydrogen peroxide, nitric acid, peracetic acid, sodium hydroxide, sulfuric acid	Starch
Yeast foods	Ammonium, calcium, potassium and zinc salts of various acids such as phosphoric, carbonic, and citric	Flour, bread, some alcoholic beverages, bacterial starter cultures

Abbreviations: BHA, butylated hydroxyanisole; BHT, butylated hydroxytoluene; EDTA, ethylenediaminetetraacetic acid.

[a]In reading this table, it is important to recognize that regulations regarding food additives (1) vary from country to country, (2) vary both with the levels of use permitted in foods and with the foods to which they may be added, and (3) are constantly being reviewed regarding their need and safety as new research emerges and newer and better additives are developed (Smith, 1993). Information provided here should not be interpreted as indicating that any food application is permissible in any specific country.
[b]The listing of examples of additives is not complete.
[c]The listing of examples of products is not complete.

Electron micrograph of a crystal of monosodium glutamate. MSG is one of the most widely used additives in food, and some people suffer reactions to it, especially a swollen liver, which extends the stomach and creates the discomforting sensation of having overeaten. COURTESY OF PHOTO RESEARCHERS, INC.

Many enzymes are derived from natural sources, for example, rennet from stomachs of calves, sheep, and goats; bromelain and papain from pineapples and papaya, respectively; ficin from latex of fig trees; pancreatin from the pancreas of pigs and oxen. However, an ever-growing number of enzymes are derived from microorganisms such as *Bacillus subtilis*, various species of molds especially *Aspergillus* varieties, and yeasts.

Carriers, extractants, and solvents. Carriers and extractants are used to extract flavoring compounds from spices and herbs to produce oleoresins; soluble solids from tea leaves; and coffee beans for the preparation of soluble drinks and for the selective extraction of caffeine in decaffeinated coffees; preparing hop extracts for beers; and extraction of cocoa powder. They are also used to extract fats and oils from oil seeds (defatting) and to dissolve oil-soluble dyes and flavorings, thereby serving as carriers to be added to other foods.

Sweeteners. There are two types of sweeteners: caloric sweeteners that provide minimal calories (usually only 1 or 2 calories) based on their sweetening power compared to that of sucrose, the sweetener they are replacing, and noncaloric sweeteners, which provide no calories. In U.S. regulations, caloric sweeteners as defined here are referred to as "non-nutritive sweeteners" and further defined as "substances having less than 2 percent of the caloric value of sucrose per equivalent unit of sweetening capacity."

Preservatives. A wide variety of additives are used for preventing or delaying spoilage and are closely restricted in respect to the foods they can be used with and the levels at which they can be used. Some preservatives, such as acetic acid, wood smoke, ascorbic and erythorbic acids, lecithin (component of egg yolk and soybeans), citric acid, and tartaric acid, are generally permitted according to good manufacturing practice. However, sulfurous acid and its salts (sulfites) cause serious problems in some asthmatics and regulations permit only low levels to be used. Nitrite and nitrate salts, used in meat curing, have been determined to be potential sources of cancer-causing agents and only minimal levels are permitted to be used.

Bleaching, maturing, and dough conditioning agents. These agents are used for whitening flour and improving (maturing and conditioning) flour's baking characteristics in the many varieties of bakery products.

Anticaking agents. These agents reduce the tendency of granulated products (dry mixes, dried egg powders, salt, and so forth) to stick together and help them keep their free-flowing properties.

Emulsifying, gelling, stabilizing, and thickening agents. Emulsifying agents are used in the formation of stable oil-and-water or oil-and-vinegar mixtures. Gelling, stabilizing, and thickening agents form soft gelled structures, thicken suspensions of particulate foods and prevent their separating, and provide mouth feel as bulking agents in low-calorie foods. They are also used to prevent or slow crystallization (staling) in foods.

Firming agents. These agents prevent or inhibit the softening of processed fruits and vegetables, especially during the process of canning in which they receive a severe heat treatment.

Glazing and polishing agents. These agents put a protective surface or coating or polish on a food, particularly confectionery products but also some vegetables and fruits.

pH-Adjusting, acid-reacting, and water-correcting agents. These agents maintain the acid-alkali balance (that is, pH) of foods at a desired level. Many delicate products such as artichokes must be acidified in order to be thermally processed (canned) with a less severe heat process because the usual high temperatures used for canning vegetables would destroy their shape and texture. Acids are also required to release carbon dioxide from leavening agents.

Sequestering agents. These agents act as sponges to gather or reduce in concentration any trace metal ions (especially copper and iron) that might, for example, promote oxidation or otherwise cause spoilage in foods. They improve the quality, color, and stability of canned products.

Starch-modifying agents. These agents can be used only to modify the properties of starch for its use in mixes, sauces, and custards.

Yeast foods. As their name suggests, these agents are used in fermentations with yeast and serve as a food for the yeast in the preparation of the inoculum. An inoculum is a highly concentrated suspension of yeast (or other microorganisms) to be added to malt mashes for beer-making or to bread doughs for leavening purposes or wherever fermentation is desired.

Miscellaneous additives. Propellant gases for the dispensing of foams or aerosol foods are also additives.

Regulation, Control, and Safety of Food Additives

Countries with well-developed food manufacturing industries have food legislation and associated regulations governing the use of food additives. In trade, where regulations between countries may differ, countries may allow conditional entry (where safety is not a concern) requiring relabeling of an offending product or specify compliance to Codex Alimentarius Commission standards before permitting importation.

The process for revoking approval or modifying the conditions of approval of existing food additives or for approving new ones varies from country to country. As problems of public health significance emerge that are attributable to the use of an additive, that information is assessed by panels of experts in the fields of epidemiology and toxicology. Should questions of safety emerge regarding the use of any prior approved additive, an evaluation must be made of the risk/benefit problems associated with continued use (Institute of Food Technologists, 1978). An excellent example of such a risk/benefit assessment can be found in the continued use of nitrate/nitrite salts in cured meat products. Banning the use of the salts in cured meats would most certainly expose the consuming public to the greater danger of botulism poisoning. The absence of these salts would permit the growth of *Cl. botulinum* in the cured meat and certainly the associated development of the *botulinum* toxin. On the other hand, these salts are also able under some circumstances to form nitroso-compounds, which are very active carcinogens.

However, there are general principles to guide the use of food additives and the assessment of new ones. No food additive is permitted for use until its safety has been assessed by expert panels of specialists. It is up to the petitioner for use of an additive to supply toxicological data to the government-appointed panel. Evaluations, based on a generally accepted protocol, must be made of the toxicological effect of the additive (Winter and Francis, 1997). Animal testing is required to determine levels of toxicity which are then used to determine human toxicity

GENERAL PRINCIPLES GUIDING THE USE OF FOOD ADDITIVES

Requirement for Uses of Additive
- The additive must serve a useful purpose in preparing, processing, storage, and handling of the food
- The use of the food additive should not deceive, mislead, or defraud the consumer
- The use of the additive should not pose a health hazard either to the general population or to any special segment within the population

levels, but if the additive is substantially the same as the natural prior sanctioned or GRAS product, animal testing may not be required.

Toxicity data that are submitted for evaluation are based on assessment of exposure; such data must also determine the level of exposure. This will be influenced by the level used in foods (which is kept to the minimum level to produce the desired effect) and the level that remains in the food after processing. Other factors affecting the dose level are the age and gender of the consumer eating the food; the physical state of that individual (that is, pregnant, lactating, convalescent, with reduced immune system, with allergies, with special diet requirements, and so on); frequency of eating the food to which the additive is added; and the composition of the rest of the diet, which can have a protective effect on the toxicity.

Prior sanctioned additives are regularly reviewed for safety. Submissions for the approval of new additives may take several years and cost many hundreds of thousands of dollars to the petitioner. Such submissions are not undertaken lightly. The consumer's demand for innovative foods with new properties and enhanced safety will certainly see the food industry develop more and functionally better additives that are safe.

See also **Adulteration of Food; Codex Alimentarius; Consumer Protests; Food, Composition of; Food Safety; International Agencies; Toxins, Unnatural, and Food Safety.**

BIBLIOGRAPHY
Beuchat, Larry, and David Golden. "Antimicrobials Occurring Naturally in Foods." *Food Technology* 43(1) (January 1989): 134–142.

Canadian Food and Drugs Act and Regulations with amendments 1999, Part B, Food, Division 1, General, B.01.001, p 16.

(U.S.) Code of Federal Regulations, Title 21—Food and Drugs (Cite 21CFR170.3). Introduction. Food and Drugs. This document may be found at the U.S. Food and Drug Administration's home website http://www.fda.gov/. Section 201 (s) can be found at http://www.fda.gov/opacom/laws/fdcact/fdcact1.htm.

Codex Alimentarius Commission. Preamble to the General Standard for Food Additives, Codex Stan 192-1995 (Rev. 2-1999). This can be found at http://www.codex alimentarius.net/.

European Union. Council Directive 89/107/EEC; amended 10.9.1994. This document can be found at http://europa.eu.int/comm/food/fs/sfp/addit_flavor/additives/index_en.html#1.

Farrer, Keith T. H. "Fredrick Accum (1769–1838)—Consultant and Food Chemist." *Food Science and Technology Today* 10 (1996): 217–222.

Farrer, Keith T. H. "Dr A H Hassall—and Food Technology." *Food Science and Technology Today* 11 (1997): 81–87.

The (U.K.) Food Labelling Regulations 1996 (Statutory Instrument 1996 No. 1499; Crown Copyright 1996). The full text of these regulations can be found at http://www.hmso.gov.uk/si/si1996/Uksi_19961499_en_2.htm.

Hartley, Dorothy. *Food in England*. London: Futura, 1985.

Institute of Food Technologists. "Benefit/Risk: Consideration of Direct Food Additives." A Symposium. *Food Technology* 32 (8) (August 1978): 54–69. This symposium, held in 1978 and comprising five papers, still provides one of the more thorough and accessible discussions on risk/benefit assessment available.

Rundell, Elisa Maria. *A New System of Domestic Cookery*. London: John Murray, 1828. A recipe book on cookery and household economics primarily but with interesting insights into food, nutritional knowledge, and home economics.

Skuse, E. *Skuse's Complete Confectioner: A Practical Guide*, 10th ed. London: W. J. Bush & Co., Ltd., ca. 1900.

Smith, J., ed. *Technology of Reduced Additive Foods*. London: Blackie Academic & Professional, Chapman & Hall, 1993.

Winter, C. K., and F. J. Francis. "Assessing, Managing, and Communicating Chemical Food Risks." *Food Technology* 51 (5) (May 1997). A comprehensive exploration of the technical aspects of risk assessment.

Gordon William Fuller

ADULTERATION OF FOOD.

"Adulteration" is a legal term meaning that a food product fails to meet federal or state standards. Adulteration usually refers to noncompliance with health or safety standards as determined, in the United States, by the Food and Drug Administration (FDA) and the U.S. Department of Agriculture (USDA).

Definition of Adulterated Food

The Federal Food, Drug, and Cosmetic (FD&C) Act (1938) provides that food is "adulterated" if it meets any one of the following criteria: (1) it bears or contains any "poisonous or deleterious substance" which may render it injurious to health; (2) it bears or contains any *added* poisonous or *added* deleterious substance (other than a pesticide residue, food additive, color additive, or new animal drug, which are covered by separate provisions) that is unsafe; (3) its container is composed, in whole or in part, of any poisonous or deleterious substance which may render the contents injurious to health; or (4) it bears or contains a pesticide chemical residue that is unsafe. (Note: The Environmental Protection Agency [EPA] establishes tolerances for pesticide residues in foods, which are enforced by the FDA.)

Food also meets the definition of adulteration if: (5) it is, or it bears or contains, an unsafe food additive; (6) it is, or it bears or contains, an unsafe new animal drug; (7) it is, or it bears or contains, an unsafe color additive; (8) it consists, in whole or in part, of "any filthy, putrid, or decomposed substance" or is otherwise unfit for food; or (9) it has been prepared, packed, or held under unsanitary conditions (insect, rodent, or bird infestation) whereby it may have become contaminated with filth or rendered injurious to health.

Further, food is considered adulterated if: (10) it has been irradiated and the irradiation processing was not done in conformity with a regulation permitting irradiation of the food in question (Note: FDA has approved irradiation of a number of foods, including refrigerated or frozen uncooked meat, fresh or frozen uncooked poultry, and seeds for sprouting [21 C.F.R. Part 179].); (11) it contains a dietary ingredient that presents a significant or unreasonable risk of illness or injury under the conditions of use recommended in labeling (for example, foods or dietary supplements containing aristolochic acids, which have been linked to kidney failure, have been banned.); (12) a valuable constituent has been omitted in whole or in part or replaced with another substance; damage or inferiority has been concealed in any manner; or a substance has been added to increase the product's bulk or weight, reduce its quality or strength, or make it appear of greater value than it is (this is "economic adulteration"); or (13) it is offered for import into the United States and is a food that has previously been refused admission, unless the person reoffering the food establishes that it is in compliance with U.S. law [21 U.S.C. § 342].

The Federal Meat Inspection Act and the Poultry Products Inspection Act contain similar provisions for meat and poultry products. [21 U.S.C. §§ 453(g), 601(m).]

Poisonous or Deleterious Substances

Generally, if a food contains a poisonous or deleterious substance that may render it injurious to health, it is adulterated. For example, apple cider contaminated with *E. coli* O157:H7 and Brie cheese contaminated with *Listeria monocytogenes* are adulterated. There are two exceptions to this general rule. First, if the poisonous substance is inherent or naturally occurring and its quantity in the food does not ordinarily render it injurious to health, the food will not be considered adulterated. Thus, a food that contains a natural toxin at very low levels that would not ordinarily be harmful (for instance, small amounts of amygdalin in apricot kernels) is not adulterated.

Second, if the poisonous or deleterious substance is unavoidable and is within an established tolerance, regulatory limit, or action level, the food will not be deemed to be adulterated. Tolerances and regulatory limits are thresholds above which a food will be considered adulterated. They are binding on FDA, the food industry, and the courts. Action levels are limits at or above which FDA *may* regard food as adulterated. They are not binding on FDA. FDA has established numerous action levels (for example, one part per million methyl mercury in fish), which are set forth in its booklet *Action Levels for Poisonous or Deleterious Substances in Human Food and Animal Feed.*

If a food contains a poisonous substance in excess of a tolerance, regulatory limit, or action level, mixing it with "clean" food to reduce the level of contamination is not allowed. The deliberate mixing of adulterated food with good food renders the finished product adulterated (FDA, *Compliance Policy Guide* [CPG § 555.200]).

Filth and Foreign Matter

Filth and extraneous material include any objectionable substances in foods, such as foreign matter (for example, glass, metal, plastic, wood, stones, sand, cigarette butts), undesirable parts of the raw plant material (such as stems, pits in pitted olives, pieces of shell in canned oysters), and filth (namely, mold, rot, insect and rodent parts, excreta, decomposition). Under a strict reading of the FD&C Act, any amount of filth in a food would render it adulterated. FDA regulations, however, authorize the agency to issue Defect Action Levels (DALs) for natural, unavoidable defects that at low levels do not pose a human health hazard [21 C.F.R. § 110.110]. These DALs are advisory only; they do not have the force of law and do not bind FDA. DALs are set forth in FDA's Compliance Policy Guides and are compiled in the *FDA and Center for Food Safety and Applied Nutrition (CFSAN) Defect Action Level Handbook.*

In most cases, DALs are food-specific and defect-specific. For example, the DAL for insect fragments in peanut butter is an average of thirty or more insect fragments per 100 grams (g) [CPG § 570.300]. In the case of hard or sharp foreign objects, the DAL, which is based on the size of the object and the likelihood it will pose a risk of choking or injury, applies to all foods (see CPG § 555.425).

Economic Adulteration

A food is adulterated if it omits a valuable constituent or substitutes another substance, in whole or in part, for a valuable constituent (for instance, olive oil diluted with tea tree oil); conceals damage or inferiority in any man-

ner (such as fresh fruit with food coloring on its surface to conceal defects); or any substance has been added to it or packed with it to increase its bulk or weight, reduce its quality or strength, or make it appear bigger or of greater value than it is (for example, scallops to which water has been added to make them heavier).

Microbiological Contamination and Adulteration

The fact that a food is contaminated with pathogens (harmful microorganisms such as bacteria, viruses, or protozoa) may, or may not, render it adulterated. Generally, for ready-to-eat foods, the presence of pathogens will render the food adulterated. For example, the presence of *Salmonella* on fresh fruits or vegetables or in ready-to-eat meat or poultry products (such as luncheon meats) will render those products adulterated.

For meat and poultry products, which are regulated by USDA, the rules are more complicated. Ready-to-eat meat and poultry products contaminated with pathogens, such as *Salmonella* or *Listeria monocytogenes*, are adulterated. (Note that hotdogs are considered ready-to-eat products.) For raw meat or poultry products, the presence of pathogens will not always render a product adulterated (because raw meat and poultry products are intended to be cooked, and proper cooking should kill pathogens). Raw poultry contaminated with *Salmonella* is not adulterated. However, USDA's Food Safety and Inspection Service (FSIS) has ruled that raw meat or poultry products contaminated with *E. coli* O157:H7 are adulterated. This is because normal cooking methods may not reduce *E. coli* O157:H7 below infectious levels. *E. coli* O157:H7 is the only pathogen that is considered an adulterant when present in raw meat or poultry products.

Enforcement Actions against Adulterated Food

If a food is adulterated, FDA and FSIS have a broad array of enforcement tools. These include *seizing* and *condemning* the product, *detaining* imported product, *enjoining* persons from manufacturing or distributing the product, or *requesting a recall* of the product. Enforcement action is usually preceded by a Warning Letter from FDA to the manufacturer or distributor of the adulterated product. In the case of an adulterated meat or poultry product, FSIS has certain additional powers. FSIS may *suspend* or *withdraw* federal inspection of an official establishment. Without federal inspection, an establishment may not produce or process meat or poultry products, and therefore must cease operations. With the exception of infant formula, neither FDA nor FSIS has the authority to require a company to recall an adulterated food product. However, the ability to generate negative publicity gives them considerable powers of persuasion.

State regulators generally have similar enforcement tools at their disposal to prevent the manufacture and distribution of adulterated food. In addition, many states have the authority to immediately embargo adulterated food and to impose civil fines. Federal agencies often will coordinate with state or local authorities to remove unsafe food from the market as quickly as possible.

See also **Additives; Botulism; Food, Safety; Genetic Engineering; Government Agencies, U.S.; Herbicides; Inspection; Microbiology; Microorganisms; Pesticides; Poultry; Toxins, Unnatural, and Food Safety; Water: Safety of Water.**

BIBLIOGRAPHY

Statutes:

Federal Food, Drug, and Cosmetic Act, U.S. Code, vol. 21, section 342.

Federal Meat Inspection Act, U.S. Code, vol. 21, section 453(g).

Poultry Products Inspection Act, U.S. Code, vol. 21, section 601(m).

Regulations:

21 C.F.R. Parts 109–110

FDA Materials:

Food and Drug Administration, Center for Food Safety and Applied Nutrition. *Defect Action Level Handbook*. Washington, D.C.: Government Printing Office, 1995. Revised 1997, 1998. Available at http://www.cfsan.fda.gov/dms/dalbook .html.

Food and Drug Administration, Office of Regulatory Affairs. *Compliance Policy Guides Manual*. Washington, D.C.: Government Printing Office, 2000; updated 2001. Available at http://www.fda.gov/ora/compliance_ref/cpg/default.htm.

Food and Drug Administration. *Action Levels for Poisonous or Deleterious Substances in Human Food and Animal Feed*. Washington, D.C.: Government Printing Office, 2000. Available at http://www.cfsan.fda.gov/lrd/fdaact.html.

Richard L. Frank
Robert A. Hahn

ADVERTISING OF FOOD. The word "advertising" is derived from the French *avertissement*, a giving notice or announcement. An advertisement is information that is publicly communicated through mass communication. The business of advertising is an aspect of commerce that is an integrated part of industrialized and affluent societies that can afford to purchase goods. Advertising brings notice to a wide range of consumer products, including food, a major consumer of advertising. In the United States in the 1990s, food and beverages together formed the most heavily advertised type of product: approximately 40 to 50 percent of television commercials are for food products, amounting to between ten and fifteen commercials every hour. Advertising takes place at a number of levels in the food marketing chain. Advertisements—ads in the United States and adverts in Britain—may be issued by manufacturers individually or as a group, by a marketing board representing a generic product, and by wholesalers, retailers, and distributors.

Although advertising has a long history, modern advertising began with the invention of printing in the six-teenth century. Early advertisements for foods, which were presented alongside those for books, medicines, cures, and remedies, tended to be for foods and drinks that were at first consumed by the upper classes. English weeklies first reported coffee in 1652, chocolate in 1657, and tea in 1658. The widespread expansion of print advertising did not take place until the eighteenth and nineteenth centuries. Its spread was stimulated and encouraged by changing and developing trade patterns, especially the rail network and the improvement of roads. Improved means of transportation allowed for the expansion of extended regional and national trade networks. As the production of goods increased, they had to be more efficiently and effectively distributed and marketed. As much of the early advertising was contained in print media, the spread of literacy, together with the steep rise in the development of newspapers and magazines, especially after 1850, stimulated its development. It is in the last hundred years that advertising has developed into a major industry. So important has it become that it is central to the production of general communications and provides the economic basis that enables them to exist. It is also central to the development and existence of many products.

Functions of Advertising

Advertising has a number of functions. It is used to launch new food products. The advertising campaign for Nescafé instant coffee granules in the 1950s allowed it to gain a foothold in a market that had strong competition from other brands such as Maxwell House, "America's favorite coffee." It is used to extend the sale of products that are already established in the marketplace. In 1956 the advertising campaign for the biscuit Snack, manufactured by Cadbury, caused an immediate increase in sales. Although its initial impact was not maintained, sales remained higher than the earlier unadvertised level for a year or so, even when there was almost no advertising support given to it. Advertising is used to promote the growth of a product. A marketing campaign for Callard & Bowser Butterscotch in 1959 and 1960 caused its consumption to expand by around 20 percent. Advertising also created a continued demand for a product when the original need to consume it had become redundant due to changing social and economic conditions. Bovril, fluid beef, was developed in the 1870s as a convalescence food and was later used as an energy food on expeditions and during sporting events. With higher incomes, better eating, changing drinking habits (for example, the increased consumption of coffee over tea, and the popularity of carbonated, or "fizzy," drinks), and the availability of new drinks, the original rationale for the consumption of Bovril had declined by the post–World War II years. An advertising campaign was introduced to remove the idea that it was an old-fashioned drink and to suggest that it was a "contemporary" one. Advertising has been used to slow down the decline in the consumption of a product. When milk consumption was falling in the postwar period in Britain, especially in the mid-1950s, the National Milk Publicity Campaign succeeded in slowing down the rate of decline and in introducing new outlets that served to stimulate consumption.

Costs of Advertising

Large sums of money are spent on food advertising. In Great Britain in 1999 the top food advertiser was Mars, a confectionery firm, which spent $99,488,921 (£63,629,000) on its advertising; the second, spending $82,966,590 (£53,062,000), was Kelloggs (GB), followed by the supermarket chain J. Sainsbury with $76,846,990 (£49,151,000). The top brand was McDonald's fast-food restaurants, which spent $66,260,524 (£42,379,000). Other highly advertised brands include the other fast-food restaurants, Kentucky Fried Chicken $19,279,797 (£12,331,000) and Burger King $17,604,550 (£11,259,000). Among the high food advertisers were supermarkets that promoted both their stores and their branded products. Sainsbury's was the top supermarket brand ($45,528,848, or £29,118,000) followed by Tesco ($28,564,912, or £18,286,000), then Asda ($25,034,171, or £16,010,000).

As these figures suggest, not all foodstuffs are advertised to the same extent. In Britain in 1999, highly advertised foods include cereal products, confectionery, ice cream, potato crisps, snacks and nuts, margarine, low-fat spreads, and cheese. By comparison, small sums are spent on herbs and spices, excluding pepper and curry. Advertising-to-sales ratios vary greatly between products. For herbs and spices and fresh vegetables the figure may be as low as 0.06 percent and 0.07 percent respectively. Many foods had less than a 1 percent ratio. Intensive advertising at 11.31 percent was noted for cereals. Generally, advertising of food products shows a lower percentage of expenditure than that of other products, including alcoholic drinks and tobacco.

Advertising Media

Food is advertised through a number of channels. As new technologies have become available, the opportunities for advertising have broadened. A number of these are especially important. Newspapers and magazines have long been a significant vehicle for advertising. Newspapers in Britain published advertisements in the seventeenth century, and, as the provincial press expanded, greater opportunities became available for food advertising. In the later nineteenth century, magazines increasingly started to carry advertisements: In the United States in the 1930s, some 20 percent of products advertised in the major print advertising media of women's and domestic magazines were for food and drink products. When radio networks were established (in 1926 and 1927 in the United States), they used advertising to bring in revenue. Food and drink manufacturers sponsored programs and also advertised their products in short "commercial breaks." In the 1950s television introduced a further medium that owes its ef-

fectiveness to the wide range of means that can be used to promote a product: moving pictures, sound (voice and music), and the written word. In the late twentieth century the introduction and extended use of the World Wide Web and e-commerce had an enormous initial growth. In the United Kingdom, growth rates for online marketing since the mid-1990s have been consistently well in excess of 100 percent, year after year. Internet advertising is undertaken through a number of means. In the year 2000, the majority (81 percent) of advertising took place through banners, and small numbers through sponsorship (9 percent), classified advertisements (7 percent), and other means (3 percent). Internet advertising includes sites from manufacturers, product manufacturing boards, supermarkets (which allow for online shopping and home delivery), and food enthusiast sites (for example, for British products in the United States).

Other media have provided further means of advertising food. Billboards and hoardings were first used for this purpose in Britain in the 1890s and are found over a wide geographical area. Light displays in cities, such as those for the carbonated drink Irn-Bru in Glasgow and Coca-Cola in London, have presented advertisements as visual images within central cityscapes. Buses and electric cars (especially since the 1890s in the United States) have carried advertising, usually on their sides or rear. Manufacturers advertise their products on their distribution vans; some also have special promotional vehicles that they use in campaigns where they take their product to public places or special shows to advertise it. Sponsorship of major public popular and sporting events is undertaken by a number of manufacturers. Flora margarine, made from sunflower oil, which is high in essential polyunsaturates, has been the sponsor of the London marathon in the late 1990s; the Bell's open golf championship is sponsored by Bell's, the whiskey manufacturer.

Advertising and promotion of foods is undertaken within the retail industry. Fancy displays draw attention to one or a range of products. In Britain, displays from the 1860s included decorative tins with hinged lids developed by the biscuit manufacturer Huntley and Palmers of Reading. As self-service supermarkets developed, largely after World War II, products could be displayed to draw special attention to them. Three-dimensional displays promoted a single product or a range, and tended to be developed by manufacturers. Supermarkets sometimes hold special testing events where customers can sample a product, thereby encouraging them to buy it. Food is also sold in special promotional packets, sometimes at a "special introductory price" or a "special promotional price." These may hold a sample of the product that can be packaged in a way that reflects the packaging on the regular-sized product.

A range of ephemeral material is distributed to food wholesalers and retailers by manufacturers and others involved in processing and distribution. Some of this, including calendars, pens, and pads of headed note paper, is intended to remind the consumer of the product on a daily basis.

Coupons, which allow the consumer to receive a discount on the product when they present one to a retailer, are found in a range of print media, especially newspapers and magazines.

The medium that is used to advertise a product is selected for its appropriateness to that product, the nature and scope of the advertising campaign, and its desired target audience. Each medium has its own values and qualities. When television started to become widely adopted in Britain in the mid-1950s, Bird's Eye decided to use this new medium to advertise its frozen food products. The company was aware that families with televisions were more likely to be interested in new ideas such as Bird's Eye's products. At that time it was recognized that there was a potentially large market for frozen food, which was a relatively new phenomenon. In the 1920s daily newspapers were best suited to advertise foods and other products that were bought on a regular basis. Magazines that were to be read by a particular social class or group carried advertisements for foods and other products that would likely be consumed by them.

Advertising Targets

Much food advertising is targeted at women, the main buyers of food in the household. As children are recognized as important persuaders in that process and as they may accompany their mothers to buy the family food, advertising is also targeted at them. Recent studies of food advertising in South Africa show the need of advertisers to monitor social changes because food advertising, like advertising in general, reflects social and cultural trends, values, and attitudes. Cultural differences are also reflected in advertising. Chinese television advertisements tend to signify family values, tradition, and technology, whereas themes in American advertisements tend to symbolize the importance of enjoyment, cost savings, and individualism. With the emergence of global culture, specific values such as global cosmopolitanism and modernity (often symbolized by the hamburger) will be spread around the world.

Food advertising reflects changing food tastes, diet, and dietary habits. The extent of the references to nutrition, health claims, and weight loss has altered in advertisements in recent decades. Research has indicated that in the United States from the 1960s to the 1980s there was an increase in references to health and weight loss in advertisements for hot and cold cereals, bread and cake mixes, frozen and pre-prepared entrees, peanut butter, canned and instant dry soup, and carbonated beverages in a range of women's magazines. There was a significant rise in health claims in the 1980s, higher than in the 1960s, and the percentage of diet claims that appeared in food advertisements in the 1980s was significantly higher than the percentage reported in the 1960s and 1970s. At the same time, between 1960 and 1980,

there were substantial decreases in claims of quality, taste, status, and consumer satisfaction. These may have resulted from changes in women's consumption and dieting behavior and the increased demand for food that is low in calories but high in nutrition. Concerns about increasing prevalence of obesity in the United States and campaigns against fast-food artificiality—both within the United States and beyond—will likely influence food advertising.

Brand Names

Central to the advertising of food is the promotion of brand names and trade names that distinguish between one manufacturer's product and that of another. As the survival of these names depends on advertising, some brands and trade names have large advertising budgets allocated to them so that they can maintain their status as products and their place in the marketplace. Brands and trade names arose in the nineteenth century as a response to increased production and the need to efficiently and effectively market products. Brand names started to be promoted in the 1870s, after which their use spread quickly. Significant increases were especially noted in the early twentieth century. Even after they were rapidly adopted, the extent of their use varied geographically and throughout time. During World War II, when widespread restrictions caused materials and food shortages, brand names were abandoned in Europe and were replaced by utility products. They came into operation again once peacetime conditions were restored. In some cases this was not until well after all controls on food and other raw products were lifted. Especially developed in Western Europe, brand names were, however, prohibited in Eastern Europe.

Brand names and trademarks are consciously devised by manufacturers. They are based on existing names, mainly personal names or words, or a combination of the two; few have no recognizable origin. The most common are word names that include personal names of manufacturers such as Nestlé (confectionery manufacturer) and Campbell's (the soup manufacturer), names of food-chain stores (Safeway), and the names of food products such as Mother's Pride (bread). Arbitrary names include Saxa table salt. Names often have an association with prestige and a range of desirable attributes, such as quality (Ambrosia rice pudding); wholesomeness (Eden Vale dairy products, Just Juice tropical fruit juices, and Lean Cuisine low-calorie frozen foods); and nutritional value (Marathon confectionery bars). Other names describe ingredients, as with Coca-Cola, a drink made from coca leaves and cola nuts, and Bovril, a drink of concentrated essence of beef.

Each brand name has a number of functions: it ensures consistency and quality; it has a personality that makes the consumers identify with the product; it is a social and cultural marker that helps the consumers to identify who they are and the social group they belong to; it allows the consumers to gain esteem within their consumer group. These values or aspects of them are reflected in advertising campaigns and advertisements.

Because of the importance of brands and trademarks in identifying foods and other products, they have become legally protected. The first protective legislation in the United States was passed by Congress in 1870. It was altered with different juridical rulings and received its final codification in 1905. Legislation has also been introduced throughout the world. In Britain it has included the Trade Marks Act of 1938.

Food advertisements use a range of appeals to promote a product. Rational appeals tend to be used for healthy foods. Emotional appeals, which are more likely to be remembered, are used for a range of products that includes fun products, or "sin foods," such as candy or desserts. Taste claims are especially important. Products are compared with similar products in side-by-side tests that point out the qualities their competition does not have (for example, the "Pepsi challenge"); these tests distinguish the product from its competitors by the ways in which it is beneficial to the consumer or puts the consumer at an advantage over those who do not use the product. Further, these tests suggest that the product is like an advertised brand in some way; they refer to the competition, state that the brand is at least as good as any other in a set, and they use experts to endorse the quality, taste, or value of the product so that it is given a heightened status. Nutritional claims are used particularly in advertisements for foods that benefit health and have health-giving qualities. Such claims may state that a product is "low" or reduced in calories, that it is "cholesterol-free" or has "reduced cholesterol"; food and drinks may be "lite" to distinguish them from standard foods. In the United States and some other countries, there are regulations governing the allowable fat content in foods billed as "low fat" and "reduced fat."

Especially for branded foods, advertisements often use slogans to help the consumer remember the product. They link the product and its function. For many years, the slogan for the Mars candy bar has suggested that it gives the consumer energy to undertake a range of activities throughout the day: "A Mars a day helps you work, rest, and play." The slogan "Bridge that gap with Cadbury's Snack" suggested that the biscuit could be eaten to fill in the gap between meals.

Celebrity Endorsements

Food advertisers use a range of figures who enjoy public recognition to endorse or act as spokespeople for a product and recommend it to the public. Especially after 1920 advertisers were aware of the relationship between popular culture idols and their audiences. Important early endorsers included movie stars and popular entertainers. The list was later extended to include television stars and individuals from occupations such as politics, sports, the

"And now, a word from our sponsor." If radio stars George Burns and Gracie Allen endorsed Spam, it had to be good. ("Spam" has since become a derogatory term for another kind of advertisement, in the form of unwanted e-mail.) COURTESY OF THE ADVERTISING ARCHIVE LTD.

arts, and business. In an endorsement, an endorser makes the product familiar to the public. It can be done in a number of ways: explicitly ("I endorse the product"); implicitly ("I use this product"); imperatively ("You should use the product"); and copresently (where the endorser appears with the product). In an endorsement, celebrities transfer meaning from themselves (their values, status, class, gender, age, personality, and lifestyle) to the product, and through it, to the consumer. Through that process, people consume a product that is associated with the star and their star image. Celebrities are chosen to represent values that are embodied in the product they endorse. The comedian Bill Cosby endorsed the soft drink Coca-Cola. Although there is a close relationship between the star and the product, not all star and product relations have successfully increased product sales. John Houseman failed as an endorser for McDonald's although he had been successful in other endorsement campaigns. Endorsements fail when they do not succeed in transferring meaning: the values between the celebrity and the product are too wide for the meaning to move between the endorser and the product.

Controls on Advertising

All food advertising is governed by a number of controls. Some of these regulate advertising in general. Defamatory statements, false representations, offers to contract, incitements to crime, contempt of court, breach of copyright, and infringement of trademarks are covered by legislation that governs libel, deceit, contracts, crime, and the infringements of rights. More specifically, in Britain in the late nineteenth and early twentieth centuries, legislation included the Indecent Advertisements Act of 1889 and the Advertisements Regulation Act of 1907, which was amended in 1925. At a wider level, the general law also affects all advertisements.

Codes of advertising have been issued as guidelines to advertisers. In the United States from 1911, steps were taken to provide codes of practice. Early codes were issued by the Associated Advertising Clubs of the World. Guidelines have also been expressed in a number of codes such as the British Code of Advertising. The Code, issued in 1979, embodies the principles that "all advertisements should be legal, decent, honest and truthful"; "all advertisements should be prepared with a sense of responsibility both to the consumer and to society"; and "all advertisements should conform to the principles of fair competition as generally accepted in business." The codes contain specific rules that govern food advertising, packaging, and labeling of foodstuffs. They define how foods can be described and the nature and scope of the nutritional information presented on the packaging. Nutritional information has become increasingly widespread in the European Community and the United States. In Britain, sections of the Customs and Excise Act 1952 prohibit misdescription in advertisements of beer and spirits. The Food and Drugs Act (as subsequently amended) contains certain requirements as to advertising and labeling of food. A number of regulations deal specifically with the representation of food claims. Diet foods are particularly regulated, for example in the 1970 British Labeling of Food Regulations, which require that "where a claim is made in an advertisement or on a label that any food is an aid to slimming, it must be substantiated, and a statement must be included that the food cannot aid slimming except as part of a diet in which the total intake of calories is controlled, whether by calorie counting, low carbohydrate/high protein or other means." Other aspects of "slimming" that are regulated include diet plans, aids to dieting, foods, appetite depressants, and weight-loss products in general. Parallel regulations and advertising codes have also been introduced in other countries such as the United States. In the 1980s in the United States, consumer protection remained the major rationale for the regulation of advertising. Other forces included new media technologies, issues of privacy and fairness, environmentalism, religion, changing economic conditions, the deregulation movement, and foreign regulatory initiatives made necessary by international trade agreements.

See also **Anorexia, Bulimia; Food Marketing: Alternative (Direct) Strategies; Food Politics: United States; Marketing of Food; Naming of Food; Obesity**.

BIBLIOGRAPHY

Alden, Dana L., Jan-Benedict E. M. Steenkamp, and Rajeev Batra. "Brand Positioning through Advertising in Asia, North America, and Europe: The Role of Global Consumer Culture." *Journal of Marketing* 63 (1999): 75–87.

Ambler, Tim. "Do Brands Benefit Consumers?" *International Journal of Advertising* 16 (1997): 167–198.

Barr, S. "Nutrition in Food Advertising: Content Analysis of a Canadian Women's Magazine, 1928–1986." *Journal of Nutrition Education* 21 (1989): 64–71.

Benson, John. *The Rise of Consumer Society in Britain, 1880–1980.* Harlow: Longman, 1994.

Brown, B. W. *Images of Family Life in Magazine Advertising, 1920–1978.* New York: Praeger, 1981.

Buchanan, Bruce, and Ronald H. Smithies. "Taste Claims and Their Substantiation." *Journal of Advertising Research* 31, no. 3 (June/July 1991): 19–35.

Fowles, Jib. *Advertising and Popular Culture.* Foundations of Popular Culture 5. Thousand Oaks, Calif.: Sage Publications, 1996.

Harris, Ralph, and Arthur Seldon. *Advertising in Action.* London: Hutchinson, 1962.

Klassen, Michael L., Suzanne M. Wauer, and Sheila Cassel. "Increases in Health and Weight Loss Claims in Food Advertising in the Eighties." *Journal of Advertising Research* 30, no. 6 (December 1990/January 1991): 32–37.

Kotz, K., and M. Story. "Food Advertisements during Children's Saturday Morning Television Programming: Are They Consistent with Dietary Recommendations?" *Journal of the American Dietetic Association* 94 (1994): 1296–1300.

Lears, Jackson. *Fables of Abundance: A Cultural History of Advertising in America.* New York: Basic Books, 1995.

Nevin, Terry R. *Advertising in Britain: A History.* London: Heineman, on behalf of the History of Advertising Trust, 1982.

Norris, J. D. *Advertising and the Transformation of American Society, 1865–1920.* Westport, Conn.: Greenwood, 1990.

O'Meara, M. A., ed. *Brands and Their Companies.* Detroit: Gale Research, 1994.

Pease, Otis. *The Responsibilities of American Advertising. Private Control and Public Influence, 1920–1940.* New Haven, Conn.: Yale University Press, 1958.

Rijkens, Rein. *European Advertising Strategies: The Profiles and Policies of Multinational Companies Operating in Europe.* London: Cassell, 1992.

Robinson, Jeffrey. *The Manipulators: A Conspiracy to Make Us Buy.* London: Simon and Schuster, 1998.

Schudson, Michael. *Advertising, the Uneasy Persuasion: Its Dubious Impact on American Society.* New York: Basic Books, 1984.

Heather Holmes

AFRICA.

This entry includes four subentries:
Central Africa
East Africa
North Africa
West Africa

CENTRAL AFRICA

Central Africa is broadly defined as the Congo River basin, plus adjoining areas in equatorial Atlantic-coast Africa. It comprises all (or parts) of Burundi, Cameroon, Central African Republic, Chad, Congo (Brazzaville), Congo (Kinshasa), Equatorial Guinea, Gabon, and Rwanda. (The list varies from one authority to another.) Where it meets Africa's Northern and Southern regions there are grassy savannas and veldts, at its juncture with East Africa, mountain ranges and great lakes. Central Africa's dominant feature, however, is equatorial rainforest and numerous rivers and swamps.

Central African gastronomy is the least known of any other similarly sized region, due partly to lack of documentation, as most Central African languages were not written down until the colonial era of the eighteenth and nineteenth centuries. Slaves, ivory, rubber, and minerals, not the region's cuisine, interested most non-Africans (Europeans and Arabs) who went there.

The First Inhabitants

The equatorial forest of Central Africa has remained unchanged by the cycles of global warming and cooling that, over tens of thousands of years, have frozen Europe and dried the Sahara. It is the home of the descendents of the first human inhabitants of the region: the Mbuti, Aka, and Efe people of the Ituri forest, the Twa of the Lake Kivu region, and related peoples. (Collectively these groups are called "Pygmy," a term that has fallen from favor, yet no other collective appellation has emerged.) When the forest people first arrived in Central Africa is unknown. One of them, taken to Egypt by an expedition that explored the area south of Egypt, is mentioned in Egyptian texts from between 2255 to 2152 B.C.E.

Unmatched in their ability to survive in the forest, the forest people live, for the most part, as they have for millennia. Using bows and poison-tipped arrows, nets, or spears—sometimes with the aid of Basenji dogs—the men hunt everything from antelope and birds to elephants and hippopotamuses. The women gather berries, fruits, insects, leaves, mushrooms, nuts, and roots. To move from campsite to campsite, they must have lightweight household goods. The most basic cooking methods are appropriate: roasting, smoking, and drying meats, and stewing meats and vegetables. When they kill a large animal, it is easier for them to move to the meat than vice-versa. The Mbuti brew a beverage called "liko" from berries, herbs, and kola nuts. A favorite sweet is wild honey.

Fishermen on the shore of Lake Victoria near Nyamazugu. © PAUL ALMASY/CORBIS.

The Arrival of Agriculture and New Foods

Over the past two millennia, because they have had increasing contact with other Africans—trading with them (exchanging forest products for agricultural foods and manufactured goods) and partially adopting their languages and cultures—forest peoples also eat foods such as the leaves and tubers of cassava (manioc, *Manihot esculenta*), rice, beans, peanuts, and tomatoes, from which they prepare stews and sauces.

The "other Africans" are the present-day Kongo, Mongo, Luba, Bwaka, Kwango, Lulua, Lunda, Kasai, Douala, and related peoples (there are hundreds of Central African ethnic groups). Collectively, they are called Bantu speakers, as their languages are part of the Bantu language group. (Bantu is a linguistic designation, not a racial one, and can be misleading because many people who speak Bantu languages are not related to the original speakers.) Bantu speakers began migrating into Central Africa from around the Nigeria-Cameroon border approximately two to three thousand years ago.

Over the course of several centuries, the population of Bantu speakers increased and they spread throughout Central and Southern Africa because they did two things that the original forest inhabitants did not: they worked iron into tools and weapons (Central Africa completely skipped the Bronze Age), and they obtained food from agriculture and, to a lesser extent, domesticated animals. (Diseases carried by Africa's tsetse fly prevent keeping livestock.) The forest people had lived in and with the forest; the Bantu speakers turned forests into farms. However, food obtained by hunting and gathering remained

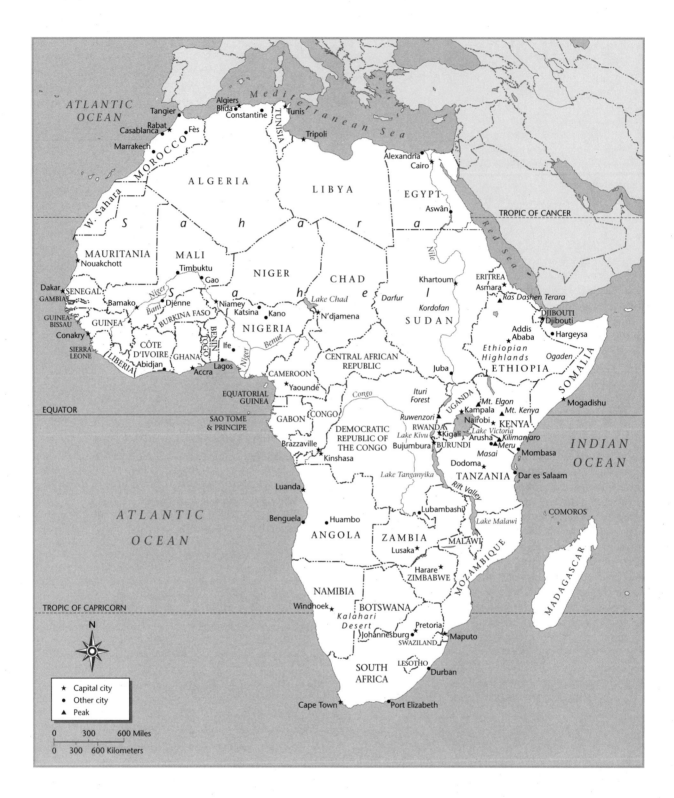

(and continues to be) an important part of their diet. In many Bantu languages, the words for "animal" and "meat" come from the same root, attesting to the close association of the two.

Contributing to Bantu expansion were Asian food crops that arrived in Africa at roughly the same time (circa the first century C.E.): bananas, plantain, and tuber crops such as yam and taro, which have been staple foods ever since. African varieties of millet, rice, sorghum, other yam species, and okra were also cultivated. Agricultural production of these high-yield crops enabled the Bantu speakers to increase their population dramatically, and they are now the overwhelming majority. More increases in population, and further migrations, occurred after the 1500s, when crops from the Americas were introduced to Africa: cassava, corn (maize), peanuts (groundnuts), tomatoes, chili peppers, sweet potatoes, papaya, pineapple, and avocado.

Central Africans have practiced swidden (slash-and-burn) agriculture for centuries. Men clear the forest and prepare the ground, but women do the rest of the work on the "plantation" or "shamba" (cultivated fields): planting, weeding, and harvesting.

Not every crop grown in Africa has been imported, but foreign crops have replaced many indigenous crops. The American peanut (*Arachis hypogaea*) replaced the Bambara groundnut (*Vigna subterranea*); Asian rice (*Oryza sativa*) replaced African rice (*Oryza glaberrima*); the chili pepper (*Capsicum*) replaced melegueta pepper (grains of paradise, *Aframomum melegueta*); and onions and garlic replaced various herbs and roots. Even the salt changed. In the Central African interior, the only salt once widely available came from various plants. It was obtained by burning leaves or bark, soaking the ashes in water, and evaporating the water in pans. Some cooks still use *sel indigène* (indigenous salt) or substitute baking soda to approximate its taste. Thus, foodways have not been static throughout history, and the larder was stocked for contemporary Central African cuisine.

Stews and Starches

Stewing has probably been the most common cooking method in Central Africa for centuries. Central African kitchens are located apart from the living and sleeping quarters. In each a large pot or cauldron for making stews rests on three stones above a wood fire. These dishes are usually simple, made with only a few ingredients. Stews are usually thickened with African oil palm fruit or crushed peanuts, but other thickeners are also used: crushed seeds of *Cucurbitaceae* (gourds, melons, and pumpkins), known by the West African name, *egusi*, and called *mbika* in Central Africa; crushed seed kernels of the *mangue sauvage* (wild mango) fruit (*Irvingia gabonensis*), called *odika*, *dika*, or *etima*; and okra, which is called *ngumbo*.

It is difficult to know whether to call these dishes stews, soups, or sauces. Part of the confusion is that they are eaten with a starchy staple dish. Many Africans believe that the only real meal is one that combines a stew or sauce with a starch. In West Africa, *fufu* is boiled pounded yam or plantain. In Central Africa the same process, pounding with mortar and pestle (often made from an entire tree trunk and limb), followed by boiling

and vigorous stirring or steaming, is used to make similar starchy staples. The word *fufu* refers to a dish made by boiling any sort of flour: maize, sorghum, millet, or cassava. (Cassava flour is dried ground cassava tuber; tapioca is the same thing.) These foods, called "dumplings" or "porridges" by English speakers, are comparable to East Africa's *ugali* and Southern Africa's *nsima*, or *sadza*. Another fufu-like staple is prepared by soaking cassava tubers in water for a few days, pounding them, then wrapping the resulting pulp in leaves and steaming it. The soaking and steaming breaks down poisonous cyanide compounds in the tubers. The finished product is called *kwanga*, *chickwangue*, *bobolo*, *mboung* or *placali* (usually ball-shaped), or *baton de manioc* (manioc stick). Women prepare *kwanga* in large batches to sell, ready-to-eat, in the market. They make the flour-based dumplings and porridges, as needed, in the home. These foods are heavy and thick, much more so than mashed potatoes. Many non-Africans do not like them at first, but they often make the mistake of taking a bite of such starches without sauce. Africans eat these bland starchy foods with a stew or sauce, usually heavily seasoned. As with West African *fufu*, a bite-sized piece of the *kwanga* (or something similar) is pulled off, dipped into the stew, then eaten. Rice and European-style bread, especially French baguettes, are also eaten with stew.

Greens

One distinguishing characteristic of Central African cooking is the use of edible leaves, which Americans call "greens." Indeed, the greens of the southeastern United States—collard greens, kale, and mustard greens—have their roots in Africa. In French-speaking Central Africa these are commonly called "feuilles" (leaves). It is hard to overstate the amount and variety of greens consumed. Oftentimes greens are the main ingredient in the daily stew, cooked with only a little onion, hot pepper, meat, fish, or oil for flavoring. Some of the greens consumed in Central Africa are bitterleaf, cassava, okra, pumpkin, sorrel, sweet potato, and taro. People cultivate greens and gather them from the wild. Cassava leaves ("feuilles de manioc") are the most commonly farmed. In many tropical areas of the world cassava is grown primarily for its tubers, but Africans have a long tradition of eating both the leaves and the tubers of this plant. *Gnetum africanum*, called *okok*, *koko*, or *eru*, is a variety of greens that grows wild. Before cooking, women pound greens in a mortar and pestle, or roll them like giant cigars and use a sharp knife to shred them finely. *Saka-saka*, or *pondu*, is a dish made from cassava leaves, onion, and a bit of dried fish. *Saka-madesu* is cassava leaves cooked with beans. Another recipe, variations of which are found all over sub-Saharan Africa, calls for greens to be cooked with tomato, onion, and mashed peanuts. Other greens dishes are made with tomato, onion, chili pepper, and fresh, salted, or smoked fish, or even canned sardines. Greens and meat are also often cooked together.

CENTRAL AFRICAN CUISINE

Richard Francis Burton, the nineteenth-century traveler and writer, is famous for his efforts to discover the source of the Nile and his account of a visit to Mecca. He could have been describing Central African cuisine when he described the food he encountered in Bonny River, in present-day Nigeria, near the boundary between Central Africa and West Africa . In the first sentence, Burton gives the "Anglicé" (English) names for African foods: "obeoka" = fowl; "nda" = fish; "fufu" = mashed yam; "fula" = soup; and "tomeneru" = tombo, or palm wine.

> breakfast is served. It is a little dinner, ordinarily consisting of obeoka, nda, fufu, fula and tomeneru,—Anglicé, fowl, fish, mashed yam, soup i.e. (the liquid in which stews have been boiled), and tombo, or palm-wine the latter however, hard, tasting like soapsuds, and very intoxicating. The cooking is excellent, when English dishes are not attempted. . . . Most of the dishes are boiled, and copiously peppered with cayenne and green chili pods to induce thirst. There are many savoury messes of heterogeneous compounds, fish, fresh and dried, oysters, clams, and cockles, poultry, goat and deer, salt beef or ship's pork, yams, plantains and palm oil. Smoked shrimps are pounded in a wooden pestle and mortar, with mashed yam for consistency, and are put into the soup like forcemeat balls.
>
> A dinner similar to breakfast is eaten at 4 to 5 P.M. Soup and stews are the favorite ménu, and mashed yam acts as a substitute for bread. It is also made into a spoon by a deep impression of the thumb, and thus it carries a thimblefull of soup with every mouthful of yam. The evening is passed with the aid of music, chatting with the women, and playing with the children.

SOURCE: Richard F. Burton. *Wanderings in West Africa*. Vol. 2. New York: Dover, 1991, p. 289.

Red Palm Oil

Another distinguishing characteristic of Central African cuisine is the use of red palm oil, obtained from the fruit of the African oil palm, *Elaeis guineensis* (not to be confused with the clear oil pressed from the hard kernel). Reddish and thick, it has a distinctive flavor for which there is no substitute. Women make red palm oil, or palm butter, at home by boiling and hand-squeezing fresh palm nuts. The oily pulp is cooked with chicken, onion, tomato, okra, garlic, or sorrel leaves, and chili pepper to produce a stew called *moambé* or *poulet nyembwe* (also *gnemboue*). *Moambé* is also made with other meats. This is one of many Central African dishes related to West African counterparts, in this case the West African palm oil chop, though the Central African versions tend to be simpler and made with fewer ingredients. Outside of Africa, canned palm soup base (also called *sauce graine*, *noix de palme*, or cream of palm fruit) can be used.

Peanuts

Peanuts are roasted and eaten as snacks, but they are used more interestingly in stews and sauces. The chicken-groundnut stew—made from chicken, peanuts, tomato, onion, and chili pepper—is common in Central Africa, as it is throughout sub-Saharan Africa. Peanut sauces are served with roasted meats or fried fish, or boiled yams, sweet potatoes, or rice. Greens are cooked in groundnut sauce; meat, fish, or fowl can be added to produce a variety of stews.

As with red palm oil, there are similarities between the ways peanuts are used in Central African and West African cooking. West Africa's groundnut chop is similar to the *muamba nsusu* (chicken soup) of the Kongo people, though the Central African version—made with chicken, onion, palm oil, tomato, ground peanuts, and hot chili pepper—is the less elaborate of the two. It is also the source of the peanut soups served in colonial North America. Many Americans mistakenly believe that peanuts are indigenous to Africa and were brought by Africans to the United States. After all, an American name for the peanut, "goober," comes from its Kongo name, "nguba." Africans may have brought peanuts to North America, but in fact they are indigenous to South America and were introduced to Africa in the early 1500s. (Diffusionist historians, who posit that Africans sailed between Africa and the Americas before Columbus, challenge this.) Africans quickly adopted the American peanut because it resembles an indigenous African plant, the Bambara groundnut. Like the American peanut, the seeds (legumes) of the Bambara groundnut grow and ripen underground. Africans used the Bambara groundnut in the same way they use the peanut. For various reasons, farmers and consumers preferred the American peanut, and the Bambara groundnut is a nearly forgotten crop.

Banana Leaves

An interesting Central African cooking method is steaming or grilling food wrapped in packets fashioned from the leaves of banana trees or other plants. This is an old cooking method, predating the use of iron, maybe even clay cooking pots. It is very practical when camping or traveling as it eliminates the need to carry pots, and the leaves can also be used as plates and bowls.

Certain leaves are especially favored because they give a particular flavor to food. *Kwanga*, for example, is wrapped in leaf packets before its final steaming. *Maboké* (singular *liboké*, also called *ajomba* or *jomba*)—leaf-wrapped packets of meat or fish, with onion, tomato, maybe okra, seasoned with lemon juice or hot chili pepper—are grilled over hot coals or steamed in a pot. Crushed peanuts, or *mbika*, are

DIFFUSIONISM: DID ANCIENT AFRICANS SAIL TO THE AMERICAS?

Who came to the Americas, and when, is a subject of debate between scholars who believe that ancient peoples, including Africans, sailed the world's oceans to the Americas, and others who say there is no evidence of pre-Columbian contact between the Old World and the New.

The traditional view is that Native Americans, after migrating into North America from Asia (via Beringia) tens of thousands of years ago, gradually spread south and east, developing their civilizations without input from the Old World until Christopher Columbus (or Leif Erickson) sailed across the Atlantic in recent historical times. Likewise, the traditional view holds that plants, foods, and cultural artifacts of the Western Hemisphere did not reach the Old World (and vice versa) until the post-1492 era of European conquest.

The diffusionist view of history challenges traditional scholarship. Diffusionist historians maintain that, in addition to the Asian incursion across Beringia, there were many transoceanic contacts between the Old World and the New, beginning in ancient times and continuing until the era of Columbian exploration. Supporting the diffusionist position is the life's work of Thor Heyerdahl, who proved that it is possible to sail great distances using ancient shipbuilding and navigational technology (in 1947 sailing from Peru to eastern Polynesia and in 1969 sailing from North Africa to Barbados on balsam rafts).

Further support comes both from the existence of Old World artifacts in the New World (and vice versa) that evidently predate the Columbian era and from oral history. Opponents of diffusionism argue that because ancient peoples could have sailed across the ocean is no proof that they actually did, that other evidence is either coincidental, occurred after Columbus, or has not been correctly dated, and that oral history is only myth. Complicating the debate are charges of prejudice from both sides.

As concerns Africa, diffusionist scholars believe that Egyptians and Phoenicians sailed to the New World in ancient times, as did Malians (of the former Sudanese Republic) in medieval times, observing that the design of Mesoamerican pyramids is strikingly similar to those found in Egypt and that Mesoamerican statues depict African explorers. If regular trade relations between Africa and the Americas are assumed, American plants such as cassava, chili, maize, tomato, and tobacco may have been known in Africa hundreds of years before they were introduced by Europeans. Likewise, African foodways may have been brought to the Americas before Columbus. It has been a quarter century since the publication of the important (though by no means only) work in this field: *They Came before Columbus* by Ivan Van Sertima. More research and evidence are needed before this debate can be resolved.

---

sometimes included in the packets. Filling the leaf packets with mashed beans (such as black-eyed peas) and sautéed peppers, then steaming, produces *koki* (also called *ekoki* or *gâteau de haricots*).

Meat, Fish, and Fowl

Generally, people in Central Africa eat meat, fish, or fowl whenever possible. Every village has domesticated chickens (or guinea fowl) and goats. Wild game, *viande de brousse* or bushmeat, is very common: antelope, birds, buffalo, crocodiles, fish, monkeys, pangolins, wild boars, and many other species are hunted. Almost every type of wildlife—from insects to primates—is hunted and eaten in Africa, though individual ethnic groups have their own traditions regarding what is edible and what is not. Some will eat snake meat, for example, while others will not. There are many traditional beliefs concerning who should eat certain foods and who should not: for example, a certain food may be reserved for men because it is believed that women who eat it cannot become pregnant or will suffer other ill effects. Women in the Odzala re-

gion of the Congo Republic do not eat gorilla meat, fearing that doing so would cause their husbands to become as brutal as gorillas.

Killing a large animal means a feast for everyone. Where there is no refrigeration, drying, salting, or smoking meat or fish is used to preserve it. All sorts of bushmeat—antelope, buffalo, crocodiles, hippopotamuses—as well as fish, are preserved in this way. When meat is not plentiful, a small amount is added to stews for flavor.

Beverages, Snacks, and Desserts

Bottled beer and soft drinks, sometimes unrefrigerated, are available throughout Central Africa. Traditional beverages include *vin de palme* (palm wine), self-fermented palm tree sap. Beer is made from corn, millet, plantains, and sorghum. Cassava, yam, or plantain porridges are thinned with water to make breakfast beverages, weaning foods for infants, and nutritious drinks for convalescents. Coffee and tea are also popular beverages. Central Africans are great snackers. Vendors selling hot beignets (French-style doughnuts), fried plantain, grilled corn-on-the-cob,

BUSHMEAT

"Bushmeat" (or, in French, *viande de brousse*) is wild game, meat taken from wild animals of the African forest or savannah, often called "the bush." Bushmeat can come from nearly any species of wildlife including antelope, boar, buffalo, cane rat, chimpanzee, crocodile, elephant, gorilla, hippopotamus, monkey, pangolin, and porcupine, as well as various birds and reptiles. Each ethnic group has its own traditions and taboos concerning which animals can be eaten and which cannot, but hunting wild animals for meat (and other products) is an extremely old tradition, predating the development of agriculture. Certain African peoples are herders and farmers, but in parts of Africa afflicted with the tsetse fly or poor forest soil and climate the food produced from domesticated animals and plants may not be sufficient to replace what hunting can provide.

Traditionally, hunting is a sign of manhood in much of Africa, and it is considered "men's work," whereas women are expected to tend the fields and care for children. Also, as is the case with horsemeat in France, people believe that certain types of bushmeat are especially healthful or possess curative properties. Bushmeat is an important protein source in the diet of rural people; when they do not eat it, the money they earn from selling it is a significant portion of their income.

Like loss of habitat and poaching animals only for their hides or tusks (leaving the meat for vultures and insects), hunting for bushmeat threatens African wildlife with extinction. In the past, human populations were small and hunting was less of a threat to the survival of any given animal species; also, certain types of bushmeat were reserved only for the chief. Modern times have brought larger populations, the development of urban elites willing to pay high prices for favorite bushmeat, roads connecting rural villages to large cities, and airports connecting Africa to the outside world. The resultant commercial trade in bushmeat has caused many ecologists to be concerned about the possible extinction of certain species. As populations and incomes grow, the demand for bushmeat is likely to increase. Logging activities in virgin forests, which bring roads and trucks to undeveloped areas, have the unintended consequence of connecting rural hunters to urban markets, and many logging workers supplement their income by being bushmeat middlemen, in addition to consuming bushmeat themselves. Hunting is generally a laissez-faire enterprise, and national and international regulations concerning wildlife and hunting are usually ignored. Any awareness among rural people of the need to preserve wildlife is outweighed by their need for food and money. It is easy for people outside of Africa to criticize their customs and actions, but it should be remembered that Africans are not the first to hunt an animal to extinction, as the history of aurochs, dodo birds, passenger pigeons, and other species makes clear.

kola nuts, brochettes (shish kabobs), roasted peanuts, soft drinks, and various fruits are seen on urban streets and near bus and taxi stops and train depots.

Generally, the traditional Central African meal is not followed by a dessert course. Sweet snacks include sugar cane, fruits, and European-style candies.

Food and Eating Customs

Traditionally, women and girls do the cooking. Men and guests eat apart from women and children. Oftentimes, breakfast is leftovers from the prior evening, a snack is eaten during the day, and a large meal is eaten in the early afternoon. People have adopted the Western custom of three meals a day, with certain foods, like bread and coffee, eaten primarily for breakfast.

Many other Western influences are seen in Central African cuisine. In urban areas, much of the diet of well-to-do consumers would be familiar to any European or American: hamburgers, pizza, and ice cream. Even in small towns, people can obtain imported spaghetti, canned meats and vegetables, and L'Arome Maggi® bouillon cubes (which seem to be essential for cooking). In both urban and rural areas, farmers and traders sell locally produced foodstuffs in open-air markets. Cities also have sprawling markets that are busy from sunrise until late at night, while small-town markets may be open only one day a week. In rural areas, households sell farm produce and bushmeat on the roadside, displaying it on a barrel or table. It is common to see urban dwellers lugging home large sacks of food after a visit to the countryside.

Festivals and Celebrations

People in Central Africa celebrate Christmas, New Year's, the end of the school year, and marriage with parties and family gatherings. African religious festivals and ceremonies, however, vary from one group to another. Many ethnic groups celebrate the *nkanda* or *mukanda*, which are initiations for young people. They signify the beginning of adulthood and may include ceremonial songs and dances, special teachings given in seclusion, induction to secret societies, circumcision, and symbolic death and rebirth. There may be special foods that are consumed only on these occasions, and there is always an emphasis on having plenty of food, preparing elaborate dishes, and, perhaps, obtaining imported food and drink. The African-influenced Christian Kimbanguist Church prohibits eating pork or monkey or drinking alcohol.

Central African cuisine will no doubt continue to adapt to new circumstances and adopt new influences. More attention should be paid to this relatively little-known area.

See also **Banana and Plantain; Game; Hunting and Gathering; Nuts; United States: African American Foodways**.

BIBLIOGRAPHY

Conrad, Joseph. *Heart of Darkness and Selections from The Congo Diary.* New York: Modern Library, 1999. Classic account of the Congo Free State.

Food and Agriculture Organization. *FAO Global Information and Early Warning System on Food and Agriculture.* Special Report. Rome: FAO. Available at http://www.fao.org/giews/.

Food and Agriculture Organization. *Crop and Food Supply Situation in Kinshasa and the Provinces of Bas-Congo and Bandundu of the Democratic Republic of Congo.* Rome: Food and Agriculture Organization, 2000.

Forbath, Peter. *The River Congo: The Discovery, Exploration, and Exploitation of the World's Most Dramatic River.* Boston: Houghton Mifflin, 1991.

Grace, M. R. "Cassava Processing." FAO Plant Production and Protection Series No. 3. Rome: Food and Agriculture Organization of the United Nations, 1977.

National Research Council (U.S.), Board on Science and Technology for International Development. *Grains.* Lost Crops of Africa, vol. 1. Washington, D.C.: National Academy Press, 1996.

Hachten, Harva. *Kitchen Safari: A Gourmet's Tour of Africa.* New York: Atheneum, 1970.

Hochschild, Adam. *King Leopold's Ghost: A Story of Greed, Terror, and Heroism in Colonial Africa.* Boston: Houghton Mifflin, 1998.

Kingsolver, Barbara. *The Poisonwood Bible: A Novel.* New York: HarperFlamingo, 1998. Missionary family in Belgian Congo, as colonial era ends.

Meditz, Sandra W., and Tim Merrill, eds. *Zaire: A Country Study.* Washington, D.C.: Federal Research Division, Library of Congress, 1994.

Naipaul, V. S. *A Bend in the River.* New York: Vintage Books, 1980. Novel set in early independence-era Kisangani, Zaire.

Post, Laurens van der. *First Catch Your Eland.* New York: Morrow, 1978.

Reader, John. *Africa: A Biography of the Continent.* New York: Knopf, 1998.

Turnbull, Colin M. *The Forest People.* New York: Simon and Schuster, 1961.

Tayler, Jeffrey. *Facing the Congo.* St. Paul, Minn.: Ruminator Books, 2000. Recent voyage down Congo River.

Van Sertima, Ivan. *They Came before Columbus.* New York: Random House, 1976.

Viola, Herman J., and Carolyn Margolis, eds. *Seeds of Change: A Quincentennial Commemoration.* Washington, D.C.: Smithsonian Institution Press, 1991.

Winternitz, Helen. *East Along the Equator: A Journey up the Congo and into Zaire.* New York: Atlantic Monthly Press, 1987.

Ed Gibbon

EAST AFRICA

East Africa comprises ten countries: Tanzania, Burundi, Rwanda, Uganda, Sudan, Ethiopia, Eritrea, Djibouti, Somalia, and Kenya. Among residents of this region, the name Eastern Africa usually refers to these ten countries, while the name East Africa means the political region comprising Kenya, Uganda, and Tanzania. In this article East Africa refers exclusively to the ten countries mentioned. This region covers an area of about 2.3 million square miles and in 2002 had a population of about 190 million people. East Africa has over 500 linguistically distinct communities, which fall into five distinct groups: the Bantu, Nilotic, Cushitic, Sudanic, and Semitic peoples. This area is also home to many people of Arabian, Indian, and European origin.

Besides being ethnically diverse, East Africa is extremely geographically diverse. Bounded to the east by the Red Sea and the Indian Ocean, the land rises (often on a plateau) to the Ethiopian and East African highlands, which contain five of the highest mountain peaks in Africa, such as Mount Kilimanjaro. Dividing these highlands is the Great Rift Valley. In East Africa, where it forms two arms (eastern and western), the Great Rift Valley has a series of lakes on its floor and all around it. All these geographical features have a heavy influence on the climate of the region, which has extremes of temperatures, humidity, and precipitation. Most of the lowland areas are hot and dry. Djibouti, regarded as the warmest city in the world, has a mean annual temperature of 86°F. Seventy-five percent of the region is either arid or semiarid, the Horn of Africa and upper half of Sudan being extremely arid. Rainfall is erratic, and there is a high incidence of famine in the region. The highlands are generally cooler and receive more precipitation. Near the equator, the rainfall has two peaks per year.

Much of the agriculture is concentrated in the highlands and around the Great Lakes of East Africa, and these areas contain the highest concentration of people. Ninety percent of East African people are employed in agriculture and livestock, with the highlands being used mainly for crop production and the dryer lowlands for animal production.

The great diversity in East Africa's climate, physical features, and ethnic groups is reflected in its food culture. This culture is further enriched by the long history of interactions with people from other continents, especially the Arabian and Indian peninsulas.

Introduction to East African Food Culture

Perhaps some of the best and oldest evidence of what human ancestors ate can be found in Olorgesailie, a historical site on the floor of the Great Eastern Rift Valley that is about 40 miles (66 kilometers) south of Nairobi, Kenya. This hot, dusty site located in a semidesert scrub was once (during the Stone Age) a lake in a lush environment that teemed with wildlife. At this site, thousands of wedgelike stone tools (handaxes, cleavers, scrapers, knives) of varying sizes litter the ground. These were the tools that human ancestors fashioned skillfully and used to dig for food and to tear up their kill, probably antelopes, giraffes, and other ungulates that came to drink water at the shores of this lake.

About five thousand years ago, much of East Africa was occupied by hunters and gatherers, commonly referred to as *ndorobo*. Although a few of these people still exist, most of these groups were assimilated by later migrants and therefore lost their identity, including their food culture. With spears, snares, and poisoned arrows they hunted big and small game—from rabbits and dik-diks to buffalo, giraffes, and elephants, and in some cases stray cat and dog families, as well. The practice of hunting still exists in East Africa, but only at low levels since it is forbidden in most countries. Gathering wild foods—such as fruits, nuts, tubers, honey, grasshoppers, caterpillars, termites, eggs, and some birds—was also an important way of acquiring food for ancestors who lived in this region. Today the contribution of gathering is less significant but many aspects of it remain. For example, during the rain season, the flying reproductive forms of termites (*tsiswa* in Luhyia) emerge from termite mounds. These are trapped, dried or roasted, and eaten or preserved in honey, or used as a snack and occasionally in sauce. A variety of caterpillars (*maungu* in Giriama) are also harvested and eaten. Wild birds that resemble a small chicken, such as *tsisindu* in Luhyia or *aluru* in Luo, are considered delicacies. Tubers and nuts obtained from the ground are a source of energy and water among people who herd livestock. The Maasai potato (*oloiropiji* or *Ipomoea longituba*), which is characterized by a flat taste, may weigh up to nine pounds and contains enough water to last a herder a whole day.

The key animals that are raised in East Africa are cattle, sheep, goats, camels, pigs, and donkeys. Cattle, which are the most important of these, were introduced into the region from North Africa in 3000–2000 B.C.E. and are the economic base for livestock keepers/ pastoralists who live in drier regions. The foods of livestock-raising groups are animal based, with milk products being by far the most important. Milk is obtained from camels, cows, goats, and occasionally sheep. It is taken fresh or is fermented in containers—mainly gourds

(*kuat* in Sudan or *kibuyu* in Swahili) or hollowed-out wood, as is the case with many pastoralists to the north and east of the region. The milk is then churned to make butter and sour milk (*rob* in Arabic or *chechirot* in Dinka), which are very popular foods in southern Sudan and among pastoralists. A variety of sticks are burned in such milk containers to disinfect and to impart a nice flavor to the milk. A popular tree for this purpose is the African olive (*oloirien* in Maasai or *Olea europaea* ssp. *africana*). The Somali community adds the aromatic hoary basil (*Ocimum americanum*) to milk as a flavoring. Butter, which was a major item of barter trade in the past, is used in preparing other foods or is mixed with other foods to add flavor. Milk, which people often drink sweetened with sugar, may be used as an accompaniment for *ugali* or *sima* (*asida* in Sudan), which is a type of stiff porridge.

To most pastoralists, fresh blood obtained by darting the jugular vein of an animal (usually a cow) is an important food, especially during times of food shortage. Blood is normally mixed with milk and stirred vigorously into a uniform brown mixture. Among the Somali, fresh blood from goat (*diik*) is recommended for women after delivering babies. A more common use of blood is stuffing it in the intestines of an animal (with spices) and cooking or roasting them. This dish, called *mutura*, is usually served in the form of large sausagelike segments. Bone soup is also popular among pastoralists. Plant parts such as bark of *olkiloriti* (Maasai for *Acacia nilotica*) are used both as a flavoring for soup and as medicine. Pork is not allowed in most of Ethiopia and among the Muslim communities, and is not tolerable in many communities. Its consumption, however, is well established in fast foods.

Agriculture is, by far, the most important production system in East Africa. Agriculture in Eastern Africa was pioneered by Cushitic speakers from the Ethiopian highlands. Other cultivators came in from the south, west (Bantu), and northwest (Nilotes). The earliest food crops of most agriculturalists included sorghum, finger and pearl millets, hyacinth (lablab) beans, Bambara groundnuts, bottle gourds, cowpeas, and yams. East African farmers eventually acquired a number of Asian crops such as banana, cocoyams, and sugar cane, as well as crops from South America, such as pumpkins, cassava (manioc), groundnut, and sweet potato. In the years following the explorations of Christopher Columbus, East Africa began to receive American crops such as maize, peanuts (groundnuts), kidney beans, and potatoes, as well as European cabbage and kales. Such foods quickly spread in popularity during the colonization era (c. 1850–1960) and became the most important foods in the region. In spite of these more recent introductions, many cultural groups retained their traditional foods, but with modified preparations.

Common Foods of the East African Peoples

Over the years, East African communities have developed and adopted specific recipes. In southern Sudan the more common foods are milk (sour or fresh), *kisira* (a type of pancake), rice, *asida* (*ugali*, or stiff porridge), and fish. In Ethiopia, typical foods would be *injera/firfir*, *kichah* (spiced pancake), *dabo* (bread), and *bula* (*ensete*, or stiff porridge). These are normally served with a variety of hot sauces (*wat*, or *watt*) on one large tray for the entire family. In Somalia the more common foods include milk (camel and cow), *canjeero* (a type of *enjera*), pasta, *otkac/nyirnyir* (dried meat), *xalwa* (a type of dessert), and *labee* (blood). In Kenya the most common foods include *ugali*, *githeri* (a mixture of maize and a pulse—that is, seeds of legumes, such as chickpeas, lentils, field peas, peanuts), *pilau* (spiced rice cooked with meat), and *chapati*. In Tanzania, *wali/pilau* and *makande* (a mixture of maize and beans) are common dishes. In Uganda, a common food is steamed *matooke* (banana) and also sweet potato and cassava products served with groundnut sauce. In Uganda *ugali* is a rather recent dish and is not very popular. In Rwanda and Burundi, beans cooked with vegetables and other starchy foods such as sweet potatoes, cassava, and green bananas are most popular. A type of ugali made from cassava—*ubuswage*—is also common.

In the inland part of Kenya, food preparations tend to be simple. Frying with oil and onion is the most popular way of improving food flavor. However, preparations are more complex and time-consuming in coastal parts of Kenya and Tanzania, where the use of coconut as a flavoring is widespread. Consequently, the foods in these regions are tastier than in inland regions. In Sudan some preparations, especially those involving food fermentation, are quite elaborate and may take up to two weeks to complete. In Uganda, steaming food that is wrapped in banana leaves is popular for preparing things such as sweet potatoes, *ugali*, bananas, cassava, vegetables, yams, and cocoyams. Of all the East African countries, Ethiopia seems to have the most elaborate food preparation methods, usually involving fermentation and spicing, especially with hot pepper.

Maize, sorghum, and millets. In the last quarter of the twentieth century, maize replaced sorghum as the most important cereal in East Africa. It is common to see people in urban areas fanning a charcoal fire in the streets and roasting fresh soft maize. Passersby buy this roasted maize (*mahindi ya kuchoma*) and eat it as they walk. Green maize is also boiled in water (*amakhaye* in Kisa), with or without the inner covers, and is salted and eaten just like roasted maize. Alternatively, fresh maize is removed from the cob and boiled fresh or when dry (*inete*). Among the Somali, fresh maize (*galeey*) is fried in oil and taken as a snack. Dry maize is fried in sesame oil to make popcorn (*salol*), which is often served with coffee to men as they chew khat (*miraa*).

Another popular East African food is *githeri*. This is basically a boiled mixture of fresh or dry maize with seeds from beans, garden peas, lablab beans, groundnuts, cowpeas, and pigeon peas. *Githeri* may be consumed alone or mixed with leafy greens or stews, especially meat stew.

When *githeri* is cooked with potatoes or cocoyams and occasionally leafy greens (mainly leaves of pumpkin, cocoyams, or Malabar gourd) and mashed, the sticky green substance that results is called *mukimo*. Among the Taita of Kenya, mukimo is made by mashing cooked cassava, sweet potatoes, or plantain with leguminous seeds, and it is known as *kimanga* or *shibe*.

Muthokoi (*naamis* in Mbulu) is a dish similar to *githeri*, but it is prepared from dry maize that has been processed to remove the tough seed coat (testa). In the Arusha region of Tanzania, cooked maize (*makande*) and rice are mixed with sour milk and served. A dry mashed mixture of maize and beans is mixed with smoked, nearly ripe bananas and mashed. This food, called *mangararu* by the Meru of northern Tanzania (*makukuru* in Swahili), can last for several days.

Ugali (sima). Probably the most important food in East Africa is *ugali* or *sima* (*asida* in Arabic, *kun* in Dinka, *kawunga* in Baganda, *akaro* in Banyankore, *buro* in Banyoro). *Ugali* is a sticky, moist dish that is made by mixing flour from a starchy food (mainly cereal and usually maize, but it can also be sorghum, finger millet, pearl millet, wheat, and occasionally cassava, or a mixture of any of these) in hot water and cooking as one mixes the substance to a paste that varies in consistency from place to place. *Ugali* by itself has a mild taste. It is usually eaten with one's fingers. It may be eaten with sour fermented milk, a vegetable stew (for example, beans, cowpeas, pigeon pea, green gram), meat stew, green vegetables, chicken, or fish. In the Lake Victoria region, fish is a common accompaniment. The combination of roasted meat (commonly known as *nyama-choma*) and *ugali* is considered a delicacy in beer-drinking places. *Ugali* is very filling and is known for its ability to make people sleepy; hence it is good for the evenings.

Ugali made from finger millet (sometimes mixed with sorghum) is popular among the Banyankore, Bakiga, Batoro, and Banyoro of western Uganda. Among the Karimojong of northeast Uganda and the neighboring Turkana of Kenya, a soft type of *ugali* (locally known as *atapa*) is often made from sorghum or pearl millet and is usually taken with sour milk, which may occasionally be mixed with animal blood.

Ugali made from cassava is common in the Lake Victoria region and in Burundi (*ubuswage/ubutsima bw'imyumbati*). Large balls of this *ugali* are wrapped in banana leaves (*imitoto*) and stored in a basket. These are picked and served with fish (*ifi*). Among the Lugbara and Madi of northwest Uganda, cassava flour is often mixed with millet or sorghum flour to prepare a type of *ugali* known as *enya* (Lugbara) or *linya* (Madi). The Iteso of Eastern Uganda and neighboring Kenya make a similar type of *ugali*, which is often eaten with groundnut paste.

In Ethiopia's Oromia region, a soft type of *ugali*, locally known as *genffo*, is prepared from wheat or maize flour and is served on a plate. A hole is then made in the

A bounty of colorful, fragrant fruits and vegetables await buyers in this African market. PHOTO BY DAVID K. O'NEIL.

middle and butter and powdered pepper and some salt are added. A more elaborate preparation is that of a breakfast food known as *kijo*. These are balls or lumps of fine, half-fermented maize starch wrapped in maize leaves and cooked by dipping the balls in boiling water. Each ball is given to one person and it is eaten with fresh or sour milk, tea, or coffee.

Another type of *ugali* is *chenga*, which is made from coarsely ground maize. Chenga is usually eaten with sour milk. In southern Sudan, sorghum is used to prepare a type of chenga, which is served with sour milk (*amok*, *chekipiu*), fish (*rech*), or meat (*ring*). This food is served at weddings and special ceremonies surrounding the event of a woman's first menstruation. Among the Kamba of Kenya, cleaned sorghum seeds are boiled with pigeon peas (*ngima ya munyala*). In southern Sudan, millet is also used to prepare a type of chenga known as *dukun* (Arabic) or *awuo* (Dinka). It is served with groundnut sauce (*mulaa keimot*) and mixed with fish stew.

Sour *ugali* is popular among peoples of southern Sudan. It is made from fermented maize or sorghum flour (*akilamuat* or *kun ayupwach*) or sour milk in water (*akileben* or *kuncha*) or tamarind water (*asidamot/akilamot kunchuei*). *Ugali* is occasionally eaten with ghee (*zet*, *miok*) instead of milk. This is popular in southern Sudan (where it is called *kundiung*) and among pastoralists. It is common to find the Wambulu of Tanzania eating this dish (*faa*) as they sit on mats.

Porridge (gruel).

Porridge (*uji* in Swahili) is a popular breakfast food in East Africa. It is a healthy food, especially for children and breast-feeding mothers, as it is easy to digest and provides both water and energy in readiness for the day. However, tea has replaced porridge as a breakfast food in most parts of East Africa, which has further complicated the problem of malnutrition.

Porridge is mainly made from cereals. Depending on the area, porridge may be thin or thick and may be flavored with sugar, salt, lemon, tamarind, baobab, coconut, cow ghee/butter, or milk. Probably the most delicious type of porridge is the fermented type, *obusera obupuute* (Kisa). Preparation of this dish, however, is tedious and time-consuming. In some areas this dish has cultural significance: Among the Kikuyu of central Kenya, a circumcised boy stayed in seclusion for a certain period, after which a caretaker (*mutiili*) led him to his mother's house, where the boy was served fermented porridge (*ucuru wa mukio*) as a sign of welcome. Finger millet (*wimbi*) porridge is the most popular of all porridges in East Africa.

Rice (wali).

Rice is an important dish for the Ethiopian, Asian, and Muslim communities in East Africa. A common dish is *wali usambara*, which is rice prepared with coconut milk, salt, and a bit of oil. *Biriani* is a very spicy dish composed of rice (usually spiced) and spiced meat or chicken stews. *Pilau* is a spicy mixture of meat stew and rice that is popular both inland and in coastal areas. Spices in this dish include coriander, cardamom, cumin, pepper, cinnamon, cloves, onion, and garlic. *Pilau* is a popular dish in ceremonies all over the region. Preparing pilau is a delicate undertaking that requires a lot of patience and is usually performed by several women working together. *Pilau* is often eaten with spiced stews. *Wali ubwabwa* is a soft type of rice that cooks as one stirs it. *Mkate wa sinia* is made from rice flour mixed with yeast, water, sugar, and coconut milk and heated from below and above. All of these dishes are common in coastal areas.

Wheat products.

Some amount of wheat is grown in the dryer highlands of East Africa, especially in Ethiopia and Kenya. Probably the most popular wheat food in the region is the Asian flat, round, thin bread widely known as *chapati*. Chapati is mainly served with stews, hot beverages, and soft drinks. In general, bread (*mkate* in Swahili, *dabo* in Amharic) has gained increasing importance in East Africa and now is the most popular starchy food for breakfast in urban areas.

The greatest variety of wheat products is found in Ethiopia. These include *kichah*, a dish made from a mixture of onions fried in oil and wheat flour. Another wheat product is *chechebsa*, which is cooked with *teff* (a type of cereal grass). Small pieces of salted dough (*lite*) are cooked on a pan without oil to a brown bread. This is buttered and spiced with pepper. *Fettira* is a thin breakfast bread made from wheat and egg and eaten with butter or yogurt.

Arakip (Arabic) or *ayup* (Dinka) is a type of dry bread prepared from maize, sorghum, wheat, or millet flour in Sudan. This bread is popular with people looking after cattle. *Kisira* (*kun pioth* in Dinka) is a Sudanese pancake like *enjera* that is prepared from maize or sorghum flour mixed with a little wheat and water. This pancake is served with beans, okra, or okra mixed with meat or *ayak* (*Corchorus*), a mucilaginous vegetable.

A whole range of wheat products, generally of European or Asian origin, are available in East African restaurants and homes. Common products include samosas (*sambusa, isambusa*), *kaimati, mandazi* and the related *mahamri*, and French bread, to name a few. *Mandazi* (*imandazi, ibitumbula* in Burundi), as they are called in Kiswahili, and the related mahamri are very popular types of buns served in restaurants. *Mandazi* are made by mixing dough with baking powder and sugar, while in mahamri the dough is mixed with yeast and often coconut milk. Both are cooked briefly in oil. In Dar es Salaam it is customary to eat *mandazi* with cooked beans (*maharage*). The mixture is called *zege*, and it is eaten along with tea for breakfast. *Kaimati*, on the other hand, is spherical and more solid than *mahamri*.

Cakes are most popular in formal ceremonies, especially weddings. Among the Luhyia, a popular cake is made by mixing ripe banana and maize flour, which is then kneaded into a dough, cut into balls, and wrapped in banana leaves and steamed in water. This sweet traditional cake (*omukati kwe lisotsi*) is served with tea or porridge.

Barley. *Cheko* (Ethiopia) is a type of spiced bread made from barley. Barley is also used to make a type of porridge known as *baso*. This is often flavored with honey, sugar, salt, and butter.

Teff. Teff (*Eragrostis tef*), a type of cereal grass, is grown traditionally only in Ethiopia, particularly in the western region. Most teff is made into *enjera* (*injera*), a huge, flat, flabby, rather elastic, and slightly sour pancake that is eaten with spicy meat or vegetable stews such as *doro watt* (hot, spiced chicken curry), *sega watt* (lamb sauce), and *key watt* (hot, spiced beef sauce). One tears off pieces of the pancake and uses them to scoop or roll the stews. Enjera is a typical food in Ethiopian restaurants all over the region. The Somali type of *enjera* (*canjeero*) is usually made from a mixture of maize and wheat and is often flavored with garlic and *iliki*. Sugar and milk cream are usually added to breakfast enjera. Enjera may also be made from a mixture of rice and wheat.

Cassava. Cassava is important at the coastal areas and among the Iteso and Luo of Lake Victoria basin and their relatives in Uganda, the Acholi, Langi, and Alur. Dry cassava can be roasted or boiled or eaten fresh. In the coastal region, fried cassava is flavored with lemon and powdered pepper and eaten with tea. Cassava is also deep-fried (*mgazija wa kukalanga* in Giriama). Cassava leaves (*mchicha kisamvu*) are used as a vegetable throughout the region.

Potato (English/Irish potato). Potatoes are used to make a popular stew (called *karanga* in Kenya) of carrots, tomatoes, meat, and onions. These are usually served with *ugali*, *chapati*, or *wali* (rice). Chips, or french fries, are the most popular foods in fast-food kiosks and are usually served with pork or beef sausages. In Burundi,

chips are also prepared from green bananas (*ibitoke*) and sweet potatoes (*ibijumbu*).

Tannia and cocoyams or taro. Tannia (*Xanthosoma sagittifolium*, called *Marumi* in the Meru region of Tanzania) is commonly used in Uganda and parts of Tanzania, especially among the Chagga, Ameru, and Arusha peoples. The tubers may be cooked with meat, beans, and maize or boiled and eaten with tea.

Cocoyams or taro (*Colacasia esculenta*), on the other hand, are widespread in the region and are commonly planted along water courses. The tubers are prepared in the same manner as tannia. Both tannia and cocoyams are popular breakfast foods.

Yams. In East Africa yams (*Dioscorea*) come in various types and include such varieties as the aerial yam or air potato, whose tubers are borne on the stems. Yams are prepared in the same ways as tannia and cocoyams.

Bananas and plantains. Many varieties of bananas exist in East Africa. Different varieties are used for brewing beer and cooking, and others are eaten when ripe, such as *kisukari* (Swahili) or *igisukari* (Burundi). *Kisimiti* and *kibungara* (found in the Mount Meru section of Tanzania) are varieties used to make traditional beers called banana and *mbege*. Also in Mount Meru, the soft varieties of bananas called Uganda and *ng'ombe* are preferred for meat and maize dishes. A cooked mixture of *ndizi ng'ombe* and maize meal, served with milk, is known as *loshoro* and is a favorite food for the Arusha. In Tanzania, mashed beans and bananas (*kishumba*) are often served as a wedding cake with *dengelwa* (local sugar cane beer).

Green bananas (*matooke*) are the most important foods of the Baganda of Uganda. They are usually wrapped in banana leaves, steamed, and then mashed and eaten with a variety of steamed sauces usually containing groundnuts.

Ensete. Ensete (*enset*) is a bananalike plant (*Ensete edule*) exploited in southern Ethiopia for its pseudo-stem and leaf midribs—a source of a starchy product that is the staple food of parts of Ethiopia. This starch is fermented in the ground for periods lasting weeks or months. It is made into several products, including *kocho* (bread) and *bula* (porridge). *Kocho* is usually eaten with *kittifo* (*kitfo*)—hand-minced beef mixed with butter and pepper and served raw or cooked. A major disadvantage of ensete is its low protein content.

Beans (kidney bean, common bean) and peas. In Rwanda and Burundi beans are eaten for breakfast, lunch, supper, and as a snack. They are cooked with starchy foods such as sweet potatoes, green bananas, cocoyams, and cassava, as well as leafy green and fruit vegetables. In coastal parts of Tanzania, beans (*maharage*) are cooked in coconut milk (*tui*) and served with *ugali*. Among the Giriama of Kenya this stew is known as *borohowa ya maharagwe*.

Other pulses commonly made into stews are cowpeas and green grams, locally known as *pojo* or *ndengu*. Pojo stew (*borohowa ya pojo*) goes well with chapati, but it is also eaten with ugali and rice. In Ethiopia meat is prohibited during fast days. In such times, chickpeas, lentils, field peas, peanuts, and other pulses are used to make the local sauces and stews, *watt*, and *alechi*.

Bambarra groundnuts. Bambara (*Vigna subterranea*) seeds are boiled with maize (usually after overnight soaking) to make a type of githeri (*amenjera ke tsimbande* in Luhyia) usually eaten as a snack. These seeds are also fried like groundnuts.

Groundnuts and other nuts. Groundnuts (*ibiyoba* in Burundi) are the most widely grown nuts in the region and are eaten raw, roasted, boiled, or in stews. In southern Sudan, ground roasted groundnuts are mixed with honey and eaten.

Groundnuts are extremely important in Uganda as they are used to make the most commonly used sauce—groundnut sauce—that is used to eat most starch foods. The sauce is usually mixed with meat, mushrooms, fish, chicken, or just tomatoes.

Among the Somali, a mixture of *iliki*, roasted groundnuts, and sugar is fried in ghee (*subag*) to make a sticky jellylike substance called *xalwa*, which is usually served with coffee or as a dessert after meals. Cashew nuts are grown in coastal areas and are a popular snack.

Gild (*Cordeauxia edulis*) is an evergreen shrub in the bean family that produces seeds called *yeheb* (*yihib*), which are eaten like nuts. These are very popular with Somali pastoralists. The inner part of marula fruit seeds (*Sclerocarya birrea*) is eaten fresh or roasted.

Fish. The most popular type of fish (*samaki*, *rech*) in East Africa is the tilapia (mainly *Oreochromis niloticus*) or *ngege*. People along the shores of Lake Victoria often enjoy this dish with ugali. The large Nile perch (*Lates niloticus*) is not as popular as talapia, but it provides large quantities of meat, which are usually made into fish balls. Another common fish is the small sardinelike fish (*Rastrineobola argentea*) known by the names *omena* (Luo) and *dagaa* (Swahili). These cheap sources of protein are dried and sold in tins in most urban markets.

Meat. Meat (*nyama*, *ring*) is used to prepare a variety of sauces and stews (*mchuzi* in Swahili and *watt* in Amharic). In Ethiopia, *quanta* is meat that is cut in long pieces, smeared with powdered pepper, salted, and dried by hanging it above the fireplace for five to seven days. This meat is used to make a hot stew, *quanta watt*, which is served with enjera or mixed with broken pieces of enjera and eaten as *quanta firfir* (Amharic) or *sukume* (Oromic). Among the Luo of Kenya, such dried meat is known as *aliya* and is made into a stew that is eaten with ugali. Among the Somali, dried meat (*otkac* or *nyirnyir*) is usually prepared from camel meat (*hilib gel*). Strips of sun-dried meat are cut into small pieces that are fried (usually in oil with garlic and *iliki*) and immersed in camel ghee (*subag*). Nyirnyir can last for several months and is usually served with tea, honey, chapati, and enjera. During breakfast, nyirnyir is served only to men. Preserved camel's meat and dates are served during Somali weddings. The date pulp is separated from the seed, mashed, and put around the preserved meat. On the wedding day, the meat basket is covered with a white cloth as a sign of purity or virginity. The dates and meat are served by the bride's mother to her new in-laws.

In Sudan, most of the meat from a slaughtered animal is dried (*shermout*). The layer of fat around the stomach is also dried and is called *miriss*. Internal organs may also be dried, pounded, mixed with some potash, and molded into a ball that is allowed to dry slowly to make *twini-digla*. The large intestine may also be cleaned and stuffed with fat and hung to dry as a type of sausage.

A common way of serving meat is to pile pieces of meat and sweet pepper on a stick and roast them. This type of meat, known as *mshikaki* (*mshakiki*, *umushikaki* in Burundi), is very common in the streets of coastal towns in the evening.

Chicken. Most households in East Africa raise chickens, which are usually prepared for guests. The various parts of the chicken hold significance in different regions. In western Kenya, for example, the tail part of the chicken is reserved for the male head of a family. Among the Kamba of Kenya, a gizzard is served to the most important person in a group of visitors, while among the Luhyia the gizzard (*imondo*) is never shared. If two people did share it, it is believed they would always be in disagreement.

Milk and milk products. The nomadic tribes of Sudan make a type of cheese called *kush-kush* eaten with sorghum porridge. Camel herders put milk into a skin bag that is fastened to the saddle of a camel, and the milk (*gariss*) is allowed to ferment. This is a major source of food for the herders as they roam with their animals in remote areas.

In the twentieth century many dairy products entered the Sudan from the North, including *jibnabeida* (white cheese), *zabadi* (yogurt), and black cumin-flavored *mish* (Dirar, Harper, and Collins, p. 20).

Meat substitutes. In rural western Sudan, a popular substitute for the meat flavor is *kawal*, a strong-smelling product derived from a two-week long fermentation of the pounded green leaves of the wild legume *Cassia obtusifolia*. In the same region, the oil seedcake remaining after oil extraction from sesame seed (*Sesamum orientale*) is fermented for a week to make *sigda*, another meat substitute. Sigda is usually consumed in a vegetable stew. *Furundu*, a similar meat substitute, is prepared from the seeds of *karkade* or red sorrel (*Hibiscus sabdariffa*). All these products are dried after fermentation in the form of hard, irregular, small balls and may keep for a year or so.

Leafy vegetables. Many leafy vegetables are used as an accompaniment for starchy foods such as ugali. These vegetables are prepared in a variety of ways—in many cases as a mixture. Common traditional leafy vegetables include baobab, cowpea, amaranth, vine spinach (*Basella alba*), Ethiopian kale (*Brassica carinata*), spiderplant (*Cleome gynandra*), jute (*Corchorus olitorius*), crotalaria, sweet potato, water spinach (*Ipomoea aquatica*), African nightshades (*Solanum* species), hibiscus (*Hibiscus sabdariffa*), *Oxygonum sinuatum*, African eggplants (*Solanum* species), pumpkin, cocoyam, bean, and cassava. Ethiopian kale (*gommen*) is important during fast days in Ethiopia when meat is prohibited. It is used to make local sauces, alecha. A few nontraditional leafy vegetables like cabbage have gained importance in the last few decades. Kale (*Sukuma wiki*), introduced in the twentieth century, is now the most highly consumed vegetable in urban parts of Kenya.

Fruit. A wide range of traditional and exotic fruits are consumed in East Africa, usually as snacks. Mango, citrus fruits, banana, jackfruit, papaya, melons, guava, passion fruit, custard apple, and avocado pear are all common market fruits. Many of the traditional fruits are picked in the wild, such as baobab (*Adansonia digitata*), wild custard apple, saba, carissa, dialium, flacourtia (Indian plum), marula, vangueria, tamarind, vitex, and jujube.

The dry cream-colored pulp of baobab, which is sour-to-sweet in taste, is eaten raw or may be dissolved in water and stirred to a milky state, at which time the seeds are sieved off and the juice is used as a sauce or for sour porridge. The pulp-coated seeds (*mabuyu*) are colored, sugar-coated, and sold as sweets in coastal towns (Swahili).

Beverages. In general, traditional East African cultures do not favor the use of juices. Juice made from ripe banana (*umutobe*) is commonly served in Rwanda, and a hot drink and juice made from *karkade* (*Hibiscus sabdariffa*) are common in Sudan, but these are exceptions. However, a great variety of alcoholic drinks are made in the region. *Muratina* is a common weak beer served in rural parts of Kenya. It is prepared from honey, sugar, or sugar cane and is named after the fermenting agent, the sausage tree fruit (*Kigelia africana*). The Maasai use aloe root (*osuguroi*) in place of sausage tree fruit for fermentation.

Busaa (Luhyia) or *amarwa* (Baganda) is an alcoholic drink as well as a food. It is made mainly from sorghum, maize, or millet flour. In Rwanda, a similar type of drink—*ikigage*—is consumed as a drink and as food. Among the neighboring Bakinga of southwest Uganda, a similar drink called *omuramba* is made from sorghum. However, a more popular drink in Rwanda is *urwangwa*, which is made from ripe banana. It is popular in ceremonies and among men when discussing important issues.

In Ethiopia, *berize* (Amharic, Oromic) is prepared with honey and the boiled stems of a tree called *gesho* (*Rhamnus prinioides*). Berize is fermented to a weak,

A Kenyan woman is shown chopping mallow leaves to make a traditional stew that is eaten with fish and *ugali*. *Ugali* is stiff cornmeal dough pressed against the elbow to make a cup, which is then used as an edible scoop. PHOTO BY Y. MORIMOTO.

amber-colored wine called *tej* (*t'ej*). It is served in special long-necked bottles after meals in ceremonies. *Tella* (*talla*) is similar to Kenyan busaa but is prepared by fermenting roasted maize flour and barley.

Mnazi or *pombe ya mnazi* is palm wine. It is a popular drink in all coastal areas where coconut trees grow. *Chang'aa* is a popular but illegal spirit made by distilling fermented grain (such as maize) or banana. It has a variety of local names, such as *kumi kumi* in Nairobi and *waraj* in western Kenya and in Uganda. The Ethiopian version of it is *katikala* (in Amharic) or *areq* (Arabic) and is usually made from finger millet. Chang'aa has over the years been responsible for a number of deaths due to unscrupulous sellers who add illegal chemicals to the beverage to increase its potency.

Sorghum is used in Sudan to brew a large variety of opaque and clear beers using complex methods. Common examples are *merissaan* (opaque beer) and *assaliya* or *um-bilbila* (clear beer). Traditional wines include *sherbot*, *nebit*, and *dakkai* made from dates that are normally found in the northern dry parts of the country. In southern Sudan, *duma* (a type of wine) is made by fermenting diluted honey.

Liralira is a local spirit of the Acholi and Lango in Uganda. It is made from finger millet and cassava flour. The neighboring Sudanic communities of Lugbara and Madi have their own brew made from cassava, known locally as *ngoli*, while the Iteso of Kenya and Uganda have a version called *ajono* that is made from finger millet. Many other alcoholic drinks are found in East Africa and go by such names as *mbege* and *karubu*.

Coffee. Although Eastern Africa is one of the largest producers of coffee, the beverage is not very popular except in its original home—Ethiopia. Among the Muslim communities of the coastal region, very strong coffee (*kahawa chungu*) is served in small cups along the streets in the evenings and early in the morning.

In Ethiopia, raw coffee (*bun*) is roasted on a pan until it turns brown. It is then spiced and ground into flour on a stone. The coffee is served in an earthenware kettle (*jebena*). Coffee-drinking is an important occasion in many communities in Ethiopia, Sudan, and Somalia. Among the Somali, coffee is served in small cups with date fruits or *xalwa*.

Tea. Tea has replaced porridge as the morning drink in many homes in East Africa. In many rural restaurants it is customary to serve tea as soon as one sits down. The common way of preparing tea in homes and in most restaurants is by boiling water and adding tea leaves and milk, all mixed together (*chai ya maziwa*). Tea without milk is popularly known as *strungi* (from "strong tea") and as *shaah biiges* in Somali. The Maragoli and Taita of Kenya value tea highly.

Stimulants. Khat (also known as Abyssinia tea or *miraa*) is a popular stimulant in East Africa. The bark from fresh young shoots is peeled off and chewed. Khat is an important plant during wedding ceremonies among the Somali and Boran of Kenya and Ethiopia.

Spices/flavorings. Probably the most widespread item used for flavor is salt. In many traditional societies, salt is a filtrate of ashes from dry bean leaves, banana peels, water reeds, sorghum head, and normal ash. Most communities used samli or ghee to flavor food. In Tanzania and most coastal parts of the region, coconut milk is also used to flavor food. Grated coconut and water are squeezed in a woven bag to produce concentrated milk.

Tea and a few other beverages are flavored with a number of things, the common being ginger (*tangawizi*) and *masala* (a mixture of spices but usually containing coriander). Tea can also be flavored with lemon grass (*Cymbopogon citratus*), lemon (*Citrus limon*), and *mjafari* (*Zanthoxylum chalybeum*). The art of flavoring is most established in Ethiopia and among the Asian community in the region. The sauces are therefore extremely hot. In Ethiopia, the powdered spice *berbere* (also *berberi* or *awaze*) has hot pepper as the main ingredient but may contain a dozen other spices. Curry powder (*bizari*), another mixture of spices (usually cardamom, turmeric,

ginger, cinnamon, and chilies) is more popular in the rest of the region. Spicing, however, seems to be more of a culture in Ethiopia and coastal regions where there has been long Islamic and Asian influence. A variety of spices are used, the more common ones being black pepper, *piper nigrum* (*pilipili manga*); cardamom, *Elettaria cardamomum* (*iliki*); chili pepper, *Capsicum annuum* (*pilipili kali*); cinnamon, *Cinnamomum verum* and *C. aromaticum* (*mdalasini*); cloves, *Syzygium aromaticum* (*karafuu*); coriander, *Coriandrum sativum* (*giligilani*); cumin, *Cuminum cyminum* (*bizari* or *nyembamba*); curry powder (*bizari*), a mixture of different spices; garlic, *Allium sativum* (*kitunguu sumu* or *kitunguu saumu*); ginger, *Zingiber officinale* (*tangawizi*); nutmeg (*kungumanga*) and mace, *Myristica fragrans* (*kungu*); sweet pepper, *Capsicum annuum* (*pilipili hoho, pilipili mboga*); tamarind, *Tamarindus indica* (*ukwaju*); and turmeric, *Curcuma longa* (*manjano*). Many of these are grown locally and for some, like cloves in Zanzibar Island, production is of world significance.

See also **Banana and Plantain**; **Cassava**; **Fermentation**; **Nuts**; **Stimulants**.

BIBLIOGRAPHY

Dirar, H. A., D. B. Harper, and M. A. Collins. "Biochemical and Microbiological Studies on Kawal, a Meat Substitute Derived by Fermentation of *Cassia obtusifolia* Leaves." *Journal of the Science of Food and Agriculture* 36 (1985): 881–892.

Maundu et al. *Traditional Food Plants of Kenya*. Nairobi: Kenrik, 1999.

Pendaeli-Sarakikya, Eva. *Tanzania Cook Book*. Dar Es Salam: Tanzania Publishing House, 1996.

Patrick M. Maundu
Maryam Imbumi

NORTH AFRICA

A Moroccan proverb says: *Mâ kainsh el-kalâm cala ettacâm*, "Where there is food, there is no talking." Indeed, as a sign of respect for the food that God has provided and the host or hostess has served, North Africans consider it impolite to converse while eating. The food itself, however, does not remain silent. Food talks. Meals convey messages. Perhaps more than anything else in North African cultural praxis, food habits constitute a rich language through which the region's history is told, social distinctions are expressed, religious feasts are celebrated, and seasonal changes and transformations in the life cycle are marked.

Historical Influences

The history of North Africa comes to the fore in both particular ingredients and dishes that are shared by most Maghrebi as well as in regional differentiation between specific dishes and ingredients. Influences from the Roman presence (200 B.C.E.–300 C.E.) can, for instance, be recognized throughout the region as wheat is the basis for the two main staple foods, bread and couscous, a steamed grain of crushed wheat or coarse flour. Islamization in the seventh century can, of course, be recognized in the prohibition of pork or wine, although flourishing vineyards can be found throughout North Africa. Arab influences that accompanied early Islamization, such as the consumption of rice, native east African vegetables such okra and *mlûkhîa* Jew's mellow (*Corchorus olitorius*) and the use of *fliyu* and mint in meat and vegetable dishes, are more pronounced in east Algeria and Tunisia than in regions further removed from the Levant, such as western Algeria and Morocco. All three countries have adopted the Arab preservation technique of drying meat, called *gedîd*, in which salt and spices are rubbed into the meat, which is then left to dry in the sun.

Morocco is the only North African country that was not occupied by the Ottoman Empire during its presence in the region (1500s–1700s). Correspondingly, dolmas, stuffed vine leaves, like Turkish and Syrian puff pastries such as baklava and *brîk*, are commonly prepared in formerly Ottoman Algeria and Tunisia, but do not feature in Moroccan cuisine. On the other hand, Algerian, Tunisian and Moroccan cookery alike have been heavily influenced by the introduction of crops from the New World such as tomatoes, courgettes, sweet peppers and potatoes. These foods were introduced to North Africa before they were introduced to central Europe. Potatoes, however, never became as popular in North Africa as they would become in Europe.

Food habits in all three North African countries discussed here have been influenced by French occupation. In Algeria, the French occupation lasted the longest (1830 to 1962). Not in the least because of the influx of a large number of French settlers, all spheres of life were influenced by it, including Algerian cuisine. Tunisia was occupied in 1881 and largely shared the same fate, at least in the cities. By the time Morocco became a French protectorate in 1912, the French occupational policy had changed. Fewer settlers were moved in, and more attention was paid to the preservation of "traditional culture." In terms of food habits, these different policies can be recognized in Morocco's being the only Magrebian country where most people still eat homemade round breads rather than bakery bought baguettes. Most city dwellers in Morocco, however, like those in Algeria and Tunisia, nowadays drink café-au-lait for breakfast. Indeed, examination of the three daily meals that are consumed throughout the Maghreb—the *ftûr* or breakfast, the *ghrdâ'* or midday meal, and the *cashâ'* or evening meal—brings to light more variations between rural and urban areas than between countries. The distinction between rural and urban food habits corresponds, albeit not exclusively, with the distinction between the poor and those who fare better economically. On the whole, for example, less meat is consumed in the countryside than in the cities, and the same is true for milk and butter. Also, in the cities, fast food chains are becoming increasingly popular and when guests come for dinner, there are always a few bottles of cola and other carbonated soft drinks on the table.

Daily Meals

In the cities breakfast usually consists of a café-au-lait with bread and butter or jam, sometimes with *La Vache Qui Rit*, wedges of processed cheese that seem to have conquered much of the developing world. The Moroccan city of Fès is famous for its *harsha*, an unleavened very thick and crusty flatbread made of crushed wheat and *arachide* or olive oil, preferably eaten with fresh cheese. Because the flatbread remains tasty for a long time, it is popular with travelers. Because it is filling, peasants are also fond of it. If leavened bread is eaten for breakfast in rural areas, it is more likely to be served with olive oil than with butter, and it is eaten with tea more often than with coffee. Heavy agricultural work demands a substantial meal, however, so that *assîda* or *bsissa*, water-based porridges of semolina or grilled barley flour, are more common rural breakfasts. Yesterday's leftovers of couscous or soup may, of course, do just as well.

Lunch. Lunch consists of a hot meal, which in Morocco is the most important meal of the day, while in Algeria and Tunisia the dishes that are served for lunch or dinner are interchangeable. Among the urban elite, especially in Algerian towns, lunch may consist of dishes from the French cuisine, such as fried meat, french fries, and salads. In Morocco and Tunisia, most people prefer to eat either a *tajîne* (tagine), a stew, also called *marqa*, or a couscous. *Marqas* tend to be more popular than couscous, especially in urban areas. Nowadays, *marqas* are almost invariably prepared in pressure cookers, but most people agree that they taste much better when prepared in a *tajîne*, the traditional cone-shaped earthenware pots that gave this kind of dish its name.

The sauce that forms the basis of a *marqa* or *tajîne* varies per region. In Morocco, saffron is traditionally used to color the basic sauce yellow. Nowadays, saffron is nearly always replaced by artificial yellow coloring powder, which is much cheaper but lacks taste. To make a *marqa*, chopped onions and garlic cloves are fried in *arachide* oil into which the (artificial) saffron is stirred. Next, fresh chopped coriander and parsley are added, then salt or "knurr," that is, stock tablets (the brand name has become the generic name) together with spices such as black pepper, paprika, cumin, and sometimes ginger and/or cinnamon. A famous mixed spice is *râs el-hânut*, "the master of the shop," which should consist of twenty spices, among which powdered rose buds and lavender, and, as tourists are meant to believe, the aphrodisiac "Spanish fly." *Râs el-hânut* is classified as a "hot" spice. Consequently, it is almost exclusively used in winter. Other "hot" spices such as black pepper, ginger, and paprika, are also used more liberally in winter than in summer, when mild spices like cumin and cinnamon are used more. After spices have been added, peeled and chopped tomatoes are put in, together with meat. Last of all, water is added, after which the sauce is left to simmer until the meat is tender.

Berber women eating traditional food from a common bowl in the Sahara Desert of Tunisia. © INGE YSPEERT/CORBIS.

Only very little water is added to the *tajîne*. The earthenware pot is placed on a charcoal burner, and it takes hours for the meat and vegetables to cook in their own juices. In Tunisia, tomatoes and *harîssa*, a chili paste, form the basis for the sauce so that the marqa is red rather than yellow. Otherwise, much the same spices are used, although cumin may be replaced with caraway. In Algeria, in regions closer to Morocco, the basic sauce is yellow, while in regions closer to Tunisia it tends to be red. Marqas are eaten with bread. In most Moroccan families, the housewife or one of her servants prepares the dough for the bread, which is then brought to the *ferrân*, the public oven, where it is preferably baked shortly before lunch, so that the bread is still slightly warm when lunch is served. Tunisian and Algerian women often reheat the bakery-bought bread before serving it.

Bread and couscous are never eaten together. While in urban areas *marqas* are prepared more often than couscous, in rural areas it is the other way around. Unlike other dishes that are associated with the countryside, however, a good couscous is considered a festive meal by urban and rural dwellers alike. Most Maghrebi eat it for Friday lunch, Friday being the most blessed day of the week. It is also a favorite dish for weddings and other big dinner parties, not in the least because it is easy to prepare in great quantities. A Friday or party couscous tends to contain more meat and a larger variety of vegetables than those eaten during the other days of the week. Meat is quite expensive in North Africa, and especially in the countryside, both daily *marqas* and different kinds of

couscous consist largely of vegetables and pulses such as chickpeas, lentils, and white beans. In coastal areas, fish, mostly deep fried, is also included.

In general, pulse-based dishes are associated with poverty. *Bisâra*, for instance, a very thick sauce of cooked dried and peeled broad beans to which lots of garlic, olive oil and cumin is added, is a much loved dish, especially in winter. Yet one would not dream of serving it to guests. The same goes for *usbân*, a Tunisian couscous with offal, the cheapest "meat" there is. Instead of these cheap—albeit delicious—meals, guests should be served dishes that consist mostly of meat, such as the originally Ottoman *l-hamm el-hlû*, cinnamon- and ginger-spiced veal, served with prunes and fried almonds, or *dajâj zîtûn*, chicken with green olives, salt lemon preserve, hard-boiled eggs, and, again, fried almonds. Throughout the Maghreb, *bstîla*, originally from Fès, has also become a favorite dish to serve guests. It is savory pie made of flaky pastry filled with pigeon or chicken that is sprinkled with cinnamon and powdered sugar before serving. The latter ingredients are also used to top off sweet couscouses that are served for dessert.

Tea and evening meal. As was mentioned before, in Algeria and Tunisia the dishes that are served for lunch or dinner are interchangeable. These meals are eaten around six or seven o'clock. In Morocco, the *cashâ'* tends to be eaten somewhere between eight and nine o'clock. This allows women to visit each other in the afternoon and have tea together, which is followed by coffee just before they go home. The green tea that is flavored with fresh mint and much sugar and may be served with *el-ghraif*, flaky pastries fried in a pan and served with honey or castor sugar, or with *beghrîr*, leavened pancakes served with honey, butter or olive oil, or *sfinj*, fritters. Although men also occasionally eat sweet pastries, throughout the Maghreb they are typically associated with women.

Because the evening meal is served rather late in Morocco, women who stay at home have tea with bread or *harsha* before they prepare dinner. Except when there are guests, dinner in Moroccan cities is light, consisting of soup, small meatballs in a tomato sauce, or milk-based porridges of rice, semolina, or pasta. In rural areas where those who work on the land have not been able to come home for lunch, dinner is the main meal and more substantial.

Meals for Special Occasions: Ramadan

During the month called Ramadan, between dawn and sunset, Muslims refrain from eating, drinking, and sexual contacts. After sunset, all this is allowed again. Ramadan is as much a month of feasting as of fasting. Indeed, many people gain weight during the fasting month. Some people save money for months in order to eat meat and luxury foods during the Ramadan nights. Much like Christmas meals in Western countries, Ramadan meals are family dinners. More often than not, friends or neighbors are invited to join in as well. Some only pop in for the sunset meal, others stay until the last meal that is served an hour before dawn. Sharing extends to strangers: every day towards sunset, people bring soup and couscous to the mosque for the poor and homeless.

Ramadan breakfast. Like most Muslims in the world, North Africans follow the example of the Prophet Mohammed (570–632), who used to break the fast by eating a date and drinking a sip of water or milk. They then perform the sunset prayers, after which the *ftûr* is served. In Morocco, *harîra*, nutritious tomato soup with meat, chickpeas and lentils, has become the national dish for breaking the fast. Besides *harîra*, what should also always be present on the breakfast table are *shebbakiyyât*, also known as *grioush*, deep-fried pastries with anise and cinnamon, which are dipped in honey or caramel when still hot and are then sprinkled with sesame seeds. *Beghrîr*, pancakes, are another favorite, as are hard-boiled eggs and olives. After having eaten two or three bowls of *harîra*, coffee with much more milk than usual is drunk.

Algerians and Tunisians also have soup for a Ramadan breakfast, but do not share the Moroccan habit of eating sweet pastries with soup. They prefer to eat large quantities of cakes and sweets with the coffee that is served later in the evening. To digest breakfast, many North African city dwellers go out to attend the open air performances and other special Ramadan festivities that are organized in town, buying orange juice, buttermilk, roasted sunflower seeds, peanuts, or chickpeas from street vendors as they stroll along.

Ramadan evening meals. Tunisians and Algerians combine the Ramadan breakfast and the evening meal. They eat a date and a bowl of soup before performing the evening prayers, after which they return for the evening meal, which in all three countries should always contain a fair amount of meat during Ramadan. *L-hamm el-hlû* (sweet veal with prunes) is a favorite Ramadan dish in Algeria, while in Tunisia *keftaji*, a stew with meatballs or a well-filled *marqa* (stew) may be served. Tunisians may also eat parched fish for a Ramadan dinner. This is frowned upon by Algerians and Moroccans: fish is easily digestible and leaves you thirsty, two qualities that are not very helpful during the fast. Ramadan dinners are served with more side dishes (eggs, olives, salads) than during other months of the year, and a larger variety of fruits appear on the table for dessert.

A typically Moroccan tradition occurs on the fifteenth night of Ramadan. That night, every family wants to eat a home-slaughtered chicken or rabbit, which gives this special dinner a connotation of a sacrificial meal. No similar tradition exists in either Algeria or Tunisia. What all three countries do share is the tradition on the twenty-seventh of Ramadan to visit the graveyard, clean the graves of relatives and have prayers said for them. On the way to and from the graveyard, children in the street and poor people who have gathered at the gates of the graveyards are given *sadaqa*, alms consisting of dates, figs and sweet bread.

Meals at night during Ramadan. People who have guests stay awake until the *shûr*, the last meal before dawn, in the meantime enjoying lots of coffee and pastries such as baklava, *brîk* (sweet puff pastries) and *sefûf*, ground and grilled sugared cereals and nuts. In the old quarters of towns, those who go to sleep are awakened for the *shûr* by musicians going through the streets. Most people have a light *shûr*: French toast, a milk-based *assîda* (porridge), or a *mesfûf*, (sweet couscous). In rural areas, however, the *shûr* may consist of a more substantial meal.

The feast meal. The last few days of Ramadan, women are very busy preparing cookies, cakes and pastries for the *cîd es-saghrîr*, the feast that ends the fasting month. In rural areas, nearly every one makes *kacak*, hard biscuit rings with anise and fennel seeds. In general, townswomen make a greater variety of cakes, cookies and pastries. In Algeria, women in Constantine are the most famous cookie makers, to be followed by those of Algiers and Blida. These cities used to have large Jewish communities, and Muslim women are said to have learned the art of cookie baking from Jewish women. Particularly popular for the concluding feast of Ramadan are *maqrûd*, date- or almond-filled fried cookies made from semolina, and *qnîdelet*, marzipan cigars. In Morocco, Fès is famous for its good pastries, such as the *kacab el-ghrazâl*, "gazelle horns," horn-shaped pies filled with almond paste.

In Morocco, many people find it important that the first meal that is eaten on the feast that ends Ramadan should be a white porridge. The color white symbolizes the purity that one has attained by fasting a whole month. The rest of the day is spent paying visits and receiving guests. In every house that they visit, people are served coffee or tea with lots of cookies and pastries. Not surprisingly, many people do not eat dinner on the first day of the feast concluding the fasting month.

The Feast of Immolation

On the tenth day of the *hajj*, the pilgrimage to Mecca two months after Ramadan, all pilgrims sacrifice a ram to commemorate how Ibrahîm (Abraham) slaughtered a ram as a last-minute substitute for the son he was willing to sacrifice as an act of obedience towards God. It is recommended by Islamic law that those Muslims elsewhere in the world who can afford it also sacrifice a ram. Voluntary fasting is recommended the day before the ritual sacrifice. Some people fast until the first meat of the sacrificed ram is served later in the day. Only men are allowed to slaughter. Female household heads call in a butcher. After the slaughtering, the rest of the day women are busy processing the meat.

Much local symbolism is attached to the various parts of the sacrificial ram. Mothers, for example, dip a finger in the blood that flows from the cut throat to mark the forehead of their children so as to ward off the evil eye. The sheepskin not only makes a perfect prayer mat, but is also thought to relieve the pain of a woman in labor who lies down on it. Of particular importance is the liver, the organ that is considered the seat of compassion. Barbecued liver is the first meat that is consumed on the day of the sacrifice. Women see to it carefully that there is a skewer for every member of the family. When someone does not make it on time for the barbecue, his or her skewer will be kept apart for them. Sharing the liver with all family members expresses and fortifies the family bond. The pieces of liver on the skewers given to girls are wrapped in the fat tissue that covered the heart of the ram, as this is believed to enhance finding a husband with a good heart.

Nowadays, pieces of meat that are not distributed among the poor can be stored in refrigerators and freezers, but the tradition of making *gedîd*, dried meat, has not disappeared. Slices of meat are put in a spicy marinate overnight. The next day, pieces of paunch are filled with the marinated chunks and then tied into bundles that are left to dry in the sun for several days. When a woman has difficulty getting pregnant, her friends may organize a lunch party for her by collecting two balls of *gedîd* from each woman who will attend, which are then served in a couscous. The chances that the honorary guest gets pregnant are thought to have improved after this ritual lunch. A tradition in Marrakesh (Morocco) is to dry the tail of the ram to save it until the *Ashûra*, the celebration of the New Year.

The *Ashûra* or Islamic New Year

Exactly one month after the Feast of Immolation, the *Ashûrâ* is celebrated on the tenth day of Muharram, the first month of the Islamic year. Traditionally this is the day on which the religious duty of performing *zakât*, the legal almsgiving, is performed. *Ashûra* concludes a transitional period of ten days between the old and new year. During this period, some people observe fasting. In Marrakesh, the fast is concluded by having a couscous with the preserved tail of the sacrificial ram, which thus comes to symbolize the farewell to the past year. In Tunisia, on the ninth day of Muharram people tend to eat chicken with very thin noodles, while on the tenth they prepare a couscous or *marqa* with mutton. In Algeria, dinner on the tenth of Muharram should be sweet, and often contains raisins, prunes and cinnamon. In Morocco, *Ashûra* is not linked to any special meal, but what is shared with the other countries is that women prepare or buy *krishlât* or *fakîya*, mix of raisins, figs, nuts, and dime-sized cookies. *Krishlât* is eaten at home and distributed among children in the neighborhood.

Despite the influence of the former French occupation, New Year celebrations according to the Christian calendar do not, as yet, receive much attention. An exception must be made for Tunisia, where people eat *mlûkhîa* or other dishes from spinach-like plants on New Year's Eve. Green is the color that symbolizes Islam. The green color of the New Year's Eve dish also symbolizes the hope for a "green," that is, prosperous, year.

The *Mûlûd* or Birthday of the Prophet

On the twelfth day of the third month of the Islamic calendar, the *mûlûd* or birth of the Prophet Muhammad is commemorated. Every country has its own special dish on this occasion. In Tunisia and Morocco, most families have *assîda* for breakfast, a semolina porridge prepared with milk and sweetened with honey. Poorer people and those in the countryside keep it simple, while people in the cities and those who are better off may add raisins and orange blossom water to the porridge. In Algeria, people in the east are known for eating *sfinj*, fritters, for breakfast, while *qatawarmi*, chicken with turnip and chickpeas, is eaten for dinner across the country. In Morocco chicken or beef with prunes and almonds is a favorite dish on the Prophet's birthday.

Life Cycle Rites

Birth. While in North African cuisine both hot and mild spices are used, the two should not be mixed. According to Tunisians, the combination of hot and sweet spices is thought to cause diarrhea, just as fish with milk is thought to cause skin diseases and tea with buttermilk stomach aches. In all three countries, dishes prepared for special occasions related to life cycle rites tend to be mild and sweet. Cinnamon, raisins, prunes, and nuts are recurring ingredients. On the occasion of a birth, for example, an Algerian new mother is offered semolina porridge with honey. In Morocco the mother is offered *sefûf*, ground and grilled cereals and nuts, flavored with sugar, anise, and fennel. *Sefûf* is considered to help her regain her strength and to pass it on to her baby through her breast milk. According to a Moroccan tradition, when the baby is a girl, a cock should be slaughtered for the first meal that the mother eats after having given birth, the cock symbolizing the future husband of the girl. If the baby is a boy, a hen is slaughtered for this dish. On the seventh day after birth, the day on which the baby is given its name, different kinds of pancakes such as *ghraif* and *beghrîr* are prepared for breakfast. In families that can afford it, a sheep is sacrificed to thank God. It is prepared for the guests who attend the name-giving party.

Marriage. According to a Moroccan custom, the last meal that a mother of a Moroccan bride prepares before her daughter leaves her parental home to join her husband should be a dish that was "stirred with no spoon," lest her husband should prove to be an easily agitated and restless man. Meanwhile, the guests at the groom's house are offered chicken with lemon preserve, almonds and hard-boiled eggs, which symbolize fertility. In Algeria, guests are served *shtetha,* "the dancing (chicken)," a name referring both to the dancing of the guests and to the movements of the chicken in the pot as is simmers in its sauce of tomatoes, potatoes, garlic, and red pepper. Often, the parents of the groom slaughter a ram or calf on behalf of the bride to serve to the wedding guests. In all North African countries the bride and groom offer each other dates and milk before they withdraw to a room to consummate the marriage. Like eggs, dates and milk symbolize fertility. For Algerians, an additional explanation is that in this way, the partners eat each other's "salt," thus becoming part of each other. On the morning after the marriage ceremony, the parents of a Moroccan bride traditionally send the newlyweds a rice porridge and *bûzelûf,* a boiled head of sheep. The whiteness of the porridge symbolizes the purity of the bride while the head expresses the wish that she uses her head in running her household. On the seventh day after the wedding, the family of the bride comes to visit her and are offered fritters (*sfinj*) and porridge (*assîda*) sweetened with honey.

Mourning. In the house where someone has died, traditionally no fire should be lit to prepare food for three days. Those who come to express their condolences bring along food for the bereaved, usually a very simple couscous and hard-boiled eggs. Besides fertility, eggs also symbolize death and mourning, particularly egg shells, which break easily. On the fortieth day after the funeral, a ram is slaughtered and its meat prepared for those who gather to recite the Qur'an on behalf of the deceased. The same ceremony is repeated a year after the death.

Jewish Food Habits

For a long time, there have been Jewish communities in North Africa. Some, such as the Algerian Bahusi have lived there since the destruction of the Temple in Jerusalem more than two thousand years ago. Others settled there after their expulsion from Spain after the Reconquista (1492). After independence in the 1960s, the majority of Jews emigrated to Israel, but all North African countries continue to have Jewish minorities.

There are only a few respects in which food habits of North African Jews differ from those of Muslims in the region, and these all pertain to religious prescriptions. Kosher cooking requires that meat and dairy products should not be mixed and that different cooking utensils should be used for each. Like most Muslims, Jews use oil to fry their meat, but unlike Muslims, they will never add *smen,* salted clarified butter. Also, when Jewish women make bread, traditionally they always throw a small piece of the dough in the fire, symbolizing the setting apart of a portion of their meals for the poor.

Furthermore, special meals are associated with particular moments in the religious calendar. On occasion of the Hebrew New Year, for example, as is the case among Algerian Muslims on the tenth of Muharram, sugar replaces salt, and sweet dishes with raisins and prunes predominate. Moroccan Jews prepare a dish with seven vegetables and a sheep's head, symbolizing merit and good fortune. During the days leading up to Yom Kippur, the fast on the tenth day of the new year, many families eat chicken, since for each family member a chicken should be sacrificed on occasion of the New Year to commemorate Abraham's sacrifice. Women also prepare "Yom Kippur bread," with almonds. To break the fast on the evening of Yom Kippur the table is set with cakes. The day after Yom Kippur, at midday Moroccan Jews eat chicken with olives, followed by *beranîya,* fried and sweetened eggplants sprinkled with sesame seeds and cinnamon.

Sukkoth, the Feast of Tabernacles, which begins five days after Yom Kippur, lasts seven days. On the first day, Jewish women in Morocco prepare a couscous. Throughout the week of the Sukkoth holiday, women serve better meals than usual. In Algeria, chicken is again a favorite, being followed by lots of fruit for dessert. On the occasion of Hanukkah, the festival of light, during which the rededication of the Temple in 165 B.C.E. is commemorated, women make their famous *qnîdelet,* marzipan cigars, and *maqrûd,* date- or almond-filled fried semolina cookies, as well as the same kind of pancakes, fritters, and puff pastries that have been mentioned above for Islamic celebrations. Tu-Bishvat, the festival of trees, is celebrated by Moroccan Jews by eating fifteen different kinds of (dry) fruits. Purim, the feast commemorating the deliverance of the Jews by Esther from a massacre, is even more a feast of pastries, and kilos of them are exchanged between women and distributed among children and the poor.

For Pesach, when the Exodus from Egypt is commemorated, the ritual meal should at least consist of a salad with *marûr,* a bitter herb, referring to the bitter life under Egyptian rule; a glass of salt water, representing the tears and sweat shed; and eggs cooked hard in ashes, a symbol of the destruction of the Temple. In Algeria,

Jews eat a lamb's leg on this occasion. The lamb symbolizes the beginning of a new life, and its leg, God's "extended arm" with which the Egyptians were hit when the ten plagues fell upon them. The lamb's leg also commemorates the fact that each Jewish family in Egypt was asked to slaughter a lamb and smear its blood on the doorposts of their houses so that these could be identified as those that were to be saved. Last of all, matzos, biscuits representing unleavened bread that was eaten during the journey through the desert are eaten, as are fresh, green vegetables, also representing a new beginning. On the evening of Mimuna, the last night of the Passover festival, many people only eat milk products, but some families place fish on the table as a symbol of fertility.

Seven weeks after Pesach, Shevuoth is celebrated. According to some this was originally an agrarian festival, but later became linked to the commemoration of the covenant of Mount Sinai. On this occasion in Morocco, "Angel's Hair," a pasta sprinkled with cinnamon and surrounded by meat or chicken, is traditionally served.

On the Sabbath, all work must cease, and no fire should be lit. Therefore, women make enough bread on Fridays for two days and prepare the fish or chicken that will be eaten on the Sabbath. A special Sabbath dish in Morocco is *skhîna*, consisting of eggs, potatoes, rice, chickpeas and meat. Traditionally, *skhîna* was prepared in earthenware casseroles that were hermetically sealed and cooked overnight in the public oven or in the still glowing ashes of the fire used to heat the public bath. This way, it was still warm when eaten for lunch on Saturday. Nowadays, most women prepare *skhîna* at home.

The meals on the Sabbath tend to be better than on other days of the week, often consisting of the same dishes that Muslims eat on Fridays. The festive meals that are served on occasions that mark the life cycle also tend to be the same as those of Muslims, such as the "dancing chicken" for marriages. Indeed, North African Jewish and Muslim cuisines overlap widely, as do the meanings of foodstuffs and ingredients used. For both Jews and Muslims, salt is purifying, bread contains *baraka*, God's blessing, dates symbolize fertility, eggs both fertility and mourning, green vegetables represent the wish for a new year of abundance, and pulses are associated with poverty.

See also **Fasting and Abstinence: Islam; Islam; Judaism; Middle East; Ramadan.**

BIBLIOGRAPHY

Bahloul Joelle. *Le Culte de la Table Dressée: Rites et traditions de la table juive algérienne*. Paris: Métailié, 1983.

Benchekroun Mohammed. *La cuisine andalou-marocaine au XI-IIe siècle d'après un manuscrit rare: Fadâlat al-khiwân fî tayyibât al-tacam wa-l-alwân, d'Ibn Razîn al-Tujîbî*. Beirut, 1984.

Bennani-Smirès, Latifa. *La Cuisine marocaine*. New edition. Casablanca: Al Madariss, 1987.

Bouayed, F. *La Cuisine algérienne*. Algiers: Entreprise Nationale du Livre, 1983.

Bruneton, A. "Bread in the Region of the Moroccan High Atlas." In *Gastronomy: The Anthropology of Food and Food Habits*, pp. 275–285, edited by M. Arnott. The Hague: Mouton, 1975.

Buitelaar, Marjo. *Fasting and Feasting in Morocco: Women's Participation in Ramadan*. Oxford, U.K.: Berg, 1993.

Carrier, Robert. *A Taste of Morocco*. London: Century, 1987.

Combs-Schilling, Elaine. "Ram's Blood: Great Sacrifice." In *Sacred Performances: Islam, Sexuality, and Sacrifice*, edited by Elaine Combs-Schilling, New York: Columbia University Press, 1989.

Dinya F. *La Cuisine marocaine de rabat, un art et une tradition*. Rabat: Publication Ribat El-Bath, 1990.

Diouri A. "Of Leaven Foods: Ramadan in Morocco." In *Culinary Cultures of the Middle East*, pp. , edited by S. Zubaida and R. Tapper. London: Tauris, 1994.

El-Ghonemy, Riad M. "Land, Food and Rural Development in North Africa." *Third World Planning Review* 16, no. 1 (1994): 27.

Fragner Bert. "From the Caucasus to the Roof of the World: A Culinary Adventure." In *Culinary Cultures of the Middle East*, edited by S. Zubaida and R. Tapper, pp. 49-63. London: Tauris, 1994.

Guinaudeau-Franc, Zetta. *Traditional Moroccan Cooking*. Paris and Saint Cloud: Editions Guinaudeau, 1976.

Hubert, A. *Le pain et l'olive: Aspects de l'alimentation en Tunisie*. Paris: Editions du Centre National de la Recherche Scientifique, 1984.

Jouin, J. "Valeurs symboliques des aliments et rites alimentaires à Rabat." *Hespéris* (1957): 299–327.

Khaldi, Nabil. *Evolving Food Gaps in the Middle East/North Africa: Prospects and Policy Implications*. Washington, D.C.: International Food Policy Research Institute, 1984.

Moryoussef, Vivianne, and Nina Moryoussef. *Moroccan Jewish Cookery*. Paris/Casablanca: Sefa International/Sochepress, 1983.

Rachik H. *Sacre et Sacrifice. Dans le haut atlas marocain*. Casablanca: Afrique Orient, 1990.

Rodinson Maxime. "Recherches sur les documents arabes relatifs à la cuisine." *Revue des Études Islamiques* (1949): 95–165.

Tamzali H. *La Cuisine en Afrique du Nord. 444 Recettes tunisiennes, algériennes et marocaines dont 33 couscous*. Hammamet: Tomkinson, 1986.

Valensi L., "Consommation et usages alimentaires en Tunisie aux xviiie et xixe siècles." *Annales*, no. 2–3 (March–June 1975): 600–607.

Virolle-Souibes Marie. "Pétrir la pâte malaxer du sens exemples kabyles." *Techniques et Cultures* 13 (1989): 73–101.

Watson, Andrew. *Agricultural Innovation in the Early Islamic World: The Diffusion of Crops and Farming Techniques, 700–1100*. Cambridge, U.K.: Cambridge University Press, 1983.

Marjo Buitelaar

WEST AFRICA

West Africa is composed of eighteen countries occupying various climate zones. The coastal region from Guinea-Bissau to Cameroon is characterized by abundant rainfall (with a rainy season of at least six months) and a thick forest of massive evergreen trees. A drier region, the savanna, lies five hundred miles north of the forest, and receives enough rainfall to sustain vast areas of rarer trees and grasses. The semiarid zone between the Sahara Desert to the north and the savanna to the south is called the Sahel, which in some years has a dry season of over nine months. North of the Sahel lies the Sahara Desert.

Ancient West Africa

Eight thousand years ago, during Europe's Ice Age, the Sahara Desert supported large populations in a lush, fertile environment dominated by savanna grassland and woodland. Fruits and vegetables, sheep, goats, poultry, and cattle provided a reliable and abundant food supply that sustained a sedentary population as it grew and developed. Fishing populations flourished along numerous rivers and streams that flowed throughout the Sahara. As the Sahara's climate changed, becoming dry and mostly desert, migrations south to arable land increased the populations of sub-Saharan Africa.

Cultivation of crops in West Africa is theorized to have originated around the headwaters of the Niger River. Millet seems to have been the first important crop, and may have been eaten in a porridge. The techniques developed for crop cultivation of fruits, vegetables, herbs, and spices were indigenous to Africa. The Diola of Guinea-Bissau, for example, transformed most of the mangrove swamps lining a number of river estuaries into a network of paddy fields. Their techniques of dyking, desalinating, ridging, and transplanting antedate all European influence. The Yoruba and Bini and other Nigerian societies have lived in settled communities on the same sites for several hundred years, evolving agricultural systems that allow continuous cultivation of their soils without significant or permanent loss of fertility.

Traditional Sources of Sustenance

In the forests of Ghana, as well as in Cameroon, traditional crops such as the cocoyam (taro) and plantain are successfully cultivated. These plants, together with raffia and oil palms, maize, cassava, African rice, and kola, thrive in the long rainy seasons, which run approximately nine months of the year.

Many West Africans who were not farmers were pastoralists or fishermen. Fish were eaten raw or pickled, fried, boiled, and prepared by "gumboing." Dried shrimp and crayfish are still essential ingredients in stews and sauces, some of which combine different types of fish with coconut milk and other ingredients. Crab, lobster, cod, mackerel, sole, pike, prawn, gilthead, eel, shrimp, sprat, flounder, carp, and other varieties of seafood provided

"fisher folk," such as the Twi of Ghana and the Muslim Bozo, with fish to sell at markets located well into the interior of the continent. In many West African cities these open-air retail markets were principally in the hands of women, who were economically independent traders.

The market streets were filled with stalls selling calabashes, palm oil, palm wine, ducks, chickens, fresh beef, mutton, and other meats, yams and yam fritters, guinea corn (sorghum) and millet beers, groundnuts, raw and cooked beans, thin brown cakes (said to smell like gingerbread), bean cakes, *karra* (meal dumplings), oblong bean buns called *jenkaraga*, and soups and stews. Some of the ready-made dishes included *enjibotchi* (rice with sauce), *ekoa* (durra [a sorghum grain] porridge), *killishi* (roasted meat, marinated and basted with oil, herbs, and spices), and *atchia-kara* (a yam and vegetable sauce ladled over chunks of beef, goat, and lamb).

An item used in Africa from antiquity, kola is indigenous to the forest zone of West Africa and is still preferred by Muslims who are prohibited from using alcohol and tobacco. It was valued as a refreshing stimulant and food by desert travelers during the trans-Saharan caravan trade and in the early stages of trade between the rain-forest regions, the Sahel, and beyond. In the sixteenth century, Askia Mahmoud supplied kola to his Songhai troops as an "energizer" before battle. Over forty species of kola are grown in the region between Sierra Leone and the Congo, with several varieties existing in Ghana alone. From ancient times, West Africans have also used different parts of the kola plant for treating swellings and fresh wounds. Ghanaians use it to reduce labor pain during childbirth and for treating guinea worm. In addition, kola nuts were used as primary flavorings in Coca-Cola and other beverages before kola substitutes were manufactured.

Culinary Taboos and the Social Significance of Cattle Raising

Although chicken, lamb, mutton, and goat were raised and widely consumed, some societies adhered to taboos relating to one or all of these meats and their by-products. Egg consumption is still forbidden in some regions, as it is believed to turn young males into thieves and make childbirth difficult for women. The Mbum women of southwestern Chad, for example, do not eat any kind of eggs, chicken, or goat for fear of pain and death in childbirth, giving birth to abnormal or unhealthy children, or becoming sterile. In societies where goats were believed to have dietary value, they were bred specifically for their milk. In others, such as in the pastoral regions of the Sahel, goat milk is less favored than cows' milk as an item of trade, but is consumed by children and herders in the field. (Lactose intolerance among some West African peoples prevents them from drinking milk.) Lamb was usually grilled or barbecued and served at special feasts. Muslims prepared whole rams for the *Id el fetr*, a major festival.

Men preparing *fufu* in a mortar in Ghana. *Fufu* is used like dumplings or like pieces of bread for scooping up mouthfuls of stew. © LIBA TAYLOR/CORBIS.

Throughout Africa, cattle assumed a great importance in social, economic, and religious affairs. Cows were slaughtered and various beef dishes prepared for special occasions such as weddings, the naming of babies, festivals, or funerals. Cattle raising among the Bororo clan of the Fulani herdspeople (Fulani are dispersed throughout West Africa, from Senegal to Cameroon) is carried out by men who are charged with the herds' daily pasturing and watering, veterinary care, and seasonal movements. Women milk the cows and market the milk. The Bororo produce enough milk to support the family year-round, living primarily on dishes made with milk, cheese, and butter. They sell their milk products (or heads of cattle, if milk production decreases) to pay for other foods. Meat is not a staple part of the diet, but sometimes male or aged cattle are slaughtered and eaten on ceremonial occasions. The people of the northern regions, however, consume large amounts of barbecued beef.

Cattle are raised by the Mande peoples (numerous West African ethnic groups, including peoples of both the savanna and forest, that speak a Mande language)

primarily for prestige, dowry payments, and sacrificial offerings. For other peoples, cattle not only provide meat, hides, manure, and milk, they are also needed for pulling loads.

The Legacy of Colonialism and Slavery

Slavery and colonialism sharply depleted the traditional abundance of meats and other foods after Europeans "discovered" Africa's wealth in the early sixteenth century. Colonialist control over African land and resources led to crop production almost exclusively for export. Profits from expanding agricultural exports went to foreign trading companies and colonial administrators, not to improve the lives of African peoples. "Cash crops," or the major exports, became palm oil from most of the coastal forest zone (a main source of lubricant for industrial machinery before the development of petroleum in the latter half of the nineteenth century), gum arabic from Senegal (a hardened resin substance extracted from acacia trees used to fix colored dyes in printed cloth in European textile factories), groundnuts from Guinea, coffee (the largest nonfuel export), and cocoa (primarily from Ghana, but Nigeria, Cameroon, and the Ivory Coast were also major producers). In the twentieth century, rubber from Firestone Tire plantations in Liberia was added to the list of exports.

The increases in production of export crops meant that production of food crops dropped and food prices rose. Sierra Leone, Liberia, and most of what was then called French West Africa were forced to import rice and other foods, even though they could grow their own. The market value of export crops also reduced the available land for staple foods at the expense of the native population. Another reason for the neglect of staple food crops was the depletion of the labor force. The slave trade drained an estimated forty million Africans from the continent between the fifteenth and nineteenth centuries. In addition, for those men between 18 and 60 years of age who remained, colonial law mandated that they labor a certain number of days for the state. Hundreds of thousands of young men left home to escape conscript labor laws in force in various parts of West Africa and found work on coffee, cocoa, and groundnut plantations in the Ivory Coast, Ghana, and Senegal.

In the late nineteenth and early twentieth centuries, urbanization and social change in some areas also pulled many people away from agricultural work, as the introduction of packaged and canned convenience foods made the traditional "from scratch" methods of food production and preparation almost obsolete. Still, West African holidays, feasts, and celebrations have been maintained, with some alterations, and continue to showcase the numerous dishes prepared with indigenous ingredients.

Festive and Everyday Dishes

Celebrations and festivities mark numerous occasions: the start of seasonal rains, new planting season ceremonies (between May and August), the "first fruits," the call for blessings for good harvests, the harvest, the start of the hunting and fishing seasons, weddings, the birth of a baby (mothers are celebrated as well on this day), the baby-naming ceremony, pubertal initiation rites, festival dances, the completion of the building of a new home, religious holidays, and funerals. Huge feasts are the highlight of such celebrations, and numerous special main dishes, meats, breads, and snacks are prepared. *Banga* and *jollof* rice (a spicy Ghanaian dish of chicken, ham, stewed tomatoes, and onions), *egusi* (melon seeds) and peanut stews and coconut soup, tiger-nut mold (a favorite pudding made with fish and yams), bean and *abala* (ground rice) puddings, roasted and barbecued meats, cassava dumplings (prepared with the leaves of the fluted pumpkin), *tiébou dienn* (pronounced "cheb-oo jen," Senegal's national dish, a fish and rice stew made with yams, okra, eggplant, cabbage, and chili peppers), vegetable side dishes (such as *akee* cooked with two or three varieties of greens), coconut candy, *chinchin* (twisted cakes), *abacha mmili* (cassava chips), *ipekere* (plantain chips), *meensa* (millet cakes), and banana fritters (rolled in groundnuts and sorghum or corn flour or cassava meal before frying) are just a few of the items on the celebration menus. *Poulet yassa*, chicken marinated in a lemon and onion mixture then grilled or sautéed, is one of Senegal's most famous dishes.

These are foods enjoyed in most of the countries within the Sahelian zone today (Mauritania, Senegal, The Gambia, Mali, Guinea-Bissau, Burkina Faso, Niger, Chad, and Cape Verde), where some of the dominant staple foods are millets, Bambara groundnuts, yams, Asian rice, sorghum, cassava, cowpeas (black-eyed peas; there are forty varieties), sesame (mixed with wheat for biscuits, used in chicken recipes, and in sesame *sucre* [sugar], a children's snack), maize, peanuts, and fonio (for hot breakfast cereal). Dominating the diets of the coastal countries (Guinea, Sierra Leone, Liberia, Côte d'Ivoire [Ivory Coast], Togo, Ghana, Benin, Nigeria, and Cameroon) are cassava, Asian rice, maize, cowpeas, lima beans, pigeon peas, sorghum, peanuts, plantains, cocoyam (taro), and yams. Plantain is the basic ingredient for many popular snack foods throughout Côte d'Ivoire, and, with bananas, bridges the gap between the dry season and harvest months of January to May, when other staples are unavailable or scarce. The cocoyam is rapidly becoming a major staple in coastal communities, while cultivation of yams in producer countries has been gradually decreasing. Nigeria is the world's largest producer of cocoyam, followed by Ghana. Served by themselves, or mixed with plantains, yams, or cassava and other ingredients, cocoyams are used to make the traditional dish called *fufu* (also *fou fou*): the staples are cooked and pounded into a smooth soft dough used to make dumplings.

In addition to being popular foods, cocoyams and yams have always carried social and cultural significance. In Nigeria, the cocoyam festival, *Alube*, is celebrated an-

nually in May. Yams are intertwined in the social, cultural, and religious life of the farming communities where they are the major crop. In remote areas of West Africa, yams were an important status symbol, conferring prestige on families who consumed large quantities. Many customs dictate that yams should be used to wean babies, and special yam dishes are prepared for birth rituals and the naming ceremony for children. In some societies, yams are also important foods for funerals as ceremonial offerings to the gods and to the spirits of the departed, in others as food during the funeral feasts.

Throughout West Africa, the yam is revered by many traditional societies including the Ibo of eastern and midwestern Nigeria. Although many of their customs have been lost or modified due to European influence, it is believed that the Ibo are more devoted to yam cultivation than any other yam producers. Their religious devotion to the food has prevented its displacement by other crops.

The New Yam Festival is, in many West African regions, the most important celebration of the year. The annual festivals are associated with planting but more particularly with the yam harvest. Some of the groups that celebrate the festival include the Ashanti of Ghana, the Ibo and Yako of eastern Nigeria, the Yoruba of western Nigeria, the peoples of the eastern Ivory Coast, the Ewe of Togo, the people of Benin, the Tiv of the Benue region of northern Nigeria, and the Kalabari of the eastern Niger Delta.

Other Indigenous Foods

Yams can be stored for six to nine months, but if they begin to run low, they are usually supplemented by fruits, seeds, and nuts that grow in abundance at different times of the year. In various regions of West Africa, these crops include the African breadfruit, the African pear, the incense tree, the star apple, the African mango, the shea butter tree (*Vitelleria paradoxa*, which produces a nutlike fruit—57 percent of its seed's weight is oil), various species of gourd (many have yamlike roots that grow deep underground), and the cultivated species of sword lily or corn-flat, the *Leguminosae*, which produces tubers and edible roots, and the all-purpose baobab tree.

The baobab grows wild in the savanna regions of Mali and other areas of West Africa. Rope was made from its bark and medicines were manufactured from extracted liquids as well as from its dried leaves; the dried leaves were also used as a thickener for stews. In addition, its fruit is not only a great source of vitamin C, but is also used to make refreshing drinks containing tartaric and other acids. A meal for making bread was derived from this plant, as was a red dye.

Sorghum, another indigenous food crop, also provides a red dye that is rubbed into animal skins to make red leather, and its stems yield large amounts of sugar. Sorghum is probably one of the world's most versatile food crops with undeveloped genetic potential. In Nigeria, young children eat the yellow varieties of sorghum to prevent blindness because their diets are deficient in vitamin A. The most common food prepared in Nigeria is *tuwo*, made by stirring sorghum flour into hot water and allowing the thick paste to cool and gel. Once cooled, *tuwo* is cut or broken up and eaten with soup. In West Africa it is generally known as guinea corn, and the grains of certain varieties are popped like popcorn. Sorghum grain is made into flour for a thick pancake batter fried in groundnut oil; sorghum beer is a favorite beverage consumed at wrestling matches as *burkutu*, an alcoholic gruel, or as *pito*, with the sediment removed. *Dawaki* are flat fried cakes made with a mixture of sorghum and bean flours, and sometimes accompany soups. A flour and water batter, *akamu*, is used to flavor and thicken porridges and cereals.

Sorghum, rice, maize, yams, plantains, cassava, and taro (cocoyam) are staples along with common ingredients such as onions, tomatoes, palm fruits, *egusi* and other melon seeds (used for thickening), okra, pumpkin, coconut, coconut milk, and a variety of nuts. Fish, meat, and vegetable dishes are heavily seasoned with numerous hot peppers and spices, such as Guinea pepper grains (*melegueta*), spicy cedar (called *atiokwo* in the Ivory Coast; the seeds are roasted, ground, and used in soups or with leafy vegetables), tea bush (known as *an-gbonto* in Sierra Leone; its fragrant leaves are used to flavor meat dishes and vegetable, *egusi*, and palm nut soups), African locust bean (harvested, boiled, and fermented to produce *dawadawa*, an indispensable condiment in Nigerian and Cameroonian cuisine), and West African black pepper (known as *fukungen* to the people of The Gambia and Senegal). Several oils are used in preparing West African dishes, such as groundnut (or peanut, sometimes preferred in stews), melon seed, sesame seed (*gingelly* or *gingili*), coconut, corn, shea butter, and palm, the favorite because it imparts a reddish color to foods. Cooking methods include frying, simmering or boiling, roasting and steaming (foods are steamed in banana, plantain, miraculous berry, cocoyam leaves, or corn sheaths), and baking, or combinations of two or three of these methods. Broiling was added in the twentieth century.

Two to three very large meals are prepared and consumed daily, and West Africans eat until they are full. Breakfast can consist of *pap* (or *ogi*, a hot beverage made with corn meal, milk or sour milk, and sugar), *akara* (bean cakes made with black-eyed peas or other beans, water, salt, onions, and peppers, then fried in peanut or palm oil), *moi-moi* (steamed bean pudding, made with black-eyed peas or other beans), roasted or fried plantains, and tea or coffee. West Africans enjoy *gari* (the dried and ground form of cassava) with soup for lunch, along with okra, *egusi* or *agbono* soup (seeds from the *egusi* melon are toasted and ground; *agbono* are the dry seeds from the African mango, ground to a smooth paste before using), and *fufu* (pounded yam). All soups contain various greens, such as *ukazi* and cassava leaves, and smoked or dried shrimp and crayfish. For dinner, there is *jollof* rice or coconut rice with roasted meats, boiled rice and a chicken, beef, or fish stew (or palm nut or pepper soup) containing okra, cabbage, groundnuts (or peanuts), and other ingredients. Vegetable side dishes, including beans and rice or rice garnished with fried plantains, are very popular. An indigenous Ghanaian dish, *kenke*, is steamed pudding made with fermented maize pulp; its two varieties are served with soups and stews. Occasionally fruits are served as appetizers, but traditionally all dishes are served at the same time rather than in courses. Fruits, nuts, and snacks, such as *chinchin* (twisted cakes sold by vendors along roadside markets), are sometimes eaten between meals.

Summary

As host for centuries to fortune hunters, colonialist regimes, and migrations from Europe and other countries, West Africa has been perceived as the recipient, not the provider, of cuisine and culture. Even as French and other foreign languages began to blend with those native to the continent, thereby changing the names of certain dishes, and as minor changes in ingredients were made in those dishes (by way of foreign influence), West African cuisine remained a significant cultural force.

Archeological excavations, together with new studies on Africa's agricultural and culinary past, demonstrate that Africa had many indigenous crops. Unfortunately, emphasis is too often placed on foods brought into Africa during the period of slavery and colonization rather than on indigenous foods consumed domestically or exported to foreign countries, and most studies limit African agriculture and diet, prior to European influence, to a small number of indigenous foods: yams, cowpeas (black-eyed peas), sorghum, millets, okra, some bush greens, and whatever items were gathered. Watermelon, *akee* (*Blighia sapida*; also *ackee* or *achee*, a bright-red tropical fruit with black seeds and a creamy white flesh), tamarind, bottle gourd, fluted pumpkin, *egusi* melon, sesame, and one or two other beans have been added in a few studies.

In Volume I of its *Lost Crops of Africa*, the National Academy of Sciences reports that Africa has produced more indigenous cereal grains, including its own species of rice (nutritionally superior to Asian rice), than any other continent. Among Africa's more than two thousand currently known native food plants are grains, such as African rice, pearl and finger millets, and fonio; cultivated fruits, such as *balanites* (desert dates), butterfruit (*africado*), horned melon, ziziphus (Rhamnaceae, the buckthorn family) and *kei* apple; wild fruits, such as chocolate berries, figs, custard apples, grapes, gingerbread plums, and star apples; vegetables such as amaranths, spirulina (a nutritious blue-green algae of fresh and brackish waters), edible mushrooms, oyster nuts, Ethiopian mustard, gherkins, mock tomatoes; legumes such as *marama*, locust and sword beans, grass peas and guar; roots and tubers such as *anchote* (*Coccinea abyssinica*), Hausa potatoes, tiger nuts, several varieties of yam, and vigna roots, and a number of spices and herbs.

These foods are endangered by "botanical colonialism," the export system of "cash crops" and "one-crop agriculture" imposed on West Africa and the rest of the continent by European colonialism. In addition, "structural adjustment programs" of the 1980s, designed by the World Bank and the International Monetary Fund to increase the role of exports in the economy and reduce Africa's deepening debt crisis, have actually intensified low agricultural productivity for domestic consumption. Poor families, in an effort to meet urgent food needs, often intensively cultivate lands and forests for subsistence or exports, frequently in areas that once yielded ancient crop species or medicinal plants, or those that are sometimes erosion-prone, where crop yields drop severely after a couple of years. Food shortages, famine, disease, and widespread poverty are the result.

West Africa has been a major contributor to world cuisine in terms of the migration of its indigenous crops, methods of production of those crops, and culinary customs. Very few of Africa's currently known native food plants have received the recognition or research deserved and warranted for so vast a larder. The scientific community has not been able to provide an exact count of foods actually native to the continent nor the age of most of its crops. The history of the continent's flora is, therefore, virtually unknown. As with environments threatened with endangered species, Africa's indigenous agricultural pantry is gradually dwindling due to lack of research and interest. Many biases exist against native African foods, biases that have kept alive perceptions of the inferiority of African crops. It is therefore hoped that there will be an eventual understanding and appreciation of Africa's endangered agricultural species, as they have much to offer, not only to Africa but the rest of the world as well in terms of solving major hunger, disease, and energy problems.

See also **Agriculture, Origins of; Anthropology; Banana and Plantain; Cassava; Cattle; Food Archaeology; Food Supply, Food Shortages; Fruit: Tropical and Subtropical Fruit; Game; Government Agencies, U.S.; Hunting and Gathering; International Agencies; Nuts; Paleonutrition, Methods of; Rice; United States: African American Foodways; Vegetables.**

BIBLIOGRAPHY

Abaka, Edmund. "Kola Nuts." In *The Cambridge World History of Food,* edited by Kenneth F. Kiple and Kriemhild Coneè Ornelas, vol. 1, pp. 684–690. Cambridge: Cambridge University Press, 2000.

Ajayi, J. F. Ade, and Michael Crowder, eds. *History of West Africa.* Vol. 1. New York: Columbia University Press, 1972.

Allison, P. A. "Historical Inferences to Be Drawn from the Effect of Human Settlement on the Vegetation of Africa." *Journal of African History* 3 (1962): 241–249.

Andah, Bassey. "Identifying Early Farming Traditions of West Africa." In *The Archaeology of Africa: Food, Metals and Towns,* edited by Thurstan Shaw, Paul Sinclair, Bassey Andah, and Alex Okpoko. London and New York: Routledge, 1993.

Ayensu, Dinah A. *The Art of West African Cooking.* Garden City, N.Y.: Doubleday, 1972.

Baker, H. G. "Comments on the Thesis That There Was a Major Centre of Plant Domestication Near the Headwaters of the River Niger." *Journal of African History* 3 (1962): 229–233.

Board on Science and Technology for International Development, National Research Council (U.S.). *Lost Crops of Africa.* Washington, D.C.: National Academy Press, 1996.

Chijioke, F. A. *Ancient Africa.* London and Accra, Ghana: Longmans, Green, 1966.

Clark, J. Desmond. "The Spread of Food Production in Sub-Saharan Africa." *Journal of African History* 3 (1962): 211–228.

Coursey, D. G. *Yams: An Account of the Nature, Origins, Cultivation, and Utilisation of the Useful Members of the* Dioscoreaceae. London: Longmans, Green, 1967.

Davidson, Basil. *The African Genius: An Introduction to African Cultural and Social History.* Boston: Little, Brown, 1970.

Davidson, Basil. *The Africans: An Entry to Cultural History.* Harmondsworth, U.K.: Penguin, 1973.

Davidson, Basil. *The African Slave Trade: Precolonial History 1450–1850.* Boston: Little, Brown, 1980.

Davidson, Basil. *Growing from Grass Roots: The State of Guinea-Bissau.* London: Committee for Freedom in Mozambique, Angola, and Guinea, 1974.

Hafner, Dorinda. *A Taste of Africa: Traditional and Modern African Cooking.* Berkeley, Calif.: Ten Speed Press, 2002.

Inquai, Tebereh. *A Taste of Africa: The African Cookbook.* Trenton, N.J.: Africa World Press, 1998.

Irvine, Frederick Robert. *Plants of the Gold Coast.* London: Oxford University Press, 1930.

Jackson, E. A. *South of the Sahara: Traditional Cooking from the Countries of West Africa.* Hollis, N.H.: Fantail, 1999.

Jones, William O. *Manioc in Africa.* Stanford, Calif.: Stanford University Press, 1959.

Mbiti, John S. *African Religions and Philosophy.* 2d ed. Portsmouth, N.H.: Heinemann, 1990.

Miracle, Marvin P. "The Introduction and Spread of Maize in Africa." *Journal of African History* 6 (1965): 39–55.

Morgan, W. B. "The Forest and Agriculture in West Africa." *Journal of African History* 3 (1962): 235–239.

Murdock, George P. *Africa: Its Peoples and Their Culture History.* New York: McGraw-Hill, 1959.

O'Laughlin, Bridget. "Mediation of Contradiction: Why Mbum Women Do Not Eat Chicken." In *Women, Culture, and Society,* edited by Michelle Zimbalist Rosaldo and Louise Lamphere, pp. 301–318. Stanford, Calif.: Stanford University Press, 1974.

Smith, Ifeyironwa Francisca. *Foods of West Africa: Their Origin and Use*. Ottawa, Ontario: I. F. Smith, 1998.

Spivey, Diane M. *The Peppers, Cracklings, and Knots of Wool Cookbook: The Global Migration of African Cuisine*. Albany: State University of New York Press, 1999.

Stanton, W. R. "The Analysis of the Present Distribution of Varietal Variation in Maize, Sorghum, and Cowpea in Nigeria as an Aid to the Study of Tribal Movement." *Journal of African History* 3 (1962): 251–262.

Wall, Joseph S., and William M. Ross. *Sorghum Production and Utilization*. Westport, Conn.: Avi, 1970.

Webster, Cassandra H. *Mother Africa's Table: A Chronicle of Celebration through West African and African American Recipes and Cultural Traditions*. New York: Doubleday, 1998.

Williams, R. Omosunlola. *Miss Williams' Cookery Book*. London and New York: M. Evans, 1957. Nigerian cuisine.

Wilson, Ellen G. *Good Food from Ghana, Liberia, Nigeria, and Sierra Leone*. New York: M. Evans, 1971.

Diane M. Spivey

AFRICAN AMERICAN FOOD. *See* **United States.**

AFRO-CARIBBEAN. *See* **Caribbean.**

AGENCIES. *See* **Government Agencies; International Agencies.**

AGRICULTURAL RESEARCH. Agricultural research has occurred continuously since humans began shifting food acquisition methods from hunter-gatherer to agrarian. The early goal of agricultural research was simply better methods of producing food. As humans and agriculture progressed, research widened to control of diseases and pests, better cultivars, productive fields or animal rearing facilities, improvement of food crops, and basic biological understanding of plants and animals. The early studies were empirical, that is, trial and error. Nevertheless, these were the forerunners of agricultural research and in many ways the forerunners of many forms of scientific investigation.

Beginnings

Most people place the beginnings of formal agricultural research in the late eighteenth century to the mid-nineteenth century. This relatively long initial phase was caused by several factors. First, many of the other basic sciences were in an early developmental stage. In fact the early agricultural scientists were trained chemists applying their skills to food production. Secondly, governments were reluctant to provide funding for agricultural research. In the United States both George Washington and Thomas Jefferson advocated formal agricultural research as a fundamental component of the newly developed country. However, Congress did not share either president's feeling and did not support a formal agriculture department until 1862. The U.S. Department of Agriculture did not achieve cabinet status until 1889.

Third, many of the world's great universities had not yet been founded or were also in early stages of development. The first colleges involved in agricultural research in the United States were Harvard, Yale, and Princeton. Several of the early endowed chairs in universities were in chemistry, agriculture, or a combination of the two. Fourth, agricultural principles developed were often not applicable to farms or crops in other parts of a country or continent. Thus an initial credibility problem existed with much of the early agricultural research. In the mid-1800s the concept of an experiment station developed in Europe. Some authors credit the Germans with development of the experiment station, while others credit the British. Regardless of the location of the first stations, the concept was to develop agricultural research sites near areas of agricultural production so results would be applicable to the local areas. This concept became common in all areas of agricultural production.

Justus von Liebig is often credited with writing the first book on agricultural research, *Organic Chemistry and Its Applications to Agriculture and Physiology*, published in both Germany and England in 1840. Liebig was an agricultural chemist in Giessen, Germany, one of the first experiment station sites. Liebig also established courses in agricultural chemistry and provided a site for foreign students to study under his tutelage. Numerous students from across Europe and the United States studied under him. The model Liebig developed for research sites near production areas, student training, and course offerings remained the standard for agricultural research around the world in the early twenty-first century.

Developments in the United States

The U.S. government did not establish a formal agricultural research agency until the middle part of the nineteenth century. Early agricultural research, from 1836 to 1862, was conducted by the U.S. Patent Office, which received, on an irregular basis, funds from Congress for specific purposes. Scientists trained in Europe were hired as faculty members by many of the universities and by other nongovernmental groups, such as the Smithsonian Institution. Thus it seems clear that universities in Europe, particularly in Germany and England, were the first to establish formal agricultural research programs.

As the scientific disciplines of chemistry and biology developed, those principles were increasingly applied to food production. In many cases chemical assays and principles were established in direct response to needs in the food and agriculture industries. In the second half of the nineteenth century agricultural research became a recognized discipline in institutes of higher education. The Hatch Experiment Station Act of 1887 established a formal linkage between the U.S. Department of Agriculture, which would supply funding, and state colleges of agriculture, where the research would be conducted. This collaboration between states and the federal government was an important model in governmental relations.

Through the first sixty to seventy years of the twentieth century, Hatch funds were sufficient to conduct research and to train students at universities. However, late in the century Hatch funding received no increases, and the funds diminished in real terms. In the twenty-first century, university scientists working in agriculture must compete for funds from a variety of funding sources, mostly federal government programs, by writing competitive proposals. Congress in collaboration with the president provides funds for the various federal research programs. Thus at times funding for research topics is influenced by political motivations instead of by the common good. Even with staffs and consultants well versed in current topics, this approach diminishes the dialogue on the most important topics that require research support. This change in research funding has positive and negative attributes. On the positive side, only the best research, on topics that have far-reaching implications and those that will have the largest impact on agriculture and society, is conducted. On the negative side, minor agricultural industries rarely receive any of this funding, and development of new opportunities in agriculture is difficult.

E. John Russell (1966) described five phases of agricultural research in Great Britain. While the years may differ, the concepts and general timing are similar to other parts of the world. Phase one began in the late sixteenth century with Francis Bacon and was characterized by numerous individuals conducting research in ancillary areas to agriculture without communication among themselves. This period lasted until the end of the eighteenth century.

The second phase coincided with the emergence of chemistry and lasted until the mid-nineteenth century. Numerous nongovernmental groups were established during the period to promote agriculture, and several universities established formal programs in agricultural sciences. The third phase lasted until the early twentieth century and included establishment of extension activities in university programs as well as expansion of teaching. The fourth stage was a short but important period because of the expansion of experiment stations, research funding from governments, and recognition of the role of agricultural development as an economic development tool. This phase lasted from 1920 to 1930. The fifth phase has lasted into the twenty-first century. Russell described this phase as the time of governmental laboratories and dissociation from farmers and their needs. While Russell's view is rather cynical, many farmers share his point.

As large, multinational companies became involved in agricultural research, much of the generated research

results became proprietary and focused on generation of revenue. However, the range of products developed during the twentieth century was extraordinary, ranging from corn syrup to lecithin and resulting in products that literally changed lives. Breakfast cereals, sliced white bread, hot dog buns, soybean meal, and more changed the way people lived in developed countries and offered the promise of alleviating hunger and malnutrition in the remainder of the world. Agricultural research in universities focused on production of crops, both plant and animal, and on improving efficiency of production. Agricultural engineers led the Industrial Revolution and are rapidly applying space-age technology to tractors. Advanced biological lines of research, including microbiology, biochemistry, molecular biology, and developmental biology, are routine in agricultural research laboratories in the twenty-first century. Practical agricultural research funding, however, is diminishing.

Agricultural research was one of the early areas of formal scientific investigation and remained the foundation for many forms of research in the twenty-first century. Results from this research led to high-quality foods that are moderately priced, significant improvements in health, elimination of various diseases, far-reaching increases in cognitive function, and many other benefits to society.

See also **Agriculture since the Industrial Revolution; Agronomy; Genetic Engineering; Green Revolution; Horticulture.**

BIBLIOGRAPHY

Harding, T. Swann. *Two Blades of Grass: A History of Scientific Development in the U.S. Department of Agriculture.* Norman: University of Oklahoma Press, 1947.

Knoblauch, H. C., E. M. Law, and W. P. Meyer. *State Agricultural Experiment Stations: A History of Research Policy and Procedure.* Miscellaneous Publication no. 904, U.S. Department of Agriculture. Washington, D.C.: U.S. Government Printing Office, 1962.

Rossiter, Margaret W. *The Emergence of Agricultural Science: Justus Liebig and the Americans, 1840–1880.* New Haven, Conn.: Yale University Press, 1975.

Russell, E. John. *A History of Agricultural Science in Great Britain, 1620–1954.* London: Allen and Unwin, 1966.

True, Alfred Charles. *A History of Agricultural Experimentation and Research in the United States, 1607–1925.* Miscellaneous Publication no. 251, U.S. Department of Agriculture. Washington, D.C.: U.S. Government Printing Office, 1937.

Paul B. Brown

AGRICULTURAL WORKERS. In the United States, workers in agriculture include agricultural inspectors, graders and sorters, and farmworkers. While some agricultural workers find permanent, full-time positions, most will work in temporary, low-paying jobs that are seasonal and often require seven-day workweeks with days that begin before sunrise. They may work indoors or outdoors. Most work with food crops or animals. However, increasing agricultural mechanization, consolidation of farms, and urbanization have led to less growth in the number of agricultural jobs in the United States. Growth in landscape and horticultural services will require a shift to fill the need for more workers in horticulture and landscaping. According to the United States Bureau of Labor, the number of jobs in agriculture was expected to grow more slowly than the average for all occupations during the 2000–2010 period.

Agricultural Inspectors

Most agricultural inspectors work in full-time, permanent positions for the federal and state governments. Inspectors frequently examine food crops, livestock, and food processing equipment and facilities for compliance with laws and regulations that govern health, quality, and safety. Inspectors also examine nursery and greenhouse crops. In order to control or eradicate pests and diseases, they collect samples of food or plants and send them to a laboratory for further examination and analysis.

Graders and Sorters

Graders and sorters of agricultural products spend their workdays grading, sorting, and classifying food and other agricultural products such as buckwheat hulls, pickles, olives, nuts, and apples. Fresh-picked fruits and vegetables must be examined and sorted by size, weight, color, or quality before packaging for markets.

Farmworkers

Farmworkers make up 90 percent of all agricultural workers. However, according to the Economic Research Service, the number of farmworkers is difficult to determine since they tend to live in unconventional housing, or are undocumented foreign immigrants who avoid enumerators. Farmworkers include laborers who work with food, greenhouse, and nursery crops, and also caretakers of farm and ranch animals. Compared to most wage and salary workers, farmworkers tend to be younger, less educated, never married, and non-U.S. citizens. Most are male and Hispanic or belong to a minority. Most farmworkers live in poverty. Between 1999 and 2000, the real average weekly earnings of hired farmworkers decreased from $331 to $319 for full-time workers and from $289 to $280 for all hired farmworkers—and the downward trend seems to be continuing.

Migrant farmworkers. Migrant farmworkers make up a large segment of all farmworkers in the United States. Migrant workers travel across state or county boundaries to do agricultural work of a seasonal or other temporary na-

An agricultural worker applies pesticides in a greenhouse in Salinas, California. CORBIS (BELLEVUE).

ture, and often must be absent overnight from their permanent place of residence. In 2000, 36 percent of hired farmworkers were not United States citizens. Almost 78 percent of the non-U.S. citizens working as hired farmworkers were employed in the West, where they accounted for 63 percent of the hired farmworker force. Crop production accounted for 72 percent of migrant farmwork.

Migrant and other farmworkers often work physically exhausting schedules: seven days a week, thirteen hours per day, in rain, heat, and high humidity. For example, while detasseling corn in Illinois in July, a group of migrant workers will likely experience insect bites, heat exhaustion, injury, fatigue, and exposure to pesticides and fertilizers. Workers earn minimum wage and may be provided with temporary housing and access to local health care. Some workers must contend with harassment when local residents mistrust the workers. Language is a barrier, especially for older workers who have not learned English. Families that travel throughout the year must keep up with schoolwork. Local school systems may provide summer school, or students may use the Internet to stay in touch with their courses at home. Sometimes, nonprofit groups will provide migrant schoolchildren with special activities such as swimming classes, library access, or tutoring.

Migrant workers have not always received the help they needed. In the 1960s—at the same time as the civil-rights movement and opposition to the Vietnam War—an effort was made to organize farmworkers in order to improve the quality of their lives. César Chávez, a migrant worker, organized agricultural workers in a successful bid for higher wages, better working conditions, and access to social services such as citizenship classes, immigration advice, and welfare counseling. In the 1970s, the United Farm Workers of America (UFWA) had 150,000 members. By the late 1900s, illegal labor or legal "green card" workers had diminished the power of the UFWA. Few twenty-first-century agricultural workers are members of a union. Some migrant agricultural workers do not have legal authorization to work in the United States.

See also **Agriculture since the Industrial Revolution; Class, Social; Division of Labor; Food Production, History of; High-Technology Farming.**

BIBLIOGRAPHY

Hurt, Douglas R. *American Agriculture: A Brief History.* Ames: Iowa State University Press, 1994.

Mines, Richard, Susan Gabbard, and Anne Steirman. "A Profile of U.S. Farm Workers: Demographics, Household Composition, Income, and Use of Services." *United States Department of Labor, Office of Program Economics Research Report #6.* Washington, D.C.: U.S. Government Printing Office, April 1997.

Runyan, Jack L. "Farm Labor: The Number of Hired Farmworkers Increased in 2000 and Most Now Come from Minority Groups." *Rural America* 16 (Fall 2001): 44–50.

United States Department of Agriculture, Office of Communications. *Agriculture Fact Book 2000.* Washington, D.C.: U.S. Government Printing Office, 2000.

Zeman, Elizabeth. "Migrant Farm Work Creates Hazards, Extra Needs." *The Daily Illini.* University of Illinois–Champaign, 30 August 2001.

Patricia S. Michalak

AGRICULTURE, ORIGINS OF. The last thirty years have seen a revolution in our understanding of the origins of agriculture. What was once seen as a pattern of unilateral human exploitation of domesticated crops and animals has now been described as a pattern of co-evolution and mutual domestication between human beings and their various domesticates. What was once seen as a technological breakthrough, a new concept, or "invention" (the so-called Neolithic revolution) is now commonly viewed as the adoption of techniques and ultimately an economy long known to foragers in which "invention" played little or no role. Since many domesticates are plants that in the wild naturally accumulate around human habitation and garbage, and thrive in disturbed habitats, it seems very likely that the awareness of their growth patterns and the concepts of planting and tending would have been clear to any observant forager; thus, the techniques were not "new." They simply waited use, not discovery. In fact, the concept of domestication may have been practiced first on nonfood crops such as the bottle gourd or other crops chosen for their utility long before the domestication of food plants and the ultimate adoption of food economies based on domesticates (farming).

The question then becomes not how domestication was "invented" but why it was adopted. What was once assumed to depend on cultural diffusion of ideas and/or crops is now seen by most scholars as processes of independent local adoption of various crops.

Patterns of Domestication

The domestication of the various crops was geographically a very widespread series of parallel events. Some scholars now recognize from seven to twelve independent or "pristine" centers in which agriculture was undertaken prior to the diffusion of other crops or crop complexes (although many of these are disputed) scattered throughout Southwest, South, Southeast, and East Asia; North Africa and New Guinea; North, Central, and South America; and possibly North America. As the earliest dates for the first appearance of cultigens are pushed back; as individual "centers" of domestication are found to contain more than one "hearth" where cultivation of different crops first occurred; as different strains of a crop, for example, maize or rice, are found to have been domesticated independently in two or more regions; as an increasing range of crops are studied; and, as little-known local domestic crops are identified in various regions in periods before major crops were disseminated, the number of possible independent or "pristine" centers of domestication is increasing, and the increase seems likely to continue.

Early Domestication of Crops

Combining patterns provided by various scholars (see the bibliography) suggest that major domesticates appear in Southwest Asia or in the Near East (wheat barley, lentils) by 9,000–12,000 B.P. or even earlier; in Thailand (rice) between 12,000 and 8,000 B.P); in China (millet, soybeans, rice) ca. 9,500 B.P.; in Mesoamerica (squash, beans, and maize) between 10,000 B.P. and 5,500 B.P.; in South America (lima beans and peppers) by ca. 8,000–10,000 B.P. and, with less certainty, potatoes and manioc by 6,000 B.P.; and in North America north of Mexico (sunflowers, may grass, chenopods, sump weed, and marsh elder) by 4000–5000 B.P.; in North Africa (pearl millet, sorghum) by 5500–6800 B.P.; in Southeast Asia (taro) by 8000 B.P. and possibly much earlier. (Root crops are presumed to have had even longer histories of domestication in the moist tropics but they are poorly preserved and difficult to document archaeologically.)

As an example of the regional complexity of incipient domestication, there may have been three centers of domestication at three altitudes in South America: a lowland complex involving manioc and sweet potato; a mid-elevation complex involving amaranth, peanut, jicama, and coca; and a high-elevation group including potato and other lesser tubers such as *ullucu*.

The agriculture of particular preferred crops also spread widely by diffusion or population movement in some areas in the prehistoric period. In perhaps the best known patterns of diffusion of agricultural economies (or displacement of indigenous hunter-gatherer populations), Middle Eastern farming economies had spread to Bulgaria by 7500 B.P.; to Italy by 7000 B.P.; and to Britain by 6000–5000 B.P. Maize diffused very widely in North and South America from Mesoamerica (apparently without the significant spread of people); and rice cultivation diffused throughout South, East, and Southeast Asia.

Despite its geographical dispersal, the adoption of the various domestic crop economies occurred within a narrow time span, between about 10,000 and 3,000 B.P. The human population entered a relationship with many different plants at about the same time, implying that human activities were the prime motivator of major economic change and entry into mutual domestication in each instance.

Domestication (genetic manipulation of plants) and the adoption of agricultural economies (primary dependence on domestics as food), once seen as an "event," are now viewed as distinct from one another, each a long process in its own right. There is often a substantial time lag between incipient domestication of a crop and actual dependence on it. That is, the adoption of farming was a gradual quantitative process more than a revolutionary rapid adoption—a pattern of gradually increasing interaction, and degrees of domestication and economic interdependence.

Moreover, the adoption of agriculture was, by all accounts, the coalescence of a long, gradual series of distinctive and often independent behaviors. Techniques used by hunter-gatherers to increase food supplies, long before farming, included the use of fire to stimulate new growth; the protection of favorite plants; sowing seeds or parts of tubers without domestication; preparing soils; eliminating competitors; fertilizing; irrigating; concentration of plants; controlling of growth cycles; expansion of ranges; and ultimately domestication. By this definition, domestication means altering plants genetically to live in proximity to human settlements, enlarging desired parts, breeding out toxins, unpleasant tastes, and physical barriers to exploitation—in short, getting plants to respond to human rather than natural selection.

Dependence on Crops

Almost all authorities describe a gradual increase in the quantitative dependence on domesticated crops. Most also see a quantitative shift from high-quality to low-quality resources (a reduction in the variety and density of essential nutrients, calories, protein, vitamins, minerals, and fatty acids per unit of bulk, desirability of foods, and ease of exploitation). Most also describe a movement downward in the trophic levels of foods exploited A common theme in almost all discussions of the origins of agriculture is the idea of increasingly "intensive" exploitation of foods (the use of increased labor to exploit smaller and smaller areas of land).

This sequence of events commonly first involved a focus on an increasing range (a "broad spectrum") of low-priority wild resources, increasing the efficiency in which space was utilized—a shift from economies focused on comparatively scarce but otherwise valuable large animals and high-quality vegetable resources to one in which new resources or different emphases included smaller game, greater reliance on fish and shellfish, and a focus on low-quality starchy seeds. There is a clear and widespread appearance of and increase in apparatus (grindstones for processing small seeds, fishing equipment, small projectile points) in most parts of the world before the adoption of agriculture, which cannot be a function of differential preservation.

Ultimately the spectrum of exploitation seems to have narrowed again as populations shifted toward more complete modification of landscapes to permit increased dependence on particular low-priority but calorically productive starches that could be obtained in large quantities per unit of space and then stored. Such modification of the land to focus on the quantity of calories per unit of space by promoting staple crops would then eliminate some calorically marginal foods, resulting in a loss of dietary variety and of some nutrients. (The major staples—rice, maize, wheat, barley, potatoes, sweet potatoes, manioc, and taro—all cause dietary deficiencies when relied on too heavily as the sole basis of a diet. The deficiencies are likely to be exacerbated by dry storage, which destroys C and B-complex vitamins.)

Intensification of Resource Use

The intensification can probably be seen best through the eyes of optimal foraging theory, much of which has focused on caloric returns for each unit of labor provided by various foods, and has argued that human groups will go first for high-ranking resources (those that yield high returns for a unit of work including preparation). Repeated studies of comparative efficiency of food-gathering techniques in various parts of the world have routinely reported that human populations should prefer resources such as large game, which, when available, can be exploited with great efficiency. Populations turn to increasing reliance on lower-ranking, that is, less efficiently exploited, resources (small game, shellfish, most nuts, individually caught fish, and small seeds) only as those of higher rank disappear or become so scarce that the time involved in finding them becomes prohibitively high (for example, as large game becomes scarce). Such calculations by scientists do not predict the behavior of individual populations perfectly (presumably because other factors such as local food preferences or inertia come into play). But they do dramatically conform to the broad trends in prehistory relating to a Paleolithic-Mesolithic-Neolithic sequence or its equivalents in the New World. And they suggest that this sequence of economic changes is one of declining efficiency in resource exploitation.

Resources used increasingly in the intensification of individual units of land—the so-called broad-spectrum revolution—typically provided fewer calories per unit of labor than the comparative emphasis on large animal exploitation that preceded them. Small seeds such as wheat, barley rice, and maize typically are among the least productive resources (and among the lowest priority as well in taste and quality) and would presumably have come into use only as preferred resources disappeared or became prohibitively scarce. Seasonal seeds, although potentially harvested quickly and in large quantity, typically involved intensive processing and the labor of storage as well as significant storage losses. A significant point is that the adoption of low-ranking resources depended not on their availability but on the declining availability of higher resources. Cereals were adopted not because they were or had become available but because preferred resources such as large game were becoming less available.

The major cereals are relatively inefficient to exploit and process, as demonstrated by Kenneth Russell with specific reference to the Middle Eastern cradle of wheat and barley cultivation. Agriculture, therefore, may not have been "invented" so much as adopted and dropped repeatedly as a consequence of the availability or scarcity of higher-ranked resources. This pattern may in fact be

Working the fields in ancient Egypt, as depicted in the Book of the Dead of Heruben, circa 1069– 945 B.C.E. © GIANNI DAGLI ORTI/CORBIS.

visible among Natufian, or Mesolithic, populations in the Middle East whose patterns of exploitation sometimes appear to defy any attempt to recognize, naively, a simple sequence of the type described above.

Technological changes were motivated by necessity or by demand, not by independent invention or technological advance. In a trend toward declining efficiency, one does not adopt new technologies simply because they are available. Such innovations may well be held in reserve until changing conditions render them the best remaining alternatives. Demand-side economics seems to have powered most of economic history; Malthusian or supply-side economics, with supply independent from demand, became the predominant pattern only when the rise of social classes prevented the needs of the poor from generating any economic "demand"—which implies not only need but entitlement (the ability to command resources).

Various sources point out, however, that such "intensification" occurred in parallel among incipient farmers and populations such as those of the West Coast of the United States, which developed an intense focus on storing starchy staples (such as acorns) but never domesticated them. The two activities may be distinguished, and centers of origin of domestication may be defined, less by human knowledge or intent as by the flexibility or recalcitrance of the intensively harvested plants toward incipient domestication. Some resources such as wheat respond readily to human manipulation; others such as acorns/oak trees defy it.

Increased demand results from population growth, climate change, and socially induced demand. Mark Cohen argues that population growth and increasing population density—or a combination of population growth and declining availability of preferred foods, which result in "population pressure" or an imbalance between population, resources, and prevalent food choices and extractive strategies—may be the main trigger of relevant economic changes. Such increasing density is ultimately traceable to the Pleistocene with the gradual density-dependent closing of cultural systems as increased density permitted groups to switch from exogamy to endogamy. According to this model, the widespread parallelism of different regions is based on the power of population flux (movement between groups) to equalize population pressure from region to region. The model has been criticized for, among other reasons, relying too much on flux as an explanatory necessity, for having the wrong time scale, and for underplaying the role of climate change.

A second category emphasizes the role of post-Pleistocene climate change in both facilitating and demanding exploitation of plants amenable to domestication. It has been argued, in fact, that farming would have been essentially impossible during the Pleistocene, but almost mandatory, at least in a competitive sense, in the Holocene. This model may provide a more powerful explanation of the regional parallelism of intensification in time than a purely population growth/flux model. The climate-based model has been criticized, however, as ignoring the fact that climate and environmental changes are zonal and therefore could not, of themselves, produce parallel economic changes in different environments undergoing different kinds of change.

A third major category that explains increased demand suggests that it resulted from enhanced social and political demand preceding and accompanying intensification. The problem is that such explanations, unless combined with data on population growth or climate change, fail to explain the parallel emergence of complex social forms.

Agriculture and the Decline in Health, Nutrition, and Food Security

Agriculture commonly has been associated with a number of social features: reduced territories, more marked social boundaries, further closing of mating systems; greater territoriality and formal definitions of property; complex social and political organization; more defined concepts of property; food storage; and sedentism. Moreover, agriculture has until recently been considered the cause or enabler of these altered social institutions. These features are only loosely bound, may be separated by long spans of time, and may occur in any of various sequences. For example, sedentism in many regions occurs long before domestication (as in parts of the Middle East), but in the New World the reverse often occurs—domesticates appearing long before settled reliance on those domesticates. Social complexity may commonly follow the origins of agriculture but precedes it in many parts of the world and, as mentioned above, occurs without domestication in some parts of the world.

Changes in Health

What was once interpreted by researchers as a transition toward improving human health, nutrition, reliability of the food supply, greater ease of food procurement, and greater longevity is now viewed as the start of declining health, nutrition, and efficiency of labor, probably declining longevity, and perhaps even declining security of food supplies. It is now commonly accepted that the adoption of farming economies and sedentism resulted in declining health and nutrition. The conclusion is based on triangulation from three sources: contemporary observation of hunting and gathering versus farming societies; theoretical patterns of nutrients and parasites in nature; and paleopathology, the analysis of health and nutrition in prehistoric skeletons representing different periods of prehistory. Many sources have found parallel trends toward declining health in prehistoric populations but challenges to quantitative methods, interpretations of some evidence, and some specific conclusions in paleopathology have been offered. Observed paleopathological trends commonly accord with expectations from other lines of evidence.

It seems probable from epidemiological considerations—and it is clear from paleopathology—for example, that farming, large concentrations of population and sedentism, the accumulation of human feces, and the attraction of stored foods to potentially disease-bearing animals markedly increased parasite loads on human populations. The increase in the prevalence of visible periostitis, osteomyelitis, treponemal infection, and tuberculosis in skeletal populations conforms both to ethnographic observations and models of probable disease history. The reduction of wild animal meat in the diet with the increasing focus on vegetable foods may initially have reduced the likelihood of food-borne diseases (of which animals are the major source). But the domestication of animals, their crowding, and their continuing proximity to human populations are likely to have raised meat-borne infections to new highs and seems responsible for epidemic diseases in human populations, many of which began as zoonotic (animal-borne) disease shared by people and domestic animals.

Consequences of Agriculture

Sedentism and farming resulted in declining quality of nutrition (or at least in the decline in the quality of nutrients available to the human populations). Indeed, some researchers have extolled the virtue of hunter-gatherer diets. Agriculture is likely to have resulted in a marked downturn in food diversity and food quality, and ultimately to a decline in nutrition. An increase in cumulative neurotoxins may have occurred as farming was adopted, the latter despite the fact that domestication itself may have bred toxic substances out of foods.

Agriculture also seems to have resulted in a change in the texture of foods toward softer foods, resulting in a decline in tooth wear but an increase in dental caries and a reduction in jaws and jaw strength. A significant advantage of soft foods based on boiling in ceramic pots, a practice largely restricted to sedentary populations, may have been the increasing potential for early weaning of children and improved food for toothless elders. But early weaning to cereals as opposed to a diet of mother's milk is well known to have serious negative effects on childhood nutrition, infection, and survival.

A dramatic increase in iron deficiency anemia (porotic hyperostosis and cribra orbitalia) is associated everywhere in the archaeological record with both sedentism, infection, and new crops. The trend is also predictable in nature, and may be observed in contemporary populations. The increased anemia probably resulted primarily from a large increase in iron-robbing hookworm associated with sedentism and with the sequestering by the body of its own iron as protection against bacterial disease.

The declining health that came with the advent of farming is also reflected in (but not universally) childhood declines in stature, osteoporosis in children, decreases in tooth size (as a result of declining maternal nutrition), and tooth defects.

Whether the adoption of broad-spectrum foraging, agriculture, storage, and sedentism increased or decreased the reliability of food supplies (and whether sedentism is itself a consequence of choice permitted by new resources or necessitated by them) is a matter of some debate. For example, it is not clear whether broad-spectrum foraging increased reliability by expanding the resource base, or decreased reliability by focusing exploitation on what had once been emergency resources.

Domestication, sedentism, and storage appear to have evened out potential seasonal shortages in resources, but they may also have reduced the reliability of the food supply by decreasing the variety of foods consumed; by preventing groups from moving in response to shortages; by creating new vulnerability of plants selected for human rather than natural needs; by moving resources beyond their natural habitats to which they are adapted for survival; and by the increase in post-harvest food loss through storage—not only because stored resources are vulnerable to rot, or theft by animals, but stores are subject to expropriation by human enemies. One possible biological clue to the resolution of this problem is that signs of episodic stress (enamel hypoplasia and microdefects in teeth in skeletal populations) generally become more common after agriculture was adopted.

Sedentary agriculture seems likely to have increased human fertility through a variety of mechanisms, including the shifting work loads for women; calorically richer diets; sedentism; and the increased marginal utility of children or the increased availability of weaning foods. Some researchers estimate that during the Mesolithic-Neolithic transition in the Iberian Peninsula fertility may have increased as much as from four to six live births per

mother, which would imply very rapid acceleration of population growth. If, in fact, fertility on average increased (possibly significantly) but population growth on average accelerated only by the trivial amount calculated below, then life expectancy must on average have declined (since growth rates are a balance of both fertility and mortality). (There is little evidence from paleopathology that the adoption of sedentary farming increased on average human life expectancy and little reason to expect that it did.)

For whatever reasons, essentially all estimates of average post-domestication population growth suggest an increase in rates of population growth (calculated as compound interest rates). But on average, the increase can have been no more than from about .003 percent per year for pre-Neolithic hunter-gatherers to about 0.1 percent for Neolithic and post-Neolithic farmers. (In both cases the averages are simple mathematical calculations of what is possible based on all reasonable estimates of world population at the period of adoption of agricultural (about 5–25 million) to estimated population in 1500 C.E. (about five hundred million). Average population growth even after the onset of agriculture would therefore have been trivial to the point where it would have been almost imperceptible to the populations involved. It would have taken such populations about one thousand years to double in size. Growth and dispersal of agricultural populations and/or diffusion of domestic crops were hardly likely to have been exuberant in most locations for that reason, particularly if arguments about declining health and very low average growth rates are considered. Owing to their low rank as resources, crops would presumably have diffused only to populations facing similar levels of demand or pressure but lacking good local domesticates of their own.

On the other hand, population growth might have been comparatively quite rapid in some areas because of increased fertility and improved life expectancy. Exuberant growth in some areas, such as Europe, must have been balanced by the decline of other populations, including those of other farmers. Exuberant growth, or diffusion, perhaps based on the relative quality of some cereals such as wheat and barley among otherwise low-ranking, intensively exploited resources, is observable in areas (such as the expansion of the Middle Eastern farming complex and probable expansion of agriculture populations into Europe). But even there, in contrast to old models assuming population expansion of hunter-gatherer "bands" into areas of very low population density, expansion would, based on observed intensity of exploitation, have been expanding into areas occupied by hunter-gatherers, who would by this time have had population densities and social complexity almost equal to their own. The pre-existing size and structure of groups of hunter-gatherers in areas of agricultural spread suggests that diffusion may have played a bigger role in the process than was once assumed.

Since health and nutrition seem to have declined, the primary advantage to farmers seems to have been both political and military because of the ability to concentrate population and raise larger armies. This would have conferred a considerable advantage in power at a time when few if any weapons were available that were capable of offsetting numerical superiority.

See also **Agriculture since the Industrial Revolution; Anthropology and Food; Barley; Food Archaeology; Horticulture; Paleonutrition, Methods of; Prehistoric Societies: Food Producers; Wheat.**

BIBLIOGRAPHY

Bogin, Barry. "The Evolution of Human Nutrition." In *The Anthropology of Medicine*, edited by L. K. Romanucci-Ross, L. Daniel E. Moerman, and Laurence R. Trancredi, pp. 96-142. Westport, Conn.: Bergin and Garvey, 1997.

Boserup, Ester. *The Conditions of Agricultural Growth.* Chicago: Aldine, 1965.

Cohen, Mark Nathan. *The Food Crisis in Prehistory.* New Haven: Yale University Press, 1977.

Cohen, Mark Nathan. *Health and the Rise of Civilization.* New Haven: Yale University Press, 1989.

Eaton, S. Boyd, Melvin D. Konner, and Marjorie Shostak. *The Paleolithic Prescription.* New York: Harper and Row, 1988.

Ingold, Tim, ed. *Companion Encyclopedia of Anthropology.* New York: Routledge, 1994.

Johns, Timothy. "The Chemical Ecology of Human Ingestive Behaviors." *Annual Review of Anthropology* 28 (1999): 27–50.

Kiple, Kenneth F., and Kriemhild Coneè Ornelas, eds. *The Cambridge World History of Food.* Cambridge, U.K.: Cambridge University Press, 2000.

Larsen, Clark. "Changes in Human Populations with Agriculture." *Annual Review of Anthropology* 24 (1995): 185–236.

Price, T. Douglas, and James A. Brown, eds. *Prehistoric Hunter Gatherers.* New York: Academic Press, 1985.

Rindos, David. *The Origins of Agriculture.* New York: Academic Press, 1984.

Wenke, Robert J. *Patterns in Prehistory.* 4th ed. New York: Oxford University Press, 1999.

Mark Nathan Cohen

AGRICULTURE SINCE THE INDUSTRIAL REVOLUTION.

It is difficult for people living in an advanced industrialized society to fully comprehend the life of a modern farmer, much less the life of farmers living before the Industrial Revolution. Up until the end of the eighteenth century, the vast majority of people were farmers who, as described by the English philosopher Thomas Hobbes in *Leviathan*, lived lives that were "solitary, poor, nasty, brutish and short." And so it had been since the beginning of time for the vast majority of people, until the advent of an agricultural revolution that started in Great Britain during the early 1700s, reached North America by the mid-1800s, and continues to this day in all but the most benighted of nations. Agriculture

had been changing since it had first appeared thousands of years earlier, but the pace quickened during the start of the Industrial Revolution in the eighteenth century, and changes that had previously taken centuries and generations began to occur within decades. By 1750, the best English agriculture was the best in the world. The most technologically advanced agriculture, it was also fully integrated into a market economy. The dominance of the British Empire in world affairs during the eighteenth and nineteenth centuries ensured that these agricultural improvements were widely distributed.

The Europe-centered Industrial Revolution of the eighteenth and nineteenth centuries accelerated an ongoing revolution in agriculture. In the industrialized West, animal power and human labor were first augmented and than almost completely replaced with mechanized sources of power. This was only part of the changes that gathered momentum in the 1700s and then transformed the world. Spectacular developments in all areas of science and nearly two centuries of exploration and conquest in the New World caused many Europeans in the early nineteenth century to reevaluate their relationship with nature. They developed an expanded worldview; it appeared to them that humanity in general, and Europeans specifically, had acquired the wisdom, knowledge, and scientific technology to dominate nature. This conviction was reinforced by the publication in 1859 of the *Origin of Species* by Charles Darwin. While the new attitude initially produced colonialism, rampant environmental pollution, and the exploitation of poorly organized workers, it also permitted the manipulation of the entire farming environment to an extent inconceivable to previous generations, and later produced for common people a standard of living previously available only to the aristocracy.

This new point of view stripped plants, animals, and soil of their mystical "vital" attributes and made of them machines to be molded to fit human needs. Physics, chemistry, and biology became tools to dissect, examine, and then reconstruct agricultural systems to make them better than any that had previously existed on earth. This process started with improved methods of crop production, advances in livestock breeding, and the invention of new farm equipment during the latter part of the Industrial Revolution. Soil, for example, ceased to contain a vital essence that must be periodically replenished by removing it from cultivation (fallowing), and became an aggregation of mineral and organic structures and chemicals whose fertility could be maintained by the application of scientific management—crop rotation, fertilizers, irrigation, pesticides, and other new methods. Adoption of new power sources, such as steam, and increased use of chemicals followed. Today, improved plant and livestock breeding through genetic engineering promises to continue the revolution well into the future.

Agricultural advances after the Industrial Revolution greatly increased food production, but increased urbanization required food to be transported long distances from producers to consumers. As with the citizens of ancient Rome, inhabitants of the ever-expanding cities became increasingly dependent on the transport, preservation, and storage of food. People starved in one part of the world, while abundant harvests spilled from granaries in another. The storage and distribution of food, rather than its production, became crucial to millions of people.

There have been periodic learned pronouncements of impending mass starvation since the English economist Thomas Malthus first proposed in his 1798 *Essay on the Principle of Population* that food production could only increase arithmetically, while population would increase geometrically. Malthus wrote that population would exceed food production at some point, and an apocalypse would ensue. While population growth has borne out his thesis for the past two hundred years, a number of scientific advances have allowed agricultural production to keep pace with it. A few major and thousands of minor refinements in agricultural practices have steadily improved productivity.

Farming Efficiency

Before the 1700s, the problem of soil fertility had been met by letting half or a third of the land go fallow for a year in two- and three-field rotations. A new four-field rotation was now based on growing specific kinds of crops in a sequence that took from or added to the soil different nutrients. Part of the field did not have to be left fallow, and the continuous use of the land greatly increased the production of forage crops used to support livestock through the winter, thereby vastly increasing the availability of meat and dairy products. The diet of even the poorest improved as they could now afford to augment their daily bread with meat and cheese.

Another major change was a rapid acceleration in the fencing of large tracts of land to produce more efficient units of production. The enclosure movement in England did away with many traditional smallholdings, combining the land into larger tracts that could be more efficiently farmed. Earlier subdividing of land among generations of sons had produced a patchwork-quilt distribution of fields. A farmer may have had access to sufficient crop area (around twenty acres) to support his family, but it would be in small strips scattered among the holdings of other farmers, in a number of fields. This was because it was thought that each field had to remain fallow for a year to recover its fertility. From 1750 to 1831, enclosures consolidated these smallholdings into fields whose size could benefit from the application of modern methods of crop production.

Until the 1700s and 1800s peasants in most European countries could not actually own the land they farmed, but held ancestral rights to work land belonging to the proprietors of large estates. When laws were passed that allowed British landowners to abrogate these traditional agreements and combine many smallholdings, thousands of farm families were displaced. Migrating to urban areas, they furnished the labor that fueled the Industrial Revolution, and the wretched characters who populated many of Charles Dickens's novels.

Throughout Europe, similar changes produced millions of restless people with a deep-seated desire to own land. Many emigrated to North America, Australia, and New Zealand, where a variety of homestead laws granted land to those who settled and worked a farm or ranch for a number of years. Based on these policies, the family farm became an institution in North America during the nineteenth and twentieth centuries, and a social and political force that continues to shape our national character. A combination of economic and demographic changes, however, has led to the steady decline in the number of functioning family farms. Although the U.S. population doubled between 1930 and 2000, the number of farms fell from 7 to 2 million. After 1987, this decline stabilized at about one percent annually. The price farmers got for commodities such as corn and soybeans remained virtually constant between 1970 and 2000, while the price they paid for everything they bought kept pace with inflation. This produced a farming population 60 percent of whom had farm incomes below the poverty line. It also discouraged the young so much that the number of farmers under the age of twenty-five decreased 50 percent between 1990 and 2000.

The large capital inputs needed to start and run a farm have transformed the production of many agricultural crops into large businesses. Ninety percent of U.S. farms, however, continue to be classified as individual operations, accounting for 71 percent of farmland and 74 percent of gross farm sales. Partnerships and corporations comprise a very small share of American farms, and people related by blood or marriage own 90 percent of them. Average acreage is higher for corporate farms (1,165 acres) and for partnerships (856 acres) than for individual operations (373 acres). Whereas the United States in the year 2000 had 2 million farms, just 60,000 of them produced 75 percent of the nation's farm output. Fewer and fewer farms were thus producing more and more of what Americans ate. The 1.3 million farms with incomes below $20,000 comprised 60 percent of the total number of farms, but cultivated only 17 percent of the total U.S. farm acreage. In contrast, the 60,000 farms with sales over $250,000 comprised only 7 percent of the total number, yet cultivated almost 30 percent of the acreage.

The many improvements in crop production up to 1935 produced only modest increases in average yield per acre in America because of deteriorating soil fertility and poor water use. Control of erosion, soil conservation, extensive government-backed irrigation developments, and better water-use efficiency reversed this trend, leading to large increases in production.

Since 1950, the gap in efficiency between the most productive mechanized agricultural systems and the least productive manual farming systems has increased twentyfold. While in small part the result of reduced soil, water, and environmental quality in developing countries, this change really reflects the spectacular advances in agricultural technology in industrialized counties. Transference of this technology to farmers throughout the world should be a major goal, and will be a major challenge to the fortunate few in the coming decades.

Livestock Breeding

Before the eighteenth century, raising animals was slow and costly; thus, meat and dairy products were usually scarce and expensive before the Industrial Revolution. The lack of sufficient forage to keep large numbers of animals over the winter often led to the slaughter of most livestock in the fall. Celebrants at many late fall festivals not only consumed the bountiful harvest of the field, but also the animals whose progeny could have supplied them with fresh meat, milk, and cheese the following year. Each spring, herds had to be rebuilt from the survivors.

Farmers had used their intuition and observations to breed animals for millennia, but the process was slow and haphazard because the inheritance of desirable traits was poorly understood. In the late 1700s Robert Bakewell, an English farmer, showed how intensive breeding for desirable traits could produce improved cattle, horses, and sheep. In Europe, sheep had been raised mainly for wool because they fattened too slowly to provide an economic source of meat. Bakewell's Leicester breed fattened quickly and could therefore be raised for both wool and slaughter. The cost of mutton dropped so low that it became the most popular meat in England, Australia, and New Zealand.

Breeding of livestock is now a science in industrial societies, with genetic analysis an integral aspect. Accurate monitoring to detect estrus, or its induction by hormones, and the use of artificial insemination allow complete control over the reproductive cycle of most livestock. Removal of ova, their in vitro fertilization, and embryo implantation promise to allow a further level of control and manipulation of the reproductive process. For example, separation of the cells resulting from the first divisions of the fertilized ovum (zygote) may be used to produce a number of embryos that, when implanted, give rise to whole herds of genetically identical animals. These techniques are being coupled with the genetic engineering of DNA in specific chromosomes, or the replacement of the entire nucleus in a zygote with a nucleus from another individual of the same, or a related, species (cloning). While possibly replete with ethical conundrums, these procedures will surely transform livestock into units of production whose fecundity, efficiency, and vigor would marvel our ancestors.

Plant Breeding

Once Mendelian genetics was rediscovered in 1900, science gave plant and animal breeders a clear under-standing of how traits were controlled by genes on chromosomes, and how they could be altered by selective breeding. Breeders made full use of this knowledge to steadily improve livestock and crops. Plants such as maize, soybeans, tomatoes, and peanuts became dietary staples in many parts of the world after their introduction from the Americas, Africa, and Asia. Identifying the sites of their origin helped locate ancestral forms of many crops, and these plants provided additional genetic resources to improve commercial varieties.

The upper limit of plant productivity is imposed by the quantum efficiency of photosynthesis and the energy content of sunlight. The photosynthate translocated from leaves not only produces the harvestable commodity, but is also used for all other plant functions. Reducing the drain of these other functions can increase yield. For example, symbiotic microorganisms in nodules on soybean roots can fix atmospheric nitrogen. It is often cheaper, however, to supply nitrogen fertilizers fixed by processes involving fossil fuels than to incur the loss of yield that would result from the soybean plant fixing a similar amount of nitrogen. Modification of the basic biochemistry and physiology underlying crop and livestock production will require levels of scientific knowledge and technical sophistication currently unavailable.

Economics of industrial-scale production require that most agriculture is monoculture, involving vast fields and herds of nearly genetically identical crops and livestock. This uniformity simplifies all aspects of production, but it also invites epidemics of plant disease. The devastating outbreak of bacterial southern corn blight in the United States in 1970, and the 2001 epidemic of viral foot-and-mouth disease in England, are examples of the seriousness of this problem. A major goal of plant and animal breeders is to stay ahead of chronic or exotic pathogens that can decimate crops and herds.

Genetic engineering has the potential to quickly create crops and livestock with unique characteristics. Rapid release of genetically modified organisms is slowed, however, because they require the same extensive field testing as new strains derived from traditional breeding. Consumer wariness has slowed the introduction of GMOs in Europe, but American consumers have readily accepted them. Most U.S. consumers have been unaware of the presence of GMOs in their food, and when they become aware, they are willing to accept claims by scientific and government sources that GMOs are safe to eat and environmentally benign. In Europe, a greater level of environmental activism and skepticism in government and scientific pronouncements has contributed to consumers' doubts about the safety and environmental impact of GMO crops. A large percentage of U.S. corn, soybean, and cotton production uses GMOs that possess pest resistance. Tailoring GMOs to the specific needs of farmers in developing countries may be the only way for food production to keep pace with their rapidly increasing populations. Crops designed with increased disease and drought resistance and better use of nutrients in the soil could supplant the strains that have been developed for use in industrialized countries and that require expensive irrigation, pesticides, and fertilizers that are unavailable in developing countries.

Development of hybrid corn was a watershed in plant breeding, heralding a change in concept from a straightforward selection of desirable characteristics to the employment of a deeper understanding of the genetics involved. Experiments by G. H. Shull in 1906 showed that crossing could reverse reductions in vigor resulting from inbreeding. Using the strategy of double-cross hybrids suggested by D. F. Jones in 1918, the first commercial corn hybrid was released in 1921. About 95 percent of the corn now grown is hybrid, and use of double-cross hybrids allows 20 percent more corn to be produced on 25 percent fewer acres than when hybrid corn first became widely available in 1930. Hybrids of many other agronomic and horticultural crops have since been developed.

The Green Revolution. The Green Revolution, a sterling example of how the development of strains suited for developing countries, and a multifaceted approach to agriculture, can greatly increase food production, was a planned international effort funded by the Rockefeller and Ford Foundations and the governments of many developing countries. In the early 1950s, wheat production in Mexico had encountered an insurmountable yield barrier because the varieties being grown became too tall, top-heavy, and lodged (fell over and were difficult to harvest) when heavily fertilized. Using short-stalked lines developed years earlier by the U.S. Department of Agriculture, Norman E. Borlaug led an effort to develop broadly adapted, short-stemmed, disease-resistant wheats that excelled at converting fertilizer and water into high yields. Mexico went from importing half its wheat in 1964 to exporting half a million tons annually within two decades.

The Green Revolution is an agricultural success story. It increased food production in Mexico tenfold from 1960 to 1990 through the use of new crop varieties, irrigation, fertilizers, pesticides, and mechanization. At the same time, famine decreased 20 percent, caloric consumption per capita increased 25 percent, and incomes and standards of living increased. The successes in Mexico led to the establishment of a rice-breeding center in the Philippines. Working at about eighteen such centers worldwide, plant breeders have produced high-yielding varieties of virtually every major crop, including potato, sorghum, maize, cassava, and beans. Increased population growth and poor husbandry of natural resources, however, have eroded many of these gains since the 1980s.

Farm Equipment

Preparing the soil with a plow, planting seeds, cultivation, harvesting, and threshing are some of the most important steps in crop production, and some of the most

labor- and energy-intensive. Inventions in the eighteenth and nineteenth centuries transferred much of farm labor to machines. Before Jethro Tull invented the precision seed drill in 1701, seeds were inefficiently planted by scattering them over a prepared field. Stands were thus often erratic and almost impossible to cultivate. The uniform placement of seeds in straight rows allowed horse-drawn cultivators to move easily up and down the rows for the control of weeds.

Little cotton was grown in the United States before the late 1790s because of the difficulty of separating the lint from the seed. Development of the cotton gin by Eli Whitney in 1793 greatly reduced the cost of producing cotton fiber for the rapidly increasing British textile industry. Slumps in production of tobacco, indigo, and rice during the 1790s had undermined the economic justification for slavery, but increased production of sugarcane and upland cotton still relied on the institution. The production of cotton in America now jumped twentyfold, from 2 million pounds in 1790 to 40 million pounds in 1800, while exports increased over 1000 percent in the same period. In less than a generation, cotton became the major crop grown in the U.S. South, and it revived the moribund slave-worked plantation system.

The first successful harvester or reaper was invented by Cyrus McCormick in 1834, as was the first modern thresher, by Hiram and John Pitts. The outbreak of the American Civil War in 1861 and subsequent conscription depleted farm labor, and forced many wheat farmers to buy reaping machines. The harvesting and threshing functions were later integrated into one machine, the combine, which did not become widely used until the early 1900s. Replacement of the cast-iron plow by the self-polishing steel plow, invented by John Deere in 1837, reduced the energy needed to plow a field because soil did not adhere to the smooth surface. To reach their full potential, most of these inventions depended on mechanical sources of power, which did not become readily available until the early twentieth century.

The major functions of a machine were often perfected over years of experimentation and modification. Sometimes mechanical limitations prevented further refinements, or an existing machine could not be easily modified to accommodate a new crop. When that occurred, it might be found easier to modify the crop to fit existing machines than to build entirely new machines. Dwarf sorghum was developed so it could be harvested with only slight modifications to an existing combine, and soybeans were developed that bore pods higher on the stalk so they could more easily be harvested. Tomatoes for processing were developed that had a more uniform set and were tough enough for mechanical harvesting using existing technology.

Integration of computers, sensors, and global positioning satellites into field equipment promises to revolutionize the planting, cultivation, and harvesting of many crops. For example, the location of each corn or tomato plant in a field can be identified using sensors and GPSs, and stored in computer memory. Subsequent operations such as weeding, applications of pesticides and fertilizers, and harvesting can then be positioned to maximize the effectiveness of every operation, thereby increasing yield and quality while at the same time reducing expenditures of time, fuel, and chemicals.

Energy and Information

In essence, farming is the conversion of sunlight and other sources of energy into food. For most of recorded history the energy to plant, cultivate, harvest, and process crops was supplied by the farmer and by domesticated draft animals (such as oxen and horses). Necessarily, the energy captured by the plant and harvested as food calories had to exceed that expended in its production. Preindustrial agriculture generally returned around twenty times more calories in the food consumed than was expended during its production. This efficiency decreases as the consumed food product requires additional processing (as for white bread versus grain potage, or cheese versus milk), conversion to other forms (cornflakes versus corn used to produce beefsteak), and shipment to distant consumers. As agriculture became mechanized, greater and greater amounts of energy were expended for each unit of food produced. Currently, mechanized agriculture in developed countries uses ten times as much energy to produce food as is returned in the food consumed. But agricultural mechanization has increased productivity so much that today's farmer can feed almost 150 people, while at the beginning of the twentieth century a farmer could feed only 2.5 people. The vast input of fossil fuels to synthesize the required fertilizers and pesticides, and to power the machinery that cultivates the fields, harvests the crops, processes them, and transports them to the consumer has so increased production that a small percentage of the population can raise enough food to keep most Americans overweight.

Before the Industrial Revolution, there was localized use of wind and water power for milling grain and pumping water, but these sources were stationary, and of no use in planting or plowing a field, or harvesting a crop. The earliest tractors were basically large stationary engines equipped with a drive system. At first, steam engines were immobile and of little use for field operations because of their enormous weight. Even in the mid-1800s steam-powered tractors were so expensive and difficult to operate that most farmers continued to use horses and mules to power farm machines. The introduction of high-pressure boilers in the 1850s lightened engines, and steam tractors enjoyed significant usage between 1885 and 1914. Tractors with internal-combustion engines eventually supplanted steam tractors because they had several advantages: they were cheaper, easier to operate, and less prone to explosions and fires.

World War I (1914–1918) did for the tractor what the American Civil War had done for the reaping ma-

chine. Soon after it began, German U-boats were sinking so many British ships that it was necessary to increase food production by bringing thousands of acres of new farmland into production or face food shortages. There were not enough horses to plow this new land, and only five hundred tractors in all of Britain. The five thousand tractors ordered by the British government from Henry Ford were delivered within five months, and were soon at work on British farms. Almost overnight, British farmers, and later their conscripted American visitors, became accustomed to seeing tractors displacing teams of horses.

The labor shortage and guaranteed market for crops during World War I stimulated U.S. tractor design and manufacture; massive industrialization led to greatly increased production. It was not until after World War II, however, that tractors became widely accepted. Many farmers bought early tractors, particularly the smaller, lighter machines that could do varied field work, but the worldwide depression of the 1930s and the fact that tractors still couldn't compete with the agility of horses in the field led to the demise of many tractor companies. Most farmers would have been thrilled to be rid of draft animals and to use mechanical devices. During the period 1908–1927 Ford built over 15 million automobiles with the Model T engine. Many farmers had a car or truck that was used to supply power for nonfield operations and for trips to town, yet continued to use draft animals for fieldwork; the Sears catalog of the time listed hundreds of accessories that could be used with the drive train of a car or truck to do everything from threshing grain and pumping water to churning butter, sawing wood, and washing clothes. Only when tractors appeared with enough power and maneuverability for fieldwork and the flexibility to furnish power for other nonfield operations were they readily adopted by most farmers. It was not until the 1920s that the all-purpose tractor made its appearance and gradually replaced steam-powered machines and draft animals. By the 1930s, seven tractor companies controlled over 90 percent of the market, and North America led the world in tractor design and production. Today, tractors using gasoline or diesel engines are ubiquitous on farms throughout the world.

Most farms in Europe and Japan had electrical power by the mid-1930s. Only 10 percent of U.S. farms were so supplied, however, at the time the Federal government established the Rural Electrification Administration in 1935. The REA supplied economic incentives that stimulated rural electrification; by 1960, over 97 percent of American farms had electricity.

Electricity brought with it better communication through the telegraph, telephone, radio, television, and eventually the Internet, all of which in turn have had tremendous effects on the farmer's life. Farms are no longer isolated from the mainstream of society. Information on weather and on commodity prices is readily available, and can assist in better planning. Farming has become such a capital-, energy-, and information-intensive business that most farmers need assistance in managing it all. Most industrialized countries have government-sponsored agricultural-research and extension services. These not only engage in practical research of immediate and local importance, but also provide significant levels of basic research to address future problems. They assist farmers, marketers, and distributors through publications, interactive websites, classes, and farm visits and demonstrations. Almost more than any other aspect of modern agriculture, the extension services are responsible for today's unmatched levels of food production, nutrition, and safety.

Agricultural Chemicals

All living things are groups of simple and complex chemicals functioning together in specific and unimaginably complex ways. Since all living things are interrelated through evolution, they are very similar at the molecular level. This means that many require roughly the same resources (thus, all plants need sunlight, carbon dioxide, water, and a few common minerals), and can be food for one another (thus, the starch stored by a potato can be used for its future growth or consumed by humans). Many organisms therefore compete for the same scarce resources and develop elaborate strategies to avoid being eaten. Weeds are simply plants that out-compete crops for the resources that limit plant growth and that we apply in profusion to cultivated crops. During domestication, the elimination of many natural defense mechanisms to produce a more easily grown, harvested, or palatable crop also produces a crop more vulnerable to pests. Reintroduction of specific natural defense mechanisms through selective genetic engineering could drastically reduce the dependence of agriculture on synthetic pesticides.

Modern agriculture is based on the establishment of a monoculture in which one specific crop or animal is grown or raised over large areas to the exclusion of all potentially competing organisms. Methods of planting, cultivation, and harvesting are all geared to the growth of uniform plants and animals. An orchard is usually composed of genetically identical (cloned) trees. Each tree will flower at roughly the same time, and produce fruits that look and taste the same and ripen at the same time. Fields are often modified to provide growing conditions that are as close as possible to being identical for all plants to further limit variability. Pruning, applications of pesticide sprays, cultivations, irrigation, and harvesting can be done over the entire orchard because all trees and fruit are at similar stages of growth and will respond similarly. An orchard composed of dissimilar seedlings would have trees that flowered at different times, and have fruit that were green or red, sweet or tart, or large or small, and that ripened at different times. The susceptibility of trees and fruits to various pests would be different, so different pesticides would have to be used at different times and rates of application. As with the other field operations, harvesting would have to be done a number of

Wheat harvest on a collective farm near Lvov, Ukraine, in 1991. © PETER TURNLEY/CORBIS.

times, and would have to be selective since the fruit on each tree would ripen at a different rate. Fruit, or any other agricultural commodity, produced in this way would be expensive and of variable quality—two attributes abhorrent to modern consumers.

Most undisturbed natural ecosystems are stable because they contain many species of plants and animals that are genetically diverse, that can exploit all the available niches, and that interact with one another to hinder the uncontrolled growth of a single pest or disease. In a monoculture the genetic and species diversity that provides stability is lacking, and control must be exerted by the farmer to maintain the health of the crops or animals and ensure an ample, high-quality yield.

Agricultural chemistry had become a recognized discipline by the mid-nineteenth century. Fertilizers and other products of the chemical industry became widely used early in the twentieth century, and have become indispensable in maintaining the yields of modern agriculture. Reliance on chemical answers to agricultural problems, however, has often obscured their deficiencies, as well as the existence of alternative solutions. Crop rotation and cultural practices have long been used to control pests. Since the end of World War II, however, farmers and ranchers have come to rely more heavily on chemical pesticides (such as insecticides, herbicides, fungicides, and nematocides). Shortly after DDT was found to be an effective insecticide in 1939, the United States began producing large quantities of it to control vectorborne diseases such as typhus and malaria. The dramatic success of DDT in controlling over five hundred insect pests diverted attention from traditional nonchemical methods of pest control. The publication of *Silent Spring* by Rachel Carson in 1962, however, made the public aware of the environmental drawbacks of using too many pesticides. Since then, there has been a complete shift in research emphasis, so that, whereas in 1925 three-fourths of published studies were on chemical pesticides, almost 80 percent of USDA pesticide research in 2000 was on alternatives to chemicals.

Environmental concerns, regulatory legislation, and increased costs were driving forces in the development of Integrated Pest Management (IPM) programs throughout the United States in the early 1970s. Bringing together experts from many fields, IPM programs strive to reduce the usage of chemical pesticides by integrating knowledge about the biology of the pest, the response of the crop to infestation, and the costs involved in applying or withholding treatment. Researchers have recognized that the pest population does not have to be completely eliminated, only kept below the point at which the farmer starts to lose money because of it. Implementation of these types of programs has significantly reduced the use of chemical pesticides while maintaining yield, quality, and economic return.

Fertilizers represent the single largest use of chemicals on the farm. Although nitrogen gas comprises 80 percent of the air we breathe, it is the element most commonly limiting plant growth. Atmospheric nitrogen must be fixed into ammonia or nitrates before a plant can use it. Lightning and biological activity (such as that of symbiotic microorganisms in nodules on legume roots) can fix nitrogen. The vast majority of nitrogen used in fertilizer, however, is fixed by the Haber process, an elegant method of combining nitrogen from air with hydrogen from natural gas under high pressure and temperature to produce ammonia. This process was invented by German scientists before World War I in response to a blockade of Chilean nitrate imposed by the British Royal Navy. During the war it was used to fix nitrogen for agriculture and to produce explosives. The inorganic ammonia fixed by this process now supplies about the same amount of nitrogen for crops as is fixed by all natural organic processes. The synthesis of ammonia consumes about 2 percent of the fossil fuel used worldwide. Overuse of cheap nitrogen fertilizer can lead to excessive runoff that pollutes groundwater and to eutrophication of bodies of water. But while inorganic nitrogen fertilizers remain cheap, it will cost less to apply them to crops than to have the plant divert its photosynthate from producing a crop to fixing its own nitrogen.

See also **Crop Improvement; Food Supply and the Global Food Market; Food Supply, Food Shortages; Green Revolution; High-Technology Farming; Horticulture.**

BIBLIOGRAPHY

Brown, Jonathan. *Farm Tools and Techniques: A Pictorial History.* London: B. T. Batsford, 1993.

Chrispeels, Maarten J., and David E. Sadava. *Plant Biotechnology, Genetics, and Agriculture.* Boston: Jones and Bartlett, 2002.

Food and Agriculture Organization of the United Nations. *The State of Food and Agriculture: Lessons from the Past Fifty Years.* Rome: Food and Agriculture Organization of the United Nations, 2000.

Grigg, David. *The Transformation of Agriculture in the West.* Oxford: Blackwell, 1992.

Heiser, Charles B., Jr. *Seed to Civilization: The Story of Food.* Cambridge, Mass.: Harvard University Press, 1990.

Jones, Eric L. *Agriculture and the Industrial Revolution.* Oxford: Blackwell, 1974.

Kelley, Hubert W. *Always Something New: A Cavalcade of Scientific Discovery.* U.S. Dept. of Agriculture, Agricultural Research Service, miscellaneous publication no. 1507, 1993.

Lee, Norman E. *Harvests and Harvesting through the Ages.* Cambridge, U.K.: Cambridge University Press, 1960.

Smil, Vaclav. *Enriching the Earth: Fritz Haber, Carl Bosch, and the Transformation of World Food Production.* Cambridge, Mass.: MIT Press, 2001.

Tannahill, Reay. *Food in History.* New York: Crown, 1995.

Vasey, Daniel E. *An Ecological History of Agiculture, 10,000 B.C. to A.D. 10,000.* Ames, Ia.: Iowa State University Press, 1992.

Mikal E. Saltveit

AGRONOMY. Agronomy embraces the branch of agriculture that deals with the development and practical management of plants and soils to produce food, feed, and fiber crops in a manner that preserves or improves the environment. The term "agronomy" represents the disciplines of soils, crops, and related sciences. In the soils area, specialties include soil microbiology, soil conservation, soil physics, soil fertility and plant nutrition, chemistry, biochemistry, and mineralogy. Specialties in the crops area relate primarily to plant genetics and breeding, crop physiology and management, crop ecology, turf-grass management, and seed production and physiology. Researchers in agronomy often work in close cooperation with scientists from disciplines such as entomology, pathology, chemistry, and engineering in order to improve productivity and reduce environmental problems. Even though less than 2 percent of the U.S. population are farmers who actively produce farm crops, the need for agronomists by other segments of society is increasing.

In the United States, field crops consist of those plants grown on an extensive scale, which differs from horticultural crops, which are usually grown intensively in orchards, gardens, and nurseries, but the distinctions are disappearing. Some of the major agronomic crops grown in the United States are alfalfa and pasture crops, peanuts, corn, soybeans, wheat, cotton, sorghum, oats, barley, and rice. Soil management aspects of agronomy encompass soil fertility, land use, environmental preservation, and non-production uses of soil resources for building, waste disposal, and recreation. Agronomists who work as soil scientists play extremely important roles

The basic idea behind agronomy is to match crops to their environment. This means following the contours of the land as well as choosing crops best suited for maintaining soil productivity. COURTESY OF THE JOHN DEERE LIBRARY.

in helping preserve water quality and preserve natural environments.

Agronomy is not a new field. As early as 7000 B.C.E. wheat and barley were grown at Jarmo, in present-day Iran. One could argue that the first farmers were in fact agronomists. In prehistoric times, humans shifted from foraging to cultivating specific crops, probably wheat or barley, for their food value. At harvest time, plants with easily gathered grain were selected first. This natural selection eventually made these food plants better adapted to continued cultivation because they were more easily harvested. Throughout the centuries, selection also occurred for other crop characteristics, such as taste, yield, and adaptation to specific soils and climates. The goal of today's production agronomists is essentially the same: to improve the quality, adaptability, and yield of our most important crops.

The Science of Agronomy

There are both basic and applied aspects of agronomy. Agronomists examine very basic components of soils and crops at subcellular or molecular levels. For example, at the basic level, agronomists use sophisticated techniques to unravel the genetic makeup of major crops in order to change their adaptation, nutritive value, or to breed medicinal benefits into agronomic crops. Genetic improve-

ment is an area where major breakthroughs are likely to occur. Agronomists have developed highly specialized computer models of crop growth in order to better understand how environmental and management components affect the way crops grow. These models help in the development of such things as precision fertilizer application techniques, which provide the crop with the correct amount of nutrients at the correct time in its life cycle. This technique helps reduce fertilizer overapplication, which is costly to the farmer, and may increase groundwater pollution. Models of how chemicals move in the soil also help assure proper application of animal manures, municipal waste, and soil amendments necessary for crop growth. Molecular components of soil constituents are studied to determine basic interactions affecting plant growth and nutrition, and soil and water quality.

Crop Production and Soil Management

Crop production consists of integrating all aspects of the field environment to assure an economically feasible and environmentally sound system of growing crops. At the applied level, agronomists use basic research information to help manage crop production systems and soil and water conservation programs. Agronomists provide a wealth of information to farmers to assure the soundness of their production programs.

Environmental and economic conditions vary dramatically, and crops must be adapted to the soils and climate for efficient crop production. Crops such as wheat grow best in the Great Plains of the United States, because wheat is well suited to the soils, rainfall, and length of growing season of the area. Likewise, crops such as cotton and peanuts are best adapted to the southern United States because these crops require warmer temperatures, a longer growing season, and more rainfall than does wheat.

Applications of sound principles of soil management are key to maintaining a healthy environment. Agronomists aid in identifying environmental risks and devise methods of reducing these risks. Management techniques developed by agronomists include terracing, strip cropping, and reduced tillage methods to reduce soil erosion. Developments in Global Information Systems (GIS) and site-specific technology are being used by agronomists to more precisely manage how, when, and where to apply soil amendments and fertilizers. GIS is also extremely useful in identifying type and extent of pest infestations. This helps reduce environmental pollution by pinpointing when and where to apply pest control and reducing the amount of pesticides used in crop production.

International Agronomy

Agronomy is an international discipline. Many of the problems, issues, and challenges faced by societies around the world are universal in nature, and require international cooperation. For example, a major problem facing the developed world is that of how best to use our land resources. Within the developing world, the same problems exist. The questions of how much and which land should be saved for food and fiber production and which land should be used for nonagricultural uses must be addressed by both developing and developed societies. Agronomists play a crucial role in assessing land quality to assure an environmentally friendly use of land. Studying how plants adapt to differing climates and environments has allowed plant scientists to increase food and fiber production in regions of the world where the necessities of life are most limited. Knowledge gained and disseminated by agronomists in the developed world has helped improve the human condition in the developing world. For example, plant geneticists and breeders use similar hybrid and variety development techniques in both developed and developing countries. Through plant breeding, for example, agronomists have developed high-yielding rice that is adapted to tropical climates. Breakthroughs in gene transfer permit plant breeders to improve grain quality and nutritional traits. These techniques have also contributed to increased production efficiency by genetically incorporating into food crops increased pest resistance and by broadening their range of adaptation.

See also **Agriculture, Origins of; Agriculture since the Industrial Revolution; Horticulture; High-Technology Farming.**

BIBLIOGRAPHY

Leonard, Jonathan N. *The First Farmers: The Emergence of Man.* Waltham, Mass.: Little, Brown, 1973.

Miflin, B. "Crop Improvement in the 21st Century." *Journal of Experimental Botany* 51 (2000): 1–8.

Pierce, Francis J., and Peter Nowak. "Aspects of Precision Agriculture." In *Advances in Agronomy.* Edited by Donald L. Sparks. Vol. 67. New York: Academic Press, 1999.

United States Department of Agriculture, National Agricultural Statistics Service, Washington, D.C. Available at www.usda.gov/nass/aggraphs/graphics.htm.

James J. Vorst

ALCOHOL. The word "alcohol" is derived from the Arabic word *al kuhul,* meaning 'essence'. The favorite mood-altering drug in the United States, as in almost every human society, continues to be alcohol. One of the reasons for the significant use of alcohol and its health impact is its feature of being (along with nicotine) a legally available drug of abuse and dependence.

Our knowledge of alcohol rests on a heritage of myth and speculation. Many health benefits have been attributed to alcohol by ancient healers who saw ethanol as the elixir of life, but almost none of its positive benefits have stood the test of time. Alcoholic beverages have been revered, more than any other substance, as mystical and medicinal agents. In recent years, however, we have stripped away much of the mystery surrounding alcohol and now recognize it as a drug with distinct pharmacological effects. However, one of the reasons that beverages containing alcohol continue to be consumed is related to the folklore and history that surround its many combinations with other flavors and its many sources of fermentation and distillation.

Chemist's View

Today one thinks of alcohol and alcoholic spirits as being synonymous, yet to a chemist an alcohol is any of an entire class of organic compounds containing a hydroxyl (OH) group or groups. The first member of its class, methyl alcohol or methanol, is used commercially as a solvent. Isopropyl alcohol, also known as rubbing alcohol, serves as a drying agent and disinfectant. Ethyl alcohol or ethanol shares these functions but differs from other alcohols in also being suitable as a beverage ingredient and intoxicant. Ethanol also differs from other alcohols in being a palatable source of energy and euphoria. It is a small, un-ionized molecule that is completely miscible with water and also somewhat fat-soluble. The remainder of this article pertains to ethanol, but refers to it simply as alcohol.

Biology of Production

Making alcoholic beverages dates back at least eight thousand years; for example, beer was made from cereal mashes in Mesopotamia in 6000 B.C.E. and wine in Egypt in 3700 B.C.E.

Ethyl alcohol is actually a by-product of yeast metabolism. Yeast is a fungus that feeds on carbohydrates. Yeasts are present ubiquitously. For example, the white waxy surface of a grape is almost entirely composed of yeast. When, for example, the skin of a berry is broken, the yeast acts quickly and releases an enzyme that, under anaerobic conditions, converts the sugar (sucrose, $C_{12}H_{22}O_{11}$) in the berry into carbon dioxide (CO_2) and alcohol (C_2H_5OH). This process is known as fermentation (if the mixture is not protected from air, alcohol turns into acetic acid, producing vinegar). When cereal grains and potatoes are used, each requires a sprouting pretreatment (malting) to hydrolyze starch, during which diastase enzymes are produced that break down starches to simple sugars that the yeast, which lacks these enzymes, can anaerobically convert to alcohol. This process makes the sugar available for the fermentation process. The yeast then continues to feed on the sugar until it literally dies of acute alcohol intoxication.

Because yeast expires when the alcohol concentration reaches 12 to 15 percent, natural fermentation stops at this point. In beer, which is made of barley, rice, corn, and other cereals, the fermentation process is artificially halted somewhere between 3 and 6 percent alcohol. Table wine contains between 10 and 14 percent alcohol, the limit of yeast's alcohol tolerance. This amount is insufficient for complete preservation, and thus a mild pasteurization is applied.

Distillation, which was discovered about 800 C.E. in Arabia, is the man-made process designed to take over where the vulnerable yeast fungus leaves off. The distilled, or hard, liquors, including brandy, gin, whiskey, scotch, bourbon, rum, and vodka, contain between 40 and 75 percent pure alcohol. Dry wines result when nearly all the available sugar is fermented. Sweet wines still have unfermented sugar. Pure alcohol also is added to fortify wines such as port and sherry. This addition boosts their percentage of alcohol to 18 or 20 percent (such wines do not require further pasteurization). "Still wines" are bottled after complete fermentation takes place. Sparkling wines are bottled before fermentation is complete so that the formed CO_2 is retained. "White" wines are made only from the juice of the grapes; "reds" contain both the juice and pigments from skins.

The percentage of alcohol in distilled liquors commonly is expressed in degrees of "proof" rather than as a percentage of pure alcohol. This measure developed from the seventeenth-century English custom of "proving" an alcoholic drink was of sufficient strength. This was accomplished by mixing it with gunpowder and attempting to ignite it. If the drink contained 49 percent alcohol by weight (or 57 percent by volume), it could be ignited. Thus, proof is approximately double the percentage of pure alcohol (an 86 proof whiskey is 43 percent pure alcohol).

Pure alcohol is a colorless, somewhat volatile liquid with a harsh, burning taste, which is used widely as a fuel or as a solvent for various fats, oils, and resins. This simple and unpalatable chemical is made to look, taste, and smell appetizing by combining it with water and various substances called congeners (pharmacologically active molecules other than ethanol, including higher alcohols and benzene). Congeners make bourbon whiskey taste different from Scotch whiskey, distinguish one brand of beer from another, give wine its "nose" and sherry its golden glow. In trace amounts, most congeners are harmless, but their consumption has been linked to the severity of hangovers and other central nervous system symptoms that include sleepiness.

Use in Food Products

Wines, liqueurs, and distilled spirits are used to prepare main dishes, sauces, and desserts, creating new and interesting flavors. The presence of alcohol in significant amounts affects the energy value of a food. Alcohol is rich in energy (29 kJ/g, or 7.1 kcal/g). It is assumed that, because of its low boiling point, alcohol is evaporated from foods during cooking. However, almost 4 to 85 percent of alcohol can be retained in foods. Foods that require heating for prolonged periods (over two hours—for example, pot roast), retain about 4–6 percent; foods like sauces (where alcohol is typically added after the sauce has been brought to a boil) may retain as much as 85 percent.

Alcohol and Malnutrition

Alcoholism is a major cause of malnutrition. The reasons are threefold. First, alcohol interferes with central mechanisms that regulate food intake and causes food intake decreases. Second, alcohol is rich in energy (7.1 kcal/g), and like pure sugar most alcoholic beverages are relatively empty of nutrients. Increasing amounts of alcohol ingested lead to the consumption of decreasing amounts of other foods, making the nutrient content of the diet inadequate, even if total energy intake is sufficient. Thus chronic alcohol abuse causes primary malnutrition by displacing other dietary nutrients. Third, gastrointestinal and liver complications associated with alcoholism also interfere with digestion, absorption, metabolism, and activation of nutrients, and thereby cause secondary malnutrition.

It is important to note that although ethanol is rich in energy, its chronic consumption does not produce the expected gain in body weight. This may be attributed, in part, to damaged mitochondria and the resulting poor coupling of oxidation of fat metabolically utilizable with energy production. The microsomal pathways that oxidize ethanol may be partially responsible. These pathways produce heat rather than adenosine triphosphate (ATP) and thereby fail to couple ethanol oxidation to useful energy-rich intermediates such as ATP. Thus, perhaps because of these energy considerations, alcoholics

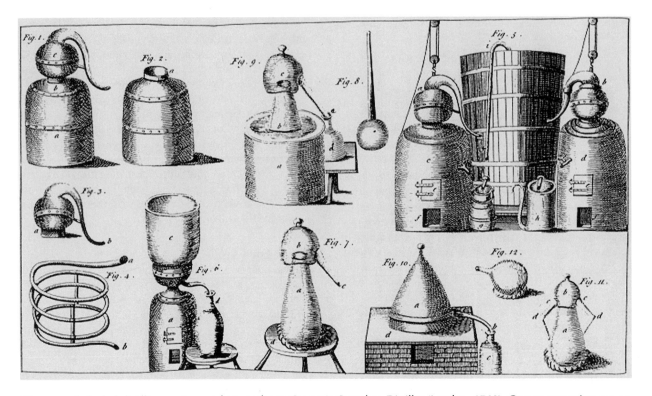

Diagrams of alcohol-distilling equipment from Ambrose Cooper's Complete Distiller (London, 1760). Copper engraving. ROUGH-WOOD COLLECTION.

with higher total caloric intake do not experience expected weight gain despite physical activity levels similar to those of the non-alcohol-consuming overweight population.

Absorption and Metabolism

Unlike foods, which require time for digestion, alcohol needs no digestion and is absorbed quickly. The presence of food in the stomach delays emptying, slowing absorption that occurs mainly in the upper small intestine.

Only 2 to 10 percent of absorbed ethanol is eliminated through the kidneys and lungs; the rest is metabolized, principally in the liver. A small amount of ethanol also is metabolized by gastric alcohol dehydrogenase (ADH) [first-pass metabolism (FPM)]. This FPM explains why, for any given dose of ethanol, blood levels are usually higher after an intravenous dose than following a similar amount taken orally. FPM is partly lost in the alcoholic. This lost function is due to decreased gastric ADH activity. Premenopausal women also have less of this gastric enzyme than do men. This difference partially explains why women become more intoxicated than men when each consume similar amounts of alcohol.

Hepatocytes are the primary cells that oxidize alcohol at significant rates. This hepatic specificity for ethanol oxidation, coupled with ethanol's high energy content and the lack of effective feedback control of alcohol hepatic

metabolism, results in the displacement of up to 90 percent of the liver's normal metabolic substrates.

Oxidation. Hepatocytes contain three main pathways for ethanol metabolism. Each pathway is localized to a different subcellular compartment: (1) the alcohol dehydrogenase (ADH) pathway (soluble fraction of the cell); (2) the microsomal ethanol oxidizing system (MEOS) located in the endoplasmic reticulum; and (3) catalase located in the peroxisomes. Each of these pathways produces specific toxic and nontoxic metabolites. All three result in the production of acetaldehyde (CH_3CHO), a highly toxic metabolite. The MEOS may account for up to 40 percent of ethanol oxidation. Normally, the role of catalase is small. It is not discussed further here.

1. *The ADH pathway.* The oxidation of ethanol by the ADH results in the production of acetaldehyde (CH_3CHO) and the transformation of nicotinamide adenine dinucleotide (NAD) to nicotinamide adenine dinucleotide-reduced form (NADH). Substantial levels of acetaldehyde can result in skin flushing. Regeneration of NAD from NADH is the rate-limiting step in this ADH pathway of alcohol metabolism. It can metabolize approximately 13 to 14 grams of ethanol per hour (the amount in a typical drink). This rate is observed when blood alcohol concentrations reach 10 mg/dL. The large amounts of reducing equivalents that are generated by the alco-

hol oxidation overwhelm the hepatocyte's ability to maintain homeostasis and as a consequence a number of metabolic abnormalities ensue. Increased NADH, the primary form of reducing equivalents, promotes fatty acid synthesis, opposes lipid oxidation, and results in fat accumulation.

2. *MEOS.* This pathway also converts a portion of ethanol to acetaldehyde. Cytochrome P4502E1 (CYP2E1) is the responsible enzyme. As other microsomal oxidizing systems, this system also is inducible, that is, it increases in activity in the presence of large amounts of the target substrate. This induction contributes to the metabolic tolerance to ethanol that develops in alcoholics. This tolerance, however, should not be confused with protection against alcohol's toxic effects. It is important to note that, even though larger amounts of alcohol may be metabolized by individuals when this capability has been induced fully, most of alcohol's harmful effects remain unabated.

Physiological Effects at Different Levels

Beneficial effects. A large variety of alcoholic beverages are available, and most people can find at least one that provides gustatory and other pleasures. Alcohol is said to reduce tension, fatigue, anxiety, and pressure and to increase feelings associated with relaxation. It also has been claimed that drinking in moderation may lower the risk of coronary heart disease (mainly among men over 45 and women over age 55), but whether that putative protection is due primarily to the alcohol or some other associated factors, such as lifestyle, remains controversial. Moderate alcohol consumption provides no health benefit for younger people, and in fact may increase risks to alcohol's ill effects because the potential for alcohol abuse increases when drinking starts at an early age.

Harmful effects. The problems of individuals who occasionally become drunk differ from those who experience drinking binges at regular intervals.

"Acute" harmful effects of alcohol intoxication: Occasional excess drinking can cause nausea, vomiting, and hangovers (especially in inexperienced drinkers). The acute neurological effects of alcohol intoxication are dose-related. These progress from euphoria, relief from anxiety, and removal of inhibitions to ataxia, impaired vision, judgment, reasoning, and muscle control. When alcohol intakes continue after the appearance of these signs and symptoms, progress to lethal levels occurs very quickly, resulting in the anesthetization of the brain's circulatory and respiratory centers.

"Chronic" harmful effects of alcohol excess: Chronic excessive alcohol consumption can affect adversely virtually all tissues. Alcoholics have a mortality and suicide rate 2½ times greater, and an accident rate 7 times greater

than average. Some of the dire consequences that are associated with alcohol abuse are:

1. *Cardiovascular problems.* Alcohol causes vasodilation of peripheral vessels (causing flushing), vasoconstriction (producing resistance to the flow of blood and increasing work load on the heart) and alcoholic cardiomyopathy (characterized by myocardial fiber hypertrophy, fibrosis, and congestive heart failure).

2. *Cancer.* Alcohol increases the risk of alimentary, respiratory tract, and breast cancers.

3. *Liver disease.* Alcohol can result in fatty liver, hepatitis, and cirrhosis.

4. *Central nervous system disorders.* Alcohol causes premature aging of the brain. Blackouts may occur (for example, those affected walk, talk, and act normally and appear to be aware of what is happening, yet later have no recollection of events experienced during the blackout).

5. *Gastrointestinal disorders.* Alcohol increases risk of esophageal varices, gastritis, and pancreatitis.

6. *Metabolic alterations.* Alcohol increases nutritional deficiencies (primary and secondary), and adversely affects absorption and utilization of vitamins. It impairs the intestinal absorption of B vitamins, notably thiamin, folate, and vitamin B_{12}. Wernicke's encephalopathy also may occur. This condition is the result of severe thiamine deficiency. It is characterized by visual disorders, ataxia, confusion, and coma.

7. *Immunological disorders.* Alcohol decreases immunity to infections and impairs healing of injuries.

8. *Others.* Alcohol causes personality changes, sexual frigidity or impotency, sleep disturbances, and depression.

Treatment

There are two major approaches that are used in the treatment of alcohol abuse: (1) correction of the medical, nutritional, and psychological problems; and (2) the alleviation of dependency on alcohol. Many sedatives or tranquilizers (for example, chlordiazepoxide) are effective in controlling minor withdrawal symptoms such as tremors. More serious symptoms include delirium tremens and seizures. For treatment of alcohol dependence, the anticraving agent naltrexone has shown promising results. Nutritional deficiency, such as lack of thiamine or magnesium, when present, must be corrected. Psychological approaches such as the twelve steps of Alcoholics Anonymous are also effective in achieving more sustained abstinence. These approaches, although helpful, too often come too late to revert the liver to its normal state. Other approaches, such as those focusing on prevention (utilizing biochemical markers), screening (through use of improved blood tests), and early detection are needed to impact on the prevalence of liver disease. The correction of nutritional deficiencies and supplementation with other substrates that may be produced in abnormally low quantities by affected patients, for example, *S*-adenosylmethionine (SAMe) and polyunsaturated lecithin have been shown to offset some of the adverse manifestations of alcohol's toxic effects. These and others are now being tested in humans.

Conclusion

Alcoholism, an addiction to heavy and frequent alcohol consumption, is a major public health issue. However, many believe that this condition does not attract attention that it merits from either the public or the health professions. Alcoholism is a multifaceted problem that cannot be solved by any single approach. The "consumption control approach" is a worthwhile endeavor with proven efficacy, but consumption control efforts by themselves are not sufficient. Prevention of alcohol misuse before it occurs also can be beneficial. Another prevention strategy includes establishing standards and guidelines for advertising and emphasizing responsibility and moderation in the serving and consumption of alcohol. "Behavioral" approaches focus on recognition of social and psychological factors and their correction. Finally, the "disease-control" approach provides new insights. Continued research into the pathophysiology of alcohol-induced disorders increases understanding of the condition and provides prospects of earlier recognition, and improved efforts for its early prevention and treatment, prior to the medical and social disintegration of its victims. By combining all of these approaches, chances to alleviate the suffering of the alcoholic are multiplied in a positively synergistic manner and the public health impact of alcoholism on our society can be minimized.

See also **Beer; Fermentation; Fermented Beverages Other than Wine or Beer; Nutrients; Nutrition; Wine.**

BIBLIOGRAPHY

Lieber, Charles S. *Medical and Nutritional Complications of Alcoholism: Mechanisms and Management.* New York: Plenum, 1992.

Lieber, Charles S. "Medical Disorders of Alcoholism." *New England Journal of Medicine* 333 (1995): 1058–1065.

Lieber, Charles S. "Alcohol: Its Metabolism and Interaction with Nutrients." *Annual Reviews in Nutrition* 20 (2000): 395–430.

Khursheed P. Navder
Charles S. Lieber

ALCOHOLIC BEVERAGES. *See* **Alcohol; Beer; Spirits; Whiskey (Whisky); Wine.**

ALGAE, TOXIC.
Marine phytoplankton, or single-cell algae, are the base of the marine food chain. Phytoplankton use sunlight to convert simple inorganic molecules, such as water and carbon dioxide, to complex organic compounds, such as protein, carbohydrates, and lipids. The ocean waters that surround continental coastlines are the home of a large number of marine algae, making them the most productive areas for the harvest of marine finfish and shellfish. Much of the time, algae are present at very low numbers, but when conditions are right, they can grow rapidly and explosively, producing a noticeable discoloration in the water called a "bloom." These blooms can cover very large areas of the coastal ocean that are often visible from satellites. Large numbers of "blooming" algae can, at times, produce toxins or result in lower oxygen levels in seawater, thereby creating significant problems for shore-based businesses (e.g., hotels, restaurants), the seafood industry, and consumers.

While many of these algal blooms are merely noxious (i.e., producing smelly odors, discolored water, gelatinous masses), some produce marine toxins that enter the marine food web when consumed by shellfish or finfish. Typically, these finfish and shellfish (particularly mussels) have a capacity to concentrate and accumulate very large amounts of these toxins without apparent harm to themselves. Toxin levels can be so high that consuming only a few mussels could be lethal. When blooms produce such deleterious effects, they are called harmful algal blooms, or HABs.

A variety of human intoxication syndromes have been characterized from the consumption of seafood contaminated with algal toxins. Five will be described here. For a detailed historical and descriptive treatment of the myriad seafood intoxications, please see the extensive monograph by Halstead, the chapter by Wekell and Liston, and *Seafood Safety* (pp. 87–110) in the bibliography. In the temperate zone, three HAB intoxications are of concern to seafood consumers and industry: paralytic shellfish poisoning (PSP), amnesiac shellfish poisoning (ASP, more correctly domoic acid poisoning), and diarrhetic shellfish poisoning (DSP). In semitropical and tropical waters, two syndromes have major impacts: neurotoxic shellfish poisoning (NSP) and ciguatera fish poisoning (CFP).

PSP and ASP present the greatest health risks due to the following factors: potency of the toxins, wide geographic distribution, and large coastal populations exposed to the toxins, thereby elevating the risk of human exposure to these toxins. In addition, shellfish production has increased to meet increasing worldwide demands. Perhaps the tropical poisonings (NSP and CFP) have disproportionately greater impacts because some of the "at-risk" populations in tropical communities are poor and dependent on seafoods for daily subsistence. In these regions, illnesses from these toxins have greater impact on daily lives than those in more developed and wealthier countries due to loss of work time and limited access to medical care. Since no antidotes are available, medical treatment for all seafood intoxications is limited to providing emergency measures (e.g., gastric lavage,

66

breathing assistance) and treating symptoms (Wekell and Liston, pp. 111–155).

The Symptoms, Toxins, and the Organisms That Produce Them

Paralytic shellfish poison (PSP). Symptoms include paralysis of the peripheral muscles including the chest, making breathing difficult (in mild cases) to impossible in the most severe cases. Along the West Coast of North America, several deaths have been reported over the past decade from recreational and subsistence shellfish consumers. The only treatment is immediate medical intervention, that is, the use of artificial respiration until the toxins are purged from the victim's body. PSP is caused by the consumption of shellfish contaminated with a suite of toxins (about a dozen individual toxins have been identified). The first toxin to be chemically identified was named "saxitoxin" because it was found in the Alaskan butter clam (*Saxidomus giganteus*). Since then, other toxins have been identified and named "gonyautoxins," after the historical name (*Gonyaulax*) for the causative organism, currently known as the *Alexandrium dinoflagellate*. The PSP toxins and associated algae are found from the sub-Arctic (and sub-Antarctic) to tropical areas, but are most common in cooler temperate waters (both in the Northern and Southern Hemispheres). In the temperate zones, the toxins are produced by the dinoflagellates in the genus *Alexandrium*: specifically *A. catenella* and *A. tamarense*. In tropical and semi-tropical areas, the dinoflagellates *Pyrodinium bahamense* var. *compressum* and *Gymnodinium catenatum* have been implicated as producers of PSP toxins.

Amnesiac shellfish poisoning (ASP or domoic acid poisoning). The first identified outbreak occurred in 1987 in eastern Canada due to the consumption of mussels contaminated with domoic acid. Symptoms varied from mild gastroenteritis to the loss of short-term memory, and in the most severe cases, death. In this incident, the elderly appeared more susceptible than younger people. The toxin binds to parts of the brain responsible for memory and learning, resulting in nerve cell death. To date, in the United States, the most common vectors of lethal levels of the toxin have been sardines and anchovies—planktivorous fish that consume phytoplankton. Consumption of these fish has resulted in the stranding and death of marine mammals and sea birds on the West Coast of the United States. So far, these are the only known poisoning victims of this toxin. Domoic acid has seriously impacted razor clam recreational fisheries (and its support industries) in Washington State and commercial crab fisheries on the West Coast of the United States. In Nova Scotia, Canada, and Maine, very high levels of domoic have been detected in mussels. However, due to an extensive and successful monitoring and surveillance programs put in place since 1987, no human illnesses have so far been reported in these areas from consumption of commercially raised shellfish. Do-

moic acid is produced by some of the diatoms in the genus *Pseudo-nitzschia*. However, not all species have been implicated in major domoic acid poisoning outbreaks, so far these include: *P. multiseries*, *P. australis*, and *P. pseudodelicatissima*. Globally, these organisms are quite cosmopolitan and have been identified in temperate waters of both the Northern and Southern Hemispheres. The genus is also fairly common in marine estuaries.

Diarrhetic shellfish poisoning (DSP). As the name implies, human consumption of shellfish containing the toxins associated with this syndrome causes diarrhea. Because symptoms are mild and similar to those in other common illnesses (gastrointestinal distress, nausea), many cases probably go largely unreported so that the true incidence of DSP is likely much higher than current epidemiological data indicates. However, there is a particular human health concern associated with DSP because the toxins involved (the dinophysistoxins or DTXs) are known potent tumor promoters (Fujiki et al., pp. 232–240). Toxic shellfish and causative organisms have been found in the Mediterranean Sea, off the Galician coast of Spain, and Ireland. *Dinophysis* cf. *acuminata* and *D. acuta* are believed to be the causative organism and are found in temperate waters worldwide. Recently, DSP toxins have been found in North America in eastern Canada and the northeastern coast of the United States but the primary source of the toxins appears to be *Prorocentrum lima* (Reguera et al., pp. 78–80).

Neurotoxic shellfish poisoning (NSP). People consuming shellfish containing the toxins report tingling fingers, numbness of lips, and reversal of temperature sensation, along with gastroenteritis. During heavy blooms of the causative organism of NSP, the dinoflagellate *Karenia brevis* (older name: *Gymnodinium breve*), aerosol dispersions of both the organism, and toxins can be caused by breaking waves and wind resulting in upper respiratory problems and distress in people. In some cases, victims may need to move inland to avoid exposure to the aerosols. The toxins involved are high-molecular-weight polyether toxins known as brevetoxins. *Karenia brevis* inhabits both temperate and tropical waters. In the United States, outbreaks are common in the Gulf of Mexico, where long-lasting blooms have been observed along the west coast of Florida. In the early 1990s, outbreaks of NSP were also reported on the North Island of New Zealand.

Ciguatera fish poisoning (CFP, or tropical fish poisoning). Symptoms, including gastroenteritis, that in most cases occur within a very short period of consuming the tainted fish. In severe cases, paresthesia or numbness occurs around the mouth, lips, and tongue. In extreme cases, burning sensations in mouth and death occur. Some victims report a reversal of the sensations of hot and cold. One victim was observed blowing on ice cream to cool it down. In some cases, symptoms reoccur years after the initial intoxication, usually during times of stress. In the most extreme cases of intoxication, death can occur within hours of consuming tainted fish. The toxin, ciguatoxin, and its congeners are complex fat-soluble, high-molecular-weight, polycyclic polyether compounds. The toxins are produced by the benthic dinoflagellate *Gambierdiscus toxicus* that grows on corals and other surfaces in tropical reefs. Virtually all tropical reef-dwelling fish are suspect (Halstead, pp. 325–402). Coral-eating fish (e.g., parrot fishes) consume algae on the coral including the associated *G. toxicus*, thereby accumulating toxin in their fatty tissues. Predators of these fish then concentrate the toxin. Top reef predators, such as barracuda in the Caribbean and moray eels (in the Pacific), are considered high-risk vectors of ciguatoxin. Tropical Pacific outbreaks of Ciguatera appear to be the most intense and have caused rapid deaths, while outbreaks in the Caribbean seem to be relatively mild. Treatment is largely symptomatic, entailing fluid replacement and other life support measures. Unfortunately, monitoring tests for Ciguatera toxins are complex and costly and have not been widely implemented.

Prevention, Control, and Mitigation

With all these intoxication syndromes, shellfish and fish show no clear outward signs that they might be poisonous. The presence of toxins can only be determined by appropriate chemical testing. Cooking, cleaning, or organ removal in fish and shellfish may reduce the toxin levels in some cases but cannot guarantee that the seafood has been rendered safe. Therefore, both recreational and commercial fishers must rely on monitoring and surveillance programs, usually operated by governmental agencies. Commercial seafoods, particularly shellfish, are usually monitored and tested for toxins (when reliable methods exist) as part of government safety and sanitation programs. It is wise for consumers to purchase only inspected shellfish from reliable, licensed retailers, since these businesses are usually required to maintain certification records for their shellfish stock.

For recreational fishers, it is vital that they obtain information about local closures or safe beaches. Necessary safety information should be posted on signs or made available by telephone "hotlines," websites, or news media. Unfortunately, depending on agency resources, recreational and private beaches are monitored in a more limited fashion, placing these fishers at a higher risk. Nevertheless, it is the recreational fishers' responsibility to obtain the needed information that will allow them to safely enjoy the sea's bounty.

See also **Crustaceans and Shellfish; Fish; Fishing; Mammals, Sea.**

BIBLIOGRAPHY

Fujiki, Hirota, Masami Suganuma, and Horoko Suguri, et al. "New Tumor Promoters from Marine Natural Products." In *Marine Toxins: Origin, Structure, and Molecular Pharmacology*, edited by Sherwood Hall and Gary Strichartz, pp. 232–240. Washington, D.C.: American Chemical Society, 1990.

Halstead, Bruce W. *Poisonous and Venomous Marine Animals of the World*. Revised edition. Princeton, N.J.: Darwin Press, 1978.

Lassus, Patrick, Geneviève Arzul, and Evelyne Erard-Le Denn, et al., eds. "Harmful Algal Blooms." In *Proceedings of the VI International Conference on Harmful Algae*. Nantes, France, October 1993. Paris: Lavoisier Publishing, 1995.

"Naturally Occurring Fish and Shellfish Poisons." In *Seafood Safety*, edited by Farid E. Ahmed, chap. 4, pp. 87–110. Washington, D.C.: National Academy Press, 1991.

Reguera, Beatriz, Juan Blanco, Ma Luisa Fernández, and Timothy Wyatt, eds. "Harmful Algae." In *Proceedings of the VIII International Conference on Harmful Algae*. Vigo, Spain, 25–29 June, 1997. Vigo, Spain: Xunta de Galicia and Intergovernmental Oceanographic Commission of UNESCO, 1998.

Smayda, Theodore J., and Yuzuru Shimizu, eds. "Toxic Phytoplankton Blooms in the Sea." In *Proceedings of the V International Conference on Harmful Algae*. Newport, Rhode Island, November 1–28, 1991. New York: Elsevier, 1993.

Wekell, John C., and John Liston. "Seafood Biotoxicants." In *Trace Substances and Health: A Handbook*, edited by Paul M. Newberne, part II. New York: M. Dekker, 1982.

John C. Wekell

ALLERGIES. Food allergy has been recognized since the time of Hippocrates. People with adverse reactions to food can be difficult to evaluate because overlap exists between true food allergy and toxic and other reactions to chemicals or other food ingredients. The incidence of food allergy is increasing in the industrialized world, raising questions about the interactive effects between environmental and genetic factors. There is a considerable burden on society in terms of cost of treatment, death from anaphylactic reactions, and the anxiety produced by real or perceived food allergy. Avoidance of the food is the current treatment, but new strategies are being developed.

Definitions

Adverse reactions to the ingestion of food that can be reproduced is termed intolerance or hypersensitivity. Since this does not imply an underlying cause, it may encompass immune or nonimmune mechanisms. For example, chemicals such as caffeine may cause reproducible symptoms, but this is not mediated by the immune system. True food allergy or food hypersensitivity is defined as a reproducible adverse reaction to food caused by the immune system creating antibodies or cellular inflammation.

Type I IgE-mediated food allergy. The classic example is immediate anaphylactic reaction to food. In susceptible individuals after exposure to the food, the immune system creates specific IgE antibodies to that food. IgE is produced by the immune system's B-lymphocytes, and is bound to receptors on the surface of mast cells. Mast cells reside in tissues at body surfaces such as the skin, eyes, nose, throat, lung, and gastrointestinal tract. Mast cells are made up of granules containing chemicals including histamine. When the food protein contacts and binds to adjacent specific IgE molecules at the mast cell surface, a cascade of events occurs leading to degranulation of mast cells and release of chemicals that cause the allergic reaction. This may include skin hives, airway swelling, wheezing, abdominal pain, vomiting and/or diarrhea. This may progress to anaphylaxis, shock, and even death. This reactivity to food can be demonstrated by skin-prick tests, which have been used to diagnose allergy since the 1870s. Food protein is placed on the skin, the skin is scratched or pricked, and a hive will develop in the presence of skin mast cells with IgE directed against the food. In the 1920s Prausnitz and Kustner showed that a substance circulating in the blood of the allergic individual was responsible for a positive skin test, because blood serum could be transferred to the skin of a nonallergic individual resulting in a positive skin test. IgE is that substance, and food-specific IgE can be measured directly in the blood, by means of the IgE RAST (radioallergosorbent) test. Diagnosis of this immediate type of food allergy rests on the history of rapid onset of symptoms, demonstration of positive skin-prick test or specific IgE RAST. Challenging an individual with the food is the ultimate way to prove a food allergy.

Non-IgE-mediated food allergy. Other immune mechanisms can be responsible for allergic reactions to foods. The classic example is celiac disease (celiac sprue or gluten-induced enteropathy). This is an immune system reaction to wheat (gluten). Patients do not have IgE antibody directed against wheat, but exposure to gluten over a period of time causes inflammation of the intestine and a characteristic atrophy or flattening of the normal intestinal villous folds. The diagnosis rests on the characteristic biopsy of the small intestine coupled with another type of antibody (IgA) against wheat protein. Any food may also cause similar intestinal inflammation, leading to varying symptoms and signs depending on the area of the intestine affected. Unlike IgE-mediated allergy or celiac disease, there are no readily available confirmatory tests for these other food allergies.

Prevalence

Food allergy is perceived as being common; however, large studies support the idea that true food allergy is less common than people think. A study of 480 infants from birth to age three revealed 28 percent were suspected by their parents as having food allergy; however, this was confirmed in only 8 percent of this group. The prevalence then decreases with age. Twenty percent of adults suspect food allergy, though allergy is confirmed in only 1 to 2 percent of adults. Although food allergies in adults tend to persist with age, many infants and children outgrow them with time.

Recently, interest has grown over the apparent increase in the prevalence and severity of food allergy. This has paralleled an increase in other atopic disorders such as asthma in industrialized nations compared with children of similar genetic background in developing countries (atopic refers to a tendency to develop allergic conditions such as hay fever, asthma, or food allergies). The "hygiene hypothesis" contends that through evolution, the human immune system has developed with a specific microbial environment, and reduced exposure to microbes in the developed world may lead to increased allergic response. Further study is needed.

Type I Immediate (IgE-Mediated) Hypersensitivity Reactions to Food

Immediate hypersensitivity reactions to foods are most common in young children, with 50 percent of these reactions occurring in the first year of life. The majority is from cow's milk and soy protein from infant formulas. Other foods begin to predominate in older children, including eggs, fish, peanuts, and wheat, and along with milk and soy account for over 90 percent of food allergy in children. Peanut, tree nut, and shellfish allergy predominate in adults. Exposures may occur inadvertently due to improper labeling, changes in product composition with time, and contamination of foods during processing. Symptoms from multiple organ systems may occur, beginning within minutes. Unfortunately, fatal anaphylactic reactions (shock) to food occur despite strict dietary avoidance and treatment of reactions. Families, caregivers, and individuals with a history of anaphylaxis to food require education in diet and in the use of self-administered epinephrine. Individuals should be observed in a hospital setting after a significant reaction. Exercise-induced anaphylaxis to food occurs when the combination of ingesting the food followed by exercise leads to anaphylaxis. Oral allergy syndrome describes symptoms of itching of the mouth and throat often attributable to eating fruits, and typically does not progress. Chronic hives or urticaria can be caused by foods, but it is a common misconception that these conditions are usually food-related; only in 1 to 2 percent of cases is urticaria or chronic hives a reaction to food. Atopic dermatitis (AD) or eczema is a chronic skin condition found in atopic individuals. Patients with AD have a 30 to 40 percent prevalence of food allergy.

Investigation and treatment of type I immediate reactions to food. The rapid onset of symptoms after ingestion correlates highly with positive skin-prick or IgE RAST tests to the offending food, making confirmation of immediate hypersensitivity straightforward. Consultation with an allergist and dietitian is recommended. Groups such as the Food Allergy and Anaphylaxis Network can provide support and educational materials.

Non-IgE-Mediated Food Allergy

The spectrum of non-IgE food allergy is quite varied, and the symptoms often parallel the area of inflammation in the gastrointestinal tract (see sidebar). Avoidance of the food will resolve symptoms and intestinal inflammation;

Manifestations of IgE Allergy to Food
  Cardiovascular (shock)
  Respiratory (wheeze, cough)
  Gastrointestinal (acute vomiting, pain, diarrhea)
  Skin (hives, atopic dermatitis)
  Eye (itching, swelling)
  Oral (itching, swelling)

Manifestations of Non-IgE Allergy to Food
  Growth delay
  Protein-losing enteropathy, edema
  Iron-deficiency anemia
  Chronic diarrhea
  Eosinophilic colitis
  Chronic vomiting/feeding intolerance
  Food protein-induced enterocolitis syndrome
  Atopic dermatitis
  Infantile colic

Manifestations of Celiac Disease (Gluten-Induced Enteropathy)
  Growth delay
  Chronic diarrhea
  Abdominal distension
  Abdominal pain
  Dermatitis herpetiformis
  Associations: Diabetes, thyroid disease, Down
    syndrome

---

rechallenge with the food will reproduce the injury. However, unlike IgE food allergy, symptoms may take days or weeks to resolve or reappear with elimination or exposure respectively, making evaluation even more difficult.

Celiac disease or gluten-induced enteropathy (see sidebar) is a chronic intestinal condition caused by non-IgE mediated allergy to gluten, a protein in wheat and other grains. Chronic exposure to gluten causes inflammation and atrophy of small intestinal folds, leading to symptoms of malabsorption of food. Typically, patients have diarrhea, weight loss, and abdominal bloating. There is a genetic predisposition to celiac disease, but onset may occur at any age, suggesting an environmental factor such as infection may be needed in some individuals to trigger the inflammatory process. The disease has a higher prevalence (up to 1 in 400–500) in individuals of eastern European descent. Celiac disease is associated with a skin condition (dermatitis herpetiformis), thyroid disease, diabetes, and Down syndrome.

Allergic or eosinophilic colitis in infants is a common manifestation of non-IgE food protein allergy. It is characterized by diarrhea with blood and mucus. It is caused by milk or soy formula and may occur in breast-fed infants from dietary antigens transmitted through breast milk. Colon biopsy shows allergic inflammation.

Food protein-induced enterocolitis is a severe reaction to food, often delayed four to six hours, without evidence of IgE. Patients present with lethargy, vomiting, and diarrhea. Recovery is within six to eight hours after fluid resuscitation. A careful history usually reveals the offending food, although this may not be appreciated unless multiple episodes occur.

Chronic enteropathy from food allergy can also lead to inflammation with villous atrophy similar to celiac disease. Most patients have diarrhea, in addition to weight loss, anemia, and low albumin from protein loss from the intestine.

Allergic gastritis is inflammation of the stomach with pain and vomiting. As with other non-IgE food allergy, biopsies of the stomach demonstrate allergic (eosinophilic) inflammation.

Allergic esophagitis is characterized by intense eosinophilia of the esophagus on biopsy. Patients complain of pain and problems with swallowing, even to the point of having food impactions in the esophagus. Treatment with hypoallergenic formula has been shown to improve esophagitis in infants; however, older children and adults may require corticosteroid medication.

Infantile colic and excessive irritability can be symptoms related to allergy in a subgroup of infants. By definition, colic is a condition with increased crying behavior in infants, for which no cause can be found. However, since allergy can potentially lead to inflammation and pain, formula allergy is often considered.

Attempts have been made to associate a variety of other problems with food allergy including joint disease, migraine, and behavioral and developmental disorders such as autism. Causal relationship between food allergy and these disorders remains unproven.

Investigation and treatment of non-IgE-mediated food allergy. The diagnosis rests on the resolution of symptoms and/or biopsy findings on an elimination diet, with a return of symptoms on rechallenge. Unlike the rapid response characteristic of IgE-mediated disease, a prolonged challenge may identify delayed reactions with predominantly gastrointestinal symptoms up to six days after exposure. Elemental diets can be used to eliminate dietary protein antigens completely, then systematic rechallenge of the patient with suspected offending foods. As with IgE food allergies, avoidance of the specific food remains the mainstay of therapy.

New Frontiers

There are a number of exciting areas of research into the prevention and treatment of food allergies. Recent reports suggest that the allergic response can be altered by promoting beneficial gut flora ("probiotic therapy"). It

---

has also been discovered that only a few sites (epitopes) on food protein molecules interact with the immune system to create an allergic reaction. Genetic engineering of foods makes it possible to alter these epitopes, creating crops that are "nonallergic." More study is needed to ensure that altering food proteins does not lead to other health concerns or different types of allergy. Other studies are under way to assess the effectiveness of promising new drug therapies for patients with food allergy.

See also **Aversion to Food; Baby Food; Health and Disease; Immune System Regulation and Nutrients; Milk, Human; Proteins and Amino Acids**.

BIBLIOGRAPHY

Justinich, Christopher J. "Food Allergy and Eosinophilic Gastroenteropathy." In *Pediatric Gastroenterology*, vol. 2, edited by Jeffrey S. Hyams and Robert Wyllie, pp. 334–347. Philadelphia: W. B. Saunders, 1999.

Metcalfe, Dean D., H. A. Sampson, and R. A. Simon, eds. *Food Allergy: Adverse Reactions to Food and Food Additives*. 2d ed, Cambridge, Mass.: Blackwell Science, 1997.

Sampson, H. A. "Food Allergy. Part 2: Diagnosis and Management." *Journal of Allergy and Clinical Immunology* 103 (1999): 981–989.

Sampson, H. A. "Food Allergy. Part 1: Immunopathogenesis and Clinical Disorders." *Journal of Allergy and Clinical Immunology* 103 (1999): 717–728.

Sampson, H. A., and J. A. Anderson. "Classification of Gastrointestinal Disease of Infants and Children due to Adverse Immunologic Reactions to Foods." *Journal of Pediatric Gastroenterology and Nutrition* 30 (suppl) (2000): 1–94.

Christopher J. Justinich

ALLIUM. *See* **Onions and Other Allium Plants**.

AMERICAN INDIANS.

This entry includes two subentries:
Prehistoric Indians and Historical Overview
Contemporary Issues

PREHISTORIC INDIANS AND HISTORICAL OVERVIEW

Native North Americans consumed a variety of foods based on the diverse plant and animal communities found throughout the continent. Regional variation in diet paralleled regional variation in the availability of these food resources. This generalization applied until around 7000 B.C.E. This entry provides an overview of Native American diet, from the northern border of Mexico to the High Arctic, from the earliest peoples in the continent to the time of European contact.

Sources of Information

How do we know about the diets of past peoples? There are three main sources of information, each with its own limitations. Working backward from the time of European contact, there is recorded information about diet. The first European people to travel to the New World provided some information about native customs, but much richer information was provided by the first Europeans to live in the New World. These people (missionaries, explorers, and early settlers) were able to record information about foods and other customs before cultural disruption altered diet and subsistence. Because contact and early settlement was more often in coastal areas or along major watercourses, there is more information about coastal peoples. By the time Europeans had made their way inland, they were already encountering cultures changed by waves of impact from coastal regions. For example, the fur trade resulted in alterations in hunting practices among northern peoples before any Europeans were able to witness daily life in some inland northern villages.

A second source of information is ethnography and oral tradition. Ethnographic information comes from anthropologists who lived among native peoples and recorded their customs, including food procurement, preparation, and storage. A vast amount of ethnographic information was collected early in the twentieth century. Since this type of study represents only one or a few points in time, it is also helpful to learn the oral traditions of people, since these can reveal long-held customs and practices.

Insights into past diets are also provided by archaeology. Archaeologists analyze remains of food items including animal bones, charred seeds and cobs, pollen, and phytoliths (siliceous secondary cell walls of certain terrestrial plants which leave a "signature" that archaeologists and paleobotanists can identify), and the tools used for food procurement and preparation (spear points, fish hooks, digging sticks, manos, and metates). Chemical analysis of human bones provides direct information on foods consumed.

There are possible errors in all of these sources of information. Historians may only record what was eaten during a particular season. Ethnographers may also miss some of the diversity of the annual round of foods due to limitations on time spent with a group of people, or variations from year to year. Some items are more likely to be preserved in the archaeological record than others (bone tools versus wooden tools; ceramic vessels versus baskets woven from fibers). However, food preferences are strongly ingrained in cultures and so it is reasonable to assume that the habits that were observed by ethnographers and early historians and that are repeated in oral traditions can be extended back into time. The exception is that a major transition, plant domestication, took place prehistorically. The timing of this transition has been studied intensively by archaeologists and physical anthropologists.

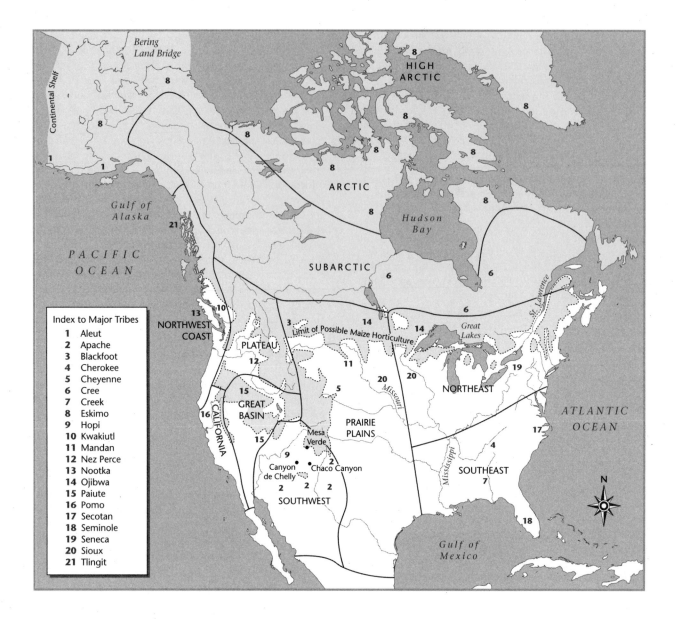

Index to Major Tribes

1 Aleut
2 Apache
3 Blackfoot
4 Cherokee
5 Cheyenne
6 Cree
7 Creek
8 Eskimo
9 Hopi
10 Kwakiutl
11 Mandan
12 Nez Perce
13 Nootka
14 Ojibwa
15 Paiute
16 Pomo
17 Secotan
18 Seminole
19 Seneca
20 Sioux
21 Tlingit

The First North Americans

The first people to enter the New World are thought to have come from northeast Asia and are usually characterized as "big game hunters." During the late Pleistocene, large terrestrial mammals such as mammoths and mastodons were hunted, as is apparent from the association of projectile points and bones from these animals. Here researchers encounter the problem of bias in the archaeological record. Did these people only eat big game? The ethnographic information on northern peoples of the boreal forest and Arctic regions points to an emphasis on meat in the diet, and indicates that animals with fatty meat (moose and beaver) were preferred over lean animals such as hare. A number of different types of berries were collected in summer and some were preserved, but they con-stituted a small percentage of the total diet. As the early Asian migrants to North America moved south, they hunted other large mammals, such as bison, and they probably learned about local plants and animals. In the arid Southwest, the archaeological record is less biased toward animal remains since wood, plant fibers, and seeds are preserved by the dry conditions. The descriptions of regional diets that follow are derived from a combination of archaeological, ethnographic, and historical information. (For additional information, the reader is referred to the *Handbook of North American Indians*, which presents information on the archaeology, ethnography, linguistics, geography, and history of various regions.)

A few generalizations can be made about the diet of North America's native peoples. The edible plants and animals that are available locally constituted the diet everywhere until the beginning of the practice of plant domestication, around 7000 B.C.E. In areas where plants were domesticated, or where domesticated plants were introduced from Mexico and Central America, locally available food resources continued to be used, but were supplemented, to varying degrees, with domesticated plants. It takes approximately 120 days for a crop of Indian corn to mature. This means that in much of Canada, where the growing season is less than 120 days, cultivation of corn was not possible, and diet continued to be based on locally available resources. There is evidence of maize cultivation in the southern portions of several provinces, including Manitoba, Ontario, and Quebec. Farther north, there was an increasingly heavy reliance on foods of animal origin. Other areas, including the Eastern Woodlands and West Coast, had plentiful and diverse foods available and continued to make use of those resources after the introduction of horticulture.

Arctic

Among Arctic peoples, diets varied depending on proximity to the coast. Those in coastal regions relied on sea mammals and fish. Sea mammals were more important in the High Arctic, where they were hunted in the frozen sea. Fish were more important in the warmer regions where there is more open water. Inland groups relied on migrating caribou, smaller terrestrial mammals (hares), birds, eggs, and berries (salmonberries, cranberries, and blueberries) and roots (cotton grass root and licorice root) (Ray, 1984). While dietary diversity was greater than is generally assumed, Arctic peoples, who are well adapted to metabolizing foods high in animal fat, relied primarily on hunting. Fat is essential as a source of lightweight, storable energy for functioning in cold climates and with periodic food scarcity. Cooking was not routinely carried out among Arctic peoples since fuel is a scarce and precious commodity. Meat was usually eaten raw and fish were dried before eating. From a nutritional perspective, this means that a number of vitamins, including vitamin C, that would otherwise be lost in cooking, were available. Internal organs were also eaten, adding to the supply of vitamins and minerals.

Subarctic

In the Subarctic boreal forest there was also a heavy reliance on animal foods in comparison to plant foods. Large terrestrial herbivores, such as caribou and moose, were hunted, along with small mammals. Fish were also an important food source. Although native people did not domesticate caribou, the migration routes were well known, and caribou drives, in which the animals were herded into enclosures, allowed for large-scale hunting. Among the Hare people of the Northwest Territories, foods were cooked either by roasting or stone boiling. Some favorite dishes included caribou tongue, caribou fetus, muskrat, and beaver tail (Savishinsky and Hara, 1981, p. 317). Meat and fish were preserved either by smoking,

drying, or freezing. A food that was common throughout the Subarctic and on the Great Plains is pemmican, which is made by pounding dried meat or fish with fat and sometimes with berries.

Northeast and Southeast

The peoples of the eastern Woodlands enjoyed a wide variety of both animal and plant foods. An assortment of nuts (hickory, walnut, and chestnut) were collected and served as one source of protein and fat. They could be stored over the winter and were used in a number of different ways. Among the Cherokee, nuts were pounded, then boiled, and the resulting milk was added to other foods such as corn. Fruits such as apple, cherry, peach, plum, and crabapple were used along with numerous wild greens, including dandelion, Solomon's seal, and bergamot, and berries (blackberry, strawberry, wild grape and huckleberries) (Chiltoskey, 1975). Animal foods included deer, rabbits, squirrels, and fish. Maize (corn) was introduced around 200 C.E., and it gradually became a staple (in breads, soups, and as roasted ears) to which other foods were added.

Researchers have determined that native plant species were domesticated prior to the introduction of maize in eastern North America. Sometime between three and four thousand years ago, indigenous plants were cultivated by people in the American mid-continent and Northeast. These plants include sumpweed (*Iva annua*), goosefoot (*Chenopodium berlandieri*), and sunflower (*Helianthus annuus*) (Smith, 1992). Goosefoot bears starchy seeds while sump weed and sunflower bear oily seeds. By 800 C.E., maize increased in importance relative to indigenous seed plants, and this was accompanied by an increase in population density in the American Midwest, Southeast, and Northeast.

Great Lakes

The area around the lower Great Lakes supported a large population of Iroquois and related groups, and has been studied extensively by early historians, Jesuit missionaries, ethnographers, and archaeologists. In addition, many descendents of those native groups still reside in the area. In 1916, F. W. Waugh published a monograph titled *Iroquois Foods and Food Preparation*, which provides detailed information on agricultural practices and utensils used in gathering, preparing, and eating foods, along with numerous preparation methods for various foods. Two commonly eaten foods among the Iroquois, historically, were corn bread and corn soup. Bread was made by pounding corn into flour. Boiling water was poured into a hollow in the flour. Additional ingredients may have included dried berries (huckleberries, blackberries, strawberries, elderberries), cooked beans, and nuts. A lump of the resulting dough was patted between the hands then dropped into boiling water. Prior to the introduction of copper kettles by Europeans, bread was more often baked under hot embers or on heated stones. The bread was

Cliffside pueblo of the Anasazi people in Mesa Verde National Park.

often eaten with maple sugar or syrup. The most common food at the time of historic contact was *sagamité*, a thick corn-based soup. From the basic corn broth, bits of meat or fish were added. Sometimes beans were also added. This meal would supply all essential amino acids and is a good source of carbohydrates.

Northwest Coast

The Northwest coast includes the land between the Pacific Ocean and the coastal mountains from the Bay of Alaska to southern Oregon. Food resources there are very rich, with abundant waterfowl, migrating sea mammals, and both marine and anadromous fish. In addition, over 550 different plant species have been documented as food items. Harriet Kuhnlein and Nancy Turner's *Traditional Plant Foods of Canadian Indigenous Peoples: Nutrition, Botany and Use* (1991) covers all of Canada but with special reference to the Canadian Northwest coast. Their detailed descriptions of plant use and the nutritional value of various plant foods provides ample evidence of an archaeological bias that overestimates the importance of animal foods in the diet. Interestingly, Native Americans did not differentiate between plants used for food and those used for medicine, since some foods were eaten as a form of medicine.

California, the Great Basin, and the Plains

Peoples of interior California and the Great Basin relied on fish, local game, and a variety of seeds. They also ate insects such as ants, roasted grasshoppers, caterpillars, fly larvae, and seventeen-year cicadas (locusts) (Bodenheimer, 1951). Food was stored in pits, and cooking was generally achieved by roasting. Pine nuts were ground into a flour that could be stored and easily transported (Kehoe, 1981). Along the southern periphery, agricultural crops included maize, beans, and squash.

The Great Plains extends from southern Canada to Texas. Along the eastern margins and along the major rivers, native people practiced small-scale horticulture. Hunting was important throughout the Plains, and there is evidence of big-game hunting among the early Clovis people, and later evidence of bison hunting through controlled drives over natural features such as cliffs and arroyos (Frison, 1998). There is archaeological evidence of long-term storage of meat from such drives. Ethnographic work as well as evidence from pollen and phytoliths indicate that a wide variety of indigenous plants were used, including plums, grapes, rose hips, berries, turnips, and camas root (Wissler, 1986).

Bison meat and fat were desirable food items. There is both archaeological and nutritional evidence for selective hunting of fatter animals (not only bison, but other large mammals as well). Meals are both more satisfying and more economical when protein is accompanied by fat and carbohydrate, a readily available source of energy that spares the higher metabolic demands required to break down protein. Other animals were also hunted for food, including deer, antelope, rabbits, and hares. Pemmican was a staple food for many Plains peoples. Foods were cooked either in earth ovens lined with heated rocks, or by boiling in hide bags with heated rocks inside.

Farming was also practiced by Plains peoples, particularly along the eastern margins and along the Missouri and Mississippi Rivers. Maize, beans, and squash were cultivated, and there is also evidence of the cultivation of the indigenous species, goosefoot, marsh elder, and sunflower, similar to the Eastern Woodlands.

Southwest

The American Southwest is of special interest for two reasons. First, the earliest evidence of domestication of maize, beans, squash, and other Mesoamerican cultigens is found there. Second, due to the hot and dry climate, plant remains are preserved in the archaeological record, providing a less biased picture of past diet than in other regions of North America. Spectacular Anasazi villages that flourished from 900–1300 C.E., such as Chaco Canyon, Mesa Verde, and Canyon de Chelly, housed people who farmed in canyon bottoms and on mesa tops with the aid of irrigation (Cordell, 1984). The Anasazi also exploited antelope, white-tailed deer, jackrabbits, cotton-tailed rabbits, and wild turkeys. Along the eastern margins, maize was traded for meat with Plains peoples. Food was prepared in earth ovens, in ceramic vessels, and on open fires. Indigenous plants used for food include piñon (pine) nuts, prickly-pear cactus buds, amaranth seeds, mesquite pods, and the heart of the agave (Cordell, 1984). *Zuni Breadstuff*, an early ethnographic account of all aspects of Zuni food, is a valuable source of information (Cushing, 1920).

Impact of European Contact

Sustained European contact altered traditional foods and food preparation throughout North America. Metal cooking pots were introduced, altering traditional roasting and boiling practices. The introduction of the horse had a profound impact on hunting techniques, particularly on the Great Plains. The fur trade altered traditional subsistence practices in the north. Displacement of native peoples by European settlers was very disruptive since an intimate knowledge of local environments was so important to obtaining food. Finally, the exchange of foods between the Old and New Worlds had a profound effect on cultures on both sides of the Atlantic Ocean (Crosby, 1972).

See also **Arctic; Canada, Native Peoples; Hunting and Gathering; Maize; Mammals; Mammals, Sea; Mexico; Thanksgiving; United States.**

BIBLIOGRAPHY

Bodenheimer, F. S. *Insects as Human Food: A Chapter of the Ecology of Man.* The Hague: Dr. W. Junk, Publishers, 1951.

Cordell, Linda S. *Prehistory of the Southwest.* Orlando, Fla.: Academic Press, 1984.

Crosby, Alfred W., Jr. *The Columbian Exchange: Biological and Cultural Consequences of 1492.* Westport, Conn.: Greenwood Press, 1972.

Cushing, Frank Hamilton. *Zuni Breadstuff.* Indian Notes and Monographs, vol. 8. Reprint, New York: Museum of the American Indian, Heye Foundation, 1974.

Frison, George C. "The Northwestern and Northern Plains Archaic." In *Archaeology on the Great Plains.* Edited by W. Raymond Wood, pp. 140–172. Lawrence: University of Kansas Press, 1998.

Katzenberg, M. Anne. "Stable Isotope Analysis: A Tool for Studying Past Diet, Demography, and Life History." In *Biological Anthropology of the Human Skeleton.* Edited by M. Anne Katzenberg and Shelley R. Saunders, pp. 305–327. New York: Wiley, 2000. A discussion of chemical methods for determining prehistoric diet.

Kehoe, Alice B. *North American Indians: A Comprehensive Account.* Englewood Cliffs, N.J.: Prentice-Hall, 1981.

Kuhnlein, Harriet V., and Nancy J. Turner. *Traditional Plant Foods of Canadian Indigenous Peoples: Nutrition, Botany and Use.* Food and Nutrition in History and Anthropology, vol. 8, edited by Solomon H. Katz. Philadelphia: Gordon and Breach, 1991.

Larsen, C. S. *Bioarchaeology: Interpreting Behavior from the Human Skeleton.* Cambridge: Cambridge University Press, 1998. Chapters on health, disease, and diet in prehistoric people.

Ray, D. J. "Bering Strait Eskimo." In *Handbook of North American Indians,* edited by William C. Sturtevant et al. Volume 5, *Arctic,* edited by David Damas, pp. 285–302 Washington, D.C.: Smithsonian Institution, 1984.

Savishinsky, Joel S., and Hiroko S. Hara. "Hare." In *Handbook of North American Indians,* edited by William C. Sturtevant et al. Volume 6, *Subarctic,* edited by June Helm. Washington, D.C.: Smithsonian Institution, 1981.

Smith, Bruce D. "Prehistoric Plant Husbandry in Eastern North America." In *The Origins of Agriculture: An International Perspective,* edited by C. Wesley Cowan and Patty J. Watson, pp. 101–119. Washington, D.C.: Smithsonian Institution Press, 1992.

Speth, John D. *Bison Kills and Bone Counts: Decision-Making by Ancient Hunters.* Prehistoric Archaeology and Ecology series, edited by Karl W. Butzer and Leslie G. Freeman. Chicago: University of Chicago Press, 1983

Speth, John D., and Katherine A. Spielmann. "Energy Source, Protein Metabolism, and Hunter-Gatherer Subsistence Strategies." *Journal of Anthropological Archaeology* 2, no. 1 (1983): 1–31.

Vanstone, James W. *Athapaskan Adaptations: Hunters and Fishermen of the Subarctic Forests.* Chicago: Aldine, 1974.

Waugh, F. W. *Iroquois Foods and Food Preparation.* Canada Department of Mines Geological Survey Memoir 86; Anthropological Series No. 12. Ottawa: Government Printing Bureau, 1916.

Winham, R. Peter, and F. A. Calabrese. "The Middle Missouri Tradition." In *Archaeology on the Great Plains,* edited by W. Raymond Wood, pp. 269–307. Lawrence: University of Kansas Press, 1998.

Wissler, Clark. *A Blackfoot Source Book: Papers by Clark Wissler.* Edited by David H. Thomas. New York: Garland, 1986.

Mary Anne Katzenberg

CONTEMPORARY ISSUES

The terms "American Indians" and "Native Americans" (both are appropriate) refer to diverse groups of indigenous peoples that have occupied the area north of Mexico and south of Canada since at least 12,000 B.C.E. With more than 550 sovereign Indian Nations currently residing within the political boundaries of the United States, summarizing their different foods and foodways is difficult. Such an undertaking would be analogous to characterizing "European foodways" as though Europeans from Italy to England were a homogeneous group. However, it is still possible to discuss some general characteristics organized along geographic lines.

Over several millennia the foodways of Native Americans were well established and included both wild and domesticated foods, traditions that have continued to evolve through the centuries of conquest, assimilation, and resistance that began with European contact in the fifteenth century. Contrary to popular stereotypes, not all Native Americans were horse-riding bison hunters who lived in tepees. Although these elements fit some historical contexts, they ignore actual regional and cultural differences.

Given the extensive ethnographic record of American Indians and the great interest the public has in their lives, it is surprising that so little research on their foodways has been done. A great deal of work on the ethnobotany of plants they used was done in the late nineteenth and early twentieth centuries, but it often focused on the potential economic importance of the plants as food and medicine, not on their importance as foods in specific cultures.

Both hunting and gathering (foraging) made important contributions to the diet of all American Indian groups at the time of contact, whether they were horticulturalists or not. The fact that no large mammals (horses, cattle, pigs, sheep, and goats) were domesticated in Native North America—only to be introduced later by Europeans—explains in part why foraging remained important. Virtually every native plant and animal species was used to some extent for food, medicine, and/or manufacture. Animal domesticates did include dogs, turkeys, and ducks, while domesticated plants included several varieties of maize (corn), beans, squash, gourds, sunflowers, sumpweed, and goosefoot (*Chenopodium*). Maize was a central food in the diets of many regional groups, and, except for California, was grown just about everywhere it was ecologically viable. The cooking traditions of Native Americans included everything from stone-boiling in leather bags to roasting and baking in earth ovens.

Because of a mixed subsistence pattern for horticultural groups, it is not surprising that both wild and domesticated foodstuffs remain traditional American Indian foods. The extent of this relationship is recognized in rights guaranteed by treaty to forage (hunt, fish, gather)

many species that are restricted by season or prohibited to non-Indians.

Traditional Native American Culture Areas

Native Americans have been traditionally divided into several culture areas related to shared geographic and environmental boundaries. This is not to say that peoples falling within these realms were all culturally the same. However, both the historical experience of these groups as well as their ways of adapting to each area have heavily influenced their traditional foodways. Regardless of academic debates about the use of the cultural-regional approach, it remains a useful way to organize the regional differences that define Native Americans and their foods. Although the focus here is the American Indian groups south of Canada and north of Mexico, there is a great deal of overlap with cultures to the north and south. Also, in addition to the hundreds of federally recognized tribes in the United States, there are dozens more who maintain cultural traditions that are not federally recognized. A few contemporary issues for each area will be discussed, but no attempt will be made to detail the foodways of specific cultural groups.

Fry bread (bread dough deep-fried in fat) is a popular food at Indian fairs and gatherings, but it is also the cause of obesity and diabetes among native Americans. The dish can actually be traced to medieval Europe. © Phil Schermeister/CORBIS.

Eastern Woodlands. Comprising the the Northeast, Great Lakes, and Southeast United States, this area extends from the Atlantic Coast west to the eastern prairies, north to the Canadian border, and south to the Gulf of Mexico. It is a place where corn, beans, and squash, all originally from Mexico, were the central staples of life and identity. Communities ranged in size from the small dispersed villages of New England to the large urbanized mound-building cities along the Mississippi and Ohio River valleys. The degree of maize dependence varied from area to area, but its central importance to this region's Native Americans is undeniable. Maize is a fundamental element of their folklore and origin myths.

Early European colonists in eastern North America rapidly incorporated various Native American dishes into their diet. Some of the best-known examples are those of Algonquin-speaking peoples, with some alterations of the original names and meanings. "Succotash," a corrupted version of the Narragansett "misickquatash," refers to whole kernels of grain. It is often a mixture of green corn cut from the cob, beans, and perhaps another ingredient, which might be anything from meat to squash. Hominy, or "rockahominy," is made by taking shelled ripened corn and soaking it in an alkaline solution made from wood ash or lye to remove the hulls. This method also enhances the nutritional value of the maize product. Throughout the United States it is sold as yellow or white hominy or under its Latin American name, "pozole." When dried and milled into course bits, it is called "hominy grits." In some areas of the Southeast, however, the term "hominy" can also refer to grits.

Although maize is an important food item in the Great Lakes region, the gathering of wild rice takes precedence there because it is essential to maintaining the identity of many cultures in this area. In fact, in many states only American Indians can legally gather true "wild" rice (*Zizania aquatica*). Given the constant demand for this product in American cooking, it continues to be a profitable resource for these communities. Many of these groups have also been in conflict with U.S. federal agencies, environmental groups, and local non-Indian communities over their legal spearfishing rights.

From the Iroquois nations of upstate New York south to the Cherokee of the Carolinas and the Seminoles of Florida, traditional foodways for nations of the Eastern Woodlands still combine locally gathered foods with the overarching importance of what the Iroquois refer to as the "Three Sisters": corn, beans, and squash. Across this region green (unripened) corn is the central element in "Green Corn" ceremonies, including the *Busk* ceremony of the southeastern cultures, which signals the beginning of a new year, and the annual *Schemitzun* (Green Corn Festival) of the Mashantucket Pequot held near Ledyard, Connecticut, which gathers nations from across the country for a huge powwow. Green corn is now a major item of American foodways when consumed as sweet corn, a mutated variety of maize that concentrates a sugar rather than a starch component.

Great Plains and Rocky Mountains. Bison, or buffalo, were a central food item and cultural symbol to many of the peoples of the central and western regions of North America. The meat was often processed into pemmican, a dried pounded meat often mixed with fat and chokecherries. This foodstuff was stored in parfleches (leather pouches) and could sustain a mobile population for long periods of time. The introduction of the horse in the eighteenth century greatly transformed the nomadic bison hunters of these regions, including groups that engaged in seasonal small-scale horticulture as well as those who did not but traded meat for maize with horticultural societies to the south and east. The horse also facilitated the migration of groups from the eastern prairies, like the Sioux, who gave up horticulture to live in tepees and become bison hunters. They were not only able to traverse great distances, but their mobility gave them the opportunity as warriors to resist assimilation well into the late nineteenth century, when almost all other Native American groups had been placed in some type of reservation system. Their dependence on bison was also their downfall because those animals were systematically slaughtered to the brink of extinction by white men, a destruction greatly facilitated by the completion of the transcontinental railroad and U.S. policies intended to starve them into submission by eliminating their food supply.

Bison remain central to Native American cultural identity. In the Dakotas and Montana some groups have begun to raise large herds of bison on the great expanses of grassland that they once occupied. A market that demands a low-fat alternative to beef, which bison meat provides (for example, buffalo burgers), has made raising them economically valuable.

Annual gatherings at the time of the traditional bison hunts in the summer months led to the importance of powwows or social get-togethers that are still held. The dance style of the plains groups is at the core of a powwow circuit that involves Indian nations from all over the United States. These events have also spread foods central to pan-Indian identities, for example, fry bread.

Southwest. Traditionally home to pueblo farming communities and bands of foragers, this desert region exemplifies Native Americans' ability to adapt to extreme environments. The same triad of corn, beans, and squash was also central to these groups, along with a host of plants gathered from the deserts and mountains. Unlike many Native American groups who were forcibly removed from their traditional homelands, Southwest farmers from New Mexico to Arizona have been able to maintain an ongoing relationship with lands that they have cultivated since prehistoric times. Groups like the Hopi continue to practice dry-land farming in the desert of northeastern Arizona, and perform cycles of elaborate rituals to bring rain and fertility to their lands. Throughout the Southwest, water rights are a major point of concern for Native Americans whose livelihood is based on range livestock and irrigated crop production. They compete for water with growing urban centers like Albuquerque, New Mexico, and Phoenix, Arizona. The use of water by mining operations exacerbated the scarcity and critical need for this finite resource.

Even peoples who were traditionally known as foragers, like the Navajo, over time incorporated horticulture. With the introduction of sheep into the region, they continued to adapt to the desert by becoming herders. Since the 1930s the Navajo have suffered through a number of government-imposed livestock reduction programs meant to limit overgrazing of the fragile desert grasses and forage, and they continue to resent and resist attempts to regulate their livelihood and important source of food. By continually adapting to both the desert environment and changing political climates, the Navajo Nation, which completely surrounds the Hopi Nation, is the largest group of American Indians in the United States, with a population of well over 300,000.

In the harsh Sonoran Desert of southern Arizona, groups like the Tohono O'odham (Papago) and Akimel O'odham (Pima) combine ancient agricultural traditions using irrigation canals with foraging for desert plants. For example, bean pods from the mesquite tree are picked and then pounded into flour, and the fruits of the saguaro cactus are collected and boiled down to make a syrup, which was also fermented and used traditionally as a ceremonial wine.

Chili peppers, a New World cultigen from Mexico, were introduced into the Southwest by the Spanish and became central to many regional cuisines.

California, Great Basin, and Plateau. Although California is known today as a major U.S. food-producing area, in the past it was home to foragers who utilized the diverse natural ecosystems of the region (e.g., their annual gathering of acorns that were processed into flour). Many groups utilized the rich coastal resources, too. This pattern ran from the Baja region in the south north to areas that overlapped with the Northwest Coast native peoples.

Native Americans from the Great Basin area survived well into the twentieth century as foragers in one of the most extreme environments that humans inhabit on earth, the Mojave Desert, including "Death Valley." Communal rabbit and grasshopper drives brought together greatly dispersed bands. A variety of desert plants were also collected. Soshonean groups in Nevada have found it difficult to maintain many of these traditions in areas where nuclear testing and uranium mining have destroyed ecosystems.

Groups from the Plateau region of the United States are located in an area that overlaps traditions from the Great Basin, Northwest Coast, and Northern Plains. The gathering and preparation of the camas tuber (*Camassia*

quamash), a type of lily, links groups like the Nez Percé to their traditional foodways.

With the vast environmental diversity of these regions, mining, logging, and commercial fishing enterprises threaten the ability of many Indian nations to continue their traditional food-getting activities. Such operations not only destroy local ecosystems but areas that are considered sacred as well.

Northwest Coast. Native American fishing and whaling communities along the Pacific coast from northern California to southeast Alaska provide a unique example of sedentary foragers who utilize both aquatic and terrestrial species of plants and animals. Salmon was a central element of their diet, smoked and also processed for oils, and provided a great source of wealth for these peoples. The anadromous nature of salmon—swimming downstream to the ocean from their birthplace and then returning to it to spawn at the end of their lives—provided an abundant and predictable source of food, allowing these foragers to become sedentary dwellers along the salmon runs. Salmon continues to be economically important to these peoples.

The operation of commercial fishing fleets as an extension of their traditional food-getting activities continually places American Indians on the Northwest Coast in direct conflict with the non-Indian commercial fishing industry as well as with U.S federal agencies regarding their fundamental right, guaranteed by treaty, to secure a livelihood. A conflict over whale hunting has also emerged. Ever since gray whales were removed from the endangered species list, some groups, like the Makah, have petitioned and won the right to conduct traditional whale hunts, to the disappointment of environmental activists who have attempted to stop them. The goal for Northwest Coast peoples is not necessarily to make whale hunting a commercial enterprise, but to engage in an important food-getting activity that has great symbolic meaning in their culture.

The Northwest Coast area is also known for the potlatch (etymologically unrelated to "potluck"), a great feast and giveaway. Wealth that was accumulated—salmon oil, for example—by the elite of a community was ceremonially given away to rival villages. Although reciprocity was an important dimension of the potlatch, gaining status and the display of a family's and community's wealth was the major point of the event. As in the past, totem poles are erected to mark the greatness of a potlatch. The potlatch remains an important community event that reinforces cultural traditions through dance, feasting, and sharing.

Contemporary Diet and Nutrition Issues

Native Americans face a host of social problems (i.e. alcohol/drug abuse and violence) at levels far above the national average, and it is alarming that the rate of adult-onset (Type 2) diabetes for American Indians is over three times that of the rest of the U.S. population as a whole.

Explanations for this phenomenon have included the "thrifty genotype" model, which posits that such a genotype would have given a genetic advantage to populations who experienced periods of feast and famine. If, during periods of feasting, they were capable of maximizing their caloric intake of fat for storage, which could be tapped during times of famine, they would have a selective advantage over other populations. Greatly increased insulin production during feasting would facilitate this process. A problem occurs when the feasting, especially in the form of high-fat, carbohydrate-rich foods, becomes full-time. The result has been high rates of obesity, insulin resistance, and diabetes.

Understanding this phenomenon is a complex issue that involves changes in diet, more sedentary lifestyles, and a movement away from traditional diets and to activities that are known to be healthier. The epidemic rise in diet-related health problems like diabetes, coronary heart disease, hypertension, and obesity has been most pronounced in the decades following World War II. The promotion of an American diet and lifestyle as one of the many facets of attempting to assimilate Native Americans into the U.S. mainstream included home economics instruction for women showing them how to utilize the surplus commodities being provided to the impoverished Indian communities. Many of these foods left out a number of micronutrients available through traditional methods of processing. For example, stone-ground maize provided a good source of iron and other minerals. Ironically, the combination of commodities—highly refined white flour, sugar, and lard—are the basis of a common Indian food, fry bread. One would be hard-pressed not to find some variant of it in communities across the United States. Go to any powwow and fry bread power will be there. A variant that includes toppings like spicy ground beef and/or beans is called an "Indian taco."

In general, the daily diet of most Native Americans does not contain traditional foods or foodways. Native Americans are just as much a part of the system of foodways as everyone else in the United States. For many, their diet reflects that of other low- to middle-income families who often buy food for its bulk, not its nutritional value. This is not to say that traditional foods are not important to their Indian identity; they are. Unfortunately, for many tribes these traditions continue to fade. The recent boom in casino gambling may benefit some groups, but the future will tell if the all-you-can-eat buffets found in most casinos represent cultural revitalization or loss.

A number of tribes have started educational programs on nutrition and campaigns that extol the benefits of their traditional foods. For example, O'odham groups (Pima and Papago) of Arizona, working in cooperation with Gary Nabhan and Native Seeds/SEARCH, have been attempting to reduce their incidence of diabetes and other diet-related health problems by promoting the growing and gathering of traditional desert foods. These programs not only stress dietary change and physical activity but also emphasize the importance of cultural traditions. The history of Native American foodways shows that, when faced with challenges, Indian peoples adapt and change while maintaining their core identities. In many cases, even when the traditional language is no longer spoken or religious rituals are no longer performed, the knowledge of traditional foods has not been forgotten.

See also **Arctic; Biodiversity; Canada: Native Peoples; Foodways; Inca Empire; Inuit; Maize; Mexico and Central America, Pre-Columbian; Potlatch; South America; United States: The Southwest.**

BIBLIOGRAPHY

Aniwaya. Available at www.aniwaya.org. Link to section on foods, Native American recipes.

Brenton, Barrett P. *Hopi Foodways: Biocultural Perspectives on Change and Contradiction.* Ann Arbor, Mich.: University Microfilms, 1994.

Calloway, Doris H., R. D. Giauque, and F. M. Costa. "The Superior Mineral Content of Some American Indian Foods in Comparison to Federally Donated Counterpart Commodities." *Ecology of Food and Nutrition* 3 (1974): 203–211.

Cox, Beverly. *Spirit of the Harvest: North American Indian Cooking.* New York: Stewart, Tabori, and Chang, 1991.

Driver, Harold E. *Indians of North America.* Chicago: University of Chicago Press, 1969.

Greenhouse, Ruth. "Preparation Effects on Iron and Calcium in Traditional Pima Foods." *Ecology of Food and Nutrition* 10 (1981): 221–225.

Kavena, Juanita Tiger. *Hopi Cookery.* Tucson: University of Arizona Press, 1980.

Moerman, Daniel E. *Native American Ethnobotany.* Portland, Ore.: Timber Press, 1998.

Nabhan, Gary P. *Gathering the Desert.* Tucson: University of Arizona Press, 1985.

Nativetech: Native American Technology and Art. Available at www.nativetech.org. Link to section on food and recipes.

Niethammer, Carolyn. *American Indian Food and Lore.* New York: Macmillan, 1974.

The North American Ethnobotany Database, University of Michigan-Dearborn. Available at www.umd.umich.edu/cgi-bin/herb.

Palmer, Edward. *Food Products of the North American Indians.* Report of the Commissioner of Agriculture for the Year 1870, pp. 404–428. Washington, D.C.: Government Printing Office, 1871.

Resources for the Anthropological Study of Food Habits. Available at www.lilt.ilstu.edu/rtdirks/. Link to section on North America: indigenous foods.

Smith, Janell, and Dennis Wiedman. "Fat Content of South Florida Indian Frybread: Health Implications for a Pervasive Native-American Food." *Journal of the American Dietetic Association* 101 (2001): 582–585.

Barrett P. Brenton

AMERICAS, PRE-COLUMBIAN. *See* **American Indians; Mexico and Central America, Pre-Columbian; Inca Empire.**

AMINO ACIDS. *See* **Proteins and Amino Acids.**

AMISH FOOD. *See* **United States: Pennsylvania Dutch Food.**

ANCIENT KITCHEN, THE. The traditional and symbolic heart of the home, the kitchen is inextricably linked with humankind's discovery of cooking food with fire. The use of fire has been known for over half a million years, as indicated by the remains of hearths in the Choukowtien cave in northern China. There "Peking Man" left traces of cooking around the hearth in the charred bones of numerous animals. Using fire for food preparation was a central culinary breakthrough. Some flavors are more palatable, and some foods are made edible, when cooked. The designs of hearths and ovens and the locations of kitchens through the millennia document the evolution of ancient kitchens. The English word "kitchen" comes from the Latin *coquere*, meaning to cook.

Kitchen Design

Several related and important areas were located near ancient kitchens, including the pantry, orchard, garden, spice and medicinal herb garden, larder, icehouse, and root cellar. Ancient Chinese clay models of a household show the kitchen located near or even over the pigsty. Pigs were a main source of meat, and they provided manure for fuel and a convenient place for cleaning up any refuse from cooking and dining. In the fifth century B.C.E. ancient Greeks designed the kitchen as a separate house, and the layout continued in ancient Rome. The Romans built street stalls for quick snacks, but these were not kitchens in the full sense. Most wealthy Romans also owned country property, where grapes were pressed into wine, wheat was harvested, and olives were pressed for oil. The city kitchens provided space for these products. Kitchens were planned with clearly defined preparation areas.

Later medieval châteaus and wealthy European homes had spacious kitchens with several adjacent anterooms, including a room for utensils, a pantry, cold storage, and a buttery. For the middle class, kitchens continued as a location for communal cooking, dining, and social activities. Renaissance kitchens were often elaborate. As is common of the privileged throughout the centuries, the wealthy boasted the most modern devices for cooking, storage, and food preparation, from the spit to gridirons, ewers, salvers, and huge cauldrons. The kitchen was viewed as a workshop for food preparation for daily dining and feasts and also for preservation of food for the winter months. Ottoman kitchens of the Turkish sultans in the sixteenth century provide another look at early kitchens of the wealthy. In the Topkapi palace in Constantinople, sultans' chefs had elaborate areas categorized for food preparation. European visitors were given a tour of the kitchen, which boasted eight-foot-wide cauldrons and large spits, and prepared food for thousands on a daily basis.

Nineteenth-century kitchens changed drastically with improvements in stoves and hearth designs. The kitchen remained a workplace, separate and distinct from the rest of the house. It was sometimes located in a separate building, in the basement (popular in Victorian times), or at the end of a long hallway. Temperate and hot climates alike moved kitchens outdoors. In India the Mogul kitchens were frequently located outdoors to remove the smells and heat of cooking from the living quarters. Moroccan kitchens placed cook pots in a "roofless kitchen," a walled enclosure off the pantry. Cool-climate Bulgarian homes have traditional summer kitchens used in the hot months.

Social Use

Traditionally a woman, sometimes an older relative or matriarch, has been the cook. A woman's domain, the kitchen was also the focal point for transmission of culture and teaching younger family members and apprentices. Even the use of kitchen servants in wealthy households was tied to the housewife or housekeeper. Often the main point of connection between master and servant was between the mistress of the house and the head cook. The kitchen became a meeting place between classes; long-time family cooks were often treated with the respect due family members. In segregated societies the kitchen was a connection between whites and blacks where orders and desires were given.

Kitchen Gods

In antiquity fire was sacred. A kitchen had an altar place for prayers and offerings to the kitchen god. Mexicans honor a patron saint of kitchens. The kitchen god Zaojing was revered in China, and Japanese cooks worshiped the god of fire. Similar examples abound.

Food Storage

A great range of food and foodstuffs is available for most kitchens, and the size of the kitchen or complexity of tools does not dictate the quality or complexity of the cuisine. The earliest storage containers were animal skins, woven baskets, or gourds. Pottery's introduction allowed more variety of shapes and types of storage in a kitchen, from double-walled cooling jugs for water to tripod pots for stews and pointed amphorae for wine. Thus the larder and pantry became central to the design and layout of early kitchens. Root cellars kept foods cool and available during hot months and provided an even, temperate climate for preserves in the winter. The smokehouse adjacent to the kitchen was crucial for meat and fish preservation. In Dutch homes the chimney had an ingenious bypass for the smoke, which allowed the cook to smoke meats at the same time. Ice and snow rooms in some cultures preserved food. Grapes were hung from rafters in Mediterranean kitchens and were preserved on the stem in water in glass jars in tsarist Russian homes. The many activities of preservation, canning, pickling, smoking, and drying all had places in early kitchens, as much of this work was done at home rather than in factories.

The Stove and Hearth

Early hearths were clay or stone, and their main purpose was to enclose the fire. The risk of fire was always a worry. Fireplaces provided heat and light, and the fire required tending. Large homes had deep hearths, and foods were cooked in pots placed in banked coals or ashes. Fireplaces had rotating spits and hooks for hanging large pieces of meat. Domes gave way to hoods, with better ventilation. Russian and Dutch homes in the sixteenth century raised the hearths and created a sleeping platform around the fire. Some flat-topped Russian stoves also accommodated steam baths and drying laundry.

The invention and mass distribution of the large cast-iron stove, called the "iron sow" in early Sweden, radically changed the design of the kitchen. In the 1870s oil lamps replaced the light a fire had given, and the risk of the open fire was contained. Gone was the hearth as a symbolic and aesthetic part of the kitchen, replaced by a modern tool that required less tending and less space.

As 1900 approached, families previously self-sufficient in food production began to purchase more marketed foods. By the 1930s the need for large kitchen staffs and large kitchens was reduced in most homes. The smaller stove, the increasing availability of mass-produced foodstuffs, and a changing workforce reduced the size of pantries, even eliminating the need for root cellars and smokehouses. The kitchen was streamlined with only a hint of design nostalgia. While the kitchen changed, it remained the symbolic center of the home.

See also **Ancient Mediterranean Religions; Gardening and Kitchen Gardens; Greece, Ancient; Hearth Cookery; Rome and the Roman Empire.**

BIBLIOGRAPHY

James, Peter, and Nick Thorpe. *Ancient Inventions.* New York: Ballantine, 1994.

Davidson, Alan, ed. *The Cook's Room: A Celebration of the Heart of the Home.* New York: HarperCollins, 1991.

Terrie Wright Chrones

ANCIENT MEDITERRANEAN RELIGIONS.

Religion shaped both the use and conceptualization of food in the Greco-Roman Mediterranean world. This was true of the consumption of animals, cereals, and other plants. Because of the central role that food played in exchanges between gods and human beings, and between human beings themselves, food contributed to social and group identity. Ethnographers such as Herodotus distinguished Greek sacrifice from Persian, Egyptian, Scythian, and Libyan sacrifice; others distinguished Jewish and Christian rites. Ancient Greek religion located the practitioner in Greek culture and in a particular Greek community. This was important because by the end of the sixth century B.C.E., Greek cities were found around the Black Sea, along the coast of Asia Minor, in North Africa and southern Italy and Sicily—and after 300 B.C.E. in Syria, Persia, and Egypt. Similarly, as Rome came to distinguish itself from its Italic and Greek neighbors and to expand first throughout Italy and then throughout the whole Mediterranean world, it became necessary to establish how Roman culture might relate to cultures indigenous to the territory it now governed. There is ample epigraphic and literary evidence that people ate together in groups with religious affiliations throughout antiquity (*orgeones* in Greek, *collegia* in Latin), and that structures of power adapted the groups to reflect their influence, but did not greatly change the practices of eating. A major example is provided by the Ptolemys, who supported their new monarchy in Egypt after the death of Alexander by reinventing the Greek civic festival of Dionysus, with the monarch now at the center.

The basis of social and political life was the animal sacrifice, for which Prometheus supplies the most important foundation myth: he brought fire, therefore culture (in Greek thought), to mortals. Greeks and Romans slaughtered animals at altars outside the temple, with all citizens or relevant parties participating in the death and the consumption of meat. The offering to the god, combined with a communal act that reinforced equality (everyone in theory had an equal share, with special parts for the priests), provided an opportunity to eat meat. It is generally thought that in Greece little meat was eaten that had not been sacrificed. In Rome, so much meat appears to have been butchered in the imperial period that commercial slaughter may have predominated. Even in the Greek world, however, the sacred and commercial were not rigidly separated. Animals were bought for sacrifice, their skins were sold, and meat that was not distributed to participants at the temple could be taken to market and sold.

Sacrifice was a major part of many civic festivals, private associations, and family occasions. Offerings of one hundred cattle (known as a hecatomb) or more were made on major state occasions, while a piglet or lamb might be offered by a small community or family. Festivals were major occasions that shaped the civic year, and calendars specifying dates, types of offering, and the names of participants and beneficiaries survive on inscriptions and in Ovid's poem the *Fasti*.

This was the form of animal sacrifice to Olympian gods. For the gods of the underworld, the whole animal

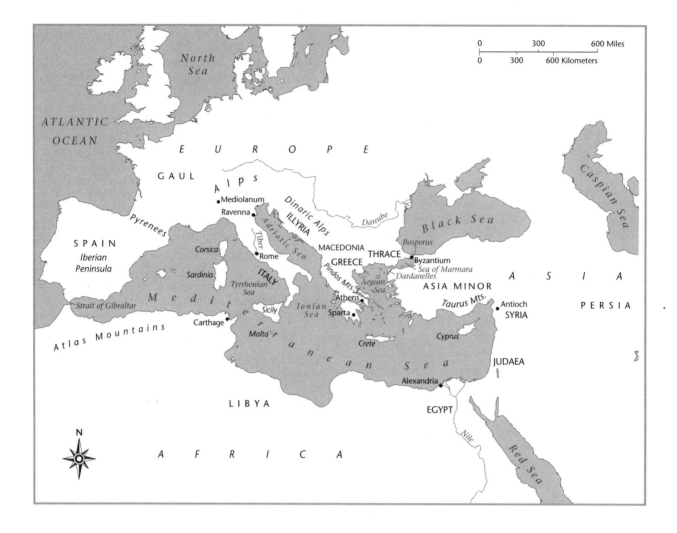

was burned, and there was no consumption by human beings. Offerings of food were, however, made to the dead, and funeral feasts in their honor were eaten. The dead were also portrayed dining on couches, as they had done in life.

Cereals as well as animals played a major role in religion. They were the responsibility of the goddesses Demeter and Persephone in the Greek world, and of Ceres and other equivalents in Rome and Italy. Persephone in the related myth represented the corn. As she was abducted by Hades and later released to the upper world, so the grain is sown and sprouts in spring. The provision of grain was a major priority in all ancient states. Major festivals of Demeter were known in Sicily and Italy; there was also the Thesmophoria in many Greek cities, a festival for women only, which promoted the growth of corn and the conception of babies. (Sex and agriculture, human and plant reproduction, were often linked in Greek culture.) This festival was one of the few in the Greco-Roman world in which fasting was an

element prior to feasting (in the myth, Demeter brought famine to mortals when her daughter was lost). There are a few other parallels to the formal fasting found in Judaism or the fasting to near death found in the early Christian church. Demeter also presided at the Eleusinian Mysteries, where corn (grain) and the afterlife were central concerns. Legumes were also linked with the dead, both in Pythagorean belief and in such festivals as the Roman Lemuria, while mixtures of grains and beans represented the precivilized diet in such Greek festivals as the Anthesteria and Pyanopsia.

The other major god of food was Dionysus (or Bacchus), who presided over the growth of noncereal plants. His cult was closely linked with agriculture, and his most important plant was the vine. Wine was central to the libation, the pouring of liquids to a god, which was a widespread practice in the Mediterranean world from early times and accompanied sacrifice, prayer, and many social-religious acts. The consumption of wine was circumscribed by ritual in the "symposium," where gods received drink-offerings of neat wine, and human drinking was in equal measures of wine and water, which were blended in the mixing bowl.

Animal sacrifice was complemented by nonblood sacrifices of cereals, honey, fruit, and vegetables, first fruits in particular. (The celebration of abundance, in art in particular, was often represented by the cornucopia.) Some cults specified nonblood offerings, particularly the Orphics and strict Pythagoreans, who abstained from the sacrifice and consumption of meat and fish. Less strict Pythagoreans allowed the sacrifice of some parts of some animals, since strict vegetarianism marked people as marginal and not participating in civic sacrifice.

New cults regularly arrived in the Greco-Roman world, such as the festival of Adonis, a Syrian god who died before maturity and was linked with the rapid growth of herbs and spices. Some foods rarely entered the sacred sphere. The most notable is fish. Greek and Roman authors noted the sacred fish of Syria and Egypt; in their own world, they often linked fish with luxury, since they belonged to the marketplace, and consumption was not regulated by religious constraints.

See also **Byzantine Empire; Greece, Ancient; Herodotus; Hippocrates; Mediterranean Diet; Pythagoras; Rome and the Roman Empire.**

BIBLIOGRAPHY

Beard, Mary, John North, and Simon Price. *The Religions of Rome*. Cambridge, U.K.: Cambridge University Press, 1998.

Burkert, Walter. *Griechische Religion der archaischen und klassischen Epoche* [Greek religion of the archaic and classical periods]. Stuttgart, Germany: Kohlhammer, 1977. Translated by John Raffant. London: Oxford University Press, 1985.

Detienne, Marcel, and Jean-Paul Vernant. *La cuisine du sacrifice en pays grec* [Foods of sacrifice in Greece]. Paris: Gallimard, 1979. Translated by Paula Wissing. Chicago: University of Chicago Press, 1989.

Deubner, Ludwig. *Attische Feste* [Attic Greek feasts]. Berlin: Akademie-Verlag, 1956.

Garland, Robert. *Introducing New Gods: The Politics of Athenian Religion*. Ithaca, N.Y.: Cornell University Press, 1992.

Latte, Kurt. *Römische Religionsgeschichte* [History of Roman religion]. Munich: C. H. Beck, 1960.

Parker, R. C. T. *Miasma*. Oxfordshire, U.K.: Clarendon Press, 1983.

Rice, E. E. *The Grand Procession of Ptolemy Philadelphus*. London and New York: Oxford University Press, 1983.

Stengel, P. *Opferbrauche der Griechen* [Sacrifice customs of the Greeks]. Munich: C. H. Beck, 1920.

Turcan, Robert. *Religion romaine* [Roman religion]. Leiden and New York: E. J. Brill, 1988.

John Wilkins

ANCIENT WORLD. *See* **Bible, Food in the; China: Ancient and Dynastic China; Greece, Ancient; Mesopotamia, Ancient; Mexico and Central America, Pre-Columbian; Rome and the Roman Empire.**

ANIMALS: PRIMATE DIETS. The daily food quest is generally the single most important activity for any animal. For this reason, natural selection should strongly favor any feature that enhances an animal's success at food acquisition. In essence, it has been suggested that different animal species can be viewed as "natural experiments" aimed at securing some portion of the always limited dietary resources available on the planet at any one time.

Humans are members of the Primate order and are placed in the suborder Anthropoidea, along with monkeys and apes. (When speaking of Primates as an order, the word is capitalized; when speaking of primates generally, the word is lowercased.) Because of our close relationship to other anthropoids, particularly the great apes (Pongidae), the dietary behavior of wild primates is of strong interest because it can provide clues about the types of dietary problems humans may have faced and resolved in their own evolution as well as insights into the probable dietary behavior of human ancestors and the nutritional composition of their wild foods.

The Role of Diet in Primate Evolution

Most primates are highly arboreal animals and carry out most activities in the canopy of tropical forest trees. Fossil evidence suggests that the earliest Primates evolved from small insectivores, initially attracted into the canopy by pollinating insects. Many morphological traits specifically associated with Primates, as, for example, keen stereoscopic vision, manipulative, grasping fingers, and a reduced dependence on the sense of smell seem to relate to selection for features associated with the efficient capture of items such as insects in an arboreal environment. However, because insects tend to be discretely distributed in the forest canopy and are also small in size, only small and relatively solitary primate foragers can be supported on such a diet.

Perhaps to circumvent these limitations, it would appear that natural selection favored a decided change in the dietary behavior of the ancestral primate, giving rise to the anthropoids. Though insects may be scarce, any animal in the tropical forest is continuously surrounded by potential plant foods. The evolution of anthropoids appears to have resulted from some early primate's ability to penetrate the arboreal plant food niche and then radiate (diversify) such that its descendents (monkeys and apes) came to dominate a strong subset of the most nutritious and energy-rich plant foods available in the forest canopy.

The idea that monkeys and apes are basically plant eaters may come as a surprise because, when we think of plant-eating animals, primates do not generally come to mind. Rather we think of cows and horses or rabbits and kangaroos. However, a wealth of field studies on many different species of wild primate show that all extant (living) monkeys and apes take by far the greatest percentage of the daily diet from plant foods, eating small to negligible amounts of animal matter. It is fair to say that primates are omnivores (taking the diet from both animal and plant foods) because most primates do eat some animal matter each day along with plant foods, but it is important to realize that most material entering the digestive tract of monkeys and apes is of plant rather than animal origin.

Primates and Plant Foods

An orientation toward plant foods is characteristic of all anthropoids irrespective of body size. Many smaller monkeys take as much as 65 percent of the diet from concentrated plant foods such as gums and ripe fruits. For example, the smallest living monkey, the pygmy marmoset (*Cebuella pygmaea*, body weight less than 2 oz.) feeds primarily on calorie-rich plant gums and saps, supplemented with ripe fruits and insects. Larger monkeys as well as all apes take most of the diet from young leaves and fruits, supplementing these with seeds, flowers, and other plant parts, and often also eggs, insects, and small vertebrates. Orangutans and gorillas are estimated to take some 99 percent of their annual diet exclusively from plant foods—wild fruits, tender young leaves, piths, and the like—while for chimpanzees, this figure is some 94 percent. Though wild chimpanzees are known to hunt, kill, and eat small mammals, including monkeys, and also to eat termites and ants, such animal foods typically contribute only a small percentage to their annual diet, most of which is made up of ripe fruits. It is likely that many monkeys and apes would eat more animal foods if they could capture them more easily. Thus the low amount of meat in the average wild primate diet may relate more to the difficulties of getting animal food than to any aversion to eating it.

When we examine the digestive tracts of most plant-eating animals, animals such as deer, cows, or rabbits, we find that their digestive tracts show notable specializations to aid them in extracting sufficient nutrition from all of the plant foods they eat. With few exceptions, however, Primates do not show such dramatic digestive specializations—yet, Primates too are plant eaters. How are primates able to exploit plant foods successfully without the extensive digestive specializations we find in most other plant-eating animals?

Primates Solve Dietary Problems with Their Heads

The answer is simple—primates tend to specialize on only the highest quality plant foods—foods that offer the most nutrition in exchange for the time and energy invested in finding and eating them. Yet, very high-quality plant foods in the tropical canopy are bound to be less abundant than lower-quality plant foods. How then are primates able to afford the costs of their high selectivity?

To put it simply, primates use their heads. An unusually large complex brain relative to body size characterizes all primates. It is hypothesized that an unusually large brain was favored in primate evolution in part to aid in remembering the types and locations of higher quality plant foods as well as when such foods were ready to be harvested. Using their large brains, monkeys and apes can keep track of when particular important food trees are producing their nutritious new leaves or sugar-rich flowers or ripe fruits and can plan the most direct travel route to reach them at the opportune moment for harvest.

Thus primates use long-term memory and planning to lower the costs associated with seeking out the best foods in the forest canopy, and because the foods they eat are of relatively high quality, elaborate digestive specialization generally is not required to digest them efficiently. A few lineages of primates do show fairly elaborate digestive specializations. These lineages—as for example, the Colobinae or "leaf-eating" monkeys—have diets composed in large part of leaves, including many mature leaves that tend to be low in nutrients and hard to digest.

Anthropoids are also characterized by extreme sociality. Most monkeys and apes live in social groups composed of various adult females and males and their immature offspring. Each group occupies a particular area in the forest and, as a general rule, its descendents will continue to occupy more or less the same area generation after generation. For this reason, the social unit so characteristic of monkeys and apes can be regarded as a type of dietary adaptation for it enables the older individuals in the group to pass on important information to young animals about the types, locations, and seasonal patterning of the higher quality plant foods in their habitat—information essential for their survival.

Each Primate Species Has a Particular Dietary Focus

Stressing that primates are largely plant-eaters is not to imply that all monkeys and apes have exactly the same diet, for they do not. Each primate species tends to have its own characteristic mix of plant (and animal) foods. In addition, each particular species typically specializes in only a certain subset of the higher-quality dietary resources in its environment. For example, the South American capuchin monkey, *Cebus apella*, has a high degree of manual dexterity and very powerful jaws. These features aid capuchins in cracking open the hard palm nuts that form an important part of their diet, which also includes ripe fruits, insects, and small vertebrates. Another monkey species often found living in the same forests as *Cebus apella* is the spider monkey, *Ateles paniscus*. Spider monkeys are characterized by a low degree of manual dexterity and small teeth, which are useless for cracking hard-shelled palm nuts. But spider monkeys specialize in soft fruits and tender young leaves, not hard palm nuts. They are also much bigger than capuchin monkeys, and if the supply of softer fruits is limited, they can chase capuchin monkeys out of fruiting trees and monopolize the fruit crop for themselves.

The Role of Diet in Human Evolution

As discussed, the closest living relatives of humans, the great apes, all eat plant-based diets. The common ancestor giving rise both to apes and humans is likewise believed to have been primarily plant-eating. All humans and apes have the same basic digestive tract—a simple acid stomach, a small intestine, a tiny cecum, and a sacculated (folded) large intestine (or colon), though the human small intestine is longer and the human colon smaller than is the case for apes. Humans and apes also show the same pattern of food digestion, indicating that, biologically, in terms of gut form and function, humans have departed little from the ancestral condition. But, unlike apes, humans eat a wide range of different foods and have many different types of diets. What factors may have contributed to this difference between humans and apes?

Some 3 million years ago, before the first evidence of human beings, we know that climatic changes caused the vegetation in many areas of Africa to shift from tropical forest to more open savanna vegetation. This produced notable changes in the types of plant foods available in these environments. In particular, finding sufficient high-quality plant foods throughout the year probably would have been difficult for a large apelike primate such as those we envision as prehuman ancestors. One solution to this problem would be to try and find some other source of high-quality food. Animal foods are such a source: they are very high quality and, because of the huge herds of grazing and browsing animals in the African savanna, animal foods are far more abundant than is the case in the tropical forest canopy.

The association of stone tools with the earliest fossil evidence for human beings (genus *Homo*, species *Homo habilis*) suggests that early humans began to include animal as well as plant foods in the diet. Rather than just being an occasional food, as is the case for chimpanzees or other apes, meat and other animal products (tongue, bone marrow, brains, fat) appear to have become an integral part of the daily human diet. Initially, the earliest humans may have lived as scavengers and relied on meat from kills abandoned by carnivores. But increasing numbers of stone tools and processed mammal bones in the archaeological record suggest that humans gradually turned to the hunting of larger animals.

Animal protein is of high quality and easy for humans to digest. It also is a rich source of many essential vitamins and minerals. In addition, and most importantly, animal foods are volumetrically concentrated relative to plant foods and thus take up much less space in the feeder's gut. By eating some meat each day and combining this animal food with energy-rich plant foods, humans evolved as large-brained, active, and social hunter-gatherers. The fossil record shows that the human brain increased substantially over the course of human evolution. It would seem that, initially, the earliest human ancestors were somehow able to include a modest amount of animal food in the diet on a routine basis along with their usual plant foods. But these animal foods provided much high-quality nutrition and also freed up space in the gut for energy-rich plant foods, thus improving the feeder's diet in terms of both nutrients and energy. This energy was required to fuel the increasingly large human brain, which requires glucose as fuel. More astute individuals doubtless were more proficient at securing animal foods as well as energy-rich plant foods and they passed these mental abilities on to their descendents. Over time, this feedback process resulted in the gradual expansion of the human brain.

Humans as Cultural Omnivores

The evolution of humans actually follows the common primate trajectory—that is, using brain power to resolve many important dietary problems. Morphologically, humans lack the huge jaws, massive teeth, and sharp claws of true carnivores. But their increasingly large and complex brains permitted early humans to substitute technology for carnivore teeth and claws and use tools and creative intellectual solutions to capture and prepare their animal and plant foods for consumption.

In addition, early humans developed a unique form of food acquisition characterized by a division of labor. Typically, male members of the social unit sought animal prey while female members sought out higher-quality plant foods. Then all of the foods collected each day were shared with all members of the social unit, giving each person a good mix of all of the different nutrients required to remain in good health. By entering the adaptive zone of culture—cultural behavior made possible by virtue of the unusually large and complex human brain—humans gradually developed the capacity to exploit dietary resources of all types in ways not possible for any other animal. The success of this uniquely human form of dietary behavior is manifested by the fact that over time, by using their wits to devise successful diets, humans have been able to colonize almost every environment on earth. As long as all of the nutrients humans require are present in their foods, humans can thrive on an amazing variety of different diets.

See also **Agriculture, Origins of; Anthropology and Food; Cuisine, Evolution of; Evolution; Food Archaeology; Hunting and Gathering; Nutritional Anthropology; Paleonutrition, Methods of; Prehistoric Societies**.

BIBLIOGRAPHY

Chivers, David J., and Peter Langur, eds. *The Digestive System in Mammals: Food, Form, and Function.* Cambridge: Cambridge University Press, 1994.

Demment, Montague W. "Feeding Ecology and the Evolution of Body Size in Baboons." *African Journal of Ecology* 21 (1983): 219–233.

Harding, Robert S., and Geza Teleki. *Omnivorous Primates: Gathering and Hunting in Human Evolution.* New York: Columbia University Press, 1981.

Lambert, Joanna E. "Primate Digestion: Interactions among Anatomy, Physiology, and Feeding Ecology." *Evolutionary Anthropology* 7 (1998): 8–20.

Milton, Katharine. "Food Choice and Digestive Strategies of Two Sympatric Primate Species." *American Naturalist* 117 (1981): 476–495.

Milton, Katharine. "Features of Digestive Physiology in Primates." *News in Physiological Sciences* 1 (1986): 76–79.

Milton, Katharine. "Primate Diets and Gut Morphology: Implications for Human Evolution." In *Food and Evolution: Toward a Theory of Human Food Habits*, edited by Marvin Harris and Eric B. Ross, pp. 93–116. Philadelphia: Temple University Press, 1987.

Milton, Katharine. "Diet and Primate Evolution." *Scientific American* 269 (1993): 86, 93.

Oates, John F. "Food Distribution and Foraging Behavior." In *Primate Societies*, edited by Barbara B. Smuts, D. L. Cheney, R. M. Seyfarth, R. W. Wrangham, and T. T. Struhsaker, pp. 197–209. Chicago: University of Chicago Press, 1986.

Terborgh, John. *Five New World Primates: A Study in Comparative Ecology.* Princeton: Princeton University Press, 1983.

Whiten, A., and E. M. Widdowson. *Foraging Strategies and Natural Diets of Monkeys, Apes, and Humans.* Oxford: Clarendon Press, 1992.

Katharine Milton

ANOREXIA, BULIMIA.

Anorexia nervosa (AN), bulimia nervosa (BN), and Eating Disorder Not Otherwise Specified (EDNOS) are three of a spectrum of conditions, commonly known as eating disorders, associated with abnormal eating patterns and a desire to be thin. The abnormal eating patterns in these eating disorders include restriction of food intake, binge eating, and purging with laxatives or by self-induced vomiting. Persons with each of these disorders may go through periods of restriction, binge eating with purging, and binge eating without purging.

The term "eating disorders" for these conditions is both correct and misleading. These disorders center around issues of eating, or, to be more exact, food consumption, and certainly can be qualified as disorders, but more than eating is disordered in these conditions: they are associated with a complex of psychological, physiological, neurological, and hormonal changes, which may be due to the disease itself, or to the changes in weight associated with inappropriate food intakes and energy outputs, or both together.

The notion that thinness is desirable, particularly in women, and that one can never be "too rich or too thin," now permeates Western societies and is becoming increasingly common elsewhere. Teenagers, who are normally preoccupied with body image, and prone to be concerned about gaining weight, may incorrectly perceive themselves as being overweight, because puberty coincides with marked changes in body shape and, for girls, increased body fat content with fat deposition in the hips. Surveys in Western countries have shown that at any one time, up to two-thirds of female high school students either are on a weight loss diet or were on one in the recent past. In the United States, eating disorders seem to be less common among African-American and Asian females than among white females, equally common among Latina females, and surprisingly common among Native Americans. Japan seems to be the country with the highest prevalence of eating disorders. Other countries seem to be catching up, wherever there is access to food and to Western modes of behavior, as exemplified in the media.

Psychological conditions associated with eating disorders include depression, affecting 50–75 percent of people with eating problems; bipolar disorder (manic-depressive illness, 4–15 percent); obsessive-compulsive disorder, affecting as many as 25 percent of people with AN, fewer in those with BN; substance abuse, in up to one-third of patients with BN; and personality disorders, particularly avoidant, in other words, mistrusting, personality. Twenty to fifty percent of patients with BN (and to a lesser extent patients with AN and other eating disorders) have experienced sexual abuse.

A syndrome called "the female athlete triad"—consisting of disordered eating, amenorrhea (disruption of menses), and osteoporosis—is becoming more common as athletic prowess has become desirable for women and as women have better access to athletic facilities in the United States because of Title IX of the Educational Assistance Act (1974). Patients with Type I diabetes mellitus appear to be more prone than the general population to eating disorders, and may use underdosing with insulin to lose weight—when they do not take enough insulin, the body fails to use and store the calories they eat and relies on breakdown of fat and muscle for fuel.

Patients with eating disorders may become parents, may have difficulties nurturing their own children, and may transmit disordered attitudes toward eating to their children. The health care team should take these difficulties into account in treatment plans for both parent and child.

Anorexia Nervosa

Anorexia nervosa (AN) represents an extreme version of the desire for thinness. The term "anorexia" is a misnomer, for a person with this condition does have an appetite, but restricts food intake and denies the desire to eat with the apparent aim of having precise control over body shape and weight. Perhaps the German *Pubertät-magersucht*—"seeking thinness at puberty"—is a more accurate term, although the disorder has antecedents in childhood and continues into adulthood.

Epidemiology. In the United States, nearly 90 percent of patients with overt, clinically recognized AN are females between the ages of twelve and twenty-three, although younger and older patients as well as males may also develop the disease. The prevalence of AN appeared to rise during the twentieth century, with a lifetime risk among women of 0.5 percent to 3.7 percent and a male to female prevalence ratio between 1 to 6 and 1 to 10. The prevalence among young adolescent males is higher, perhaps reflecting a secular trend or an increasing emphasis on male appearance and "fitness."

The only groups among whom the disease has been recognized are groups who have easy access to food, and among whom being thin is a socially desirable state. However, conditions clinically indistinguishable from AN have existed in Western cultures prior to the twentieth century, particularly during the late Middle Ages and Renaissance, when they were associated with religious asceticism—the professed goal was to demonstrate the person's ability to deny the needs and pleasures of the flesh, rather than to be thin for social acceptance. Similar conditions associated with religious practices also occur in other cultures.

Etiology. Scientific opinion concerning the etiology of AN has vacillated between a biological and genetic explanation and a sociopsychological one. The patient's complaints lie in the psychological realm, while the disease presents features that point to biological and genetic components. There is a significantly higher concordance of anorexia nervosa among monozygotic twins (identical, that is, having the same genes) than among dizygotic twins (fraternal, that is, genetically only as close as a nontwin sibling). Family members have a higher than expected prevalence of other affective (emotional) and addictive disorders.

A host of neurohormonal changes appear once starvation has set in, but it is unclear which of these changes are causal, which are due to progression of the disease, and which are due to semistarvation. A reasonable explanation for the condition is that the person first restrains eating or performs excessive exercise for psychosocial reasons, and then develops a biologically driven self-perpetuating condition.

Development, signs, symptoms and biological findings. Anorexia nervosa develops in three phases, often preceded by picky eating and digestive problems in childhood. In Phase I the patient develops an increased consciousness about physical appearance, coupled with a

Diagnostic Criteria for Anorexia Nervosa (Diagnosis Number 307.1)

A. Refusal to maintain body weight at or above a minimally normal weight for age and height (e.g., weight loss leading to maintenance of body weight less than 85 percent of that expected; or failure to make expected weight gain during period of growth, leading to body weight less than 85 percent of that expected).

B. Intense fear of gaining weight or becoming fat, even though underweight.

C. Disturbance in the way in which one's body weight or shape is experienced, undue influence of body weight or shape on self-evaluation, or denial of the seriousness of the current low body weight.

D. In postmenarcheal females, amenorrhea, i.e., the absence of at least three consecutive menstrual cycles. (A woman is considered to have amenorrhea if her periods occur only following hormone, e.g., estrogen, administration.)

Specify type:

Restricting Type: during the current episode of anorexia nervosa, the person has not regularly engaged in binge-eating or purging behavior (i.e., self-induced vomiting or the misuse of laxatives, diuretics, or enemas).

Binge-Eating/Purging Type: during the current episode of anorexia nervosa, the person has regularly engaged in binge-eating or purging behavior (i.e., self-induced vomiting or the misuse of laxatives, diuretics, or enemas).

SOURCE: American Psychiatric Association, *Diagnostic and Statistical Manual of Mental Disorders*, 4th ed. Washington, D.C.: American Psychiatric Association, 1994.

loss of self-esteem, and begins dieting and exercising to lose weight. While these beliefs and behaviors have become increasingly the norm among adolescent women in developed countries, in certain people it progresses to Phase II.

During Phase II (frank AN) the person develops an "anorectic attitude": an unreasonable fear of eating coupled with pride in the ability to loss weight. Restriction of food intake begins with "fattening," "dangerous" foods such as carbohydrates and fats, while other foods, particularly vegetables, are viewed as "safe." In an effort to rationalize their restrictions, patients may develop a sophisticated fund of nutritional knowledge. They may delude parents or other caretakers into believing that they are eating when in fact food may be hidden or vomited up. Patients may also become obsessed with preparing foods, which they then refuse to eat. Some patients may have episodes of binge eating with or without purging in addition to restriction. Patients with this form of anorexia nervosa are more likely to be depressed, suicidal, and self-harming.

Patients may persist in the belief that they are eating a lot when in fact they eat very little. Sensations of hunger and satiety are impaired, with the result that these two states become confused. Further, delayed gastric emptying due to developing malnutrition may contribute to the perception of fullness after consumption of only small amounts of food. Eventually the person may reject all or nearly all foods.

The "anorectic attitude" may be self-amplifying, in that starvation itself may lead to abnormal attitudes towards food. Semistarved persons who are otherwise in good health also develop an obsession with food, linger for hours over a meal, and may feel that once they start eating, they will not be able to stop. For persons with AN, the thought that they may not be able to stop may be a terrifying prospect, confirming their worst fears about their inability to control their appetite.

The types of food that a person with AN likes appear to be normal when ascertained by questionnaire; however, a dislike for high-fat and low-carbohydrate foods is revealed. Taste testing suggests that persons with AN have an abnormally high preference for highly sweet tastes, coupled with a dislike of fatty foods. In this phase, the person may use laxatives and enemas, in the belief that these procedures will prevent absorption of ingested food, and also because anorexics may judge themselves to be constipated since the severely reduced food intake leads to formation of smaller than normal amounts of feces. Laxatives and starvation-induced changes in gut motility lead to both constipation and complaints of abdominal pain. Patients may abuse diuretics in an attempt to lose weight, although their effect is confined to water weight loss.

Patients may participate in extreme physical activity, preferably carried out alone, although it may be expressed in organized group activities such as ballet or athletic performance. This physical hyperactivity is in direct contrast to the inactivity seen in starving subjects without AN.

Depression, anxiety, obsessional traits, perfectionism, and rigidity in thinking are all found in patients in Phase II of AN. The states are often associated with social isolation.

During Phase II, nutritional status may deteriorate steadily, and if untreated, patients may not enter the recovery phase, Phase III. Death may occur from cardiovascular collapse due to starvation and electrolyte imbalance, or due to too rapid refeeding, as well as suicide. As many as 5 percent of patients may die of AN in the acute phase, and 20 percent on long-term follow-up—the highest mortality rate for a psychiatric condition.

Phase III of this disease, which is attained only with difficulty, and in some cases not at all, is the acknowledgment by the patients that they have starved themselves, and need treatment, coupled with success at alleviating the signs and symptoms of the disease.

Management. The management of anorexia nervosa is complex, requiring a concerted effort on the part of the health care team, including physician, nurse, nutritionist, social worker, and psychologist, as well as the patient and his or her family. Because patients are capable of maintaining a state of denial, it is very difficult to engage the patient into the care process. Often the patient has to be in a state of collapse before intervention is even tolerated. Indications for hospitalization are weight loss below 40 percent of normal weight; orthostatic hypotension (low blood pressure when standing); electrolyte (sodium, potassium) imbalance; dehydration; hypoglycemia (low blood sugar); infection; and marked family disturbance.

Treatment involves refeeding and psychological rehabilitation. Refeeding is critical for all patients whose weight is 85 percent or less of that expected. Depending on the severity of the patient's malnutrition, feeding may occur in the hospital, in a clinic setting, or at home. The patient should be hospitalized well before collapse is imminent. Feeding may be oral, naso-gastric, or via intravenous lines. Oral feeding is preferred but some patients may only permit refeeding if it is through a naso-gastric tube, and thus beyond their control. Intravenous feedings may be required if cardiovascular collapse is imminent. No special diets are needed, although concentrated foods may be useful in attaining adequate caloric intakes, and vitamin and mineral supplements are required. Refeeding must be slow, and performed under close medical monitoring, lest the patient develop edema and increased circulating blood volume, which can lead to electrolyte imbalances, anemia, and cardiovascular collapse. Other fatal complications of rapid refeeding include acute stomach or large bowel dilatation. Treatment protocols may also include restriction of exercise, in order to prevent the patient from exercising away the calories. Some patients are adept at finding ways to increase physical activity in the face of exercise restriction, and some patients may become severely agitated when denied the right to exercise.

Psychological treatment varies by health care team and may combine individual, family, and group therapy. Drug therapy may be used, particularly selective serotonin reuptake inhibitors (SSRIs), especially in patients who have regained weight but still are depressed or have obsessive-compulsive symptoms.

The ideal of clinical improvement consists of a return to 90 percent of normal weight, the resumption or initiation of menses in women, normalization of eating patterns, as well as the development of a mature, self-confident outlook, with a normal body image. Few patients attain this ideal. However, the short-term prognosis with respect to weight gain, return of menses, and improvement in outlook is usually good, although the food obsession and inability to control appetite may persist for weeks to months after the patient has regained an adequate amount of weight.

Unfortunately, the long-term prognosis is not so favorable: On the average, about 40 percent of patients recover more or less completely, 27 percent have ongoing endocrine abnormalities or are mildly underweight, 29 percent have a serious recurrence of the disease within a four-year period, and up to 5 percent succeed in starving themselves to death. Those who are over twenty, have prolonged illness, are depressed, have a family history of mental disturbance, have poor family relationships, who use purgatives and diuretics and who follow binges with vomiting have the worst prognosis.

Bulimia Nervosa

People with bulimia nervosa (BN) have recurring irresistible urges to consume extremely large amounts of food at one sitting (binge). The binge leads to acute feelings of gastric distension, and to sharpening of the fear of becoming fat. To relieve both problems, patients may then proceed to self-induce vomiting or purging. Persons with this condition report a sense of "cleaning out" with vomiting and purging, which may positively reinforce these behaviors. Note that binging without purging comes under the rubric of Eating Disorders Not Otherwise Specified (EDNOS), according to the *Diagnostic and Statistical Manual of Mental Disorders*, 4th ed. (DSM-IV), and is described below.

Precipitants of a binge include hunger, being alone, feelings of anxiety, frustration, and worthlessness, and problems with a significant other.

Epidemiology. Like AN, BN primarily afflicts young females from food-rich backgrounds. Its prevalence is unknown because only the most severely affected come to health care. Estimates of the disorder vary from 2.5 to 20 percent of women and 1 to 5 percent of men from the ages of eighteen to twenty-one.

Etiology. The etiology of BN remains unknown. Causes may include a biological predisposition to obesity, depression, and metabolic disturbances (in particular neurohormonal abnormalities, such as abnormalities in the release of gut hormones after eating), coupled with a socially determined desire for thinness, and with bingeing and purging as a group activity, a phenomenon which is becoming increasingly common among women living together, for example in a sorority, or men as part of a team, for example wrestlers.

Families of BN patients have a high prevalence of disorders such as major depression, irritable bowel syndrome, obsessive-compulsive disorder, attention deficit disorder with hyperactivity, and migraine, all of which have been linked to abnormalities in the function of neu-

Diagnostic Criteria for Bulimia Nervosa (Diagnosis Number 307.51)

A. Recurrent episodes of binge eating. An episode of binge eating is characterized by both of the following:

(1) eating, in a discrete period of time (e.g., within any 2-hour period) an amount of food that is definitely larger than most people would eat during a similar period of time and under similar circumstances

(2) a sense of lack of control over eating during the episode (e.g., a feeling that one cannot stop eating or control what or how much one is eating)

B. Recurrent inappropriate compensatory behavior in order to prevent weight gain, such as self-induced vomiting; misuse of laxatives, diuretics, enemas, or other medications; fasting; or excessive exercise.

C. The binge eating and inappropriate compensatory behaviors both occur, on average, at least twice a week for three months.

D. Self-evaluation is unduly influenced by body shape and weight.

E. The disturbance does not occur exclusively during episodes of anorexia nervosa.

Specify type:

Purging Type: during the current episode of bulimia nervosa, the person has regularly engaged in self-induced vomiting or the misuse of laxatives, diuretics, or enemas.

Non-Purging Types: during the current episode of bulimia nervosa, the person has used other inappropriate compensatory behaviors, such as fasting or excessive exercise, but has not regularly engaged in self-induced vomiting or the misuse of laxatives, diuretics, or enemas.

SOURCE: American Psychiatric Association, *Diagnostic and Statistical Manual of Mental Disorders,* 4th ed. Washington, D.C.: American Psychiatric Association, 1994.

rotransmitters (chemicals such as norepinephrine and serotonin responsible for sending messages from one nerve cell to the next) in the brain. Levels of monoamine oxidase (MAO, an enzyme responsible for degrading norepinephrine and serotonin) in the blood cell clotting fragments called platelets are lower than normal in a person with BN. Low activity of MAO has been associated with impulsiveness, intolerance of boredom and monotony, and sensation seeking, also commonly seen in bulimic individuals. SSRIs, specifically fluoxetine, which increase

TABLE 1

Physical signs and symptoms associated with anorexia nervosa and bulimia nervosa

	Anorexia nervosa	Bulimia nervosa
Body weight	Usually below normal	May be below normal, normal, or above normal
Skin and hair	Dry skin; lanugo (soft down-like hair overgrown on limbs, nape of neck, and cheeks); yellowing of skin (but not whites of eyes) due to excessive consumption of carrots and other carotene containing vegetables	Scratches on the dorsum of the hand due to rubbing of the hand against the upper teeth during self-induced vomiting
Teeth	Increased caries due to acid erosion, if patient vomits frequently	Carious due to acid erosion, if patient vomits frequently
Water and electrolytes	Low blood potassium, due to vomiting; low blood sodium due to use of laxatives	Low blood potassium due to frequent vomiting
Bones	Osteoporosis leading to irreversible vertebral collapse, due to lack of estrogen, and to reduced consumption and to malabsorption of minerals and fat soluble vitamins	Incidence of osteoporosis variable
Amenorrhea	Characteristic	Variable
Brain	Brain damage in long-term disease, which may be irreversible	Unknown
Gastro-intestinal tract	Slow gastric emptying and slow intestinal transit time, due to starvation	An enlarged stomach with stomach cramping, leading to digestive difficulties; esophageal irritation, due to regurgitation of stomach acid; dysmotility of the esophagus (poor coordination of esophageal movement); slow stomach emptying; injury to the nerves in the gut wall, leading to permanent loss of bowel reactivity; constipation and diarrhea.
Metabolic rate	Reduced	Mildly reduced
Body temperature	Reduced, with difficulty maintaining a steady body temperature in cold or warm conditions; an occasional patient has an elevated metabolic rate	Variable
Cardiovascular system	Hypotension (abnormally low blood pressure); bradycardia (slow heart rate); decreased heart size and cardiac output	Variable, depending on body weight; if body weight is low, the signs are similar to those seen in Anorexia nervosa.
Blood	Anemia and leukopenia (low white blood cell count) due to inadequate mineral intake and to starvation	Anemia, due to frequent small upper gastrointestinal tract bleeds, leading to iron loss
Causes of death	Cardiovascular collapse, suicide	Cardiovascular collapse, suicide

responsiveness to endogenous serotonin, are moderately effective in treatment of BN. Abnormalities in other hormones and neurotransmitters, including cholecystokinin (CKK), which is released in response to fat in the intestine and depresses appetite, neuropeptide YY, which is involved in activating appetite, and leptin, are under investigation.

Development, diagnosis, and clinical manifestations. The phases of development of BN are far less clear than those of AN, though, as children, patients with this condition may have had pica (the consumption of nonfood items such as dirt or paint chips), and may have suffered through mealtimes in which there was a great deal of commotion and distress. Some bulimics have been severely abused physically, sexually, or both and may show signs and symptoms of post-traumatic stress disorder, including multiple personality disorder.

It is difficult to determine when bingeing becomes an overt pathological state. Binge episodes may vary from several times daily to once a month or less, and 20 percent of female college students are estimated to have participated at least once in a binge-purge episode.

A binge-purge episode starts with a craving for high-calorie food, usually those high in carbohydrates and fat but low in protein, particularly junk food, which does not have to be cooked. The food is obtained and consumed at one sitting. Thus, a patient may consume a box of cookies, a bag of doughnuts, and a half-gallon of ice cream in a single binge. The binge may then be followed by self-induced vomiting, and/or laxative use. Binges and purges most often occur in private, although there is an increase in group binge-purge episodes among young people who live in communal settings, for example in boarding school or in college. The frequency of episodes increases with increasing stress. Some patients may fast between episodes of bingeing, and may in fact have the binge-eating/ purging form of AN. Other patients may binge without purging.

In BN, eating patterns outside a binge-purge episode are usually characterized by a degree of restrained eating. Nevertheless, when bulimics perceive that they have "violated" the restraint, that is, eaten more than "allowed," they will eat more than a normal person in a test meal situation. Increased postmeal hunger is also experienced by individuals with BN. The restrained eating may therefore be the result of conscious attempts to compensate for the inability to feel satiety, and may be a mechanism for maintaining normal weight in the face of episodes of great hunger and craving. Patients have larger than normal stomachs, which results in both slower than normal stomach emptying and failure to sense fullness, due to excessive relaxation of the stomach, and lower than normal levels of the hormone cholecystokinin (CCK) after a meal. CCK is produced in the intestinal tract in response to fatty food, and signals to the brain that the person has eaten enough. As a result of these changes, the person may fail to be aware of satiety. It may be that once binge-purge episodes have begun, these anatomical and physiological changes will amplify the perceived need to binge, and the consequent need to purge.

In taste tests, persons with BN have a higher than normal preference for very sweet and very fatty foods. Normally, the more a person eats of a sweet food at a single sitting, the less pleasant it becomes. Bulimics may not experience this decrease in pleasantness, as a result of which they may be able to eat large amounts of highly sweet food.

The hypothalamus normally senses when blood glucose levels have risen following food ingestion, which also contributes to the feeling of satiety. Persons with BN appear to have mild insulin resistance, which may prevent their hypothalamus from sensing that rise in blood glucose levels.

Persons with BN are less likely than persons with AN to have a distorted body image, though persons with BN do express an overvaluation of thinness and a fear of becoming overweight. A person with BN may be depressed and agitated, but, unlike a person with AN, usually does not participate compulsively in physical activity.

The most striking complaints and physical and biochemical findings regarding BN are related to the frequent vomiting (Table 1). The ability to taste with the palate may be destroyed due to the stomach acid, although taste by the tongue is little affected. Whether these taste changes contribute to bingeing is unknown.

Management. Bulimia nervosa requires long-term, continuous, nonjudgmental psychological management, nutritional counseling, and rehabilitation, and may include medications, particularly SSRIs. Cognitive behavioral therapy approaches that redirect the person's attention away from food and eating, and which address the person's other psychological problems, are the most successful. Patients may have other conditions, such as drug abuse or personality disorders, which need to be addressed before the eating disorder. Both depressed and nondepressed patients with BN may benefit from med-

Diagnostic Criteria for Eating Disorder Not Otherwise Specified (Diagnosis Number 307.50)

The Eating Disorder Not Otherwise Specified category is for disorders of eating that do not meet the criteria for any specific Eating Disorder. Examples include

1. For females, all of the criteria for anorexia nervosa are met except that the individual has regular menses.
2. All of the criteria for anorexia nervosa are met except that, despite significant weight loss, the individual's current weight is in the normal range.
3. All of the criteria for bulimia nervosa are met except that the binge eating and inappropriate compensatory mechanisms occur at a frequency of less than twice a week or for a duration of less than 3 months.
4. The regular use of inappropriate compensatory behavior by an individual of normal body weight after eating small amounts of food (e.g., self-induced vomiting after the consumption of two cookies).
5. Repeatedly chewing and spitting out, but not swallowing, large amounts of food.
6. Binge-eating disorder: recurrent episodes of binge eating in the absence of the regular use of inappropriate compensatory behaviors characteristic of bulimia nervosa.

SOURCE: American Psychiatric Association, *Diagnostic and Statistical Manual of Mental Disorders,* 4th ed. Washington, D.C.: American Psychiatric Association, 1994.

ications such as SSRIs. These drugs may help with interpersonal functioning, mood, and anxiety symptoms.

Eating Disorder Not Otherwise Specified

Eating Disorder Not Otherwise Specified (EDNOS) is the term applied to conditions that have some characteristics of the classic eating disorders AN and BN, but which do not meet all the diagnostic criteria outlined in the DSM-IV. Multiple combinations of signs and symptoms are possible, as noted in Table 1. Persons who abuse weight-reduction medications and other regimens, and who are trying to lose large amounts of weight for reasons of beauty rather than health, as well as persons with binge-eating disorder, also fall under this rubric, as do people who use disordered eating behaviors in an attempt to correct the size of what they perceive as abnormally large (or abnormally small) body parts.

Binge-eating disorder is characterized by binges that are not followed by efforts to get rid of the extra calories. It is estimated that about 2 percent of the general population suffers from this condition, with a male to fe-

Sophie Sukup's *Iss dich schlank!* (Eat Yourself Thin!), published in Stuttgart, Germany, in 1927, promised overweight readers that they could get immediate results by eating the fat away. The cover design of the book makes it clear that the new ideal physique is no longer that of the Rubenesque maiden of pre-1918 Germany. ROUGHWOOD COLLECTION.

BIBLIOGRAPHY

American Psychiatric Association. *Diagnostic and Statistical Manual of Mental Disorders*, 4th ed. Washington, D.C.: American Psychiatric Association, 1994.

American Psychiatric Association. *Practice Guideline for the Treatment of Patients with Eating Disorders*, 2d ed. Washington, D.C.: American Psychiatric Association, 2000.

Boskind-White, Marlene, and William C. White, Jr. *Bulimia/Anorexia : The Binge/Purge Cycle and Self-Starvation*, 3d ed. New York: Norton, 2000.

Gull, Sir William W. "Anorexia nervosa (apepsia hysterica, anorexia hysterica)." *Transactions of the Clinical Society of London* 7 (1874): 22.

Hobart Julie A., and Douglas R. Smucker. "The Female Athlete Triad." *American Family Physician* 61 (2000): 3357–3364, 3367.

Virginia Utermohlen

ANTHROPOLOGY AND FOOD. What distinguishes the anthropological study of food from that of other disciplines is its focus on food within a cultural and often cross-cultural context. Anthropologists study humans and human culture across space and evolutionary time; this includes the study of their own culture and social institutions. Subfields of the anthropological study of food include cultural, linguistic, biological, and archaeological anthropology. Research in nutritional anthropology cuts across these subfields. Food requires hunting, gathering, growing, storage, distribution, preparation, display, serving, and disposal, all of which are social activities. Topics for the anthropological study of food within a cultural system include economy, inequality, gender, status, hunter-gatherers, and food as a symbol.

Of basic interest to archaeologists is the diet or subsistence pattern of the peoples they study. Since seasonal patterns of movement are often linked to subsistence regimes, archaeologists frequently study the overall settlement-subsistence pattern. Other major topics of study related to food are the origins of agriculture, the process of plant and animal domestication, and the study of foodways (food in a social and cultural setting). With the help of interdisciplinary teams of specialists, archaeologists examine a variety of evidence such as animal bones (faunal analysis or zooarchaeology), plant remains (paleoethnobotany or archaeobotany), human bones (osteology), residues (chemistry), and the settlement system. Faunal and paleoethnobotanical analyses are able to determine diet (which animals and plants were eaten) as well as hunting, gathering, butchering, and preparation techniques, the identity of preferred or high-status foods, the seasonality of site occupation and diet items, and whether the animals/plants were domesticated. The phrase "You are what you eat" is true in that what you eat forms the

male ratio of 1 to 3, in contrast with frank bulimia nervosa, where the proportion is closer to 1 in 6. Because people who have this disorder do not vomit or purge, they are often obese; they compose about a third of the patients visiting weight reduction clinics. They also may have body image dissatisfaction, low self-esteem, and depression. Active psychotherapy can reduce binge frequency, but once therapy is discontinued, relapse rates are high, and weight lost due to the decrease in binge frequency is often readily regained. Approaches that emphasize self-acceptance, improvement of body image, and better overall health, rather than focusing on weight loss, appear to have the best long-term success rate. It is likely that similar approaches may be effective for people who abuse weight-loss regimens.

See also **Aversion to Food**; **Body**; **Body Composition**; **Caloric Intake**; **Eating, Anatomy and Physiology of Eating**; **Fasting and Abstinence**; **Hunger, Physiology of**; **Obesity.**

The !Kung hunter Gumtsa digs up a plant for food. The !Kung peoples live in the Ngamiland District of Botswana. Their primitive lifestyle and simple foodways are of great interest to anthropologists. © PETER JOHNSON/CORBIS.

bones and organs in your body, leaving behind chemical signatures. Human bones reflect the general health and nutrition of the individual, and may be chemically analyzed to reveal diet through isotopic (heavy element) or chemical signatures.

Biological Anthropology

Topics in biological anthropology range from biological and nutritional questions about humans and primates (e.g., questions of nutrition, health, and evolution of human and primate physiology and diet) to cultural practices and choices that affect biology and nutrition (e.g., dietary strategies and food selection choices). Cross-disciplinary themes include the process of human adaptation, population variation, and health. In many societies, medicine is not distinguished from food. Human digestive systems, the substances upon which humans feed, and medicinal natural substances are closely intertwined and are the result of a co-evolution.

ARCHAEOLOGICAL FOODWAYS

Foodways is a subdiscipline of cultural anthropology that studies food in its social and cultural setting. Foodways studies were pioneered in the 1990s by archaeologists who study hierarchical, stratified societies in the southeastern United States. A foodways approach combines studies of food remains, the ceramic vessels used to prepare and serve food, and other aspects of the food system with settlement patterns to answer questions about cultural change and the production, storage, distribution, preparation, and serving of food within social contexts. Two examples illustrate the cultural richness that such research may provide. In her study of the people who lived in the central Mississippi River Valley between 500 and 1100 C.E., Sissel Johannessen examined multiple lines of evidence to understand the relationship between shifts in diet and social changes. Her work combines summaries of internal community patterning, food storage facilities, paleoethnobotanical remains, and ratios of different types of ceramic vessels and sets them within the six-hundred-year period during which this farming society adopted maize agriculture. Johannessen documented how change in diet, accompanied by changes in food production, distribution, storage, and consumption, reflected a basic shift in social interaction and people's perception of their place in the world. They went from living as isolated families in the sixth century to group solidarity and affiliation with mound centers. As the locus of power shifted from household to center, food storage shifted from household pits to above-ground granaries, and greater variation arose in the ways food was cooked and served.

Another example is the study by Paul D. Welch and C. Margaret Scarry, who used a foodways approach to examine the intricacies of the social relationships within a chiefdom in the southeastern United States dating between 1050 and 1550 C.E. The ratios of food processing by-products (maize cobs and nutshells) and food consumption evidence (maize kernels) differ between low-status (farmstead) and high-status (civic/ceremonial mound center) locations, as do the types and cuts of meat and the ratios of cooking to storage or serving vessels. Furthermore, analysis of the ceramic vessel ratios from the various locations allowed distinction between types of high-status activities.

Linguistic Anthropology

Linguistic anthropologists study human perception and communication, finding a close connection between how

These prehistoric flint tools were used for hunting and preparing food. © MAURICE NIMMO; FRANK LANE PICTURE AGENCY/CORBIS.

people perceive their world and the structure of their language. The field of folk taxonomy recognizes regularities in how humans perceive and categorize their natural world. A society's closeness to nature and sources of food will be reflected in how finely they are able to categorize plants and animals, and more salient plants and animals will be marked linguistically. Linguists who study folk taxonomy usually consider themselves ethnobotanists or ethnobiologists (see below).

Cultural Anthropology

Cultural anthropologists pioneered the method of ethnographic data collection wherein the anthropologist lives among and participates in the daily life of the native culture over a period of months or years. Ethnographers attempt to situate the study of food within a community or culture, seeking to explain the interrelation between food systems and human behavior. Frameworks for the study of food include but are not limited to economy, political economy, cultural ecology, inequality, gender, ethnicity, households, policy formulation, biodiversity, hunter-gatherers, urbanization, and food as symbol. Cross-cultural research compares food and food systems in different cultures, most recently through multisited studies.

Ethnobotany and Ethnobiology

Ethnobotany (study of the relationships between plants and peoples) and ethnobiology (study of the relationships between living organisms and humans) draw on the resources of each of the subdisciplines of anthropology as well as from other fields such as chemistry, botany, pharmacology, zoology, entomology, engineering, and so on. A major concern of these disciplines is intellectual property rights—who should be compensated, and how they should be compensated, for sharing their traditional knowledge about plants and animals or for sharing the results of breeding plants or animals.

See also **Agriculture, Origins of; Ethnobotany; Ethnopharmacology; Food Production, History of; Foodways; Nutritional Anthropology; Paleonutrition, Methods of; Prehistoric Societies.**

BIBLIOGRAPHY

Berlin, Brent. *Ethnobiological Classification: Principles of Categorization of Plants and Animals in Traditional Societies.* Princeton: Princeton University Press, 1992.

Counihan, Carole. *The Anthropology of Food and Body: Gender, Meaning, and Power.* New York: Routledge, 1999.

Counihan, Carole, and Penny van Esterik, eds. *Food and Culture: A Reader.* New York and London: Routledge, 1997.

Douglas, Mary. "Deciphering a Meal." *Daedalus* 10 (1972): 61–81.

Douglas, Mary, ed. *Food in the Social Order: Studies of Food and Festivities in Three American Communities.* New York: Russell Sage Foundation, 1984.

Etkin, Nina L., ed. *Plants in Indigenous Medicine and Diet: Biobehavioral Approaches.* Bedford Hills, N.Y.: Redgrave, 1986.

Goody, Jack. *Cooking, Cuisine, and Class: A Study in Comparative Sociology.* New York and Cambridge: Cambridge University Press, 1982.

Gosden, Chris, and Jon Hather, eds. *The Prehistory of Food: Appetites for Change.* One World Archaeology, vol. 32. London: Routledge, 1999.

Harris, Marvin, and Eric B. Ross, eds. *Food and Evolution: Toward a Theory of Human Food Habits.* Philadelphia: Temple University Press, 1987.

Johannessen, Sissel. "Food, Dishes, and Society in the Mississippi Valley." In *Foraging and Farming in the Eastern Woodlands*, edited by C. Margaret Scarry, pp. 182–205. Gainesville: University of Florida Press.

Lévi-Strauss, Claude. *The Raw and the Cooked: From Honey to Ashes, the Origin of Table Manners.* Translated from the French by John and Doreen Weightman. New York: Harper and Row, 1969.

Messer, Ellen. "Anthropological Perspectives on Diet." *Annual Review of Anthropology* 13 (1984): 205–249.

Stinson, Sara. "Nutritional Adaptation." *Annual Review of Anthropology* 21 (1992): 143–170.

Welch, Paul D., and C. Margaret Scarry. "Status-Related Variation in Foodways in the Moundville Chiefdom." *American Antiquity* 60 (1995): 397–419.

Gail E. Wagner

ANTIOXIDANTS

ANTIOXIDANTS. Antioxidants are specific organic compounds that are active in the prevention of very rapid harmful chemical chain reactions with oxygen or nitric oxide, that is, oxidation reactions. In the body, oxidation reactions generally involve highly reactive molecules called free radicals. Free radicals reside primarily in the mitochondria of cells. When free radicals are released from the mitochondria in numbers sufficient to overwhelm the protective biochemical systems of the body, they become a threat to some cellular structures such as lipids, proteins, carbohydrates, and nucleic acids in cell membranes. Compromised cellular structure alters cellular function, and may lead to the initiation of the disease process. In severe oxidative stress, cell death may occur. Antioxidants react with the free radicals before they are able to react with other molecules, thus providing protection from oxidation reactions (Cross et al.).

Chemistry 101: How and Why Cells and Other Molecules Interact

The human body is made up of many different types of cells that are composed of multiple diverse types of molecules. Molecules are put together in such a way that one or more atoms of one or more elements are joined by chemical bonds. Atoms have a nucleus of neutrons and protons which is surrounded by electrons. It is the number of protons (positively charged particles) in the nucleus of the atom that determines the number of orbiting electrons (negatively charged particles). Electrons are involved in chemical reactions and are the substances that bond atoms together to form molecules. Electrons orbit the atom in one or more of the atom's shells. The innermost shell is full when it has two electrons. When the

first shell is full, electrons begin to fill the second shell. When the second shell has eight electrons, it is full, and electrons begin to fill the third shell, and so on. The electrons surrounding antioxidants react with the electrons surrounding free radicals, causing them to become much less reactive. Antioxidants may be more effective when one antioxidant is used in combination with another. This synergistic relationship between several antioxidants occurs when, for example, vitamin E donates an electron from its outer shell to a free radical and vitamin C donates an electron to vitamin E, maintaining the ability of vitamin E to continue donating electrons to free radicals. Vitamin C may then receive an electron from glutathione that would enable vitamin C to remain active as an antioxidant. Therefore in this type of situation, an attack on membranes by a free radical results in the participation of three different antioxidants.

In What Forms Are Antioxidants Found and How Are They Metabolized?

Antioxidants are found in many forms. The principal vitamins with antioxidant properties are vitamins E and C, and beta-carotene. Vitamin E (*d*-alpha tocopherol) is a fat-soluble antioxidant, which means it is stored in body fat and works within the lipid portion of cell membranes to provide an alternative binding site for free radicals, preventing the oxidation of polyunsaturated fatty acids (Chow). Vitamin E is a family of eight compounds synthesized by plants in nature: four tocopherols (alpha, beta, gamma, delta) and four tocotrienols (alpha, beta, gamma, delta). Each has different levels of bioactivity in the body over quite a wide range, but generally speaking, alpha-tocopherol has greater bioactivity than beta-tocopherol, which has greater bioactivity than gamma-tocopherol, which has greater bioactivity than delta-tocopherol. Only alpha-tocotrienol has bioactivity of any significant amount, which is slightly less than that of beta-tocopherol. Digestion and absorption of vitamin E is greatly improved when consumption is accompanied with dietary lipids or fats. Absorption of vitamin E ranges from 20 to 50 percent, but may be as high as 80 percent, with absorption decreasing as intake increases (Bender, 1992). Dietary vitamin E absorption requires bile and pancreatic enzymes in the small intestine, where it is incorporated into micelles within the lumen of the small intestine. The micelles carry the vitamin E across the brush border of the small intestine and the vitamin E is then taken up by chylomicrons, which are transported by the lymph system to tissues and the liver. Vitamin E may be stored in the liver, adipose tissues, and skeletal muscle. When needed, vitamin E places itself in cell membranes. Excretion of vitamin E is by way of urine, feces, and bile (Wardlaw and Kessel).

Vitamin C (ascorbic acid) is a water-soluble antioxidant and is found in the water compartments of the body where it interacts with free radicals. It has been shown that short-term supplementation of vitamin C lasting two to four weeks can significantly reduce the level of free radicals in the body (Naidoo and Lux). Dietary vitamin C is absorbed primarily by active transport in the small intestine, with absorption decreasing as intake increases. Approximately 70 to 90 percent of vitamin C is absorbed when dietary intake is between 30 and 180 mg/day. The kidneys excrete excess dietary vitamin C in urine, but excrete virtually no vitamin C when intake of the vitamin is very low (Wardlaw and Kessel). After absorption in the small intestine, vitamin C is transported in the blood to cells in its reduced form, ascorbic acid or ascorbate. The concentration of vitamin C varies in different tissues in the body. For instance, vitamin C concentrations are highest in the adrenal and pituitary glands, intermediate in the liver, spleen, heart, kidneys, lungs, pancreas, and white blood cells, and lowest in the muscles and red blood cells (Olson and Hodges). This vitamin may also possess some prooxidant properties, meaning it can participate in oxidizing other molecules such as iron in the blood stream (Alhadeff et al.).

Beta-carotene is a precursor to vitamin A (retinol). Beta-carotene is the most widely known compound in a group known as carotenoids, which are pigment materials in fruits and vegetables that range from yellow to orange to red in color. Carotenoids are also called proformed vitamin A because they can be made into vitamin A by the body when necessary. Carotenoids are pigments that are responsible for the orange color of many fruits and vegetables such as oranges and squash. Other carotenoids present in foods include antheraxanthin, lutein, zeaxanthin, and lycopene. Dietary retinol is usually found bound to fatty acid esters, which are in turn bound to proteins, and must undergo a process called hydrolysis that frees the retinol from the esters, enabling the retinol to then be absorbed in the small intestine. Proteolytic enzymes in the small intestine, such as pepsin, hydrolyze the retinol from the proteins. Approximately 70 to 90 percent of dietary retinol is absorbed provided there is adequate (10 grams or more) fat in the meal consumed (Olson). Carotenoids are absorbed at much lower levels, sometimes at levels as low as 3 percent, with absorption decreasing as intake increases (Brubacher and Weisler). Retinol and the carotenoids are carried through the absorptive cells of the small intestine by micelles for transport through the lymph system to the liver, which then can "repackage" the vitamins to send to other tissues, or act as the storage facility for the vitamins until needed by the body.

There are also enzymes that possess antioxidant properties. Glutathione peroxidase, superoxide dismutase, and catalase are the most well known. Glutathione peroxidase breaks down peroxidized fatty acids, converting them into less harmful substances. Peroxidized fatty acids tend to become free radicals, so the action of glutathione peroxidase serves to protect cells. The activity of glutathione peroxidase is dependent on the mineral selenium, which is the functional part of this enzyme, or

the part of the enzyme that makes it have antioxidant activity. Therefore, selenium is considered to have antioxidant properties. Superoxide dismutase and catalase react with free radicals directly, reducing their ability to oxidize molecules and cause cellular damage.

A class of compounds termed isoflavones, which are derived from soy, also have antioxidant activity. Genistein, daidzein, and prunectin are all able to prevent the production of free radicals. Isoflavone activity as an antioxidant plays an important role in the aging process and cancer prevention primarily due to having estrogen-related biologic activities in humans (Shils et al.).

The polyphenols (epicatechin, epicatechin-3-gallate, epigallocatechin, and epigallocatechin-3-gallate) found in jasmine green tea also possess natural antioxidant properties. Studies have shown that these polyphenols are able to protect red blood cells from destruction upon attack by free radicals (Shils et al.). The polyphenols present in red wine have also been found to be protective against the oxidation of low-density lipoproteins and high-density lipoproteins, which are very important factors in the prevention of the development of atherosclerosis or coronary artery disease (Ivanov et al.).

A final group of compounds, synthetic antioxidants, are often added to foods to prevent discoloration and delay oxidation of the foods after exposure to oxygen. They also help protect fats from rancidity. Rancidity causes fats to develop an unappealing flavor and odor. Most of the antioxidants used in foods are phenolic compounds. There are four antioxidants that are approved for use in foods, particularly fats. They are propyl gallate (PG), tertiary butylhydroquinone (TBHQ), butylated hydroxyanisole (BHA), and butylated hydroxytoluene (BHT) (Charley and Weaver). Sulfites, which are sulfur-based chemicals, are also used as antioxidants in foods. However, because some people may be very sensitive to sulfites and have adverse reactions to them in foods, the Food and Drug Administration has required that labels on foods containing sulfites alert the public to their presence.

Dietary Sources of Antioxidants

Vitamin E is found in egg yolks, milk, plant and vegetable oils (including margarine and to a lesser extent butter), nuts, seeds, fortified whole-grain cereals, flatfish, halibut, shrimp, canned tuna in oil, asparagus, peas, tomatoes, apples, canned apricots in light syrup, blueberries, grapefruit, oranges, peaches, and pears. The milling process of whole grains causes most of the dietary vitamin E to be lost. The Recommended Dietary Allowance (RDA) as established by the U.S. Department of Agriculture currently is 15 International Units (IU) per day for men and 12 IU/day for women. In order for toxic effects to be produced, the amount of vitamin E consumed from foods would have to be 15 to 100 times the amount recommended for humans and this is extremely unlikely to occur (Wardlaw and Kessel). Symptoms and effects of toxicity are discussed in detail in Signs and Symptoms of Antioxidant Deficiency and Toxicity, below.

Vitamin C is present in large amounts in broccoli, asparagus, cabbage, cauliflower, potatoes, tomatoes, apples, applesauce, apricots, bananas, blueberries, cherries, grapefruit, lemons, oranges, peaches, strawberries, kiwi, pineapples, pears, cranberries, and the juices and jams made from these fruits. The Recommended Dietary Allowance for vitamin C currently is 60 mg/day for both males and females. Vitamin C obtained from foods rarely can be consumed in amounts large enough to be toxic to humans (Wardlaw and Kessel).

Beta-carotene is found in liver (primary storage organ in animals for vitamin A), egg yolk, fortified milk, butter, spinach, carrots, squash, sweet potatoes, broccoli, tomatoes, peaches, mangoes, apricots, papaya, cantaloupes, and fortified breakfast cereals. Because beta-carotene is converted to vitamin A by the body, there is no set requirement. However, the RDA for vitamin A is set in Retinol Equivalents (RE) at the level of 625 μg/day RE for men and 500 μg/day RE for women (Wardlaw and Kessel).

Diets High or Low in Antioxidants

Diets that are rich in antioxidants focus on high intakes of a variety of foods, especially large amounts of fruits, vegetables, and foods made from whole grains. Vegetarian diets, especially vegan diets (diets that exclude all foods from animal sources), are made up primarily from fruits, vegetables, whole grains, and legumes, and are an example of the types of diets that incorporate high levels of antioxidants. Another example of a diet that provides optimal levels of antioxidants is the Mediterranean diet. The Mediterranean diet is based on traditional eating habits in Greece, southern Italy, and Crete. This diet is rich in olive oil, foods from whole grains, and tomatoes, and minimizes the daily intake of poultry, eggs, sweets, and red meat. Red wine often accompanies meals in the Mediterranean diet and possesses some antioxidant activity (Murcia and Martinez-Tome). Furthermore, many of the spices used in Mediterranean cooking also have been observed to have some level of antioxidant properties (Martinez-Tome et al.). Asian-American diets also focus primarily on fruits, legumes, nuts, seeds, vegetables, and whole-grain food products, with liberal use of vegetable oils, while a minimum of meat is eaten. The traditional healthy Latin American diet provides beans, whole grains, nuts, fruits, and vegetables at every meal, with fish or shellfish, milk products, plant oils, and poultry being optional for daily intake.

Unfortunately, the typical American diet does not involve adequate intakes of fruits, vegetables, and whole-grain food products. This is not due to the lack of foods that fall into those categories but rather to the fact that too many Americans prefer fast foods and processed foods that are not rich sources of antioxidants. The Food Guide Pyramid developed by the United States Department of Agriculture recommends that six to eleven servings of bread cereal, rice, and pasta be consumed daily; three to five servings of vegetables per day; two to four servings of fruit per day; two to three servings of milk products per day; two to three servings of meat, poultry, fish, dry beans, eggs, and nuts per day; and that the use of fats, oils, and sweets be sparse (Wardlaw and Kessel). Most Americans do not adhere to the guidelines of the Food Guide Pyramid and therefore do not receive adequate amounts of foods that provide large quantities of antioxidants.

Certain disease states make it difficult to obtain adequate amounts of fat-soluble vitamins due to an inability to digest foods with fat properly. The digestion and absorption of fat in foods is required for digesting and absorbing fat-soluble vitamins such as vitamins A and E. Individuals with cystic fibrosis, celiac disease, and Crohn's disease absorb fat very poorly, which also means that the fat-soluble vitamins are poorly absorbed. As the unabsorbed fat passes through the small and large intestine, it carries the fat-soluble vitamins along with it, and is eventually excreted in the feces (Wardlaw and Kessel). Chronic alcoholics are also at risk for not obtaining adequate amounts of antioxidants due to a marked decrease in food intake in favor of the consumption of alcohol. Alcoholism may also result in liver disease, which leads to an inability of the liver to store the fat-soluble antioxidants.

Signs and Symptoms of Antioxidant Deficiency and Toxicity

Obtaining dietary intakes of vitamin E, vitamin C, and vitamin A from foods to meet the recommendations of the Food Guide Pyramid will prevent most healthy individuals from experiencing any deficiencies of these antioxidants. However, in diets that do not provide adequate amounts of fruits, vegetables, and whole grains, deficiencies may occur. It takes longer to develop a deficiency of the fat-soluble antioxidants, vitamins E and A, than it does to develop a deficiency of the water-soluble vitamin C.

Failure to obtain adequate vitamin E in the diet may cause certain medical conditions. Hemolytic anemia is caused by vitamin E deficiency, with an increased breakdown of red blood cells or hemolysis. Premature infants are most susceptible to vitamin E deficiency due to very small stores of the vitamin at birth and the frequently required use of oxygen to accommodate immature lungs. Premature infants are also growing very rapidly and need increased intakes of vitamin E. Special formulas are used to provide vitamin E to help prevent deficiency (Wardlaw and Kessel).

The disease caused by vitamin C deficiency is scurvy. The symptoms of scurvy are fatigue and small, purple spots or hemorrhages (petechiae) that appear around hair follicles on the back of the arms and legs. There are also bleeding gums and joints, impaired wound healing, pain in the bones, fractures, and diarrhea. Consuming a vitamin C–free diet for as little as 20 days may cause scurvy, but resuming vitamin C intake for one week can cause the reversal of the disease and accompanying symptoms (Wardlaw and Kessel).

Vitamin E toxicity may result from intakes of more than 1,500 IU/day of vitamin E isolated from natural sources and 1,100 IU/day for synthetic vitamin E for adults nineteen years or older. It is only possible to acquire such high doses of either form of vitamin E via supplementation. Use of supplemental vitamin E at such high doses in persons with a compromised health status may lead to complications such as hemorrhaging in individuals who are taking anticoagulants or are vitamin K-deficient (vitamin K is important in blood coagulation) (Wardlaw and Kessel).

Vitamin C toxicity may occur at intakes of 2 g/day or higher. The symptoms of vitamin C toxicity are nausea, abdominal cramps, and osmotic diarrhea. Because vitamin C is a water-soluble vitamin, much of excess vitamin C obtained from supplemental megadoses is excreted in urine (Wardlaw and Kessel).

Small children who do not eat enough vegetables are at an increased risk for vitamin A deficiency. In fact, individuals with very low incomes and the elderly are also at risk for deficiency due to an inability to obtain adequate intakes of foods that are good sources of vitamin A and to the decreased gastrointestinal function that may occur with age. Night blindness is a symptom of vitamin A deficiency, causing the rod cells in the eye to take a longer period of time to recover from flashes of light. Another symptom of vitamin A deficiency is dry eyes caused by deterioration of the mucus-forming cells in the body. In an individual with dry eyes, dirt and other contaminants are not washed away, and this may lead to eye infections. If vitamin A deficiency is not corrected, the condition of the eyes worsens, leading to more serious disorders of the eye; eventually irreversible blindness may result. The skin is also affected by a compromised vitamin A status. Primary symptoms are very dry skin and rough and bumpy texture of the skin surface. When vitamin A supplements are taken long-term at three times the RDA a condition called hypervitaminosis A may develop. This condition can cause spontaneous abortions in pregnant women or birth defects in infants and therefore women of child-bearing age wishing to become pregnant should avoid using high doses of vitamin A supplements (Wardlaw and Kessel).

Maintaining Antioxidant Content in the Foods You Eat

Antioxidants in foods are a valuable addition to a healthy diet and steps can be taken to preserve the antioxidant content of foods until they are ready to be ingested. Keeping fruits and vegetables refrigerated or in a cool, dry place helps to slow down the natural breakdown by enzymes that begins to occur as soon as the foods are picked. Fruits and vegetables should not be trimmed or cut until they are ready to be consumed to prevent unnecessary exposure to oxygen. Cooking by steaming, microwaving, or stir-frying in small amounts of fat for short amounts of time also helps to preserve the vitamin content of foods. If liquids are used to cook fruits or vegetables, do not add fat while cooking if you are planning to discard the liquid before eating the fruits or vegetables, to avoid losing the fat-soluble vitamins that may be in the liquids. Finally, it is important to remember that the skin of some fruits and vegetables contains a higher vitamin content than the inner parts, such as the skin of an apple (Wardlaw and Kessel).

See also: **Dietary Assessment; Dietary Guidelines; Natural Foods; Niacin Deficiency (Pellagra); Nutrition Transition: Worldwide Diet Change; Vitamin C; Vitamins: Overview; Vitamins: Water-soluble and Fat-soluble Vitamins.**

BIBLIOGRAPHY

Alhadeff, L., C. Gualtieri, and M. Lipton. "Toxic Effects of Water-Soluble Vitamins." *American Journal of Clinical Nutrition* 42 (1984): 33–40.

Bender, D. *Nutritional Biochemistry of the Vitamins.* New York: Cambridge University Press, 1992.

Brubacher, G., and H. Weisler. "The Vitamin A Activity of Beta-carotene." *International Journal of Vitamin and Nutrition Research* 55 (1985): 5–15.

Charley, H., and C. Weaver. *Foods: A Scientific Approach.* Upper Saddle River, N.J.: Prentice-Hall, 1998.

Chow, C. K. "Vitamin E and Oxidative Stress." *Free Radical Biology and Medicine* 11 (1991): 215–232.

Cross, C. E., A. vander Vliet, and C. O'Neil. "Reactive Oxygen Species and the Lung." *Lancet* 344 (1994): 930–933.

Ivanov, V., A. C. Carr, and B. Frei. "Red Wine Antioxidants Bind to Human Lipoproteins and Protect Them from Metal Ion-Dependent and -Independent Oxidation." *Journal of Agricultural and Food Chemistry* 49(9) (2001): 4442–4449.

Martinez-Tome, M., A. M. Jimenez, S. Ruggieri, N. Frega, R. Strabbioli, and M. A. Murcia. "Antioxidant Properties of Mediterranean Spices Compared with Common Food Additives." *Journal of Food Protection* 64(9) (2001): 1412–1419.

Murcia, M. A., and M. Martinez-Tome. "Antioxidant Activity of Resveratrol Compared with Common Food Additives." *Journal of Food Protection* 64(3) (2001): 379–384.

Naidoo, D., and O. Lux. "The Effect of Vitamin C and E Supplementation on Lipid and Urate Oxidation Products in Plasma." *Nutrition Research* 18 (1998): 953–961.

Olson, J. "Recommended Dietary Intakes (RDI) of Vitamin A in Humans." *American Journal of Clinical Nutrition* 45 (1987): 704–716.

Olson, A., and R. Hodges. "Recommended Dietary Intakes (RDI) of Vitamin A in Humans." *American Journal of Clinical Nutrition* 45 (1987): 693–703.

Shils, M. E., J. A. Olson, M. Shike, and A. C. Ross. *Modern Nutrition in Health and Disease.* Baltimore: Williams & Wilkins, 1999.

Wardlaw, G. M., and M. Kessel. *Perspectives in Nutrition.* Boston: McGraw-Hill, 2002.

Rebecca J. (Bryant) McMillian

APHRODISIACS. Throughout the centuries, emperors and everyday folk alike have ingested, imbibed, sprinkled, or applied almost every conceivable substance—from almond paste to zebra tongues—in the hope of arousing sexual desire. Whether to woo a reluctant lover, revive a flagging libido, or pique carnal pleasure and performance, lovers the world over have relied on aphrodisiacs to do the trick. But which ones have the greatest reputations for potency (and why?) and do any of them really work?

Aphrodisiacs through the Ages

The association between food and eroticism is primal, but some foods have more aphrodisiacal qualities than others. Biblical heroines, ancient Egyptians, and Homeric sorceresses all swore by the root and fruit of the mandrake plant. The grape figured prominently in the sensual rites of Greek Dionysian cults, and well-trained geishas have been known to peel plump grapes for their pampered customers. Fermented, of course, grape juice yields wine, renowned for loosening inhibitions and enhancing attraction (though as Shakespeare's porter wryly notes in *Macbeth*, alcohol "provokes the desire, but it takes away the performance"). Honey sweetens the nectarlike philters prescribed in the *Kama Sutra* to promote sexual vigor, and the modern "honeymoon" harks back to the old custom for newlyweds to drink honeyed mead in their first month of marriage. Grains like rice and wheat have long been associated with fertility if not with love, and *Avena sativa* (green oats), an ingredient in many over-the-counter sexual stimulants, may explain why young people are advised to "sow their wild oats." Numerous herbs and spices—basil, mint, cinnamon, cardamom, fenugreek, ginger, pepper, saffron, and vanilla, to name a few—appear in ancient and medieval recipes for love potions, as well as in lists of foodstuffs forbidden in convents because of their aphrodisiac properties.

Among other delicacies banned by the Church in centuries past were black beans, avocados, and chocolate, presumably all threats to chastity. And truffles—both earthy black and ethereal white—caused religious consternation in the days of the Arab empire. One story has it that the *muhtasib* of Seville tried to prohibit their sale anywhere near a mosque, for fear they would corrupt the morals of good Muslims. For those who held debauchery in higher esteem, the list of favored aphrodisiacs was bound only by the imagination. The herb valerian, noted for its stimulant properties at lower doses, was long a brothel favorite, and *yūjo*, professional women of pleasure in feudal Japan, supplemented their charms with the aphrodisiacal powers of eels, lotus root, and charred newts.

From Symbol to Science

How did certain foods come to be regarded as aphrodisiacs in the first place? In some cases, legendary associations play a likely role: Cleopatra is rumored to have rubbed her private parts with a honey-almond mixture that drove Mark Antony mad. Some believe that the Aztec

Aphrodisiacs flirt with the libido, and in this advertisement for vodka, the message is clear, yet subtle. Sparkling crystal, silver glasses, and caviar imply indulgent luxury, yet it is the glasses for two and the beautiful woman in the background that tells us that this intimate indulgence will also lead to love. PHOTO COURTESY OF STOLICHNAYA RUSSIAN VODKA.

ruler Montezuma fortified himself with upwards of fifty cups of chocolate before visiting his harem (though more scholarly reports contend it was the conquistadors who sought such reinforcement). Casanova famously boasted of seducing a virgin by slipping a raw oyster into her mouth. Madame du Barry is said to have used ginger in a custardy concoction that stirred Louis XV to passion. And because Aphrodite, Greek goddess of sexual love, was said in myth to be born from the sea, a beguiling array of seafoods have been deemed aphrodisiacs (her very name is the source of the word).

Symbolism, too, plays an obvious part. During the Middle Ages, the Law of Similarities, or Doctrine of Signatures, held that in God's universe "like causes like," so suggestively shaped and textured substances were believed to enhance virility and fertility by virtue of their resemblance to sexual organs. Firm, elongated asparagus, sea cucumbers, and ginseng (literally, "manroot") and moist, fleshy figs, peaches, and oysters are prime examples. Other symbolic aphrodisiacs are rhinoceros horn and deer antler and the sex organs of animals known for their virility or procreative fervor, such as the tiger or rabbit.

Some foods are exalted as aphrodisiacs by virtue of their rarity or luxury. Bird's nest soup, *foie gras*, caviar,

THE NOTORIOUS SPANISH FLY

Cantharides, a potent preparation made from the crushed dried bodies of the green blister beetle, has been famed throughout history as an aphrodisiac. The Marquis de Sade reportedly favored Spanish fly to enhance virility, and an entire legion of nineteenth-century French soldiers "stood at attention" for prolonged periods after feasting on frogs that had themselves been dining on cantharidin-laden beetles.

Spanish fly does indeed produce erections, but one might die for the pleasure: the French legionnaires in question suffered from priapism, persistent painful erections that, untreated, can result in scarring and permanent loss of erectile function. Antonio Gamoneda in *The Book of Poisons* noted that "Great injury befalls those who take the Spanish Fly, because they will feel a burning corrosion in almost all their body. . . . They will suffer from swoons, surfeit, and lightheadedness, and will fall to the floor and gnaw table legs." This urogenital-tract irritant can be deadly and should be avoided.

Fortunately, safer drugs are now available to aid impotence, and people experiencing sexual dysfunction are well advised to seek medical advice.

truffles, and champagne are all, even if no longer necessarily difficult to obtain, still suggestive of wealth and largesse, playing into the age-old association among food, sex, and the provision of resources. Certain foods also lend themselves to particularly sensual dining rituals and modes of eating. Preparing food tableside with competence and élan, consuming whole ripe fruits or succulent birds or crustaceans, eating with the hands, licking fingers coated in delectable juices, feeding one's partner, sharing food from a common platter, sucking and slurping seductively—such acts and rituals constitute true foreplay for culinarily inclined lovers.

"No one has ever succeeded at seduction by means of food alone," wrote Manuel Vázquez Montalbán in his *Immoral Recipes*, "but there's a long list of those who have seduced by talking about that which was about to be eaten." Certainly, stimulating the mind helps stoke the sexual appetite, and it is our social and cultural associations that imbue certain foods with erotic meanings. But is there solid scientific evidence to support the claims made for aphrodisiacs beyond their placebo effect?

Proponents of chocolate point out that it contains phenylethylamine, or PEA, the brain chemical believed to underlie the euphoric sensation of being "in love." But eating chocolate has not been found to actually increase PEA levels in the body. The chili pepper may have a stronger claim to its fiery reputation: it quickens the pulse and induces sweating, mimicking the state of sexual arousal, and has also been shown to stimulate the release of endorphins, naturally occurring opiates that play a role in sexual pleasure. Ginkgo biloba, said to boost both mental and sexual performance, may restore or enhance physical function by increasing blood flow to the genitals, but the safety and efficacy of this herbal enhancer are still unclear (heart patients and those on aspirin need to be especially cautious). Garlic may promote potency through a similar mechanism, with its high content of arginine, an amino acid that enhances blood flow and could thereby augment erections. The lure of the elusive truffle may derive in part from a pheromonelike chemical it contains, similar to one secreted in the saliva of male pigs to attract sows. And the oyster, that consummate aphrodisiac, is noted not only for its fleshy, briny sensuality but also for its rich supply of zinc, which may aid normal sperm production and libido (though it is unlikely that oysters make a difference in any but the most zinc-deficient diets).

The Ultimate Aphrodisiac

Overall, aphrodisiacs seem to be more the stuff of folklore than of science. But in the realm of food and love, the power of the imagination is not to be ignored—believing something's an aphrodisiac may well make it so. Yet all the oysters in the world cannot take the place of the ultimate aphrodisiac. As the Roman philosopher Seneca once promised, "I will show you a philter without potions, without herbs, without any witch's incantation—if you wish to be loved, love."

See also **Art, Food in**; **Chocolate**; **Greece, Ancient**; **Rome and the Roman Empire**; **Sex and Food**; **Symbol, Food as**.

BIBLIOGRAPHY

Ackerman, Diane. *A Natural History of Love*. New York: Random House, 1995.

Allende, Isabel. *Aphrodite: A Memoir of the Senses*. Translated from the Spanish by Margaret Sayers Peden. New York: HarperCollins, 1998.

Flandrin, Jean-Louis, and Massimo Montanari, eds. *Food: A Culinary History from Anquity to the Present*. English edition by Albert Sonnenfeld. New York: Columbia University Press, 1999.

Hopkins, Martha, and Randall Lockridge. *InterCourses: An Aphrodisiac Cookbook*. Memphis, Tenn.: Terrace, 1997.

Nordenberg, Tamar. "Looking for a Libido Lift? The Facts about Aphrodisiacs." *FDA Consumer* 30, no. 1 (January–February 1996): 10–15.

Meryl S. Rosofsky

APICIUS. The proverbial gastronomer Apicius (M. Gavius Apicius, c. 25 B.C.E–c. 37 C.E.), who lived at the time of the emperor Tiberius, gives his name to the most complete cookbook that has come down from antiquity, one that reflects an ancient Roman cuisine that survives, in part, in early-twenty-first-century Italian traditional practice and that has also shaped European cookery, whenever cooks—or their employers—wished to touch base with ancestral foodways. The book, *De re coquinaria* (On Cookery), is actually the product of a Late Antique compiler, writing about 400 C.E., who drew from an agricultural treatise, a work on household economy, and a Greek study of dietetics, in addition to two genuine publications by Apicius: a general cookbook plus a more specialized one on sauces. Over the years, scholars have been able to establish the true name of Apicius; in the past he was known as Apitius Caelius. Because of abbreviations in the headings of one of the ninth-century manuscripts that preserved the text, his identity was further confused by "ghosts" created through scribal errors of transmission (Three gourmets of that name did not exist, as some authors still have it).

Copying over 450 recipes, our anonymous "editor" organized his gleanings into ten books or chapters, giving each a pretentious Greek name: *Epimeles*, the prudent housekeeper (conserves and preservation advice); *Sarcoptes* (minced meats such as sausages, quenelles, and the like); *Cepuros*, the gardener (vegetables); *Pandecter* (compound dishes of many ingredients); *Ospreon* (legumes, such as peas, beans, chick-peas, and lentils); *Aeropetes* or *Trophetes* (fowl, both wild and domestic); *Politeles*, gourmet dishes (including eggs and limited sweets for *bellaria* or the dessert course); *Tetrapus* (quadripeds both wild and domestic); *Thalassa*, the sea (shellfish, crustaceans, cephalopods); and *Halieus*, the fisherman. An independent selection of thirty-one Apician recipes, recorded in an early medieval manuscript, represents *excerpta* made by one Vinidarius, apparently an Ostrogoth of the period of King Theodoric at the end of the fifth or early sixth century, and includes an impressive list of the herbs, roots, and seeds (spices) that should be at hand in a prosperous kitchen.

From Carolingian manuscripts of *De re coquinaria*—two of which survive in the New York Academy of Medicine and in the Biblioteca Apostolica of the Vatican—Italian Renaissance humanists commissioned numerous copies. The first printed edition of 1498 was shared in two issues between the printers G. Le Signerre in Milan and Ioannes de Legnano, the latter reprinted anonymously in Venice at the end of the century, and again by Tacuinus in 1503. Physicians stand out among subsequent editors: G. Humelberg of Zurich (1542) and Martin Lister (1705).

Seneca tells of Apicius committing suicide when he discovered that his assets—still representing considerable wealth—seemed not enough to enable him to continue dining with his accustomed extravagance, while the elder Pliny castigates his gluttony by reference to his partiality for flamingo tongues. Anecdotes accrued to his repu-

ANCIENT *CASSOULET*

Conchic[u]la à la Apicius (one of several ancestors of a cassoulet)

Conchiclam Apicianam: accipies Cumanam mundam, ubi coques pisam. Cui mittis Lucanicas concisas, esiciola porcina, pulpas petasonis. Teres piper, ligusticum, origanum, anethum, cepam siccam, coriandrum viridem, suffundis liquamen [garum], vino et liquamine temperabis. Mittis in Cumanam, cui adicies oleum, pungis ubique, ut combibat oleum. Igni lento coques ita ut ferveat et inferes. (V, iv, 2)

Take a clean Cumaean pot [earthenware from Cumae] in which you cook the [dried] peas. Into this add Lucanian sausages, cut up; little pork meatballs; and pieces of pork shoulder. Pound [in a mortar] pepper, lovage, oregano, dill, dried onion, green coriander and moisten with *liquamen* [oriental fish sauce, for saltiness]; blend with wine and *liquamen*. Put this in the Cumaean pot, to which you add [olive] oil and prick [the seasoned meats and peas] all over so that the oil is absorbed. Cook over a low fire that it may simmer, and serve.

ED. NOTE: The dried whole peas, or beans, should be soaked overnight before cooking; in other dishes of this chapter the peas are first cooked with leeks, coriander [cilantro], and mallow flowers. Elsewhere Apicius gives a recipe for preparing Lucanian sausage in which the minced meat is seasoned with pepper, cumin, savory, rue, parsley, bay leaves, and *garum* [oriental fish sauce such as *nuoc mam* etc.], plus "condiments"; the latter justifying the use of preserved duck, comparable to certain French cassoulets; finally whole peppercorns, pine nuts, and bits of fat are added before the meat is packed into intestines and hung to smoke. It is possible to use Italian sausage like that from Abruzzi, or even Chinese sausages. Bake in a slow oven.

tation long after his death, such as the tale of his storm-tossed voyage to the coast of Libya in search of the largest, most succulent prawns; when the shrimp did not meet expectations he ordered the hired ship to turn back to home port without his setting foot on land to recover from the journey. One indulgence of Apicius is enshrined in the Italian language. His invention of feeding swine on figs, thus engorging their livers, and then giving them honeyed wine (the Roman apertif *mulsum*) so that the pigs might die in ecstasy, their livers deliciously *ficcatum* (literally, "figged"), gave rise to the word for all liver, *fegato*.

Apicius's recipes, without proportions or details of procedure, reveal the extent to which Roman cookery, although lacking such New World products as quintessentially Italian as tomatoes and capsicum peppers, or medieval Arabic imports like spinach and eggplant, nevertheless survives in Italian *agrodolce* tastes, a love of pasta and farro, an ingenuity in sausage making, and the use of drastically reduced wine or must in sauces (from ancient *passum* to *sapa*, for example). It also provides both name and concept to Mediterranean dishes such as paella, tian, and cassoulet.

See also **Ancient Kitchen; Cookbooks; Rome and the Roman Empire.**

BIBLIOGRAPHY

Apicius. *Cooking and Dining in Imperial Rome.* Edited by J. D. Vehling. New York: Dover, 1977. A chef's rather than a classicist's translation. Originally published in 1936.

Apicius. *Decem libri qui dicuntur* De re coquinaria *et excerpta Vinidario conscripta.* Bibliotheca scriptorum graecorum et romanorum Teubneriana. Edited by Mary Ella Milham. Leipzig: Teubner, 1969. Critical edition, with full apparatus.

Apicius. *L'art culinaire.* Translated by Jacques André. Les Belles lettres: Paris, 1965.

Apicius. *The Roman Cookery Book.* Translated by Barbara Flower and Elizabeth Alföldi-Rosenbaum. London and Toronto: Harrap, 1958.

Bober, Phyllis Pray. *Art, Culture, and Cuisine: Ancient and Medieval Gastronomy.* Chicago: University of Chicago Press, 1999. See Chapter 6 and Appendix.

Dery, Carol A. "The Art of Apicius." In *Proceedings of the Oxford Symposium on Food and Cookery 1995: Cooks and Other People,* edited by Harlan Walker. Blackawton, Totnes, Devon, U.K., 1996, pp. 111–117.

Edwards, John. *The Roman Cookery of Apicius.* Point Robers, Wash.: Hartley and Marks, 1984.

Solomon, Jonathan, and Julia Solomon. *Ancient Roman Feasts and Recipes Adapted for Modern Cookery.* Miami: Seemann, 1977.

Phyllis P. Bober

APPETITE. Appetite is a term implying a strong desire to acquire or participate in, exemplified by terms such as sexual appetite or appetite for life. In the context of food, appetite is used to describe a wanting or liking for particular foods, usually on the basis of their sensory properties (taste and texture) or a psychological attribute (perceived value or symbolic status). In this way appetite is usually distinguished from hunger, which implies a desire or seeking for food arising from a state of need or nutritional deficit. At the beginning of the twenty-first century the understanding of appetite achieves special importance because of its potential role in the worldwide epidemic of obesity, sometimes called a pandemic. Given that, in many parts of the world, people are surrounded by a plentiful supply of food that prevents chronic hunger (though permitting normal meal-to-meal hunger), the capacity to eat food in the absence of hunger or in a low state of hunger assumes special importance. Consequently, understanding appetite and how it can be controlled are urgent tasks in the fight against the obesity epidemic.

Appetite can therefore be defined as a liking for particular foods, or an attraction for foods based on their perceived pleasantness. This is normally referred to as the hedonic dimension of food selection. This characteristic can be described as the subjective pleasure that is derived from the consumption of food; in turn, this can be measured by asking people to rate the magnitude or intensity of pleasure associated with eating or tasting foods. This pleasure arises from the interaction between the person's perceptual capacity (acuity of taste, smell, and sensory feedback from the mouth) and the physical properties of foods. The intensity of the pleasure therefore depends in part on internal (personal) and external (food-related) factors. These food factors can be natural, such as the presence of sweet carbohydrates in fruits or, and much more common now, the deliberate construction of powerful properties in the manufacturing process. It can be hypothesized that the industrial production of foods (designed to possess a combination of properties, for example, sweetness, fattiness, flakiness) has saturated the food supply in many parts of the world with an abundance of appetite-stimulating products. These products include chocolates and desserts, cheese, meat, and pastry combinations, and many types of fried snacks. The inherent attractiveness of such products can stimulate eating in the absence of any obvious need for nutrients.

Biological Basis of Appetite

Is there a biological basis for appetite and for the degree of attractiveness of specific types of foods? It does seem that human beings derive pleasure from particular food properties—the qualities of sweetness and fattiness are prominent. It is generally understood that, during the course of human evolution, a preference for foods with these properties would lead people to consume foods that possessed energy—yielding value, for example, the nutritional value of carbohydrates and the energy value of fats. Consequently the value of these traits for survival has almost certainly persisted until the present day, at which stage these genetic dispositions may be detrimental in the current "obesigenic" environment (but useful when foods with these properties were scarce). The word "obesigenic" was coined around the end of the twentieth century to suggest an environment that promoted weight gain through the abundance, attractiveness, and marketing of food consumption, together with reduced opportunities for physical activity. It is recognized that most cultures contain highly prized food habits based on foods that are either sweet or fatty, and sometimes a combination of both—when the palatability can be intense.

Do these genetic traits based on the pleasurable qualities of food have a basis in brain processes? The intrinsic sensory attractiveness of food is mediated by "reward" pathways in the brain. These pathways promote various types of pleasure and can be artificially stimulated by drugs. By using drugs as tools it has been found that particular neurochemical transmitters are involved in the process of reward; these transmitters include dopamine, opioid, and cannabinoid molecules together with their specific receptors. It can also be demonstrated empirically that the areas of the brain that subserve the most intense pleasure can be stimulated both by food sensations (arising from sensory pathways), and modulated by signals of need (arising from the body's energy stores). This means that a nutritional deficit, indicated by a low body weight, for example, can sensitize the reward system so as to increase the measured pleasantness of foods. In practice this would mean that a person who had been coerced into losing substantial body weight would display an increased rating of pleasantness for certain foods. This can be seen as a useful biological mechanism and is given credibility via the long-known phenomenon called alliesthesia, which is perceiving an external stimulus as pleasant or not, depending on internal stimuli. This concept is based on the biological notion of pleasure being a useful trait.

However, it seems certain that another mechanism must also be at work. This mechanism is based on the recognition that some people who gain weight easily and become obese possess traits that lead them to derive a high degree of pleasure from food. Consequently, foods with potent sensory properties are attractive targets for such people and this increasing pleasantness can lead to overconsumption and weight gain. There is clear evidence that obese women rate sweet/fatty foods very highly and consume substantial quantities; other studies have shown that obese people show preferences for fatty foods and for the taste of fat. After eating, obese subjects frequently rate the same food as being more pleasant than do lean subjects. In this way the expression of appetite—a heightened pleasure of eating—can be seen to contribute to increasing body weight and obesity. This arises from endogenous traits to derive pleasure from food (sometimes specific foods) in conjunction with an abundance of foods possessing a profile of pleasure-stimulating properties.

Hedonics and Hunger

The identification of the pleasure response of appetite with a neurochemical substrate also helps to differentiate the hedonic dimension of food from the hunger dimension. The term "hedonic," derived from the Greek word *hedone*, refers to the seeking of pleasure. Experimental studies in human subjects have shown that a drug called naloxone that blocks opioid receptors can reduce the perceived pleasantness of food without diminishing hunger. In contrast a drug such as fenfluramine, that acts upon serotonin receptors, can substantially reduce hunger without changing the perceived pleasantness of food. This type of pharmacological dissection indicates that the overall control of food intake depends upon both appetite (signals of pleasure) and hunger (signals of absence of food). However, the separation of the systems is not complete since experimental investigations have shown that while people are eating very good-tasting food their hunger is elevated. This elevation serves to prolong the meal so that more food is consumed. The relationship is, however, asymmetrical: although pleasantness increases hunger, a state of satiety does not reduce the perception of pleasure. Indeed, even when people report feeling full, a very palatable food can often still be eaten. Surveys have shown that foods rated as most palatable (pleasant) are associated with the largest meal sizes and with the greatest amount of food consumed. The results of scientific observations are therefore consistent with the widespread belief that people eat more of good-tasting food. However, people do not always choose to eat the most delectable or most pleasure-giving food; eating also depends on the appropriateness of the food for the particular social context. This is a good example of a cultural rule overcoming a biological response. However, much overeating in certain cultures arises from the strength of the biological response or perceived intensity of pleasure overcoming the cultural convention.

The Palatability Dilemma

The potency of appetite in stimulating food consumption creates a problem in the present climate of escalating levels of obesity. There are now strong intentions in the nutraceutical sector of the food industry to encourage the production of functional foods for appetite control; that is, foods that possess satiety-inducing or hunger-suppressing properties. The word "nutraceutical" was coined to resemble the word "pharmaceutical" and refers to those foods that may have specific functional effects generated in a manner similar to the way in which drugs work. However, advances in food technology have, over the years, been able to bring about an increase in the overall pleasantness (palatability) of foods entering the market-place. Indeed, one of the legitimate goals of the food industry is to make eating a source of pleasure. It can be observed that for many people, eating is the cheapest form of pleasure available on a day-to-day basis. However, improving palatability means increasing the sensory attractiveness of foods and the willingness of people to consume such foods. Satiety implies reducing the willingness of people to consume. The question therefore arises whether it is possible for the food industry to increase the palatability of foods without weakening satiety—and vice versa. The balance between palatability and satiety is the essence of the interaction between hunger and hedonics in the control of food intake. It remains to be determined how the interplay between these factors contributes to the current obesity epidemic.

See also **Acceptance and Rejection; Anorexia, Bulimia; Eating: Anatomy and Physiology of Eating; Hunger, Physiology of; Obesity; Sensation and the Senses**.

BIBLIOGRAPHY

Blundell, John E., and Peter J. Rogers. "Hunger, Hedonics and the Control of Satiation and Satiety." In *Chemical Senses*, edited by Mark I. Friedman and Michael G. Tordoff. New York: M. Dekker, 1991.

de Castro, J. M., F. Bellisle, and A.-M. Dalix. "Palatability and Intake Relationships in Free-Living Humans: Measurement and Characterization in the French." *Physiology and Behaviour* 68 (2000): 271–277

Mela, D. J., and Peter J. Rogers. *Food, Eating and Obesity: The PsychoBiological Basis of Appetite and Weight Control*. London: Chapman and Hall, 1998.

Mela, D. J., and D. A. Sacchetti. "Sensory Preferences for Fats: Relationships with Diet and Body Composition." *American Journal of Clinical Nutrition* 53 (1991): 908–915.

Yeomans, M. R. "Taste, Palatability and the Control of Appetite." *Proceedings of the Nutrition Society* 57 (1998): 609–615.

John E. Blundell
Joanna Le Noury

APPLE. Picking apples on a clear, crisp, sunny autumn day provides a cornucopia of pleasures. The enjoyment of being outdoors and savoring another harvest has been part of the human experience for centuries. Biting into a crunchy, sweetly flavored apple or quaffing a big glass of fresh cider reminds one why apples are a part of fairy tales and folk history. Remember Snow White and Johnny Appleseed? Apples have sustained humans with beverages—hard and sweet cider—innumerable culinary dishes, winter provisions, and even foodstuffs for hogs and cattle, and they are still an integral part of American culture and commerce. Apple pie is the quintessential American dessert, and bins of fresh apples are present year-round in every supermarket. An apple variety exists for every taste bud, and eating apples has a lot of health benefits, too. They are a good source of antioxidants and fiber, and an individual apple contains about 80 calories, 5 grams of fiber, 6 milligrams of vitamin C, and 170 milligrams of potassium.

Origin of Apples

Botanists theorize that apples originated somewhere in central and southern China. This area is home to around twenty *Malus* species, whose seeds were gradually spread by birds throughout the Northern Hemisphere. Ornamental crab apples are also descendants of these smaller, bitter-fruited species. It was thought that the edible apple (*Malus domestica*) evolved as a complex hybrid from a number of these wild apple species. However, Barrie Juniper, emeritus fellow in the Department of Plant Sciences at Oxford University, has suggested that a small population of a single *Malus* species from the wild forests of the Tian Shan (the Heavenly Mountains) along the border of western China and Kazakhstan is the progenitor of all modern apple cultivars. These Tian Shan forests became isolated by biological and climatic changes about 4.5 million years ago and evolved in isolation. Juniper theorizes that as bears and wild pigs, horses, and donkeys gradually began to occupy the area and to eat the largest and sweetest fruits, they aided in the process of natural selection for larger, sweeter fruit. Because apples do not breed "true to type" from seed, these wild plantings from dispersed seeds gradually contributed to a diversity of apple varieties from this one species. Later, around ten thousand years ago, humans began to travel through the area and also began to eat these fruits and to carry them westward. Juniper and other researchers are studying the remnants of these forests of wild fruit trees and are collecting samples for DNA analysis. These wild fruit trees are a fruit breeder's paradise for genetic material.

Ancient History

By 2500 B.C.E. apples were cultivated throughout northern Mesopotamia and Persia. The walled gardens of Persia included fruit trees for their ornamental beauty as well as for their culinary delights. The ancient Greeks and Romans also cultivated apple orchards, and their wealthy citizens enjoyed apples as part of the dessert course at banquets. The Greeks, well advanced in horticultural knowledge, understood grafting and propagated specific varieties for their orchards. The Greek writer Theophrastos knew that apples would not grow true to type from seeds, writing, "Seedlings of . . . apples produce an inferior kind which is acid instead of sweet . . . and this is why men graft." In the first century C.E. the Roman writer Pliny described over twenty named varieties in his *Natural History*. Apple orchards were established throughout continental Europe and in Britain as the Romans extended their empire, culture, and crops. An indicator of the importance of the apple in these ancient cultures is its prevalence in Greek and Roman mythology. The Roman goddess Pomona tended her orchards and bestowed gifts of fruit on her favorites as rewards for favorable acts.

After the collapse of the Roman Empire, many of the favorite dessert apple varieties of the day disappeared. Charlemagne's rise to power in 771 brought a measure of peace and prosperity and an increased interest in horticultural pursuits. His *Capitulare de Villis* (Rules of Land Use) decreed that every city should include apples, cherries, plums, peaches, and pears. Charlemagne also issued an edict that brewers (which included cider makers) should be encouraged to develop their trade. Apple cultivation and varietal development progressed in Europe during the Renaissance. Varieties were selected, named, and propagated, and orchard plantings increased. These improved varieties were included in beautiful displays of fresh fruit at Renaissance banquets, where fresh apples were enjoyed as part of the dessert course.

North American History

Apples have been part of American life from the first arrival of European settlers. One of the first documented orchards in the New World belonged to William Blaxstone, a well-known horticulturalist and clergyman. He planted his orchard around 1625 on the slope of what became Beacon Hill in Boston. Blaxstone, who was described as an eccentric, saddle-trained a bull and distributed apples to his friends on his rides. One of his apples, Sweet Rhode Island Greening, is probably the first named variety from the United States.

Colonial America. A one- to six-acre apple orchard was an important part of farmsteads in seventeenth- and eighteenth-century America. Apples were grown primarily for hard cider, which was the beverage of choice because water was regarded as unsafe. Everyone in the family drank cider, and each family produced twenty to fifty barrels of cider each autumn for its own consumption and to use as barter for needed goods and services. Cider was not considered prime until it had aged over a year. Applejack, made from distilled cider, was even stronger. The first cider mills were built around 1745. Prior to this cider was made by pounding apples in a trough and draining the pomace. By the late eighteenth century cider mills dotted the countryside. In New England one in ten farms had a cider mill.

Cider was also used in cooking apple butter. Sweet cider (the unfermented, freshly pressed juice) was combined with peeled and boiled apples and cooked until the mixture had been reduced to a thick paste through evaporation. It was then put up in earthen jars for later use. Some cider was allowed to become vinegar and was used for food preservation. Apples were also dried for winter preservation. Michel Crèvecoeur, author of *Letters from an American Farmer* (1782), described drying apple slices on wooden platforms erected on poles. The fruit was spread out on wooden boards, where it was soon covered with "all the bees and wasps and sucking insects of the neighborhood," which he felt accelerated the drying process. The dried apples were used for apple pies and dumplings throughout the year. Peaches and plums were also dried but were considered more of a delicacy and were saved for special occasions. The dried apples, also called schnitz, were stored in bags hung in the attic rafters to keep them dry and away from mice. The Pennsylvania Dutch, German settlers in eastern Pennsylvania, were prodigious apple growers and developed a brisk business in colonial America selling schnitz, apple butter, and cider. A traditional Pennsylvania Dutch apple dish, called schnitz pie, consists of dried apples first cooked in water; then sugar and spices are added to the pot, and finally the mixture is baked in a lidded pie crust. *Schnitz and knepp* is a dish of ham, potatoes, and dried apples cooked together; dumpling dough is added and cooked briefly right before serving.

After the Revolution, grafting and nurseries became more commonplace. Still, until the mid-nineteenth cen-

Cleft grafting on fruit trees according to a medieval method described by Pietro Crescenzi (ca. 1233–ca. 1320). From a woodcut in the *De Omnibus agriculturae partibus*. ROUGHWOOD COLLECTION.

tury most plantings in home orchards were of seedling trees that were not pruned. The fruit was primarily used for cider and fed to hogs. Pork was cheap, and the abundant apples and peaches were an inexpensive way to fatten pigs. Cider was even part of political campaigning and was dispensed freely during voting time. During one election, George Washington's agent is said to have dispensed 3.75 gallons of beer, wine, cider, or rum to every voter.

Insect pests and diseases were not quite as prevalent in colonial times as they later became. Some key fruit pests had not yet made the trip to the New World, and other native insects had not yet discovered apples. Pest-damaged fruit was also accepted as natural and unavoidable. Still-life paintings of fruit from this and earlier eras clearly show insect and disease damage on the fruit. In 1806 Bernard McMahon, in *The American Gardener's Calendar*, instructed readers to pick the worst of the leaves off the tree and dash the branches with water in dry weather to prevent insect damage from spreading.

Johnny Appleseed, whose real name was John Chapman, was a popular folk character in early nineteenth-century America. Born in Leominster, Massachusetts, in 1774, Johnny Appleseed started seedling apple tree nurseries throughout Pennsylvania, Ohio, and Indiana. Traveling by canoe or on foot, he gave apple seeds from cider mills to any farmer who promised to plant them and take care of them. On his travels he also planted seedling nurseries in clearings. At his death in 1847, he had established apple trees over 100,000 square miles of territory.

Nineteenth-century apple growing. Agricultural settlement of midwestern and western states by European settlers began in the mid-1820s. Home orchards were planted in Washington State by the first European immigrants from the eastern states in the mid-1800s. Commercial orchard plantings did not take hold until the

Harvested apples at Brogden Farm in Kent, England, are being boxed for distribution to the London market. Kent lies at the center of Britain's apple-growing region. © HULTON-DEUTSCH COLLECTION/CORBIS.

advent of the big irrigation projects in the late nineteenth century. By 1850 five hundred named varieties were cultivated. The seedling nurseries started by Johnny Appleseed and settlers across the country were the start of unique American varieties like Baldwin, Esopus, Spitzenburg, Green Newton, Jonathan, Hawley, Newton Spitzenburg, Swaar, Winesap, and York Imperial.

The mid-nineteenth century saw changes in American agriculture as urban populations grew and a smaller percentage of people were involved in agriculture. Apple growing was no longer primarily the purview of the self-sufficient homestead. Alcoholic cider fell into disrepute with the spread of the temperance movement, and the cider industry declined. Larger commercial orchards were established for growing and selling fresh apples. The apple industry was affected between 1880 and 1930 by the development of the refrigerated railroad car that allowed fruit growers in the western states to ship fruit east. The development between 1910 and 1920 of refrigerated storage meant that long-keeping winter apples were not as necessary, so fewer varieties were grown by commercial orchards. At the beginning of the twentieth century seven thousand named varieties of apples existed, but five thousand of these varieties were extinct by the beginning of the twenty-first century. Prior to refrigerated storage, apple cultivars grown in small orchards varied from early-season baking apples to winter-keeper types with a thick, waxy skin that would store well in root cellars.

Pest Management

Pesticides were not developed or widely used until the late nineteenth century, when growers began producing fruit more for market and for fresh eating rather than for cider and for home consumption. Orchardists experienced increasing pest damage from codling moth, a lar-

val fruit pest accidentally introduced from Europe by early settlers, and from other pests and diseases. The first arsenical insecticide, Paris green (copper acetoarsenite), was developed in the 1870s to control codling moth. Lead arsenate was developed as an insecticide in 1892. Growers also began using nicotine sulfate to fortify the lead arsenate applications. At first these broad spectrum, toxic pesticides were applied one to three times during a growing season, but the number of applications increased as codling moth became more difficult to control. By 1945 orchardists were using up to seven applications of lead arsenate each season. DDT, developed during World War II, was hailed for its effectiveness against insect pests and low toxicity to humans. Not until later did scientists discover that DDT persisted in the food chain. Still, these new pest controls were not without concerns. DDT successfully controlled codling moth but wiped out natural predators that kept other pests in check, so the number of pests that needed to be controlled greatly increased as the number of pesticides increased.

Public debate over pesticide use grew with the increasing use of pesticides. In 1937 the U.S. Congress directed the U.S. Public Health Service to investigate the possible harmful effects of spray residues on fruits and vegetables. Although the Service's report, finished in 1940, concluded that harmful effects were minimal, the dialog about pesticide use continued, reflected in various scientific studies and public debates through the decades. The 1962 publication of *Silent Spring* by Rachel Carson galvanized public opinion about the environmental consequences of pesticide use.

Apple Orchards in the Twenty-First Century

The introduction of integrated pest management in the 1970s placed more emphasis on understanding pest and disease life cycles and pest populations as the basis for pesticide applications instead of touting the benefits of applying sprays on a routine basis. Still, fruit growers must meet the demand for inexpensive, blemish-free fruit in a competitive marketplace. Pesticide use on apples remains higher than on most other crops. Researchers continue to study pest- and disease-monitoring techniques, biological controls, and new targeted pesticides to develop more ecologically based production systems and to lower the pesticide risk for agricultural workers and consumers. Consumer demand for organic fruits and vegetables produced without synthetic pesticides and fertilizers has increased. Organic apple production is growing, particularly in the Northwest, which has fewer insects and diseases than the Northeast.

In the early twenty-first century Washington State produced 50 percent of the apple crop in the United States, followed by New York, California, Michigan, and Pennsylvania. Although over two thousand varieties of apples are grown in the United States, commercial orchards produce about 90 percent of the crop from ten varieties of apples—Red Delicious, Golden Delicious,

Granny Smith, Rome, Fuji, McIntosh, Gala, Jonathan, Idared, and Empire. Controlled atmosphere storage, where the oxygen level is decreased and additional nitrogen is introduced into refrigerated storage, means apples can be stored from one season to the next and hold their quality. Approximately 50 percent of the crop is sold for fresh eating; 20 percent is processed for vinegar, cider, juice, jelly, and apple butter; 17 percent is canned as applesauce and pie filling; and 13 percent is exported. Internationally apples are the most widely cultivated tree fruit. Annual world apple production stands at approximately fifty-seven metric tons of apples. China is now the world's largest producer of apples, followed by the United States, Turkey, Italy, Germany, France, Iran, Poland, Argentina, and India.

Horticultural Requirements
Commercial apple orchards require skilled management. Apples are adaptable but grow best in cool temperate climates from about 35 to 50 degrees latitude. Most apple varieties require full sun, good soil drainage, and a chilling period (1,000 to 1,600 hours of temperatures below 45°F) and 120 to 180 frost-free days to produce a crop. Fruit quality is highest when day temperatures are warm but nights are cool. Orchardists favor trees that have been propagated on size-controlling rootstocks. These rootstocks produce smaller trees that can be planted more intensively, yield more per acre, and bear fruit earlier (two to four years) than full-sized standard rootstocks. Trees are pruned annually, and pests, diseases, soil fertility, and water needs are monitored to maximize fruit quality, size, and color. Growers must also pay attention to market demands and price fluctuations to maintain viable businesses in a highly competitive international arena.

One option for smaller family farm operations is to focus on direct marketing to the consumer. Roadside marketing, farm markets, and pick-your-own operations can emphasize locally grown, unique apple varieties. Large-scale supermarkets tend to carry only a few varieties, while the several thousand apple varieties once grown in the United States are unknown to many consumers. Apple aficionados can search out regional favorites like Smokehouse, a fine, old Delaware and Pennsylvania apple from 1837; Grime Golden, the rich, distinctive apple from the mountains of West Virginia; or Blue Permain, a large, dark purplish-red fruit that will keep all winter in a root cellar. The best baking apples are found at farmer's markets. The tart Lodi ripens early in the season, Fallawater is an old favorite for both baking and eating, and the yellow-fleshed Smokehouse is juicy and firm for pies.

Preserving the rich heritage and genetic diversity of these varieties is a concern of the Seed Savers Exchange, a nonprofit organization devoted to saving heirloom varieties of vegetables and fruits. The organization maintains a historic orchard of seven hundred apple varieties at its Heritage Farm in Decorah, Iowa, and aims to obtain cuttings of all existing nineteenth-century apples.

The U.S. Department of Agriculture also maintains an apple germ plasm collection of more than three thousand varieties in orchard plantings or in tissue culture storage. These collections offer genetic characteristics, such as insect and disease resistance, flavor, fruit size, and cold hardiness, that are important in breeding new apple cultivars.

Home Gardening
The general perception among gardeners is that apple growing is too complicated and is best left to experts. Backyard apple-growing enthusiasts know that, while apple growing does take an investment of time and knowledge, it really is not difficult. Some homework will determine the varieties and size-controlling rootstocks that thrive in an area. Local agricultural extension agents are good resources for information on which pests and diseases might present problems. The North American Fruit Explorers (NAFEX) is a network of fruit-growing enthusiasts who publish a quarterly journal of helpful varietal and growing information. Disease-resistant varieties, such as Liberty, Redfree, Gold Rush, and William's Pride, are an absolute boon for backyard orchardists. Gardeners can combine the disease-resistant varieties with insect-trapping techniques, like the apple maggot trap, which is a red apple-sized sphere coated with sticky tanglefoot to attract apple maggots, and kaolin clay, a fine clay particle spray material, to produce a good-quality apple without inundating a backyard with pesticide materials. Harvesting a basket of crisp, delicious apples from a backyard orchard should be on every gardener's wish list.

See also **Fruit: Temperate Fruit; Pie; United States: Pennsylvania Dutch Food.**

BIBLIOGRAPHY

Childers, Norman Franklin. *Modern Fruit Science.* Gainesville, Fla.: Horticultural Publications, 1983.

Fegley, H. Winslow. *Farming, Always Farming.* Birdsboro, Pa.: Pennsylvania German Society, 1987.

Fletcher, S. W. *Pennsylvania Agriculture and Country Life.* Volume 1: *1640–1840.* Harrisburg, Pa.: Pennsylvania Historical and Museum Commission, 1950.

Hedrick, U. P. *A History of Horticulture in America to 1860.* Portland, Ore.: Timber Press, 1988.

Janson, H. Frederic. *Pomona's Harvest: An Illustrated Chronicle of Antiquarian Fruit Literature.* Portland, Ore.: Timber Press, 1996.

Long, Amos, Jr. *The Pennsylvania German Family Farm.* Breinigsville, Pa.: Pennsylvania German Society, 1972.

McMahon, Bernard. *The American Gardener's Calendar.* Charlottesville, Va.: Thomas Jefferson Memorial Foundation, 1997. Facsmile edition of the 1806 work.

Morgan, Joan, and Alison Richards. *The Book of Apples.* London: Ebury Press, 1993.

Price, Eluned. "East of Eden." *The Garden* 126, no. 6 (June 2001): 456–459.

Tannahill, Reay. *Food in History*. New York: Stein and Day, 1973.

Thuente, Joanne. *Fruit, Berry, and Nut Inventory*. Edited by Kent Whealy. 3d ed. Decorah, Iowa: Seed Savers Exchange, 2001.

Upshall, W. H., ed. *History of Fruit Growing and Handling in United States of America and Canada 1860–1972*. University Park, Pa.: American Pomological Society, 1976.

Watson, Ben. *Cider, Hard and Sweet*. Woodstock, Vt.: Countryman Press, 1999.

Sarah Wolfgang Heffner

TABLE 1

The largest aquaculture industries, by volume, in 1999

Values are in million metric tons

Species	Volume
Giant tiger prawn	3,651,782
Pacific cupped oyster	3,312,713
Japanese kelp	3,023,240
Silver carp	2,837,420
Grass carp	2,743,194
Atlantic salmon	2,448,280
Japanese carpet shell	2,194,521
Roho labeo	1,493,884
Rainbow trout	1,350,168
Japanese amberjack	1,282,090
Yesso scallop	1,252,448
Nori	1,249,923
Whiteleg shrimp	1,062,774
Nile tilapia	1,025,739

AQUACULTURE. Aquaculture, the controlled or semi-controlled production of aquatic plants and animals, has increased at double-digit percentage rates since the early 1980s. This increase has been in response to declines in commercial harvests of wild stocks of fish and shellfish. Oceans of the world are currently at maximum sustainable yield. Since the late 1980s, there has been a concerted effort to maintain global commercial harvest of ocean fish at approximately 100 million metric tons (mmt). However, as global population grows, demand for fish and shellfish increases, and the percentage of aquatic products grown in aquaculture must likewise rise to meet the supply of those products. Projections for increased production are in the range of 40–100 mmt of new aquaculture production by about the year 2030. The lower range assumes only increases in world population; the upper figure represents increases in world population plus a 1 percent per year increase in per capita consumption. To put this number in perspective, the 1995 world production figures for soybeans was 137 mmt, swine was 83 mmt, and chickens was 46 mmt. Thus, to meet demand in the first part of the twenty-first century, we must realize significant growth. This increase in production will not be accomplished with a single species.

There are fewer than thirty large species-specific aquaculture industries globally, and the fourteen largest industries are listed in the table. However, there are over twenty-five thousand species of fish and there are estimates that one thousand new species are being evaluated for their culture potential. The small percentage of species raised relative to the total number available is an indication that aquaculture is a new concept in many parts of the world. As a subsistence enterprise, aquaculture has been practiced for over four thousand years. As a series of large industries, aquaculture is less than fifty years old, often stimulated by declining wild stocks of fish. The channel catfish industry, which only began in the late 1960s in the southern United States, is illustrative of a relatively young industry. Today, over 90 percent of the U.S. supply of Atlantic salmon is cultured. In 1980, that figure was a fraction of 1 percent, at most. The global supply and demand characteristics created a good deal of volatility in production, which has only increased over time. Additional factors such as identification of new dis-

eases and movement of those diseases contribute to the volatility in production. Inevitably, as new aquaculture species are brought into culture settings, new diseases are identified that were previously unknown. In the past ten years, new viral diseases have been identified in shrimp and salmon, both of which caused large-scale losses from production facilities.

Of the approximately 25 mmt of global aquaculture production, there are only a few industries that produced over 1 mmt in 1996. Several of the species of Asian carp and the common carp account for the largest industries. Silver carp production was 2.2 mmt, grass carp production was 1.8 mmt, bighead carp production was 1.1 mmt, and common carp production was 1.5 mmt. Virtually all of this production occurred in China with the exception of common carp, which is raised throughout Europe, its native range. Of the species typically available in U.S. markets, pen-raised Atlantic salmon accounted for 0.4 mmt, rainbow trout production for 0.3 mmt, channel catfish production for 0.2 mmt, and tilapia for 0.6 mmt. Production of several invertebrates was significant. Scallop production was 1.0 mmt, shrimp production was 0.9 mmt, oyster production was 1.1 mmt, mussel production was 1.0 mmt, and clam production was 1.0 mmt. Production of brown seaweeds was 4.5 mmt and red seaweed production was 1.6 mmt. Thus, the largest aquaculture industry is the production of brown seaweeds, largely for nonfood use. In the twenty-first century, greater demand will likely result in increased production.

There are only a few production systems in use for aquaculture, and they include earthen ponds, raceways, cages or net pens, and indoor recirculating systems. Earthen ponds or cages placed in existing bodies of water are the oldest production system and the indoor recirculating systems are the newest. For successful culture, considerable technical expertise is required when us-

Fish culture technicians working in a fish hatchery in the early spring. Photo courtesy of United States Department of Agriculture.

ing a recirculating system. All of the current industries use earthen ponds (catfish, tilapia, Asian carps, shrimp), raceways (rainbow trout), or cages/net pens (Atlantic salmon, yellowtail, an amberjack from Southeast Asia). Producers are experimenting with indoor recirculating systems using a wide variety of species. There are a few successful producers using indoor systems, but the number will inevitably grow as both the systems themselves and information on targeted species increase. Successful aquaculture can be viewed as the correct match of species under a certain set of market conditions with production system. Some species do not tolerate some of the production systems or do not thrive in those systems. Behavioral characteristics of the various species often point toward the appropriate culture systems. For example, sedentary fish (bluegill, catfish, and flounder) should probably be raised in systems without significant water flow (earthen ponds, cages/net pens), whereas those that typically swim a great deal (tuna, trout, and striped bass) can be raised in raceway systems with a constant flow of water.

Fish are generally considered good quality food for human consumption because of the low saturated fat levels and generally high levels of n-3 fatty acids. Fish tend to retain the fatty acids that are in their diet. Thus, we can manipulate the fatty acid concentrations of fish and produce "designer fish" for targeted markets. Further, we can control the fat concentration in muscle through selected feed and produce a low-fat or high-fat fish depending on the demands of the market. Cultured aquatic animals can be safer products for consumption than wild fish because they are raised in a defined environment, and pollutants can be eliminated. Wild fish can be exposed to environmental pollutants and retain those they encounter. Organoleptic properties (taste) of fish and shellfish raised in aquaculture can be quite different from wild stocks. Fish flavor can be manipulated by dietary ingredients fed to the target species. If the diet contains a rel-

atively high percentage of fish meal, the fish can taste fishier than if the diet contains a relatively high percentage of corn and soybean products. Fish fed the latter diets are often described as "milder" tasting, which is a desirable characteristic in certain markets. There is also a taste consideration with environment. Some species can survive both fresh- and saltwater, but osmoregulation changes to meet the challenges of those environments. This physiological change affects taste because of the chemical compounds used to regulate ionic balance. A good example of this is the freshwater shrimp. When raised in freshwater, taste has been described as mild, whereas if the shrimp is placed in saltwater for one to two weeks, it will taste more like a marine shrimp. Even with these positive attributes, aquaculture is experiencing growing pains.

Culture of aquatic animals produces the same wastes as other animal production industries. The problem is confounded by the fact that those wastes are discharged as rearing water is renewed. There have been incidences of environmental degradation resulting from aquaculture. One of the focal points of aquacultural research is waste management, focusing on phosphorus and nitrogen dynamics originating in the diet. Those efforts, as well as efforts related to siting aquaculture operations, land-use practices, and economic development, have become the focal point of sustainable aquaculture development. Along with the overall focus on sustainability, there are significant concerns about the feed used to achieve aquaculture's successes. Fish meal is a high-quality ingredient, yet it is a finite resource similar to all other species in the oceans. Ingredients made from soybeans, corn, canola, wheat, legumes, peanuts, and barley, as well as the by-products of the brewing industries and animal packing operations, are needed.

Growth of aquaculture in the twenty-first century will most likely be similar to growth in terrestrial animal production seen in the twentieth century. Fish and shellfish are the last major food item humans still hunt and gather from wild populations. The sustainable nature of aquacultural production probably will be the focal point of research in the early part of the twenty-first century and those results should facilitate the production increases necessary for sufficient quantities of fish and shellfish in the future.

See also **Crustaceans and Shellfish; Fish,** *subentries on* **Freshwater Fish** *and* **Sea Fish.**

BIBLIOGRAPHY

Adelizi, Paul D., Ronald R. Rosati, Kathleen Warner, Y. Victor Wu, Tim R. Muench, M. Randall White, and Paul B. Brown. "Evaluation of Fish Meal-Free Diets for Rainbow Trout, *Oncorhynchus mykiss.*" *Aquaculture Nutrition* 4, no. 4 (1998): 255–262.

Donahue, Darrell W., Robert C. Bayer, John G. Riley, Alfred A. Bushway, Paul B. Brown, Russell A. Hazen, Keith E. Moore, and Dorothy A. Debruyne. "The Effect of Soy-Based

Diets on Weight Gain, Shell Hardness, and Flavor of the American Lobster (*Homarus americanus*)." *Journal of Aquatic Food Product Technology* 8, no. 3 (1999): 69–77.

Floreto, Eric A. T., Robert C. Bayer, and Paul B. Brown. "The Effects of Soybean-Based Diets, with and without Amino Acid Supplementation, on Growth and Biochemical Composition of Juvenile American Lobster, *Homarus americanus*." *Aquaculture* 189 (2000): 211–235.

New, M. B. "Aquaculture and the Capture Fisheries—Balancing the Scales." *World Aquaculture* 28 (1997): 11–30.

Riche, M., and P. B. Brown. "Incorporation of Plant Protein Feedstuffs into Fish Meal Diets for Rainbow Trout Increases Phosphorus Availability." *Aquaculture Nutrition* 5 (1999): 101–105.

Twibell, Ronald G., and Paul B. Brown. "Optimum Dietary Crude Protein for Hybrid Tilapia *Oreochromis niloticus* x *O. aureus* Fed All-Plant Diets." *Journal of the World Aquaculture Society* 29 (1998): 9–16.

Twibell, Ronald G., Bruce A. Watkins, Laura Rogers, and Paul B. Brown. "Dietary Conjugated Linoleic Acids Alter Hepatic and Muscle Lipids in Hybrid Striped Bass. *Lipids* 35 (2000): 155–161.

Wu, Y. Victor, Ronald R. Rosati, and Paul B. Brown. "Effects of Lysine on Growth of Tilapia Fed Diets Rich in Corn Gluten Meal." *Cereal Chemistry* 75 (1998): 771–774.

Wu, Y. Victor, Kerry W. Tudor, Paul B. Brown, and Ronald R. Rosati. "Substitution of Plant Proteins or Meat and Bone Meal for Fish Meal in Diets of Nile Tilapia. *North American Journal of Aquaculture* 6 (1999): 58–63.

Paul B. Brown

"The Waiter," an anthropomorphic assembly of objects related to winemaking by Giuseppe Arcimboldo. © CHRISTIE'S IMAGES/ CORBIS.

ARAB SOCIETIES. *See* **Iran; Islam; Middle East; Africa: North Africa; Ramadan.**

ARCIMBOLDO, GIUSEPPE. Giuseppe Arcimboldo (also spelled Arcimboldi), was an Italian artist in Milan, Italy, between 1527 or 1530 and 1593. A painter, he also designed the stained glass windows for Milan's duomo. Arcimboldo's artwork, especially famous for its fragments of landscapes, flowers, herbs, vegetables, noodles, and cookware, was fashionable during the sixteenth century. His work became especially well known throughout Europe after the Austrian Holy Roman Emperor Rudolf II exhibited Arcimboldo's paintings in the many residences of the Habsburg imperial family. In fact Arcimboldo's bizarre pieces and grotesque portraits pleased the Habsburg emperor so much that he appointed the Italian painter Habsburg court painter at Vienna and Prague and also made him a count palatine. Arcimboldo also created the illusionistic sceneries for the Habsburg court theater.

Arcimboldo's most famous paintings had contemporary allegorical meanings and were unique compositions of edibles and culinary objects placed together in such a way as to represent the contours or heads of cooks, innkeepers, fishmongers, and symbolic figures related to the world of arts and sciences. He was not prolific, but his paintings of fantastic heads and social satirical subjects were popular. Many surrealists, including the Spanish artist Salvador Dalí, claim Arcimboldo as a surrealistic ancestor.

Arcimboldo's paintings and drawings in Austria are in Vienna's Kunsthistorisches Museum, in Graz, and in Innsbruck's Habsburg Schloss Amras. In Italy his works are preserved in Cremona, in Brescia, and in Florence's Uffizi Gallery. In the United States the Wadsworth Atheneum in Hartford, Connecticut, houses some of Arcimboldo's work.

See also **Art, Food in: Painting and the Visual Arts; Italy.**

Elisabeth Giacon Castleman

ARCTIC. The Arctic lies north of 70° latitude, marked by the tree line of the Subarctic. Few cultural groups occupy the Arctic: the Inuit live across the circumpolar region from northern Siberia throughout Greenland; the Aleuts and Yu'pik live on the coast and

110

islands of southwestern Alaska; and six major Saami groups live in the northern reaches of Scandinavia and western Russia. Arctic diets are unique because animal products are staples and plants are seasonal supplements. Inuit diets traditionally are composed of marine mammals, fish, caribou, small game, birds, and plants, while Saami depend on herded reindeer for milk and meat, fishing, gathering plants, and hunting small game and birds. The diets of Aleuts and Yu'pik are similar to that of the Inuit.

Inuit Food Lists and Categories

Inuit are famous for eating marine mammals, mostly seal (*natsiq*). Bearded seal (*oodguk*), walrus, polar bear (*nanuk*), narwhal (*tuugalik*), beluga (*qilalugaq*), and the large plankton-eating whales are preferred foods. Seabird, goose, and duck eggs (*maniq*), ptarmigan, ducks, and geese are also eaten. Arctic char (*iqaluk*), an anadromous fish, is preferred above sculpin (*kanuyak*) and cod (*oogak*). Shellfish are consumed, but are not a major food resource. Land mammals, caribou (*tuktu*, or reindeer), and Arctic hare are eaten to achieve a culturally desirable balance in the diet. Commonly eaten plants include kelp, sorrel, willow, blueberry, crowberry, soapberry, wintergreen, lichens, Eskimo carrots, and Eskimo peanuts. The vegetable matter from herbivore's stomachs is also consumed.

Animal foods are divided into those associated with the sea or ice and those associated with the land. Inuit are subsistence hunters and divide themselves into two categories, *Sikumiut* are "people of the ice" and *Taramiut* are "people of the land." These categories relate as well to hunting on the sea and on the land. For a community to maintain an ecological balance in the animals, subsistence rules are practiced. One rule is that, whenever possible, hunters seek to provide a mixed diet with animals of the sea and animals of the land. If this balance is not maintained in hunting, it is believed that the animals may disappear. Some years the seal are more prolific and available, so more seal is eaten. Other years more caribou or char will be abundant and consumed. The diet reflects this balance among land and sea animals. Hunters carefully respect the animals by maintaining the balance and thus ensure their future harvests. Plants are considered separately in the diet as treats that complement the standard animal fare when they are available. The most culturally desirable diet of the Inuit varies by mixing sea mammals, caribou, and Arctic char. The relative proportion of these three staples in the diet depends on the geographic location and local foraging practices of the group.

During the contact periods, European dry and canned staples were introduced as trade items across the Arctic. These new foods were slowly adopted into the Inuit diet. Foods became divided into two categories, "country" or foraged food produced by Inuit themselves, and store-bought or imported foods, obtained by trading furs or for cash. Common store-bought foods include tea, sugar, flour, biscuits, and breads. Other imported foods include canned fruit and jam, meats, fish, and vegetables. Store foods are considered inferior and incapable of sustaining health for anyone raised eating country food.

Meal customs and food distribution. Hunting and food sharing form the core of Inuit society. When hunters return with fresh game or fish, it is distributed for consumption according to social rules. This occurs at least several times a week. Meals are communal and all animal foods are shared, distributed first within the community and then within the household. During the distribution, fresh, or uncooked, meats are eaten by anyone who is hungry. The remaining portions are distributed according to the kinship or friendship relationship of the receiver to the hunter. The hunter, his wife, father, mother, or a related elder conducts this process. While this food remains in the household, family members eat it communally at least once a day.

The typical traditional meal includes fresh, boiled, fried, or grilled meats, organs, and soft bones. The food is served on the ground outdoors or on the floor of the shelter. The animal food is cut away from the butchered carcass with the personal knife of the individual and eaten without any other utensils. If the animal food is boiled, its broth is drunk after eating the meat. Everyone is expected to eat until hunger subsides. All visitors to a home are expected to partake of whatever game is available. Hoarding or overeating food is not acceptable. Birds, eggs, plants, and small fish or shellfish are usually eaten by individuals, but are shared on demand with anyone who is hungry.

As a result of contact with Europeans, drinking heavily sugared tea and eating bannock or some form of bread has come to follow the consumption of animal food. The bannock is made from flour, water or milk, and fat (lard, vegetable shortening, or caribou or seal fat) and baked on a rock or in a frying pan over a fire. Tobacco is then shared. Before black tea was introduced, herbs were collected for making teas.

Meal patterns are guided by hunger and age. Young children and babies are fed frequently on demand until they reach five or six. The adult demand for food varies, but fewer meals are eaten in winter than in spring, summer, and fall. On average, one full meal and two or three tea breaks are taken between sleeping. Elders eat less as they grow older, but drink sweetened tea more often. Immature seal, cached meat, and fish are favored by the very old individuals.

Men, women, and children eat together. The men eat with long knives (*sevik*) as they squat near the animal food, and women use the *ulu*, the traditional curved knife of Inuit women. Children use smaller versions of adult knives as soon as they can control them. Older infants and toddlers eat premasticated foods from their mothers, but are typically breast-fed until they are four or five. Orphaned or adopted babies are fed seal broth.

Food preparation. Food preparation varies by season and environment. At camp, Inuit share the communal feast daily. "Fresh" (uncooked) seal (*mikiayak*) or other marine mammals are prepared within a short time after the animal is captured. Camp dwellers are called by children to the feast. The hunter or a designated relative, typically his wife, opens the animal after the body has had time to "cool." Those who are feeling cold would eat first, as the rich blood (*auok*) and warm chunks of exposed liver (*tingook*) warm the individuals' bodies and restore health and well-being. The blood not consumed is drained and

the animal gutted. Organ meats, especially kidney (*taktu*), are eaten or fed to dogs along with the fat scraped from the skin and other waste. Intestines are saved, and the outer covering chewed. A delicacy among the North Baffin Inuit is chopped fat and brains mixed with the animal's blood (*allupiauoq*) in the body cavity before the meat is eaten. Eyeballs are sucked but not swallowed. The skin is saved for household and clothing use. During hungry periods, when animals are scarce, the skin, scraped on both sides, can also be eaten. Seal "hips" are preferred by men in the Eastern Arctic, while women enjoy the tenderloin

112

along the spine, the backbone, and the ribs. Shoulders, flippers, and forelimbs are eaten by both men and women.

Marine mammals can also be eaten frozen (*quok*), sliced thin as the individual eats from the carcass, or the meat can be aged. To prepare aged seal, for example, seal is packed in its skin and stored a few days or as long as three weeks. Rotted seal is cached in the fall for consumption the next spring or summer. *Ooyuk* is soup made by boiling meat in fresh water, and seasoned with kelp. Salt or dry soup mix often replaces kelp. Chunks of meat are eaten out of the pot, which is usually set over a seal oil lamp or an open hearth. Cupfuls of rich broth (*kiyuk*) are drunk. Seal is deep-fat fried in the summer or grilled on flat rocks over heather fires. Seal oil is produced by pounding the fat. This rendered oil is then stored in a seal bladder to be eaten with plants or raw or dried fish. In spring and summer, foods are cooked on heather fires, which gives them a wonderful herbal taste. Polar bear and walrus were once consumed fresh, or raw, but they are only eaten cooked, due to concern about Arctic trichinosis. Narwhal and beluga whale are prized for their sweet skin (*muqtuq*). The meats of these animals and other whales can also be eaten prepared as other meats are. Polar bear organ meats are never eaten.

While seal typically dominates the diet, caribou (*tuqtu*) is also widely consumed, prepared in ways similar to the seal. Caribou meat is also cut into pieces and hung to air-dry for storage. Birds are captured, their feathers plucked, and then eaten uncooked. Eggs are sucked. Arctic hare is boiled as *ooyuk*, never eaten uncooked. Arctic char are eaten fresh, filleted into three boneless pieces hung from the head, or partially air-dried (*serata*) or freeze-dried (*pisi*). The fish can be boiled as *ooyuk* or fried (*satoya*), or grilled as well. Shellfish are eaten raw or boiled, but are rare in the Eastern Arctic.

Seasonal variation. Seal, walrus, and polar bear typically dominate winter foods. *Ooyuk* is popular in winter, as are frozen foods. As the sun returns daylight to the land, spring begins and groups of related Inuit begin to congregate for camping and hunting seal. Short hunting trips include fresh seal picnics. Easter is marked by the spring caribou hunt and feast. Once the ice begins to break up, Inuit cannot travel safely. Whatever foods can be captured near land-based camps are eaten. When dried caribou, fish, and cached marine mammals are exhausted, the diet is aged seal oil with plants and, perhaps, fresh fish. Summer continues with full daylight, marked by open-water sealing and whale hunts, and *muqtuq* is prepared and consumed. Summer fish camps produce large numbers of char to eat fresh, frozen, or dried. Plants are gathered during long walks, mostly by women and children. Seal and caribou are fried and grilled. In August, the sun begins to leave the northern sky and early fall begins. A fall caribou hunt culls the migrating herds. Bulls are especially desired because of their rich fat. The quiet winter season returns and the annual cycle begins again.

Foods of the Saami

Saami occupy the Arctic and Subarctic. These people were colonized in the thirteenth century and little is known about their indigenous foodways prior to colonization.

Saami lived traditionally by following the herds of reindeer seasonally as the animals fed on lowland lichens and mushrooms in early spring and winter and highland grasses in summer. The bulls were culled from the herds in October, December, and January to provide meat for fall and winter feasting and storage by smoking and drying.

Saami, like Inuit, eat caribou, or reindeer, using all the edible parts of the animal. Like the Inuit, they eat their foods cooked, boiled, smoked, and roasted. Reindeer meat is boiled in a thick soup that resembles Inuit *ooyuk*. Meat is eaten out of hand from the pot and the gravy scooped up in a cup to be drunk. Saami drink reindeer milk and use it to make cheese, which is often smoked, something Inuit do not do. While some Saami are known for reindeer herding, other groups and frequently eat fish. Both Saami groups, however, consume fish, land mammals, plants, and birds. Saami diets have been greatly influenced by northern European cooking patterns and foods for the past seven hundred years.

See also **Canada: Native Peoples**; **Fish**; **Fishing**; **Inuit**; **Lapps**; **Mammals, Sea**; **Siberia**.

BIBLIOGRAPHY

Balikci, Asen. *The Netsilik Eskimo.* Garden City, N.Y.: Natural History Press, 1970.

Berti, P. R., S. E. Hamilton, O. Receveur, and H. V. Kuhnlein. "Food Use and Nutrient Adequacy in Baffin Inuit Children and Adolescents." *Canadian Journal of Dietary Practice and Research* 60, 2 (1999): 63–70.

Birket-Smith, Kaj. *The Eskimos.* Translated from the Danish by W. E. Calvert. Revised by C. Daryll Forde. London: Methuen, 1959.

Feldman, Kerry D. "Subsistence Beluga Whale Hunting in Alaska: A View from Eschscholtz Bay." In *Contemporary Alaskan Native Economies,* edited by Steve J. Langdon, pp. 153–171. Lanham, Md.: University Press of America, 1986.

Fienup-Riordan, Ann. *The Nelson Island Eskimo: Social Structure and Ritual Distribution.* Anchorage: Alaska Pacific University Press, 1983.

Ingold, Tim. *The Skolt Lapps Today.* New York: Cambridge University Press, 1976.

Jorgensen, Joseph G. *Oil Age Eskimos.* Berkeley: University of California Press, 1990.

Kuhnlein, H.V., R. Soueida, and O. Receveur. "Dietary Nutrient Profiles of Canadian Baffin Island Inuit Differ by Food Source, Season and Age." *Journal of the American Dietetic Association* 96 (1996): 155–162.

Kuhnlein, Harriet V., and Nancy J. Turner. *Traditional Plant Foods of Canadian Indigenous Peoples: Nutrition, Botany, and Use.* Volume 8, *Food and Nutrition in History and Anthropology,* edited by Solomon Katz. Philadelphia: Gordon and Breach, 1991.

Lowenstein, Tom. *Ancient Land, Sacred Whale: The Inuit Hunt and Its Rituals.* London: Bloomsbury, 1993.

Matthiasson, John S. *Living on the Land: Change among the Inuit of Baffin Island.* Peterborough, Ont.: Broadview Press, 1992.

Smith, Eric Alden. *The Inujjuamiut Foraging Strategies: Evolutionary Ecology of an Arctic Hunting Economy.* New York: Aldine de Gruyter, 1991.

Wolfe, Robert J. "The Economic Efficiency of Food Production in a Western Eskimo Population." In *Contemporary Alaskan Native Economies,* edited by Steve J. Langdon, pp. 101–120. Lanham, Md.: University Press of America, 1986.

Kristen Borré

ART, FOOD IN.

This entry includes five subentries:
Film and Television
Literature
Opera
Painting and the Visual Arts
Poetry

FILM AND TELEVISION

Food has been a popular and versatile film prop since the silent film era. It's a perfect cinematic prop—simple to prepare, readily understood by the viewer, and able to provide countless ways to move a story line along and advance the theme of a film, be it political, sexual, interpersonal, historical, or even mystery. At times food plays a supporting role enabling the main character to further the plot. At other times food itself plays a starring role.

The first and most enduring food prop is probably the pie, largely because it is easy to make and easily aimed at a person we don't necessarily want to hurt but whose dignity is at stake. According to Lorna Woodsum Riley's *Reel Meals Movie Lover's Cookbook,* Mabel Normand launched the first pie in film when she spontaneously threw someone's custard cream pie at Fatty Arbuckle in a Keystone Studio silent film, *A Noise from the Deep* (1913). This act garnered lots of laughs so Keystone studios, under the direction of Mack Sennett, repeated it in numerous other films, as did such silent film stars as Laurel and Hardy, Buster Keaton, the Three Stooges, and Charlie Chaplin. Blake Edwards, in an homage to the silent era, placed Tony Curtis in the midst of an enormous number of flying pies in *The Great Race* (1965), and Nora Ephron in *Heartburn,* her semiautobiographical novel that was made into a film in 1986, tells her philandering husband just what she thinks of him by squishing a Key lime pie in his face.

Pies weren't the only food used in early films. Laurel and Hardy were major advocates of food in film, as best revealed in *A Swank Dinner Party.* Since they were the waiters at that party, it was, of course, anything but

swank. Hardy slips on a banana peel while carrying a huge cake, and even the swanky guests wreak havoc trying to nab the cherry in their fruit cocktail.

The scenes most remembered in some films are those in which food has played a supporting role. In *The Gold Rush* (1925, reedited in 1942) writer, director, and star Charlie Chaplin best demonstrated the dramatic possibilities of food. Finding himself freezing, starving, and snowbound in an Alaskan cabin with another prospector at Thanksgiving, Chaplin is unwilling to spend the holiday without an appropriate meal. So he boils one of his boots, carves and delicately plates it, offers his companion the choice of "sole" or "boot," and proceeds to eat the shoelace as though it were spaghetti. Simultaneously funny and touching, it is the film's most remarkable scene. Chaplin used food to make a political statement in *Modern Times* (1936) by showing the plight of the worker, in this case an assembly-line worker, and the heartlessness of management. To speed things up, a robot is devised to feed workers so they can continue working. In a hilarious scene Chaplin is given a meal of soup and corn on the cob by a robot that eventually runs amok.

The seduction scene in the Oscar-winning *Tom Jones* (1963) created a big stir because of the way in which food was used in an overtly sexual manner. Albert Finney, at his best as the womanizing Tom Jones, seduces actress Joyce Redman whom he has just met. Dining together, they consume chicken, oysters, and wine in a manner that grows more deliberate and increasingly sensual.

Woody Allen used food in *Annie Hall* (1977) to illustrate the cultural and ethnic differences of the film's protagonists. Midwestern WASP Diane Keaton is shown ordering a pastrami sandwich on white bread with mayo and tomatoes—a shock to Allen's New York Jewish character (pastrami sandwiches are always on rye with mustard). In *Five Easy Pieces* (1970), restaurant dining was difficult for Jack Nicholson, who had to use convoluted means just to get some toast, while Meg Ryan in *When Harry Met Sally* (1989) dictated in no uncertain terms exactly the way she wanted food served to her during lunch in a deli with Billy Crystal. This same dining scene also provided the perfect background for the film's most memorable scene—the fake orgasm.

Food and murder occur in equal proportion in Mafia movies. Francis Ford Coppola used lots of food in the first (1972) and third (1990) installments of *The Godfather.* Marlon Brando playing Don Corleone is shot while choosing fruit at an outdoor stand. And, after a rubout, Clemenza shows his priorities when he tells his partner "leave the gun, take the cannoli." Later Clemenza shows young Michael Corleone how to cook spaghetti with meatballs and sausage just in case he goes to jail and needs to know how. Near the end of the third *Godfather* film, Eli Wallach as Don Altobello waxes nostalgic about the virtues of olive oil just before he dies from eating a poisoned cannoli.

Director Martin Scorsese in *GoodFellas* (1990) presented a jail scene with actor Paul Sorvino carefully slicing garlic with a razorblade while a cellmate is preparing spaghetti sauce with beef, veal, and pork. Also on the menu are bread, cheese, prosciutto, steak, salami, peppers, and onions. This well-fed group of Mafia jailbirds sits down to eat a lavish meal with Frank Sinatra crooning in the background. Scorsese also showed he could film elegant dining. In *The Age of Innocence* (1993) there is a well-researched banquet scene resplendent with a floral and ice sculpture centerpiece, elaborate English bone china and silver tableware, impeccable service, and restrained table manners reflective of the late 1800s. The diners enjoyed oysters, fish, and other perfectly presented delicacies.

A septet of films has had particular success in casting food in a starring role. First among them is *Babette's Feast* (1987). Drawing from Isak Dinesen's short story, Gabriel Alex directed and wrote the screenplay for this Oscar-winning best foreign film set in nineteenth-century Denmark. Two adult sisters, the daughters of a pastor, live in a remote village where they have dedicated themselves to the service of God and relinquished all worldly desires. Babette, played by Stéphane Audran, is a French political refugee who is taken in by the sisters in return for working as their housekeeper and cook. Their meals consist largely of a humble gruel of bread soaked in ale. Some years after Babette's arrival, the sisters decide to hold a dinner to honor the hundredth anniversary of their father's birth and ask Babette to cook. She has recently won the lottery and sends her nephew to Paris to collect the necessary ingredients. Unknown to the sisters, she is a former chef, and she cooks for the sisters and the members of their little church the best feast ever shown on film. It begins with Potage à la Tortue, followed by Blini Demidoff aux Caviar Russe, Caille en Sarcophage avec Sauce Perigourdine, La Salade, Les Fromages, Baba au Rhum et Fruits Confit, Champagne Veuve Cliquot 1860, Clos de Vougeot 1845 wine, and coffee. Although her humble and religious diners had vowed to remain unaffected by the food, they are quickly overwhelmed by the mastery of this culinary artist who forever changed their lives.

Tampopo (1986), kind of a spaghetti western with a culinary theme, which was directed by Juzo Itami, demonstrated Japan's seriousness about food. Tampopo, a widow with a son, seeks the recipe for the perfect noodle to serve in her restaurant. Assisted by a truck driver who would have looked more comfortable on a horse, there is much intrigue along the way to noodle perfection. What makes this such a good food movie is the inclusion of a series of unrelated but very smart food vignettes ranging from sexual seduction to a lesson in the proper way for the Japanese to eat Italian noodles.

Taiwanese writer and director Ang Lee serves up a multitude of enticing dishes in *Eat Drink Man Woman* (1994). The film opens with five minutes of master chef

Charlie Chaplin in the 1925 movie *The Gold Rush* demonstrates the art of eating a boiled shoe. © BETTMANN/CORBIS.

Chu, played by Sihung Lung, chopping, dicing, steaming, and frying in what is, to date, the best sequence of food preparation on film. Chef Chu, a widower with three grown daughters, tries to keep his family together by serving sumptuous Sunday dinners. He prepares enormous meals including steamed deer spareribs with ginger in a pumpkin pot and lotus flower soup plus one hundred other dishes all prepared for the film by famous Taiwanese chefs. Lee said he had to shoot each dish within eight seconds to capture perfect steam, a requirement he found very stressful.

La Grand Bouffe (1973) is a French film in which four men gather at a country house to eat themselves to death with fabulous food prepared by one of them who, fortunately, is a chef. A nonstop display of gorgeous food both cooked and uncooked includes the best wild boar, lamb from Mont-Saint-Michel, oysters, calves' heads, cod, beautiful pâtés, tarts, quail on skewers, pastas, pizzas, pullets, and pigs to name just a few. This film is an amalgam of beautiful food, ongoing sex, and a dismaying array of bodily reactions to too much food. Although it remains unknown why these four successful men want to eat themselves to death, the film does portray the horrors of excess. A food credit is given to the French store Fauchon.

Master chef Paul Bocuse is credited for the beautiful food in *Who Is Killing the Great Chefs of Europe?* (1978), a whodunit filmed in some of Europe's best restaurants. Worth viewing just to see Robert Morley play Max Vandevere, the disdainful and pretentious editor of *Epicurious Magazine*, the film portrays the trouble that begins when he selects four chefs to prepare a dinner for the queen of England. Jealousy sets in, murder ensues, and chefs are killed in the manner in which they prepare their signature dishes. There are beautiful shots of baked pigeon en croûte, pressed duck, the fish market in Venice, and the interiors of legendary restaurants

The Cook, the Thief, His Wife, and Her Lover (1989) is a complex and beautiful film in every way. Directed by Peter Greenaway, each frame looks like a Dutch genre painting. Costumes designed by Jean Paul Gaultier and a haunting musical score add to the film's lavishness. Here food provides the basis for magnificent still life frames while the lush red restaurant and eerie kitchen provide ongoing tableaux and the setting for a story about a loutish thief who thinks that dining in a fine restaurant elevates him to a higher social class. Not all is beautiful, however, in this film that also portrays denigrating sex scenes and cannibalism.

Laura Esquivel's novel *Like Water for Chocolate* (1993) was written as a prelude to a screenplay and includes recipes. In the film, directed by Alfonso Arau, Mexican family food is the star, and much of it has mystical properties that can start fires and evoke passion, sorrow, and uncontrollable yearning when it is cooked by the romantically unfulfilled Tita.

The decade of the nineties brought hefty expense accounts and ambitious restaurant dining in the United States. Coincident with this came three American films that explore restaurant life in remarkably different ways. *Big Night*, produced by Stanley Tucci in 1996, again explores the cook as an artist, much as *Babette's Feast* did, but within the difficult framework of cooking authentic ethnic cuisine in 1950s America. In 1998 Shari Springer Berman and Robert Pulcini directed a documentary entitled *Off the Menu: The Last Days of Chasen's*. Filmed just before the closing of the famed Los Angeles restaurant, it is a close look at a bygone era of Hollywood glamour when stars and movie moguls, dressed to the nines, made nightly appearances at their regular tables in this family restaurant where they were treated like valued family members and catered to in ways unimaginable in today's restaurant. *Dinner Rush* captured a very different restaurant scene, that of New York circa 2001. Directed by Bob Giraldi and shot in his own Tribeca restaurant, Gigino, *Dinner Rush* forthrightly portrays the downside of the restaurant business with its intrigues, food fads, trendiness, fickle customers, power struggles, critic corruption, and more. What with all of this, the film is edgy and fascinating and most likely tells it like it is.

Television

Food in television has mostly been of the "how to" cooking show genre. Gerry Schremp notes in *Celebration of American Food* (p. 99) that James Beard led the parade of cooking shows with weekly appearances in 1946, followed by Dione Lucas in 1947. Television pictures were black-and-white then, and only eight thousand homes had sets. Julia Child jump-started cooking shows with her 1963 inaugural series for public television, which was the leader in the production of such programs. Popular among viewers were the *Victory Garden* series and Jeff Smith as the *Frugal Gourmet*. Public television tends to feature cooking teachers and cookbook writers who are basically home cooks, creating food meant to be replicated at home. Capitalizing on an undeniable interest in good food, the genre catapulted to new and different levels when an entire cable network devoted only to food, the Television Food Network, was launched in November 1993, initially reaching three million homes and expanding to more than sixty million by the year 2002. The network experimented with a restaurant review show, a call-in show devoted to dieting and healthy eating, and, most notably, a one-hour live news show entitled "Food News and Views" that was, as its name suggests, devoted solely to the topic of food and drink. As the genre has matured, more attention has been given to the entertainment value of "cooking" shows, giving way to contests such as *Ready, Set, Cook* and Japan's entry, called *Iron Chef*, which features some unusual food video and involves a panel that judges the best dishes created during the time frame of the show. Attractive and youthful celebrity chefs have replaced home cooks on these shows, and celebrity food with refined ingredients and architectural presentation has replaced the homier presentations of earlier public television shows. A notably successful Food Network show has been that of Emeril Lagasse, whose catch phrases and natural good humor have made him its star. The Food Network, in turn, has given Emeril a live audience with which to interact, a band, and numerous other gimmicks to hold viewer attention. Martha Stewart became a television network cooking star in the late 1990s, combining her talents into a multimedia television, radio, cookbook, and magazine package.

Cooking shows are rarely done in real time. The standard format has the cook combining ready-to-cook ingredients, then going to a finished dish to show how it should look—which is usually splendid since television studios have state-of-the-art kitchens staffed with professional cooks and stylists who turn out elegant creations that either inspire or intimidate the viewer.

The History Channel broke new ground by presenting a series of documentaries entitled *America Eats: History on a Bun* (1999). More than just bun food, the histories of fried chicken, ice cream, soda pop, and pizza were explored with excellent use of archival footage showing how food and eaters alike used to look in America.

See also **Beard, James**; **Child, Julia**; **Humor, Food in**; **Styling of Food**.

BIBLIOGRAPHY

International Movie Data Base. Available at www.IMDB.com

Maltin, Leonard. *Leonard Maltin's 2002 Movie & Video Guide.* New York: Penguin Putnam, 2002.

Poole, Gayle. *Reel Meals, Set Meals: Food in Film and Theatre.* Sydney: Currency Press, 1999.

Riley, Lorna Woodsum. *Reel Meals Movie Lover's Cookbook.* Lombard, Ill.: Wallace-Homestead, 1987.

Schremp, Gerry. *Celebration of American Food: Four Centuries in the Melting Pot.* Golden, Colo.: Fulcrum, 1996.

Doris Weisberg

LITERATURE

François Rabelais in his irreverent and influential sixteenth-century novel *Gargantua and Pantagruel* writes "[t]he satirist is correct when he says that Messer Gaster—Sir Belly—is the true master of all the arts. . . . To this chivalrous monarch we are all bound to show reverence, swear obedience, and give honour" (pp. 570–571). According to twentieth-century literary critic Mikhail Bakhtin, Gaster is portrayed by Rabelais not as the creator of society, but more as the embodiment of the organized human collective. Because appetite is located in the viscera, "[t]he bowels study the world in order to conquer and subjugate it" (p. 301).

What better place to begin a discussion of food in literature than with Rabelais's novel in which references to food appear on nearly every page. This novel pokes fun at the sanctimoniousness of the hierarchy of the Catholic Church and the feudal elite by drawing on the humorous and vulgar language of the marketplace and the carnivalesque imagery of clowns, fools, giants, and dwarfs that were an integral part of medieval society. In carnival, the social hierarchy of everyday life is leveled, and individuals become united in a festival in which all participants are actors, and communal laughter mocks everyday society.

It is the belly and its appetites that give rise to the festival, and feasts of course inevitably accompany any festival. Such feasts celebrate the human encounter with and triumph over the world, in which food represents the entire process of cultivation, harvest, storage, trade, and preparation. Humanity devours the products of nature without being devoured by the world. This encounter takes place in "the open, biting, chewing, rending mouth" during carnival festivities (Bakhtin, p. 281).

Because of the excesses characteristic of celebratory feasting, Rabelais portrays his larger-than-life characters as capable of devouring much more than was humanly possible. Listen, for example, as the giant Pantagruel calls forth a feast for his men—with their grotesque bellies and wide-open throats—after a military victory in which only one opponent survived:

> He had refreshment brought and a feast spread for them on the shore with great jollity; and he made them drink too, with their bellies to the ground, and their prisoner as well . . . except that the poor devil was not sure whether Pantagruel was not going to devour him whole; which he might have done, so wide was his throat . . . and the poor fellow, once in his mouth, would not have amounted to more than a grain of millet in an ass's throat. (p. 250)

Food imagery in *Gargantua and Pantagruel* is just one of the more extreme examples of the feast in literature.

The jovial, celebratory feast, the culmination of the process of growing food, in which humankind in social solidarity encounters the world with an open mouth, naturally gives rise to excellence in conversation, to wise speech, and therefore to literature.

In Plato's *Symposium*, for example, a group of prominent Athenians gather to discuss the nature of love over an elaborate meal, during which Socrates is both lauded for his wisdom and mocked for his homeliness. The feast also is a celebration and validation of a community, and a celebration of victory, such as a successful marriage, military victory, or treaty. Feasts, therefore, bring to a close several of Shakespeare's romantic comedies, such as *As You Like It* and the *Tempest*.

In Fielding's eighteenth-century novel *The History of Tom Jones, a Foundling*, for example, the hero's general lust for life is portrayed through his appetite for food and sex together. In the nineteenth century, when Victorian British society developed ambivalent feelings toward human appetites in general, Charles Dickens portrays one of his best-known characters, Oliver Twist, being thrown out of an orphanage for having more of an appetite than the authorities deem fitting.

Food in Culture and Memory

Feasts and food in literature, however, portray more than the mere physical appetite for food and a human triumph over nature in festivals. Each culture, with its own tradition of literature, also maintains its own distinct cuisine and distinct traditional rules that govern acts of eating. The food traditions of a community are composed not just of recipes, but of the methods and technologies by which foods are grown, gathered, stored, prepared, served, and thrown out. Such traditions include also culturally transmitted rules that govern ideas of health and cleanliness as related to food. Furthermore, each community that gives rise to a distinct literature necessarily also maintains culturally specific rules governing foods that are especially valued and foods that are especially shunned and controlling the contexts in which particular foods may or may not be eaten.

In events that involve the serving of food—from snacks to meals to festival feasts—networks of reciprocity among food preparers, as well as the relationships between those doing the cooking and those being served, become articulated. Food and events in which food is served, therefore, help define the social organization and cultural identity of the very communities that give rise to distinct literary traditions.

Because food customs call forth such a labyrinth of associations on the part of individual writers, and because the inherent sensuality of food involves not only the senses of smell and taste, but also the other senses, food is capable of evoking an avalanche of memories and feelings. Food imagery may appear, therefore, in literature as a source of deeply embedded associations that lead into the depths of individual and cultural memory. Perhaps showing the influence of Freudian thought, Marcel Proust's *In Search of Lost Time* (commonly known as *Remembrance of Things Past*) evolves from the narrator's memories brought out of the unconscious and into his conscious mind as he ate crumbs of "squat, plump little cakes called 'petites madeleines'," that he had dipped in a cup of tea:

> And soon, mechanically, disspirited after a dreary day with the prospect of a depressing morrow, I raised to my lips a spoonful of the tea in which I had soaked a morsel of the cake. No sooner had the warm liquid mixed with the crumbs touched my palate than a shudder ran through me and I stopped, intent upon the extraordinary thing that was happening to me. . . .
>
> Undoubtedly what is thus palpitating in the depths of my being must be the image, the visual memory which, being linked to taste, is trying to follow it into my conscious mind. . . .
>
> And suddenly the memory reveals itself. The taste was that of the little piece of madeleine which on Sunday mornings at Combray (because on those mornings I did not go out before mass), when I went to say good morning to her in her bedroom, my aunt Léonie used to give me, dipping it first in her own cup of tea or tisane. (pp. 60–63)

The Meal as Communion

Despite the availability of individual associations about food to a writer, it is the sharing of food within distinct food cultures that continues to be the major focus of literature about food. Furthermore, this sharing of food continues to be commonly portrayed in literature as a communion, even though the public festival of the late Middle Ages has, in modern society, become private. The famous Christmas feast that concludes Dickens's sentimental children's story, *A Christmas Carol*, with its flaming plum pudding and its transformation of the miserly Ebenezer Scrooge into a more generous soul, is a prototype.

The family dinner as a private religious festival is perhaps more clearly seen in Virginia Woolf's novel *To the Lighthouse*, in which a private dinner of *boeuf en daube* gives a well-housed coherence to an otherwise dark and fragmented world outside of the home. The cook and main character, Mrs. Ramsay, leads in this communion. In preparation, Mrs. Ramsay lights the candles,

> and the faces on both sides of the table were brought nearer by the candlelight, and composed, as they had not been in the twilight, into a party round a table, for the night was now shut off by panes of glass, which, far from giving any accurate view of the outside world, rippled it so strangely that here, inside the room, seemed to be order and dry land; there, outside, a reflection in which things wavered and vanished, waterily. (p. 108)

Expanding on the idea of the meal as a private festive occasion, Woolf writes that Mrs. Ramsay serves the main course of beef:

> And she peered into the dish, with its shiny walls and its confusion of savoury brown and yellow meats, and its bay leaves and its wine, and thought, This will celebrate the occasion—a curious sense rising in her, at once freakish and tender, of celebrating a festival. (p. 111)

A description of a fruit basket in the center of the table—the literary equivalent of a painting of a still life, writes Bettina Knapp, author of an essay about this dinner scene—concludes the description of the whole meal. The still shapes and the rich textures and colors in the basket of fruit represent, in peaceful form, the emotional complexities contained within the character of Mrs. Ramsay herself, and the serenity born of that particular meal.

Meals portrayed in literature as moments of light and warmth in the dark and cold are not uncommon. In Herman Melville's *Moby Dick*, Ishmael and Queequeg, the Fijian cannibal, share a meal of clam chowder in a jovial inn in cold and wintry Nantucket, Mass., just as they had shared a warm bed together earlier in New Bedford on a bitter New England night. Ishmael comments that to appreciate warmth it is best to feel as if you are "the one warm spark in the heart of an arctic crystal" (p. 48).

In perfect contrast to the social solidarity of the shared meal, Captain Ahab compares the life of isolation that he has led with the life of community that could have been his had he not been obsessed with the white whale. He states this contrast in the language of food as metaphor, and shared food—in this case, the breaking of bread—as communion:

> When I think of this life I have led; the desolation of solitude it has been; the masoned, walled-town of a Captain's exclusiveness, which admits but small entrance to any sympathy from the green country without—oh, weariness! heaviness! . . . and how for forty years, I have fed on dry salted fare—fit emblem of the dry nourishment of my soul!—when the poorest landsman has had fresh fruit to his daily hand, and broken the world's fresh bread to my mouldy crusts . . . aye, aye! What a forty-years' fool—fool—old fool has Ahab been! (pp. 477–78)

The Feast as a Focal Point of Plot

While plot in literature most often focuses on the vicissitudes of human relationships, on love, conquest, betrayal, and loss, rather than food, the feast—as both the culmination of one process and the beginning of another—naturally appears as a fulcrum on which plots can turn. Meals and feasts, then, often provide the framework for events. Meals that are not portrayed as placid communions, therefore, reveal the contradictions brewing in the plot. In Homer's *Odyssey*, it is just after a feast of the suitors, which the hero attends disguised as a beggar, that Odysseus announces his return and slaughters his rivals. In Shakespeare's *Hamlet*, the juxtaposition of the wedding of the bereaved queen too soon after the funeral of her husband elicits from Hamlet himself the ominous quip that "the funeral bak'd meats did coldly furnish forth

118

the marriage tables" (Act I, scene ii, lines 180–181). By juxtaposing two antithetical feasts, Shakespeare warns the reader that foul play, yet to be revealed in full, has taken place.

In *Beloved*, the 1987 novel by Toni Morrison, the central tragic episode of the story—an escaped slave's murder of her own young daughter to prevent her from being taken back into slavery—is immediately preceded by a feast that celebrates the young mother's freedom. This feast begins innocently enough when the man who ferried the woman across the Ohio River to freedom brings two buckets of blackberries to the family to be made into pies. To the pies, the family incrementally adds turkey, rabbit, fried perch, corn pudding, peas, various breads, and desserts, and invites the whole community to attend. "Ninety people . . . ate so well and laughed so much, it made them angry," Morrison writes (p. 136). They were angered that this family would celebrate so proudly while others still suffered. Yet the reader knows from the beginning that the celebration is premature and therefore doomed: the young woman's husband, the son of the older woman with whom she has come to live, remains in slavery and in danger. The plot turns from victory to tragedy on the fulcrum of the feast.

An excessive meal can betray other excesses latent in the personalities of the characters. In *Anna Karenina* by Leo Tolstoy, the characters Levin and Oblonsky share a meal that seems vulgar in its quantity. During this meal of three dozen oysters, *soupe printanière*, turbot with sauce Beaumarchaise, roast beef, *poulard à l'estragon*, parmesan cheese, *macédoine de fruits*, vodka, champagne, and two bottles of Chablis—a gustatory metaphor for Tolstoy's opinion of the excesses of nineteenth-century Russian aristocrats—Levin speaks of his desire to propose to a woman half his age. Oblonsky, who himself has just been caught being unfaithful to his wife, encourages him. The food and conversation at the table encapsulate the magnitude of human desire that Tolstoy lays out in his novel as a whole, and cautions of the price that all pay for seeking the satiation of their desires.

Meals, Communion, and Counterculture in the American Novel

While in modern Western literature communion and meaning can be found around the dinner table, in the tradition of the American antihero, the bourgeois dinner table has sometimes been portrayed as stuffy and stultifying. Mark Twain perhaps began this tradition in *Huckleberry Finn* when he describes Huck complaining about having to abide by social manners at the Widow Douglas's house:

When you got to the table, you couldn't go right to eating, but you had to wait for the widow to tuck down her head and grumble a little over the victuals, though there warn't really anything the matter with them,— that is, nothing only everything was cooked by itself. In a barrel of odds and ends it is different; things get

mixed up, and the juice kind of swaps around, and the things go better. (p. 4)

Countercultural characters similar to Huck appear recurrently in American literature. In this tradition, the wild out-of-doors, away from the social conventions of the dinner table, engender their own religious sensibility. In its suspicion of conventional modernity, this countercultural sensibility relates to the conventional the way that the carnivalesque related to feudal culture. Sometimes this suspicion of the conventional can also be symbolized by food, by a countercultural communion of sorts.

Ray Smith in Jack Kerouac's *Dharma Bums* speaks of himself as a religious wanderer, hops a train going north from Los Angeles, and shares a counter-communion in the freight car with an old hobo:

The little bum was sitting crosslegged at his end before a pitiful repast of one can of sardines. I took pity on him and went over and said, "How about a little wine to warm you up? Maybe you'd like some bread and cheese with your sardines?" (p. 4)

The communion on the freight train ends with the little bum "warming up to the wine and talking and finally whipping out a tiny slip of paper which contained a prayer by Saint Teresa announcing that after her death she will return to the earth by showering it with roses from heaven, forever, for all living creatures." (p. 5).

Whether in a public festival, a private bourgeois home, or in a distinctly nonbourgeois boxcar, the sharing of food in harmony is indeed a blessing, as the saintly shower of roses ending this one literary meal indicates.

Food and Social Healing

Finally, another strand of food literature in the United States is represented by *Dinner at the Homesick Restaurant* by Anne Tyler and *Home at the End of the World* by Michael Cunningham. In Tyler's work, Ezra, the youngest child of a broken home, opens a restaurant called Homesick Restaurant, where he fervently hopes the world's emotionally wounded will find healing in the nurturing environment of a restaurant that serves home-style cooking. In *Home at the End of the World*, a nontraditional family opens the Home Café in Woodstock, N.Y., hoping to offer the world honest, home-cooked food, when traditional fare has become so processed and standardized that it fails to meet the needs of a materialistic, spiritually bereft American nation.

See also **Brillat-Savarin, Anthelme; Etymology of Food; Feasts, Festivals, and Fasts; Folklore, Food in; Herodotus; Language about Food; Luxury; Metaphor, Food as; Petronius; Rabelais, François; Sensation and the Senses; Shrove Tuesday; Symbol, Food as.**

BIBLIOGRAPHY

Bakhtin, Mikhail. *Rabelais and His World.* Translated by Helene Iswolsky. Bloomington, Ind.: Indiana University Press, 1984. Originally published in 1968.

Bevan, David, ed. *Literary Gastronomy*. Amsterdam: Rodolpi, 1988.

Cunningham, Michael. *Home at the End of the World*. New York: Farrar, Straus, and Giroux, 1990.

Dickens, Charles. *A Christmas Carol*. New York: Penguin, 1990. Originally published in 1843.

Dickens, Charles. *Oliver Twist*. Edited by Fred Kaplan. New York: Norton, 1993. Originally published between 1837 and 1839.

Fielding, Henry. *The History of Tom Jones*. Edited by R. P. C. Mutter. Baltimore, Md.: Penguin, 1966. Originally published in 1749.

Homer. *The Odyssey*. Translated by Robert Fitzgerald. Garden City, N.Y.: Anchor Books, 1963.

Kerouac, Jack. *The Dharma Bums*. New York: Viking Press, 1958.

Knapp, Bettina. "Virginia Woolf's *boeuf en daube*." In *Literary Gastronomy*, edited by David Bevan, pp. 29–35. Amsterdam: Rodolpi, 1988.

Melville, Herman. *Moby Dick*. New York: Albert and Charles Boni, 1939. Originally published in 1851.

Morrison, Toni. *Beloved*. New York: Knopf, 1987.

Plato. *The Symposium*. Translated by Christopher Gill. New York: Penguin, 1999.

Proust, Marcel. *Swann's Way*. Translated by C. K. Scott Moncrieff and Terance Kilmartin and revised by D. J. Enright. New York: Modern Library, 1992. Originally published in 1913 and revised in 1981.

Rabelais, François. *The Histories of Gargantua and Pantagruel*. Translated by J. M. Cohen. New York: Penguin Books, 1982. The five books originally appeared between 1542 and 1564.

Rouyer, Marie-Clair, ed. *Les avatars de la nourriture* (Food for thought). Bordeaux: Université de Montagne, 1998.

Schofield, Mary Anne, ed. *Cooking by the Book: Food in Literature and Culture*. Bowling Green, Oh.: Bowling Green State University Popular Press, 1989.

Shakespeare, William. *As You Like It*. Edited by S. C. Burchell. New Haven, Conn.: Yale University Press, 1954.

Shakespeare, William. *Hamlet*. Edited by Tucker Brooke and Jack Randall Crawford. New Haven, Conn.: Yale University Press, 1947.

Shakespeare, William. *The Tempest*. Edited by David Horne. New Haven, Conn.: Yale University Press, 1955.

Shapiro, Anna. *A Feast of Words: For Lovers of Food and Fiction*. New York: Norton, 1996.

Theophano, Janet. "It's Really Tomato Sauce but We Call It Gravy." Ph.D. dissertation, University of Pennsylvania, 1982.

Tolstoy, Leo. *Anna Karenina*. Translated by Constance Garnett. Garden City, N. Y.: Doubleday, 1944. Originally published between 1875 and 1876.

Twain, Mark. *Huckleberry Finn*. New York: Harper and Row, 1923. Originally published in 1884.

Tyler, Anne. *Dinner at the Homesick Restaurant*. New York: Knopf, 1982.

Woolf, Virginia. *To the Lighthouse*. San Diego, Calif.: Harcourt Brace Jovanovich, 1990. Originally published in 1927.

Yoder, Don. "Folk Cookery." In *Folklore and Folklife: An Introduction*, edited by Richard M. Dorson, pp. 325–350. Chicago, Ill.: University of Chicago Press, 1972.

Jonathan C. David

OPERA

Just as one cannot separate words and music to get at the mystery of opera, food and opera are more compelling together than they are apart. The most immediate connection between the two is at the mouth and throat. Singers are understandably focused on these areas and seek gustatory gratification as a means of dealing with preperformance jitters and postperformance elation and exhaustion. It is not uncommon for a singer to lose five pounds during a long evening of exertion while wearing a thirty-pound costume under hot lights.

Singers and audience members both have their dining traditions. Each tends to eat sparingly before a performance: singers to avoid feeling full (although Beverly Sills famously ate steak before going onstage) and operagoers so that they will not doze off while digesting a large meal. At intermissions some audience members have a light snack and a refreshment. Singers will seek liquid refreshment during performances—Birgit Nilsson often had a beer waiting at the side of the stage to slake her thirst. American tenor Richard Leech chomps on ice cubes to keep his mouth and throat cool.

Following performances, there is—especially in Europe—a tradition known as "souper." This is late-night eating in which the food is more festive than gastronomically challenging. The idea is to continue the sense of occasion that a night at the opera can foster. At a souper meal, whether attended by musicians, audience members, or both, dishes might include smoked fish, boiled shrimp with piquant sauces, rollmops, broths, risotto or pasta with truffles and cheese, boiled beef, and cakes, all washed down with copious amounts of wine, beer, and, especially, sparkling wine. The goal is that the food be tasty and arrive quickly. The most famous operatic depiction of souper is in the second act of *Die Fledermaus* by Johann Strauss Jr., in which party guests dance, sup, and sing in praise of champagne.

It is not surprising that chefs vied to create dishes to honor singers, composers, and opera characters. While performing at Covent Garden in London, the famous Australian opera singer Dame Nellie Melba dined at the nearby Savoy Hotel where the French chef Georges-Auguste Escoffier created in her honor both a form of well-browned, very dry "Melba" toast and a dessert he called "Peach Melba," consisting of a poached peach covered with vanilla ice cream and a special raspberry sauce and a garnish of chopped pistachios. Escoffier also created Sole Otello, combining the dark hues of truffle and mushroom (for Othello) with the pure white fish (for Desdemona). Luisa Tetrazzini had her famous turkey and noodles, and Gioacchino Rossini (opera's greatest gourmand) lent his name to any dish that featured truffles and foie gras. Enrico Caruso loved chicken livers, so preparations that included them bore his name. Wagner, a vegetarian, did not inspire chefs. Nor did Beethoven, who resented having to periodically stop composing to seek sustenance.

Although many operas seem to have drinking songs and choruses (in part because singers willingly consume thirst-quenching beverages onstage), there are not many eating scenes for the simple reason that food would obstruct the singers' vocal equipment. Mozart's Don Giovanni, who satisfies many appetites in the course of the opera, does dine heartily in the second act, although most interpreters of the role mime eating and ingest very little. Puccini's Tosca plays with her food in the second act until she discovers the knife that she will use to kill Scarpia. The funniest eating scene in opera comes in Rossini's *L'Italiana in Algeri*, in which the Italian Isabella feeds copious amounts of spaghetti to Mustafà, her Algerian captor, to distract him as she engineers her escape. As she runs to a ship in the harbor, Mustafà is dutifully twirling his pasta as he has been instructed. Surely the mezzo-soprano, once the curtain falls, will seek a bowl of noodles all her own.

See also **Escoffier, Georges-Auguste; Italy.**

BIBLIOGRAPHY

Plotkin, Fred. *Opera 101: A Complete Guide to Learning and Loving Opera.* New York: Hyperion, 1994.

Fred Plotkin

PAINTING AND THE VISUAL ARTS

Within the purview of world cultures, the vast majority do not address the subject of food in art in a gustatory manner or, at least, not to any great extent. When the subject emerged in the Mediterranean Basin, it was the Italians—one of whose bequests was the very concept of *cives* (or civilization)—who have had the longest history of a preoccupation with food. This being said, all art about food for eating in the West can be divided into three parts: leftovers on the floor, food displayed in preparation for the meal, and completed dishes, whether cooked or ripe, set out on a table, ledge, or some other flat surface. The ancient Greek beginnings were preserved by the Romans and feature the *rhopoi*, the trivial remains of a meal found in a floor mosaic that call to mind the excesses imagined by Petronius for the feast of the ex-slave Trimalchio in the *Satyricon*. Alternatively, there is the *xenion*, the gift of food laid out on a ledge and painted on the wall in trompe l'oeil to tempt and tease a tired traveler.

With the establishment of Christianity as the official religion of a declining Roman Empire, secular subject matter went into eclipse. However, there was still food on the table in the proper sanctified contexts, such as the *Feast in the House of Levi*, the *Wedding at Cana*, *Christ in the House of Mary and Martha*, the *Last Supper*, and the *Supper at Emmaus*. Medieval renderings of these subjects feature food only in its rudiments. But from the Renaissance through the Baroque periods, there is a resurgence of worldliness, manifesting itself in a considerable interest in the menu and the table setting. Tintoretto's *Last Supper*, in the Church of San Giorgio Maggiore, Venice, is a case in point. Here, the serving of a wide range of foodstuffs by assembled servants distracts from Christ's proleptically offering the Host to his disciples. Another example is Veronese's huge *Last Supper* for the Monastery of Santi Giovanni e Paolo, Venice. Wine in large bottles, wrapped in leather or raffia, is poured into hand-blown Murano goblets. A large bowl holding fowl is set before Jesus; a mercenary walks away from the table with a plate full of food, tipping his head back to down his wine. Veronese even records that cutlery invention borrowed from Byzantium, the fork. When the Inquisition objected, Veronese pled artistic license, but changed the title to *Christ in the House of Levi*.

A very important entrepôt for the depiction of food and its cultivation is found in the calendar pages and borders of the Books of Hours of the early Renaissance. In the *Book of Hours* of Catherine of Cleves, the cooked, pricked biscuits and pretzels, and the raw mussels, a crab, and fish eating fish, border the images of individual saints. A notable instance of calendar events is found in the Limbourg Brothers' *Les Très Riches Heures du Duc de Berry*. In January, Berry sits at a groaning board to celebrate the Feast of the Epiphany; in September, the grapes are harvested at his favorite chateau. A second broadcasting of seed occupies a peasant in October, while by November, peasants are tasked with shaking down acorns to fatten the boars that will be consumed at Christmas. This tradition of seasonal occupations and festivities carried over into oil painting in the five great landscapes by Pieter Brueghel the Elder. His *Return of the Hunters* illustrates a perennial activity in the dead of winter, the slaughtering and singeing of a hog. Brueghel also essayed the novel subject of Carnival battling with Lent, who proffers the fasting foods of pretzels and herring on a peel in opposition to the skewered viands of gluttony.

In the secular realm, Renaissance Italy set the tone for the rest of Europe in art, in horticulture, in cuisine, and in prolonged, elaborate feasting that was both a political statement and a gastronomic assault. Paintings of interiors of vast noble kitchens filled with activity provide visual complements to the descriptions of state banquets set down by the professional cook Bartolomeo Scappi in his monumental *Opera* (1570). At the opposite end of the spectrum are the exquisite watercolors on parchment created by Giovanna Garzoni, many of them for the Medici, who were avid innovators in gardening. Frequently, her figs, broad beans, artichokes, or cherries, painted life-size, are set out in bowls lined with grape

Still life with artichokes in a Chinese dish by Giovanna Garzoni (1600–1670). Collection of the Pitti Palace, Florence. PHOTO COURTESY OF DR. PHOEBE LLOYD.

leaves that are placed on Mother Earth to honor the Tuscan preference for rustic food fresh from the land. A contemporary foil to Italy's gastronomic bliss is Anthonius Claesson's painting of an English family of ten saying grace at a table, where a roast of beef holds center stage framed by two great salts. There is a round loaf of bread on the table, but no vegetables, and an old-fashioned cut of bacon is being carried to the table.

It is this Italian absorption with food that prompted Annibale Carracci to invent the first genre paintings in the 1580s. Although he excelled as a history painter, Carracci departed from this exalted calling when he painted two scenes of meat stalls, where butchers were plying their trade, and another of a peasant *mangiafagiolo* (bean eater), mouth agape, hungrily shoveling in beans. Following on the heels of Carracci, the archrebel Caravaggio revived the *xenion* tradition in the 1590s with his *Basket of Fruit*. The fruit is piled high in a wicker basket that extends over a ledge. A similar basket of fruit at the table's edge graces his *Supper at Emmaus*, where the realism of the well-accoutred table is balanced against the miraculous moment of Christ's revelation.

By the seventeenth century, the Dutch, whose country was arguably the wealthiest in Europe at that time, rivaled the Italians in prolonged feasting and in paintings about comestibles characterized by spillage and overabundance. That Dutch still life of the interrupted meal and genre paintings of market scenes and the stalls of fishmongers and butchers may be vanitas symbols or al-

legories of gluttony, or the five senses, respectively, is much debated. Whatever their symbolic charge, they, nevertheless, reveal what went onto the Dutch table and into the Dutch stomach. In stark contrast to these paintings that become touchstones for everyday experience is Rembrandt's depiction of the *Slaughtered Ox*, where the stilled life of the carcass, slit down the belly, splayed and hung, functions on the level of metaphor.

The Dutch and the Spanish, who were united under Habsburg rule until 1581, diverge in their depictions of food. Spanish art's distinctive contribution is the *bodegón*, where food is displayed on a ledge in stark raking light. The *bodegón* replicates the environment in which Spanish food was often placed, since in that hot Mediterranean country the kitchen was located in the basement with windows placed high in the wall. Outstanding examples of the *bodegón* aesthetic are found in the oeuvre of Sanchez Cotan, whose works have been rightly pronounced "solemn, magical larders." *Bodegóns* are for contemplation, not consumption.

The French, who from Gallic times had displayed an especial affinity for food's preparation, did not produce distinctive still lifes and genre paintings with foodstuffs until the eighteenth century. Then Chardin, whose subject matter so often addresses the domestic worlds of working-class maids and middle-class mothers, masterfully crafted works that reflected their domain in the kitchen and at table. Some of his still lifes can even be read as a list of ingredients that make up a particular dish.

The Bean Man shows an Italian peasant enjoying a bowl of beans. Painting in the collection of the Galleria Colonna, Via della Pilotta, Rome. REPRODUCED BY PERMISSION.

Concurrently, Boucher introduced the subject that was destined to become a French preoccupation, the *déjeuner*.

Although the Philadelphia still life painter Raphaelle Peale probably did not know the work of Chardin, he, too, assembled and painted raw ingredients for a meal. His other specialty was depicting a variety of skillfully decorated cakes. It is germane that, by the Federal era, Philadelphia was not only America's most culturally sophisticated and ethnically diverse city, but also her culinary capital.

On the Spanish front, the early nineteenth century witnessed Napoleon's Peninsular War and the retaliatory tactics of guerrilla warfare. In this brutal atmosphere, Francisco Goya also pursued the idea of still life as metaphor. His three gutted salmon slices, rendered a pulsating deep pinkish red, are not set forth in anticipation of a meal. The painting is about evisceration.

By contrast, there are numerous instances when it becomes clear that artists have been preoccupied with food's pleasures. The record goes back to Michelangelo. His illustrated list for a Lenten menu, though restricted to bread, fish, and wine, expands as he contemplates the happy possibilities. Not surprisingly, it is in nineteenth-century France, in the era when French haute cuisine was perfected, that the joys of the table begin to proliferate

in art. Renoir's *Luncheon of the Boating Party*, which takes place at the Restaurant Fournaise on an island that divided the Seine at Chatou, celebrates a meal that has advanced to the dessert course. Renoir's friend Monet was equally taken with the subject of mealtime; it is significant in this regard that at one point Renoir stole bread so that the Monet family would not go hungry. Early in his career, Monet depicted the *déjeuner* as it was consumed by family or friends on four occasions. Later in life, when Monet was established in his career and could afford to buy a house in Giverny, he would give special consideration to the interior decoration of the chrome yellow dining room, down to the detail of two sets of china. His cooking journals record what was placed on those plates. Bonnard is another French artist who depicted the pleasures of the table. Nor should it be forgotten that the painting that launched the Impressionist rebellion was about—and not about—lunch: Édouard Manet's *Le Déjeuner sur l'Herbe*.

Matisse helped usher in modern art by serving up the resplendent *Harmony in Red* (1908–1909). Against a red wall decorated with blue floral arrangements, a motif that flows onto a red table holding two wine decanters, fruit, and rolls, a maid bends slightly to arrange more fruit on a compote. A riveting instance of a Surrealist's preoccupation with food on the table is René Magritte's

1935 *Portrait.* Magritte's scene is set in a bistro with a bottle of wine and a place setting for one gracing the table. In keeping with his conviction that images are treacherous, Magritte fills the plate with a round slice of ham containing one centered eye looking up at the diner, hence the artist's title. Another Surrealist contribution is Meret Oppenheim's *Objet: Déjeuner en fourrure,* a fur-lined teacup and spoon that has become a veritable icon.

As the twentieth century progressed and people became more removed from food's involved preparation, art about food lost its celebratory aspect. Edward Hopper's *Night Hawks* (1942), though set in a diner, is hardly about the enjoyable consumption of food. Rather it exudes the grim impersonality found in film noir. As the availability of food came to be taken for granted on account of mass production, art about food dwindled into banality. Several 1960s Pop artists addressed the topic. Wayne Thiebaud's deliberately monotonous pies and cakes, so synthetic looking, are reminiscent of the days of the Automat. A further distancing of food from contexts of nurture and nature is found in Andy Warhol's obsession with highly commercialized processed food in his images of soup cans and bottles of Coke that unfold repetitiously. Claes Oldenberg's response was to transmogrify junk food. In 1979, Judy Chicago completed *Dinner Party,* a tribute to famous women that took the form of a particularized place setting representing each woman, the settings themselves laid out along the raised rim of a triangular table. It fell to a farm girl born in Sun Prairie, Wisconsin, in 1887, to hold to tradition. Although Georgia O'Keeffe never painted food and did not cook herself, she appreciated others who did and would prepare superbly the fresh, simple foods she relished; and she enshrined their recipes just as Monet or Alice B. Toklas had, by keeping a food journal.

See also **Arcimboldo, Giuseppe; France; Italy; Low Countries; United States.**

BIBLIOGRAPHY

Bergström, Ingvar. *Dutch Still-Life Painting in the Seventeenth Century.* Translated by Christina Hedström and Gerald Taylor. New York: Hacker Art Books, 1983.

Braudel, Fernand. *Capitalism and Material Life, 1400–1800.* London: Weidenfeld and Nicolson, 1973.

Braudel, Fernand. *The Mediterranean World in the Age of Philip II.* New York: Harper and Row, 1972.

Bryson, Norman. *Looking at the Overlooked: Four Essays on Still Life Painting.* Cambridge, Mass.: Harvard University Press, 1990.

Florentines: A Tuscan Feast: Giovanna Garzoni, 1600–1670. Foreword and recipes by Lorenza de'Medici. London: Pavilion, 1992.

Guy, Christian. *An Illustrated History of French Cuisine from Charlemagne to Charles de Gaulle.* New York: Orion Press, 1962.

Jordan, William B. *Spanish Still Life in the Golden Age, 1600–1650.* Los Angeles: Perpetua Press, 1985.

Joyes, Claire. *Monet's Table: The Cooking Journals of Claude Monet.* 2d English ed. New York: Simon and Schuster, 1989.

Kleiner, Fred S., Christin J. Mamiya, and Richard G. Tansey. *Gardner's Art Through the Ages.* 11th ed. Fort Worth: Harcourt, 2001.

Lloyd, Phoebe. "Philadelphia Story." *Art in America* (November 1988): 154–171, 195–203.

Riley, Gillian. *Painters & Food: Renaissance Recipes.* San Francisco: Pomegranate Artbooks, 1993.

Sambrook, Pamela A., and Peter Brears. *The Country House Kitchen, 1650–1900.* London: Sutton Publishing in Association with the National Trust, 1997.

Sterling, Charles. *Still Life Painting from Antiquity to the Twentieth Century.* 2d ed. New York: Harper and Row, 1981.

Sullivan, Margaret A. "Aertsen's Kitchen and Market Scenes: Audience and Innovation in Northern Art." *The Art Bulletin* 81 (June 1999): 236–266.

Wood, Margaret. *A Painter's Kitchen: Recipes from the Kitchen of Georgia O'Keeffe.* 2d ed. Santa Fe: Red Crane Books, 1997.

Phoebe Lloyd

POETRY

Food has been a topic of poetry for many centuries and in many cultures; the notion that food writing and poetry writing are totally separate ventures is a recent development. Much of our knowledge of eating habits, culinary practices, and food taboos throughout history and around the world comes from poetry. Food in poetry also functions as a powerful symbol of spiritual and moral states, and at other times it is used as a sexual symbol.

The Chinese have a long tradition of including food in poetry, going as far back as the Chou Dynasty (from the 12th century B.C.E. to 221 B.C.E.). There are Chou poems celebrating festive foods of the time, including stewed turtle, fried honey cakes, duck, quail, and good wine, and discussing the preparation of rice. The *Shih Ching* (Book of Songs) includes food scenes such as lamb sacrifice, in which the aroma of the roasting meat is described and fruit and wine are offered; verses on a feast of rabbit and plenty of wine; a song rejoicing in family togetherness at a feast including such meats as lamb, ox, and tripe, and an abundance of wine; agricultural songs celebrating wheat, millet, barley, plums, cherries, dates, melons, gourds, beans, garlic, and rice (from which wine is made). The culinary abundance of the T'ang Dynasty (618–907) is strongly evident in its poetry, which contains paeans to plums, pears, persimmons, jujubes, many kinds of melons, spring wine, and peaches, which were a traditional symbol of immortality in Chinese poetry and painting. Poems were also forums for discussing differences between foods. For instance, the eighth-century poet Chang Chiu-ling used poetry to address the many ways in which lychees and longans are not similar fruits at all, despite their superficial similarities. Poems written during another prosperous period, the Ch'ing Dynasty (1644–1922), link food and sex, with female beauty and sexuality compared to melons, cherries, and grapes.

Food is also an important presence in classical Western poetry. Homer's *Iliad* and *Odyssey* are rich with scenes of feasting, as well as of ordinary eating. In a famous scene from the *Odyssey*, Odysseus and his crew, trying to return by sea to Ithaca, stop at an unknown land whose inhabitants, the Lotus Eaters, offer a lavish banquet to the three men who are sent to explore. The fruit (or the juice from the fruit) that the men consume gives them great pleasure and also makes them forget all thoughts of home and family so that the other crew members must drag them away by force. Homer also describes the feast of roast meat served to Odysseus by Achilles. The Greek poet Hesiod wrote about enjoying good wine with meat and bread. The Roman poet Martial wrote a great deal about foods, such as figs, olives, parsnips, chicken, fish, cheese, eggs, chives, shallots, and onions, to name a few. Virgil described milk and cheese in his *Georgics*, which celebrates the agricultural life and mourns the dissolution of Italy's farms after famers were sent to war. Ovid wrote about olives and grapes in the *Amores*. In Greek mythology, the six pomegranate seeds eaten by Persephone (daughter of Demeter, goddess of agriculture) in the underworld after her abduction by Hades, are the mythical reason for winter: For each seed consumed, Persephone must spend a month of the year in the underworld, causing her mother to grieve and neglect her work. The story of Persephone and the pomegranate seeds continues to influence contemporary writers. In her collection *Mother Love*, the American poet Rita Dove writes of a modern young woman's journey to Paris that parallels Persephone's descent into the underworld. Her meal at "the Bistro Styx" includes Chateaubriand, Camembert, pears, figs, parsley, bread, and Pinot Noir. A mourning modern Demeter has a Spartan breakfast of cereal and raisins and puts stones into it.

Roman poets, including Catullus, Horace, and Martial, also wrote dinner-invitation poems. In the invitation poem, the poet cajoles the addressee into coming for dinner. He may describe the foods that are going to be served, talk about the wine that is going to be poured, and describe the entertainments that will be offered. Invitation poems are not only a source of information on what the Romans ate, but also literary documents in themselves. This tradition did not end with the Roman Empire. In the style of the classical invitation poem, Ben Jonson's "Inviting a Friend to Supper" describes a meal of salad, mutton, fowl, cheese, fruit, pastry, and wine. Another, more extensive food catalogue occurs in Jonson's "To Penshurst," which includes pheasant, carp, eels, cherries, plums, figs, grapes, quinces, apricots, peaches, cake, nuts, apples, cheeses, pears, beer, bread, and wine.

In the medieval Arab world, among those with sufficient resources, poetry and food were enjoyed in tandem, in lavish fashion. At banquets given by the caliphs,

FOOD IN OVID'S *ART OF LOVE*

The Roman love poetry of Ovid (43 B.C.E.–17 C.E.) reminds us of the ways in which food can serve erotic or aphrodisiac purposes. He talks of signals exchanged between secret lovers across a dinner table, and of messages written with a finger in spilt wine. He imagines a rival carefully mixing wine for a girlfriend, selecting the tastiest morsels from a serving dish for her to enjoy (Ovid, *Amores*, book 1 poem 4, and book 2 poem 5; see Ovid, *The Erotic Poems*, translated by Peter Green, Harmondsworth and New York: Penguin, 1982).

Ovid makes fun of aphrodisiac foods in a tongue-in-cheek didactic poem on love and seduction, in which he conscientiously lists several of such foods that Romans believed to be effective:

> Some old women will tell you to take dangerous herbs and salep (I judge these to be poisons), or they will mix for you pepper and stinging-nettle seed and pellitory chopped into vintage wine. But the Love Goddess . . . does not permit her pleasures to be forced in that way. You can try the white bulb that comes from Megara; try the lascivious rocket leaf grown in gardens; try eggs; try honey from Mount Hymettus; try the nuts that are found in prickly pine-tree cones (Ovid, *Art of Love*, book 2, lines 415–424. Translation by Andrew Dalby).

Salep is the ground root of an orchid (*Orchis mas* and other species) that is familiar as a hot winter drink in Turkey and the Balkans. Pellitory-of-Spain or Spanish chamomile is an ancient medicinal herb (*Anacyclus pyrethrum*). Rocket leaf (*Oruca sativa*) is the spicey-leafed plant arugula. The grape-hyacinth bulb (*Muscari comosum*), once a speciality of Megara in central Greece, is often served as an appetizer: it is known as *volvi* in modern Greek and *lampascioni* in Italian. Mount Hymettus, near Athens, is a source of fine honey.

Andrew Dalby

poems naming each dish—and recounting the spices and herbs used in its preparation, as well as the method of cooking—were recited during the dinners, so that the guests might savor the poetry along with the food.

There is food poetry in the Bible, as well. Throughout the Song of Solomon, the male and female narrators compare one another to fruits and other foods. The man's cheeks are compared to a "bed of spices"; the woman's breasts are described as "clusters of grapes" and her nose

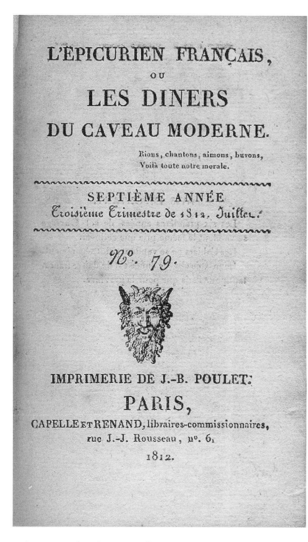

Title page of *L'épicurien français,* a popular collection of poems and stories with food themes from early-nineteenth-century Paris. ROUGHWOOD COLLECTION.

come, / Come, butter, come, / Peter stands at the gate / Waiting for a buttered cake, / Come, butter, come."

In the sonnets, Shakespeare invokes appetite and eating as metaphors for human behavior, beginning with images of famine and gluttony in Sonnet 1, "From fairest creatures we desire increase." In Sonnets 56 ("Sweet love, renew thy force") and 110 ("Alas! 'tis true, I have gone here and there"), appetite represents desire. In Sonnet 75, which opens with "So are you to my thoughts as food to life," appreciation of the beloved is compared to feasting, and the speaker without the beloved is "starvèd for a look." In Sonnet 52, infrequency of "feasts" gives them meaning, and in Sonnet 118, the eating of "eager compounds" and "bitter sauces" is contrasted with the sweetness of the beloved.

Jonathan Swift, whose concern with matters of hunger reached its most famous height with "A Modest Proposal," the essay in which he ironically suggests fighting hunger by eating children, saw fit to write poetry about onions, oysters, and fishmongers. Robert Burns's "Address to a Haggis" is traditionally recited with the serving of the Scottish dish. The English writer Sydney Smith composed recipes in verse, giving instructions for preparing salad dressing and roasting mutton, for instance.

In the twelfth-century Celtic poem "The Vision of Mac Conglinne," Mac Conglinne helps a king overcome his gluttony. The poem, delectable not only to poetry lovers but also to scholars of medieval Ireland, catalogues an outrageous abundance of foods, including salmon, kale, hazelnuts, sausages, bread, cheese, bacon, and especially milk, which is described as being so thick that it must be chewed.

Food in poetry sometimes carries moral significance. In an archetypal episode in Ovid's *Metamorphoses,* the poor couple Baucis and Philemon share their meager food supply with beggars, who turn out to be gods in disguise and reward the couple with abundance. The biblical story of Eve's eating of the forbidden fruit, said to be an apple but possibly a pomegranate, is portrayed as the first human sin and the reason for man's state of sin. The story of Eve's giving in to the tempting fruit also starts off John Milton's epic on the fall of mankind, *Paradise Lost.* In Chaucer's *Canterbury Tales,* food is an important element in maintaining the balance of bodily humors, and gluttony is addressed as one of the Seven Deadly Sins. Gluttony is severely punished in Dante's hell. And food taboos are part of the human struggle: In Byron's *Don Juan,* a starving crew of seamen resort to cannibalism, but only after a long and horrible effort to avoid it.

Food in poetry can have transformative, and sometimes destructive, powers. In the English epic *Beowulf,* feasting (which always involves plenty of drinking) is generally followed by sleep, which makes the men vulnerable to attacks by the monster Grendel, who feasts on men. (Feasts in *Beowulf* are also given to honor people, and are the backdrop against which many discussions and con-

as smelling like apples. Figs, grapes, vines, and pomegranates are used to describe their love for each other. The apple tree, standing out among other trees, represents the beloved's standing out among men. Other foods mentioned in the exchange include honey, milk, saffron, and cinnamon.

Food is inherent to many traditional songs and poems of the Celtic world and in England. For instance, an Irish saying goes: "Rye bread will do you good, / Barley bread will do you no harm, / Wheat bread will sweeten your blood, / Oat bread will strengthen your arm." Early Celtic poems tell of affection for such foods as mushrooms, milk, and colcannon, the Irish dish of mashed potatoes with cabbage or kale. In England, a song once accompanied the churning of butter: "Come, butter, frontations take place.) In Samuel Taylor Coleridge's "Kubla Khan," the consumption of milk and honey is linked to an altered state of mind. John Keats paid close attention to food in his poems and letters; in his poem "La Belle Dame Sans Merci," the beautiful woman destroys a knight by feeding and seducing him. The food, like the sexual attraction, is central to his undoing.

Some poets invoke food to convey matters of the spirit. T. S. Eliot's question "Do I dare to eat a peach?" conveys the jaded frame of mind of the speaker of "The Love Song of J. Alfred Prufrock." Emily Dickinson uses hunger metaphorically; in the poem "Hunger," hunger and dining express loneliness and love. Another poem, "Forbidden Fruit," makes a pithy statement about human nature: "Forbidden fruit a flavor has / That lawful orchards mocks; How luscious lies the pea within / The pod that Duty locks!"

Some poets simply delight in the discussing of food. Pablo Neruda, in his *Elemental Odes*, writes about artichokes, lemons, and olive oil (and the use of the oil in mayonnaise and salad dressing). Ogden Nash has a book of light verse about food. D. H. Lawrence wrote poems entitled "Pomegranate," "Peach," "Medlars and Sorb-Apples," "Figs," and "Grapes." A. E. Housman celebrates the cherry tree in "Loveliest of Trees, the Cherry Now." William Carlos Williams's famous "This Is Just to Say" has immortalized some irresistible plums in an icebox; the savoring of plums occurs also in his "To a Poor Old Woman." The contemporary American poet Robert Hass weaves lush California cuisine into many poems.

Poetry and food may be coming back together, as they were in ancient times. Enough contemporary poets have written poems about food to fill a number of anthologies of food poems, including one devoted exclusively to poems about potatoes (*Spud Songs*, ed. Gloria Vando and Robert Stewart).

See also **Bible, Food in the; Folklore, Food in; Myth and Legend, Food in.**

BIBLIOGRAPHY

Asala, Joanne. *Celtic Folklore Cooking*. St. Paul, Minn.: Llewellyn Press, 1998.

Chang, K. C. *Food in Chinese Culture*. New Haven: Yale University Press, 1977.

Dalby, Andrew. *Empire of Pleasures*. New York: Routledge, 2000.

Furst, Lilian R., and Peter W. Graham, eds. *Disorderly Eaters: Texts in Self-Empowerment*. University Park, Penn.: Pennsylvania State University Press, 1992.

Gowers, Emily. *The Loaded Table: Representations of Food in Roman Literature*. New York: Oxford University Press, 1993.

Mahon, Brid. *Land of Milk and Honey*. Boulder, Colo.: Mercier Press, 1998.

Neruda, Pablo. *Selected Poems*. Translated by Ben Belitt. New York: Grove Press, 1961.

Root, Waverley. *Food*. New York: Simon and Schuster, 1980. Reprint: New York: Smithmark, 1996.

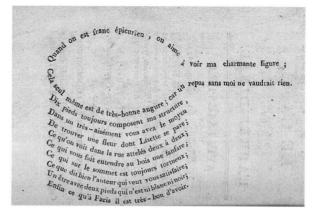

A poem about food in the shape of a saucepan. From *L'épicurien français* (Paris, 1812). ROUGHWOOD COLLECTION.

Silverman, Jeff. *The First Chapbook for Foodies*. Emeryville, Calif.: Woodford Press, 2000.

Tannahill, Reay. *Food in History*. Great Britain: Penguin, 1973. Reprint: New York: Crown, 1988.

Visser, Margaret. *Much Depends on Dinner*. New York: Collier, 1986.

Waley, Arthur. *The Book of Songs*. New York: Grove Press, 1987.

Adrienne Su

ARTHROPODS: INSECTS, ARACHNIDS, AND CRUSTACEANS. Arthropods are animals with exoskeletons (external skeletons), segmented bodies, and jointed legs. They are the largest group of animals on Earth and include insects, crustaceans, and arachnids. Insects include organisms such as beetles, grasshoppers, and butterflies. They are mostly terrestrial, small in size, and typically herbivorous. Many species of insects are used as food, and they are traditional food sources in many areas of the tropics. Crustaceans include lobsters, crabs, crayfish, and shrimp. They are mostly aquatic animals, and some, like lobsters and crabs, are relatively large animals. (Crustaceans are discussed below, and are covered in further detail in the article "Crustaceans and Shellfish.") Throughout history, the larger crustacean species have been highly prized food sources. Arachnids include spiders and scorpions, some forms of which are used as food.

The arthropod's exoskeleton is a tough cuticle made of chitin that protects the organism and provides anchor points for muscles. The exoskeleton in crustaceans is rich with calcium carbonate and is particularly hard and thick. The exoskeleton limits an organism's ability to grow in size and must be periodically shed (molted) as the organism grows. Most arthropods go through a series of molts and become more adultlike with each succeeding one.

Some insects, like flies, wasps, beetles, and butterflies, go through larval and pupal stages that are quite different from the adult stages of those species. As embryos, these organisms develop into a larva that is relatively immobile and specializes in eating and storing fat. The larva then transforms into a pupa (an intermediate stage between larva and adult), and finally into an adult that is highly mobile and specializes in reproduction. In insects that undergo such a metamorphosis, the larva is generally the largest form and the one that humans typically prefer as food. The advantage, for humans, of consuming larval insects is that during immature stages of development, insects are soft-bodied and typically high in fat; in addition, the larval stage is often the stage of the life cycle in which individual insects can be found in the greatest aggregations. For example, in the order Lepidoptera (butterflies and moths), insects are in their largest form and have the highest energy (caloric) value during the larval stage of the life cycle. In contrast, the adult forms of Lepidoptera have lower body mass, a hardened exoskeleton, and are more mobile and widely dispersed than larvae.

The crustaceans used as food are aquatic animals that are widespread geographically. Shrimp, lobsters, and crabs inhabit marine ecosystems, and crayfish inhabit freshwater ecosystems. Shrimp are the smallest crustacean and range in size from that of a small insect to over twenty centimeters (seven to eight inches). They tend to live close to the bottom, or in midwater, and feed on plants and small animals. They are food for predatory fish like cod, pollock, and flounder. Lobsters, crabs, and crayfish are larger than shrimp and are important benthic (bottom-dwelling) predators in local ecosystems. The American (*Homarus americanus*) and European (*Homarus gammarus*) species of lobster are found in the northern Atlantic Ocean. Adults feed on plant material, shellfish, sea urchins, and crabs. They are solitary animals that defend territory around their shelter (spaces under rocks or large crevices), and they are most active in foraging at night. Spiny (rock) lobsters are found in warm tropical and temperate seas. They feed on snails and clams and small crustaceans and are prey for sharks, octopus, and finfish. They lack the larger claws of the American and European lobsters and are gregarious animals that sometimes migrate long distances.

Crabs are the rounder bodied (compared to shrimp and lobsters) crustaceans that walk sideways; some even swim. The species of crab used as food vary in size from less than two pounds for the Dungeness crabs (*Cancer magister*) to up to twenty-five pounds for the Alaskan king crab (*Paralithodes camtschaticus*). Adult crabs are omnivores and dominant predators in local food webs. They feed on shellfish, finfish, and other crustaceans, as well as on detritus (debris). Crabs are widely distributed geographically: Species like the gazami crab (*Portunus tritu-*

berculatus), the swimming crab (*Portunus pelagicus*), and the blue crab (*Callinectus sapidus*) are tropical or subtropical in distribution. The snow or queen crab (*Cheonoecetes opilio*) is found in the cold seas of the North Atlantic and Pacific Oceans and the Sea of Japan. The most spectacular crabs are the king crabs that live off the coast of Alaska. The red king crab (*Paralithodes camtschaticus*) is the largest: males of this species can grow to up to twenty-five pounds and have a leg span of five feet across. The blue and the golden king crabs (*Paralithodes platypus* and *Lithodes aequispinus*) are somewhat smaller than the red king crab, but they are still king-sized.

Crayfish (or crawfish) look somewhat like lobsters, but they inhabit freshwater ecosystems and are primarily temperate in distribution. North America contains the greatest species diversity of crayfish. They feed on aquatic and semiaquatic vegetation, invertebrates, and detritus. North American species range in size from two to three ounces (50 to 80 grams), but much larger species exist in Australia.

History of Consumption

European populations and European-derived populations in North America historically have placed taboos on entomophagous eating practices (the consumption of insects) and continue to do so. This is notwithstanding the repeated attempts by entomologists to make insects more appealing. One of the best-known attempts is Ronald Taylor's 1975 book *Butterflies in My Stomach*, and the accompanying recipe guide, *Entertaining with Insects* (1976).

Although entomophagous eating practices have ceased in Europe, insects were at one time frequently eaten throughout the continent. Rural inhabitants of Europe consumed Cockchafer grubs until the 1800s, and these grubs were an important source of protein in Ireland during the famine of 1688. The Greeks and Romans also held some insects in high esteem as a food source. Ancient Greeks considered grasshoppers a delicacy, and even Aristotle wrote of eating cicadas. He considered them tastiest just before the final instar (stage between two molts), but females laden with eggs were also considered to be very good. The Greeks and Romans also ate a large Melolonthid grub, possibly *Lucanus cervus*, which Pliny wrote was fattened before consumption.

For many other populations the consumption of insects has continued into the early twenty-first century, or not long before that time. In Mexico a well-known example of cuisine involving insects is *ahauatle*, a mixture of hemiptera eggs, that Francisco Hernandez first described in 1649. The eggs were also dried and used as a condiment in the preparation of a traditional Christmas Eve dish, *revoltijo*. In Colombia the giant queen ants of the genus *Atta* are considered a gastronomical delicacy. There the consumption of giant queen ants can be traced to precolonial times: Gonzalo Jimenez de Quesada, founder of the Colombian capital city Santa Fe de Bogotá, first described their use by local peoples in the highlands in 1555.

The consumption of a wide variety of insects has been reported among Amerindian groups in South American rain forests, and insects have probably been part of that region's diet for a very long time. The insects that appear to be consumed most commonly are ants of the genus *Atta*, palm grubs, and caterpillars of various sorts. The naturalist Alfred Wallace first described the consumption of Atta queen ants in 1854:

> They are eaten alive; the insect being held by the head as we hold a strawberry by its stalk, and the abdomen being bitten off, the body, wings and legs are thrown down to the floor, where they continue to crawl along apparently unaware of the loss of their posterior extremities.

Palm grubs, the large, fatty, legless larvae of woodboring weevils (*Rhynchophorus*) found in the pith of felled palm trees, are a highly esteemed food among Amerindians. Bancroft, writing in the eighteenth century, claimed that palm grubs were equally highly esteemed by Europeans in Surinam, particularly by the French.

In Africa the use of insects as food is quite widespread and probably has deep historical roots. The mopane worm (*Gonimbrasia belina*), the so-called snack that crawls, is one of the best known edible caterpillars. Termites are also utilized as food, especially in the early rainy season when the reproductive forms swarm from the nest. At one time, termites were such an important addition to the diet that their mounds were often disputed as property. Locusts (grasshoppers that go into a swarming phase), in particular the desert locust (*Schistocerca gregaria*), also play a large role in the diet of Africans. In African history the locusts were so popular that people actually welcomed the arrival of swarms.

In the Middle East the desert locust was also a major source of food historically. Perhaps the most well-known incident involving locust eating was John the Baptist's ordeal in the desert during which he survived on locusts (St. John's bread) and honey. By using locusts as food he was observing the decree of Moses, "These ye may eat; the locust after his kind and the bald locust after his kind, and the cricket after his kind and the grasshopper after his kind" (Leviticus 9:22).

In Asia the consumption of insects as food was described from the Chung-Qiu dynasty (770–475 B.C.E.) and continues to the present day. The most commonly consumed food insects in that region are bee brood (larvae and pupae), beetles such as *Dytiscid* and *Hydrophilid* beetles, and the giant water beetle (*Lethocerus indicus*), the larvae of weevils like *Rhynchophorus*, and locusts of the genera *Oxya* and *Locusta*. Perhaps the most well-known insect eaten in the region is the pupa of the silkworm *Bombyx mori*.

In Australia the black honey ant (*Camponotus inflatus*) is a highly sought-after food of Aboriginal Australians

Collecting bamboo grubs for food in rural Thailand. © MICHAEL FREEMAN/CORBIS.

and is even considered a totem animal by some clans. It is similar to the honey ant found throughout North and Central America: a modified worker ant with an enlarged body the size of a grape that is full of nectar. Digging up these ants is still considered an important traditional practice and is still taught to children. Witchetty grubs were also an important food of Australian Aborigines. The name witchetty grub refers to any number of root-boring larvae and probably includes Cossid moth larvae (*Xyleutes leuchomochla*), giant ghost moth larvae (*Hepialidae*), and longicorn beetle larvae (*Cerambycidae*). One of the most unique and well-documented examples of entomophagous eating habits in Australia was the annual feast of bugong moths (*Agrotis infusa*), which occurred until the 1890s. These moths migrate from the plains to aestivate (the summer equivalent of hibernation) in the rock crevices of the Bugong Mountains. Aboriginal Australians from many different tribes traditionally gathered to feast on them. Evidence of these feasts has been carbon-dated as early as 1000 C.E.

Procurement and Capture

The harvesting of insects varies greatly by species because it is tailored to the ecological and behavioral characteristics of different species, as well as the stage of the life cycle sought. Harvesting is typically done for subsistence or to satisfy the demands of a local market.

The harvesting of larval forms like grubs and caterpillars is relatively easy as long as the food source is known. Caterpillars like mopane worms can be picked from their host trees (mopane trees), or for species like the Pandora moth (*Colorado Pandora lindseyi*), gathered as they descend from their host trees to pupate in the soil. The larva of wood-boring weevils like *Rhynchophorus* can be harvested by splitting open the palm trees they inhabit, and the larva of root-boring grubs like wichetty grubs can be harvested from the roots of their host plant.

Harvesting mobile adults is more of a challenge. One strategy is to harvest at a point of high aggregation. The giant queen ants of the genus *Atta* can be collected as they swarm from the nest on nuptial flights early in the rainy season. Some termites, like *Macrotermes*, can be harvested in the same way. The bogong moths are smoked out of the rock crevices where they gather to aestivate. Social insects that live in large colonies, like ants and termites, can be dug out or lured out by intruding smoke or by inserting a probe, which the soldiers defending the colony will attack. At least one arachnid, the tarantula, can also be attracted out of its burrow using a probe.

Another strategy is to create an aggregation. For grasshoppers and crickets this is done by surrounding them by hunters carrying sticks and driving them into holes or trenches. They can also be captured by dragging bags or nets along the ground and collecting them. A third strategy is to attract the insects to a flame or a light. One species of giant queen ants, as well as some termites and dragonflies, can be attracted to a flame that conveniently singes their wings and makes them very easy to collect. At lease one species of beetle can be attracted to a black light.

Preparation and Consumption

In areas where insects are a traditional part of the diet, they are typically consumed raw or are prepared like other foods, especially other animal food. For example, in Japan grasshoppers, silkworm pupae, and bee pupae are cooked in soy sauce and sugar and served as appetizers. In other parts of Asia, larvae of various sorts, beetles, scorpions, and tarantulas are served fried or stir-fried with vegetables and typical seasonings. In Africa, mopani worms are eaten raw, fried, or cooked in a typical stew after they have been squeezed to remove gut contents.

In general, soft-bodied forms like larvae and pupae are typically fried, grilled, or stewed with local vegetables and seasonings. Larger, hard-bodied forms (such as adults with exoskeletons) like grasshoppers and locusts are typically soaked or cooked in salted water and then sun-dried, or even grilled like shrimp. The legs and wings are typically removed before they are consumed. The exoskeleton of these organisms is retained and provides a certain crunchiness. Smaller organisms with exoskeletons, like ants and termites, are often roasted or fried. In the past, Native North Americans roasted both grasshoppers and crickets and pounded them together with seeds and berries to make a cake called a "desert fruitcake," which could be sun-dried and stored.

Relations to Human Biology

Arthropods are animals and are therefore generally comparable to other animal foods in terms of their nutritional composition. Insects have protein content similar to that of meats like beef and pork. The quality of the protein, however, appears to vary greatly among species; in most cases it is better in terms of amino acid composition than that of plant foods like grains and legumes. The larval stages of arthropods like palm grubs and wichetty grubs are quite high in fat and are similar in that regard to U.S.-style hot dogs. Caterpillars tend to be more muscular and, hence, higher in protein. In terms of micronutrients, insects generally have reasonable quantities of iron, calcium, and B vitamins. As mentioned earlier, the crunchy exoskeleton of insects like grasshoppers is partially composed of chitin, a substance not digested by humans. Little is known about the potential toxic or anti-nutritional factors of insects, although in areas where pesticides are used, toxicity may be of serious concern for all species.

Contemporary Issues

There is a worldwide general trend towards the reduction of entomophagous eating practices. This may be due to the increased use of pesticides to control insects in agricultural zones or the trend toward the adoption of westernized diets (in other words, diets like those of North Americans and Europeans) in which insects have extremely low status as food or are taboo. Despite the general reduction in the consumption of insects as food, there have been efforts to commercialize some food insects. Entrepreneurs in Australia have introduced some local delicacies like black honey ants, witchetty grubs, bardi grubs (the larvae of a Cerambycid beetle), and Trigona bees to the commercial food market, and some Australian restaurants include insects on their menus. Entrepreneurs in South Africa market mopani worms, and the appearance of caterpillars as ingredients has been a general trend on menus in Africa. Some Asian countries also export food insects as specialty items: Thailand exports frozen steamed ant larvae and pupae, Korea exports pupa of the silkworm *Bombyx mori*, and Japan exports bee pupae in soy to the United States.

There has also been research and development into the rearing of insects as "mini-livestock" in order to meet the subsistence needs, especially the protein needs, of impoverished rural populations. The idea of purposefully raising insects for food is not as far-fetched as it might

130

seem: for example, many societies have been raising bees for a long time.

See also **Australian Aborigines; Crustaceans and Shellfish; Hunting and Gathering; Proteins and Amino Acids**.

BIBLIOGRAPHY

Caddy, John F., ed. *Marine Invertebrate Fisheries: Their Assessment and Management.* New York: John Wiley and Sons, 1989.

Chaffin, Yule. *Alaska's Southwest: Koniag to King Crab.* Anchorage: Chaffin, 1967.

DeFoliart, Gene R. "Insects as Food: Why the Western Attitude Is Important." *Annual Review of Entymology* 44 (1999): 21–50.

Goddard, J. S. "Food and Feeding." In *Freshwater Crayfish: Biology, Management and Exploitation,* edited by D. M. Holdich and R. S. Lowery. London and North Ryde: Croom Helm, 1988. Portland, Ore.: Timber Press, 1988.

Paoletti, Maurizio, and Sandra G. F. Bukkens, eds. "Minilivestock." Special issue of *Ecology of Food and Nutrition* 36, no. 2–4 (1997).

Phillips, B. F., and J. Kittaka, eds. *Spiny Lobsters: Fisheries and Culture.* 2d ed. Malden, Mass.: Fishing News Books, 2000.

Pitre, Glen. *The Crawfish Book: The Story of Man and Mudbugs Starting in 25,000 B.C and Ending With the Batch Just Put on to Boil.* Jackson: University Press of Mississippi, 1993.

Tannahill, Reay. *Food in History.* New York: Stein and Day, 1973.

Taylor, Ronald L. *Butterflies in My Stomach.* Santa Barbara, Calif.: Woodbridge Press, 1975.

Taylor, Ronald L., and Barbara J. Carter. *Entertaining with Insects.* Santa Barbara, Calif.: Woodbridge Press, 1976.

Toussaint-Samat, Maguelonne. *A History of Food,* translated by Anthea Bell. Paris: Bordas, 1987. New York: Barnes and Noble, 1998.

Darna L. Dufour

ARTIFICIAL FOODS. The term "artificial" refers to something produced to imitate nature. Some artificial foods created with rubber or similar materials are incredibly lifelike. People have even placed them on a table when they are away to fool robbers into believing someone is home and ready to eat. These food models are more commonly used in educational settings to help people understand reasonable portion sizes. They are also used in displays, such as restaurant windows, as food spoilage is not an issue. A computer search using the term "artificial food" will locate retail vendors of these food models.

Edible Food

The term "artificial food" also creates images of edible food made from substances that do not occur naturally. No wholly artificial foods exist in the strict sense, but

TANG®

Tang®, a powdered orange drink meant to mimic orange juice, was introduced in 1957 and went into national distribution in 1959. It rose in popularity in 1965, when it became part of the diets of the astronauts in the space program. Tang® has been on every manned space flight since *Gemini 4,* including Apollo flights, *Sky Lab,* and the space shuttles. The National Aeronautics and Space Administration (NASA) chose it because of its compact nature as a powder, its convenience, its storage qualities, and its required nutrients, such as vitamins A and C.

Tang® obviously appealed to kids who wanted what astronauts were eating, and hundreds of other powdered beverages followed. Sugar-free Tang became available in March 1985, driven by consumer demand for sugar-free low-calorie beverages.

The popularity of the powdered orange juice substitute gradually dwindled as the convenience of fresh orange juice at a reasonable price rose. For a brief time in the 1990s the popularity of Tang® increased with "Generation X" due to a "Tang and Toast" advertising campaign. Tang® is popular when a convenient dried food is required, such as on camping trips and in the military. It is usually carried by suppliers of dried and dehydrated foods for long-term food storage or specialty grocery stores with a nostalgic supply. The original purpose of Tang® as a convenient, inexpensive powdered drink has been forgotten. After 1999 it was available in pouches, ready to drink, in flavors such as Fruit Frenzy and Orange Uproar.

Rumors abound that some consumers have used Tang® Drink Mix to clean their dishwashers. Tang® does contain citric acid, which can act as cleaning agent. Kraft Foods has taken the position that Tang® Drink Mix is intended to be a food product, and the company does not advocate its use for any other purpose.

some foods are called artificial or seem artificial to some people. Viewing a food as artificial is most likely if it contains ingredients, such as colorings or flavorings, that are not inherent in the food. An example is artificial strawberry flavoring created in the laboratory to mimic the natural taste of fresh strawberries.

Foods may also be "artificial" for medical reasons or to suit personal beliefs. For example, artificial milk is created for infants born with a genetic disease called phenylketonuria (PKU). The artificial milk replicates the

Artificial foods are popular in Japan, where they are widely used in restaurant window displays to help customers make decisions. The food is often so realistically made that it cannot be differentiated from the actual product it is imitating. Shown here is an elaborate window display in the Shinjuku District of Tokyo. © MICHAEL S. YAMASHITA/CORBIS.

nutritional content of real milk but lacks a specific amino acid, phenylalanine, not tolerated by an infant with PKU. Without this artificial milk, infants with PKU would develop severe mental retardation.

Vegetarian food substitutes, such as imitation bologna, may be viewed as "artificial" by some because they imitate nature. They may look and taste similar to a meat product, yet they contain no meat. Others argue that the term "artificial food" may not apply here, as many vegetarian meat substitutes contain only all-natural ingredients. Most would conclude that the consumer definition of artificial food relates more to the presence of any artificial ingredient, such as nutrients, artificial coloring, or artificial flavoring, that possesses ingredients or attributes that simulate another food.

Sometimes artificial ingredients are added to provide a nutrient that would be in the food in its natural state. For example, orange juice has vitamin C, so Tang® Drink Mix is fortified to contain at least 100 percent of the daily value for vitamin C (see sidebar on Tang®). Sometimes ingredients are added but not to the same level the natural product would contain. For example, potassium is added to Tang®, primarily in the form of potassium citrate. A small amount of potassium is contributed by orange juice solids and other ingredients. The body uses the potassium in Tang® from potassium citrate just as it would use the naturally occurring potassium in foods and beverages. The quantity, though, is different from that of natural orange juice. The potassium content of Tang®

Drink Mix is 50 milligrams per 8 fluid ounces. Orange juice contains approximately 470 milligrams per 8 fluid ounces.

Foods Containing Artificial Flavor or Color
The consumer looks for the term "artificial" on food labels to distinguish between foods that are in their natural states and those that have been modified in some way. On the label the term "artificial" is applied to flavor or color as defined by the federal government. For example, this is the federal definition of artificial flavor:

> The term artificial flavor or artificial flavoring means any substance, the function of which is to impart flavor, which is not derived from a spice, fruit or fruit juice, vegetable or vegetable juice, edible yeast, herb, bark, bud, root, leaf or similar plant material, meat, fish, poultry, eggs, dairy products, or fermentation products thereof. Artificial flavor includes the substances listed in Secs. 172.515(b) and 182.60 of this chapter except where these are derived from natural sources (*Code of Federal Regulations*, Title 21, vol. 2, 2001, pp. 73–78).

In simpler terms, for the purposes of nutrition labeling, artificial flavor means anything added to food for flavor that is not taken directly from whole foods.

The federal definition of artificial color or artificial coloring means any "color additive" as defined in Sec. 70.3(f) of the food code. Some food colors obtained largely from mineral, plant, or animal sources may be listed on the label with the general term "artificial color." Regulations require certification of colors derived primarily from petroleum, known as coal-tar dyes. Some color additives must be listed by name on the label. These are additives that are safe for most people but have been identified as a problem for a small number of consumers. For example, FD&C Yellow No. 5, listed as tartrazine on medicine labels, must be individually labeled because it causes hives and itching in a small proportion of consumers.

Though reactions to color additives are rare, the Food and Drug Administration (FDA) wants to know about them. The agency operates the Adverse Reaction Monitoring System (ARMS) to collect and act on complaints concerning all food ingredients, including color additives. Consumers can register complaints by contacting the FDA district offices in their local phone directories or by sending written reports to the ARMS at the Food and Drug Administration in Washington, D.C.

Determining if Food Has Artificial Flavor or Color
Artificial ingredients in the food supply are generally considered safe for individuals without specialized medical conditions such as specific food allergies. Some consumers prefer to avoid foods deemed artificial anyway, as a precaution that fits with their own beliefs. Thus nutrition labeling assists these consumers in following their personal preferences.

Grocery stores usually have mechanisms that allow consumers to decide if they want to purchase the food. For example, if a strawberry shortcake contains flavoring from strawberries enhanced by artificial flavor, the box will be labeled "natural and artificial strawberry flavor." If the food contains solely artificial flavors, it will be labeled "artificial strawberry flavor."

Foods packaged in bulk containers for retail stores may not contain a nutrition label. The labeling information for the food, however, should be displayed plainly in view or on a counter sign. Restaurant food is more challenging, as restaurants are not required to provide nutrition labeling.

See also **Additives; Allergies; Coloring, Food; Fads in Food.**

Irene Berman-Levine

ASIA. *See* **Asia, Central; China; India; Japan; Korea; Southeast Asia.**

ASIA, CENTRAL. The mention of Central Asian foodways usually conjures up competing images of nomadic and sedentary lifestyles. In one, the roving sheepherder astride a brawny steed, between base camp and mountain pasture, clutches a leather pouch of fermented milk. The other vision includes the long-beard in his colorful robe and headdress, enjoying perfumed pilaf in a tranquil teahouse. While scholars quibble over cultural and physical boundaries of Central Asia, culinary cultures of the region represent an intriguing mix of steppe and settlement, highlands and lowlands, Turkic and Iranian.

Culinary Culture and Geographic Setting
Generally speaking, hospitality is the defining feature of this underpublicized cuisine. For all the ethnic and geographic variations in Central Asia, the food of the region exhibits more homogeneity than disparity. Basic methods of preparation, main ingredients, common dishes, and predominant cultural traditions of Islam all reflect the enriching exchange along the heart of the storied Silk Road. The regional larder consists of mutton, rice, cumin, coriander, cilantro, dill, nuts, tea, dried fruits, and yogurt, distinguishing it from Chinese and European fare. Meal preparation is often conducted outside over fire, with cast-iron cauldrons (*kazan*) for frying, simmering, and steaming; open-flame braziers for grilling; and *tandir* ovens for roasting meats and baking breads. Customary dishes throughout the region include soups and stews, pilafs, noodles, steamed dumplings, grilled meats on skewers, flatbread, savory pastries, and halvah.

The geographical limits of Central Asia, once called Turkistan, include the Soviet successor states (Uzbekistan, Turkmenistan, Tajikistan, Kazakhstan, and Kyrgyzstan), and Xinjiang in northwest China. Others do not hesitate to add other Turkic-language areas, like the Caucasus, Turkey, and parts of Siberia, while some embrace Mongolia, Iran, Afghanistan, northern India, Pakistan, and even Tibet in the Central Asian cultural orbit.

The thriving culture of Iran was the primary influence on Central Asian society, with later Arabic and Mongol contributions. One hundred and fifty years of Russian power and fifty years of intensive Chinese subjugation of the region have considerably altered the foodways. Well-documented Soviet problems of collectivization and distribution homogenized local diets. The turbulent history of Xinjiang continues, with Chinese migrants and laborers, particularly from Sichuan, flooding the region after the 1960s, dropping the Turkic Uighur population from roughly 75 percent to less than 50 percent. In China proper, Uighur cuisine is segregated and disparagingly referred to as Muslim food.

Diet and Foodstuffs
Greek humoral theory, as propagated by ibn Sina of the eleventh century, still affects the diet of millions in the region. Combined with traditional Chinese thought, Central Asians consider food to have either "hot" or "cold" (Farsi, *sardi* or *garmi*) qualities, serving both medicinal and nutritive functions. Three meals a day are standard, each including tea and flatbread (*nan* or *naan*). The largest meal is usually taken in the evening.

The spirited bazaars of Central Asia—part marketplace, part carnival, and part town square—capture the Silk Road mystique. Aromatic spices take center stage, though only cumin, red and black pepper, and coriander seeds are used in abundance. Herbs of distinction include cilantro, dill, parsley, and celeriac leaves. Seasoning is generally mild, but sauces, relishes, and even whole peppers are added for punch. Other flavor enhancers are white grape vinegar and fermented milk products. Rendered sheep fat is the general cooking oil, though vegetable oil and cottonseed oil are widely used. Olive oil and butter are not traditional cooking fats.

The Asian sun sweetens market produce. Delicious tomatoes, peppers, onions, cucumbers, and eggplants comprise the basic vegetables. The area also offers unique varieties of pungent green radishes (*turup*), yellow carrots (actually turnips), and a prodigious selection of pumpkin and squash. Dolma, meaning "stuffed" in Turkish, may be created from any vegetable—cabbage, grape leaves, peppers, tomatoes, and so forth—by hollowing it out or wrapping it around a filling. Spring fruits traditionally include grapes, apricots, strawberries, cherries, figs, and peaches. The tree harvest in autumn brings apples, quinces, persimmons, and pears. Winter delivers lemons, mandarins, pomegranates, and smooth-skinned melons. Melon slices are also sun-dried and braided into long ropes to take their place alongside dried apricots, figs, dates, and raisins.

Core Cuisine

Meat and rice. Lamb and mutton, mainly fatty-tailed sheep, are the favorite protein of Central Asians. The fat, which imparts a sweet and rich quality to a dish, is valued more than the meat itself. Beef and chicken are consumed in substantial quantities, and horse, camel, and goat are not uncommon. Fish, though not eschewed, is rarely available, and Islamic dietary law forbids pork. *Shashlyk* (shish kebab), the standard street food, is prepared with beef, mutton, or minced meat and served with flatbread and lightly pickled onions. A kebab of fresh sheep liver and tail fat is a true luxury. While Westerners forget their charcuterie traditions, no part of an animal in Central Asia is ever wasted. There are still dishes made of lungs, intestines, and sheep's head and trotters.

Pilaf (*palov*) epitomizes Central Asian cuisine. A ceremonial dish for guests and family days, pilaf is so ubiquitous that there is sometimes a mistaken impression that it is their only dish. Meat, onions, and carrots are sautéed, then simmered to a broth, and covered with rice. Raisins, barberries, chickpeas, or dried fruit may be added for variety. Cumin is often the sole spice, while turmeric is added on special occasions for its golden color. Similar to an American barbecue, pilaf preparation is considered a manly challenge. Working with only a woklike *kazan* and spatula (*kapkir*), an *oshpaz*, master pilaf chef, can serve up to a thousand people from a single cauldron, making him much in demand for festivals and weddings.

Bread and noodles. Flatbread is baked daily at home or in communal ovens. Bread is considered holy and accompanies each meal. Most baked goods are made with wheat flour, though mung bean and corn flour are used also. Some flatbreads are topped with onions, pieces of sheep's fat, or even meat. Others are glazed with *kalonji*, anise, poppy, or sesame seeds. In Xinjiang the round plump breads astoundingly resemble New York City bagels. *Katlama*, related to the Indian *paratha*, is flaky unleavened bread cooked on a skillet.

The steppe nomads have added flour and dough to their soups for centuries. A dish of square flat noodles topped with boiled meat is called *beshbarmak* in Kazak-Kyrgyz areas. From farther east come steamed dumplings, *manty* (Korean *mandoo*), vying with pilaf for the national dish in Kyrgyzstan, Kazakhstan, Uzbekistan, and Chinese Turkistan. Uighurs have mastered hand-pulled noodles, common in Korea and China proper. Made with only soft wheat, water, and salt, the transformation of a ball of dough into noodle threads in a mat-

PROVERBIAL LAND OF MILK AND HONEY

Although God did not mention Central Asia when promising Moses a "good and spacious land, a land flowing with milk and honey," the region certainly fits the description. The Eurasian herders, having domesticated sheep and goats roughly ten thousand years ago, realized that milk, in addition to the meat and wool of their flocks, was essential to their survival. The pastoralists took advantage of microbiology to improve the flavor of fresh milk, make it more digestible and nutritious, and increase its shelf life. The resulting dairy product is determined by controlling the action of bacteria, enzyme, or yeast. Milk, either fresh or skimmed of cream, may be of several sources—ewe, goat, cow, camel, mare, and dri (yak). The first step is simply separating fresh cream from the milk to make a soured clotted cream, or *kaimak,* enjoyed with flatbread and honey. The honey is imbued with a marvelous flavor due to the nectar gathered from cotton and grape blossoms and the varied mountain valley flowers, grasses, and trees.

Fresh milk quickly sours through fermentation in warm conditions, essentially the same bacterial process employed for pickles, olives, or sourdough bread. Yogurt *(katyk)* is used in soups, beverages, and even doughs to add a pleasant sourness, with the lactic acid produced by bacteria breaking down the milk sugar. With reduced lactose, the cultured products become more digestible

for most Central Asians, who, along with 70 percent of the world, have a dairy intolerance. Fermented camel milk is *shubat,* and *agaran* is its cream. Mixing *katyk* and water creates a refreshing salty drink, *ayran* or *chalop* (Kyr), similar to the Indian *lassi.* Drained yogurt results in *suzma,* a fresh curd cheese eaten plain, in salads, or with soups and main courses as a garnish. Adding a rennet enzyme to milk makes *panir* or soft cheese, unaged, white, and rindless.

Kumys, fermented camel's or mare's milk, made famous by numerous Western travelers, including Marco Polo, has been subjected to both bacterial and yeast fermentation. Caucasian kefir is made with a similar process. *Kumys* or *ayrag* (Mongolian), primarily made with mare's milk, is the mildly alcoholic drink (up to 4 or 5 percent) of the nomads and may also be slightly fizzy with carbonic acid. *Saba* is a Kazak leather sack for making *kumys* that imparts a smoky, earthy quality. Refusing an offer of *kumys* may cause offense. Mare's milk has four times more vitamin C than cow's milk, aiding a pastoral diet scarce in fruits and vegetables. The remaining milk or whey from *kumys* or *suzma* is salted and sun-dried, formed into balls or bricks, and called *qurut* or *qurt.* This form, which is eaten often as a snack, lasts the winter months and may be added to soups or reconstituted as a drink.

---

ter of minutes is both compelling performance art and a dying culinary method.

A casing of dough with a typical filling of fatty mutton and onions becomes a number of other dishes simply by varying the cooking technique. If the dough is fried, the dish is called *belyashi* (Kazan Tartar) or *chebureki* (Crimean Tartar). The Turkish *borek,* also a fried savory pastry, may be related to the Slavic *pirog, piroshki,* and *pierogi.* Baked in a *tandir,* the dish is called *samsa* (Uzbek) or *sambusa* (Tajik), like Indian *samosa.* Steamed *manty* or *hoshan* (Kazak) are usually topped with a sauce of tomatoes, potatoes, and diced mutton. Smaller boiled versions of *manty* are *chuchvara, pelmeni* (Siberian), *tushbera* (Tajik), and *joshpara* (Farsi).

Hospitality and Traditions

Meals and customs. Central Asian cookery often requires great sacrifices on the part of the host. The Uzbek adage "*Mehmon otanda ulugh*" (the guest is greater than the father) remains accurate for most of the Muslim East. Generally, guests remove their shoes before entering the

house and are seated at a low table *(takhta)* or on the floor with a *kurpacha,* or cushion. Diners gather around a *dastarkhan* (literally, tablecloth), which is an enormous assortment of food offered to the honored guest. On some occasions, men and women are separated. Special meals are eaten commensally by hand and can last for several hours with multiple courses and endless cups *(piala)* of tea. Though most of the region embraces Islam, alcohol is widely accepted in the successor states.

In addition to the ever-present pilaf, some distinct dishes are served during Islamic holidays. Navrus, the Muslim New Year, corresponds to the spring equinox. *Halim,* wheat porridge, is prepared from boiled meat and wheat grains, seasoned with black pepper and cinnamon. A children's favorite, *nishalda,* popular during Ramadan, is made with whipped egg whites, sugar, and licorice flavoring. *Sumalak,* symbolic of friendship and tolerance, is among the most traditional dishes. Prepared only by women, overnight, wheat sprouts are blended with oil, flour, and sugar and cooked on low heat. Eid-ul-Fitr marks the end of Ramadan with three days of feasting.

Collecting mare's milk in Tourgut, Kyrgyzstan. PHOTO COURTESY OF GLENN R. MACK.

Tea and dessert. Freshly made green tea, the drink of hospitality, complements every meal. Teatime, which may occur at the slightest cause, often includes flatbread, sweets, fruits, and pastries. Dried fruit with nuts—walnuts, pistachios, and almonds—is also a perfect accompaniment. Black tea is common in the Russian regions. Both teas are served with sugar, milk, salt, butter, or even fruit preserves. Uzbeks have a custom called *shapirish*, whereby the hostess returns the first two cups back into the teapot to stir the infusion. Thus the tea is described as going from mud *(loy)* to tea *(choy)* to wine *(moy)*.

As sugar cane originated in India, sweets are a gift from the south, via Iran. This tradition produces tea sweets such *chakchak*, fried dough with honey; *urama*, fried spiraled strips of dough with powdered sugar; sugar-coated almonds; and *novvot*, crystallized sugar. More familiar halvah and *paklava* are also common desserts. *Sharbat* is fruit juice that migrated to Europe as frozen sherbet.

Food available outside the home includes street food and that from cafés, modern restaurants, and the traditional *chai-khana* (tearoom). Ideally near a poplar-lined stream or in a cool courtyard orchard, it is a gathering place for fraternity and socializing. The *chai-khana* in many ways functions like a community center and helps preserve certain aspects of Central Asian identity obscured by colonial powers.

Regional Variations and Specialties

The cuisines of Central Asia may be divided into three overlapping groups: Tajiks, Turks, and nomadic Turko-Mongol tribes. However simplistic, this categorization provides a more coherent approach to understanding the culinary cultures of Central Asia than organization along the arbitrary national boundaries. Numerous subcuisines from other ethnic minorities, such as Koreans, Tartars, Dungans (Chinese Muslims), Slavs, and Germans add to the culinary diversity of the area.

Sedentary cuisine. The Iranian-Tajik influence extends from Tajikistan and southern Uzbekistan to Iran and Afghanistan and beyond to northern Pakistan and Jammu-Kashmir in India. These cuisines employ more vegetables and legumes, resort to complex seasonings, and boast elaborate sweets. Years of civil strife in Tajikistan and Afghanistan have devastated food supplies and interrupted traditional foodways. Generally, the farther away from the nomadic steppe, the more complex the spice blends and seasoning of the dishes. In Tajikistan and Uzbekistan, an unusual dish is *tuhum barak*, an egg-filled ravioli flavored with sesame-seed oil. Tamerlane and his entourage of craftspeople from Samarkand, cooks included, brought the meat-eating tradition to India along with many fruits, particularly the melon and grape. The descendants of these cooks—the Wazas—are the master chefs of Kashmir.

The Turkic group of languages claims roughly 125 million speakers and stretches from Siberia to the Balkans. Uzbeks and Uighurs, as settled Turks, favor pilafs, noodles, and stews. Since the oasis civilization is a middle ground, literally and figuratively, between the Iranian courtly cuisine and the pastoral nomads, their food has become most representative of Central Asian cuisine. In Uzbekistan, *moshkichiri* and *moshhurda* are common meat and mung bean gruels. *Dimlama* is braised meat and vegetables cooked in a pot sealed with dough. Its origins may be tied to *dumpukht* in Farsi, signifying food cooked in its own steam, shortened also in India to *dum*, as in *dum-aloo*. Apricot seeds are specially treated and roasted in ash to produce an exceptional snack. Because of linguistic ties, Azerbaijan and Turkey are often included in Central Asian culinary culture, as these countries share roots, not to mention cooking methods and many dishes, with the Eurasian nomads.

Nomadic cuisine. Of all the Central Asian peoples, none has experienced such dramatic cultural upheaval due to colonization, industrialization, and urbanization as have the nomads. The traditional meal of steppe and highlands was meat on occasion, milk products, and the stray onion. As Turkmenistan is mostly desert, vegetable and grain cultivation is challenging. *Chorek* (flatbread), gruel, and tea remain typical for most meals.

In Soviet times the Turkmen, Kazaks, and Kyrgyz were forcefully settled into dreary apartment blocks. Separated from the land and their herds, the nomads adopted many Russian or Uzbek foods and customs. Kazaks and Kyrgyz claim as national dishes *beshbarmak* and *kumys*, fermented mare's milk. Horsemeat sausage *(kazy)*, when served with cold noodles, is called *naryn*. Barley, wheat, and millet are quite common; from them comes *dzarma*, fermented barley flour. *Boso*, or fermented millet, and *boorsak*, a ritual dish made from small pieces of deep-fat-fried dough, are also found in Tibet by the same name. When the Uighurs and Dungans fled China in the late nineteenth century, they brought *laghman*, other noodle dishes, and spicy peppers that were quickly embraced by the Kazaks and Kyrgyz.

The diminished state of traditional foodways in Central Asia is often decried, particularly when judging the cuisine through the distorting prism of Western restaurant culture. These Eurasian civilizations were completely transformed during the colonial experience. However, the trend of globalization triggers entrenchment of cultural heritage and local foodways. As borders open, outside interest is countered with a pronounced revival and demonstration of ethnic identity. If domestic traditions and hospitality persevere, the Central Asian culinary arts and its foodways are bound to flourish.

See also **China; Iran; Islam; Middle East; Noodles of Asia; Rice; Russia; Tea.**

BIBLIOGRAPHY

Arsel, Semahat, ed. *Timeless Tastes: Turkish Culinary Culture*. Istanbul: Vehbi Kooc Vakfi: DiVan, 1996.

Dunn, Ross E. *The Adventures of Ibn Battuta: A Muslim Traveler of the Fourteenth Century*. Reprint. Berkeley: University of California Press, 1990.

Frye, Richard N. *The Heritage of Central Asia from Antiquity to the Turkish Expansion*. Princeton, N.J.: Markus Wiener, 1996.

Makhmudov, Karim. *Uzbekskie bliuda* (Uzbek dishes). Tashkent: Uzbekistan, 1982.

Pokhlebkin, V. V. *Kukhni zakavkazskikh i sredneaziatskikh narodov* (Cuisine of the Caucasus and Central Asia). Moscow: Tsentrpoligraf, 1997.

Pokhlebkin, V. V. *Sobranie Izbrannykh Proizvedenii: Natsional'nye Kukhni Nashikh Narodov: Povarennaia Kniga* (Collected works: National cuisines of our people: Recipes). Moscow: Tsentrpoligraf, 1996.

Zubaida, Sami, and Richard Trapper, eds. *Culinary Cultures of the Middle East*. London: Tauris, 1994.

Glenn R. Mack

ASIA, SOUTHEAST. *See* **Southeast Asia.**

ASSESSMENT OF NUTRITIONAL STATUS.

Nutritional status is the balance between the intake of nutrients by an organism and the expenditure of these in the processes of growth, reproduction, and health maintenance. Because this process is highly complex and quite individualized, nutritional status assessment can be directed at a wide variety of aspects of nutriture. These range from nutrient levels in the body, to the products of their metabolism, and to the functional processes they regulate. Nutritional status can be measured for individuals as well as for populations. Accurate measurement of individual nutritional status is required in clinical practice. Population measures are more important in research. They can be used to describe nutritional status of the group, to identify populations or population segments at risk for nutrition-related health consequences, and to evaluate interventions.

The choice of nutritional status assessment method must be made mindful of the level at which one wants information, as well as of the validity and reliability of the method. All methods have error. All methods produce imperfect measures that are indirect approximations of the process. Whatever method is chosen for assessment of nutritional status, the data obtained must be compared with reference data to produce an indicator of nutritional status. The quality of the available reference data is, therefore, another factor that affects the assessment data.

Ideal methods are sensitive and specific. Unfortunately, it is difficult to achieve both in the assessment of nutritional status. Sensitivity refers to the ability of a technique to correctly identify those affected by a condition (for example, undernutrition) as having that condition. Specificity refers to the ability of a technique to correctly classify normal individuals as having normal nutritional status. Body mass index (wt/[ht]^2) is a global measure of nutritional status that illustrates the difference between these two constructs. Most persons who consume insufficient energy have low body mass index, so the measure is sensitive. However, there are other causes of low body mass index, including genetics and disease, so body mass index is not specific to nutritional status.

The assessment of nutritional status is commonly summarized by the mnemonic "ABCD," which stands for anthropometric measurement, biochemical or laboratory tests, clinical indicators, and dietary assessment. This review will focus on anthropometric and dietary techniques.

Anthropometric Approaches to Nutritional Status Assessment

Anthropometric approaches are, for the most part, relatively noninvasive methods that assess the size or body composition of an individual. For adults, body weight and height are used to evaluate overall nutritional status and to classify individuals as at healthy or nonhealthy weights. In the United States of America and other industrialized countries, the emphasis for unhealthy weight is overweight and obesity. The standards for these have changed over time. The most recent classification is to use body mass index (BMI, in kg/m^2) (Kuczmarski and Flegal, 2000). BMI, regardless of age or population, is normal at 18.5 to 25.0 kg/m^2, overweight at 25.0 to 29.9 kg/m^2, and obese at over 30.0 kg/m^2 (USDA & USDHHS, 2000). In general BMI greater than 30 is assumed to be due to excessive adiposity.

In children, growth charts have been developed to allow researchers and clinicians to assess weight- and height-for-age, as well as weight-for-height. For children, low height-for-age is considered stunting, while low weight-for-height indicates wasting. In addition to weight and height, measures of mid-arm circumference and skinfold measured over the triceps muscle at the mid-arm are used to estimate fat and muscle mass. Anthropometric measures of nutritional status can be compromised by other health conditions. For example, edema characteristic of some forms of malnutrition and other disease states can conceal wasting by increasing body weight. Head circumference can be used in children 36 months and younger to monitor brain growth in the presence of malnutrition. Brain growth is better spared than either height or weight during malnutrition.

To interpret anthropometric data, they must be compared with reference data. The choice of the appropriate reference has been discussed by Johnston and Ouyang.

Because well-nourished children in all populations follow similar patterns of growth, reference data need not come from the same population as the children of interest. It is of greater importance that reference data be based on well-defined, large samples, collected in populations that are healthy and adequately nourished. Reference growth charts (Kuczmarski et al., 2002) have been compiled from cross-sectional data collected from population surveys of U.S. children. These have been adopted as international standards by the World Health Organization.

Choosing a Dietary Approach to Nutritional Status Assessment

Several techniques exist for collecting dietary data with which to estimate nutritional status. Because these techniques vary in cost for data collection, burden on the respondent, and which aspects of diet they are designed to measure, it is important to clearly articulate the goals of dietary assessment of nutritional status before choosing an assessment strategy.

The primary consideration in choosing a dietary assessment method is the specific type of data needed. Is the research intended to document intake of "foods" or of "nutrients"? If the answer is foods, the method must take account of the population's foodways. These include variability in food intake patterns (for example, day-to-day, seasonal, ritual cycles); differences in food consumption by sex, age, and ethnicity; and what items the population considers to be legitimate "food." If the objective is to measure nutrient intake, the method must take into account several additional factors: food preparation techniques, including the addition of condiments and the effects of the technique on nutrient composition of the food; sources of error in the determination of amounts of foods consumed; differentiation distribution of nutrients among foods; and the contribution of "nonfood" consumption (such as betel nut, laundry starch, and vitamin and mineral supplements) to total nutrient consumption.

Another important consideration is the time period the data are intended to represent. If the period is a relatively discrete one, it may be possible to document diet quite precisely. However, if the interest is in measuring "usual" diet, the methods must allow this abstract concept to be estimated statistically.

Population measures of dietary status can be derived either from data describing the entire population or population sub-group, or from data describing samples of individuals. Population-wide data include food availability figures, which allow the assessment of food balance—the amount of food produced or imported by a population less that exported or used as nonhuman food. Such measures are necessarily crude, as they do not measure consumption directly. Another approach to measuring dietary status of groups has been to focus on the household. Indirect data on household food intake can be derived from records of foods brought into the household or from pantry inventories. Because of variations in intrahousehold distribution of foods, such techniques cannot be used to estimate individual intakes.

By far the most precise way of measuring dietary intake is to gather data on individuals. These methods depend on identifying a period of time for which data are needed, measuring food quantities consumed, and then translating these into nutrient amounts, either through direct chemical analysis or (more commonly) using food composition tables.

Common Methods for Dietary Data Collection

The most valid, or accurate, dietary methods are prospective methods. These involve keeping records of foods consumed over the period of time of interest. This can be done by individuals themselves, or by others observing them. Sometimes the foods are weighed before eating and then plate waste is weighed and subtracted. A similar method is to prepare two duplicate meals; one is consumed by the subject and the other is analyzed for nutrient content. Another method is the dietary record, in which the subject records estimated amounts of foods consumed. In any case, these methods are highly reactive because individuals may alter usual behavior to make their diet more socially desirable or to simplify the process of record keeping.

Recall methods are the most widely used type of dietary data collection method. They are less reactive, but also less accurate than record methods. Twenty-four hour recalls, in which the previous day's intake is queried in detail (for instance, foods, amounts, preparation techniques, condiments) are easiest for individuals to complete. The data reported are converted from foods to nutrients with the use of food composition tables. Because a single day is not representative of usual intake, multiple twenty-four hour recalls are frequently used. These multiple recalls can be thought of as sampling from an individual's ongoing food behavior. The number necessary to reliably measure diet depends on the nutrient of interest. Nutrients widely distributed in food (such as carbohydrates) require fewer days than nutrients not widely distributed (such as cholesterol). The number of recalls needed also depends on the nature of the diet. In societies where day-to-day and season-to-season food intake varies, more days are needed than where diets are more monotonous.

The semiquantitative food frequency is a recall method in which an individual summarizes the diet to produce a measure of usual intake. For a list of foods commonly eaten, the individual estimates how frequently the food has been eaten in the time period in question (often, one year) and in what amount. Food composition tables are then used to estimate the usual daily intake. This method combines low burden on the individual with low cost. It has been widely used and studied, as it is the foremost method used in nutritional epidemiology. Research has examined how best to formulate a list of foods,

how to present the foods to the subject, and whether portion sizes should be included.

Because the act of estimating frequency of intake is assumed to be based on cognitive processes, research has examined how best to maximize reliability and validity of food frequency data by focusing on the cognitive tasks experienced in the course of completing a food frequency questionnaire. This includes questions such as whether a long list of individual foods should be presented (for example, skim milk, 2 percent milk, whole milk) or whether foods should be nested (for example, questions about the presence or absence of milk in the diet separated from the variety of milk). The results of these analyses have been mixed but suggest that incorporation of formatting changes based on cognitive theory will enhance the accuracy of reporting.

There has also been recent discussion of the actual task of summarizing and estimating intake experienced by the subject. The traditional explanation that persons completing a food frequency questionnaire actually retrieve and integrate past behavior to achieve an average dietary intake has been challenged by arguments that persons answer food frequency questionnaires in terms of a composite image of themselves and their diet, rather than a statistical estimate. If the latter is the case, one might expect that attempts to minimize error will reach a threshold of error that is unlikely to be crossed without a major conceptual shift in dietary data collection techniques for nutritional status assessment.

See also **Caloric Intake; Dietary Assessment; Food Consumption Surveys; Nutrition.**

BIBLIOGRAPHY

Beaton, G. H., J. Milner, P. Corey, V. McGuire, M. Cousins, E. Stewart, M. de Ramos, D. Hewitt, P. V. Grambsch, N. Kassim, and J. A. Little. "Sources of Variance in 24-hour Dietary Recall Data: Implications for Nutrition Study Design and Interpretation." *American Journal of Clinical Nutrition* 32 (1979): 2546–2549.

Buzzard, Marilyn. "24-Hour Recall and Food Record Methods." In *Nutritional Epidemiology*, 2d ed., edited by Walter Willett. Oxford: Oxford University Press, 1998.

Drewnowski, Adam. "Diet Image: A New Perspective on the Food-Frequency Questionnaire." *Nutrition Reviews* 59 (2001): 370–372.

Dwyer, Johanna. "Dietary Assessment." In *Modern Nutrition in Health and Disease*, 9th ed., edited by Maurice E. Shils, James A. Olson, Moshe Shike, and A. Catherine Ross. Baltimore: Williams and Wilkins, 1999.

Johnston, Francis E. "Reference Data for Physical Growth in Nutritional Anthropology." In *Training Manual in Nutritional Anthropology*, edited by Sara A. Quandt and Cheryl Ritenbaugh. American Anthropological Association, Special Publication no. 20, 1986.

Johnston, Francis E., and Z. Ouyang. "Choosing Appropriate Reference Data for the Anthropometric Assessment of Nutritional Status." In *Anthropometric Assessment of Nutritional*

Status, edited by John H. Himes. New York: Wiley-Liss, 1991.

Kuczmarski, Robert J., and Katherine M. Flegal. "Criteria for Definition of Overweight in Transition: Background and Recommendations for the United States." *American Journal of Clinical Nutrition* 72 (2000): 1074–1081.

Kuczmarski, Robert J., C. L. Ogden, and S. S. Guo. 2000 CDC Growth Charts for the United States: Methods and Development. National Center for Health Statistics. Vital Health Statistics 11 (246), 2002.

Quandt, Sara A. "Intracultural Variation in American Infant Diet: Patterns in Diversity and Consequence for Research Design." *American Behavioral Scientist* 31 (1987): 250–265.

Thompson, F. E., A. F. Subar, C. C. Brown, A. F. Smith, C. O. Sharbaugh, J. B. Jobe, B. Mittl, J. T. Gibson, and R. G. Ziegler. "Cognitive Research Enhances Accuracy of Food Frequency Questionnaire Reports: Results of an Experimental Validation Study." *Journal of the American Dietetic Association* 102 (2002): 212–225.

U.S. Department of Agriculture and U.S. Department of Health and Human Services. Nutrition and Your Health: Dietary Guidelines for Americans. Washington, D.C.: U.S. Government Printing Office, 2000. Home and Garden Bulletin No. 232.

Willett, Walter. *Nutritional Epidemiology*, 2d ed. Oxford: Oxford University Press, 1998.

Sara A. Quandt

ASSYRIA, ANCIENT. *See* **Mesopotamia, Ancient.**

AUSTRALIA AND NEW ZEALAND.

Australasian neighbors, once part of the same vast land mass known as Gondwanaland, Australia and New Zealand share a similar recent history. Both were British colonies settled largely by emigrants from England, Scotland, and Ireland, and both experienced rapid agricultural expansion in the 1800s. The initial prosperity of both was built on primary production, a high proportion of which—wool, meat, wheat, dairy products, fresh fruits such as apples and pears, and dried fruits such as raisins, sultanas, and currants—was exported, principally to Britain (until the formation of the European Economic Community).

One significant difference between the two countries is in their indigenous populations; the original inhabitants of Australia, for over forty thousand years before white settlement, were nomadic hunter-gathering Aborigines, while in New Zealand the first people were relatively stable semiagrarian communities of Maoris who arrived from eastern Polynesia in the seventh or eighth century. Both groups exploited indigenous food resources, but the Maoris also brought with them plant foods such as yams, taro, and kumara (sweet potato), which they cultivated.

Early Colonial Food and Cooking

The convict colony of New South Wales, founded in 1788, was at first heavily reliant on imported rations. Gradually, however, emancipated convicts and free settlers, many with farming experience, settled the land, often establishing orchards and gardens around the homesteads and becoming largely self-sufficient. These initial farming experiences benefited later colonies, including New Zealand.

The success and profitability of sheep grazing, which saw sheep numbers in New South Wales increase almost fivefold between 1803 and 1813, meant that meat was abundant and very cheap in the colonies, and a pattern of "meat three times a day" was firmly established by the 1840s. The standard weekly ration for Australian farm laborers in the 1830s was ten pounds of meat, ten pounds of flour, two pounds of sugar, and four ounces of tea.

Mutton, tea, and damper formed the basis of a sustaining, if monotonous, diet for many rural workers. Damper was a yeastless substitute for bread, made of flour, salt, and water and cooked in the embers. In *A Summer at Port Phillip* (1843), Robert Dundas Murray wrote: "You have mutton and damper today,—mutton and damper will appear tomorrow, and from that day till the end of the year, your dinner is mutton, boiled, roasted or stewed." Even in landowners' homesteads, mutton was ubiquitous. It was generally cooked as Robert Dundas Murray described, but in both Australia and New Zealand at least one new dish became popular—Colonial Goose, a roasted boned leg or shoulder of mutton with a sage-and-onion stuffing.

In both Australia and New Zealand, the early white settlers made only limited use of the indigenous food resources, preferring to choose those foods that resembled familiar fare. Seafood, including the oysters of Sydney harbor, and shellfish such as *toheroa* and *paua* (abalone) in New Zealand, were readily accepted and eaten, as were freshwater fish and crustaceans. In Australia kangaroo was rated equal to hare and venison, and kangaroo tail soup was often featured on menus; game birds such as quail, pigeon, duck, and wild turkey were also hunted and eaten. Of the vast range of plant foods consumed by the indigenous inhabitants, only a few, such as native fruits made into preserves or desserts, appeared on colonial tables.

Urban Lifestyles

The gold rushes of the mid-nineteenth century brought great prosperity, especially to the cities, which, by the 1870s, could boast sophisticated restaurants and a wide range of imported luxury foods, from caviar to Gorgonzola cheese. In domestic kitchens, however, plain, homely, English-style cooking prevailed, though with local adaptations. The roast (or baked) dinner serves as an example of how Australia and New Zealand developed their own variations of English traditions; the joint, beef or lamb, was baked in the oven with drippings, sur-

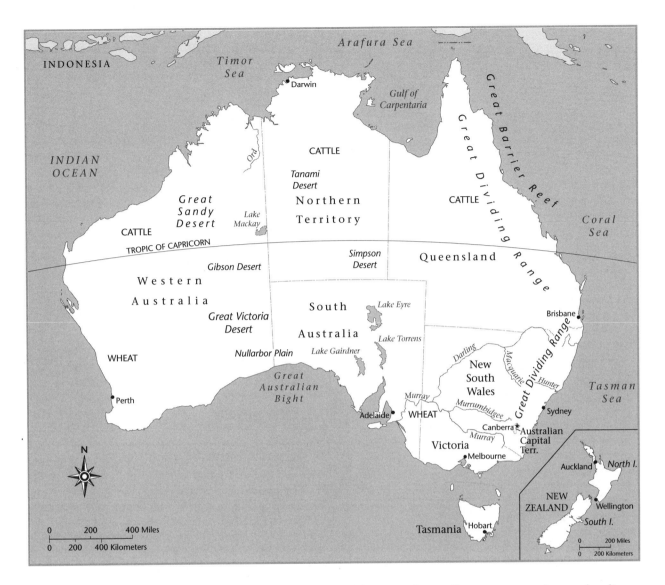

rounded by a variety of vegetables—the obligatory potatoes and pumpkin, plus onions, parsnips, orange-fleshed kumara in New Zealand, sometimes carrots, and white-fleshed sweet potato—and served with gravy and a green vegetable, usually peas or beans.

By the turn of the century food was no longer cooked in the hearth but on wood-burning ranges or, in the cities and large towns, gas stoves, which were introduced in the 1870s. Ice chests were also becoming common at this time, favoring the growing popularity of cold puddings such as jellies, flummeries, and molded custards which also took advantage of commercially manufactured gelatin.

Large quantities of meat were still being eaten, despite success with the first shipment of frozen meat from Australia to England in 1880 and subsequent development of a profitable export trade, and despite increasingly loud denunciations of overconsumption of meat by the medical profession. The Sydney physician Dr. Philip Muskett, in particular, railed against the eating habits of a nation of meat worshipers and tried to persuade Australians to adopt a diet more appropriate to the climate by eating more vegetables, particularly salads. At this time, according to the evidence of recipe books, vegetables were typically overcooked and salads rare; tomatoes did not become popular until the 1880s and even then tended to be cooked rather than eaten raw.

Most Australian and New Zealand households at the end of the nineteenth century began the day with a substantial breakfast: porridge, bacon and eggs, sausages or chops (particularly on farms that raised their own meat), toast or bread, tea or coffee. Dinner, the principal meal, was often served in the middle of the day and was centered on the main course of meat and vegetables, sometimes preceded by soup, and followed by dessert of some sort—a hot or cold pudding, custard, tart, or pie. (See the menus sidebar.) The evening meal generally featured meat again, but was less substantial. In cities and towns dinner was often eaten in the evening, after the return from work of the (male) head of the household, and the midday meal, lunch, was reduced to sandwiches and fruit

AN ECONOMICAL DINNER, 1891

Shoulder of mutton, onion sauce
Baked potatoes
Boiled cabbage
Oxfordshire pudding
Stewed fruit, cheese, biscuits

SOURCE: Wicken, Harriet. *The Australian Home, a Handbook of Domestic Economy.* Sydney: Edwards Dunlop, 1891, p. 260

* * *

FAMILY DINNER MENU, 1940

Vermicelli & Parsnip Soup
Triangles of Toast
Baked Stuffed Shoulder of Mutton
Brown Gravy, Red Currant Jelly
Baked Potatoes, Boiled Celery
Stewed Peaches, Baked Custard

SOURCE: Osborne, W. A., and E. Howell. *What Shall We Have for Dinner?* Melbourne: Albright & Wilson, n.d., p. 11

* * *

FOUR ECONOMY MENUS, 1965

Beef curry; Lemon-drop pancakes
Hamburgers; Lemon cream rice
Potato meatloaf; Caramel meringue pie
Brawn, potato salad; Apple snow

SOURCE: *Australian Women's Weekly,* 2 February 1965

* * *

BUDGET STRETCHERS— INEXPENSIVE FAMILY DISHES, 1991

Tomato and spinach lasagne
Chickpea casserole with potato dumplings
Spicy baked eggplant
Glazed chicken wings
Beef and vegetable curry
Tuna and corn frittata
Ham and vegetable fried rice

SOURCE: *Australian Women's Weekly,* August 1991

or to the quasi-national dish of both countries, the meat pie (accompanied by tomato sauce).

Scones, Sponges, and Afternoon Teas

In addition to the three daily meals was afternoon tea, which could be particularly lavish on Sundays. Until about the mid-twentieth century, afternoon tea was the accepted way of entertaining guests; it was a particularly feminine form of entertaining, and gave women the opportunity to display their flair and imagination.

Many of the dishes that Australians and New Zealanders claim as their own belong to the world of the afternoon tea. Adapting a British tradition, Australians developed pumpkin scones (with the addition of mashed pumpkin) and fried scones. Lamingtons, cubes of butter cake coated with a thin chocolate icing and rolled in desiccated coconut, were invented in the early 1900s. Anzac biscuits, made with rolled oats, flour, coconut, butter, sugar, and golden syrup, and named after the forces that served in World War I, are common to both countries, as are afghan biscuits, melting moments, and hokey pokey biscuits. Cooks in both Australia and New Zealand specialize in light, airy sponge cakes, often served as a four-inch-high sponge sandwich filled with jam and cream.

Another antipodean invention is the Pavlova, a crisp-shelled, soft meringue cake spread lavishly with whipped cream and decorated with fresh fruit, such as strawberries or passion fruit pulp. Its origins are still disputed, but it seems likely that the cake originated in New Zealand, even if today's standard recipe reflects a later Australian version.

Multicultural Influences

In both Australia and New Zealand, postwar food and eating reflects multicultural influences. Since the 1960s, increasing numbers of Australians and New Zealanders have traveled in Europe and Asia and experienced different cuisines, while at the same time an influx of immigration, particularly from Mediterranean countries—Greece, Italy, the former Yugoslavia, Turkey, and the Middle East—has resulted in the availability of a vast diversity of foods and restaurants. Many Vietnamese settled in Australia at the end of the conflict in that country, further diversifying the range of Asian foods and ingredients available. The tropical city of Darwin, in particular, has a large population of Asian and Pacific Island peoples whose foods and cuisines can be sampled at the weekly (in the dry season) Mindil Beach Market. Among successful "new" foods are Cervena (farmed deer) in New Zealand and kangaroo in Australia, harvested in the wild under license. New Zealand has also effectively commercialized the kiwifruit, a fruit of Chinese origin (and formerly known as the Chinese gooseberry) imported into New Zealand in the early 1900s.

The changes in eating habits since around 1950 demonstrate a convergence of different trends. Supermarkets have replaced individual specialists and convenience foods—prepared soups and sauces, instant cakes and puddings, frozen pastries and ice creams—have largely replaced the raw ingredients from which such dishes used to be made. Relaxation of licensing laws, together with greater appreciation of wine, led to a blossoming of restaurants, often run by immigrants; today's opportunities for dining out range from silver-service

Shepherd Peter Coble at the Narra Allen sheep station north of Boorowa, Australia, prepares to dose Merino sheep in the paddock. Sheep raising is one of Australia's major agricultural industries. © PAUL A. SOUDERS/CORBIS.

restaurants to casual cafés to fast-food franchises. Thanks to both the food manufacturing industry and restaurants, people are familiar with a wide range of cuisines, both European and Asian. Emphasis on the links between health and eating has made people increasingly aware of dietary advice. Finally, a greater recognition of vegetarianism is obvious, with most cafés and restaurants including vegetarian options in their menus.

Domestic menus, while becoming more simplified, also show the influences of many different cuisines and a willingness to accept nonmeat meals. (See the menus sidebar.) Meat consumption declined dramatically in the 1970s when the cholesterol–heart disease connection was announced, though the cooked breakfast had already begun to wane in the presence of a proliferation of ready-to-eat breakfast cereals. In Australia the consumption of meat is less than two-thirds what it had been one hundred years earlier, and consumption of lamb and mutton has halved. In fact, there is more chicken, and almost as much pork, eaten as lamb and mutton (both chicken and pork are the products of intensive factory farming).

The last years of the twentieth century also saw greater awareness of indigenous food resources, such as the Australian flavorings of lemon myrtle and native pepper leaf, which are increasingly used in restaurants and by the food industry.

See also **British Isles**; **Pacific Ocean Societies**.

BIBLIOGRAPHY

Burton, David. *Two Hundred Years of New Zealand Food & Cookery.* Wellington: Reed, 1982.

Farrer, K. T. H. *A Settlement Amply Supplied: Food Technology in Nineteenth Century Australia.* Melbourne: Melbourne University Press, 1980.

Pascoe, Elise, and Cherry Ripe. *Australia the Beautiful Cookbook.* Sydney: Cumulus, 1995.

Santich, Barbara. *What the Doctors Ordered: 150 Years of Dietary Advice in Australia.* Melbourne: Hyland House, 1995.

Symons, Michael. *One Continuous Picnic: A History of Eating in Australia.* Adelaide: Duck Press, 1982.

Barbara Santich

AUSTRALIAN ABORIGINES.

Australian Aborigines are believed to have first arrived in northern Australia forty to sixty thousand years ago. They gradually spread throughout the continent, adapting to a vast range of environments from coastal tropics to inland desert, from temperate grasslands to mountainous highlands and riverine plains. In view of the diversity of plant and animal resources available in such a variety of settings, it is difficult to generalize about Aboriginal food, diet, and cooking practices. Nevertheless, some fundamental features were common to virtually all of the five hundred "tribes" or language groups believed to have been living in Australia at the time of European settlement at the end of the eighteenth century.

Hunter-Gatherers

Aborigines practiced a highly mobile hunter-gatherer lifestyle, moving frequently from place to place in accordance with seasonal availabilities of food resources. At the same time, they manipulated the environment in such a way as to favor certain species of flora and fauna. Their management of the land and its resources included setting light to dry grass and undergrowth in specific areas at certain times of the year in order to drive out small animals that they could easily capture. This practice has since been termed "firestick farming." It had a secondary benefit in that the new green growth which followed rain attracted small marsupials and other animals to the area, thus ensuring food supplies.

Typically, men hunted large game such as kangaroos and emus, and speared, snared, or otherwise procured smaller animals (opossums, bandicoots), birds (wild ducks, swans, pigeons, geese), and fish. Men tended to operate individually, while groups of women and older children collected plant foods (fruits, nuts, tubers, seeds), small game such as lizards and frogs, and shellfish. There were variations to this pattern; around coastal Sydney, the principal food-gathering task of women was fishing, and men also collected vegetables. The relative contributions of men and women to the communal meal varied according to season and location, but women's gathering activities could provide from 50 to 80 percent of a group's food. The time taken to collect a day's food varied similarly, but rarely would it have occupied the whole day.

The Aboriginal diet was far from monotonous, with a very wide range of food resources exploited. In northern Australia, thirty different species of shellfish were

An Australian Aborigine prepares to throw a boomerang while hunting in the Outback. Photo dated 1930. © BETTMANN/CORBIS.

collected throughout the year from seashore and mudflats; in Victoria, about nine hundred different plant species were used for food. Whatever the available resources, Aborigines did not always and necessarily eat everything that was edible; in some coastal regions fish and sea animals were preferred as sources of protein, and land animals were relatively neglected. On the other hand, Tasmanian Aborigines ate lobsters, oysters, and other shellfish but did not eat scaly fish; they avoided carnivorous animals and the monotremes platypus and echidna, though in other regions echidnas were eaten.

Tools were basic: a digging stick for women, spear and spear thrower for men. Fish, birds, and small game could be caught in woven nets or in conical basket traps. Many Aboriginal groups used lines, with crude shell or wooden hooks, to catch fish; alternatively, fish traps were sometimes constructed in rivers and along the coast to entrap fish, or temporary poisons were placed in waterholes to stun fish or bring them to the surface.

Food Distribution and Taboos

Complex rules determined food sharing arrangements. Men were usually treated preferentially in the distribution of game, with the hunter distributing the various portions among his male relatives who might then pass some to the women; if the hunter himself had a share it was an inferior cut. Offal—heart, liver, kidneys, brains—tended to be particularly prized, and often went to senior men. Women's gathering was for themselves and their immediate family rather than for the whole group, and there were certain plant foods that men apparently ignored.

Because of Aboriginal spiritual beliefs that people, plants, animals, and, indeed, the land are all part of a system created by ancestral spirits, all united and having equal rights to the resources of the country, totemic relationships existed between human and nonhuman species. The rules governing these relationships varied; for some groups killing and eating the totem was always taboo, while for others it might have been prohibited only at specific times or in special ceremonies. Thus some language groups of Aborigines may not have eaten emu while neighboring groups did.

Particular taboos, usually involving animal foods, applied to women during pregnancy or lactation, to young girls at their first menstruation, and to young boys at the time of their initiation. Wallaby and two species of bandicoot were sometimes forbidden to girls, because they would cause premature puberty, and to young boys, because they would favor brownish rather than black beards. Some foods, such as bitter tubers, were prohibited to children but sweet foods, such as plant galls and the edible gums that exude from kurrajong and other trees, were regarded as special treats and preferentially left to the young.

Food Preparation and Cooking

Many fruits and nuts and a few plant foods could be eaten raw and did not require cooking, but generally roots, bulbs, and tubers were roasted in hot ashes or hot sand. Some required more or less lengthy preparations to improve their digestibility or, in some cases, to remove bitterness or leach out quasi-poisonous components. In the central Australian desert, Aborigines relish the honey sucked from the distended bellies of underground worker ants; in effect, these "honey ants" serve as live food stores for other worker ants.

The principal means of removing toxins were pounding, soaking, and roasting, or a combination of any of these. One particular variety of yam, *Dioscorea bulbifera*, was subjected to a series of treatments to remove bitterness. First it was scorched to shrivel the skin, which was removed; then it was sliced and the slices coated with wet ashes and baked in a ground oven for twelve hours or more, and the ashes were then washed off before eating.

The kernels of the cycad palm (*Cycas armstrongii*), highly toxic in their unprocessed state, were treated by pounding, soaking in still or running water until fermented, and pounding again between stones to produce a thick paste that was cooked in hot ashes, sometimes wrapped in paperbark, yielding a kind of damper or bread.

Aborigines did not have sophisticated cooking equipment; basic culinary techniques included baking in hot ashes, steaming in an earth oven, or roasting on hot coals, this last method typically used for fish, crabs, small turtles, and reptiles. Oysters, too, were often cooked on hot coals until they opened, but in northern Australia large bivalves were "cooked" by lighting a quick fire on top of the closely packed shells arranged on clean sand, hinge side uppermost.

Cooking in hot ashes was the most common method of preparing tubers, roots, and similar plant products including yams (*Dioscorea* spp.) and the onion-shaped tubers of spike rush (*Eleocharis* spp.), both of which were important foods for Aborigines in northern Australia. Witchetty grubs (*Xyleutes* spp.) and similar grubs from other trees were also cooked in hot ashes, if not eaten raw, as were the flat cakes, commonly called dampers, made from the seeds of wild grasses such as native millet (*Panicum* sp.). The relatively complicated preparation involved threshing, winnowing, grinding (using smooth stones), the addition of water to make a paste, then baking in the ashes. Seeds of other plants, such as wattles (*Acacia* spp.), pigweed (*Portulaca* spp.), and saltbush (*Atriplex* spp.), as well as the spores of nardoo (*Marsilea drummondii*), were treated similarly.

Earth ovens were essentially pits, sometimes lined with paperbark or gum leaves, heated with coals or large stones previously heated in a fire. Foods to be cooked were placed in the oven, covered with more paperbark, grass, or leaves and sometimes more hot stones, then enclosed with earth or sand. Roots and tubers were sometimes placed in rush baskets for cooking in an earth oven, and when clay was available, such as near the edge of a river, fish were enclosed in clay before baking.

Large game such as kangaroo and emu was gutted immediately after killing and carried back to camp where the carcass was thrown onto a fire for singeing. After the flesh had been scraped clean, the animal was placed in a pit in which a fire had previously been lit to supply hot coals, covered with more hot coals plus earth or ash or sand, and baked. The cooking time depended on how long hungry people were willing to wait.

Ceremonial Foods

When special occasions such as initiation brought large numbers of Aborigines together, it was essential that food resources in the vicinity of the meeting place were both adequate and reliable. Ceremonial foods, therefore, were less associated with particular qualities than with seasonal abundance. In the mountainous regions of southern New South Wales and Victoria, bogong moths (*Agrotis infusa*) were profuse and easy to collect in late spring and summer, and at this time Aboriginal groups converged in the mountains where ceremonies took place. The prevalence of shell middens suggests that shellfish provided ceremonial sustenance in coastal areas. In Arnhem Land (Northern Territory) cycad nuts were plentiful at the end of the dry season, when travel was still possible, and the kernels, once heated to remove toxins, were ground to yield a thick paste, and subsequently baked in the ashes to serve as a special ceremonial food for men participating in sacred ceremonies and forbidden to women and children unless authorized by older men.

Many Aborigines today have lost touch with their foods and foodways, preferring instead the convenience of Western-style foods. Nevertheless, recognition of the health benefits to Aborigines of their traditional diet has resulted in active encouragement of hunter-gatherer practices, even if only to supplement store foods. In many areas, Aborigines have special hunting and fishing rights for species that are otherwise protected or subject to limits—though today their hunting typically involves firearms rather than clubs and spears.

See also **Hunting and Gathering; Pacific Ocean Societies.**

BIBLIOGRAPHY

Bryce, Suzy, comp. *Women's Gathering and Hunting in the Pitjantjatjara Homelands.* Alice Springs, Northern Territory, Australia: IAD Press, 1997.

Crawford, I. M. *Traditional Aboriginal Plant Resources in the Kalumburu Area: Aspects in Ethno-economics.* Perth: Western Australian Museum, 1982.

Isaacs, Jennifer. *Bush Food: Aboriginal Food and Herbal Medicine.* Sydney: Weldons, 1987.

Low, Tim. *Bush Tucker: Australia's Wild Food Harvest.* Sydney: Angus and Robertson, 1989.

Meehan, Betty. *Shell Bed to Shell Midden.* Canberra: Australian Institute of Aboriginal Studies, 1982.

Rose, Frederick G. G. *The Traditional Mode of Production of the Australian Aborigines.* Sydney: Angus and Robertson, 1987.

Stewart, Kathy, and Bob Percival. *Bush Foods of New South Wales: A Botanic Record and an Aboriginal Oral History.* Sydney: Royal Botanic Gardens, 1997.

Zola, Nelly, and Beth Gott. *Koorie Plants, Koorie People: Traditional Aboriginal Food, Fibre, and Healing Plants of Victoria.* Canberra: Koorie Heritage Trust, 1992.

Barbara Santich

AUSTRIA. *See* **Germany, Austria, Switzerland.**

AVERSION TO FOOD. Food aversions are far more common, far more diverse both within and across cultures, and far stronger than is often realized. Examination of the characteristics and origins of food aversions can help to illustrate the many contributions of genes and environment to behavior. Further, an understanding of food aversions can be useful in understanding, as well as treating, many eating and drinking disorders.

Classification of Food Aversions

Food aversions have been classified into four types: foods that are rejected because they are dangerous, inappropriate, disgusting, or distasteful. We consider foods to be dangerous, and therefore do not eat these foods, if eating them has previously resulted in physical harm, or if eating these foods is reputed to cause physical harm. However, a dangerous food, such as poisonous mushrooms, would be eaten by someone if there were some medication to prevent any illness from occurring.

Inappropriate foods are items that we consider not to be food. An example of an inappropriate food would be Kentucky bluegrass. Although deer and other herbivores might eat this grass, we would consider it inappropriate for humans to do so. Similarly, there may be an item, such as a particular kind of berry, that is considered to be a food by one culture but not by another.

There are several reasons why someone might treat an item as an inappropriate food. One involves the taste of the item. From birth, humans find certain tastes, notably the taste of bitter, to be aversive, and therefore may not consider items with those tastes to be appropriate foods. For example, many wild plants taste extremely bitter. Given that poisonous plants are often bitter, scientists believe that humans who avoided bitter tastes were more likely to survive and therefore humans evolved to have an innate aversion to bitter tastes. Direct experience with an item may also contribute to its classification as an inappropriate food; attempts to chew some wild plants can be fruitless. Finally, someone may consider an item to be an inappropriate food because of information passed on by someone else. For example, caregivers may tell children that grass is not food.

Disgusting foods are those that most of us would not want in our meals or stomachs no matter how the foods were disguised and no matter how small the amount. Some examples of items classified as disgusting foods are urine and feces. Foods can become disgusting because of someone's having observed others' reactions to these foods, because of contact of a previously nondisgusting food with something considered disgusting, or because a food looks similar to something disgusting. Thus, because most American children learn from others that insects are disgusting foods, we consider a glass of milk that used to have a cockroach in it to be disgusting, and we find fudge that looks similar to feces to be disgusting. Similarly, cultural beliefs can result in certain foods being considered disgusting. For example, many vegetarians consider meat to be disgusting, and Jews who keep kosher may find meal combinations of meat and dairy products to be disgusting.

Probably the most studied is the fourth and final category: distasteful foods. These are foods that most of us would not mind eating if the taste of the food were covered up by another taste, or if we only found out that we had eaten it after we had finished eating. An example is warm milk. Once again, an innate dislike of certain tastes can contribute to food aversions of this sort. However, many members of the distasteful food category are illness-induced food aversions (also known as taste aversions). Humans and many other species exhibit illness-induced food aversions when they eat something, become ill, and then do not want to eat that food again. This is an extremely powerful type of learning. Study of the acquisition of illness-induced food aversions has proved extremely important to the development of general learning theory, and has resulted in a number of different applications outside of the laboratory. Therefore, the following sections discuss illness-induced food aversion learning in some detail.

Taste Aversion Learning: Basic Observations

Prior to scientists' conducting any investigations of taste aversion learning, farmers were aware of this phenomenon, which they called bait shyness. The farmers found that it was difficult to kill rats by putting out poisoned bait. The rats would take only small samples of any new food, in this case the bait, and if they then became ill, they would subsequently avoid the bait.

Laboratory experiments on taste aversion learning began in the 1950s. Researchers noticed that rats eat less after being irradiated. Apparently irradiation makes rats gastrointestinally ill and they associate the illness with food, resulting in a taste aversion to the food.

In 1966 John Garcia and Robert A. Koelling used a taste aversion paradigm to show learning theorists that it is easier to learn some associations than others. In their experiment, rats more easily learned to avoid licking flavored water when that licking was followed by illness than by shock, and they more easily learned to avoid licking water accompanied by clicks and light flashes when that licking was followed by shock than by illness. Garcia and Koelling concluded that it is easier for rats to associate tastes with illness and audiovisual events with shock than vice versa. It was due to results such as these that this type of learning was labeled taste aversion learning.

Odors may also play an important role in food aversions linked to illness, yet the term "taste aversion learning" has persisted. The fact that tastes and odors are more easily associated with illness than with other sorts of events helps us to survive. The presence of a poison is more likely to be indicated by a particular odor or taste than by a particular appearance or sound.

Subsequent experiments found that taste aversion learning has some other special properties that may help animals to survive. For example, taste aversions can be acquired with up to twenty-four hours between consumption of the food and illness. This is advantageous because it may take hours before a poison will result in illness. In addition, in taste aversion learning, the taste actually seems to come to taste bad. This also helps animals to survive because a poison should be avoided no matter under what circumstances it is encountered. Finally, taste aversions are more likely to form to novel foods, and often form after just one pairing of a taste with illness. These characteristics help to ensure that, as much as possible, animals learn quickly to avoid new poisonous foods. Animals appear to have evolved so that they easily acquire long-lasting aversions to cues associated with poisonous foods.

Taste aversion learning has been studied in a great many species, including humans. Surveys have found that most college students report having acquired at least one taste aversion. In general these aversions are strong and have persisted a long time. Laboratory experiments have shown that taste aversions are acquired similarly across species.

Applications of Taste Aversion Learning

Research on taste aversion learning can help us to understand, and possibly modify, many food aversions and preferences. For example, taste aversion learning may cause what are termed specific hungers. These are preferences for specific foods containing a nutrient, such as thiamine or sodium, in which an animal's diet has been deficient. Animals may feel ill when deficient in these nutrients, and thus form taste aversions to their usual foods. New foods, or foods associated with recovery from the illness, are therefore preferred.

In a very different application, taste aversion learning has been used for wildlife management—to prevent coyotes from attacking sheep on ranches in the western part of the United States. Many ranchers choose simply to kill the coyotes. However, coyotes are a valuable part of the ecosystem (for example, by decreasing the rabbit population). Researchers reasoned that, if they could train the coyotes to avoid sheep but not rabbits, this would preserve the ecosystem. They therefore placed lamb bait laced with an illness-inducing drug on the range in areas frequented by coyotes. The coyotes appeared to acquire an aversion to eating or even approaching sheep. In fact, after aversion training, coyotes behave submissively toward sheep, running the other way when a sheep approaches.

Taste aversion learning has also been helpful in understanding the life-threatening anorexia that can accompany cancer. Some cancer treatments, such as radiation and chemotherapy, can cause gastrointestinal illness. When this illness is paired with food consumption, taste aversions can result. Ilene L. Bernstein and Mary M. Webster gave child and adult patients a novel-tasting ice cream prior to their chemotherapy and the patients acquired an aversion to that ice cream. These findings and others have resulted in the development of the "scapegoat technique." This technique involves giving cancer patients a novel food along with some familiar food just prior to their chemotherapy. The patient forms an aversion to the novel food and not to the familiar, usual food.

Although it might seem that taste aversion learning could be useful in decreasing overeating, it is not employed for this purpose. Taste aversions form to specific foods, and it is too easy for a patient to switch to overeating a different food once an aversion has been acquired to a previously overconsumed food.

In contrast, taste aversion learning has been successfully employed in treating alcohol abuse, although the pairing of alcohol and illness must be done carefully in order for strong taste aversions to develop. In addition, it is necessary for illness to be paired with a variety of alcoholic beverages in order to ensure that an alcoholic does not switch to new alcoholic beverages following aversion training.

Conclusion

There are a great many different types of food aversions in humans and other animals. Some of these aversions help animals to survive, and others can be extremely debilitating. Continuing research will help to maximize the

Martin E. P. Seligman (president of the American Psychological Association in 1998) has described how, in 1972, he ate sauce béarnaise on steak and then became ill with what was definitely stomach flu (his colleague at work who had not eaten the steak came down with the same affliction, and his wife who had eaten the steak did not). Yet, even though he was absolutely convinced that the sauce béarnaise did not cause his illness, Seligman acquired an aversion to it.

*

Some children and pregnant women repeatedly consume nonnutritive substances such as paint, plaster, and dirt. Because such food cravings are most likely to appear in people who need a lot of nutrients, it has been proposed that these cravings are the result of specific hungers for minerals such as iron.

positive effects of these aversions, and minimize their negative effects.

See also **Additives**; **Anorexia, Bulimia**; **Bioactive Food Components**; **Disgust**; **Food Safety**; **Sensation and the Senses**; **Taboos**; **Toxins, Unnatural, and Food Safety**.

BIBLIOGRAPHY

American Psychiatric Association. *Diagnostic and Statistical Manual of Mental Disorders*. 4th ed. Washington, D.C.: APA, 1994.

Barnett, Samuel Anthony. *The Rat: A Study in Behavior*. Chicago: Aldine, 1963. Description of bait shyness.

Bernstein, Ilene L., and Mary M. Webster. "Learned Food Aversions: A Consequence of Cancer Chemotherapy." In *Cancer, Nutrition, and Eating Behavior*. Edited by Thomas G. Burish, Sandra M. Levy, and Beth E. Meyerowitz. Hillsdale, N.J.: Lawrence Erlbaum, 1985.

Garcia, John, and Andrew R. Gustavson. "Carl R. Gustavson (1946–1996) Pioneering Wildlife Psychologist." *APS Observer* (January 1997): 34–35. This paper and ones by C. R. Gustavson describe work on training coyotes to avoid sheep.

Garcia, John, Donald J. Kimeldorf, and Robert A. Koelling. "Conditioned Aversion to Saccharin Resulting from Exposure to Gamma Radiation." *Science* 122 (1955): 157–158.

Garcia, John, and Robert A. Koelling. "Relation of Cue to Consequence in Avoidance Learning." *Psychonomic Science* 4 (1966): 123–124. Paper showing it is easier to associate tastes than audiovisual stimuli with illness.

Gustavson, Carl R. "Comparative and Field Aspects of Learned Food Aversions." In *Learning Mechanisms in Food Selection*. Edited by L. M. Barker, M. R. Best, and M. Domjan. Waco, Tex.: Baylor University Press, 1977.

Gustavson, Carl R., Linda P. Brett, John Garcia, and Daniel J. Kelly. "A Working Model and Experimental Solutions to the Control of Predatory Behavior." In *Behavior of Captive Wild Animals*. Edited by H. Markowitz and V. J. Stevens. Chicago: Nelson-Hall, 1978.

Logue, A. W. *The Psychology of Eating and Drinking: An Introduction*. 2d ed. New York: W. H. Freeman, 1991. General text including information on origins, characteristics, and applications of food aversions.

Logue, A. W. "Taste Aversion and the Generality of the Laws of Learning." *Psychological Bulletin* 86 (1979): 276–296.

Logue, A. W., Iris Ophir, and Kerry E. Strauss. "The Acquisition of Taste Aversions in Humans." *Behavior Research & Therapy* 19 (1981): 319–333.

Nakajima, S., H. Ka, and H. Imada. "Summation of Overshadowing and Latent Inhibition in Rats' Conditioned Taste Aversion: Scapegoat Technique Works for Familiar Meals." *Appetite* 33 (1999): 299–307.

Rozin, Paul. "The Selection of Foods by Rats, Humans, and Other Animals." In *Advances in the Study of Behavior*, edited by J. S. Rosenblatt, R. A. Hinde, E. Shaw, and C. Beer. Vol. 6. New York: Academic Press, 1976. Description of specific hungers.

Rozin, P., and April Fallon. "The Psychological Categorization of Foods and Non-Foods: A Preliminary Taxonomy of Food Rejections." *Appetite* 1 (1980): 193–201.

Seligman, Martin E. P., and Joanne L. Hager, eds. *Biological Boundaries of Learning*. New York: Appleton-Century-Crofts, 1972. Description of sauce béarnaise phenomenon.

Wiens, Arthur N., and Carol E. Menustik. "Treatment Outcome and Patient Characteristics in an Aversion Therapy Program for Alcoholism." *American Psychologist* 38 (1983): 1089–1096.

Alexander W. Logue

AZTECS. *See* **Mexico and Central America, Pre-Columbian.**

BABY FOOD. The consumption of food is an extraordinarily social activity laden with complex and shifting layers of meaning. Not only what we eat but how and why we eat tell us much about society, history, cultural change, and humans' views of themselves. What, when, and how we choose to feed infants and toddlers, the notion of "baby food" as opposed to "adult food," and whether or not these foods are nourishing and satisfying reveals how mass production, consumption, and advertising have shaped attitudes about infancy and corresponding parenting philosophies and practices. From the late 1920s to the postwar baby boom of the 1950s, mass-produced solid infant food, especially fruits and vegetables, shifted items of rarity into a rite of passage, a normal, naturalized part of an infant's diet in the United States. In the early twenty-first century commercially produced infant food not only remained a mainstay of an infant's diet in the United States but manufacturers also sought new markets, including developing countries.

Preindustrial First Foods

Historically, semisolid mixtures of grains and water, animal milk, or broth, variously known as "pap," "panada," or "gruel," have been the first semisolid food (also known as "beikost") an infant receives. (Cone, 1984, p. 12; Quandt, 1984). In many cultures mothers chew food, making it similar in consistency to gruel, then feed it to their infants. The earliest known infant feeding devices date back to the second or third centuries, though few specifics regarding their use are understood (Fildes, 1995, p. 116). Commonly infants have been introduced to pap mixtures as a supplement to breast milk. The pap then becomes an increasingly prominent part of infants' diets until they are completely weaned, which varies from several months old to three to four years of age.

Mass-Produced Baby Food

The industrialization of the food supply laid important groundwork for dramatic changes in infant feeding. By the 1920s in the United States canned goods were mass-produced in sufficient quantity to be affordable for most, allowing Americans to consume, among other things, more fruits and vegetables year round. Also at this time the discovery and promotion of vitamins helped change Americans' wary attitude toward fruits and vegetables.

These foods previously were not fed to children before two or three years of age as they were thought to cause cholera and dysentery.

Thus the market was ripe for the introduction of commercially canned food for babies, especially produce. In 1928 the Michigan-based Fremont Canning Company, owned by the Gerber family, began producing strained vegetables for infants, which proved so successful that the company changed its name to the Gerber Products Company and became the exclusive maker of baby foods. By 1935 Gerber's biggest competitors, Beech-Nut, Heinz, and Libby's, entered the baby food market. Despite these competitors' quick development of their own mass-produced strained baby foods, Gerber managed to maintain its dominance of the market (Nisbet, 1954). Mothers, both those at home full-time and those with paid employment, embraced and benefited from commercially prepared solid infant food, and within a matter of decades the product became a common part of an infant's diet. The easy availability of, prominent advertising for, and increasing use of commercially prepared infant formulas acclimated mothers and doctors alike to infants' ingestion of substances other than breast milk.

Increasingly Earlier Introduction of Solids

In the late 1920s, just as Gerber began its national advertising and distribution of canned baby foods, the prevailing wisdom advocated introducing strained fruits and vegetables around seven months. The market for baby food increased with the idea that babies could eat solids, especially fruits and vegetables, at an earlier age. During the 1930s the recommended age was four to six months, and by the 1950s it was four to six weeks, with some doctors advocating feeding infants strained cereals and vegetables within days of birth. As this early introduction of solids became standard advice and practice, solid baby food, like infant formula, functioned not only as a supplement to but as a substitute for breast milk.

Commercial Baby Food: Modifications over Time

While mass-produced baby food increased infants' year-round consumption of fruits and vegetables and provided a welcome efficiency in preparation, it also had its deficiencies. Throughout most of the twentieth century commercially canned baby food was overcooked and contained added salt, sugar, starches, fillers, artificial preservatives, and even, though infrequently, dangerous contaminants, such as lead, glass shards, or pesticides. Moreover until the 1990s baby food manufacturers did not have to list the precise percentage of each ingredient on the label (Stallone and Jacobson, 1995).

Mass-produced baby food was created and became successful in response to an emerging industrialized society, meeting the needs of changing work patterns and an increasingly fast-paced lifestyle. It remained a rite of passage for most American babies at the advent of the twenty-first century, though with modifications. During the 1970s the return to breast-feeding and the renewed popularity of homemade baby foods were products of the public's more skeptical attitude toward corporate capitalism and institutions in general. In the 1980s and 1990s, mostly in response to consumer demand, baby food manufacturers eliminated sugar, salt, and modified starch from most products, introduced organic lines, and eschewed the use of any foods containing genetically modified organisms. Because of an overall declining birthrate in the United States at the beginning of the twenty-first century, baby food manufacturers, to maintain and even increase market share, began to forge new markets, targeting Latino and African American populations in the United States and trying to expand market share in developing countries around the globe.

See also **Lactation; Milk, Human; WIC (Women, Infants, and Children's) Program.**

BIBLIOGRAPHY

Cone, Thomas E., Jr. "Infant Feeding: A Historical Perspective." In *Nutrition and Feeding of Infants and Toddlers*, edited by Rosanne B. Howard and Harland S. Winter. Boston: Little, Brown, 1984.

Fildes, Valerie. "The Culture and Biology of Breastfeeding." In *Breastfeeding: Biocultural Perspectives*, edited by Patricia Stuart-Macadam and Katherine A. Dettwyler. New York: Aldine de Gruyter, 1995.

Nisbet, Stephen S. *Contribution to Human Nutrition: Gerber Products since 1928.* New York: Newcomen Society in North America, 1954.

Quandt, Sara A. "The Effect of Beikost on the Diet of Breast-fed Infants." *Journal of the American Dietetic Association* 84 (1984): 47–51.

Stallone, Daryth D., and Michael F. Jacobson. "Cheating Babies: Nutritional Quality and the Cost of Commercial Baby Food." Center for Science in the Public Interest (CSPI) Report, April 1995. Available at www.cspinet.org.

Strasser, Susan. *Never Done: A History of American Housework.* New York: Pantheon, 1982.

Stuart-Macadam, Patricia. "Breastfeeding in Prehistory." In *Breastfeeding: Biocultural Perspectives*, edited by Patricia Stuart-Macadam and Katherine A. Dettwyler. New York: Aldine de Gruyter, 1995.

Tice, Patricia M. *Gardening in America, 1830–1910.* Rochester, N.Y.: Strong Museum, 1984.

Amy Bentley

BABYLONIA. *See* **Mesopotamia, Ancient.**

BACTERIA, LACTIC ACID. *See* **Microorganisms.**

BACTRIA, ANCIENT. *See* **Indus Valley.**

BAGEL. A specialty of East European Jews, the classic bagel is a small ring of dough made of white flour, yeast, and water. The dough is first boiled and then baked.

The Bagel in Europe

According to Mordecai Kosover in *Yidishe maykholim*, the earliest mention of the bagel is in the 1610 statutes of the Jewish community of Cracow, which state that it is permissible to make a gift of bagels to the woman who has given birth, the midwife, and the girls and women who were present (Kosover, p. 129). Even earlier sources indicate that the father would send *pretsn*, or pretzels, which are historically related to the bagel, to everyone on the occasion of a circumcision. Legends that trace the first bagel to the Ottoman siege of Vienna in 1683 are apocryphal. The very same story is told about the origin of the croissant, the pretzel, and the coffeehouse.

A relatively affordable treat, the East European bagel was portable and small. According to a Yiddish proverb, only by the third bagel would one feel full. Bagels made with milk or eggs were known from at least the nineteenth century, and almond bagels were among the prepared foods exchanged on the holiday of Purim. Bagels and other round foods were eaten before Tisha B'av, a fast day commemorating the destruction of the Temple, and in the twenty-first century bagels are served after a funeral and during the seven days of mourning that follow. The round shape symbolizes the round of life. The *beuglich* described in Israel Zangwill's *Children of the Ghetto* (1892) as "circular twisted rolls" suggest the *obwarzanek*, a twisted, fresh ring pretzel dating from the Middle Ages and still sold by street vendors in Poland and the large twister bagels sold in Toronto in the twenty-first century.

The Bagel in the United States

The bagel arrived in the United States with Jewish immigrants from eastern Europe at the end of the nineteenth century. From the 1890s until the 1950s bagel bakers struggled to form their own union, a process that began in 1907 with the establishment of a benevolent society for bagel bakers. With the influx of younger and more radical immigrants after World War I, the process of converting the benevolent society into a union intensified. Local 338, the International Beigel Bakers Union of Greater New York and New Jersey, coalesced in 1925

150

and was finally recognized as an autonomous local in 1937. Thanks to the union, bagel bakers in the New York metropolitan area won the best working conditions in the baking trade.

While radical in their politics, these bakers were conservative in their craft. Bagel bakers resisted technology because mechanization of the rolling process would eliminate jobs. As a result the bagel industry in the New York metropolitan area was one of the last of the baking industries to become fully automated. As late as the 1960s bagels were still made by hand in small bakeries by Jews for Jews, and Local 338 controlled the industry. Water bagels plain or salted were the basic varieties.

From 1955 to 1984 bagel bakeries outside New York and outside the jurisdiction of the bagel bakers' union found ways to distribute this highly perishable product far beyond the freshness radius of the bakery. They modified the dough, introduced flavors, packaged bagels in plastic bags, froze them, and shipped them to groceries and supermarkets across the country. Frozen bagels were marketed primarily to non-Jews. Once the bagel was packaged, it could be branded. The bagel began its shift from a generic product to a branded commodity.

With distribution channels in place and demand growing, the bagel industry was ready to increase production. Thompson Bagel Machine, which had been in development since World War I, was patented in 1960 by the Thompsons, an East European Jewish family in Los Angeles. In 1963 the first automated bagel-forming machines were introduced in New Haven, Connecticut; Buffalo, New York; and St. Louis, Missouri. As the growing bagel industry outside New York started penetrating the New York market, the union weakened and automation entered, thereby transforming the bagel baking business and fueling its exponential growth. By 1984 Lender's Bagels, which started as a family bakery in New Haven in 1927 and was the first to use a bagel-forming machine, had become so successful that it was acquired by Kraft and then Kellogg, who saw the bagel outpacing and even supplanting croissants, doughnuts, cereals, and other breakfast foods.

The Bagel Boom

The bagel has become one of the fastest-growing sectors of the food industry. The bagel industry, with relatively low barriers to entry, has attracted a wide range of people. H&H Bagels, the icon of the New York bagel, has been owned by Herman Toro, who was born in Puerto Rico, since the 1970s. Hand-rolling is largely a specialty of Egyptian and Thai immigrants. During the 1980s, with growing national awareness of the bagel and the introduction of bagel-steaming equipment, the developing bagel category became dominated by rapidly expanding chains, franchises, and privately held as well as publicly traded bagel companies. By the mid-1990s the bagel boom peaked, and a shakeout followed. Some of the companies that grew fastest showed the most serious losses.

The bagel as Americans know it today evolved in the Jewish community in the United States. It has also become an icon of New York food, especially the onion bagel shown here. PHOTO BY ANDRÉ BARANOWSKI.

Meanwhile the bagel had spread to such places as Germany, Turkey, Japan, Taiwan, Australia, and Bali.

The Bagel as Icon Food

After the Holocaust American Jews came to identify the bagel with the Old World and with immigrant Jewish culture. The bagel became a lightening rod for their ambivalent feelings. While Irving Pfefferblit declared in "The Bagel" that "the Jewish bagel stands out like a golden vision of the bygone days when life was better," upscale Miami hotels during the 1950s served lox on English muffins or tartines rather than on lowly bagels (Pfefferblit, p. 475).

With the suburbanization of Jews and secondary migration of Jews to California and Florida during the postwar years, the bagels and lox brunch became a Sunday morning ritual with its own equipage, including bagel slicers and decorative bagel platters with compartments for smoked salmon, cream cheese, butter, olives, radishes, and slices of onion and tomato. So important did this meal become that "bagel and lox Judaism" became a metaphor for the gastropiety of suburban Jews.

The close identification of the bagel with New York City arises in no small measure from its labor history, though some claim the secret to the New York bagel is the water. Paradoxically the further the bagel traveled from New York, the more it became identified with New York and with all that is metropolitan and cosmopolitan. However, other cities with large Jewish communities also have long bagel histories and distinctive bagels. The Montreal bagel has a narrow coil and a big hole. It is rolled by hand, boiled in water sweetened with honey, sprinkled with sesame seeds, and baked in a wood-fired oven, which gives it a slight smokiness.

Bagel Innovations

New bagel eaters with no prior loyalties are a prime market for bagel innovations. With but a few concepts (size, shape, flavor, topping, stuffing, and carrier or platform), it is possible to produce combinations, permutations, and improbable hybrids. The early Lender's frozen bagels weighed two ounces. Bagels in the twenty-first century range from three to more than five ounces. There are cocktail minibagels and overstuffed party bagels the size of a tire. Cosi recently introduced the squagel, a square bagel. Where there were once only a few varieties (poppy seed, pumpernickel, and eventually cinnamon raisin), by the twenty-first century there were unlimited flavors (from cranberry granola to piña colada), toppings (everything from poppy seeds, sesame seeds, caraway seeds, and garlic to streusel), and fillings (from cream cheese to bacon and eggs).

At bagel shops offering twenty types of bagels, which is not uncommon, and even more varieties of spreads and fillings, customers can create hundreds of combinations. Bagel eaters from birth tend to be disdainful of what might be called the random bagel effect. "Turkey, tomato, sprouts, avocado, and cream cheese on a peanut butter and chocolate chip bagel" at Goldstein's Bagel Bakery in California is an ungrammatical culinary sentence for those fluent in the language.

The bagel replaces bread, pizza, croissant, and tortillas as the preferred carrier or platform for their fillings and toppings. New hybrid bagel products include the *bagelwich* (bagel plus sandwich), *bragel* (bagel plus roll), *bretzel* (bagel plus pretzel), *fragel* (fried bagel), and *flagel* (flat bagel) as well as the Bageldog, pizza bagel, UnHoley Bagel (ball injected with cream cheese), bagel chips, bagels for birds and dogs, and bagel bones for people. The bagel is distilled into a flavor of its own for bagel-flavored rice cakes and matzoh.

The bagel has become not only a platform for other foods but also a carrier for meanings and values as diverse as those who eat them. For many it is an icon of East European Jewish culture, for others it is quintessentially New York, and for many around the world, including in Israel, it is American.

See also **Bread**; **Breakfast**; **Judaism**; **United States: Ethnic Cuisines**.

BIBLIOGRAPHY

Kosover, Mordecai. *Yidishe maykholim: A shtudye in kulturgeshikhte un shprakh-forshung.* New York: YIVO, 1958.

Pfefferblit, Irving. "The Bagel." *Commentary* 7 (May 1951): 475–479.

Barbara Kirshenblatt-Gimblett

BAHÁ'Í. Originating in Persia in the mid-nineteenth century, the Bahá'í Faith is the youngest of the independent world religions. It is also one of the fastest growing and most widespread of religions with about 7 million adherents in over 220 countries. Founded by the prophet Bahá'u'lláh, the faith is built on the fundamental principles of unity and justice and the necessary convergence of spiritual and social development. The faith embraces a concept of progressive revelation that assigns equal status to previous prophets, who are known as "manifestations of God." There is only one God. As perfect reflections of God the manifestations occupy a status between the human and the divine. Each prophet brings the same core message as well as new teachings suited to the time and place of his particular revelation and the stage of development of humanity. Bahá'u'lláh's purpose, as the latest of these manifestations of god, is to usher in a new world order of peace and prosperity for the human race.

Dietary codes and prohibitions are absent in the Bahá'í sacred writings. Rather than rules there is an emphasis on guidance and on the responsibility of individual believers to live a virtuous life. Food rules and practices are often used as boundary markers in religions and as a way for believers to assert their faith identities. The absence of such prescriptive dietary codes in Bahá'í teachings exemplifies the Bahá'í concept of the unity of humankind by removing one boundary between races, cultures, and religions. There is no symbolic value attached to particular foods, nor are there foods that are associated with specific rituals or celebrations. Generally speaking Bahá'ís follow local dietary custom. Nevertheless, there are three aspects of food that are explicitly addressed in Bahá'í sacred writings: the relationship of diet to health, fasting, and commensality as exemplified in the Nineteen Day Feast.

Role of Religion in Shaping Daily Diet

There is a special concern for the strength and well-being of the body as the temple of the human spirit. The body should be a willing, obedient, and efficient servant, kept in good health so that the Bahá'í can devote all his or her energy to serving Bahá'u'lláh's purpose. To this end, Bahá'ís are expected to take responsibility for looking after their own health, in which diet plays an essential role. Both asceticism and hedonism are to be avoided; the former because it is an inappropriate withdrawal from the world and a rejection of what God has provided, and the latter because one should not be preoccupied with material possessions. Instead, moderation is advised as a means to achieve a state of "detachment" necessary to attain true understanding of God's will.

The ideal regime is a balanced natural diet that is adapted to local climate and to the type of work in which the body is engaged. Although animal food is not forbidden, meat-eating is considered to be only a temporary necessity of the current age, one that will give way in the future to vegetarianism. Vegetarianism is portrayed as being a compassionate practice, for the killing of animals blunts the spiritual qualities of the human race. A meatless diet is also natural in that it uses simple foods that grow from the ground. Finally, vegetarianism is just; one should not eat lavishly while others starve.

Food is not only seen to be the chief way of maintaining health, but also the preferred means for treatment of disease. Health and disease are conceived of in terms of balance and bodily equilibrium reminiscent of Greek humoral theory and Ayurvedic conceptions of hot and cold. Disease arises from disturbances to the balance of the body, which can be restored through consumption of food containing the necessary elements to bring it back to health. Although a time is foreseen when improved medical knowledge and understanding will enable all illness to be treated by food, Bahá'ís are enjoined to take full advantage of the best that current medicine has to offer and to seek the services of competent physicians when they are ill.

Fasting and Feasting

There is only one annual fast prescribed for Bahá'ís. The precepts of the fast are laid down in the Kitab-I-Aqdas, or Most Holy Book, of Bahá'u'lláh and along with obligatory prayer it is the most important of Bahá'í ritual obligations. The fast bears a marked resemblance to Islamic practice, the context in which it emerged. The Bahá'í fasting period lasts nineteen days from the second to the twentieth of March, and requires complete abstention from food and drink between the hours of sunrise and sunset. It is a period of meditation and prayer, a chance to renew one's spiritual self, and a reminder of the need to abstain from selfish desires. The fast is binding on Bahá'ís in all countries but it is an individual obligation, not enforceable by Bahá'í administrative institutions. It applies to all believers from the age of maturity (thought of as age fifteen) until seventy, with exemptions for travelers under specified conditions; the sick; women who are menstruating, pregnant, or nursing; and those engaged in heavy labor, who are advised to be discrete and restrained in availing themselves of this exemption. Unlike in the Islamic model, fasters who are unable to meet their commitment do not have to offer any sort of restitution or make up the missed days later. Nor are sexual relations prohibited during fasting periods. Bahá'ís are allowed to fast at other times of the year but this is not encouraged, and is rarely done. Fasting itself is only acceptable if it is done purely out of love for God. This is reminiscent of the importance of *niyyah* or intent in the Islamic fast of Ramadan.

SELECTION FROM *SOME ANSWERED QUESTIONS* BY 'ABDU'L-BAHÁ

The science of medicine is still in a condition of infancy; it has not reached maturity. But when it has reached this point, cures will be performed by things which are not repulsive to the smell and taste of man—that is to say, by aliments, fruits and vegetables which are agreeable to the taste and have an agreeable smell. . . . All the elements that are combined in man exist also in vegetables; therefore, if one of the constituents which compose the body of man diminishes, and he partakes of foods in which there is much of that diminished constituent, then the equilibrium will be established, and a cure will be obtained (Sec. 73).

Feast has a particular meaning in the Bahá'í Faith, referring to the monthly community meeting known as the Nineteen-Day Feast. The original purpose of the Bahá'í feast was a means of creating fellowship, and is rooted in the Persian tradition of hospitality. Bahá'u'lláh enjoined believers to entertain nineteen people every nineteen days even if only water was provided. Over time the feast shifted from being a display of personal hospitality to becoming an institutional event. The modern Nineteen-Day Feast is held in each Bahá'í community on the first day of each Bahá'í month, and consists of three parts. The first is devotional and consists of readings from the Bahá'í sacred writings; the second is a consultative meeting where administrative and community issues are discussed; the third is a social gathering at which food is served. What is served is at the discretion of the host and is guided by personal preference and local custom. The Nineteen-Day Feast is intended only for the members of the Bahá'í community; however, non-Bahá'í visitors should be received hospitably at the social portion of the feast only.

The sharing of food is an important feature of Bahá'í social events. Food sharing also occurs through charitable activity and social action. However, where local community development projects supported by Bahá'ís involve food, these usually take the form of agricultural development rather than food distribution.

See also **Fasting and Abstinence: Islam; Iran; Vegetarianism.**

BIBLIOGRAPHY

'Abdu'l-Bahá. *Some Answered Questions.* Wilmette, Ill.: BPT, 1964. Section 73. Passages on food, health, and the body.

Paul Fieldhouse

BAKING. Baking refers to two culinary processes: cooking by dry heat in an enclosed oven and making up flour-based goods (breads, cakes, pastries) that are cooked by baking. By extension a baking day is devoted to making breads and cakes and includes the idea of a batch bake or tray bake made up in quantity for cutting into smaller pieces. Cooking flour-based items using a griddle is also considered a form of baking. "Roasting" meat or vegetables such as potatoes in the oven is also in practice baking. The idea is also implied in the clambake of shellfish, using layers of heated stones and seaweed.

Two trades are directly concerned with baking, the baker using yeast to make breads and the pastry cook producing delicate pastries and cakes. The demarcation is unclear in English, which often applies the word "baker" to someone who makes cakes. French distinguishes more sharply between the *boulanger* and the *pâtissier*, as does German between the *Backer* and the *Konditor*.

The technique has a wide geographical spread. It is used throughout North America and Europe, across the Middle East and North Africa, and into central Asia and northern India. The concept was introduced by Europeans to their former colonies, many of whom have continued the practice. Baking is exceptionally important in cultures that rely on wheat as their primary cereal. Methods and technology have developed principally to exploit and enhance the properties of the gluten it contains. Others (rye, barley, oats) contain less gluten but are used in northern and western European baking, usually as residual traditions from times when wheat was expensive and difficult to obtain. Maize does not lend itself to baking, although North American settlers managed to develop corn breads, and the Atlantic communities of northern Portugal and Spain also use it in breads and cakes.

The history of baking is one of interaction between ingredients, fuels, and oven technology. On a basic level virtually any food can be "baked" by burying it in hot ashes or placing it on a stone beside the fire, something that must have been known from the earliest times. Developing control to the point of producing items as diverse as breakfast rolls, soufflés, and chocolate brownies has taken thousands of years.

Enclosed Ovens

Early advances included the development of enclosed ovens. One type was a pit oven in the ground with a fire in the bottom. These were known by about 3000 B.C.E. in Egypt, where they were hollow cones of clay that contained a layer of coals. The modern tandoor, a large ceramic oven sunk into the ground and fired with wood or charcoal, echoes this idea. Tandoors have limited applications for baking but are essential for breads such as the flat, leavened wheat nan of Persian and northern Indian traditions. The dough is slapped onto the clay sides of the tandoor and cooks fast. Tandoors become very hot, and the fire remains in the base throughout cooking. This

along with their shape makes them unsuitable for complex baking.

Another type was the beehive oven, a domed structure situated above ground. An early version is in an Egyptian tomb model of about 1900 B.C.E. Early ones were made of clay and had the advantage of enclosing food in a hot environment but allowing the baker the opportunity to make more than flat shapes. Stone or brick ovens of similar shape evolved later and can be seen at Pompeii. They were used for baking with wheat flour and sour dough leaven. Beehive ovens fired with wood became the primary means of baking in medieval and early modern Europe. They were used for wheat or rye breads and the sweet, enriched festive breads and cakes that developed from these breads.

To heat a beehive oven, a fire was lit inside. After a while the oven was cleaned out, leaving heat stored in the walls. This heat diminished slowly over time. It could not be controlled, but by the sixteenth century a sequence had evolved. Coarse breads were baked first, followed by white breads, pastries, and joints of meat (often in pastries or pies), and progressing to cakes that would burn at high temperatures. Residual heat was used for drying fruit or for confectioneries. It was a time-consuming and complex operation. The size of the ovens and scarcity of fuel led to the idea of baking communally. For a small charge customers could bake their own dough or meat in an oven owned by a village baker. Such habits were noted in southern England during the eighteenth century and were still observed in some Mediterranean countries, for instance Greece, in the early twenty-first century. Small clay ovens were also still used in some regions, such as the Iberian Peninsula.

Wood-fired ovens produce unique, much-liked textures and tastes. Italian restaurants sometimes use wood-fired pizza ovens, and French bakers advertise *cuit au feu de bois* (cooked with a wood fire). Baking in these ovens requires a peel, a special implement with a long handle and a flat plate at one end for lifting food into or out of these large and often extremely hot structures.

Griddle Baking

Little is known about the history of griddle baking. An ancient and widespread technique, it was available to anyone with a fire and a flat stone. At some stage specially made griddles—heavy metal plates—developed. Although it does not use enclosed heat, its association with cooking flour-based items links it firmly to the idea of baking.

Griddle baking is associated with Scotland and Ireland, where locally dug peat is used for fuel. Peat gives a slow, gentle heat unsuited to oven baking. The tradition continued in South Wales where cheap coal was burned in open kitchen grates, over which the griddle was balanced. Typical products include Welsh cakes, like small biscuits, and Scottish griddle scones or drop scones, small

French print showing the interior of a nineteenth-century bakery. © GIANNI DAGLI ORTI/CORBIS.

thick pancakes. British crumpets and muffins (made from bread dough) are baked on modern versions of the griddle, gas or electrically heated hotplates.

Another item used for baking with a open fire was the Dutch oven, which could be regarded as a form of covered griddle. It consisted of a heavy iron pot with a lid, both of which were preheated before use. Food was placed inside the pot, the lid was put on, and hot coals were heaped over it. They were used for baking bread, biscuits, and cakes as well as for roasting meat and other cooking. Both griddles and Dutch ovens were easy to carry and were much used by North American pioneers. Baking with these implements was enhanced in the mid-nineteenth century by the development of bicarbonate of soda, leading to the development of Irish griddle-baked soda bread. Bicarbonate of soda and baking powder were promoted through recipe booklets and rapidly became popular for making biscuits, quick breads, and cakes in parts of Europe and North America.

Due to regional poverty and the availability of slow-burning fuel, the East retained a form of griddle baking. Chapatis, the thin flat breads of Pakistan and India, are baked on metal plates over fires of dried cow dung, a fuel that gives slow heat.

Kitchen Ranges

Controllable heat was the key to modern baking. Initially this took the form of the cast-iron coal-fired kitchen range, an idea patented by Thomas Robinson, a London ironmonger, in 1780. Over the next century designs evolved to control the heat, partly through the work of the American statesman Count Rumford. Ranges became fixtures in many European and North American houses. For the first time convenient and controllable ovens existed, although they still needed skill for good results. However, gas was used as a fuel for domestic cooking by the 1880s, and electricity was introduced about a decade later, giving even more accuracy and ease. By this time numerous regional baked specialties had developed, including tortes and gâteaux in central Europe, Christmas *Lebkuchen* in Germany, and teatime cakes in Britain. North America inherited baking traditions from all European countries in the form of festive breads, cakes, and cookies. In turn, by the twenty-first century North Americans grew much of the wheat that sustained the baking traditions in their native countries.

Utensils

Baking requires many utensils. Measuring is important, so most kitchens and all professional bakers possess spoons, cups, and scales. Bowls are needed for mixing, sieves and sifters for flour or sugar, rolling pins for pastry, cutters and molds for cookies, and forcing bags and nozzles for soft mixtures. Paper is used to line trays and molds and to hold cake and muffin mixtures. Flat metal baking sheets are used to support anything from a round loaf without a pan to a batch of cookies.

Many loaves of bread are baked in oblong pans. Common cake pan shapes include square, round, and tube pans. Many cultures have special forms as well, such as the German *Rehrücken* (a ribbed half cylinder for baking a chocolate cake in a "saddle of venison" shape) and the Alpine and Rhine areas' *Gugelhupf* (a tall, fluted tube pan). Novelty shapes run to Santa Claus and Easter lambs. Cake pans affect the rate at which mixtures heat, and ideally they should match the final volume of the cakes baked in them. Professional pastry cooks use many sizes, from the one-bite petit four up to cakes for large parties. Small shapes in special molded trays include patty pans for baking cupcakes or British mince pies and shell shapes for French madeleines. Pies and tarts, too, have special shapes, including plain round plates and tart rings with fluted edges. Cylindrical formers are used in England for raising pork pies.

In contrast, the only essential for baking meats or vegetables is a metal or earthenware container, although various patent "roasting tins," intended to be self-basting for cooking joints of meat, were developed in the twentieth century. The use of a thermometer designed to show the internal temperature of a piece of cooking meat is often recommended by cookery books.

Physanges

Despite the fact that it typically uses temperatures ranging from 300 to 500°F (150 to 260°C), baking is an inefficient method of heat transfer. It relies on a combination of radiant heat from the oven walls and air convection. What it does effectively is dehydrate the surface of food at a high temperature, producing delicious flavors and aromas. These are due to the Maillard reaction, in which amino acids contained in the food react with sugars during heating, producing the typical smells of baking bread and roasting meat.

Physically, three stages can be identified during the baking of bread. They were summarized by Harold McGee (1984) as, first, when the yeast cells have been killed by heat; second, when the maximum temperature has been reached inside the loaf, gelatinizing the starch and coagulating the protein; and third, when the Maillard reaction induces surface browning, producing the characteristic flavor. Cakes follow a similar basic pattern. Yeast is not involved, but the first stage includes the expansion of minute air cells in the mixture and the release of carbon dioxide from any chemical leavening present. In the second, flour, egg, and milk proteins coagulate, and starch gelatinizes as the batter sets into a solid foam. Browning reactions set in during the third.

Nutritionally, baking has little effect on cereal foods, although it reduces the thiamin (vitamin B_1) content. Many baked items are energy-dense because of the quantities of starch, fat, and sugar they contain. Some keep better than others. French baguettes stale quickly, but English fruitcake keeps so well it can almost be regarded as a form of preserved food.

Baking meat has the effect of coagulating the proteins of which it is composed. They shorten and toughen, squeezing out some of the water they contain, leading to weight loss in the cooked item. Most cooks aim at a compromise when oven-baking meat. Muscle proteins coagulate at about 160°F (71°C) and after that become dry and tough. But connective tissue requires long cooking at high temperatures to convert it to tender gelatin. As with cereal foods, the thiamine content is reduced, and the Maillard reaction develops the flavor and aroma. While this has no nutritional effect, it is important in provoking appetite. Baking vegetables, a relatively slow way of cooking them, reduces their vitamin C content significantly.

See also **Bread**; **Hearth Cookery**; **Pastry**; **Roasting**; **Utensils, Cooking**.

BIBLIOGRAPHY

David, Elizabeth. *English Bread and Yeast Cookery*. London: Allen Lane, 1977. Ovens and baking, especially in England.

Davidson, Alan. *The Oxford Companion to Food*. Oxford: Oxford University Press, 1999.

Eveleigh, David J. *Firegrates and Kitchen Ranges*. Shire Album 99. Princes Risborough, U.K.: Shire Publications, 1983. The development of the kitchen range.

Fussell, Betty. *The Story of Corn*. New York: Knopf, 1992. Development of corn breads.

Kelly, Sarah. *Festive Baking in Austria, Germany, and Switzerland*. London: Penguin Books, 1985. Northern and central European traditions.

McGee, Harold. *On Food and Cooking*. London: George Allen and Unwin, 1984; New York: Scribners, 1984. Physics and chemistry.

Mason, Laura, with Catherine Brown. *Traditional Foods of Britain: An Inventory*. Totnes, U.K.: Prospect Books, 1999. Baked goods in Britain.

Wigginton, Eliot, ed. *The Foxfire Book*. Garden City, N.Y.: Anchor, 1972. Dutch ovens and wood-fired stoves.

Wilson, C. Anne. *Food and Drink in Britain*. Chicago: Academy Chicago, 1991; London: Constable, 1991. Background information for the United Kingdom.

Laura Mason

BALKAN COUNTRIES. Countries on the Balkan Peninsula, a region in southeastern Europe, are bounded by the Adriatic and the Ionian seas in the west, the Mediterranean and the Aegean seas in the south, and the Sea of Marmara and the Black Sea in the east. The penin-

sula includes Slovenia, Croatia, Bosnia and Herzegovina, Yugoslavia, Macedonia, Bulgaria, Albania, Greece, and European Turkey.

The region was already settled in the Stone Age. The oldest people living there were the Thracians, the Illyrians, the Greeks, and the Celts. When the Romans invaded Illyria in 168–167 B.C.E., the area was politically and culturally united for the first time in history. The division of the Roman Empire into its Eastern and its Western parts in 375, and the split within the Christian church in 1054 furthered the gap between the peoples of the area (Eastern Orthodox, Catholic), influencing its political and cultural development.

Between the fourteenth and the end of the nineteenth centuries, a great part of the Balkan Peninsula was united in the Ottoman Empire, influenced by its feudal system and civilization, which have strongly marked the culture of the Balkan countries even up to the present.

Principal Characteristics of the Balkan Food Culture

The food culture of the Balkan Peninsula depended upon the historic, geographical, climatic, social, and religious elements. There are three main food culture areas: the Mediterranean, the continental lowland, and the continental mountain areas.

The Mediterranean area is divided into the coastal and the continental parts. People living along the coast tend their vineyards, grow olive trees, different kinds of vegetables, citrus fruits, spices, and they fish. Wine, olive

Housewife preparing vegetables for a meal. Note the traditional raised hearth and the modern stove in the background. © CAROLINE PENN/CORBIS.

oil, cabbage, kale, different kinds of salad greens, cauliflower, figs, grapes, almonds, cherries, marascas, and different fishes are their main staples.

The continental part of the Mediterranean area has a well-developed agriculture. Farmers breed mostly sheep, goats, and poultry, to a lesser extent also cattle and pigs. Fields yield crops of wheat and corn, in some places also rice, cotton, sesame, and poppy. Fertile valleys are sprinkled with vineyards. Meals, therefore, consist mostly of meat dishes, but also of milk, milk products, and vegetables. Lakes provide freshwater fishes.

The continental lowland area, which is distinctly agricultural, starts north of the Balkan Mountains and Šarplanina. Vast fields of corn and wheat give plenty of food. Farmers grow oats, barley, rye, millet, and buckwheat. Since wheat is mostly sold for profit, dishes consist mainly of corn; corn bread is eaten in most places. Because of an abundance of corn, which is very important as fodder, cattle and pig farming are very developed; in the north, sheep and goats are bred as well. The meat of these animals plays a very important role in the food culture of the local population. Farmers also grow fruit, especially apple, pear, plum, and they cultivate walnut trees.

Sheep farming is important in the mountainous part of the Dinaric Alps and in the Rhodope Mountains; less important is cattle breeding. Meals generally consist of milk and different kinds of cheese, corn bread (*proja*), and polenta (*kaèamak*). Many dishes are prepared from cornmeal, eggs, and the *kajmak* cheese; one of these dishes is *èimbur*, boiled eggs covered with *kajmak*. Also popular

are vegetable dishes made from cabbage, beans, onions, green peppers, and eggplant. Vegetables pickled in vinegar (*turšija*) are consumed in winter. Meat dishes consist mostly of lamb and sheep meats, usually roasted or prepared in a number of different ways. Beef and pork, which are usually dried in the air and made into prosciutto, or smoked, are eaten during the winter months (*pastrma*).

Individual Groups of Dishes

The food culture of the Balkan Peninsula displays Asian as well as west European influences. Even though the Oriental influence has been very strong in the last several centuries, ethnic characteristics and traditions have been preserved. Dishes consumed in this region therefore contain many similar elements, but may also greatly differ from each other. One of the characteristics shared by most is the use of numerous spices, onions, garlic, tomatoes, parsley, paprika, and capers.

Soups are prepared from vegetables, meat, herbs, or different kinds of fish. Meat soups usually contain a variety of vegetables, as well. Throughout the Balkans, spring is the time for a thick lamb soup (*mayiritsa*). Other popular vegetable soups are potato, leek, corn, or bean soups, or a soup made of zucchini with milk or eggs. Along the Danube River, fishermen prepare thick soups (*Alaska èorba*), while in coastal areas, they make soup from sea fishes (the Greek *khakhavia*).

In the past, meat did not play a central role in the food culture of the Balkans. It was, nevertheless, a highly esteemed food, which could be prepared in a variety of ways. Grilling and spit roasting are characteristic of the Balkan region, and lambs, kids, or pigs are roasted on spits on prominent occasions, such as weddings and New Year's Day. People grill seasoned minced meat shaped in different forms (*èevapèièi*, *pleskavica*), kabobs (*vešalica*, *šaši kebasi*), lamb and veal cutlets, beefsteaks, or small pieces of meat with vegetables and mushrooms (*muèkalica*, *krzatmas*).

Also very popular are meatballs (*èufte*), be it in or without a sauce, for instance, the *pasha* of Turkey or the Greek *kreftaidakiya*. Minced meat is also used for the preparation of meat pie (*burek*), which can also be filled with cheese or vegetables. Meat can be served in a stew (goulash, paprika). Chicken is roasted with an addition of spices and vegetables, such as olives, peppers, tomatoes, zucchini, and eggplant. Duck or goose is most often served roasted, sometimes with filling.

In Balkan cuisine, vegetables are often prepared as a main or side dish, usually consisting of legumes, cabbage, kale, root crops, zucchini, peppers, tomatoes, and eggplant. These vegetables are made into a ragout, or filled with rice, meat, corn, vegetable, or cheese, or stewed with rice and meat (*ðuveè*). Very popular dishes are those which are made from a mixture of vegetables, meat, and rice (*sarma*), or those prepared with vine leaves (*jalanci dolmasi*), or other leaves (cabbage, kale, chard). There are different casseroles in which meat is prepared together with vegetables, for instance, the Albanian shepherd's pot, or the Bosnian pot. The Turkish moussaka, a baked dish consisting of layers of sautéed vegetables, meat, rice, or potatoes, is prepared throughout the Balkan Peninsula.

Oriental influence is most strongly felt in the great variety of pastries, which have always been an important part of festive meals in all Balkan countries. Among the most popular are different pastries drenched in sugar syrup, and strudels. Most of the sweets contain walnuts and almonds, which are also put into stuffed apples (*tufahije*), or fill walnut pies, cakes, and the famous baklava cakes made from paper-thin dough. Nuts are sprinkled on sweet noodles (*kadaif*). *Žito*, wheat with walnuts, is a festive dish from Serbia. On Christmas and Easter, which are among the most prominent holidays in the region, different kinds of cakes are still served; one of them is the *pinca* from the Croatian coastal area, or Greek *melomacarona*, and another is *kourabiethes*. *Vasiljica* or *badnjaèa* are prepared in Serbia and Bosnia. Tables filled with festive dishes display a great variety of the Balkan cuisine and a strong attachment to the traditional culinary tradition.

See also **Central Europe**; **Greece and Crete**; **Rome and the Roman Empire**.

BIBLIOGRAPHY

Biluš, Ivanka, and Zvonimir Mršic, eds. *Hrvatska za stolom*. Zagreb: Alfa, 1996.

Bogićevič, Mirko. *Vukova trpeza*. Belgrade: Naučna knjiga, 1988.

Cvijić, Jovan. *Balkansko poluostrvo*. Belgrade: Srpska akademija nauka i umetnosti, 1991.

Gavazzi, Milovan. "Zur Herkunft eines Südslavischen Brauchtumsgebäckes." In *Serta Slavica in Memoriam Aloisii Schmaus*. Munich, 1971.

Katičić, Jelena. *The Balkan Cookbook*. Belgrade: Jugoslovenska knjiga, 1987.

Maja Godina-Golija

BANANA AND PLANTAIN.

Bananas, including the dessert banana and the cooking types or plantains, are cultivated in more than 120 countries throughout the tropics and subtropics, according to the Food and Agriculture Organization of the United Nations (FAO) current statistics. In terms of total production the banana ranks after oranges, grapes, and apples, but when plantain production is added, it becomes the world's number one fruit crop. While commercial production of bananas is oriented to the fresh export trade destined mainly for temperate-zone markets, plantains and even unripe bananas—consumed boiled, fried, roasted, or even brewed—are a major staple food throughout the tropics.

The origin of the word "banana" probably derives from languages spoken in the coastal regions of Sierra Leone at the beginning of the sixteenth century. It is important to note that none of the major producing regions seem to have incorporated clear linguistic distinctions between dessert and cooking bananas in their languages. The Spanish word *plátano*—from which the English term "plantain" may have derived (Simmonds, p. 57)—does not have a precise origin but is employed throughout the Spanish-speaking world and its meaning changes with location: in most of Central and South America, while the word *banana* is used as in English, *plátano* is reserved for the plantain, whereas in Mexico and Spain—the latter including the Canary Islands, from which the banana is thought to have been carried to the New World (Galán Saúco, p. 9)—it is used for either bananas or plantains. The situation in Southeast Asia is somewhat different, where vernacular names do not differentiate between dessert and cooking bananas (*kluai* in Thailand, *pisang* in Malaysia and Indonesia, *saging* in the Philippines, *chiao* in China, or *choui* in Vietnam) (Valmayor et al., p. 13).

Taxonomy

According to Chesman, who in 1948 pioneered the modern classification of bananas (Simmonds, p. 53), most edible bananas and plantains belong to the *Eumusa* section of the genus *Musa* (family Musaceae) and derive from the species *Musa acuminata* Colla and *M. balbisiana* Colla, which correspond roughly to two species originally described by Linnaeus in his general botanical work *Systema Naturae* (1758) to which he gave the names *M. sapientum* and *M. paradisiaca*, the first referring to a plant producing horn-shaped fruit and similar to the modern "French

In nature all species, plants and animals, are diploids; that is, they have a chromosome number of $2n$, formed by the contribution of n chromosomes (genome) from each progenitor. For diverse reasons and by various natural genetic paths, plants with different levels of ploidy do appear sporadically (e.g., n = haploids; $3n$ = triploids; $4n$ = tetraploids, etc.), and a side effect of this natural process is the loss of fertility. In the case of the banana, the appearance of triploids has proven beneficial to the consumer, as seedless fruits are produced.

Plantain," and the second to a type similar to the most popular dessert banana of the tropics, the "Silk Fig." Both of Linnaeus's designations were soon widely applied, with any plantain being referred to as *M. sapientum* and all dessert types being referred to as *M. paradisiaca*. This outdated nomenclature is still used in some modern reference books and papers.

A completely different group evolved from the *Australimusa* section of the *Musa* genus, the so-called Fe'i bananas, common in the Pacific and composed of a group of cultivars characterized by the red sap of the plant and, chiefly, the fact that its fruit is produced in erect bunches rather than the hanging bunches typical of all *Eumusa* types. It is likely that several species, most particularly *M. maclayi* Muell., are involved in the origin of the Fe'i group.

In purely commercial terms, the most important dessert bananas are those of the Cavendish subgroup— sterile, seedless triploids (AAA) of *M. acuminata*, of which the best known cultivars are "Grande Naine" and "Dwarf Cavendish." Others include AA diploids (such as "Pisang Mas" in Southeast Asia and "Bocadillo" in Latin America, both well known because of their excellent taste, which makes them highly prized by European gourmet fruit retailers), various AB diploids (*acuminata* × *balbisiana*), AAA triploids (the best known is "Gros Michel," at one time the world's leading commercial cultivar but now virtually absent from cultivation because of its high susceptibility to Panama disease, a fungal wilt of serious economic importance), and AAB triploids such as "Silk Fig" (also known as "Pome" and "Manzano"), and the recently obtained AAAB tetraploid "Goldfinger."

Cooking bananas are usually hybrids, mainly AAB or ABB triploids, with the exception of the so-called "Highlands bananas," AAA triploids used in Africa mainly for beer production.

Area of Origin and Main Historical Developmental Facts

Wild bananas were probably used in prehistoric times for, among other non-food purposes, cloth, shelter, and dyes. Interest in them as a food crop appeared early in agricultural history, doubtless linked to the appearance of parthenocarpy (i.e., development of fruit without pollination) and consequent lack of seeds in the primitive types of *M. acuminata* from which the modern edible triploids evolved. Many wild banana diploids and triploids are still abundant throughout southeastern Asia, with a primary area of origin in Malaysia and Papua New Guinea, while most of the plantains originated in India and the Philippines. In any event, both spread quickly to other tropical and subtropical regions of the world. The Fe'i bananas evolved throughout the Pacific islands from Indonesia to the Marquesas and still remain closely confined to the area.

The main recognized milestones of these movements are:

- c. 500 C.E. — Introduction to Africa from Indonesia (via Madagascar)
- c. 1000 C.E. — Distribution throughout Polynesia and introduction to Mediterranean areas during Muslim expansion
- 1300s–1400s — Introduction to the Canary Islands from West Africa
- 1516 — First recorded introduction to the New World (Santo Domingo) from the Canary Islands
- 1500s–1800s — Distribution of bananas and plantains throughout tropical America
- Early 1800s — Introduction to the New World from Southeast Asia of the cultivars Dwarf Cavendish and Gros Michel
- Late 1800s — Beginning of the international trade
- 1900s — Banana becomes a major food item in the temperate-zone markets of the Western world as well as in Asia

Many authors question some of these dates: particularly at issue is the well-documented distribution of the banana in South and Central America shortly after Columbus's first trip, leading some historians to speculate on its presence in the New World prior to 1492. But until proof becomes available, the accepted explanation is that its rapid foothold and spread ran parallel to the slave trade, for which the banana was considered a staple food. The relative durability of banana propagation material and the rapidity with which the plant produces fruit favor this hypothesis, although the archaic uses of the plant's materials still practiced today by some native communities of the Amazon basin, as well as the increasing body of knowledge pointing to the Asiatic ancestry of Native Americans—whose forebears could conceivably have brought banana seeds with them—also support the idea of an early introduction to Latin America (Moreira).

Legends and Myths

The banana plant has been associated with the religions, folklore, traditions, and social customs of many cultures. In most cases these refer to the special botanical characteristics of the plant. A good example is the Indonesian myth "The banana and the rock," which in short recounts how in the beginning, God gave humans a rock as a gift. Not at all pleased, the humans clamored for a different gift, whereupon God gave them a banana plant but with the caveat "You choose the banana and not the rock. Your life will be like this plant, in that soon after it has borne descendants the mother plant will die and the young shoots at its base will come into their own. If you had chosen the rock, your life would be eternal." (Frazer, as cited in *Infomusa*, 1999). The banana is regarded in many cultures as a symbol of fertility and prosperity; thus, it is frequently planted in the corner of subsistence fields of rice, yam, and other basic crops to "protect" them. Throughout Southeast Asia and the Pacific the plant is an important part of the dowry, ensuring food for the newlyweds' future family.

In New Caledonia the Fe'i banana, given its typical blood-red sap, is considered to be the reincarnation of ancestors, with different clones identified with the diverse clans and others considered privileges of the chiefs. The Yanomami tribe of the Brazilian Amazon use the fruit in their funeral rituals, eating a paste of ripe bananas to which the ashes of the deceased are added (http://www.kah-bonn.de/ausstellungen/orinoko/texte.htm).

In the East African highlands, the care and cooking of bananas are tasks reserved for women, with each elderly woman undertaking the responsibility to provide for ten men; beer bananas, on the other hand, are part of the male domain. In Tanzania, however, women prepare the beer and proceeds from sale are their only socially acceptable form of revenue. Hawaiian women, by contrast, were forbidden, under pain of death, from eating most kinds of bananas until the early 1800s (http://hawaii-nation.org/canoe/maia.html).

The Qur'an holds that the banana is the *Tree of Paradise*, and the notorious *forbidden fruit* that tempted Eve in the Garden of Eden could conceivably have been a banana rather than an apple, to say nothing of the leaf—certainly larger than that of the fig tree—with which she later covers her modesty. Simmonds provides some support for this, reminding us that Linnaeus did give the banana its scientific species name of *paradisiaca* (paradise), as well as that the frequent inclusion of "fig" in the common and cultivar names given to certain banana varieties cannot be purely coincidental.

Perhaps one of the best examples of the strong relationship between the banana and humans is the fact that in many languages the banana plant is referred to using terms that indicate people consider it as a family unit: "mother plant" referring to the plant while it is producing a bunch and that will become the "grandmother"

FIGURE 1

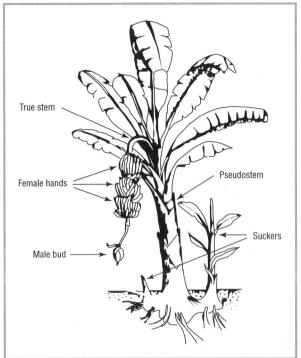

once that bunch has been cut; "son" or "daughter" plant referring to the sucker growing at the mother's base, which will produce the next crop; the "parent crop," referring to the plants that will provide the first harvest. In the same anthropomorphic line, the terms "hands" and "fingers" are assigned to the fruit (see Botanical Description).

Botanical Description

Bananas and plantains are evergreen herbaceous tropical plants that can be considered giant herbs, as some varieties reach up to ten meters in height, although most commercial types grow to between two and five meters (see Fig. 1). The external "trunk" is in fact a *pseudostem* formed by the concentric assemblement of the leaf sheaths crowned by a rosette of large, oblong-to-elliptic–shaped leaves (ten to twenty under healthy conditions), conferring on the plant the aspect of a herbaceous tree. The *true stem* is a subterranean organ that extends upward at the core of the *pseudostem* until culminating in the inflorescence (the fruiting organ of the plant), which emerges from the top of the plant, and it is responsible for producing all the other parts of the plant: roots, leaves, and shoots or suckers. Leaves are produced successively until the inflorescence is cast, and in variable quantity depending on the specific variety of banana or plantain, climate, and cultural practices.

Although the plant dies after producing fruit, it can be considered perennial in as much as suckers successively replace the senescent aerial parts without need for

Banana ripening facility for Chiquita Brands International in Costa Rica. The bananas are ripened artificially and processed for export. COURTESY AP/WIDE WORLD PHOTOS.

replanting. Several suckers emerge consecutively from buds located at the axil of leaves; under commercial cultivation, they are regularly eliminated, leaving either the most vigorous sucker, or the one capable of producing a bunch when better prices can be obtained, to replace the mother plant.

The large and complex inflorescence is composed of double rows of flowers, called hands, and covered by bracts, usually red or reddish in color, grouped helixoidally along the inflorescence axis, reproducing the pattern of the leaf system. All flowers are hermaphroditic, but only the female or so-called "first" hands (in most cases between four and nine, but sometimes up to fifteen) will give rise to the edible fruit—technically known as fingers; the other hands are of an intermediate or even male character and do not produce edible fruit (these rudimentary fruitlets usually fall before the edible fingers mature). Commercial fruit develops parthenocarpically, although some varieties produce seed in the wild or can be forced to do so in specialized breeding work.

Depending mainly on climate, cultivation conditions, and varieties, the time lapse between emission of the inflorescence and harvesting of the bunch can be anywhere from three to ten months. Bananas are harvested year-round, with normal commercial bunch weights of 15–30 kg, although bunches of more than 45 kg are not unusual when properly cultivated (exceptional cases of bunches of

more than 125 kg have been recorded). A medium-sized dessert banana finger weighs around 160 g.

Nutritional Value and Uses

Banana fruit is composed mainly of water (around 65 percent for banana and 75 percent for plantain) and carbohydrates (from 22 percent for banana and 32 percent for plantain). It contains several vitamins, including A, B, and C, and is very low in protein and fat but rich in minerals, particularly potassium (around 400 mg/100 g). It is cholesterol free, high in fiber, and low in sodium. Chemical composition varies not only among cultivars but also according to climatic and other conditions (values are widely available in most of the texts cited in the Bibliography).

Ripe fruit is usually consumed fresh—simply peeled and eaten as a snack or dessert, in salads mixed with other fruit, and with breakfast cereals, but it also lends itself to more elaborate dishes ranging from ice cream to pie fillings.

Plantains, being starchier than bananas, can be eaten ripe or unripe, but many countries have developed commercial processes to provide a wide variety of products from both fruits (in several cases, green bananas can also be used): puree, flour, jam, jelly, chips, crisps, flakes, dried, catsup, relishes or spreads, preserves, vinegar, and even wine. Banana flour, both from green and ripe fruit, has a great industrial potential and, enriched with sugar, powdered milk, minerals and vitamins, and artificial flavoring, is much used in baby foods. In several areas of Southeast Asia, young fruits are pickled. Puree is used in the manufacture of dairy products, such as yogurt and ice cream, in breads and cakes, banana-flavored drinks, baby food, and diverse sauces.

In Uganda—the country with the highest per-capita consumption of bananas and plantains in the world in 1996: 243 kg while people in most European countries only averaged between 7 and 15 kg—an important part of the diet comes from unripe plantains that are first peeled, then steamed wrapped in their own leaves, and finally pounded to a starchy paste called *matoke* that constitutes the main dish. Both Uganda and Tanzania produce and consume large quantities of beer brewed from local Highlands bananas. A plantain and soybean mixture, SOYAMUSA, combining carbohydrates and proteins, has been recently developed in Nigeria to be used as a weaning food for toddlers. All told, bananas and plantains represent more than 25 percent of the food energy requirements of Africa (Frison and Sharrock, p. 30).

Tostones is a very popular dish in the Caribbean: slices of green plantain are double-fried (flattening slices with a wooden press between fryings), producing a tasty side dish used in lieu of the ubiquitous french-fried potato. *Mofongo* is a typical Puerto Rican dish made from fried green plantain, pork, and garlic. Finely ground and roasted dried green plantain has been utilized as a coffee substitute in some countries (Morton, 1987, p 43).

Although the fruit is the main economic product, many parts of the banana plant can be used as food, fodder, or for industrial purposes. Throughout the tropics, male buds, young flowers, and even the pseudostem of some cultivars are eaten cooked as vegetables. Flowers and ashes from burned green leaves and pseudostems are used in curries in Southeast Asia. The possibility of using the raquis to prepare a flour for human consumption and of making a marmalade from plantain peel is being studied in Colombia. Leaves are used for wrapping other food during steaming or other cooking, such as in preparing the Venezuelan *hallaca* and many pit-steamed or pit-roasted meats and vegetables typical among the Pacific Islanders. Banana leaves are also used as environmentally friendly "disposable plates" in southern India, where in fact several cultivars (mainly AAB or ABB plantain types) are grown exclusively for leaf production (Singh, p. 27).

Green and commercially rejected ripe bananas are currently used as animal feed. Leaves, pseudostems, bunch raquis, and peels are also commonly used in fodder. In the Canary Islands (Spain), fresh, chopped banana leaves make up about 80 percent of the diet of Pelibüey sheep.

Medicinal and Therapeutical Value

The easy digestibility and nutritional content make ripe banana an excellent food, particularly suitable for young children and elderly people. In the green stage (and after liquefying) it is used in Brazil to treat dehydration in infants, as the tannins in the fruit tend to protect the lining of the intestinal tract against further loss of liquids. In general, the banana is appropriate for consumption when a low-fat, low-sodium, and/or cholesterol-free diet is required, making it particularly recommendable for people with cardiovascular and kidney problems, arthritis, gout, or gastrointestinal ulcers (Robinson, p. 216).

As the fruit is easy to carry and peel, it is of great value to athletes as a quick and healthy method of replenishing energy because of its high energy value: 75–115 kCal/100 mg of pulp (the lower range for banana and the higher for plantain). Both bananas and plantains contain complex carbohydrates capable of replacing glycogen and important vitamins, particularly B_6 and C, and minerals (potassium, calcium, magnesium, and iron). Ripe fruit has been used to treat asthma and bronchitis, and, as mentioned, in the control of diarrhea. Boiled and mashed ripe fruit, especially when mixed with other appropriate plants, is also cited as a good remedy against constipation.

The juice extracted from the male bud is thought to be good for stomach problems. The peel of ripe bananas has antiseptic properties and can be used to prepare a poultice for wounds or even applied directly to a wound in an emergency. The banana pseudostem is also cooked in India as a dish called "Khich Khach," to be taken monthly to prevent constipation. Fresh leaves have reportedly been used medicinally for a whole range of disorders from headaches to urinary tract infections—at one time, stem juice was considered a remedy for gonorrhea. Many of these purported remedies are not well documented and require further investigation.

Modern History, Commercialization, and Trade

The greatest development of the international banana trade occurred in Latin America during the second half of the nineteenth century, with exports from the West Indies and Central America to markets in North America. It was linked inexorably to railway and port expansion and to land concession policies. The founding in 1899 of the United Fruit Company—of Chiquita brand renown—is generally considered to be the fundamental milestone in this process. According to several sources, over the course of many decades this company wielded considerable power over the governments of several Central American countries, to which it allegedly "contributed" around 30 percent of its net operating profit. Thus the term "banana republic" came into use to define a country whose government was manipulated, and presumably corrupted, by the economic clout of a private enterprise.

From harvesting to consumption, bananas require careful handling as the fruit is very susceptible to physical damage and needs proper (cool) storage to avoid quick ripening and decay. After the bunch arrives at the packing house, it is dehanded and broken into clusters of 4–6 fingers each. Both hands and clusters are washed, usually by passing through tanks containing disinfectant solutions, and packed in cardboard boxes holding 12–18 kg on average. Modern refrigerated ships, equipped with holds that feature controlled temperature and humidity, transport the boxed fruit from the producing countries to distant markets. Temperature during transport is extremely critical: between 13 and 14°C guarantees that fruit will reach its destination in optimum conditions, whereas a short exposure to 12°C or colder temperatures will damage the fruit beyond repair by deteriorating its taste.

According to export trade figures, the major supplying countries can be divided into three groups: 1) the Dollar area, including most Latin American countries (where the trade is largely in the hands of multinationals like Chiquita, Dole, or Del Monte); 2) the ACP area, named for the African-Caribbean-Pacific countries that were signatories of the 1975 Lomé Convention and later treaties with the European Union (EU) designed to protect their economy, largely based on agricultural products; and 3) European producers, particularly the Canary Islands (Spain), the French West Indies, and the Portuguese islands of Madeira.

The main importers are Japan (mostly served by the Philippines), the United States, and Canada (supplied almost exclusively by the Dollar area countries), and the European Union (shared among all the major supplying groups by virtue of the Common Market Organization's banana regulations, which broadly follow the World Trade Organization precepts regarding free trade while safeguarding the traditional economies of ACP countries and EU ultraperipheral regions). Organic production is of increasing importance to import markets and, as is happening with other products, its impact on world trade should be felt in the near future.

About 95 percent of the world export trade is based on Cavendish bananas, but plantains are also the subject of recent interest, especially in Europe because of the burgeoning immigrant population of chiefly African and Latin American origin. Other specialty or exotic bananas, particularly those with red peels and/or flesh, but also *apple* ("Manzano"), *baby banana* ("Bocadillo" or "Pisang Mas"), and *ice cream* ("Lady Finger") types are commercialized on a small scale to satisfy niche markets.

See also **Africa**; **Caribbean**; **Fruit**.

BIBLIOGRAPHY

Champion, J. M. "Botanique et Génétique des Bananiers." Tome I. *Notes et Documents sur les Bananiers et leur Culture.* I.F.A.C. Setco. Paris, 1967.

Davies, G. "Banana and Plantains in the East African Highlands." In *Bananas and Plantains*, edited by S. Gowen, 493–508. London: Chapman and Hall, 1994.

Frazer, J. G. *citant* A. C. Kruijt. *The Belief in Immortality*, 1. [London, 1913], excerpted in *Infomusa* 8 (1) (1999): 30.

Frison, E. A., and S. L. Sharrock. "Introduction: The Economic, Social and Nutritional Importance of Banana in the World." In *Bananas and Food Security*, edited by C. Picq, E. Fouré, and E. A. Frison, 21–35. International Symposium, Douala, Cameroon, 10–14 November, 1998. Montpellier, France: INIBAP, 1999.

Galán Saúco, V. *Los Frutales Tropicales y Subtropicales en los Subtrópicos. II. Plátano (Banano).* Madrid: Mundi-Prensa, 1992.

Giraldo, G., L. L. Carvajal, M. L. Sánchez, and M. I. Arcila. "Diseño de un Producto Alimenticio para Humanos (Hojuelas) a partir del Raquis de Plátano Dominico-Hartón (*Musa* AAB Simmonds)." In *Postcosecha y Agroindustria del Plátano en el Eje Cafetero de Colombia*, edited by D. G. Cayón Salinas, G. A. Giraldo Giraldo, and M. I. Arcila Pulgarín, 217–223. CORPOICA, Universidad del Quindío, Asiplat, Comité Departamental del Quindío, COLCIENCIAS. Fudesco, Armenia, Colombia, 2000.

Gopinath, C. Y. "How to Cook a *Musa* Pseudostem." *Infomusa* 4 (2) (1995): 31.

Guevara, C. B., Giraldo, M. Ivonne, G. Giraldo, and M. I. Arcila. "Diseño de un proceso de producción de mermelada a partir de la cáscara de plátano Dominico-Hartón." In *Postcosecha y Agroindustria del Plátano en el Eje Cafetero de Colombia*, edited by D. G. Cayón Salinas, G. A. Giraldo Giraldo, and M. I. Arcila Pulgarín, 223–228. CORPOICA, Universidad del Quindío, Asiplat, Comité Departamental del Quindío, COLCIENCIAS. Fudesco, Armenia, Colombia, 2000.

Kagy, V. "Importance Alimentaire, Socio-économique et Culturelle de la Banane dans la Société Kanak de Nouvelle-Calédonie." In *Bananas and Food Security*, edited by C. Picq,

E. Fouré, and E. A. Frison, 437–445. International Symposium, Douala, Cameroon, 10–14 November, 1998. Montpellier, France: INIBAP, 1999.

Moreira, R. S. *Banana, Teoria e Prática de Cultivo.* Fundação Cargill. Sao Paulo, Brazil. CD-ROM, 1999.

Morton, J. F. *Fruits of Warm Climates.* Winterville, N.C.: Creative Resources Systems (distributors); Miami, Fla.: J. F. Morton, 1987.

Robinson, J. C. *Bananas and Plantains.* Wallingford, U.K.: CAB International, 1996.

Simmonds, N. W. *Bananas.* 2d ed. London: Longmans, 1966.

Singh, H. P. "Growing Banana for Leaf." *Infomusa* 5 (1) (1996): 27–28.

Soto Ballestero, M. S. *Bananos: Cultivo y Comercialización.* San José: Litografíc e Imprenta, 1992.

Thompson, A. K., and O. J. Burden. "Harvesting and Fruit Care." In *Bananas and Plantains*, edited by S. Gowen, 403–433. London: Chapman and Hall, 1995.

Valmayor, R. V., S. H. Jamaluddin, B. Silayoi, S. Kusumo, L. D. Dahn, O. C. Pascua, and R. R. C. Espino. *Banana Cultivar Names and Synonyms in Southeast Asia.* Los Baños, Laguna, Philippines: INIBAP, 2000.

White, Lynton Dove. *Canoe Plants of Ancient Hawaii: Mai'A.* (1994). Available at http://www.hawaii-nation.org/.

Víctor Galán Saúco

BARBECUE. While meat grilled over a charcoal or wood fire is common to many cultures around the world, American barbecue is distinguished from these other dishes because of the cuts of meat it traditionally involves, the cooking techniques it employs, and the definitive sauces and side dishes that accompany it. Barbecue is cooked slowly at temperatures ranging from about 175 to 300°F with more smoke than fire. The meat involved varies from region to region. Traditional barbecue most often is pork, beef, lamb, or goat. However, chicken is also a popular barbecue meat.

The word "barbecue" is generally thought to have evolved from the word "barbacoa," which first appeared in Gonzalo Fernández de Oviedo's 1526 book *De La Historia General y Natural de Las Indias*. He describes the technique of skewering meat on sticks and then roasting it over a pit dug in the ground. The writing of Bernardino de Sahaún, who accompanied Hernán Cortés in his conquests of Mexico, uses the word "barbacoa" in references to meats roasted under the ground. References to barbecue cooking technique are also found in the 1698 memoirs of Père Labat, a French priest who wrote about his travels in the West Indies.

Several countries have culinary traditions that, to greater or lesser extents, could be called barbecue. For example, in India, meats are often roasted over charcoal in tandoor, a clay oven. In Jamaica, pork and chicken are barbequed "jerk" style over a slow fire of wood from the all-spice tree. In Mexico, whole goats are often butterflied, skewered, and cooked over a slow fire. In South Africa, the word *braai* is used to refer to the metal or brick pit over which meat is grilled, or to the event at which such meat is served. In Cuba, pit-roasted pigs are the traditional Christmas Eve dinner. In Brazil, *churrasco* refers to the technique of cooking meat on skewers over open pits. That country's *churrascaria* restaurants are famous for their all-you-can eat style of service. American barbecue enthusiasts generally refer to the technique involved in cooking steaks, hamburgers, or fish over an open fire as "grilling" rather than "barbecueing."

The word "barbecue" can be employed as a verb when it refers to the cooking technique. It is also an adjective, as in the phrase "barbecued ribs." And it is a noun when it refers to the gathering at which barbecue is served, as in the sentence, "We are going to a barbecue." Barbecue is important in the American culinary lexicon for two main reasons. First, it takes place outdoors, the cooking is often a public if not a communal event, and it is closely associated with family gatherings and such holidays as Independence Day and Labor Day. Second, barbecue is closely associated with particular regions of the country. The cultural identity of those regions and the people who live in them are inextricable from the style of barbecue served there.

Several theories have been advanced about how roasted meat evolved into American barbecue. The writings of Thomas Jefferson and George Washington include references to barbecue. The event is clearly related to the pig roasts common in Great Britain. While pig roasts may have been common in New England, barbecue did not take root there. Rather, in the eastern United States barbecue is most closely associated with states in which enslaved Africans did much of the cooking. Many of these people were transported from Africa via the Caribbean islands, where they may have learned some of the barbecue techniques of Native Americans. Mexican-Americans continue to use the barbacoa technique described in the writings of Bernardino de Sahagún today.

Barbecue is primarily associated with the American South and is cooked and eaten by most of the region's ethnic groups. But the food was taken to other regions by African-Americans as they fled the South for factory work in the Midwest and other regions in the middle decades of the twentieth century. Barbecue ultimately became common in the area from Virginia over to Kansas, down to Texas, and across to Florida and in African-American enclaves in California.

Barbecue geography can be tricky in that often barbecue styles do not conform to the lines on maps. In the Carolinas, Georgia, and other parts of the Southeast, barbecue means pork, either whole hogs or pork shoulders, generally cooked over hickory or oak wood. It is then chopped, sliced, or pulled and served on buns. Sauces vary widely within the region. Parts of South Carolina are unique in that they use mustard as the basis of their sauce. Parts of North Carolina and Kentucky are similarly unique in that they use a thin sauce that tastes like Worcestershire sauce. The most popular sauce throughout the Southeast is a thin vinegar-based recipe flecked with flakes of dried red pepper and sometimes sweetened with sugar. The most popular barbecue sauce in the country, a thicker, sweeter, tomato-based sauce, is also popular in parts of the Southeast.

Though coleslaw and hush puppies are common side dishes throughout the Southeast, the definitive side dishes are regional stews. In South Carolina and parts of eastern Georgia barbecue is often accompanied by rice and hash, a stew made with some combination of pork and pork organ meats. In Virginia, North Carolina, and Georgia, Brunswick stew is served. The ingredients in this dish vary considerably and can include wild game, corn, lima beans, potatoes, and tomatoes, depending on the locale. In Kentucky, where mutton is the preferred meat for barbecuing, burgoo, a stew similar to Brunswick stew, is the popular accompaniment.

In Tennessee the basic barbecue dish is pork served on a bun with mayonnaise coleslaw. There as in many parts of the barbecue belt significant differences exist between urban and rural barbecue. In urban areas the sauces tend to be thicker and sweeter, and barbecued ribs are a standard part of the menu.

The distinctions in Texas barbecue are based largely on proximity to Mexico. Barbacoa, cow's head cooked in underground pits with mesquite wood and served with salsa on tortillas, is a common Sunday morning meal. While beef brisket is the standard barbecue meat in most of Texas, people along the border often refer to this as "American barbecue" to distinguish it from barbacoa. In southern Texas pinto beans generally accompany barbecue, and the meat is usually seasoned with cumin and chili powder. Eastern Texas barbecue is primarily beef brisket, but baked beans are more common than pinto beans there. Potato salad often replaces coleslaw as a side dish in eastern Texas, and spicing of the meat is influenced less by Mexican flavors.

In Arkansas, Oklahoma, Kansas, and Missouri, where the southeastern and southwestern traditions merge, beef and pork are equally popular. The sauces in those places tend to be sweet, thick, ketchup-based recipes. In Chicago and other cities where African Americans settled, pork ribs are the staple rather than whole hogs or pork shoulders.

Unlike most home cooking, barbecue is generally cooked by men. Sociologists have several theories for this. Men may be attracted to the fact that barbecue is cooked outdoors and in public rather than in a closed kitchen. Also at the root of barbecue is a primitive technique, often involving chopping wood, taming a fire, and butchering large cuts of meat. These tasks are traditionally viewed as masculine, and the technique is passed down from father to son.

With an increasing emphasis on faster, simpler cooking, some commercial establishments have replaced wood and charcoal pits with electric or gas ovens. Additionally the popularity of barbecue sauce as a condiment has meant that sometimes any meat slathered in a sweet, ketchup-based sauce is improperly called barbecue.

See also **United States,** *subentries on* **African American Foodways** *and* **The South.**

BIBLIOGRAPHY

Bass, S. Jonathan. "'How 'bout a Hand for the Hog': The Enduring Nature of the Swine as a Cultural Symbol of the South." *Southern Culture* 1, no. 3 (Spring 1995).

Browne, Rich, and Jack Bettridge. *Barbecue America: A Pilgrimage in Search of America's Best Barbecue.* Alexandria, Va.: Time-Life Books, 1999.

Egerton, John. *Southern Food: At Home, on the Road, in History.* New York: Knopf, 1987.

Elie, Lolis Eric, and Frank Stewart. *Smokestack Lightning: Adventures in the Heart of Barbecue Country.* New York: Farrar, Straus and Giroux, 1996.

Hilliard, Sam Bowers. *Hog Meat and Hoecake: Food Supply in the Old South, 1840–1860.* Carbondale: Southern Illinois University Press, 1972.

Johnson, Greg, and Vince Staten. *Real Barbecue.* New York: Harper and Row, 1988.

Perdue, Charles L., Jr., ed. *Pigsfoot Jelly and Persimmon Beer.* Santa Fe: Ancient City Press, 1992.

Raichelen, Steve. *The Barbecue Bible.* New York: Workman, 1998.

Smith, Steve. "The Rhetoric of Barbecue: A Southern Rite and Ritual." *Studies in Popular Culture* 8, 1 (1985): 17–25.

Taylor, Joe Gray. *Eating, Drinking, and Visiting in the South.* Baton Rouge: Louisiana State University Press, 1982.

Wilson, Charles Reagan, and William Ferris, eds. *Encyclopedia of Southern Culture.* Chapel Hill: University of North Carolina Press, 1989.

Lolis Eric Elie

BARLEY. Barley is recognized as one of the very first crops to be domesticated for human consumption. It remains one of the major cereal crops grown in the world: barley is grown on every continent on which crops are grown. It is well adapted to diverse environmental conditions and thus it is produced across a broader geographic distribution than most other cereals. Relative to other cereal crops, barley ranks fourth in total grain production. The grain of barley enters the human food chain via distinctly different routes. First, barley is used as an animal feed and therefore makes an essential contribution to the human diet indirectly through meat production. Second, barley serves as a substrate for the production of alcoholic beverages, in particular beer. Third, a minor amount of barley is used to produce a diverse range of foodstuffs eaten by humans.

The Biology of the Barley Plant

The scientific name of barley is *Hordeum vulgare L.* Barley is a flowering plant belonging to the family Poaceae (the grasses). In addition to barley, the grass family includes the crops most important to human existence, including rice, wheat, and maize, and other species such as sorghum, oats, rye, millet, and sugarcane. In European contexts, barley grain is often referred to as "corn." The genus *Hordeum* includes approximately thirty species that are indigenous to at least four continents. Barley is the only domesticated species to have emerged from the genus *Hordeum*, in contrast to other crop genera such as *Triticum* (the wheats) and *Phaseolus* (the dry beans), which each contain several domesticated species. The other members of the genus *Hordeum* exist as wild plants.

Growth and development. The life cycle of the barley plant first begins with seed germination underground. The first visible sign of germination is root emergence, followed by the emergence of the cylindrically shaped coleoptile, which is the first structure to appear above ground. Interestingly, most above-ground tissues of the barley plant initially develop from the crown, a structure located below ground. The first leaf grows upward within the cylinder of the coleoptile, and emerges above the soil. This and other leaves do not expand along their entire length; rather the outer section (the blade) does so, while the base (the sheath) remains formed in a hollow cylinder. New leaves emerge in succession up through the sheaths of the older leaves.

The barley plant is not restricted to the development of one main stem, as observed in maize. Rather, like most other small-grain cereals such as wheat and rice, barley produces several additional secondary stems termed tillers that emerge up from the crown beginning a few weeks after the emergence of the main stem. The number of tillers produced varies depending upon the barley genotype and the environment. For instance, under highly fertile conditions, plants will produce more tillers than if nutrient starved.

Reproduction. Barley varieties are classified as spring or winter types, depending on whether they need a cold treatment, ranging from two to several weeks before making the transition to the reproductive phase of growth. When barley switches to its reproductive phase, the true stems of some of the tillers, called culms, elongate upward. The flowering structure, known variously as the spike, ear, or head, is borne upward, ultimately emerging from the "boot," which is the sheath of the uppermost leaf on the culm (the flag leaf). The height of a barley plant when the spike has emerged varies greatly, but averages approximately eighty centimeters. The spike consists of a large number of individual flowers called florets, which are present in individual spikelets that are attached to a central stemlike structure called the rachis. Spikelets are attached in groups of three on opposite sides of the rachis. The total number of spikelets on a spike varies, but averages approximately sixty. The awns are a notable feature of the spike. They are hairlike extensions that emerge upward from the lemma, one of two thin sheets of cells that surround the floret (the other is the palea). Awn length varies considerably among barley varieties.

Barley is also classified based upon the fertility of the florets on the spike. In six-rowed barleys, all of the florets are fertile, leading to six vertical rows of seeds on the spike. In contrast, in two-rowed types only the central floret of the three at each node is fertile, and thus just two rows of seeds develop on opposite sides of the rachis. The fertile florets consist of both male and female reproductive structures, and fertilization occurs as the spikes are emerging from the boot. Barley is thus predominantly self-pollinated. Between twenty-five and sixty seeds per spike are produced, and for spring barley the seed matures three to five months after planting.

Characteristics of the barley grain. Barley seeds are approximately eight millimeters in length and weigh approximately fifty milligrams when mature, though there is a considerable range in these values between varieties. In most cases, the harvested barley grain includes the seed, a small structure called the rachilla, and both the palea and lemma, all of which adhere firmly to the seed. Barley grain in which these structures remain attached is referred to as covered barley, with the palea and lemma, collectively termed the hull. However, barleys in which the palea and lemma do not adhere to the seed are also well known. These hulless barleys share harvesting features similar to wheat, because when harvested the seed is cleanly separated from all other components of the spike.

The barley seed consists of the embryo, a series of outer layers of cells called the pericarp, and the endosperm. The endosperm contains different nutrients that the embryo draws upon as it grows into a plant. The principal compound found in the endosperm is starch, which represents about two-thirds of the mass of the seed. This starch serves as an energy source for the seedling. Another significant carbohydrate, the β-glucans, are components of the endosperm cell walls. The second largest component of the barley endosperm is protein. The amount of protein present is generally inversely proportional to the amount of starch. This protein provides a source of amino acids that can be used for protein synthesis by the seedling. The amount of protein present in a seed is positively correlated with the amount of nitrogen fertilizer applied when the parent plant is being grown. Additionally, the barley grain contains a large variety of other compounds present in minor amounts, including mineral nutrients and different organic compounds, including various vitamins.

The History of Barley Use

The progenitor of cultivated barley is *Hordeum vulgare* subspecies *spontaneum*, or wild barley. Wild barley is still

Barley spikes from two-rowed and six-rowed types. PHOTO COURTESY OF DAVID GARVIN, USDA–ARS.

widely distributed in a large geographic region ranging west from Israel, Turkey, Syria, and Egypt, eastward to Pakistan, India, and into western China. It is particularly prevalent in the Fertile Crescent region of the Near and Middle East. Biological evidence for wild barley as a progenitor of cultivated barley is suggested by the fact that they both have the same base chromosome number (seven), and can be easily crossed to produce fertile offspring. Wild barley is two-rowed, and thus the first domesticated barley was two-rowed. Six-rowed types and hulless barley emerged not long afterward from the domesticated two-rowed types, due to a few chance mutations. Several traits have been selected in barley compared to wild barley, which facilitate harvest, storage, and utilization. The most important of these are nonshattering spikes where the seeds adhere to the rachis and allow easy harvesting, increased straw strength, larger seeds, and reduced grain dormancy.

Along with wheat, barley was one of the first crops to be domesticated by humans and thus it played an important role in the emergence of agriculture in the Old World. There is rich evidence of barley in the archaeological record from numerous sites throughout the Near and Middle East, supporting the notion that it was a common and important crop in ancient times. It is likely that barley was already domesticated and being cultivated as early as ten thousand years ago, though wild barley was likely being harvested as a food long before this. Further, early written records from various cultures bear frequent mention of barley, as does the Bible, reinforcing the fact that barley was an important crop. Indeed, barley remained an important human food crop for many millennia, but it was gradually supplanted by wheat. The rapid spread of agriculture from the Near East into Europe and Asia led to the broad dissemination of barley and its cultivation. In more recent history, barley was brought to the New World as far back as the explorations of Columbus. Barley was introduced to the eastern United States early in the seventeenth century, and the west coast of the Americas in the eighteenth century.

Barley Production

Barley is grown on nearly sixty million hectares of land worldwide, resulting in the production of approximately 140 million metric tons of grain. The top ten barley producing countries include Russia, Germany, Canada, Ukraine, France, Australia, the United Kingdom, Turkey, United States, and Denmark. Barley producers select the appropriate varieties to be grown and crop management schemes to produce grain well suited to a particular end use. Specific producer considerations vary widely, but include the choice of variety to plant, the timing of planting and grain harvesting, and agricultural inputs such as fertilizers, herbicides, fungicides, and insecticides. In the Northern Hemisphere, in regions where winters are too severe to allow winter barleys to survive overwintering, spring barleys are planted, usually in April or May. In warmer regions where winter barleys can overwinter, planting is done in September or November.

Given that the producer obtains only a small profit margin for barley produced, additional agricultural inputs are minimized. For instance, nitrogen fertilization is managed to maximize yield without compromising end-use quality. Barley is also subject to damage by a range of diseases, including powdery mildew, stem and leaf rust, smuts, leaf blotches, viral diseases, and head blights. Thus these diseases are managed by a combination of strategies including the use of disease-resistant varieties, application of fungicides, tillage practices, timing of crop planting, and crop rotation.

When the barley crop is mature, harvesting is accomplished either by direct combining or by first swathing, which entails cutting the culms and allowing the grain to dry in the field, and then harvesting. Technology for harvesting ranges from a simple sickle in developing countries to sophisticated mechanical combines that cut the culms above the soil, move the harvested plants between rollers to dislodge seeds, and pass this over mesh screens, allowing the grain to fall into a collection bin and the chaff to blow back out to the ground. Once the grain is harvested, it may either be stored in bins on the farm, or delivered to a local grain elevator where it is purchased from the producer. The price paid for barley grain depends on its intended end use. After purchasing the grain, the elevator cleans, dries, and stores it, and ultimately resells the grain to the various businesses that use barley (feed, food, and malt industries).

Barley Consumption

Animal feed. The principal use of barley grain is as feed for poultry, swine, sheep, and cattle. Worldwide, 60 percent or more of the barley that is produced is used for animal feed. The particular barley varieties used as animal feed are sometimes specially developed "feed barleys" with attributes such as high protein that are geared specifically toward this end use. Sheep can be fed whole barley; however, before barley is fed to other animals it is ground using a hammer mill or rolling mill, or may be flaked with steam-heated rollers. Thus, the final feed product may be whole, ground, flaked, or pelleted barley. Since the phosphorus in barley is generally more readily absorbed by animals than it is from other feed grains, the use of barley as animal feed tends to result in less potential environmental phosphorus contamination from the animal waste runoff. While barley grain is the principal part of the plant used as animal feed, in some instances barley plants themselves may be used as a forage hay for animals.

Human consumption of barley. Less than one-half of the barley produced throughout the world is used for the preparation and production of products directly consumed by humans. Only a minor amount of barley is actually used in the production of foods for human consumption, though the range of uses for barley within this context are diverse. In some regions of the world, barley is grown for human consumption where other grains do not grow well. When consumed as grain, hulless barley is generally used because the absence of the hull makes the product more palatable and easier to process. Barley can be pearled, which removes the outer layers of the seed and the embryo, followed by processing to produce small rounded pieces of the endosperm. Covered barley can also be dehulled, milled, and polished to remove the bran layers, to produce a ricelike product. Pearled and polished barley are used in porridges and soups and as rice substitutes. Other food uses include barley flakes, flour for baking purposes (either alone or in mixtures with wheat flour) to produce breads and crackers, grits, breakfast cereals, pilaf, noodles, and baby foods. Lastly, some barley is used for the production of distilled spirits such as whiskey, vodka, and gin, and for making vinegar and malted beverages.

Beer: the main use of barley for human consumption. The truly unique feature of barley that sets it apart from other small-grain cereals such as wheat is that the vast majority of barley that humans consume is not in the form of solid food derivatives, but rather in the form of a single product, the alcoholic beverage beer. The production of beerlike alcoholic beverages dates back several thousand years, and beer may be the oldest fermented beverage consumed by humans. Many barley varieties are developed specifically to possess the chemical and biochemical properties desirable for this purpose; such barleys are called malting barleys. In contrast to feed barley, malting barley has a high starch content. Because of the greater value of the end product of malting barley compared to feed barley, malting barley brings the producer more money. However, barley must meet stringent specifications of the malting and brewing industries before it will be used for this purpose. Both two-rowed and six-rowed barley are used to make beer, with six-rowed types preferred in the United States and two-rowed varieties preferred elsewhere. Beer production is divided into two processes, barley malting and brewing, which are undertaken by independent industries.

The beer-making process. Beer production requires just four ingredients: barley, water, hops, and yeast. Barley provides sugars and amino acids for yeast growth, and the yeast converts the sugars to ethyl alcohol in a process called fermentation. Before barley is used to make beer, it is converted to "malt" to render it a better substrate for brewing. Malting is essentially a process of truncated seed germination. When grain enters a malt house, it is first steeped in water for two to three days. After steeping, the barley is transferred to germination beds for three to four days. Here the grain begins to produce enzymes capable of degrading the starch, protein, and the cell walls of the endosperm, and degradation of protein and cell walls proceeds. The barley grains are then subjected to heat that kills the growing seedling and dries the remnant grain, but leaves intact the components of the endosperm as well as the enzymes capable of degrading them. The product that emerges is malt. Major malt producing countries include the United States, Germany, and France, while major importers of malt include Japan, Germany, and Brazil.

Malt is used by breweries for beer production. The malt is first milled and mixed with water in a process called mashing. This mash is allowed to rest at temperatures that encourage degradation of starch from the endosperm into sugars, by the enzymes present in the malt. The mash is then transferred to a container with a sieve on the bottom, called a lauter tun. Here the liquid fraction of the mash, called wort, is separated from the residual solids by filtration. Traditionally, covered barley is used for beer production because the hulls of the barley malt settle in the lauter tun and participate in filtering out residual solids. The resultant wort contains the soluble components derived from the malt, such as sugars and amino acids liberated by enzyme action. Hop plant flowers (or a derivative of them) are added to the wort and boiled. The hop oils add certain bitter flavors to the beer and protect it from bacterial contamination. The wort is then cooled, transferred to a fermentation vessel, and inoculated with yeast. The yeast use the sugars and amino acids from the malt to grow, and as it grows the metabolism of the sugar maltose leads to the production of ethyl alcohol and carbon dioxide as by-products of the fermentation process. After fermentation, the yeast and other solids are allowed to settle out. This is followed by an aging period, carbonation, and final packaging to produce the finished beer. Thus, the role of barley grain in beer production is similar to its role in the barley life cycle: to provide nutrients for growth. However, in beer production the benefactor of the nutrients is the yeast and not the growing seedling.

Worldwide, well over one billion hectoliters of beer are produced annually, from approximately sixty million metric tons of barley. It takes approximately fifty grams of malt to produce a 375-milliliter bottle of beer, though this amount can be less depending on the type of beer and whether adjuncts (nonbarley sources of sugars, often rice or corn) are used. The largest beer producing countries include the United States, China, Germany, Brazil, Japan, the United Kingdom, and Mexico.

Traditions. The principal barley product consumed by humans, beer is produced and drunk in large quantities worldwide. Beer is probably recognized as the beverage most strongly associated with celebration, relaxation, and social interaction, and has become a ubiquitous component of recreational activities. Beer is commonly consumed in a diverse range of settings, including the home, restaurants, and bars, and for a broad range of occasions, particularly social gatherings. For instance, beer is a fixture at professional sporting events of all kinds held around the world. The increasing demand for beer is reflected in the rapid expansion in the number of microbreweries, and in the growth in popularity of home brewing. Beer consumption continues to grow in popularity, with production doubling over the last thirty years to keep up with demand. In addition, barley plays a ceremonial role in some societies. For instance, in India barley is often used in marriage and other ceremonies.

See also: **Beer; Cereal Grains and Pseudo-Cereals; Grain Reserves; Livestock Production; Maize; Rice; Wheat.**

BIBLIOGRAPHY

Bamforth, Charles. *Beer: Tap into the Art and Science of Brewing.* New York: Plenum Press, 1998.

Barley: Origin, Botany, Culture, Winter Hardiness, Genetics, Utilization, Pests. Agriculture Handbook No. 338. Washington, D.C.: U.S. Department of Agriculture, 1979.

Briggs, D. E. *Barley.* London: Chapman and Hall, 1978.

Cook, A. H., ed. *Barley and Malt: Biology, Biochemistry, Technology.* New York: Academic Press, 1962.

Davies. M. S., and Gordon C. Hillman. "Domestication of Cereals." In *Grass Evolution and Domestication*, edited by G. P. Chapman, 199–224. Cambridge: Cambridge University Press, 1992.

Heiser, Charles B., Jr. *Seed to Civilization. The Story of Food.* Cambridge, Mass.: Harvard University Press, 1990.

Lewis, Michael J., and Tom W. Young. *Brewing.* London: Chapman and Hall, 1995.

Rasmussen, Donald C., ed. *Barley.* Madison, Wisc.: The American Society of Agronomy, 1985.

Renfrew, Jane M. *Paleoethnobotany: The Prehistoric Food Plants of the Near East and Europe.* London: Methuen, 1973. Good illustrations of barley seed morphology and additional useful information on archaeological record in Near East, though barley taxonomy is outdated.

Shewry, Peter R., ed. *Barley: Genetics, Biochemistry, Molecular Biology, and Biotechnology.* Wallingford, U.K.: CAB International, 1992.

U.S. Department of Agriculture (USDA) Foreign Agricultural Service Website. This website is a gateway to a wealth of information on global agriculture, including world production of crops including barley (see crop production tables at http://www.fas.usda.gov/wap/circular/2002/02-01/grains.pdf).

Zohary, Daniel. "The Origin and Early Spread of Agriculture in the Old World." In *The Origin and Domestication of Cultivated Plants*, edited by C. Barigozzi, pp. 3–20. Amsterdam: Elsevier, 1986.

Zohary, Daniel, and Maria Hopf. *Domestication of Plants in the Old World: The Origin and Spread of Cultivated Plants in West Asia, Europe, and the Nile Valley.* 2nd ed. Oxford, U.K.: Clarendon Press, 1993.

David F. Garvin
Harsh Raman
Kevin P. Smith

BEANS. *See* **Legumes.**

BEARD, JAMES. Born in Portland, Oregon, Beard (1903–1985) spent most of his life in New York, spanning the continent as the father of American cooking and as the larger-than-life champion of American foods, reveling in their glorious abundance and variety. His father was a "Mississippi gambler type" who skipped town while his English mother, Mary Elizabeth Jones, an émigré to Portland, firmly ruled her son, her Gladstone Hotel, and the Chinese chefs in its kitchen. In his culinary memoir *Delights and Prejudices* (1969), Beard gives a fine account of growing up amid the backstairs comedy of the Glad-

James Beard in his New York kitchen. PHOTO DAN WYNN/© RITA WYNN

stone, a drama which no doubt influenced his lifelong passion for the theater.

At nineteen he went to London to become an opera singer and then to New York to become an actor. To keep from starving, he opened a catering shop called Hors d'Oeuvre with friends in 1937 and three years later published his first cookbook, *Hors d'Oeuvres & Canapes*, followed by *Cook It Outdoors* in 1941. By combining food with showmanship, he channeled his theatrical energy into writing and single-handedly created the drama of American food. Over the next four decades—after a stint in the army and the United Seamen's Service, opening navy canteens—he would publish more than twenty books in addition to making extensive contributions to *House & Garden*'s single-subject cookbook series and writing numerous articles for newspapers and magazines. With the publication of *The James Beard Cookbook* in 1959, he became America's leading food guru, preaching the gospel of honest American food to those who had earlier looked exclusively to Europe for guidance in all things culinary.

At six feet four inches, weighing 310 pounds at his heaviest, he was as large as his subject, and his persona matched his message. He was among the first to promote both on television, when he appeared with Elsie the Cow for the Borden Company on NBC in 1946. He also initiated a new style of domestic cooking school to urge ordinary home cooks to take pleasure in their food. In 1955, he began the James Beard Cooking School in New York and soon added one in Seaside, Oregon. By teaching in all sorts of venues across the country, he created a network of devoted followers who continued to spread the word after his death.

That word was "fun." During the postwar decades of affluence, he taught Americans, who had survived the Depression, World War II austerity, and native Puritanism, to have fun with cooking, eating, and living in the American way. His 1972 *American Cookery* defined and celebrated the tradition of American cooking he had inherited from a body of cookbooks that began before the Civil War with Mary Randolph and Eliza Leslie and stretched to his contemporaries Irma Rombauer and Helen Evans Brown. While his appetite for traveling was as large as his girth, and while he spent much time in France, he sieved the flavors of other countries through his own American palate to create a menu that was always exciting because of the new combinations it offered. While his meals and menus were eclectic, he would say that it was the cook, not a country or a culture, that unified a meal. His culinary library in the 12th Street townhouse he owned in Greenwich Village was vast, and he was instrumental in directing his cooking students toward the literature of cooking.

In 1986, his house became a living theater honoring his name and his mission as the headquarters for the James Beard Foundation, where chefs from around the world showcase their skills. Through events such as the

"It has always been my contention that the people of the Western European countries ate pretty dull food until the discovery of America."

"Like the theater, offering food and hospitality to people is a matter of showmanship, and no matter how simple the performance, unless you do it well, with love and originality, you have a flop on your hands."

"The kitchen, reasonably enough, was the scene of my first gastronomic adventure. I was on all fours. I crawled into the vegetable bin, settled on a giant onion and ate it, skin and all. It must have marked me for life, for I have never ceased to love the hearty flavor of raw onions."

—*Delights and Prejudices*

annual celebration of Beard's Birthday and Beard Awards for members of the food industry, the Foundation has established a generous scholarship fund and a national network of chefs, writers, and restaurateurs.

See also **Child, Julia; Cookbooks.**

BIBLIOGRAPHY

Beard, James. *Love and Kisses and a Halo of Truffles: Letters to Helen Evans Brown.* Edited by John Ferrone. New York: Arcade, 1994.

Clark, Robert. *James Beard: A Biography.* New York: HarperCollins, 1993.

Jones, Evan. *Epicurean Delight: The Life and Times of James Beard.* New York: Knopf, 1990.

Betty Fussell

BEEF. *See* **Cattle; Meat.**

BEER.

This entry includes four subentries:
Origins and Ancient History
From Late Egyptian Times to the Nineteenth Century
The Twentieth Century
Production and Social Use

ORIGINS AND ANCIENT HISTORY

The Origin of the "Cereal Wine"—Beer

The origin of beer lies far back in prehistory; there is evidence that it was being made at least eight thousand years ago in Mesopotamia, but it had probably been produced

ONION SANDWICHES

Brioche loaf or good white bread, sliced very thin
White onions, peeled and sliced very thin
Mayonnaise, preferably homemade
Chopped parsley

Cut the brioche or bread into rounds with a biscuit cutter. Spread the rounds lightly with mayonnaise. Divide into two batches. Arrange a layer of onion slices on one batch and top with the other. Press together gently. Roll the edges in mayonnaise and then in the chopped parsley. Pile on a serving dish and refrigerate for several hours before serving.

—*Love and Kisses*, p. 364

for many thousands of years before, and perhaps in many different places. Its great success must be closely related to the development of cereal agriculture, which occurred about ten thousand years ago. The sequence of events might well have been:

1. Making a dough of grain (whether crushed or uncrushed), which then underwent spontaneous fermentation.

2. Baking dough into bread, soaking the bread in water, heating the result, and allowing it to cool and then to undergo spontaneous fermentation. (A similar process would have occurred if the grain had been mixed with water and boiled into porridge: after cooling, it would have undergone spontaneous fermentation.)

3. Steeping the grain induces sprouting and the synthesis of amylase enzymes that decompose the starch of the grain into sugar, a process that is aided by heated water and/or baking. After cooling in water, the spontaneous fermentation will start. Barley has the advantage of having a rather large excess of amylases in comparison with other cereals such as millets and sorghum.

When people learned to steep grain in water and then heat it slowly, the overall product was greatly improved. Another improvement to the process that was invented was to bake bread from crushed or malted grain and then immerse it in water and heat the result. If bread was the intended product, more crushed or malted grain could be added to the dough; if beer was desired, all that was needed was the addition of more water instead. It is unknown when the use of a starter (a small amount saved from a previous fermentation for use in the next fermentation) began.

All these primitive beers were, technically, ales (that is, top-fermented)—spontaneously fermented both by yeasts and by *Lactobacillus*, which gave the beverage a sour taste.

Domestication of Barley, Wheat, and Rye

Domestication of the most important beer cereals—barley, wheat, and rye—started at least ten thousand years ago at the transition from the Pleistocene to the Holocene period in the Fertile Crescent, the region from the eastern Mediterranean Sea to the eastern part of the Tigris and Euphrates area. When the glacial ice finally started to withdraw in the Northern Hemisphere, the climate of the Fertile Crescent was mild, wet, and ideal for early man, and numerous species of wild cereal grasses (grains) available for gathering flourished. Subsequently, the climate got warmer and drier and agriculture, a more prolific and dependable source for grains and other foods, was developed through the domestication of wild plants. The exact course of this domestication is complex, and is based in part on climatic changes, plant availability, preadaptive technology, population pressure, and resource stress.

All three cereals, barley (*Hordeum*), wheat (*Triticum*), and rye (*Secale*) are grasses in the tribe *Triticeae*, and they have all in different varieties played a great role in the development of beer in the Eurasian region. In other parts of the world, other cereals have had the corresponding importance, for example, sorghum (*Sorghum bicolour*) in Africa, rice (*Oryx sativa*) in Asia, corn or maize (*Zea mays*) in America, and millets. Cereals not belonging to the wheat, barley, oats, maize, or rice genera are commonly referred to as millets and are found in America, Africa, India, and Eurasia.

All domesticated varieties of barley belong to the same species, *Hordeum vulgare*, and its wild form *H. vulgare spontaneum* crosses easily with all domesticated forms. The major morphological difference between the wild and the domesticated forms is a tough rachis (the main stem holding the seed clusters) in the latter. In principle, there are three forms of barley, the two-rowed, the six-rowed, and the naked-grain form.

In connection to beer, the most important domesticated wheat varieties have been einkorn (*Triticum monococcum*), emmer, and the bread wheat, *Triticum aestivum*. Einkorn is a diploid form close to its wild ancestor, emmer is tetraploid, and the bread wheat is hexaploid.

Domesticated rye, *Secale cereale*, is very closely related to wild rye, *Secale montanum*, which still grows in the mountains of Turkey, northwestern Iran, and the Caucasus. Wild rye is more cold- and drought-resistant than are wild wheat and barley. Cultivated rye is predominantly a winter crop and it can succeed under less favorable climatic and soil conditions than can wheat.

There was probably a close connection between the production of beer and bread, the domestication of barley, and the social and ceremonial importance of the alcohol in beer. Beer was produced from bread, and barley is a very suitable cereal for both bread and beer production. Additionally, alcohol has been emphasized to have an important role in social relationship, in matters of reciprocity and obligation. The archaeologists Solomon Katz and Mary Voight have proposed that the development of settled agriculture was dependent on the desire to brew beer.

Mesopotamia

The oldest documentary evidence of beer brewing comes from Uruk in Mesopotamia and dates to about 3500 B.C.E.; it is found on clay tablets that tell the story of Gilgamesh in Sumerian, written in cuneiform with accompanying pictures. The tablets describe in great detail how beer was prepared, the different varieties of beer, how its brewing and selling was arranged, and how it was consumed. Röllig (1970) gives an excellent review of most of the details from the historic periods in Mesopotamia from the old Sumerian period (about 3000 B.C.E., which is the most interesting period for our present purposes) until about 1000 B.C.E.

At this time in Mesopotamia, barley was the most important cereal for both humans and animals. The grain was steeped into water and then either air- or oven-dried. After removal of the sprouts, the malt was milled. For brewing, various kinds of beer-breads or *bappir* were baked from unmalted barley or other cereals and added, along with sweeteners and spices; it has been proposed by some investigators that hops were sometimes used also. (The amount of emmer used was taken as indicative of the quality of the beer.) Then the malt and the beer-breads were probably mixed with water and heated, after which the vessel was removed from the oven to cool. It has been pointed out by Katz and Maytag (1991) that the "cooked mash" was spread out on mats to remove the spent grains and to allow the liquid to drain. By the time of the hymn to Ninkasi, from about 1800 B.C.E., a "filter" had become the symbol of the brewers. Consequently, long straws were not necessary any longer, and the beer could be consumed directly from cups. Before fermentation, spices, herbs, and sweet plant extractives with effects that were believed to be medicinal were added; the augmented sugars and microorganisms from the herbs helped to induce fermentation. (It is known that the brewers saved some of the wort from one fermentation to use it as a starter for the next brew, as has often been done in sour-bread fermentation.) Katz and Maytag (1991) also found in the hymn of Ninkasi that date juice and grapes or raisins were added to the wort to induce fermentation. The entire concoction was then transferred, with more water, into a fermentation vessel, which was long and narrow-necked to minimize the mixture of inside and outside air and decrease infection from outside. We do not know how long fermentation lasted, but probably most of the beer was quickly top-fermented into weak ale, which was tapped from the bottom of the vessel through a filter after a few days.

In early Sumerian times, beer was drunk through long straws, with the remnants of all the ingredients still present in the beer; such a straw, made of gold, has been found in a tomb at Ur. In later times, the beer was filtered as described above and then drunk from small vessels.

Many different recipes and descriptions are preserved from the Mesopotamian period: "strong beer," "red-brown beer," "pressed beer," "dark beer," and "good dark beer," for example. These beers were very heavy and thick—almost like syrup—and very nutritious. Although they were very strong and heavy, they could not stand long storage in the warm climate, and so the people had good reason to complain about sour beer. The goddess of beer of the Sumerians was Ninkasi, who was in charge of everything concerning beer, one of the most important ingredients of life in Mesopotamia, both as a food and socially. A Sumerian proverb says: "Who does not know beer, does not know what is good. Beer makes the home pleasant." It is interesting to note that the first very important king of Babylonia, Hammurabi, who reigned between 1792 and 1750 B.C.E., issued a set of laws (known as the Code of Hammurabi) that governed civil and criminal matters, included in which are rules for making and serving beer. (One copy of the code can be viewed on a column made of green diorite that is housed at the Louvre Museum in Paris.)

Egypt

For the ancient Egyptians also, beer was the preeminent beverage and was more popular than water, which often was contaminated; and although beer had a lower social status than wine, beer was a necessity for the household and the kitchen. Brewing was the woman's task, as it was in Mesopotamia. The divinities presiding over it were goddesses and some kind of chief brewer (the official Kha-bau-Seker, who bore the title of "Controller of the Brewing Women"). According to Egyptian religious tradition, Osiris, the god of agriculture, taught the people to prepare beer. The Greeks connected Osiris with Dionysus, the wine god, who in turn was associated with the earlier Thracian god Sabazius. The connection between the Egyptian people, beer, and their gods—for instance, Hathor-Sekhmet—was very close. The intimate relation between baking and brewing in Egypt and in Mesopotamia is supported both by the use of the Sumero-Akkadian word *lahamu*, originally meaning "loaves" (compare Hebrew *laham*, "bread"), to indicate brewing and by the constant association of baking and brewing in Egyptian art. "Bread and beer" was the symbol of food and a greeting formula.

Artifacts dating from about five thousand years ago found in the ancient tombs of Beni Hassan in Egypt show an established practice of brewing, serving beer to the public, and exportation of beer through the city of Pelusium to many Mediterranean ports. *The Book of the Dead,*

Wooden figurine of a female brewer, ca. 2465–2323 B.C.E. This carving is located in the Egyptian Museum, Cairo. © GIANNI DAGLI ORTI/CORBIS.

1. Steeping the grain in water, and then aerating it, re-moistening it, grinding it, working it into a dough, and adding yeast. Finally, after fermentation, the whole mass was strained though a cloth or a sieve, and the filtrate recovered.

2. Drying bread, soaking it in water, and leaving it to ferment in a warm place, which is identical to the traditional method for making *kvas* ("kvass," in English—a beer made in Russia, typically from rye).

The preparation of *bouza* in modern southern Egypt and the Sudan consists of the following steps:

1. Ground wheat, barley, or other cereal is kneaded with water and yeast.

2. After a short leavening, the dough is lightly baked into thick loaves.

3. Another fraction of wheat is moistened, exposed to air for some time, crushed, and then added to the previously prepared loaves after they have been crumbled.

4. The fermentation is initiated by adding some old *bouza*.

Flavorings are not added. The result is a thick beverage with a strong yeasty odor.

Beer was consumed primarily for pleasure and nutrition, but it was also used for cooking and for medicinal purposes, often as a constituent of mixtures. The beer given to the slaves was unfiltered and crude, but was very nutritious because it contained residual grain proteins and vitamins.

See also **Barley; Cereal Grains and Pseudo-Cereals; Wine.**

BIBLIOGRAPHY

Arnold, J. P. *Origin and History of Beer and Brewing*. Chicago: Wahl-Henius Institute of Fermentology, 1911.

Cantrell, Philip A., II. "Beer and Ale." In *The Cambridge World History of Food*, edited by Kenneth F. Kiple and Kriemhild Coneè Ornelas, vol. 1, pp. 619–625. Cambridge: Cambridge University Press, 2000.

Corran, H. S. *A History of Brewing*. London: David and Charles, 1975.

Darby, William J., Paul Ghalioungui, Louis Grivetti. *Food: The Gift of Osiris*. London: Academic Press, 1977.

Eberlitz, Erich, and Bruno Meissner. *Reallexikon der Assyriologie*, vol. 2, pp. 25–28. Berlin and Leipzig: Walter de Gruyer and Co., 1938.

Hardwick, William A., "History and Antecedents of Brewing." In *Handbook of Brewing*, edited by William A. Hardwick. New York: M. Dekker, 1995.

Kahn, Lisa C. "Beer and Brewing." In *The Oxford Companion to Archaeology*, edited by Brian M. Fagan. Oxford: Oxford University Press, 1996.

Katz, Solomon H., and Fritz Maytag, "Brewing an Ancient Beer," "Hymn to Ninkazi," "Secrets of the Stanzas," and "A Thrilling Link with the Past." *Archeology* 44:4 (1991): 24–33.

which dates from the same era, depicts beer being made from barley and offerings of cakes and beer to various deities.

The process of malting and dehusking the malted grain is probably thousands of years old, and the methods of today are very similar. In general, the preparation of beer, as described in late Egyptian documents and in tomb art of all periods, did not materially differ from the methods of preparing present-day *bouza* or its African analogues; however, Egyptian beer was often flavored by such plants as skirret (*Sium sisarum*—a member of the water-parsnip genus).

The Egyptians used either malts of various grains (principally emmer), which were formed into dough, or dried bread, and yeast (*Saccaromyces winlocki*), which was fermented in a rather warm place. In principle, there were two methods:

Katz, S. H., and M. Voight. "Bread and Beer: The Early Use of Cereals in the Human Diet." *Expedition* 28:2 (1987): 23–34.

Küster, Hansjöng. "Rye." In *The Cambridge World History of Food*, edited by Kenneth F. Kiple and Kriemhild Coneè Ornelas, vol. 1, pp. 149–152. Cambridge: Cambridge University Press, 2000.

Lohberg, Rolf. *Das grosse Lexikon vom Bier* [The great encyclopedia of beer]. 3rd ed. Stuttgart: Scripta Verlags-Gesellschaft, 1984.

McCorrison, Joy. "Barley." In *The Cambridge World History of Food*, edited by Kenneth F. Kiple and Kriemhild Coneè Ornelas, vol. 1, pp. 81–89. Cambridge: Cambridge University Press, 2000.

McCorrison, Joy. "Wheat." In *The Cambridge World History of Food*, edited by Kenneth F. Kiple and Kriemhild Coneè Ornelas, vol. 1, pp. 158–174. Cambridge: Cambridge University Press, 2000.

Olsson, Sven-Olle R. "Kvass." In *Gastronomisk Kalender 1978*, pp. 94–115. Stockholm, 1977: 94–115.

Röllig, Wolfgang. *Das Bier im Alten Mesopotamien* [Beer in Old Mesopotamia]. Berlin: Gesellschaft für die Geschichte und Bibliographie des Brauwesens EV, Institut für Gärungsgewerbe und Biotechnologie, 1970.

Toussaint-Samat, Maguelonne. *History of Food.* Oxford: Blackwell, 1992.

De Wet, J. M. J. "Millets." In *The Cambridge World History of Food*, edited by Kenneth F. Kiple and Kriemhild Coneè Ornelas, vol. 1, pp. 112–121. Cambridge: Cambridge University Press, 2000.

Sven-Olle R. Olsson

FROM LATE EGYPTIAN TIMES TO THE NINETEENTH CENTURY

Late Egyptian to Roman Times

The Egyptians exported beer to the Greeks, who traded it to Gaul, to Spain, and to the east coast of the Adriatic; it then spread to Germania (what is now Germany and some portions of central Europe), where it became very popular. Beer may also have been established in non–wine-producing areas at an earlier date. It is rather probable that beer production originated close to the geographic expansion of agriculture, which implies that beer could have been present in Europe at least around 3000 B.C.E., when use of the plow spread in Europe. In a female grave in Egtved in Denmark from about the year 1357 B.C.E. rests from an alcoholic beverage were found in a vessel made of birch bark. It contained rests of wheat, cranberry, honey, and bog myrtle (sweet gale). (Corresponding remains have been found in the Hallstatt beer amphora found at Kulmbach dated 800 B.C.E.).

In China, alcoholic beverages seem to have been present since 4000 B.C.E. in Dawenkou in Shandong; the oldest written documents come from the Shang dynasty, 1324–1066 B.C.E., written by Du Kang and describing the production of *jiu*. *Jiu* meant all alcoholic beverages, usually of 10–15 percent alcohol, obtained by fermentation of cereals, millet, and wheat. The process was first to make a ferment cake, which provided molds and yeasts that then started the fermentation process in a mash of cooked cereals. During the T'ang dynasty, 618–907 C.E., the cereals for this process were either glutinous millet or glutinous rice. These processes later spread to Japan, Korea, and all of Southeast Asia. Prior to the introduction of this process in Japan, brewers saccharified the rice by chewing boiled and raw rice.

Beer was a considered a barbaric drink by the Greeks and Romans, though, according to Pliny, beer was known in the Mediterranean countries before viticulture (the cultivation of grapes) became popular. There are frequent references—in Tacitus, for example—early in the common era to malt beverages being consumed by the tribes of Germania (as well as by the Saxons, Celts, Thracians, and Scythians), and even to the establishment of *tabernae*, or taverns. Originally, beer was produced from a variety of malted and unmalted grains such as millet, barley, wheat, oat, and rye, with different supplements such as honey, juniper, mushrooms, and bark—but without hops. In the Greek and Roman world, wine was the beverage of the upper classes and beer was the drink of the common people, as was the situation in pre-Ptolemaic Egypt. (For more details see Arnold [1911] and Hoffman [1956].)

Medieval Times to the End of the Nineteenth Century

Home brewing. From the year 719, when the Lex Alemannorum (a code of laws formulated by the Franks) was promulgated, all people in the Germanic area were entitled to brew their own beer. Home brewing began in Great Britain in about the twelfth century. With the growth of towns, commercial operations started brewing and selling in the same establishment. Later, the point of sale was centrally located in a town or city. Growth of brewing was slow until the industrial revolution made large breweries possible.

The types of beer and brewing techniques of the Middle Ages survived until recent years in the Nordic countries, as has the old method of spontaneous lactic and alcoholic fermentation of *kvas* ("kvass," in English—a beer made typically from rye) in eastern Europe.

Monasteries. Monasteries have had an active role in the brewing and sale of beer, and in the improvement of brewing processes. Two of the first beer-brewing monasteries—with brewing activities dating back to the seventh to eighth centuries—were St. Gallen (in Switzerland) and Weihenstephan (in Bavaria), both of the Benedictine order. Beer was a substitute for wine, a good nutrient during Lent, and an excellent base for spices used medicinally. In the year 1000, forty of the houses of the monastery of St. Gallen were devoted to brewing; they produced strong beer, oat beer, and light beer for themselves, guests, and pilgrims, and for sale. In the early Middle Ages, there were four to five hundred monasteries brewing beer in Germany; the practice was international and a large source of income for the monasteries. The famous Trappist beer is still made in Belgium by Trappist monks, whose order has developed from the Benedictine and Cistercian orders.

Cities. In southern Germany, Bavaria was a wine-drinking area until the Thirty Years' War (1618–1648), and the monasteries were the main producers of beer. During the twelfth and thirteenth centuries, cities were burgeoning and they created licenses to produce beer, which could be heavily taxed by the authorities. In the northern part of Germany, many competing breweries were developed and great volumes of beer were exported by members of the Hanseatic League to other parts of Europe. In the northern city of Hamburg, there were six hundred brewers in the sixteenth century, as contrasted with only thirty in the southern city of Munich in the fifteenth century. Some of the most famous breweries in the sixteenth century were in Erfurt, Einbeck, Zerbst, Naumburg, and Braunschweig.

After the Thirty Years' War, which destroyed the northern cities and Bavarian viticulture, most of the brewing shifted from the north to Bavaria, where by 1420 the monasteries had developed the method of bottom fermentation that produces lager beer. Before this development, all beers were top-fermented—that is, ales. In 1516 the *Reinheitsgebot* (Purity Law) was approved for Bavaria, which decreed that only barley malt, hops, and water were allowed for beer brewing. In 1551 another law was approved in Munich saying that bottom-fermenting yeast should be used. Northern Germany was opposed to the new law, and Baden and Württemberg did not accept it until 1896 and 1900, respectively. In 1906 it was accepted for lager throughout the German Empire. The only exception made was to allow wheat malt in the specialty ales *Alt, Kölsch,* and *Berliner Weisse* and in wheat beer.

Grut and hops. Ancient beer was flavored by many different spices, even medically active ones, during the centuries, and Hildegard von Bingen mentions in her *Physica,* which dates from about 1156, both hops and *grut* as additives to beer, which is the first documentation of the use of hops in beer. *Grut* was a mixture of several spices, chief among them being the leaves of bog myrtle or sweet gale (*Myrica gale*). It was used mainly during the thirteenth to fifteenth centuries and it survived in the northwestern part of Germany and in the Netherlands until the eighteenth century. In many areas, the authorities sold the right to use *grut* (*Grutrecht*). During these times, hops and *grut* were used for beer simultaneously.

Hops had been introduced for beer brewing sometime between the years 764 and 1156, when the first hop agriculture was found in Geisenfeld in the Allertau area in Bavaria, and when Hildegard wrote her *Physica,* respectively. The introduction of hops probably came via contacts of the Germans with Slavic peoples in central Europe. The acceptance of hops in beer was very slow and even forbidden in certain areas. By the year 1400,

the Dutch had already introduced hops, but it was not until the sixteenth century that the use of hops in beer was gradually accepted in England. One reason for this slow acceptance could have been the difference in taste of the beer, from a rather strong and sweet beer without hops to a less strong and somewhat bitter beer. The great advantage of hopped beer was the better storage capabilities it afforded.

Ale and lager. Ales were the only beer type in Europe before the advent of lager, beginning in the fifteenth century in Bavaria. In 1603 lager was forbidden by the city of Cologne. However, it slowly spread through Germany together with the Purity Law, and during the nineteenth century, production volume increased dramatically. The most important types of lager were the dark from Munich, the pale from Dortmund, and the pale and heavily hopped from Pilsen (pilsner). Dortmund Export became world-famous in the nineteenth century, and pilsner became the great winner in the world of the twentieth century. In the northern and western parts of Germany, ales dominated until the start of the twentieth century.

In England, Professor Charles Graham became interested in lager in 1888 and started a discussion about the two types of beer. It was not until the end of World War II that lager was accepted by the British people. One significant impediment to the success and spread of lagers was their great need for cooling.

In Britain, ales have been the popular beers and have influenced tastes in both British colonies and other countries through export. At the end of the seventeenth century, most of the export of ale from Britain went to America and the West Indies, but the trade of strong, sweet ale, "Russian Imperial Stout," and porter (a heavy, dark-brown ale) to Russia and the countries around the Baltic had begun. In the beginning of the nineteenth century, half of the ale exported by Britain went to Asia and Australia. That type was called Indian Pale Ale (IPA); it was strong, sweet, and highly hopped.

Development in America. Brewing in America started with the early British and Dutch settlers. As early as 1587, Sir Walter Raleigh malted maize (corn) for brewing, and hops were grown by 1637 in Charlestown, Massachusetts. Malt and ale were imported from Britain, and New York and Philadelphia became the main brewing centers in the eighteenth century. In Canada, brewing was initiated in 1620 by the monastery of Notre Dame des Anges. The first steam engine was installed in Philadelphia in 1819. At the beginning of the nineteenth century, there were 150 breweries in the United States, producing 160 thousand Imperial barrels (7.2 million U.S. gallons).

From 1840 onward, German immigrants began brewing lager, and the number of breweries increased to 4,131 in 1873; this number decreased to 1,092 in 1918 and 230 in 1961. In 1850, ale brewing was dominant, and in 1860, lager production was less than twenty-five percent of the total production of 3.8 million barrels. Hop culture spread to California in 1851, Wisconsin in 1860, Washington State in 1866, and Oregon in 1880. After 1850, lager began to prevail, but brewing it required ice, and machines to make that ice. This requirement was met by the introduction of the refrigerator. The first one was installed in New Orleans in 1867.

Brewing companies and the science of brewing. By the beginning of the eighteenth century, three items had been invented that later had very great importance for the brewing industry: the hydrometer, the thermometer, and the steam engine. Both the hydrometer (along with its offshoot, the saccharometer) and the thermometer gave the brewer instruments to measure and monitor processes more exactly, and the steam engine—which replaced horses—opened possibilities of working with greater volumes in the brewery. All the vessels of the brewery were still of wood except the brew kettle, which was made of copper. The technical revolution during the eighteenth and nineteenth centuries, as well as the beginning of free trade among both cities and states, had a great impact on the development of the brewing industries in Europe and the United States, and it was during this time that most of the big brewing companies were started and formed.

However, the most important inventions for the breweries were made in the biological and biochemical fields. In 1833 Anselme Payen and Jean-François Persoz discovered an enzyme, diastase, that can split starch. In the late 1830s, Franz Schulze discovered the yeast cells, *Saccaromyces;* his discovery was confirmed by Louis Pasteur in 1857. The final synthesis explicating the fermentation process was performed by Eduard Buchner in 1897; he demonstrated that fermentation could proceed with just the juices of the yeast cells—without the living cells—showing that a complex of enzymes (zymase) is responsible for the conversion of carbohydrates to alcohol and carbon dioxide.

Before these discoveries, people did not know why and how fermentation occurred. Often they ascribed it to supernatural forces, and many used the same equipment from fermentation to fermentation; sometimes sourdough from bread baking was used to initiate the fermentation. In any case, most of these beers and ales were also lactic-fermented and thus sour. In 1883, E. C. Hansen from the Carlsberg Laboratories of Carlsberg Brewery in Copenhagen isolated the active yeast culture from bottom-fermentation yeast, which J. C. Jacobsen, the founder of the brewery, had brought there from Munich. This species was called *Saccaromyces carlsbergensis* (it was later renamed *Saccaromyces ovum*) and today is considered a variety of *Saccaromyces cerevisiae*, the common yeast organism. Jacobsen's method of isolation and pure-culture propagation of yeasts from single cells was rapidly adopted. By 1896 it was in wide use in lager breweries in many countries and has become the standard method.

Germany became unified during the nineteenth century, and it was then possible for breweries to sell their products over a wider area than before. The first limited brewing company was formed in Dresden in 1838. Between 1831 and 1865, because of the great success of lager, there was a dramatic fall in the numbers of breweries producing ales in Prussia, from 16,000 to 7,400. The first scientific brewing research institutions were formed in Bavaria (Munich and Weihenstephan) in 1880, and in Berlin in 1883.

BIBLIOGRAPHY

Arnold, J. P. *Origin and History of Beer and Brewing.* Chicago: Wahl-Henius Institute of Fermentology, 1911.

Barnett, J. A., R. W. Payne, and D. Yarrow. *Yeast Characteristics and Identification.* 2nd edition. Cambridge: Cambridge University Press, 1990.

Brockhaus Enzyklopädie in zwanzig Bänden (Brockhaus encyclopedia in twenty volumes). 17th ed., vol. 2, pp. 706–709. Wiesbaden: F. A. Brockhaus, 1967.

Brothwell, Don R., and Patricia Brothwell. *Food in Antiquity.* London: Thames and Hudson, 1969.

Corran, H. S. *A History of Brewing.* London: David and Charles, 1975.

Darby, William J., Paul Ghalioungui, Louis Grivetti. *Food: The Gift of Osiris.* London: Academic Press, 1977.

Davidson, Alan. *The Oxford Companion to Food.* Oxford: Oxford University Press, 1999.

Hardwick, William A. "History and Antecedents of Brewing." In *Handbook of Brewing,* edited by William A. Hardwick. New York: M. Dekker, 1995.

Hoffman, M. *5000 Jahre Bier* [5000 years of beer]. Frankfurt am Main and Berlin: Alfred Malzner Verlag, 1956.

Ishige, Naomichi. "Food and Drink Around the World, Japan" In *The Cambridge World History of Food,* edited by Kenneth F. Kiple and Kriemhild Coneè Ornelas, vol. 2, pp. 1173–1183. Cambridge: Cambridge University Press, 2000.

Jackson, Michael. *The Great Beers of Belgium.* Antwerp, Belgium: Media Marketing Communications, 1991.

Lohberg, Rolf. *Das grosse Lexikon vom Bier* [The great encyclopedia of beer]. 3d ed. Stuttgart: Scripta Verlags-Gesellschaft, 1984.

Nesbitt, Mark C. "Agriculture." In *The Oxford Companion to Archaeology,* edited by Brian M. Fagan. Oxford: Oxford University Press, 1996.

The New Encyclopaedia Britannica in thirty volumes: Macropedia. 15th ed., vol. 3. Chicago: Encyclopaedia Britannica, 1982.

Nordland, Odd. *Brewing and Beer Traditions in Norway: The Social Anthropological Background of the Brewing Industry.* Oslo: Universitetsforlaget, 1969.

Olsson, Sven-Olle R. "Kvass." In *Gastronomisk Kalender 1978,* pp. 94–115. Stockholm, 1977.

Räsänen, Matti. *Vom Halm zum Fass: Die volkstümlichen alkoholarmen Getreidegetränke in Finnland* [From straw to vessel: The traditional low-alcoholic cereal beverages in Finland]. Helsinki: Kansatieteellinen Arkisto 25, 1975.

Sabban, Francoise. "Food and Drink Around the World, China." In *The Cambridge World History of Food,* edited by Kenneth F. Kiple and Kriemhild Coneè Ornelas, vol. 2, pp. 1165–1175. Cambridge: Cambridge University Press, 2000.

177

Salomonsson, Anders. *Gotlandsdricka*. Karlstad: Press' Förlag AB, 1979. Contains an English summary.

Schafer, Edward. "T'ang." In *Food in Chinese Culture*, edited by K. C. Chang, pp. 87–140. New Haven and London: Yale Universtity Press, 1977.

Toussaint-Samat, Maguelonne. *History of Food*. Oxford: Blackwell, 1992.

Von Hofsten, Nils. "Pors och andra humleersättningar och ölkryddor i äldre tider" [Sweet gale (*Myrica gale*) and other substitutes for hops in former times]. *Acta Academiae Regiae Gustavi Adolphi* XXXVI, pp. 1–245. Uppsala: AB Lundequistska Bokhandeln, 1960.

Sven-Olle R. Olsson

THE TWENTIETH CENTURY

Beer in 1900

The central area for modern beer development and beer culture is the portion of Europe from Austria in the southeast to the British Isles in the northwest. The Nordic nations are also beer countries, but, with the exception of Denmark, they have not played a significant role. At the beginning of the twentieth century, ales dominated the market in the United Kingdom, the northern and western part of Germany, and Belgium. Lager had started its spread from Bavaria to the big cities in Germany and to the neighboring countries. It had also become rather well established in the United States, but the populace of the United Kingdom had not yet accepted it.

Beer Around the World

Around the world, Australia got Foster's beer, a lager, from the United States in 1888. East Africa received beer from the United Kingdom in 1922, and today, lager, ale, and sorghum beer are all brewed by African breweries. One of the best-known beers from that region is Tusker lager from Kenya. Guinness and Heineken also have large breweries in the area. In South Africa, lager is dominant. In 1904, China got its first lager, Tsingtao, and in 1916 the company was acquired by the Dai Nippon Beer Company in Japan. The Japanese then spread the beer-brewing culture to other parts of East Asia.

Beer in the United States

The United States—where the brewing industry was well established before 1900, with a very wide production of different kinds of beers such as ales, stouts, and lagers—experienced a golden age of brewing between about 1870 and 1919. This, however, came to a halt on January 16, 1919, when the Eighteenth Amendment to the United States Constitution, which prohibited all alcoholic beverages, was ratified. Prohibition lasted from January 16, 1920, to December 5, 1933, when its repeal by the Twenty-first Amendment took effect. During this period, breweries had to survive on nonalcoholic products such as near beers, malted milk, ice cream, and so forth. Two of the surviving companies, Anheuser-Busch and Miller, ended up being two of the top three breweries of the

world. The top ten breweries produced about one-third of the world production of 1.25 billion hectoliters (hL, equivalent to 33 billion gallons) in 1995.

World Production

During the twentieth century, world beer production increased from about 250 million hL (6.6 billion gallons) in 1900 to about 1.306 billion hL (34.5 billion gallons) in 1998, an increase of 522 percent. In 1900, production volumes in Germany and the United States were about equal and together constituted about half of the world production. In 1998, the United States produced 238 million hL (6.29 billion gallons) and Germany 112 million hL (2.96 billion gallons), which together represents only 27 percent of the world production. World production of beer was distributed by region in 1997 as follows: the Americas, 37%; Europe, 34%; the Far East, 23%; Africa, 4.5%; the South Pacific, 1.8%; and the Near East, 0.1%. The greatest increase in beer production is found in areas far away from the traditional beer countries—such as China, countries in Latin America, South Africa, and Turkey (an Islamic country). It is evident that they have evolved a new way of life. Two of the traditional beer countries, Germany and the United Kingdom, are still in the top ten in production, but they will probably soon be overtaken by some of the countries mentioned above.

World Per Capita Consumption

Per capita consumption of beer in different countries shows which people have beer as their natural and central beverage. The top ten countries in 1999, each with a per annum consumption of at least 88.1 liters (23.3 gallons) per person, are still from the old beer center of Europe, which stretches from the British Isles to Austria and up to Denmark (Table 1)—except for Australia, which got its beer traditions from the British colonization of the continent. The newcomers are Turkey, some Latin

TABLE 1

The top ten countries in per-capita beer consumption in liters, 1999

	Consumption 1999, e = estimated	% change 1970–1999	No in top-ranking list of % change 1970–1999
1 Czech Rep.	159.4 e	13.9	27
2 Rep Ireland	154.7	53.8	20
3 Germany	127.5	-9.6	37
4 Luxembourg	109.0	-14.2	38
5 Austria	108.9	10.3	28
6 Denmark	101.9	-6.1	32
7 U.K.	99.0	-3.9	31
8 Belgium	97.5 e	-26.4	43
9 Australia	91.2 e	-24.6	41
10 Slovakia	88.1 e	-16.0	39

SOURCE: *World Drink Trends 2000*, p. 15

American countries, South Africa, and several European countries (including some that have traditionally been considered "wine countries"). Except for the Czech Republic, the Republic of Ireland, and Austria, the traditional beer countries show a decrease in per capita consumption (Table 1).

Lager and Ale

During the twentieth century, a variant of pale lager, pilsner, became the big winner all over the world—in Australia, the United States, and even the old ale area of the British Isles. Only northwestern Europe is bucking the trend: In Belgium, Trappist-Abbey and brown ales are increasing in production, as are *Altbier*, *Kölsch*, and wheat beer in Germany. In the British Isles, bitter ale, pale ale, mild ale, Scotch ale, sweet stout, and barley wine are decreasing in consumption; only bitter stout is increasing. Consumption of draft beer in Great Britain for 1999 is as follows: lager, 44.8 percent; ale, 42.2 percent; stout, 6.3 percent. The remaining 6.7 percent of the total consumption concerns packaged beer of all types. It was not until after World War II that lager truly began to succeed in Great Britain, and it took about fifty years for it to achieve approximately 50 percent of the British market.

Beer Developments in the Twentieth Century

Characteristic of the development of beers and breweries during the twentieth century is the worldwide success of the American variant of the Bohemian lager, pilsner—crystal-clear pale-dry beer, often of the light type, with a low taste of malt and a low bitterness, frequently served very cold. Another trend is that the number of breweries has decreased, individual breweries have become bigger and bigger, and different companies have merged into great brewing conglomerates. In the United States, there were 750 brewing companies and plants in 1936; this number had decreased to 26 companies and 215 plants in 1989, despite a 440 percent increase in volume. Still another trend is the increase of popularity and consumption of beer in nontraditional beer-drinking areas such as Latin America, South Africa, and various parts of Asia. The exportation of beer is a huge worldwide business; Table 2 lists volumes for countries with large exports and imports.

The establishment of microbreweries, which started in 1981 and had increased to 500 breweries by 1992 in the United States, and has spread to other countries as well, is an interesting development that demonstrates the desire for high quality and diversity of beer. Other important developments are ice beer (made by freezing off some of the water); dry beer, with a very low content of residual sugar; light beer, with a low content of dextrins in the beer; low-alcohol beer (less than 1.5 percent alcohol by volume); and nonalcoholic beer (less than 0.5 percent alcohol by volume). Most important are the advances in biochemistry, which have allowed brewing to become an industry based on science and technology. The industry has progressed to the use of stainless steel vessels and containers, and all processes are fully automated and all by-products are taken care of. The expenses for beer production are dominated by costs for packaging, sales, production, and taxes; only a very small proportion of the costs is needed for raw materials.

Beer and Health

Calories, vitamins, and minerals. The effects on health of beer drinking depend to a large degree on which beer is consumed, how much, and by whom. Contents of alcohol, carbohydrates, and proteins differ greatly between low- and high-alcoholic beer. The nutritional value of heavy beer is significant, especially if the beer is unfiltered and contains yeast cells. The caloric value of beers varies from 276 kcal/L in alcohol-free beer, to 428 kcal/L in pilsner, to 660 kcal/L in a *Doppelbock* (double-strength bock beer—a heavy dark beer). For example, 360 ml (just over 12 fluid ounces) of ordinary beer with 419 kcal/L, 4.5% alcohol and 38 g/L carbohydrates will give about 5–12% of the Recommended Dietary Allowance (RDA) of folate, niacin, vitamin B_6 (pyridoxine), riboflavin, and pantothenic acid; 10.3% RDA of magnesium; and 13.5% RDA of phosphorus. Thiamine and pantothenic acid amounts are rather low in beer in relation to the caloric content. This implies that other dietary sources of B-complex vitamins are needed. Beer also contains some chromium, which is needed for glucose and lipid metabolism. The amount of chromium present can be significant for chromium-deficient people. Further, the low content of sodium tends to counteract the water retention seen in heavy drinkers, which, in fact, may typically result from their additional salty food intake. Aside from the caloric content of modern filtered beer, it cannot be

TABLE 2

The top ten countries in beer importation and exportation in 1995

Worldwide in million hectoliters

Importation		Exportation	
Country	Million hL	Country	Million hL
1 U.S.	13.2	Netherlands	10.4
2 U.K.	5.2	U.S.	9.8
3 France	3.5	Germany	7.6
4 Italy	3.0	Belgium + Luxembourg	4.5
5 Japan	2.7	Canada	3.6
6 Germany	2.6	Ireland	3.3
7 Russia	2.0	Denmark	3.1
8 South Africa	2.0	U.K.	3.1
9 China	0.9	France	1.4
10 Canada	0.66	Czech Rep.	1.12

SOURCE: Bamforth, 1998, pp. 10–11.

Menu in the shape of a Bierstein for Eitel's Old Heidelberg restaurant in Chicago, 1934. The restaurant served beer only from the Blatz brewery in Milwaukee, much like the pub and brewery arrangements in England. ROUGHWOOD COLLECTION.

regarded as an important nutrient, since the vitamin and mineral contents are relatively low, but it does make a contribution. To make a complete meal with beer, a source of protein and fiber-rich vegetables should accompany the beer.

Medical effects of beer. Although beer is a low-alcoholic beverage of less than 10% alcohol by volume (typically about 5 to 7 percent) in comparison with wine and spirits (about 10 to 50 percent), all the effects of alcohol must be considered. For reviews on this subject, see Cox and Huang (1991, 165–176) and Owades (2000, 19–26). Generally, beer has not been found to differ specifically in its physiological effects on a short- or long-term basis from other alcoholic beverages, if the effects are related to the amount of alcohol consumed. Beer also has the advantage of filling the stomach more quickly than wine and spirits and will give a slower increase of blood alcohol level. Heavy drinking may provoke diarrhea or vomiting and cause excessive urination, all of which flush vitamins and minerals out of the body. Heavy drinkers of alcohol may get dilated cardiomyopathy with specific intracellular changes, which is a kind of congestive heart failure. In 1884, it was described as *Münchener Bierherz* (Munich beer-heart) by Bollinger. This type of disease also occurred during the period of addition of cobalt to beer to stabilize its head.

In the past, alcohol has, in the medical literature, usually been connected to negative and hazardous effects on the body; however, in recent decades, a large number of clinical studies have shown that moderate drinking (about two to three drinks or twenty-five to eighty grams [about 0.88 to 2.8 ounces] of alcohol per day) decreases the risk for cardiovascular morbidity and mortality in comparison with both a higher and a lower alcoholic consumption, and most studies indicate that there are no beneficial differences among alcoholic beverages (but see below). Subjective health has also been shown to be highest in persons with a moderate alcoholic consumption (100 to 199 grams [about 3.5 to 7.0 ounces] per week). The beneficial effects of alcohol might be explained by an increase of HDL-C (high-density lipoprotein-C), decreased levels of prothrombotic factors such as fibrinogen, and reduced platelet aggregability, vessel contractility, and pulmonary artery pressure in heart failure patients. Antioxidative compounds—which may decrease the oxidation of LDL (low-density lipoprotein) and the risk for atherosclerosis—such as polyphenols, gallic acid, rutin, epicatechin, and quercetin in red wine and in full-bodied and darker beers may have additional beneficial effects. The question of whether some alcoholic beverages have more prominent effects in these respects remains to be elucidated in further clinical studies. However, red wine has been proposed to be more efficient than other alcoholic beverages in a number of studies.

Hops and medical effects. Other effects of beer, such as the central nervous arousal and the sedative effects, can be explained by the general effects of alcohol. It has often been discussed whether compounds from hops might influence the physiological effects of beer. It is interesting to note that hops—dried, liquid extract, and tincture—are recommended by health-food specialists for various conditions: "Hops are stated to possess sedative, hypnotic, and topical bactericidal properties. Traditionally, they have been used for neuralgia, insomnia, excitability, priapism, mucous colitis, topically for crural ulcers, and specifically for restlessness associated with nervous tension headache and/or indigestion." (Newall, Anderson, and Phillipson 1996, 162–163). Antibacterial activity toward gram-positive bacteria is documented, but the sedative effect needs to be documented, as most of the studies are made with hops in combination with other herbs. Recurring suggestion has been made that hops and beer have estrogenic activity and that the infection of molds producing estrogenic mycotoxins is a significant problem. Recently, a potent phytoestrogen, 8-prenylnarigenin, has been identified in hops and shown to have a concentration in beer of about 100m/L, which is equivalent to a few mg/L estradiol or less. This concentration in beer is not considered to be detrimental, but handling and ingestion of hops might have estrogenic effects in humans. It is also possible that 8-prenylnaringin might contribute to the health-beneficial effects of moderate beer consumption.

See also **Alcohol; Barley; Vitamins; Wine.**

BIBLIOGRAPHY

Asp, Nils-Georg. "Dricka bör man annars dör man: Drycker som näringskälla" [You need to drink, otherwise you will die: beverages as nutrients]. In *Våra drycker till vardags och fest* [Our beverages for weekdays and festivities], edited by Bengt W. Johansson and Anders Salomonsson. Stockholm: Carlssons, 2000.

Bamforth, Charles. *Tap into the Art and Science of Brewing.* New York: Plenum Press, 1998.

Barth, Heinrich J., Christiane Klinke, and Claus Schmidt. *Der Grosse Hopfenatlas: Geschichte und Geographie einer Kulturpflanze* [The great hop atlas: history and geography of a cultivated plant]. Nuremberg: Joh. Barth & Sohn, 1994.

Bollinger. "Über die Häufigkeit und Ursache der idopathischen Herzhypertropie in München" [Concerning the abundance and cause of idopathic myocardial hypertrophie in Munich]. *Deutsche Medizinische Wochenschrift* 12 (1884): 180–181.

Cantrell, Philip A., II. "Beer and Ale." In *The Cambridge World History of Food*, edited by Kenneth F. Kiple and Kriemhild Coneè Ornelas, vol. 1, p. 625. Cambridge, U.K.: Cambridge University Press, 2000.

Corran, H. S. *A History of Brewing.* London: David and Charles, 1975.

Cox, W. Miles, and Wei-Jen W. Huang. "Alcohol Toxicology." In *Encyclopedia of Human Biology*, edited by Renato Dulbecco, pp. 165–176. San Diego: Academic Press, 1991.

Ensminger, Audrey H., M. E. Ensminger, James E. Konlande, and John R. K. Robson. *Foods & Nutrition Encyclopedia.* 2nd ed., vol. 1, p. 192. Boca Raton, Fla.: CRC Press, 1993.

Grant, Herbert L. "Microbrewing." In *Handbook of Brewing*, edited by William A. Hardwick. New York: M. Dekker, 1995.

Grönbeck, Morten N., Ulrik Becker, Ditte Johansen, Adam Gottschau, Peter Schnor, Hans Ole Hein, Gorm Jensen, and Thorkild I. A. Sörensen. "Öl, vin, spiritus og dödelighed" [Beer, wine, spirits, and mortality]. *Läkartidningen*, 98 (2001): 2585–2588.

Hardwick, William A. "Commercial and Economic Aspects." In *Handbook of Brewing*, edited by William A. Hardwick. New York: M. Dekker, 1995.

Lohberg, Rolf. *Das grosse Lexikon vom Bier* [The great dictionary of beer]. 3rd ed. Stuttgart: Scripta Verlags-Gesellschaft, 1984.

Milligan, S. R., J. C. Kalita, A. Heyerick, H. Rong, L. De Cooman, and D. J. De Keukeleire. "Identification of a Potent Phytoestrogen in Hops *(Humulus lupulus L.)* and Beer." *The Journal of Clinical Endocrinology & Metabolism* 84:6 (June 1999): 2249–2252.

Mukamal, Kenneth J., Malcolm Maclure, James E. Muller, Jane B. Sherwood, and Murray A. Mittleman. "Prior Alcohol Consumption and Mortality Following Acute Myocardial Infarction." *Journal of the American Medical Society* 285:15 (2001): 1965–1970.

Narziss, Ludwig, and Werner Back. *Abriss der Bierbrauerei* [Outline of beer brewing]. 6th ed. Stuttgart: Ferdinand Enke Verlag, 1995.

Newall, Carol A., Linda A. Anderson, and J. David Phillipson. "Hops." In *Herbal Medicines: A Guide for Health-Care Professionals*, pp. 162–163. London: Pharmaceutical Press, 1996.

Nielsen, A. C. *The Drink Pocket Guide 2001.* Henley-on-Thames: NTC Publication, 2000.

Oakland, S. "Beer, Ales and Stout." In *Encyclopedia of Food Science, Food Technology, and Nutrition*, edited by R. Macrae, R. K. Robinson, and M. J. Sadler. London: Academic Press, 1993.

Olsen, E. G. J., "Non-ischemic Myocardial Diseases, 12.10" (in "The circulatory system"). In *Oxford Textbook of Pathology*, edited by James O'D. McGee, Peter G. Isaacson, and Nicolas A. Wright, vol. 2a, *Pathology of Systems.* Oxford: Oxford University Press, 1992.

Owades, Joseph L. "Alcoholic Beverages and Human Responses." In *Encyclopedia of Food Science and Technology*, edited by Fredrik J. Francis, 2nd ed., vol. 1. New York: Wiley, 2000.

Parker, Jim. *BRD, North American Brewers Resource Directory 1997–1998.* 14th edition. Boulder, Colo.: Brewers Publ., 1999.

Piendl, Anton. *Biere aus aller Welt* [Beers from all the world]. Schloss Mindelburg: Brauindustrie, 1970–1990. An impressive analytical work of most of the individual brands of beer in the world.

Poikolainen, Kari. "Alcohol and Mortality: A Review." *Journal of Clinical Epidemiology* 48:4 (1995): 455–465.

Poikolainen, Kari, Erkki Vartiainen, Heikki Korhonen. "Alcohol Intake and Subjective Health." *American Journal of Epidemiology* 144:4 (1996): 346–350.

Reid, Peter. *Modern Brewery Age Blue Book.* 57th edition. Norwalk, Conn., 1997/1998.

Rimm, Eric B., Arthur Klatsky, Diederick Grobbee, and Meir J. Stampfer. "Review of Moderate Alcohol Consumption and Reduced Risk of Coronary Heart Disease: Is the Effect Due to Beer, Wine, or Spirits?" *British Medical Journal* 312 (1996): 731–736.

Teuber, M., and A. F. Schmalreck. "Membrane Leakage in *Bacillus subtilis 168* Induced by the Hop Constituents Lupulone, Humulone, Iso-humulone and Humulinic Acid." *Archives of Microbiology* 94 (1973): 159–171.

World Drink Trends 2000: International Beverage Consumption & Production Trends. Produktschap Voor Gedistilleede Drenken. Henley-on-Thames: NTC Publications, 2000.

Sven-Olle R. Olsson

PRODUCTION AND SOCIAL USE

Beer may be defined as a cereal wine: an alcohol-fermented (and sometimes concomitantly lactic-acid-fermented) beverage, produced from one or more malted cereals, such as barley, wheat, rye, oats, corn, or rice, or from mixtures of these and unmalted cereals. In the following, the product is called "beer" if barley is at least one of the main constituents of the malt; otherwise, it is called "wheat beer," "rye beer," "oat beer," etc., as appropriate.

The Basic Beer-Production Process

To ferment the starch inside the grains of the cereals, it is malted (softened by soaking in water and allowed to germinate) and mashed with warm water; this allows the diastases of the grains, which are activated by the malting and mashing processes, to break the starches into shorter carbohydrates, upon which yeasts can act. After separation, a clarified liquid, known as wort, is produced, which is then boiled with hops; this adds a note of bitterness to the beer's flavor while killing microorganisms. After chilling, yeast is added (either naturally from the environment or as an intentional addition), and fermentation takes place. After clarifying and storage, the beer is ready for consumption.

Classification of Beers

Beers can be categorized according to the type of cereal used, but it is more common to use the type of fermentation for this purpose: spontaneous fermentation, top fermentation, or bottom fermentation.

Spontaneous fermentation. Spontaneously fermented beers are produced without the active addition of any microorganisms to the wort. The microorganisms come from the surrounding air and the equipment used in the brewing process and are a mixture of yeast species and lactic-acid bacteria, a mixture that produces alcohols and lactic and other organic acids, and gives the product a sour taste. Examples are the Russian beverage kvass, which is typically made of rye, and Belgian Lambic beer and the old *Berliner Weisse*, which are both produced partly from wheat. All beers made before the introduction and knowledge of pure yeast cultures were in a sense made via spontaneous fermentation. However, most such beers (as well as wines) were made inside containers that were repeatedly used for this purpose. Such containers rapidly become infected with spores that continue to maintain the original species of yeast—that is, the ones that produced fermentation in the first place. The use of the same vessel and associated equipment from one batch to the next causes the cereal grains employed to continue to be cross-infected between brewings. Recent scientific studies indicate that these spores remain alive for decades, or even longer. Moreover, many beer-making traditions include the step of adding fruit, such as raisins, to the mixture; this practice assures that the yeasts that naturally reside on the surface of the fruit will become a significant part of the microorganisms that infect the mixture.

These types of beer are technically ales—that is, they are all top-fermented.

Top fermentation: ales. Top-fermented beers, ales, are fermented at a rather high temperature, about 64–72°F (18–22°C), letting the yeast float on the surface of the wort.

Typical ales are British and Irish pale ales, bitters, stouts, and porters; Belgian ales, such as Trappist and abbey beers; and western German ales, such as *Alt Bier* and *Kölsch.* The Bavarian wheat beers—*Weissbier* (*Weizenbier*)—are also top-fermented and are produced in different varieties: pale and dark, with and without yeasts remaining, and as bock and *Doppelbock.* Some of the British and Belgian ales can be very strong, up to about 12–17 percent alcohol by volume, while common ales have a concentration of 3.5–6.0 percent alcohol by volume. Ales were predominant before the great expansion in popularity of bottom-fermented beers, the lagers, in the nineteenth century.

It should be noted that the term "ale" has also been used to signify unhopped beer, as contrasted with hopped beer (Cantrell, p. 619).

Bottom fermentation: lagers. Bottom-fermented beers, lagers, originated in Bavaria, where a cold-adapted yeast strain had been developed over a period of many years in the cold caves used for fermentation and storage. A temperature of about 45–59°F (7–15°C) is typical for bottom fermentation. The cold fermentation and the location of the yeast cells at the bottom of the container yield better storage capabilities and a cleaner, more purely malty taste in lagers, in comparison with ales, which are usually more fruity and bloomy in flavor. The name "lager" implies it is stored in cold conditions. Lagers are the dominating beers of the world today: pilsner; Bavarian; Vienna; *Münchener,* pale and dark; *Dortmunder;* bock; and *Doppelbock* beers. The difference between them depends principally on the brewing liquid, the type of hops, and the type of malt used. Bock and *Doppelbock* beers have a higher alcoholic content, 6.0–7.0 percent by volume and 6.0–8.0 percent by volume, respectively, in comparison with the other lagers, 3.8–6.0 percent by volume. Bocks and *Doppelbocks* are spring beers; their high levels of alcohol were originally produced to compensate for Lenten fasting.

Raw Materials

Barley. Barley is a grass of the genus *Hordeum* and of the family Gramineae; it is one of the most important cereals of the world, after wheat, maize (corn), and rice. Barley is mainly used for livestock feed and for beer malting. The world production for 1999 was 130 million tons, with the greatest producers being Germany (13.3 million tons) and Canada (13.2 million tons) (FAO, *Production Yearbook,* 1999). Barley is produced all over the world up to 70°N latitude; it prefers reliable rainfall, a long growing season, and deep rich soils, but it can stand much more difficult conditions. It is not as cold-resistant as wheat, and in some regions it is sown in the autumn (Kendall, pp. 109–111).

For malt production, the two-rowed form of barley is often preferred over the six-rowed, although both give excellent malts. The advantages of barley for malting are principally the following:

- The husk gives each individual grain of barley microbiological protection during malting, thereby helping to prevent the growth of mold.

- The husk provides a useful filter during traditional wort separation. The filtered material, spent grains (trub), is composed of husks, proteins, a little starch, and minerals. The trub is used for animal food (Narziss, 1995, p. 176).

- The gelatinization temperature of malt starch is lower than the inactivation temperature for α-amylase, which is one of the main enzymes breaking down the starch into shorter carbohydrates. (Gelatinization accelerates the transformation to sugars and makes it more thoroughgoing.) (MacLeod, pp. 50–51)

For more detailed reviews see Hough, Briggs, and Stevens (1971) and Adamic (1977).

Water. The different composition of natural brewing water, or production water, from Pilsen, the Czech Republic; Burton upon Trent, England; Munich; Dortmund, Germany; and Vienna characterizes five types of different beers. Pilsen water has low concentrations of ions and is suitable for highly hopped lager beers with pale malt. Burton upon Trent water has high concentrations of calcium, bicarbonate, and particularly sulfate, and this combination has been shown to be perfect for highly hopped ales with dark malt. The waters from Munich, Dortmund, and Vienna have rather high concentrations of alkaline ions, and Dortmund water in particular has rather high concentrations of calcium and sulfate. Vienna water is more highly mineralized than Munich water, with a rather low sulfate but a higher bicarbonate concentration. The waters from Munich and Vienna give a lager that is not heavily hopped and is used with both light and dark malts. The *Dortmunder* lager is more highly hopped and has a slightly higher alcohol content and a pale malt.

Brewing water must be of potable-water quality. The ion composition and pH can be adjusted by ion exchanges, for example. The pH before wort boiling should be 5.4, so as to obtain a pH after boiling of 5.2 (Moll, pp. 138–139). The different ions of the brewing water have profound effects on the malting and brewing processes, the fermentation, the flavor, and, as a result, the type and quality of the beer. The previously mentioned famous beers are distinguished by the effects of geological conditions of their wells on the brewing water. The important cations are calcium, magnesium,

sodium, potassium, iron, manganese, and trace metals. The anions are carbonate, sulfate, chloride, nitrate and nitrite, phosphate, silicate, and fluoride. Their concentrations in the brewing water should comply with those found in water suitable for drinking (for standards, see Moll, pp. 134–135).

Some of the many effects of the ions are pH adjustments made by calcium, magnesium, carbonates, and sulfate from the brewing water and phosphate and organic acids from the malting. If calcium chloride is added, insoluble calcium carbonate, phosphate, and free hydrogen ions will form, which will decrease the pH. In contrast, pH can be increased when the brew is boiled, forming carbon dioxide from carbonate and hydrogen carbonate, which binds hydrogen ions. Many of the different anions such as carbonates, phosphates, and all the organic acids in the brew have buffering capacities (they minimize changes in the pH).

Besides these pH effects, many of the cations, including trace metals, work as coenzymes for many different enzyme systems. For example, magnesium is a cofactor in the metabolic enzymes necessary to produce alcohol and protect yeast cells by preventing increases in cell membrane permeability elicited by ethanol and temperature-induced stress. Other critical trace element cofactors are cobalt and chromium, which enhance the kinetics of alcohol fermentation.

Calcium, along with phosphates, provides thermal protection for mash enzymes and is the principal factor for pH adjustments during wort boiling. It also tends to inhibit color formation during the boil, and facilitates protein coagulation, oxalate sedimentation, yeast flocculation, and beer clarification. Magnesium works similarly to calcium and causes harsh bitterness (Fix, p. 5). Sodium, together with chloride, causes a salty taste in higher concentrations (>400 mg/l), but in lower concentrations it can be used to increase the "mouthfullness." Sodium is also very important for sodium/potassium transport across cell membranes. The amount of potassium should not be excessive as it inhibits many enzymes in the wort preparation. Iron should be avoided as it inhibits the malting, gives color to the wort, decreases the "mouthfullness," and causes a bitter taste. Iron is essential for the oxidative processes of the yeasts, especially terminal oxidation. Manganese works as a coenzyme in many enzyme systems and stimulates cell division and protein generation.

Sulfate, with calcium and magnesium, decreases the pH and stimulates the carboxyl and amino peptidases. The sulfate concentration in the brewing water determines the concentration of sulfate in the final beer (malt and hops also contribute to the amount of sulfate) but does not increase the amount of sulfur dioxide. Sulfate also increases the flower flavor of hops and gives beer a dry, bitter taste. Chloride stimulates α-amylases and gives a soft and full beer taste as calcium chloride. Often, the chloride/sulfate concentration ratio is used to describe the ratio of body and fullness in relation to dryness.

Nitrates and nitrites are the last stage in the oxidation of organic material and give beer a bad taste. Nitrites are toxic for the yeast cells. Phosphate ions in the brewing water are not acceptable because they indicate organic contamination. Silicates of calcium and magnesium have negative effects on the proteins and cause protein-unstable beers. Fluorides have no negative effects on the fermentation but cause the beer to become a little darker and have a broader taste (Narziss, 1992, pp. 17–52). For more details about the effects of the ions in brewing water, see Narziss, 1992; MacLeod; and Moll.

Hops. The cultivated hop plant, *Humulus lupulus*, with its relatives *H. japonicus* and *H. yunnanensis*, belongs, along with species of the genus *Cannabis* (e.g., *C. sativa*, hemp), to the family Cannabinaceae. Together with the nettle family, Urticaceae, they form the order Urticales. Hops are dioecious (i.e., there are individual male and female plants) and perennial and are indigenous throughout much of the Northern Hemisphere between 35° and 70° N, though mostly cultivated today between 43° and 54° N, and 37° and 43° S. The most important regions for hop cultivation are in South Africa, Australia, Argentina, the United States, Germany, the Czech Republic, and England, having an amount of daylight during the growing season of 15:27–18:42 hours, a mean temperature of about 50–66°F (10–19°C), and average rainfall of between 2.5 and 22.4 inches during the period of April to September in the Northern Hemisphere and October to March in the Southern Hemisphere (Barth, Klinke, and Schmidt, p. 49). The world production in 1999 was about 98,000 tons, with Germany contributing about 28,000 tons, the United States about 29,000 tons, and China about 15,000 tons (FAO, *Production Yearbook*, 1999). Many different varieties of hops with different contents of humulone (an antibiotic) and hop oils have been developed, particularly in Germany, England, and the Czech Republic. (For more details about the varieties, the history, and the trade, see Barth, Klinke, and Schmidt, pp. 1–383.)

Both pollinated and unpollinated cones (strobili) from the female plants are used, with the unpollinated ones used in Germany thought by some to yield a better taste than the seed (MacLeod, p. 80). Inside the infolded bases of the bracteoles (the small leaves from which the flowers grow) and on the seed are the resin-producing lupulin glands, which contain the essential compounds for use in beer: the resins humulone (the α-acids) and lupulone (the β-acids), and the aromatic hop oils. The α-acids yield, after boiling and isomerization, iso-α-acids, which contribute bitterness to the beer, and hop oils, which contribute to the aroma. In addition, hops also benefit beer by improving clarity and foam stability, and, most important, flavor stability because of bacteriostatic activity of the iso-α-acids (flavonoids) (Grant, pp. 157–167). Hops are the major preservative of beer.

Other herbs and spices. Down through history many types of herbs and spices have been added to beer (von Hofsten, pp. 208–221; Rätsch, pp. 28–40), and many of them have been considered to be remedies. Besides hops, sweet gale (*Myrica gale*) and marsh tea (*Ledum palustre*), two of the constituents of the old European mixture of beer additives, *grut*, are believed to have been in widespread use. Placotomus mentions in his book from 1543 the use of more than twenty plants as additives for beer (von Hofsten, p. 212).

Since 1516, when the *Reinheitgebot* (Purity Law) was approved in Bavaria, the use of additives other than hops in beer has been prohibited there; this inhibited the use of new herbs and spices, and new combinations of old ones, in beer in Bavaria. However, in Belgium and its surrounding areas, and in Great Britain, other types of beers using wheat and herbs and spices were developed. Many of the recipes are secret, but we know of the use of coriander leaves and seeds, cardamom, camomile, clover, grains of paradise (the seeds of the West African plant *Aframomum melegueta*), cinnamon, plums, peaches, cherries, coffee, chilies, and chocolate (Jackson, 1998, pp. 16–17).

Yeast. The living microorganism producing beer from wort by anaerobic degradation of sugars to alcohol is a yeast species, *Saccaromyces cerevisiae*, which is also used for baking and wine fermentation. The species has at least a thousand different strains (Barnett, Payne, and Yarrow, pp. 595–597). Two of them are *S. cerevisiae cerevisiae* used for top-fermentation of ales and *S. cerevisiae uvarum* (*carlsbergensis*) used for bottom-fermentation of lagers. They differ from each other by the temperature used: as noted above, 64–72°F (18–22°C) for the ales and about 45–59°F (7–15°C) for the lagers. Further, *S. c. uvarum* (*carlsbergensis*) has the ability to ferment the disaccharide melibiose, which *S. c. cerevisiae* is unable to do, due to lack of the enzyme melibiase (α-galacoidase) (Russel, pp. 169–170). Different breweries have developed their own strains or mixtures of strains of yeast to maintain the distinctive qualities of their beers. Important requirements for a good brewing yeast are flocculating power (i.e., the capability of forming loose, fluffy clumps), ability to ferment maltotriose (a complex sugar found in the wort), head-forming potential, fermentation efficacy, interaction with isohumulones (forms of the antibiotic α-acids produced by hops), response to fining (clarifying and purifying), and propensity for producing important individual flavor components (MacLeod, p. 84). In the San Francisco beer Anchor Steam, lager yeast is used for fermentation at a high ale-fermentation temperature, which gives a very interesting beer with the roundness and cleanness of a lager and the fruitiness and some of the complexity of an ale.

Outline of Modern Brewing Procedures

Detailed descriptions of this highly technological and scientifically based process can be found in de Clerck (1957–1958); MacLeod (1977); Hardwick (*Handbook of Brewing*,

Hop-sampling warehouse at the Guinness brewery, Dublin, Ireland, circa 1915. To maintain the quality of hops used in brewing, samples were taken from various lots of newly purchased hops and tested. ROUGHWOOD COLLECTION.

1995); Hough, Briggs, Stevens, and Young (1982); Narziss (1992–1999); and Narziss (1995).

An outline of the different procedures is given by Hardwick ("An Overview of Beer Making," 1995, p. 88).

Beer Chemistry

Malting. The process of malting grain starts with steeping it in water. After several hours, the embryo begins to take up water and to grow. To produce energy, the growth hormone giberellinic acid is formed and transported to the aleurone cells around the starch-rich endosperm to start the formation of hydrolytic enzymes such as α-amylase, endo-β-glucanase, and peptidase. The cell walls of the endosperm contain β-linked glucan and pentosan, which are degraded by the endo-β-glucanase and pentosanases. The net action is to solubilize and break down the cell walls and the small starch granules in the endosperm. The peptidases break down the peptides into amino acids, which are essential for yeast nutrition; the large polypeptides, which have not been used by the yeast cells during fermentation, are important for foam stability in the final beer, but in conjunction with polyphenols have the potential to form undesirable haze in the beer.

When the malting is completed, the malt has to be kiln-dried to stop the enzymatic activities and to reduce the water content so as to allow storage of the finished malt. The kilning is divided into two steps: the drying, at temperatures up to 176°F (80°C), giving a moisture content of 4 percent; and the curing process, at higher temperatures, yielding flavor components through the Maillard reaction. This reaction browns the malt, producing amino acid–carbonyl compounds, which undergo further transformations to yield the colored, aromatic compounds known as melanoidins. The higher the temperature, the darker the malt will be and the more the enzymes will be inhibited (Kendall, pp. 117–118; Fix, pp. 41–45). These compounds contribute both to dark color and to different varieties of burnt-sugar or caramel taste. The malt type and the mixture of malts forms the body or the "mouthfullness" of the beer and produces the basis of classification into pale, medium, and dark beers. If the malt is kilned over an open fire, it will acquire a definite smoky taste like the Bavarian *Rauchbier,* "smoke beer." The feeling of "mouthfullness" can be decreased by splitting the residual sugar of the beer, the α-glucans, dextrins, by exogenous enzymes during the malting process. The resulting carbohydrates will finally be fermented by the yeast. The process is used to produce diet, lite, light, and dry beers.

Mashing. The type of brewing liquid used for beer production plays a very great role. However, with modern technology, any type of liquid with the optimal concentrations of the different ions can be created from any water. Calcium ions contribute to a more acid mash by precipitating as calcium phosphate and thus setting hydrogen ions free from phosphate ions. The pH obtained in this way, 5.4, is favorable for the activities of amylases. Bicarbonate ions act in the opposite way and give a more alkaline mash, which is unfavorable, and thus they should typically be removed. Calcium sulfate is often added to the mash to decrease the pH and to give bitterness to ale. Nitrates and iron ions have deleterious effects on yeasts. For detailed discussions on brewing liquids and salts, see Moll (pp. 133–156).

Germany complies with the *Reinheitsgebot*, the Purity Law, which, except for *Weissbier*, permits only barley malt, hops, and water for beer brewing. In most other countries, however, adjuncts up to 50 percent by volume are added to the mash to decrease the cost and to balance the taste of the beer. The adjuncts can be sugar solutions, other malts, or other unmalted cereals, such as rice, maize, wheat, or barley (though both rice and maize must be precooked before their incorporation into the mash, as their starches have high gelatinization points) (Stewart, pp. 121–132).

The mashing can be performed by either infusion or decoction. Infusion mashing is performed in a single vessel at a uniform temperature of about 150°F (65°C), and after the mashing, filtration is performed in the same vessel. The decoction system starts with a low temperature, which is then raised by the removal, boiling, and return of a part of the mash. The whole mash finally is transferred to a separate vessel, the lauter tun, for filtration. In Britain, the infusion is used with well-modified and coarsely ground malt, whereas in continental Europe the larger decoction method is used with a finer grind and less well-modified malt. Decoction mashing is a more versatile procedure for different malts and also has the advantage of low temperature, which helps to maintain the stability of such heat-labile enzymes as proteinases, β-glucanases, and β-amylase (MacLeod, pp. 59–73; Narziss, 1999; Rehberger and Luther, pp. 247–322).

The objective of the mashing is to produce fermentable sugars from the degradation of solubilized starch, amylose, and amylopectin. The sugars obtained are glucose, maltose, maltotriose, maltotetraose, and higher dextrins to a total of about 70 to 75 percent, with the higher values coming from decoction malting. Unfermentable dextrins persist to the finished beer and are an important part of the mouth-filling experience of the beer. Proteins, peptides, and amino acids, as well as vitamins, inorganic ions, fatty acids, organic acids, tannins, and lipids, are extracted during the mashing and all are important for yeast fermentation.

The amount of malt used is directly proportional to the alcoholic concentration of the finished beer. About one-fourth to one-third of the weight of the malt is metabolized to alcohol.

Wort boiling. The filtered sweet wort from the mashing is transferred to the wort vessel for boiling, which inactivates the enzymes, sterilizes the wort, lowers the pH via precipitation of calcium phosphate and removal of carbon dioxide from bicarbonate, concentrates the wort, denatures and precipitates proteins, dissolves any additional sugars used, isomerizes hop α-acids, and removes unwanted flavor components. A long boiling process increases the shelf life of beer. Elimination of high-molecular-weight material (i.e., flocculation of the proteins) is increased by stirring and adding carrageen, a colloid typically extracted from the red alga *Chondrus crispus*. It has also been shown that the malty full-bodied flavor of beer declines and sharper notes are enhanced with rising temperature of heat treatment. The color of the wort is also increased with higher temperatures, aeration, and higher contents of soluble nitrogen. The process is the same as the one that occurs during kilning, the Maillard reaction (MacLeod, pp. 73–81).

During the wort boiling, hops, whole or powdered, are added to give their characteristic bitterness and aroma to the beer and, because of their antimicrobial action, to increase its shelf life. Principally, there are two types of acids contributed by the hops: α-acids such as humulone, cohumulone, and adhumulone; and β-acids such as lupulone, colupulone, and adlupulone. The bitter taste of fresh hops derives almost entirely from the α-acids, but they have only limited solubility in the wort. However, during the boiling, the α-acids are transformed into soluble, bitter iso-α-acids, which contribute to the hoppy bitterness of the beer. There are at least six cis- and trans-iso-α-acids and their overall level in beer is about 0.0002 to 0.0005 oz/gal (Neve, pp. 33–38). The β-acids are largely unchanged during boiling.

The aroma of the hops comes from a very complex mixture of compounds and most of the volatile hop oils are lost in boiling, but a late addition of aroma hops increases the flavor. A discussion and list of the hop compounds in beer is found in Hardwick ("The Properties of Beer," pp. 573–577).

Fermentation. The principal pathway for carbohydrate metabolism is the Embden–Meyerhof–Parnas pathway, which is the anaerobic metabolism of glucose to pyruvates and alcohol by the yeast cells:

1 mole of glucose gives 2 moles of pyruvates, which will give 2 moles of alcohol and 2 moles of carbon dioxide (CO_2).

A more comprehensive equation that describes a brewery fermentation is given by Bamforth (p. 143):

Maltose (100 g) + amino acid (0.5 g) → yeast (5 g) + ethanol (48.8 g) + CO_2 (46.6 g) + energy (50 kcal)

Glucose and fructose are the first carbohydrates to be absorbed by the yeast cells from the wort. For the up-

186

take of maltose, the principal sugar of the wort, maltose permease must be synthesized, and before maltotriose can be used, the maltose of the wort has to be almost completely depleted. The formation of maltose permease is the time-limiting effect on the speed of fermentation of the wort. This enzyme is also inhibited by glucose, thus yielding a longer lag period in glucose-supplemented wort (MacLeod, pp. 81–103).

Amino acids can be divided into four groups according to their uptake into the yeast cells: A, B, C, and D in that sequence for both *S. c. cervisiae* and *S. c. carlsbergensis*. The A and C amino acids appear to compete with the same permease. Proline, which is the only member of the D group, disappears very slowly, implying that a substantial amount of this amino acid will remain in the final beer: about 0.003 to 0.004 oz/gal.

Unwanted products from the fermentation process, which are closely related to amino-acid metabolism, are certain higher alcohols: 3-methylbutanol, fusel alcohol, and vicinal diketones (diacetyl). Presence of diacetyl seems to depend on a deficiency of the amino acid valine. A deficiency of methionine or an excess of threonine gives unacceptable levels of hydrogen sulfide (MacLeod, p. 91). Consequently, careful control of the amino-acid composition of the wort is essential. Esters (e.g., ethyl acetate) are also important as taste- and aroma-producing compounds. Their formation is favored by high-gravity brewing followed by dilution, ample supplies of assimilable nitrogen, and relatively high concentrations of alcohol (MacLeod, pp. 81–103). For further discussion on fermentation, see Munroe (1995, pp. 323–353).

The wort is rather rich in B vitamins, but this content, particularly the content of thiamine, is decreased during fermentation by the yeasts (Hardwick, pp. 576–577).

Aging and finishing.

Newly fermented beer, often referred to as green beer, has to mature in flavor through storage at low temperatures and should be removed from the yeast. It may also require being clarified, stabilized, carbonated, blended, or standardized. The processes involved include filtrations, CO_2 additions, pasteurization, and additions of tannic acid and proteolytic enzymes for clarification of the product. For a more detailed discussion, see Munroe (pp. 355–379). Storage of green beer together with its yeast cells decreases the amount of diacetyl and 2,3–pentanedione, which have a buttery taste that is undesirable in lighter beers. Sulfur-containing compounds, such as hydrogen sulfide, sulfur dioxide, and dimethyl sulfide, may also show up in the beer, producing unattractive flavors and aromas.

During storage, a secondary fermentation can be performed to accelerate aging and the maturation of taste. A secondary fermentation can also be performed in the bottle, as is done in many Belgian ales and Trappist beers, for example. Another method used is to add up to about 20 percent of highly fermenting primary beer (high-*kräusen)* to the green beer in storage. Also during storage, aroma hops may be added to increase the aroma of the beer, and iso-α-acids from hops can be added to help control bitterness in the beer.

Modern industrial processes of aging and finishing beer, with ultrafiltrations, pasteurization, and total separation of yeast cells, give the modern-style clear, "dead" beer, which has a long shelf life. This contrasts with "real" beer or ale, which retains living yeast cells and thus exhibits richer taste and aroma, but has a shorter shelf life and often greater variation in taste and aroma. Most lagers do not contain yeast cells, but many bottom-fermented beers such as *Weissbier mit Hefe* (literally, "wheat beer with yeast"), Belgian beers, and British ales and stouts do. A comprehensive summary of the chemical constituents and the physical properties of beer can be found in Hardwick, "The Properties of Beer" (pp. 551–585).

Beer aging and oxidation.

Beer is a fresh food product, which undergoes chemical changes during storage. Some of these are expressed as sensory changes shown in the schematic graph given by Bamforth (p. 68). The progression of these changes has been described by Dalgliesch (1977, cited in Fix):

Stage A is the period of stable, "brewery-fresh" flavor.

Stage B is a transition period in which a multitude of new flavor sensations can be detected.

Stage C products exhibit the classic flavor tones of beer staling.

Stage D, not included in Dalgliesch, "is the development of 'kaleidoscopic flavors,'" as exemplified in Rodenbach's Grand Cru and in Trappist beers, "recalling the subtlety and complexity of great wines" (Fix, pp. 127–128).

Most of these changes are due to a range of oxidative reactions in the beer. Hence, it is extremely important for the quality and shelf life of beer that the beer be oxygen-free. The alcohols in beer can be oxidized to aldehydes and acids, and the iso-α-acids can also be oxidized, with the formation of free fatty acids. All these compounds have prominent effects on aroma and taste. Free fatty acids can also form esters with the alcohols and the unsaturated fatty acids as well as the melanoidins produced via browning of the malt can undergo autooxidation. The fatty acids will give fatty and soapy flavor notes. Melanoidins may oxidize alcohols to aldehydes or acids. However, melanoidins can also be reduced by the oxidation of iso-α-acids and work as antioxidants, thereby protecting the beer from oxidation, as is the case in dark beer. The same effects are seen from malt- and hop-based phenols. Together with fatty acids, they interact in a complex electron exchange system.

The different kinds of phenols, from cathecin to polyphenols (also called tannins and flavonoids), which originate from the malt, the hops, and also from the fermentation process itself play a large role in these chemical reactions. They can act as useful antioxidants in the beer and add to the sensory impression of freshness. However, if they themselves become oxidized, they contribute astringency and harshness. Another very important result of the chemical reactions is the reduction of unsaturated fatty acids. This inhibits the development of long-chained unsaturated aldehydes, such as trans-2-nonenal, which is a prominent factor for the development of staling and cardboard and/or papery notes. Because of these reactions, highly hopped beer is less prone to develop the staling effect (Fix, pp. 127–139).

Beer and Social Use

Throughout history, beer-drinking peoples have considered beer an essential part of both their food supply and their enjoyment of life. Bread and beer—food and beverage—were two parts of nutrition united via having almost the same process of fabrication. In earlier times, beer was thought of as liquid bread. As a beverage, it was also preferred over water, partly because water was often contaminated by bacteria, whereas beer became almost sterilized through the boiling of the wort and the antiseptic qualities of hops.

Beer and other alcoholic beverages have played a very important religious and social role: maintaining ties within groups and between people and their deities. It is not surprising that man has considered intoxicated humans to be in close contact with the deities and acquiring spiritual and supernatural forces from them. In Old Norse mythology, mead (an alcoholic beverage fermented from honey) gave humans immortality, wisdom, and poetic abilities. Mead and beer were considered to contain the spirit of the gods, and hence people ingested the gods by drinking the beverages in the same way as Christians drink the blood and eat the flesh of Christ at communion, in the form of bread and wine (Thunaeus, vol. 1, pp. 17–24; Wiegelmann, pp. 533–537).

At the ceremonial feasts of the Nordic people in the tenth century, the beer and food were first blessed and then highly ornamented horns of beer went to everybody to make toasts to the gods: to Odin for victory and power for the king, and then to Njord and Frej for a good harvest and peace. Then they drank *minne*, memory, for their ancestors and relatives. The ceremony formed and strengthened bonds both between the gods and men, and among men (Thunaeus, vol. 1, pp. 17–24; Wiegelmann, pp. 533–537). In medieval times and persisting until the nineteenth century, important ceremonies such as baptisms, weddings, funerals, and harvest celebrations had *öl*, beer, in their names; there were, for instance, *dopöl*, the celebration of baptism, and *gravöl*, the funeral feast. For the various celebrations, a strong beer was produced. On other days, a much weaker beer was consumed, which was sometimes even mixed with milk. People showed their hospitality by having a tankard with beer standing on the table, and everyone was welcome to take a sip.

These examples from the Nordic countries exemplify the general pattern of mankind using alcoholic beverages as ceremonial links to the gods and a method of creating and increasing social contacts among people. Many of these ceremonies and social implications of drinking together are still active today.

Mixtures of Beer and Other Beverages

In *Berliner Weisse*, juices of red raspberry, green sweet woodruff, or, more recently, pineapple may be added. To Belgian Lambic, different fruits can be added to the second fermentation to create, for example, *Kriek* (using cherries) and *Framboise* (using raspberries) (Jackson, 1991, pp. 95–100).

The English shandy (beer mixed with lemonade or ginger beer) and the German *Radler* and *Alsterwasser* (beer mixed with a clear soft drink, typically lemon or lemon–lime soda) are quite popular today. Shandy has a tradition that dates back to the tenth century (Zotter, pp. 222–223). *Alsterwasser* has also become popular with cola and tequila (Pini, pp. 88 and 788). *Radler* was earlier a common mixture for children and young people in Germany. In southern Sweden, the mixture of beer (*svagdricka*) and milk called *drickablandning* (mixture of drinks) was very popular until about the middle of the twentieth century.

Food and Beer

Beer is used as an ingredient in food preparation in soups and stews, for marination of meat, as a liquid for boiling, and in sauces. Many German examples are given by Lohberg (pp. 269–331). Traditional soups with beer in northern Europe are *Biersuppe*, *Öllebröd*, and *Ölsupa*, which are boiled mixtures of beer and meal and/or milk and egg, with ginger, cinnamon, and fruits. *Carbonade*, beef stewed in beer, is a favorite dish in northern France, Belgium, and the Netherlands.

The specific types of beer used traditionally in an area almost always fit very well with traditional local food. The most popular type of beer in the world today, pilsner or light lager, which is served cold and has low levels of bitterness and maltiness, is a good partner with almost any kind of food, which may well be an important reason for its popularity.

Other types of beers, which have a more complex taste, should be paired with different foods using some care, as the combination should not overpower the individual flavors of either the beer or the food, but enhance the positive features of both. A nice introduction with illustrative food and beer combinations has been presented by Jackson (1998). In general, beer can be paired with different kinds of food as well as wine can be, and sometimes better.

Service Traditions

Drinking vessels and beer containers. In Latin America, the Incas and the Mayas developed very elaborate containers both for the production of *chica* and for storage and ritual drinking. The malting and fermentation took place in hollow tree trunks that were often decorated and covered with carpets or palm leaves. The bottles were ceramic stirrup vessels with a long neck, sometimes two joined into one, with a round bellow that could be formed as a human head. Ordinary ceramic cups were also used. The ceramics were painted with many different scenes, often with a strong erotic touch. Bottles filled with *chicha* were buried with the dead (Rätsch, p. 103).

The serving of beer in Mesopotamia and in ancient Egypt was from ceramic containers, both large ones from which people drank with straws (primarily to penetrate the top-fermenting yeast and floating husks) and smaller ones like our cups. For ceremonial drinking, elaborate bull's horns were used in northern Europe. After the ceramic period and persisting into the twentieth century, the wooden barrel and the wooden tankard were the principal storage and drinking containers. In Scandinavia, it was common to have elaborate drinking bowls, often in the form of a goose, for ceremonial feasts, and during the sixteenth century, the upper class used ornamental wooden drinking vessels (Hirsjärvi, pp. 57–68; Cleve, pp. 15–42; Gjærder). Drinking vessels were also later made of lead, tin, copper, silver, stoneware, ivory, china, or glass. Tankards usually had the same general design whether or not they were lidded. Lids were usually metallic, and the rest of the tankard was made of glass, ceramic, or wood. There were very elaborate, expensive tankards and also simple and practical ones (Jung; Lohberg).

Although its history is very long, perhaps as long as the history of beer itself, before the nineteenth century the beer glass was seen only among the upper classes. It was the technique of glass pressing in great industrial scale in the nineteenth century that made the glass available to everyone. The design of the beer glass has developed in some distinctive ways, with special sizes and shapes for specific types of beers and special glasses displaying the names and logos of the brewers for almost every brand of beer (Lohberg; Jackson, 1998). Jackson includes color images of both the glass and the bottle for each type of beer presented in the book.

The original wooden barrel was generally replaced in the twentieth century by the steel barrel. At the end of the nineteenth century, glass bottles were introduced, and beginning in 1935, they were joined by metallic containers—beer cans.

Serving temperature. There is a correct serving temperature for every beer. The richer the flavor and aroma of a beer is, the higher its serving temperature should be. A very low temperature is suitable if taste is secondary. The only beers that are appropriate to serve cold, about 39°F (4°C), are light, pale lagers. More tasty lagers should be served between 43 and 50°F (6 and 10°C), and ales between 54 and 64°F (12 and 18°C). Jackson (1998) is a good source for recommendations of serving temperatures for specific beers.

DRINKING ESTABLISHMENTS IN EUROPE

The establishments for serving beer in Europe have developed into three different lines or beer-serving cultures:

- The Central European in the area of South Germany, the Czech Republic, and Austria: The *Bierkeller* or *Biergarten* has no bar but rather big wooden tables, chairs, or benches; the beer (only a few brands) is served from barrels. The glasses are specific for the type of beer served. In Munich the beer could be served in a tankard of glass or ceramics, *ein Mass* (which means one tankard) of either one or two liters.
- The British: The pubs have a bar around which most of the people gather. Some real ales, a stout, and a light lager from kegs are served in pint glasses.
- The Belgian: The typical cafés have some resemblance to the French or the Austrian cafés serving wines and coffee. The number of brands of beer offered is great—up to the hundreds in some cafés in Belgium.

In all three types of establishments the food served is simple but in most cases nourishing.

Beer and Traditional Medicine

Hans Zotter's book (pp. 222–223) contains medical recommendations and rules from Ibn Butlan from the tenth century. It illustrates how beer was looked upon medically in the old tradition of Hippocratic medicine, a tradition that prevailed until about the seventeenth century. Its view was that

Beer is "hot and humid"; or "cold and humid."
The best beer is sharp and spicy.
Beer drinking relieves the sharpness of heat and drunkenness.
It dilates the vessels and creates discomfort.
In contrast, the mixture of beer and lemon juice or citric acid helps.
Beer drinking creates "malicious body fluids," which are good for people with hot "complection" and for young people, especially during hot weather and in hot countries.

In 1614, the philosopher and alchemist Paracelsus wrote: "Cerevisia malorum divina medicina" (Beer is a divine medicine against harms) (Rätsch, pp. 12–14). Beer was also used as a carrier or solvent for many different folk remedies (Rätsch, pp. 28–40). The use of herbs and spices, such as hops and sweet gale, in beer may well have its origin in folk medicine.

Interestingly, beer is still prescribed today in the United Kingdom as a medication for the elderly.

See also **Alcohol; Fermentation; Fermented Beverages Other than Wine or Beer; Wine.**

BIBLIOGRAPHY

Adamic, E. B. "Barley and Malting." In *The Practical Brewer: A Manual for the Brewing Industry*, edited by H. M. Broderick, 2d ed. Madison, Wis.: Master Brewers Association of the Americas, 1977.

Bamforth, Charles. *Tap into the Art and Science of Brewing.* New York: Plenum Press, 1998.

Barnett, J. A., R. W. Payne, and D. Yarrow. *Yeast Characteristics and Identification.* 2d ed. Cambridge, U.K.: Cambridge University Press, 1990.

Barth, Heinrich J., Christiane Klinke, and Claus Schmidt. *Der Grosse Hopfenatlas. Geschichte und Geographie einer Kulturpflanze* (The great hop atlas: History and geography of a cultivated plant). Nuremberg: H. Carl, 1994.

Cantrell, Philip A., II. "Beer and Ale." In *The Cambridge World History of Food*, edited by Kenneth F. Kiple and Kriemhild Coneè Ornelas, vol. 1, pp. 619–625. Cambridge, U.K.: Cambridge University Press, 2000.

de Clerck, Jean. *A Textbook of Brewing.* Translated by K. Barton-Wright. 2 vols. London: Chapman and Hall, 1957–1958.

Cleve, Nils. *Till Bielkekåsornas genealogi* (On the genealogy of the kosa from the Bielke family). Stockholm: Fataburen, 1965.

Dolphin. Richard. *The International Book of Beer Can Collecting.* London: Hamlyn, 1978.

Fix, George. *Principles of Brewing Science: A Study of Serious Brewing Issues.* Boulder, Colo.: Brewers Publications, 1999.

FAO. *Production Yearbook.* Geneva: 1999. Available at http://www.fao.org.

Gjærder, Per. *Norske Drikkekar av Tre* (Norwegian drinking vessels in wood). Bergen, Norway: Universitetsforlaget, 1975.

Grant, Herbert L. "Microbrewing." In *Handbook of Brewing*, edited by William A. Hardwick. New York: Marcel Dekker, 1995.

Grant, Herbert L. "Hops." In *Handbook of Brewing*, edited by William A. Hardwick. New York: Marcel Dekker, 1995.

Hardwick, William A. "An Overview of Beer Making." In *Handbook of Brewing*, edited by William A. Hardwick. New York: Marcel Dekker, 1995.

Hardwick, William A. "The Properties of Beer." In *Handbook of Brewing*, edited by William A. Hardwick. New York: Marcel Dekker, 1995.

Hardwick, William A., ed. *Handbook of Brewing.* New York: Marcel Dekker, 1995.

Hirsjärvi, A. *Hur de nordiska ölkåsorna kommit till* (How the Nordic beer kosas have been developed). Stockholm: Fataburen, 1947.

von Hofsten, Nils. "Pors och andra humleersättningar och ölkryddor i äldre tider" [Sweet gale and other substitutes for hops in former times]. In *Acta Academiae Regiae Gustavi Adolphi* 36. Uppsala, Sweden: AB Lundequistska Bokhandeln, 1960.

Hough, J. S., D. E. Briggs, and R. Stevens. *Malting and Brewing Science.* London: Chapman and Hall, 1971.

Hough, J. S., D. E. Briggs, R. Stevens, and T. W. Young. *Brewery Fermentations: Malting and Brewing Science.* London: Chapman and Hall, 1982.

Jackson, Michael. *Beer.* London: Dorling Kindersley, 1998.

Jackson, Michael. *The Great Beers of Belgium.* Antwerp, Belgium: Media Marketing Communications NV, 1991.

Jung, Hermann. *Bier, Kunst und Brauchtum* (Beer, art, and custom). Wiesbaden, Germany: English Verlag, 1981.

Kendall, N. T. "Barley and Malt." In *Handbook of Brewing*, edited by William A. Hardwick. New York: Marcel Dekker, 1995.

Lewis, Michael J., and Tom W. Young. *Brewing.* Gaithersburg, Md.: Aspen, 2001.

Lohberg, Rolf. *Das grosse Lexikon vom Bier* (The great encyclopedia of beer). 3d ed. Stuttgart: Scripta Verlags-Gesellschaft, 1984.

MacLeod, Anna M. "Beer." In *Economic Microbiology: Alcoholic Beverages*, edited by A. H. Rose, vol. 1. London: Academic Press, 1977.

Magnus, Olaus. *Historia om de nordiska folken* (History of the Nordic people), Book 13, Chap. 32, 1555. Reprint, edited by John Granlund, Vol. 3, p. 74. Stockholm: Gidlunds, 1951.

Moll, M. M. "Water." In *Handbook of Brewing*, edited by William A. Hardwick. New York: Marcel Dekker, 1995.

Munroe, James H. "Fermentation." In *Handbook of Brewing*, edited by William A. Hardwick. New York: Marcel Dekker, 1995.

Munroe, James H. "Aging and Finishing." In *Handbook of Brewing*, edited by William A. Hardwick. New York: Marcel Dekker, 1995.

Narziss, Ludwig. *Die Bierbrauerei in drei Bänden* (Beer brewing). 3 vols., 7th ed. Stuttgart: Ferdinand Enke Verlag, 1992–1999.

Narziss, Ludwig. *Abriss der Bierbrauerei* (Outline of beer brewing). 6th ed. Stuttgart: Ferdinand Enke Verlag, 1995.

Neve, R. A. *Hops.* London: Chapman and Hall, 1991.

Owades, Joseph L. "Alcoholic beverages and human responses." In *Encyclopedia of Food Science and Technology*, edited by Fredrik J. Francis, vol. 1, 2d ed. New York: John Wiley, 2000.

Pini, Udo. *Das Gourmet Handbuch* (The gourmet handbook). Cologne, Germany: Könemann, 2000.

Rätsch, Christian. *Urbock: Bier jenseits von Hopfen und Malz; Von den Zaubertränken der Götter zu den psychedelischen Bieren der Zukunft* (*Urbock:* Beer beyond hops and malt; From the magic potions of the gods to the psychedelic beers of the future). Aurau, Switzerland: AT Verlag, 1996.

Rehberger, Arthur, and Gary E. Luther. "Brewing." In *Handbook of Brewing*, edited by William A. Hardwick. New York: Marcel Dekker, 1995.

Russel, Inge. "Yeast." In *Handbook of Brewing*, edited by William A. Hardwick. New York: Marcel Dekker, 1995.

Stewart, Graham G. "Adjuncts." In *Handbook of Brewing*, edited by William A. Hardwick. New York: Marcel Dekker, 1995.

Thunaeus, Harald. *Ölets historia i Sverige* (The history of beer in Sweden). 2 vols. Stockholm: Almqvist och Wiksell, 1968–1970.

Wiegelmann, Günther. "Bier im germanischen Bereich" (Beer in the Germanic area). In *Reallexikon der Germanischen Altertumskunde*, edited by Johannes Hoops, vol. 2. Berlin and New York: Walter de Gruyter, 1976.

Zotter, Hans. *Das Buch vom Gesunden Leben* (The book of the healthy life). *Die Gesundheitstabellen des Ibn Butlan in der illustrierten deutschen Übertragung des Michael Herr. Nach der bei Hans Schott erschienenen Ausgabe Strassburg 1533*. Graz, Austria: Akademische Druck- u. Verlagsanstalt, 1988.

Sven-Olle R. Olsson

BEETON, ISABELLA. Isabella Beeton (1836–1865), author of *Beeton's Book of Household Management*, was born at 24 Milk Street, Cheapside, London, as Isabella Mary Mayson, one of four children of Benjamin and Elizabeth Mayson. Isabella was educated at Heidelberg, Germany, and became an accomplished pianist.

When she returned from Germany, and while visiting family and friends in London, she met the wealthy publisher Samuel Orchart Beeton. Samuel Beeton, a publishing genius, possessed a talent for capitalizing on Victorian market trends. Part of the new and prosperous middle class, he published popular literature and *Beeton's Book of Garden Management* and *Beeton's Book of Universal Information*. Isabella and Samuel were married on 10 July 1856 and settled in the London borough of Harrow.

Their marriage was a fruitful professional collaboration: He was enthusiastic and creative, while she was a meticulous, level-headed researcher with an eye for detail. Beeton encouraged Isabella to compile her recipes and household management tips into articles written for *The Englishwoman's Domestic Magazine: An Illustrated Journal Combining Practical Information, Instruction, and Amusement* (EDM). She eventually assumed editorial responsibilities for *EDM*, and also for the Beetons' new journal, the *Queen*. She was soon working regularly at Samuel's office at the Strand, in an era when very few women worked in an office. While writing and editing for Samuel's magazines, and despite the loss of her first child, Isabella was already researching and gathering data for her magisterial work, *The Book of Household Management*. She also found time to open a soup kitchen at her house in the winter of 1858 to feed the poor children of Hatch End and Pinner.

According to Nicola Humble, the editor of the 2000 edition of *Mrs. Beeton's Book of Household Management*, the book remains one of the great unread classics of our time, though a highly collectible one. Published in October 1861, *Mrs. Beeton's Book of Household Management* (BHM) sold 60,000 copies and nearly 2 million by 1868. Originally published as monthly supplements in *EDM*, the first installment appeared in September 1859 when Isabella was twenty-three.

The *BHM*, as Humble notes, is much more than a cookery book. Its comprehensive range of recipes and household management techniques (2,751 entries) speaks to a culture that was caught up in the social changes of mid-nineteenth-century urban England. The *BHM* is also a sort of window into the Victorian social life of kitchens and household, giving all manner of instructions on etiquette, on the handling of servants, the economic spaces of kitchens, child rearing, medical advice, and animal husbandry. The book is also noted for some famous maxims, including, "A place for everything and everything in its place." Isabella Beeton herself never claimed that the recipes were original, and her preface acknowledges correspondents from Great Britain and Europe for their ideas. She adapted recipes from Alexis Soyer's *Modern Housewife* and Eliza Acton's *Modern Cookery for Private Families*, and, though she cites Soyer, she does not give credit to Acton. What Isabella Beeton did do was test the recipes herself, and any recipe she found uneconomical, impractical, and difficult, she discarded. If she was not an original cook, she was supreme in her organizational skills, arranging the recipes in alphabetical order, listing estimated costs, and producing clear, concise instructions for all food preparation and cooking as modern cookbooks do. It is worth noting that the *BHM* is not the first of its kind, and that Hannah Glasse's *The Art of Cookery Made Plain and Easy* (1747) also included household improvement tips and simplified cooking techniques.

Isabella Beeton became ill after the birth of a child, and died of puerperal fever at age twenty-eight—but not before completing the editorial work on *Mrs. Beeton's Dictionary of Cookery*. Samuel Beeton died of tuberculosis twelve years later, in June 1877. The Beetons are remembered by a road, Beeton Close, near their old home at Hatch End, which was bombed out during a German air raid in September 1940. The *BHM* has since been reprinted numerous times, and Isabella Beeton's life has been turned into the one-woman show *Bella* by Alison Neil and adapted for BBC radio in 2002 by Tony Coult.

See also **Cookbooks**.

BIBLIOGRAPHY

Beeton, Isabella. *Mrs. Beeton's Book of Household Management*, edited by Nicola Humble. Oxford: Oxford University Press, 2000. The original edition was published in 1861.

Freeman, Sarah. *Isabella and Sam: The Story of Mrs. Beeton*. New York: Coward, McCann, and Geoghegan, 1978.

Yoke-Sum Wong

BELGIUM. *See* **Low Countries**.

BERIBERI. Beriberi is a disease that usually begins with a loss of feeling in the feet and then weakness and pain in walking. In many, but not all, cases the body then becomes swollen and in the most serious cases the heart begins to fail, and the patient becomes breathless and soon dies. The problem stems from an insufficient intake of the vitamin thiamin (or "thiamine") even though we require each day only about 1 milligram, which is equivalent to one 32,000th of an ounce. The word "beriberi" comes from Indonesia and may mean "weak" or "swelling," but there have been many other suggested meanings.

The disease used to be a serious problem in Far Eastern countries where white rice was the staple food and people ate only small quantities of supplementary foods. Husked rice grains provide a reasonable amount of this vitamin, but further processing, or "polishing" to rub off the bran and germ, removes most of the remaining thiamin. Washing the grains and boiling them leaves even less thiamin in the final cooked food. Unfortunately, brown (unpolished) rice goes rancid more quickly under tropical conditions and so has only a short storage life. In traditional peasant communities, where enough paddy (unhusked grain) would be pounded and winnowed each morning for the day ahead, this was not a problem. When inexpensive power machinery for milling and polishing rice was developed, this made the provisioning of the armed forces in particular much more convenient, but in Japan and other Asian countries it was followed by serious outbreaks of beriberi in the army and navy.

Infantile beriberi also has been a major cause of death among breast-fed infants in the Philippines and other communities where mothers are in a state of borderline, subclinical thiamin deficiency. Affected infants typically cease to pass urine and experience difficulty in breathing. Even those near death, however, respond dramatically to a dose of thiamin.

It is technically possible now to mix in with white rice a few vitamin-rich pellets manufactured to resemble rice grains. However, where rice-growing communities each have their own small village mill, it has been found impracticable to control such additions, which slightly increase the millers' costs. As an alternative, communities at risk can be supplied with inexpensive vitamin pills.

In developed countries thiamin deficiency is still a problem among alcoholics, partly because such addicts have highly abnormal diet patterns and partly because they seem to absorb the vitamin less efficiently. They also may show acute heart problems without any early symptoms of traditional beriberi. A small proportion progress to a syndrome with irreversible brain damage that requires indefinite hospitalization.

In many Western countries, millers are required to fortify white wheaten flour with thiamin (along with other micronutrients). Thus, even the population groups, such as alcoholics, who are eating an unbalanced diet are less likely to become deficient. It also has been suggested that alcoholic drinks should be fortified with thiamin. This would not be prohibitively expensive, but authorities have felt that, on balance, it would be undesirable because it would allow them to be marketed as "health drinks" despite the injurious effects associated with or caused by alcohol consumption, that is, automobile accidents, disruption of families, and a wide range of health problems.

See also **Dietary Assessment**; **Dietary Guidelines**; **Disease: Metabolic Diseases**; **Rice: Rice as a Food**; **Rice: The Natural History of Rice**; **Vitamins: Overview**; **Wheat.**

Kenneth John Carpenter

BIBLIOGRAPHY

Carpenter, K. J. *Beriberi, White Rice, and Vitamin B.* Berkeley: University of California Press, 2000.

Williams, R. R. *Toward the Conquest of Beriberi.* Cambridge, Mass.: Harvard University Press, 1961.

BERRIES. Wherever humans have lived, berries have been a part of their diet. Most of these have never developed beyond local markets but some have become globally important crops. Historically, berries were eaten fresh or processed into dried or fermented products. Many descriptions of indigenous American culture describe smoking and/or drying berries that are mixed with some sort of meat product to form Pemmican. As sugar became commonly available as a preservative, jams, preserves, and jellies became popular. With the development of the canning industry in the late 1800s, the freezing industry in the mid-1900s, and the global transportation system in the late 1900s, long-distance distribution and long-term storage began to spread a handful of berry crops throughout the world. Today, in any large grocery, fresh berries are available year round. Whereas berries used to be found only in the fresh produce and dessert sections, they are now found in every section as well as in the adjacent health food store as a nutritional supplement and in the liquor store as wine and distilled spirits. Historically, berries were welcomed as a pleasing and nutritious addition to a drab table. While this has not changed, the increased value placed on nutraceutical foods is likely to expand berry consumption even further. (Nutraceutical foods, also called functional foods, are foods that provide a medical or health benefit beyond the traditional nutrients they contain.)

Market globalization has led to the development of a group of major crops, often at the expense of still popular regional crops. This discussion is largely limited to the most economically important and well-known temperate "berry" crops that are produced on a shrub or a perennial herbaceous plant, including: strawberry (*Fragaria* X *ananassa*), blueberry (*Vaccinium corymbosum* and *V. angustifolium*), cranberry (*V. macrocarpon*), black currant (*Ribes nigrum*); red raspberry (*Rubus idaeus*), black raspberry (*Rubus occidentalis*), and blackberry (*Rubus* sp.).

Strawberry (*Fragaria*)

Plant biology. The cultivated strawberry (*Fragaria* X *ananassa*) is a low-growing, herbaceous perennial in the rose family (Rosaceae). Trifoliate leaves are produced from a crown as are the flowering trusses and runners. The hermaphroditic (both sexes present) flowers have white petals with many stamens surrounding a pistil-covered receptacle. The showy flowers are insect pollinated. Following successful pollination and fertilization, the achenes (seeds) set, and the receptacle tissue below the achenes swells and ripens. The crown also produces runners, which are elongated stolons that can root and form new "daughter" plants.

History. Strawberries are believed to have been cultivated in Greek and Latin gardens and they were mentioned by Pliny the Elder (23–79 C.E.) in his *Natural History*. Darrow reprints many examples of the use of strawberry in Christian religious art of the 1400s. The "X" in the Latin name for the cultivated strawberry, which indicates that it is a hybrid between two species, points to its interesting background. The Mapuche and Huilliche people of Chile were cultivating the native *F. chiloensis* at the time of the Spanish conquest in the mid-1500s and the plant was counted by the Spaniards as a spoil of war that they carried north into Peru and Ecuador. In 1711, Amédée François Frézier was commissioned by King Louis XIV of France to sail to Chile on an intelligence mission. In addition to mapping and observing Spanish activities, he explored the botany of the region. Five plants from Concepción survived the six-month voyage back to France in 1714. Frézier did not realize that the wild species are largely dioecious (separate male and female plants) and he had only collected female plants. As a result, these Chilean treasures were very uneven in their performance, producing little if any fruit in France. After many years of observation, gardeners realized that the plants were productive when grown with *F. virginiana*, the meadow strawberry, which the Europeans brought back from their colonies in eastern North America. Regardless of whether the hybridization of these two American species in France was intentional or happenstance, the result was the cultivated strawberry.

Fragaria chiloensis, the beach strawberry, ranges from Alaska to the central California coast in North America and Chile, primarily on dunes within the fog zone adjacent to the Pacific Ocean. *Fragaria virginiana* ranges throughout much of temperate North America except for the drier regions. New germ plasm (wild representatives of a species) from these two species have been used over time to introduce new traits into the cultivated strawberry and, in one case, this led to a revolution in the industry. While most strawberries produce flower buds in response to the shortening days of late summer and go

The *Witte Hollander* or White Dutch Currant, one of the oldest strains of white currants surviving from the late 1600s. It was developed in Holland and introduced into English and American gardens in the 1720s. ROUGHWOOD SEED COLLECTION, PHOTO WILLIAM WOYS WEAVER.

on to fruit the following spring, one population of *F. virginiana* from the Wasatch Mountains in Utah was found in the 1960s that, when grown in California, flowered and fruited regardless of day length. This "day-neutral" trait was incorporated into commercial cultivars and allows for nearly year-round production of fruit throughout the world.

Production, processing, and distribution. California is the most important production area in the world, and cultivars and production techniques developed there are commonly used throughout the world. Strawberries for the wholesale fresh market are grown on fumigated soils with plastic mulch and drip irrigation. The plants are primarily grown as an annual crop. Fruiting begins about two months after planting and continues for seven to nine months, after which the plants are removed. Fresh market strawberries are harvested directly into plastic clamshell packages that are then shipped under refrigeration. Strawberries for the processed market are either a by-product of the fresh market, that is, those that are too small or malformed, or they are harvested from cultivars specifically designed for the processed market. Processing cultivars have intense color and flavor, and maintain their integrity after processing. Strawberries are canned and dried but the primary raw processed products are as frozen IQF (individually quick frozen) berries, sugar and sliced packs, purees, or as juice. A tremendous diversity of consumer products are made from these primary raw products.

Strawberries, as with most berries, once had to be consumed locally due to perishability; however, with improved cultivars, production practices, packaging, and transportation, fresh fruit can be shipped long distances from the growers' fields.

Strawberries are a valuable source of vitamin C, fiber, folic acid, and anthocyanins (red pigment). Anthocyanins have been recently recognized for their nutraceutical benefit as antioxidants in human nutrition.

Red Raspberry, Black Raspberry, Blackberry, Caneberry, Bramble (*Rubus*)

Red (*Rubus idaeus*) and black raspberry (*R. occidentalis*), and blackberry (many diverse *Rubus* species), are the most important crops in the genus *Rubus*. In addition, some of the hybrids between red raspberry and blackberry such as "Boysen" and "Logan" and other species such as the cloudberry (*R. chamaemorus*) in Scandinavia, the wineberry (*R. phoenicolasius*) in Japan, the mora (*R. glaucus*) in Andean South America, and the trailing raspberry (*R. parvifolius*) in Asia have become regionally important crops. As a group, these species are often referred to as "caneberries" or "brambles."

Plant biology. Members of the Rosaceae discussed above have perennial root systems and biennial canes. With one exception, these biennial canes are vegetative the first year (primocanes) and produce fruit the second year (floricanes) before dying. The primocane/fall fruiting raspberries and, in the near future, blackberries are the exception, as they flower and produce fruit late in the season on first-year canes. Floricanes break bud in the spring and produce flowering branches with many insect-pollinated flowers. Flowers have white or light pink petals with a ring of many stamens that surround a pistil-covered receptacle (also called torus). After pollination and fertilization, each of the individual ovaries develops into a drupelet, which collectively form the aggregate fruit. Raspberries are differentiated from blackberries based on whether the torus remains on the plant when the fruit is picked (raspberries) or whether it is picked with the fruit (blackberries).

Raspberry history. Red raspberry is native throughout the colder temperate regions of the Northern Hemisphere and black raspberry throughout the midwestern and mid-Atlantic regions of the United States. The first red raspberries were introduced into cultivation in Europe about 450 years ago, according to Hedrick, and European cultivars were brought to North America prior to 1800. Black raspberries were commonly picked from the wild in North America and the first named cultivars began appearing in the 1850s.

Red raspberry. While raspberries today are grown throughout the world in temperate regions, their production is concentrated in eastern Europe and the Pacific Northwest of North America. Berries from these two regions are primarily processed as IQF, purees, or juice, and these basic raw products serve as the basis for innumerable consumer products. Trellised, irrigated, long-term, perennial plantings that are mechanically harvested are standard for the processing industry. Production for the fresh market is evolving rapidly, with California and Mexico as the production centers for the Americas and Germany in Europe. Chile, New Zealand, and Australia are the major suppliers of fresh fruit during winter in the Northern Hemisphere. For the fresh market, plants are grown either in a perennial system or, as in California, for one and a half years, during which two crops are produced, and then the plants are removed. Fruit for the fresh market are hand-picked and generally produced under protective plastic hoop structures.

Black raspberry. While there are many scattered small plantings of black raspberries throughout North America to serve local fresh market needs, the bulk of the industry is concentrated in Oregon's Willamette Valley. Black raspberries are grown in hedges about one by one meter in short-term (three- to four-year) perennial plantings that are machine harvested. While some black raspberry jam is produced, the berries are primarily processed as juice and often used as a natural colorant.

Blackberry. Blackberries are native throughout Eurasia and the Americas, although the primary commercial cultivars were developed from species native to North America. Erect and semierect cultivars were derived from eastern North American species and these can be characterized by being upright-growing, firm-fruited, large-seeded, and more suitable for the fresh market than for processing. These types are generally grown in small, long-term, perennial plantings throughout the United States, with a higher concentration of acreage on the western coast of the United States. For the processing market, the trailing blackberry cultivars, particularly "Marion" (often called Marion berry), are grown in long-term, trellised plantings that are harvested by machine for the processing market. This industry is concentrated in Oregon's Willamette Valley, although Mexico is expanding production. Fruit is processed as IQF, purees, and juice, and these are used to produce many consumer products.

Variations in regional demand. Demand for the various types of caneberries shows marked geographical trends. Since the caneberries have always been picked from the wild near where people have lived, there are many small but regionally significant industries that have developed around these crops. While red and black raspberry and blackberry dominate the worldwide market, travelers in Andean South America or Scandinavia will find an abundance of products made from the regionally grown mora or cloudberry, respectively. In North America, the region where one grew up often influenced what kind of caneberry one preferred, with southerners preferring blackberry and northerners preferring red raspberry.

Uses and nutrition. Until the late part of the 1900s, raspberries and blackberries were primarily used to make jams and jellies or desserts. Now these crops have been incorporated into myriad products that require juices. Blackberries and raspberries are an excellent source of vitamin C, calcium, fiber, iron, and folic acid. The increased interest in nutraceutical products focuses special interest on these crops. While blueberries and cranberries have been touted for their proven health benefits, the anthocyanins (pigments that give the fruits their red and purple colors), which are powerful antioxidants, are even more concentrated in blackberries and raspberries, especially in black raspberries.

Blueberry, Cranberry, Lingonberry (Vaccinium)

Plant biology. Blueberry, cranberry, and lingonberry are all long-lived perennial crops in the Ericaceous family. These crops were originally native to acidic and moist soils with high organic matter levels in cool temperate regions of the Northern Hemisphere. Blueberries are upright-growing plants with long-lived perennial canes. Highbush blueberry (*Vaccinium corymbosum*), native to the eastern United States, is a shrubby, crown-forming bush (1–2.5 m) and is the basis for most of the cultivated blueberry industry. Lowbush blueberry (*V. angustifolium*), native to the northern United States and southern Canada, is a small bush (0.5 m) that spreads by underground stems. Managed wild stands of the lowbush in eastern Canada and eastern Maine are the basis for the "wild" blueberry industry. Cranberry (*V. macrocarpon*) is a creeping plant that produces fruiting uprights and is native to boggy areas of the northern United States and southern Canada. Lingonberry (*V. vitis-idaea*) is a short-statured (0.3 m) plant that spreads by underground stems, and while it is found circumboreally, it has been primarily developed into a crop in Scandinavia and northern Europe.

Blueberry. Blueberries produce clusters of hanging bell-shaped white or light pink flowers in the spring. The insect-pollinated flowers swell to form a true berry that contains many very small seeds. When ripe, the fruit have a bluish black skin covered by a waxy bloom that gives them their bright blue appearance.

Blueberries are truly an "all-American" crop, as they were native to this continent, developed as a crop on this continent, and, until the late 1900s, were not well known outside of this continent. In the early 1900s, a grower in New Jersey began to work with the U.S. Department of Agriculture (USDA) to develop improved blueberries. From these modest beginnings, the USDA went on to release all of the cultivars, which led to highbush blueberries' rise from a little-known "swamp plant" to one of the most important berry crops worldwide. While lowbush blueberries have not been changed by breeding, the production practices have become highly developed since the first Europeans harvested the expanses of mixed lowbush blueberry and forest lands in Maine and eastern Canada that Native Americans had harvested for generations.

Highbush blueberry production is concentrated in North Carolina, New Jersey, Michigan, and the Pacific Northwest, and the much smaller European industry is primarily in Germany and France. Chile, New Zealand, and Australia are major suppliers in the winter months in the Northern Hemisphere. Today plants are grown on ridged plantings, with irrigation and pest control, and they are harvested by machine for processing markets. The berries for the fresh market are harvested, cooled, packed in plastic clamshells, and shipped around the world. Fresh blueberries are often stored for up to two months in a controlled atmosphere.

Early growers and commercial canners recognized that if they burned their "wild" lowbush fields every other year, they could more easily harvest the abundant fruit in the intermediate year. Field burning not only managed growth, but it eliminated many of the competing plants, insects, and diseases. While lowbush blueberries were never planted by man, they are really no longer "wild" since the larger commercial operations are intensively managed, as are the highbush blueberries. Lowbush blueberries are harvested by hand with rakes and, where the ground surface area permits, by machines for processing.

Lowbush and highbush blueberries are processed as IQF, purees, juice, and dried products. One of the reasons that blueberry consumption and production rose so dramatically at the end of the twentieth century was their suitability for many processed products (for example, they have no noticeable seeds or pits, they blend well with other products, and their flavor is not intense so they can be used very widely).

Blueberries are an excellent source of vitamin C and fiber. Anecdotal stories from World War II attributed the supposedly better night vision of British pilots to their consumption of bilberry (*V. myrtillus*) jam. Decades later, in the 1990s, the benefits of bilberry to the health of microcapillaries and as a powerful antioxidant were documented by medical research. Subsequently, blueberry, which is more readily available for mass consumption than bilberry, was studied and was found to have a similar chemical constituency, although sometimes at a lower concentration than in bilberry.

Cranberry. Cranberry, originally called "craneberry" by early immigrants to North America due to the shape of the flower, was used by Native Americans as a food, a medicine, and a dye long before Europeans arrived. Native to northern temperate areas from Minnesota to the Atlantic Ocean, cranberries were first cultivated in Massachusetts in the early 1800s. While many cultural changes have improved production, most of the cultivars grown today are selections from the wild or superior plants found in growers' bogs. Bog establishment is a very expensive process that involves land leveling, water system management, soil amendments, and diking. Since the development of wetlands is tightly regulated in North America, establishing new bogs there is becoming increasingly difficult. The vining plants produce uprights that produce flowers. With insect pollination, the flowers are fertilized and the fruit develop. In early fall, the fields are flooded and specialized machines beat the fruit off the plant where they can float to the surface and be skimmed off into trucks. While many have the image of cranberries growing in water, they are actually not tolerant of flooding for extended periods, so fields are drained immediately after harvest. For commercial bogs in very cold climates, water is layered into the fields in early winter, and after each layer freezes, another is added, eventually covering the plants and protecting them from the harsh climate. Fruit is primarily processed into juice. A small portion of the crop is sold fresh for the Thanksgiving and Christmas holiday season, and there is a growing market for dried, sweetened cranberries ("craisins"). Cranberries have a long association with holidays, particularly American Thanksgiving. In 1959, just before the holiday season, a pesticide scare swept the United States, closing all outlets for fresh cranberries, and much of the crop was dumped. This disaster further spurred the development of a wider variety of products. The Ocean Spray growers cooperative, formed in the 1930s, did a remarkable job of expanding cranberry demand in the late 1900s, particularly through their well-known fruit juices.

Cranberry juice has been a well-known home remedy for women seeking relief from yeast infections in their urinary tract. In the 1990s, medical research documented that consumption of cranberry juice could cure yeast infections. In addition, cranberries are a rich source of vitamin C, fiber, and anthocyanins, which are powerful antioxidants.

Lingonberry. Lingonberries have always been closely tied with the people of Scandinavia and northern Europe, where much of the commercial crop is still harvested from wild stands. When cultivated, the plants are established in rows that fill in quickly with growing underground stems. Two crops are produced in long season areas; the summer crop is usually not harvested, but the fall crop is harvested for holiday sales. While machines are being developed to harvest lingonberries, hand raking is still the predominant method of harvest. Lingonberries most often remind people of a "mild" cranberry. As such, they can usually be used in similar applications to fresh cranberries and are popular as preserves and relishes.

Black Currant, Gooseberry, Red Currant (Ribes)

Gooseberries and currants are members of the Saxifrage family that have been prized in Europe and Russia for centuries but have not developed a strong market elsewhere. Gooseberries and red currants have very interesting histories, but their production is tiny compared to black currant and they will not be discussed in detail. Part of the reason that currants and gooseberries have not developed a following in the United States is that growing them has been banned in many states, as they are an alternate host for white pine blister rust, which can be devastating to the white pine timber trade.

Plant biology, history, and production. These crown-forming, long-lived perennial shrubs produce their fruit on woody, one-year-old, smooth canes (gooseberries have thorns). Buds along the cane produce strigs that have from eight to thirty flowers in the spring. The flowers are not showy, typically light green or yellow colored, but are attractive to insects for pollination. Black currants (*Ribes nigrum*) are native to the cooler regions of Eurasia and can tolerate extremely cold winter temperatures. Despite being found in close association with humans for a long time, they were largely used as a medicinal plant until fairly recently. Hedrick quotes an herbal from 1633 that says black currants are "of a stinking and somewhat loathing savour."

Uses and nutrition. Beginning in the 1900s, juice products from currants were developed, the most famous being Ribena, as it was recognized that the high vitamin C content of black currants could be maintained when juiced. In a sense, black currant juice has been to Europeans what orange juice was to Americans. In addition to vitamin C, black currants are a rich source of antioxidants, vitamin A, and calcium. Black currants are grown almost exclusively for processing as juice. Plants, primarily cultivars developed in the United Kingdom or Russia, are cultivated in hedgerows that are mechanically harvested. Fruit is bulk frozen and then juiced.

Lesser-Known Crops

As was first mentioned, wherever humans have lived they have made berries a part of their diet, and as such there are innumerable berries not mentioned here that are part of the human diet. Some examples of other berries that have generated renewed or new interest, in addition to red currant and gooseberry, include aronia (*Aronia melanocarpa*), elderberry (*Sambucus nigra/S. canadensis*), sea buckthorn (*Hippophae rahmnoides*), juneberry/serviceberry/saskatoon (*Amelanchier* sp.) and edible honeysuckle (*Lonicera caerulea*) (Finn). However, unless they have unique characteristics, such as high nutraceutical value, they are unlikely to significantly impact the production and consumption of the major crops.

See also **Fruit; Nutraceuticals; Pesticides; Wine.**

BIBLIOGRAPHY

Darrow, G. M. "Strawberry Improvement." In *Yearbook of the United States Department of Agriculture, 1937.* Washington, D.C.: Government Printing Office, 1937.

Finn, Chad. "Temperate Berry Crops." In *Perspectives on New Crops and New Uses,* edited by Jules Janick. Alexandria, Va.: ASHS Press, 1999.

Hedrick, U. P. *The Small Fruits of New York.* Albany, N.Y.: J. B. Lyon Co., 1925.

Chad Elliott Finn

BETTY CROCKER. Betty Crocker, an American cultural icon, was created in 1921 by the advertising department of the Washburn Crosby milling company just before it merged with General Mills. The consummate homemaker who could answer any cooking question with ease, Betty Crocker was based upon several real women, the two most notable being home economists Janette Kelley and Marjorie Child Husted.

Neither her name nor her face, which has been updated numerous times, was real. Both, however, became synonymous with good cooking and competent homemaking through newspaper columns, radio programs, television spots, and the publication of over 150 cookbooks. Betty Crocker's most significant contribution came in 1951 with the publication of *Betty Crocker's Picture Cookbook,* which remains a top-selling cookbook today. Unlike the extremely thorough *The Joy of Cooking* by Irma Rombauer, *Betty Crocker's Picture Cookbook* helped women cook by including both large illustrations and recipes on one page.

Betty Crocker's image and what it represents has created an automatic acceptance by consumers of numerous General Mills products from breads to cake mixes. Perhaps more important, her icon status has given her an active role in American life. Betty Crocker has helped generations of American women over the years deal with challenges including food scarcity during the Depression and World War II, a renewed emphasis on homemaking in the postwar years, and the increasing sophistication of American taste. From cutting food costs to increasing women's satisfaction through cooking to adding new ingredients to update old recipes, Betty Crocker continues to keep her finger on the pulse of American life and to respond accordingly.

See also **Advertising of Food; Baking; Cake and Pancake; Cookbooks; Cooking; Marketing of Food.**

BIBLIOGRAPHY

DuSablon, Mary Anna. *America's Collectible Cookbooks: The History, the Politics, the Recipes.* Athens: Ohio University Press, 1984.

Levenstein, Harvey. *Paradox of Plenty: A Social History of Eating in Modern America.* New York: Oxford University Press, 1993.

Erika A. Endrijonas

BETTY CROCKER MAKEOVER

1936   1955   1965   1968

1972   1980   1986   1996

General Mills created Betty Crocker in 1921 as a kind of mother figure to promote the company's food products. Over the years, Betty has undergone a number of makeovers to keep her in tune with changing perceptions about homemakers and cooking. These eight pictures show how she has changed since 1936. One thing has remained consistent: she is always dressed in red. © AP/WIDE WORLD PHOTOS.

BIBLE, FOOD IN THE. Food and drink are everywhere in the Bible. Among the best-known scenes are the Last Supper (Mark 14:17–25; Matthew 26:20–29; Luke 22:14–23; John 13:1–14, 13:31), the feeding of the five thousand (Mark 6:30–44, 8:1–10), the feast for the lost son (Luke 15:11–32), and the wine miracle in Cana (John 2:1–12) from the New Testament and the first Pesach meal in Egypt (Exodus 12:1–13, 12:16); Abraham's sacrifice of Isaac, for whom a wild goat was substituted (Genesis 22:1–19); the manna in the desert (Exodus 16:31–35); and the recurring mention of the land flowing with milk and honey from the Old Testament. The function of food in the Bible is twofold. First, it offers information on what was produced and consumed in the area in biblical times, including how food was prepared and its meaning; second, it conveys messages to the reader.

Attitudes toward Food in the Bible

Scientific interest in food in the Bible always has focused on, among other things, sacrifice and abominations (Bolle; Bourdillion and Fortes; Douglas; James; and Smith). The biblical sacrificial animal is rarely burnt entirely, as indicated in the descriptions of some specific sacrifices in Numbers 28 and 29 or Abraham's sacrifice. The majority of a sacrifice is consumed either by those who offer the sacrifice or by the priests (1 Samuel 1–2). Each food offering (the meat) is accompanied by a grain offering (flour and olive oil) and a drink offering (preferably wine,

One of the most popular food scenes in the Bible is the Marriage of Cana, which has allowed Christian artists down through the centuries to employ their creative talents on imagery drawn from their own life experience. Italian Renaissance painter Giotto di Bondone (d. 1337) created this dinner scene as it would have appeared in a nobleman's house around the early 1300s. © ARCHIVO ICONOGRAFICO, S.A./CORBIS.

but in some cases beer is acceptable) (Numbers 28–29). Sacrifices, usually offered at feasts, distribute precious animal protein evenly among the population and over time. A feast occurs on each new moon, and others follow in the middle of at least every second month.

The nature of the sacrifice follows the rules of purity described in Leviticus. No restrictions apply to the consumption of plants, but elaborate rules govern animal food. Animals are divided into three groups: animals on land, creatures in the water, and birds. Of these only a small sample are considered clean: "You may eat any an-

imal which has a parted foot or a cloven hoof and also chews the cud; . . . all those that have fins and scales," and birds with two legs who fly and do not eat carcasses (Leviticus 11). The purity rules conform with the animals well adapted to the local climate and easily domesticated. Furthermore the food taboos keep the Israelites distinct from other peoples of the region, supporting their group identity. When Christianity starts to convert other peoples, the strict food rules become an obstacle and therefore are removed. According to Acts 10 it was revealed to Peter that nothing is unclean.

Meat is always in the foreground of biblical narratives on food, and it is the highly esteemed center of any festive meal, religious or secular. During their wanderings in the wilderness, the Israelites yearn for the fleshpots of Egypt (Exodus 16:2); in 1 Samuel 2:12–17 the priests demand a piece of good roast from the sacrifice instead of being content with whatever their forks catch from the cauldron; it is a sign of honor to be fed a piece of meat by the host (1 Samuel 9:23); and meat is essential to a covenant. Nevertheless, the staples are cereals (barley, wheat, emmer, spelt, millet, and sorghum). Barley, the most important, is mainly consumed as grits (porridge); wheat is valued higher and is baked into bread. The highly valued fruits include olives for oil, which is easy to store, and dates, which provide energy. Vegetables (leek, orache, onion), pulses (fava bean, pea, lentil, chickpea), fruits (apple, fig, pomegranate, melon, mulberry, grape), and herbs and spices (cassia, cinnamon, coriander, cumin, dill, garlic, ginger, laurel, mint, mustard, saffron, turmeric) are abundant.

Situations of Consumption

Among the most prominent situations for consuming specific foods are feasts, covenant meals, carouses, and fasts. The majority of religious feasts consist of the sacrifice of animals—usually birds, sheep, goats, or cattle, depending on the means of the family—and the communal meal of the family. The important religious feasts are Pesach (Passover), Massot (Feast of Unleavened Bread), Shavuot (Pentecost), Rosh Hashanah (New Year), Yom Kippur (Day of Atonement), Succoth (Feast of Tabernacles), Hanukah (Festival of Lights), and Purim (Feast of Lots). Life-cycle festivals mentioned in the Bible include weddings, birthdays, and burials. For the wedding of Jacob and Leah, "Laban gathered all the men of the place together and gave a feast" (Genesis 29:22); when Samson marries, the party lasts seven days (Judges 14:12); Raguel tells his wife Edna "to bake a great batch of bread" and has two oxen and four rams slaughtered for the two weeks of celebrating the marriage of Tobias and Sarah (Tobit 8:20); Jesus compares heaven to the wedding feast of a king's son (Matthew 22:1); the wedding party at Cana-in-Galilee runs short of wine, and Jesus turns water to wine (John 2:1–12). The only birthday party mentioned in the Bible is the Egyptian pharaoh's, which turns out to be the day of destiny for the chief baker and the chief butler when one is hanged the other restored to his service (Genesis 40:20). The bread to console and the cup of consolation are the frugal nutrients for mourners, who often refuse to eat and drink for a short time after the death of a beloved or fast for a longer period to display their mourning.

The covenant meal as a pact between people or between God and his followers is a recurrent theme. This meal makes the oath binding forever by threatening the partners' bodies with a curse. In case of perjury, the curse "may seep into his body like water and into his bones like oil" (Psalms 109:18). God's covenants with Abraham and Moses are sealed by the ritual slaughtering of several animals (Genesis 15; Exodus 24). When Jacob leaves Laban's home, they swear an oath regarding the respective territories and have a feast with their kinspeople (Genesis 31:43–54). Joseph is sold to the passing tradesmen while his brothers "sat down to eat some food" (Genesis 37:25). Sharing provisions with the inhabitants of Gibeon, Joshua settles a pact with the Gibeonites (Joshua 9:14–15). Those who share a meal are obligees, but they frequently betray each other (Psalms 41:9; Proverbs 23:7; Mark 14:18). The New Covenant is made at the Last Supper (Matthew 26:17–30; Mark 14:12–26; Luke 22:7–39; John 13:1–30).

Biblical authors highly value wine and beer but oppose any abuse. Nevertheless, carousals are frequently mentioned and are often connected with licentiousness. Lot's two daughters intoxicate their father with wine "and then lie with him" (Genesis 19:32). The author of the book of Ecclesiasticus (also known as Sirach) dissuades a man from sitting with a woman and drinking wine (Ecclesiasticus 9:13). Holofernes wants to dine with Judith and intends to seduce her. When he drinks too much, he falls asleep, and Judith decapitates him (Judith 12–13).

Important figures like Moses, Jesus, and Paul fast at times of particular spiritual, psychological intensity.

THE STORY OF JUDITH

The story of Judith in the book of Judith exemplifies the meaning the Israelite society accorded to food. The behavior of the two protagonists presupposes their respective fates. Judith, the shining heroine who finally saves the Israelites from the Assyrian siege, always does the right things. She fasts except on religious feasts, she only eats pure food, and she is never drunk. On the other hand Holofernes, the commander in chief of the Assyrian army, is a glutton and drunkard who gives dinner parties every day. This is the starting point for Judith's project to rescue her people. She goes to Holofernes's tent dressed in her best clothes and prettily adorned, but she sits at her own table and consumes her own pure food, only pretending to be his guest. Holofernes is blinded by the beauty of the Israelite lady and does not realize she is not truly participating in his party. He eats and drinks until he is so drunk he is incapable of seducing her. When he falls asleep, Judith cuts his head off. Deprived of their leader, the Assyrians withdraw, and Judith is celebrated as the savior of the Israelites.

Moses abstains from eating and drinking for forty days before he climbs up Mount Sinai to bring down the Ten Commandments (Exodus 34:28; Deuteronomy 9:9). These forty days recur in the New Testament when Jesus goes to the desert before he starts to preach (Matthew 4:2–11; Mark 1:12–13; Luke 4:1–13). The Christian interpretation is that everything Jesus says afterward is comparable to Moses' commandments. Paul fasts as a sign of a new beginning after his conversion (Acts 9:9). Whenever the Israelites are at war, they proclaim a general fasting (Judges 20:26; 1 Samuel 14:24–32; 2 Chronicles 20:3; Ezra 8:21–23; Esther 4:15–16; 1 Maccabees 3:46–60). The mourner refuses to eat (Genesis 49:10; Numbers 20:29; 2 Samuel 1:12, 3:35). The preparatory fasting before a religious feast is meant to purify the individual and the community (Leviticus 16:29, 23:26; Numbers 29:7; 2 Kings 25:4–8; Zechariah 7:5, 8:19).

Preparation of Food

On most biblical occasions it is the women's domain to prepare food. They pound the grains in mortars or use hand mills (Numbers 11:8). From barley they prepare the grits (Leviticus 2:14), sometimes after roasting the barley (Ruth 2:14). They grind the wheat and then bake bread, cake, or biscuits (Genesis 18:6; Leviticus 2:2; 1 Kings 5:2). Bread is leavened or unleavened (Exodus 12:15; Numbers 9:11; Deuteronomy 16:2; Joshua 5:11). Butter and cheese are made from the milk of cows and sheep (Genesis 18:8; 2 Samuel 17:29; Isaiah 7:22). Meat is boiled in a cauldron (1 Samuel 2:13) or roasted on a fire and seasoned with herbs and spices (Exodus 12).

Meanings of Food in the Biblical Text

Food is integral to communicating the biblical message. Food characterizes situations and persons, and it structures and marks the dramatic development of the text. Metaphors frequently consist of gastronomic terms, and many of Jesus' parables are connected with food. Two important culinary fantasies active in modern texts or imaginations are Cockaigne and cannibalism.

Naming is a simple way to convey something about a person. Biblical figures often have figurative names, many derived from food. Adam, the ancestor of all humankind, is made "from red clay," a soil good for growing certain crops. Adam is described in a close relationship to agriculture, and the moment he leaves paradise he starts farming: "So the Lord God drove him out of the garden of Eden to till the ground from which he had been taken" (Genesis 3:23). Names like Leah, Rachel, Rebecca, Egla, and Tamar express the qualities of the women bearing them. Leah, which means "cow," and Rachel, which means "mother sheep," become the mothers of the twelve tribes (Genesis 29). Rebecca, "cow," is Isaac's wife and Jacob's mother (Genesis 24, 25, 26). Tamar, "date palm," is the name of a number of influential women from Genesis to Matthew. The women important to Israel are named after animals and plants fundamental to subsistence in the Near East, part of

everyday experience, and available, tame, and reliable. They guarantee survival, and they provide milk, meat, and fruit. In contrast, women and men named after wild animals, often favorite game animals, do not play any important role in the history of Israel. Associated with sexual situations, their names indicate they are beautiful, elegant, charming, and erotic. Examples include Dishon, Epher, Tabitha, and Zibiaha, which mean "gazelle"; Hoglah, which means "partridge"; and Zipporah, which means "bird" (Genesis 36:21; Exodus 2:16–22; Numbers 12:1; Judges 11:25; 1 Chronicles 1:38; 2 Kings 12:2; Joshua 17:3; Acts 9:36–41).

A person's character is revealed in his or her good behavior at table. A negative figure is usually depicted as lacking good table manners, such as eating and drinking too much, consuming impure food, choosing a wrong seat according to the hierarchy, and general immoderateness. Frequently such people are killed, and their bodies become food for the dogs (1 Kings 14:11, 21:23; Psalms 68:24; Jeremiah 15:3). Good and ideal people eat and drink moderately. They are modest and hospitable, and they carefully choose their food and their company at table.

Feasts and fasts not only structure the year of the community and the life cycles of individuals, they also mark climaxes and happy events, for instance, when people meet after a long separation (Genesis 43:25–34; Luke 15:11–32), on the occasion of a wedding (Genesis 29:22; Judges 14; Matthew 22:1; John 2:1–12), before people part for some time (Genesis 31:54; John 13; Acts 20:7), and when a war is won (Genesis 14:17; 1 Samuel 14:32; Esther 9:17; 1 Maccabees 4:23). Plenty of food and drink is typical of every feast, often indicating that the story is over and everything went well (Judith 16:18–20; Nehemiah 8:10; 2 Maccabees 10:6). Hunger moves people from one place to another, as when Abraham moves to Egypt (Genesis 12:10), when Jacob's family does the same (Genesis 46), and when hunger brings David's pious ancestor Ruth to the family (Ruth). Fasting marks turning points, as when the sterile Hannah prays, fasts, and finally conceives Samuel (1 Samuel 1:7) when the warriors fast before the decisive battle, they will win (Judges 20:26; 2 Chronicles 20:3; Ezra 8:21–23).

The recurrent combination of "milk and honey" can be called a biblical leitmotif and is one of the best-known biblical gastronomic metaphors. Milk and honey are highly valued products, symbols of the wealth of a country. The land God promised to Abraham and his children, usually identified with Canaan, "is a land flowing with milk and honey" (Exodus 3:8, 3:17, 13:5, 33:3; Leviticus 20:24; Numbers 13:27, 14:8; 16:13–14; Deuteronomy 6:3, 11:9, 26:9, 26:15, 27:3, 31:20; Joshua 5:6; Ecclesiasticus [Sirach] 46:8; Jeremiah 11:5, 32:22; Ezekiel 20:6, 20:15). The cup is a metaphor for life or death (Isaiah 51:17–23; Jeremiah 25:15–29, 49:12, 51:7; Ezekiel 23:31–34; Obadiah 16; Habakkuk 2:15–16; Zechariah 12:2; Psalms 16:5, 23:5; Mark 10:38; Matthew 23:25; Revelation 17:4; 1 Corinthians 10:21), and the cup of the

Eucharist is the culminating point in the New Testament (Matthew 26:26–29; Mark 14:22–25; Luke 22:19–20). Psalms 23 is the poetically outstanding citation of the metaphor for the relation between Israel and God, the shepherd and his herd.

Pictures of the other world are deeply rooted in worldly experiences, of which food and eating and drinking are most important. Good and evil, heaven and hell are described with an abundance of excellent food and drink or with hunger, starvation, and cannibalism respectively. The promised land Canaan is expected to produce plenty of food, and paradise is the place without hunger. The Garden of Eden is described in contrast to the place where Adam must work hard to eat his bread (Genesis 2–3). The garden is lost forever, but after death the good will be rewarded. Job states that for the wicked the other world will not "swill down rivers of cream or torrents of honey and curds" (20:17), implying that it will for the good. The New Testament promises all those who believe in Jesus will be invited to the never-ending heavenly feast with Abraham, Isaac, and Jacob or to "the wedding-supper of the Lamb" (Matthew 8:11, 22:2–14, 26:29; Luke 12:37, 13:29, 14:15, 22:16, 22:30; Revelation 3:20, 19:9, 19:17).

If Israel conforms to the commandments, the reward will be fertility and abundance (Leviticus 26:3–13; Deuteronomy 28:1–4). But if the people do not hold the commandments, God will curse them with infertility of the land and the people (Leviticus 26:20–39; Deuteronomy 28), thistles and thorns will grow instead of corn [wheat, not maize] and fruit in the fields (Genesis 3:18; Job 31:40; Wisdom 24:31; Isaiah 5:6, 32:13; Jeremiah 12:13; Hebrews 6:8). People will be driven to eat unclean food (2 Kings 6:25; 2 Maccabees 6:18–20, 7:1; Isaiah 65:4, 66:3, 66:17; Ezekiel 4:9; Daniel 1:8), they will suffer from hunger and will starve to death (Deuteronomy 28:48, 32:24; 2 Samuel 24:13; 1 Chronicles 21:12; Psalms 34:11, 105:16; Isaiah 32:6; Jeremiah 11:22, 42:16; Luke 6:25; Revelation 18:8), and worst of all they will eat their own children (Leviticus 26:27–29; Deuteronomy 28:53–57; Lamentations 4:10; Zechariah 11:9). Eating one's own children on the one hand is the worst of sins and on the other hand is the strongest punishment for sinning. Eating the children is the reversal of giving birth. Instead of propagating humankind and the family, society is endangered. If people do this willingly, they violate God's wish to have a great number of followers, but if they violate his commandments, he will end their existence. To be without children means to be without a future, the name of the family extinguished forever. Living on in Israel means living on in future generations, as the many genealogies show (Genesis 4:20, 10:21, 17:4–16, 19:30–38, 25:12–18, 36:9; Exodus 1:5; Ruth 4:18–22; 1 Chronicles 2–8; Matthew 1:1–17).

See also **Christianity; Fasting and Abstinence; Feasts, Festivals, and Fasts; Judaism; Religion and Food; Sacrifice; Sin and Food.**

BIBLIOGRAPHY

Bolle, Kees W. "A World of Sacrifice." *History of Religions* 23 (1983): 37–63.

Bourdillion, Michael F. C., and Meyer Fortes, eds. *Sacrifice.* London: Academic Press, 1980.

Douglas, Mary. "The Abominations of Leviticus." In *Purity and Danger.* London: Routledge and K. Paul, 1999.

Douglas, Mary. *Leviticus as Literature.* Oxford: Oxford University Press, 1999.

Feeley-Harnik, Gillian. *The Lord's Table: Eucharist and Passover in Early Christianity.* Philadelphia: University of Pennsylvania Press, 1981.

Ferguson, Walter W. *Living Animals of the Bible.* New York: Scribner, 1974.

James, E. O. *Sacrifice and Sacrament.* London: Thames and Hudson, 1962.

Schmitt, Eleonore. *Das Essen in der Bibel* [Eating in the Bible]. Münster: LitVerlag, 1994.

Smith, Denis Edwin. "Table Fellowship as a Literary Motif in the Gospel of Luke." *Journal of Biblical Literature* 106 (1987): 613–638.

Smith, William Robertson. *Lectures on the Religion of the Semites.* Edinburgh: Black, 1889.

Zohary, Michael, and Naomi Feinbrun-Dothan. *Flora Palaestina.* 4 parts. Jerusalem: Israel Academy of Sciences and Humanities, 1966–1986.

Eleonore Schmitt

BIOACTIVE FOOD COMPONENTS. The term "bioactive food component" refers to nonessential biomolecules that are present in foods and exhibit the capacity to modulate one or more metabolic processes, which results in the promotion of better health. Bioactive food components are usually found in multiple forms such as glycosylated, esterified, thiolyated, or hydroxylated. Bioactive food components also have multiple metabolic activities allowing for beneficial effects in several diseases and target tissues. In general, it is thought that bioactive food components are predominantly found in plant foods such as whole grains, fruit, and vegetables. However, probiotics, conjugated linolenic acid, long-chain omega-3 polyunsaturated fatty acid, and bioactive peptides are most commonly found in animal products such as milk, fermented milk products and cold-water fish.

Table 1 summarizes the biological function and food sources for both plant- and animal-based bioactive food components. However, a review of both plant- and animal-based bioactive food components is beyond the scope of this article. Therefore, this article will focus on plant-based bioactive food components.

Common Forms Found in Foods

There are myriad bioactive food components in plant-based foods. A partial list includes the polyphenols, phytosterols, carotenoids, tocopherols, tocotrienols, organosulfur compounds including isothiocyanates and diallyl- (di, tri)sulfide compounds, soluble and insoluble fiber, and fruto-ogliosaccharide. It is most common to find mixtures of these compounds within a plant food rarely is one class of bioactive food component found singly.

Polyphenols are the most numerous and widely distributed group of bioactive molecules. Polyphenols are a diverse group of plant substances that contain one or more benzene rings and varying number of hydroxyl (OH), carbonyl (C=O), and carboxylic acid (COOH) groups. These commonly exist with one or more attached sugar residues (that is, conjugated). The most common class of polyphenols is the flavonoids. Other types of polyphenols include catechins, thearubingens, theaflavins, isoflavones, and over eight thousand others. Food sources of polyphenols and flavonoids include vegetables, fruits, cereals, legumes, nuts, tea, wine and other beverages made with fruit, vegetables, and grains. The polyphenol content can vary tremendously between food sources and within foods of the same type. For example, Bravo (1998) reported the following ranges for total polyphenols in barley and millet as 590 to 1,500 mg/100 g dry matter, 8.7 to 30.9 mg/100 g dry matter for oats and corn, 20 to 2,025 mg/g fresh onions and leeks, and 6 to 15 mg/100 g fresh brussels sprouts. For blueberries, strawberries, cranberries, and raspberries the total polyphenol content is 37 to 429 mg/100 g berries.

The organosulfur compounds are commonly found in cruciferous vegetables such as broccoli, cauliflower, and brussels sprouts or allium vegetables such as garlic, leeks, and onions. Organosulfur compounds contain sulfur atoms that are bound to a cyanate group or a carbon atom in a cyclic or noncyclic configuration. The bioactive components of foods containing organosulfur compounds are obtained only after cutting, chewing, or crushing has damaged the vegetable. In cruciferous vegetables various isothiocyanates such as sulforaphane, phenethyl-isothiocyanate, and benzyl isothiocyanate are formed from glucosinolyates by the action of myrosinase. In alliums, allicin is formed from alliin and then rapidly converted to diallyl sulfide, diallyl disulfide or diallyl trisulfide by the action of allinase. In both cruciferous and allium vegetables, these hydrolytic breakdown products are the health-promoting bioactive food components.

Phytosterols are the plant counterparts of cholesterol in animals. The structures are similar, however; the side-chain in plant sterols contains additional double bonds and methyl and/or ethyl groups. The most common bioactive phytosterols are beta-sitosterol, campesterol, and stigmasterol. The nonvegetarian diet contains approximately 250 mg/day of unsaturated phytosterols while a vegetarian diet contains over 500 mg/day. The best food sources include nuts, seeds, unrefined plant oils, and legumes. The saturated derivatives of plant sterols are plant stanols, the most common being sitostanol. Plant stanols occur naturally in wood pulp, tall oil, and soybean oil, but are most commonly obtained in the diet by chemical hydrogenation of plant sterols. Western diets contain approximately 20 to 50 milligrams of plant stanols.

The carotenoids are lipid-soluble plant pigments that are either oxygenated or non-oxygenated hydrocarbon containing at least forty carbons and an extensive conjugated double bond system. Beta-carotene, alpha-carotene, and lycopene are the predominant nonpolar bioactive carotenoids and lutein is the primary polar bioactive carotenoid. Carotenoids can be found esterifed to fatty acids or unesterifed in plant tissue. Carrots, squash, sweet potato, and spinach are abundant in both beta- and alpha-carotene and the dark green leafy vegetables such as kale, spinach, mustard greens, and green beans are good sources of lutein. Lycopene is found predominately in tomatoes. The total carotenoid content of fruits and vegetables varies with age and storage (Parker).

The tocopherols and tocotrienols are lipid-soluble bioactive compounds that contain a phenolic-chromanol ring linked to an isoprenoid side chain that is either saturated (tocopherols) or unsaturated (tocotrienols). There are also four primary forms of tocopherols and tocotrienols—alpha, beta, gamma, and delta—that differ in the number and position of methyl groups on the phenolic-chromanol ring. In addition, the tocopherols have three asymmetrical carbons at position 2, 4', and 8' of the isoprenoid side chain. Consequently, there are eight isomeric forms of tocopherols, of which RRR-a-tocopherol has the greatest bioactivity and is also the most abundant in human blood and tissues. Typical dietary sources of both tocopherol and tocotrienols include vegetable oils; nuts and the germ portion of grains are rich sources of both these compounds.

Biological Actions

There is a significant lack of understanding of the precise biological mechanism(s) of how plant-based bioactive food components impart health-promoting benefits. It is clear that bioactive food components act simultaneously at different or identical target sites. Bioactive food components have been shown to have the potential to reduce the risk of cancer, cardiovascular disease, osteoporosis, inflammation, type 2 diabetes, and other chronic degenerative diseases.

Bioactive food components have health-promoting roles at various stages of diseases that are associated with multiple progressive steps, from initiation to development. For example, in cardiovascular disease, isoflavones may reduce circulating oxidized low-density lipoproteins in the plasma, bind cholesterol in the intestinal tract thereby reducing absorption of dietary cholesterol, enhance bile excretion thereby reducing endogenous cholesterol levels, and modulate arterial elasticity thereby improving blood vessel dilation and constriction response.

As antioxidants, polyphenols, carotenoids, tocopherols, and allyl sulfides quench free radicals and reactive

202

oxygen species. A free radical is a carbon or oxygen atom that has an unpaired electron and is highly unstable. Free radicals can form in lipids, proteins, and carbohydrates. The primary actions of antioxidants include the regulation of the redox potential within a cell and the reduction of potential initiators of carcinogenesis. The redox potential refers to the balance of the reducing and oxidizing reactions that occur within the cell. Redox changes within a cell are able to trigger various molecular responses such as induction of apoptosis (cell death) and activation of signal transduction (the transfer of messages between cells and within a cell). Therefore, redox and antioxidant regulation of physiological and pathological processes is important in optimizing health and disease prevention.

Other bioactive compounds are able to bind to toxins or carcinogens in the intestinal tract thereby preventing transformation or even absorption such as the binding of N-nitroso compounds in the intestinal tract by polyphenols in tea. The lipid-lowering mechanism of dietary fiber and phytosterol/stanols occurs by sequestering cholesterol in the intestinal tract and reducing cholesterol absorption. Dietary fiber is the indigestible parts of plant foods; it provides structure to the plant cell walls and is composed of long straight chains of carbohydrate molecules held together by bonds that cannot be broken by human digestive enzymes. This long fibrous structure allows dietary fibers to entrap harmful toxins and carcinogens in the digestive tract. There are two types of dietary fiber: soluble and insoluble. Soluble dietary fiber can dissolve in or absorb water and is effective in binding toxins and cholesterol in the intestinal tract. Insoluble dietary fiber, on the other hand, cannot dissolve in water and is effective in adding bulk and increasing the rate of passage of food through the intestinal tract. Insoluble dietary fiber, therefore, acts by diluting out potential carcinogens and decreasing contact of toxins and carcinogens with the intestinal tract by speeding their passage out of the body. Foods rich in soluble dietary fiber include apples, cranberries, mango, oranges, asparagus, broccoli, carrots, peanuts, walnuts, most legumes, oats, and psyllium. Rich food sources of insoluble dietary fiber include apples, bananas, berries, broccoli, green peppers, spinach, almonds, sesame seeds, most legumes, brown rice, whole-wheat breads, and cereals.

The structural similarity between several isoflavone metabolites and the metabolite of estrogen, estradiol, suggests the possibility of estrogen-like biological activities. Isoflavones or phytoestrogens, however, exhibit antagonist estrogen activity resulting in lower overall exposure to estrogen in premenopausal women and reducing breast cancer risk (Cassidy et al. 1994, 1995; Shimizu et al.). In postmenopausal women phytoestrogen-rich diets reduce the hormone-sensitive increases in plasma cholesterol levels and bone loss (Potter et al.; Setchell and Cassidy).

The induction of enzyme systems that detoxify toxic chemicals such as the phase I and phase II detoxifying enzymes is thought to reduce one's susceptibility to mutagenic effects. Bioactive food components with antioxidant functions are able to activate phase II detoxifying enzymes via an antioxidant-responsive element (Mukhtar and Ahmad). Isothiocyanates, in particular sulforaphane, are potent mono-inducers of phase II detoxifying enzymes (Zhang et al.). Diallyl sulfides from garlic preparations, on the other hand, are inducers of both phase I and phase II detoxifying enzymes (Yang et al.).

A primary mechanism for immune-modulation is the multiple antioxidant capability of polyphenols, tocopherols, carotenoids, isothiocyanates, and allyl sulfides. Together these compounds are able to reduce the deleterious effects of reactive oxygen species and free radicals, which cause premature death of immune cells (Brennan et al.). Bioactive food components have also been shown to stimulate the phagocytic action of macrophages and synthesis of several immune cell types, which increases the protection against infection. Among the foods that have been shown to have beneficial immuno-modulatory effects are broccoli, garlic, onions, vegetable oils, almonds, walnuts, and others that are listed in Table 1.

Effects of Food Processing
In general, processing of fresh fruits and vegetables results in changes in composition of the bioactive food components. These changes can be beneficial or detrimental to the total content of health-promoting phytochemicals. It has been shown that coarseness of cutting, length of storage post-harvest, steam blanching, and thermal processing all influence the retention of bioactive compounds in cruciferae and allium vegetables (Howard et al.; Song and Milner). Reported losses of 30 percent to 80 percent of bioactive isothiocyanates have been reported (Howard et al.). Temperatures of 212°F (100°C) and higher result in the inactivation of key enzymes, myrosinase in cruciferae and allinase in allium vegetables, thereby reducing the amount of bioactive components. However, temperatures associated with normal cooking have shown little evidence of substantial loss of isothiocyanates. Leaching of glucosinolates and hydrolysis products also results in a reduction in total phytochemical content following cooking. Research has shown that heating garlic to a temperature of 140 to 212°F (60 to 100°C) or microwave heating for 30 to 60 seconds results in significant losses of the anti-inflammatory, anticancer, antimicrobial, and antioxidative activities of garlic (Song and Milner). However, the protective effect of garlic was nearly restored if the garlic preparation was allowed to sit for 10 minutes at room temperature prior to any heat treatment.

The bioavailability of carotenoids and other lipid-soluble bioactive food components has been shown to be improved with processing that increases surface area, such as cutting and chopping, and heat treatments that break down the protein and carbohydrate matrix that bind carotenoids (Stahl and Sies; Parker). The brewing

TABLE 1

Summary listing of various bioactive food components, common food sources, and biological functions

Bioactive component	Food source	Function
Glucosinolates, diallyl sulfides, isothiocyanates	Broccoli, cauliflower, brussels sprouts, garlic, onions	Induction of detoxifying enzyme systems, antimicrobial, immunomodulator, anticancer
Tocopherols and tocotrienols	Vegetable oil, nuts, seeds	Antioxidant, immunomodulator
Isoflavonoids and polyphenols	Grapes, red wine, tea, fresh fruit, and vegetables	Antioxidant, lipid-lowering, immunomodulator, antiosteoporotic, anticancer
Phytoestrogens (genistein, daidzein)	Soybean and other soy-based products, flaxseed, cabbage, legumes, tea	Antiestrogen, antiosteoporotic, antiproliferative
Phytosterols	Vegetable oils, nuts	Lipid-lowering
Dietary fiber	Whole grains, oats, fresh fruit with skin	Lipid-lowering
γ-linolenic acid, α-linolenic acid, and omega-3 fatty acids	Evening primrose or borage oil, walnuts, rapeseed, flaxseed, fish, microalgae	Anti-inflammatory, lipid-lowering
Lutein	Green leafy vegetables	Reduction in age-related macular degeneration
Carotenoids	Carrots, corn, squash, green leafy vegetables, oranges, papaya, red palm oil	Antioxidant immunomodulators
Lycopene	Tomatoes	Antiproliferative, anticancer
Bioactive peptides: lactoferrin, glycomacropeptide	Milk and fermented milk products	Immune system enhancing, antiproliferative, antimicrobial
Probiotics	Fermented milk products	Immunomodulators, anticancer, gastrointestinal health modulators

of tea leaves, whether black or green, releases 69 to 85 percent of bioactive flavonoids within 3 to 5 minutes in hot water (Trevisanato and Kim).

Dietary Recommendations

Clearly, bioactive food components will play an important role in health maintenance in the future. However, information is needed in regards to the bioavailability of bioactive food components and the effective dosage required in humans to optimize health benefits. Current information suggests that to obtain and maintain blood levels of beneficial polyphenols, especially phytoestrogens and isoflavonoids, and carotenoids one needs to consume on a daily basis 25 to 60 grams of soy protein,

five to nine servings of fruits and vegetables, one fresh clove of garlic, and four to six cups of green or black tea (Klotzbach-Shimomura). To achieve optimal phytosterol/stanol and fiber levels a daily intake of 25 to 35 grams of fiber is recommended by consuming seven to eleven servings of whole grains, legumes, pastas or nuts, and five to nine servings of fruits and vegetables.

The average American diet consists of two to four servings of fruits and vegetables and only five to seven servings of whole grains. Consequently, there is still a need to provide information and food choices to consumers to aid in the selection of a diet that contains optimal levels of health-promoting bioactive food components.

See also **Antioxidants; Assessment of Nutritional Status; Dairy Products; Dietary Assessment; Dietary Guidelines; Fiber, Dietary; Fish; Fruit; Lipids; Nutrient Bioavailability; Vegetables.**

BIBLIOGRAPHY

Bravo, L. "Polyphenols: Chemistry, Dietary Sources, Metabolism, and Nutritional Significance." *Nutrition Reviews* 56 (1998): 317–333.

Brennan, L. A., G. M. Morris, G. R. Wasson, B. M. Hannigan, and Y. A. Barnett. "The Effect of Vitamin C or Vitamin E Supplementation on Basal and H$_2$O$_2$-Induced DNA Damage in Human Lymphocytes." *British Journal of Nutrition* 84 (2000): 195–202.

Cassidy, A., S. Bingham, and K. D. R. Setchell. "Biological Effects of Isoflavones Present in Soy in Premenopausal Women: Implications for the Prevention of Breast Cancer." *American Journal of Clinical Nutrition* 60 (1994): 330–340.

Cassidy, A., S. Bingham, and K. D. R. Setchell. "Biological Effects of Isoflavones in Young Women—Importance of the Chemical Composition of Soya Products." *British Journal of Nutrition* 74 (1995): 587–590.

Howard, L. A., E. H. Jeffery, M. A. Wallig, and B. P. Klein. "Retention of Phytochemicals in Fresh and Processed Broccoli." *Journal of Food Science* 62 (1997): 1098–1104.

Klotzbach-Shimomura, K. "Functional Foods: The Role of Physiologically Active Compounds in Relation to Disease." *Topics in Clinical Nutrition* 16 (2001): 68–78.

Mukhtar, H., and N. Ahmad. "Tea Polyphenols: Prevention of Cancer and Optimizing Health." *American Journal of Clinical Nutrition* 71 (2000): 1698S–1702S.

Parker, R. S. "Phytochemicals: Carotenoids." In *Wiley Encyclopedia of Food Science and Technology*, 2nd ed., vol. 3, edited by F. J. Francis, pp. 1909–1915. New York: John Wiley and Sons, 2000.

Potter, S. M., J. A. Baum, H. Teng, R. J. Stillman, N. F. Shay, and J. W. Erdman. "Soy Protein and Isoflavones: Their Effects on Blood Lipids and Bone Density in Postmenopausal Women." *American Journal of Clinical Nutrition* 68 (1998): 1325S–1379S.

Setchell, K. D. R., and A. Cassidy. "Dietary Isoflavones: Biological Effects and Relevance to Human Health." *Journal of Nutrition* 129 (1999): 758S–767S.

Shimizu, H., R. K. Ross, L. Bernstein, M. C. Pike, and B. E. Henderson. "Serum Estrogen-Levels in Postmenopausal Women—Comparison of American Whites and Japanese in Japan." *British Journal of Cancer* 62 (1990): 451–453.

Song, K., and J. A. Milner. "The Influence of Heating on the Anticancer Properties of Garlic." *Journal of Nutrition* 131 (2001): 1054S–1057S.

Stahl, W., and H. Sies. "Uptake of Lycopene and Its Geometrical Isomers Is Greater from Heat-Processed Than from Unprocessed Tomato Juice in Humans." *Journal of Nutrition* 122 (1992): 2161–2166.

Trevisanato, S. I., and Y.-I. Kim. "Tea and Health." *Nutrition Reviews* 58 (2000): 1–10.

Yang, C. S., S. K. Chhabra, J.-Y. Hong, and T. Smith. "Mechanisms of Inhibition of Chemical Toxicity and Carcinogenesis by Diallyl Sulfide (DAS) and Related Compounds from Garlic." *Journal of Nutrition* 131 (2001): 1041S–1045S.

Zhang, Y., T. W. Kensler, C.-G. Cho, G. H. Posner, and P. Talalay. "Anticarcinogenic Activities of Sulforaphane and Structurally Related Synthetic Norbornyl Isothiocyanates." *Proceedings of the National Academy of Sciences* 91 (1994): 3147–3150.

Joy Emilie Swanson

BIODIVERSITY AND THE CORNUCOPIA OF FOODS.

Whenever you take up a bowl of paella, or a salad plate of mixed greens, nuts, and fruits, you are enjoying the benefits of biodiversity. There is something intrinsically pleasurable about a heterogeneity of vegetable varieties, shellfish species, or the ecological mosaic of marine and terrestrial landscapes sampled to prepare such dishes. Biodiversity can be simply defined as the "variety of life on Earth," and it includes both the richness of habitats found within different regions as well as the richness of species, varieties, and genes.

In a world where agricultural and aquacultural practices correspond to the growth rates and population densities of edible plants and animals, biodiversity can be sustained, without depleting harvests or degrading ecological habitats. But where traditional practices of food production and harvesting have been displaced, or species-rich landscapes have been degraded or converted to urban or industrial uses, this diversity is imperiled. In other words, the continued availability of this cornucopia of foods can no longer be taken for granted, and the term "biodiversity" is increasingly used in the context of loss of biodiversity or the extinction crisis. The number of species doomed to extinction each year of this coming

Biodiversity is evident in the large range of grass and flower species occupying this prairie at the National Bison Refuge in Montana. © PHOTO RESEARCHERS, INC.

Biodiversity includes not just the mix of different species but also the unique variations within species, as in the case of these heirloom turnips. The flat-rooted variety is Purple Top Milan, the white one in the center Goose Egg, and the ones beneath it Orange Jelly. Each variety also exhibits a very different flavor and storage qualities. PHOTO BY L. WILBUR ZIMMERMAN. COURTESY OF THE ROUGHWOOD SEED COLLECTION.

century is projected by Harvard professor E. O. Wilson to be on the order of 27,000 unique and irreplaceable life forms. This extinction rate is the highest rate since humankind began manipulating life on earth.

Although the term "biodiversity" first came into vogue around 1988, during a conference on this theme sponsored by the National Academy of Sciences of the United States, synonyms such as "biological diversity" and "biotic diversity" had already been in currency among scientists and conservationists for some four decades. However, most people erroneously equated the term with species diversity or species richness, as if the number of plant and animal species in a given area served as the only indicator of biodiversity. "Biodiversity" is now considered to include the variety of life considered at all levels, from genetic variants belonging to the same species, through arrays of species and lifeforms, to the variety of habitats and ecosystems found within an ecological landscape including both wildlands and farmlands.

Let us first consider how our cornucopia of foods is filled with the genetic variation found within a single species. Consider, for example, the astonishing variety of vegetables and fruits grown and stored on just one patch of land, such as that of the Heritage Farm of the Seed Savers Exchange in Decorah, Iowa. The dozen or so members of the Seed Savers Exchange staff grow and maintain the genetic diversity represented by some 4,100

named varieties of tomatoes (one species), 3,600 varieties of beans (six species), 1,000 varieties of peas (one species), 1,200 chili peppers (four species), 1,200 squash and pumpkin varieties (four species), 400 melons (two species), 650 varieties of maize (two species), and 200 varieties of garlic (one species). Each of these varieties, whether it is a land race developed exclusively by traditional farmers and gardeners, or a cultivar developed by scientifically trained plant breeders, has been selected for its unique flavor, texture, color, size, shape, keeping time, as well as for its maturation rates, productivity, and resistance to pests, diseases, droughts, and freezes.

Unfortunately, many varieties such as these have already been lost from future use by gardeners, chefs, brewers, and the public at large. For example, it is estimated that 60 percent of the crop land races grown by indigenous tribes in North America at the time of first European colonization have been lost over the following five centuries. Several threats have led to losses of genetic replacement by modern commercial cultivars, and genetic contamination through accidental hybridization with modern cultivars, including genetically modified organisms (GMOs). Further consequences include genetic erosion due to the decline in traditional farming, along with reductions in planting areas and crop population sizes, and genetic extirpation resulting from the genocide or displacement of traditional farming communities, and termination of their agricultural practices.

In addition to genetic variation below the species level, biodiversity is influenced by the number of crop species grown in a given area and how they are intercropped. For example, some fifty botanical species of fruits, vegetables, and nuts can be found in some indigenous dooryard gardens, intermixed in what agroecologists term "polycultures." These crop mixtures often outyield the harvests that a single crop would produce on the same area of land, and harbor a variety of beneficial insects, such as predators on pests and pollinators.

At the landscape level, an ecological mosaic of fields, gardens, orchards, hedgerows, and managed wildlands provides what is now termed "agrobiodiversity," which includes habitat for both wild and domesticated organisms. It is at this level that land conservation organizations interested in protecting the diversity of foods desired by the public must succeed, for this diversity can be easily lost without the cultural landscapes that sustain species, their interactions with one another, and traditional ecological knowledge about how to manage them.

Gary Paul Nabhan

BIODYNAMIC GARDENING. *See* **Organic Agriculture; Organic Farming and Gardening.**

BIOTECHNOLOGY. Biotechnology, in its broadest sense, is the use of biological systems to carry out technical processes. Food biotechnology uses genetic methods to enhance food properties and to improve production, and in particular uses direct (rather than random) strategies to modify genes that are responsible for traits such as a vegetable's nutritional content. Using modern biotechnology, scientists can move genes for valuable traits from one plant into another plant. This way, they can make a plant taste or look better, be more nutritious, protect itself from insects, produce more food, or survive and prosper in inhospitable environments, for example, by incorporating tolerance to increased soil salinity. Simply put, food biotechnology is the practice of directing genetic changes in organisms that produce food in order to make a better product.

In nature, plants produce their own chemical defenses to ward off disease and insects thereby reducing the need for insecticide sprays. Biotechnology is often used to enhance these defenses. Some improvements are crop specific. For example, potatoes with a higher starch content will absorb less oil when frying, and tomatoes with delayed ripening qualities will have improved taste and freshness.

Paving the Way to Modern Biotechnology
Advances in science over many years account for what we know and are able to accomplish with modern biotechnology and food production. A brief review of genetics

REGULATORY OVERSIGHT

Three government agencies monitor the development and testing of biotechnology crops: the Food and Drug Administration (FDA), the U.S. Department of Agriculture (USDA), and the Environmental Protection Agency (EPA). These agencies work together to ensure that biotechnology foods are safe to eat, safe to grow, and safe for the environment.

U.S. Food and Drug Administration (FDA): Lead agency in assessing safety for human consumption of plants or foods that have been altered using biotechnology, including foods that have improved nutritional profiles, food quality, or food processing advantages.

U.S. Department of Agriculture: Provides regulatory oversight to ensure that new plant varieties pose no harm to production agriculture or to the environment. USDA's Animal and Plant Health Inspection Service (APHIS) governs the field testing of biotechnology crops to determine how transgenic varieties perform relative to conventional varieties, and the balance between risk and reward.

Environmental Protection Agency (EPA): EPA provides regulatory and safety oversight for new plant varieties, such as insect-protected biotechnology crops. EPA regulates any pesticide that may be present in food to provide a high margin of safety for consumers.

and biochemistry is useful in evaluating the role of biotechnology in our food supply.

Proteins are composed of various combinations of amino acids. They are essential for life—both for an organism's structure, and for the metabolic reactions necessary for the organism to function. The number, kind, and order of amino acids in a specific protein determine its properties. Deoxyribonucleic acid (DNA), which is present in all the cells of all organisms, contains the information needed for cells to put amino acids in the correct order. In other words, DNA contains the genetic blueprint determining how cells in all living organisms store, duplicate, and pass information about protein structure from generation to generation.

In 1953 James Watson and Francis Crick published their discovery that the molecular structure of DNA is a double helix, for which they, along with Maurice H. F. Wilkins, won a Nobel Prize in 1962. Two strands of DNA are composed of pairs of chemicals—adenine (A) and thymine (T); and guanine (G) and cytosine (C). A segment of DNA that encodes enough information to

GENETICALLY MODIFIED ORGANISMS: HEALTH AND ENVIRONMENTAL CONCERNS

There is really little doubt that, at least in principle, the development of genetically modified organisms (GMOs) can offer many advantages. Genetically modified organisms have included crops that are largely of benefit to farmers and not clearly of broad public value. Plans for development of GMOs include foods that have far greater nutritional and even pharmaceutical benefit; crops that can grow in regions that currently cannot provide enough food for subsistence; and foods that are more desirable in terms of traits that the public wants. The market forces that largely determine which products are developed are complicated, and there are important trade-offs: the traits that may be needed to feed a starving world are different from the traits farmers in the United States want, and both may differ from the characteristics the paying public supports.

Most criticisms of genetic engineering focus on food safety and environmental impacts. What impact will GMOs have on the health of those who eat them? Will some individuals develop allergic reactions? The new technology makes it possible to cross species barriers with impunity. A scare over StarLink corn is instructive of this kind of problem. "*Bt* corn," a common GMO, includes a gene from *Bacillus thuringienis*, which produces a pesticide that kills the European corn borer. StarLink is a variety of *Bt* corn that includes a protein (Cry9C) that does not break down as easily in the body, which increases the risk of allergic reactions in some people (though there are no verified cases of this). StarLink corn was approved for animal feed but not for human consumption. Unfortunately it is difficult if not impossible to keep the food supply for animals and humans separate. The result has been the discovery of small amounts of StarLink corn throughout the food supply. (Of course, there is also the question whether a small trace of Cry9C in a fast-food taco is the greatest health problem involved in such a meal.)

A second set of concerns arises over the environmental impact of GMOs. There are several different concerns. First, there are worries about gene flow. The same genes that may one day make it possible for plants to grow in poor, salty soil or in relatively arid regions could create an ecological nightmare by allowing these crops to spread beyond their normal range as a result of the gene(s) that have been transferred into the crop itself, or if those same genes should be introduced to other plants. This can happen through outcrossing between the GMOs and closely related plants. For example, GM wheat could cross with native grasses in South America to alter the makeup of the ecosystem and potentially create "super weeds," a possibility that has raised concerns in the "Wheat Belt" of the United States and elsewhere. Even in the absence of gene flow, the GMOs themselves could become super weeds (or the animal equivalent) as a result of the traits that make them better suited to new habitats. The environmental trade-off for technology that

make one protein is called a gene. It is the order of DNA's base pairs that determines specific genes that code for specific proteins, which determines individual traits.

By 1973 scientists had found ways to isolate individual genes, and by the 1980s, scientists could transfer single genes from one organism to another. This process, much like traditional crossbreeding, allows transferred traits to pass to future generations of the recipient organism.

One Goal, Two Approaches

The objective of plant biotechnology and traditional crop breeding is the same: to improve the characteristics of seed so that the resulting plants have new, desirable traits. The primary difference between the two techniques is how the objective is achieved. Plant breeders have used traditional tools such as hybridization and crossbreeding to improve the quality and yield of their crops with a resulting wide variability in our foods. These traditional techniques resulted in several benefits, such as greatly in-creased crop production and improved quality of food and feed crops, which has proven beneficial to growers and producers as well as consumers through a reduction of the cost of food for consumers. However, traditional plant breeding techniques do have some limits; only plants from the same or similar species can be interbred. Because of this, the sources for potential desirable traits are finite. In addition, the process of crossbreeding is very time-consuming, at times taking ten to twelve years to achieve the desired goal—and complications can arise because all genes of the two "parent" plants are combined together. This means that both the desirable *and* undesirable traits may be expressed in the new plant. It takes a significant amount of time to remove the unwanted traits by "back crossing" the new plant over many generations to achieve the desired traits. These biotech methods can preserve the unique genetic composition of some crops while allowing the addition or incorporation of specific genetic traits, such as resistance to disease. However, development of transgenic crop varieties still requires a significant investment of time and resources.

makes it possible to produce sustainable agriculture or aquaculture in regions where it cannot "naturally" flourish is the significant risk of loss of biodiversity and the unchecked spread of plants or animals into unintended regions. (The argument is made, however, that biotechnology can be used to increase yields on the land that is currently used for agricultural production, allowing nonfarm land to be retained as forests and reserves and thereby conserve biodiversity.)

In addition to these concerns over the ecosystem and the creation of superweeds, there is a worry over the potential impact of some GMOs on nontarget organisms. Cornell University researchers found that pollen from *Bt* corn could kill the larvae of monarch butterflies that ingested it. This raised the fear that these engineered crops could kill butterflies and other nontarget organisms in addition to the corn borer. The consensus from subsequent field research is that *Bt* corn does not pose a major threat to monarch butterfly populations—loss of habitat in Mexico, where the butterflies overwinter, is a more serious threat. Nevertheless, the *Bt* corn–butterfly issue showed that it is not always possible to predict the consequences that may arise from the introduction of these crops.

Genetically engineered microorganisms present even greater environmental and health concerns. It will soon be possible to engineer bacteria and viruses to produce deadly pathogens. This could well open a new era in biological weapons in addition to the environmental problems that could result from the release of organisms into the environment. The environmental assessment of the widespread introduction of engineered microorganisms has only barely begun to receive attention (Cho et al., 1999).

These concerns are exacerbated by some inadequacies in the regulatory framework for GMOs. There is a growing sense that the Food and Drug Administration, the U.S. Department of Agriculture, and the Environmental Protection Agency are not sufficiently rigorous or consistent in how they regulate GMOs and that there should be a single set of standards, including a mandatory environmental assessment. The opposition to GMOs in Europe is much more widespread than in the United States, and the single most important factor for the differences between European and American attitudes is the level of confidence in the regulatory institutions that protect the food supply. After "mad cow disease," Europeans do not trust their governments to provide safe food. A similar loss in confidence among U.S. consumers could have a similar effect. In spite of these concerns, however, there have so far been no documented food safety problems resulting from the introduction of GM crops in the mid-1990s and their large-scale consumption by the American public. There have also been no ecological disasters, although the time since their introduction has been too brief for the absence of disaster to be very meaningful. In some crops, notably in *Bt* cotton, there have been significant reductions in the use of pesticides.

David Magnus
with contributions by Peter Goldsbrough

The Many Applications of Biotechnology

Since the earliest times, people have been using simple forms of biotechnology to improve their food supply, long before the discovery of the structure of DNA by Watson and Crick. For example, grapes and grains were modified through fermentation with microorganisms and used to make wine, beer, and leavened bread. Modern biotechnology, which uses the latest molecular biology technology, allows us to more directly modify our foods. Whereas traditional plant breeding mixes tens of thousands of genes, biotechnology allows for the transfer of a single gene, or a few select genes or traits. The most common uses thus far have been the introduction of traits that help farmers simplify crop production, reduce pesticide use in some crops, and increase profitability by reduction of crop losses to weeds, insect damage, or disease.

In general, the early applications of crop biotechnology have been at points in our food supply chain where economic benefit can be gained. The following are examples of modern biotechnology where success has been achieved or is in progress.

Insect resistance. Crop losses from insect pests can cause devastating financial loss for growers and starvation in developing countries. In the United States and Europe, thousands of tons of pesticides are used to control insects. Using modern biotechnology, scientists and farmers have removed the need for the use of some of these chemicals. Insect-protected plants are developed by introducing a gene into a plant that produces a specific protein from a naturally occurring soil organism. *Bacillus thuringiensis (Bt)* is one of many bacteria naturally present in soil. This bacterium is known to be lethal to certain classes of insects, and only those organisms. The *Bt* protein produced by the bacterium is the natural insecticide. Growing foods, such as *Bt* corn, can help eliminate the application of chemical pesticides and reduce the cost of bringing a crop to market. The introduction of insect-protected crops such as *Bt* cotton has allowed reduced use of chemical pesticides. This suggests that genetically engineered food crops can also be grown with reduced use of pesticides, a development that would be welcomed by the general public.

Herbicide tolerance. Every year, farmers must battle weeds that compete with their crops for water, nutrients, sunlight, and space. Weeds can also harbor insects and disease. Farmers routinely use two or more different chemicals on a crop to remove both grass and broadleaf weeds. In recent years new "broad-spectrum" chemicals have been discovered that control all these weeds and therefore require only one application of one chemical to the crop. To provide crops with a defense against these nonselective herbicides, genes have been added to plants that render the chemicals inactive—but only in the new, herbicide-resistant crop. Many benefits come from these crops, including better and more flexible weed control for farmers, increased use of conservation tillage (involving less working of the soil and thereby decreasing erosion), and promoting the use of herbicides that have a better environmental profile (that is, that are less toxic to nontarget organisms).

Disease resistance. Many viruses, fungi, and bacteria can cause plant diseases, resulting in crop damage and loss. Researchers have had great success in developing crops that are protected from certain types of plant viruses by introducing DNA from the virus into the plant. In essence, the plants are "vaccinated" against specific diseases. Because most plant viruses are spread by insects, farmers can use fewer insecticides and still have healthy crops and high yields.

Drought tolerance and salinity tolerance. As the world population grows and industrial demand for water supplies increases, the amount of water used to irrigate crops will become more expensive or unavailable. Creating plants that can withstand long periods of drought or high salt content in soil and groundwater will help overcome these limitations. Although genetically engineered crops with enhanced drought tolerance are not yet commercially available, significant research advances are pointing the way to creating these in the future.

Food applications. Research into applications of biotechnology to food production covers a broad range of possibilities. Examples of food applications also include increasing the nutrient content of foods where deficiencies are widespread in the population. For example, researchers have successfully increased the amount of iron and beta-carotene (the precursor to vitamin A in humans) in carrots and "golden rice"—a biotech rice developed by the Rockefeller Foundation that may help provide children in developing nations with the vitamin A they need to reduce the risk of vision problems or blindness.

Another example of food biotechnology is crops modified for higher monounsaturated fatty acid levels in the vegetable to make them more "heart-healthy." Efforts are also under way to slow the ripening of some crops, such as bananas, tomatoes, peppers, and tropical fruits, to allow time to ship them from farms to large cities while preserving taste and freshness.

Other possible food applications for which pioneering research is under way include grains and nuts where naturally occurring allergens have been reduced or eliminated. Potatoes with higher starch content also promise to have the added potential to reduce the fat content in fried potato products, such as french fries and potato chips. This is because the starch replaces water in the potatoes, causing less fat to be absorbed into the potato when it is fried.

Edible vaccines. Vaccines that are commonly used today are often costly to produce and require cold storage conditions when shipped from their point of manufacture in the developed world to points of use in the developing world. Research has shown that protein-based vaccines can be designed into edible plants so that simple eating of the material leads to oral immunization. This technology will allow local production of vaccines in developing countries, reduction of vaccine costs, and promotion of global immunization programs to prevent infectious diseases.

Global food needs. The world population has topped six billion people and is predicted to double by 2050. Ensuring an adequate food supply for this booming population is going to be a major challenge in the years to come. Biotechnology can play a critical role in helping to meet the growing need for high-quality food produced in more sustainable ways.

What Are Consumers Saying?

Crops modified by biotechnology (also known as genetically modified or GM crops) have been the subjects of public discussion in recent years. Considerable public discussion may be attributed to the public's interest in the safety and usefulness of new products. Although biotechnology has a strongly supported safety record, some groups and organizations abroad and in the United States have expressed a desire for stronger regulation of biotechnology-derived products than of similar foods derived from older technology. The assessment of the need for new regulation is related to an understanding of the science itself, as was detailed in the sections above; this is a continual process of development.

Consumer acceptance is critical to the success of biotechnology around the world. Attitudes toward biotechnology vary from country to country because of cultural and political differences, in addition to many other influences.

In the United States, the majority of consumers are supportive about the potential benefits biotechnology can bring. Generally, U.S. consumers feel they would like to learn more about the topic, and respond favorably when they are given accurate, science-based information on the subject of food biotechnology.

See also **Agriculture since the Industrial Revolution; Agronomy; Crop Improvement; Ecology and Food; Environment; Food Politics: United States; Food Safety; Gene Expression, Nutrient Regulation of; Genetic Engineering; Genetics; Government Agencies; Green Revolution; High-Technology Farming; Inspection; Marketing of Food; Toxins, Unnatural, and Food Safety.**

BIBLIOGRAPHY

Arntzen, Charles J. "Agricultural Biotechnology." In *Nutrition and Agriculture*. United Nations Administrative Committee on Coordination, Subcommittee on Nutrition, World Health Organization. September 2000

Borlaug, Norman E. "Feeding a World of 10 Billion People: The Miracle Ahead." Lecture given at De Moutfort University, Leicester, England, May 1997.http://agriculture .tusk.edu/biotech/monfort2html International Food Information Council (IFIC). "Food Biotechnology Overview." Washington, D.C.: February 1998. Available at http:// ific.org.

Cho, Mildred, David Magnus, Art Caplan, and Daniel McGee. "Ethical Considerations in Synthesizing a Minimal Genome." *Science* 286 (10 December 1999): 2087–2090.

Charles J. Arntzen
Susan Pitman
Katherine Thrasher

BIRDS. *See* **Poultry; Seabirds and Their Eggs.**

BIRDSEYE, CLARENCE. Clarence "Bob" Birdseye (1886–1956), American businessman and inventor, was originally an Amherst biology major, but dropped out and became a U.S. field naturalist in Labrador in 1920. There he became impressed with the well-

Photograph of Clarence Birdseye, shown using a Dictaphone in his office. PHOTO COURTESY OF THE LIBRARY OF CONGRESS.

preserved cellular structure of cooked fish that was frozen naturally in the Arctic outdoors. He noted that this quick freezing process caused less crystallization within the fish tissue. Once he returned to the United States, Birdseye developed his crude Multiplate Quick Freeze Machine: tightly sealed cartons, encased in metal, that were filled with food and then lowered into a low-temperature brine solution that froze the foods. Later, he froze foods with calcium chloride brine chilled to −40°F. In 1924 he organized the General Seafood Corporation and turned his attention to developing refrigerated railroad boxcars to transport frozen foods nationwide. In 1929 Birdseye sold his company to Postum, Inc., which became General Foods Corporation. His line of frozen foods was renamed Birds Eye.™ Ultimately, in 1949, using the anhydrous freezing process, Birdseye managed to cut freezing time from 18 hours to 90 minutes.

Though his process was not the first to freeze foods, distinction came to him for the quickness of his method for producing tasty, well-preserved fresh fish, fruits, and vegetables in retail-sized containers. The restaurant business profited greatly from his work. Birdseye held three hundred patents, in addition to a patent for a process of converting crushed sugarcane residue into paper pulp.

FROZEN PEAS

Birdseye's process indirectly improved the diet of the industrialized world by making possible the freshest frozen foods, frozen at or near farm sites, year round. This later led to the packaging of ethnic foods and meal combinations such as TV dinners. One of his most popular frozen products is green peas, the second largest vegetable crop in the United States. In the early twenty-first century more than 90 percent of all peas are sold as frozen peas. Frozen peas retain their brightest color and original shapes when placed in boiling water and removed from the heat.

See also **Fish; Frozen Food; Peas; Preserving; Storage of Food; Vegetables.**

BIBLIOGRAPHY

"Alpert's Heated. Birdseye's Frozen." Safe Food Organization. 27 May 2002. Available at http://www.safefood.org/history.html

Davidson, Alan. *The Oxford Companion to Food.* Oxford: Oxford University Press, 1999.

Elan, Elissa. "Clarence Birdseye." *Nation's Restaurant News* 30 (February 1996): 32.

Fucini, Joseph, and Suzy Fucini. *Entrepreneurs: The Men and Women behind Famous Brand Names and How They Made It.* Boston: G. K. Hall, 1985.

Wallechinsky, David. *The People's Almanac Presents the Twentieth Century: History with the Boring Parts Left Out.* Woodstock, N.Y.: Overlook Press, 1999.

Marty Martindale

BIRTHDAY FOODS. Food is almost always a significant part of the observance or celebration of a birthday in the Western world. It may play several roles: as refreshments for those attending a celebration; as a gift, such as a box of candy for the honoree; as sweets or cupcakes taken to school by the birthday child; or the candy in a piñata at a party. Families often have their own favorite festive food that is served on birthdays of family members, or a favorite food of the birthday celebrant will be served in his or her honor.

In some cultures, a birthday food is an important cultural symbol recognized by the entire community. Wheat noodles, a symbol of longevity, are stretched to great lengths and served in soup to birthday celebrants in Northern China. Another symbol of longevity there, the peach, appears for birthdays as a bun, shaped and colored like a peach, with a sweet paste filling.

Food may be offered to the gods as a part of the religious celebration of a birthday. In Thai communities it is taken to the temple on the birthday morning, to receive a birthday blessing from a monk. In Sri Lanka, children go to the temple on their birthdays to receive a special blessing and to give money to the priest for a special offering of a traditional food, such as rice porridge, to the gods. This is also shared with the family.

Other traditional festive foods include the French *croquembouche*, a cone-shaped tower of small cream puffs fastened together with caramel, or the Norwegian *kransekaka*, a pyramid of as many as twenty-six pastry rings, gradually decreasing in size from bottom to top, and iced and decorated. These may be part of a birthday celebration but are more likely to be the centerpiece for a wedding or, perhaps, a christening. In Korea, steamed rice cakes of various kinds, usually made of layers of ground rice alternating with a bean paste, are served on birthdays but also on other special days.

However, in many parts of the world and especially in the West and countries influenced by Western traditions, by far the most popular food for celebrating a birthday is the birthday cake, complete with decorative icing and glowing candles. In the United States, birthday cakes, especially for children, are essential to the celebration. The custom cuts across all economic, racial, and religious lines. Although elaborately decorated cakes also are used to mark events like weddings, farewell parties, and other major events, the birthday cake is distinctive because of its candles. Any depiction of a circle topped by a one or more candles is recognized at once as a birthday cake.

Birthday Celebrations

Birthdays of powerful and wealthy individuals have been celebrated for millennia. The Bible's book of Genesis (ch. 40:20) indicates that Egyptian pharaohs organized festive events around their birthdays and, according to Dalby and Grainger in *The Classical Cookbook* (p. 32), so did Romans in far-flung parts of the Empire. After the Middle Ages, birthdays began to be celebrated by others of wealth and position. Eventually, a growing middle class in the United States in the post–Civil War period began to emulate the customs and manners of their more affluent fellow citizens.

Although there are a number of cultures in which birthdays are not observed, particularly in Africa and the Middle East, usually a birthday is regarded as a rite of passage marking an individual's progress through the life cycle. Certain points along the way may be regarded as more important than others: for example, a first birthday or a sixtieth for a Korean; a fifteenth for a girl in the Latino community or a sixteenth in some other cultures in the United States, a twenty-first, fiftieth, or seventy-fifth for an American, or any birthday year which ends in a zero for a Dane. For such occasions a cake with candles usually is considered essential and extraordinary efforts may be made to provide it. A birthday cake requires a social gathering and ordinarily would not be eaten without others being present.

Cakes and celebrations. The birthday cake tradition in the United States is little more than a century old, but the relationship of cakes and celebration has a much longer history. It was traditional in Roman times, especially for those reaching fifty years of age, to be feted with special cakes, according to Toussaint-Samat in *History of Food* (p. 32), but the cakes of Roman times, and for many centuries after, consisted mainly of cereal grain meal moistened with water or wine, and perhaps leavened with some form of yeast. Like small pancakes, they were baked on a griddle and picked up and eaten like cookies.

The Development of Modern Cakes

During the Middle Ages in Northern Europe there was little distinction made between bread and cake. Both were leavened with yeast and sweetness was not an important

212

characteristic. Alan Davidson has written in *The Oxford Companion to Food* (p. 123) that it was not until the late fourteenth century in Europe that professional cooks were able to create immense yeast-leavened cakes filled with dried fruits for special occasions. In the sixteenth century, Italian and French pastry cooks began to develop lighter baked goods using batters based on egg-and-sugar foam instead of yeast. As their methods spread to other parts of Europe, cakes began to change rapidly, although still requiring a professional baker.

Chemical leavens.   Leavening baked goods with chemical substances, particularly pearlash, a refined form of potash, was in use by professional bakers in Europe by the mid-seventeenth century, according to Witteveen in *Petits Propos Culinaires #21* (pp. 66–68). But pearlash, saleratus, ammonium carbonate, and other substances known as "yeast powders," also used by home cooks in the United States by the end of the eighteenth century, imparted an unpleasant taste, particularly to delicately flavored baked goods. In 1863 two pharmacists in Indiana finally succeeded in developing the right blend of baking soda and cream of tartar to produce baking powder. Much earlier in the nineteenth century, the cast iron stove had come into use, and as home bakers learned to employ it in concert with chemical leavens, the modern-day layer cake became possible.

At that time, preparing cake ingredients still involved a lot of tedious work, but later in the century, many labor-saving devices for cooks—egg beaters, standardized baking pans, measuring cups and spoons, and ice boxes—appeared. What once was accessible only to a person wealthy enough to hire and outfit a professional cook had become possible for home cooks everywhere to produce successfully.

Twentieth-century cakes.   By early in the twentieth century, women's magazines and their advertisers were spreading the word not only about modern kitchen equipment and products that made baking a cake quick and easy, but were introducing their readers to recipes for layer cakes with glorious frostings and luscious fillings as popular desserts, especially in the American South. Since then, except for the introduction of the chiffon cake in 1948, and cake mixes at about the same time, the contemporary cake has not changed substantially. It is a baked, sweetened creation leavened with eggs or chemical leavens perhaps with the addition of eggs so that it is tender, light, and porous in texture. Usually, but not always, it contains wheat flour or a substitute like finely ground nuts. It may contain a substantial amount of fat or none at all.

Birthday Cakes

The great cake, a large, lavish creation, was the centerpiece for any Early American party at which it appeared. Making it was difficult, time-consuming, and costly. As Louise Conway Belden points out in *The Festive Tradi-*

First birthdays are a rite of passage for most American children, and part of the fun is to get down into the food. © ARIEL SKELLY/CORBIS.

tion: Table Decoration and Desserts in America, 1650–1900 (pp. 184–190), its appearance made the event special and festive.

Lavishly decorated cakes continue to be symbolic of life's festive and dramatic moments, and birthday cakes are expected, above all, to be dramatic in appearance. Only wedding cakes are more elaborate. Besides highlighting an individual's birthday as an important event, today they often are used as spectacular centerpieces for public occasions in order to provide a photo opportunity or other publicity. Size and appearance are the first consideration; the cake's flavor and texture may be of less concern.

A contemporary American birthday cake is usually tall, composed of two or more layers or baked in an angel food, bundt, or other tube pan. It often is a unique creation, shaped and decorated to please the birthday celebrant (a clown cake for a child, or a hobby-related cake for an adult). Icing with elaborate decorations of gum paste (which has been made in the Middle East since before the end of the twelfth century) and the generous use of color, borrowed by medieval Europeans from Arab cuisine, add to the dramatic effect, but are not essential. The cake's primary distinguishing characteristic is that it is topped with candles.

Candles. Light from the sun or from fire had very early religious and mystical significance, and rituals using light in the form of candles became part of religious ceremonies surrounding weddings, funerals, and other important human events, according to O'Dea's *Social History of Lighting* (pp. 34, 139–143). Candles also are associated with the measurement of time, and were used in the late ninth century by England's King Alfred to measure the hours of the day. In the Judeo-Christian tradition they have been used to symbolize the passage of time (at Advent or Hanukkah). The candles, rather than the cake itself, connote a long span of time.

Using very small tapers to light a special cake, with the number of tapers equal to a birthday child's age, seems to have begun in Germany in the late eighteenth century or earlier, judging by a letter written in 1799 by the German poet and dramatist Johann Wolfgang von Goethe, in which he referred to the tradition of *Kinderfest* (Goethe, pp. 114–115).

Birthday cake rituals. During the twentieth century, birthday celebrations spawned a host of traditions, rituals, and objects related to the festive cake. Although these vary among families and groups, when the cake appears, it is almost always accompanied by the singing of the "Happy Birthday" song, usually in English, even in non–English-speaking countries in Europe and Asia. In Spanish-speaking countries of the Western Hemisphere, it often is sung in both Spanish and English. Spain and Denmark have their own birthday cake songs, with other words and tunes.

The honoree is encouraged to make a secret wish and attempt to blow out all the candles with one breath to ensure that the wish will be realized. Despite various theories that have been advanced, the true origins of this custom are unknown. After the candles are extinguished, the cake is cut and distributed to guests. For young children, whose celebrations are more focused on their ages and growth, there may be attempts by child guests, particularly in Spain and Northern Italy, to pull the birthday child's earlobes, once for each year of age, just as in the United States, spanks may be administered, finished off with "and one to grow on."

Development of an Industry

A global industry has grown up around the birthday cake tradition. Hundreds of kinds of cake decorating supplies are sold, in small shops and from huge warehouses: retail, wholesale, by mail and on the Internet. The techniques, supplies, and equipment are available to residents of even the most isolated rural areas. The industry also has published hundreds of profusely illustrated instruction books describing how to use the tools and supplies to create fanciful cakes. Women in many parts of the

world have learned by using books or taking classes to decorate cakes for family and friends and many have gone on to establish a career in cake decorating.

Bakeries, pastry shops, and supermarkets in the United States do a thriving business in birthday cakes that can be decorated with frosting, gum paste flowers, or little plastic figures and carry a standard piped-on icing message like "Happy Birthday," or they can be customized for special orders in as elaborate a form as any purchaser's imagination and purse will permit, including having color photos reproduced on the iced cake's top surface.

Birthday candles reflect the global nature of birthday cakes. Some candle boxes carry safety directions in as many as five languages, and list manufacturing sites in Asia, Europe, and the United States. They are available in many sizes and lengths, all colors, metallic finishes, stripes, polka dots, and fanciful shapes such as cowboy boots, toy trains, or clowns. There are candles shaped like numbers for use when one taper for each year would be impractical, musical candles, and trick candles that relight magically after being blown out.

See also **Cake and Pancake; Candy and Confections; Christmas; Epiphany; Wedding Cake; Weddings.**

BIBLIOGRAPHY

Belden, Louise Conway. *The Festive Tradition: Table Decoration and Desserts in America, 1650–1900.* New York: W. W. Norton, 1983.

Dalby, Andrew, and Sally Grainger. *The Classical Cookbook.* London: British Museum Press, 1996.

Davidson, Alan, ed. *The Oxford Companion to Food.* Oxford: Oxford University Press, 1999.

Goethe, Johann Wolfgang von. *Goethe's Werke: Weimarer Ausgabe,* vol. 35. Weimar, 1892.

McFeely, Mary Drake. *Can She Bake a Cherry Pie?: American Women and the Kitchen in the Twentieth Century.* Amherst: University of Massachusetts Press, 2000.

O'Dea, William T. *The Social History of Lighting.* London: Routledge and Kegan Paul, 1958.

Smallzreid, Kathleen Ann. *The Everlasting Pleasure: Influences on America's Kitchens, Cooks and Cookery, from 1565 to the Year 2000.* New York: Appleton-Century-Crofts, 1956.

Toussaint-Samat, Maguelonne. *History of Food.* Translated by Anthea Bell. Cambridge, Mass.: Blackwell Publishers, 1992.

Wilson, C. Anne, ed. *The Appetite and the Eye: Visual Aspects of Food and Its Presentation Within Their Historic Context.* Edinburgh: Edinburgh University Press, 1991.

Witteveen, Joop. "Notes and Queries." In *Petits Propos Culinaires,* no. 21. London: Prospect Books, 1985.

Shirley E. Cherkasky

BISCUITS. The word "biscuit" is derived from the Latin *panis biscoctus,* "twice-baked bread." From the sixteenth to the eighteenth century, forms of the word included *besquite* and *bisket*. Similar forms are noted in many European languages. "Biscuit" covers a wide range of flour baked products, though it is generally an unleavened cake or bread, crisp and dry in nature, and in a small, thin, and flat shape. It has a number of cultural meanings. In the United States, a biscuit is a soft, thick scone product or a small roll similar to a muffin. The British biscuit is equivalent to the American cookie and cracker. These latter terms are relatively modern. "Cookie" comes from the eighteenth-century Dutch word *koekje*, a diminutive of *koek* (cake). "Cracker" is a North American term that also came into use in the eighteenth century, connoting the sound of the wafer as it was chewed or broken (at this time, "cracker" was also used to mean a firecracker or a noisy person or object).

Biscuits have evolved from different aspects of baking practices such as tarts, pastries, short cakes, and sugar confectionery. They have given rise to the wafer, macaroon, cracker, sandwich, snap, gingerbread, honey cake, rusk, and water biscuit. Some, like the wafer, were baked in the Middle Ages; others are of more recent origin, such as the "fancy biscuit," an early-nineteenth-century invention of British bakers that led to the development of a biscuit industry, which was later exported throughout the world. Biscuits are divided into two main groups. The first are plain or have a savory flavoring. The second type are sweet or semi-sweet in character.

Biscuits are made from a number of ingredients. Flour is the most basic and important. Different types give a range of textures and crispness. Wholemeal wheat flour is used in the "digestive," "sweetmeal," or "wheatmeal" type of biscuits. Oatmeal forms the basis of oatmeal biscuits. Rice flour and corn flour add flavor. Fats give the biscuits their "shortness." Butter and lard are the main fats, though these are augmented by vegetable and other refined fats. For fancy biscuits, sugar is an important ingredient, and introduces a range of tastes. It is added in several forms: processed as caster and Demerara sugars, syrups, honey, and malt extract. These have a range of consistencies and may help to bind together other ingredients. Aerating and raising ingredients, such as baking powder (bicarbonate of soda and tartaric acid), make the biscuit light. Flavorings are also added. These include dried fruit, nuts, chocolate (powder or chips), spices, herbs, and flavoring essences such as vanilla. The dry ingredients are bound together with eggs and milk (fresh, condensed, or dried) or water. Biscuits have a high energy content, ranging from 420 to 510 kcal per 100 g.

The mechanized process of biscuit-making is rapid and continuous. The ingredients are mixed into a dough that is then kneaded and rolled to a uniform thickness. Biscuit shapes are cut from it, and placed in a traveling oven. Some biscuits require special preparation and cooking techniques. Biscuit-making has become increasingly and highly mechanized since the early nineteenth century, when technological aids were limited and it was

A circa 1896 chromolithograph showing "Zoological Biscuits," the original name for animal crackers, which were introduced in England in the late 1870s. ROUGHWOOD COLLECTION.

highly labor-intensive. They can be baked commercially or in the home.

Most biscuits are distinguished by their appearance: round, square, oblong, finger-shaped, or fancifully impressed with designs. Plain biscuits are normally punched with a cutter or docker, to increase crispness during baking. Fancy biscuits can be covered with sugar, icing, or coated (fully or partially) with chocolate. Each type of biscuit also has its own commercial name, which refers to ingredients, a designation (sandwich, wafer, macaroon, or cracker), texture, eating qualities, and the time when it was to be eaten. The range of biscuits has increased over the past 150 years. Huntley & Palmers, of Reading, England, a world leader in biscuit production, sold around 130 varieties in 1870; by 1898, this increased to over four hundred. Some became well established and have a long history. For example, the "Abernethy biscuit," a proprietary biscuit based on the captain biscuit, was devised by Dr. John Abernethy (1764–1831), chief surgeon at St. Bartholomew's Hospital, London. Some biscuits have been eaten in large

The American Biscuit—A Divergent Tradition

In Britain and most of Europe, the biscuit follows a direct lineal descent from the Latin *panis biscoctus* (literally twice-baked bread), but in North America broad inconsistencies have emerged in the way this term is used in advertising and in common speech. For light baked goods with a crisp, brittle texture, two terms are in common use: "cracker" and "cookie." Historically Americans also used the word "biscuit" like their British cousins, as in the case of the ship biscuits or water biscuits of the early 1800s. Both of these foods are called crackers in the United States.

The old water biscuit of the nineteenth century has become the oyster cracker of seafood restaurants and oyster houses. The ship biscuit, with its light sprinkling of salt, has become the boxed cracker of the supermarket. Nabisco Saltines were one of the first of this type marketed commercially on a national scale.

However, Americans call the soft crackers of Maryland's Chesapeake Bay area "beaten biscuits." This is a cracker made with high-gluten flour and water that is beaten (the technical term is "broken") until the dough becomes soft and spongy. When baked, the biscuits are tender and fluffy as though made with yeast. Out of this species of cracker evolved the fluffy raised biscuits made with baking powder that are popular in the South. These soda biscuits, as they were once called, represent a type of bread substitute served with gravies and various fricasseed foods. In the American South they are almost universally eaten at breakfast.

Two common denominators unite all types of American crackers. The first is that they are not sweet, and therefore they are not considered dessert foods. The second is that they are "docked," the baking term for punching tiny holes into the dough so they become light and brittle once they are baked. Docking prevents the dough from shrinking and becoming tough. The old baker's tool used for making the holes was called a biscuit dock, normally a wooden handle attached to a stamp featuring numerous spikes arranged in whatever pattern the baker wanted for his or her crackers. Many docks featured the baker's initials or a simple pattern, such as a ship's anchor for a ship's biscuit.

When sugar is added to these simple recipes, American terminology changes. The crackers become wafers, and if fat of any kind enters into the recipe, the wafers graduate to cookies. The term "cookie" was borrowed from the Dutch, who settled in New York in the early 1600s. The word simply means a little cake, and "little cake" is what most cookies were called in early American cookbooks, just as they were in England. By the 1790s, however, the New York term began to show up in many places outside of that state.

The popularity of the term increased because of its connection with the fashionable New York New Year's cookies, highly ornamented stamped cookies served during New Year's Day entertainments. The word moved into American cookbook literature and eventually came to encompass any crisp, sweet finger food. But one further distinction has developed. "Cookie" is applied to foods of this kind that are either homemade or intrinsically American. How is this known? Chinese fortune cookies were invented in the United States in the 1840s under the name of motto cookies. They are not foreign. By this same rule, imported French champagne biscuits are not called cookies. Likewise the Italian *biscotti* served at nearly every coffee bar would never be characterized as cookies. Cookies are comfort food. Cookies are what children are allowed to eat. The word separates what is recognizable and American from all the rest.

William Woys Weaver

---

quantities. The Digestive (or Wholemeal) and Rich Tea became market leaders in Britain from 1949 onward. Other sorts fell out of favor, but new varieties are being continually developed as a result of consumer demand, changing tastes, and innovations in production techniques. Chocolate-coated biscuits started to become popular in the first decade of the twentieth century.

Some biscuits have become cultural markers. The snickerdoodle, flavored with nutmeg, nuts, and raisins, is a speciality of the Pennsylvania Dutch. The gingersnap, a thin ginger biscuit, is popular in Sweden. Povorone is a Spanish and Mexican biscuit of pastry dough flavored with nuts or cinnamon, rolled in icing sugar after baking. Shortbread, a rich, short biscuit that is a speciality of Scotland, is exported throughout the world. Traditionally, it was a festive food eaten at Hogmanay (the eve of New Year's Day), though it is now eaten on everyday occasions.

Biscuits are sold in several distinctive ways. They are marketed either as a single variety or as an assortment. Some of these, such as Victoria Assortment, are well-known in England and Canada. Originally, fancy biscuits were sold as novelties. They were kept in highly decorated tins, which are still sold, but have been largely replaced by other forms of packaging. The earliest tins held 228 g; later ones extended to 4.5 kg. They were sold in tens of thousands, especially at Christmastime. Biscuit tins have become something of a cultural phenomenon quite separate from the biscuits themselves, since the empty tins are commonly reused as household furniture, for storage, or as decoration.

The role of the biscuit in the diet has also changed. In the early nineteenth century, the fancy biscuit was an expensive novelty, eaten only by the upper classes, and played a relatively minor role in popular diet. Only when the time of meals altered did the role of biscuits increase, being eaten at luncheon and afternoon tea. However, it was not until the 1960s that quality biscuits were within the range of most family incomes, especially in Britain. Biscuits have adapted to a range of uses. They have become health foods (sold in pharmacies), as well as slimming or digestive aids. They are now accompaniments to hot drinks, alcoholic beverages, courses of a meal (usually with cheese), snacks, or substitutes for bread, like the old ship's biscuit, eaten by men on long sea journeys. Biscuits have also assumed a place in popular folklore, for they surface in such expressions as "take the biscuit," which in Britain means the most surprising thing that could have occurred.

See also **Baking; Bread; Cake and Pancake; Digestion; Pastry; Wedding Cake.**

BIBLIOGRAPHY

Adam, James S. *A Fell Fine Baker: The Story of United Biscuits: A Jubilee Account of the Men and the Companies Who Pioneered One of Britain's Most Celebrated Industries.* London: Hutchinson Benham, 1974.

Brown, Catherine. *Scottish Cookery.* Edinburgh: Mercat Press, 1999.

Corley, T. A. B. "Nutrition, Technology and the Growth of the British Biscuit Industry 1820–1900." In *The Making of the Modern British Diet*, edited by Derek J. Oddy and Derek S. Miller. London: Croom Helm, 1976.

Corley, T. A. B. *Quaker Enterprise in Biscuits: Huntley & Palmers of Reading 1822–1972.* London: Hutchinson, 1972.

Manley, D. J. R. *Biscuit Packaging and Storage: Packaging Materials, Wrapping Operations, Biscuit Storage, Troubleshooting Tips.* Cambridge, U.K.: Woodhead, 1998.

Wolf-Cohen, Elizabeth. *The Complete Biscuit & Cookie Book: Creative and Delicious Ideas for Making and Decorating Biscuits.* London: Apple, 1994.

Heather Holmes

BISON. *See* **Cattle; Mammals; Meat.**

BODY. The intricate relationship between food and the human body finds expression in virtually all dimensions of human existence: from physiology to psychology, from the domestic sphere to that of political economy, from the societal to the symbolic. In exploring the ways in which food and its consumption are articulated in the forms and images of corporeality, it bears note that the human body, per se, is an abstraction. As gender studies scholars have maintained, there is no such thing as a neutral "human body": every human body is individually unique in a multiplicity of ways (most basically, at the genetic level). In addition, all human bodies are sexed—be they female, male, or born hermaphrodite. For heuristic purposes only, then, it is convenient to generalize about "the human body."

Human Growth and Development

The size and shape of an individual human body (what biologists call "phenotype") is the product of the interactions over time of the genetic makeup ("genotype") and environmental influences, including behavior. Morphology, or physical form, derives from hereditary, endocrinological, metabolic, maturational, environmental, and lifestyle factors, yet the relative weight of these effects may vary depending on the somatic trait in question. For example, adult height is under rather high genetic control, whereas adult weight has a relatively low degree of heritability. There is strong evidence, however, that both energy expenditure and the basal metabolic rate enjoy a significant genetic component; likewise, gene regulation is pronounced in the distribution, or patterning, of body fat at all stages of the life span.

Growth, in terms of the progressive development of adult proportions, is measured linearly (by height or length of limb bone); in the expansion of girth, or surface area (by quadratic measures); and in terms of volume, or mass (by cubic measures). Aberrations in any of these dimensions can arise from genetic abnormalities or environmental stress, in the form of malnutrition, disease, toxins, accidents, psychosocial stress, and/or other insults to the developing organism. Human growth is so highly sensitive to environmental forces that it provides a reliable indicator of the quality of the environment, although even under stress the body maintains proportionality, in what has been called the "harmony of growth." Moreover, short-term or seasonal sources of stress need not permanently compromise the developing body, since humans possess the capacity for "catch-up" growth—a rapid increase in growth velocity that restores a child to predicted size—in weight and to a lesser degree in height. Despite its sensitivity, human growth thus appears to be a "target-seeking process" that seeks to move back to its individual trajectory when driven off course (Johnston, p. 318). The ability to recover is a function of the timing, duration, and intensity of insult, plus the quality of the post-insult environment. Data suggest that weight recovery from severe caloric and/or protein shortages can be achieved (in both children and adults), with lean muscle tissue synthesized first, followed by the laying down of adipose tissue. However, weight gain in itself does not necessarily guarantee a return to normal health, as the body's chemical composition and anatomy may be in danger of disequilibrium without attention to key micronutrients during the recovery process. With respect to stature, chronic stress in childhood can lead to permanent stunting in adult height. It is estimated that approximately one-third of the world's children are stunted in height in comparison with averages compiled for children in North America alone.

Under normal circumstances, human growth and development from conception to maturity follow a patterned trajectory. This trajectory is characterized by a rapid velocity of post-natal growth (with growth rate at its fastest in the first year of life); a steady growth rate with a lower, decelerating velocity during childhood; a juvenile growth spurt around the age of seven or eight (in about two-thirds of healthy children); and the onset of adolescence, with a markedly accelerated growth spurt, beginning for girls at age ten, on average, and for boys at age twelve years (in Western societies, yet later in stressed ecosystems). With the onset of adolescence, the relatively similar childhood body shapes and compositions of the two sexes undergo maturational processes that lead to marked differentiation. Maturation involves skeletal changes, such as the female's wider pelvic girth relative to shoulder width; muscular changes, with males exhibiting a more dramatic increase in accretion of muscle than do females; changes in adipose tissue and fat patterning, with females adding both central body and limb fat, and males losing fat from the subcutaneous layers (superficial under-the-skin fat, as opposed to deep body fat); and changes in secondary sexual characteristics, such as pubic hair and breast development. Growth ceases on completion of puberty after the period of peak growth velocity, whereupon the human body attains adult stature and achieves full reproductive maturity.

The most striking features of the adult stage of life are its stability (homeostasis) and its resistance to pathological influences. With advances in nutrition, medicine, and hygiene and a resulting increased life expectancy at all ages, more humans today live sufficiently past the reproductive years to experience chronic disease and failing physiology. Senescence—defined as cumulative, universal, progressive, irreversible, and degenerative aging—does not appear to be under tight genetic control. Rather, aging is a multi-causal process, and most pathologies relating to age (for example, cancers, heart disease, and late-onset diabetes) are probably culturally and environmentally specific. However, there is a general tendency for both sexes to experience age-related losses in stature and in muscular (lean body) mass, coincident with a decline in total energy requirements. Biological aging in non-Western populations tends to be associated with declining fatness as a percentage of total body composition; in contrast, industrialized populations tend to experience age-related increases in fat.

Human Morphological Variation

As a result of the dynamic gene-environment interactions taking place from birth to maturity, body size and morphology exhibit a wide range of variation within and between populations. Variation in body shape at a population level may, in part, mark a phenotypic manifestation of the evolutionary forces of natural selection, wherein statistically normal adult morphology is regulated by genetic adaptations to specific ecosystemic and other environmental constraints. For example, there exists a clear geographical pattern that, in colder habitats, mean body weight is greater, which might assist in the maintenance of core body temperature. Likewise, low weight may confer a thermoregulatory advantage in tropical climates, where, too, greater skin surface area (with pores) as a proportion of weight can assist with the dissipation of heat through perspiration.

In addition to genetic differences, there are many environmental and behavioral factors that influence body shape. Nutrition and overall dietary intake play central roles, as do energy-expenditure activities, disease, lifestyle, and socioeconomic status. Variance in basic caloric intake (measured as an excess or deficit in energy balance) is a major determinant of visible differences in body morphology, mainly in the ways that caloric excess shapes subcutaneous fat deposition. Simply put, eating plays an increasingly prominent role in determining what we look like, and the kinds of cross-population and intra-individual variations we see. Fat is one of the most labile tissues of the body and alters according to both genetic and environmental factors. Ethnic differences in subcutaneous fat thickness suggest genetic variation in fat patterning among populations, with peoples of European ancestry exhibiting a more peripheral than central pattern of fat distribution (limb fat over visceral fat) than those of African and Asian ancestry. Across all ethnic groups, there is marked sexual dimorphism with regard to total body fat and fat patterning, with post-adolescent females averaging approximately 20 percent in body fat composition, whereas males average 12 percent. Fat patterning is related to health status in direct and indirect ways; for example, there is strong evidence that body fat at greater than normative values (relative to gender), especially in the form of central body depositions of adipose tissue, correlates with increased risk for cardiovascular diseases and for the metabolic malady of late-onset diabetes (non-insulin-dependent diabetes mellitus).

Processes of societal "modernization," including increased population mobility, provision of social services, and industrialization (the transition from a predominantly agricultural mode of subsistence to a cash-based economy) have all influenced body shape and size, in both positive and negative ways. Positive effects have come through improved health care and education; negative effects through the growing preponderance of Western lifestyles and consumption of highly processed, energy-dense foods (such as candy and "fast food"). Widespread

218

increases in levels of obesity (often coupled with malnutrition) have been common in low-income as well as middle- and upper-income communities, and throughout urban, peri-urban, and rural areas. Medical obesity (generally defined as an individual who weighs 25 percent more than the expected weight for a given height and body frame) has become particularly acute among recently modernizing populations of the so-called New World regions, that is, the Amerindians of the Americas, the Aborigines of Australia, and the Polynesians of the Pacific islands. It is unclear whether these populations may be genetically susceptible to late-onset diabetes triggered by rapid social and economic change, or whether undernutrition during fetal and infancy years may be an underlying factor. While in the developed (some might say overdeveloped) countries excess energy (caloric) intake relative to expenditure presents the greatest food-related health problem, in much of the world undernutrition is still a major cause of morbidity and mortality.

Culture and Excess Food Consumption

Ideologies about the body and beliefs concerning ideal body size and shape are highly culture specific and, as such, transform over time, as cultures themselves undergo changes in subsistence, politics, religion, aesthetic tastes, and cross-cultural contact.

Contrary to the medical diagnosis of obesity, social definitions of obesity vary cross-culturally and across different historical eras. In traditional societies, excess body weight has generally been regarded in positive terms. Its value may even be culturally elaborated to such an extent that certain members of the group are deliberately fattened, especially in communities living in environments experiencing extreme seasons or marginal subsistence. For example, in past times when food supplies were irregular among the Nauru peoples of the Pacific, young women were fattened to improve their reproductive performance. Herein, the reproductively viable woman "was supported in her role as the creator of new life, in a community which perceived itself to be under demographic threat" (Ulijaszek et al. 1998, p. 410). Even when Nauru puberty ceremonies involving fattening practices diminished in importance as a result of the introduction of a cash economy, food as a marker of prestige persisted. Likewise, ritual fattening of Annang women in Nigeria is believed to enhance fertility, whereas, among the Azande of Central Africa, fatness is still associated with higher social status as well as greater fertility.

In some cultures, fatness has not only been desirable, it has been evocative of desire, particularly sexual desire. During the Chinese Tang Dynasty (618–907) and for long thereafter, plumpness was the standard of beauty for women; wealthy women were over-fed to levels of excessive obesity. Today, Chinese phrases still equate plumpness with health and good fortune; conversely, phrases associated with thinness indicate poor physical and social position.

Turning to prehistory in this context, it is worth noting the numerous Paleolithic statuettes of obese, voluptuous female figures that have been found over a broad geographical region of present-day Europe. The remarkable uniformity of female figurines, which are almost invariably obese and far outnumber male figurines (none of which are corpulent), suggests that a shared perception of a particular female form existed during Paleolithic times. The most famous of such figurines—the Venus of Willendorf—dates from 26,000 to 22,000 years ago. While we may never know whether the Venus of Willendorf was an actual woman, a fertility-cult idol, or a "mother" goddess, she likely represented a widespread ideal of femaleness, one that emphasized obesity. Based on the life-like depiction of the fat patterns and other features of the statue, it has been suggested that she must have been modeled on a real human subject. If so, she would most likely have been exempt from food-gathering and other high-energy exertion activities, implying that collective food resources were devoted to her care.

The positive value accorded to fatness in some cultures has generally been interpreted as a response to the vagaries of uncertain food supply, wherein individuals with larger body size represented better reproductive potential, higher social status, economic success, and/or better survivability during times of shortage. Body fatness does in fact confer considerable advantages in buffering adversity and promoting female reproductive success: the energy store of body fat in adequately nourished women is usually equivalent to the energy cost of a pregnancy. There is thus a direct, biological equation between body size and individual health, and by extension between the body size of group members and group welfare. Since physical strength derives from food (that is, adequate nutrition and caloric intake), controlling a secure food supply is a source of power, and a marker of such, resulting in a symbolic connection: food not only converts into, but comes to symbolize, fat, flesh, mass. Excess body size might reflect food security, signaling the endurance of the collective and its demographic (hence, politico-military) strength. The obese, voluptuous female may literally embody the practical and ideological values of food. Likewise, the pregnant or lactating female figure is a corporeal sign of the body as life-giving food, itself a source of survival for future generations.

With the rise of industrialization, the majority of the population has become emancipated from direct engagement in the food quest and food production, while at the same time food has become more readily available to all.

The positive value and the aesthetic desirability of obesity common in traditional societies tend eventually to subside with modernization. In late-twentieth-century Western societies, fatness became associated with sloth and laziness, and the cultural ideal emphasized a slender body form and even implied a moral virtue related to thinness. In spite of these new ideals and well-documented negative health effects of being overweight, obesity has nonetheless emerged as an epidemic health problem worldwide (reaching levels as high as 60 percent of adults in the contemporary United States). Tragically, moreover, the excessive ideals of thinness allowed to perpetuate in the fashion and cosmetics industries have contributed to the rise of another major public health crisis in Western societies, in the form of eating disorders, such as self-starvation, or anorexia nervosa.

Ideologies of the Anorexic Body

Food's central role in mediating the cultural construction of the body is as true in the case of such wasting diseases as anorexia nervosa as it is for obesity. An extremely complex psychological and somatic illness, anorexia nervosa is a life-threatening eating disorder defined as a refusal to eat that results in a body weight of less than 85 percent of the individual's expected weight for height and age. Features of anorexia that shed light on the relationship between the body, the self, and culture include an intense fear of gaining weight, a distorted body image of being fat (even when the anorexic may be emaciated in actuality), absence of regular menstrual periods, and in some cases, binge eating followed by self-induced vomiting or laxative abuse. Anorexia predominantly strikes females, especially in their teenage years; only 10 percent of sufferers are males. Conservative estimates suggest that 1 percent of females in the contemporary United States develop anorexia, and approximately 4 percent of college-age women in the United States suffer from the binge-eating disorder of bulimia.

Anorexia in its contemporary form is generally regarded as a negative symptom of the current popular culture ideal of female slenderness that valorizes an emaciated and androgynous supermodel-type of figure, characterized by an unrealistically thin waist, willowy limbs, and small breasts. The disease is thus shaped by the cultural concept of the female body in the West, a concept in which food and food symbolism play a central role alongside gender roles and expectations. According to feminist theories, patriarchal ideologies juxtapose the masculine body as an active working thing (energized by caloric intake and a very carnal, consuming relationship to the external world at large) against the feminine body as a passive vehicle intended to provide gratification, which exists in order to be used, to be itself consumed. In short, the masculine subject depends for its existence on the construction of the feminine object as an arena for action and penetration.

In this context, anorexia has been interpreted as both a symptom of a woman's imprisonment to patriarchal society and as an attempt to resist its pressures. On the one hand, an anorexic woman enslaves herself to the impossible ideals of thinness, and by practicing self-starvation literally internalizes and embodies dominant culture's tacit attempts to minimize and control her. On the other hand, by not eating, the anorexic attempts to assert autonomy over her body and body boundaries, and thereby

free herself of external incursions. In both events, food acts as a metaphor for all foreign (contaminating) substances, and food abstinence becomes a measure of self-discipline, self-reliance, and purity: the anorexic shuts out the world, with an autonomy on display and visibly performed in the figure of her thin, model-like body. Yet food consumption is also an expression of desire. If women threaten to become active subjects through the expression of desire in the form of a voracious appetite, then the patriarchal definition of womanhood is undermined. In the logic of this equation, "flesh is appetite made concrete" (MacSween) and appetite is a form of voice (Brumberg, p. 19). Female fat thus becomes an external sign of female desire that intrudes into masculine space. While power might commonly be equated with size, it has been noted that, as women become more powerful and visible in society, they also paradoxically become less massive. In other words, the successful woman is a thin woman. On the surface, the dominant theme reads that a successful woman has the willpower to not eat; at the same time, however, there exists a hidden and contradictory subtext: that women should really not be visible or powerful. With a rise in female power, then, there is a corresponding loss of female flesh, and, paradoxically, a symbolic cancellation of female presence.

Hence, by not desiring food, a modern anorexic makes her body desirable according to the norms of dominant society. By making her body a mirror of starvation, she simultaneously makes herself less threatening to patriarchy. These parallels between desire and food, modesty, and morality also underpin a type of "holy anorexia" that pious medieval women were known to practice. In Europe in the early Christian Middle Ages, asceticism—including abstinence from food consumption—was considered a form of religious piety, and anorexia in particular was a chosen path for women wishing to express their religious fervor. Like its modern counterpart, medieval anorexia may have served to order women's behavior according to dominant values, but also to exercise a kind of resistance. In a historical epoch with few or no birth control options, medieval women anorexics (whose symptoms generally included irregular menstruation) could free themselves of the burden of fertility, while manipulating the powerful imagery of female fertility. For both the medieval and the modern anorexic, then, self-starvation has been part of a larger struggle for liberation from a patriarchal family and society, in the former case, to achieve greater spiritual purity and in the latter, to succeed in the secular public sphere.

Food and Body Connections

For a variety of reasons, males are less associated with food and food symbolism than are females, a situation that largely holds across cultures. Ideologies about the ideal male body in contemporary Western societies tend to focus on muscular body build achieved through energy expenditure and exercise regimes, rather than through food intake or abstinence. Men who suffer from anorexia athletica (compulsive exercise) may abuse food in the form of undereating or binge eating, along with steroids or laxatives, in attempts to achieve a model physique.

Perhaps because of the ideological links between musculature and virility, red meat (primarily beef) has popularly been regarded as "man's food" in contemporary society. The common cliche "real men don't eat quiche" captures such gender assignment of food in a Western "you are what you eat" cultural paradigm. Salads are seen, by contrast, as the preserve of women, though not simply based on caloric levels, since while meat has higher calories than lettuce, salad dressings are likely to be calorie-rich. Chinese culture provides another pronounced example of food categorization schemes, wherein most foods possess either a *yin* or *yang* nature, categories that also align with female or male connotations, respectively.

In sum, culture-specific body image plays a prominent role in consumption patterns and types of food consumed, based on gender and dominant ideologies. As food consumption is "worn" by the body through processes of human growth and development, it might be said that beliefs about food are "worn" by the body as a reflection of cultural norms. In various cultural and historical contexts, the body, as an index for food, has come to symbolize individual and collective welfare, fertility, morality, sexuality, power, and/or resistance.

See also **Anorexia, Bulimia; Aversion to Food; Body Composition; Consumption of Food; Eating; Evolution; Gender and Food; Obesity; Women and Food.**

BIBLIOGRAPHY

Beckett, Chris. *Human Growth and Development.* London: Sage, 2002.

Bell, Rudolph. *Holy Anorexia.* Chicago: University of Chicago Press, 1987.

Bogin, Barry. *Patterns of Human Growth and Development.* Cambridge, U.K.: Cambridge University Press, 1988.

Bordo, Susan. *Unbearable Weight: Feminism, Western Culture, and the Body.* Berkeley: University of California Press, 1993.

Brumberg, Joan Jacobs. *Fasting Girls: The Emergence of Anorexia Nervosa as a Modern Disease.* Cambridge, Mass.: Harvard University Press, 1988.

Bynum, Caroline Walker. *Holy Feast and Holy Fast: The Religious Significance of Food to Medieval Women.* Berkeley: University of California Press, 1988.

Crews, Douglas E., and Ralph M. Garruto. *Biological Anthropology and Aging: Perspectives on Human Variation over the Life Span.* Oxford: Oxford University Press, 1994.

de Garine, Igor, and Nancy J. Pollock, eds. *Social Aspects of Obesity.* New York: Gordon and Breach, 1995.

Gabaccia, Donna R. *We Are What We Eat: Ethnic Food and the Making of Americans.* Cambridge, Mass.: Harvard University Press, 1998.

Johnston, Francis E. "The Ecology of Post-Natal Growth." In *The Cambridge Encyclopedia of Human Growth and Development,* edited by Stanley J. Ulijaszek, Francis E. Johnston, and Michael A. Preece, pp. 315–319. Cambridge, U.K.: Cambridge University Press, 1998.

MacSween, Morag. *Anorexic Bodies: A Feminist and Sociological Perspective on Anorexia Nervosa.* London: Routledge, 1993.

Sobal, Jeffery, and Donna Maurer, eds. *Weighty Issues: Fatness and Thinness as Social Problems.* Hawthorne, N.Y.: Aldine de Gruyter, 1999.

Ucko, Peter J. *Anthropomorphic Figurines of Predynastic Egypt and Neolithic Crete, with Comparative Material from the Prehistoric Near East and Mainland Greece.* London: A. Szmidla, 1968.

Ulijaszek, Stanley J., ed. *Health Intervention in Less Developed Nations.* Oxford: Oxford University Press, 1995.

Ulijaszek, Stanley J., Francis E. Johnston, and Michael A. Preece, eds. *The Cambridge Encyclopedia of Human Growth and Development.* Cambridge, U.K.: Cambridge University Press, 1998.

Kyra Landzelius

BODY COMPOSITION. The term body composition describes the various components that make up a person's body. The absolute and relative amounts and distribution of these components are relevant to diverse body functions and, thus, influence the state of health and various disease risks. A commonly used body composition model organizes the body to five levels of increasing complexity: from atomic to molecular, cellular, tissue-system, and whole body.

At the atomic level, the body is made up of chemical elements essential for life. Four major elements, oxygen, carbon, hydrogen, and nitrogen, collectively account for more than 96 percent of adult body weight. The remaining are minerals present in the form of salts. Calcium and phosphorus make up the major bulk of remaining minerals, found mostly in bone.

The four elements, oxygen, carbon, hydrogen, and nitrogen, are present at the molecular level in water and as organic compounds. Water serves as a solvent where chemical reactions take place. Protein and phospholipids serve as major structural components of the body. Proteins, glycogen, and lipids that include phospholipids and fats are all organic compounds. Protein, in the form of enzymes and hormones, performs important biochemical and physiological roles in the body. Glycogen reserves are small and used mainly as metabolic fuel. Fat serves as insulation and as an energy store. The two major organic compounds, protein and fat, plus water are usually grouped with the mineral component (osseous and nonosseous) to form the four-compartment model, a model used most often when considering the nutritional status of a person.

Two alternate groupings of these components used to describe body composition at the molecular level are the division of the body into a fluid and a dry component. The latter is comprised of proteins, minerals, and fat. The second alternative, also referred to as the classic two-compartment model, divides the body into fat and fat-free masses. Fat mass is the most variable as it is affected by energy balance. The fat-free mass is composed of water, proteins, and minerals. This term is used synonymously with lean body mass. This compartment also includes essential lipids. It is metabolically important and its chemical composition is assumed to be constant in a healthy adult.

At the cellular level, the chemical compounds are assembled into either the cellular component (the body's main functional components) or the extracellular supporting components; for example, extracellular fluid and solids, of which the skeleton makes up its major bulk. Because living cells consist of metabolically important structures and an inert fat component, the cellular component is further subdivided into a body cell mass and fat. This three-compartment model of body cell mass, fat, and extracellular components presents a physiological view of the body.

The tissue system level is also of structural and functional importance. Tissues contain cells that are mostly similar in appearance and function. Tissues and organs are categorized into adipose tissues, skeletal muscles, skeleton, blood, and a "residual" category that includes the skin and visceral organs. Adipose tissue includes fat cells, blood vessels, and structural elements. White adipose tissue is located mainly in the subcutaneous and visceral compartments. Subcutaneous fat provides insulation, and most visceral fat serves as an energy store. Brown fat is present in small quantities in discrete locations and plays an important role in heat production in neonates during cold exposure.

The whole body level of organization involves physical characteristics, such as body size and shape.

Normal Changes Throughout the Life Cycle

Growth. The growth process involves an increase in body size and compositional changes of tissues and organs, physiological changes during adolescence, and finally, chemical maturation of tissues and organs to reach a "stable" composition in adulthood (Table 1). Growth in height, weight, tissues and organs, and changes in chemical composition are not uniform. Thus, the relative proportions of various tissues and organs vary at different stages of growth (Table 2).

Length and weight increase rapidly during the second half of gestation and continue to change rapidly through the first year of postnatal life. There is a relative slowing in growth rates as gestation approaches term,

TABLE 1

Anthropometry and body composition of fetus, neonate, and adult

Parameter	28-week fetus	Neonate Boy	Neonate Girl	20- to 29-year-old adult Male	20- to 29-year-old adult Female	60- to 69-year-old adult Male	60- to 69-year-old adult Female
Body weight (kg)	1.015	3.530	3.399	78	64	83	71
Length/height (cm)	36	50	49	176	163	174	160
Body mass index (BMI)	–	–	–	25.2	24.2	27.4	27.7
Components of whole body (% body weight)							
Fat	4	14	15	11	29	31	45
Water	84	69	69	65	51	52	43
Protein	9	13	13	18	15	14	11
Bone mineral mass	1.2	2.1	2.1	4.2	3.7	3.5	2.7
Components of fat-free mass (% fat-free mass)							
Water	88	81	81	73	72	75	77
Protein	9	15	15	20	21	20	20
Bone mineral mass	1.3	2.4	2.5	4.7	5.2	5.0	4.9

Data on fetuses were calculated from those of Widdowson and Dickerson, and those of Ziegler and coworkers.
Data on neonates were those of Fomon and coworkers.
Bone mineral mass for fetuses and neonates were calculated using the equation of Koo and coworkers.
    BMC (g) = 24.2 * body wt (kg) − 11.1.
Data on body weight and stature in adults were from NCHS for all race/ethnicity groups in the United States.
Data on body fat and fat-free mass in adults were those of Reference Man.
Data on water, protein, and bone mineral mass of adult Caucasian males and Caucasian females in the United States were calculated from their relative proportion in fat-free mass using the data of Ellis.
Data on water, protein, and bone mineral mass in fat-free mass of adult Caucasian males and Caucasian females in the United States were those of Ellis.

TABLE 2

Weight distribution of organs and tissues

	Neonate	Adult	
		Male	Female
Body weight (kg)	3.4 kg	70 kg	58 kg
Organs or tissues (percent body weight)			
Adipose tissue	27%	21%	33%
Skeletal muscle	22%	40%	29%
Skeleton	9–18%	9–18%	9–18%
Visceral*	8%	7%	7%
Skin (excluding hypodermis)	6%	4%	3%

Data were those of Reference Man.
*Visceral organs include heart, lung, stomach, intestines, liver, gall bladder, pancreas, and spleen.

due to the physical constraints imposed on the fetus. Rapid growth in skeletal muscle and adipose tissue causes a concomitant surge in the relative protein and fat contents in the fetus and a decrease in its relative water content. At the same time, a progressive fluid shift occurs from the extracellular into the intracellular compartment. Progressive mineralization of the skeleton also occurs during this period.

After the first year, growth rate slows until the second major growth spurt at adolescence. Hormonal changes during adolescence cause major physiological differences between sexes. The "adolescent growth spurt" lasts about two to three years and begins earlier in females. In females, there is a larger accretion of body fat. In males, the increase in skeletal muscle mass is more intense and of longer duration. This sex difference in skeletal muscle and fat content persists throughout the adult years. "Chemical maturation" of the fat-free mass is completed during adolescence, when there is a relative decrease in water and a relative increase in fat, protein, and bone mineral mass.

Normally, adult height and weight are reached at about eighteen years of age by females, and twenty years of age by males. The height and weight is 170 cm and 70 kg respectively for the reference adult male, and 160 cm and 58 kg for the reference female. Relative weights of skeletal muscles and adipose tissue are higher, and that of viscera lower, in adults compared with infants. Although relative weight of the skeleton is similar between infants and adults, the adult skeleton has a higher mineral content.

Aging. The aging process produces a decline in height, lean weight, muscle mass, and skeletal size. Loss of skeletal muscle and bone mass is related to the age-associated decline in physical activity and to the decline in various hormonal secretions.

BODY MASS INDEX

Body Mass Index (BMI) is a useful guide for assessing adiposity. BMI is weight/height^2 (kg/m^2). It is related positively with body fat content. A high BMI is associated with an increased risk of cardiovascular disease, diabetes, osteoarthritis, and other conditions. However, a high BMI may also reflect a high muscle mass. Thus, other assessments should be performed, and BMI is only one of several risk factors associated with the diseases noted above.

A range of values for BMI has been used to help adults assess their health status. According to the Centers for Disease Control and Prevention (CDC), a healthy BMI for adults is between 18.5 and 24.9 kg/m^2. An individual with a BMI value of less than 18.5 is considered to be underweight. A BMI value of between 25.0 and 29.9 is considered to be overweight, and obesity is designated by values of 30 or higher.

It is more difficult to interpret BMI values for children and adolescents because of changes in body fat content that vary normally with age and sex in these life stages. As with growth references for weight and height, sex-specific preferences for BMI-for-age are available for ages two to twenty years. Limits have been established to identify undesirable weights in children and adolescents. Those under the fifth percentile on the BMI-for-age references are classified as underweight; those equal or over the eighty-fifth percentile are considered to be at risk of becoming overweight; and those equal or over the ninety-fifth percentile are considered to be overweight.

Changes in Body Composition under Different Conditions

Weight loss. Prolonged food deprivation causes growth faltering in children and weight loss in adults. Recurrent infections due to poor hygiene and health care may exacerbate food deprivation. Severe weight loss also occurs in diseases, such as malignant cancers, hepatic and renal diseases, and those involving the gastrointestinal tract. Loss in weight in severe undernutrition is due to loss in both body cell mass and fat mass.

Loss in body cell mass and preservation of the extracellular fluid results in an increase in water content in the fat-free mass and an increase in the ratio of extracellular fluid to intracellular volume.

Weight gain. Most weight gain involves a mixture of fat and lean tissues with their relative contribution depending on the initial body composition, physiological

METHODS OF MEASUREMENT

Because of the implications of changes in body composition to health and disease, there is a need for their measurements. Virtually all the major elements—oxygen, carbon, hydrogen, nitrogen, sodium, chlorine, calcium, and phosphorus—can be measured directly by *in vivo* neutron activation analysis techniques. Total body potassium (K) can be measured by whole-body counting of the naturally occurring radioisotope ^{40}K. These techniques are expensive and are available in only a few centers.

The four-compartment model (fat, water, protein, and mineral) is ideal for assessing growth and nutritional status. Theoretically, fat mass can be assessed from the distribution volume of inert gases; but in practice, it is problematic, and its use remains a challenge. Water can be estimated by measuring the dilution volume of water labeled with stable-isotopes of hydrogen, ^{2}H$_2$O, or oxygen, H$_2$^{18}O); protein may be estimated indirectly from measurements of total body nitrogen by assuming that 16 percent of protein is nitrogen; and the total body mineral contents calculated from total bone minerals which are estimated by whole-body dual-energy X-ray absorptiometry (DXA).

Although fundamentally important, methodological constraints often limit the use of the four-compartment model. Thus, the classic two-compartment model that compartmentalizes the body into fat mass and fat-free mass is used more widely by physicians and exercise physiologists. Fat-free mass, which includes water, proteins, and minerals, can be determined by various indirect methods if one assumes that the relative composition of this compartment is relatively constant in healthy adults. The established "constant" values for the various components of fat-free mass are population- and ethnic group–specific, and applicable only to healthy young white adults. Successful application of the two-compartment model to the young, sickly, elderly, and different ethnic groups requires determination of group specific "constants."

The earliest method, and one considered to be the "gold standard," for estimating fat-free mass, is densitometry. The body density is obtained by underwater weighing and assuming a density of 1.100 g/cm^3 for fat-free mass and 0.900 g/cm^3 for fat mass. A more modern air-displacement method has been used to measure body density. Its advantage is its applicability to infants, the sickly, and the elderly. Fat-free mass can also be estimated from measurement of either total body water or potassium, and by assuming that the water content of fat-free mass is 73.2 percent, and that its potassium content is 68.1 mmol/kg in adults. Other noninvasive methods for measuring body composition include total body electrical conductivity (TOBEC) and bioelectrical impedance analysis (BIA) techniques. These methods use the principle that the fat-free mass conducts an electrical current better than does the fat mass.

Although information at the cellular level is important, quantifying the compartments may be technically difficult. Attempts have been made to assess the size of cellular compartments in healthy adults by using "constant" values. Body cell mass has been estimated from measurements of potassium multiplied by a factor of 8.33, and extracellular solids from estimates of total body calcium and the assumption that 17.7 percent of extracellular solids is calcium. Dilution volume of bromine or chlorine has been used to estimate the extracellular fluid volume.

Most of our knowledge of the composition of specific tissues and systems comes from studies of cadavers and tissue biopsies. Computed tomography (CT), magnetic resonance imaging (MRI), and ultrasound imaging provide information on subcutaneous and visceral adipose tissues, and DXA provides information specific to the skeleton. Skeletal muscle mass can be estimated indirectly from measurements of total amount of creatinine in the urine over a 24-hour period. Radiology is useful to assess the proportions of bone, fat, and muscles in limbs.

Commonly used techniques at the whole body level are anthropometric measurements of body weight, height, body circumferences, and skinfold thicknesses. These techniques are simple and easy to perform and are well suited for field work or for large-scale studies. Sex-appropriate clinical growth charts available from the National Center for Health Statistics (NCHS) are used routinely for clinical assessments of growth by pediatricians. Two sets of sex-appropriate weight-for-age, length-for-age, and weight-for-length percentile references are available: one for infants from birth to thirty-six months, and another for older children from two to twenty years of age. Two often-used methods that reflect fatness are measurements of skinfold thickness and estimates of the body mass index (BMI). Regional subcutaneous fat distribution can be estimated from skinfold thickness measured with specifically designed calipers. The approximate ratio of upper–body adiposity to lower-body adiposity may be estimated by measuring waist and hip circumferences. Body mass index, calculated from weight/height^2 (kg/m^2), is often used to assess adiposity.

status, and physical activity. For example, an obese person gains a larger proportion of fat than lean tissues than does a lean person.

Overweight and obesity, and their associated health risks, are of increasing prevalence in affluent societies. In the United States, the incidence of obesity has increased from 12 percent in 1991 to 17.9 percent in 1998.

The significant consequences of increase in adiposity are not limited to net changes in body composition. Specific regional fat distributions appear to be associated with diverse levels and types of morbidity. Higher levels of upper-body obesity, especially of the visceral, is associated with abnormalities of fatty acid metabolism and is related to the higher risks of hypertension, premature coronary death, and type 2 diabetes mellitus.

Physical training. In general, physical training increases muscle and bone mass, and decreases fat mass. Gains in muscle mass and losses in fat mass vary with the intensity and duration of usual physical activity. Changes in body composition associated with physical activity are mediated by increases in the secretion of anabolic hormones. These increase lean body mass. Increases in catecholamines facilitate fat loss.

Immobilization. Reduction or loss of mobility increases the nutritional risk of obesity or sarcopenia, an abnormally low lean body mass. Prolonged immobilization causes loss of body nitrogen and calcium, hence a decrease in muscle mass accompanied by decreases in muscle strength and decreases in bone density.

Osteoporosis. The high prevalence of osteoporosis in the elderly, especially in females, is a major public health concern. Loss of bone mass and deterioration of bone tissue is a feature of the normal aging process that is attributable to an intrinsic deterioration of the ossification process. It leads to increased bone fragility and, consequently, increased risk of bone fracture. Although reduction in bone density affects every individual, in some, loss in bone mass is severe. The skeleton is not uniformly involved; the spine and other trabecular bone are more affected commonly and severely than is the cortical bone of the axial skeleton. The greater severity of osteoporosis in females is attributed to a lower peak bone mass achieved at puberty and estrogen withdrawal at menopause. Other factors causing loss of bone mass are a lack of physical activity and decreased calcium intake.

BIBLIOGRAPHY

Bloomfield, Susan A. "Changes in Musculoskeletal Structure and Function with Prolonged Bed Rest." *Medicine and Science in Sports and Exercise* 29 (1997): 197–206.

Centers for Disease Control and Prevention. Available at www.cdc.gov/nccdphp/dnpa/bmi/bmi-for-age.htm.

Ellis, Kenneth J. "Human Body Composition: In Vivo Methods." *Physiological Reviews* 80 (2000): 649–680.

Fomon, Samuel J., Ferdinand Haschke, Ekhard E. Ziegler, and Steven E. Nelson. "Body Composition of Reference Children from Birth to Age 10 Years." *American Journal of Clinical Nutrition* 35 (1982): 1169–1175.

Jensen, Michael D. "Health Consequences of Fat Distribution." *Hormone Research* 48 Suppl 5 (1997): 88–92.

Koo, Winston K., Jocelyn Walters, Andrew J. Bush, Russell W. Chesney, and Susan E. Carlson. "Dual-Energy X-Ray Absorptiometry Studies of Bone Mineral Status in Newborn Infants." *Journal of Bone Mineral Research* 11 (1996): 997–1002.

Mokdad, Ali H., Mary K Serdula, William H. Dietz, Barbara A. Bowman, James S. Marks, and Jeffrey P. Koplan. "The Spread of the Obesity Epidemic in the United States, 1991–1998." *Journal of the American Medical Association* 282 (1999): 1519–1522.

National Center of Health Statistics. www.cdc.gov/nchs/about/major/nhanes/datatblelink.htm.

Raisz, Lawrence G. "Osteoporosis: Current Approaches and Future Prospects in Diagnosis, Pathogenesis, and Management." *Journal of Bone and Mineral Metabolism* 17 (1999): 79–89.

Snyder, W. S., M. J. Cook, E. S. Nasset, L. R. Karhausen, G. Parry Howells, and I. H. Tipton. *Report of the Task Group on Reference Man.* ICRP Publication 23. New York: Pergamon Press, 1984.

Wang, Zi-Mian, Richard N. Pierson, Jr., and Steven B. Heymsfield. "The Five-Level Model: A New Approach to Organizing Body-Composition Research." *American Journal of Clinical Nutrition* 56 (1992): 19–28.

Widdowson, Elsie M., and John W. T. Dickerson. "Chemical Composition of the Body." In *Mineral Metabolism*, vol. 2, edited by Cyril L. Comar and Felix Bronner. Orlando: Academic Press, 1972.

Ziegler, Ekhard E., Alejandro M. O'Donnell, Steven E. Nelson, and Samuel J. Fomon. "Body Composition of the Reference Fetus." *Growth* 40 (1976): 329–341.

Hwai-Ping Sheng

BODY IMAGE. *See* **Anorexia, Bulimia; Body; Eating: Anatomy and Physiology of Eating; Obesity.**

BOHEMIA. *See* **Central Europe.**

BOILING. The admission of the novice cook that he or she "cannot even boil water" has perpetuated the idea that boiling water is one of the simplest tasks in the kitchen. In reality, it is also a frequently misunderstood and mislabeled culinary technique. Boiling is one of the moist (as opposed to dry) heat processes of cooking, which include pressure cooking, scalding, simmering, poaching, stewing, fricasseeing, braising, casserole-making, double-boiling, and steaming, as well as partial moist-heat processes, like blanching. Through the years, however, these traditional terms for different kinds of moist heat cooking have been variously interpreted and,

Photo showing the physics of boiling water and its change to steam. COURTESY OF PHOTO RESEARCHERS, INC.

Hot: 130 to 135°F. The water is too hot to touch without injury.

Poach: 160 to 180°F. The water is beginning to move, to shiver.

Simmer: 185 to 200°F. There is movement, and little bubbles appear in the water.

Slow boil: 205°F. There is more movement and noticeably larger bubbles.

Real boil: 212°F. The water is rolling, vigorously bubbling, and steaming.

Boiling is affected by altitude. At sea level, water boils at 212°F; at 3,000 feet, it boils at 205°F; 5,000 feet, at 203°F; and 7,500 feet, at 198°F. Because certain foods, like soup, pasta, and vegetables, will cook at a lower temperature, they will take longer to cook.

The boiling process serves two purposes: it destroys organic impurities, and it transforms raw ingredients into cooked foods. Boiling water hardens the albumen in eggs; toughens fibrin and dissolves tissues in meat; and bursts starch grains and softens cellulose in cereals and vegetables. One of the great advantages of water as a cooking medium is that it needs only a vessel and heat to reach and maintain its boiling point, no matter how long or how hard it is heated.

The food scientist Harold McGee maintains that during the boiling process, it is the convection currents in hot water that heat food. The "moist" cooking methods, however, cannot brown foods; consequently, meat and vegetables are normally sautéed in a frying pan before they are simmered in broth or water. Despite this limitation of the technique, by which boiling in water is conducted at a substantially lower temperature level than that of broiling, baking, and frying, boiling is a very efficient process. As McGee notes in *On Food and Cooking*, "The entire surface of the food is in contact with the cooking medium, which is dense and turbulent enough that the water molecules continuously and rapidly impart their energy to the food" (p. 615).

The old adage "a stew boiled is a stew spoiled" can be applied to almost every other kind of food because lengthy cooking at high temperatures toughens the proteins in meats, fish, and eggs, and the rapid bubbling breaks up delicate foods. While recipes either call for foods to be immersed in cold water and brought to the boiling point or plunged into boiling water, they almost never indicate boiling for a protracted period of time. Even so-called "boiled" eggs should be simmered after the initial contact with boiling water. Simmering, then, is often used in tandem with boiling because simmering liquid gently cooks fragile foods and tenderizes tough ones.

Only certain foods, such as vegetables, pasta, cereals, and other grains, are truly boiled in water. In these cases, it is necessary to maintain the boil to ensure their proper cooking. Because adding foods to boiling water lowers the boiling point, it is usually stipulated that the

of necessity, combined with other culinary methods. For example, a braise, fricassee, and brown stew have their origin in dry heat sautéing but are finished by long moist-heat cooking in stock. Even foods that are specifically labeled "boiled," such as boiled eggs, boiled potatoes, and boiled coffee, are not entirely cooked in boiling water but rather simmered after being brought to a boil. The pores of food are sealed by being dropped into rapidly boiling liquid, but then the temperature is usually reduced to a simmer (185–200°F)—the suitable temperature for cooking soups, stews, and braises.

Boiling, or *bouiller*, is cooking in boiling water. Water boils at 212°F (sea level), and simmers at 190°F. To fully understand the heating process, Julia Child advises the cook to observe water in its various cooking stages, from tepid to real boil, by testing it and using an immersable thermometer and noting the following temperature changes:

Tepid: 85 to 105°F. The water is comparable to the temperature of the human body.

Warm: 115 to 120°F. The water is touchable but not hot.

quantity of water must be at least three times the volume needed to cover the ingredient to offset the lower temperature caused by their addition. In cooking vegetables, particularly, the amount of salted water will insure rapid boiling, thereby shortening the time of cooking and preserving color.

According to Fannie Merritt Farmer, milk should never be allowed to boil because at boiling temperature the casein is slightly hardened, and the fat is rendered more difficult to digest. She advises the use of a double boiler to "scald (196 degrees)" milk heated over boiling water.

History of Boiling

McGee theorizes that, as a culinary technique, boiling probably followed roasting and preceded baking. Because boiling requires containers that are both water- and fireproof, the development of pottery at least ten thousand years ago had to precede boiling. And the large pots hanging in the fireplaces of the earliest kitchens attest to the fact that many meals were slowly simmered, sometimes over a period of days. In Taillevent's *Viandier* (c. 1364) the cook's activities centered on a fireplace that featured an adjustable pothook from which large cooking pots hung filled with meats, poultry, game, and vegetables. To control temperatures, the pot's position could be stationary over temperate ashes or could be swung over the hottest coals. Hot coals or logs could also be moved beneath it. This method of hearth cooking continued into the eighteenth century and even later in rural areas. Chef and author John Thorne eulogizes the pot as the emblem of the kitchen and quotes the noted French chef Alain Senderens, who suggests in his *Figues sans barbarie* (1991) that unlike "spit cooking" or the kind of roasting associated with the early "gatherers," "the cooking of the pot symbolized the feminine domain of the kitchen, family, economy, and, by extension, the civilizing process itself." By preparing food in boiling water in a pot, the cook took what nature provided and transformed it into thoroughly cooked food. "From this instant," Senderens believes, "cooking came to indicate the cultural, intellectual, and technological level of a society" (Thorne, p. 239).

Whether gender driven, as Senderens implies, or a matter of historical temperament, the cooking process became more complex and varied because of the invention of pottery at least ten thousand years ago. Furthermore, the word "pot," contrary to popular belief, does not seem to reflect the Latin *potare* (to drink) or be related to the Spanish *olla* or Italian *pentolone* or *marmitta*—the words for large cooking vessels. Etymologically, "pot" can be traced to Celtic origins: Irish *pota*; Gaelic *poit*; and Welsh *pot*, and there is reason to believe that the word "pot" may have developed initially in northern lands.

Traditionally, boiled dinners and one-pot cooking seemed to be a congenial way of dining in cold climates. From broth-based fondues in Switzerland to the soup kettle that used to hang over the open hearth in the old farmhouses of Japan's snow country, variations on sustaining one-pot meals can be found in almost every ethnic cuisine, including the Italian *bollito misto*, Spanish *cocido*, and the French *potee lorraine*. The cold regions of China had a communal dish known in the West as the Mongolian hot pot, named for its distinctive cooking utensil, and a popular contemporary Japanese modification is called *shabu-shabu*.

Asian cooking also has a communal one-pot meal, called *nabemono*, literally "things in a pot," which is served at home and in restaurants. Diners do their own cooking, choosing whatever meat, poultry, fish, and vegetables they like from platters overflowing with raw ingredients that they cook over a communal pot of sizzling broth. The broth is continually enriched in flavor as the ingredients are dipped into it. Although the *donabe*, an earthenware casserole with thick pottery walls and distinctive shape, requires a portable and substantial heat source to maintain the temperature of the dipping broth, everything from gas rings to an alcohol or canned-heat burner can be used effectively during the traditional lengthy meal.

Pot-au-feu, or "pot on the fire," consisting of meat, poultry, and vegetables in their cooking liquid, has also been a fixture of French gastronomy since the Middle Ages, and it was dramatized by King Henri IV, who promised his subjects a chicken in their pot every Sunday. In some French cookbooks a distinction is sometimes made between a pot-au-feu, a boiled beef and vegetable dinner; and a *poule-au-pot*, in which a whole stewing hen was used; and a *potée* or mixed pot of ingredients, including pork and veal shoulder and various sausages. Used in every French household, the tall earthenware cylindrical pots known as marmites were the ideal cooking utensils for this meal of meat, poultry, and vegetables, which was brought to a boil in water and then simmered for hours over the fire. A good consommé was thereby produced and a full-course dinner served—clear broth first, the boiled meat and vegetables presented separately. A dish called petite marmite was almost identical with pot-au-feu except that its primary purpose was to be served and eaten all together.

By the time Pierre François de la Varenne's cookbook was published in 1651, the fine broth that hours of simmering had produced in these one-pot meals had an intrinsic value, and separate recipes for bouillon began to appear for the purpose of enhancing soups and entrees. As did medieval cooks before him, La Varenne kept in reserve one meat stock and one fish stock to make a roux, flavor a soup or stew, and combine with other ingredients for a sauce.

On the other side of the Atlantic, boiled dinners have always been popular in New England, Pennsylvania, and other parts of the country. Prepared like a pot-au-feu, the New England boiled dinner is made traditionally with either corned or fresh beef, and boiled beets on the side, while other sections of the country feature an Irish boiled dinner that includes cabbage, onions, and new potatoes simmered with the corned beef. Boiled crab dinner, the signature seafood dish of the Chesapeake Bay region, consists of blue crabs placed into seasoned boiling water, cooked, cracked open, and accompanied by melted butter. And Wisconsin boasts a famous Door County whitefish boil.

Among the nutrition conscious, there is growing concern about whether cooking, especially the lengthened cooking of boiling, robs foods of their vitamins and enzymes. The cult of raw food, for instance, has rapidly gained momentum. For such adherents, 116°F is the point beyond which components of the original human diet become "dead," unhealthy victuals. But nutritionists generally come down on the side of cooked food, both to rid ingredients like mushrooms and meats of toxins and to enhance the pleasures of the table. Boiling and its related moist heat cooking techniques, therefore, are worthy of mastering and a challenge to the cook.

See also **Child, Julia; Cooking; La Varenne, Pierre François de; Nutrients; Packaging and Canning, History of; Poaching; Preparation of Food; Taillevent; Water: Water as a Resource.**

BIBLIOGRAPHY

Child, Julia. *From Julia Child's Kitchen*. New York: Knopf, 1975.

Corriher, Shirley O. *Cookwise: The Hows and Whys of Successful Cooking*. New York: William Morrow, 1997.

Culinary Institute of America. *The New Professional Chef*. Edited by Linda Glick Conway. New York: Van Nostrand Reinhold, 1991.

Farmer, Fannie Merritt. *The Original Boston Cooking-School Cook Book*. New York: New American Library, 1988. The original edition was published in 1896.

McGee, Harold. *On Food and Cooking: The Science and Lore of the Kitchen*. New York: Scribners, 1984.

Peterson, James. *The Essentials of Cooking*. New York: Artisan, 1999.

Thorne, John, with Matt Lewis Thorne. *Pot on the Fire: Further Exploits of a Renegade Cook*. New York: North Point, 2000.

Tsuji, Shizuo. *Japanese Cooking: A Simple Art*. Tokyo: Kodansha International, 1980.

Joan Reardon

BOTANICALS. Botanicals are fresh or dried plants, plant parts, or plants' isolated or collective chemical components, extracted in water, ethanol, or other organic solvents, plus essential oils, oleoresins, and other extractives used for flavoring, fragrance, functional health benefits, medicine, or other biological and technical activities. Many botanicals, broadly speaking, also can be classified as herbs, plants used for flavor, fragrance, or medicinal qualities, such as caraway, parsley, rosemary, sage, and

thyme. Other botanicals fall under the classification of spices, piquant aromatic plant materials, usually of tropical origin, used to season food. Examples include cloves, cinnamon, nutmeg, and pepper. Botanicals commonly are used in foods, drugs, and cosmetics. The cosmetic industry uses over 360 botanical ingredients, classified as "biological additives," to enhance the fragrance, performance, or consumer appeal of products. Botanicals, either in crude form (whole dried plants or plant parts) or in their isolated or modified chemical constituents, also are used in prescription and nonprescription (over-the-counter) drugs. In addition, over 1,600 botanicals and their derivatives are sold in the United States in a special food category called "dietary supplements." In commercial trade, botanicals, though not defined as such, generally refer to dried materials of plant origin sold in bulk form as whole, cut-and-sifted, or powdered ingredients.

Botanicals in Human Experience

Botanists conservatively estimate that 250,000 species of flowering plants exist on Earth. At least 85,000 plant species worldwide have been documented as being used as medicinal botanicals, at least in folk medicine. The World Health Organization estimates that as much as three-quarters of the world's population relies on traditional forms of medicine, chiefly herbal or botanical medicine. Botanicals used in foods, drugs, and cosmetics are an integral part of daily life.

The human experience in the use of botanicals is inextricably interwoven with human history. The first known historical evidence for the use of plants comes from the Middle Paleolithic burial site in Iraq known as Shanidar IV, a Neanderthal grave containing remains of yarrow flowers (*Achillea* spp.), marshmallow (*Althaea* spp.), and ephedra (*Ephedra* spp.), all of which are botanicals still in use in the twenty-first century.

The Ebers papyrus, dating to 1500 B.C.E., was discovered in 1876. This ancient Egyptian manuscript mentions 876 medicines, most of which are of botanical origins. Undoubtedly, ancient Greek scholars learned from their Egyptian predecessors about the use of botanicals in medicine. The writings of Hippocrates (466–377 B.C.E.) refer to many botanical substances. The starting point for Western medicine, and in particular botanical ingredients used in the West in the nineteenth and twentieth centuries, is the first-century work *De Materia Medica of Dioscorides of Anazarba in Cilicia*. For more than fifteen centuries, all Western cultures depended on this source for information on botanicals. It includes over six hundred botanicals, most of which are in use in the twenty-first century.

Botanicals as Food Additives

Over 250 botanical substances are added during food product manufacturing for flavor, fragrance, or technical characteristics, such as coloring, thickening, or preservative activity. These botanicals are used commonly and extensively, often in the form of concentrated extracts at parts per million levels, as natural ingredient additives for many categories of food products, including baked goods, canned goods, meat products, dairy products, nonalcoholic beverages, and alcoholic beverages. Many botanical ingredients have a long history of use and generally are recognized as safe. However, for a new ingredient, not previously marketed materially in the United States, to enter the American market, it must receive prior approval by the Food and Drug Administration (FDA). The manufacturer (or industry trade organization) may submit toxicological data to the FDA in support of the ingredient's safety.

Botanicals as Dietary Supplements

In 1994 the U.S. Congress passed the Dietary Supplement Health and Education Act, which created a special food regulatory category for dietary supplements, including vitamins, minerals, herbs or other botanicals, amino acids, or other dietary substances used to supplement the diet by increasing the total dietary intake. Concentrates, metabolites, constituents, extracts, or their combinations also are included in the definition. Dietary supplements are regulated as foods rather than as drugs despite the fact that most such products are intended to provide a health benefit. The vast majority of botanicals available on the American market, from over 1,600 plant species, are sold as dietary supplements.

Many well-known botanicals sold as dietary supplements in the United States also are available in other Western countries, notably Germany, where they are regulated as drugs under a special category called phytomedicines. By definition, phytomedicines include the totality of chemical constituents within a botanical or plant part rather than a single isolated chemical component. Well-known botanicals in this category are garlic (*Allium sativum*), ginkgo leaf extracts (*Ginkgo biloba*), echinacea (*Echinacea purpurea*, *E. angustifolia*, and *E. pallida*), ginseng (*Panax ginseng*), kava kava (*Piper methysticum*), saw palmetto (*Serenoa repens*), St. John's wort (*Hypericum perforatum*), and valerian (*Valeriana officinalis*). In the European markets for these botanicals, quality is strictly regulated. In the United States, it is not; therefore dietary supplements are perceived as "unregulated."

Botanicals in Modern Medicine

Prescription and nonprescription drugs of botanical origin are used widely in modern medicine, primarily as purified derivatives or partially modified secondary chemical compounds. Remarkably it is estimated that approximately 25 percent of drugs in the average American pharmacy are botanical derivatives. Of 121 prescription drugs in use in the early twenty-first century that originate from 90 plant species, 74 percent were discovered in scientific follow-up of historical or folkloric claims of medicinal value. Botanical derivatives used in chemotherapy include paclitaxel (taxol), extracted from yew species (*Taxus* spp.),

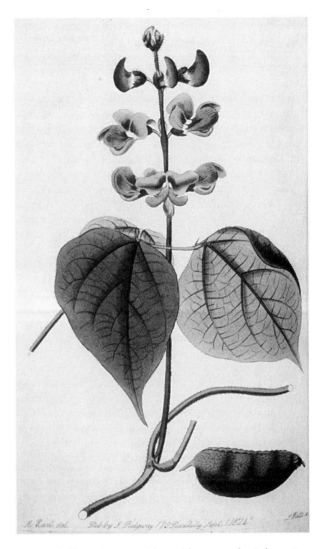

Botanical illustrations provide a rich source for information about historical food plants. This picture of the purple hyacinth bean (*Dolichos labab*) appeared in *Edward's Botanical Register* in 1824 and represents one of the most beautiful scientific renderings of this bean. It was grown as an ornamental in the United States, but the white flowering variety provides an important source of food in India. The bean was also known to the ancient Greeks and Egyptians. ROUGHWOOD COLLECTION.

used for certain forms of breast and ovarian cancer; vincristine and vinblastine, purified alkaloids extracted from the Madagascar periwinkle (*Catharanthus roseus*), used in the treatment of leukemias and Hodgkin's disease; and semisynthetic compounds from mayapple (*Podophyllum* spp.), used in the treatment of testicular and small-cell lung cancers. Nonprescription botanical ingredients include the laxatives psyllium seed (*Plantago* spp.) and senna leaves (*Senna* spp.). Some botanicals are the source of both drugs and foods. Morphine, codeine, and other chemical analogs from the opium poppy (*Papaver somniferum* L.) are used for the management of pain. The opium poppy is also the source of poppy seeds, used as a decorative and flavoring component in the culinary arts.

Foxglove: From Folk Medicine to Modern Botanical

The cardiac glycosides digoxin and digitoxin, extracted from several species of foxglove (*Digitalis* spp.), are used in the treatment of heart diseases, such as atrial fibrillation and congestive heart failure. This botanical was not well known to the ancients as a medicinal plant. Instead, it was considered a poisonous plant. A British physician, William Withering, introduced the drug to medicine in 1785 in *An Account of the Foxglove and Some of Its Medical Uses: With Practical Remarks on Dropsy and Other Diseases*, published in Birmingham, England, where Withering served as a physician at the general hospital. In 1775 Withering became aware of the secret family recipe of an elderly patient, Mrs. Hutton, in Shropshire, England. She had developed a reputation for curing "dropsy" (congestive heart failure) when physicians had failed. Withering discovered that the active ingredient was foxglove. Crude extracts of the botanical were prescribed widely in the 1800s, although exact dosing requirements sometimes resulted in fatal overdoses. The crude drug and its preparations have a narrow therapeutic ratio. A small increase in dose, only slightly above that necessary for therapeutic results, can produce toxicity. The discovery and isolation in the leaves of the glycosides responsible for the botanical's pharmacological cardiac effects led to more exact controlled dosage forms with lower risks of toxic effects.

"The Dose Makes the Poison"

Foxglove and its isolated chemicals are a good example of a fundamental principle in the response of a cell, organ, or organism to a botanical drug or food ingredient. The response or expected activity is proportional to the dose. Therefore, research on the effects of a substance on an organism requires measurement of a dose-response relationship. Such information is gathered by measuring responses to appropriately variable amounts of the active agent (usually in laboratory animals). Doses are increased incrementally until 80 percent of the maximal response is achieved. Above the level of 80 percent, usually only small changes in activity are observed. Higher doses also may result in toxic effects. Quantitative analyses of the dose-response curve measure the relative potencies of a drug or extract and help determine at what levels a beneficial or a toxic reaction may occur.

Inhibition or potentiation of a response often involves attachment of a molecule to a cellular receptor site. Targeting cell receptor sites helps direct research to specific activities, such as anti-inflammatory or analgesic (pain-relieving) effects, or to diseases, such as diabetes mellitus or cancer. Mechanisms of action of potential interest often relate to cell receptor site competition. Sometimes effects are mechanical. For example, psyllium seed works as a bulk laxative by absorbing moisture in the intestines, thus increasing bulk and stimulating mechanical peristalsis.

A common adage in toxicology is "the dose makes the poison." In pharmacology, the measure of a substance's margin of safety is known as the "therapeutic index." This index is expressed as the ratio of the dose causing harmful effects to the dose causing a therapeutic effect in a specific proportion of individuals. The amount of a substance that causes death in 50 percent of laboratory animals is expressed as LD50 (dose lethal to 50 percent).

Botanicals Withdrawn Due to Safety Concerns

Most botanicals have a long history of apparent safe use. Ingredients may be withdrawn when new information raises safety concerns. Sassafras (*Sassafras albidum*) is an example. Sassafras derives its flavor and fragrances from an essential oil comprised of up to 80 percent safrole. In the late 1950s safrole, then used as a primary root beer flavoring, was banned as a food additive due to concerns over serious liver toxicity and carcinogenicity. The ban was subsequently extended to dried sassafras bark sold for the intended purpose of making an herbal tea. Dried sassafras leaves (used as a base for gumbo filé) must also be free of safrole. Another example of a botanical no longer considered safe is comfrey (*Symphytum* spp.). Popular in the 1970s and 1980s, comfrey leaves and roots were regarded as a virtual cure-all, earning it the name "all-heal." Apparently used safely for centuries, comfrey was found to contain significant amounts of a class of pyrrolizidine alkaloids that cause a condition known as veno-occlusive disease of the liver (resulting in the occluding or clogging of the major veins in the liver). The rare disease can only be diagnosed with a liver biopsy; thus it went unrecognized for decades. Internal use of comfrey products is restricted or prohibited in many countries.

See also **Additives; Flowers; Herbs and Spices; Hippocrates; Processing of Food.**

BIBLIOGRAPHY

American Herbal Products Association. *American Herbal Products Association's Botanical Safety Handbook*, edited by Michael McGuffin, Christopher Hobbs, Roy Upton, and Alicia Goldberg. Boca Raton, Fla.: CRC Press, 1997.

Aronson, J. K. *An Account of the Foxglove and Its Medical Uses, 1785–1985*. London and New York: Oxford University Press, 1985.

Barrett, Bruce, and David Kieffer. "Medicinal Plants, Science, and Health Care." *Journal of Herbs, Spices & Medicinal Plants* 8, no. 2–3 (2001): 1–36.

Blumenthal, Mark, Alicia Goldberg, and Josef Brinckmann, eds. *Herbal Medicine: Expanded Commission and Monographs*. Austin, Tex.: American Botanical Council, 2000.

Duke, James A. "Foreword." In *Plants Used against Cancer: A Survey*, edited by Jonathan L. Hartwell. Lawrence, Mass.: Quarterman, 1982.

Foster, Steven, and Varro E. Tyler. *Tyler's Honest Herbal: A Sensible Guide to the Use of Herbs and Related Remedies.* 4th ed. Binghamton, N.Y.: Haworth Herbal Press, 1999.

Hill, Albert F. *Economic Botany: A Textbook of Useful Plants and Plant Products.* New York: McGraw-Hill, 1937.

Leake, Chauncey D. *An Historical Account of Pharmacology to the Twentieth Century.* Springfield, Ill.: Thomas, 1975.

Leung, Albert Y., and Steven Foster. *Encyclopedia of Common Natural Ingredients Used in Food, Drugs, and Cosmetics.* 2d ed. New York: John Wiley, 1996.

McGuffin, Michael, John T. Kartesz, Albert Y. Leung, and Arthur O. Tucker. *Herbs of Commerce.* 2d ed. Silver Spring, Md.: American Herbal Products Association, 2000.

Nikitakis, Joanne M., ed. *CFTA Cosmetic Ingredient Handbook.* Washington, D.C.: Cosmetic, Toiletry, and Fragrance Association, 1988.

Williamson, Elizabeth M., David T. Okpako, and Fred J. Evans. *Selection, Preparation, and Pharmacological Evaluation of Plant Material.* New York: John Wiley, 1996.

Steven D. Foster

BOTULISM. Botulism is a paralytic illness caused by a nerve toxin produced by the soil bacterium *Clostridium botulinum* and spread by contaminated food or by infection of a wound. The term comes from the Latin *botulus* (sausage), but the vehicle in food-borne cases today is usually vegetables or other food improperly canned at home. Commercial canning is almost never implicated, although a notable case in 1971 left one person dead and several others seriously injured. The illness is rare, with only twenty-five to thirty food-borne cases reported annually in the United States.

C. botulinum is a spore-forming bacteria that can lie dormant in the soil for months or years. In a warm, moist, low-oxygen environment, however, the spores can produce vegetative cells that multiply rapidly and secrete a deadly toxin, which attacks the nervous system of the person ingesting contaminated food.

Symptoms of botulism include double vision, blurred vision, drooping eyelids, slurred speech, difficulty in swallowing, dry mouth, and muscle weakness. An antitoxin can be used with early diagnosis, but otherwise treatment involves supportive care, sometimes including a ventilator. A severe case can require months of medical and nursing care and may leave the patient with permanent impairments. Botulism is fatal in about 8 percent of cases, usually from respiratory failure.

Thorough washing can remove the spores and proper heating will destroy them. If, however, the food being canned is not washed properly and fails to reach the necessary temperature for the required time, the spores can germinate and produce toxin in the canned goods.

A pH in the acid range will also kill the spores, so acidic foods such as fruit and tomatoes are less likely to be vehicles than low-acid food such as corn, green beans, or asparagus. Canners are often advised to raise the acidity of food by adding an acid source such as lemon juice or citric acid.

To avoid the danger of botulism, home canners of low-acid foods are advised to use a pressure canner instead of the unpressurized, boiling-water-bath systems used previously. A temperature of up to 250°F is needed, which can be reached with pressure canners operated at ten to fifteen pounds per square inch. The time required ranges from twenty to one hundred minutes, depending on the food and the size of the jars. Detailed instructions are available with home canning systems, either from the U.S. Department of Agriculture or from an extension agent.

Industrial quality control makes it highly unlikely that commercially canned food will be contaminated with *botulinum* toxin. However, consumers should reject any commercial canned goods that appear swollen or bulging and any canned food with a bad smell or flavor.

In recent years, scientists have recognized an infant form of botulism in which infants ingest spores that germinate and produce toxins in the intestines. This appears to be linked mainly to the ingestion of raw honey, so authorities urge parents never to feed raw honey to babies. There is little danger of this variant of the disease after the age of one year.

See also **Packaging and Canning, History of; Packaging and Canning, Modern; Safety, Food.**

BIBLIOGRAPHY

Centers for Disease Control and Prevention. "Botulism." At http://www.cdc.gov/health/botulism.htm.

Silliker, J. H., ed. *Microbial Ecology of Foods.* Vol. 1. New York: Academic Press, 1980.

U.S. Department of Agriculture. *Complete Guide to Home Canning.* Washington, D.C., 1994.

Richard L. Lobb

BRAZIL. The only Portuguese-speaking country in South America and the largest Portuguese-speaking country in the world, Brazil has been called "a country without a memory" by one of the leading guidebooks. Lack of memory, though, should not be interpreted as lack of history, as the mix of cultures in the country's gene pool is rich indeed, with a complexity and variety that show nowhere more than in the food.

Portuguese seaman Pedro Alvares Cabral was thousands of miles from his stated destination of the Cape of Good Hope when he arrived on 22 April 1500 and became the first European to walk on the land that would be named Brazil in 1511. The treaty of Tordesillas, signed in 1494, had divided up the globe and given all lands known and unknown east of an imaginary north-south line 370 leagues west of the Cape Verde Islands to

the Portuguese. By 1532, when the first substantial Portuguese settlement was founded, the die had been cast based on Portuguese experiences in Asia and in Africa. Brazilian sociologist Gilberto Freyre notes in *The Masters and the Slaves: A Study in the Development of Brazilian Civilization* that Brazil was "a society agrarian in structure, slave holding in its technique of economic exploitation, and hybrid in composition, with an admixture of Indian and later of the Negro." Almost five hundred years later, these three major groups—Indian, Portuguese, and African—continue to form the matrix threads of Brazil's culinary culture.

Native Influences

French chronicler Jean de Lery's 1770 *Histoire d'un voyage fait en terre du Bresil* offers insights into the daily life of the native peoples and reminds readers that the women were responsible for much of the agriculture, the management of the entire house, and all of the cooking. Many of these culinary creations are still a vital part of the country's menu. Manioc or cassava (*Manhiot esculenta, Manhiot aipi,* or *Manhiot dulcis*) remains a major staple. The bitter cassava tuber, which required time-consuming preparation to remove the prussic acid (also known as hydrocyanic acid), was processed into a meal, which formed the basis of the diet. The liquid was also used and became the basis for *tucupi,* a condiment of cassava water, garlic, chili, chicory, and seasonings that is still prized today in the Amazon region. The Portuguese colonists at first confused the manioc with the true yam that they were familiar with from Africa. Soon, though, they were eating such Indian dishes as a form of cassava cake known as *mbeieu* or *beiju,* a cassava porridge or paste known as *mingau,* and *pacoka* or *pacoca,* a pulverized fish and cassava meal that has given its name to a popular contemporary pulverized peanut and sugar candy. Maize (*Zea mays*) was known, but never assumed the importance in Brazil that it had in other parts of Central and South America. Fish was also abundant and played a major role in the diet, with the pirarucu (*Arapaima gigas*) having the place of primacy. Fish was frequently prepared by roasting it in its own fat over a slow fire, then sealing it in earthenware jars. Other varieties of Amazon fish were prepared in this manner as was manatee, which was called *peixe boi* or ox fish.

Green vegetables were scarce, but nuts were consumed, particularly the cashew, as were the sweet potato, peanut, and cacao. Papaya (*Carica papaya*) and guava were eaten, as were pineapples. When the Portuguese brought bananas and citrus fruits, they were immediately adopted by the natives. Ripe fruit was eaten raw and green fruits grilled or roasted. Seasoning was done with chili; in fact the Indians were known for their overuse of the fiery capsicum as well as their abundant use of ginger and of lemon. Freyre cites a Jesuit account that cautions that excessive usage of the three resulted in frequent attacks of dysentery. Another of the lasting contributions of the native Brazilians to the cooking of today's Brazil has been the cooking utensils. The mortar, earthenware water jug, and wicker sieve, along with calabash utensils large and small, all hark back to the first Brazilians.

Portuguese Colonization

Portugal at the time of the colonization of Brazil was a nation recovering from a lengthy period of Moorish occupation. Old Portuguese cookbooks like *Arte de Cozinha,* published in 1692 by "a royal cook," list numerous recipes for "Moorish lamb," "Moorish fish," and the like. The everyday diets of the Portuguese in the years after the Moors fluctuated between feast and famine. The upper classes hovered between the excesses required on religious feast days, when meals had to be provided to royal retainers, rent collectors, and religious persons for show and status, and the far more frequent days when bread and radishes were the norm. For the poor, bread and onions were typical fare, and meals of sardines or other fish were a treat; meat was rarely tasted. Much of the agricultural wealth of the country was maintained in the convents and monasteries.

In the new land, the colonists began to shape their diet with the foods they knew either in their Iberian home or in the Asian and African colonies. They brought figs, citrus fruits, coconuts, rice, watermelon, the pumpkin called Guinea pumpkin (West Indian cooking pumpkin or *Cucurbita maxima Duchtre*), mustard, cabbage, lettuce, coriander, cucumbers, watercress, eggplant, carrots, and more. Gabriel Soares de Sousa, in his *Tratado descriptivo do Brasil em 1587,* offers a seemingly exhaustive listing of the plants brought. He adds that a green belt of one to two leagues encircled Salvador and provided much of the fruits and vegetables for the capital. Olive oil, butter, chickens, and eggs all arrived, as did pigs and the art of preserving pork and other meats.

Although the colonists brought an abundance of ingredients with them, they were so preoccupied with acquiring fortunes in the new land that their diets did not markedly improve. All was sacrificed to King Sugar. Cattle were banished because they destroyed the cane, and domestic agriculture was neglected. By the seventeenth century, travelers were astonished to note that large cities had no slaughterhouses as there were no cattle to send to them. The colonists, though, did have a major influence on the cooking pots of contemporary Brazil, not only by transporting and acclimatizing countless plant species, but also by establishing a countrywide culture—that of Portugal, with its abundant use of cabbage and kale, its hearty soups and rich stews, its traditions of grilling, and the Iberian fondness for sweets. (The Iberian "sweet tooth" combines the North African love for sugar and a tradition of intricate confections developed in Roman Catholic convents.) It is to the mother country that Brazil owes dishes such as the dense, rice-filled chicken soup known as *canja*, the strips of leafy kale greens that accompany the *feijoada* that is the national dish, and a national taste for meat and potatoes.

African Influence

The African hand in the Brazilian cooking pot completes the triptych, most noticeably in the northeastern states, where the plantation system held greatest sway. There, from virtually the inception of colonization, Africans were in control of the kitchens of the Big Houses. In Bahia, they were from the Bight of Benin and the Sudanese regions of West Africa. In Rio and Pernambuco, they were mainly Bantu. All brought their own tastes in food. The religious traditions of the African continent crossed the Atlantic as well, and in the hands of the Big House cooks, many ritual dishes were secularized and joined the culinary repertoire. The *akara*, a bean fritter fried in palm oil by the Yoruba people of southwestern Nigeria, was transformed into the Brazilian black-eyed pea fritter, or *acaraje*; *fon akassa* changed only its spelling to become the *acaca*, and the Angolan cornmeal porridge known as *funji* kept its name and its spelling as the dishes of the African continent were turned into Brazilian standbys.

African cooks embellished dishes with ginger, chilies, and pulverized cashew nuts and maintained the tastes of coastal Africa in the continued use of dried smoked shrimp and palm oil. They adapted recipes and adopted the ingredients of the new land to create a cooking so unique that the food of the state of Bahia is considered by many the linchpin that connects the cooking of Africa with that of the Western Hemisphere.

In the late nineteenth and early twentieth centuries, new immigrants joined the cultural mix that is Brazil: Japanese arrived to work on the coffee plantations, Syrians and Lebanese arrived and became shopkeepers and merchants, German and Swiss farmers settled in the

Brazil's long coastline has blessed it with a rich fish cookery. These fishermen are sorting their catch on the beach at Ceara, Brazil. © STEPHANIE MAZE/CORBIS.

southern states, and Italians established themselves in São Paulo. Each group brought its own dishes, and soon stroganoff and sushi, risotto and sauerbraten could claim pages in any Brazilian cookbook. The result is a country where the regional cuisine is as distinctive as it is varied.

Regional Cuisines

The Amazon region still recalls the country's first inhabitants in dishes like *beijus*, cassava flour crackers that are sometimes flavored with coconut, and *pato no tucupi*, duck cooked with *tucupi*, a condiment prepared from cassava liquid with garlic, chicory, and the leaves of the *jambu* plant, which produce a slight numbing effect on the tongue. The condiment also turns up in *tacaca*, a soup that also contains dried shrimp and tapioca. Fish from the river abound, with the enormous *pirarucu* and the flavorful *tuncare*. Tropical fruits range from the little known, like the *guarana* (the seeds of which make a highly caffeinated beverage), *cupuacu*, a relative of cacao, and the fragrant *jambo*, or rose apple, to the more familiar *maracudja*, or passion fruit, and cashew. There are also Brazil nuts, called *castanha do para*.

Culinary historian Luís da Câmara Cascudo claims that the food of the country's northeast region can be broken down into that of Bahia and the rest of the region. The tastes of the rest of the region are simple ones, featuring dried meats called *charque*, *carne seca*, or *carne do sol*. Stewed with beans and served with rice and abundant sprinklings of cassava meal, the meals are as stripped of pretense as the cowboys and hard-scrabble farmers who inhabit the arid inland region known as the Sertao. The rich tastes of Bahia reflect the area's exuberance. The tastes of sugar, coconut, *cachaca*, chili, and orange-hued

The biodiversity of Brazil's native fruits is one of the largest in the world. These fruits were photographed in the market at Angra, Brazil. © Richard Bickel/CORBIS.

palm oil called *dende* abound in dishes where the African hand is evident. Dishes with the gustatory complexity of *vatapa*, a puree of dried, smoked shrimp, ground peanuts and cashews, bread crumbs, ginger, chilies, coconut milk, and palm oil, are popular. The *acaraje*, or black-eyed pea fritter, is traditional street food, often slathered with *vatapa*, and sweets prepared from coconut, sugar, and tropical fruits are traditional.

The two major cities of São Paulo and Rio de Janeiro revel in international dining that knows few borders, with restaurants owned by three-starred Michelin chefs and local notables. Specialties include Rio's Saturday *feijoada*, the country's national dish of black beans, rice, stewed meats, greens, and sliced oranges. São Paulo offers Japanese fare in the Liberdade district as well as German-style beer halls and *rodizio*-style churrascarias (Brazilian barbecue), where waiters circulate constantly with a never-ending procession of skewers of meat that is sliced at the table.

The heartlands of Minas Gerais and Goiás are marked by their love of beans. They celebrate with dishes like *Tutu a Mineira*, mashed black beans served with pork chops and kale, and a version of *feijoada* prepared with pink beans instead of black ones. Mineros pride themselves on their wood-burning ovens called *fogao de lenha* and their cheeses, which are prized throughout the country.

The southern states are more European in focus, with large settlements of Italians and Germans. They are also the home of Brazil's gauchos and boast a meat culture centered on spit-roasting meat *churrasco*-style. The prairies of Mato Grosso and Mato Grosso do Sul are made up of huge ranches called *estancias* or *fazendas*, where cattle farming is a major industry. Beef, pork, and fish dominate the regional menu, and as settlement increases there, the newcomers are sure to add another chapter to the rich and ongoing history of the food culture of Brazil.

See also **Africa: North Africa; Cassava; Central America; Columbian Exchange; Iberian Peninsula; Mexico; Mexico and Central America, Pre-Columbian; South America; Sugar and Sweeteners.**

BIBLIOGRAPHY

Cascudo, Luís da Câmara. *História da Alimentação no Brasil.* 2 vols. São Paolo: Companhia Editora Nacional, 1967–1968.

Freyre, Gilberto. *The Masters and the Slaves (Casa-Grande & Senzala): A Study in the Development of Brazilian Civilization.* 2d English Edition. Trans. Samuel Putnam. New York: Knopf, 1964.

Harris, Jessica B. *Tasting Brazil: Regional Recipes and Reminincences.* New York: Macmillan; Toronto: Maxwell Macmillan Canada, 1992.

Peterson, Joan B., and David Peterson. *Eat Smart in Brazil: How to Decipher the Menu, Know the Market Foods, and Embark on a Tasting Adventure.* Madison, Wisc.: Ginkgo, 1995.

Jessica B. Harris

BREAD. What is bread? At its simplest it is merely a paste of flour or meal and water cooked over or surrounded by heat. More complex breads are leavened in various ways and contain salt and other ingredients, particularly fat and sugar. Although bread is usually thought of as being made from wheat, it can be made from virtually any grain—rye, corn (tortillas), barley and oats (bannocks), teff (injera), amaranth, millet, and rice. Only wheat, however, has the gluten that is essential to a risen loaf, so unless these other grains are mixed with wheat, the loaves will be flat. Many, such as oat, barley, and pure rye bread, will be heavy and dense as well.

Plant Biology

The kernel of wheat is the grain used in most breads. Wheat is the single grain that contains enough gluten to allow the development of the protein strands that are the foundation of bread. These strands form layers and pockets that trap the steam from the water and the carbon dioxide released by the yeast during the fermentation process and thus give the bread its rise. Since other grains do not have this capability, they are usually combined with wheat flour to increase the gluten level of the mixture.

Wheat is not actually a seed but rather a true fruit. The wheat grain has three parts. Bran is the outer layer of the wheat kernel and is high in fiber and nutrients. The germ is the "embryo" of the kernel, and when sprouted, it reproduces new wheat plants. The endosperm makes up most of the kernel and is the food reserve for the germ. The endosperm is extracted during the milling process to make common white flour.

Plant Nutrition

Wheat is rich in complex carbohydrates, which are an excellent source of energy for the human body. It also contains many essential B vitamins and the key minerals iron and calcium. After the milling process, in which the bran and germ, which contain most of the vitamins and minerals, are separated from the endosperm, enrichments frequently are added to the flour to restore the grain to its nascent nutritional levels. The two most common enrichments are folic acid, which prevents heart disease and neural deformities, and the other B vitamins, including niacin, thiamin, and riboflavin, which prevent beriberi, pellagra, and nutritional anemia.

Types of Wheat

Many different types and strains of wheat are grown conventionally or organically worldwide. In the United States wheat is classified into four categories. Hard wheat is used for breads and similar baked goods; soft wheat is preferred for cakes and pastries; winter wheat, which includes hard wheat varieties, is planted in the late fall to over-winter in harsh climates and is harvested in the spring; and spring wheat is planted in the spring and is harvested in the late summer or early fall. Wheat is fur-

ther categorized as red wheat, that is, hard, red winter wheat; or white wheat, that is, soft, white spring wheat. The thousands of varieties of wheat grown in the United States break down into six classes: hard, red winter; hard, red spring; soft, red winter; durum, primarily used in pasta making; hard white; and soft white.

In the late 1990s the artisanal baking world developed an interest in wheat's particular profile. This profile is generally indicated by a farinograph, which displays such important factors as protein (gluten) levels, ash content (a measure of extensibility, related to fiber), and falling number. Each of these elements plays an important role in the overall baking process, and each farinograph number tells the baker what type of results to expect. The baker's knowledge of the specific flour's profile dictates how much water to add, how long to knead the dough, and how long the fermentation time should be.

Identity preserved (IP) wheat has also attracted interest. Traditionally, when the wheat is harvested, it is stored in large silos prior to distribution to the mill. The mélange of different strains of wheat, even within a single category, present in the silo makes it virtually impossible to know how the flour will perform once it is milled. Yet these "blends," as they are called, are the most prevalent grains in the marketplace. Using the IP methodology, only one type of wheat is stored in a particular silo, thus giving the discerning baker more control over the outcome of the final product. While this IP methodology will probably never rule the marketplace due to silo space limitations and lack of general interest, it will continue to gain market share as the artisanal side of the baking industry continues to flourish.

The History of Bread

It is widely believed that the domestication and cultivation of wheat and other grains directly influenced human transition from nomadic people to domesticated, stationary people. In most parts of the world this transition was completed as wheat and subsequently bread became significant dietary staples. However, people continued nomadic ways where cultivation of grains was either not feasible or not desirable.

The earliest breads were more like porridges and flat cakes. Grains were mashed with water or milk and were eaten either raw or cooked, providing nutrition and sustenance. The porridge became thicker and more paste-like, and eventually this paste was cooked either on a hot rock or in an early subterranean oven, creating a more mobile product. Twenty-first-century descendants of those earliest breads include Middle Eastern pita bread, Indian naan, and pizza.

The first leavened breads were invented nearly seven thousand years after flatbreads were introduced into the diet. To put the history of bread on a timeline continuum, it is necessary to start nearly ten thousand years ago. About 8000 B.C.E. the first grinding stone, called a

Bread is indeed the staff of life in most wheat-consuming countries. The great variety of North African breads is evident in this Tunisian bread shop. © MICHELLE GARRETT/CORBIS.

quern, was invented in Egypt, and the first grain was crushed. The modern Indian chapatis, made from unleavened whole wheat flour, and Mexican tortillas, made from corn, resemble the breads produced at that time. Between 5000 and 3700 B.C.E. Egypt began organized grain production along the Nile River Valley. At this time bread became a staple food that often was used in trade and barter, and it began to migrate to other cultures.

About 3000 B.C.E., also in Egypt, varieties of wheat that were tougher, that is, more tolerant of weather and environment, were developed. It is widely thought that, owing to the Egyptian skill with brewing beer and the warm climate, wild yeasts attracted to the flour mixtures created the first sourdough. Recognizing the fermentation process, bakers began to experiment and developed the first purposefully leavened breads. By about 2500 B.C.E. the first true sourdoughs were in regular production in the Middle East and Mediterranean regions.

In about 2300 B.C.E. the cultivation of grain began in India along the Indus Valley. Around 1500 B.C.E. horses took over the task of plowing and the first iron plowshares were introduced. In about 1000 B.C.E. yeasted breads became popular in Rome. The circular quern, the basis for milling until the Industrial Revolution and the

basis for so-called stone-ground flours in the twenty-first century, was developed by about 500 B.C.E. The water mill was invented in Greece around 450 B.C.E. Consequently culinary historians credit the Greeks with ushering in bread baking as an art form.

In Rome the first bakers guilds were formed as a means of unifying the craftspeople around 150 B.C.E. Well-to-do Romans insisted on the more exclusive and expensive white breads. Darker whole wheat and bran breads were for the masses, an attitude that persisted well into the twentieth century in Europe and North America. By about 100 C.E. Mexican natives made the first stone-ground corn tortillas. By 300 C.E. the Greeks had developed more than seventy different types of bread, showing their penchant for furthering the bread baking craft. Around 600 C.E. the Persians developed a windmill prototype that changed the face of bread production.

In medieval times bread baking became a status symbol in Britain. The upper classes preferred fine, white loaves, while those of poorer status were left with the whole wheat, bran, and coarser breads. By 1066 hair sieves were employed to sift the flour, producing a finer white flour. In 1569 in England, Queen Elizabeth I united the "white and brown" bread bakers to form the

Worshipful Company of Bakers. The Great Fire of London in 1666 reportedly was started by a baker. In 1683 the bagel was introduced in Vienna as a thank-you gift to the king of Poland.

Wheat was first planted in the United States as a hobby crop in 1777. During this century the earl of Sandwich gave his name to the sandwich, originally meat between two slices of bread. In 1789 mobs calling for bread helped trigger the French Revolution. In 1834 the roller mill was invented in Switzerland. Rather than crushing the grain as in stone-ground methods, the steel roller mill breaks open the grain, allowing easier separation of the germ, bran, and endosperm. This invention drastically changed milling around the world and increased the consistency of milled flour.

Bread in Modern Times

Leavened bread was generally prepared outside the home, and this led to the development of communal bake houses. Usually situated by rivers or streams, these bake houses presented serious fire hazards due to the construction materials of the buildings and ovens. The proximity to water put them near the mills and close to natural fire suppression. Bake houses were usually owned by land barons and lords. Bakers and bakery owners used the ovens on a communal basis for a fee paid either in money or in kind. The very nature of the bake house allowed bakers to bake more bread, thus increasing their ability to distribute it and keep prices down.

The same innovations of the industrial revolution that made white wheat breads more plentiful also made mass production the norm. By 1825 German bakers created the first cakes of commercial yeast, which expedited the process and consistency of yeast activity and influenced taste and visual appeal as well. In the twentieth century hydrogenated oils, artificial preservatives, emulsifiers, and other chemical additives entered the dough to soften the crumb (texture) and to lengthen the shelf life of mass-produced breads. Factory bread has become standard in most industrialized countries.

By the early twentieth century bread flour was largely replaced by bleached, bromated, and enriched flour. The grain is bleached and sterilized with chemicals to make it white and soft. It is then enriched by adding back the vitamins and minerals destroyed in the processing. Obviously this industrialization of bread methodology and production altered the taste and appearance of bread. Some authorities feel this methodology is largely responsible for the mid-century decline of bread consumption in the United States. In 1910 the per capita consumption of bread products was roughly 210 pounds. By 1971 consumption had been cut nearly in half, to approximately 110 pounds per person. This trend turned around with the rediscovery of artisanal breads and methodologies. The trend back to more wholesome and historical breads began in the United States in the 1980s. Some bakers who wanted to be more mindful of the

As bread baking became industrialized during the nineteenth century, professional bakers turned to baking aids like this cream loaf pan of tinned sheet iron, which simultaneously makes six large sandwich "batons." The loaves are perfectly round for slicing. Manufactured about 1890 by Thomas Mills Brothers of Philadelphia. ROUGHWOOD COLLECTION. PHOTO CHEW & COMPANY.

process and their ingredients returned to their baking roots. They produced freshly baked, wholesome, rustic breads that benefited from longer fermentation periods, and they eschewed all chemicals and additives. The result is a more flavorful and nutritious loaf similar to those baked over a thousand years ago. Led by the Bread Bakers Guild of America (modeled after the first European bakers guilds) this reinvention of bread permeated baking cultures throughout the industrialized world.

Buying Bread

By the twenty-first century bread products were sold on three major levels. The first is the traditional neighborhood bakery, still in existence in large urban centers in the twenty-first century. The second is the grocery store, or supermarket. Third is what might be called the bakery café, along with the specialty foods store.

The neighborhood bakery. The neighborhood bakery has its roots in western Europe and is known for its local roots and outreach as well as the freshness of its products. This is particularly true in France, where local boulangeries are numerous. Each one offers local residents their daily bread, fresh, uncommercialized, and unique to that particular bakery.

Local bakeries build their client base from the immediate neighborhood, especially in larger urban centers, where population density and foot traffic allow the independent baker to make a living by directly connecting to his or her customer. Breads are baked fresh daily and are meant to be consumed that day or the following day at the latest. Even though, as a result of the extended fermentation used, many of these breads have a longer shelf life than one or two days, it is the freshness that sells the bread.

Grocery stores. The amount of bread purchased at grocery stores and supermarkets is the largest portion by far primarily because of the convenience of one-stop shopping. These bread products have been developed and baked with a longer shelf life in mind than breads baked in a neighborhood bakery. Frequently made with dough conditioners, emulsifiers, and mold inhibitors, they are meant to withstand plastic bags and to last for several days in the store.

In general the types of breads found in the grocery store are a result of the bread industrial revolution that took place at the beginning of the twentieth century. Consumer desire for white bread with a soft crust along with mechanized developments in the milling and baking industry made it possible not only to mass produce a homogeneous product but also to distribute it over a wide geographic area. While exceptions exist, most of these factory-produced breads have taken a formula detour from similar products produced in neighborhood bakeries. Dough conditioners make it easier for the wholesale bakery's machinery to handle the dough without damaging it and to soften the crumb of the bread. Emulsifiers homogenize the dough (in some cases it is nearly batterlike) so each loaf of bread resembles the ones before and after it. Mold inhibitors are used in the actual formula and are sprayed topically as the bread exits the oven to delay the onset of bread mold.

Bakery departments have also been created in the grocery store itself to reach the customer who wants a fresher product. Breads are baked throughout the day, and in addition to being fresher they generally have a more pronounced flavor. Where the baker gives care and attention, the in-store product can come close to the quality of breads produced by the local neighborhood bakery. However, when the baker is working from a base or mix or even with a par-baked product (a frozen, partially baked bread that is finished off in the store), the overall quality is usually only a slight improvement over the bread on the store's shelves.

Bakery café and specialty foods stores. Bakery cafés and specialty food stores have experienced widespread growth since the early 1980s. Both typically provide a higher-quality product than that found in the grocery store. Whether purchased from a high-quality wholesale bakery or baked in-house from a fresh or par-baked product, baked goods comprised a wide selection.

Bread Preparation: Yeasted Dough

Yeast dough production requires twelve basic steps no matter what type of dough is produced. Dough types are generally classified as lean dough (low in fat and sugar), including French baguettes, rustic breads, Tuscan breads,

hard rolls, and pizza; rich dough (with sugar, fats, or eggs added), including brioche, challah, and egg breads; and rolled-in dough (with fat incorporated in many layers using a rolling and a folding procedure), including croissants, Danish pastries, and cinnamon rolls.

The Twelve Steps of Yeast Dough Production

Scaling is the exact measurement of all ingredients (professional bakers and dedicated amateurs measure by weight) and the French term, *mise-en-place*, applies to having all the ingredients scaled or prepped and ready before starting production.

Mixing and kneading involve the incorporation by hand or by machine of the ingredients in proper sequence to form the bread dough, which is then further kneaded. Kneading or working the dough by hand or by machine further disperses the ingredients and develops the gluten in the dough.

Fermentation, also referred to as the first rise, is the process whereby the gluten (protein) in the dough is allowed to relax while the yeast grows and reproduces. The yeast digests the sugars in the flour and produces alcohol and carbon dioxide (CO_2). The carbon dioxide gets trapped in the pockets that result from the kneading process and causes the bread to expand or rise and develop flavor. At this point the dough can be left at room temperature if it is to be baked that day, or it can be retarded; that is, the fermentation period can be extended in a cool environment, usually a specialized refrigerator. Doughs that have been retarded for twelve to twenty-four hours generally have more complex flavors and are easier to fit into the baker's production schedule. There is also a noticeable buildup of natural acidity, which helps extend shelf life.

Punching down or deflating the dough, also called turning, refers to the general deflating of the dough mass by either gently pushing down or folding the dough, not hitting it as implied. The purpose is twofold, to increase the strength and tolerance of the gluten and to de-gas the dough prior to scaling. After punching, the dough is allowed to rest before moving on to the next step.

Scaling is cutting and weighing individual pieces of dough, which will become the actual loaves of bread.

Rounding occurs once the dough has been scaled. Each piece is gently shaped into a round ball before moving on to the next step. This rounding allows uniformity in subsequent steps.

Benching is allowing the dough pieces to rest, usually for fifteen to twenty minutes. The time varies with each type of bread and with the amount of leavening used. Clean, dry towels placed over the dough during this period prevent a dry crust from forming on the dough.

Make-up is forming the individual pieces of dough into their final shapes, free-form loaf, pan loaf, dinner rolls, and so forth.

Proofing, also referred to as the final rise, allows the dough to rise one last time before baking. The yeast is still alive and continues to leaven the dough. Proofing generally takes place in a warm, draft-free environment either at room temperature or in a proof box, where temperature and humidity are controlled. At this point shaped loaves can be retarded for twelve to twenty-four hours and baked at a later time.

Baking is the actual cooking of the bread. When the dough is put in the hot oven, it undergoes oven spring, one last push of the yeast to make the dough rise. The actual temperature and time depend on the oven type (deck, rotary, convection, rack, and so forth) and the use of steam, although yeast breads are generally baked at a high temperature. Technically speaking, this is when the starches gelatinize and sugars caramelize, giving the loaf its final appearance.

Cooling begins when the finished bread is removed from the oven. The bread cools completely before it is packaged or sliced. Cooling racks are usually nothing more than wire shelves that allow air circulation on all four sides of the bread. Even breads baked in or on pans are quickly removed to a cooling rack so the bread bottoms do not become soggy from continued steaming.

Storing prevents the staling or starch retrogradation that begins as soon as the bread is removed from the oven. To preserve their thin, crisp crusts, some breads are best not packaged (lean breads in particular), but modern baking and distribution practices require many bakers to do so. Once a loaf has been put into a bag, the staling process is somewhat slowed down and the crust becomes soft. Wrapping and freezing help maintain quality for a longer period of time. Refrigeration, on the other hand, speeds up staling.

Methods of Preparation

While the twelve steps of baking are virtually constant for almost any bread form, three predominant production variations exist. Each is a means of manipulating the key ingredients to produce a predictable loaf of bread. Production timing is also influenced. The key difference is fermentation, the natural process that occurs after the ingredients have been mixed and the dough has been kneaded. The length of fermentation time has a significant effect on the overall flavor profile, on the end product, on the baker's production life.

Straight dough method. The straight dough method is perhaps most familiar to all bakers, professional and amateur alike. It incorporates the twelve steps in a direct fashion as dictated by the ambient temperature of the bakeshop, proceeding through the steps with no break. The total time of the cycle would be about four hours from start to finish. Because of the relative shortness of the baking cycle, a higher proportion of yeast is used than in other methods so that fermentation can run its full course. The result is a bread with a stronger yeast flavor than other breads.

In its most rustic form, bread was often baked in the hot ashes of a fire, hence the term "ash bread" or "ash cake." This cattle hand in Pugal, India, has just baked flat bread on a griddle over a small fire. © ZEN ICKNOW/CORBIS.

Sponge method. The sponge method follows the same twelve production steps with a few exceptions. Initially a percentage of the total flour, water, and yeast are mixed to form a sponge or pre-ferment. The sponge method enhances the flavor profile of the final product. Since less yeast is used, a longer, cooler fermentation can be applied, ranging anywhere from three to twenty-four hours. During this time the lactic acid bacteria in the water-flour mixture have full time to develop. The resulting buildup of organic acids and alcohols contributes to a more developed flavor profile. When the sponge is ripe, it is incorporated into the remaining flour, water, salt, and other ingredients. The twelve steps are followed from this point on.

Typical pre-ferment types. Poolish, one of the first pre-ferments made with commercial yeast, originated in Poland and is widely used by French bakers. Made with a higher percentage of water as opposed to flour than other pre-ferments, poolish has a batterlike texture. Biga, a pre-ferment of Italian origin, is more doughlike than a poolish and is commonly made with equal parts (by weight) of flour and water. Old dough is a piece of dough from an earlier batch of bread that is allowed to ferment and then is incorporated back into a fresh batch of dough. Called *pâte fermentée* (fermented dough) by the French, it can be fermented for up to six or eight hours at room temperature or longer under refrigeration.

Sourdough uses wild yeast to build a culture. Wild yeast, the flora, is present in the air and on the skins of fruits and vegetables. The baker basically harvests those wild yeast organisms and creates a culture that will leaven bread dough.

First, a culture is created using water and flour. This mixture is left covered with cheesecloth or another porous material at room temperature until it begins to ripen. At this point, the wild yeasts, having found the food (primarily natural sugars) in the flour, begin to feed and reproduce. A slightly acid smell and bubbling indicate that the culture is alive. The culture is continually fed to increase its volume and leavening strength until there is enough starter (*levain*) to leaven a batch of dough with enough left over to perpetuate the culture. Under the right conditions, cultures can be kept vital and alive for many years. The sourdough method is a time-intensive method, since no commercial yeast is used to speed up production. The benefits are many, however. Due to the lower yeast levels, the slower activity produces a stronger flavor profile and more noticeable sour aroma, an increased level of organic lactic acids, and a greater array of naturally occurring bacteria. It is primarily due to the abundance of naturally occurring acids, alcohols, and bacteria that breads baked with the sourdough method become stale more slowly, have a better shelf life for the vendor and the consumer, and have less molding.

Traditions: A Historical Perspective

Bread and traditions pertaining to it are deeply ingrained in lore and language worldwide. From its beginnings bread has held a special, even sacred sway on humankind. As bread is the staff of life, it is truly all-pervasive.

Challah is the Jewish bread served on the Sabbath and on holidays in which the twelve tribes of Israel are represented by twelve braids on each loaf. For Rosh Hashanah, the Jewish New Year, the challah is wound in a ring to symbolize the continuity of life. Some loaves have a ladder on top, representing the ascent of God on high.

According to legend, a baker alerted the forces of Vienna to the approach of the Turks in the siege of 1683. The bakers commemorated the Viennese victory with a crescent-shaped roll, precursor to the croissant, as the symbol of the Turks was a crescent.

In France a law prevented bakers from increasing the price of bread beyond a point justified by the price of the raw materials. Tuscan bakers, during the time of papal dominance, were subjected to an extremely high salt tax. As a result Tuscan bakers decided to abolish salt in their breads. Tuscan tastes adapted to this custom, and a traveler will note, for example, that Tuscan prosciutto is considerably saltier than its regional counterparts.

Several cultures celebrate the Epiphany (6 January) with a ring cake with a tiny doll representing the Christ child baked in it. Whoever gets the piece with the doll is crowned king or queen for the day and is obliged to reciprocate by giving a party on Candelmas (2 February).

Bread in the Lexicon

Bread has been a part of language for many thousands of years. Because of the importance of bread worldwide, it should come as no surprise that bread talk has permeated the everyday vocabulary. In 1933 nearly 80 percent of the bread sold in the United States was sliced. The expression "the best thing since sliced bread" was coined from this market predominance. The term "break bread," meaning to dine together, highlights the reverence given to bread and its importance at mealtime.

The expression "bread upon the water" describes resources risked without expectation of return. Bread was a form of currency in ancient Egypt, and the term "bread" is colloquially used as a term for money. "Breadwinner" designates the person who earns the better part of the household income.

Bread has long been called the staff of life. This metaphor of the wheat stalk expresses the importance of wheat, grains, and in turn bread. The term baker's dozen refers to a count of thirteen, rather than to twelve, a traditional dozen. Dating back to the Middle Ages, some bakers cheated with undersize and occasionally adulterated loaves. An extra loaf or item was thrown in to reduce suspicion.

Bread and Human Biology

Bread is a great source of energy because it is rich in complex carbohydrates. The human body slowly turns these carbohydrates into sugars, which the body utilizes for energy. Breads and grain products occupy the first and largest rung of the widely accepted Food Pyramid. The Food and Drug Administration (FDA) has indicated that all adults should eat six to eleven servings of carbohydrates daily (depending on age and gender), and bread can make up a large segment of this daily intake. As approved by the FDA and the U.S. Department of Agriculture (USDA), breads rich in whole grains can advertise that they help fight heart disease and cancer. Breads (and grain-based foods in general) that contain 51 percent or more whole grain ingredients by weight can use the following health claim on labels: "Diets rich in whole grains and other plant foods low in total fat, saturated fat, and cholesterol may reduce the risk of heart disease and certain cancers." Whole grain breads are also a great source of fiber and roughage, which aid the body's digestive and waste elimination systems.

Grain products are enriched with iron, folic acid, and other B vitamins, including niacin, thiamin, and riboflavin. Over the years enrichment has helped eliminate nutrition-related diseases, such as beriberi, pellagra, and severe nutritional anemia. Research has shown that folic acid helps prevent heart disease. Women of childbearing age also need folic acid. The daily minimum requirement of four hundred micrograms is essential in preventing birth defects of the spinal cord and brain.

See also **Bagel; Beriberi; Bread, Symbolism of; Judaism; Metaphor, Food as; Niacin Deficiency (Pellagra); Pizza; Symbol, Food as; Wheat.**

BIBLIOGRAPHY

Balkan Info.com. "Balkan Easter Traditions." Available at www.b-info.com.

CyberSpace Farm. Available at www.cyberspaceag.com.

Edgar, Jeffrey, and Robert Kunkel. "Kinds of Wheat." Available at www.kings.k12.ca.us.

Elizabeth Botham and Sons Ltd. Available at www.botham.co.uk.

Federation of Bakers. Available at www.bakersfederation.org.uk.

Flour Advisory Bureau. "Bread Superstitions and Traditions." Available at www.wheatintolerance.co.uk.

Gislen, Wayne. *Professional Baking.* 2d ed. New York: John Wiley, 1994.

Guglhupf Bakery and Patisserie. Available at www.guglhupf.com.

History of Bread. Available at www.breadinfo.com.

"Italian Breads." Milioni Magazine Online. Available at http://milioni.com.

Kansas Wheat Commission. Available at www.kswheat.com.

Moorshead, Halvor. *History Magazine* 1 (1999).

Nestlé Corporation. "The History of Bread." Available at www.oror.essortment.com.

Northmont Area Community Network. "Mexican Traditions for Christmas." Montgomery County, Ohio: 2002.

Phillips, Carole. "Passover and Easter Traditions." *Cincinnati Post*, 31 March 2001.

PolStore, Inc. "Polish Traditions." Available at www.polstore.com.

"Preferments and Fundamentals of Fermentation." National Baking Center, Dunwoody Institute, 2000.

"Ukrainian Culture and Traditions." San Diego Insider. Available at www.sdinsider.com.

Wheat Foods Council. Available at www.smartbread.com and www.wheatfoods.com.

Peter S. Franklin

BREAD, SYMBOLISM OF. Bread is among the most popular foods in the world. Whether it is leavened or unleavened, made into loaves or cakes, baked, steamed, or fried in oil, bread is universal. Whatever the grain, bread occupies an important place in every civilization. It has exceptional nutritional value, and as the only nearly perfect product for human nourishment, can be consumed by itself. It is made from flour, water, salt, yeast, and sometimes additives.

Farming has had a profound affect on the religious beliefs of agricultural communities, and the symbolism of wheat is deeply associated with the symbolism of bread. Since the Neolithic period, mythology and ritual representation have tended to be identified with plant life because the mystery of human birth and death was in many respects similar to the life cycle of plants.

The growth of settlements, which ethnologists refer to as the "great turning point for humanity" and which was indirectly inspired by the search for bread (agriculture was only a means to this end), helped define social and economic institutions (the growth of property rights, the use of wheat as a form of exchange value, and so on). Planting and harvesting as well as the events that endanger crops (flood, drought) were perceived as key events in agricultural life.

During its life cycle the grain of wheat dies and is reborn months later in the form of a spike capable of providing sustenance to human beings. Wheat is the quintessential nutritional plant. It was believed to contain the mystery of life and death and thus it became a sacred plant. One of the essential features of the Neolithic era was plant cultivation. This led to a way of life that had previously been unimaginable and gave birth to new beliefs that completely altered the spiritual universe of humankind.

Religious connections with the animal world were replaced by what might be called a mystical solidarity between humankind and vegetation. Moreover, female sacredness and the female principle in general assumed greater importance because of women's influential role in agriculture. Women's fertility was associated with that of the earth, and women were responsible for the abundance of the harvest because of their knowledge of the mystery of creation. During the fertility festivals in Syracuse (Sicily), loaves of sesame bread shaped like female genital organs were handed out.

This sacred and divine dimension of the wheat spike helped associate it with the symbolism of resurrection. Examples survive on bas-reliefs from the temple of Isis, the Egyptian nature goddess and wife and sister of Osiris, in Philae, an island in the Nile, in which the mummy of Osiris, god of the underworld, presents spikes of wheat watered by a priest, symbolizing the new wheat that will soon grow. This same symbolism is found on clay statuettes of Osiris that contain wheat kernels, which were placed in graves to ensure the survival of the dead.

This close relationship between the celebration of the seasons, the death and rebirth of the god, and the possibility of a life beyond the grave clearly illustrates the connection between wheat and Osiris and the manifest symbolism of resurrection, which he represented in

241

In this 1883 promotion for Wonder Flour (the ancestor of Wonder Bread) the lightness of the bread is weighed against an ostrich feather, implying that airy bread from processed flour is better than the old hearth-baked kind, a point most artisanal bakers would dispute. The flirtatious woman in red, white, and blue, dressed like a cancan dancer, would have raised eyebrows with her leg-exposing attire. The second implied message, then, is that light bread is sexy. ROUGHWOOD COLLECTION.

Egyptian religion. Ancient Egypt was far from unique, however, for cereal plants were associated with divinities in nearly all cultures, such as the Greek goddess Demeter and the Roman goddess Ceres.

In the Old Testament wheat and bread are symbols of the fecundity of the earth. The New Testament associates the fruits of the earth—a gift of God to humankind—with the symbolism of wheat and associates the gifts of God with the hearts of humans (grace), especially in the parable of the good seed and the bad seed. Bread becomes the symbol of the supreme gift from God to humankind—eternal life, the body of Christ in the Eucharist: "Take this and eat, for this is my body."

In Hebrew "Bethlehem" means 'house of bread'. The city is located seven kilometers (five miles) south of Jerusalem and is considered the place of origin of the house of David and the birthplace of Jesus. In the Old Testament the Eternal sends manna to the Hebrews when they are crossing the desert (Exodus). Manna symbolizes bread and prefigures the Christian Eucharist. It is a sign of the generosity of God toward humankind. Jewish matzoh is an unleavened bread that is eaten to commemorate this event. In the Roman Catholic faith, unleavened bread is used to prepare the hosts for the Eucharist. The Orthodox Church uses leavened bread.

In imperial Rome bakers (*pistores*) celebrated 9 June, the Vestalies, in honor of the Roman goddess Vesta. In the *Fastes* the Roman poet Ovid describes how the Romans came to worship Jupiter Pistor or Jupiter the Baker. According to Ovid, when the Gauls attacked Rome in 387 B.C.E., the Romans invoked Jupiter, and the great god counseled them to throw what was most precious to them over the walls. While praying to Ceres, they prepared small loaves of bread with the remains of their flour and threw the loaves at their assailants. Seeing this, the Gauls believed Rome was well provisioned and had the wherewithal to withstand a lengthy siege, so they abandoned their assault of the city. In recognition the Romans built a temple to Jupiter Pistor that associated the symbolism of wheat (life, death, and rebirth) with the destiny of the city.

Bread is not associated only with spirituality and the afterlife, however. Even in antiquity the production of bread was associated with procreation. The process of loading, baking, and unloading the oven parallels copulation, pregnancy, and childbirth. In Hebrew and Chaldean the word *zera* has several meanings referring to the seed of the plant, to sperm, and to human progeny. Hebrew *zera* became the Greek *sperma*, Latin *semen*, and English "seed." Latin *placenta* was the name of a much appreciated pastry served on feast days in ancient Rome. Leaven, which plays the role of the grain or seed, is also referred to as "mother" in English and *madre* in Spanish. In Egypt the basket in which dough is left to rest is known as a *coffin*. Various popular expressions associate bread with the concept of procreation. In France a young woman who found herself pregnant before marriage was said to have "borrowed a loaf from the batch." In England the expression "a bun in the oven" refers to a woman's pregnancy. Bread symbolizes the forces of life, and an element of eroticism is associated with its manufacture. The French word *four* (once *forn*) for oven is derived from church Latin *fornicatio*, in turn derived from *fornix*, which literally meant a vault but figuratively meant a prostitute. In ancient Rome, prostitutes fornicated with clients in vaulted rooms that resembled ovens.

The French word *miche*, used for a round bread loaf, also signifies breast or buttocks, and a *bâtard* is a thick French baguette. In English buns refer to the buttocks as well as various small round rolls. In Italy, in the region around Naples, a small bread loaf is known as an "angel's penis," and in Germany *Brotleib* can refer to the female body.

While bread is itself a symbol of life, shaped breads carry multitudes of additional meanings. One of the oldest shaped breads is the ring shown here in an Athens market. This is the *bracellus* of ancient Greece and Rome, a form of bread associated with abstinence and even death. In the oldest surviving manuscript of the *Aeneid* (sixth century C.E.), Aeneas and Dido are shown breaking a *bracellus* prior to her self-immolation. © NEIL BEER/CORBIS.

The sickle is often associated with wheat and bread because of its role in the harvest, but it is also associated with the god Saturn, the mistletoe of the Druids, and the silver bow that belonged to Artemis, the sister of the sun god Apollo. That is why, in connection with grain, the sickle fulfills one of the functions of the moon, for the harvest ends a life cycle that begins with the death of the kernel of wheat. Like the scythe, the sickle serves as a positive end to the cycle for it signifies the harvest and nourishment, both physical and spiritual. It also prefigures the symbolism of wheat, the bread of the future, and other promises of transformation.

Bread is an object of belief and superstition in many cultures. The Hittites believed that the bread served to soldiers preserved them from impotence and that leavened bread helped ward off epidemics (providing it was placed in a special barrel). In Belgium during the Middle Ages, bread kneaded on Christmas Eve protected the home against lightning. In many places people give newlyweds bread and salt to express the hope for health and prosperity. In Russia a saltcellar is placed on top of the loaf of bread, which is presented to the couple by one of their mothers.

Many other ancient beliefs have continued into the twenty-first century. In Sweden it is customary to prepare a flat round bread pierced with a hole when a daughter is born, and the bread is eaten the day she gets married. In Hamburg, Germany, a highly suggestive, triphallic

bread is offered to the bride and groom on their wedding day. For centuries Christians have made the sign of the cross on the crust of a loaf of bread before cutting it.

Throwing bread out or placing it upside down on the table supposedly brings bad luck. This superstition is connected to an ancient belief that bread turned toward the entrails of the earth, therefore toward hell, attracts evil spirits. In another medieval belief, bakers refused to have any physical contact with or even to serve the executioner of Paris, a man who inspired fear and was held in contempt by the people of the city. Ultimately the king was forced to issue an edict that compelled the bakers to serve the executioner. In protest and as a sign of their dissatisfaction, the bakers turned the executioner's loaf upside down on the rack to distinguish it from the others.

Various powers are attributed to bread blessed by a priest. At the end of the feast in honor of Saint Joseph in Sicily, guests are sent home with a piece of consecrated bread to keep in the house to bring fertility and good fortune in the coming year. On the Feast of Saint Calogero, Sicilians bring ex-votos made of bread covered with poppy seeds to church to be blessed. Islanders keep consecrated bread to throw upon the stormy waters for the safe return of fishermen at sea. *Kulich* (Russian Easter bread), a domed cylindrical loaf, is decorated with religious Easter symbols (notably *XB* for *Khristos Voskrese* or Christ is Risen), surrounded with dyed eggs, topped with a beeswax candle, and taken to church to be blessed.

According to popular belief, the sign of a perfectly baked *kulich* is that it will never mold; some say it will last for a year. *Kulich* is shared with the departed when, on Easter Monday, families go to the cemetery to picnic on the gravesites. In Russia true *bliny*, yeast-based pancakes prepared only once a year during *Maslenitsa* or Butter Week (Mardi Gras), represent the sun—round, golden, and warm—and symbolize the arrival of spring. One is always left in the window for the departed.

Kutya, a sweetened wheat-berry pudding, is traditionally the first or last food eaten on Christmas. Though more of a porridge than a bread, *kutya*, which is decorated with a cross of almond slices on top, is taken to gravesites or even thrown into the open grave. It is also given to propitiate Father Frost. *Kutya* bears an uncanny resemblance to *cuccìa*, a Sicilian wheat-berry pudding served on the feast of Saint Lucy, when traditionally no milled grain is eaten. (Saint Lucy was a blinded martyr, and under the Julian calendar her feast day was on the darkest day of the year, the first day of winter; it is celebrated on 13 December under the Gregorian calendar.)

For centuries bread has been a formidable political and economic weapon, and from ancient Rome onward, those in power have always kept a watchful eye on its availability. Roman bakers, for example, were closely regulated and under the control of the state. The Roman state went so far as to nationalize the baking industry. In France over a millennium and a half later, repeated famines triggered the French Revolution. Napoleon's letters during his campaigns attest to the emperor's extreme preoccupation with the supply of bread to Paris. The weight and price of bread was still regulated by the state in France in the twenty-first century.

Ancient breads have been a source of inspiration. They are a rich trove of ideas for bakers in the twenty-first century. While the techniques for making bread have changed, the human stomach has not. Industrial methods of production and freezing have led to the creation of new bread types, but industrially produced bread will never replace artisanal bread, which has undergone something of a renaissance in the United States in the early twenty-first century. The new gastronomy emphasizes quality much more than quantity.

A symbolic foodstuff international in scope, bread is the quintessential human food. Its history underlies a large part of the history of the human race, the simplest perhaps in the history of everyday life and eating. It connects people to culture, to tradition, and sometimes to religion.

See also **Baking**; **Bread**; **Metaphor, Food as**; **Symbol, Food as**; **Wheat**.

BIBLIOGRAPHY

Armengaud, Christine. *Le diable sucré*. Paris: Editions de La Martinière, 2000.

Fabiani, Gilbert. *Petite anthologie culinaire du pain*. Barbentane France: Equinoxe, 2001.

Jacob, Heinrich Eduard. *Six Thousand Years of Bread: Its Holy and Unholy History*. New York: Doubleday, Doran, 1944.

Macherel, Claude. *Une vie de pain: faire, penser et dire: le pain en Europe*. Brussels: Crédit Communal, 1994.

Poilâne, Lionel. *Guide de l'amateur de pain*. Paris: Robert Laffont, 1981.

Rousseau, Marguerite. *Pains de tradition*. Paris: Flammarion, 2001.

Sheppard, Ronald, and Edward Newton. *The Story of Bread*. London: Routledge & Kegan Paul, 1957.

Ziehr, W. *Le pain à travers les âges: paysan, meunier, boulanger*. Paris: Hermé, 1985.

Lionel Poilâne

BREAKFAST. Breakfast, the first meal of the day, can mean many things to many different people. The English term comes from a Middle English word meaning 'breaking the fast'. Any meal that breaks the overnight fast that occurs while we sleep is considered "breakfast."

Breakfast throughout History

From archaeological evidence at Neolithic sites we know that there was an early reliance on cereal grains; what people consume at breakfast, however, has changed considerably over time and place. Wild emmer and einkorn wheats and a variety of barley were first gathered and then cultivated in the Middle East around 7000 B.C.E. (McGee, p. 233). Maize (corn) was grown in South America and rice in Asia starting around 4500 B.C.E., and rye and oats were cultivated in Europe from about 400 B.C.E. Neolithic peoples used stone querns to grind the hulled grains, then boiled them to make a kind of porridge.

Roman soldiers woke up to a breakfast of *pulmentus*, a porridge similar to the Italian polenta, made from roasted spelt wheat or barley that was then pounded and cooked in a cauldron of water. On the march, they ate *bucellatum*, dried bread similar to Holland rusk (Renfrew, p. 22). People in the Middle East made and grilled flatbreads of all kinds, perhaps accompanied by green onions or another easily cultivated vegetable and a soft cheese, a tradition that carries through to the present time.

When other types of wheat were introduced throughout the Middle East and Europe, higher-rising breads could be baked. Only the wealthy could afford wheat bread because the cultivation of wheat required the most fertile lands. Oats and barley could grow in poorer soils and a colder, wetter climate and provided the basis for heavy breads that peasants ate. Barley was also used to make malt and thus to brew beer from Neolithic times onwards. Water was regarded as unsafe to drink from ancient times through the Renaissance, so beer was the beverage of choice for breakfast. People living in what is now Europe broke their fast with a mug of beer and an oatcake, a heavy bread made from barley and oats, or a bowl of porridge.

In warmer climates, rice became a breakfast staple. In Hong Kong, chicken *congee*, or rice cooked in a rich chicken stock, has been eaten with tea for breakfast for centuries. Likewise in southern India, rice is cooked with fresh ginger, chilies, and spices and served with eggs cooked in ghee or clarified butter.

In South America, maize kernels were soaked in lime to remove the hulls and then ground into a moist *masa* to make corn tortillas—the flatbreads of South America. These are still served with eggs, salsa, refried beans, plantains, avocados, and spiced pumpkin seeds or pepitas and other accompaniments for breakfast.

By the end of the 1600s, breakfast throughout most of Europe and the American colonies was a simple affair similar to the current "continental breakfast" offered in hotels in America and Europe. Less affluent households still drank beer for breakfast with their bread or porridge, but wealthier households began to include coffee or tea. Bread and butter, a selection of cold meats, perhaps porridge on a cold day, and coffee, tea, or another hot beverage was the breakfast norm by the early 1800s. In 1821, English writer William Cobbett complained in *Cottage Economy* that "The drink, which has come to supply the place of beer, has, in general, been tea. It is notorious, that tea has no useful strength in it; that it contains nothing nutritious; that it, besides being food for nothing, has badness in it, because it is well-known to produce want of sleep in many cases, and in all cases, to shake and weaken the nerves." England imported 20,000 pounds of tea in 1700 and 20 million pounds by 1800.

Arabs in Ethiopia had been cultivating coffee beans and making the dark, rich beverage since 1000 C.E. Coffee traveled to Turkey, then, by the 1500s, to Venice as part of the spice trade, where it was discovered by the English. Enterprising planters smuggled coffee beans to create plantations in the East Indies and later in South America. By the mid-1650s, coffee was the main attraction at cafés, named after the French word for coffee, in London and Paris. Today, coffee and tea remain breakfast fixtures all over the world.

By Victorian times, when abundance was enjoyed by Americans as well as the British at the height of the British Empire, breakfast was a lavish affair, whether served at a table in a farm kitchen or in an elegant city dining room. Cookbooks from the period provide insight into the breakfast served by affluent households. In the 1861 *Book of Household Management*, Isabella Beeton suggested a daily breakfast buffet that included a cold joint of meat, game pies, broiled mackerel, sausages, bacon and eggs, muffins, toast, marmalade, butter, jam, coffee, and tea.

In the 1877 *Buckeye Cookery and Practical Housekeeping*, the anonymous American compilers suggested breakfast menus for every season. In spring, they recommended fried brook trout, eggs on toast, baked beans and Boston brown bread, rice waffles, coffee, tea, and milk. In summer, the menu included fresh Nutmeg melons, fried fish,

Photographer Michael Neveux has played visual games in this picture called "Balanced Breakfast," which tosses a humorous volley at both nutritionists and gravity. © MICHAEL NEVEUX/CORBIS.

Saratoga potatoes, and sliced tomatoes. The fall menu called for oatmeal mush, fried salt pork, corn oysters, baked potatoes, and stewed peaches. In winter, the recommendation was for pork tenderloin, fried apples, buckwheat cakes with syrup, and sliced oranges.

During the nineteenth century, cooks also made breakfast dishes that were a combination of cereals and meats. Scrapple, a blend of pork and cooked cornmeal mush, is sliced and fried for breakfast in Pennsylvania. In Cincinnati, breakfasters still love *goetta* (pronounced "get-uh"), a savory blend of cooked whole oats with pork and onions, also sliced and fried. At this same time, there was a movement against these lavish eating habits, which resulted in the birth of the breakfast cereals we are familiar with today. On 25 December 1865, Ellen White had a vision at her home in Battle Creek, Michigan. She saw the ailing members of her husband Elder James White's congregation returned to blooming health and was convinced that a better diet consisting of more whole grains and fiber was the missing component. And since Battle Creek was the national headquarters for the Seventh-Day Adventists, the Whites' religious affiliation, she wanted all Seventh-Day Adventists to be restored to health. She persuaded her husband to offer a medical scholarship to John Harvey Kellogg, who then set about studying nutrition in New York City.

As a student who wanted a healthier diet, Kellogg cooked for himself and knew how long it took to first soak and then cook whole or cracked grains. He wanted an easier way to eat a nutritious breakfast, and the idea of precooked cereals came to him. However, it took two years of trial and error before he introduced the first ready-made cereal—"Granola," as he called it—to the patients at the Seventh-Day Adventist health sanitarium in Battle Creek. Soon to follow were Grape-Nuts, so named because they were sweetened with dextrose or grape sugar and the product had a nutty flavor, in 1898; they were developed by Dr. Kellogg and his brother Will. Corn flakes flavored with malted barley debuted in 1902. Alexander P. Anderson of the Quaker Oats Company developed the technology for puffed cereals, and puffed rice was introduced to the American consumer at the St. Louis World's Fair in 1904. Today, 66 percent of Americans still eat cold cereal for breakfast (Perryman). Even those who skip breakfast still might drink a glass of orange juice, another breakfast staple.

Breakfast around the World

Americans also enjoy other types of breakfast foods, some more healthy than others. In addition to fruit juices, particularly orange juice, pancakes, biscuits, eggs, bacon, sausages, and other breakfast meats, Americans also consume hash brown potatoes and breakfast pastries such as coffee cakes, donuts, and muffins. About 7 percent of Americans enjoy a Southern-style breakfast with eggs, sausage, grits, and biscuits. On-the-go breakfasters—now about 68 percent of the population—might stop at a fast-food restaurant for a cup of coffee, a breakfast sandwich, a bagel, or a doughnut. Fast-food restaurants have expanded their breakfast offerings while the number of bagel emporiums and coffee shops has greatly increased to meet the growing needs of these breakfasters on the way to work or school. Health-conscious eaters favor breakfast cereal bars, plain bagels, yogurt, and herbal tea or fresh-squeezed carrot juice, and have prompted this segment of the prepared foods market to burgeon (Lach). About 32 percent of Americans currently eat toast for breakfast.

Unlike the sit-down family breakfast of the past, the early-twenty-first century American breakfast is eaten at different times before parents and their children leave for work and school. This trend also fuels the need for easy-to-eat breakfast items such as breakfast bars, yogurt, cereals, toaster pastries, and microwavable frozen breakfast entrees.

In England, the typical English breakfast or "full fry-up" includes fruit juice, a bowl of cereal, eggs with fried streaky bacon or sausages, sometimes grilled tomatoes and mushrooms, perhaps a kipper or other smoked fish, fried bread or toast or scones, and marmalade. In France, a croissant or a baguette with fresh butter and a cup of

café au lait (coffee with milk) is common. Italians enjoy a light breakfast of pastry or bread and butter with coffee, while the Germans, Swiss, Dutch, and Scandinavians prefer a breakfast of cold sliced meats and cheeses, bread and butter, jam, and perhaps a boiled egg. Dutch and Belgian breakfasters might enjoy a touch of chocolate—as a filling in a croissant or chocolate sprinkles known as *hagel* over buttered toast.

In other parts of the world, breakfast is equally simple. In India, it might mean flatbread with cardamom-scented tea or steamed dumplings with a spicy sauce and coconut chutney (Sahni, p. 104). Mexicans eat *huevos rancheros*, or scrambled eggs with chilies and salsa, or even *menudo*, braised tripe, and burritos. In Saudi Arabia, families eat eggs, baked beans, cheese, olives, and *ma'soub*, or pancakes with bananas, but are also including American cereals.

Breakfast as a Social Ritual

Apart from the necessity of breaking the fast, the first meal of the day can also function as an important social ritual. Retired businessmen and farmers, networking men and women in management, mothers of young children, or singles often meet at a designated restaurant for an early morning breakfast. Schools, churches, and other organizations offer pancake breakfasts as fundraisers. Tailgate breakfasts served from the back of a car or van feed fans at weekend football games; hunt breakfasts served buffet-style feed those about to saddle up.

The wedding breakfast, a more formal affair, brings together the wedding party and the families for an elegant first meal to start the couple's big day—or, often, their first day as a married couple on the day after the wedding. Less hearty foods, such as champagne, smoked salmon, shirred eggs, eggs Benedict, steamed asparagus, and Danish pastries would be on a wedding breakfast menu.

Brunch, a combination of breakfast and lunch served later in the morning, is often a relaxed social occasion, most often held on Sunday in private homes or restaurants. Savory bread puddings, egg casseroles, omelets, waffles, coffee cakes, and fruit compotes are typical brunch fare. Alcoholic drinks such as Bloody Marys (vodka with spiced tomato juice), Mimosas (champagne with orange juice), or screwdrivers (vodka with orange juice) might also be served.

The Best Way to Start the Day

No matter what is on the menu, research shows that breakfast is still a very important meal. In a 1998 study of schoolchildren published in the *Archives of Pediatric and Adolescent Medicine*, researchers found that children who eat breakfast perform better academically and also behave better. The children who ate breakfast functioned intellectually at almost a grade level higher than those who did not, and were less likely to fall asleep at their desks or disrupt class because of hunger. The same goes for adults. Eating breakfast improves the ability to concentrate, reduces the risk of heart disease, improves weight control, and increases strength and energy. Generally, health professionals recommend that we eat a healthy breakfast consisting of protein, whole grains, and fruits that totals about one-third of our daily caloric intake (Maynard).

See also **Beeton, Isabella; Cereal Grains and Pseudo-Cereals; Cereals, Cold; Dinner; Fruit; Kellogg, John Harvey; Lunch; Vegetables; Vitamin C.**

BIBLIOGRAPHY

Beeton, Isabella. *The Book of Household Management.* London, 1861.

Black, Maggie. *Food and Cooking in Medieval Britain: History and Recipes.* London: Historic Buildings and Monuments Commission for England, 1985.

Brears, Peter. *Food and Cooking in 17th Century Britain: History and Recipes.* London: Historic Buildings and Monuments Commission for England, 1985.

Buckeye Cookery and Practical Housekeeping. Minneapolis, Minn.: Buckeye Publishing Company, 1877.

Lach, Jennifer. "What's for Breakfast?" *American Demographics* (May 1999).

Maynard, Cindy. "Start Your Day with a Breakfast Boost." *Current Health* 2, no. 26 (September 1999): 16.

McGee, Harold. *On Food and Cooking: The Science and Lore of the Kitchen.* New York: Scribners, 1984.

Murphy, J. Michael, et al. "The Relationship of School Breakfast to Psychosocial and Academic Functioning: Cross-sectional and Longitudinal Observations in an Inner-City School Sample." *Archives of Pediatrics and Adolescent Medicine* 152 (September 1998): 899–907.

Perryman, M. Ray. "Changes in the American Palate." *Dallas Business Journal* 25, 3 (31 August 2001): 55.

Renfrew, Jane. *Food and Cooking in Roman Britain: History and Recipes.* London: Historic Buildings and Monuments Commission for England, 1985.

Sahni, Julie. *Classic Indian Vegetarian Cooking.* London: Dorling Kindersley, 1987.

Stead, Jennifer. *Food and Cooking in 18th Century Britain: History and Recipes.* London: Historic Buildings and Monuments Commission for England, 1985.

Judith M. Fertig

BRILLAT-SAVARIN, JEAN ANTHELME. The author of the best-known work of gastronomy, Jean Anthelme Brillat-Savarin (1755–1826), was born in Belley in the region of Bresse, studied law in Dijon, became a lawyer and president of the civil court at Ain, a mayor of Belley, and a commander of the National Guard. In 1789 he was chosen to be a deputy to the National Assembly. In 1793 the Revolutionary Tribunal accused him of "moderatism" and he fled to Switzerland, Holland, and finally America. In New York he supported himself for

Nineteenth-century print based on a portrait of Anthelme Brillat-Savarin, author of *The Physiology of Taste* (*Physiologie du goût*). © GIANNI DAGLI ORTI/CORBIS.

three years by teaching French and playing the violin in the John Street Theatre, but he also traveled north through New England, where he hunted game in good company, and south to Philadelphia where he met Thomas Jefferson. Returned to France in 1796, he was appointed judge to the Supreme Court of Appeals in Paris.

As a bachelor gourmand, he entertained often in his home on the Rue de Richelieu and frequented such stylish restaurants as Grand Véfour and Beauvilliers. Known to be a learned and witty man, he wrote treatises on a number of different sciences and wished to make a science of culinary art.

In 1826, he published anonymously the *Physiologie du goût: Méditations de gastronomie transcendante, ouvrage théorique, historique et à l'ordre du jour, dédié aux gastronomes parisiens* (Physiology of Taste, or Meditations on Transcendental Gastronomy: a theoretical, historical and contemporary work, dedicated to the gastronomes of Paris), a collection of aphorisms, epigrams, anecdotes, and essays on subjects as diverse as chemistry, physiology, nutrition, obesity, appetite, gourmandism, digestion, dreams, frying, and death. He even included a miniphilosophic history of cuisine from man's discovery of fire to the tables of Louis XVI.

THE PHYSIOLOGY OF TASTE

"Tell me what you eat, and I shall tell you what you are" (Fisher, p. 3).

"The discovery of a new dish does more for human happiness than the discovery of a star" (p. 4).

"A dinner which ends without cheese is like a beautiful woman with only one eye" (p. 4)

"Let one open any book of history, from Herodotus to our own days, and he will see that, without even excepting conspiracies, not a single great event has occurred which has not been conceived, prepared, and carried out at a feast" (p. 54).

"Whosoever pronounces the word "truffle" gives voice to one which awakens erotic and gastronomical dreams equally in the sex that wears skirts and the one that sprouts a beard" (p. 93).

Although his aim was didactic, his gift was for storytelling—his anecdotes rather than his analyses make his work live. His timing and his tone were right for the new bourgeoisie of Paris and the form of his *Physiology* helped establish the popularity of a new essayistic genre, the profile. Translated into many languages, his work has enjoyed a wide readership because of his light and easy style, his facility with a phrase—so quotable that his aphorisms have become clichés—and finally his intellectual solidity in placing the physical and aesthetic pleasures of food in the social–scientific context of human behavior.

In short, he took the subject of food seriously in a new way. Instead of elaborating an aesthetics of taste, based on the idiosyncrasies of individuals in the manner of his aristocratic contemporary Grimod de la Reynière, Brillat-Savarin attempted to find general principles that would liberate taste from autocratic authorities. His attempt to provide a scientific basis for all the pleasures of the table was compatible with the reasoned conservatism of the Enlightenment that had earlier sent him into exile. His *Physiology* is a remarkably egalitarian work.

At the same time, he epitomizes the urbane civility of a man born in the country who rose to high office in the city in the new ranks of the Parisian bourgeoisie. Others, striving to improve their social standing, could identify with him. As Brillat-Savarin outlined them, his standards of excellence were no longer defined by professional chefs of the court or by grand banquets of court cuisine, but by the quality of ingredients and a care of preparation that anyone could learn. He rhapsodizes over cheese, eels, or truffles not because they are extravagant luxuries but because they are part of a well-stocked larder that any man of means could buy and serve at home. For the convenience of his readers, he took care to include the names and addresses of his favorite Parisian suppliers of groceries, pastries, and breads. In effect, although a habitué of the best restaurants in town, he was essentially addressing the home cook and the home diner.

Although writing almost two centuries ago, he describes a culinary world that seems familiar to any inhabitant of a large cosmopolitan city in the early twenty-first century. In praising the Parisian table, he does not ascribe its virtues to an indigenous French character, but rather to the fruits of an increasing internationalism. He lists which ingredients come from France, which from England, Germany, Spain, Italy, Russia, Africa, Holland, and America. He concludes: "a meal such as one can eat in Paris is a cosmopolitan whole in which every part of the world makes its appearance by way of its products" (Revel, *Culture and Cuisine*, p. 218). He fancied himself a citizen of the world and as a result his name has become synonymous, at least in the Western world, with food's most civilized expression of wit and humanity.

See also **Cookbooks**; **Fisher, M. F. K.**; **France**; **Gastronomy**; **Grimod de la Reynière.**

BIBLIOGRAPHY

Boissel, Thierry. *Brillat-Savarin, 1755–1826: Un chevalier candide.* Paris: Presses de la Renaissance, 1989.

Doucet, Henri. *Un Brillat-Savarin du XXe siecle.* Vienne, Isère: Doucet, 1994.

Fisher, M. F. K., trans. *M. F. K. Fisher's Translation of Brillat-Savarin's* The Physiology of Taste. New York: Knopf, 1971. Valuable glosses.

Lalauze, Adolphe, trans. *Brillat-Savarin's* Physiologie du goût: *A Handbook of Gastronomy, New and Complete Translation with Fifty-Two Original Etchings by A. Lalauze.* New York: Bouton, 1884. Preface by Charles Monselet.

MacDonogh, Giles. *Brillat-Savarin: The Judge and His Stomach.* London: Murray, 1992.

Betty Fussell

BRITISH ISLES.

This entry includes four subentries:
England
Ireland
Scotland
Wales

ENGLAND

Since the 1970s, English food appears to have undergone a transformation. A postwar cuisine of plainly cooked meat and vegetables supplemented with baked goods and puddings has apparently given way to multiculturalism. Restaurants serve fusion food. Supermarkets sell chilled meals based on Italian or Asian recipes. The cookery sector of publishing is buoyant. This seems astonishing for a country whose eating habits evolved little between the

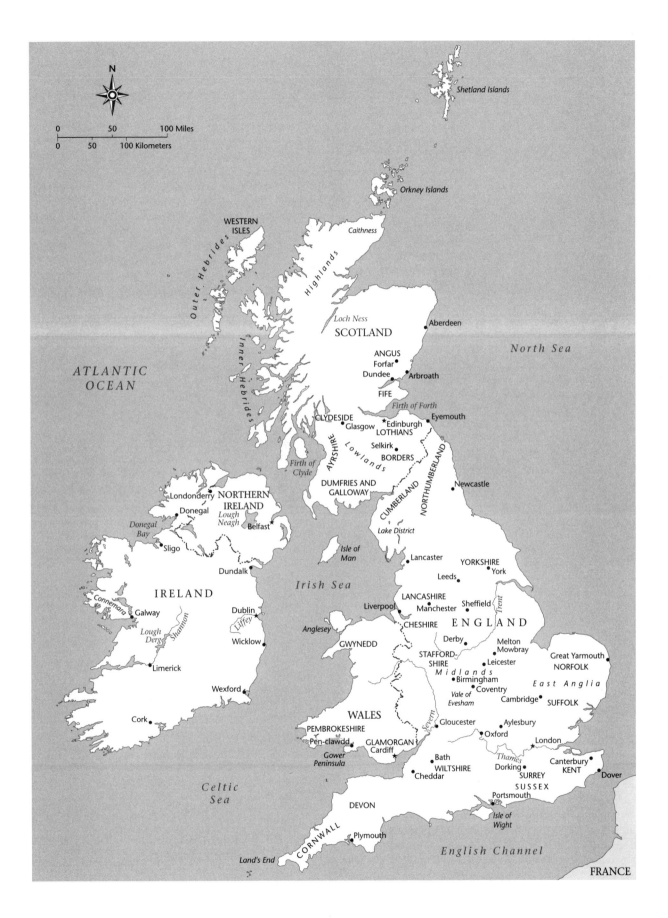

The interior of Covent Garden in London, circa 1920. This market hall was one of the largest in England as well as the center of London's food distribution system until after World War II, when it was closed due to traffic congestion. ROUGHWOOD COLLECTION.

mid-nineteenth century and 1953, when Second World War rationing ended; but beneath the metropolitan froth, old ideas about plain cooking live on.

Background

England has an unpredictable but generally benign maritime climate, without extremes; relief is low, the highest mountain standing 3210 feet (978 meters). A basic topographic division runs from northeast to southwest, along the watershed of the Trent and Severn rivers. North and west of this, the land tends to be higher, and the climate colder and wetter. To the south and east, hills are generally low, and summers warmer and drier. Annual rainfall ranges from about 97 inches (2,500mm) in the hills of the northwest to about 23 inches (600mm) in the driest parts of the east; winter temperatures rarely drop more than a couple of degrees centigrade below freezing and the summer maximum is about 86°F (30°C).

England's political and cultural dominance of the United Kingdom makes it difficult to disentangle Eng-

lish food habits from those of the Welsh, Scots, and Irish. Successive waves of settlers have brought ideas about food, but few attributions can be made until the twentieth century. Foreign trade has been important to English cuisine since at least the late Middle Ages. Spices came from the East Indies; sugar and currants were initially imported from the Mediterranean, and later from colonial possessions. A dependence on tropical crops— tea, coffee, chocolate, sugar—developed in the nineteenth century; and the idea of curry came home with the nabobs of the East India Company.

Meat

Localized breeds of cattle, sheep, and pigs developed in the nineteenth century. Grass-fed beef from Aberdeen Angus, Hereford, and other traditional breeds is considered best. Most sheep meat is eaten as lamb, under the age of a year; mutton, from older sheep, formerly important, is now almost unobtainable. Fresh pork was and is popular, as is bacon. Wiltshire became an important center for curing meat in the nineteenth century. Bacon provided a relish for the otherwise monotonous diets of the poor. It remains an English favorite, though much is now imported from Denmark. Regional ham cures that became famous include those of York (or, more properly, Yorkshire), Cumberland, Devon, and Suffolk.

Poultry has long been important for both meat and eggs. In the nineteenth century, the counties around London produced Sussex and Dorking chickens; Surrey was famous for capons, and the town of Aylesbury produced ducks. Turkeys and geese were reared on corn (grain) stubble in East Anglia for sale in the capital. Poultry production is now an intensive industry, though small businesses based on high-quality traditional poultry production are appearing. Only geese have not succumbed to intensive systems.

Game has always featured on the aristocratic menu. Venison was most sought after; deer farming has made this more accessible, but it remains a minority taste, as do hares. Rabbits, nurtured in warrens in the Middle Ages, escaped, naturalized, and became pests, and the only wild creatures easily accessible to the poor. Wildfowl of all descriptions were eaten up to the eighteenth century, but subsequently the choice narrowed to about a dozen species, of which pheasants are most common, yet grouse from heather moorlands, and partridges are most prized.

Meat Cookery

Meat cookery demonstrates a preference for plain roasted (or, strictly speaking, baked) meat. Traditional accompaniments are horseradish sauce for beef; mint sauce (finely chopped mint mixed with sugar and vinegar) for lamb, and sage and onion stuffing and applesauce for fresh pork, which is generally roasted with the skin on to make crackling. Roast potatoes and boiled green or root vegetables are also served. Boiled meat dishes, such as salt beef with carrots, or mutton with caper sauce have almost vanished, though some people still marinate beef with salt, spices, and sugar for several days to make spiced beef. Steaks and chops are used for grilling.

Other meat dishes include pies or steamed suet puddings of beefsteak and kidney; oxtail is made into stews and soups. Skirt of beef is mixed with chopped potato, onion, and turnip in Cornish pasties, popular everywhere but closely identified with Cornwall itself. Northern butchers make a paste of cooked beef beneath a layer of fat; this potted beef is a remnant of an eighteenth-century tradition of potting all kinds of meat. Lancashire hotpot is a traditional stew of lamb or mutton chops with layers of onions and potatoes. It evolved in an area where a high rate of female employment led to a reliance on slow-cooked and ready-prepared foods.

Pork products include fresh sausages of lean and fat meat and some type of grain; the Cumberland type, with a high meat content and distinctive coiled presentation, is considered particularly good. Pork pies, survivors of a

PUDDINGS

Pudding has two different but linked meanings. It can indicate any sweet food considered suitable for dessert, ranging from fresh fruit to the most elaborate of sweet dishes. This usage developed after puddings, a fairly neutral staple food in the seventeenth century, evolved a subset of heavily sweetened dishes eaten for the second course at dinner.

Older meanings relate pudding to specific groups of dishes, some savory, some sweet. The oldest group is represented by sausage-type products such as black puddings (blood, fat, and grain) and white puddings, well documented since the sixteenth century. Bag puddings, mixtures of suet and flour or breadcrumbs, wrapped in a cloth and boiled, were known by the seventeenth century, and developed two distinct types. One was the sweet suet pudding with lemon peel, currants, sugar, and spice. Plum pudding, a heavily enriched version with raisins, candied peel, and sugar, has become a symbol of Christmas and remains essentially unchanged since the eighteenth century. Other sweet puddings include versions filled with fresh seasonal fruit, or jam roly-poly, suet crust spread with jam and rolled up, which became a school dinner staple. The second type was the savory suet pudding with a meat filling. These were recorded by the nineteenth century: steak and kidney remains a favorite, though puddings made with steak and oysters, mutton, and game such as partridges are also recorded.

Other ancient pudding types are pease pudding, based on a puree of dried peas, eaten with boiled bacon or ham, and Yorkshire pudding, made from batter baked in a popover pan, the principal survivor of numerous recipes for batter puddings boiled or baked.

In the eighteenth century, many sweet puddings using pastry and fruit or nuts became fashionable. Mixtures of rice or sago with milk and sugar also became common. These remain popular, though often in debased "nursery" versions. Puddings, steamed or baked, based on sponge-cake mixtures, flavored with lemon, ginger, or cocoa, became popular in the mid-nineteenth century, as did summer pudding, based on bread and fresh summer fruit.

great tradition of raised pies, are made with a lard-based hot-water crust. Melton Mowbray in the Midlands is famous for a fine version. Black puddings (blood sausages), highly seasoned mixtures of blood, grain, and cubes of fat, are known everywhere but have a strong association with the industrial towns of south Lancashire (as does ox

Salted kippers from Cumbria, England, are one of the traditional breakfast specialties of the country, but they are an acquired taste for outsiders. They are salted prior to smoking, hence the distinctive flavor. © JACQUI HURST/CORBIS.

tripe). Hog's puddings, of seasoned grain and fat, are popular in the southwest. Other items include faggots, chopped offal wrapped in squares of caul; haslet, a kind of loaf made from scraps of lean and cured pork; and brawn, a cold jellied dish made from meat picked from the head. Lard, beef suet, and drippings are important in traditional cookery.

Chicken, once an expensive treat roasted for special occasions, is now ubiquitous. It is much used in dishes of foreign origin. Rabbit stews and pies became poverty food, and the taste for them has waned. Hare soup and jugged hare—cooked slowly with wine and herbs, the sauce thickened with the blood of the animal—are classic dishes of English game cookery.

Fish

Cod and haddock, though becoming scarce, are staples of fish and chip shops; grilled Dover sole is a standard of English restaurant cookery. Oysters, until the mid-nine-

teenth century a cheap food, suffered from pollution and disease and are now a luxury. Morecombe Bay shrimps (*Crangon crangon*), potted in spiced butter, are a traditional teatime delicacy. Eels, until the 1970s, were closely associated with the food habits of the London poor. Eel pie, and mash (mashed potatoes) shops sold them cold as jellied eels (boiled and allowed to cool in their liquid) or hot with mashed potato and "liquor," a green parsley sauce. Herrings were important until a recent decline in fish stocks. Some were eaten fresh, but most were preserved. Red herrings (heavily salted and smoked for long-term keeping) were superseded in the nineteenth century by lighter cures: kippers (split and cleaned before smoking) evolved in Northumberland, while Yarmouth favored bloaters (whole, lightly salted smoked herrings). Salmon, which became expensive when rivers were polluted during the nineteenth century, is cheap again because of fish farming, and poached salmon with cucumber is an English summer favorite.

Bread and Baking

White wheaten (wheat) bread is of primary importance. Traditional oblong tin loaves have become degraded under industrial production, and foreign influence makes it easier to buy croissants, ciabatta (a bread of Italian origin with a chewy, open texture), pita, or nan bread than a traditional cottage loaf (two-tiered round loaf). Historically, bread grains included rye, barley, and maslin (mixed grain). In the northern hills, oats, the only reliable grain crop, were used for flatbreads. By the seventeenth century a preference for wheat had developed in the London area. Variety diminished as the taste for wheat spread and grain imports grew in the nineteenth century. Now, only the oat-bread tradition survives. Haverbread (from Old Norse *hafre*, oats), flat ovals about a foot long, can occasionally be found in towns on the Yorkshire-Lancashire border. A stronger custom of baking floppy oatcakes about ten inches in diameter continues in Staffordshire. Barley is now grown for brewing.

There are many small regional breads. Kentish huffkins, Cornish splits, and Yorkshire teacakes are all round and flattish, enriched with a little sugar, lard, and dried fruit. Hot plates are used to bake muffins (made from soft bread dough), and also crumpets, and pikelets (both made from thick, yeast-leavened batter). This trio of foods are all eaten toasted and spread with butter for breakfast or tea. Scones, of flour, sugar, egg, and dried fruit, are common. Chelsea buns and Bath buns are rich and sweet. Hot cross buns, marked with a cross on top, are plainer and spiced; formerly made only on Good Friday, they are now produced for several weeks around Easter.

Lardy cakes made from bread dough folded with lard, sugar, and dried fruit are typical of southern England. Currants, raisins, and candied peel feature in yeast-leavened Guernsey gâches, Cornish saffron cakes, and Yule loaves (sweetened Christmas breads made in the north). Rich fruit cakes are related to these breads historically. Modern versions are heavy with sugar, butter, raisins, currants, and candied cherries. Covered with almond paste and sugar icing, they are essential for Christmas or weddings; baked with a marzipan layer in the middle, they become simnels, for Easter.

The taste for dried fruit extends to Eccles, Chorley, and Banbury cakes—spiced currant mixtures wrapped in puff pastry. Small mince pies, filled with a mixture of dried fruit, spices, and sugar, are eaten all over the country throughout the Christmas season. Originally the mincemeat filling did contain veal, mutton, or beef; now, an enrichment of beef suet is all that survives of this. Such dried fruit and pastry confections have been popular for at least four hundred years.

Ginger is popular in baking. Grasmere gingerbread comes from the Lake District, where local ports were active in the West India trade and a taste for brown sugar, rum, and ginger survives. Parkin is a north-country gingerbread that often contains oatmeal. Cornish Fairings and Ashbourne cakes are also ginger-flavored, and have a crisp, biscuity texture. The diversity of modern British biscuits (cookies) is a product of nineteenth-century industry, but Shrewsbury cakes (related to shortbread) were recorded in the seventeenth century, and Bath Olivers (plain biscuits) in the early nineteenth.

Vegetables and Fruit

The English have never been renowned for sensitivity in cooking vegetables, which were generally boiled and served with butter. Cabbages, carrots, parsnips, spinach, and salads such as lettuce and watercress have a long history of use, as has asparagus: the Vale of Evesham and Norfolk are particularly associated with this crop. One

FISH AND CHIPS

Fish and chips, a favorite take-away (takeout) food in England, are sold in their own specialized restaurants and shops. There is some debate about when the combination became popular, but fried fish was being sold as street food in London as early as the 1830s, when Charles Dickens mentioned a fried-fish warehouse in *Oliver Twist*. Chips (french fries) appear to have joined the fish by the 1880s, and the pairing has remained popular ever since.

Cod is most commonly used, though haddock is preferred in some areas; the fillets are dipped in batter before deep-frying. For chips, the potatoes are cut in thick fingers and deep-fried. Vegetable oil is the usual frying medium in the south. Beef drippings are often used in the north. On purchase, the cooked fish and chips are seasoned with salt and vinegar as the customer desires. A pot of mushy peas (cooked marrowfat peas) is sometimes added to the order. Traditionally, newspapers are used for wrapping fish and chips, and the smell of deep-frying combined with hot newsprint is part of the experience. Health regulations now demand layers of greaseproof paper to insulate the food from printer's ink.

The center of English social life is the village pub, where all manner of truths and confessions are part of the daily fare. Oftentimes the food is minimal, but at the best establishments it vies with high-class home cookery, as in the case of this famous pub in Boston, England. © JAMES L. AMOS/CORBIS.

vegetable almost uniquely used by the English is sea kale (*Crambe maritima*); wild plants were overexploited in the nineteenth century but sea kale is now cultivated in small quantities. Potatoes first gained wide acceptance in the north; by the nineteenth century they were eaten everywhere by everyone, and have continued to be so.

Apples, pears, cherries, and plums are traditional fruit crops of the southeast and southwest. Cobnuts are grown in Kent; soft fruit is grown across much of the country, strawberries and raspberries being favorites. Historically, the north, with a more challenging climate, relied on gooseberries, damsons, and rhubarb, the latter mostly grown in West Yorkshire, where it is forced as an early spring crop. Traditional fruit puddings and jams are a strength of the English kitchen. One vital item, the bitter orange, is grown in southern Spain and imported specifically for making breakfast marmalade. A taste for sugar confectionery has led to numerous boiled sugar sweets, many using fruit flavorings.

Dairy Products

Dairy products were considered food for the poor in the seventeenth century, but have become progressively more important. Cream is mixed with fruit purees for fools, and beaten with wine and lemon for syllabubs. Clotted cream,

MUFFINS AND MUFFIN-MEN

As late as the 1930s, muffins were sold in London by muffin-men, street vendors who announced their presence by ringing a bell. In 1851, Sir Henry Mayhew recorded in *London Labour and the London Poor* that muffin-men bought their wares fresh from the bakers. The muffins were kept warm by wrapping them in flannel; they were then carried through the streets in baskets for resale door-to-door. The custom apparently derives in part from genteel ladies who did not keep servants who could be sent on errands, but who liked a slap-up (lavish) tea. The muffin-men recognized this, and made their rounds in mid-afternoon, convenient for tea time. Muffins were most popular in winter. To eat them, they were toasted, pulled apart around the circumference, spread with butter, and the halves put back together to allow the butter to melt.

The origin of the name is a mystery. Recipes appear in the mid-eighteenth century, but the idea is probably much older. Muffins enjoyed great popularity but were considered old-fashioned by the early twentieth century, and had almost vanished by the Second World War. In the 1980s, they were revived by industrial bakeries, and are once again available, in varying degrees of quality. Muffins in England—quite unlike sweetened muffins and what people in North America call "English muffins"—are disks about four inches in diameter and an inch thick, and made from plain, soft bread dough. Size and the use of yeast as a leaven relates them to the many other small breads of English traditional baking, while the use of a hot plate puts them in the same category as crumpets, pikelets, and several Welsh and Scottish specialties.

heated gently to produce a thick crust, is a specialty of Devon and Cornwall. Butter is essential for spreading on bread and toast, as well as in cooking generally. Cheese-making in Britain was centralized during the Second World War, concentrating on "territorial" cheeses—Stilton, Cheddar, Gloucester, Cheshire, Lancashire, Wensleydale, Derby, and Leicester. All named for their areas of origin, they became generic (apart from Stilton, the manufacture of which was restricted to a small area in 1910). A dwindling nucleus of farm cheese-makers was boosted in the 1980s as "new wave" artisans who injected new creativity and energy into the industry.

Meal Times and Names

The British all recognize the early morning meal as breakfast, but after that a division becomes apparent. One pattern is a light midday lunch, perhaps afternoon tea, and a large dinner in the evening. The other is midday dinner and a substantial tea in the early evening. Sometimes this is called high tea or supper, though "supper," confusingly, is also used to indicate a light, late-evening repast. This divide originated when dinner, once a midday meal, slipped first to the early evening and then as late as 8:00 P.M. in the early nineteenth century. Lunch and afternoon tea developed to fill the long hours between breakfast and dinner. Wealthy younger people and southeasterners tend toward the lunch and dinner pattern. Poorer people, older ones, and northerners follow, to a diminishing extent, the dinner and tea pattern.

The "full English" breakfast. There is much nostalgia for the full English breakfast, a meal now mostly encountered in hotels, guesthouses, and cafés. Fried bacon and eggs are essential. Tomatoes, mushrooms, baked beans, fried bread, sausages, and black pudding are often added. Toast and marmalade generally follow. In cafés this meal is often available at any time. Time-consuming to prepare and eat, it is rarely made at home on a workday, when breakfast usually consists of cereal or toast, or coffee and a pastry bought on the way to work. However, cooked breakfasts are often made as a weekend treat.

Other items sometimes found at breakfast are oatmeal porridge (now closely identified with Scotland, but a survivor of a general British tradition of grain pottages) and kippers. In India, the British took *khichri*, spiced rice and lentils eaten with dried fish, and transmuted it into kedgeree, a mixture of rice, onions, and smoked haddock, still popular. Substantial breakfasts were most fully developed in country houses in the mid-nineteenth century, when huge buffets including such delicacies as deviled kidneys, raised pies, and cold tongue were laid out.

Lunch. Lunch has few special foods linked with it; though large formal lunches are sometimes eaten, a collation of odds and ends is more frequent. Sandwiches are a popular choice. The English have found sandwiches a convenient handheld meal since the mid-eighteenth century, when the Earl of Sandwich is said to have asked for his meat between two slices of bread, so as to avoid leaving the gaming table. Currently enjoying a zenith of popularity and variety, numerous specialty shops sell them filled with anything from conventional cheese and pickles or roast beef and horseradish combinations to chicken *tikka* or prawns and avocado. For those who want a hot lunch, soup or "something on toast"—cheese, eggs, fish, baked beans—are popular.

Dinner. Dinner is a substantial hot meal, whether taken at midday or in the evening. The traditional pattern is cooked meat or fish with vegetables. A sweet course, usually referred to as pudding, follows. Food may come from the prepared-food counter in a supermarket, and home cooks are as likely to choose dishes from the Mediterranean or the Indian subcontinent as traditional English ones. Take-away (takeout) food, from traditional fish and

English country fare has undergone a revolution, in part due to high-end tourism and to a process of rediscovery among English food enthusiasts who want to see more of the country's culinary treasures showcased to visitors. Here, traditional English veal shin is baked in a clay pot with various root vegetables at Le Manoir, Great Milton, Oxfordshire, England. © Michael Boys/CORBIS.

chips to kebabs, curries, or "a Chinese," are possible choices.

Confounding the lunch-dinner division are the special cases of Sunday dinner and Christmas dinner. These phrases still imply a large midday meal. Sunday dinner is often roast beef and Yorkshire pudding, served with gravy made from the meat juices or a commercial mix. Roasted or boiled potatoes and other vegetables, typically boiled cabbage and carrots, are also served. Lamb, pork, or chicken may take the place of the beef. Pudding choices include trifle (sherry-soaked sponge cake covered with layers of custard and cream); treacle tart (filled with golden syrup, lemon, and breadcrumbs), or lemon meringue pie. Steamed suet or sponge puddings are seen as old-fashioned but remain popular, as do fruit pies.

Christmas dinner usually centers on turkey or goose accompanied by sage and onion stuffing. Bread sauce, milk infused with cloves and shallot, thickened with breadcrumbs, is a classic accompaniment and a survival of a medieval tradition of bread-thickened sauces. Brussels sprouts are generally among the vegetables. This is followed by Christmas pudding flambéed with brandy, served with rum or brandy butter. Turkey is now the general choice, a reflection of centuries of great feasts involving various bird species, though roast beef was also a standard Christmas dish until the nineteenth century.

Afternoon tea and high tea. Tea is overlaid with social nuances. Apart from tea to drink (a beverage of primary importance in England since the mid-eighteenth century), afternoon tea is a dainty meal: bread and butter, small sandwiches filled with cucumber, a cake. Cream tea is a variant on this, with scones, jam, and cream. Elaborate afternoon teas are now most often taken in a café. High tea is a substantial meal, for people returning from work, or for children after school. It involves hot food such as kippers, eggs, pies, or sausages, or, in summer, cold ham or tinned canned salmon and salad. Bread and butter is always on the table, together with jam, and a selection of cakes—large ones, such as fruit cake or a Victoria sandwich (sponge cake filled with jam and cream), and small fairy cakes (similar to cupcakes or miniature muffins), jam tarts, and cookies.

Recent Developments

A trend toward vegetarianism and concern about animal welfare has become apparent since the 1970s, leading to a growth in consumption of organically produced and vegetarian foods. Another development is a taste for ethnic food. Though imitations of Asian food, such as curry, piccalilli, and mushroom ketchup, have been made since the eighteenth century, in the last hundred years immigrant communities have introduced numerous new ideas. Chinese restaurants were widespread by the 1960s and Italian restaurants soon followed. Indian restaurants began to penetrate beyond major centers of immigration in the 1970s, putting dishes such as chicken *tikka masala* on the national menu, especially after pub closing time. West

Indian, Hispanic, Turkish, and Thai restaurants can now be found in most cities.

London restaurant culture now has a global reputation for excellence, and interest in eating healthily has increased; but London is not England, and the high incidence of cardiovascular disease throughout the country is partially attributed to poor diet. Writers, guides, and chefs have raised the variety and quality of ingredients and of ready-prepared food, and cookery is a popular subject for television. But the best traditional English food remains a specialty found mostly in the homes of dedicated cooks.

See also **Custard; Fish and Chips; Pastry; Tea (Meal).**

BIBLIOGRAPHY

Ayrton, Elisabeth. *The Cookery of England*. London: André Deutsch, 1974.

Burnett, John. *Plenty and Want: A Social History of Diet in England from 1815 to the Present Day*. London: Scolar Press, 1979. Newton, Mass.: Biscuit Books, 1994.

Davidson, Alan. *North Atlantic Seafood*. London: Macmillan, 1979; New York: Viking, 1980. A book that covers far more than just England, but contains much information about fish as used in Britain.

Davidson, Alan. *The Oxford Companion to Food*. Oxford: Oxford University Press, 1999. Though this book covers food globally, it contains much information on English food habits and includes a useful article on early English cookery books (cookbooks).

Drummond, J. C., and Anne Wilbraham. *The Englishman's Food: A History of Five Centuries of English Diet*, with a new introduction by Tom Jaine. London: Pimlico, 1994.

Grigson, Jane. *English Food*, with a foreword by Sophie Grigson. London: Penguin, 1992. Classic English recipes, updated for a modern audience.

Hartley, Dorothy. *Food in England*. London: MacDonald and Jane's, 1954; Boston: Little, Brown, 1996. A slightly romantic but well-observed picture of traditional English cookery from information gathered between the two world wars.

Mason, Laura, and Catherine Brown. *Traditional Foods of Britain: An Inventory*. Totnes, Devon, U.K.: Prospect Books, 1999. Based on information gathered for Euroterroirs, a European Union study of local foods.

Walton, John K. *Fish and Chips and the British Working Class 1870–1940*. Leicester, U.K., and New York: Leicester University Press, 1992.

Wilson, C. Anne. *Food and Drink in Britain: From the Stone Age to Recent Times*. Chicago: Academy Chicago Publishers, 1991. Still the standard reference on the history of food in the British Isles.

Wilson, C. Anne, ed. *Luncheon, Nuncheon, and Other Meals: Eating with the Victorians*. Stroud, U.K.: Alan Sutton, 1994. This book contains much information on meal times, patterns, and content as social change affected them in the nineteenth century.

Laura Mason

IRELAND

The first settlers, the Mesolithic people, came to Ireland about 7000 B.C.E. and lived by hunting, fishing, and gathering. Neolithic colonists introduced domestic animals and crops about 4000 B.C.E. Cultivated cereals included emmer wheat *(Triticum dicoccum)*, bread wheat *(Triticum aestivum)*, and barley. Wild foods, such as hazelnuts and dried crabapples, were stored. Farming, crops and livestock, continued during the Bronze Age (2000–700 B.C.E.) and the pre-Christian Iron Age (700 B.C.E.–500 C.E.), as is evident from faunal remains and from the range of quernstones for saddle, beehive, and disk querns used to process cereals for domestic use.

In the historical period literary data of various kinds supplement the archaeological record. Religious texts in Old Irish and Latin from the Early Christian period (500–1000 C.E.) describe monastic and penitential diets, and the Old Irish law tracts of the seventh and eighth centuries provide insight into food-production strategies, diets, and hospitality obligations. Prestige foods are correlated with social rank according to the general principle that everyone is to be fed according to his or her rank. Persons of higher social status enjoyed a greater variety and quality of food than those of lower rank. Milk and cereal products were the basis of the diet, and a distinction was sometimes made between winter and summer foods. The former apparently consisted of cereals and meat and the latter mainly of dairy produce.

Milk and Milk Products

Milk, "good when fresh, good when old, good when thick, good when thin," was considered the best food. Fresh milk was a high-status food of sufficient prestige to be served as a refreshment to guests in secular and monastic settings. Many milk products are mentioned in the early Irish legal tracts and in *Aislinge Meic Con Glinne* (Vision of Mac Con Glinne), an early medieval satirical text in the Irish language rich in food imagery and probably the most important source of information about food in medieval Ireland. Butter, curds, cheese, and whole-milk or skim-milk whey were common elements of the diet. Butter was often portrayed as a luxury food. It was part of the food rents a client was obliged to give to his or her lord and a festive food for monastic communities. Curds, formed naturally in milk or by using rennet, were a common summer food included in food rents and apparently a normal part of the monastic diet. Cheese, in soft and hard varieties, was of great importance in the early Irish and medieval diet. Whey, the liquid product of the preparation of curds and cheese, was rather sour, but diluted with water it was prominent in the stricter monastic diets of the early Irish Church. Goat's milk whey, considered to have medicinal properties, was still in regular use in parts of Ireland in the early nineteenth century.

These milk products held their ancient status in the diet to varying degrees until the threshold of the eighteenth century, when forces of commercialization and modernization during the modern period altered levels of consumption and ultimately the dietary status of some milk products. Milk and butter remained basic foodstuffs, and their dietary and economic significance is reflected in the richness of the repertoire of beliefs, customs, and legends concerned with the protection of cows at the boundary festival of May, traditionally regarded as the commencement of summer and the milking seasons in Ireland, when the milch cows were transferred to the lush green pastures. Cheese making, which essentially died out in the eighteenth century, probably due to the substantial international butter and provisions trade from Ireland, made a significant comeback in the late twentieth century.

Cereal Products

Wheat products were consumed mainly as porridge and bread in early and medieval Ireland. Porridge was food for children especially, and a watery type figured prominently as penitential fare in monasteries. Wheaten bread was a high-status food. Climatic conditions favored barley and oat growing. Barley, used in ale production, was also a bread grain with monastic and penitential connotations. Oat, a low-status grain, was probably the chief cereal crop, most commonly used for oaten porridge and bread. Baking equipment mentioned in the early literature, iron griddles and bake stones, indicates flat bread production on an ovenless hearth. Thin, unleavened oaten bread, eaten mostly with butter, was universal in medieval Ireland and remained the everyday bread in parts of the north and west until the nineteenth century. Barley and rye breads or breads of mixed cereals were still eaten in parts of eastern Ireland in the early nineteenth century.

Leavened wheaten bread baked in built-up ovens also has been eaten since medieval times, especially in strong Anglo-Norman areas in East Ireland, where commercial bakeries were established. English-style breads were available in cities in the early seventeenth century, and public or common bake houses are attested from this period in some urban areas. Built-up ovens might be found in larger inns and prosperous households, but general home production of leavened bread, baked in a pot oven on the open hearth, dates from the nineteenth century, when bicarbonate of soda, combined with sour milk or buttermilk, was used as a leaven.

A refreshing drink called sowens was made from slightly fermented wheat husks. Used as a substitute for fresh milk in tea or for sour milk in bread making when milk was scarce, it replaced milk on Spy Wednesday (the Wednesday of Holy Week) and Good Friday as a form of penance. A jelly called flummery, procured from the liquid by boiling, was widely used.

Meat, Fowl, and Fish

Beef and mutton have been eaten in Ireland from prehistoric times, and meat was still considered a status food

Wrought iron oatcake drier or hardening stand, Ireland, nineteenth century. Thin, unleavened oatcakes were baked on a griddle then placed upright on the stand to dry before the open fire. COURTESY OF THE DEPARTMENT OF IRISH FOLKLORE, UNIVERSITY COLLEGE, DUBLIN.

in the early twenty-first century. Pigs have been raised exclusively for their meat, and a variety of pork products have always been highly valued foodstuffs. Domestic fowl have been a significant part of the diet since early times, and eggs have also figured prominently. Wild fowl have been hunted, and seafowl provide seasonal, supplementary variations in diet in some seacoast areas.

Fish, including shellfish, have been a food of coastal communities since prehistoric times. Freshwater fish are mentioned prominently in early sources and in travelers' accounts throughout the medieval period. Fish were included in festive menus in the nineteenth century and were eaten fresh or cured in many ordinary households while the obligation of Friday abstinence from flesh meat remained in force.

Beverages

Milk and whey were the most popular drinks in early and medieval Ireland, but ale was a drink of great social importance. It was also regarded as a nutritional drink suitable for invalids and was featured in monastic diets at the celebration of Easter. Mead made by fermenting honey with water apparently was more prestigious than beer. Wine, an expensive import, was a festive drink in secular and monastic contexts. Whiskey distillation was known from the thirteenth century. Domestic ale and cider brewing declined drastically after the eighteenth century in the face of commercial breweries and distilleries.

Nonalcoholic beverages, such as coffee, chocolate, and tea, were consumed initially by the upper sections of society, as the elegant silverware of the eighteenth and nineteenth century shows. But tea was consumed by all sections of society by the end of the nineteenth century.

Vegetables and Fruit

From early times the Irish cultivated a variety of plants for food. Garden peas and broad beans are mentioned in an eighth-century law text, and it appears that some member of the allium family (possibly onion), leeks, cabbages, chives, and some root vegetables were also grown. Pulses were significant in areas of strong Anglo-Norman settlement in medieval times but were disappearing as a field crop by 1800, when vegetable growing declined due to market forces. Cabbage remained the main vegetable of the poor. Apples and plums were cultivated in early Ireland, and orchards were especially prominent in English-settled areas. Exotic fruits were grown in the walled gardens of the gentry or were imported for the large urban markets. A range of wild vegetables and fruits, especially crabapples, bilberries, and blackberries, were exploited seasonally.

Edible Seaweeds

Edible algae have been traditionally used as supplementary food products along the coast of Ireland. Duileasc (*Palmaria palmata*), anglicized as "dulse" or "dilisk" and frequently mentioned in the early Irish law texts, is one of the most popularly consumed seaweeds in Ireland. Rich in potassium and magnesium, it is eaten raw on its own or in salads, or it is stewed and served as a relish or a condiment for potatoes or bread. Sleabhach (*Porphyra*), anglicized as "sloke," is boiled, dressed with butter, and seasoned and eaten as an independent dish or with potatoes. Carraigin (*Chondrus crispus*), or carrageen moss, has traditionally been valued for its medicinal and nutritional qualities. Used earlier as a milk thickener and boiled in milk to make a blancmange, it has come to be regarded as a health food.

Collecting shore foods, such as edible seaweeds and shellfish, was a common activity along the Atlantic Coast of Ireland on Good Friday, a day of strict abstinence. The foodstuffs collected were eaten as the main meal rather than as an accompaniment to potatoes.

Potatoes

Introduced in Ireland toward the end of the sixteenth century, the potato was widely consumed by all social classes, with varying degrees of emphasis, by the nineteenth century. Its widespread diffusion is evident in the broad context of the evolution in the Irish diet from the seventeenth century. In the wake of the English conquest of Ireland, the seventeenth and eighteenth centuries were a time of sustained transition in Irish economic, demographic, and social life. Demographic expansion beginning in 1600 led to a population in excess of 8 million by 1800. The food supply altered strikingly during that period. The diet of the affluent remained rich and varied, while commercialization gradually removed milk and butter from the diet of the poor and resulted in an increased emphasis on grain products. The commercialization of grain and the difficulty in accessing land during the eighteenth century forced the poorer sections of society to depend on the potato, which was the dietary staple par excellence of about 3 million Irish people by the early nineteenth century. Fungus-induced potato crop failures from 1845 to 1848 caused the great Irish famine, a major human disaster.

Diets changed gradually in the postfamine years, and while the potato was but one of many staples by the end of the nineteenth century, it never lost its appeal. The ripening of the new potato crop in the autumn remained a matter for celebration. In many parts of the country the first meal of this crop consisted of mashed potatoes with scallions and seasoning. Colcannon, typically associated with Halloween, is made of mashed potatoes mixed with a little fresh milk, chopped kale or green cabbage, fresh onions, and seasoning with a large knob of butter placed on the top. In some parts people originally ate it from a communal dish.

Boiled potatoes are also the basic ingredient for potato cakes. The mashed potatoes are mixed with melted butter, seasoning, and sufficient flour to bind the dough. Cut into triangles, called farls, or individual small, round cakes, they are cooked on both sides on a hot, lightly floured griddle or in a hot pan with melted butter or bacon fat. Apple potato cake or "fadge" was popularly associated with Halloween in northeast Ireland. The potato cake mixture was divided in two, and layers of raw sliced apples were placed on the base, then the apples were covered with the remaining dough. The cake was baked in the pot oven until almost ready. At that point the upper crust was peeled back, and brown sugar was sprinkled on the apples. The cake was returned to the oven until the sugar melted. "Stampy" cakes or pancakes were raw grated potatoes sieved and mixed with flour, baking powder, seasoning, a beaten egg, and fresh milk and cooked on the griddle or pan.

The menus of restaurants that offer "traditional Irish cuisine" include such popular foods, which also were commercially produced by the late twentieth century. But as Irish society becomes increasingly pluralistic, the so-called "international cuisine" and a wide range of ethnic restaurants characterize the public provision of food in major urban areas. In the private sphere, however, relatively plain, freshly cooked food for each meal is the norm. Milk, bread, butter, meat, vegetables, and potatoes, though the last are of declining importance, remain the basic elements of the Irish diet.

See also **Potato; Sea Birds and Their Eggs.**

BIBLIOGRAPHY

Cullen, L. M. *The Emergence of Modern Ireland, 1600–1900.* London: Batsford, 1981.

Danaher, Kevin. *The Year in Ireland.* Cork, Ireland: Mercier, 1972.

Flanagan, Laurence. *Ancient Ireland: Life before the Celts.* Dublin, Ireland: Gill and Macmillan, 1998.

Jackson, Kenneth Hurlstone, ed. *Aislinge Meic Con Glinne* (Vision of Mac Con Glinne). Dublin: School of Celtic Studies, Dublin Institute of Advanced Studies, 1990.

Kelly, Fergus. *Early Irish Farming: A Study Based Mainly on the Law-Texts of the 7th and 8th Centuries A.D.* Dublin: School of Celtic Studies, Dublin Institute of Advanced Studies, 1997.

Lucas, A. T. "Irish Food before the Potato." *Gwerin* 3, no. 2 (1960): 8–40.

Lysaght, Patricia. "Bealtaine: Women, Milk, and Magic at the Boundary Festival of May." In *Milk and Milk Products from Medieval to Modern Times*, edited by Patricia Lysaght, pp. 208–229. Edinburgh: Canongate Academic, 1994.

Lysaght, Patricia. "Food-Provision Strategies on the Great Blasket Island: Sea-bird Fowling." In *Food from Nature: Attitudes, Strategies, and Culinary Practices*, edited by Patricia Lysaght, pp. 333–336. Uppsala: The Royal Gustavus Adolphus Academy for Swedish Folk Culture, 2000.

Lysaght, Patricia. "Innovation in Food—The Case of Tea in Ireland." *Ulster Folklife* 33 (1987): 44–71.

Ó Danachair, Caoimhín. "Bread in Ireland." In *Food in Perspective*, edited by Trefor M. Owen and Alexander Fenton, pp. 57–67. Edinburgh: John Donald, 1981.

O'Neill, Timothy P. "Food." In *Life and Tradition in Rural Ireland*, edited by Timothy P. O'Neill, pp. 56–67. London: Dent, 1977.

Ó Sé, Michael. "Old Irish Cheeses and Other Milk Products." *Journal of the Cork Historical and Archaeological Society* 53 (1948): 82–87.

Sexton, Regina. *A Little History of Irish Food.* Dublin, Ireland: Gill and Macmillan, 1998.

Patricia Lysaght

SCOTLAND

In Scotland food and food traditions have, as elsewhere, changed over time while regional influences have had a major effect. In addition, both Europe and Scandinavia have introduced changes in the food of the country. Geography has played a central role in determining the basic foodstuffs and their place in the diet. The country is divided into two areas, the Highlands in the north and west, and the Lowlands in the south and east. Each has its own distinct language and culture. The Highlands are generally a mountainous region, with an emphasis on pastoral activities, livestock husbandry, crofting (small acreage farming), general agriculture, and maritime activities. The Lowlands are the chief agricultural area.

Beginning with the Agricultural Revolution of the late eighteenth and early nineteenth centuries, the area developed specialized agricultural districts. The east is predominantly an area of arable and crop production; the climate of the west makes it suitable for the raising of

Oat cake roller for breaking up oat cakes into coarse crumbs for use in puddings and porridge, circa 1800. ROUGHWOOD COLLECTION. PHOTO CHEW & COMPANY.

livestock. The major towns and cities are located in this region, between the Firths of Forth and Clyde. These two areas are divided into smaller ones. The South-West, including the Inner Hebrides, is a dairying area; the East and South-East are advanced grain-cropping areas with a European reputation for farming; the North-East is a stock rearing area, especially for beef; the Highlands and Islands are another stock area.

A number of foods and foodstuffs have been important in the Scottish diet. Cereals have played a central role, especially in rural areas. Bere, a barley, was the traditional grain. By the end of the seventeenth century, it was being rapidly supplanted by oats. Beginning in the eighteenth century oats came to be recognized as a mark of Scottish nationality. As its consumption grew, bere fell down the social scale, though it continued to be eaten in Caithness and Orkney in the early twentieth century. Bere and oats were eaten in a number of ways. Oatmeal was milled into a number of "cuts" or grades, used for specific dishes. It was the basis of brose (mixed with water to make an instant food), porridge (cooked with water or milk), and such foods as sowens and skirley (mixed with fat and onion). Oatmeal was an ingredient in dishes such as haggis (mixed with liver and suet, traditionally cooked in a sheep's stomach). It was baked into bannocks and oatcakes, often toasted over an open fire.

Wheat was a grain grown in only the most favored areas and sold as a cash crop. Wheat bread was at first a prestigious food, eaten by the higher classes; for the lower classes it was eaten on special occasions such as harvesting. In the late eighteenth century, it spread from

Scottish shortbread stamp with swan motif circa 1870. These stamps, or "prints" as they were called, were carved by craftsmen who traveled from village to village selling them during the summer months. ROUGHWOOD COLLECTION. PHOTO CHEW & COMPANY.

the towns and cities, where it was accompanied by the rise in baker's shops. Peas and beans were bread crops. Especially in the Lowlands, they were made into meal, but also put into dishes such as broths. These grains also indicated social class, and by the seventeenth century they were confined to the poorer people.

Baking

These grains, especially oats and wheat, were used in the tradition of baking, for which Scotland has become renowned. From oats, bannocks, scones, and oatcakes were baked. These did not use raising agents. From wheat, cakes, pastry, and shortbread were oven-baked. This was a later development, owing to the late introduction of the oven and the initial high cost of sugar.

Potatoes

The potato was introduced as a novelty in the late seventeenth century. In the 1740s there was resistance against eating it. By the 1790s when the "Statistical Account of Scotland" was compiled, it had become an important element of the diet, especially in Highland areas and among the poorer classes of the Lowlands. It was a principal food in the diet and was a cheap and healthy food and a substitute for bread. The potato continued to be an important element and only declined in status in the 1990s in the face of increased use of pasta and rice. Traditionally potatoes were boiled, with or without their skins. In the urban diet of the late nineteenth century and throughout the twentieth century and beyond, they were sliced and deep-fat fried as chips. They were eaten as a

meal, as a side dish in a main meal, or as an ingredient in a wide range of dishes such as soups and stews; they were also used in baking, as in potato scones.

Fruits and Vegetables

Fruit and vegetables had a relatively small role in the diet. The traditional staple vegetable was kale, a member of the *Brassica* varieties. Vegetable gardening around the houses of noblemen and lairds, and the rise of market gardening in the vicinity of the large towns, especially from the eighteenth century onwards, meant the development of a wide range of vegetables. Like other foodstuffs, they were at first eaten by the wealthy classes, then spread to the social classes below. Traditionally they were consumed as broth. Fruit was not extensively grown, and a limited number of varieties were raised. Orchard fruit was little cultivated, though soft fruit, especially strawberries and raspberries, has been commercially grown from the late eighteenth century; fruit was supplied from kitchen gardens. Especially where domestic production was limited or not undertaken, fruit growing wild in nature provided an important source. It could be a fruit substitute, as were rosehips during World War II. Fruit was eaten raw, or made into dishes, puddings, sauces, and drinks, including alcoholic ones. When sugar became available, it was made into conserves, jams, and jellies, or was bottled.

Dairy Products

Milk and dairy products have had a number of roles. Much of the supply has been from cows; that from ewes and goats has been minor. Milk has always been an important element in the rural diet. In urban areas and near towns, the supply was traditionally inadequate, though small town dairies filled a gap. Supplies had a seasonal fluctuation. Milk could be processed into dishes such as Corstorphine cream, made from frothed whey. Cheesemaking enabled surplus quantities of milk to be utilized, especially in districts located away from centers of population. A large number of regional recipes and varieties exist, some developed during the expansion of the dairy industry in the nineteenth century. The Highlands are associated with soft cheeses for rapid consumption such as crowdie; the Lowlands have longer-keeping hard cheeses. Butter was the only source of fat in the rural diet, though beef or mutton fat could be obtained.

Meat, Fowl, and Fish

Meat was a foodstuff associated with social status. Among the rural population in the 1790s, it was rarely eaten. Even by the 1840s, it was still not an everyday foodstuff, especially among the poor. Before the Agricultural Revolution, livestock were slaughtered at Martinmas (November 11) as not all animals could be overwintered. Meat from domesticated livestock was supplemented by wild game and animals such as rabbits and hares. Sea fowl was caught in coastal areas. The nobility consumed large quantities of meat, especially on days when rents were paid: payment was made in-kind, of which livestock formed a major element.

There were regional variations in the types of meat consumed. The keeping of pigs became prevalent with the spread of potato growing in the eighteenth century. At that time, mutton became a meat of social distinction, being confined to the higher classes in the Lowlands, and the lower classes in the Highlands and Islands.

All parts of animals were utilized, as food, or as non-food items, such as tallow for lighting or hides and leather goods. Mealy puddings were made from entrails; blood was mixed with oatmeal to form blood puddings (black pudding); heads and trotters from sheep were made into pie and soup stock (powsoddie). Meat was rarely eaten fresh. It was salted, dried, or pickled in brine.

Fish was primarily eaten in coastal regions. With the improvement of transport networks in the nineteenth century, consumption spread to inland regions. Fish was a central element of the diet: it was a subsistence food, it filled the hungry gap before harvest when food was in short supply, and it was a delicacy. The Western Isles and Islands had large quantities of herring, haddock, whiting, and mackerel. Other fish included salmon, cod, ling, and shellfish such as cockles and oysters; around the Orkney Islands, whale was plentiful. Coalfish was widely eaten among the working classes. Inland fish such as trout were caught. Fish were eaten fresh, dried, or smoked. A number of fish dishes, many local in nature, are food identity markers: kippers, salted and smoke-cured fish, usually herring, first developed in Newcastle in the 1840s; salt-pickled herring or Finnan haddock, a lightly salted and smoked haddock; Arbroath smokies, salt-dried and smoked haddock.

Birds and poultry include domestic poultry, especially hens and geese. Their eggs were eaten, as were those of wild fowl. In some districts such as Ness, in the Outer Hebrides, wild bird flesh was eaten from gannets.

Some foods have become associated with geographical areas (see Table 1).

Beverages

The traditional drink crop was bere or barley. Ale was drunk, especially in Lowland areas; in the Highlands, whiskey was distilled, both legally and illicitly. Hot drinks spread from the upper classes. Tea drinking started to become increasingly widespread by the 1790s, though for some time afterwards it remained a drink for special occasions among lower social classes. Cocoa was drunk, as were coffee substitutes such as chicory. Coffee was not a drink of the working class, and even among industrial workers in Edinburgh in the 1950s it was consumed rarely, if at all. In recent decades coffee has increasingly taken the place of tea, among all social classes.

Special Foods for Special Occasions

Special foods were eaten during festivals. They were specially prepared; they often had ingredients with a certain

TABLE 1

Area	Foods and dishes
Edinburgh and the Lothians	Midlothian oatcakes Edinburgh rock (sugary confection)
Angus and Fife, Forfar	Bridies (pastry filled with steak), Dundee marmalade, Dundee cake, Arbroath smokies, Pitcaithly bannock
Glasgow and Clydeside	Glasgow broth
Ayrshire	Cheese and Ayrshire shortbread
Borders	Selkirk bannock (rich yeasted bannock with sultanas and raisins); Eyemouth fish pie
Dumfries and Galloway	Galloway beef
North-East	Butteries, Finnan haddock, Aberdeen Angus steak, skirlie
Highlands and Inner Hebrides	Fried herring, game soup, tatties and crowdie (potatoes and soft cheese), Highland oatcakes, Atholl brose (whisky mixed with oatmeal).
The Outer Hebrides	Whelk soup, barley bannocks, kale soup
Orkney and Shetland	Oatmeal soup, fried herring and onions, potatoes with milk, beremeal bannocks

significance (such as flour from the last sheaf) or were made with ingredients that were expensive, difficult to obtain, or not eaten at other times of the year. Some dishes were served only at a festive occasion, or during part of it, others were not.

Festivals took place around the Celtic Calendar. They were held at the quarters that marked the passing of one season to another (Beltane, Lammas, Whitsun, and Martinmas). Foods included bannocks and oatcakes. Others were associated with the Gregorian Calendar. Hogmany, New Year's Eve, on December 31, was and probably still is the most widely celebrated of all the calendar festivals. Many of its foods were sweet in nature. Shortbread was a rich textured biscuit of flour, sugar, and butter. This could be decorated with a sugar iced or embossed pattern. Pitcaithly bannock was decorated with crystallized lemon and orange peel, caraway comfits, and almonds. Black bun is a rich and spiced dried fruit cake enclosed within a thin casing of bread dough or pastry. During harvest, harvesters were given wheat bread and ale; harvest meals also celebrated the end of harvest.

Rites of passage had foods associated with them. These included many common foods, with special attributes, such as bread, cheese, bannocks, and whiskey.

Meal Times and Menus

Meals had distinct patterns. Eating times were shaped by class, occupation, work hours, and days of the week. In rural areas meals were arranged around the feeding of livestock.

Three main meals were eaten: breakfast in the morning, dinner in the middle of the day, and tea or supper at

The traditional Scottish *quaich* or drinking vessel derives its form from the Late Antique *condy*, a drinking bowl without feet. The Gaulish god Lugh is often depicted holding a *quaich* in one hand, indicating that there may have been religious or ritual associations with this vessel in ancient Scotland and on the Continent. This ceramic *quaich* dates from about 1680. ROUGHWOOD COLLECTION. PHOTO CHEW & COMPANY.

five or six in the evening. The main meal was dinner; supper was fairly light but could also be substantial. Although traditionally no food was eaten between meals, changing mealtimes led to the evolution of the high tea, taken in the late afternoon, around four o'clock. It filled the gap between dinner and the evening meal. It developed as tea drinking became popular, especially among the upper classes. By the 1890s sweet and chocolate biscuits were becoming popular additions to the high tea. Meals had a number of courses. Dinner was three courses: a soup, a main course, and what was called a pudding. This varied: if there was soup, there might be no pudding; if there was no soup, the pudding was more substantial.

The eating of dishes, especially the main meal, had a weekly cycle. Sunday, the Sabbath, was reserved for churchgoing for Protestants and Catholics. (Other faiths had their Sabbaths on different days.) On this day meat was eaten. It was roasted, served with dumplings, and accompanied by potatoes and cooked vegetables. The by-products and leftovers of the Sunday dinner were eaten throughout the working week.

Menus of daily meals are recorded in household accounts, personal and travel diaries, letters, and cookery books. According to Alexander Fenton, house-servants in the 1790s had "breakfast of oatmeal porridge or sowens with milk; dinner of broth and boiled meat warm twice a week, or of re-heated broth, or milk, with cold meat, or of eggs, cheese, butter, and bread of mixed barley and pease-meal; supper was for breakfast, or in winter there might be boiled potatoes mashed with a little butter and

milk" (*Scottish Country Life*, p. 170). Ian Carter notes that in North-East Scotland during the 1840s, "the usual food of the farm servants [farm workers] is porridge and milk for breakfast: for dinner, potatoes, bread and milk with perhaps oatmeal brose made with greens, for supper. They do not have beer, except when there is a deficiency of milk. In harvest time an allowance of beer is given then" (*Farm Life in Northeast Scotland*, 1979, pp. 132–133).

Food and the diet have been influenced by a number of factors. Agriculture and changes within it led to changes in agricultural practices and the introduction and spread of new crops and markets. These affected the crops and livestock raised, their quantities, and seasonal availability. Trade and contact with other countries introduced foods, dishes, food habits, names of dishes, and methods of cooking. These were especially noted from the Netherlands during the sixteenth and seventeenth centuries. Political and cultural links have been important, like those from the Auld Alliance with France, which started in the eleventh century and had its greatest impact in the seventeenth and eighteenth centuries. It introduced dishes cooked "in the French way," such as "beef alamonde," dishes such as "omlit of eggs," terminology such as "gigot," a leg of mutton or lamb, and cooking utensils such as the "ashet," a dish for serving meat.

Union with England

Scotland was politically influenced by its larger neighbor, England. The two countries were joined in 1603 by a union of Crowns, then a Union of Parliaments in 1707. These brought the countries closer and shifted the power structure. The English Court influenced the food and eating habits of the nobility. Cultural influences came from the English diet and the introduction of such dishes as roast beef, mutton, and lamb.

Immigrants influenced the native food culture. From those of the sixth to the twelfth centuries, the Scandinavians influenced the use of resources from the sea and introduced dishes such as fish and mustard. Large-scale immigration took place in the nineteenth and twentieth centuries from Ireland, Italy, and India. Italians were noted for fish and chips and ice cream, with all their traditions of these foods. Italian specialty shops such as Valvona and Corolla are a noted feature of some cities such as Edinburgh, where there is a large Italian population.

Social changes created a demand for new foods. Food substitutes, such as margarine, developed around 1870, allowed for greater variation in the diet. So too did new methods of food preservation, such as canning, from the 1860s; refrigeration was first applied to meat imported from the United States in the 1880s; pasteurization was first used in the dairy industry around 1890. These also reduced the influence of season and locality.

See also **Barley; Cereal Grains and Pseudo-Cereals; Fish: Overview; Tea (Meal); Wheat; Whiskey (Whisky).**

BIBLIOGRAPHY

Baker, T. C., J. C. McKenzie, and J. Yudkin, eds. *Our Changing Fare: 200 Years of British Food Habits*. London: MacGibbon and Kee, 1966.

Brown, Catherine. *Broths to Bannocks: Cooking in Scotland 1690 to the Present Day*. London: John Murray, 1990.

Brown, Catherine. *Feeding Scotland. Scotland's Past in Action Series*. Edinburgh: National Museums of Scotland, 1996.

Brown, Catherine. *Scottish Cookery*. Edinburgh: Mercat Press, 1985, 1990.

Brown, Catherine. *Scottish Regional Recipes*. 1981; Glasgow: Richard Drew, 1985.

Brown, Catherine. *A Year in a Scots Kitchen. Celebrating Summer's End to Worshipping its Beginning*. Glasgow: Neil Wilson Publishing, 1996.

Cameron, David Kerr. *The Ballad and the Plough. A Portrait of the Life of the Old Scottish Fermtouns*. London: Victor Gollancz, 1978.

Carter, Ian. *Farm Life in Northeast Scotland 1840–1914*. Edinburgh: John Donald, 1979; 1997.

Fairlie, Margaret. *Traditional Scottish Cookery*. London: Hale, 1973.

Fenton, Alexander. *Country Life in Scotland. Our Rural Past*. Edinburgh: John Donald, 1987.

Fenton, Alexander. "Milk Products in the Everyday Diet of Scotland." In *Milk and Milk Products*, edited by Patricia Lysaght. Edinburgh: Canongate, 1994.

Fenton, Alexander. *The Northern Isles. Orkney and Shetland*. Edinburgh: John Donald, 1978.

Fenton, Alexander. "Receiving Travellers: Changing Scottish Traditions." In *Food and the Traveller. Migration, Immigration, Tourism, and Ethnic Food*, edited by Patricia Lysaght. Nicosia, Cyprus: Intercollege Press in association with the Department of Irish Folklore, University College Dublin, 1998.

Fenton, Alexander. *Scottish Country Life*. Edinburgh: John Donald, 1976.

Fenton, Alexander. "Wild Plants and Hungry Times." In *Food from Nature. Attitudes, Stategies, and Culinary Practices*, Acta Academiae Regiae Gustavi Adolphi, 71, edited by Patricia Lysaght. Uppsala: The Royal Gustavus Adolphus Academy for Swedish Folk Culture, 2000.

FitzGibbon, Theodora. *A Taste of Scotland: Scottish Traditional Food*. London: Dent, 1970. New ed., Glasgow: Lindsay Publications, 1995.

Geddes, Olive M. *The Laird's Kitchen: Three Hundred Years of Food in Scotland*. Edinburgh: Her Majesty's Stationary Office and National Library of Scotland, 1994.

Gibson, Alexander, and T. C. Smout. "Scottish Food and Scottish History, 1500–1800." In *Scottish Society 1500–1800*, edited by R. A. Houston and I. D. White. Cambridge, U.K.: Cambridge University Press, 1989.

Holmes, Heather. "Official Schemes for the Collection of Wild Brambles and Rosehips in Scotland during the Second World War and Its Aftermath." In *Food from Nature. Attitudes, Stategies, and Culinary Practices*, Acta Academiae Regiae Gustavi Adolphi, 71, edited by Patricia Lysaght.

Uppsala: The Royal Gustavus Adolphus Academy for Swedish Folk Culture, 2000.

Holmes, Heather. "Tourism and Scottish Shortbread." In *Food and the Traveller. Migration, Immigration, Tourism, and Ethnic Food*, edited by Patricia Lysaght. Nicosia, Cyprus: Intercollege Press in association with the Department of Irish Folklore, University College Dublin, 1998.

Hope, Annette. *A Caledonian Feast. Scottish Cuisine through the Ages*. Edinburgh: Mainstream, 1997.

Lerche, Grith. "Notes on Different Types of 'Bread' in Northern Scotland: Bannocks, Oatcakes, Scones, and Pancakes." In *Gastronomy. The Anthropology of Food and Food Habits*, edited by Margaret L. Arnott. The Hague: Mouton, 1975.

Lochhead, Marion. *The Scots Household in the Eighteenth Century*. Edinburgh: Moray Press, 1948.

Lockhart, Wallace. *The Scots and Their Fish*. Edinburgh: Birlinn, 1997.

Lockhart, Wallace. *The Scots and Their Oats*. Edinburgh: Birlinn, 1997.

MacLeod, Iseabail, ed. *Mrs McLintock's Receipts for Cookery and Pastry Work (Scotland's First Published Cookbook 1736)*. Aberdeen: Aberdeen University Press, 1986.

Marshall, Rosalind K. "The Queen's Table." In *Tools and Traditions. Studies in European Ethnology Presented to Alexander Fenton*, edited by Hugh Cheape. Edinburgh: National Museums of Scotland, 1993.

McNeill, F. Marian. *Recipes from Scotland*. Edinburgh:1972.

McNeill, F. Marian. *The Scots Kitchen, Its Traditions and Lore with Old-Time Recipes*. London: Blackie and Son, 1929; Edinburgh: Reprographia, 1973; London: Grafton, 1988.

Oddy, Derek J., and Derek S. Miller, eds. *The Making of the Modern British Diet*. London: Croom Helm, 1976.

Robertson, Una. "Orange Marmalade: Scotland's Gift to the World." In *Food and the Traveller. Migration, Immigration, Tourism, and Ethnic Food*, edited by Patricia Lysaght. Nicosia, Cyprus: Intercollege Press in association with the Department of Irish Folklore, University College Dublin, 1998.

Smout, T. C. "Early Scottish Sugar Houses, 1660–1720." *Economic History Review*, 2d series XIV (1961–1962): 240–253.

Sprott, Gavin. "From Fowling to Poaching." In *Tools and Traditions. Studies in European Ethnology Presented to Alexander Fenton*, edited by Hugh Cheape. Edinburgh: National Museums of Scotland, 1993.

Steven, Maisie. *The Good Scots Diet: What Happened to It?*. Aberdeen: Aberdeen University Press, 1985.

Storrie, Susan. "Jewish Cuisine in Edinburgh." *Scottish Studies* 31 (1993): 14–39.

Turnbull, Michael, with Paul V. Rogerson. *Edinburgh a la Carte: The History of Food in Edinburgh*. Edinburgh: Scottish Cultural Press, 1997.

Wolfe, Eileen, ed. *Recipes from the Orkney Islands*. Edinburgh: Gordon Wright, 1978.

Yellowlees, Walter. *Food and Health in the Scottish Highlands: Four Lectures from a Rural Practice*. Old Ballechin, U.K.: Clunie Press, 1985.

Heather Holmes

WALES

Archaeological and documented evidence show that the early Welsh economy was based on mixed farming. When journeying through Wales in 1188, Giraldus Cambrensis (also known as Gerald de Barri or Gerald of Wales) noted that most of the population lived on its flocks and on milk, cheese, butter, and oats. Numerous references to foods in literary works establish that this was generally how the Welsh subsisted until well into the nineteenth century.

Ingredients of the Traditional Diet

The Report of the Royal Commission on Land in Wales (London, 1896) shows that small farmers and tenants survived on home-cured meat from domestic animals, home-grown vegetables, dairy products, and cereal-based dishes. Farmers and cottagers would fatten and slaughter at least one pig a year to provide a constant supply of salted bacon. On larger farms, a bullock or barren cow was also butchered and the meat shared between neighboring

Traditional Welsh cakes were baked in a small reflector oven on the hearth. The bottle jack to the right of the mantlepiece was used for roasting meat. COURTESY OF THE NATIONAL MUSEUM OF WALES.

farms. Keeping cattle provided sufficient milk to produce butter and cheese; vegetables were grown in the kitchen garden and fields, mostly leeks, carrots, cabbages, herbs, and, from the eighteenth century onward, potatoes. Wild fruits, plants, berries, wild animals and birds were utilized in season, and communities living close to coastal regions varied their diet by fishing and collecting shellfish such as cockles, mussels, periwinkles, and limpets. Inhabitants along the coastal regions of the Gower peninsula, Pembrokeshire, and Anglesey gathered the edible seaweed laver (*porphyra umbilicalis*). Prepared as a commercial product by Glamorgan families, it was sold along with cockles and mussels in the market towns of south Wales, famously Pen-clawdd. It was usually tossed in oatmeal and fried in bacon fat; today laverbread is a recognized Welsh delicacy, sometimes known as Welsh caviar.

Traditional Dishes

The topography determined that oats and barley were the most commonly grown cereal crops, with wheat confined to the fertile lowlands. Oatmeal in its various forms was one of the basic elements in the diet of the Welsh. *Llymru* (flummery) and *sucan* (sowans), consisting of oatmeal steeped in cold water and buttermilk, boiled until thickened and served cool with milk or treacle, as well as *bwdram* (thin flummery), *uwd* (porridge), and *griwel blawd ceirch* (oatmeal gruel) were among the everyday fare served in most rural districts until the early twentieth century. The bread most regularly eaten throughout Wales until the late nineteenth century was oatbread, formed into wafer-thin circular loaves and baked on a bakestone or griddle over an open fire. It was used in the counties of north Wales as a basic ingredient in cereal pottages such as *picws mali* (shot) or *siot* (shot); a popular light meal consisting of crushed oatbread soaked in buttermilk. *Brŵes* (*brose*) was a common dish in the agricultural areas of the north and regularly prepared as a breakfast dish for the menservants. It was made from crushed oatbread steeped in meat stock and sprinkled with crushed oatbread before serving.

Welsh rural society was largely self-supporting with the exception of sugar, salt, tea, rice, and currants, which had to be purchased. Sundays and special occasions usually merited a roast dinner for which a joint of fresh meat would be purchased from the local butcher; this was followed by homemade rice pudding. Very little fresh fruit was purchased, and eggs were eaten only on very rare occasions. The limited range of supplies also demanded great resourcefulness to provide an assorted menu. The ability to prepare an assortment of stews from one basic ingredient, namely oatmeal, required considerable dexterity. Similar skill was required for broths such as *cawl* and *lobsgows* using home-cured meat.

The open fire with its many appliances was central to cooking throughout the eighteenth and nineteenth centuries, and, in many rural homes, well into the twentieth century. Such limited cooking facilities also governed what could be prepared. Stews, joints of meat, and puddings were boiled in a cooking pot or cauldron. Pot ovens were used for roasting meat and baking cakes and fruit tarts, and the bakestone was widely used to bake oat-cakes, drop scones, soda bread, pancakes, and griddle-cakes (such as Welsh Cakes). Additionally, spits, Dutch ovens, and bottle-jacks, clockwork implements in the shape of a bottle that were hung in front of the fire, were used for roasting meat.

The preparation and consumption of traditional foods were closely integrated with patterns of life in rural Wales. Before labor-saving agricultural machinery, farmers were dependent on the cooperation of their neighbors to fulfill seasonal work. Corn (grain) or hay harvesting, corn threshing, and sheep shearing were essentially communal efforts requiring communal meals and celebrations. By the end of the nineteenth century, the *Boten Ben Fedi* (harvest pie), consisting of mashed potatoes, minced beef, bacon, and onion was served for the corn harvest supper. Threshing and shearing days were also marked with plentiful meals of cold lamb or beef, potatoes, and peas followed by rice pudding for dessert. *Tatws popty*—beef, onions, and potatoes—was a favorite in parts of Gwynedd, and afternoon tea consisted simply of home-baked bread, butter, cheese, and jam; while rich yeasted fruitcake and gooseberry pie were considered as shearing specialties in most regions.

In the industrial towns and villages during the late nineteenth century and early twentieth century, wives would often help to support their families in periods of hardship by preparing and selling home-cooked dishes, considered delicacies by members of the local community. Coal-miners' wives or widows prepared dishes of minced seasoned liver and pork fat called *faggots*, which were served with peas and sold from the women's homes or from market stalls. Pickled herrings were a comparable savory dish sold by women in the slate-quarrying communities of north Wales and consumed with home-made oatcakes by quarrymen and farm servants.

Although the tradition of living off the land survived until a later period, in the rural areas change came with improved roads, modern shopping facilities, refrigerators, and freezers. By the early twenty-first century, the majority of the above-mentioned dishes are mostly eaten on special occasions as traditional food.

See also **Cake and Pancake; Cattle; Cereal Grains and Pseudo-Cereals; Dairy Products; Herding; Hearth Cookery; Meat, Salted; Stew.**

BIBLIOGRAPHY

Evans, R. M. "*Bwydydd Sir Aberteifi*" [Cardiganshire foods]. *Cardiganshire Antiquarian Society Transactions* 12 (1937): 52–58.

Evans, Hugh. *The Gorse Glen*. Translated by E. Morgan Humphreys from the Welsh *Cwm Eithin*. Liverpool: Brython, 1948.

Freeman, Bobby. *First Catch Your Peacock: A Book of Welsh Food*. Pontypool: Image, 1980.

Rees, T. Kenneth. "Prophyra the Laver Bread Seaweed." *Swansea Scientific and Field Nature Society Journal* 1, part 8 (1934): 248–255.

Peate, Iorwerth C. "The Pot-Oven in Wales." *Man* 43 (1943): 9–11.

Peate, Iorwerth C. *Tradition and Folk Life: A Welsh View*. London: Faber and Faber, 1972.

Thomas, J. Mansel. "The Weed of Hiraeth." *Journal of the Gower Society* 12 (1959): 26–27.

Tibbot, S. Minwel. *Baking in Wales*. Cardiff: National Museum of Wales (Welsh Folk Museum), 1991.

Tibbot, S. Minwel. "Cheese-Making in Glamorgan." In *Folk Life*, edited by Roy Brigden, vol. 34 (1995): 64–79.

Tibbot, S. Minwel. *Cooking on the Open Hearth*. Cardiff: National Museum of Wales (Welsh Folk Museum), 1982.

Tibbot, S. Minwel. "Going Electric: The Changing Face of the Rural Kitchen in Wales." In *Folk Life*, edited by William Linnard, vol. 28 (1989): 63–73.

Tibbot, S. Minwel. "Liberality and Hospitality, Food as a Communication in Wales." In *Folk Life*, edited by William Linnard, vol. 24 (1985): 32–51.

Tibbot, S. Minwel. "*Sucan* and *Llymru* in Wales." In *Folk Life*, edited by J. Geraint Jenkins, vol. 12 (1974): 31–40.

Tibbot, S. Minwel. *Welsh Fare*. Cardiff: National Museum of Wales (Welsh Folk Museum), 1976.

Williams, A. J. Bailey. "Bread Making in Montgomeryshire." *Montgomery Collections*, vol. 49 (1946): 262–265.

Mared Wyn Sutherland

BROASTING. "Broasting" is a trademarked term for frying chicken, potatoes, and other food in a pressure cooker using equipment and ingredients obtained under license from the Broaster Company of Beloit, Wisconsin. More broadly speaking, pressure frying is a technique for frying foods in oil under pressure, which is intended to seal the surface of the food and hold in its natural moisture while producing a crisp exterior.

Broasting is found only in food-service settings, since Broaster Company sells equipment and ingredients and licenses its name and program only to retail operations, such as restaurants, fast-food outlets, and grocery stores. Broaster Company, which was founded in 1954, had about five thousand licensees in 2002. Pressure frying is also used by some of the larger food-service operations, such as KFC (formerly known as Kentucky Fried Chicken) and Chick-Fil-A. These companies do not use the term "broasted," however, since it is trademarked by Broaster Company.

Pressure frying can be attempted at home using special equipment. The manufacturers of pressure cookers, however, do not recommend using them as pressure fryers. Manufacturers specifically advise the user not to put more than ¼ cup of oil in a pressure cooker, which is less than needed for frying. Use of a large amount of oil under high heat can damage the pressure seal of the lid and lead to the escape of steam or hot oil. A few companies manufacture units specifically designed to contain hot oil under pressure, and only these pressure fryers should be used at home.

Commercial units use gas or electricity to heat oil in a fry pot sealed to hold in steam. The pressure builds up to about fourteen pounds per square inch, with the food reaching an internal temperature of approximately 250°F (120°C) as compared with the 215 to 220°F (about 100°C) that occurs in conventional frying. Cooking time is reduced nearly in half as compared to conventional units, which is a significant advantage in the quick-service setting. A single unit can cook several racks of pork ribs in one batch in seven minutes, for example.

If all goes well, the cooked product will retain less than half as much oil as food cooked in a conventional open fryer. It is believed that this occurs because natural moisture escapes through the oil in the form of steam in conventional frying. In pressure frying, steam is locked into the fry pot, and natural moisture is forced to stay inside the food, which also prevents oil from getting in and producing a greasy product. Beck Sales Company, which makes the Fagor Classic brand of pressure fryer for home use, says its fryer will produce chicken with 44 percent more moisture than open-fried chicken, with 40 to 70 percent less fat and fewer calories.

The pioneer in pressure frying was "Colonel" Harland Sanders, founder of Kentucky Fried Chicken (KFC). At his restaurant in Corbin, Kentucky, Sanders sold fried chicken prepared in the traditional southern method of frying in a skillet. He preferred this to deep-fat frying because skillet frying produces a less-greasy product, but the method takes considerably longer than deep-fat frying. When the pressure cooker was marketed in the late 1930s as a time-saving device, Sanders purchased one and experimented with using it as a fryer. He eventually came up with the right combination of time, pressure, amount of oil, and temperature, and he began to use a pressure cooker in his restaurant. By the twenty-first century, all KFC restaurants used pressure frying to cook the company's Original Recipe Chicken. Various KFC outlets use several different types of pressure cookers.

The procedure specified by the Broaster Company is typical of pressure frying operations. The chicken is marinated and breaded, in both cases with proprietary ingredients, and oil is heated in the fryer pot to 360°F. A stainless steel basket is then lowered into the boiling oil, and pieces of chicken are loaded, up to fourteen pounds per load. Since dark meat takes longer to cook, thighs are loaded first, followed by legs, breasts, and wings. The cover is then locked in place, and the pressure valve is closed, allowing pressure to build up quickly. The chicken is cooked at 360°F for eight to nine minutes, at which time the pressure valve is opened to release the steam, the cover is removed, and the chicken is drained.

It is considered important to keep the oil in the pressure fryer as clean as possible, which can be a problem when breaded products are cooked. Loose breading can create smoke and an off flavor due to the intense heat of the operation. Commercial units therefore have systems that recirculate the oil and filter out breading, carbon, excess moisture, and other impurities. This also extends the useful life of the oil. Steam can be used to force the oil out of the cooking pot and into the filter at the bottom of the cooker when the cooking cycle is completed, thus reducing the oil retained in the food and also lessening the chance of injury from hot oil when the pressure is released and the pot is opened. Pressure frying is safe when conducted according to manufacturer's instructions, but some units are equipped with built-in fire suppression systems. These systems, plus the heavy-duty construction needed for pressurized operation, make pressure fryers more expensive than conventional open fryers. Generally, pressure fryers are found only in restaurants that sell large amounts of fried chicken or other fried items.

While chicken is the best-known product in broasting or pressure frying, other foods can also be cooked in the same type of unit. Broaster Company provides its licensees with recipes, cooking instructions, coatings, seasonings, and marinades for potato wedges, catfish, pork chops, ribs, fish, shrimp, and mushrooms, among other items. While pressure frying normally uses fresh food, frozen items can also be pressure fried successfully. The finished chicken product should have a crispy, golden-brown exterior and should be tender and juicy throughout.

See also **Chicken; Fast Food; Frying; Poultry; United States: The South.**

BIBLIOGRAPHY

Bendall, Dan. "How to Buy a Fryer." *Restaurant Hospitality* 84, no. 11 (November 2000): 97.

Townsend, Rob. "Frequent Fryers Share Ideas." *Restaurants and Institutions* 100, no. 17 (27 June 1990): 123.

Richard L. Lobb

BROCCOLI. *See* **Cabbage and Crucifer Plants.**

BROILING. Broiling is a dry-heat method of oven cooking meats and vegetables in which the food is exposed to direct, radiant heat from a gas or electric element at about 550°F. The food is placed in a special pan and set several inches below the heating element until the desired state of doneness is achieved. Because little or no fat is added, broiling is considered a good method of cookery for those who are counting calories.

In Europe, broiling is considered virtually synonymous with grilling, but in America, the term "broiling" is usually applied to cooking in an oven, while "grilling" usually denotes the use of an outdoor or indoor grill.

In broiling meat, the objective is to sear the outside of the piece and seal in its natural juices or moisture, producing a browned, crusty exterior while bringing the interior to the doneness desired by the cook. In beef, this ranges from a state so rare that it appears to be tinged blue, to "well done," with no hint of pink. The classic beefsteak is cooked medium rare. Beefsteak, pork chops, chicken, and fish are the most commonly broiled foods, but a wide variety of foods can successfully be broiled, even fruit, such as bananas.

Broiling uses a sturdy, two-part pan that fits well in the oven and is normally provided with the oven when new. The top part is the cooking surface and is slotted to permit juices to drip into the bottom part, which can be lined with aluminum foil to make cleaning easier. Either gas or electric heating elements can be used. While restaurants almost always use gas, many home kitchens are equipped with electric broilers. An electric broiler can be an advantage for some foods, such as fish, for which a temperature lower than 550°F is desirable, since the broiler can be set to the desired temperature. Some, but not all, gas broilers can be similarly adjusted.

Since heat rises, it may seem odd that the food is put under the heating element. However, broiling works by radiant energy, in which the heat is applied directly from the gas flame or red-hot electric element, rather than by convection, in which hot, moving air carries the energy.

While the broiler should always be pre-heated for ten to fifteen minutes before the cooking begins, the broiling pan should be left out so that the food is put on a cold surface and then put in the oven. This is to ensure that the food is cooked on one side at a time; otherwise, a hot pan would begin an inadequate cooking process on the "down" side before the piece is turned and becomes the "up" side, exposed to the heating element.

No moisture is added in broiling. To assist in the browning process, however, a thin film of oil can be brushed onto the food piece. Salt and pepper should be added after each side is cooked, but not before; salt can draw out moisture and slow down the browning process, while pepper will burn at high temperatures.

Before broiling beefsteaks and pork chops, most of the external fat should be trimmed, since it will create smoke and contribute nothing to the cooking of the meat. (The juiciness of beef comes from the internal fat known as marbling and a substance called myoglobin rather than from its external fat.)

Basic Technique

Adjust the rack so that the surface of the food will be the desired distance from the broiler (see "Position," below). Keep in mind that the pan and the food together will be

"Broiling" used to mean bringing food into contact with an open flame. The term has been largely replaced by "grilling." These Thai sausages are being broiled on a broiling screen in Lap Lae, Thailand. © MICHAEL FREEMAN/CORBIS.

two or three inches deep at least. Slash the external fat vertically at several points to keep the steak from curling up as the fat shrinks. Place the food on the broiler pan and put it in the oven; sear one side, add salt and pepper to the cooked side, and turn the piece to cook the other side. Remove when the desired state of doneness is reached; let stand for a few minutes to allow the juices to settle, and serve with sauce or a pat of butter.

Position. The distance of the food piece from the broiler depends on the thickness of the piece. Pieces of meat that are an inch or less thick should be placed about two or three inches from the broiler, with thicker cuts set farther away. Very thick steaks (three or four inches thick, such as a filet mignon) should be broiled on one side about four inches from the broiler, and then the pan should be moved to a lower rack, eight or nine inches from the boiler, to finish.

Time and doneness. While a well-done steak was once considered a mistake if not a tragedy, many restaurant patrons and home cooks have come to tolerate this cooking method. The reasons for this may have to do with the fact that the best steaks—those labeled "prime" according to the grading system of the U.S. Department of Agriculture—are expensive and sold mainly to restaurants or high-end food stores, so that most supermarket shoppers have little acquaintance with steaks whose flavor is at its peak before they are thoroughly cooked. Also, some people believe that undercooked steak is dangerous. In fact, harmful bacteria, if present at all, are present only on the surface and are quickly destroyed by the heat of normal cooking. Deep muscle meat is sterile except under very unusual circumstances, such as extreme illness in the animal, or mishandling of the food. This observation does not apply, however, to hamburger,

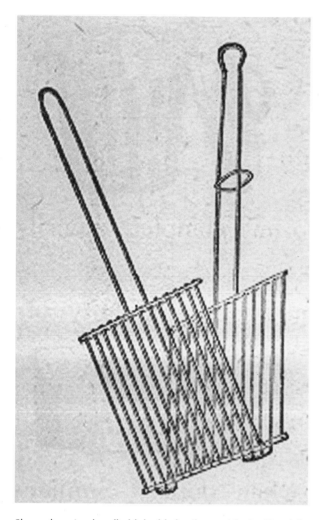

Shown here is a handheld double broiler used for broiling fish, sausages, oysters, and small pieces of meat. The broiler was called "double" because it could be flipped over so that food could be cooked on both sides. From a wood engraving, circa 1880. ROUGHWOOD COLLECTION.

which consists of ground meat that could include contaminated portions; the USDA recommends thorough cooking of hamburgers and other ground meat products.

The timing for beefsteaks of about one inch thick, placed two inches from the broiler is: very rare, one to two minutes per side (the interior will be purple with a hint of blue); rare, two to three minutes per side (red inside); medium, three to four minutes per side (pink in the center); well done, broil three minutes per side, then lower the rack several inches and cook six to ten minutes more (the steak will be grayish or brown all the way though).

Suitable foods. Beef cuts suitable for broiling include the tenderloin or fillet (the center part is used for châteaubriand, and the tip is the filet mignon); rump steaks; flank steak (for London broil); sirloin, rib-eye, and round steak.

Chicken legs, thighs, and wings can be broiled. Bone-in chicken breasts, as a result of their bulk, are better roasted or grilled than broiled in the oven; boneless chicken breast, however, is perfect for the broiler. The pan should be coated with oil to keep boneless breast from sticking, since it has almost no fat of its own.

Broiling is a good method for pork tenderloin but can easily dry out leaner cuts, such as pork chops, which usually benefit from cooking in liquid on the stovetop. Lamp chops broil well but will cook very quickly, taking two or three minutes per side for medium rare.

Fish fillets are thin enough to be broiled on a single side. Whole, cleaned fish (such as bluefish or mackerel) and fish steaks (such as salmon or tuna) can be broiled on both sides. A whole fish should have the head and tail left on for cooking and should be slashed in two places in the thickest part of the fish to let the heat reach the middle.

Some fruits and vegetables can be broiled, including asparagus; firm tomatoes, cut in half; and peppers. Broiling separates the skin from the pepper, leaving soft, cooked meat. Broiled grapefruit and bananas make tasty side dishes or desserts. Grapefruit, cut in half and topped with sugar, can be broiled until bubbling. Bananas can be peeled, cut lengthwise, and dotted with butter and sugar before broiling.

See also **Barbecue**; **Cooking**; **Grilling**; **Hamburger**; **Iron Cookstove**; **Meat**; **Roasting**.

BIBLIOGRAPHY

Bittman, Mark. *How to Cook Everything: Simple Recipes for Great Food.* New York: Macmillan, 1998.

Conran, Caroline, Terence Conran, and Simon Hopkinson. *The Essential Cook Book: The Back-To-Basics Guide to Selecting, Preparing, Cooking, and Serving the Very Best of Food.* New York: Stewart Tabori & Chang, 1997.

Hillman, Howard. *Kitchen Science: A Guide to Knowing the Hows and Whys for Fun and Success in the Kitchen.* Boston: Houghton Mifflin, 1989.

Kamman, Madeleine. *The New Making of a Cook: The Art, Techniques, and Science of Good Cooking.* New York: William Morrow, 1997.

Robuchon, Joel. *Larousse Gastronomique.* New York: Clarkson Potter, 2001.

Wright, Jeni, and Eric Treuille. *Le Cordon Bleu Complete Cooking Techniques.* New York: William Morrow, 1997.

Richard L. Lobb

BRUNCH. *See* **Breakfast**; **Lunch**.

BRUSSELS SPROUTS. *See* **Cabbage and Crucifer Plants**.

BUDDHISM. Buddhism originated in India in the fifth century B.C.E. and from there spread to many lands. The historic Buddha, born around 563 B.C.E., spent most of his eighty years traveling throughout north India preaching the way to salvation by reaching Nirvana and the cessation of rebirths. In some Buddhist traditions, respect for earth deities continues as a reflection of earlier cults of the soil. Animal sacrifices can still be seen in rituals requesting a boon from deities, ancestral spirits, and guardian spirits of localities. Food offerings may be left at stone monuments often containing relics commemorating the life and teachings of the Buddha. But these food practices are not Buddhist.

Buddhism is divided into several branches or ordination traditions. The Mahayana tradition, based on Sanskrit texts, spread into China, Korea, Vietnam, and Japan. The Buddhism of Tibet, Nepal, and Mongolia is also known as Vajrayana. Theravada Buddhism, "the way of the elders," is the form of Buddhism found in Sri Lanka, Burma, Thailand, Laos, and Cambodia. It is based on Pali texts. More recently, Buddhism has spread to Europe, Australia, and North America, where people are converting in large numbers, partly out of interest in Buddhist meditation practices.

The kneeling women are giving donations of rice to a procession of monks in Luang Prabang, Laos, March 1993. The monks collect rice every morning. © MICHAEL S. YAMASHITA/CORBIS.

Food Rituals

Food rituals transmit collective and individual messages about religious principles. Religion influences dietary intake by prescribing or proscribing certain foods, providing ritual foods or meals, and reinforcing key cultural and social values. Unlike Hinduism, Islam, and Judaism, Buddhism has less rigid dietary laws defining what people can eat and with whom they can dine. However, fasting and feasting are integral parts of most religious traditions, and Buddhism is no exception. The special foods used in the annual cycle of Buddhist holidays and festivals differ by country. Food is both a marker of religious affiliation and a marker of ethnic identity. It is therefore impossible to identify foods as specifically Buddhist, as opposed to Thai Buddhist or Japanese Buddhist, for example.

In rice-growing Asian communities where Buddhism is practiced, food in rituals reflects the rhythms of food production, including its scarcity or abundance during the year. In some countries, it is possible to see a contrast between ascetic approaches to food (for example, during the rains' retreat from July to October) and festive excess (for example, after harvest in November and December).

Food rites mark changes in personal status as well, serving as temporal boundary markers through the life cycle. Special foods may be prepared for birthdays, weddings, funerals, tonsures, and ordinations, for example, particularly if monks officiate. In Theravada traditions, some of these rituals are Brahmanic in origin and feature rice and milk-based dishes. Harvest celebrations also make confections from foods such as rice, peanuts, sugar, sesame seeds, and coconut, possibly related to the sweet offerings of South India, called *panchakadjaya* (five foods). Puffed rice is used at funerals to symbolize rice that cannot be grown again.

Monastic Traditions

Dietary abstinence relates to a very widespread idea that giving up something desirable increases spiritual potency. In many religious traditions, food refusal also represents a denial of social relationships, a denial of sociability. Fasting is not central to Buddhist practice except for the monastic community. Most Theravada monks eat only once or twice a day, in the early morning and just before noon, as a part of monastic discipline and their dedication to following the path of the Buddha. The Sanskrit term *sambhogakaya* refers to the monastic practice of eating together. Theravada monks fast after noon and all night, often joined by pious laypersons who partially withdraw from the lay life of the householder on special holidays.

Monks are expected to show moderation and control in all things, including eating. They are warned that wrong mental states easily come to the surface when collecting or eating food. When Theravada monks go on begging rounds, giving people an opportunity to put food into their bowls, they are expected to show no interest in the qualities of the food and even mix the food donations together.

Chinese Buddhism regulates communal meals as part of monastic discipline. Rather than food being collected from begging or donations as in Theravada communities, food in Chinese monasteries is often prepared at the temple by lay devotees. Mahayana monasteries used to grow their own food to provide vegetables for simple meals with rice or rice porridge. Occasionally lay donors might provide a vegetarian feast to celebrate Buddha's birth, enlightenment, and death, or *parinibbana*, in order to gain merit.

Zen cooking (*shojin ryori*) is a style of vegetarian cooking developed by Zen monks that acts as an aid to meditation and spiritual life. Food is prepared as a spiritual exercise with attention to balance, harmony, and delicacy. Some Zen and Chinese Mahayana temples practice the three-bowl eating style, making eating a ritual training. The three bowls contain rice, vegetables, and soup. In fact, eating can be a kind of meditation—remembering to let go of evil, to cultivate good deeds, and to save sentient beings—as each food is put into one's mouth. In such events, food is consumed according to need with no waste and no overconsumption.

Theravada Buddhists believe that by feeding monks they obtain religious merit that assures them of a good rebirth. Laypeople advance on the path to Nirvana by striving for moral purity and doing good works, especially by giving food to the monks. People also believe that giving food to the monks transfers merit to the dead. By going to the temple on the holy day and giving food to the monks, people hope to help their dead relatives who may be wandering the earth as hungry ghosts or living in hell.

Food as Metaphor

Food is often used in Buddhist texts to explain complex ideas in an easily understood manner. Buddhism rejects the asceticism of fasting and denial found in many religious traditions. After the Buddha fasted for six years, he rejected the extreme of starvation as a route to salvation. Instead, he used the experience of eating and digesting food as a means to understand the instrumentality of food. The element of heat transmutes food into body during the process of digestion. Thus, eating is an important metaphor for understanding bodily existence and the transformation of matter and substance. Eating literally makes us human and embodies us.

The Buddhist path is the middle way requiring monks and laity to eat to maintain life and nourish the body but not to cling to the sensual pleasures of eating. In this philosophical interpretation, it is not material substances such as food that block salvation but the craving for them. When Buddhists gain right understanding, they can use this analytical knowledge to guide daily life, as well as for meditation. Food as an object of meditation is a metaphor for the foulness of the body. Monks concentrate on the repulsiveness of food in order to reduce their craving for food. The cessation of craving food is equated with the cessation of the body and the end of the cycle of rebirths.

Commensality

For the laity, eating, particularly eating rice, is a means of orienting oneself in relation to all sentient beings whose lives are sustained by food and religion. Reciprocal food giving sustains lay communities as well as the monastic community. In general, Buddhist rituals imbue food with sanctity; the sanctity remains in the food after it has been received by the monks. Communal eating is one means of experiencing Buddhist precepts and concepts in a direct and sensory way.

In some Buddhist communities, members of the laity serve monks and the community by preparing and serving food from a communal kitchen. Mahayana services and ritual events are likely to be vegetarian. Most Chinese gods and goddesses are presumed to be vegetarian, but they may be offered meat in an attempt to provide the best, most valued food. Chinese Buddhism honors a number of deities, such as Kwan Yin, the Goddess of Mercy. A home altar might contain incense, flowers, tea, and fruit to be consumed later. The Kitchen Goddess helps one eat and drink healthily, and representations of her may be seen in household and restaurant kitchens.

Food given to Chinese deities is considered blessed; its essence is consumed by gods and Buddhas before it is eaten by the worshipers. Following chanting services in many temples, a communal meal is served, which may include beans, bean sprouts, vegetables, fruit, and always rice for prosperity.

Food Distribution in Theravada Communities

Four times in the lunar month, or weekly, the following practices might be seen repeated in Theravada communities throughout the rural areas of Southeast Asia. On a holy day, people bring such food as rice and dishes to eat with rice to the temple. Although the food is the best a household can prepare, people bringing the food cannot taste or even smell the food. A true gift that will gain religious merit must be well intentioned, and only by denying themselves even the smell of the food will the offering bear fruit. The monks chant to accept the food and confer blessings on those who have given food.

At the end of the morning service, after the monks have eaten, the laypeople consume the remaining food offered to the monks. By giving to monks who must follow rules of celibacy and denial, religious merit is increased at a greater rate. Generally, everyone who participates in the service shares in consuming the food that has been accepted or blessed by the monks. Even those who have not contributed food are actively encouraged to share the meal, as if the sharing of food may cause the intention to give generously to arise among all partaking of the meal. Following the meal, participants share the merit accrued from feeding monks with all sentient beings.

Buddhism and Vegetarianism

Buddhism in North America is widely associated with vegetarianism, although not all Buddhists are vegetarian and vegetarianism is not part of canonical Buddhism. This association with Buddhism developed because the key principles of Buddhism include ahimsa, or nonviolence and the avoidance of suffering. Theravada Buddhists in Southeast Asia are not generally vegetarian, although their daily meals may not include much meat. Meat dishes are even given to monks since meat is not explicitly forbidden to them by the rules of monastic conduct. Buddhist texts such as the *Majjhirma Nikaya* refer to the Buddha eating the proper proportion of curry to rice, experiencing flavor but not greed for flavor.

As more Westerners become Buddhist and as more Buddhist immigrants and refugees settle in North American and European cities, Buddhist vegetarian restaurants have prospered, offering devotees and secular vegetarians an opportunity to consume food exemplifying the Buddhist principle of nonviolence. Practicing Buddhist chefs prepare vegetarian feasts for events such as meditation retreats and cater meals for vegetarian practitioners and health-conscious diners. They may also perform *dana*, or selfless giving, by providing free food to the hungry.

Values of reciprocity and sharing are extremely important to Buddhists. In the strongly individualized and materialistic communities of North America, it is particularly difficult to maintain models of generosity and reciprocity. Commensality—the shared meal of Buddhist merit makers—is a model of reciprocity, redistribution, and generosity. The act of eating together and sharing each other's food is a concrete and reliable means of establishing a moral community where people know they can develop relations of trust with others and cooperate in joint activities within the domain of religion and in other domains.

See also **Fasting and Abstinence: Hinduism and Buddhism; Feasts, Festivals and Fasts; Hindu Festivals; Hinduism; Metaphor, Food as; Religion and Food; Rice; Sensation and the Senses; Southeast Asia; Vegetarianism.**

BIBLIOGRAPHY

Khare, Ravindra S. *The Eternal Food: Gastronomic Ideas and Experiences of Hindus and Buddhists.* Albany: State University of New York Press, 1992.

McLellan, Janet. *Many Petals of the Lotus: Five Asian Buddhist Communities in Toronto.* Toronto; Buffalo: University of Toronto Press, 1999.

Van Esterik, Penny. "Feeding Their Faith: Recipe Knowledge among Thai Buddhist Women." *Food and Foodways* 1 (1986): 197–215.

Van Esterik, Penny. *Taking Refuge: Lao Buddhists in North America.* Tempe: Arizona State University, Program for Southeast Asian Studies; Toronto: York Lanes Press, Centre for Refugee Studies, York University, 1992.

Warren, Henry Clarke. *Buddhism in Translations.* New York: Atheneum, 1969. Original ed. Cambridge, Mass.: Harvard University, 1896.

Penny Van Esterik

BUFFALO. *See* **Cattle; Mammals; Meat.**

BUTTER. Butter is made by churning milk fat. It has a solid, waxy texture and varies in color from almost white to deep yellow. It is mostly made from cow's milk, but water buffalo milk is used in the Indian subcontinent, yak milk in the Himalayas, and sheep milk in central Asia. Butter is an important food in North America, Europe, and western and central Asia but is of lesser importance in the rest of the world.

Butter Making

Until the late nineteenth century, butter was made by traditional small-scale methods. Milk was "set" in bowls until the cream rose and could be skimmed off. It was used fresh for sweet cream butter or "ripened" (soured) as the bacteria it contained converted the lactose (milk sugar) to lactic acid. Sometimes clotted (scalded) cream was used, and milk fat retrieved from whey after cheese making can also be used for making butter.

Once or twice a week the cream was churned in a standing churn with a plunger or in a barrel turned end-over-end. Eventually, granules of butter separated out, leaving buttermilk, which was drained off and used for drinking and baking. The butter was washed and worked (kneaded with a paddle) to get rid of excess liquid, then salted. Butter-making implements were wooden; they included bowls, butter paddles, and prints carved with motifs, such as swans or wheat ears, used to stamp finished pats.

In modern industrial manufacture, cream is separated by a centrifugal process to give a fat content of 30 to 38 percent. It is always pasteurized, and ripening is induced by adding a bacterial culture. The cream is churned at a temperature of 53 to 64°F (12 to 18°C). High-speed continuous churns were introduced after World War II. In these the cream is mixed by revolving blades, which induces granulation quickly. The butter granules are forced through a perforated plate and are worked mechanically. Salt and annatto (coloring) are added if desired. About twenty liters of milk are needed to make one kilogram of butter.

Physical Descriptions

The mechanism of butter production is not fully understood. The process inverts cream, an emulsion of minute fat globules dispersed in a liquid phase (water), to become butter, an emulsion in which minute drops of liquid are dispersed in a solid phase (fat). Churning first traps air in

FLAVOR IN BUTTER

Flavor in butter is influenced by many factors. Two basic types exist in European and North American tradition: sweet cream, churned from fresh cream, with a mild, creamy flavor and ripened; or lactic butter, made from soured cream, which should have a fuller, slightly nutty flavor. Salt butter can be of either type. Regional tastes in this vary widely. In Europe, Welsh butter is noted for being very salty, whereas French butter is often not salted at all. Under modern conditions, salt is only added for flavor, its original preservative function now obsolete.

The characteristic butter flavor comes partly from the high proportion of short-chain fatty acids milk fat contains, especially butyric acid. Ripening gives a "lactic" flavor derived principally from a substance called diacetyl, produced by the bacterial species involved. In the United States, most butter has a mild lactic flavor, although it is stronger in "cultured" butter, which is closer to that produced in Germany and central Europe, where strongly flavored butters are preferred.

Differences in butter flavor were far more apparent in the past. Factors that influenced the flavor of farm-made butter included the food the cattle ate. Turnips, introduced as a fodder crop in eighteenth-century England, were notorious for giving a characteristic and much-disliked taint to butter. Some pastures, such as those of Normandy, are recognized as producing excellently flavored butter. Poor storage conditions for milk or butter also led to taints, as fats pick up odors quickly. Storage in rooms that also contained, for instance, onions was not recommended. Care during handling is also important. Length of ripening time, hygienic handling, and complete expression of the buttermilk from the finished product influence flavor.

Finally, from the moment it is finished, butter is susceptible to rancidity of two types. Hydrolitic rancidity is produced by the presence of moisture and is hastened by enzymes and microorganisms, and consumers have developed a taste for some forms. Oxidative rancidity, produced by reaction with oxygen in the air, is found unacceptable by everyone.

Finished butter has a complex structure of minute water droplets, air bubbles, and fat crystals distributed through amorphous fat. Proportions of solid and liquid fats present in butter vary. A lower churning temperature increases the proportion of crystalline fats, giving a harder, almost crumbly product. Higher temperatures produce a softer butter. Butter can also be whipped after churning to make it softer and easier to spread. Flavor is influenced by many factors (see sidebar).

Salt was originally added as a preservative. Butter made from unpasteurized milk is susceptible to bacterial spoilage. Even under modern conditions of hygiene, it is susceptible to oxidative rancidity. One way of extending shelf life is clarification, which includes two basic methods. One is to melt the butter gently and pour the fat off, discarding the milky residue. The second, used in India, is to simmer the butter until the water evaporates and the protein and milk sugar form a solid brown deposit. The fat, now with a nutty flavor, is strained off and stored as ghee, which keeps for months. Butter and ghee are significant in Indian cookery and Hindu religious ritual. In the Arab world *samneh*, a form of clarified butter, is also used for cookery. In Morocco it is mixed with herbs to make *smen*, a strongly flavored aged butter.

Nutrition

Nutritionally the composition of butter is roughly 80 percent fat (mostly saturated), 12 percent water, 2 to 3 percent nonfat milk solids (lactose, protein), and 2 percent added salt. It is the most concentrated of dairy products, containing about 740 kilocalories per 100 grams (210 kilocalories per ounce). Butter is a valuable source of vitamin A, plus it has a little vitamin D. It is also a source of dietary cholesterol. Vitamin content is higher in summer, when the cattle feed on fresh grass.

Nutritional debates over saturated fatty acids and cholesterol in relation to coronary heart disease have centered on butter. High fat consumption can be related to raised blood lipids, but the relationship of dietary cholesterol to blood cholesterol is less easy to demonstrate. Evidence for or against is seized in the debate between butter and margarine manufacturers over which is superior. The two groups have competed since margarine was invented in the 1870s. Their arguments were originally couched in terms of economics but subsequently obscured important health issues. In the United States butter consumption stands at about 500,000 metric tons per annum, as opposed to the European Union, which consumes almost 1.5 million tons with only about one-third more population than the United States. Much of the difference is probably due to preferential consumption of margarine for perceived health benefits by U.S. consumers.

Development of Production

Annual world production of butter (including ghee) rose from about 5.35 million metric tons in 1961 to about 7.551 million metric tons in 2001, during which time the

the cream, producing a foam. Continued agitation destabilizes the fat globules, disrupting the fine membranes that surround them and releasing naturally occurring emulsifiers such as lecithin. As agitation continues, the foam collapses, and the fat droplets are forced together in grains. Gradually they increase in size and become visible.

TABLE 1

Butter and ghee production

Butter and ghee production (mt)	Year							
	1961	**1971**	**1981**	**1991**	**1998**	**1999**	**2000**	**2001**
World	5,344,948	5,712,823	6,846,762	7,230,231	6,842,943	6,991,151	7,201,428	7,551,093
Latin America & Caribbean	129,415	155,307	206,855	191,692	204,587	209,485	210,840	219,718
Canada	165,107	134,309	116,915	101,059	90,600	92,060	92,060	92,060
European Union (15)	1,825,529	1,916,890	2,396,300	1,931,824	1,794,111	1,768,090	1,738,656	1,730,629
India	433,000	432,000	670,300	1,050,000	1,600,000	1,750,000	1,950,000	2,250,000
Japan	13,214	47,699	63,636	75,922	88,931	85,349	87,578	82,000
New Zealand	213,500	230,800	247,200	250,881	343,658	317,000	344,000	384,000
United States	696,629	520,268	557,095	621,500	529,800	578,350	578,350	578,350

© Copyright FAO 1990–1998

Butter imports

Butter imports—qty (mt)	Year						
	1961	**1971**	**1981**	**1991**	**1998**	**1999**	**2000**
World	566,571	786,113	1,524,808	1,333,061	1,214,011	1,213,135	1,256,727
Latin America & Caribbean	15,092	61,809	71,324	87,551	65,778	70,056	71,217
European Union (15)	467,074	527,783	705,015	615,223	657,293	668,492	698,404
Canada	0	1,399	28	164	3,275	5,820	14,477
India	100	2,951	18,675	3,192	4,311	10,255	6,535
Japan	376	923	1,734	20,524	565	548	391
New Zealand	0	11	27	14	822	500	652
United States	390	320	938	2,381	40,096	29,468	22,160

© Copyright FAO 1990–1998

Butter exports

Butter exports—qty (mt)	Year						
	1961	**1971**	**1981**	**1991**	**1998**	**1999**	**2000**
World	629,535	842,045	1,473,373	1,364,364	1,322,174	1,301,421	1,311,496
Latin America & Caribbean	14,799	8,612	10,088	8,126	17,380	25,654	24,249
European Union (15)	260,405	446,090	1,087,809	983,892	718,992	692,079	660,345
Canada	3	2,029	61	12,415	12,077	10,932	6,711
India	7	181	240	340	909	1,700	1,815
Japan	10	1,108	313	3	0	17	7
New Zealand	165,690	194,463	203,058	176,148	315,850	298,034	358,528
United States	2,597	43,006	54,207	32,006	9,024	3,536	8,906

© Copyright FAO 1990–1998

global population doubled. By the twenty-first century, India was the world's largest butter and ghee producer. Its production increased fivefold between 1961 and 2002, whereas the country's population increased about 2.25 times. The European Union, an area in which butter has enormous importance in traditional eating habits, is the next most important producer, followed by the United States. New Zealand, with a small population, produces much butter for export, but production in Canada, formerly an important exporter, has fallen.

The origins of butter are unknown. One theory is that migrating nomads discovered that milk they carried with them became butter (much as American pioneers made butter by allowing the motion of the wagons to churn milk as they traveled). Butter has been known in Eurasia since ancient times, although the classical Greeks regarded it as barbarian food. Later friction arose over Lenten food prohibitions by the church in medieval Europe. Oil, a southern staple, was allowed, but butter, derived from animals, was forbidden, creating difficulties for northerners who had to buy expensive imported oil or pay a fine to use butter.

In northern and western Europe, butter was an integral part of the pastoral economy. It was churned from surplus summer milk and was stored in wooden barrels. Butter production was women's work and in many places,

Traditional Chinese butter sculpture. Some of the butter has been dyed to create brilliantly colored images. © JOHN SLATER/ CORBIS.

clined rapidly. Canada and New Zealand developed butter as an export commodity for the British market. Most butter produced in the developed world is made in creameries.

Butter is important in European food habits and cuisines derived from them. It is used as a spread for bread, crackers, and toast and to dress cooked vegetables and pasta. In baking it adds flavor and shortness to cakes and some pastries. Butter has a privileged position in French cookery, especially in sauces, such as beurre blanc, hollandaise, and béarnaise. It is not ideal for frying as the protein it contains burns at about 250°F (120°C), but clarified butter can be heated to about 375°F (190°C) and is often used for shallow frying fish. Butter or ghee also gives character to northern Indian food. For instance, a small amount heated with spices is added to pulse dishes for richness and to finish the cooking process. In Tibet butter is floated on bowls of tea, the residues of which are mixed with *tsampa* (barley flour) and eaten.

See also **Dairy Products; Margarine.**

BIBLIOGRAPHY

Davidson, Alan. *The Oxford Companion to Food.* Oxford: Oxford University Press. 1999.

Garard, Ira D. *The Story of Food.* Westport, Conn.: AVI Publishing, 1974.

McGee, Harold. *On Food and Cooking.* London: George Allen and Unwin, 1984; New York: Scribners, 1984.

Visser, Margaret. *Much Depends on Dinner.* London: Penguin Books, 1986.

Laura Mason

such as early modern England, provided an income for farmer's wives, hence the frequency of Butter Market as a street name in English towns. Certain areas developed dairy food production as a specialty. By 1750 the Low Countries exported butter and cheese to neighboring regions. In Ireland butter is the most esteemed of all dairy products. In the Middle Ages it was used to pay taxes and was buried in peat bogs for preservation. Archeologists still find the occasional cache of "bog butter," which made Irish oat cake and later potatoes palatable. Migrants from the Low Countries, Britain, and Ireland took their taste for butter to North America, where observers remarked on the lavish use of it in cookery and at the table.

Creamery production of butter, in which milk collected from a large number of farms was taken to a central point for processing, began in the late nineteenth century. It gave benefits in economies of scale and quality control but reduced regional nuances. An important step toward the process was the introduction of a mechanical cream separator by Gustav de Laval in Denmark in the 1870s. In 1881 Alanson Slaughter built a creamery in Orange County, New York, using the milk produced by 375 cows. By 1900 a creamery in Vermont used the milk from thirty thousand cows to make over ten tons of butter a day, and the production of country butter de-

BYZANTINE EMPIRE. Constantine I, the first Christian emperor of Rome (reigned 306–337), established a new eastern capital in 330 at a site unrivaled for its beauty and unmatched as a center for administration and trade. The Greek colony of Byzantium had prospered on its exports of salted bonito and other seafood. Now renamed Constantinopolis (modern Istanbul), it was destined to be the capital of the later Roman or Byzantine Empire for eleven hundred years.

The civilization of Constantinople is sometimes misunderstood as a poor imitation of classical Greece and Rome. From the perspective of medieval western Europe, however, Constantinople was a city of magic and mystery. Early French epics and romances tell of the wondrous foods, spices, drugs, and precious stones that could be found in the palaces of Constantinople.

Byzantine culture never ceased to develop and to innovate, and this is certainly true of its cuisine. Among favored game were the gazelles of inland Anatolia, and wild asses, of which herds were maintained in imperial parks. The seafood most appreciated by the Byzantines was bo-

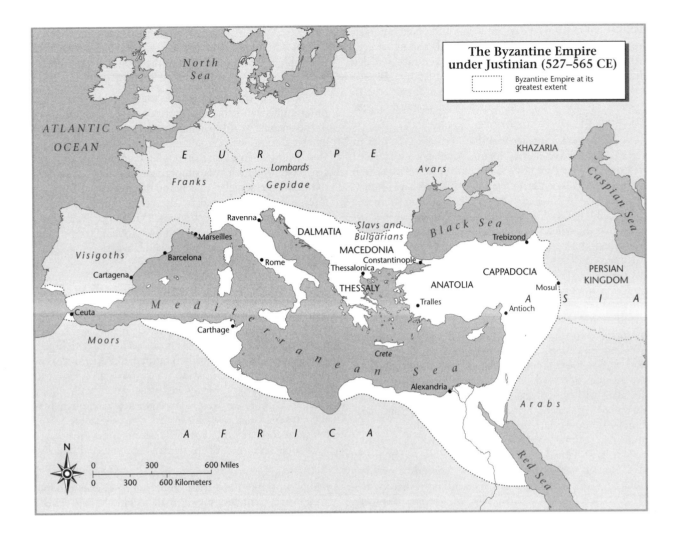

The Byzantine Empire
under Justinian (527–565 CE)

Byzantine Empire at its
greatest extent

targo (salted mullet roe), and by the twelfth century they were familiar with caviar. Fruits largely unknown to the ancient world but appreciated in Constantinople included the aubergine (eggplant), lemons (via Armenia and Georgia), and the orange. The Byzantines were the first to try rosemary as a flavoring for roast lamb; they first used saffron in cookery. These aromatics, well known in the ancient world, had not previously been thought of as food ingredients.

Byzantine cheeses included mizithra (produced by the pastoral Vlachs of Thessaly and Macedonia) and Cretan prosphatos. As for bread, the bakers of Constantinople were in a most favored trade, according to the ninth century Book of the Eparch, a handbook of city administration: "bakers are never liable to be called for any public service, neither themselves nor their animals, to prevent any interruption of the baking of bread." Mastic and anise were among the aromatics used in baking.

The distinctive flavor of Byzantine cookery is best represented by sweets and sweet drinks. There are dishes that we would recognize as desserts: *grouta*, a sort of frumenty, sweetened with honey and studded with carob

seeds or raisins; and rice pudding served with honey. Quince marmalade had been known to the Romans, but other jellies and conserves now made their appearance, based on pear, citron, and lemon. The increasing availability of sugar assisted the confectioner's inventiveness. Rose sugar, a popular medieval confection, may well have originated in Byzantium.

Flavored wines, a variant of the Roman *conditum* (spiced wine), became popular as did flavored soft drinks, which were consumed on fast days. The versions that were aromatized with mastic, aniseed, rose, and absinthe were especially popular; they are distant ancestors of the mastikha, vermouth, absinthe, ouzo, and pastis of the modern Mediterranean. A remarkable range of aromatics, which were either unknown to earlier Mediterranean peoples or used only as perfumes or in compound drugs, were added to Byzantine spiced wines: spikenard, gentian, yellow flag, stone parsley, spignel, valerian, putchuk, tejpat, storax, ginger grass, chamomile, and violet.

Two influences combined to produce the great range of powerful flavors at the heart of Byzantine cuisine. One was the Orthodox Christian church calendar, with its numerous fast days on which both meat and fish were proscribed: the rich (including rich abbots and ecclesiastics) gave their cooks full rein to produce fast-day dishes as piquant and varied as could be imagined. Byzantine pease pudding, a fast-day staple, was aromatized with nutmeg, an eastern spice unknown to the classical Greeks and Romans.

The second influence was that of dieticians. Ancient Greek and Roman dietary manuals had been addressed to experts. The Byzantine ones, however, were written for nonspecialists. As in classical Greece and Rome, physicians relied on the theory of the "four humors" (blood, phlegm, yellow bile, black bile) and prescribed diets aimed to achieve a proper balance of humors in each individual. The effect of each ingredient on the humors was therefore codified so that the desired balance could be maintained by a correct choice of dish and by a correct adjustment of ingredients, varying for the seasons, the weather, the time of day, and each individual's constitution and state of health. Dieticians sometimes recommended vegetarian meals, eaten with vinegar or other dressing. Spices and seasonings became ubiquitous, used both during the cooking process and at the table to amend the qualities of each dish. Fresh figs, if eaten in July, must be taken with salt. A daily glass of conditum, strong in spikenard, was recommended in March; anisaton, anise wine, was appropriate for April. These Byzantine dietary manuals are important sources of culinary history; botargo is first named in the eleventh century by the dietician Simeon Seth, who notes that it "should be avoided totally." The earliest work in this tradition is Anthimus's *On the Observance of Foods*, compiled by a Byzantine physician for a gothic monarch in the early sixth century.

The food of the poor of Constantinople was no doubt limited, though a poetic catalog of a poor family's larder (*Prodromic Poems* 2.38–45, probably twelfth century) includes numerous vegetables and locally grown fruits along with a considerable list of flavorings: vinegar, honey, pepper, cinnamon, cumin, caraway, salt, and others. Cheese, olives, and onions perhaps made up for a scarcity of meat. *Timarion*, a satirical poem of the twelfth century, suggests salt pork and cabbage stew as being a typical poor man's meal, eaten from the bowl with the fingers just as it would have been in contemporary western Europe. The staple of the Byzantine army was cereal food—wheat or barley—which might be prepared as bread, biscuits, or porridge. Inns and wine shops generally provided only basic fare. However, in the sixth-century *Life of St. Theodore of Syceon*, a Byzantine text, there is a reference to an inn that attracted customers by the quality of its food.

Annual fairs were a focus for the food trade. Important fairs were held at Thessalonica and Constantinople around St. Demetrius's day. Constantinople was known for specialized food markets. Sheep and cattle were driven to market to Constantinople from pastures far away in the Balkans, and eastern spices followed long-established trade routes through Trebizond, Mosul, and Alexandria. The populist emperor Manuel (1143–1180) liked to sample the hot street food of the capital, paying for his selection and waiting for change like any other citizen.

Medieval travelers to Byzantium did not always like the strange flavors they encountered. Garos, the fish sauce of the ancient world, which was much used as a flavoring by the Byzantines, was unfamiliar and often unappreciated. Many disliked resinated wine (comparable to modern retsina), which was simply "undrinkable" according to one Italian traveler, Liutprand of Cremona. However, foreigners were seduced by the confectionery, the candied fruits, and the sweet wines. William of Rubruck, a thirteenth-century diplomat who was looking for presents to take from Constantinople to wild Khazaria, chose dried fruit, muscat wine, and fine biscuits.

The cuisine of the Byzantine Empire had a unique character of its own. It forms a bridge between the ancient world and the food of modern Greece and Turkey. In Constantinople astonishing flavor blends were commonplace. For example, roast pork was basted with honey wine; skate was spiced with caraway; wild duck was prepared with its sauce of wine; there was garos, mustard and cumin-salt, and black-eyed peas served with honey vinegar. Old recipes were adapted to new tastes; whereas ancient cooks had used fig leaves, *thria*, as edible wrappings for cooked food, during Byzantine times vine leaves were used in recipes, the precursors of modern dolmades.

When the future emperor Justin II (reigned 518–527) walked from his Dalmatian homeland to Constantinople in 470 as a penniless young man seeking service in the Imperial guard, we are told that he had nothing but army biscuits to keep him alive on his long march. This *paximadion*, or barley biscuit, makes the perfect link from the ancient, via the Byzantine, to the modern period. A classical Roman invention, popularized in the Byzantine Empire, it has many modern descendants: the Arabic *bashmat*, *baqsimat*, the Turkish *beksemad*, the Serbo-Croat *peksimet*, the Romanian *pesmet*, and the modern Greek *paximadi*.

Beyond the old boundaries of the Byzantine Empire, Byzantium's greatest legacy to western cookery may be summed up in these four things: the table fork, which entered Europe through Italy; marzipan, which appears to have originated in Armenia (the word is of Armenian origin); the samovar, which moved northward into Russian culture via the Greek Church; and the Cult of St. Nicholas, together with the gingerbread cookies associated with this Christmas saint.

See also **Balkan Countries; Greece, Ancient; Mediterranean Diet; Middle East; Rome and the Roman Empire**.

BIBLIOGRAPHY

Few Byzantine texts relevant to food are available in English translation. They include the following, cited in the text of the article: *The Book of the Eparch* [text, translation and studies] ed.

by I. Dujcev. London: Variorum Reprints, 1970. *The Works of Liudprand of Cremona*, tr. by F. A. Wright. London: Routledge, 1930. Anthimus, *De observatione ciborum: On the Observance of Foods* edited and translated by Mark Grant. Totnes, Devon, U.K.: Prospect Books, 1996. *Three Byzantine Saints*, translated by E. Dawes and N. H. Baynes. Crestwood, N.Y.: St. Vladimir's Seminary Press, 1977. [Includes the Life of St. Theodore of Syceon.] The following, also cited above, are at present available only in Greek: *Poèmes prodromiques en grec vulgaire*, edited by D.-C. Hesseling, H. Pernot. Amsterdam: Müller, 1910. *Simeonis Sethi syntagma de alimentorum facultatibus*, ed. B. Langkavel.

Leipzig: Teubner, 1868. *Timarion*, tr. by Barry Baldwin. Detroit: Wayne State University Press, 1984. *The Mission of Friar William of Rubruck*, translated by P. Jackson. London, 1990. For more information see: Dalby, Andrew. *Siren Feasts*. New York: Routledge, 1996. Chap. 9. Dalby, Andrew. *Flavours of Byzantium*. Totnes, Devon, U.K.: Prospect Books, 2003. A. Kazhdan, et al. *The Oxford Dictionary of Byzantium*. New York: Oxford University Press, 1991.

Andrew Dalby

C

CABBAGE AND CRUCIFER PLANTS. The cole crops broccoli, brussels sprouts, cabbage, cauliflower, collards, kale, and kohlrabi belong to the same species (*Brassica oleracea* L.) in the Brassicaceae or mustard family. Kale most closely resembles the progenitor to this group of vegetables. Native to European coasts, wild *B. oleracea* and related species are one to two meters in height with large lobed leaves and a terminal inflorescence of yellow flowers. Different portions of the plant were emphasized during domestication. Broccoli and cauliflower were selected for large edible inflorescences, kohlrabi for an enlarged basal stem, and brussels sprouts and cabbage for leafy buds (axillary and terminal buds, respectively). These vegetable crops grow best in cool climates with adequate soil fertility and ample water. *Brassica* species are unique in producing glucosinolates, the compounds that impart pungency to various cole crops. Certain forms of these compounds are antinutritional while others are beneficial. On the balance, consumption of cole crops has a positive influence on human health. Cole crops are used fresh, may be canned, frozen, dehydrated, pickled, and fermented. Sauerkraut, made from fermented cabbage, is an ancient process that was used to preserve this vegetable as a source of vitamins and minerals during the winter months.

Plant Biology

Plant description. The cole crops are members of the Brassicaceae family (formerly Cruciferae). This family includes over three thousand species in more than three hundred genera. Plants are usually herbaceous annuals, biennials, or perennials. Cabbage and related cole crops belong to the species *Brassica oleracea* L.

With exception of certain cabbages and some types of kale, this group has smooth, alternate leaves with lobed or wavy to highly dissected margins. Leaves may be thick and succulent, with or without a waxy bloom. Some types grow to over two meters on a shallow and fibrous root system. The inflorescence is a terminal raceme of showy yellow or white flowers. Flowers possess four perpendicular petals that the medieval Europeans thought resembled a crucifix (thus the former family name Cruciferae). Flowers also have four sepals, a two-celled, superior ovary with a single stigma and style, and six stamens, two of

which have shorter filaments than the others. The fruit (seed pod) is a silique with a persistent, beaked style. At maturity, siliques dehisce longitudinally to release the small round brown or black seeds. Seeds mature fifty to ninety days after fertilization. The species is insect cross-pollinated with self-pollination prevented by a sporophytic self-incompatibility system. All naturally occurring *B. oleracea* are diploid with nine pairs of chromosomes.

With the exception of some cauliflower and broccoli cultivars, the cole crops have a biennial reproductive cycle. Broccoli and cauliflower may be either annual or biennial (Table 1). Except for tropical cauliflowers, vernalization is required for flowering.

During domestication, different plant organs were emphasized. Kale and collards are the least modified from the ancestral form. Cabbage possesses a head composed of overlapping leaves formed on a shortened stem. Brussels sprouts form smaller heads in the leaf axils of the stem. The edible portion of kohlrabi is a shortened and swollen stem. Broccoli has been selected for an enlarged stem and inflorescence that is consumed when flowers are fully developed but have not yet opened. Like broccoli, the head of cauliflower is eaten. However, the head consists of a highly branched mass of undifferentiated shoot apices (curd) that only later may differentiate into floral primordia.

Growth requirements. The *B. oleracea* are cool season crops, with optimum growing temperatures of about 59–68°F (15–20°C), but plants will grow slowly even at 14°F (5°C). Cole crops are cold and frost tolerant, but developmental stage and type of crop affects the degree of cold tolerance. Young plants are more tolerant than are older plants, and crops whose vegetative parts are eaten are generally more tolerant of low temperatures than crops whose reproductive parts are consumed. Kale and brussels sprouts are the most cold hardy, and can withstand temperatures as low as 14 to 23°F (−5 to −10°C). High temperatures (>77°F or >25°C) will inhibit or impair head development in broccoli. Almost no broccoli cultivars can be grown in the warm tropics because plants fail to form heads. Winter, summer, and tropical cauliflower cultivars have been developed, each of which has a different optimal temperature range. For summer types, the optimum temperature for curd development is 62 to 64°F (17 to 18°C) with small "button" heads induced at temperatures above 68°F (20°C). Some winter types develop curds even at 50°F (10°C) while some tropical types will tolerate temperatures up to 86°F (30°C).

Botanical types and horticultural characteristics. *Brassica oleracea* vegetables show amazing diversity in form that is reflected in the different botanical variety names assigned to them (Table 1). These names generally describe the origin of the crop, or the edible part that has been accentuated.

The cabbage group is differentiated based on head shape and color, leaf texture, and intended use. Savoy types, with crinkled leaves and looser heads, are used primarily fresh in salads. Smooth-leafed, firm-headed cabbages are used for fresh market and processing. Fresh market types are typically small-headed and may be green or purple. Fresh market types are further differentiated into those sold immediately, and those stored for several months before sale. Processing types (mainly used for sauerkraut) have large heads (up to 4 kg) that are high in dry matter. Cabbage heads can vary in shape from pointed, to round, to oblate.

Firm heads (which depends on the arrangement and thickness of leaves, leaf angle, and freedom from axillary cavities) are preferred. The core (main stem within the head) should be small in diameter and less than half the height of a mature head. A dark-green or purple external color is preferred for market. Fresh market and storage cabbage can have white, green, or purple internal color, but for sauerkraut, white internal color is essential. Uniform size and maturity are necessary for efficient harvest and packing.

While the term "broccoli" is commonly used in the United States to refer to *B. oleracea* var. *italica*, elsewhere this crop may be called "sprouting broccoli" or "calabrese" (after a landrace, or farmer-selected variety, from the Calabria district of southern Italy). Other crops that use the name "broccoli" are "broccoli rape" (turnip or *B. rapa* inflorescences), "heading broccoli" or "cauliflower broccoli" (*B. oleracea* var. *botrytis*), and "Chinese broccoli" (*B. oleracea* var. *alboglabra*). Broccoli may have purple or green heads, be single or multiple-headed, and have annual or biennial (winter type) habit. Cultivars also vary in plant height, head shape, size of flower buds, and stem length.

Important horticultural characteristics for broccoli include yield (which is related to uniform field matu-

TABLE 1

The cole crops, their uses and plant biology

Crop	Species and botanical name	Part used as food	Flowering habit	Internodes elongate in first year	Temperature requirements for flowering
Kale	*Brassica oleracea* var. *acephala*	Leaves	biennial	yes	Approximately 6 weeks at 4.5°C after reaching a minimum stem diameter (3–4 mm)
Collards	*B. oleracea* var. *acephala*	Leaves	biennial	yes	Similar to kale
Cabbage	*B. oleracea* var. *capitata*	Leafy head or apical bud	biennial	no	Approximately 8 weeks at 4.5°C after reaching a minimum stem diameter (usually 6-8 mm)
Brussels sprouts	*B. oleracea* var. *gemmifera*	Axillary heads or buds	biennial	yes	Similar to cabbage; specific data not available
Kohlrabi	*B. oleracea* var. *gongylodes*	Fleshy stem	biennial	no	Little juvenile period; one week at 10°C sufficient to cause bolting
Cauliflower	*B. oleracea* var. *botrytis*	"Curd"	annual	yes	Summer and tropical varieties: Will form curds without cold and proceed to develop flowers. Late varieties may not have time to flower during growing season.
			biennial	no	Winter varieties: Low temperature exposure after about 6 weeks of age will cause curd formation; flowering follows without additional chilling.
Broccoli or Chinese kale	*B. oleracea* var. *italica*	Young inflorescence	annual	yes	Low temperature hastens heading but not required for head formation and flowering.
Kai lan, Chinese broccoli, or Chinese kale	*B. oleracea* var. *alboglabra*	Leaves, young inflorescence	annual	yes	Specific data not available

280

Cabbage figures prominently in the diet of Caribbean and Central American countries. These cabbage fields are in the mountainous region of Valle Nueva near Constanza, Dominican Republic. © RICHARD BICKEL/CORBIS.

rity, and head size and stem weight), and head and stem color (dark green is preferred for processing). Heads should be firm and supported by a deeply branched stem. Domed heads shed water and are less susceptible to head rot than are flat heads. Smooth heads are needed for fresh market, whereas processors prefer segmented heads. The individual branches or florets should be small, firm, and even in maturity and color. Small flower buds (called "beads") are preferred. Defects include uneven flower bud development ("rosetting"), large bead size, loose heads, depression in center of the head, dead flower buds, leaves in head, and yellow color.

Cauliflower cultivars are differentiated mainly by maturity as previously described. Curds are commonly white, but may also be green, orange, or purple. Summer and some winter types have been selected for leaves that wrap tightly about the head to facilitate curd blanching, while tropical types may lack adequate wrapper leaves for self-blanching. For some cultivars, field workers must break or band the wrapper leaves to provide adequate

covering for the curd. Cauliflower is perhaps the most fickle of the cole crops to grow because of its exacting climatic requirements.

Important horticultural characteristics include head size (medium is preferred for fresh market, but it can be large for processing), head weight (less cavity space is better), and large, clasping wrapper leaves that prevent curd exposure. Yield depends on good cover, which permits heads to grow larger before exposure. Heads must be pure white for processing and fresh market. Uniform maturity is important but difficult to achieve, even in F_1 hybrids. Over-mature heads will begin to show curd differentiation ("riciness"). Heads should be free from leaves.

Brussels sprouts are late maturing biennials. The main difference among cultivars is in stem length and maturity. Shorter types, while earlier maturing, also tend to be lower yielding than the tall types. For processing, sprouts should be firm and about 1.5 to 3 cm in diameter. Cultivars may have green or purple sprouts.

CULTIVARS

The term "cultivar" is used to distinguish a kind of vegetable from a botanical variety. Cultivars are things like "Excelsior" broccoli or "Snow Man" cauliflower. Cultivars may be open-pollinated, pure lines or inbreds, or F₁ hybrids. A botanical variety refers to a group of similar cultivars. For example, broccoli is classified as *Brassica oleracea* var. *italica* (the botanical variety of the cole family that comes from Italy). Sometimes the term "variety" is used interchangeably with "cultivar." For example, many garden seed catalogs use the term "variety." The terms "open-pollinated," "pure line," "inbred," and "F₁ hybrid" refer to the genetic structure of a cultivar. Open-pollinated varieties (often referred to as OPs) are usually a mix of genetically heterozygous plants forming a heterogeneous population. OPs are usually cross-pollinated and can be variable for horticultural traits. If a plant from an OP population is self-pollinated for several generations, it becomes an inbred line. With approximately six generations of self-pollination, a line will become genetically homozygous, and the population will be homogeneous. Crops that are normally self-pollinated (such as beans or peas) are called "pure lines" when inbred. F₁ hybrids are developed by crossing two inbred lines. The cross must be repeated to produce F₁ hybrid seed because selfed or crossed seed from the F₁ hybrid will not breed true. F₁ hybrids are genetically heterozygous but form homogenous populations.

Cultivar types. Cole crop landraces and cultivars were originally open-pollinated populations, consisting of genetically heterogeneous individuals. Such populations are subject to inbreeding depression in subsequent growing seasons if the grower saves seeds from too few individuals. Some open-pollinated cultivars are still grown, but the majority of contemporary cultivars are F₁ hybrids. Breeders develop inbreds, which are then planted in isolation in pairs to produce the F₁ hybrid seed, relying on self-incompatibility or cytoplasmic male sterility to enforce outcrossing.

Isolation of one-half to one mile between seed fields is required to prevent unwanted cross pollination. Any combination of *B. oleracea* crops and their wild forms may cross with one another and produce contaminants in a seed lot. *B. oleracea* does not need to be isolated from *B. rapa*, *B. juncea*, *B. nigra*, *B. napus*, and *Raphanus sativus* because these species will cross only with great difficulty.

Phytonutrient constituents. The Greeks and Romans recognized the nutritional and medicinal benefits of cole crops. Today, cole crops are recommended for increased consumption by people in developed countries. Cole crops supplement staple foods of higher caloric value with protein, vitamins, minerals, and dietary fiber. While epidemiological studies have demonstrated the health benefits of cole crops, they do contain some antinutritional constituents.

The vegetable parts of the cole crops have a high water content, are low in lipids and carbohydrates, and as a consequence, have relatively low caloric value (Table 2). They are most notable as a source of soluble and insoluble fiber, calcium and potassium, vitamin C, folate, and carotenoids (b-carotene [beta-carotene] and lutein) when compared to other vegetables of similar water content. Although the protein level is low, cole crops do contain significant levels of the essential sulfur-containing amino acid methionine, but not cysteine.

Several compounds give cole crops their characteristic flavor, and affect health and nutrition (Table 3). Glucosinolates and their breakdown products are the best characterized of these compounds. Glucosinolates are a class of sulfur-containing glucosides of which about fif-

TABLE 2

Nutritional composition of the major cole crops. Comparisons based on 100 grams edible product. Cabbage and cauliflower are raw; broccoli and brussels sprouts are cooked.

Crop	Water	Calories	Protein	Fat	Total carbohydrate	Vitamin A	Vitamin C	Fiber
	(%)	kcal	g	g	g	IU	mg	g
Cabbage	94	22	1.0	0.4	4.5	132	20	2.3
Savoy cabbage	92	24	1.8	0.1	5.4	889	17	2.8
Broccoli	91	28	3.0	0.4	5.1	1,388	75	2.9
Cauliflower	93	23	1.8	0.5	4.1	17	44	2.7
Brussels sprouts	87	39	2.6	0.5	8.7	719	62	2.6

SOURCE: USDA Nutrient Database for Standard Reference (http://www.nal.usda.gov/fnic/cgi-bin/nut_search.pl)

teen occur in significant quantities in the Brassicaceae. Within a given species, only three or four glucosinolates may be present in high concentrations. Glucosinolates are found in all *Brassica* tissues, and are generally highest in seeds, intermediate in young vegetative tissues, and lowest in older vegetative tissues. Myrosinase metabolizes glucosinolates to various isothiocyanates. Normally stored apart from glucosinolates in myrosin cells, myrosinase only comes into contact with its substrate when cells are ruptured. The type of isothiocyanate formed depends on the composition of the precursor glucosinolates, the pH, and the presence of certain cofactors such as ferrous iron. Glucosinolates have little flavor; rather, the breakdown products are responsible for the characteristic flavors of the cole crops. In their most extreme form and concentration, isothiocyanates cause the pungency of horseradish. In the cole crops, these compounds in too high a concentration may impart a bitter or "spicy" flavor. The wild cole crop progenitor has fairly high glucosinolate concentrations, which have been reduced in the domesticated species.

Glucosinolate-derived compounds have both positive and negative nutritional effects. Isothiocyanates are goitergenic in animals and people if consumed in sufficient quantities. In brussels sprouts, degree of bitterness correlates with level of the isothiocyanate goitrin, so named because of past association with goiter.

On the positive side, epidemiological studies have demonstrated that a diet high in fruits and vegetables, and in *Brassica* vegetables in particular, limits the risk of certain cancers. Glucosinolates may prevent cancer by acting as metabolic detoxicants to facilitate alteration and excretion of cell carcinogens. Sulphoraphane, a sulphinyl-containing isothiocyanate, is a strong inducer of the phase II enzymes responsible for anticarcinogenic activities. While sulphoraphane is found in most cole crops,

GLUCOSINOLATE-DERIVED COMPOUNDS

Glucosinolate-derived compounds have also been implicated in plant defense against pathogens and vertebrate and invertebrate pests. While they may deter generalized predators and pathogens, certain pathogens and insects can detoxify these compounds, and they may in fact serve as an attractant. Further research is needed to clarify the complex and varied roles played by glucosinolate-derived compounds. If consumed in moderation, the beneficial effects of cole crops on health far outweigh deleterious effects.

sprouted broccoli seeds have the highest concentrations. This finding by Paul Talalay's group at John Hopkins University has stimulated the commercial production of broccoli sprouts.

Glucosinolate-derived indole compounds are inducers of liver and intestinal enzymes that reduced tumor formation in rats. Timing is critical, in that while these compounds were effective when ingested prior to the carcinogen, administration after introduction of the carcinogen increased carcinogenesis in rainbow trout.

Other compounds of nutritional importance are flavonoids and S-methylcystine sulfoxide. Broccoli contains relatively high levels of the anticarcinogenic flavonoids kaempfrol and quercetin. Purple cabbage and other purple- or red-pigmented cole crops contain various anthocyanins. While anthocyanins in other crops

TABLE 3

Secondary nutritional compounds found in various raw cole crops[z]

Crop	Total glucosinolates (mmoles 100g⁻¹)	Carotenoid	mg 100g⁻¹	Flavonoid	mg 100g⁻¹	a-amino acid	mg 100g⁻¹
Brussels sprouts	367.2–553.0	Lutein	610	—	—	SMCSO[x]	68.0
		β-carotene	441				
Broccoli	161.9–248.4	Lutein	1,614	Quercetin	1.8	SMCSO	19.1
		β-carotene	800	Kaempferol	2.5		
White cabbage	68.6–238.3	Lutein	80	—	—	SMCSO	18.5
		β-carotene	51				
Savoy cabbage	164.5–461.3	Lutein	103	—	—	—	—
		β-carotene	50				
Savoy cabbage (outer leaves)	—	Lutein	14,457	—	—	—	—
		β-carotene	10,020				
Cauliflower	94.6–178.2	Lutein	trace			SMCSO	14.3
		β-carotene	none	—	—		

[z]Data compiled from Gomez-Campo, 1999.
[x]S-methylcystine sulfoxide.

The world's most famous cabbage dish is doubtless Alsatian *choucroute garni*, sauerkraut buried under a mountain of sausages and meats. © NIK WHEELER/CORBIS.

have shown anticarcinogenic properties, similar studies have not been carried out for cole crop anthocyanins. S-methylcystine sulfoxide is hydrolyzed by cystine lyase to methyl methanethiosulphinate, a compound that is similar to allyl thiosulphinate found in garlic. These compounds influence flavors, and are anticarcinogenic. Because of the similarities, and the health benefits found associated with these compounds in *Allium*, further study is warranted in the *Brassica*.

History

Original extent and domestication.
The wild progenitor of *Brassica* is found on the rocky Atlantic coasts of Europe (Bay of Biscay) and Britain. Researchers now believe that the free living *B. oleracea* populations found along the Mediterranean coast are feral and weedy escapes from cultivation. Related wild Mediterranean species (*B. cretica*, *B. insularis*, *B. montana*, and *B. ruprestris*) may have contributed genetically to the domesticated crops, al-

though molecular data does not support this hypothesis. Definitive archaeological evidence is lacking, but the crop was almost certainly a late domesticate compared to the primary domesticates of the Near East center such as emmer wheat, barley, pea, and lentil.

Different cole crops were likely domesticated in different places at different times, and multiple domestication within a type cannot be ruled out. More recent hybridizations among different types further complicate the picture. Leafy kales and nonheading cabbages were most likely the first domesticates, with some researchers hypothesizing that separate domestications occurred from Greece to Wales. "Stemkales" and headed and sprouting cabbages were described by Greek and Roman writers, although it is unclear whether these crops were the ancestors to the modern cabbage and broccoli. Domestication occurred prior to 1000 B.C.E., and possibly a millennia or more earlier. Broccoli and cauliflower are recent domesticates (possibly as old as 500 B.C.E.) from the eastern Mediterranean, and perhaps as localized as Cyprus and Sicily. The first clear description of broccoli and cauliflower was written about 1100 C.E. in Spain. Brussels sprouts were domesticated in northern Europe (some say Belgium) in about the fourteenth century. Early herbals depicted a kale with enlarged leaf axil buds, inferring that brussels sprouts were derived directly from kale. Kohlrabi may have been derived from marrowstem kale, or from a cross of marrowstem kale with cabbage. The origin of collards is closely associated with cabbage; whether collards are an ancestor or descendant of cabbage is unknown.

Historical diffusion.
From Europe and the Mediterranean, cabbage and kale dispersed into Mesopotamia and Egypt. These crops later spread throughout the Old World along trade routes, eventually reaching China where distinctive kale and broccoli types were to compete with the *B. rapa* cabbages of East Asian origin. When trade with the New World began, all of the cole crops were taken to the Americas. In the tropics, cole crops were widely accepted, except for broccoli, which does not form heads under tropical conditions.

Broccoli and cauliflower diffused from the Mediterranean (cauliflower earlier than broccoli) to elsewhere in the Near East, northern Africa, and Europe. Cauliflower was mentioned in Turkey and Egypt in the sixteenth century and in England and France in the seventeenth century. Both broccoli and cauliflower were first described in the United States in 1806, but production did not flourish until the 1920s. The broccoli industry became established about 1923 when the D'Arrigo Brothers Company began growing broccoli in California and catering to the large Italian immigrant population on the East Coast. Interest in broccoli in central and northern Europe increased after the crop became popular in the United States, and worldwide, broccoli production is increasing.

Procurement

Agriculture and crop husbandry. The majority of cole crop hectarage is found in the milder growing areas. The optimum growing season is determined by an interaction among latitude, altitude, and time of the year, as well as proximity to temperature-moderating oceans and lakes. In the United States, most of the cole crops for processing are produced at northern latitudes (New York, Wisconsin, Oregon, and Washington), the exception being California. The leading state for fresh market production is California, followed by New York, Georgia, Arizona, Texas, and Florida. Winter production in the United States of cole crops is done in Florida, Texas, and California. In the subtropics and tropics, cole crops are generally produced at higher altitudes. Commercial cauliflower production is restricted to the maritime climates of the United States because of its sensitivity to heat during curd formation.

For commercial production, the crops are generally grown in monoculture in 50–75 cm rows with within row spacing of 15–30 cm. Crops may be direct seeded or transplanted. Direct seeding is cheaper, but transplanting generally produces a more even stand with more uniform maturity. Cole crops require about 2.5 cm per week of moisture applied regularly throughout the season. In most production areas, natural precipitation is supplemented with irrigation.

Optimum soil pH is 5.5–6.5. Liming low pH fields improves micronutrient uptake and reduces incidence of club root. Plentiful amounts of nitrogen, potassium, and phosphorus are required for optimum plant growth. Nitrogen may be applied as a split application. Cole crops require adequate quantities of boron, calcium, and magnesium.

Harvesting and packing. Cabbage may be hand- or machine-harvested. Generally, heads intended for fresh market are hand-harvested, while those destined for storage or sauerkraut are mechanically harvested.

Broccoli and cauliflower are entirely hand-harvested. The greatest impediments to automating harvest are lack of cultivars with suitable plant architecture and a nonuniform maturity across a field. Even with F_1 hybrids and transplants, microenvironment differences will cause differential maturation in different parts of the field. Growers typically harvest two or three times at several-day intervals to maximize harvest of heads at optimum maturity. Attempts to develop a selective harvester for these crops have not been successful to date.

Brussels sprouts may be hand- or partially machine-harvested. The lower buds on the plant mature before those on the upper portion of the stem. Sprouts are harvested by hand at three or four-week intervals during the growing season by breaking the petioles of the lower leaves, then snapping the mature sprouts. If a single harvest is desired, the terminal growing point is removed

SAUERKRAUT

Fermenting cabbage to make sauerkraut is an ancient practice. The process is simple, and facilitated long-term storage of the crop. Sauerkraut is made by salting shredded cabbage and placing the mixture in an anaerobic container to ferment. Salt draws moisture from the cabbage leaves to produce a brine solution (ideally 2.25 percent). The brine inhibits growth of most microorganisms but allows certain anaerobic bacteria to propagate. *Leuconostoc mesenteroides* initiates the process, while others (primarily *Lactobacillus*, *Streptoccocus*, and *Pediococcus* spp.) continue fermentation. There are a number of conditions that need to be met, or a poor quality product will result. Salt must be evenly distributed, otherwise soft or pink kraut will form. Temperature will affect the composition of the microbial population, which in turn determines the pH and mix of flavor components. Temperatures below 18°C will produce sauerkraut with the best flavor, highest acidity, and ascorbic acid. Nonanaerobic conditions will allow yeast and molds to grow, which will impart undesirable flavors and odors, and will cause spoilage. Sauerkraut is preserved by canning. Sauerkraut is typically consumed with meat or poultry, but may also be used in salads. Sauerkraut juice may be blended with other vegetable or fruit juices to produce a novel and pleasing product.

Today, many people mainly associate sauerkraut with a condiment served on their hotdog bun at a baseball game. In northern Europe during the winter and on Western sailing ships, sauerkraut was an essential staple. The pickling process preserved about one-third of the vitamin C contained in the cabbage leaves, and provided a source of this essential vitamin at times when it was unavailable from other foods. For example, Captain Cook carried sauerkraut on his voyages of exploration as a preventative for scurvy. Fermented products, such as kimchi in Korea, which is made with Chinese cabbage (*B. rapa*) or Daikon radish (*Raphanus sativus*) serve a similar purpose in the temperate Asian world.

when sufficient height and lower bud development has been achieved. Upper buds will then catch up with lower buds in growth, resulting in near-uniform-sized sprouts along the stem. Plants are then cut in the field; the leaves are removed and sprouts are sheared from the stalk using a sprout cutter.

In large-scale operations, broccoli, cauliflower, and cabbage harvested for fresh market are packed in the field.

After broccoli heads are cut from the plant, leaves are removed and a mechanical cutting and banding machine is used to trim the stems to 15–20 cm in length. Two to four heads are bundled using rubber bands or a twist-tie. The prepared heads are then packed in a box and quickly cooled to 32°F (0°C) using slurry ice (40% ice and 60 percent water), which is hosed directly into the box. Cauliflower heads are harvested for fresh market when they grow to 15–20 cm in diameter. They are trimmed of most leaves (leaving a few basal leaves to protect the heads from damage), sorted to uniform size (typically six, twelve, or twenty-four heads per crate), and packed into crates or cartons. Individual heads may be wrapped with perforated film. Cauliflower is cooled to 32–36°F (0–2°C) for shipping and storage. Cabbage heads are harvested when firm and 1–1.5 kg in weight. Wrapper leaves are trimmed and heads are sorted and packed into crates or cartons and cooled to 32–36°F (0–2°C). Vacuum cooling, rather than slurry ice, is used to cool cabbage and cauliflower. Hand-harvested brussels sprouts are carried from the field in containers, washed and sorted for size and firmness, and quickly cooled (usually vacuum cooling) to 32°F (0°C). Sprouts are packaged in cellophane bags or baskets.

Storage and Processing. All of the cole crops are stored at near freezing, typically 30–36°F (−1–2°C) and at high (90–100 percent) relative humidity. Cabbage can be stored up to four months under ambient conditions and up to six months in modified atmosphere storage. Broccoli can be stored for only one to two weeks, cauliflower for two to three weeks and brussels sprouts for three to four weeks under optimal conditions in normal atmosphere storage.

The cole crops may be preserved by canning, freezing, pickling, dehydration, or fermentation. Broccoli, cauliflower, kale, collards, and brussels sprouts are usually processed by freezing. Cabbage may be dehydrated, or fermented to produce sauerkraut. Brussels sprouts, cabbage, and cauliflower may also be pickled. Kale and collards may be canned.

Seeds of the cole crops, especially broccoli, are consumed as sprouts. Extracts of cabbage-derived anthocyanins are being used commercially as red food colorants.

BIBLIOGRAPHY

Decouteau, Dennis R. *Vegetable Crops.* Upper Saddle River, N.J.: Prentice-Hall, 2000.

Dickson, Michael H., and D. H. Wallace. "Cabbage Breeding." In *Breeding Vegetable Crops.* Edited by Mark J. Bassett, pp. 395–432. Westport, Conn.: AVI Publishing Company. 1986.

Fahey, Jed W., Yesheng Zhang, and Paul Talalay. "Broccoli Sprouts: An Exceptionally Rich Source of Inducers of Enzymes That Protect Against Chemical Carcinogens." *Proceedings of the National Academy of Sciences, USA* 94 (1997): 10367–10372.

Gómez-Campo, C., ed. *Biology of* Brassica *Coenospecies.* Amsterdam and New York: Elsevier, 1999.

Hedrick, U.P., ed. *Sturtevant's Edible Plants of the World.* New York: Dover, 1972.

Luh, Bor Shiun, and Jasper Guy Woodroof, eds. *Commercial Vegetable Processing.* 2nd ed. New York: Van Nostrand Reinhold, 1988.

Nieuwhof, M. *Cole Crops: Botany, Cultivation, and Utilization.* London: L. Hill, 1969.

Peirce, Lincoln C. *Vegetables: Characteristics, Production, and Marketing.* New York: Wiley, 1987.

Rubatsky, Vincent E., and Mas Yamaguchi. *World Vegetables: Principles, Production, and Nutritive Values.* 2d ed. New York: Chapman and Hall, 1996.

Sauer, Jonathan D. *Historical Geography of Crop Plants: A Selected Roster.* Boca Raton, Fla.: CRC Press. 1994.

James R. Myers

CACTUS. Cacti are succulent perennials that are native to arid and semi-arid regions and are cultivated extensively, except where freezes regularly occur. The land area devoted to cactus cultivation in 2001 was about 1.8 million hectares (4.4 million acres), mostly for fodder, and over half of which was in northern Africa and northeastern Brazil. Cacti are also cultivated in over twenty countries for their fruits, which commercially fall into three categories: cactus pears, which are the fruits of the prickly pear *Opuntia ficus-indica* and certain other cacti with flat stems (cladodes), and represent over 90% of the cactus fruits sold; pitahayas, which are the fruits of vine cacti in the genera *Hylocereus* and *Selenicereus*; and pitayas, which are the fruits of columnar cacti. Young cladodes are consumed as a vegetable *(nopalitos)*, particularly in Mexico. Nearly all cacti employ a photosynthetic pathway known as Crassulacean acid metabolism (CAM), in which the stomates (shoot pores that allow CO_2 entry) open primarily at night, when temperatures are lower and water loss is lower than for the overwhelming majority of plants, whose stomates open during the daytime. The best known edible CAM plant is pineapple, which is cultivated on about half as much area as cacti. Because of their lower water loss, cacti and other CAM plants thrive in dry regions (and also require little or no irrigation when cultivated in other regions).

History

Although evidence for cacti in human diets goes back more than 8,000 years in present-day Mexico, worldwide consumption has developed only in the last few hundred years. Cacti were introduced into Europe in 1495 from the second trip of Christopher Columbus to the New World. *Opuntia ficus-indica* spread across the Mediterranean region in the sixteenth century, where it readily grew under the local semi-arid conditions. Also in the sixteenth century, Spaniards introduced *Hylocereus undatus* into the Philippines, whence it spread throughout southeast Asia. In the nineteenth century, it became established in Viet Nam and is now extensively cultivated in the Mekong Delta, where its tasty fruit with red peel and white pulp is called "dragon fruit." Also in the nineteenth century, the columnar *Stenocereus queretaroensis* was domesticated in Jalisco, Mexico. None of these species received much agronomic attention until the end of the twentieth century, and even then the money for research and development was meager. Both fruit crops and young cladodes used as vegetables require much hand labor. Although machines have been developed to remove the irritating small spines (termed "glochids") from cactus pears, many improvements in their cultivation await future research.

Fruits

Fruits of many cacti are edible. Indeed, the Seri Indians of the southwestern United States and northwestern Mexico consumed fruits from over twenty species, including those of the saguaro cactus (*Carnegiea gigantea*), used by various Native Americans for fruits and wine. Fruits collected from the wild influenced the species selected for domestication. Such selections involved various species of *Opuntia* in Mexico, eventually leading to the presently planted cultivars.

Cactus pear. The fruits of *Opuntia ficus-indica* and a few other prickly pears are harvested in the summer from plants that are one to three meters tall. Harvest can be delayed by removing the early flowers, as is commonly done in Sicily, leading to a second harvest in the autumn that is more valuable per fruit due to lessened competition from other species. One-year-old cladodes can bear five to fifteen fruits each; terminal cladodes with fewer fruits tend to bear larger ones (over 150 g each), which command higher prices. After harvesting, the fruits must have the glochids removed mechanically, after which they are often packaged by color and weight. Fruits with red pulp are prized in the United States and certain European countries, whereas greenish pulp for mature fruits is generally preferred in Mexico. Although sold in supermarkets worldwide, fruits are also sold by street vendors, who slice the peel and provide the exposed pulp directly to the consumer. The relatively large seeds are a detriment to fruit consumption by many, but the seeds are harmless and readily swallowed by aficionados.

The country with the greatest land area devoted to cactus pear cultivation is Mexico (Table 1). Annual production can be over fifteen tons fresh weight per hectare under intensive management. In Mexico, Sicily, Israel, and the United States, most production is from commercial plantations, whereas in other Latin American countries and in northern Africa, a large amount of the fruit is collected from hedges and other informal plantings.

Pitahayas and pitayas. The most widely cultivated pitahaya is *Hylocereus undatus*, which in 2001 was cultivated on about 12,000 hectares in many countries, including Viet Nam, Taiwan, the Philippines, Mexico, Guatemala,

TABLE 1

Land areas and harvests for fruit production by *Opuntia ficus-indica* and closely related species in 2001

Country	Area (hectares)	Annual harvest (tons fresh weight)
Argentina	900	8,000
Bolivia	1,300	3,500
Chile	1,200	9,000
Israel	400	7,000
Italy	7,500	80,000
Mexico	70,000	400,000
Northern Africa (Algeria, Morocco, Tunisia)	~20,000	—
South Africa	200	1,500
United States	200	3,600

Peru, Colombia, and Israel. It is a vine that is trained to grow on posts, trellises, or arbors. Its relatively large fruits (generally 250 to 500 g) are harvested after the peel, which has no spines or glochids, turns red. The pulp is

Vendor selling cactus pads in Guanajuato, Mexico. © DANNY LEHMAN/CORBIS.

whitish with small black seeds. Other species of *Hylocereus* and *Selenicereus megalanthus* have peels and pulps of various colors, leading to a wide choice of tasty and visually appealing fruits.

Although their cultivation is expanding rapidly, in 2001 pitayas were harvested on only about 3,000 hectares worldwide, mostly in Mexico, from species like *Cereus peruvianus*, and especially *Stenocereus queretaroensis* and other *Stenocereus* species. Fruits grow along the main stem and branches about two to six meters above the ground, requiring a pole with a basket-like attachment for harvest of individual fruits. Fruits of *Stenocereus queretaroensis* have an attractive and tasty dark red or purple pulp with small seeds (like those in kiwis) that are easily swallowed. However, the fruits tend to split within two or three days after harvest, requiring rapid local consumption.

Vegetables

Tender young cladodes about 10 to 15 cm long of *Opuntia ficus-indica*, *Opuntia robusta*, and a few related species are used in Mexico as *nopalitos*. About 6,000 hectares were cultivated for this purpose in 2001, and *nopalitos* are also prepared from plants in the wild or growing around houses, or as hedges. The raised portions of the stem containing spines and glochids are readily removed with a knife or by machine. The cladodes are then generally sliced or diced and blanched in a weak saline solution for a few minutes to remove excess mucilage. After draining, the material can be cooked, yielding a vegetable with a taste not unlike string beans or okra. Because of their high fructose and mucilage content, *nopalitos* are highly recommended for people with type II diabetes. Often the blanched material is pickled and used as a relish or in salads. More than thirty companies sold pickled *nopalitos* in Mexico in 2001, and this product is in supermarkets worldwide.

Other Uses

Other uses of cacti range from candy made from the stems of barrel cacti that have been infused with a sugar solution to peyote from dried stems of *Lophophora williamsii*, used by Native Americans for ceremonial purposes. Flowers have been used for medicinal purposes and to make perfume. The seeds of cacti such as *Opuntia ficus-indica* have been dried, ground, and then used as a flavoring paste for cooking. Carminic acid, an important red dye for food coloring, can be extracted from dried cochineal insects that feed on *Opuntia ficus-indica*. Although most cactus pears are consumed fresh, sorbets and marmalades are also prepared from the fruits. The strained pulp of fresh fruits is used as a fruit drink or fermented to make wine. Fruits of cactus pears are also partially dried and sold in brick-sized blocks in Mexico. More than thirty brands of dried and powdered cladodes are sold in Mexico as a dietary supplement. The range of edible products from cacti is indeed great and their use is steadily increasing, as more people become willing to try new and natural foods, and growers search for crops that do not need irrigation.

BIBLIOGRAPHY

Mizrahi, Yosef, Avinoam Nerd, and Park S. Nobel. "Cacti as Crops." In *Horticultural Reviews* 18 (1997): 291–319.

Nobel, Park S. *Los Incomparables Agaves y Cactos.* Translated by Edmundo Garcia Moya. Mexico City: Editorial Trillas, 1998.

Nobel, Park S. *Remarkable Agaves and Cacti.* New York: Oxford University Press, 1994.

Nobel, Park S., editor. *Cacti: Biology and Uses.* Berkeley, California: University of California Press, 2002.

Valles Septién, Carmen, editor. *Succulentas Mexicanas/Cactáceas.* Mexico City: CVS Publicaciones, 1997.

Park S. Nobel

CAJUN CUISINE. *See* **United States.**

CAKE AND PANCAKE. The cake, as we now understand it in Anglo-American cookery, is the product of western European culture, with few parallels in non-European cookeries. It is commonly expressed in French by the word *gâteau*, a term without specific meaning (*gâteau de pomme* is both an apple cake and a molded apple jelly) and whose origin remains undetermined. Nevertheless, since the nineteenth century, the culture of the cake has spread to many parts of the world as the result of colonialism and the internationalization of French, English, and more recently of American cookery.

In Latin America, for example, American-type layer cakes are called *queques*, but the more traditional Spanish term *pastel* is often employed for birthday cakes of similar shape and structural arrangement. The use of conflicting terminologies for cakes, and the multitudes of types of foods defined as cakes, make it difficult to create a standard logic and a simple definition. No scholarly undertaking has thus far tackled the cake to create a unifying thesis about its diverse evolutionary forms. This would require a detailed analysis of the huge vocabularies for cake and cakelike pastries that exist in many European languages both ancient and modern. The discussion here will focus on the cake in relation to American cookery.

The concept itself is quite basic: cake is bread, if bread is defined as something baked from flour or meal, as in Welsh oatcake. However, this basic idea has evolved in English to cover a number of preparations also generally categorized as sweet and normally considered dessert or special occasion foods. While nearly all types of modern cakes are thought to have evolved out of some form of enriched bread, that course of evolution is highly varied from culture to culture and encompasses a great many regionalized forms and colloquial names. Both the word *cake* and the preparations associated with it have experienced sometimes separate and convoluted histories.

The word is generally assumed to have entered English via Old Norse *kaka*, although this line of derivation is doubtful, since the Norse word itself was assimilated from Vulgar Latin, for a similar root may be observed in such terms as the Dutch *coeke* and *koek*. *Koekje*, the diminutive of *koek*, was corrupted in colonial American English as cookie (literally a "little cake"), yet it preserves the essential concept that the cake is flat and baked, regardless of size—an important point. Since a similar term *kuoche* appears in medieval German, also for a type of enriched bread flat in shape, it is quite probable that cake entered modern English as a Latin loan word via ancient British or Anglo-Saxon rather than Old Norse, although literary documentation does not surface until the 1300s. Neither Billy (1993) nor Lambert (1997) has ascertained Celtic roots for the term; thus a Latin origin must be presumed.

Whatever the route of assimilation, the root meaning of cake is quite clear, for it is expressed in the Latin verb *coquere*, to cook or prepare food in the limited sense of baking or exposing it to heat it in some way. German and the other languages that assimilated this verb-concept also extended it to mean something baked that is both flat and made with or covered with ingredients that differentiate it from common flat bread, hence terms like *Kuchen*, *Fladen*, *Wähe*, and *Zelten* in German-speaking Europe. *Torte*, a word derived from Latin *tortum*, moved into German and other northern European languages (such as Polish) via French or Italian during the Renaissance and entered English as tart. The fruit tart of Renaissance England evolved into the colloquial fruit pie of colonial America and there departed from its ancient flat cake ancestry, which may be said to linger on only in the shape of the bottom crust.

However, very primitive types of cake do survive in the form of the Alsatian *quiche* (derived from German *Kuchen*)—where the rim of the cake dough is turned up to allow for a deeper covering or filling (common cheesecake also belongs to this category). Another type is like the so-called *galette bretonnaise* (Breton flat cake), which is round, flat, sweet in taste, and enriched with butter. It is baked on a griddle or bake stone and thus shares a common lineage with the bannock and *scon* of the insular Celts. A Mediterranean counterpart would be the *karydopita nistisimi* (Lenten walnut cake) of Greece eaten with syrup. The sweet johnnycake of colonial America is a New World extension of this primitive flat cake concept. The hoecake (a flat bread baked on a shovel) and the ashcake (a flat bread baked under hot coals) are both variants of this basic type.

It is also clearly evident from surviving written evidence that medieval cakes were not necessarily sweet, for they could include such ingredients as cheese and herbs, a batter of cheese and eggs, a few slices of sausage,

Cake stand and glass bell cover manufactured by Whitehall & Tatum, Millville, New Jersey, circa 1840. ROUGHWOOD COLLECTION. PHOTO CHEW & COMPANY.

or even a mixture of fruit and vegetables. In their original dietary contexts, such cakes were not viewed as everyday fare, but were reserved for special occasions such as time of harvest, a village fair, a saint's day, or some similar event. The most festive cakes were those enriched with fat and fruit, or sweetened with fruit and honey, and out of that tradition of elaborately flavored bread evolved most of the rich cakes we know today. French pastry cooks generally divide cakes into eight categories based on the type of doughs employed, but these are merely terms of convenience. There are only four structural families.

The Galette or Short Bread
The galette or short bread is the type described above in connection with *galette bretonnaise* and American sweet johnnycake. The unifying features include an enriched, stiff unleavened dough—which may be molded or flattened by hand or with a rolling implement—a round shape, and a brittle texture once baked. The cake may be further ornamented by impressing images or patterns into the surface. These cakes rely for their tenderness or soft texture on a combination of fat (usually butter) and specially selected flours, such as soft wheat flour or a mixture of barley flour and wheat, or even to some extent on breaking the dough by beating it. They are now commonly categorized as pastries, especially since this type of dough is now employed to make cookies, but historically, such short doughs were treated as cakes as long as they conformed to a flattened shape. When the short breads are stacked and interfilled with rich ingredients, they are almost always referred to as *tortes* or *gâteaux*. An example of the former would be the linzer torte of Austria, while the French *gâteau mille-feuille* would be an

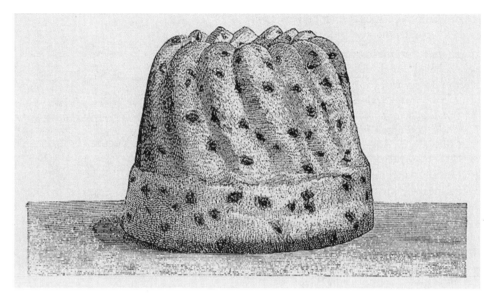

A yeast-raised Gugelhopf cake with raisins, as depicted in a nineteenth-century German wood engraving. ROUGHWOOD COLLECTION.

example of the latter. This French cake is perhaps the most fragile of all, since it is constructed of layers of round sheets of puff pastry interfilled with various sorts of cream and jam.

Bread Cakes or Loaf Cakes

These may be further divided into sweet and savory types. An example of the latter would be the common Italian *foccacia* covered with herbs, cheese, and sliced tomatoes. An example of the sweet type would be the early American Moravian sugar cake, which is essentially a sweetened yeast-raised dough into which is inserted a mixture of brown sugar, cinnamon, and butter. This is accomplished by making holes in the surface of the dough and pressing the mixture in with the index finger. The common thread is that these cakes are yeast-raised and therefore most like bread in texture. Furthermore, they were meant to be eaten out of hand like a piece of bread. Many sweetened festive breads of the Mediterranean preserve this old form, especially in the elaborate preparations of Greek *Vasilopita* (St. Basil's cake) for the New Year and the numerous traditional Cypriot breadlike cakes ornamented with dried fruit, almonds, and brightly colored comfits.

The yeast-raised *Gugelhopf* or *Napfkuchen* of southern Germany and Austria are further extensions of this basic idea, with the additional refinement that the bread is baked in a form so that it acquires an impressive ornamental shape. Rather than sticking fruit into the surface, it is chopped and worked into the dough itself. The Worcester loaf cake of New England, which was similarly baked in a shaped cake pan, provided early Americans with an equivalent example. Its vernacular name, however, indicates that originally (in the 1600s) it was baked round to resemble a loaf of bread, and like bread, it was not made too sweet since it was served with jam or preserves on ceremonial occasions such as funerals. This type of yeast-raised cake achieved its most monumental and most vertical expression during the Renaissance and Baroque periods in such phallic shaped cakes as the Russian Easter cake and the Polish baba.

Baked Pottages or Plum Pudding Cakes

Plum pudding cake was once found in many parts of medieval Europe, but quickly disappeared during the Renaissance in favor of lighter and sweeter preparations. Since the plum cake was associated with traditional fall butchering and Christmas feasting in England (and may be traced to pagan times), it has lingered on in British cookery to this day. It was also brought to colonial North America, where it continues as a feature of Christmas fare under the name of fruitcake. Fruitcake is especially popular in the American South.

In order to understand the origin of this cake, we must start with something similar to mincemeat thickened with meal, cracked wheat, or flour, to which is added a variety of rich ingredients. These would include blood from butchering (hence the term black cake), suet, butter, dried fruits, honey, and a variety of spices. This could be served freshly made as a festive pottage, or baked thick in a pan or shallow crock and later turned out like a wheel of cheese. The use of pottery for such purposes is attested to by Michael Hero, who illustrated something similar called *Scherbenbrodt* (crock bread) in his *Schachtaffeln der Gesuntheyt* (Strasbourg, 1533).

At this point, the baked mass becomes a cake due to its round, flattened shape and solid texture, and black cake it is indeed. Furthermore, it can be sliced and eaten with the fingers; thus it migrates from the medieval pottage course to an *entremet* for the final course, when various sweets and delicate foods are served. From here, the cake undergoes rapid metamorphosis, with increasingly more eggs, sugar, spices, candied fruits, and other ingredients associated with luxury, leaving the homey pottage altogether to evolve along a separate line into plum pudding. One unifying feature, however, is the dark color that came initially from blood, but which is later derived from molasses or brown sugar. Both plum pudding and fruitcake retain this visual allusion to their ancient association with butchering. And to some extent, both have retained their medieval role as visual centerpieces during the course of the meal.

The festive nature of this type of cake, which eventually comes to rely on beaten eggs for its lightness, is preserved in names like rich bride cake, Twelfth Night cake, and Christmas plum cake. More refined (less dark) versions developed into tea cakes, such as Dundee cake and Cumberland fruit cake. The latter preparation has many counterparts in Victorian cookery books. Both the bride and Twelfth Night cakes were similarly ornamented with elaborate icings, but the bride or wedding cake has since evolved into something quite different, having crossed over the line into the next category of cake discussed below.

The traditional bride cake made with fruit as described here probably fell out of fashion due to its dense weight, since it could not be stacked to a great height without crushing the layers underneath. Furthermore, there is considerable work involved in icing it, since it must be coated with a hard layer of marzipan to keep moisture from seeping out into the highly ornamented royal icing encasing the whole creation. Such seepage would stain the work or dissolve it altogether. This telling detail is evident in the fact that most commercial American fruitcakes are no longer sold iced, since this requires a level of competence now dispensed with in large-batch operations.

Pancakes and Batter Cakes Baked in Pans

This takes us into a realm of research that on one level is refreshingly simple, yet on another, perplexing and ambiguous. Let us deal with the ambiguities first. Most of the cakes in the category of pancakes and batter cakes cooked in pans are referred to in French as *gâteaux*, since they are now of a large and impressive sort. Unfortunately, the origins of the word *gâteau* are obscure, although the *Viandier* of Taillevent (1380s) mentions something called a *gaitellet*, which has been glossed as a little cake. This would imply that there were cakes larger than a *gaitellet* and known by another closely related name (*gaitelle*). If this has a Gaulish root (which is possible), it may derive from a cognate of the Latin *catinus*, a deep dish or bowl, or more specifically from *catillus*, the diminutive for a dish or plate (here again the inference

Stacked tube pans for *gâteau breton*. Made by E. Dehillerin, Paris, ca. 1912. White metal. ROUGHWOOD COLLECTION. PHOTO CHEW & COMPANY.

is something flat in shape). This is, of course, quite speculative, but leaves one fact beyond doubt: the cake in question is created from batter, from something liquid that is first beaten light.

We are on firmer ground with the 1398 observation of John of Trevisia who saw in England a cake "tornyd and wende" at the fire. He even said that it was called a cake and his comment is in fact considered one of the earliest documented uses of the word. What he observed was the preparation of the once popular spit cake (*Spiesskuchen*) much depicted in the paintings of Bruegel and other north German artists. This is created by dripping well-beaten batter onto a hot spit as it turns before the fire, thus spinning out a series of flat irregular cakes in accordion fashion. This was served set on end as a type of wedding cake, one of the few ways in which medieval cooks could raise a batter cake to great heights. Verticality is a feature of many cakes of a highly festive nature, and this cake is still made today by professional bakeries in France, Belgium, Holland, and Germany.

The spit cake is an anomaly in its unusual method of baking. Most batter cakes were created in a much more straightforward manner: down hearth in a bake kettle (Dutch oven). However, this takes us into yet another region of ambiguity concerning the origin of the cake, since we must now confront the pan and the ways in which it dictated the evolution of all cakes composed of batter. It would seem logical to presume that the *pan-* in "pancake" refers to Vulgar Latin *panna*, which is normally glossed as a shallow pan or vessel. But all things did not flow from Rome. Thus we might also look to words such as the Belgic and Treverian Gaulish *panna* (a likely source for the Vulgar Latin in any case) for a more basic explanation and a richer understanding of the batter cake.

The meaning of *panna* is well attested to by its survival in Westphalian German under the name *Pannas*, a festive pot pudding made during the butchering season that is solidified in a pan, then sliced and fried in little cakes. One of the original Belgic meanings of *panna* was a cauldron or kettle (in which the pudding was boiled), but more abstractly a cooking implement or ceramic form of varying depth. These alternative meanings survive in German as *Pfannkuchen* or *Pfannzelten* (south German), cakes that are hearth-baked in a kettle—a concept that survives in the form of the Dutch oven and colonial American spider corn cake.

The thinnest sorts of batter cakes are those most like the pancakes and crepes made from milk, flour, and egg and served today as breakfast foods. They evolved out of omelets to which flour, fat, and other ingredients were added in ever-increasing amounts. The next immediate stage would be cakes resembling the Italian *fritatta*, then soufflés (cakes that deflate), and finally batters that actually contain enough structural material to bake firm and retain their shape. Such pan-baked delicacies were known even in the early Middle Ages, for in his *De honesta voluptate et valetudine* (1465) Platina published a recipe for a Byzantine *artolaganos* (pan or layer cake) prepared with eggs, sugar, cheese, and finely ground millet. His recipe came from Milanese chef Martino di Rossi under the name *migliaccio* (millet cake), proof that delicate, batter-based cakes were already a feature of Italian court cookery by that time.

At this point, the pancake moves further along two separate lines of evolution. Since thickness and lightness were increasingly sought after, the pan itself became taller and taller to contain the new heights being achieved. More closely controlled results could be expected in an oven, so batter cake cookery was soon transferred to the bake oven. It is important to remember that Rossi's *migliaccio* was baked in a kettle down hearth, as most peasant variants of this type of cake continued to be baked well into the nineteenth century. However, cakes with heavy ingredients, like the *migliaccio*, soon evolved into delicate pound cakes once freed of the smoky, drafty atmosphere of the hearth, while batters with reduced fat and more beaten egg whites followed the *fritatta* to its ultimate conclusion in Savoy and sponge cakes. Denser batters were baked in pans—at first round, like hearth implements, then square; finally, during the late Renaissance we witness the cake evolving into the multitudes of shapes depicted in many French cookery books of the period.

The replacement of flour with highly refined commercial starches and the replacement of eggs with chemical leavenings allowed the development of lighter and lighter cakes during the nineteenth century. The angel

food cake invented in the 1870s by Linus Dexter of Vineland, New Jersey, was the product of just such a technological shift. Likewise, American cooks began to stack one cake upon the other to create the thick layer cake, a response no doubt to a similar evolution in the wedding cake, which soared to great heights once freed of its old fruit cake foundation. The opposite may be said for chocolate cakes, which now vie for density and richness. They may have replaced the sinfully greasy baked pottages of the Middle Ages (although still dark in color), and they may be relegated to dessert carts in the scheme of many modern restaurants, yet fine cakes still command a place of high esteem by virtue of their sheer voluptuousness. They have become the alter ego of a society obsessed with the ills of overabundance.

See also **Bread; Pastry; Wedding Cakes.**

BIBLIOGRAPHY

Billy, Pierre-Henri. *Thesaurus Linguae Gallicae.* Hildesheim: Olms-Weidmann, 1993.

Charsley, S. R. *Wedding Cakes and Cultural History* London: Routledge, 1992.

Hausen, Hans Jürgen. *Kunstgeschichte des Backwerks.* Oldenburg, 1968.

Hörandner, Edith. *Model: Geschnitzte Formen für Lebkuchen, Spekulatius, und Springerle* Munich: Callwey, 1982.

Jakob, Heinrich. *6000 Jahre Brodt.* Hamburg, 1954.

Kyphre, Theophano, and Kalliope Protopapa. *Paralosiaka Zymomata tes Kyproy.* Nicosia: Cyprus Research Centre, 1997.

Lambert, Pierre-Yves. *La langue gaulois: Description linguistique, commentaire d'inscriptions choises.* Paris: Editions Errance, 1997.

Rhiner, Oskar. "Dünne, Wähe, Kuchen, Fladen, Zelten: Die Wortgeographie des Flachkuchens mit Beilag und ihre volkskundliche Hintergründe in der Schweiz." *Beiträge zur schweizerdeutschen Mundartforschung* 9 (1958).

Weaver, William Woys. *America Eats: Forms of Edible Folk Art.* New York: Perennial Library, 1989.

Wiswe, Hans. *Kulturgeschichte der Kochkunst: Kochbücher und Rezepte aus zwei Jahrtausenden.* Munich: H. Moss, 1970.

Wurmbach, Annemarie. "Kuchen-Fladen-Torta: Eine wort- und sachkundliche Untersuchung." *Zeitschrift für Volkskunde* 56 (1960): 20–40.

William Woys Weaver

CALCIUM. Calcium (Ca^2) is a silver-white metallic element of the alkaline-earth group. Ninety-nine percent of calcium in the human body is in bone and teeth. The remaining one percent is in blood and body fluids. In addition to its role in maintaining strength of bone and teeth, calcium is involved in nerve cell function, control of muscle tone, and blood clot formation. Calcium is also necessary in order for many important proteins to properly perform critical metabolic functions throughout the body.

Functions

Cells. Calcium concentrations in the fluids outside cells are much larger than calcium concentrations inside cells (the cytosol). Unequal calcium concentrations in the extracellular fluid and cytosol are required for cells to carry out many crucial functions. For example, when a hormone in the blood binds to a receptor on the cell, calcium pours into the cytosol from extracellular fluid. This change in the amount of calcium in the cytosol signals the cell to perform some critical function. The critical function that is triggered depends on the type of cell. (In muscle cells, for example, a nerve signal triggers the release of calcium into the cytosol, allowing muscle contraction to occur.) After the critical function is performed, calcium is rapidly pumped out of the cell, and the calcium concentration in the cytosol returns to the normal (low) level.

Structural. In addition to cellular functions, calcium's more familiar role is a structural one—as a component of bones and teeth. Blood calcium levels are maintained strictly even if calcium has to be taken from bone. Bone mineral (hydroxyapatite) is made up primarily of calcium, phosphate, and carbonate. Bone constantly changes during growth and throughout adulthood. Changes in bone occur through balancing activities of bone-destroying cells (osteoclasts) and bone-forming cells (osteoblasts), which act together to remove and replace bone, respectively. During growth, bone formation generally exceeds destruction, yielding net bone-mass gain in the whole skeleton.

Bone-mass accumulation continues until peak bone mass is achieved, generally during the third decade of life. The age at which peak bone mass is reached varies by gender and differs by skeletal site. Males achieve peak bone mass later than females and gain more bone during puberty than females, resulting in larger bones. Although peak bone mass at all skeletal sites is generally reached by age thirty, bone accumulation is nearly complete by age twenty in the lumbar spine and in portions of the hip for both males and females. Genetic, environmental (for example, physical activity or mechanical "loading" of the skeleton), hormonal, and nutritional factors interact to influence peak bone-mass levels. Failure of an individual to reach the maximum peak bone mass permitted by his or her genetic makeup can be related to low calcium intake or a sedentary lifestyle without adequate physical activity. Parathyroid dysfunction, genetic or nutritional skeletal disorders, or medication use may affect peak bone-mass accumulation and overall bone health adversely. Smoking and excessive alcohol consumption also are likely to be detrimental to skeletal health.

After an individual reaches peak bone mass, net bone gain in the whole skeleton generally does not occur. Age-related bone loss occurs in both genders, but the rate of bone loss increases with estrogen loss at menopause in females. Age-related bone loss is caused by increased osteoclast (bone-destroying) activity compared to osteoblast (bone-building) activity. Physical activity during adulthood, combined with adequate overall nutrition and calcium intake, can help to maintain bone strength.

Metabolism

Absorption. Calcium absorption across the intestinal wall into the blood occurs by different mechanisms. Two major mechanisms include passive diffusion and active transport. Vitamin D is required for the active transport mechanism but not for the passive diffusion mechanism. The percent of calcium that is absorbed into blood generally decreases with higher calcium intakes; however, the total amount of calcium absorbed is usually greater with higher calcium intakes. The percent of calcium absorbed into blood is highest in infants, spikes again at the start of puberty, then gradually declines with age. The percent of calcium absorbed into blood also increases during the last two trimesters of pregnancy.

Homeostasis. The body keeps tight control (homeostasis) of blood calcium concentration by continuously changing various factors. When blood calcium concentration falls below normal, the parathyroid gland releases parathyroid hormone (PTH). PTH stimulates increased removal of phosphate into urine by the kidneys. This increased phosphate removal triggers the kidneys to keep calcium in the blood rather than excrete it in the urine. PTH also stimulates osteoclasts to remove calcium from bone in order to help restore normal blood calcium concentration. Finally, PTH is involved in making certain that enough vitamin D is present in the intestine to allow for increased calcium absorption from the gut into the blood. PTH decreases to normal once calcium homeostasis is reached. Another hormone, calcitonin, is responsible for stopping bone breakdown by osteoclasts when blood calcium concentration is above normal. Thus, the hormones PTH and calcitonin work together to keep blood calcium concentration within a very narrow range.

Dietary Requirements

Bioavailability. Both dairy products and most dietary supplements provide adequate amounts of calcium. Calcium is present in smaller amounts in grains, fruits, and vegetables. Because grains are eaten in high amounts, however, they are an important source of calcium. Other calcium-rich foods include bok choy (Chinese cabbage), kale, cabbage, and broccoli. Calcium from some foods containing high levels of oxalic acid (spinach, sweet potatoes, rhubarb, beans) or phytic acid (unleavened bread, nuts and grains, seeds, raw beans) is absorbed poorly due to formation of insoluble calcium salts. The ability to enhance dietary calcium intake by consuming calcium-fortified food sources is increasingly common.

Although high protein intake temporarily increases urinary calcium excretion, there is no evidence to indicate that calcium intake recommendations should be adjusted according to protein intake. Although caffeine has a slightly negative impact on calcium retention, the modest calcium loss can be offset by a similarly modest increase in calcium intake. High salt (sodium chloride) intake usually results in increased urinary calcium loss because excretion of sodium and calcium at the kidney are linked. High salt intake triggers increased urinary sodium loss and, therefore, increased urinary calcium excretion. However, as with protein and caffeine, there is no evidence to indicate that calcium intake recommendations should be adjusted according to salt intake.

Dietary requirements and bone mass.

Because circulating calcium levels are so strictly controlled, blood calcium concentration is a poor indicator of calcium status. Chronic inadequate calcium intakes or poor intestinal absorption leads to reduced bone mass as PTH acts to maintain homeostatic blood calcium at the expense of skeletal strength. Bone mineral content (BMC) and bone mineral density (BMD) are common measures of bone strength and fracture risk. BMC is measured in grams, the amount of bone mineral at the selected site (for example, whole skeleton, lumbar spine, hip, forearm) and BMD (g/cm^2) are calculated as BMC divided by bone area in the region of interest. An adult is defined as osteoporotic by the World Health Organization if his or her BMD is more than 2.5 standard deviations below gender-specific normal young adult BMD. Osteoporosis and related spine, hip, and wrist fractures are major public health concerns.

Recommended daily calcium intakes (measured in milligrams) increase from infancy through adolescence. The rate of calcium accretion relative to body size is greatest during infancy. Infants accrete approximately 140 mg of calcium per day during the first year of life. This need for calcium during the first year of life is reflected in the amount of milk consumed by human milk-fed infants. Although evidence indicates that feeding of formula results in greater bone mineral accretion than human milk feeding during the first year of life, there is no indication that this effect is beneficial either short- or long-term.

Calcium accretion continues in childhood, and maximal accretion occurs during puberty. Children of ages one to eight years accrete 60 to 200 mg of calcium per day. Peak calcium accretion occurs during puberty for both males (mean age 14.5 years) and females (mean age 12 years). Accordingly, calcium intake requirements are highest during adolescence.

Calcium retention and bone turnover decline after menarche in females, but the amount of calcium women need does not change because the percentage of calcium absorbed into the blood decreases. In males, bone mineral accretion occurs until mean age 17.5 years. Evidence from clinical trials indicates that calcium supplementation in children can increase BMD, but the effect occurs primarily among populations who usually have low calcium intake, is not apparent at all skeletal sites, and probably does not persist when supplementation is stopped. Apparently the benefit is short-term only.

Dietary calcium requirements decline for both males and females once adulthood is reached and remain constant throughout the reproductive years. Intestinal calcium absorption, however, also decreases with age. At the end of the reproductive years (approximately age fifty), bone-mass loss occurs in both males and females. Bone-mass loss is particularly pronounced in females during the first few years following menopause. The bone loss that occurs with the loss of estrogen at menopause cannot be reversed simply through increased calcium intake. Reductions in age-related bone loss through calcium supplementation have been demonstrated in postmenopausal women, but the effects vary by skeletal site, usual calcium intake, and postmenopausal age. Because of the reduction in intestinal calcium absorption with age in all individuals and the potential of increased calcium intake to offset bone loss due to estrogen depletion, increasing the amount of calcium in one's diet is recommended for all individuals over fifty years of age.

Maternal calcium requirements increase during the third trimester of pregnancy in accordance with fetal growth needs and to prepare for lactation, and the mother's intestinal calcium absorption efficiency increases in order to meet her increased need for calcium. If this need for more calcium is not met, the mother's skeleton will be depleted to meet the calcium demands of the fetus. Furthermore, calcium loss from the mother's skeleton occurs during lactation and cannot be prevented by calcium supplementation. However, evidence indicates that maternal bone density is recovered to prelactation levels within approximately six months after the recurrence of menses.

Toxicity.

Calcium toxicity is uncommon but can occur if too much calcium is taken in through dietary supplements. In susceptible individuals, excess calcium intake can lead to the formation of kidney stones (renal calcium deposits); however, dietary calcium is not a common cause of kidney stones. Hypercalcemia from ingestion of large quantities of calcium supplements is rare but the resulting kidney problems and ramifications to cell function affect major tissues and organs. In the United States, the maximum daily calcium intake judged likely to pose no adverse health effects—Tolerable Upper Intake Level (UL)—is set at 2,500 mg per day for all ages beyond one year of age. There are insufficient data to determine a UL for calcium for infants less than one year of age.

Summary.

Changes in dietary calcium requirements throughout the lifespan reflect concurrent alterations in growth rate, intestinal absorption efficiency, and reproductive and estrogen status. Because calcium plays vital roles in critical cell responses, plasma calcium levels are strictly homeostatically controlled at the expense of skeletal integrity, if necessary. Homeostatic control of circulating calcium involves PTH, vitamin D, and calcitonin.

Appropriate lifestyle choices (for example, physical activity) and adequate calcium nutrition promote optimal bone-mass accretion during growth and young adulthood, possibly resulting in reduced current and future fracture risk. Dairy products and dietary supplements provide similarly adequate amounts of calcium to the body. Grains, fruits, and vegetables contain smaller amounts of calcium, and calcium absorption from foods high in oxalic acid or phytic acid is limited. Calcium-enriched products such as bread and fruit juice are becoming increasingly important sources of dietary calcium.

See also **Dairy Products; Lactation; Milk, Human; Nutrition; Phosphorus and Calcium; Trace Elements.**

BIBLIOGRAPHY

Abrams, S. A., K. O. O'Brien, and J. E. Stuff. "Changes in Calcium Kinetics Associated with Menarche." *Journal of Clinical Endocrinology and Metabolism* 81 (1996): 2017–2020.

Aloia, J. F., A. Vswani, J. K. Yeah, P. L. Ross, E. Flaster, and F. A. Dilmanian. "Calcium supplementation with and without Hormone Replacement Therapy to Prevent Postmenopausal Bone Loss." *Annals of Internal Medicine* 120 (1994): 97–103.

Barger-Lux, M. J., R. P. Heaney, and M. R. Stegman. "Effects of Moderate Caffeine Intake on the Calcium Economy of Premenopausal Women." *American Journal of Clinical Nutrition* 52 (1990): 722–725.

Bonjour, J. P., G. Theintz, F. Law, D. Slosman, and R. Rizzoli. "Peak Bone Mass." *Osteoporosis International* 1 (1994): S7–S13.

Dawson-Hughes, B., G. E. Dallal, E. A. Krall, L. Sadowski, N. Sahyoun, and S. Tannenbaum. "A Controlled Trial of the Effect of Calcium Supplementation on Bone Density in Postmenopausal Women." *New England Journal of Medicine* 323 (1990): 878–883.

Heaney, R. P. "Protein Intake and Bone Health: The Influence of Belief Systems on the Conduct of Nutritional Science." *American Journal of Clinical Nutrition* 73 (2001): 5–6.

Heaney, R. P., R. R. Recker, M. R. Stegman, and A. J. Moy. "Calcium Absorption in Women: Relationships to Calcium Intake, Estrogen Status, and Age." *Journal of Bone and Mineral Research* 4 (1989): 469–475.

Heaney, R. P., R. R. Recker, and C. M. Weaver. "Absorbability of Calcium Sources: The Limited Role of Solubility." *Calcified Tissue International* 46 (1990): 300–304.

Heaney, R. P., P. D. Saville, and R. R. Recker. "Calcium Absorption as a Function of Calcium Intake." *Journal of Laboratory and Clinical Medicine* 85 (1975): 881–890.

Heaney, R. P., and T. G. Skillman. "Calcium Metabolism in Normal Human Pregnancy." *Journal of Clinical Endocrinology and Metabolism* 33 (1971): 661–670.

Kalkwarf, H. J., B. L. Specker, D. C. Bianchi, J. Ranz, and M. Ho. "The Effect of Calcium Supplementation on Bone Density during Lactation and after Weaning." *New England Journal of Medicine* 337 (1997): 523–528.

Kurtz, T. W., H. A. Al-Bander, and R. C. Morris. "'Salt Sensitive' Essential Hypertension in Men." *New England Journal of Medicine* 317 (1987): 1043–1048.

Lu, P. W., J. N. Briody, G. D. Ogle, K. Morley, I. R. Humphries, J. Allen, R. Howman-Giles, D. Sillence, and C. T. Cowell. "Bone Mineral Density of Total Body, Spine, and Femoral Neck in Children and Young Adults: A Cross-Sectional and Longitudinal Study." *Journal of Bone and Mineral Research* 9 (1994): 1451–1458.

Martin, A. D., D. A. Bailey, and H. A. McKay. "Bone Mineral and Calcium Accretion during Puberty." *American Journal of Clinical Nutrition* 66 (1997): 611–615.

Prince, R. L., M. Smith, I. M. Dick, R. I. Price, P. G. Webb, N. K. Henderson, and M. M. Harris. "Prevention of Postmenopausal Osteoporosis: A Comparative Study of Exercise, Calcium Supplementation, and Hormone-Replacement Therapy." *New England Journal of Medicine* 325 (1991): 1189–1195.

Recker, R. R., K. M. Davies, S. M. Hinders, R. P. Heaney, M. R. Stegman, and D. B. Kimmel. "Bone Gain in Young Adult Women." *Journal of the American Medical Association* 268 (1992): 2403–2408.

Riis, B., K. Thomsen, and C. Christiansen. "Does Calcium Supplementation Prevent Postmenopausal Bone Loss?" *New England Journal of Medicine* 316: 173–177.

Specker, B. L., A. Beck, H. Kalkwarf, and M. Ho. "Randomized Trial of Varying Mineral Intake on Total Body Bone Mineral Accretion during the First Year of Life." *Pediatrics* 99 (1997): e12.

Wallace, B. A., and R. G. Cumming. "Systematic Review of Randomized Trials of the Effect of Exercise on Bone Mass in Pre- and Postmenopausal Women." *Calcified Tissue International* 67 (2000): 10–18.

World Health Organization. *Assessment of Fracture Risk and Its Application to Screening for Postmenopausal Osteoporosis.* Geneva, Switzerland: World Health Organization, 1994.

World Health Organization, Institute of Medicine. *Dietary Reference Intakes for Calcium, Phosphorous, Magnesium, Vitamin D, and Fluoride.* Washington, D.C.: National Academy Press, 1997.

Wosje, K. S., and B. L. Specker. "Role of Calcium in Bone Health during Childhood." *Nutrition Reviews* 58 (2000): 253–268.

Karen S. Wosje

CALIFORNIA. *See* **United States.**

CALORIC INTAKE. The calorie is a unit of heat energy required to raise the temperature of 1 gram (1 milliliter) of water 1°C from 14.5° to 15.5°C. The calorie is a very small unit; and although it is used colloquially, the energy measured is 1,000 gram calories or kilocalories (kcal). Another unit of energy is the joule: 1 kcal = 4.184 kJ. Calories are used as a unit to measure the energy in food as well as the energy produced, stored, and utilized by living organisms.

Calories in Food

Foods are comprised of carbohydrates, fats, proteins, vitamins, minerals, and water. The energy-yielding nutrients

TABLE 1

Caloric content of common foods

Food	Serving size	Weight (grams)	Calories
Beer	12 fl. oz.	356	146
Cheddar cheese	1 oz.	28	114
Margarine	1 Tbsp.	14	50
Apple	2³/₄ in. diameter	138	80
White bread	1 slice	25	65
Doughnut, cake plain	3¹/₄ in. diameter	50	210
Rice, white	1 cup cooked	205	264
Beef patty	3 in. X ⁵/₈ in., 21 percent fat	85	236
Chicken breast, fried	1 piece batter dipped	140	364
Broccoli	1 cup cooked	180	50
Corn	On cob, 5 in. long	77	83

are carbohydrates, fats, and proteins. When foods are oxidized or burned, they yield approximately 4.0 calories/gram for proteins and carbohydrates and 9.0 calories/gram for fats. Most foods contain mixtures of the three macronutrients but are classified by the predominant nutrient. For example, protein-riched foods such as beef also contain fat. Table 1 presents a sample of ten common foods, their weights, serving sizes, and calories. Daily caloric consumption is assessed in a number of ways: 24-hour dietary recalls, food intake diaries, weighing food before it is eaten, and using food labels on packaged foods.

In the early to mid-1990s, world food supply estimates of available calories per person per day ranged from 2,099 kcal in sub-Saharan African countries to 3,600 kcal in North America with averages of 2,573 kcal for developing countries and 3,356 kcal for industrialized countries. The percentages of calories are estimated to be 70.4 and 52.3 from carbohydrate, 19.6 and 35.4 from fat, and 10.0 and 12.3 from protein for developing and industrialized countries, respectively.

The energy requirements for humans are established by national and international organizations (for example, World Health Organization). The Recommended Dietary Allowances (RDAs), or more recently, the Dietary Reference Intakes (DRIs) are shown in Table 2. These caloric recommendations are based on the average needs for an individual based on age and sex with additional allowances for pregnancy and lactation. Restricted intakes lead to growth faltering in weight and height; and conversely, a surfeit of calories leads to excess energy stores and obesity. For example, a short and thin, preadolescent child with a slow rate of growth along the fifth percentile requires about 17 percent less dietary energy than a child following the average growth trajectory at the fiftieth percentile.

Energy Expenditure

Caloric needs are based on energetic demands related to body size and activity. Overall caloric demands per kilo-gram of body weight are extremely high from conception through infancy, and decrease thereafter. Total Daily Energy Expenditure (TDEE) is a combination of the Basal Metabolic Rate (BMR) sometimes called the Resting Metabolic Rate (RMR) and Physical Activity Level (PAL). The BMR is the minimum energy expenditure for maintenance of respiration, circulation, body temperature, and other vegetative functions. It is based on body size, growth, reproduction, diurnal hormonal variation, other physiological conditions, and thermoregulation related to environmental temperature. The BMR accounts for approximately two-thirds of the TDEE. In addition, about 10 percent of energy intake is expended in dietary thermogenesis or the energy costs of processing food.

Metabolic rate can be obtained by direct calorimetry that measures the total quantity of heat liberated from the body in a specially constructed chamber. With direct calorimetry, a young male with an average American diet generates 4.82 calories for every liter of oxygen consumed. Because direct measurements involve expensive equipment in a laboratory setting, most of the calculations for caloric needs are done with indirect calorimetry. Indirect calorimetry uses the differences in the concentrations of inhaled and exhaled oxygen to estimate energy use. The law of conservation of energy states that there must be a balance between all forms of energy expended or absorbed.

Reference equations are used most frequently to estimate energy needs and expenditures. Sets of reference

TABLE 2

Recommended dietary allowances for energy

Age (year)	Energy (kcal)
Infants	
0.0–0.5	650
0.5–1.6	850
Children	
1–3	1,300
4–6	1,800
7–10	2,000
Males	
11–14	2,500
15–18	3,000
19–24	2,900
25–50	2,900
51+	2,300
Females	
11–14	2,200
15–18	2,200
19–24	2,200
25–50	2,200
51+	1,900
Pregnant	+300
Lactating	
1st 6 mo.	+500
2nd 6 mo.	+500

equations for BMR and standard energy expenditures for activities or PAL are routinely used in assessing an individual's TDEE. For adults, PAL ranges from 1.4 to 2.10 for light to very heavy work. For example, daily energy expenditure for a 120-pound (54.4-kg) woman who has a sedentary office job would be approximately:

BMR = 14.7(54.4) + 496 = 1,296 kcal
TDEE = PAL × BMR = 1.56 × 1,296 = 2,022 kcal.

Body weight is a key variable in energy expenditure. Walking at 3.5 miles/hour expends 0.035 kcal/min which would be 3.9, 5.2, and 7.0 kcal/min for individuals weighing 110, 150, and 200 pounds, respectively.

Individual differences in metabolic mechanisms are not well understood. Remarkably, for most adults, the sensitivity of the energy balance system for change is less than one percent per year. The "average" American adult male contains 140,000 kilocalories of energy in body fat, 24,000 kilocalories in protein, and only about 800 kilocalories in carbohydrate. Consequently, an individual consuming 2,000 kilocalories per day of which 40 percent is carbohydrate will ingest an amount of carbohydrate comparable to body stores, protein intake will average only about one percent, and fat intake will be considerably less than one percent of total body stores.

Weight Control and Energy Balance

Caloric intake and expenditure are factors in the growing worldwide epidemic of obesity. It is estimated that in the United States, 35 percent of adults eighteen years of age and older are overweight or obese based on weight for height standards. The rising prevalence of obesity is due to an increase in intake of calorically dense foods and a decrease of energy expenditure with modernization, including increases in transportation, decreases in subsistence activities, increases in thermally regulated environments, and decreases in energy demands due to chronic illness. Weight reduction hinges on reducing caloric intake while maintaining micronutrient balance and fiber and water intake. Traditionally, recommended diets were labeled by their caloric content, such as the "1,200 calorie diet." Some diets have focused on the reduction of fat because each gram of fat is twice as calorically dense as a gram of carbohydrate or protein. Interventions also emphasize increased voluntary energy expenditure through daily routines such as walking or formal exercise programs. Pharmacological interventions directly influence energy balance by increasing BMR, decreasing absorption of fat calories, or decreasing transit time through the gut, and indirectly by altering hunger and satiety.

Low-energy intake compromises growth in vital tissues, lowers basal metabolic rate, and reduces work capacity relative to individuals with sufficient energy intake. People develop behavioral strategies to reduce muscular activity to conserve energy. For undernourished populations, interventions target increasing caloric intakes and reducing macro- and micronutrient deficiencies.

Finally, energy in kilocalories or joules has been used for measuring the flow of energy through ecological systems. Energy flow analyses measure time and task allocations in various subsistence activities as well as the biological characteristics of human and nonhuman populations in an ecosystem.

See also **Assessment of Nutritional Status; Composition of Food; Dietary System: A Historical Perspective; Eating: Anatomy and Physiology of Eating; Nutrient Requirements; Nutrition; Obesity; Physical Activity and Nutrition.**

BIBLIOGRAPHY

Bray, George A. "Obesity—A Disease of Nutrient or Energy Balance?" *Nutrition Reviews* 45 (1987): 33–43.

FAOSTAT. *Computerized Information Series: Food Balance Sheets 1961–1994.* Rome: Food and Agricultural Organization, 1996.

Food and Agricultural Organization. *World Food Supplies and Prevalence of Hunger.* Rome: Food and Agricultural Organization, 1992.

Food and Agricultural Organization/World Health Organization/United Nations University. *Energy and Protein Requirements.* Geneva: WHO Technical Report Series No. 724, 1985.

Food and Nutrition Board. *Recommended Dietary Allowances.* 10th ed. Washington, D.C.: National Research Council/National Academy of Science, 1989.

Ulijaszek, Stanley J. *Human Energetics in Biological Anthropology.* Cambridge: Cambridge University Press, 1995.

U.S. Department of Agriculture. *Nutritive Value of Foods.* Home and Garden Bulletin No. 72. Washington, D.C.: USDA, 1986.

Leslie Sue Lieberman

CALORIE. The calorie is a unit for measuring heat energy, and it is usually used as the unit for food energy and of energy expenditure. Media and lay attention to food, exercise, and health, as well as the greater prevalence of obesity during the past few decades, has resulted in a cultural preoccupation with caloric intake and expenditure in industrialized nations. Heat is that which produces a change in temperature. Heat was formerly regarded as a substance called "caloric," but it came to be viewed as the random motion of molecules.

The calorie has traditionally been defined as the amount of heat required to raise the temperature of 1 gram of water by 1.8°F (1.0°C), usually defined as from 58.1°F to 59.9°F (14.5°C to 15.5°C), under normal atmospheric conditions. Because electrical measurements can be standardized more accurately than heat measurements, a calorie is officially defined as equivalent to 4.186 joule. A joule is defined, in "force × distance" units, as 1 Newton meter, which is equal to (1 kg m/s^2) × (1m) or 1 kg m^2/s^2. Energy values are expressed as joules when the Système International d'Unités, which is recommended for all scientific purposes, is required.

Food energy values and energy expenditures are commonly expressed as the number of kilocalories (kcal). One kcal is equal to 1000 calories or 4.186 kJ or 0.004186 MJ. Although the terms "calorie" and "large calorie" have frequently been used in place of kilocalorie in the nutrition literature and for food labeling purposes, these alternative terms are confusing, and their use is discouraged.

Measurement of Energy Values of Foods

The energy in foods is present as chemical energy; it can be measured by the heat evolved when the food is oxidized or combusted. Although energy transformations normally involve friction and heat conduction, which cause the changes of one form of energy to another to be incomplete, various forms of energy normally can be converted completely to heat. The caloric value of a food may be determined by burning weighed samples of the food in an oxygen atmosphere in an apparatus called a calorimeter, which is designed to allow measurement of the heat released by combustion of the fuel or food. The total amount of heat produced or consumed when a chemical system changes from an initial state to a final state is independent of the way this change is brought about (the law of Hess or the law of constant heat sums). Thus the complete oxidation of a compound, such as glucose, to CO_2 and H_2O produces the same amount of heat whether the process is carried out in a calorimeter or by metabolism within the body.

Heats of combustion are not accurate reflections of the amount of energy available to the body, however, because the body does not completely absorb and metabolize ingested nutrients. The energy lost in the excreta (feces and urine) must be subtracted from the total energy value of the food to obtain the amount of energy available to the body from consumption of the food. The caloric values of foods reported in food composition tables are "physiological fuel values," also referred to as "available energy" or "metabolizable energy" values. They are not total energy values.

Physiological Fuel Values of Foods

The physiological fuel value of a food or a food component may be determined by measuring the heat of combustion of the food in a calorimeter and then multiplying the heat of combustion by correction factors for incomplete digestion and incomplete oxidation of the food in the body. In about 1900, Wilbur Olin Atwater and his associates at the Connecticut (Storrs) Agriculture Experiment Station used this approach to determine the physiological fuel values of a number of food components (i.e., the protein, fat, and carbohydrate isolated from various foods). They determined factors appropriate for individual foods or groups of foods, and they proposed the general physiological fuel equivalents of 4.0, 8.9, and 4.0 kcal per gram of dietary protein, fat, and carbohydrate re-

spectively for application to the mixed American diet. These factors are commonly rounded to 4, 9, and 4 kcal per gram (17, 36, and 17 kJ per gram) respectively for protein, fat, and carbohydrate. The conversion factors determined by Atwater and his associates remain in use in the twenty-first century, and energy values of foods are calculated using these factors. The energy values (physiological fuel values) reported in food composition tables are commonly estimated by determination of the proximate composition of each food (i.e., the water, protein, fat, carbohydrate, and ash contents) followed by multiplication of the amount of each energy-yielding component by the appropriate conversion factor.

See also **Caloric Intake**; **Dietary Assessment**; **Nutrition**.

BIBLIOGRAPHY

Kleiber, Max. *The Fire of Life: An Introduction to Animal Energetics.* New York: Wiley, 1961.

Kriketos, Adamandia D., John C. Peters, and James O. Hill. "Cellular and Whole-Animal Energetics." In *Biochemical and Physiological Aspects of Human Nutrition*, edited by Martha H. Stipanuk. Philadelphia: Saunders, 2000.

Merrill, A. L., and B. K. Watt. *Energy Values of Foods . . . Basis and Derivations.* USDA Agriculture Handbook No. 74. Washington, D.C.: U.S. Government Printing Office, 1973.

Martha H. Stipanuk

CANADA. Canada is a vast country touched by three oceans, and it holds within its boundaries prairies, hills, mountains, semidesert and desert country, rocky thin-soiled lands, a multitude of lakes, enormous forests, and Arctic tundra. While the terrain varies greatly, there is a commonality across Canada, and that is the severity of winter. Few European immigrants in Canada's early history were prepared for the cold, and from the beginning, Canadians struggled with the elements for their survival. This was a defining factor in the development of Canadian cuisine. But it is the people of Canada who, more than the land and weather, created Canada's cookery. From the First Nations people to the waves of immigrants from every country in the world, Canada's cuisine became distinctly regional.

Diversity has been a characteristic of Canadian cuisine from the beginning of settlement. In the seventeenth century, the first Europeans in Canada encountered a highly varied population of Native Peoples, for example, hunters and gatherers including the Inuit in the Arctic; agricultural people in parts of southern Quebec and Ontario; buffalo hunters on the plains; and fishermen on the West Coast among the nearly sedentary Pacific North Coastal people.

By the end of the eighteenth century, the dominant groups in Canada were British (particularly English and Scots), French, and American Loyalists. The cuisine that

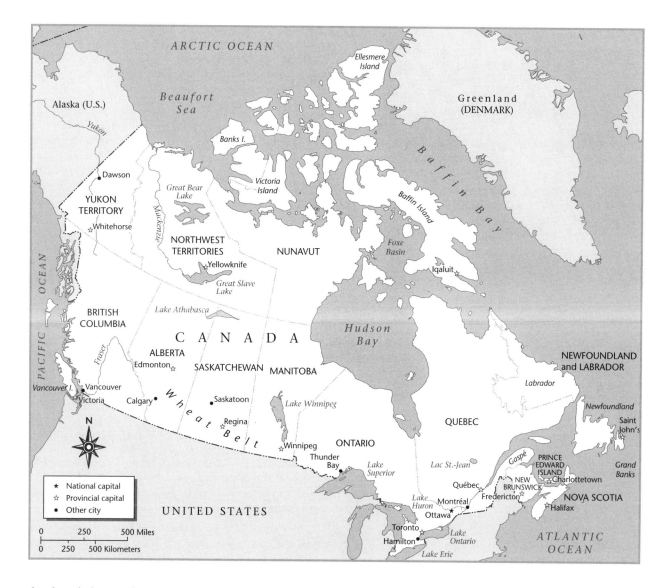

developed during the nineteenth and first half of the twentieth century reflected these influences. There were strong overtones of French cookery in Quebec, British influences in English-speaking Canada, and a strong import of culinary culture from the United States. While there were many ethnic groups in Canada by the end of World War II, British-American cookery dominated Canadian cookery. A partial exception to this generalization was the Chinese influence. Peasants from southern China immigrated to "Golden Mountain" (Canada or, more specifically, British Columbia) beginning in the 1850s. Many were employed in construction and the building of the railroad. As with other cultural groups, they were discriminated against, but they introduced Canadians to Chinese cuisine by opening Chinese restaurants in nearly every village and city across Canada.

In spite of the cultural dominance of English-speaking Canadians, other ethnic immigrant groups often settled in regional pockets where they maintained their language and their culinary traditions. Coming from different regions in their home countries, they melded traditions together. For example, in the Ukraine, women made *pysanky* (eggs decorated with ritualistic symbols) according to their local traditions, but in Canada, they drew designs from many regions of Ukraine. Northern and Southern Italian foods such as pasta and polenta, likewise, were simply "Italian" in Canada.

Until after World War II, ethnic foods were rarely written about in Canadian food magazines or cookbooks, and ethnic recipes were highly modified. In a 1920s community cookbook, for example, a chop suey recipe was a mixture of fried hamburger, rice, tomatoes, and onions, baked for an hour; and spaghetti was cooked meat, spaghetti, onion, butter, green pepper, and canned tomato soup, baked with buttered bread crumbs; both were seasoned only with salt and pepper. In the 1970s the milieu changed when, under the leadership of Pierre Trudeau, Canada adopted a policy of multiculturalism. It then became the fashion to share ethnicity, and the easiest way was through cookery. The foods that ethnic

Like the United States, Canada is home to many ethnic communities. These Greek Canadians are preparing traditional Easter pastries in Vancouver, British Columbia. © ANNIE GRIFFITHS BELT/CORBIS.

groups had eaten in the privacy of their homes became de rigueur.

After World War II, fast-food eateries and chain restaurants serving inexpensive, mass-produced foods swept across North America. Franchises on the U.S. model were adopted and Canadians quickly developed their own fast food restaurants for hamburgers, fried chicken, and pizza. A favorite fast-food chain is Tim Horton Donuts, a coffee and donut shop. Popular Canadian restaurant chains that developed were "road houses" serving grilled foods and pasta. The Americanization of Canadian foods and foodways was influenced also by food articles in American magazines and by television food shows.

Canadian cuisine is strongly regional in character with American influences. The eating pattern of three meals a day, the popularity of many foods, the importation of fresh produce and manufactured foods, and the eating of particular foods at the feasts of Thanksgiving, Christmas, and Easter are common denominators of the cuisine of both the United States and Canada. The real difference is the highly visible regional cuisines of Canada, based on the available ingredients and the ethnic groups who settled in these regions. Canadian cuisine cannot be understood without examining these regional traditions.

Newfoundland: A Survival Cuisine

From the early sixteenth century, the huge and lucrative cod fisheries on the coasts surrounding this island province and the Grand Banks offshore attracted fishing vessels manned by Basque, Portuguese, French, and British sailors. Before settlement, these groups salted cod in summer fish-drying camps, and then dried it on "flakes." A product that could keep indefinitely, salt cod was eaten in Europe for centuries. Eventually the Eng-

lish settled in the north and west, followed by the Irish, in St. John's and the east coast, and French along the south shore. Newfoundland's environment is harsh and demanding with deceivingly warm but short summers. The cuisine that developed was simple and entrenched.

Only a few ingredients are needed to make rib-sticking, hearty, and soul-satisfying meals. Fish (cod) and root vegetables form the basis of the Newfoundlanders' diet. There is little agriculture on the island, but root vegetables can be grown there, and tiny vegetable garden plots are often found along the roadside on the western coast. Potatoes, carrots, onions, turnips, parsnips, and cabbage are mainstays.

In 1992 the cod stocks crashed on the Grand Banks, and a moratorium was placed on commercial fishing in Canadian waters on the Banks. Although a way of life for Newfoundlanders seemed to have been lost, cod remains their favorite food. While the major cod fisheries are still closed, some fish is available on the southern coast, and local inhabitants are allowed to "jig" for cod two weekends a year. When a Newfoundlander says the word "fish," he or she means "cod," which, over the centuries, has been the preferred dish. A fresh cod dinner is Newfoundland comfort food. A thick piece of cod, usually grilled or poached, is served with mashed potatoes, mixed peas and carrots, coleslaw and fluffy white rolls. Delicacies are cod tongues and cheeks, either sautéed or deep-fried. Salt cod is prepared most commonly as fish 'n' brewis (also called "fisherman's brewis"). The salted fish is soaked, shredded, and cooked with dried bread chunks (hardtack) until thick, and schruncheons (fried diced salt pork) with its fat is poured over the mixture.

Pea soup (a thick potage of yellow split peas with diced turnips, carrots, and potatoes) can be traced back to the daily fare of sixteenth-century fishermen—with salt beef added on Sundays. Split peas are also used to make pease pudding by dropping a pudding bag of peas into Jigg's dinner, a boiled dinner of salt beef, onions, potatoes, carrots, and turnips.

To supplement and vary the fish and salt-beef diet, many men hunt partridge, ptarmigan, rabbits, turr (a seabird), moose, caribou, and deer. Moose is preferred only because it will fill the hunter's freezer—and his neighbors'—and last through the winter. A traditional wild-game dish is flipper pie made from seal flippers, carefully prepared and cooked in a pastry. The wilds also provide berries in abundance, eaten fresh and preserved for the long winter, either frozen for pies and other desserts or made into jams. Favorites are blueberries, strawberries, blackberries, raspberries, partridgeberries (lignonberries), and yellow baking apples (cloud berries).

More than anything else, Newfoundlanders are known for fun: parties, Newfoundland fiddling, and rum. Screech, a dark rum, was named because American servicemen during World War II found it made them "screech." Those "from away" may undergo a Newfoundland initiation by tossing back Screech and reciting an intonation, always with good humor, and sometimes accompanied by kissing a cod.

The Maritime Provinces: An Entrenched Cuisine

The cuisine of the Maritime provinces of Nova Scotia, New Brunswick, and Prince Edward Island (P.E.I.) is a bittersweet one—bitter because so many people were dislocated, either within the Maritimes or because they had to leave their homelands, sweet because the Maritime cuisine was a result. Early migration into the Atlantic provinces generally took place of necessity. Power struggles between France and England led to the forced displacement of the French Acadians in 1755, and American planters took over their rich farmlands. Scattered to many countries, some Acadians returned after 1763, not to their rich farmlands but to less desirable land, or they turned to fishing. Settling in parts of New Brunswick, Nova Scotia, and Quebec, they developed a distinct cuisine in each area: buckwheat pancakes, *poutine râpée* (dumpling stuffed with salt pork), *râpure* (grated potato and chicken or seafood pie), *fricots* (stews), rabbit pies, and many other traditional dishes.

Later in the century, in 1783, United Empire Loyalists, scorned in the United States, made their way into the Maritimes. These American Loyalists brought New England food traditions, popularizing corn in many forms (corn-on-the-cob, johnnycakes, corn puddings, and Anadama or Yankee bread), and the Saturday night custom of baked beans and brown bread. Freed African loyalists and others of African descent also came north. Blacks settling in the Shelburne area brought Southern American cooking: deep-fat frying, barbecued meat, the use of corn meal and hominy, pork, rice, and fish. Germans left for Lunenberg, Nova Scotia, in 1753 and contributed Solomon Gundy (pickled herring), soused eels, and sauerkraut. Scots in Cape Breton brought oat cakes and porridge bread. These early settlers created distinct regional cuisines. But the one traditional meal common to the Maritimes is Dutch mess, also called hugger-in-buff, fish and schrunchions, or house bankin, depending upon where one lives. Salt cod is soaked, then cooked; potatoes are boiled in the fish broth; salt pork and onions are fried, vinegar and cream added and poured over the cod and potatoes. The next day, leftovers are mashed and made into fish cakes.

The abundant fish and shellfish were the key ingredients defining early Maritime cuisine, and they continue to do so today. These seafoods, along with root vegetables, dried peas, cabbage, and trade goods from Britain formed the basic components used in early eastern Canadian cookery. Early English colonists were dependent upon Great Britain for food, and these supplies grew into a thriving trade of tea, sugar, spices (ginger was a favorite), and dried fruits. The triangular trade between England, New England, and the Caribbean brought molasses, rum, and ginger from the Caribbean. Halifax, the

THE ORDER OF GOOD CHEER

The small band of French explorers at Port Royal, Nova Scotia, anticipated the winter of 1606 with dread. The previous winter many of their men had died from a mysterious "land-sickness." The illness was thought to be caused by ill-temper, idleness, and discontent. Samuel de Champlain, a member of the band, founded *L'ordre de bon temps* (the Order of Good Cheer) to prevent the illness. The object of the society was to go hunting and fishing for wild game and seafood that could be served up in a series of feasts held throughout the winter.

The feasting was met with great enthusiasm by Chief Henri Membertou and his Mi'kmaq followers, who joined the hunting forays and were invited to the grand dinners. It was the custom of the Mi'kmaq to share their food with whoever was in the vicinity, and the French reciprocated this generosity. The variety of raw ingredients for their meals was extensive—venison, moose, beaver, ducks and geese, salmon and trout caught through the ice, scallops, cockles, sea urchin, crabs, and lobster. In addition to these foods, there was plenty of wine and provisions from France.

Although we do not know the dishes prepared for the feasts, the gentlemen in the group were accustomed to sophisticated food. Champlain had been a visitor to the court of Henry IV; one of the men wrote in his diary that their food was as good as roastmeats from the cook shops of Paris. As well, Champlain kept stocked fish ponds near the Habitation.

The Order did help to fend off the illness (scurvy) during the winter. More than anything else, however, the lasting benefit of the dinners was an enduring friendship between the Mi'kmaq and the French. As others have found, the dining table is much better than a negotiating table for mediating conflicts between cultures. The spirit of the Order of Good Cheer is a culinary legacy to Canadians.

early center of British social life, retains a distinct English character. Gaily signed pubs serve meat pies and fish and chips. British dishes linger—roast beef with Yorkshire pudding, trifle, and gingerbread.

Each Maritime province has vast coastal areas, and cod is common to all. Products of the sea vary somewhat in each province. Prince Edward Island is associated with lobster fisheries, aqua-cultured blue mussels, Malpeque oysters, and Irish moss. Nova Scotia is known for Digby scallops and dulse (a reddish seaweed). New Brunswick

POOR MAN'S FARE

Pâté à la râpure (or rappie pie, the English name) is a traditional Acadian dish with its roots in the frugality of French women. After the British victory in Nova Scotia in the late eighteenth century, some families who had been expelled from the fertile Annapolis Valley returned, but to fishing or to farming marginal land. Times were extremely hard, but they were able to cultivate potatoes—and the men liked their white shirts starched. The women made starch by grating potatoes, squeezing out the starch, and boiling the white shirts in the extract. Since they couldn't waste the potato gratings, they put them into a pan with lobster or fish and baked this mixture. The result, distinctly different from sliced and baked potatoes, was a gelatinous, translucent mixture flavored with seafood, called *râpure.* Today the tradition continues and, although they still squeeze out the starch to give *râpure* its distinct character, the starch is seldom used for stiffening white shirts.

fishes for Fundy salmon, smelt, trout, and shad. Samphire greens (eaten locally) are harvested from the shores of each of these provinces. In countryside Nova Scotia, roadside "canteens," one-room buildings, sell some of the region's best seafood: lobster or clam rolls, fried scallops, or fried fish—all seafoods cooked fresh from the sea.

The harvest from the land is also regional. Nova Scotia is known for its Annapolis Valley apple orchards, New Brunswick for its maple syrup and wild chanterelles, and P.E.I. for its potatoes. New Brunswick fiddleheads from the Ostrich fern are a gourmet delicacy picked in early spring before the fronds open, and are cooked as a vegetable.

By the early 1800s, established food traditions had become associated with a way of life, and to a great extent, have remained impervious to change. Even the large migrations of ethnic groups after World War II were insufficient to displace these three-hundred-year-old culinary traditions.

Quebec: A Distinct Cuisine

Quebecois consider themselves a distinct society, and this is reflected in their cuisine. Restaurant menus are written in French, and the cuisine is distinctly French, but with a difference: most of all, the love of—even obsession with—good food and its celebration, the use of flavorful sauces, the elaboration of courses, the use of fresh ingredients, and the respect for their chefs. The first European settlers in Canada in the early seventeenth century were French. They maintained close ties with their mother country until after the English conquest in the mid-eighteenth century. At that time, communication with France was cut off.

Thus, many traditional Quebec dishes resemble those prepared in medieval and early Renaissance France. Well-known favorites across Quebec are *cretons* (a rich pork pâté), *tourtière* (meat pie), *ragoût de pattes et de boulettes* (pigs' feet and meatball stew), *les cipaille* or *cipâte* (baked casserole made by layering pastry with meat, poultry, and/or seafood), and *galettes de sarrasin* (buckwheat pancakes). A hearty fare, originally cooked for fishermen, farmers, and loggers, they are today reserved for family gatherings and holidays.

The abundance of wild game and the land available to provide forage for it probably influenced Quebec's cuisine more than any other factor. This provided ordinary settlers with meat and gave them an equality with royalty unknown to the seventeenth-century French peasant. Indeed, in France at that time, food was frequently scarce. It is not surprising that the Quebecois' diet was rich in meat, poultry, and fish and that regional dishes were made with these ingredients.

Although maintaining their French heritage, the Quebecois incorporated ingredients and dishes from other cultures. From the beginning, the French had close ties with aboriginal peoples whose culture dictated that they share game and fish with their friends. The Native Peoples showed them the edible wild flora and fauna, and the French were quick to incorporate wild game, berries, and maple sugar into their diet. It should be noted that corn, beans, and squash had already been introduced into France before Quebec was colonized, and potatoes are thought to have been introduced by the British. American Loyalists and British immigrants after 1755 also influenced Quebec cookery; the French especially liked sweet British desserts, many of them made with molasses. Cultural influences continue today as with the Middle Eastern innovation *mechoui*, a popular party at which a whole animal is barbecued, usually wild game like buffalo or wild boar. Quebec cities, like other Canadian centers, have a multicultural character. This is especially true of Montreal, where there are more French-speaking immigrants than in other major Canadian cities: Haitians, Lebanese, and Vietnamese have all influenced Quebec's cookery, particularly in their family-owned restaurants and their ingredients in small grocery stores. Moreover, Montreal's population contains a mix of people speaking a multitude of languages who have contributed their foodways to the cultural mix of this city.

Quebec's cuisine is a highly regional one. The Institut de Tourisme et d'Hôtellerie du Québec has identified at least seventeen gastronomical regions within the province and has searched out more than 30,000 regional recipes. In the Gaspé, for instance, salt is used liberally and salmon layered with pastry is their version of *cipâte*. People from the Lac Saint-Jean area are called "*les Bluets*" (blueberries), and these berries are made into *grandpères* (dumplings cooked in blueberry sauce) or a blueberry *cipaille*. Gourgane beans brought from Europe are unique to this area and are often made into *soupe aux gourganes*, a filling bean, barley, and vegetable potage.

Today, young Quebec-trained chefs search out local ingredients, experiment with them, and to some extent are turning to France for inspiration. Artisanal breads, soft cheeses, goat cheeses, Normandy-style apple cider, local wines, organically grown vegetables, white asparagus, fresh herbs (especially summer savory), wild mushrooms, rabbits, caribou, and wild game birds are some of the ingredients finding their way onto the Quebec table. The Quebec diet is changing but the accent remains distinctly French Quebec.

Ontario: A Dynamic Cuisine

The French and then the British and, shortly thereafter, American Loyalist immigrants had close contact with members of the Iroquoian tribes. From these original farming inhabitants, the immigrants learned how to plant corn, beans, squash, Jerusalem artichokes, and sunflowers, and to tap the maple trees for their sweet sugar. In the early days of settlement, wild game and fresh fish from the streams and the many lakes in Ontario were plentiful. The French left little impact upon Ontario's cuisine, but the English foodways became dominant: their style of eating and especially their love of sweets, roasted beef and pork, cooked root vegetables, white bread, and tea. One of the first tasks the settlers had was to build grist mills to grind wheat for their cakes and breads. They found the farmland in southern Ontario to be fertile, and most of the crops from their homelands flourished. Dairy herds were established, which led in the nineteenth century to a significant trade in cheddar cheese with England and the popularity of this cheese in Ontario.

There were two influential groups who came north with the Loyalists at the end of the eighteenth century. The Iroquois under the leadership of Joseph Brant settled near Brandford to form the Six Nations. An agricultural people, they grew the "Three Sisters"—corn, beans, and squash—and reinforced the growth and use of these crops in Ontario. The other group was the Pennsylvania German Mennonites who took up farming in the Waterloo area. When the Ontario Mennonites chose their food preparations from the Pennsylvania German recipe repertoire, a difference appeared. While the recipes they loved best were still distinctly Mennonite, the choices of foods changed. In Ontario, they are known for summer sausages, *Nusschinken* (cool-smoked ham), smoked pork chops, *Koch Käse* (a runny cooked whey cheese flavored with caraway seed, smeared on bread with apple butter), shoofly pie made with maple syrup, Dutch apple pie, doughnuts, and mint tea.

CABIN AU SUCRE

Where the sugar maples grow in Quebec, there will be "sugar shacks." From the beginning of settlement, colonists tapped the clear maple sap to produce sugar for the year's use as a sweetener. "Spiles," originally wooden tubes with sharpened ends and now metal tubes with hooks for buckets or tubing, were placed in holes drilled into the sugar maple trees. When the nights were cold and days warm, the sap flowed. In the old days, horses hauled tubs of the clear liquid to a covered shed where the sap was boiled down day and night. It took thirty to forty buckets of sap to produce one bucket of golden maple syrup. Men and boys stayed for weeks in the bush tending the fires and watching the syrup so that it would not burn. Today, when one drives through Quebec in the early spring before the snow melts, buckets adorning maple trees and smoke billowing from the bush are a common sight. From this, today's *cabin au sucre,* or sugar shack, has become a Quebec feature that anyone can enjoy. City folk today flock to the *cabins au sucre* to feast on maple-drenched dishes, to dance, and to drink. Outdoors, children are treated to *la tire,* syrup boiled down to a taffy and hardened on snow, and horses draw wagons of fun-seekers into the bush to view the miles of plastic tubing collecting the clear sap—Quebec "gold."

In the nineteenth century, southern Ontario was the terminus of the "underground railroad," offering shelter to American blacks escaping slavery. They brought Southern American cookery to Ontario. Irish, Scots, English, and other groups streamed into Ontario during this century, reinforcing British cuisine. Rutabagas (called turnips) were standard winter fare. Steamed carrot pudding became a Christmas tradition. China tea cups were given to brides, and the prescribed wedding cake was a dark fruit cake.

Some ethnic groups entering Ontario in the nineteenth and twentieth centuries formed communities around Ontario: the Poles in Wilno, the Portuguese in Strathroy, the Italians in Guelph, the Scots in the Renfrew valley near Ottawa, the Finns in Thunder Bay, and Ukrainians and Eastern Europeans in Hamilton. This is not to say that myriad cultural groups are not found in these areas; the point is that in these areas, the home cuisine and the language of these settlers was maintained.

Coming primarily from politically troubled parts of the world, approximately 175,000 immigrants annually enter Canada. Of these, about half locate in Ontario, the majority moving into the Toronto area. Immediately after World War II came Italians, Eastern Europeans, British war brides, and many others. In the 1970s, after Canada's newly entrenched multicultural policy, immigrants streamed in from Hong Kong, Vietnam, Somalia, Ethiopia, Croatia, Serbia, India, Sri Lanka, the Middle East, and other countries. Ontario had long served up a meat, potato, and root vegetable table, but the influx of new people and their culinary traditions meant a developing and rapidly changing gastronomy in Ontario, led by Toronto.

Toronto, the most culturally diverse city in Canada, is a reflection of Canadian multiculturalism in the make-up of its population and in its cuisine. There are five Chinatowns in the Toronto area, most recently settled by affluent Chinese from Hong Kong, and Chinese restaurants represent every region in China. Upscale restaurants serve Italian, Portuguese, Greek, Indian, Lebanese, Caribbean, and American cuisine, but the neighborhood dining spots are the best places to find the comfort food of nearly every nation in the world and at a reasonable price.

As a result of this diversity, Ontario is somewhat fragmented in its cuisine, but people in Ontario pride themselves on a receptivity to the flavors of the world. Hoisin sauce, *garam masala, baba ghanoush*, phyllo pastry, flat breads, *tzatziki*, pierogies, rice and beans, Jamaican meat patties, and espresso are, if not daily fare, part of Ontario's food repertoire.

The Prairies: Bread and Beef

Traveling west through the provinces of Manitoba, Saskatchewan, and Alberta, seemingly endless fields of wheat dominate the landscape. The wheat belt runs through all three prairie provinces, and wheat is an important economic export. Canadian cuisine has been affected by this bountiful crop since it was first planted on the Prairies in the last half of the nineteenth century. Canadians have a history of baking. In 1913 Five Roses Flour Company published a cookbook of recipes collected from women across Canada. By 1915 this book was found in 950,000 or nearly half of the homes in Canada. In addition to bread and pastry flours, durum wheat that is made into semolina flour for making pastas is grown here.

Prairie history, however, was not one of farming. Native Americans who dominated the plains lived primarily on buffalo, which they preserved by drying and mixing it with buffalo fat and berries, usually Saskatoon berries, and storing the mixture, known as pemmican, in containers made of buffalo skin. French and Scottish voyagers of the fur trade were provisioned with pemmican by Native People, and early settlers relied upon it. When overhunting led to the demise of the huge buffalo herds, beef took its place. A favored method of beef cookery is

grilling, and some cook it outdoors year round. For community barbecues, a hole is dug with a backhoe large enough for several cords of wood and an entire beef animal. After twelve hours of underground cooking, the beef is sliced and served with baked beans, fresh breads, salads, pickles and relishes, pies and cakes. Calgary, the home of the Canadian cowboy, glorifies the chuck wagon at "stampede," the annual rodeo. Chuck wagon races are an awaited event; the wagons dash pell-mell around a circle and at the finish line the cowboy "cook" must be the first to light the campfire. Chuck wagon expressions humorously included "baked wind pills" (baked beans), "CPR (Canadian Pacific Railroad) strawberries" (prunes), "dough-gods" (dumplings), "paperweights" (hot biscuits), and "yesterday, today and forever" (hash).

Until the 1950s, British settlers strongly influenced prairie cuisine. Stews, roast beef with Yorkshire pudding, and cakes named after British royalty (Prince of Wales, Prince Albert, King George and King Edward cakes) were popular. Today, Alberta is dotted with English tea houses, in as unlikely locations as a grain elevator.

While British cookery dominated the great wave of immigration (over a million) in the early part of the twentieth century, immigrant groups did not sacrifice their culinary traditions. Russian Mennonites settling in Manitoba, Icelandic immigrants in Grimli, Manitoba, Hutterites in Alberta, and the French who came early in settlement, particularly in Winnipeg, continued to cook their favorite recipes, as had their families before them.

Ukrainians, however, influenced prairie cookery. From the time they arrived at the end of the nineteenth century, they brought with them a tradition of wheat farming and cuisine. Mothers taught daughters the ancient art of making traditional breads and pysanky. They introduced *varenyky* or pierogies (flour-based rounds of dough stuffed with a unique Canadian potato and cheddar cheese mixture), stuffed cabbage rolls, *psyrizhky* (baked stuffed buns), and *paska* (Easter bread).

Newer immigration waves have made their mark on Prairie cuisine, particularly in the cities. In Winnipeg there is the largest Philippine population outside of that country. West Indian *roti* shops, Middle Eastern foods, and other ethnic foods add to the culinary flavors of Winnipeg, Edmonton, Saskatoon, and Calgary.

British Columbia: Aboriginal, English, Chinese, and California Fusion

Because of settlement patterns in British Columbia, Canada's westernmost province, its cuisine is different from the rest of Canada. The aboriginal people included many bands of North Coastal and Interior Coastal Peoples living in small villages along the Pacific Ocean and in the interior mountainous areas. By the 1860s there was a genteel English colony on Vancouver Island enjoying garden parties and afternoon tea. Chinese laborers arrived in the last half of the nineteenth century, and in addition to opening restaurants, frequently became cooks in English homes. In the twentieth century, the Californian free-spirited cookery spread up the coast, espousing the use of fresh local ingredients and healthy cooking, including vegetarianism. Many other cultural groups added to this mix but the dominant cuisine is Aboriginal, English, Chinese, and Californian.

As the cuisine in British Columbia developed, locally grown or harvested ingredients from land and sea respectively were adopted by all groups and each modified them according to their backgrounds. The Pacific harvest focuses on salmon: coho, chinook, pink, chum, and red sockeye salmon. Halibut, black cod, lingcod, tuna, rockfish, and eulachon are also favored fish. Shellfish include crabs (especially Dungeness) oysters, scallops, shrimp, prawns, abalone, and many varieties of clams. Agricultural areas in the beginning were developed in the Fraser River delta, supplying produce for Victoria and Chinese vegetables for early Chinese immigrants. Further inland, microclimates characterize the agricultural areas of the Okanagan and Similkimen Valleys, the fruit-growing regions of British Columbia. This climate is ideal for viticulture, and some grapes left on the vine until January are made into Eiswein. Soapberries, thimbleberries, salmonberries, huckleberries, and many other berries are harvested from the wild, as are pine mushrooms growing in evergreen forests.

The first inhabitants who influenced British Columbian cookery were the North Coast Native Peoples. Salmon was and continues to be their primary foodstuff: it is baked, poached, barbecued, and smoked. Family smokehouses are common in the coastal villages. Women also preserve salmon by canning for times when it is not in season. Eulachon oil and herring eggs are prized foods. Eulachon, a small oily fish (also called "candle fish" because when dried it can be lighted), can be eaten fried or baked, but is prized more for its oil, used as a dip for foods and as a seasoning. Spruce boughs are placed in the ocean water and become a spawning site for herring. The branches are harvested with the eggs still clinging to them and are then dried. It is not uncommon to see these boughs drying on the sides of houses. Roots were gathered in the past but are not as commonly used today with the exception of roasted camas bulbs. Indian ice cream is made by whipping the indigenous soapberries into a froth. These local ingredients still dominate aboriginal cooking, particularly since food must be brought to many native villages by ferry. However, the overall cuisine of the Native Peoples has been affected by Canadian culinary culture and their daily menus are as likely to include pizza, burgers, donuts and coffee, stews, pies and cakes as that of any other Canadian. But they value their distinct culinary traditions.

Victoria on Vancouver Island, more than any other Canadian city, has a decidedly English character. Afternoon tea is still a tradition, and locally brewed ales can be found at English-style pubs. In the warm climate (by

French Canada is noted for its distinctive cookery, and the Old City of Quebec has capitalized on food tourism. Shown here is the Auberge du Tresor, a restaurant and hotel in the historic part of the city. © WOLFGANG KAEHLER/CORBIS.

Canadian standards), growers around Victoria are able to successfully harvest such fruits as kiwi and figs. Their small farms are often organic, and herbs are grown year-round.

Vancouver, the largest city in British Columbia, although multicultural, has a character all its own. Here there are English, Chinese, Pacific Coast Native, Italian, and Japanese, as well as Californian influences. The Chinese influence is strongest in Vancouver. The Chinese community demands fresh produce and fish—evident in Vancouver food stores. Chinese vegetables such as *gai lohn* have long been grown in the Fraser River delta. Live fish and shellfish from the Pacific are kept in tanks (goeduck clams, Dungeness crabs, and rockfish). Recent wealthy immigrants from Hong Kong created a demand for imported Chinese foods and medicines such as ginseng (grown commercially in British Columbia and Ontario), dried abalone, shark's fin, and bird's nest.

Young, well-trained chefs are combining this cooking in various adaptations, creating a fusion cuisine. These young people revere local ingredients, ethnic ideas and styles, organically grown foods, herbs, edible flowers, whole grains, and enjoy the good life.

The North: Finding Food for Survival
Canada's agricultural belt as well as its population is concentrated in approximately the lower one-third of its land mass. The "North" includes the territories of the Yukon, the Northwest Territories, and the newest territory, Nunavut. For purposes of describing the regional cuisines of Canada, the forest land south of the tundra and north of the agricultural belt are also included, as are parts of the Prairie provinces, Ontario, Quebec and Labrador.

Indigenous ingredients distinguish the cuisine of northern Canada from other regions. Because food supplies are difficult to transport, there is more of an emphasis upon local foods than in southern Canada.

Caribou, muskoxen, moose, deer, ptarmigan, and arctic char are hunted or fished. Today aboriginal people supply wild game to restaurants and the luxury market, particularly caribou, muskoxen, and arctic char. Migratory ducks and geese provide variety to the larder in the fall. Berries grow profusely—blueberries, partridge berries, cranberries, and black currants are made into pies, preserves, jellies, and sauces. These foods all have local habitats—not all are found in every part of Canada's north.

The aboriginal population comprises about two-thirds of the northern population. Before European settlement, the Inuit occupied the Arctic, that is, the tundra beyond the tree line that encompasses the northern third of Canada's land mass. The aboriginal tribes of the Mackenzie and Yukon River basins and the Northern Cree occupy the northern wooded areas. Before contact with Europeans, these Peoples of the First Nations were self-sufficient and lived seasonally, either following herds of caribou or moving from place to place where food could be found. Their diet was rich in protein, with plant materials making up an estimated five percent of their food. This diet was healthy and supplied all their nutritional needs. In the twentieth century, attempts to assimilate Native Peoples into white society changed the native culture dramatically. Many were moved to permanent settlements (especially the Inuit) and were no longer able to resume their migratory food patterns. They began to live on foods that could be transported into their villages, usually by plane. These foods were much different from their traditional diet. Carbohydrates were introduced, particularly white flour and refined sugar. Manufactured foods like potato chips and soft drinks became popular, especially because the traditional pattern was to eat when hungry rather than at set mealtimes. Rich in fat and starch, these new foods were detrimental to the health of Native Peoples, leading to diabetes and other dietary diseases. While there is a trend among Native Peoples to return to their traditional diet, permanent settlements make this difficult.

The largest white settlements in the north are in the Yukon and Northwest Territories. Dawson and Whitehorse were settled during the gold rush, and Yellowknife was established as the capital of the Northwest Territories. The Yukon today has predominately British roots. The center of the gold rush beginning in 1897, Dawson drew miners, honky-tonk girls, and the Royal Canadian Mounted Police (RCMP). To prevent starvation, miners were required to pack in a year's supply of food before they were allowed into the territory. Provisions were basic and affected the cuisine of the territory: beans, flour, dried fruit, sugar, bacon, and tea were common items. Wild game supplemented their plain diets, but if they struck it rich they could buy luxury foods such as chocolate, champagne, and fresh eggs. Prospectors became known as "sour-doughs" because they craved white bread so much they baked it in their camps. Legend has it that they kept the yeast starter alive by carrying it in their armpits when traveling in the bitter cold.

Today procurement of food for the north still requires a great deal of planning. Winter is unpredictable, and even where there are logging trails or water access to northern communities, food supplies are sometimes delayed. Nearly any food can be shipped in by air, but that option is expensive. With modern communications with the rest of the world, there is demand for many more food products, especially in increasingly popular luxury fly-in hunting and fishing lodges. Overall, diets in the North are simpler than elsewhere, but definitely Canadian in style.

From coast to coast, diverse regional cuisines dominate Canadian cooking. Canadians today value their ethnic origins highly and take pride in preserving their culture, particularly their cuisine. Overlying these regional cuisines is a dominant North American influence, which is not surprising since there was American immigration into Canada early in its history, the language is understood by most Canadians, and the cultural influence of the media has brought trends and new foods to Canada. Canadians also take advantage of fruits and vegetables grown south of the border that lend variety to winter meals. One cannot say that there is a national cuisine, as there is in Mexico, but one must experience and enjoy the diverse regional cuisines of Canada, which together create a diversity of foodways that reflect Canadian society.

BIBLIOGRAPHY

Aitken, Julia, and Anita Stewart. *The Ontario Harvest Cookbook: An Exploration of Feasts and Flavours.* Toronto: Macmillan, 1996.

Armstrong, Julian. *A Taste of Quebec.* Toronto: Macmillan, 1990.

Barer-Stein, Thelma. *You Eat What You Are: People, Culture and Food Traditions.* 2nd ed. Toronto: Firefly Books, 1999.

Canadian Historical Association. *Canada's Ethnic Groups*, series of booklets. Ottawa: Canadian Historical Association, 1982–1991.

Driver, Elizabeth. *A Bibliography of Canadian Cookbooks (1825–1949).* Toronto: University of Toronto Press, forthcoming.

Ferguson, Carol, and Margaret Fraser. *A Century of Canadian Home Cooking: 1900 through the '90s.* Scarborough, Ontario: Prentice Hall, 1992.

Five Roses Cook Book. Montreal: Lake of the Woods Milling Co., 1913.

Institut de Tourisme et d'Hôtellerie du Québec. *Cuisine du Québec.* Montreal: Les Éditions TransMo, 1985.

Lafrance, Marc, and Yvon Desloges. *A Taste of History: The Origins of Québec's Gastronomy.* Montreal: Les Éditions de la Chenelière, 1989.

Nightingale, Marie. *Out of Old Nova Scotia Kitchens.* New York: Scribners, 1971.

Ontario Historical Society. *Consuming Passions: Eating and Drinking Traditions in Ontario*. Toronto: Ontario Historical Society, 1990.

Powers, Jo Marie, ed. *Buon appetito! Italian Foodways in Ontario*. Toronto: Ontario Historical Society, 2000.

Powers, Jo Marie, ed. *From Cathay to Canada: Chinese Cuisine in Transition*. Toronto: Ontario Historical Society, 1998.

Powers, Jo Marie, and Anita Stewart, eds. *Northern Bounty: A Celebration of Canadian Cuisine*. Toronto: Random House of Canada, 1995.

Stechishin, Savella. *Traditional Ukrainian Cookery*. Winnipeg: Trident Press, 1957.

Stewart, Anita. *The Flavours of Canada: A Celebration of the Finest Regional Foods*. Vancouver: Raincoast Books, 2000.

Turner, Nancy J. *Food Plants of Interior First Peoples*. Vancouver: University of British Columbia Press, 1997.

Jo Marie Powers

CANADA.

NATIVE PEOPLES

There are over half a million Peoples of the First Nations scattered across Canada. Divided into more than 600 bands, nearly 60 percent live on reserves, the majority on the plains and the West Coast. Greatly differing in their background, culture, and traditional cuisine, the Peoples of the First Nations can be divided into cultural groupings, each with a distinct cuisine: the Woodland First Nations, the First Nations of Southeast Ontario, the Plains People, the Pacific Coastal Nations, the First Nations of the Plateau, and the First Nations of the Mackenzie and Yukon River basins. The Inuit, occupying one-third of the landmass in Canada, are another important aboriginal group with a different and distinct cuisine.

Inhabitants of Canada for thousands of years before European contact, the Native Peoples created markedly different cuisines from the raw ingredients available: local wildlife and indigenous plants. Although basic cooking methods varied from tribe to tribe, most peoples roasted food over hot coals and used the "stone-boiling" method of cookery. Food and water were placed in a wooden, bark, or skin container and hot rocks were dropped into the vessel to heat the water and cook the food. It was not surprising that iron kettles were highly prized when offered in trade by Europeans because they simplified this method of cookery. Salt was absent from their traditional food preparations as was frying food in fat. Both were introduced by Europeans along with new ingredients and preparations. Wheat flour was one of the first widely accepted foods and bannock became the traditional bread that spread to every tribe across Canada. New root vegetables such as carrots, onions, and turnips were readily added to their cooking pots for flavor and nourishment. It is thought that potatoes, brought to Eu-

BANNOCK

Bannock is a bread universally loved and prepared in the homes of every aboriginal tribe in Canada. The Scottish fur traders are thought to have introduced this preparation. Folklore tells its probable origin. Scottish men, carrying a bag of flour in their canoe and not caring about amenities, made a well in the center of the flour, poured in water, and stirred it with their fingers to make a dough. Wrapped around a stick and roasted over the campfire, this bannock was shared with aboriginal guides.

Today bannock has many variations. Flour, a small amount of baking powder and salt, and sometimes a little fat, are placed in a large bowl and an indentation is made in the center. Buttermilk, milk, or water is poured in and the liquid is deftly and gently worked into the flour to form a soft dough. This is rolled out and cut into rounds and baked. The result is a tender, unleavened bread about two inches thick. It is also cooked in an ungreased skillet on top of the stove. When the bannock dough is fried in fat, it is called "fry bread" or "fried bread." In the out-of-doors, bannock is still baked over a campfire, either wrapped around a stick in the traditional manner or in a heavy iron skillet placed on hot coals. For variety, blueberries, saskatoon berries, or raisins are added to the dough before it is baked.

At powwows, bannock is a featured food. It is rolled into large rounds and deep-fried as a base for Indian tacos. This recipe first appeared on the powwow circuit between twenty and thirty years ago, and the fry bread base is topped with a seasoned bean or meat mixture, shredded cheese, chopped lettuce, and tomato. The fry bread can also be served hot with butter and honey.

rope from Peru by the Spaniards, were carried to Canada by Irish immigrants and these easy-to-grow tubers were quickly accepted in aboriginal communities. Refined, cheap sugar was a valued commodity and enjoyed in its many uses in sweet desserts and, later, in soft drinks. In the twentieth century, aboriginal people, like other North Americans, became enamored with manufactured foods including snack foods, rich in salt, fat, and sugar, and began to shop at their band or grocery stores for most of their food supplies. However, nutritional research has shown that their native diet was healthier than the new diet to which they were introduced. The incidence of diabetes and other dietary diseases is high among Native Peoples.

After initial contact, Europeans attempted to assimilate the Peoples of the First Nations into white culture, most recently by taking children from their families and placing them in residential boarding schools. Children were taught English and ate the white people's diet, but the Peoples of the First Nations remembered their past. There is a strong force within their communities to prepare traditional foods, and, at the same time, to improve their diet. Young aboriginal chefs are making their mark on Canadian cuisine. Specifically trained in courses on aboriginal cuisine and native culture, these young people are putting native cuisine on Canadian menus.

Although diverse in their foods and foodways, there is a commonality that crosses from Nation to Nation, and that is a deep spiritual relationship with the land and the life forms that inhabit it. The Peoples of the First Nations have a great respect for all living things and believe that human beings participate in a world of interrelated spiritual forms. Moreover, toward the end of the twentieth century, aboriginal peoples across Canada began a concerted effort to control their lands and resources.

The Woodland Peoples

The Woodland Peoples include Mi'kmaq, Montagnais, Ojibway, Algonquin, Odawa, and Cree, the tribes who first met the French and formed alliances with them in the seventeenth century. Spread across the eastern provinces from Nova Scotia to Manitoba, they were hunting and gathering societies, migrating from place to place, following the seasonal movements of wild game animals. Moose, venison, beaver, rabbit, and caribou in the north were their quarry. Wild waterfowl and fish were also part of their diet, as well as berries that could be gathered. Wild game was prepared by the women, who either roasted the food or boiled it by dropping heated stones into water-filled bark containers.

Sharing food was part of their culture and many an early settler would not have survived had it not been for the native people who gave them part of the meat they hunted and taught them how to track game and use snowshoes. They introduced the French to maple sap, which they prized as a spring tonic and which could be boiled down to sugar. They showed them fiddleheads, the fronds of the ostrich fern, a gourmet delicacy in twentieth-century Canada. An important grain, part of the Ojibway diet, was wild rice, gathered in shallow bays by canoe. The Woodland Peoples no longer depend upon wild game, although hunting and trapping are still important.

The spiritual part of their culture remains integral to their life. For example, the Ojibway observe the seasons with festivals, beginning in the spring with the strawberry festival and the drinking of strawberry juice, giving thanks to their creator.

Peoples of Southeast Ontario

At the time of contact, the aboriginal people who were farmers in Canada lived in Ontario (members of the Iroquoian tribes), and there were occasional farming settlements in Quebec. Fifteen varieties of corn, sixty of beans, and six of squash, including pumpkins, were grown. Jerusalem artichokes and sunflowers were also cultivated. Maples were tapped in the spring and the sap boiled down to sugar, used sparingly as a sweetener and sold to early settlers. The most important of their crops were corn, beans, and squash, the "Three Sisters," which together provided a complete diet. Food was cooked by the women in pottery containers, which they made. Fish and meat were added for flavoring but were a small part of their diet. Three festivals were held to honor corn: the corn planting, the green corn, and the harvest festivals.

The largest band in Canada is the Six Nations of the Grand River Iroquois in Ohsweken, Ontario, who came north with British Loyalists in the late eighteenth century. Their ceremonies are held in a modern building resembling a long house in style. For traditional ceremonies families bring food, fragrant sweet grass is burned, and the food is blessed. Corn soup is served at ceremonies and in homes. To make this special soup, women begin preparing it in late summer, first slowly drying white flint corn kernels in the oven and then storing them in containers. The soup is made by simmering the dried corn with fresh pork, kidney beans, and a little salt. Corn soup is also served at the "Snow Snake" in the winter, a contest in which the men throw a javelin-like spear down an icy groove (the spear may travel almost 3,300 ft., close to 1,100 yds.).

The Plains Peoples

The Plains Peoples (Blackfoot, Blood, Peigan, Gros Ventre, Cree, Assiniboine, Sioux, and Sarcee [Tsuu T'ina]) followed buffalo migrations. Depending upon the tribe, after the slaughter the kidney, heart, or liver (all were considered sacred) was eaten first, raw. Animals were always slaughtered as needed, not for sport. Every bit of the buffalo was utilized for food, clothing, or shelter. The fresh meat was either roasted or cooked in a skin bag by the stone-boiling method. Jerky was prepared by sun-drying strips of meat, which were pounded almost into a powder and then mixed with buffalo fat and berries to make pemmican. Stored in a buffalo skin, it remained edible for years, and early European settlers and fur traders depended upon it. After the buffalo had all but disappeared, its meat was replaced by beef. Today, the Plains Peoples' favorite method of cooking beef is boiling it with potatoes, and the boiled meat is often served with pork cracklings. Tongue is a delicacy eaten during the Sun Dances. Kidneys, lightly grilled on the outside, are eaten by the Siksika of the Blackfoot. Intestines are stuffed with raisins, cooked, and eaten. Their tradition of not letting any part of the animal go to waste continues. Men of these tribes still consider themselves meat eaters and continue to hunt wild game for food and sport—deer, antelope, rabbits, and, near the Rockies, elk and mountain sheep, as well as other animals and birds.

The Pacific Coast First Nations

The Pacific Coast First Nations (Haida, Tsimshian, Nootka, Coast Salish, Kwakiutl, and Bella Coola) live on the coast of British Columbia. By the time Columbus had reached the Americas, these people had developed an elaborate social structure. They lived in semipermanent communities in homes built with cedar boards, had extensive trade networks, and had sufficient leisure time for artisan carvers to develop.

A unique feature of these people was the potlatch, an elaborate feast publicly declaring and legitimizing a change in state—birth, marriage, death, or inheritance of rights. The chief who gave the potlatch provided enormous quantities of food, served in intricately carved containers, and invited guests from other tribes were expected to consume food until they could eat no more. During the feast the chief gave away his possessions, and the more generous he was, the more powerful he was thought to be. The potlatch was outlawed from 1884 until 1951, but was still held in secret. Potlatches today are held for the same reasons as in the past, and the potlatch ceremonies—singing, drumming, dancing, and speechmaking—all reaffirm the community's cultural identity.

The planning for a potlatch may take several years. The community participates in preparing feast foods, which are a combination of their favorite traditional dishes and North American foods. Entire families attend the potlatch, including infants. Generally, two meals are served each day of the potlatch, a dinner and then a late supper break after midnight. Some of the traditional foods that are served include dried herring roe, grease from the eulachon (an anadromous marine food fish found along the north Pacific coast), seaweed soup with salmon eggs, and, always, salmon. These foods are accompanied by tossed salads, vegetables, pickles, bannock, and cakes. Speechmakers reiterate the "plentifulness of the food." Rituals are observed at the feast: elders and chiefs are served first, guests are considered rude if they refuse food during the meal, and all are invited to take food home. On the last night of the feast, boxes and boxes of goods are given to the guests. Today these gifts consist of a variety of goods such as mugs, glasses, housewares, T-shirts with the family crest, towels, and blankets. Valued foods such as dried herring eggs and eulachon grease are given to special guests, as are envelopes of money. The revitalized potlatch reinforces community cohesiveness and support for the leaders of the community.

The First Nations of the Plateau

The First Nations of the Plateau (Interior Salish, Kottenay Tribe, Chilcotin, Tahltan, Tagish, and Carrier Sekani) occupy the great valley between the Rocky Mountains and the coastal ranges in British Columbia. These peoples, along with the coastal Nations, were the most numerous of any aboriginal group before European contact. Within these cultural groups, staple foods varied from northern to southern British Columbia. In the central area, salmon, which spawned in the Fraser River, were the staple food, while in the north wild game, especially moose, deer, and caribou, was hunted. Researchers have identified more than 150 plants that were gathered and, in the southern area, supplied 50 percent of the calories consumed. Families or chiefs owned gathering areas and, although agriculture, per se, was not practiced, the grounds were tended and cared for so that plants would flourish and could be harvested annually. Roots were an important staple, especially Yellow Avalanche Lily, Spring Beauty tubers ("Indian Potato"), and bitterroot. Pit cooking was favored for cooking roots. A hole was dug, rocks added, a fire built to heat the rocks, and a protective layer of vegetable matter was placed over the coals. Foods were placed on top of this layer and carefully covered with more greenery and then with soil. Some water was added, and the whole cooked for hours. Wild berries, gathered by women, were eaten fresh or cooked and dried in wooden frames to make berry cakes, then stored for later use. These cakes were soaked and mixed with eulachon oil. The Interior Peoples had extensive trade with the Coastal Peoples and exchanged their roots, berries, and other goods for eulachon "grease," herring roe, and other goods. When potatoes, rice, flour, sugar, and other foods were introduced, they were readily accepted by the Interior Peoples. They still gather berries, root vegetables, and wild mushrooms. Their traditional foods are greatly valued even though many of their ancestral gathering grounds have been destroyed by cattle or development.

The First Nations of the Mackenzie and Yukon River Basins

Small in numbers, the twelve tribes of the Mackenzie and Yukon River basins occupy one-fourth of Canada's landmass. They include the Chipewyan, Beaver, Slave, Yellowknife, Dogrib, and Hare tribes. Their traditional hunting lands, located just below the tundra, provided sparse vegetation for game animals, so family units had their own hunting grounds. Seminomadic, they followed migratory animals such as caribou. Where available, they hunted moose, mountain sheep, wood buffalo, and bear. Hunting was often a winter activity that required snowshoes, and snares were set to trap game. Fish were important, caught either through the ice in the winter or by canoe after the ice broke up in the spring. Game was boiled in birch bark containers using the stone-boiling method. All of the Yukon tribes held memorial feasts for their dead on the first anniversary of their death. Today, hunting is still an important part of their life and snowmobiles have allowed them to have a wider range in their winter hunting territory. However, permanent settlements and the decrease in caribou herds in some parts of their territory have diminished the emphasis on game as their major food supply.

In the twenty-first century, Native Peoples eat much like other North Americans. They buy their foods from grocery or band stores, frequent fast-food restaurants and pizza parlors, get Chinese takeout, and drop into coffee and donut shops.

See also **American Indians; Arctic; Canada; Inuit; Potlatch.**

BIBLIOGRAPHY

Hungry Wolf, Beverly. *The Ways of My Grandmothers.* New York: Morrow, 1980.

"Indian and Northern Affairs Canada." Section on Culture and History. Available at http://www.ainc-inac.gc.ca/ch/index_e .html

Kuhnlein, Harriet V., and Nancy J. Turner. *Traditional Plant Foods of Canadian Indigenous Peoples: Nutrition, Botany, and Use.* Volume 8: *Food and Nutrition in History and Anthropology,* edited by Solomon Katz. Philadelphia: Gordon and Breach, 1991.

Skye, Bertha. "Traditional Cree and Iroquois Foods." In *Northern Bounty: A Celebration of Canadian Cuisine,* edited by Jo Marie Powers and Anita Stewart, pp. 113–120. Toronto: Random House, 1995.

Stewart, Anita. "Potlatch Revival," *Canadian Living* (April 1993): 31–36.

Turner, Nancy J. *Food Plants of Interior First Peoples.* Vancouver: UBC, 1997.

Jo Marie Powers

CANCER. *See* **Health and Disease.**

CANDY AND CONFECTIONS. Candy is a collective name for sugary treats such as fudge, taffy, bright colored gumdrops, and boiled sugar. Originally, "sugar candy" meant sugar concentrated to the point that it formed a hard crystalline mass on cooling. The term (derived ultimately from a Sanskrit root, through Arabic *sukkar quandi*) was first recorded in English in the late fourteenth century; the word "candy" used alone appeared in the eighteenth century. The equivalent word in British English is "sweets." "Confection" is a word with a wider meaning. Sugar-based candy represents one category of confections (and is the sense mostly discussed here). Chocolate is another category (though the fillings of bars may be candy). The idea of a confection extends to pastry, cookies, and cakes. The trade of the confectioner, who is skilled in making delicate sweet things, links these different areas of expertise together.

Five hundred years ago, "confection" meant a mixture made to enhance health. Confection originally had the sense of 'something put together', and confections in the fourteenth century were medicinal preparations made from combinations of various drugs. It was very quickly discovered that "a spoonful of sugar makes the medicine go down," and sweetening agents were added to the medicines. "Confection" was being used to mean 'a preparation of spices, sugar, fruits, etc.' by the middle of the

CANDY CANES AND PULLED SUGAR

Striped candy canes, used for decorating the Christmas tree, are made by a technique known as pulling. For this, a concentrated hot sugar syrup is worked by stretching and folding, either by hand over an iron hook set in the wall or on a specially designed machine. After a short time, the sugar becomes opaque and white as pockets of air are folded into the mass and stretched. The basic lump of pulled sugar is made into a rough cylinder and decorated lengthwise with stripes and patterns made from colored boiled sugar (usually red). Then the mass is pulled out again (often by spinning on a machine) into long thin pieces. This process extends the sugar into thin ropes with decoration running through the whole length. Once the required diameter, usually about half an inch, is reached, the ropes are cut into shorter sticks. Candy canes are given an extra flourish by bending the top to give a shepherd's crook shape. Pulling is known in many other countries. In Britain it is used for "seaside rock," sold as a souvenir in seaside resorts. This is a sugar stick with letters or patterns running the length. In Sweden it makes the traditional mint-flavored *polkagrisar.*

Pulling is also used to make a more friable textured candy. The best-known example is probably Edinburgh rock, sold in the Scottish capital. For this, the sugar syrup is boiled to a lower temperature, and the sugar is allowed to grain after the candy is shaped. Similar confections include cinnamon-flavored *kaneel-brokken* (The Netherlands) and *peinir schekeri* (Turkey). Pulled sugar has an ancient and obscure origin. A description of the process is given in the *Kitab-al-Tabikh,* a collection of recipes written down in thirteenth-century Baghdad, but, as with other candy techniques, the skill was probably developed at a much earlier date somewhere farther east and transmitted westward with sugar cane and the knowledge of refining sugar itself.

fifteenth century. Confectioners preserved fruit, made sugarplums, marzipan, cordials, and light cakes. Sugar was important in these: it was expensive, exotic, sweet, and considered to be a spice with health-giving qualities. It was used to decorate other foods. In the English-speaking world, sugar became steadily cheaper through the eighteenth and nineteenth centuries. Chocolate candies were known in the late 1600s but only became common when large-scale production developed at the end of the nineteenth century. Pastry making (*patisserie* in French) became a specialty divorced from sugar-working. Candy-making also became an industry, helped by glucose (from corn syrup), and cheap penny candies emerged as the most obvious sugar confections.

Special uses of the word "candy," such as sugar candy, rock candy, and candied fruit, hint at the history of confections. Sugar candy is a hard mass of tiny crystals. It is now seldom made (although fudge is a softer version, and maple candy can be considered a special type). To make rock candy, large sugar crystals are allowed to grow slowly on sticks suspended in syrup. Candied (or crystallized) fruit is preserved by soaking in syrup. Concentration is gradually increased until it is strong enough to prevent decay. This was formerly an important preservation method for fruit, stems, and roots, including medicinal items such as lettuce stems and marshmallow roots. These techniques and other candies such as candy canes and jelly beans were brought to North America by European settlers. They can be traced back through the Middle Ages to traditions of sugar-working transmitted westward from the Byzantine and Islamic worlds.

Modern chemistry shows that early candy recipes exploit special properties of ordinary white crystal sugar (known chemically as sucrose) when boiled as syrup. This skill of sugar-boiling is of fundamental importance to the confectioner. First, the crystals are dissolved in water and brought to the boil. Although water boils at 100°C, sucrose does not melt until it reaches a temperature of around 160°C. As weak syrup boils, it becomes more concentrated, and the temperature rises above 100°C. More water evaporates. This increases the sugar concentration, which raises the temperature further, so that more water boils off and the syrup becomes more

The interior of a confectionery shop showing a confectioner making candied comfits. From Balthasar Schnurr's *Kunst- und Wunderbüchlein* (Frankfurt, 1615). ROUGHWOOD COLLECTION.

HALLOWEEN

Halloween in North America is celebrated by the custom of "trick or treat," in which collecting candy plays a vital part. The use of the colors orange and black and the images used on the packaging add to the general theme of witches, ghouls, and pumpkins. The festival of Hallowe'en, or "All Hallows Eve," has its roots in the Christian celebrations of All Saints and All Souls on November first and second; scholars believe this date was originally a pagan festival of the dead that was taken over by the church. Yellow- and orange-striped candy corn (first devised in the 1880s) recalls the idea of harvest, also important at this time of the year.

In Mexico, the Day of the Dead features a particularly vibrant and lavish selection of human and animal figures and skulls made from hard sugar candy or sugar paste sold at local fairs. These appear to have arisen from a fusion of European techniques of sugar-working, Christianity, and elements of native tradition.

In Europe, Halloween and All Saints have some special associations with candy. In southern Europe, All Saints is remembered as a special time when people visit the graves of relatives, and perhaps eat one special seasonal confection, for instance the Spanish *huesos de santo* (almond candy rolls filled with sweetened egg yolk). One place in which many candies are traditional to this date is Sicily. Here, marzipan fruit, *torrone,* and *cubiata* (the latter two local versions of nut or sesame brittle) are sold in special fairs together with *pupi di cena*—statuettes made of hard sugar candy with gaudy foil decorations. These figures recall a general Renaissance tradition, now mostly forgotten elsewhere to the east of the Atlantic, of decorating banquet tables with sugar models.

In the United Kingdom, toffee was traditionally made around the beginning of November, but All Souls traditions to do with candy or other special foods had almost disappeared by the twentieth century. However, the American trick or treat custom has recently been discovered by British children, and candies aimed specifically at this market now appear in the shops.

concentrated until it is entirely molten sugar. The basis for candy-making lies in cooking the syrup to varying temperatures—relatively low for chewy candies, higher for hard candy. These are measured on a special thermometer or by observed "stages" such as the "ball" test used when making fudge.

The art of confectionery is divided into a number of specialized professions, one of them cake decorating. Cake decorations are mostly sugar or sugar-based, and it takes an expert hand to achieve the fine points of piping and design. This confectioner in Knightsbridge, London, is putting the final touches on a Christmas cake in 1958. © HULTON-DEUTSCH COLLECTION/CORBIS.

Another part of the story of candies lies in the chemical structure of sucrose. This consists of two smaller sugar molecules, glucose and fructose, linked together. Dissolved in syrup, the links between the smaller molecules break, giving a mixture of sucrose, glucose, and fructose in water. The original candy was syrup boiled to a temperature of about 115°C, and then stirred, poured into a mold, and cooled. Stirring encourages the mixture to grain: the glucose and fructose bond again as sucrose, and crystals form, giving a hard texture. This is now used only for a few special items such as some of the figures made for the Mexican Day of the Dead and English Kendal Mint Cake. But the same basic technique gives the solid-yet-melt-in-the-mouth textures of fudge, penuche, New Orleans pralines, peppermint patties, and fondant. In these candies, the industry uses numerous technical devices to control crystal size, giving very small crystals and a creamy texture. Careful control of temperature and "seeding" syrups with preprepared crystals of the desired size are two methods.

Syrups boiled to 154°C and cooled quickly remain transparent and glassy and are the basis of hard, clear candies such as fruit drops and golden barley sugar sticks.

Confectioners knew that acid from fruit juice helped to keep clear candies translucent, and in the nineteenth century, they discovered that newly available ingredients, such as tartaric acid (from grapes) or glucose (in corn syrup) were more reliable. These "doctors" alter the chemistry of the syrup so that the relative proportions of glucose and fructose are unequal, inhibiting graining and encouraging a clear candy. Glucose, used to control texture in most industrially produced candies, is a vital ingredient in modern confectionery. Sugar syrups boiled to high temperatures can also be used for pulling, a method for such favorites as peppermint sticks and candy canes.

A third category of candies, which includes jelly beans, red-hots, and M&Ms, is made by panning in a special revolving drum like a large concrete mixer. This is a low-temperature process, using weak syrups cooked to only a few degrees above 100°C. Nuts (especially almonds), seeds (such as caraway or aniseed), and pellets of chocolate or fruit paste are coated with small amounts of syrup and tumbled until the sugar has dried on their surface. Eventually this builds up in thin layers to make a shell. Jelly beans as now made originated in the late nineteenth century but older recipes used bits of fruit paste. The Italian name for candies such as sugar almonds is *confetti*, and a tradition of throwing handfuls of these during festivities is commemorated in the paper confetti thrown at weddings.

Other ingredients add flavor, color, and texture to candies. Sugar paste is a mixture of confectioner's sugar and soaked gum arabic or tragacanth. Through the centuries, this was valued for modeling flowers and figures and is still popular for cake decoration. It is also an excellent vehicle for medicines and perfumes. Pastes were made up containing strong drugs such as opium or fragrances such as violet to sweeten the breath. Lifesavers and English Polo Mints echo this tradition, although high pressure is now used to compress the sugar.

Fruit confections often rely on pectin for their jellied texture. Gelatin and plant-derived gums provide alternatives in candies such as gum drops and pastilles. Chewing gum was devised in the late nineteenth century as a sweetened confection based on chicle, an elastic latex derived from a Mexican tree. Foundations for the success of this were laid in the 1890s by a dynamic young salesman named William Wrigley. Flour gives a characteristic chewy toughness to licorice candies, and cornstarch is used in Turkish delight (replacing the wheat-derived starches originally employed).

Almonds are used in many confections. Ground with sugar, they make marzipan. In caramelized sugar, they make brittle, although peanuts have become a more usual base for this candy. Almonds are also combined with sugar that has been boiled with egg whites to make French nougat and its relatives *turron*, *torrone*, and numerous other Mediterranean and Middle Eastern variations. Divinity, a softer version of this, developed in the southern United States. Egg whites gave the spongy texture to early marshmallow recipes; gum or gelatin are now used.

Milk, butter, and cream provide delicious textures and flavors in caramels, butterscotch, and toffee. The ancestor of these seems to have been taffy, unrefined sugar boiled with butter and then pulled. It was made in both England and North America in the nineteenth century, but the traditions have diverged on opposite sides of the Atlantic. In England, taffy has been forgotten, and modern toffee is brittle, hard, and brown. In America, taffy has developed into soft, multicolored salt-water taffy. Chewy caramels, boiled with milk, probably developed from the taffy tradition in the eastern United States. Milk is also important in confections from other cultures. Thick condensed milk is the *dulce de leche* of Hispanic cultures. Similar preparations provide the basis for many Indian and Bangladeshi confections including fudge-like *barfi* and cake-like *gulab jamun*.

The principal contribution that candies and confections make to the diet is concentrated energy. Consumption of candy is high in North America and Europe. According to the National Confectioner's Association, total U.S. consumption hovered around 7 billion pounds per annum for candy and 3.3 billion pounds for chocolate during the late 1990s. Debates continue over the relationship between confections and health problems such as diabetes and heart disease. The consensus is that too much sugar, whatever the source, is bad for the human body. The relationship of sugar and candy to dental cavities is direct and has been noticed for centuries; a visitor to the court of Elizabeth I in England observed that her teeth were black and attributed it to eating too much sugar.

The complex history of candies and confections has seen them go from being expensive luxuries to something consumed every day by everybody. Much of this is due to cheap sugar and industrial production methods. Despite this, they are still considered treats, valued for decorative qualities as well as their intrinsic sweetness. They retain strong links with celebrations such as weddings, christenings, Christmas, and Easter in many countries.

See also **Chocolate; Christmas; Day of the Dead; Desserts; Easter; Feasts, Festivals and Fasts; Halloween; Sugar and Sweeteners; Syrups.**

BIBLIOGRAPHY

American Craft Museum. *The Confectioner's Art.* New York: American Craft Council, 1988.

Carmichael, Elizabeth, and Sayer, Chloë. *The Skeleton at the Feast: The Day of the Dead in Mexico.* London: British Museum Publications, 1991.

Davidson, Alan. *The Oxford Companion to Food.* Oxford: Oxford University Press, 1999.

Hendrickson, Robert. *The Great American Chewing Gum Book.* Radnor, Pa.: Chilton Book Co., 1976.

Mason, Laura. *Sugar Plums and Sherbet: The Prehistory of Sweets.* Totnes, Devon: Prospect Books, 1998.

Time-Life Books. Gillian Boucher, series editor. *The Good Cook: Confectionery.* Amsterdam: Time-Life Books, 1981.

Laura Mason

CANNIBALISM. There is certainly no shortage of information on cannibalism. A search at any good library will net twenty to thirty books on the topic, and, at the time this encyclopedia went to press, the World Wide Web contained no fewer than 850 sites. Books on the topic range from popular surveys by Askenasy (1994) to anthropological treatments by Brown and Tuzin (1983), Goldman (1999), and Petrinovich (2000) to anthropological critique by Arens (1979) to postcolonial and literary critique by Barker and others (1998). A superficial examination of post–World War II films lists a variety of both serious and humorous treatments of cannibalism, many of them first-rate (*Fires on the Plain* [Japan, 1959], *Soylent Green* [U.S., 1973], *Survive!* [Mexico, 1976], *Eating Raoul* [U.S., 1982], *Silence of the Lambs* [U.S., 1991], *Delicatessen* [France, 1991], *The Cook, the Thief, His Wife, and Her Lover* [1993/1989, France/Netherlands.], *Alive* [U.S., 1993]). The fact that cannibalism is a powerful taboo in most human societies undeniably contributes to our fascination with tales about organisms eating conspecifics (others of the same species), especially humans.

THE GREEKS

The ancient Greeks' fears of cannibalism were reflected in the writings of Homer and others. For example, the Titan god Kronos ate his sons Hades and Poseidon and tried to eat Zeus in the fear that they would supplant him. Zeus, the future leader of the Olympian gods, forced his father to disgorge Hades and Poseidon. In another story, the curse on the House of Atreus was brought about by a deceptive form of endocannibalism. Atreus and Thyestes were brothers. In a series of deceptions, Atreus, having killed his own son without knowing who he was, exacted revenge against his brother, Thyestes, by killing Thyestes' own sons and serving them to him at a feast. A final example is in the tale of Odysseus' return from Troy to Ithaca. He stopped at an island in search of food and stumbled on the cave of Polyphemus, a Cyclops. Odysseus escaped from Polyphemus, but not before the Cyclops had devoured a number of his men.

The practice of human cannibalism is highly variable and can be defined in a number of ways: (1) Endocannibalism is the consumption of deceased individuals who live within the group, such as kin and friends. (This pattern was common in New Guinea as an act of veneration.) (2) Exocannibalism is the consumption of outsiders as an act to gain strength or demonstrate power over the vanquished, who had usually been murdered. (3) Starvation or survival cannibalism is the consumption during actual or perceived starvation. (This is well documented in numerous historical sources.) (4) Gastronomic cannibalism is nonfunerary, nonstarvation cannibalism, that is, routine cannibalism for food. (This is not well documented.) (5) Medicinal cannibalism is the consumption of human tissues such as blood, powdered bone, or dried tissue for medicinal purposes. (6) Sadistic cannibalism is the killing and eating of individuals out of sadistic or psychopathological motives. (There is considerable evidence for this pattern of cannibalism.) In exocannibalism, gastronomic cannibalism, and sadistic cannibalism, the victims are murdered before being eaten; in endocannibalism, starvation cannibalism, and medicinal cannibalism, they are not.

Cannibalism in Nonhuman Animals

Cannibalism occurs in a wide variety of invertebrate and vertebrate species and includes: infanticide, mating and courtship, competitive encounters, eating the old, and eating eggs. Among nonhuman organisms, cannibalism may be either ecological or social. Ecological factors include a limited food supply or the recovery of reproductive investment when food is scarce for infant survival; social factors include competition for reproductive resources or food resources. A general principle is that older individuals usually consume younger ones or eggs; it is relatively rare for adults to eat other adults. Elgar and Crespi (1992) define cannibalism in nonhuman organisms only in cases where an individual is killed (rather than dying a natural death) before being eaten.

In a comprehensive survey of cannibalism in primates in the wild, Hiraiwa-Hasegawa (1992) observed only five species in this practice: *Cercopithecus ascanius* (redtail monkey), *Papio cynocepharus cynocephalus* (baboon), *Macaca fuscata* (Japanese macaque), *Gorilla gorilla beringei* (mountain gorilla), and *Pan troglodytes* (common chimpanzee). In each episode observed, infants were eaten after being killed, and this custom appeared to serve a nutritional (therefore, ecological rather than social) purpose in animals who ordinarily consumed meat as a part of their diets. Chimpanzees, our closest evolutionary relatives, have the highest rates of cannibalism among nonhuman primates; chimpanzees also have the highest rates of predation (of red colobus monkeys) among nonhuman primates.

Cannibalism in History and Prehistory

Identification of cannibalism in the distant past is, according to Tim White (1992), based on very specific indicators in fossilized or unfossilized human bones: (1) similar butchering techniques for human and animal remains; (2) similar patterns of long bone breakage (for marrow extraction); (3) identical patterns of processing and discarding after use; and (4) evidence of cooking (White, 1992). Based on these criteria, there is good evidence for cannibalism from the southwestern United States; New Guinea, Fiji, and other sites in the Pacific; and Europe; there is limited evidence at other sites around the world. Ann Gibbons (1997) has reported that very early paleoanthropological specimens dating back hundreds of thousands of years are increasingly being identified as showing signs of cannibalism.

There is abundant evidence from historical accounts of cannibalism in the Caribbean (the term was defined for Carib Indians; the Spanish word *Canibales* is a form of the ethnic name *Carib*) and in Spanish accounts of Mesoamerican ritual sacrifices and cannibalism. Many historical accounts have been challenged within the past few decades because most information was derived from enemies of the groups identified as "cannibals," where the term was used to denigrate the other group. Also, during periods of exploration from the sixteenth century onward, Europeans were likely to accept the identification of "cannibal" in a group that was thought to be "savage" and "primitive." Hence, there is probably some exaggeration in the historical literature.

A storm of controversy has arisen over new evidence for cannibalism in Anasazi populations of the southwestern United States from the period between 900 and 1200 C.E. White (1992) and the Turners (1999) have identified skeletal remains from a number of populations that lived in the Four Corners area that show clear signs of persistent and regular cannibalism (White, 1992; Turner and Turner, 1999). The controversy has been fueled by

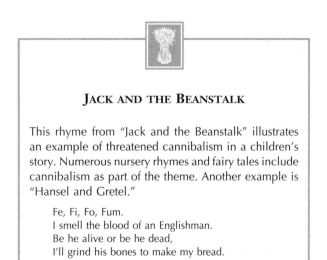

JACK AND THE BEANSTALK

This rhyme from "Jack and the Beanstalk" illustrates an example of threatened cannibalism in a children's story. Numerous nursery rhymes and fairy tales include cannibalism as part of the theme. Another example is "Hansel and Gretel."

> Fe, Fi, Fo, Fum.
> I smell the blood of an Englishman.
> Be he alive or be he dead,
> I'll grind his bones to make my bread.

Cabbage and Crucifer Plants Cabbage figures far more prominently than lettuce in the diet of Caribbean and Central American countries. These cabbage fields are in the mountainous region of Valle Nueva near Constanza, Dominican Republic. © Richard Bickel/CORBIS.

Left: **Cuisine** Black truffles from southern France prepared in the style of nouvelle cuisine. This style of food preparation has become so abstract and internationalized that the food has lost a sense of place and cultural identity. Photo by André Baranowski.

Below: **Cooking** Smoke rising from the hearth of a Guyami hut in the jungle near Chiriqui Grande, Panama. In medieval Europe, the presence of a hearth (and by implication the smoke it produced) provided a legal definition of the household regardless of the number of people it served. In contrast to the image of black truffles prepared according to the tenets of nouvelle cuisine, this hut and its abundant smoke provides an image of cooking at its most down-to-earth simplicity. © Danny Lehman/CORBIS.

Feasts and Festivals Pastor Robert J. Urffer officiates during the observance of Harvest Home at Union Church, Neffs (Lehigh County), Pennsylvania, in 1945. Harvest Home was at one time a far more common observance than Thanksgiving in the United States. The ending of World War II added poignancy to this particular occasion. Roughwood Collection.

Feasts and Festivals St. Patrick's Day party for children from Marion Jane Parker's *The Children's Party Book* (Chicago, 1923). Irish culture is celebrated with a game called "Kissing the Blarney Stone," a soap bubble contest (the green bubbles seen over the table), and St. Patrick's Ice Cream—colored green, of course. Roughwood Collection.

the traditional view of these peoples as peaceful and non-violent and the belief that, if cannibalism did exist, it resulted from periodic famine and hunger, which must have commonly struck prehistoric peoples of the arid Southwest. A new image of these peoples, under the purported cultural influence of Mesoamerican traditions of violence from the south, is one of human sacrifice, cannibalism, and social pathology—quite different from the earlier view.

Cannibalism and Survival

Some of the best-documented examples of cannibalism have been based on the conditions that take place during widespread famines and on accounts of shipwrecked, marooned, or stranded groups of people who have gone for long periods without food. Two of the best-documented of many cases are the pioneer Donner party's isolation in the Sierra Nevada Mountains in the fall and winter of 1846–1847, and the crash of the Uruguayan rugby team in the Chilean Andes in October 1972. In these and other well-documented cases, it is unquestionable that the food acquired by means of cannibalism enabled some individuals to survive rather than starving to death.

A more controversial issue is whether regular cannibalism in groups of people makes the difference between inadequate and adequate dietary intake. The Aztecs of Mexico practiced regular ritual sacrifice of captives and consumed the victims. Michael Harner (1977) and Marvin Harris (1977) argued that this food provided a protein-rich source of nutrients to a large Aztec population that was suffering from limited protein intake due to the absence of Native American domestic animals during pre-Hispanic times. This argument has been countered on the grounds that (1) population density was somewhat lower than estimated and (2) protein sources were available from a variety of plant and wild animal food that, when considered together, provided an adequate protein intake for most of the people.

Garn and Block (1970) argued that the meat yield from an average human body (50 kg) would only provide about 4.0 kg of protein, and that this would meet the daily minimum protein requirements of only sixty adults. However, Dornsteich and Morren (1974) presented a more convincing argument for New Guinea cannibalism in several highland populations. They noted that the consumption of human flesh by the Miyanmin people provided between 5 and 10 percent of the daily intake of protein, which was equivalent to or greater than the protein derived from domestic and feral pig consumption. This basic issue seems to relate to the primary motives that people have for consuming human flesh. It is probably not correct to state that some people practice cannibalism solely as a source of food. There are many other human motives for cannibalism. On the other hand, human tissue has the same nutritional value as any other mammalian tissue when it is eaten, whether by a human or nonhuman predator.

KURU

Kuru can be used as an example of how endocannibalism led to a disastrous epidemic of a degenerative encephalopathic disease, the discovery of a whole class of diseases called prion diseases, a Nobel Prize won by D. Carleton Gajdusek, and the beginning of our understanding of mad cow disease, which led to the mass destruction of livestock in the United Kingdom.

A popular account of the early discovery of kuru is given in a book by Michael Howell and Peter Ford (1985). The Fore people, who live in the central highlands of New Guinea and practiced a form of endocannibalism, were reported to have a disease that had a gradual onset (imbalance) but then progressed rapidly to an inability to stand or sit upright, dementia, and a general neurological deterioration that always ended in death. The Fore attributed the lethal disorder to sorcery, but Western officials believed the epidemic had natural causes, perhaps hysteria. Following work by Vincent Zigas, a district medical officer, and Carleton Gajdusek, a young American scientist, it was discovered that endocannibalism, as practiced by the Fore, contributed to the familial transmission of the infectious agent. By handling and consuming the incompletely cooked remains of the kuru victims, especially the highly infectious brain and nervous tissue, members of the family contracted the disease but did not show symptoms until many years later. The first connection with an animal disease was suggested in 1959 when a veterinary scientist suggested that kuru in humans seemed similar to symptoms of a disease called scrapie that was found in sheep. The most recent epidemic of a prion disease is mad cow disease (bovine spongiform encephalopathy), which is a livestock disease that has been transmitted to humans. This is the second example of a livestock prion disease that has somehow been transformed and become infectious in humans (the first is the probable transmission of scrapie to humans in kuru). Finally, the kuru epidemic in the Fore population was brought to a halt when the Australian government outlawed cannibalism in what is now Papua-New Guinea, and the practice slowly began to decline.

Cannibalism and Disease

The Fore tribe of the highlands of Papua New Guinea was investigated at length beginning in 1957 by D. Carleton Gajdusek, who won a Nobel prize in 1976 for his study of the neurological-degenerative disease kuru, which he determined was caused by human contact with infected human brain tissue. Kuru, Creutzfeldt-Jakob disease, and bovine spongiform encephalopathy are all transmissible spongiform encephalopathies (TSE) and were formerly believed to be caused by a slow virus infection; recent evidence indicates that they are conveyed by proteins called prions. Among the Fore, the principal pattern of contact with infected human tissue was during the mortuary preparation associated with endocannibalistic consumption of dead kin. In 1979 William Arens challenged Gajdusek's explanation for the spread of kuru on the grounds that there were no direct observations of cannibalism in the Fore people.

Whether cannibalism reflects pathological behavior depends on the circumstances of consumption. Starvation cannibalism appears to be tacitly condoned by Western societies, and other societies have sanctioned a variety of exocannibalistic practices. But perhaps the most abhorrent practice is that of sadistic or psychopathological murder and consumption of human tissue. Jeffrey Dahmer is a most recent example. A deranged young man who did not appear to be abnormal, he was arrested in Milwaukee in 1991 for the murder, dismemberment, and partial consumption of seventeen individuals. There are many other examples of such bizarre and pathological behavior in the literature.

BIBLIOGRAPHY

Arens, William. *The Man-Eating Myth: Anthropology and Anthropophagy.* Oxford: Oxford University Press, 1979.

Askenasy, Hans. *Cannibalism: From Sacrifice to Survival.* Amherst, N.Y.: Prometheus Books, 1994.

Barker, Francis, Peter Hulme, and Margaret Iversen, eds. *Cannibalism and the Colonial World.* Cambridge, U.K.: Cambridge University Press, 1998.

Brown, P., and D. Tuzin, eds. *The Ethnography of Cannibalism.* Washington, D.C.: Society for Psychological Anthropology, 1983.

Dornstreich, Mark D., and George E. B. Morren. "Does New Guinea Cannibalism Have Nutritional Value?" *Human Ecology* 2 (1974): 1–12.

Elgar, M. A., and B. J. Crespi. "Ecology and Evolution of Cannibalism." In *Cannibalism: Ecology and Evolution among Diverse Taxa,* edited by M. A. Elgar and B. J. Crespi, pp. 1–12. Oxford: Oxford University Press, 1992.

Gajdusek, D. Carleton. "Unconventional Viruses and the Origin and Disappearance of Kuru." *Science* 197 (1977): 943–960.

Garn, Stanley M., and W. D. Block. "The Limited Nutritional Value of Cannibalism." *American Anthropologist* 72 (1970): 106.

Gibbons, Ann. "Archaeologists Rediscover Cannibals." *Science* 277 (1997): 635–637.

Goldman, L. R., ed. *The Anthropology of Cannibalism.* Westport, Conn., and London: Bergin and Garvey, 1999.

Harner, Michael. "The Ecological Basis for Aztec Sacrifice." *American Ethnologist* 4 (1977): 117–135.

Harris, Marvin. *Cannibals and Kings: The Origins of Cultures.* New York: Random House, 1977.

Hiraiwa-Hasegawa, M. "Cannibalism among Non-Human Primates." In *Cannibalism: Ecology and Evolution among Diverse Taxa,* edited by M. A. Elgar and B. J. Crespi. Oxford: Oxford University Press, 1992.

Howell, Michael, and Peter Ford. *The Beetle of Aphrodite and Other Medical Mysteries.* New York: Random House, 1985.

Petrinovich, L. *The Cannibal Within.* New York: Aldine de Gruyter, 2000.

Turner, Christy G., II, and Jacqueline Turner. *Man Corn: Cannibalism and Violence in the Prehistoric American Southwest.* Salt Lake City: University of Utah Press, 1999.

White, T. D. *Prehistoric Cannibalism at Mancos 5MTUMR-2346.* Princeton: Princeton University Press, 1992.

Michael A. Little

CANNING. *See* **Packaging and Canning.**

CARAMELIZATION. Caramelization is the familiar browning of sugars through exposure to heat. The most common form of sugar—table sugar or sucrose—is a disaccharide, a combination of two monosaccharides: glucose and fructose. The two sugars can be easily separated using the enzyme invertase, which is essentially what bees do when they make honey from nectar. Fructose caramelizes more readily than glucose, so baked goods made from honey are generally a bit darker than those made with sucrose.

When sugar syrups are heated, they pass through several distinct stages, each having characteristics that are very useful to confectioners. Different sugars reach these stages at varying temperatures. The following table is for sucrose:

Caramelization of sugar begins around 310°F. When it reaches the light caramel stage (at 356°F for sucrose), many complex chemical reactions change simple sugars into a host of different flavoring compounds. Scissions (the breaking of long molecular chains into shorter segments), rearrangements of molecular components, and subsequent reactions between the resulting new compounds all occur in rapid succession. One of the compounds created during caramelization is biacetyl ($C_4H_6O_2$), which has a warm buttery scent, but there are also traces of as many as one hundred sweet, sour, and bitter compounds. The complexity of the resulting mixture makes the flavor of butterscotch more interesting than the mere sweetness of sugar. Of course, a number of yellow and brown water-soluble polymers are also produced, which accounts for caramel's coloration. These polymers are often used as colorants in commercial food products, from colas to soy sauce, and even in the variety of pumpernickel known as "black bread."

316

TABLE 1

Stages in the caramelization of sugar

Stage	Temperature	Characteristics and uses
All water evaporated	212°F	Sugar is melted and impurities rise to the surface.
Small Thread	215°F	No color; cools soft; no flavor change. Used in buttercream frostings.
Large Thread	219°F	No color; cools soft; no flavor change. Used in preserves.
Small Ball	230–240°F	No color; cools semisoft; no flavor change. Used in cream candy fillings, Italian meringue, fondants, fudge, and marshmallows.
Large Ball	246–252°F	No color; cools firm; no flavor change. Used in soft caramels.
Light Crack	264°F	No color; cools firm; no flavor change. Used in taffy.
Hard Crack	300–331°F	No color; cools hard; no flavor change. Used in butterscotch and hard candies.
Extrahard Crack	334°F	Slight color; shatters like glass when cooled; no flavor change. Used in nut brittles and hard candies.
Light Caramel	356°F	Pale amber to golden brown; rich flavor.
Medium Caramel	356–370°F	Golden brown to chestnut brown; rich flavor.
Dark Caramel	370–400°F	Very dark and bitter; smells burned. May be used for coloring, but has little sweetness left.
Black Jack	410°F	Known to Carême as "monkey's blood." At this point, the sugar begins to breaks down to pure carbon.

Many cooks assume that all the browning done in the kitchen is the result of caramelization, and it is common to see recipes that describe the "caramelization" of seared meats. However, that browning is actually the result of another set of chemical processes known, collectively, as the Maillard reaction. Maillard reactions are similar to caramelization, except that they involve the interaction of sugars and proteins—specifically, fructose, lactose, and one form of glucose with the amino acid lysine—at higher temperatures than those at which caramelization occurs. More complex carbohydrates, such as the starches found in flour, will also break down when heated into simpler sugars that can interact with the protein. That is one of the reasons that meats are often dusted with flour or cornstarch before searing. Since the Maillard reaction begins with a greater variety of chemical compounds than is required for caramelization, the resulting chemical complexity is greater. These reactions account for the wonderfully savory browning of baked breads, roasted coffee beans, and some cooked meats. If one considers the three differing flavor and aroma profiles of beef when raw, boiled, or roasted, the satisfyingly complex flavor produced by the Maillard reactions in the roasted meat is immediately apparent.

Crème caramel, dulce de leche, and similar desserts owe their flavor and color to both caramelization and the Maillard reaction. It the case of flan, the sauce for the custard is actually a thin coating of hard caramelized sugar used to line the mold before the custard is cooked—the caramel dissolves in water expressed from the cooked custard. In crème brûlée, the caramel topping remains crisp because it is browned à la minute under a broiler or small hand-held torch. Soft "caramel" candies are usually milk-based products that are merely flavored with caramel (but not brittle as true caramel would be).

Caramelization and Maillard reactions require temperatures that cannot be reached when water is present (the boiling point of water limits the cooking temperature to 212°F or less). Caramelization starts around 310°F, Maillard reactions even higher. When the sap of maple trees is boiled to make syrup, caramelization takes place even in the presence of water—because, while the average temperature is below 310°F, the temperature where the liquid is in contact with the hot metal of the evaporating pan is high enough for caramelization to occur. Similarly, the surfaces of roasted meats become dehydrated during cooking, allowing Maillard browning to take place while the interior remains moist.

These reactions (along with similar effects caused by enzymatic processes) can sometimes lead to undesirable browning. For example, when fruit preserves are prepared, the bright color of the ripe fruit must be maintained. Ascorbic or citric acids interfere with enzymatic browning, so they are typically added to low-acid fruits. Similarly, sulfur dioxide prevents the low-temperature Maillard reactions that often occur when carbohydrates and amino acids are present in high concentrations. Sultanas, or golden raisins, are merely raisins in which natural browning reactions have been prevented by sulfur dioxide.

See also **Candy and Confections; Carême; Dessert; Processing of Food; Sugar and Sweeteners; Syrups.**

BIBLIOGRAPHY

Davidson, Alan. *The Oxford Companion to Food.* Oxford: Oxford University Press, 1999.

McGee, Harold. *On Food and Cooking; The Science and Lore of the Kitchen.* New York: Scribners, 1984.

Richardson, Thomas, and John W. Finley, eds. *Chemical Changes in Food during Processing.* Westport, Conn.: AVI Pub. Co., 1985.

Waller, George R., and Milton S. Feather, eds. *The Maillard Reaction in Foods and Nutrition.* Washington, D.C.: American Chemical Society, 1983.

Gary Allen

CARBOHYDRATES.   Plants manufacture and store carbohydrates as their main source of energy through photosynthesis. Once consumed, these organic compounds can be digested, absorbed, and metabolized, supplying humans or animals with energy. Carbohydrates provide roughly half of the total caloric intake of the average human diet. These calories may be used immediately for energy metabolism or may be transformed and stored as glycogen or fat to be used as an energy source as demanded. Dietary carbohydrates are comprised of a wide array of compounds ranging from the simple one- or two-unit sugars to the long chain starches, glycogen and cellulose. Carbohydrates can be classified as monosaccharides, di- and oligosaccharides, and polysaccharides.

TABLE 1

Carbohydrate classification

Classification	Number of sugar units**	Examples
Monosaccharides	1	Glucose, galactose, fructose
Disaccharides	2	Sucrose, lactose, maltose
Oligosaccharides	2–10	Includes the disaccharides
Polysaccharides	> 10	Glycogen, starch, cellulose

**A "sugar unit" is one monosaccharide—each unit is not necessarily the same monosaccharide. For example, sucrose consists of one glucose unit and one fructose unit.

Monosaccharides, often referred to as simple sugars, are the simplest form of carbohydrates and are seldom found free in nature. The three that can be absorbed by the human body include glucose, galactose, and fructose. Glucose is the most abundant of the monosaccharides and the most important nutritionally. It is the repeating monosaccharide unit in starch, glycogen, and cellulose, and is found in all edible disaccharides.

Oligosaccharides are short chains of monosaccharide units that are joined by glycosidic bonds. They generally have between two to ten units, with the disaccharides, those chains containing two units, being the most abundant. The most common disaccharides include:

Sucrose (from table, cane, and beet sugars), consisting of glucose and fructose

Lactose (from milk sugar), consisting of glucose and galactose

Maltose (from malt sugar), consisting of two glucose units

Polysaccharides are long chains of monosaccharide units. The major polysaccharides include the digestible forms (glycogen and starch) and nondigestible forms (cellulose, hemicellulose, lignin, pectin, and gums).

Starch is the most common digestible polysaccharide found in plants. It can be found in two forms—amylose and amylopectin. Amylose is a linear, unbranched molecule that is bound solely by a-1,4 glycosidic bonds. Amylopectin, which makes up the greatest percent of the total starch content, is branched with a-1,6 bonds at the branch points.

Glycogen is the major storage form of carbohydrates in animals, found primarily in the liver and skeletal muscle. When energy intake exceeds energy expenditure, excess calories from fat, protein, and carbohydrate can be used to form glycogen. It is made up of repeating glucose units and is highly branched. During times of fasting or in between meals, these chains can be broken down to single glucose units and used as an energy source for the body. Although found in animal tissue, animal products do not contain large amounts of glycogen because it is depleted at the time of slaughter due to stress hormones.

Cellulose is the major component of cell walls in plants. Just as starch and glycogen, it too is made up of repeating glucose molecules. However, the glycosidic bonds connecting the units are b-1,4. These bonds are resistant to mammalian digestive enzymes rendering cellulose, and other substances containing these bonds, indigestible. Thus, cellulose is not considered to be a significant source of energy for the body. However, as a fiber, it is important for intestinal bacteria.

Since cellulose is a major part of the plant cell wall, it also encases some of the starch, preventing the digestive enzymes from reaching it and decreasing the digestibility of some raw foods such as potatoes and grains. Cooking causes the granules to swell and also softens and ruptures the cellulose wall, allowing the starch to be digested.

Dietary Fiber

Fiber can be classified as soluble and insoluble. Soluble fiber, which includes pectin and gums, dissolves in water to form a gel in the digestive tract. This increases the time the food is in the small intestine, thus increasing the chance of nutrients being absorbed. It is believed that soluble fiber plays a role in lowering blood LDL cholesterol. This could be due to the binding and increased excretion of fat and bile acid (a derivative of cholesterol) or other mechanisms not yet understood. Bacteria in the bowel can use fiber as a food source. These bacteria can degrade the fiber and release some components that can then be absorbed and used by the body. The increased nutrition for the bacteria can increase microbial growth, which can then lead to increased stool bulk, with little of the fiber actually found in the stool.

Insoluble fiber, including cellulose, hemicellulose, and lignin (a noncarbohydrate component of the cell wall that is often included as dietary fiber), absorbs water, thereby increasing the bulk and volume of the stool. It helps to speed the movement through the intestinal tract, preventing constipation, and is prescribed in the treatment of irritable bowel syndrome. It has also been shown that insoluble fibers bind fat-soluble carcinogens and re-

318

move them from the gastrointestinal tract, helping to decrease cancer risk.

Refined and processed foods have not only most of the fiber removed, but along with it many of the vitamins, minerals, and phytochemicals (chemicals found in plants believed to contain protective properties) that contribute to the health benefits of whole grain foods. The federal government's Dietary Guidelines for Americans encourage individuals to include whole grain foods in their diet to ensure adequate fiber to promote proper bowel function, as well as to receive other added health benefits.

Digestion, Absorption, and Transportation

In order for carbohydrates to be absorbed by the intestinal mucosal cells, they must first be converted into monosaccharides. The digestive process begins in the mouth with salivary a-amylase that partially breaks down starch by hydrolyzing some of the a-1,4 bonds. However, the digestion that takes place here is of little significance since food remains in the mouth for only a brief period, although this may differ depending on chewing time. The enzyme continues to work for a short time in the stomach until the pH is lowered due to hydrochloric acid that inhibits the enzyme.

STARCH

Starch from plants makes up about half of our dietary carbohydrates. Starch molecules can aggregate to form granules that differ by size and shape depending on the source of the starch, for example, corn, potato, and manioc. Although there is no difference in the nutritional value between the starches since all cooked starches are broken down in the body into glucose molecules, they do differ by characteristics such as solubility, flavor, and thickening power. Because of these characteristics, starch is often removed from the source to use commercially. For example, the starch can be removed from tubers such as potatoes and manioc (also known as cassava) through a wet milling process, or in the case of manioc, through leaching and drying. The potato starch is often used as a thickener or instead of cornstarch in recipes, while manioc is best known as tapioca.

The bulk of carbohydrate digestion occurs in the small intestine by pancreatic a-amylase. The pH of the small intestines is increased due to the addition of bicarbonate and bile, allowing the enzyme activity to occur. Specific disaccharidases located on the intestinal mucosal cells help to further break down the carbohydrates into the monosaccharides: glucose, fructose, and galactose.

Once the carbohydrates have been broken down, the monosaccharides can be absorbed by the mucosal cells. Glucose and galactose enter by active transport, which requires energy as well as specific receptors and carriers. Fructose is absorbed by facilitated diffusion. Like active transport, facilitated diffusion requires a specific carrier, but instead of needing energy, it relies on the low levels of fructose inside the cell to "pull" the fructose inside. Once transported through the intestinal wall, the monosaccharides enter the blood through the capillaries and are carried to the portal circulation and then to the liver.

Metabolism of Carbohydrates

The liver is the major site of galactose and fructose metabolism, where they are taken up, converted to glucose derivatives, and either stored as liver glycogen or used for energy immediately when needed. Although glucose is metabolized extensively in the liver, unlike galactose and fructose, it is also passed into the blood supply to be used by other tissues. Tissues like skeletal muscle and adipose tissue depend on insulin for glucose uptake, whereas the brain and liver do not. This dependence on insulin becomes a problem for diabetics who either cannot make insulin

TABLE 2

Examples of carbohydrate food sources

Monosaccharides

Glucose	Fructose	Galactose
Fruit	High-fructose corn syrup	Milk
Vegetables	Honey	Milk products
Honey	Fruit	

Disaccharides

Sucrose	Lactose	Maltose
Table sugar	Milk	Beer
Maple sugar	Milk products	Malt liquor
Fruit		
Vegetables		
Honey		

Polysaccharides

Starch (rye, oats, wheat, rice, potatoes, legumes, cereals, bread)

Dietary Fiber

Soluble

Pectin	Gums
Fruits (apples, berries)	Oats, barley
Jams and jellies (additive)	Ice cream (additive)
	Legumes

Insoluble

Cellulose	Hemicellulose	Lignin
Whole wheat foods	Whole grains	Fruit
Bran		Seeds
Leafy vegetables		Bran, wheat
		Vegetables

(IDDM) or are resistent to insulin (NIDDM). For individuals left untreated, dietary carbohydrates cause glucose levels to rise, resulting in hyperglycemia, which will lead to serious consequences if steps are not taken to correct it.

Once in the tissues, the fate of glucose depends on the energy demands of the body. Glucose can be metabolized through the glycolysis pathway to pyruvate where it is either converted to lactate or completely oxidized to CO_2, H_2O, and energy. Liver and skeletal muscle can convert excess glucose to glycogen through a pathway known as glycogenesis. The glycogen is stored after meals to be used as an energy source when energy demands are higher than intake. At this time the glycogen is broken down into individual glucose units, a process known as glycogenolysis, and the glucose can be metabolized further. Excess carbohydrates also can be used as a substrate for fat synthesis.

Carbohydrates are an essential part of a healthy diet. They provide an easily available energy source, are an important vehicle for micronutrients and phytochemicals, help to maintain adequate blood glucose, and are important in maintaining the integrity and function of the gastrointestinal tract. Table 2 contains examples of foods that contain the various types of carbohydrates.

See also **Digestion**; **Fiber, Dietary**; **Starch**.

BIBLIOGRAPHY

Ettinger, Susan. "Macronutrients: Carbohydrates, Proteins and Lipids." In *Krause's Food, Nutrition, and Diet Therapy*, edited Kathleen L. Mahan and Sylvia Escott-Stump. 10th ed. Philadelphia, Pa.: W. B. Saunders, 2000.

FAO/WHO. *Carbohydrates in Human Nutrition: Report of a Joint FAO/WHO Expert Consultation, Rome, 14–18 April 1997*. Rome: World Health Organization, Food and Agriculture Organization of the United Nations, 1998.

Guthrie, Joanne, and Joan Morton. "Food Sources of Added Sweetners in the Diets of Americans." *Journal of the American Dietetic Association* 100 (2000): 43–48, 51.

Kiens, B., and E. A. Richter. "Types of Carbohydrates in an Ordinary Diet Affect Insulin Action and Muscle Substrates in Humans." *American Journal of Clinical Nutrition.* 63 (1996): 47–53.

Macdonald, I. A. "Carbohydrate as a Nutrient in Adults: Range of Acceptable Intakes." *European Journal of Clinical Nutrition.* 53 (1999): S101–S106.

Debra Coward McKenzie
Rachel K. Johnson

CARDIOVASCULAR DISEASES. *See* **Health and Disease**.

CARÊME, MARIE ANTOINE. Marie Antoine Carême was born into a working class family in Paris in

1784. When he died in 1833, he was recognized as the greatest chef of his time, and his name was familiar to the rich and famous throughout Europe.

Carême's colleagues, and the public at large, first discovered his talents with the publication of *Le Pâtissier royal parisien* in 1815. It was only the third French treatise devoted entirely to French pastry, following *Le Pâtissier françois* (1653) and *La Pâtisserie de santé* (1790). Carême's approach to pastry was innovative in more than one way. Not only did he perfect and diversify the uses of now classic preparations, such as *génoise* and *biscuit* (sponge cakes) or cream puff pastry, but appears to be the first to give recipes for *fromage bavarois* (pastry cream lightened with whipped cream and stiffened with gelatin) and its elegant derivative, the *Charlotte russe*.

In addition to presenting a far greater number of preparations than his predecessors, *Le Pâtissier royal parisien* was also one of the first to include a profusion of engraved plates throughout. Until then, French cookbooks contained very few illustrations, and when they did, they were almost exclusively devoted to table settings, some of which, nevertheless, included instructions for building very elaborate centerpieces for dessert tables. Carême's engravings, on the other hand, were for finished dishes. To the modern eye, they look less like pictures of food than elaborate architectural constructions: temples, helmets, waterfalls, all made of cooked sugar, almond paste, nougatine, and so on, to serve not only as centerpieces, but also as presentation pedestals for his elaborate pâtés and desserts. For Carême, the way food was served was as important as the way it tasted. He criticizes the way his predecessors seasoned and served "mountains of food," and he even attacks the size and shape of the china they employed.

In his great work on cookery, *L'art de la cuisine française au XIXe siècle* (1847), Carême carries his love of extravagant decoration to new heights for savory dishes, as well, standing cutlets and poultry on end and presenting them in a circle, turban style, or sticking whole fish and roasts with a wide array of decorative skewers garnished with truffles, crayfish, and mushrooms. More important, he entirely revamps the art of cookery itself, arguing, among other things, for a cuisine based on "velvety" sauces, rather than the thin, watery sauces favored in the past and for developing a series of basic preparations (brown and white sauces, court-bouillons, forcemeats, etc.) that would become the building blocks of classic French cuisine upon which entire families of preparations could be constructed by combining them or changing the main ingredient or a flavoring.

Despite all of his modernism, Carême preferred the monumental *service à la française*—in which all the dishes of a given course were placed on the table at once—to the newly-introduced *service à la russe*, in which they were kept hot in the kitchen, then served sequentially from platters passed by waiters. "Certainly this method of serving is conducive to good eating," he wrote, "but our ser-

Portrait of Marie Antoine Carême, from a nineteenth-century wood engraving. ROUGHWOOD COLLECTION.

vice *à la française* is more elegant and lavish." His influence on French cuisine was enormous, and succeeding generations of chefs continued in the paths he had traced. It was not until 1903, when Auguste Escoffier published his *Guide Culinaire*, that Carême's authority was finally challenged, but his name is revered to this day as a great master whose contributions irrevocably shaped the course of French cuisine.

See also **France,** *subentries on* **Food and Cuisine in France** *and* **Tradition and Change in French Cuisine.**

BIBLIOGRAPHY

Hyman, Philip. "Culina Mutata: Carême et l'ancienne cuisine." In *L'Art culinaire au XIXe siècle: Antonin Carême.* Exhibition catalogue. Paris: Délégation à l'action artistique de la ville de Paris, April 1984.

Hyman, Philip, and Mary Hyman. "La première nouvelle cuisine." In *L'Honnête volupté: Art culinaire, Art majeur,* pp. 73–74. Paris: Editions Michel de Maule, 1989.

Rodil, Louis. *Antonin Carême.* Marseille: Laffitte, 1980.

Mary Hyman
Philip Hyman

CARIBBEAN. The Caribbean is generally thought to include the Greater and Lesser Antilles in the Caribbean Sea, as well as the mainland French Guiana, Guyana (formerly colonial British Guiana), and Suriname (formerly Dutch Guiana) in South America, and the Central American nation of Belize (formerly British Honduras). It is a geographic nexus between Old and New Worlds, and as such has been global since its inception as a region. Boasting no distinguishable population of direct pre-Columbian descendants apart from a small Carib community in Dominica, its inhabitants are otherwise composed of a highly diverse ethnic and cultural mix of descendants from the Americas, Africa, Europe, and Asia.

Spain was the initial colonizer of the entire Caribbean, but contiguous Spanish settlement in the Caribbean was limited largely to Puerto Rico, the Dominican Republic, and Cuba. Still, one should talk of the Caribbean as a region distinct from Latin America. The Spanish Caribbean islands have been shaped by experiences similar to those of their non-Spanish neighbors. While their cultural connections to Latin America are apparent—in language, culture generally, and perhaps in political philosophy—their Caribbean experience of slavery, plantation agriculture, and the rise of peasantries accord more with the Antilles. It is food (sugar in particular, but also coffee, cocoa, citrus, spices, and bananas), and not language that culturally unifies the Caribbean as a region historically.

Caribbean food, like the people who have come to inhabit the region, is not homogeneous, nor can we accurately talk about an indigenous diet without accounting for the effects of the Columbian conquest of the Americas. There were indigenous American food plants and tobacco, but there were also scores of new cultivars, from Africa, Europe, and Asia, as well as domesticated animals, which played a major role in the constitution of the region after 1492. But these two categories were not, however, isomorphic with the categories of domestically consumed and exported categories of post-conquest Caribbean food products. Instead, there are two categories of Caribbean food that better account for its history as a region. One encompasses those products that are responsible for constituting the region through a transatlantic system of trade. These products shape the way in which the region is defined by European and North American tastes. The other includes products grown as a direct response to the rigidities of this global system through culturally elaborated alternative systems of production, exchange, and consumption.

Repopulating the Region: Foundations of Exploration and Imperialism

Before the seventeenth century, the rights of Spain and Portugal to have colonial monopolies were established by several papal decrees issued in the fifteenth century. *Inter Coetera* of Pope Calixte III in 1456 gave Portugal the right to colonize lands "discovered" while circumnavi-

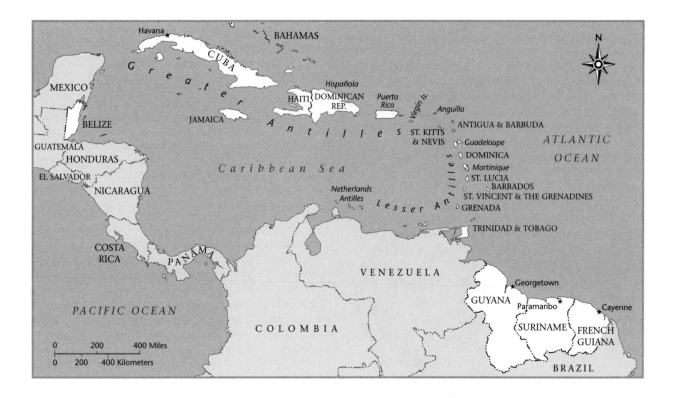

gating Africa on South Asian exploration. Later bulls, for instance *Inter Coetera II* of Alexander VI in 1493, affirmed Spanish rights to colonization west of the Azores. Colonization rights, as conveyed by God's earthly representative, were in effect divided hemispherically. The 1493 Tordesillas Treaty, for instance, recognized Portuguese colonization rights up to 270 leagues west of the Azores, thus establishing Brazil as Portuguese but the rest of what is now regarded as the Caribbean and Latin America as Spanish (Mudimbe, 1995).

A common denominator in Spanish and Portuguese colonization should be noted. *Rominus Pontifex*, a papal bull of Nicolas V in 1454, is explicit that the central mission of colonization was proselytization. Non-Christians could be dispossessed of their lands under the doctrine of *terra nullius* (no man's land) or even killed for resisting conversion to Christianity. In fact, as Valentin Mudimbe has documented well in his study of these papal instruments, "if [colonial subjects] failed to accept the 'truth' and, politically, to become 'colonized,' it was not only legal but also an act of faith and a religious duty for the colonizers to kill the natives" (Mudimbe, 1995, p. 61). The grounding of New World colonization by the Spanish in such a religious dictum is responsible in part for the violent character of transatlantic contact, both in the Caribbean region and in mainland Latin America. Disease (particularly smallpox), genocide, and enslavement eliminated most of the indigenous populations of the larger settled islands by the end of the sixteenth century. Beginning in the seventeenth century, settlements by other European nations had a similar effect on the smaller

islands of the Lesser Antilles. Today, only the small eastern Caribbean island of Dominica boasts any bona fide "Carib" Indian population, amounting to no more than two thousand persons.

Spanish settlements had been established, mainly on the islands of Hispaniola and Cuba. A production system using Amerindian slave labor was attempted, but after subsequent failures, some slaves were imported from Africa. Still, within seventy-five years, these settlements had become largely peasant-oriented and insular. Spain had turned its attention to the mainland of Latin America, pursuing a policy of resource (particularly gold) extraction. In the early seventeenth century, various European nations began to challenge Spain's monopoly on colonization in the Americas on the grounds that many of the islands claimed by Spain were not, nor had they ever been, occupied by Spain. British, French, Dutch, Danish, and Swedish explorers began to settle the smaller islands of the Lesser Antilles. Though the colonizers differed, there was one common trait on these newly settled lands—the plantation.

The Sweet Taste of Colonialism

Columbus's inadvertent happening onto the Americas in 1492 is responsible for a shift of Europe's center from thalassic (focused on the Mediterranean Sea) to oceanic (focused particularly on the Atlantic) (Mintz 1991, p. 112). McNeill has noted the impact of this shift on Europe:

> The principal historical impact of the American food crops, I suggest, was that they undergirded Europe's rise to world dominion between the eighteenth and

twentieth centuries. No other continent of the Old World profited so greatly. That was because Europe's climate, and especially its comparatively abundant rainfall, fitted the needs of the American food crops better than anywhere else, except China; and in China rice was so productive that the new crops had less to offer than potatoes and maize did in Europe" (McNeill, 1991, p. 52).

The Peruvian potato, for instance, was extraordinarily important to Europe, as it produced four times the caloric intake of rye bread. Potatoes never replaced grain completely: they do not store nearly as well as grain. But the efficient use of acreage is credited with population booms in Germany and Russia and the quick adoption of industry each experienced.

The constitution of an Atlantic epicenter is reflected not merely in the exchange of commodities between the Old and New Worlds. It is defined by the manner in which the demands made by Europe's growing populations were accommodated. Taste is essentially what defined the Caribbean as a region. The Caribbean provided a hospitable climate for the cultivation of sugar cane, particularly on the flatter, drier islands of the Antilles and coastal South America. The Spanish had initially developed sugar cane production in Cuba in the seventeenth century (Ortiz, 1947) but had not taken an interest in the mass production of the product. British colonization in the sixteenth century began to exploit sugar cane production using existing regional techniques, as well as methods learned from the Dutch occupation of Brazilian sugar estates. French interest in sugar production quickly followed and was equally influential by the eighteenth century. What was most significant about sugar was not the growing pancolonial interest in the cultivation of another New World commodity, but its rapid transformation from a luxury item to a sweet, tempting product demanded by a growing European working class: "...as sugar became cheaper and more plentiful, its potency as a symbol of power declined while its potency as a source of profit gradually increased" (Mintz, 1985, p. 95).

Production of sugar in the Caribbean multiplied to keep up with metropolitan demand. The need for a cheap source of physical labor led to the forced relocation of at least five million African slaves to the Caribbean during this same period. Revolts, slave maroonage (flight from plantations followed by the establishment of communities in remote terrains), and other forms of resistance both on the slave ships and in the colonies did little to slow European expansion of the sugar industry. In fact, at the time that Western Europe began to industrialize in the late eighteenth century, the importation of slaves to the Caribbean, particularly to the French colony of Saint-Domingue on the western third of the island of Hispaniola, was at its highest. Saint-Domingue was so valuable a colony to the French that at the Treaty of Paris they ceded their entire claim to Eastern Canada (now Quebec) in exchange for retaining it, Martinique, and Guadeloupe. During a protracted conflict of 1791 to 1803 in this colony, which in 1804 would be declared the republic of Haiti by revolting slaves, France and England both endured enormous military losses. France lost nineteen generals, including Leclerc, the husband of Napoleon's own sister Pauline, in the conflict. The "unthinkability" of losing the Haitian Revolution helps explain the silence on the subject in West European and American historiography (Trouillot, 1995). It was the profitability of Caribbean sugar colonies that had shaped the military and economic might of Europe generally and of France and England in particular.

Following the loss of Saint-Domingue, France retracted its New World interests, selling its remaining North American claims to the newly formed United States under the Louisiana Purchase in 1803. Britain's interest in sugar cane production declined along with global prices in the late nineteenth century, as beet sugar production proved more profitable. Prior to its contraction, however, the British employed a number of labor management devices aimed at reducing the costs of labor on their plantations. Between the end of apprenticeship in 1838 and 1917, about 500,000 East Indians were brought, mainly as indentured laborers, into the Caribbean (Williams, 1970, p. 348). The cultural influence is particularly strong where the concentrations of Indians were highest, in Trinidad and Guyana. Chinese laborers were brought, particularly to Cuba. Javanese were brought to Surinam, and African indentured servants to the French West Indies as well.

By the mid-nineteenth century, Cuba emerged as the dominant sugar producer in the Americas. Cuban reintegration into sugar production had begun following the British occupation of Havana in 1762 and the concomitant massive importation of slave labor into Cuba by enterprising merchants. Sugar production in Cuba essentially demonstrates an adaptation of the plantation system to a transition from mercantilist to capitalist interests in the New World. American merchant interests in the Cuban sugar industry developed throughout the nineteenth century and serve to explain, in part, American military intervention in the Cuban-Spanish War in 1898.

American military and financial involvement in Cuba thereafter typifies the manner in which foreign tastes shape the Caribbean's definition as an area in the twenty-first century. Rather than merely serving to satiate the European taste for sugar, the region has been used to satisfy new tastes: for sun, sex, and sin. The elimination of tropical diseases from the Caribbean by the early twentieth century, coupled with the devastation of Europe during World War I, made the Caribbean an attractive tourist destination. Casinos, brothels, and beaches were set up specifically to pander to North American and European interests.

A foreign traveler to the Caribbean is likely to come into contact with a broad range of dishes professing to be authentic in character. Most food produced for tourists reflects the particular tradition of transatlantic shipping from which these contemporary relations emerge: imported goods today compared to the dry provisions of the colonial period; Bacardi, yet another imported rum consumed over locally produced brands. Even the origins of the Daiquirí come from a drink that was consumed on slave ships to prevent scurvy: it was the name of the place where soldiers from the United States first tasted it (Ortiz, 1947, p. 25). As much as Europe's addiction to sugar defined the Caribbean culturally as a region from the seventeenth to the nineteenth centuries, so too does this new addiction affect it today. Even the concept of a Caribbean nation itself must endure the hungers of North American college students on spring breaks, en route to a "Bacardi Nation" that has petitioned for United Nations membership (Cohen, 1998).

Biting Back: Local Food Economies

Perhaps the most contentious debate among contemporary scholars of the Caribbean concerns the origins of the region's cultural influences. Many argue that African cultural influences define the region culturally (Herskovits, 1990; Brathwaite, 1993). Others have suggested the rigidities of the colonial system were so severe as to preclude the survival of any culture (Frazier, 1966). But one thing can be said about the Caribbean over any other region of the world. The Caribbean embodies all of the elements of what we today might call globalization: rapidity and movement of labor and capital; the amalgamation and negotiation of diverse and worldly cultural influences; and integral development of technology and communications. This, however, should not imply that the region is more culturally manufactured than other regions of the world, or that the late establishment of formal national or regional identities (beginning with the failed West Indies Federation from 1958–1962) is reflected in a lack of cultural distinctiveness. A few scholars have correctly noted that the Caribbean is best defined culturally through processes negotiated by its own inhabitants, and not determined by the mere movement of one or another traits from Europe, or Africa or Asia, to the region (Mintz and Price, 1992; Scott, 1991).

Inasmuch as the plantation system sought to define its inserted inhabitants in the Caribbean region as a monolithically defined production matrix, there were responses in the production, exchange, and consumption of food. Plantation owners were required by the late seventeenth century to provide rations to their slaves, but these tended to be inadequate. Slaves responded by establishing their own provision grounds adjacent to the plantations, on which they grew a wide range of products, not only for their own consumption but for sale as well (Mintz, 1978a; Mintz, 1978b; Gaspar, 1991; Mintz, 1995). So important were these provision grounds that some even revolted to keep them. The 1831 abolition of the Sunday market for the barter and exchange of slave-produced goods in Antigua sparked uprisings and the burning of several plantations (Gaspar, 1991). During the early years of the Haitian Revolution, "the leaders of the rebellion did not ask for an abstractly couched 'freedom.' Rather, their most sweeping demands included three days a week to work on their own gardens and the elimination of the whip" (Trouillot, 1995, p. 103).

Often the surplus of these gardens was sold in slave markets, some reaching off-island destinations. Though the available historical record seems unwilling to acknowledge the fact, slaves were, in a strict sense internationally mobile. Market women ("hucksters" in the Eastern Caribbean, "higglers" in Jamaica, "Madan Sara" in Haiti) would traffic agricultural products both in local markets and to other islands in the region, either individually or through third parties. An eighteenth-century soldier's diary establishes that nonproduce, even manufactured items—including textiles, "syrup beer and a country drink called mawbey" (Aytoun, 1984, p. 28)—are being exchanged in local markets in the small Eastern Caribbean island of Dominica by these market women, and legitimated through the payment of an often hefty fee to their owners. The ability of the market women to meet this fee (rumored to be as much as a dollar and a half a week—an immense sum by the standards of the day) in cash payments suggests that slave markets were significantly broader than the historical record has typically suggested. Dry goods such as rice, wheat flour, beans, corn, and salted meats we know were imported, both from Europe and the United States, except during interruptions caused by the American Revolution. Similarly, a number of agricultural products were being cultivated on provision grounds: "ground provisions" (tubers, including yams, potatoes, dasheen, tannia, eddoes), citrus, bananas and plantains, breadfruit, cassava (the flour of which is used to make farina), and various herbs, used as a spice, for medicinal purposes, and in Obeah, Voudun, and other Afro-Caribbean religious ceremonies, particularly as a poison against slavemasters and in rebellions.

Until emerging national governments established and enforced customs regulations in the 1960s, the regional circulation of agricultural produce and dry provisions remained primarily a locally constituted economy. Ascendant merchants and entrepreneurs following emancipation began to formalize the importation of dry and canned goods in particular. Local agricultural products continue to have symbolic meanings that reflect the historic articulation of ground provision production with the transatlantic plantation system. In islands where certain agricultural products are abundant, it is not uncommon to see surpluses of certain products—bananas and breadfruit are common in the Eastern Caribbean for instance—given away rather than sold. Land, no matter how small in area, has enormous meaning "as a symbol of personhood, prestige, security, and freedom for descendants of former slaves in the face of plantation-engendered land scarcity" (Besson, 1987, p.15). The South Asian and Far

Eastern contemporary cultural and cuisine influences—for instance in the curry dishes, such as the *roti* associated with Trinidad, Guyana, and Jamaica but abundant through the Caribbean—are in fact the result of colonial responses to labor shortages on plantations following emancipation. British emancipation implemented a four-year period of apprenticeship designed to reorient slaves to wage labor. Yet freed slaves continued to demonstrate a stronger desire to work provision grounds.

An interesting case in which the attachment to provision grounds and transatlantic production intersect involves the emergence of the Eastern Caribbean banana economies from the 1950s onward. Bananas, produced mainly in Dominica, St. Lucia, St. Vincent and The Grenadines, and Grenada, were under exclusive license for sale to Britain during this period. Farmers, most of whom were cultivating plots of no more than a few acres, were required to produce exclusively for sale in British supermarkets in exchange for guaranteed markets. Trouillot has noted the reluctance of Dominican banana farmers to diversify their production cycles because of the symbolic qualities that bananas impart: "We can always eat our fig" was the response. While still green, bananas are a starch, and thus an excellent carbohydrate source. Green bananas (or "fig") are frequently used in local Caribbean cooking, as a porridge, used with other ground provisions in a stew (*bouyon*), or even used in certain festive cooking dishes, for instance in *sankouche* (with salted codfish, Creole, and curry seasonings). Bananas require about nine months to come to fruition, and the comparisons to a child's gestation period are sometimes invoked in the care of banana plants.

Gobbling Globalization and Globalization Gobbled
Despite an ideological commitment to local produce, and the proactivity of some small-scale producers, Caribbean tastes are hardly defined by some kind of peasant ethic or veneration of local products. Tubers, once key carbohydrates in the Caribbean diet, are declining in importance. And while even the most prototypical of Caribbean dishes have always to some extent been the product of a Creolization (blending) of locally grown products with imported items such as salted codfish, rice, and flour, imported items, particularly canned items, are gaining as status symbols. Former Jamaican Prime Minister Michael Manley once lamented: "How can we build agriculture if our middle class believes it will surely rot if it can't buy tin mushrooms from abroad?" (Manley, 1988, p. 37). Monetary remittances from Caribbean persons living and working in more lucrative wage employment in Europe, Canada, and the United States has a long tradition in the Caribbean, and has been responsible for infusing cash into these economies. More recently, the remittance of actual packaged food products is becoming more prevalent (Palacio, 1991).

The retention of land, particularly for agricultural purposes, by small-scale producers and plantations alike,

continues to be under threat, not just by hurricanes, agricultural diseases, and declining prices for many agricultural products, but by a growing nonagricultural sector. Plantations have declined in importance through most of the Caribbean during the last century, and, accordingly, many former estates have been sold off. Supplementing one's wages on a plantation with the maintenance of a provision garden has thus become increasingly difficult. Golf courses, mining expeditions, and hotel development not only acquire or degrade land, but draw Caribbeans into low-paying service-sector wage positions, making them "a stranger in we own land" (Pattullo, 1996). As labor has gradually been drawn out of the agricultural sector, and land for gardens is increasingly abandoned, sold, or not maintained, many Caribbean people have become increasingly reliant on wages in a highly volatile and unstable service sector to buy these packaged, imported food items.

Local cuisine in some ways has become increasingly foreignized, not merely by the inclusion of foreign products in Caribbean diets, which has always occurred in varying degrees, but through substantial changes in the ways in which Caribbean fare is internationally recognized. Foreign investment interests increasingly appropriate local cuisine for commercial purposes. Hotels throughout the Caribbean are notorious for hiring European chefs to cook "authentic" Caribbean dishes, which are often flashy reinterpretations or fusions of Caribbean fare—*accras* (fried codfish) are marked up as much as ten times in price in foreign owned restaurants for the mere addition of tartar sauce. And the local dishes historically consumed by Caribbean people are likewise affected by these changes. Fried chicken is now ubiquitous, so much so that Kentucky Fried Chicken is the only franchise on many of the more sparsely populated islands. The longest lines in any Caribbean capital will be at the fast-food chains. Locally, Ovaltine has far more cachet than the Blue Mountain Coffee of Jamaica sought by upper-class American consumers. And apart from national celebrations in which folk recipes predominate, most celebrations throughout the Caribbean are overcome by, as some complain, "rum and coke and smoke," the smoke being from the barbecue.

Despite the dramatic changes to Caribbean food through the postwar period of modernization and international development, local responses to these changes continue to be informed by an ongoing process of Creolization. Foreign phenomena continue to be incorporated into local dishes. *Peleau* (a specifically Creole dish, but ostensibly the same rice and beans–based dish found throughout the Caribbean) was once regarded in the Eastern Caribbean as a dish that usually included fish. Declining fishery production and the rapid growth of frozen chicken imports have changed the content but not the underlying Caribbean form. Caribbean food has established its distinctiveness historically by creatively and strategically incorporating diverse elements into a localized answer to the rigidities imposed by foreign consumer demands.

See also **Africa; Banana and Plantain; Central America; France; Fruit; Iberian Peninsula; Potato; South America; United States: African American Foodways.**

BIBLIOGRAPHY

Aytoun, James. *Redcoats in the Caribbean.* Published for the East Lancashire Regiment Museum. Darwen, England: Wardleys Printers, Ltd., 1984.

Besson, Jean. "A Paradox in Caribbean Attitudes to Land." In *Land and Development in the Caribbean.* Edited by Jean Besson and Janet Momsen. London: Macmillan, 1987.

Brathwaite, Kamau. *Roots.* Ann Arbor: University of Michigan Press, 1993.

Cohen, Colleen B. "This is de test': Festival and the Cultural Politics of Nation-Building in the British Virgin Islands." *American Ethnologist* 25, 2 (May 1998): 189–214.

Crosby, Alfred W. "Metamorphosis of the Americas." In *Seeds of Change: A Quincentennial Commemoration.* Edited by Herman J. Viola and Carolyn Margolis. Washington, D.C.: Smithsonian Institution Press, 1991.

Frazier, E. Franklin. *The Negro Family in the United States.* Chicago: University of Chicago Press, 1966.

Gaspar, David Barry. "Antigua Slaves and Their Struggle to Survive." In *Seeds of Change: Five Hundred Years Since Columbus.* Edited by Herman J. Viola and Carolyn Margolis. Washington, D.C.: Smithsonian Institution Press, 1991.

Hall, Robert L. "Savoring Africa in the New World." In *Seeds of Change: Five Hundred Years Since Columbus.* Edited by Herman J. Viola and Carolyn Margolis. Washington, D.C.: Smithsonian Institution Press, 1991.

Herskovits, Melville J. *Myth of the Negro Past.* Boston: Beacon Press, 1990. Originally published in 1958.

McNeill, William H. "American Food Crops in the Old World." In *Seeds of Change: Five Hundred Years Since Columbus.* Edited by Herman J. Viola and Carolyn Margolis. Washington, D.C.: Smithsonian Institution Press, 1991.

Mintz, Sidney W. "Caribbean Marketplaces and Caribbean History." *Nova Americana* 1, 1 (1978): 333–344.

Mintz, Sidney W. "Pleasure, Profit, and Satiation." In *Seeds of Change: Five Hundred Years Since Columbus.* Edited by Herman J. Viola and Carolyn Margolis. Washington, D.C.: Smithsonian Institution Press, 1991.

Mintz, Sidney W. "Slave Life on Caribbean Sugar Plantations." In *Slave Cultures and the Cultures of Slavery.* Edited by Stephan Palmie. Knoxville: University of Tennessee Press, 1995.

Mintz, Sidney W. *Sweetness and Power: The Place of Sugar in Modern History.* New York: Viking, 1985.

Mintz, Sidney W. "Was the Plantation Slave a Proletarian?" *Review* 2 (1): 81–98, 1978.

Mintz, Sidney W., and Richard Price. *The Birth of African American Culture: An Anthropological Perspective.* Boston: Beacon Press, 1992.

Mudimbe, Valentin Y. "Rominus Pontifex (1454) and the Expansion of Europe." In *Race, Discourse, and the Origin of the Americas: A New World View.* Edited by Vera Lawrence Hyatt and Rex Nettleford. Washington, D.C.: Smithsonian Institution Press, 1995.

Ortiz, Fernando. *Cuban Counterpoint: Tobacco and Sugar.* New York: Knopf, 1947.

Palacio, Joseph. "Kin Ties, Food, and Remittances in a Garifuna Village in Southern Belize." In *Diet and Domestic Life in Society.* Edited by Anne Sharman, Janet Theophano, Karen Curtis, and Ellen Messer. Philadelphia: Temple University Press, 1991, 121–146.

Patullo, Polly. *Last Resorts: The Cost of Tourism in the Caribbean.* London: Cassell, 1996.

Scott, David A. 1991. "That Event, This Memory: Notes on the Anthropology of Diasporas in the New World." *Diaspora* 1, 3 (1991): 261–284.

Trouillot, Michel-Rolph. *Peasants and Capital: Dominica in the World Economy.* Baltimore: Johns Hopkins University Press, 1988.

Trouillot, Michel-Rolph. *Silencing the Past: Power and the Production of History.* Boston: Beacon Press, 1996.

Williams, Earl. *From Columbus to Castro: The History of the Caribbean.* New York: Vintage, 1984. Originally published in 1970.

Jeffrey W. Mantz

CASSAVA. Cassava, or manioc (*Manihot esculenta*), is a root crop native to tropical America that is now consumed by millions of people throughout the tropics, and is used in food preparation in many industrialized processes. Although it is not well known outside the tropics, cassava now accounts for about 30 percent of the world production of roots and tubers. It is an exceptional producer of carbohydrates and a plant better able to tolerate seasonal drought than other major food crops.

Plant Biology

The cassava plant is a perennial woody shrub that grows from about one to three meters in height. The leaves are palmate (hand-shaped) and dark green in color. The cone-shaped roots are starch storage organs covered with a papery bark and a pink to white cortex. The flesh ranges from bright white to soft yellow. Over five thousand varieties of cassava are known, each of which has its own distinctive qualities and is adapted to different environmental conditions.

The cassava plant is hardy and better able to tolerate drought and poor soil conditions than most other food plants. It can grow in extremely poor, acidic soils because it forms a symbiotic association with soil fungi (mycorrhizae). It is also one of the most productive food plants in terms of carbohydrate production per unit of land, and unequalled in its ability to recover when foliage is lost or damaged by diseases or pests.

The cassava plant is somewhat unusual, and even infamous, because both the roots and leaves can be toxic to consume. The toxicity of cassava is due to the presence of cyanogenic glucosides (compounds of cyanide and glucose) which liberate hydrogen cyanide (HCN)), a potent toxin, when the plant tissue is damaged. Cyanogenic glucosides are found throughout the plant and in all varieties of cassava. Varieties referred to as "sweet," or low-cyanide, have low levels of cyanogenic glucosides in the flesh of the root and can be peeled and cooked like other root vegetables. Those referred to as "bitter," or high-cyanide, have higher levels of cyanogenic glucosides throughout the root (peel and flesh) and require more extensive processing before they are safe to consume. A number of different processing techniques are used (grating, fermenting, sun drying), all of which serve to damage the plant tissue and hence cause the liberation and volitalization of HCN. The potential toxicity of cassava foods depends on the effectiveness of processing and preparation techniques; high-cyanide roots can be processed to remove all most all traces of cyanide-containing compounds. Many farmers prefer to cultivate the high-cyanide varieties for reasons that are not entirely clear.

History

Cassava was domesticated sometime in the distant past, maybe five thousand years ago. Exactly where is not known, but the current consensus is that domestication took place somewhere in Central or South America, perhaps along the southern border of Brazil, where wild relatives of cassava are currently found.

Cassava was the staple crop of the Amerindians of South America when the Portuguese arrived in 1500 just south of what is known as Bahia, Brazil. The Amerindians living in the area were the Tupinamba, who relied on cassava as a dietary staple, processing it into bread and meal using techniques similar to those still used by Amerindians in the twenty-first century.

When the Portuguese began to import slaves from Africa in about 1550, they used cassava in the form of meal (farinha) to provision their ships and began cultivating cassava at their stations along the coast of West Africa soon afterward. From their stations near the mouth of the Congo River, cassava diffused to all of central Africa. The Portuguese were also responsible for introducing cassava to East Africa, Madagascar, India, Ceylon, Malaya, and Indonesia by the 1700s.

Cassava was probably first introduced into Asia during Spanish occupation of the Philippines and was distributed throughout tropical Asia by the beginning of the nineteenth century. Expansion of cassava cultivation was pushed by colonial administrators who saw cassava as a famine reserve (especially the Dutch in Java, and the British in India), and as an export commodity (Malaya and Java in the 1850s).

Procurement and Production

Cassava is typically grown by small-scale farmers using traditional methods, and farming on marginal lands not well suited to other crops. It is propagated by planting stakes cut from the woody stems of mature plants. These plantings require adequate moisture during the first two to three months, but after that they are relatively drought resistant. Cassava roots mature to harvestable size in six to twelve months depending on variety and ecological conditions, and can be harvested at any time in the following two years, a harvest window that provides farmers an unusual degree of flexibility. To harvest the plants, farmers typically cut off the top three-quarters of the plant, and then pull up the roots and separate them from one another. Mechanical harvesting is still relatively rare.

Because fresh cassava roots deteriorate rapidly (within three to four days) after harvesting, they are usually consumed immediately or processed into a form that has better storage characteristics. Fresh roots (low-cyanide) destined for distant markets can be sealed in wax, packaged in plastic bags, or frozen to prevent deterioration. Leaves can be harvested at any stage of the growth of the plant, but typically only the youngest leaves are picked. The leaves deteriorate rapidly after harvesting and so are generally cooked the same day.

Cassava Foods

Cassava roots are prepared into an amazing variety of foods. Traditional preparation techniques vary by region, and by ethnic group within a given region.

South America. For Amerindians, the most common ways of preparing high-cyanide cassava were as a bread (*casabe, cazabe, beiju*), a roasted granular meal (*fariña*, farinha), and as a beer (*chicha*). In the northwest Amazon the bread is a large, thick (one inch or more) flat bread made by peeling and grating the roots, and then sieving the grated mash with water to separate the liquids and starch from the more fibrous portion. The starch is allowed to settle, and the liquids decanted off the top, then boiled to make a drink (*manicuera*). The starch and fibrous portion of the roots are stored separately and allowed to ferment for forty-eight hours before being dewatered, and then recombined and baked on a large clay griddle. In Venezuela and Guyana the bread is a thinner, hardtack-like bread made without the starch extraction step.

Farinha is made by soaking the roots of yellow-fleshed, high-cyanide varieties in water until they ferment. The roots are then peeled, grated, mixed with fresh grated roots and the mixture allowed to ferment for a week or more. The mash is then dewatered, sprinkled onto a hot griddle, and roasted while being stirred. The resulting product is a dry granular meal that can be stored almost indefinitely. It is most commonly consumed as *chive*, a drink that is made by putting a handful of meal in water and swirling to mix. Well-made meal can expand five times in volume and results in a full feeling.

Cassava bread being baked on a stone griddle at Dritabiki, Suriname. The bread, which is drying in the sun in the foreground, is paper-thin and brittle when eaten. Among the Djuka peoples of Suriname, the bread is crumbled to make a dried cereal called *kwak*. © ADAM WOOLFITT/CORBIS.

Chicha, a mildly alcoholic beer, is made from both low-cyanide and high-cyanide cassava. With low-cyanide varieties it is prepared by peeling, cooking, and mashing the roots, then adding water and some masticated roots and allowing the mixture to ferment. With high-cyanide varieties it is prepared from *manicuera* (the cooked juices) and a very thin bread, some of which is masticated, and other cooked roots or tubers.

In the national cuisines of South America, low-cyanide cassava is used as a vegetable (boiled, or boiled and fried). In Brazil, farinha is part of a number of traditional dishes, and in Colombia several breads are made with the fermented starch of high-cyanide cassava.

Africa. Cassava is the second most important food crop in sub-Saharan Africa. The majority of the cassava-based foods made in Africa rely on fermentation in one form or another. Two common products are *gari*, a granular meal similar to farinha, and *fufu*, a sticky dough made by pounding cooked or fermented roots into a paste. Other products include *chikwange* or *baton de manioc*, a steamed/boiled paste made from soaked roots, and *lafun*, a flour made from soaked roots.

Asia. Cassava roots are prepared in most Asian countries by boiling, baking, and frying. Another widespread practice is to peel, slice, and sun dry the roots and then grind them into a flour. The flour is then used to make porridge, or other traditional foods like *chappatis* and *dosas* (India), *bibingka* (Philippines), and a rice-like product called *landong* (Philippines). Commercially produced cassava starch is exported as tapioca.

South Pacific. Boiling and baking are the most common techniques for preparing cassava roots. On some islands cassava is also used to prepare *ma*, a traditional fermented product typically made from breadfruit.

North America and Europe. The pure starch, or tapioca, extracted from cassava roots is commercially available as a flour, flakes, or pellets (pearls) and is used to thicken a wide variety of food products such as sauces, gravies, pie fillings, pudding, and baby foods. The well-known dessert tapioca pudding is made with the pearls, which become gelatinous, semi-transparent balls in the finished product, affectionately referred to as "frog spawn" by British schoolchildren.

Relations to Human Biology

Fresh peeled cassava roots are rich in carbohydrate (30–35 percent), and low in protein (1–2 percent) and fat (less than 1 percent). They have nutritionally significant amounts of calcium (50 mg/100g), phosphorous (40 mg/100g) and vitamin C (25 mg/100g). The quality of the protein is relatively good, and the starch is highly digestible. Fresh cassava leaves are a good source of protein (23 percent), vitamins, and minerals.

The cyanide-generating potential of cassava roots and leaves has been of considerable concern. Although traditional methods of processing are effective in reducing cyanide content to innocuous levels, inadequate processing, as sometimes occurs during famine and periods of social upheaval, or the rush to market, can lead to health problems, particularly cyanide poisoning.

In South America there is no evidence of acute or chronic cyanide toxicity associated with cassava consumption by Amerindians for whom cassava is a traditional dietary staple, even though some groups rely on varieties of cassava with a very high cyanide content. In other parts of the world, however, cassava consumption has been associated with cyanide toxicity and other disorders. Acute cyanide poisonings are relatively rare, but can be fatal. The cases typically involve the consumption of raw or inadequately processed cassava. The symptoms are dizziness, headache, nausea, vomiting, and diarrhea.

In Africa, cassava-based diets have been associated with two neurological disorders: tropical ataxic neuropathy (TAN) and konzo. Both occur among the rural poor on diets largely restricted to high-cyanide cassava. TAN is a disease characterized by ataxia (muscular incoordination), reduced sensory perception, and deafness. The onset is slow and the course progressive, and it is found primarily in adults over the age of forty. Konzo is a disease characterized by the sudden onset of spastic paralysis in both legs, which results in a slightly spastic gait in mild cases and a complete inability to walk in severe cases. It primarily affects children and women under forty, and tends to occur in areas under conditions of famine or near-famine when people have nothing to eat but cassava and their nutritional status is poor. Both of these disorders are relatively rare given the millions of people on cassava-based diets in Africa.

The cyanide found in cassava-based diets is metabolically detoxified to thiocyanate and therefore cassava consumers have higher than normal levels of thiocyanate in body fluids. This is thought to be beneficial in areas of West Africa where sickle-cell anemia is present because thiocyanate inhibits the tendency of hemoglobin molecules to sickle. It is problematic in areas of Africa where the dietary iodine intake is low because thiocyante blocks iodine uptake by the thyroid gland. In these areas, cassava consumption is associated with iodine deficiency disorders including goiter, cretinism, mild mental disorders, and other related conditions.

Cassava as a Symbol of Identity

Important food plants like cassava tend to be powerful symbols of social and cultural identity. These symbolic associations can be clearly seen in South America.

For the native people like the Tukanoan, cassava is one of the most important and highly valued foods, and is consumed with meals and most snacks. They believe that cassava was the first food; it was planted by the first woman to make bread for the first man. They consider the extracted starch, *weta*, to be the purest, whitest, and more nourishing of foods. The term *weta* also means the essence of something. For non-Indian subsistence farmers in the Amazon, farinha is an essential component of everyday meals and snacks, as well as an ingredient in special dishes. People will go to considerable trouble and expense to obtain it from the market when home-produced supplies run out because cassava is part of the fabric of everyday life, and consuming it part of their identity. In contrast, for Brazil's urban elite, farinha is only occasionally consumed as part of certain traditional dishes, and the everyday consumption of farinha is seen as a marker of lower class status and poverty.

Global and Contemporary

Cassava now provides about 30 percent of worldwide production of roots and tubers, and is the staple crop of over 200 million people in Africa alone. World production increased more than four-fold in the last two decades of the twentieth century, with most of this increase being in Africa. Cassava is a crop with enormous potential to provide food energy, and a crop that will play a particularly important role in areas like Africa where the production of adequate food is a serious challenge.

It is also a crop that has received relatively little attention from researchers in comparison to the dominant food crops of the green revolution—wheat, rice, and maize. However, efforts are underway to rectify the situation, and find ways to capitalize on cassava's strengths (high productivity, tolerance of poor soils and low rainfall, and relatively good resistance to pests and disease) and to improve its major shortcomings (rapid postharvest deterioration), and address its cyanide content. The following areas are particularly promising:

1. The use of microbial biotechnologies (technologies that utilize organisms like fungi and bacteria) to improve production and the processing of traditional products and to develop new products. Cassava production depends on soil mycorrhiza (fungi), and processing technologies depend on a variety of fungi (*Aspergillus*, *Saccharomyces*, and others), and bacteria (mostly *Lactobacillus* and *Corynebacterium*) to reduce toxicity, improve storage qualities, and achieve the desired taste and texture of cassava foods.

2. The use of micropropagation (culturing of tiny masses of dividing cells) for the exchange of varieties. This is particularly important for cassava because the plant is traditionally propagated from vegetative stakes that can transmit disease.

3. The use of genetic biotechnology for inserting new genetic material (DNA) into cassava varieties in order to improve quality and disease resistance.

See also **Africa; Brazil; South America.**

BIBLIOGRAPHY

Balagopalan, Cherukat, Gourikkutty Padmaja, Saroj K. Nanda, and Subramoney N. Moorthy. *Cassava in Food, Feed, and Industry.* CRC Press, Inc.: Boca Raton, Fla., 1988.

Cock, James H. *Cassava: New Potential for a Neglected Crop.* Boulder, Colo., and London: Westview Press, 1985.

Dufour, D. L. "The Bitter is Sweet: A Case Study of Bitter Cassava (*Manihot esculenta*) Use in Amazonia." In *Food and Nutrition in the Tropical Forest: Biocultural Interactions.* Edited by A. M. Hladik, A. Hladik, O. F. Linares, H. Pagezy, A. Semple, and M. Hadley. Man in the Biosphere, vol. 15, pp. 575–588. Paris: UNESCO and Parthenon Publishing, 1993.

Dufour, D. L. "Cassava in Amazonia: Lessons in Safety and Utilization from Native Peoples." *Acta Horticulturae* 375 (1994):175–182.

Dufour, D. L. "A Closer Look at the Nutritional Implications of Bitter Cassava Use." In *Indigenous Peoples and the Future of Amazonia: An Ecological Anthropology of an Endangered World.* Edited by Leslie E. Sponsel. Tucson: University of Arizona Press, 1995.

Dufour, D. L. "Cyanide Content of Cassava (*Manihot esculenta*, Euphorbiaceae) Cultivars Used by Tukanoan Indians in Northwest Amazonia." *Economic Botany* 42 (1988): 255.

Dufour, D. L. "Effectiveness of Cassava Detoxification Techniques Used by Indigenous Peoples in Northwest Amazonia." *Interciencia* 14, no. 2 (1989): 86–91.

Jones, William O. *Manioc in Africa*. Stanford: Stanford University Press, 1959.

Lancaster, P. A., J. S. Ingram, M. Y. Lim, and D. G. Coursey "Traditional Cassava-Based Foods: Survey of Processing Techniques." *Economic Botany* 36, no. 1 (1982): 12–45.

Wigg, David. *The Quiet Revolutionaries: A Look at the Campaign by Agricultural Scientists to Hunger and How the Much-Needed Cassava Could Help*. Washington, D. C.: The World Bank, 1993.

Darna L. Dufour

CATSUP. *See* **Condiments.**

CATTLE. The history of the domestication of cattle, their use as key elements of human survival systems, their biology, how and when they are currently raised, and how they are processed and marketed for consumption are all issues that help us understand beef as a part of different food systems. "Cattle" refers to live animals, including the young (calves), females before giving birth (heifers), females that have given birth (cows), fertile males (bulls), and castrated males (steers). Beef is the meat of all these animals while specialized terms for beef, such as veal (the

meat of young, milk-fed calves), relate to food preferences in different cultures.

Beef is produced and consumed worldwide, and, like that of many commodities, its production is increasing. It is consumed not only as hamburgers, roasts, and steaks, but meat by-products including hides, horns, hoofs, intestines, and brains are used in a variety of products including: shampoo, marshmallows, ice cream, gelatin, cement, chalk, chewing gum, makeup, matches, margarine, and strings for musical instruments and tennis racquets. Beef is raised in three phases before it is processed: calves are raised on pasture and range land, as feeder cattle they feed on pasture, crop residue, and range land, and finally they go to feedlots, where they are fattened for slaughter. The slaughterhouse (packer) is also the disassembly plant, where the carcass is divided into "cuts." Since the advent of boxed beef, most of the disassembly occurs at the plant itself, whereas previously sides of beef went to wholesale or retail butchers who divided it further. After slaughter, the commodity chain diverges. A portion goes directly to wholesalers, who distribute to institutional users or grocery stores, although grocery chains are increasingly linked directly to the packer. Another portion goes into further processing for sausages, bologna, hot dogs, and other processed meats, or is used for canned and frozen "heat and eat" meals. The carcass is rendered and the by-products are used in a wide variety of products. For example, hooves can be made into gelatin, hides into leather, bones and cartilage into bonemeal for plant nutrition, and intestines and some organs and other parts not usually used in meat markets go to pet food. Up until the mid-1980s, the

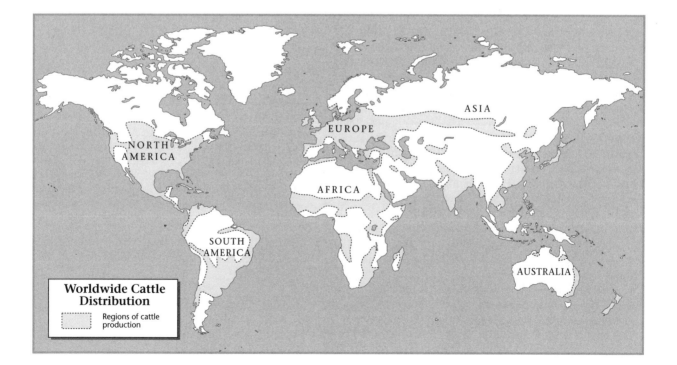

Worldwide Cattle Distribution
Regions of cattle production

bones and nerves were ground into bone meal and fed as a supplement to cattle and other animals, until this practice was banned. Beef is increasingly consumed in restaurants, from steakhouses to fast food establishments. There is enormous variety in the use of all parts of the animal for delicacies prepared for home use and street food sale, from the stomach (tripe soup in many cultures) to the tail. Lower-quality beef and inferior parts are used in Japan in a simple dish called *nimono* as a kind of seasoning.

Biology

Description. Cattle are large ruminants of the family Bovidae and the genus *Bos*. Ruminants are mammals whose stomach has four parts—rumen, reticulum, omasum, and abomasums. The rumen provides a pouch where fibrous plant materials are broken down by bacteria so their nutrients can be digested. Because they are ruminants, cattle can digest plant materials that serve no other human use. As herbivores, they are selective eaters, but consume a variety of types of plants.

From the time of their original domestication, cattle were selectively chosen to meet multiple human needs, including providing traction and transportation, meat, and milk. Cattle have provided fuel for cooking and heating, plaster for walls, manure for gardens and fields, strings for musical instruments, and clothing—from hats to shoes. Originally valued for docility, cattle are increasingly bred to meet specific needs of those who raise them, process them, and eat them.

The systematic development of cattle breeding began as a part of the industrial revolution and the renaissance of British agriculture. The enclosure movement in England in the sixteenth century not only forced rural peasant farmers from the land to work in factories, but left privatized lands in the hands of a few landed gentry who could breed the stock they desired. Breed formation started with a useful local type that was then inbred until it showed uniformity. Breeds were then shown at livestock fairs that were part of the country lifestyle of the landed classes. Heredity was carefully recorded in herd books, and sires and mating were carefully controlled. Pure breed associations were formed. It was in this context, between 1750 and 1850, that the Angus, Hereford, and Shorthorn breeds were developed.

In other regions of Europe, inbreeding had produced uniform and locally adapted breeds, although specialization in rearing and feeding cattle for beef occurred long after it had in Great Britain. In the United States, interest in breeding began around the turn of the twentieth century (numbers had been important up to that point). In particular, Herefords were imported because they matured early, which allowed for the slaughter of yearlings rather than the four-year-olds prevalent at that time. In parts of France, five- to six-year-olds are still preferred for their flavor, particularly if they are fattened on grass.

In the course of seeking early maturing animals, many lines and traits have been lost. However, the introduction of new breeds has transformed the appearance—and probably the taste, nutritional qualities, and tenderness—of cattle in beef-exporting nations, particularly the United States and Canada.

Original extent. Cattle may have originated at about the same time in Europe, Asia, and Africa. Surviving relatives are present on all three continents. Seldom kept solely for beef production, cattle were beasts of burden as well as critical providers of milk and butter. They were only slaughtered when their ability to produce these ongoing products was reduced, at which point their hides, hooves, horns, bones, intestines, and other non-edible parts were valued as much as their meat, which generally supplemented that provided by wild game. Modern domestic cattle are believed to descend from *Bos taurus*, which includes European breeds such as Shorthorn and Jersey and *Bos indicus*, which includes Zebu breeds from South Asia and Africa. Cattle in much of the world were primarily used for traction for crop agriculture and for transportation.

Nutritional and nonnutritional constituents. Bovine flesh is called beef when the animal is mature and referred to as veal when it is a calf. Beef provides high levels of energy and protein. Proteins found in beef have a higher digestibility than most plant proteins and a wider range of amino acids. The bioavailability of important minerals (including calcium, phosphorous, iron, zinc, magnesium, and manganese) as well as vitamins (including thiamine, riboflavin, niacin, pyridoxine [B6], and B12) is high in beef. In many parts of the world, beef is viewed as the most fortified and most nutritious butcher's meat. High in iron, it can also be high in cholesterol and highly saturated fatty acids, as for many years cattle were bred for weight gain. Corn-fed cattle have higher levels of omega-6, which is a coagulant, in their meat. Grass-fed animals, in contrast, have much higher concentrations of omega-

TABLE 1

Characteristic	*Bos taurus*	*Bos indicus*
Ears	Short and erect	Long and drooping
Hump	Absent	Well-developed and fleshy
Skin	Relatively tight	Very loose
Hair	Long and thick	Fine and short
Horns	Short and turned down or hornless	Long and turned up
Call	Bellow	Grunt
Body	Wide through barrel and hindquarter	Narrower throughout
Temperament	Relatively docile	Nervous
Heat tolerance	Poor	Good
Birth weight	High	Low

These distinguishing characteristics have been combined and recombined in over a hundred different registered breeds.

3 fatty acids, which have anti-inflammatory properties and are anticoagulants. Too much omega-6 leads to clogged arteries, while omega-3 fatty acids do not. Fat content in general depends on the cut of beef, genetics, and the feeding of the animal prior to slaughter.

History

Domestication. Among early transhumant populations, which moved seasonally to find food, herds of hoofed mammals that were the ancestors of our current breeds moved with them. Initially roaming to find grass as seasons changed, cattle were later driven to provide a constant source of fuel and milk. As human life became more sedentary, cattle were an important part of the move to agriculture, providing traction for plowing in many sites in the Old World. In the New World, cattle were introduced with European colonization.

Historical diffusion and trade. Cattle husbandry was a part of Roman culture and spread with the Roman Empire. Norman conquerors brought beef-eating to the British Isles, although cattle were already serving many other functions for farm households. Cattle culture was an early part of complex social organization, often representing wealth. For example, the Celts based their wealth on cattle prior to 1066. In fact, in a number of languages the root word for cattle and for money is the same. In parts of Africa, wealth is judged by number of cattle, and dowries are paid in cattle.

South American grasslands did not have large ruminants before the Spanish and Portuguese introduced cattle to the grasslands from Argentina and Chile to Mexico and the southern part of what is now the United States. Raised on large *estancias, faezendas,* or *haciendas,* they were valued primarily for their hides, hooves, and horns, which could be exported to Europe. The owners of the large estates employed *vaqueros, gauchos,* or cowboys to undertake the day-to-day care of the cattle and to drive them to the appropriate place for shipping or slaughter. Thus, cattle imported to the New World from Spain were primarily beef cattle, the famous long-horns, tough for eating but resilient, and able to utilize the meager feed available in the dry plains of the central North American continent.

Australia and New Zealand grasslands were the last to have cattle introduced. The first cattle, black Africander, arrived in 1788 and Zebu cattle arrived from India in 1795, followed by English breeds. While settlers introduced cattle, it was large companies that exploited the great potential of the early cattle industry in Australia. The early cattle were driven to follow forage and water availability and then to slaughter. Wire fencing in the 1860s and bore wells and the railway book in the 1880s allowed for the establishment of permanent cattle stations. With the first shipment of frozen beef to England in 1879, the cattle industry became export-oriented.

Europeans who came to the North American continent and the Antipodes (New Zealand and Australia) brought their livestock with them. There was much genetic diversity in the livestock that arrived with migrants from different rural areas of Europe. The cattle from northern Europe tended to be triple-purpose cattle—for traction, milk, and meat—and they tended to be either family cows or small herds of beef raised on family farms outside population settlements.

The coming of the railroad transformed cattle production in North and South America, allowing both livestock and sides of beef to travel further faster. Beef was produced primarily in the plain states. Cattle drives to railheads gave rise to the myths of the cowboy. Railroads transported the cattle to population centers, where they could be butchered nearer to the consumer. The wide dispersal of cattle and their seasonal migrations was gradually cut back as the plains were fenced and other forms of agriculture competed with cattle for the land.

Yet even in the east, the ability of ruminants to convert plant materials of all kinds into food meant that land unfit for agriculture, because it was too steep or too poorly drained, was used for grazing cattle. As farmers moved into the plains in the 1830s and 1840s, before the lands of the majority of states like Iowa and Illinois were drained for agriculture, cattle were an important part of the farming mix using land that was unfit for cultivation or homesites. As soil was drained, however, less land was used for pasture, and more was used for crops.

Cattle were still the cheapest way of shipping the course grains, particularly corn. Meadows changed to pasture, and then were drained and became cropland. The farmers who moved to these reclaimed areas were almost all commercial rather than subsistence. As cities grew, the demand for meat increased.

James Whitaker argues that "through a combination of availability of railroads, type of land tenure, cost of drainage, and price of beef in the 1880s and early 1890s," many of the states shifted to producing cash grains rather than fat cattle (1975, p. 14). Mechanization in particular helped bring about this change, as did the ability to open up the prairie with chisel plows.

During the nineteenth century, cow/calf operations and fattening cattle were further differentiated. By 1819, cattle feeders from Indiana, Ohio, and Kentucky were traveling as far west as Missouri and Oklahoma in search of young animals to take home for fattening on corn in preparation for the overland drive to the eastern markets. But some cattle producers believed they could raise cattle *and* corn more cheaply in Iowa and Illinois than in Ohio or Kentucky. Those cattle were driven to eastern markets or shipped south to New Orleans on the Mississippi.

Those who first drove feeder cattle east to fatten brought the cattle-feeding pattern to Iowa and Illinois when they returned to settle after seeing the advantages

Detail of a fresco from a tomb in the Valley of the Kings, Egypt. Dating from 1306 to 1209 B.C.E., this scene shows a man and his wife (she is following him) plowing fields with cattle. In some cultures, cattle were far more valuable as draught animals than as food. © ARCHIVO ICONOGRAFICO, S.A./CORBIS.

of cheap prairie grass and corn. Until the Civil War, these cattle went primarily to the eastern markets.

Farmers had to go greater distances to find the feeder cattle they needed to fatten for market. Cow/calf operations, which thrived on smaller farm units, encouraged settlement. Large-scale operators gathered their herds from farmers who felt that feeding cattle was not profitable with less than two dozen head (Whitaker, 1975, p. 22). Thus, small operators produced the calves, while larger operations fed them out and fattened them.

After the Civil War, feeders again returned to Texas and the plains. The increasing use of the western range as a source of feeder cattle brought significant changes to the cattle feeding industry in the Corn Belt. There were two available feeding strategies: 1) purchase cheap western cattle, feed them for a year, and then sell for a small profit margin per animal hoping to make money on the large volume of sales; or 2) pursue a low-volume business of better quality of cattle bringing a larger profit per head. Improved cattle provided a way to get the most profit out of good grass and good corn while not robbing the land of its fertility as the cattle recycled the nutrients they consumed.

Those who followed the second strategy were more interested in improved beef breeds. Farmers were slow to improve their herds, but those who did generally profited from it. Because cow/calf operations were a small part of many farms, breed and pasture improvements were not quickly or widely adopted.

By the end of the 1850s, cattle were being fattened in Iowa and Illinois rather than being calved and weaned and driven east to be fattened. In the years after 1865, technological advances contributed to the continued growth and expansion in the beef industry. Illinois and Iowa became leading producers of corn-fattened cattle and Chicago became one of the world's leading cattle markets. The organization and expansion of a central market in Chicago was a result of the new railroad network, the concentration of meat packers in Chicago, the development of refrigeration facilities, the reorganization of retail meat marketing, and growth of the export trade in live and dressed beef. Demand for dressed beef increased, and the Corn Belt states met that demand with the combined production of cattle and corn.

The Civil War and the railroads brought centralization of market facilities, as increased receipts of livestock created chaos in handling transactions between several markets in the city. Formation of the Union Stockyards in 1865 was critical to bringing order out of chaos and in concentrating power. Demands of the new end market, created by the expansion of the railroads, gave rise to the dressed beef industry and the major packers who controlled it.

Although the technology existed before the Civil War, it was only in the late 1860s that refrigeration was effectively used to prevent the early spoilage of fresh meat, lengthening the time and distance from point of slaughter that fresh beef could be consumed. At first, consumers distrusted the quality of meat shipped hundreds of miles after being slaughtered; but, because dressed beef was sufficiently cheaper than local butcher stock, people were willing to try it.

The Swift Company was critical in moving this conversion forward. Swift and other companies fought with the railroad about whether dressed beef could be shipped at the same rate as live cattle. The invention of the hermetically sealed tin meant that corn-fattened cattle from Illinois and Iowa could be packed and shipped to domestic and foreign markets.

Soon after the Civil War, in the early 1870s, Chicago packers replaced packing pickled beef in barrels with canning. A court ruling that invalidated patented claims on the canning process triggered the expansion of canned meat. Western beef tended to be canned, as the quality was inferior to the corn-fed beef of the Midwest.

The great expansion of the market through technological and marketing changes in the dress beef trade created large vertically organized Chicago-based corporations. These corporations controlled, for the most part, both the wholesale and retail domestic markets for beef products. Known as the "big five," Armour & Company, Patrick Cudahy, Nelson Morris, Swift & Company, and Wilson & Company frequently acted together in buying cattle in the Union Stockyards and dividing retail trade among themselves. They also set prices and attempted to eliminate some of the less profitable aspects of competition.

As these companies were expanding rapidly due to the sharp increase in demand, they were pressed for cash and, thus, worked hard to lower both the price of labor in the packing plants and the cattle they purchased. To compound the problem of vertical integration and monopoly, a number of the packers went into the cattle feeding business.

By 1900 the concentration, if not the ownership of packing plants, had become decentralized. The major leading packing centers, with the same packers owning most of the capacity, were located in Chicago, Kansas City, Omaha, East St. Louis, and St. Joseph. There were lesser centers in Des Moines, Sioux City, St. Paul, and Fort Worth. The packers had so revolutionized the meat trade that butchers in some circles in the 1920s claimed that "not a retail butcher has made a fair profit and a living in the last ten years" because of packer branch houses (Whitaker, 1975, p. 54).

A major transformation of beef packing, which had previously been located near consumers and the transportation centers of larger cities, occurred with the founding of Iowa Beef Packing in Denison, Iowa, later renamed IBP. To lower buying costs, shorten transportation distances, and eliminate intermediaries, IBP put its plants near large feed lots, which tended to be located near sources of feed grains and away from large population centers.

Work on the plant floor was organized to require less skilled and less experienced workers. Thus wages could be considerably lower than in Chicago, Kansas City, or even Des Moines. Focusing on primal cuts, they became know as "kill and chill" plants, shipping to meat processors all the specialty items that were once part of traditional packing plants. Hot dogs, sausages, processed meats, and even hamburger were shipped to other sites for further elaboration and additional value. That also kept work standard and wages low compared to the plants that were closing in the Midwest.

In 1967, IBP perfected an innovation that dramatically changed the industry—boxed beef. Instead of shipping beef to customers in whole carcass form, as the industry had done for years, IBP mastered a process in which the packer breaks down the carcass into smaller portions. These cuts are then vacuum-packed and shipped out in boxes. While boxed beef was initially sold to the hotel, restaurant, and institutional trade, they soon shipped it to retail groceries as well.

Through this "butcher friendly" concept, it became possible to eliminate more than 250 pounds of fat, bones, and trimmings, which were of very little value to the retail and food service customer. Boxed meat improved quality, provided easier merchandising at the retail level, improved shelf life, and saved energy, transportation, and labor costs. This major innovation in beef processing came with the 1967 opening of a boxed beef operation at IBP's new Dakota City plant complex. It was the first large-scale beef processing plant in the nation. Dakota City also became the new location of the company's headquarters.

The advent of boxed beef changed the structure and geography of the entire meat industry. Now, instead of shipping carcasses, the packing plants cut the beef down into wholesale pieces and vacuum packed them into boxes. This greatly reduced the amount of work for wholesale butchers and also decreased the amount of space needed for shipping. In the 1970s, fuel and transportation costs were at an all-time high in constant dollar terms. Boxed beef allowed the packer to add more value to the product at the plant, to reduce transaction costs in shipping, and it reduced labor costs for urban retail grocery chains. It also reduced the power of grocery store cutters, as the retooling of the plants in rural areas reduced the power of the workers on the floor. Stores were able to bypass the skilled labor union members for meatpacking and distribution by hiring low-skilled workers to do repetitive tasks that were relatively quickly learned; turnover was high due to poor working conditions but labor was plentiful as long as unemployment was relatively high or there was a plentiful supply of immigrant workers. That strategy that linked new technology to new workers lowered costs and pushed the balance of power in the industry in favor of the packers and the grocery chain and against cattle growers and packing plant workers.

Procurement

Husbandry. Calves are generally conceived either through artificial insemination (increasingly the case in developed countries) or by bulls, in the case of larger herds, or borrowed for the occasion for smaller herds. Calves are raised on grassland or rangeland with their mothers until weaned, then usually sold to a stocker feeder who will bring them up to around nine hundred to a thousand pounds on rangeland, pasture, or crop residues. Prior to slaughter, cattle often enter a feedlot, where they are fed high-protein feed and fattened.

Artificial insemination (AI) is little used in cow/calf operations in the western half of the United States. Most herds depend on bulls. One bull for each twenty to thirty cows is usually recommended. The biggest deterrent to using AI is the extra labor needed to detect cows in heat on open range and then to confine them for individual insemination. The problem was partially overcome with the approval for use of hormonal materials that can be injected to synchronize estrus. More than half of an entire cowherd may be bred successfully during a single day by a skilled inseminator using AI and estrus stimulation.

Birthing difficulties are one of the most costly problems in calf production. As a result, American ranchers typically breed their heifers to Longhorns in order to get low birthweight calves—but this results in substandard beef.

Cow/calf producers normally rely on grazing. Nutrients obtained through grazing are usually less costly than those provided through harvested forages, grains, or other processed feeds. In addition, the dispersion of cattle grazing helps to minimize other problems, such as disease epidemics. Lowering the risk of disease decreases production costs and also reduces the need for labor. The western United States dry native range, on which agricultural operations are minimal, provides an overwhelming share of the grazing. The area necessary to support a cow depends on the amount of rainfall—the less the rainfall, the more acres required to support each head of livestock.

The stocker feeder generally uses pasture and rangeland as well as crop residues for feeding. The cattle still harvest most of their own food. Increasingly, stocker feeders are using rotational grazing (particularly in Australia and New Zealand), which helps them raise more cattle better on less land and keep the land in better condition.

There is a disjunction between the cow/calf operator or stock feeders and the feedlots/packers, which results in a very fragmented commodity chain with a great deal of distrust between the stages. The first two stages manage the resource. The last two stages manage the market.

While much of the world prefers grass-finished beef, the United States and Canada have focused on corn-fattened beef. Grain farmers who raised cattle on their uncultivable land fed their cattle using their own

The use of cattle as draught animals has declined considerably since the introduction of tractors, but in rural Romania it is still a common sight. This team of bullocks is at work in fall plowing in the village of Hobbitza. © ADAM WOOLFITT/CORBIS.

grains. While farm feedlots were dominant through the 1960s, changes in the tax laws in the 1970s made investment in "agricultural" enterprises extremely profitable. Capital moved into stand-alone feedlots, first from rural professionals, then from their urban kin and friends, and finally from corporations. The relocation of the feedlots, in turn, impacted corn production. As the large feed lots moved to more arid areas, where waste management was easier and population less dense, demand for corn increased. Beef fattening became more concentrated and shifted west.

Biological and mechanical technology worked together to standardize beef production in order to maximize packer convenience. Packing plants demanded uniform-sized carcasses to maintain the speed of the disassembly line. Adjusting the height of the chain that carried the carcass around the plant was time consuming. At the same time, hormones were being introduced to increase rate of growth and improve feed conversion. While there is some evidence that the injection or implanting of hormones or steroids may toughen the meat and affect flavor, it does add extra weight. Animals were slaughtered at the same age and much higher weights, in essence increasing the supply of beef.

Slaughter and processing. Traditionally, small farmers around the world raised cattle from calf to slaughter (although in many parts of Africa, as in North and South America, beef cattle were not herded by their owners). Once the productivity of the animal had declined or feed supply became scarce, it was either slaughtered for home consumption or taken to an *abattoir* or butcher to be slaughtered, disassembled, and sold.

The division of labor between cow/calf operations, stock feeder operations, and fattening operations was established in the early part of the twentieth century. By that time, the industry had taken on its current form—very centralized packing operations with close ties to wholesale and retail distributors linked to feedlots, feeders, and cow/calf operations. Industrial concentration increases as the animals grow older. There are a great many cow-calf operations, slightly fewer stock feeder operations for the weaned calves, many fewer feedlots, many fewer packers, and a decreasing number of wholesalers, now mostly linked to retail chains.

Before World War II, retail stores bought quarters and sides of beef and cut them into "primal cuts" and retail cuts. After the war, consolidation of the retail grocery industry proceeded very rapidly, as local butcher shops and single-store operations were closed. One of the major ways supermarkets had of increasing profits was decreasing labor costs. Self-service, which required less labor to gather customer orders, now included meats, replacing the butcher who had previously cut and wrapped meat to each customer's specific request. Supermarket corporations particularly welcomed the central processing of meat, which allowed them to reduce the number of meat cutters who were their highest paid workers. Box beef was an innovation that met the needs of supermarket chains, as net profits declined between 1967 and 1974 to 0.8 percent, 60 percent of their previous level, and real wages grew over 7.5 percent per year, or 50 percent faster than before (Walsh, 1991, p. 452). Thus the retail part of the beef industry was ready for packaging innovation. That innovation, boxed beef, impacted the geography as well as the structure of the meat-packing industry by moving beef processing from urban centers, where, as a mature industry, it was highly unionized, to rural areas near feedlots and sources of grain, particularly corn. As these areas were sparsely populated, it was necessary to recruit a labor force, and new migrants from Asia (particularly Southeast Asia), Latin America (particularly Mexico), and Africa (particularly Somalia) moved to the rural packing plants to take the jobs.

Storage. Consumers prefer fresh beef to frozen beef. Yet beef has a relatively high spoilage rate. Spoilage is averted by keeping bacterial counts low, which is accomplished through plant cleanliness, careful slaughter procedures that prevent *E. coli* from the intestines from coming into contact with the carcass as it goes to be disassembled, and keeping temperatures low so that the bacteria multiply at low rates. Reducing the oxidation of the meat after aging, that is, minimizing contact with oxygen in the atmosphere, is also a factor. Refrigerated cars and trailer trucks help reduce spoilage, as does consuming the meat shortly after it is produced and slaughtered. Irradiation of beef is now highly promoted by the industry to increase shelf life, but meat processors have been reluctant to introduce this procedure because of consumer concerns related to its impact on beef quality and safety.

Aging the carcass adds tenderness and flavor, but adds cost in terms of storage space and time in inventory. After slaughter and initial disassembly, beef is moved within the packing plant to a refrigerated room kept at a temperature between 34°F and 38°F. This cools the meat and firms it prior to shipment. The meat is generally kept refrigerated for 24 to 36 hours. Fresh beef can be held for several weeks at this temperature, and prime beef is sometimes held for five or six weeks long to "age" it. Fresh chilled beef must be shipped in specially refrigerated cars and ships in order to arrive in good condition.

Distribution. There is increasing vertical integration between the international companies who own the packing plants and retail grocery chains. While beef has traditionally gone through a series of brokers and wholesalers, the links in the commodity chain have been reduced for a number of major grocery chains such as Walmart. This vertical integration has been coupled with an increase in branded beef for supermarket sales, which was unheard of in the early 1990s. Restaurant chains are also forming tighter linkages with packers and even feedlots, stock feeders and cow/calf operators, as consumer demand for particular qualities in appearance and taste, as well as how an animal is raised, become more important.

Changes in the means of procurement over time. Carcasses are graded for quality, which is assumed to be related to taste and tenderness. The price paid by the packing house depends in part on the grade the carcass receives and that day's demand for the different grades. Different nations have their own grading standards. Grading standards change over time, but relatively slowly. In part, that is because each stage of the system defines quality differently.

Despite increasing concentration in feeding and packing, the beef cattle industry is disjointed and dispersed because of its dispersed resource base. There are over one million cow-calf herds in the United States, down 2 percent between 1996 and 1997. The average cowherd consists of fifty cows. Thirty percent of calves come from 700,000 herds, averaging fifteen heads of cattle. Sixty percent of cattle end up in 215 different feedlots. This dispersed base funnels through the auction markets, which still play a dominant role in the cattle industry, into gross economies of scale in the form of feedlots and packing. The cattle industry is a scavenger industry, in that its nutrient fuel base varies widely and ranges extensively, and includes grass, crop residue, and wheat that otherwise might not be used for commercial purposes. And there are difficulties in linking the different parts of the value chain when one part is based on managing the available resources (cow-calf operations and feeder cattle operations) and another is based on responding to market timing (feed lots and packers).

American beef exports have increased from less than one percent of production in the 1970s to around 9 percent by 2000. In general, imported beef competes with U.S. dairy cull cows in the production of hamburger. Imports have averaged 9 to 11 percent of beef consumed in the United States since the mid-1980s, with the level in any year depending on the phase in the American cattle cycle. For example, at the peak of the cattle cycle in 1996, less than 8 percent of the beef consumed in the United States was imported, compared to over 11 percent in 2000.

Preparation and Consumption

Preparation. Beef can be preserved and prepared in many ways. Early preservation involved salt: meat was salted and dried or placed in a brine of salt water. Beef is still salted and dried in many parts of the world, providing portability and flexibility in storage and consumption. The dried beef can be eaten dry or reconstituted in sauces. Prior to the advent of canning, corned beef was shipped across continents to feed armies stationed abroad. But with the advent of the canning process, corned beef could be more easily shipped and stored for a wide range of purposes. Relatively large pieces of fresh beef are preferred in Europe, Australia and New Zealand, and the Americas. In Asia and Africa, beef is eaten more often, but in smaller quantities than in the West. In some cultures, beef is a condiment, served in highly flavored sauces with grains and legumes.

Different cultures have different ways of cutting beef and defining beef quality. In France, where hormone injections and implants are illegal, male cattle are not castrated until they gain full size. The preferred animal is older, slow growing, grass-fed, and the meat is darker in color. In North America, animals are killed younger, grow faster through the use of hormones and nutrient-rich feeding, and the meat is lighter in color in the meat case. These cuts of beef are often grilled (requiring marbling) or fried. Groups of European origin also bake and boil various cuts of beef. Braising, simmering, roasting, broiling, soups, and stews are other ways that specific cuts of beef are made palatable. Beef is also eaten raw, chopped fine for beefsteak tartare and beefsteak *à l'americaine*. Beef is often cooked with alcoholic beverages, such as beer and wine, to tenderize it and add flavor.

The introduction of European genetics led to four modern Japanese breeds that are known as *wagyu*. They are valued because of their wonderful taste and extreme tenderness. The meat is thinly sliced and placed in boiling water along with a variety of vegetables, resembling a traditional method for cooking fish and vegetables for *shabu-shabu* and *sukiyaki*. High marbling is required to maintain its tenderness during the boiling process. Beef in served in many cultures with a wide variety of root crops and vegetables

Types of beef. Almost all parts of the animal are used as food. Western cookbooks include recipes for brains, blood, heart, kidneys, liver, lights (lungs), sweetbreads (thymus gland), tongue, and tripe (the lining of the third stomach), which are particularly used in regional cooking. In addition, beef heads were made into head cheese and the feet used in soups in many cultures. Use of these less desirable cuts came from peasant households, who invented delicious but labor-intensive ways to utilize the parts rejected by the upper classes.

Consumption

Traditions. Because of the multiple functions of cattle and their breeding potential to increase wealth, many societies in Asia and the Pacific developed strong taboos against killing cows or healthy bulls. Only worn-out work animals, barren cows, and unwanted calves were sold for slaughter or consumed within the household. Thus many of the ways of cooking beef involved long, slow cooking.

Many cultures around the world consume beef. Its consumption is permitted by all major religions of the world except Hinduism, although Buddhism discourages the eating of the meat of four-legged animals, including beef. For many years, in India, which had a very high cattle population (and even higher if one counts water buffalo), it was illegal to kill cattle, and slaughter of buffalo was highly restricted. Japan only revoked the ban against eating meat in 1882, soon after the Meiji Restoration. Shinto also had strong norms against showing of blood. Thus butchers cut the beef very thinly. Christianity views eating meat, particularly beef, as highly desirable and a sign of self-indulgence. Thus the giving up of meat during holy seasons, such as Lent, and on Fridays becomes a symbol of sacrifice, replicating that of Christ for the world.

Generally, beef is a meat for the wealthy. Nations that are large producers of beef also tend to eat very large pieces of beef relatively often. As nations' fortunes rise and fall, so does their per capita beef consumption. For example, the economic slowdown of the 1980s decreased Peruvian beef consumption, and the economic problems at the end of the twentieth and the beginning of the twenty-first century have reduced the traditionally high consumption of beef in Argentina.

Nourishment

While beef provides important nutrients, particularly iron and key amino acids, it is also a source of fat and cholesterol, although the concentration varies, depending on the cut of beef and how the animal was raised.

Symbolism

Ritualism and traditions. Cattle worship was widespread in the cattle cults of the Mediterranean basin. The crescent of the cow horns was seen as imbued with the life-giving power of the crescent moon. Cows, in particular, figure as symbols of fertility in parts of Asia and Africa.

Cattle are viewed as sacred in the Hindu tradition. Beef is not consumed, nor are cattle unduly constrained.

But the by-products of cattle form an important part of peasant survival strategies in many rural areas. Their manure provides building materials, fuel, and fertilizer, and the animals themselves provide traction to raise the grains and pulses that are the staples of the South Asian diet. The prohibition against killing cattle ensures that even in times of hunger, the means to produce the following year will be in place.

Cattle have a paramount and pervasive symbolic value in many parts of East Africa, where they represent social status as well as wealth. As a result, the supply of cattle exceeds the demand for their meat, milk, hides, traction, or other uses to which they are put. In particular, the use of cattle for meat and hides or their sale for cash reduces the status of the head of household. More recently, the size of cattle corrals has proven to be an excellent proxy for the household wealth and status in communities in much of Africa. Cattle have critical symbolic importance in ritual, dance, marriage, and other aspects of social relations. For example, in many cultures the marriage contract calls for the payment of bride price to compensate for the loss of the services of the young woman to her parents. This is often negotiated in terms of number of cattle, delivered in installments: at marriage, the birth of the first child, and at the birth of the second child, at which time the marriage process is seen to be complete.

Global and Contemporary Issues

Commercialization. Over 48 million metric tons of beef were consumed globally in 2000, an increase of slightly over a million-and-a-half tons since 1995. Beef production worldwide exceeded consumption in 2000 by over a million metric tons, a pattern of overproduction that has marked the end of the twentieth and the beginning of the twenty-first century.

Generally, beef consumption increases with a rise in middle class incomes. The Argentina consumes the most beef per capita, followed by the United States, Australia, and Canada. The United States consumes the largest total amount of beef annually (around 12 million metric tons a year), followed by the European Union, the People's Republic of China, and Brazil. Canada, Mexico, Colombia, Argentina, and the Russian Federation are also major beef consumers.

Between 1995 and 2000, beef consumption increased 49 percent in India and 32 percent in the People's Republic of China. In contrast, during the same period it declined 28 percent in the Russian Federation and 19 percent in Poland. It did not decline further in the Russian Federation because of beef that came in the form of food aid. Unlike Europe, the United States does not have a direct subsidy program for beef, although it often steps in as a buyer to help keep market prices up. That beef is exported as food aid, and used domestically for school lunches and at military bases.

The United States trades an increasing amount of dressed beef internationally. The U.S. had a cattle inventory of 99.5 million head in January of 1998 (USDA/NASS, 1998), compared to a world cattle inventory of 1,323.3 billion head (FAO, 1998). While the numbers of American cattle rise and fall in approximately 18-year cycles, with numbers increasing with each cycle, world cattle numbers have shown a general increase since 1961. The current cycle peaked in 1996. With the large herd destruction in Europe in 2001 due to animal diseases, the herd shrink will increase.

Australia exports the most beef, followed closely by the United States, which is the second largest international beef exporter (primarily high quality beef) and the largest beef importer (primarily low quality beef to be made into hamburger). The United States consistently imports more beef than it exports. Japan is the second largest importer of beef. Between 1995 and 2000, beef exports increased the most in Canada and Brazil, followed by India and Uruguay. China and Australia decreased beef exports during this period, perhaps related to the increased consumption in both those countries. Mexico's beef imports increased over five times during the six-year period, as its economy gained a solid footing. However, imports dropped in many countries during that time period. In South Africa, decreasing imports was coupled by increased production. But in both Poland and the Russian Federation, both imports and production dropped substantially.

Consumption patterns. Beef is increasingly consumed in institutions and restaurants rather than at home, following the trend of most foods. Many cuts of beef require long cooking times, whereas restaurants tend to offer quick cooking cuts such as hamburger and steaks. Condiments and sauces give the meat flavors once provided by long cooking with herbs and spices. A variety of tenderizers are used to substitute for lack of aging, unreliable genetic origins, and short cooking times.

Beef is often eaten in the form of hamburgers, as the whole place and pace of eating changes in America and other places of the world. Where the ritual of family dining continues, beef often has an honored place, but the shift of women's work from the home to the factory and office has reduced that practice. Beef for home consumption is increasingly ground beef, with a growing market in packaged foods that can augment the ground beef and give it a homemade gourmet patina.

Beef that has been prepared to be carried out or home delivered, particularly as pepperoni or hamburger pizza, is increasingly popular, not only among the young but among working couples who would like to eat at home but have no time to cook. Increasingly, work place cafeterias are providing after work take-home meals for company or agency employees.

Institutions serve beef often, including in school lunchrooms (increasingly through franchisers, including fast food purveyors), hospitals, nursing homes, and prisons. There are fewer dietary restrictions on beef than pork among ethnic groups, increasing its utility in many institutional settings.

While beef has long been part of ready-to-eat soups and entrées, there are increasing attempts to make beef easier to cook and tastier—perhaps in response to the use of less tasty, less tender, quick-maturing breeds and hormone use to speed growth in the United States, where, unlike in Europe and Japan, early maturity is preferred over taste and tenderness. (However, the USDA firmly states that hormone-raised beef is extremely tasty and tender.) Beef is thus available at retail in stir-fry or fajita slices that have been marinated in a wide array of herbs, spices, and tenderizers. This cuts cooking time and gives a wider menu variety to the working chef and eater.

Types of consumption. Cattle and calf meat is consumed directly as meals and snacks, and its by-products are used in a wide number of foods, from gelatin to ice cream. In the United States, direct per capita beef consumption declined from 81.7 pounds to 63.8 pounds in 1997. More recent data suggests that U.S. beef consumption is increasing from the low in the years 1992–1996 of 63.5 pounds, in part in response to economic expansion.

Issues surrounding consumption. Cattle have proven to be a source of conflict at all stages of their production and consumption. On rangelands and pasture, there is great concern about: 1) overgrazing and its negative impact on biodiversity, soil quality, and hydrology; and 2) contamination of streams when cattle are allowed to freely wander in them. While research and practical experience have shown that cattle can enhance grassland and rangeland, that is often not the case, and cattlemen and women are generally extremely suspicious of environmental constraints, since they are seen as potentially infringing on the rights of the cattle operators to use their land and the land they rent (whether from the government or from their neighbors) as they see fit.

Cattle raising has been the cause of a great deal of deforestation in tropical areas of the world. Settlers clear land, selling valuable timber to transnational companies. The newly cleared soils are planted with fast-growing pasture that often is relatively impervious to water, increasing runoff. Cattle are grazed for the low end of the beef market, ending up in fast food outlets in developed countries.

In Europe and increasingly in America, there is concern about how cattle are raised and treated. There is growing concern about the stress animals undergo in large feedlots, which some believe affects the taste of the meat. Modern packing plants have tried to decrease stress at the time of slaughter to reduce the adrenalin in the muscle tissues, which toughens the meat and gives it an off-putting flavor. Concern for animal welfare is coupled with health and environmental concerns surrounding large feedlots and packing plants.

Europe does not allow injection or implantation of hormones, which is a standard practice of most producers in the United States. In fact, stocker feeders inject their cattle with hormones on penalty of not being able to sell them to a feedlot. If the cattle are not injected in the neck, meat quality will be negatively impacted around the site of injection, which is often easiest to administer into the prime cuts. Hormones increase the rate of growth and nutrient utilization, but increasing evidence suggests that they negatively impact meat taste and tenderness. They are also viewed as a health hazard in Europe, as well as having a negative impact on animal health, as the use of these steroids puts additional stress on the animal. As a result, Europe banned American beef produced with artificial hormones in 1989, which has resulted in a continuing trade battle.

Mad cow disease (bovine spongiform encephalopathies, or BSE) has been linked to the fatal Creutzfeldt-Jakob Disease (CJD) through human consumption of meat from cattle with the prion disease. It is thought to be transmitted from one animal to another through the consumption of bone meal from sick but undiagnosed cattle or sheep and from animals to humans by eating meat that contains prions transferred by the nervous system. Thus the brains and the meat that is in contact with the spinal column are particularly suspect. In parts of Europe, the sale of meat on the bone has been forbidden. As a result, beef consumption has dropped precipitously and exports have been banned altogether.

Foot and mouth disease outbreaks can cripple production and exports, as occurred in Britain, Argentina, and Europe in 2001. In contrast to BSE, foot and mouth disease is not transferable to humans, but it is easily passed among hooved species and greatly reduces the productivity in infected cattle herds. Increased globalization of the food system may be related to both outbreaks.

See also **Ecology and Food; Goat; Mammals; Meat; Pig; Sheep; United States: Midwest.**

BIBLIOGRAPHY

The Council of Agricultural Science and Technology. *Animal Agriculture and Global Food Supply.* Ames, Iowa: Council of Agricultural Science and Technology, 1999.

Economic Research Service, U.S. Department of Agriculture. *Livestock, Dairy and Poultry Situation and Outlook. LDP-M-80.* Washington, D.C., 2001.

Foutz, C. P., H. G. Dolesal, T. L. Gardner, D. R. Gill, J. L. Hensley, and J. B. Morgan. "Anabolic Implant Effects on Steer Performance, Carcass Traits, Subprimal Yields, and Longissmus Muscle Properties." *Journal of Animal Science* 75 (1997): 1256–1265.

Higgins, L., and R. A. Jussaume, Jr. "The Viability of Niche Marketing with Global Commodity Chains: An Example from Beef." *International Journal of Sociology of Agriculture and Food* 17 (1998): 45–66.

Pillsbury, Richard. *No Foreign Food: The American Diet in Time and Place.* Boulder, Colo: Westview Press, 1998.

Putnam, Judith Jones, and Jane E. Allshouse. *Food Consumption, Prices and Expendituetres, 1970–97.* Statistical Bulletin No. 965. Food and Rural Economics Division/Economic Research Service/USDA.Washington, D.C. 1999.

Rouse, John E. *World Cattle.* Norman: University of Oklahoma Press, 1990.

Walsh, John. "The Social Context of Technological Change: The Case of the Retail Food Industry." *The Sociological Quarterly* 32, 3 (1991): 447–468.

Whitaker, James W. *Feedlot Empire: Beef Cattle Feeling in Illinois and Iowa, 1840–1900.* Ames: Iowa State University Press, 1975.

Willham, R. L. "Genetic Improvement of Beef Cattle in the United States: Cattle, People and Their Interaction." *Journal of Animal Science* 54 (1982): 659–666.

Cornelia Butler Flora

CAULIFLOWER. *See* **Cabbage and Crucifer Plants.**

CENTRAL AMERICA.

Central America is an isthmus, or land bridge, that unites the two continents of North and South America. It consists of seven countries: Belize, Guatemala, Honduras, El Salvador, Nicaragua, Costa Rica, and Panama. Except for Belize, all of these countries were first settled by the Spanish in the early 1500s and remained part of the Spanish colonial empire until they revolted for independence in 1821. The culinary history of the three-hundred-year colonial period has not been studied as thoroughly as it has in Mexico or in South America, in part because many documents relating to the area are housed in Spain rather than in local archives. Furthermore, while Central America attempted to unite politically following independence, that effort eventually failed. This political fragmentation has left a distinctive imprint on the culinary profile of the region. In spite of this, however, there are certain unifying features.

Common Features

Geographically, the countries have a great abundance of volcanoes. This has had an important influence on the cuisine because the volcanoes have fertilized the soil with mineral nutrients that have made this one of the richest areas of biodiversity in the world. The gold the Spanish conquistadors had hoped to find was made up for by an exquisite natural beauty and an abundance of unusual food plants, both cultivated and wild. Due to this rich soil, the region has become a center of coffee production.

Another unifying feature is the composition of the people themselves. The population of Central America consists mainly of four groups: mestizos, a mixture of Spanish and native peoples and the largest group; small pockets of indigenous populations; Africans; and people of unmixed European descent sometimes referred to as Creoles. Throughout much of the region, African populations are concentrated along the Atlantic coastline, while mestizos populate the Pacific side. The central area of the isthmus is home to a lush rainforest sparsely populated by small groups of indigenous tribes.

The African population descends mainly from runaway slaves who escaped from Jamaica and neighboring Caribbean islands. They have preserved a dialect of English infused with African vocabulary. This group has made Central America more diverse in language as well as in cookery, since its cooks have blended together African and indigenous food preferences. One of the typical ingredients is coconut: shredded coconut, coconut milk, or coconut oil. Except for smaller indigenous tribes like the Miskitos of central Nicaragua, coconut is not widely favored by the other ethnic groups.

In terms of cookery, the mestizos have mixed traditional indigenous dishes, mainly preparations of Mayan origin, with old Spanish prototypes, but in some instances the two cooking traditions have been kept separate. The smaller indigenous tribes still remaining in Central America rely mainly on hunting and gathering and have not influenced the cookery as much as larger groups, such as the Mayans.

One of the characteristics of all Central American cooking is the use of fresh ingredients, from fresh meats and vegetables, to tortillas and breads made to order, even dairy products prepared the same day. The markets abound with the sweet aromas of tropical fruits and vegetables displayed in an endless sea of colors. The market is especially important as a stage for lively social exchange, and since the cooking traditions of Central America are mostly oral rather than based on cookbooks, recipe discussions in the marketplace serve as a major conduit for ideas and the comparison of family cooking preferences.

Oral tradition is a key to understanding Central American cookery: most recipes are handed down from generation to generation by word of mouth. In middle- or upper-class families, it is customary to have an in-house cook, but someone in the family is assigned the task of teaching the cook the way a dish should be prepared. Special instruction and attention are required for dishes that have been handed down within the family and are usually prepared only on special occasions. Although the choice of recipe ingredients may vary within each country and family, there are still quite a few standard national dishes that have been maintained over a long period of time and have not undergone much variation. Outside the region, little is known about the cookery of Central America because many of the key recipes are not written down, except perhaps in a small number of local cookbooks of very recent date.

Beef is an important meat in Central American cooking because of the large number of cattle ranches, which

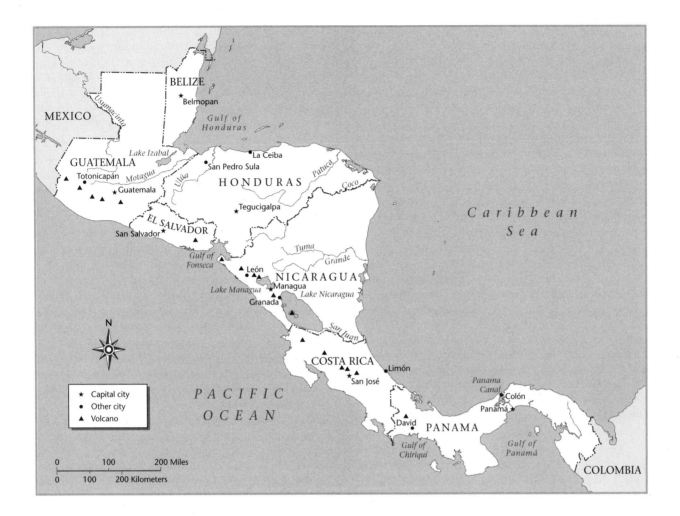

provide beef both for local consumption and for export. The flavor of Central American beef is very different from that of the beef of North and South America, in part because the animals are grass-fed and thus leaner, but also because the Criollo breed of cattle is itself quite distinctive. The flavor and texture of its meat more closely resemble veal than beef.

It was customary for a middle- or upper-class family to have beef at least once a day, especially in Nicaragua. New dietary trends have changed a few old traditions so that now people mindful of their health are eating less red meat, yet beef is still a luxury for the poor. For those who prefer to eat less red meat, beans are a common substitute. Beans are said to be one of the staple foods of the poor, but they are very popular among all social classes. Once boiled, the beans may be sautéed with onions, sweet peppers, garlic, salt and pepper, and some of the cooking broth may be added. The result is a simple yet tasty dish. A common preparation consisting of beans, boiled plantains, and cheese forms a one-pot vegetarian meal that is nutritionally balanced as well as pleasing to the palate. Many of the most popular dishes of the region are studies in simplicity, since light food is a welcome reprieve in the hot climate.

Contrary to popular belief, Central American cookery is not spicy, except in Guatemala where the chili pepper plays an important role as a spice. Elsewhere, chili pepper is an optional ingredient, except in some dishes where it is considered critical, but one is always given the option to choose between something spicy or not. At most meals, a bowl of hot sauce or a salsa consisting of a mixture of tomatoes, garlic, onions, and sweet and hot peppers marinated in lime juice provides added spice and flavor for many dishes. There are many other variations of salsas containing chili peppers, such as *encurtido*, a mixture of chopped vegetables pickled in vinegar with hot peppers. In this case, the spicy vinegar brings out a variety of subtle flavors in the dishes eaten with it. Most meat preparations are marinated in a mixture of black pepper and sour orange or lime juice, giving them a cleaner and more complex taste. The sour juice is important in tenderizing, flavoring, and sterilizing the meat.

The annatto is another important ingredient in the cookery of this region. Annatto is the seed of an indigenous tree (*Bixa orellana*), better known in other parts of the world for coloring cheese; it is this ingredient that dyes the cheese orange or yellow. The cultural importance of annatto dates back to pre-Columbian times when it was used for special rituals. The Mayas and other indigenous populations employed it as body paint during religious ceremonies, and also for coloring pottery, for monetary purposes, and for flavoring certain foods. Known as *achiote* in Central America, the seeds are ground and mixed together into a paste of black pepper, salt, and vinegar that is then diluted in either sour orange juice or lime juice and used to marinate or preserve meat. Historically, *achiote* was used to preserve meats from spoiling in the tropical heat. Today, *achiote* creates a delicious marinade for grilled meats. It seems to have little taste as a raw paste, but when heated, it undergoes a chemical change that releases a complex array of flavors. While *achiote* lengthens cooking times, it also prevents meats from scorching or drying out while they are being grilled.

Rice is a key element in every Central American meal and is one of the important culinary contributions from Spanish cookery. After careful rinsing, rice is usually sautéed in oil with onions until toasted; water is then added, with a little salt to taste. Toasting causes the grains to remain fluffy, and the onions impart a subtle aroma and flavor that complements many entrees. In fact, Central Americans commonly judge the abilities of cooks based on the fluffiness of their rice, for it is said that if one masters the art of cooking rice, one has mastered the art of cooking.

There are numerous rice dishes in the region that are similar to Spanish paellas, such as *arroz a la Valenciana* in Nicaragua. This consists of a mixture of chicken, pork, shrimp, and sausage cooked together with rice and vegetables. *Arroz con pollo* is another popular dish served throughout the region from Guatemala to Panama. Although the recipe varies, the essential mixture and texture is common, consisting of chicken and vegetables cooked together in a stew; rice is then added. This recipe has much more broth than the Nicaraguan *arroz a la Valenciana*, and *achiote* is added as the substitute for saffron.

Throughout Central America, maize is doubtless the single most important culinary element in all of the regional cookeries. Maize was so important to the indigenous peoples before the arrival of Columbus that in Mayan mythology man and woman were created from two maize kernels. It was seen as a life-giving element and it has greatly influenced the cookery of Central America. The tortilla, made from maize flour and water, is usually present in at least one daily meal. It is traditionally eaten while still warm and accompanied by several types of salty cheese. There are people who specialize in making tortillas and can shape the dough between their hands in a matter of seconds, until it reaches a circumference of approximately 10 inches (25 centimeters). The tortillas are then placed on a hot griddle, lightly scorched, and rushed to the table while still steaming.

Maize is also the ingredient for many refreshing drinks and is fermented to create an alcoholic drink known as *chicha*, which can also be consumed before full fermentation takes place. This old indigenous beverage has changed very little over time, except that now sugar is used as a sweetener rather than honey. *Chicha* is a generic term used by the early conquistadors to describe any alcoholic beverage in the New World, but there are actually many variations of *chicha* throughout Latin America.

Atole is another drink made from maize that is mainly a feature of Guatemalan cuisine, but is present throughout Central America under many local variations. It is a filling, high-energy drink that can be either sweet or salty. *Atole*, typically served hot or warm, has a thick consistency and can be made from a wide variety of ingredients, the most common being milk, sugar, ground maize kernels, cinnamon, and cloves. In Nicaragua, *atole* vendors always seem to show up after a heavy afternoon rainstorm, making sure everyone warms up by drinking plenty of the beverage. It is especially popular in the cool mountainous areas of the region.

Tamales made from maize are popular throughout the isthmus and are prepared in a variety of ways, depending on the local cultures. Each country has a special variation of tamales, but aside from the different ingredients, they are always wrapped in either cornhusks or plantain leaves and steamed or boiled. Tamales can be eaten on any occasion, but in some countries, such as El Salvador, Costa Rica, and Panama, they are generally prepared for holidays. Traditionally, they are consumed during the Christmas season or at Easter. They can also range in size from dainty handheld appetizers to large main-course dishes. The most common forms consist of ground dried maize or the raw mashed kernels shaped into a thick, rectangular dough that is filled with different vegetables or meats, or simply sweetened with sugar. They are then wrapped in leaves and boiled or steamed.

Just as there are variations in ingredients, there are also variations in nomenclature. For example, in El Salvador, *tamales rellenos* are similar to the Honduran and Nicaraguan *nacatamales*. In both Honduras and Nicaragua, there are tamales (boiled in corn husks) and *nacatamales* (boiled in plantain leaves), which vary from one another in their fillings. *Nacatamales* are difficult to prepare not only because of the complexity of the ingredients, but also because of the length of time they take to cook. In Nicaragua, there are people who specialize in making them since they are always in demand for parties or for traditional Sunday brunch.

Another way of using ground maize is as a thickener for stews or for giving a distinctive flavoring to certain dishes. Ground maize can also be toasted and used to flour meats or fish for deep frying. Water and sugar can be added to toasted maize to make *pinolillo*, a chocolate-like drink that is filling yet refreshing. In Honduras, *pinolillo* is also prepared with a touch of ground chocolate, thus giving it a more complex taste.

Central America is a paradise for natural fruit drinks, since it has a seemingly endless variety of fruits that can be mixed together to produce deliciously healthy and refreshing beverages. One can find a natural fruit juice stand on almost every street corner on hot, sunny days. Many Central Americans take a break before lunch and sit for a few minutes under the shade of a tree to cool off and relax with a tall glass of *refresco*, literally "refreshing," with plenty of ice. The best drinks are made with ripe fruits, so that there is no need for sugar. These fruits can also be used for creating an enormous variety of sorbets, which are popular on hot, humid afternoons.

The plantain plays a much more important role in Central American cuisine than the potato. It is more or less a staple vegetable, and green or ripe plantains can be prepared in a number of ways. Although the plant is not native to the continent, it adapted very quickly to the climate and soil of this tropical region. Its leaves are used in wrapping foods, such as tamales and *nacatamales*, for grilling, and sometimes as eating utensils. The plantain leaves give the food a subtle yet rich flavor, and, when grilling fish, keep it from scorching and impart flavor to the meat. It is said that Nicaraguan *vigorón* is not authentic unless it is served on the plantain leaf, which functions as a plate. When the leaf is folded, some of the juice is released into the food, perhaps giving it its "authentic" flavor. The old colonial Nicaraguan city of Granada is well known for its *vigorón*, consisting of boiled yuca (cassava), a sour and spicy shredded cabbage salad, and crunchy pork rinds.

Another way of cooking the unripe plantain is to cut the fruit into paper-thin strips and fry them at a high temperature, thus making them crunchy yet not oily. This is a popular way of preparing plantains throughout Central America. They can also be grilled or boiled in water and accompanied by a salty cheese. The ripe plantains can also be boiled and baked with cinnamon, cloves, and cheese, resulting in a tasty dessert sweetened by the vegetable's own natural sugars.

As a general rule, the indigenous peoples of Central America were originally vegetarian, eating meat only on special occasions and cooking with little or no oils or fats. The European method of frying and cooking with animal fat quickly changed the native cuisine, but it also made room for a new and inventive style of cooking. Besides the better-known meats such as pork, beef, chicken, and fish, other animal meats are also part of Central American cookery. The *gibnut* or paca, a large rodent that feeds mainly on wild nuts, is consumed in Belize. The *cusuco* (*Dasypus novemcinctus*), a species of armadillo, is eaten in several countries, but it is most popular in El Salvador, where it is mainly a feature of rural cookery. This meat is marinated in lime juice, then grilled, following the same method used for cooking iguana.

Iguana is eaten throughout the region, but, again, it is mainly consumed by country people. The iguana is

Central Americans have developed a special breed of cattle to withstand the hot, humid climate. This herd is grazing near Tegucigalpa, Honduras. PHOTOEDIT. REPRODUCED BY PERMISSION.

known to have a rich flavor because it feeds on fruits, and it is especially fond of papaya, which gives the meat a tender texture and sweet flavor. Many people consider the meat an aphrodisiac, and it can also be boiled in soup, an old home remedy for strengthening those who are sick. Furthermore, iguana was an important meat substitute during the colonial period, since the Catholic Church declared it a type of fish for consumption on meatless days. There are numerous methods of cooking iguana, but those who eat it generally prefer it grilled.

Guatemala

Guatemala was once part of the heartland of Mayan civilization. The Mayan imprint on modern Guatemala's culinary riches is present in its numerous traditional dishes, especially those with corn as the predominant ingredient. The country is well-known for the great variety of its *atoles*. One of these *is atole de arroz*, a sweet beverage with corn, rice, cinnamon, sugar, and chocolate as ingredients. In the cool and mountainous area of Totonicapán, there is an unusual (and probably very old) *atole* made with beans, salt, and ground chili pepper.

Recados, pastelike mixtures, are important in Guatemala and are used for marinating meats or as condiments to bring out complex flavors in cooked dishes. The most common of these is *recado colorado*, which uses ground annatto as a base mixed with garlic, black pepper, cumin, and other ingredients depending on the local recipe. Of all Central American countries, Guatemala is the only one that uses the chili pepper almost as an essential part of its cuisine. Peppers are used as a condiment, or as a main dish such as *chiles rellenos* (stuffed peppers). The chilies are first fire-roasted, next filled with a traditional mixture of pork and beef, onions, tomatoes, cabbage, and herbs. They are then dipped in a batter, covered with breadcrumbs and fried, blending indigenous and European methods of food preparation.

Belize

Located to the east of Guatemala, Belize is a country with a large native-born population of African descent. Formerly a British colony, it attracted immigrants from other parts of the Caribbean due to an extensive lumbering industry. It is also the only Central American country where English is the official language. In the western part of the country, the food is similar to that of Guatemala because of the border they share. This cuisine is a blend of Spanish and Mayan influences, yet the coconut is an important ingredient because of the predominating African influence.

One of the local delicacies is conch soup in which the meat from the giant conch, a mollusk, is cooked with okra, green plantains, onions, lime juice, chili peppers, and coconut until it acquires a thick consistency. Belizeans are as proud of their conch soup as they are of their popular stewed beans with pork or beef. Stew beans are prepared by boiling meat with the beans, onions, coconut milk, herbs, and spices (depending on personal tastes); they are served with rice. *Garnaches* and *salbutes* are common dishes and can be served either as a main meal or as appetizers. These are thin, crispy deep-fried tortillas served with beans, cheese, and cabbage on top and may also be accompanied with chicken. In May, the cashew festival, which evolved out of the English May Day celebration, takes place. This festivity includes plenty of food and live music, as well as locally made cashew wine.

Honduras

Honduras has a diverse cuisine that shares many similarities with that of Nicaragua, its neighbor to the south, including the influence of African-Caribbean culture. An outstanding Honduran dish is the popular *sopa de caracol*, or conch soup. In this recipe, fresh carrots, chayote, chickpeas, celery, onions, plantains, and baby corn are sautéed in butter and added to a clear broth flavored with *culantro*, a native herb similar in flavor to cilantro, but stronger-tasting. Coconut is then added to the broth along with some milk, the conch meat, achiote, and parsley as the garnish. The result is a flavorful soup with an African-Caribbean touch.

Capirotadas, commonly eaten during Lent, are small dumplings made from maize flour and water, filled with cheese, and then lightly fried until brown. The dumplings are subsequently added to a vegetable broth and enjoyed as a main meal. Another variation is to add syrup cooked with cinnamon and cloves, which is then served on the dumplings, creating a tasty yet simple dessert. *Pinole*, a slightly coarse, ground maize, is used as a thickener in dishes such as *gallina en pinol* and *iguana en pinol*. In both recipes—the first made with chicken or (preferably) hen and the second with iguana—toasted maize gives the meat a light nutty taste that complements the mixture of meat, herbs, broth, and vegetables.

El Salvador

El Salvador is the smallest Central American country and the only one without an Atlantic coastline. The cuisine of El Salvador is popular throughout the isthmus because of its famous *pupusas*. Although there are similar variations of these tortillas in most Latin American countries, El Salvador has gained recognition for having what are generally considered the best recipes. *Pupusas* are basically tortilla dumplings filled with either cheese, small pieces of *chicharrón* (pork rinds), a mixture of both, or beans. The dumplings are then covered with *curtidos*, a combination of cabbage, shredded carrots, and chilies infused in vinegar.

Nicaragua

Nicaragua is the largest country in Central America, and until the 1970s it was also the wealthiest. Its cuisine varies greatly from region to region, from old Spanish dishes such as *relleno*, *salpicón*, or *indio viejo*, to more indigenous preparations like *nacatamales*. *Relleno* literally means "stuffing" and in its original Old World form was probably used for stuffed fowl or empanadas. Like many Spanish dishes of medieval origin, it uses ingredients now associated with desserts: dried fruit, milk, nutmeg, sugar, and shredded bread as a thickener. Along with these ingredients, pork, olives, finely diced carrots, onions, mustard, capers, and vinegar or wine are blended into the mix. The result is a sweet and sour dish in which the diverse ingredients seem to come together harmoniously. Due to long, slow cooking and hours of constant stirring, this dish is so time-consuming to make that it is only eaten once a year, during the Christmas holidays. The large outlay of expensive ingredients, many of which must be imported, once set this dish apart as a class symbol of the old ruling families of the country during the colonial period, but today *relleno* has assumed the character of a national icon, especially to expatriate Nicaraguans.

Another dish of Spanish origin is *salpicón*, which is thought to have come to Nicaragua during the 1500s. The basic concept involves making a complete meal out of the basics for soup. It begins with beef boiled with an assortment of vegetables, most importantly ripe plantains. The meat is then taken out of its broth and finely chopped

The market at Chichicastango, Guatemala, is rich in local produce and in colorful native costumes. © TIBOR BOGNAR/CORBIS. CENTRAL EUROPE

with onions, sweet peppers, bitter orange juice, salt, and pepper. The boiled plantain is mashed, having already given the soup a subtle sweet flavor, and is then used as the dough for making empanadas. The empanadas are filled with the chopped beef and cooked rice that is to accompany the meal. A complete dinner is thus created by using as many ingredients as possible with little waste.

Indio viejo is similar to *salpicón* in that beef is boiled to create soup, but different in that the meat is then shredded and cooked again in its own broth with maize flour, spearmint, tomatoes, and, depending on family, recipes, *achiote*. The result is a complementary blend of Old World and indigenous flavors. *Nacatamales* also blend the Old World with the New, but the basic recipe has indigenous roots. Best described as fairly large dumplings made from maize flour, they are filled with capers, potatoes, onions, prunes, meat (pork, chicken, or turkey) marinated in *achiote*, tomatoes, and chilies. The dumplings are then wrapped in plantain leaves and boiled in water for several hours until all the ingredients are fully cooked. *Nacatamales* are usually enjoyed as Sunday brunch with strong black coffee.

Costa Rica
Costa Rica is well-known worldwide for its natural beauty and perhaps also for its excellent coffee. Ecotourism has helped the country's economy, but it has also greatly changed the local food culture. Aside from the more popular Americanized fast-food restaurants that are now common, the true cuisine of the Costa Rican people is the one prepared at home. Without a doubt, most Costa Ricans crave the popular *gallo pinto*, a mixture of white rice and beans cooked with a variety of fresh herbs and vegetables, creating a tasty meal of its own. This dish is eaten in most parts of the country at least once a day.

Olla de carne is another popular recipe that blends together a variety of vegetables and beef. This one-pot dish consists of squash, corn, yuca, ayote, and potatoes cooked together with beef in its broth, creating a very hearty stew. Round pieces of lightly mashed green plantains, known as *patacones*, are served during most meals and act as a substitute for the now ubiquitous french fries. During the Christmas holidays, Costa Ricans enjoy elaborate tamales, very similar to the Nicaraguan *nacatamales* in the variety of ingredients used as well as in the manner of preparation.

Panama
Panama is a country defined largely by the Panama Canal, which has created a trading link between the Atlantic and the Pacific. During pre-Columbian times, the country was a center of older civilizations that specialized in gold

craftsmanship, using native animals as models for their works of art. Panama's culinary connection to this indigenous past was largely severed during the colonial period, when the region was part of what is now Colombia.

Created by the United States during the early 1900s, Panama and its canal attracted many immigrants seeking employment and new opportunities. This migration shaped modern Panamanian culture because of the large numbers of black laborers arriving from English-speaking islands in the Caribbean. The result was a blending of the local mestizo cuisine with that of the newly arrived immigrants. Panamanians keep their traditional cuisine alive at home, but they assimilated many African elements, especially the use of coconut as a main ingredient.

One example of the strong African influence is the popularity of *fufu*, particularly along the northern Atlantic coast of the country. Elsewhere in Latin America, *fufu* is a dumpling made of plantains or yams, but in Panama the term is applied to the entire stew. It is composed of a coconut milk base, boiled plantains, chilies, yuca, yams, and fried fish added at the end. *Saos* is yet another African-influenced dish adapted from the Jamaican kitchen. It consists of boiled calf's or pig's feet marinated in plenty of lime juice, onions, chilies, salt, and pepper.

In spite of the prevalence of these African influences, most Panamanians identify their national cookery with indigenous and Spanish preparations, especially *sancocho*, which is treated as a national culinary symbol. This dish consists of chicken cooked with vegetables, including yuca, corn, plantains, chayote, and potatoes, served with rice on the side. Panamanians seek relief from the mid-morning heat by enjoying the popular and refreshing beverage known as *chicheme*, which resembles *atole* because it is a maize-based beverage blended with sugar and cinnamon. Before lunch time, Panamanians like to enjoy a drink of *chicheme* with the tasty *carimoñolas*. These lightly fried dumplings consisting of boiled mashed yuca filled with ground beef, sweet peppers, tomatoes, and herbs can be eaten either as appetizers or as a main course.

See also **Banana and Plantain; Caribbean; Iberian Peninsula; Inca Empire; Maize; Mexico; Mexico and Central America, Pre-Columbian; South America.**

BIBLIOGRAPHY

Burns, E. L. *What's Cooking in the Belizean Kitchens.* Belize City: Graphics One, 1984.

Campabadal, Isabel. *Nueva cocina costarricense.* San José, Costa Rica: University of Costa Rica Press, 1997.

Coe, Sophie D. *America's First Cuisines.* Austin, Tex.: University of Texas Press, 1994.

Conzemius, Eduard. *Ethnographical Survey of the Miskito and Sumu Indians of Honduras and Nicaragua.* Washington, D.C.: U.S. Printing Office, 1932.

Cox, Beverly, and Martin Jacobs. *Spirit of the Earth: Native Cooking from Latin America.* New York: Stewart, Tabori, & Chang, 2001.

Figueroa vda. De Balsells, Catalina. *Cocina Guatemalteca: arte, sabor, y colorido.* Guatemala City: Editorial Piedra Santa, 2000.

Franco de Alvarez, Aurora Sierra. *Cocina regional Guatemalteca.* Guatemala City: Editorial Piedra Santa, 1999.

Martínez Campos, Gabriel, and Esperanza Salazar Zenil. *Recetario colimenense de la iguana.* Mexico City: Conaculta, 2000.

Prats de Dávila, Dolores. *Reviviendo la cocina Hondureña.* San Pedro Sula, Honduras: Impresora del Norte, 1999.

Vivas, Angélica. *Cocina Nicaragüense.* Managua, Nicaragua: Vanguardia, 1991.

Vivas, Angélica. *50 Años en la cocina.* Cali, Colombia: Carvajal, S.A., 1995.

Weaver, William Woys, and Enrique Balladares-Castellón. "Salpicón Nicaragüense: A Latin American Culinary Puzzle." *Radcliffe Culinary Times* 1 (Winter 1999): 12–14.

Williams, L. O. "The Useful Plants of Central America." *Cieba* 24 (1981): 1–4, 3–381.

Enrique Balladares-Castellón

CENTRAL ASIA. *See* **Asia, Central.**

CENTRAL EUROPE. For the purposes of this encyclopedia, Central Europe will be defined as the Czech Republic, Slovakia, Hungary, Romania, and Poland, although technically Austria and Germany played a critical role in the cultural development of the region. All of these countries were at one time completely or partly incorporated into the Prussian or Austro-Hungarian Empires and therefore shared in the transcultural culinary exchanges during the eighteenth and nineteenth centuries. Central Europe is a region represented by huge ethnic diversities, a complicated political history, and a wide range of microclimates, from Poland's cold Baltic winters in the north to the mild Black Sea climate of coastal Romania in the south.

From a geographic standpoint, most of the region is drained by the Danube River. The Carpathian Mountains form a natural barrier, cutting off Poland to the north and Romania to the east. The Transylvanian Alps in central Romania divide the region even further, and the Wallachian Plain stretches south across the Danube into Bulgaria. Hungary occupies a vast windy plain roughly corresponding to the ancient Roman province of Pannonia. The southernmost parts of this region were once under the political domination of the Byzantine Empire. This was followed by nearly five hundred years of Ottoman Turk influence.

The Czech Republic's kingdoms of Bohemia, Hungary, and Poland were all at one time major political and

cultural forces as well. The traditional foods of these three kingdoms were gradually incorporated into the court cuisine of the Austrian Empire, so by the nineteenth century they had become "Viennese." The Wiener schnitzel (Viennese veal cutlet) would never have been possible without Hungarian beef; the famous *Kolatschen* (custard-filled pastries) of the Vienna coffeehouses would never have existed without the ancient *kolace* of Bohemia. As a political coequal to Austria, Hungary evolved a distinctive cuisine of its own inspired by nationalistic themes. Since Slovakia and Romanian Transylvania were once part of the Hungarian Kingdom, they experienced Hungarian influences most, but, by the same token, they gave back to Hungarian cookery added regional nuances and many specialized dishes.

While all of these countries were once unified in some manner under Austro-Hungarian rule, that unity disintegrated with the fall of the empire in 1918, after which they became independent states. At the close of World War II, and under the coercion of the occupying Soviet forces, all of the Central European nations were brought into the Soviet empire and remained within that cultural and political sphere until the fall of communism in 1989. Each of these nations became independent again with an earnest desire to rediscover the culinary past that was largely ignored for almost forty-five years. However,

the communist governments of all the Central European countries took considerable interest in ethnographic research and established many open-air museums and research institutes where rural life could be studied. While the motivation was political, the end result was a body of valuable archival materials much better organized than in some Western countries.

If there is a common theme to this discussion, it would be that linguistic and religious boundaries of Central Europe do not coincide with political boundaries. There are large minority populations in each country, and before the mass expulsion of Jews during World War II and of Germans at the end of the war, the diversity of minority populations was even greater than in the twenty-first century. This diversity created a patchwork quilt of foodways and local cookeries, all of which must be considered when viewing the region from a historical perspective. Yet regardless of the ethnic diversity, there are certain universal foods common to all the Central European cuisines. These include sour cream, dried mushrooms, poppy seeds, sauerkraut, horseradish, and smoked bacon. Bacon and bacon drippings provide one of the distinctive flavors of this region. On a par with this is the generous use of dill.

During the nineteenth century, movements for national independence turned toward rural peasant culture to find a national cultural identity, and certain traditional peasant dishes became symbols of national styles of cooking. Hungarian *gulyás* (goulash) is a classic example. Originally it was a stew prepared by cattle drovers, herders whose occupation was essentially the same as the gaucho of Argentina and the cowboy of the American West. Their unfettered lifestyle and distinctive eating habits became a symbol of Hungarian identity; thus, the food they ate was elevated to a national icon.

This process occurred in all of the Central European countries and was in many respects random since it overlooked the fact that there were numerous ethnic groups who did not aspire to form states of their own, among them the Jews, Armenians, and gypsies. While the Central European Jews belong to the Ashkenazim, their traditional food culture represents elements of Spanish Sephardic traditions combined with South German flour-based dishes and such Slavic features as borscht or *blinz*.

Periodization of Culinary History

The food culture of Central Europe may be broken down into historical periods corresponding with the rest of Europe, although, in general, development has lagged behind western Europe. The medieval period lasted until about 1500, followed by a period of political upheaval and consolidation from 1500 to 1680. Ottoman invasions occupied the political stage, and the countryside experienced vast destruction and loss of populations. The era from 1680 to 1850 may be viewed as one of reconstruction and political reorganization under the Habsburg monarchy. Political unification brought with it cultural repression and an institutionalizing of German as the lingua franca of the region. In the 1780s all Jews living within the Austrian Empire were forced to Germanize their names. German became such a dominant language that in some regions, such as Bohemia, it nearly replaced the local tongue.

The foods and foodways of medieval Central Europe represent an area of research largely unexplored by scholarship, in part due to the lack of surviving records. Maria Dembińska's pioneering work on medieval Poland (1963) has pointed the way for similar studies of Bohemia and Hungary, but published research is limited. In spite of this, some generalities can be made. The kingdoms of Bohemia and Hungary were powerful in the early Middle Ages, and Bohemia in particular became the epicenter for many culinary influences in the region. Likewise, the Danube River served as a conduit for new foods and dishes emanating from Byzantium. The strudel, the cucumber, and red beets moved into Central Europe by this route. The lack of written records has been addressed through medieval archeology, especially since World War II.

Meal Systems in Central Europe

The medieval meal systems of Central Europe are key to understanding meal systems of the region, even in the twenty-first century. Traces of the medieval two-meal system (a light meal in the morning about 9:00 A.M. and an evening meal about 5:00 P.M.) still survive in parts of Central Europe, and this eating pattern defines the type of foods consumed. During the summer half of the year (from spring plowing to fall plowing), field workers eat three times a day, but during the winter they revert to the medieval two-meal system. In grain-growing regions, the first meal eaten in the early hours of the day was generally bread with lard or cottage cheese, since it was easy to transport. A midday meal of hot cooked food was brought to the field hands during their break. In the crescent-shaped mountainous zone surrounding the Carpathian Basin as well as in the Carpathian areas of the Ukraine and Transylvania (Romania), the morning meal was a hot cooked dish, such as Romanian *mamaliga* (cornmeal mush). The midday meal consisted of remnants from the morning, while a cooked evening meal was eaten at home. It was also a general custom to eat from a common bowl. Until the late nineteenth century, children normally stood to eat at the dinner table, and men and boys ate separately from women and girls. Once children reached the age of puberty, they were given a place to sit at the farmhouse table in accordance with their status in the family. For example, younger boys of lesser rank sat lower down the table than their older brothers, who had first choice of the food after their father.

Another unifying feature of Central European cookery is the widespread use of gruels made from hulled, whole, or cracked grains. The grits can also be made from lentils, peas, fava beans, and in more recent times from New World beans. All levels of Central European society ate grits, but the proportion varied. Wealthier people consumed more meat, while the poorest individuals subsisted on an essentially vegetarian diet. In medieval Poland the inevitable gruel for king and peasant alike was millet. In modern-day Romania it is *mamaliga* made from maize. Rice has never played a significant role in the cookery and has always been associated with luxury foods and urban cuisine. Only the Bulgarians grew rice on a large scale, mostly for provisioning the Ottoman army. Rice did not become integrated into Bulgarian food culture until the eighteenth century.

Along with grain-based gruels, bread soup was another universal food throughout the region. This is a dish of medieval origin in which pieces of bread are soaked in hot broth, then puréed, or the broth is simply poured over a slice of bread. Nearly every country in Central Europe possesses a long list of local variations on this theme. More elegant preparations replaced the bread with roux, flour fried in lard or bacon drippings. A close relative of this soup was a dish made from small balls or crumbs of dough produced by rubbing the dough against a sieve or grater. The dough was then boiled in water, milk, meat stock, or vegetable puree until thick. The most typical dish of this kind prepared in Hungary is called *tarhonya*, a term borrowed from Turkish in the eighteenth century.

During the Middle Ages it was called *vágott étek*, *vagdalt étek*, and *gombóta*, terms all referring to the shape of the dough or to the action of rubbing the flour. In mountainous areas of Slovakia, Poland, and Romania, this dish is made with buckwheat flour.

The introduction of maize via the Balkans was perhaps the most important addition to the gruel-based diet of the countryside. In most areas it was first introduced as a fodder crop, but poor farmers in mountainous areas soon adopted it as a foodstuff since it was much easier to grow than wheat. The most common method of preparing it was in the form of mush, but it was also used as a filling in sausages, as dumplings mixed with meat or vegetables, and as a stuffing in steamed cabbage leaves. The mush is known as *mamaliga* in Romania and *puliszka* in Hungary.

Shifts in Taste Preferences

In terms of general taste preferences, there have been a number of important shifts in Central European diets. Pickled vegetables (especially cabbage and root crops), vinegar preparations, and sour milk are found everywhere, especially in areas where beer is the most common beverage. The sweet-and-sour or tart and spicy foods preserved in peasant cuisine began to disappear in urban cookery during the eighteenth century in favor of more neutral tastes. This shift occurred directionally from west to east and from the upper classes to the lower ones. Sugar at one time represented a prestige food consumed only by the aristocracy and rich merchants, and it reached peasant cookery only in the nineteenth century. The preference for food highly spiced with black pepper shifted in the late eighteenth century to a widespread use of paprika. This shift began in the lower Balkans and emanated out of Bulgaria, where New World peppers had been introduced in the 1600s. The Bulgarians have always been the market gardeners of Central Europe, and it was through them that many new foods, such as beans, maize, and tomatoes, were disseminated into the Slavic regions.

Drinking Habits

Central Europe can be divided into three large zones according to the predominant drinking habits. The northeastern region, including the Czech Republic and Poland in particular, are beer-drinking countries. In the northwest, brandy and spirits predominate, while the southern area is largely wine-drinking. The centers of wine production lie in Slovakia, Hungary, and Romania. The Romans introduced viticulture into these countries, and many grape varietals are peculiar to central Europe, among them the famous Tokay of Hungary.

Among the nonalcoholic beverages, buttermilk, whey, and a light beer made with birch sap (*Betula pendata*) were popular in many parts of the region, as were herbal teas, especially medicinal teas made with Saint-John's-wort. Coffee drinking spread from the Balkans

The idealized kitchen of the Austro-Hungarian Empire. Frontispiece from the 1833 Polish adaptation of Franz Zelena's *Wiener Kochbuch* (Viennese Cookbook), first published in Vienna in 1828. ROUGHWOOD COLLECTION.

due to Turkish influence. Coffee is consumed with milk as an early morning beverage or is taken black after meals. The peasants first served it at the beginning of feasts and weddings and only later incorporated it into their everyday diet.

Poland

Poland's culinary history did not begin in 1364 with the famous Congress of Kings held in the ancient capital city of Cracow, but it was during that event that Poland's distinctive cuisine was showcased to the world. The host of this gathering, which included hundreds of nobles and several thousand retainers, was King Casimir III, who had positioned the kingdom as a world power and who was himself a connoisseur of Italian cooking. Present at this congress was Peter I de Lusignan of Cyprus, who brought

Poppy seeds are used extensively in Central European cooking. During the Middle Ages poppy seeds were associated with fasting dishes, but today they are enjoyed in traditional cakes like the one shown here. PHOTO BY ANDRÉ BARANOWSKI.

with him Byzantine cooks, a troupe of gypsy musicians, and eating habits of the East. The culinary watershed of this event has not been studied in great detail, but after that, Polish dishes are mentioned frequently in cookery books of the 1400s and 1500s as one of the recognized "national" styles of cooking. Elements of Poland's medieval cuisine have also been preserved in the countryside, as the Polish ethnographer Zofia Szromba-Rysowa has pointed out in her study of village foodways *Przy wspólnym stole* (At the common table, 1988).

Poland's culinary identity may be divided into four broad regional styles: the cuisine of the mountainous south; the cookery of the Baltic coastal region; the foods of the east, principally dishes emanating from Lithuania and Russia; and the classic cookery of the great estates and urban restaurants. The influence of Germany was also pervasive, especially in the period before 1700. The first cookbook written in Polish, the *Kuchmistrzostwo* of 1532, was a translation of a popular German cookbook called the *Kuchenmeisterei* that first appeared at Nürnberg in 1485. The first truly Polish cookbook was published at Cracow in 1682 by Stanislaw Czerniecki under the Latin title *Compendium Fercolorum*. Czerniecki was a petty noble who served as royal secretary to King Jan III So-

bieski. Parallel to the German influence was the Yiddish-speaking Jewish community, one of the largest in Europe.

When the elector of Saxony ascended the Polish throne in the early eighteenth century, he brought with him French cooks. This blend of French and Polish themes in the court cuisine of the country helped to create the Polish cookery that has survived into the twenty-first century. Poland's haute cuisine has always differed from that of other European nations in that it has drawn its inspiration from the peasantry and recreated these foods not only as symbols of Polishness but also as a political reminder that Poland's most ancient monarchs and noble families were themselves the children of peasants. These dishes include *bigos* (a game stew); the baba cake; *sauce polonaise* (a sauce originally served with boiled pike); and a host of sausages (the Polish word *kielbasa* simply means 'sausage'), the most famous of which are *kielbasa krakowsaka* (pressed ham sausage), *kasza gryczana* (buckwheat kasha), and pierogi, the Polish equivalent of Spanish empanadas. Polish beer and vodka are also well-known outside the country.

The Czech Republic

Although small in size, the Czech Republic is one of the wealthiest and most industrialized of the Central European countries. It is also blessed with a rich culinary history tracing back to the early Middle Ages. The country consists of two major regions, Bohemia and Moravia, each with its distinct local cooking style. The capital, Prague, is situated on the Vlatava River, which flows north into Germany. This geographic link brought the city and its culinary culture in constant contact with German Saxony and the Baltic port city of Stettin at the mouth of the Oder. However, due to its political domination by Austria, Prague became a melding place for many exotic culinary ideas and the location of a number of well-known cooking schools and restaurants. Prior to World War I, the company of Bohuslav and Vydra was internationally known for its culinary equipment, especially gingerbread and pastry supplies. In the area of pastry, the Czech Republic is perhaps best known as the home of the layer cake (torte) and *koláce* (sweet buns with a variety of fillings). Both terms evolved from Latin.

Other important culinary centers in the country are Karlovy Vary (the former Karlsbad), which was a famous spa resort during the Austro-Hungarian Empire, and Plzen (Pilsen). Plzen is a scenic town noted for its Pilsner beer. Until 1945 the town was situated in the heartland of the Sudeten German region. After the expulsion of the Germans, the Czechs continued the famous brewery and maintained an international standard for high-quality brewing.

As a counterpoint to the heavy Germanization of the country under the Austrians, Bohemia produced Magdalena Dobromila Rettigová (1785–1845), a cookbook writer whose recipes were widely circulated in Czech and

Polish family in Upper Silesia enjoying a dessert course of traditional homemade cakes and fruit wines. PHOTO BY ANDRÉ BARANOWSKI.

were translated into German. Rettigová also wrote juvenile literary fiction that championed the national language. She was followed by Božena Němcová (1820–1862), whose semiautobiographical novel *The Grandmother* (1855) described the foods and daily life of Bohemia and offers a detailed look into the mind-set of a culture besieged by foreign and mostly Germanizing influences with a long list of foods the author considered typical of Czech culture. Some of this nostalgia for the past is present in Marie Rosická's *Bohemian-American Cook Book* first published in Omaha, Nebraska, in 1915. In print off and on since its first appearance, the book is an important culinary link to the homeland for Czech immigrants in the United States.

Slovakia

While Slovakia speaks the same language as the Czech Republic, it has experienced a different history. The an-

cient capital city of Pressburg (now Bratislava) on the Danube has oriented the country southward, and for much of its history Slovakia was a territory of the kingdom of Hungary. Like Hungary, Slovakia is a wine-growing region, thus it forms a cultural line of demarcation between the beer-drinking Slavs to the north and the wine-drinking central Europeans to the south. The country's wines are mostly white, consisting of Pinot Gris (Rulandske to Slovakians), Sylvaner, and a few others. The main wine-growing area centers around Modra, north of Bratislava.

Slovakia is also a country where fish play an important role in the diet, especially trout and carp. During the Middle Ages, Slovakian towns along the Danube were involved in an extensive fish-pickling industry, once critical to the Roman Catholic dietary calendar. Since it lay on trade routes with Poland and Bohemia, Slovakia also served as a conduit for culinary ideas flowing out of

Hungary and the Ottoman Empire. Maize is significant in the diet, and Hungarian *gulyás* is prepared in myriad ways. The Carpathian Rocombole garlic, popular among American growers, came from the eastern part of this country.

Hungary

Most food historians do not realize that Marcus Rumpolt, the author of *Ein New Kochbuch* (1581), was Hungarian by birth, not German. While his cookbook is viewed as a classic of German Renaissance printing, a number of the recipes incorporated in the book are Hungarian. The book was also translated into Hungarian. Rumpolt is just one example of the pervasive influence Hungary has had on the cookery of Central Europe. On the international level, Hungarian cookery is perhaps the best-known of all the cuisines of Central Europe, and so are its wines.

Hungary experienced the fate of being a great medieval power, only to suffer defeat and invasion by the Ottoman Turks. The medieval kings of Hungary enjoyed a long association with Italy, especially southern Italy and Sicily, thus Hungarian cookery early developed a distinctiveness best characterized as a blend of Slavic and Mediterranean Europe. The Turkish occupation of the country devastated it, and not until the 1680s were the Turks driven back, after their defeat at Buda. Through dynastic marriage, the kingdom of Hungary became part of the Habsburg Empire, but Turkish influences lingered and blended with local culinary traditions, coffee drinking among them. However, Austrian rule meant that both upper-class and middle-class cooking became heavily Germanized. Many of the foods associated with Hungarian cuisine came from the countryside, among them *pörkölt* casseroles, *guylás*, *palacsubták* (a type of pancake), and *Liptó* cheese made with goat milk.

In contrast to this, Budapest became a great center for pastry baking, in part due to the proximity of wheat-growing districts and constant contact with the Viennese court. Two of the best-known nineteenth-century cafés were Gerbaud's in Pest and Russwurm's in Buda, but the most famous of all was run by József Dobos, whose Dobos Torte is found in every cookbook devoted to elaborate cakes.

Nothing about Hungarian cuisine, however, is better known than paprika. Introduced in the eighteenth century from Bulgaria, paprika gradually made such inroads into Hungarian cookery that it became a defining element. The Hungarians have also become the unrivaled masters in pepper breeding, so in any given farm market it is possible to see vast quantities of unusually shaped peppers, both sweet and hot, piled in heaps or hanging in endless strings among braids of garlic and other local produce. Hungarians enjoy peppers with every meal, even at breakfast. One popular breakfast dish consists of hot peppers stuffed with bacon drippings. The peppers are sliced and eaten on rye bread.

Romania

Romania's borders have moved considerably throughout history. The western part of the country was once the Principality of Transylvania and part of the Austro-Hungarian Empire. It is difficult for a country that speaks a romance language to look west toward Vienna for culinary inspiration when it has the Black Sea lapping at its feet. This mixture of Slav and Latin, of Orientalism and self-conscious Francophilia, characterized the flowering of Romanian haute cuisine during the interwar period. It was the product of literati, and it was decidedly sybaritic.

This is not the Romanian cookery of modern cookbooks, yet in reality there are probably two distinct Romanian cookeries, one created exclusively in the restaurants, an important aspect of Romanian social life, and the simpler foods made at home. Much unites both of these cookeries with the Mediterranean and the Near East. Spit-roasted meats, stuffed vegetables, rice pilafs, an abundance of eggplants, and a good array of local red and white wines all work together to give the food a peculiarly Romanian character. Food is often served *mezze* fashion, in an array of small dishes, and there is a widespread preference for hot pepper.

Mamaliga, Romanian polenta, is well-known and has already been mentioned, but not as well-known are Romanian *ghiveci* (a dish resembling ratatouille), *mititei* sausages (garlic-flavored beef sausages), carp's roe paste (*icre*), sour winter soups, and *sarmale* (stuffed cabbage leaves). In Transylvania the cookery changes due to the presence of a large German minority that settled there in the Middle Ages and to an even larger Hungarian community. Both of these groups have distinctive local cuisines that have had an important influence on Slovakia and Hungary to the west.

See also **Germany, Austria, Switzerland**; **Judaism**; **Middle Ages, European**; **Sausage**; **Stew**.

BIBLIOGRAPHY

Chamberlain, Lesley. *The Food and Cooking of Eastern Europe.* London: Penguin, 1989.

Dembińska, Maria. *Food and Drink in Medieval Poland.* Edited by William Woys Weaver. Philadelphia: University of Pennsylvania Press, 1999.

Kisbán, Eszter. "'The Noodle Days': Early Modern Hungary and the Adoption of Italian Noodles in South Middle Europe." *Ethnologia Europaea* 23 (1993): 41–54.

Komlos, John. *Nutrition and Economic Development in the Eighteenth-Century Habsburg Monarchy: An Anthropometric History.* Princeton, N.J.: Princeton University Press, 1989.

Livi-Bacci, Massimo. *Population and Nutrition: An Essay on European Demographic History.* Cambridge: Cambridge University Press, 1990.

Petránová, Lydia. "Development and Possibilities of Historical Studies of Meals and Nourishment in Bohemia." In *European Food History*, edited by Hans J. Teuteberg. Leicester, U.K., and New York: Leicester University Press, 1992.

Szromba-Rysowa, Zofia. *Przy wspólnym stole* (At the common table). Wroclaw, Poland: Zaklad Norodowy im. Ossoli'-skich, 1988.

Vaduva, Ofelia. "People's Food in the Iron Gate Zone." In *Ethnologische Nahrungsforschung—Ethnological Food Research*, pp. 293–301. International Symposium for Ethnological Food Research, Helsinki, Finland, 1973. Helsinki, Finland: Suomen muinaismuistoyhdistys, 1975.

Kara Kuti

CEREAL GRAINS AND PSEUDO-CEREALS.

Cereals and pseudo-cereals are the primary carbohydrate supply for the world's human population. Nearly half of the annual cereal production is used for human food. Cereals also serve as the primary food for dairy and draft animals, poultry, and wild birds, and are the main ingredient in the production of alcohol. The primary cereals include wheat, rice, corn, sorghum, millets, oats, barley, and triticale. Wheat and rice provide nearly 50 percent of the world's food energy. Millet is a term that refers to small-seeded grain and has been applied to many unrelated species. The primary millet involved in world trade is proso millet, which is grown mostly in northern China. Foxtail millet and pearl millet, totally unrelated species, are also widely grown for grain on subsistence farms in Asia and Africa, respectively. Three other unrelated millets—finger, brown-top, and Japanese—are locally important cereals on subsistence farms throughout the world. Pseudo-cereals include amaranth and buckwheat.

Defining Cereals and Pseudo-Cereals

Cereals are members of the grass family (Gramineae) that are grown for their edible starchy seeds. Pseudo-cereals are grown for the same purpose, but are not members of the grass family. Since they are grouped based on use rather than the biology of the plant, this aspect will be considered separately. Initial development of cereal plants involves seminal roots that vary from three to eight in number. They arise directly from the hypocotyl. Further plant development includes the development of a second set of roots which are permanent and arise from the point just a little below the surface of the ground. These roots are fibrous rather than tap and are noted for their ability to control soil erosion through an extensive network of root hairs. They extend outward and downward in all directions from the crown, providing the primary nutrition for the plants.

Cereals are identified by alternate two-ranked leaves that are frequently formed near the ground. The leaves are composed of a sheath that encloses the stem (culm) and is split down the side opposite the blade. Identification of vegetative plants is usually based on the shape and size of the ligule, which is an appendage extending upward at the juncture of the sheath and the blade, and on the presence or absence of hairs in this region. The stems are composed of nodes and internodes that elongate to varying degrees as the crop matures. The nodes associated with leaf blades are the most apparent and are identified as the swelling in the stems. Nodes lower on the plant have the potential to develop additional stems, which are frequently referred to as tillers. The grain is produced on a spikelet that varies significantly from corn to wheat to millet in size, shape, and appearance.

The cereals and pseudo-cereals are essentially a starchy crop. However, they may contain significant quantities of protein and oil, and it is frequently these constituents that determine suitability for a specific end use. Structurally the seeds are composed of three main parts including the endosperm, embryo, and seed coat. The endosperm is the primary starch storage portion but also contains some protein. The embryo is the oil storage portion, high in protein and minerals. The seed coat, also called pericarp or bran, consists mainly of cellulose and hemicellulose with some protein and lignin. Relative proportions of the three components vary among the different cereals with the embryo of "small grains" such as wheat and barley making up less than 4 percent of the total seed, while in corn it averages 12 percent. There is also large variation from variety to variety.

Buckwheat and amaranth are two of the most widely used pseudo-cereals, but their production is dwarfed by the true cereals. Buckwheat is in the Polygonaceae family and amaranth is in the Amaranthaceae family. Neither has been the primary energy source for large regions, but both have played significant roles in food use. They both have a tap root rather than a fibrous root system and have two cotyledons rather than one as is true for the grasses. The root system consists of a tap root (central or primary root) that extends downward to a considerable distance. This root is thicker and stouter than the lateral roots that arise from it. The lateral roots may be divided several times. The tap root first penetrates the soil for some distance, forming no laterals. Laterals are then formed, beginning at the upper portion of the tap root. Buckwheat and amaranth are herbaceous, erect growing annuals. Under ordinary conditions buckwheat attains a height similar to wheat. Amaranth is typically twice the height of wheat, but there are some dwarf varieties that seldom grow taller than four feet. Both plants adjust themselves very efficiently to surroundings, such as fertility of soil and rate of seeding, by sending out branches from the main stem. The buckwheat kernel is in the form of an achene, being a single seed enclosed in an indehiscent pericarp that fits tightly around the seed. The achene is three-angled, the angles being acute, and has the form of a pyramid with the base rounded. The hull or pericarp varies from silver gray to brown or black in color and is hard and thick, with the surface polished and shining. It separates readily from the mealy endosperm. The relatively large embryo is central, dividing the soft, white endosperm into two parts, the cotyledons being broad. The surrounding testa is membranous and light yellowish-green in color.

Buckwheat groats, called kasha, are sold in whole and granulated form. Kasha can be baked, boiled, or steamed to serve as an alternative to rice and potatoes. Buckwheat flours have been used extensively in pancake mixes as well as in various breads. The Japanese mill buckwheat groats into flour for use in the production of soba noodles, a major part of the Japanese diet. Buckwheat flour is the primary ingredient in such European dishes as polenta and Zganci.

Reliance of the world population on one or more of the cereal grains as a primary food material is not just happenstance. They contain the main food essentials for the human and animal body, although they are deficient in vitamins and may be low in particular amino acid portions of the protein. Pseudo-cereals frequently have a unique amino acid profile and can be used to supplement cereals for a more balanced amino acid diet. Starch, the primary constituent of cereal grains, breaks down in the digestive tract into simpler and more easily digested sugars to supply the body with its primary source of energy. While varying in oil percentage, the oil plays a significant role in total energy supply in the diet and some varieties have been selected with amounts adequate for processing and selling as vegetable oil.

While rich in thiamine, riboflavin, niacin, and pantothenic acid, the cereals do not meet all of the vitamin and mineral requirements for food or feed. Frequently foods and feeds that are used to supplement these needs are considered more important than the cereals themselves, but as a proportion of total food and feed consumed, none come close. The role of fiber in the diet has recently been studied extensively and has altered somewhat the thought on the value of the seed coat, which contains the highest portion. This portion is also high in vitamins and minerals and many recipes have been altered to include higher proportions of whole grain or bran to take advantage of the health benefits.

Cereals and pseudo-cereals are not often used as human food without some preparation to convert them to a more edible and digestible form. Modern processing methods utilize grains to produce everything from tortillas to macaroni, as well as breakfast food, flour, bread, and vegetable spreads.

Origins of Cereals

The origins of some cereals are obscure. More than one had its cultural beginning before recorded history. The development of cereal grains, probably more than any other factor, permitted the earliest tribes to change from nomadic life to full or partial agricultural subsistence. They provided more food with less effort than did any other crop. They were important for their ability to provide subsistence and security of subsistence over time. Cereals can be easily stored to provide food between harvests. Their role in reducing the time spent by people in hunting and gathering allowed humankind to develop other pursuits.

The various cereals probably developed in different parts of the world. Corn is likely the only cereal native to the Americas, while wheat and barley may have been cultivated first in the Fertile Crescent area of the Middle East. The pseudo-cereal amaranth is also native to the Americas, and the earliest identification of amaranth as a grain comes from archaeological digs at a cave in Tehaucan, Puebla, Mexico, where seeds of *Amaranthus cruentus* were dated as six thousand years old. Aztec writings are the first recorded indication of its use and mention collection of large quantities of amaranth along with corn and beans in annual tribute to the ruling class. Although the origin of proso millet has not been ascertained, it is one of the first cultivated cereals, most likely prior to wheat. Proso millet has been known for many thousands of years in eastern Asia including China, India, and Russia. The genus *Setaria* is widely distributed in warm and temperate areas. Foxtail millet, the most widely grown food of this genus, is one of the world's oldest cultivated crops. Its planting was mentioned in Chinese records as early as 2700 B.C.E. Foxtail was the most important plant food in the Neolithic culture in China, and its domestication and cultivation constituted the earliest identifiable manifestation of this culture, the beginning of which has been estimated at over four thousand years ago. Buckwheat is native to temperate east Asia, where it was grown in China before 1000 C.E.

Modern Cereal Production

Development of mechanization for planting, harvesting, shipping, and processing of cereals during the first half of the twentieth century led to the greatest advancement in cereal production since the dawn of history. Practically all labor involved in modern cereal production involves mechanized operation. Mechanization—along with improvements in weed, disease, and insect control, improved nutrient management, and variety improvements—increased production potential and led to the Green Revolution in the second half of the twentieth century. Today, one farmer typically provides cereals that feed more than one hundred people. The average yield per unit of land of cereals has increased by more than 50 percent in the last fifty years. Increases in corn and rice have been more dramatic than those of the other cereals, but all have shown steady improvements. The dramatic yield improvements in corn have led to a production area increase in corn at the expense of oats, millet, rye, and barley. Especially in China, millet production has been pushed to more marginal areas with the best land being dedicated to corn and rice, with higher yield potential.

The sickle or reaping hook was used for cutting cereals during the Stone Age. In biblical times the blades were made of bronze or iron. Steel sickles were made in the nineteenth century. The sickle is still a part of harvesting in many developing countries. Typically a man with a sickle can cut, bind, and shock an acre of grain in around forty hours. A scythe was more common in the Roman Empire and areas of the Orient. With attached cradle frames, harvesting time was cut to twenty hours per acre. In the first century of the common era, Pliny the Elder described a grain stripper that was pushed by oxen and used by inhabitants of Gaul. Between 1775 and 1840 reapers were developed in Europe and the United States, but this was quickly replaced by combines by 1950. The combine not only replaced the reaper, but also replaced the thresher that was developed in the latter half of the nineteenth century. Before then, grain had been flailed out by hand or threshed by treading out the grain under the feet of people or livestock. With a flail a man can thresh seven or eight bushels per day. A form of threshing machine still used in Asia and Africa consists of stone-studded planks, stone rollers, or metal disks on a shaft drawn by animals over the grain stalks that are spread on a threshing floor. Today, modern combines cut, thresh, and clean more than one hundred acres per day.

The mechanical corn picker was not developed until World War II and replaced the age-old tradition of husking by hand from the standing stalk. If the stalks were being harvested for forage, some cut them by hand and placed them in shocks to cure. Today the corn picker has been replaced by the modern combine used on other small grains with only modifications of the header.

Storage and Transportation

Compared with many other crops, cereals and pseudo-cereals are extremely amenable to storage. The moisture content at harvest is typically below 15 percent and their composition and seed coats are such that deterioration is slow. Seasonal harvest with a continuous demand means that storage between harvests is required. Under typical conditions this need can be met easily; with care, storage for many years without serious loss of quality is possible. Storage during times of surplus is a part of human history, and with benefits of modern technology, cool dry conditions can be maintained and storage can be successful for extended periods of time. There are, however, problems with storage, including excessive moisture content at the time of storage, excessive temperature, microbial, insect, and arachnid infestation, rodent and bird predation, mechanical damage, and biochemical deterioration. The latter is especially important for cereals and pseudo-cereals with higher than normal oil content because the oil becomes rancid over time.

The distribution system for cereals is frequently criticized as there is a surplus of production and yet hungry people around the world. However, the infrastructure that moves cereals by truck, train, barge, and ship is one of the most complex and efficient systems in the world. It is estimated that rail shipments from Kansas and Nebraska—the heart of winter wheat production—to the Pacific Coast, or a combination of truck and barge shipments to the Gulf Coast, cost less than $0.50 per bushel, including less than $0.15 for transportation from the field

to a local destination, and that loading on a ship and delivering to a handling facility in Southeast Asia or Africa adds only $0.50 per bushel. Getting from one village of the developing world to the next can double the total value of the wheat.

Processing

Cereals are processed in many ways, but the methods are broadly grouped into wet milling, dry milling, oil processing, fermentation, and feed processing. Characteristic features of milling processes include separation of the endosperm from the embryo and seed coat, and reduction of the endosperm into flour or grits. Milling schemes are classified as wet or dry, but this is a relative classification because water is used in almost all separations. Few generalizations can be made about cereal milling. For example, most rice is milled in two stages to remove the husk and then the bran, however, some is milled into flour. There are dry milling processes that change the shape and size of cereal. Fractions produced by this step are frequently separated in another step. An additional milling process can be completed by changing the temperature or water content. Unlike dry milling, which primarily just fractionates, wet milling is a maceration process in which physical and chemical changes occur in the basic constituents: starch, protein, and cell wall material. The objective is complete dissociation of the endosperm cell contents with the release of the starch granules from the protein network. Processing has taken a huge step from Stone Age grinding stones for dry milling to soaking processes to remove starch, described by Cato in the second century B.C.E., to modern milling and extrusion processes. Milling processes today are almost entirely based on meeting end product specifications by the most efficient means possible with almost all steps controlled mechanically and electronically.

The other primary processing method is production of alcohol from cereal grains through a fermentation process. This two-step process includes the conversion of starch to soluble sugars by amylolytic enzymes, followed by the conversion of the sugars into alcohol. In the first step the enzymes may be derived from the grain itself (malting), from other organisms present or added as extracts. The malting process has also been used for the production of some breakfast foods. It is comprised of a controlled germination during which enzymes capable of catalyzing hydrolysis of starch are produced. The fermentation process results in the development of alcoholic drinks, including beer and sake. Further processing by evaporating and condensing increases the alcohol content and produces whiskey, scotch, bourbon, and neutral spirits, including those used for production of fuel. Today production of gasohol ranks as one of the largest uses of corn following its use as animal feed. The by-products of fermentation are primarily used as livestock feed.

The number of foods prepared from a base of cereals is the largest of all food crops. Cereal grains are largely interchangeable for different uses and are, therefore, mutually competitive. They can substitute for one another in a number of food and nonfood uses. In their use as feeds they are almost completely interchangeable. That allows more latitude within which available grain supplies can satisfy a series of demands.

As raw materials in major processing industries, however, grains are not always so interchangeable. Technology of a particular process often requires a specific combination of chemical and physical characteristics in the raw material, which can be met fully by only one type of grain. This has been extended to variety specificity for many products and has led to the development of identity-preserved marketing systems that are quite distinct from the bulk transportation systems discussed earlier. Some predict that with greater use of biotechnology for adding trait specificity, the identity-preserved marketing systems may become increasingly important.

Cereal uses for food are largely defined by cultural context, but with the greater global movement of people, there is now a greater dispersion of foods. For example, rice-based products are now a common food item in places with no rice production. The same is true of amaranth.

The Aztecs used amaranth, which they called *huautli*, in a beverage, a sauce, for a type of tortilla, and for various medical uses. Popped or ground amaranth often was mixed with honey or other sweet, sticky plant materials, and then shaped into a variety of figures and shapes that were used in celebrations and religious ceremonies. Unlike most cereals, amaranth leaves are used as a vegetable, similar to spinach, and certain types have been selected almost exclusively for their leaf production. Most commercial production of amaranth is for types selected primarily for grain or forage production.

Both cereals and pseudo-cereals have a long history of use as forage crops for livestock. The small grains have been used extensively for hay, grazing, green-chop (fresh fodder harvested and used as cattle feed), and silage. Foxtail millet, pearl millet, and some other millets are perhaps better known for their forage use than for their grain production. Corn and sorghum are utilized extensively for silage. Almost all stover of all cereals and pseudo-cereals has potential utilization by livestock even though it may require supplementation with higher-protein feeds. Prior to the soft dough stage, when the kernel is still immature and has not yet hardened, most cereals meet or exceed nutrient requirements of livestock. Cereal forages are used as supplemental feed for cow and calf herds, support major elements of the stocker cattle industry, and have potential to produce finished beef. Cereal improvement programs, while directed at improved seed production, have improved disease resistance, stress resistance, insect resistance, and general adaptability to specific climates. This has led to significant improvements in consistency and quantity of forage production as well.

Cereal silage is an important part of the dairy industry. Corn silage alone makes up over 40 percent of the value of the forage fed to dairy cows in the United States. Corn silage is noted for its palatability, consistent quality, high yields, and energy content compared with alternative forages. The cost of production tends to be lower for corn silage than for most other forages, but this is partially offset by the large transportation costs of relatively wet material. Transportation costs have largely limited use to livestock production near the field from which the silage was harvested.

While the cereals and pseudo-cereals are primarily known as a source of energy, they have played important roles in other ways throughout history. Cereal sprouts have long been known for their cleansing properties and are a common part of health food stores. Amaranth and buckwheat have been evaluated extensively for their vitamin E, B_1, and B_2 activity in reducing arteriosclerosis. Oats and buckwheat are recognized as cholesterol-lowering foods. The pseudo-cereals have a different amino acid composition than the cereals and when combined in the diet produce a much more ideal amino acid balance.

Perhaps because of their importance in meeting daily sustenance and perhaps for other reasons, the cereals have been a symbol of human life and culture throughout recorded history. Amaranth played a major role in pagan rituals. Wheat and wheat harvesting are a part of world symbolism from the flags of major countries to churches and cemeteries. So much emphasis was placed on grain production by Roman peoples that the protection of grain was the primary concern of Ceres, one of the powerful Roman goddesses. The name cereal was derived from this association. With the huge supply of human energy coming from a few major cereals, and a few minor cereals in some regions, one of the big concerns for the world population is the risk of a major crop failure. This possibility has received increasing attention as selection and major gene improvements have narrowed the genetic base within crops to a few major varieties. It is particularly important that the diversity within major crops is conserved effectively, available for use, and managed wisely.

See also **Barley; Bread; Cereals, Cold; Horticulture; Maize; Mexico and Central America, Pre-Columbian; Pastry; Porridge; Rice; Rome and the Roman Empire; Wheat.**

BIBLIOGRAPHY

Baltensperger, David D. "Foxtail and Proso Millet." In *Progress in New Crops*. Edited by Jules Janick. Alexandria, Va.: ASHS Press, 1996.

Brenner, David M., et al. "Genetic Resources and Breeding of Amaranthus." In *Plant Breeding Reviews*, vol. 19. Edited by Jules Janick. New York: John Wiley & Sons, Inc., 2000.

Carleton, Mark Alfred. *The Small Grains*. Edited by L. H. Bailey. New York: Macmillan, 1923.

Conrad, H. R., and F. A. Martz. "Forages for Dairy Cattle." In *Forages, The Science of Grassland Agriculture.* 4th ed. Edited by Maurice E. Heath, Robert F. Barnes, and Darrel S. Metcalfe. Ames: Iowa State University Press, 1985.

Edwardson, Steven. "Buckwheat: Pseudocereal and Nutraceutical." In *Progress in New Crops.* Edited by Jules Janick. Alexandria, Va.: ASHS Press, 1996.

Food and Agriculture Organization of the United Nations. *The State of the World's Plant Genetic Resources for Food and Agriculture.* Rome: Food and Agriculture Organization of the United Nations, 1998.

Hitchcock, A. S. *Manual of the Grasses of the United States.* Revised by Agnes Chase. Vols. 1–2. New York: Dover Publications, Inc., 1971.

Horn, F. P. "Cereals and Brassicas for Forage." In *Forages: The Science of Grassland Agriculture.* 4th ed. Edited by Maurice E. Heath, Robert F. Barnes, and Darrel S. Metcalfe. Ames: Iowa State University Press, 1985.

Kent, N. L., and A. D. Evers, eds. *Kent's Technology of Cereals.* Exeter, U.K.: 1994.

Leonard, Warren H., and John H. Martin. *Cereal Crops.* New York and London: Macmillan and Collier-Macmillan Ltd., 1963.

Majors, Kenneth R. "Cereal Grains as Food and Feed." In *Crops in Peace and War: The Yearbook of Agriculture 1950–1951.* Edited by Alfred Stefferud. Washington, D.C.: U.S. Government Printing Office, 1952.

Myers, Robert L. "Amaranth: New Crop Opportunity." In *Progress in New Crops.* Edited by Jules Janick. Alexandria, Va.: ASHS Press, 1996.

Roth, Greg, and D. J. Undersander, eds. *Corn Silage Production, Management, and Feeding.* Madison, Wis.: American Society of Agronomy, 1995.

Sprague, G. F., and J. W. Dudley, eds. *Corn and Corn Improvement.* 3d ed. Madison, Wis.: American Society of Agronomy, 1988.

Stubbendieck, James, Geir Y. Friisoe, and Margaret R. Bolick. *Weeds of Nebraska and the Great Plains.* Lincoln: Nebraska Department of Agriculture, 1994.

Vail, Gladys E., Jean A. Phillips, Lucile Osborn Rust, Ruth M. Griswold, and Margaret M. Justin. *Foods: An Introductory College Course.* 6th ed. Boston: Houghton Mifflin, 1973.

David D. Baltensperger

CEREALS, COLD. Cold cereal has been a favorite breakfast of millions of Americans for several generations. Ready-to-eat cold cereal started as a healthy snack in the early 1900s. By the twenty-first century more than 2.7 million pounds of cold cereal were consumed by children and adults each year in the United States.

Cold cereal makes a quick, nutritious, low-cost, and portable breakfast. Ready-to-eat cereal products supply important nutrients. When combined with low-fat milk, cold cereal makes a meal that is high in protein and low in cholesterol and fat. Milk and grains compliment each other nutritionally since they are from different food

Fresh corn and a pretty face are used to promote Kellogg's new breakfast cereal in this 1907 advertisement. COURTESY OF JANET CAMERON.

groups. Most cereals are fortified with at least 25 percent of the daily recommended intake of essential vitamins and minerals and may provide up to twenty-six grams of fiber per cup of cereal.

Hot, cooked grains started long ago, but cold, ready-to-eat cereals were not available until Will Keith Kellogg and his physician brother John Harvey Kellogg began experimenting with flaked wheat in the early 1900s in Battle Creek, Michigan. While John Harvey Kellogg sought a nutritious food for his patients, Will Keith Kellogg recognized the sales potential of the crunchy, flaked grains that offered taste and convenience. Based on their experiments, Will Keith Kellogg founded the Battle Creek Toasted Corn Flake Company, later renamed the W. K. Kellogg Company. He is credited with transforming American breakfast habits and pioneering the mass advertising campaign in the United States. Competition among cereal manufacturers spurred marketing creativity. Cheerios, developed and marketed in 1941 as Cheerioats, supplied World War II soldiers with Yank Paks, special one-ounce packages available to the military. Cheerios also sponsored the *Lone Ranger* radio and

Most cold breakfast cereals are eaten with milk, but the addition of fresh fruits, nuts, or raisins is also popular. © ARTHUR BECK/CORBIS.

television shows during the 1940s and 1950s and featured premiums, such as deputy badges.

Cold cereal has gone through many changes since the Kellogg brothers' time. Most cereals are made from one grain or a combination of several grains, including wheat, corn, rice, oats, and barley. Ready-to-eat cereals fall into three main categories: whole grain, enriched, or restored. Whole grain cereals include the bran, germ, and endosperm—parts of the grain or "seed"—and the nutrients they naturally contain. Enriched cereals contain grains supplemented with vitamins and minerals above the level found in them naturally. For example, most grains are low in vitamin D, so enriched cereals have added vitamin D to meet the body's requirement. Restored cereals contain whole or refined grains plus nutrients that were lost during processing, such as B vitamins and iron. Some cereal manufacturers add 100 percent of the recommended daily value of nutrients; most add just 25 percent.

Experts disagree on the value of cold cereal. Some nutritionists feel that unfortified, natural whole grains are healthier than prepared cereals made from fortified, refined grains. Others argue that consumers are likely to eat more of the sweet-flavored cereals and therefore will eat sufficient quantities to meet dietary requirements. But

cold cereals have more than vitamins and minerals. Fiber is an important part of whole grains and of the human diet. Cereal ingredients such as oats, wheat, and psyllium, contain fiber and help reduce the risk of heart disease. Scientific research indicates that a diet including wheat bran may help reduce the risk of colon cancer.

Cereal boxes note that "diets rich in whole grains and other plant foods and low in total fat, saturated fat, and cholesterol, may help reduce the risk of heart disease." When shopping for cold cereal, read the nutrition facts on the box. Most nutritionists agree that the best cold cereal contains one or more whole grains, no partially hydrogenated oils, no added sugar, no added salt, and plenty of fiber (at least 3 grams of fiber per 100 calories or 3 to 5 grams of fiber per 1-ounce serving). Some cereal makers add BHT or other artificial ingredients to preserve flavors. Other companies avoid artificial ingredients and depend instead on heat processing at low temperatures or the addition of oil to preserve cereal quality.

Responding to customer concerns, cold cereals are likely to begin to include more plant-derived ingredients, such as cornstarch or herbal blends. Cornstarch helps keep cereal flakes crunchy in milk and helps hold together clusters of fruit, nuts, and grains. Some consumers want their breakfast cereal to supply herbal extracts, such as gingerroot, elderberries, or green tea, as well as whole grains. Look for nontraditional cereal grains, such as triticale, spelt, kamut, quinoa, flax, and soybeans. Sprouted grains offer a sweet, maltlike flavor. Substitutes for refined sugar include honey and fruit-juice concentrates; however, these ingredients add sugar, too. Cereals have also become more portable for on-the-go consumers without the time for a sit-down breakfast.

See also **Breakfast; Cereal Grains and Pseudo-Cereals; Kellogg, John Harvey; Wheat: Wheat as a Food.**

BIBLIOGRAPHY

Kuntz, Lynn A., ed. "Building a Better Breakfast Cereal." Food Product Design. Available at http://www.foodproductdesign.com.

Leonard, David. "How Healthy Is Your Breakfast Cereal?" University of New Hampshire Cooperative Extension Service. Available at http://ceinfo.unh.edu/Common/Documents/gsc10130.htm.

Machado, M. Fátima, Feranda A. R. Oliveira, and Luis M. Cunha. "Effect of Milk Fat and Total Solids Concentration on the Kinetics of Moisture Uptake by Ready-to-Eat Breakfast Cereal." *International Journal of Food Science and Technology* 34 (1999): 47–57.

Smith, Andrew P. "Breakfast Cereal Consumption and Subjective Reports of Health." *International Journal of Food Science and Technology* 50, 6 (1999): 445–449.

W. K. Kellogg Foundation. Available at http://www.wkkf.org/WhoWeAre/Founder.asp.

"Will Keith Kellogg." Available at http://www.netstate.com.

Patricia S. Michalak

CHEESE.

Cheese, which has been described as "milk's leap toward immortality," can be more dispassionately defined as a product of milk fermentation. Yet part of our fascination with cheese may come from the sheer number and diversity of cheeses worldwide. They number into the thousands, although an exact count is difficult, as cheeses are notoriously difficult to classify. A classification of cheese only in terms of bacteriological processes neglects the symbolism of ancient mythologies, regional pride, and artistic ingenuity that are embedded in this, one of the simplest and most complicated of foods. The mythology of cheese is shared by disparate groups: the Greeks gods and mortals, the conquerors and conquered of the Roman Empire, a delighted Napoleon and the waitress who first served him Camembert. The legends are compelling, but not as much as the product itself.

History

The beginnings of cheesemaking are unknown, but it has been generally reasoned that the knowledge of how to turn milk into cheese closely followed upon the domestication of lactating animals. Some of the earliest archaeological evidence of cheesemaking comes from the Fertile Crescent, where animals were domesticated around 8000 B.C.E. A Sumerian relief (c. 3500–2800 B.C.E.) portrays cattle and dairying practice. Pots that had likely contained cheese were discovered in the tomb of Horus-aha, the second king of the Egyptian First Dynasty (c. 3000–2800 B.C.E.). And perforated bowls (c. 3000–1000 B.C.E.) made from pottery or rushes have been found in more than one European location. These bowls were designed to drain the liquid whey from the solid curds.

Cheesemaking was an efficient means of preserving an extremely perishable food (milk) from the spoiling effects of the Near East climate. The art and science of cheesemaking spread into Europe, and quickly became a regular part of the diet and a symbol of strength in ancient Greece, where Olympians trained on diets of cheese. Polyphemus, the brutal Cyclops of Homer's *Odyssey*, milks his animals amid the racks of cheese in his cave, while Odysseus watches quietly nearby. According to Greek mythology, the knowledge of cheesemaking was a gift to mortals by the gods of Mount Olympus. Roman soldiers carried cheese rations with them as the Roman Empire grew, though cheesemaking was highly developed in the Celtic parts of Europe. The Feast of Imbolc (2 February) was a celebration of the approach of spring: the new lambs and the milk of the ewes represented the changing seasons and were honored as a first sign of spring.

Artisanal cheesemaking might have been lost after the fall of the Roman Empire if not for the Christian monasteries. The monks not only preserved cultural traditions during the Dark Ages, but spent much time reworking and improving cheese recipes. Their creations, among them French Munster and Epoisses, are still referred to as "monastery" or "trappist cheeses."

In the following centuries, cheesemaking grew as an art and industry. The first commercial cheese factory in the United States was established in Rome, New York, in 1851. Innovations like the kind of cream cheese popularly known as Philadelphia Cream Cheese and pasteurizing whole cheese (patented in the United States by James Kraft in 1916) followed. Almost a century of pasteurized process cheese sales in the United States and abroad have demonstrated their popularity, but a growing number of cheesemakers and cheese-eaters are committing to the preservation and production of artisanal (made by hand) and farmstead (made from the animals of a farm on that farm) cheeses. Several books about specialty cheeses have been published in the last few years, and wider selections of domestic and imported cheeses are available in supermarket, and restaurants.

Milk

When confronted by the vast number of cheeses, the different shapes, colors and aromas at a well-stocked cheese counter, it is astonishing to remember that all these endless varieties come from only one basic ingredient. Although a cheesemaker makes many decisions throughout the cheesemaking process that will affect the finished product, the first step is always to select the raw material, milk.

Cheese can be made from any animal that produces milk: cow, sheep, goat, camel, mare, buffalo, or yak. With the exception of Italy's mozzarella *di bufala*, made from the milk of herds of water-buffalo, cheeses in the Western world are typically made from the milk of cows, goats, and sheep. Of the three animals, sheep produce the lowest volume of milk, but because it is so much higher in fat and protein content than either goat's or cow's milk, less of it is needed to make cheese. On average, ten pounds of cow's or goat's milk or about half that amount of sheep's milk is required to make one pound of cheese. In contrast to the rich, concentrated flavor of sheep's milk, goat's milk is slightly sweet and fresh-tasting; cow's milk is the lightest of the three. The milk of individual breeds of the same species also has a unique flavor profile. Consequently, the laws governing many name-controlled cheeses specify the breed of animal from which the milk is to come. Cheesemakers have the further choice of how to use the milk they collect: full fat, partly skimmed, or with extra cream added.

Free-grazing animals feast on a bounty of wild grasses, flowers, and other vegetation during the warmer months. This gives their milk a complexity of flavor that is easily distinguishable from the milk of grain-fed animals in winter. Some cheesemakers insist that they can

Red-painted cheese press, Connecticut, ca. 1835. Tulip poplar and oak. The press creates a wheel of cheese inside the tub, while excess whey drips from the drain into an earthenware pot. ROUGHWOOD COLLECTION. PHOTO CHEW & COMPANY.

perceive slight flavor adjustments daily—as the animals move from one pasture to another.

Pasteurization

Milk used for cheese may or may not be pasteurized. Pasteurization is a process of heating milk that destroys most of the naturally present bacteria (see Cheese Safety below). Current U.S. law requires that cheeses be pasteurized or, if made from unpasteurized milk, aged for at least sixty days at 35°F before sale for consumption. Milk may be pasteurized in one of two ways: by heating it to 161°F for fifteen seconds, or by heating it to 145°F for thirty minutes (the latter method is sometimes called "heat treatment"). These laws apply to both domestically produced and imported cheeses. When cheese is made from unpasteurized milk, it is frequently referred to as "raw milk" cheese, connoting that the milk has not been

"cooked." Most cheesemakers believe that the brilliant nuances of flavor found in raw milk, with its naturally present "good" bacteria, simply cannot be duplicated in a pasteurized milk cheese, though some well-respected cheeses, including British Stilton, are made only from pasteurized milk.

The Principles of Cheesemaking

An oft-repeated legend has it that the first cheesemaker fell into the role by accident. A nomadic tribesman prepared for a long desert journey, he carried a bag made from the dried stomach of a young sheep and filled with milk. As he walked steadily under the relentless sun, the milk began to curdle. Noting that this "fresh cheese" had a pleasant taste and did not spoil as easily as milk, the nomad later drained off the whey and salted the curds to enhance these qualities. The cheesemaking tradition had begun.

While modern cheesemaking techniques are more refined and recipes have become standardized, the basic principles remain the same now as when the (possibly apocryphal) nomad of cheese legend opened his sheep's stomach bag (which supplied the coagulating rennet), warmed by the sun and agitated by his rhythmic trek.

The Steps of Cheesemaking

There are as many recipes for cheese as there are cheeses, but all of them follow some combination of these steps.

Acidification: souring the milk. The milk is gently warmed to encourage the growth of lactic acid bacteria, Streptococci and Lactobacilli. These bacteria feed on the milk sugar lactose, changing it to lactic acid. As the acidity rises, the solids in the milk (casein protein, fat, some vitamins and minerals) clump together, forming curds in the watery whey (milk is approximately 85 percent water). This is the first step for making all cheeses; in ancient times, cheeses were most likely the result of leaving pots of milk to sour naturally in the sun, affected by bacteria in the air. Some cheesemakers still wait for these process to begin with free, airborne lactic acid bacteria, but most use a starter culture. Starters are widely available commercially, but cheesemakers can also use a bit of the previous day's milk (unless it is pasteurized)—the same principle as with a sourdough bread starter.

Renneting: coagulating the curd. Cheesemaking has been referred to as "controlled spoiling" because of the need to efficiently form curds before undesirable bacteria cause the milk to become rancid. The enzyme rennin, traditionally removed from the stomach lining of a young animal (usually the same species of animal that supplied the milk), hastens and completes the curdling process. The renneting property of some plants has been recognized nearly since the dawn of cheesemaking; these vegetable rennets are the traditional agents in several cheeses. Other vegetarian rennets, made from a yeast or fungus, are also used today.

The curd is left to "set," forming a network of protein that traps the other milk solids inside. As the solids bind more tightly together, they begin to push out the liquid whey, a process the cheesemaker may continue by cutting, cooking, and pressing. The whey is sometimes used to make cheese as well (Italian ricotta and Cypriot hallumi are two examples), but usually it is discarded.

Treating the curds. After renneting, cheese recipes diverge. Some soft cheeses, like fresh goat's milk cheese, are gently transferred to molds. The curd's own weight will continue to press out whey. These cheeses might be labeled "hand ladled" to indicate that they were created using this time-consuming method. The Greeks called the molds that held the curds *formos*, which became the root for cheese in Italy (*formaggio*) and France (*fromage*). Our English word "cheese" has its root in the Latin *caseus*, which became *Käse* in German and *queso* in Spanish.

In contrast to the light touch required for soft cheeses, which derive their creamy texture from a higher water content, the curds for other cheeses are sliced and chopped, by hand or machine, to release more whey. The smaller the curds are cut, the firmer the resulting cheese. Cheddar and some other cheeses undergo a unique process called "cheddaring," which results in its firm, flaky texture. Blocks of curd are stacked, turned, and restacked to press out as much whey as possible. Then the dry curds are milled, ground into tiny pieces, and packed into molds.

Some hard cheeses are "cooked," that is, the curds are reheated during processing. This causes the curds to release even more whey and alters the texture of the cheese. Examples of cooked cheeses include Emmentaler, Appenzeller, and Gruyère.

Preparation for aging: salting, molding, and pressing. Cheeses can be salted in four different ways. For some cheeses, the salt is stirred directly into the curd. A second method involves rubbing or sprinkling dry salt onto the rind of a cheese. This helps to form the rind, protecting the inside of the cheese from ripening too quickly. Some large cheeses are soaked in a pool of brine. The fourth option is to wash the surface of the cheese with a brine solution. In the case of washed-rind cheeses, the salt does not protect the cheese from bacteria—it invites them. The cheeses must be regularly rubbed with water, brine, or alcohol to encourage the growth of the bacteria that give them their sticky orange rinds and distinctive aroma.

Cheese is then transferred, if it has not been already, to a mold where the final cheese will take shape. The whey of soft cheeses drips through the holes in their molds, pressed out by the cheese's weight. Other, firmer cheeses are pressed by hand or machine to extract the last bits of whey.

Ripening. During the ripening or aging stage, the cheesemaker cares for the cheese at a precise temperature and humidity level until it is ready to eat; this can range anywhere from a few weeks for a soft-ripened cheese to a few years for a wheel of Parmigiano-Reggiano. Depending on the variety, ripening cheeses need to be turned to equally distribute the butterfat and brushed to maintain the rind quality.

Name-controlled Cheeses

Before the 1951 Stresa Convention in Stresa, Italy, it was impossible for traditional, regional cheesemakers to protect their products from inauthentic forgeries. The delegates to this international conference accomplished two goals: they created a uniform definition of "cheese" to facilitate international trade, and protected by law the names and origins of a select group of treasured traditional cheeses. Protected cheeses fall into two categories. A few cheeses, including France's Roquefort and Switzerland's Sbrinz, are given absolute protection—the cheese cannot be made outside of its designated region. A second group of cheeses may be produced in nontraditional areas, but must be clearly labeled with its region of origin. Camembert produced in the United States is a good example of this second group.

"Name-controlled" cheeses must meet stringent laws that go beyond the international standards for processing and safety. The departments and associations that supervise these cheeses differ from country to country (and from cheese to cheese), but generally emphasize the unique, regional quality of the cheese. In Switzerland, for example, cheeses must be native to the area in which they are made. France has the most specific cheese production laws of any country. The Appellation d'Origine Contrôllée (AOC) designation indicates that a cheesemaker has complied with regulations that include the type and breed of animal from which the milk comes, location of production of both milk and cheese, production techniques (including pasteurization), the final composition of the cheese (its fat and moisture content, for example), and the physical and sensory attributes of the cheese, which include its shape, size, and of course, flavor. Spain, Portugal, Italy, and Great Britain are also home to name-controlled cheeses.

The effort to control cheese quality through government standards of identity can be related to similar efforts with wine. Purchasing a French cheese with the AOC designation on the label does not necessarily guarantee quality, however. Subtle differences between individual producers, milk quality, or aging time and conditions can make the difference between a great cheese and a not-so-great one.

Classifying Cheese

As Pierre Androuët asserts in his fundamental text *Guide du Fromage* (Guide to Cheese), a cheese should simply be what it is—its appearance, aroma, texture, and flavor

Traditional baskets for straining cheese curds. Cyprus, 20th century. Myrtle twigs. The use of myrtle for cheese strainers dates to classical antiquity. ROUGHWOOD COLLECTION. PHOTO CHEW & COMPANY.

should be characteristic of the variety to which it belongs. But how does one determinate a cheese's "type"? There are innumerable cheeses, and no single, standardized method for grouping them; rather, authorities employ different classification systems.

General characteristics, such as the type of milk (or whey) used or the country of origin, provide a starting point for discussing broad topics; for example, the relative unpopularity of sheep's milk cheese in the United States compared to European countries, or the social implications of cheese consumption in England as opposed to France. More specific classifications—the moisture content of the cheese (hard, semi-hard, soft, or fresh), whether it was made from pasteurized or unpasteurized milk, or the length of aging—may serve scientific inquiries concerned with bacterial development rates in different cheeses.

When cheese is classified by "type," it is grouped by similar characteristics like taste, smell, and appearance. The rind type and the method of production are often used as determining factors. Steven Jenkins describes eight different cheese "families" (including processed cheese) (*Cheese Primer*, pp. 11–13). These very common categories may help when choosing a cheese at the cheese counter, but a particular cheese may fit into more than one category, or not seem to fit in any.

Fresh cheese. After the formation of curds, the cheese (and also, sometimes, the whey) is usually transferred to plastic tubs and covered. The cheeses are eaten fresh, not ripened, and do not have a rind. Cottage cheese, cream cheese, and feta—a pickled cheese—are some common examples of fresh cheeses. Sometimes fresh Mozzarella is also included in this category because it does not form a rind, but this is problematic because Mozzarella curds are heated and stretched.

Bloomy rind cheeses. Also called simply "soft ripened cheese," this category includes cheeses like French Camembert and Brie, which are covered with velvety white molds that ripen the cheese from the outside in.

Washed-rind cheese. These orange, sticky, stinky cheeses are rubbed with a water, brine, or alcohol solution to invite the growth of ripening bacteria and molds on their rinds. Examples include the French Livarot (nicknamed "The Colonel" because it is ringed with raffia stripes) and Alsatian Munster.

Natural rind cheese. These cheeses are self-sufficient, naturally forming their rinds from air contact. Surface-molded goat cheeses and British Stilton are good examples. British farmhouse cheeses are sometimes included in the natural rind category because their permeable cheesecloth wrapping allows them to develop a thick protective rind. Likewise, Parmigiano-Reggiano and other cheeses are helped to form a rind that still develops largely from air contact.

Blue-veined cheese. To allow the growth of their distinctive bluish or greenish interior molds, these cheeses are never pressed. They are typically injected with a mold strain, and then pierced to expose the insides to air. They may be wrapped in foil like Italian Gorgonzola or form natural rinds like British Stilton.

Uncooked, pressed cheese. This is a category defined by processing type. These cheeses are pressed to remove whey, but are not cooked (see Treating the Curds).

Cooked, pressed cheese. Cheeses such as Swiss Emmental (sometimes Emmentaler) and Gruyère are cooked and pressed in the processes described above.

Processed cheese. There is another type of cheese that, because of its overwhelming presence in supermarket refrigerator cases, should not be overlooked. Pasteurized processed cheese is created by heating and mixing a blend of natural cheeses and emulsifiers. These cheeses—American cheese certainly being the best-known in the United States—can retain their flavor and texture qualities in a much broader range of temperature and moisture conditions than can natural cheeses, and for a longer period of time. They are also easy to use in a variety of dishes, and are typically less expensive than natural cheeses. Because the entire product, not just the milk, is pasteurized, and because processed cheeses are often vacuum-packaged, they are uniformly and consistently safe. The nutrient content of processed cheese remains very close to that of natural cheese, although the sodium content may be higher. All of these characteristics make them popular choices not only in the United States but in other countries as well.

Processed cheese food and cheese spread both contain natural cheese and emulsifying agents, but add other ingredients like whey, skim milk, milk powders, or water that raise the moisture content of the product. This causes them to melt or spread more easily. There are also imitation cheese products that contain little or no milk protein. Soy cheese is one example of an imitation cheese product.

Nutritional Value

The fat content of cheese is noted on its package as a certain percent butterfat. This can be misleading, however, because the fat content is evaluated as a percentage of the solids in the cheese (fat-in-dry-matter), not the overall weight of the cheese. Even a very hard, aged cheese like Parmigiano-Reggiano contains a significant amount of water, about 30 percent. As a cheese ages, it loses moisture, and the fat percentage relative to weight increases, though the fat-in-dry-matter remains the same. Soft cheeses typically have a high fat-in-dry-matter percentage, but they also contain more water than hard cheeses;

their overall fat percentage is much lower, as much as half, the fat-in-dry-matter percentage.

Cheese's greatest nutritional advantage is its high protein content and the digestibility of that protein. In addition, cheese is a valuable source of vitamin A, vitamin B2, and vitamin B12, and the minerals calcium and phosphorus.

People who suffer from lactose intolerance often believe that they must forego cheese altogether. In fact, many cheeses (especially aged, hard cheeses like Parmigiano-Reggiano) contain very little or no lactose, as the lactose is expelled along with the whey. The small amounts of remaining lactose are mostly converted into lactic acid during the aging process.

Cheese Safety

Cheese has been cited as the vehicle for several bacterial outbreaks—defined as an illness from a common source that affects two or more people. Organisms communicated to humans through cheese have included Salmonella, *Listeria monocytogenes*, *Brucella melitensis*, and *Escherichia coli* (including *E. coli* O157). Nearly all of these bacteria are destroyed during the pasteurization process. Raw milk cheeses seem to have been the cause of reported outbreaks more often than pasteurized cheeses. In the interest of public safety, the United States requires that milk for cheesemaking be pasteurized or that the cheese be aged for sixty days. However, recent concerns about the effectiveness of pasteurization, coupled with alarm and confusion over animal disease outbreaks like mad cow disease and hoof-and-mouth disease (which do not affect milk safety) have prompted scientists and government officials to reevaluate the current policy.

A close review of the reported outbreaks reveals that current laws are probably adequate to prevent cheese-borne illnesses, provided that they are strictly enforced and the starting quality of the milk is high. Reports and studies of cheese-borne outbreaks often include "unpasteurized" and "improperly pasteurized" cheese in the same category, implying that milk that has not completed the pasteurization process is of the same quality as raw milk. Traditional cheesemakers would argue that this is not the case. When milk is intended for pasteurization, its initial bacterial quality need not be as high as that of raw milk, as all bacteria will be destroyed in the pasteurization process. However, if the pasteurization process were ever to fail, or if, as some researchers have hypothesized, pasteurization is not effective against all bacteria, milk of low initial bacterial quality increases the risk of cheese-borne illness. Cheesemakers who use raw milk, on the other hand, must take special care to keep it free of dangerous bacteria.

Few outbreaks have been caused by unpasteurized dairy products in which there was not at least one flaw in the production process. Curds from unpasteurized milk have been mislabeled as pasteurized, raw milk cheeses have been sold before the minimum required aging time, and fresh, unpasteurized Mexican soft cheese has been illegally imported and sold. All of the above cases involved raw milk cheeses, demonstrating the danger that can be associated with that product. Yet, they also show that the existing standards governing raw milk cheese could have prevented the outbreaks, if they had been carefully followed.

Bacterial levels in raw milk will always be higher than in properly pasteurized milk, even when the greatest of care is taken. Aging a cheese for at least sixty days has long been thought to neutralize harmful bacteria, but this may not be true for all types of cheeses and all types of bacteria. Certain groups of people, those with weakened immune systems or special concerns, should not consume raw milk products, particularly soft and semi-soft cheeses. A consumer choosing a raw milk cheese needs to do so fully aware of the possible risks. New labeling requirements could help make sure that people are informed of the risks and the pleasures when they purchase cheese.

See also **Dairy Products**; **France**; **Italy**; **Wine**.

BIBLIOGRAPHY

Androuët, Pierre. *Guide to Cheeses.* With the help of N. Roche and G. Lambert, translated by John Githens, and new cheeses by Anthea Bell. Henley-on-Thames, U.K.: Aidan Ellis, 1993. New and revised edition. Originally published as *Guide du fromage* (Paris: Stock, 1971).

Fox, Patrick F., ed. *Cheese: Chemistry, Physics and Microbiology.* 2d ed. 2 vols. London: Chapman & Hall, 1993.

Harbutt, Juliet. *Cheese: A Complete Guide to Over 300 Cheeses of Distinction.* Minocqua, Wis.: Willow Creek Press, 1999.

Jenkins, Steven. *Cheese Primer.* New York: Workman, 1996.

Jones, Evan. *The World of Cheese.* New York: Knopf, 1978.

Kosikowski, Frank V., and Vikram V. Mistry. *Cheese and Fermented Milk Foods.* 3rd ed. 2 vols. Westport, Conn.: F. V. Kosikowski, 1997.

Masui, Kazuko, and Tomoko Yamada. *French Cheeses.* New York: DK Publishing, 1996.

McCalman, Max and David Gibbons. *The Cheese Plate.* New York: Clarkson Potter, 2002.

Nantet, Bernard, et al. *Cheeses of the World.* Translated by Clio Mitchell, Rob Jamieson, and Daniel Wheeler. New York: Rizzoli, 1993.

Pearl, Anita May, Constance Cuttle, and Barbara B. Deskins. *Completely Cheese: The Cheeselover's Companion.* Edited by David Kolatch. Middle Village, N.Y.: Jonathan David, 1978.

Rance, Patrick. *The French Cheese Book.* London: Macmillan, 1989.

Rance, Patrick. *The Great British Cheese Book.* London: Macmillan, 1982.

Sardo, Piero, Gigi Piumatti, and Roberto Rubino, eds. *Italian Cheeses: A Guide to Their Discovery and Appreciation.* Translated by Giles Watson, Helen Donald, and Michael Farrell. Bra, Italy: Slow Food Editore, 1999.

Simon, André. *Cheeses of the World.* 2d ed. London: Faber and Faber, 1960. Reprint, 1965.

Stamm, Eunice R. *The History of Cheese Making in New York State: The History of Cheese Making in the Empire State from the Early Dutch Settlers to Modern Times.* New York: Lewis Group, 1991.

Tewksbury, Henry. *The Cheeses of Vermont.* Woodstock, Vt.: Countryman Press, 2002.

Werlin, Linda. *The New American Cheese: Profiles of America's Great Cheesemakers and Recipes for Cooking with Cheese.* New York: Stewart, Tabori & Chang, 2000.

Sara Firebaugh

CHEF, THE. This entry focuses on the emergence of the *chef de cuisine* with the rise of restaurants in the public sphere. Until recently, well-known chefs working in restaurants in Britain and the United States were French or French-trained (for example, Alexis Soyer at the Reform Club in London and Charle Elme Francatelli at Delmonico's in New York City). Japan and China did not have fine dining-style restaurants or the western-style kitchen organization until more recently. African Americans were usually cooks, primarily in domestic settings or as caterers.

The role of "chef" emerged initially from the homes of European nobility, beginning as early as the medieval period. In these grand estates, kitchens were large and populated with numerous workers whose jobs were to help the nobility execute the large, complex banquets important to the maintenance of social position and power during this period. These banquets were about excess, elaborately decorated fish, fowl, and game on platters, dramatic interludes, and massive goblets of wine. As Europe entered the early modern period (1500s and 1600s), the link between social power and social display began to revolve more around exhibits of refinement. Civility and elegance took precedence over excess. The table increasingly became a site for such assertions, hence the kitchen also became more important.

The position of "chef," which comes from *chef de cuisine*, or chief of the kitchen, signifies the highest-ranking worker in a grand hierarchy. Initially he was in charge of running the kitchen, and, like the butler, reported in turn to the head of the household. In twentieth-century parlance, the "chef" traditionally has been a department head. *Chefs de cuisine* were part of the guild system, which regulated artisan practices in France until the French Revolution. Guilds controlled apprentices, the only means available for acquiring training in artisanal crafts and becoming an established craftsperson. Guilds also supervised aspects of production. In France up until the nineteenth century, *maître queux*, or master cooks in noble houses, were treated under a separate set of guild statutes. *Cuisiniers* and *traiteurs*, who worked alongside the urban streets, were considered another corporate

No evidence exists that women were ever appointed *chefs de cuisine* in any kitchen setting before well into the twentieth century. From the medieval period women worked as domestic cooks throughout Europe, but their roles were clearly defined as servants. In the move from private to public sphere, women were left behind to work in smaller, nonprofessional venues.

Chefs de cuisine historically came from France or were trained under French chefs due to the importance of the French court as the seat of "civility" and "culture" for European courtly life, more generally beginning in the early modern period. French haute cuisine symbolized, along with porcelain dishes, ornate silverware, and table decorations, and other French artisanal products, the heights of refinement. Throughout Europe a courtly banquet displaying these items revealed the sophistication and social status of the noble hosts. French chefs were hired to work for the nobility throughout Europe, including the Russian tsar and the king and queen of Britain among others.

French *chefs de cuisine* capitalized on the powerful reputation of French haute cuisine. By the 1600s they began to simultaneously promote and codify their cuisine with the publication of cookbooks, for example Pierre François de La Varenne's *Le Cuisinier français* (1651), which he dedicated to his noble patron, the Marquis d'Uxelles. Antonin Carême, another *chef de cuisine* who worked in various noble households, created *Le Cuisinier parisien, ou, l'art de la cuisine française au dix-neuvième siècle* (1828), heralded by many as the first cookbook to document the modern approach to French haute cuisine, an approach that focused on refined sauces, extremely elaborate set pieces, and an integrated system of skills and methods. By the late nineteenth century, the ever growing popularity of French chefs both inside and outside of France, the increasingly literate bourgeoisie, and greater possibilities for printing books meant that many chefs, including Urbain Dubois, Georges-Auguste Escoffier, and Jules Gouffe, wrote cookbooks in which they advocated for their mastery of French haute cuisine and its importance in the culinary pantheon. *Chefs de cuisine* managed large kitchens, but they also advocated for a certain culinary sensibility and approach. This approach was disseminated to all the apprentices and cooks working in their kitchens.

Apprenticeship was traditionally the primary means of training cooks. Only after a minimum three-year apprenticeship could a young boy, who generally began his apprenticeship between the ages of ten and thirteen, be called a "cook." The early years were usually spent cleaning vegetables, scrubbing copper pots, and generally obeying the orders of the cooks, *sauciers, poissoniers, sous chefs*, and *chefs de cuisine*, all higher up in the hierarchy of kitchen work. After completing an apprenticeship, a young journeyman cook could stay in the establishment where he was trained or search for work elsewhere. The arduous and long journey to becoming a *chef de cuisine*

Drawing by Franz Freiherr von Lipperheide (1835–1906) showing the type of clothing worn by court cooks during the 1400s. From a hand-colored print published in Berlin in 1884. ROUGH-WOOD COLLECTION.

group. Only after the revolution did these two groups meld, eventually leading to the identification of the *chef de cuisine* or head of any large establishment, public or private.

Without question, the most dramatic shift in both identity and practice for the chef was the move from the private to the public sphere as the primary locale for plying the trade. Up until the middle of the eighteenth century, all those with the title *chef de cuisine* worked for the nobility. With increased urbanization, the decline of the monarchical state, and the rise of bourgeois city life, the tables turned on the appropriate sites for asserting social rank. Power shifted to the new domain of the restaurant as fine dining became available to a new social class. *Chefs de cuisine* came to oversee these kitchens. An example is Antoine Beauvilliers, who worked for numerous noble houses but eventually moved to Paris, opened an early fine dining restaurant, La Grande Taverne de Londres, and wrote a cookbook, *L'Art du cuisinier* (1814). The shift from the private to the public sphere took years to complete. Auguste Escoffier, who worked from the 1860s to the 1930s, was the first renowned *chef de cuisine* who trained or worked only in public restaurants.

was not over; years went by before an aspiring cook could hope to become a chef.

Even though the official guild system was abolished after the French Revolution, until the 1870s all culinary training continued to occur within the confines of work establishments. As the culture of work changed in France and in Europe more generally, cooks and chefs began to reconsider this approach. The industrialization of many artisanal production forms on one hand and the increasingly elite status of certain occupations (engineer, pharmacist, doctor) on the other began to concern those involved in the food and beverage trades. Artisanal training was beginning to shift from the workplace to schools supported by the state. The elite alimentary craftspeople, the *chefs de cuisine*, decided the culinary training system needed to change. From 1870 through 1900 a dedicated group of French chefs worked to create a professional culinary school to replace the traditional apprenticeship program. Unfortunately their efforts did not succeed due to much resistance by those in charge of establishments used to the free labor of apprentices and the general belief in the apprenticeship model. Thus in the food trades the link between formal schooling and professional training did not occur until well into the twentieth century. Vocational schools designed to train cooks eventually capable of achieving the status of *chef de cuisine* were founded in Europe and North America by the 1930s and 1940s and throughout the world by the 1960s. However, apprenticeship was the dominant mode of culinary education for entry into professional kitchens through the late twentieth century.

The lineage of the French remained powerful in the organization of work in professional kitchens in the twentieth century. Such dominance is seen in the types of food prepared, the organization of the kitchen, and the identity and training of the head chefs running the kitchen. The imprint of the French on public fine dining meant that the *chef de cuisine* position retained the flavor of that culture.

As the modern restaurant became more a part of the economic culture, however, *chefs de cuisine* were as often found outside the kitchen, promoting their restaurants, dealing with customers, and reading and responding to profit and loss statements. The traditional tasks of overseeing menu and recipe development and supervising the production of food as it goes out of the kitchen into the restaurant remained a vital part of their job descriptions but did not encompass them totally. In larger, more corporate environments, such as hotels, chain restaurants, and college food services, the title *chef de cuisine* was often replaced with "executive chef." Managing a professional kitchen revolves around a corporate-style identity as much as or more than any cultural or culinary allegiance.

After the 1990s the identity and practice of the *chef de cuisine* began to shift even more, particularly in the United States and England. Chefs have gone from anonymous blue-collar workers sweating without much acclaim in big, hot kitchens to celebrities with their own cooking shows, product lines, and cookbooks and memoirs. Much like aspiring stars in the movie industry, aspiring cooks go into the profession because they hope to be famous one day. Why has fame come to the once lowly cook and chef? There are many possible answers, but one would have to be the decline of domestic cooking resulting from the increased number of women entering the work force since around 1970. Another answer may be found in the tremendous increase in disposable income for a certain segment of the urban population, which, combined with less cooking at home, has made going to restaurants a combination of high theater and spectator sport. Meanwhile, the expectation that the most powerful and high-ranking people working in public kitchens should be French or at least French-trained began to dissipate. The chef can come from anywhere and creates food that is indebted to but not dominated by French haute cuisine. The *chef de cuisine* has become a citizen of the globe and a respected professional.

See also **Carême, Marie Antoine; Escoffier, Georges-Auguste; France; Kitchens, Restaurant; La Varenne, Pierre François de; Places of Consumption; Restaurants.**

BIBLIOGRAPHY

Beauvilliers, Antoine. *L'Art du cuisinier*. Paris: Pilet, 1814.

Carême, Marie Antonin. *Le Cuisinier parisien, ou, l'art de la cuisine française au dix-neuvième siècle*. Paris: Auteur, 1828.

Elias, Norbert. *The Civilizing Process*. Translated by Edmund Jephcott. New York: Pantheon, 1982.

Escoffier, Auguste. *Auguste Escoffier: Memories of My Life*. Translated by Laurence Escoffier. New York: Van Nostrand Reinhold, 1997.

Spang, Rebecca L. *The Invention of the Restaurant*. Cambridge, Mass.: Harvard University Press, 2000.

Trubek, Amy B. *Haute Cuisine: How the French Invented the Culinary Profession*. Philadelphia: University of Pennsylvania Press, 2000.

Wheaton, Barbara Ketcham. *Savoring the Past: The French Kitchen and Table from 1300 to 1789*. Philadelphia: University of Pennsylvania Press, 1983.

Amy B. Trubek

CHEMICAL CONTAMINANTS. *See* **Additives; Environment; Food Safety; Toxins, Unnatural, and Food Safety; Water: Safety of Water.**

CHICKEN SOUP. Since prehistoric times, chickens have been mainly kept for their eggs. However, capons and old tough chickens were boiled by a wide variety of groups in Asia, Polynesia, Africa, and Europe. Boiling permitted the fuller use of chicken parts, such as bones, giblets, feet, neck, and pinions. Consumption of the liquid expanded the quantity of food available, added variety to the diet, and extracted nutritional components that otherwise would have been lost.

Broth was considered a restorative in the ancient world. Chicken broth's special identification with health may have been due to the humoral system of medicine. According to the theory, broth had qualities that eased digestion. As thin foods were believed to be easier to digest, broths were specifically recommended for the sick. Also, the color of chicken soup was similar to the human complexion and was consequently considered nourishing. Whatever the cause of the original belief, it survived into the Middle Ages: Chicken broth was commonly believed to be healthful throughout the Mediterranean and Western Europe. Moslems were particularly taken with chicken broth, as were the Jews. For instance, the classical Persian philosopher and physician Avicenna (980–1037) and the Jewish rabbi, physician, and philosopher Maimonides (1135–1204) regarded chicken soup as beneficial for the ill. This belief survived in Western culinary traditions, particularly those of Jews in Eastern Europe. Jews boiled chickens on Friday. The water in which the chicken was boiled was converted into soup and consumed during the week. Added to the broth were other ingredients, such as carrots, onions, celery, parsnips, kreplach, noodles, and matzoh balls. It was offered to those who were ill as a restorative.

Recipes for using chickens in soups were present in cookery manuscripts and were published in early printed cookbooks, such as Platina's *On Right Pleasure and Good Health* (1470), which contains a recipe that recommends chicken broth for the old and infirm. Chickens were employed in soup-making in England from the earliest days, and soup recipes containing chicken were regularly published as medical prescriptions.

Europeans introduced chickens into the Americas, and chickens were used in soup-making from the sixteenth century onwards. In the United States, recipes for soups containing chicken were published since 1824. However, the actual term "chicken soup" was not commonly used until the late nineteenth century. American manufacturers produced and promoted various commercial chicken soups, the most common of which was chicken noodle soup.

Today, chicken soup is particularly associated with Jewish cookery and is popularly known as the "Jewish penicillin." In 1993 Jack Canfield and Mark Victor Hansen compiled a book titled *Chicken Soup for the Soul*, which built on chicken soup's healthy reputation and set in motion the publications of dozens of "chicken soup" books, including the first cookbooks solely focused on making chicken soup. Some scientific evidence has surfaced to support the belief in the healthful qualities of chicken soup: In addition to protein and vitamins, recent research has suggested that chicken soup does have a naturally occurring peptide that has positive influence on health.

See also **Poultry; Soup; Stew.**

BIBLIOGRAPHY

Canfield, Jack, and Mark Victor Hansen, comps. *Chicken Soup for the Soul: 101 Stories to Open the Heart & Rekindle the Spirit.* Deerfield Beach, Fla.: Health Communications, 1993.

Cooper, John. *Eat and Be Satisfied: A Social History of Jewish Food.* Northvale, N.J.: Jason Aronson, 1993.

Myra, Chanin. *Jewish Penicillin: Mother Wonderful's Profusely Illustrated Guide to the Proper Preparation of Chicken Soup.* San Francisco: 101 Productions, 1984.

Wilen, Joan, and Lydia Wilen. *Chicken Soup and Other Folk Remedies.* Rev. ed. New York: Ballantine Books, 2000.

Andrew F. Smith

CHILD, JULIA. Possibly more than any other person, from the 1960s onward, Julia Child (1912–) revolutionized American attitudes toward cooking and eating by embodying two principles: cooks are made, not born, and the pleasure of food comes first. With the supreme confidence of a born clown who grew to six-foot-two, she turned America on to food by entertaining her audience as well as instructing them, making her an icon of the American spirit of energy and good humor. Combining the skills of a highly organized engineer with those of a slapstick comedian, she brought all of America into her home kitchen, through the doubled media of books and television, to wish them *"bon appétit."*

Born Julia McWilliams in Pasadena, California, to a family who had their own cook, Child did not set foot in a kitchen until she married at thirty-four. A graduate of

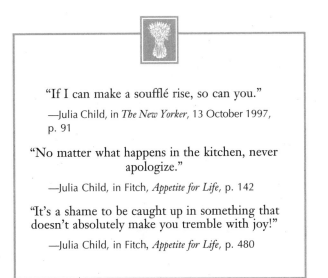

"If I can make a soufflé rise, so can you."
—Julia Child, in *The New Yorker*, 13 October 1997, p. 91

"No matter what happens in the kitchen, never apologize."
—Julia Child, in Fitch, *Appetite for Life*, p. 142

"It's a shame to be caught up in something that doesn't absolutely make you tremble with joy!"
—Julia Child, in Fitch, *Appetite for Life*, p. 480

Julia Child has become an icon of modern American cooking. She is shown here holding a bowl of tomatoes. Courtesy of AP/Wide World Photos.

Smith College and a veteran of World War II, she wed a fellow member of the Office of Strategic Services (OSS) whom she had met in Ceylon, Paul Child, who loved art, good living, and good food. When her husband was assigned to the Paris office of the United States Information Service in 1948, Child quickly enrolled in the *Cordon Bleu* school of cooking. There she joined with Louisette Bertholle and Simone Beck to found *l'École des Trois Gourmandes* (the school of the three gourmets). The first volume of *Mastering the Art of French Cooking* appeared in 1961. The second volume, coauthored by Child and Beck, followed in 1970. Together, the encyclopedic volumes introduced "the servantless American cook" to the classic techniques and terminology of French bourgeois cooking translated into American terms and American kitchens.

While the success of the first volume was phenomenal, it was but a prelude to Child's success as a television performer in 1962, in which her infectious enthusiasm and natural clowning were simultaneously embraced and parodied. She followed *The French Chef* series for Boston's public station WGBH, from 1963 to 1973, by eight more series over the next decades, where she often served as interlocutor to guest chefs. Usually a series such as *In Julia's Kitchen with Master Chefs* was followed by a book of similar title, so that her publishing output was as prolific

as her broadcasting. To date she has published eleven volumes.

Like James Beard, Child linked America's East to West, with houses in both Cambridge, Massachusetts, and Santa Barbara, California. She was among the first to establish an American food community with a national educative mission and proselytized universities to recognize gastronomic studies as part of a liberal arts curriculum. With California winemakers Robert Mondavi and Richard Graff, she founded the American Institute of Wine and Food in 1981 and helped transform the International Association of Cooking Professionals (IACP) into a comprehensive trade organization.

Her personal generosity and breadth of spirit brought amateurs together with professionals and made her a goodwill ambassador, not just between America and France, where the Childs built a house in Provence, but also internationally. She has fulfilled in her own life her admonition in her first book to "above all, have a good time." By taking what she called the "lah-de-dah" out of French cooking, she has made the pleasures of food available to ordinary Americans everywhere.

See also **Beard, James; Chef; Cookbooks; Fisher, M. F. K.; Gastronomy; Wine**.

BIBLIOGRAPHY

Child, Julia. *The Way to Cook*. New York: Knopf, 1989.

Fitch, Noel Riley. *Appetite for Life: The Biography of Julia Child*. New York: Doubleday, 1997.

Reardon, Joan. *M. F. K. Fisher, Julia Child, and Alice Waters: Celebrating the Pleasures of the Table*. New York: Harmony, 1994.

Betty Fussell

CHILI PEPPERS. Chili peppers (genus *Capsicum*) can be eaten fresh or dried, raw or cooked, alone or mixed with other foods. They add zest to any food—meat, poultry, seafood, starch, vegetable, fruit—whether eaten by themselves or as an ingredient in a prepared dish. Peppers are the most popular spice and condiment in the world. They are consumed daily by one-quarter of the world's population, and the rate of consumption is growing. Nonpungent or sweet peppers are also consumed as a vegetable, but are the less popular spice. All capsicums were pungent before being domesticated by prehistoric New World peoples and before the breeding of nonpungent (sweet) types. Peppers, both pungent and nonpungent, are the fruit of perennial shrubs that were unknown outside the tropical and subtropical regions of the Western Hemisphere before 1493, when Christopher Columbus returned from the first of his voyages in search of a western route to the East Indies. Although he did not reach those exotic spice lands as he had proposed, his return to Spain with examples of a new pungent spice

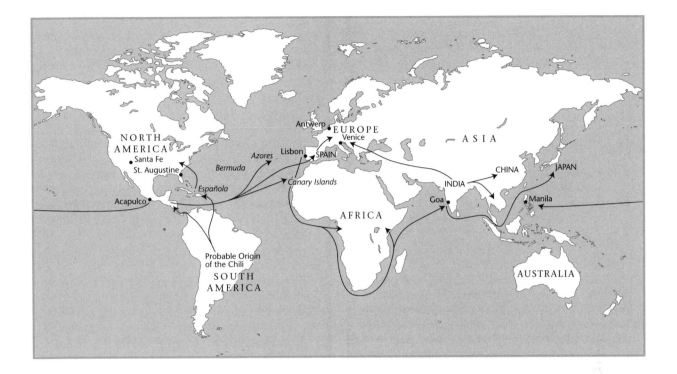

discovered during his first voyage to the eastern coast of the Caribbean island of Española (Dominican Republic and Republic of Haiti) is well documented in his journal. Today capsicums are not only consumed as a spice, condiment, and vegetable; they also have many other uses—as coloring agents, in landscape design, as ornamental objects, in decorative design—and have great potential in the field of medicine.

Nutrition

Nutritionally, capsicums are a superior food. They are an excellent source of the B vitamins, are superior to citrus as a source of vitamin C when eaten raw, and they contain more vitamin A than any other food plant by weight. Vitamin A increases as the fruit matures and dries but is not affected by exposure to oxygen, while the production of vitamin C in peppers diminishes with maturity and drying and is, as in all plant foods, destroyed by exposure to oxygen. Capsicums also contain significant amounts of magnesium, iron, thiamine, riboflavin, and niacin. Even though chili peppers are not usually eaten in large quantities, small amounts are important where traditional diets provide only marginal amounts of vitamins. However, ripe nonpungent varieties, such as bell peppers, can be eaten as painlessly as an apple while providing more food value.

Capsaicin: The Pungent Principle

A unique group of mouth-warming, amide-type alkaloids containing a small vanilloid structural component known as capsaicin act directly on the pain receptors of the mouth and throat to produce the burning sensation as-

sociated with peppers. This vanilloid element is also present in pungent spices such as ginger and black pepper. Birds and a few other creatures such as snails or frogs do not have neuroreceptors for pungent vanilloid compounds and thus capsaicin does not cause them pain.

V. S. Govindarajan (1985) has suggested "pungency" as the proper term for the perception of the hot or burning sensation humans have in response to such foods rather than to others. Consequently, the response to chili peppers should be defined as pungent rather than hot, stinging, irritating, sharp, caustic, acrid, biting, burning, and spicy. He also suggests that pungency be given the status of a gustatory characteristic of food, as are sweet, sour, bitter, saline, astringent, or alkaline.

The vanillyl amide compounds or capsaicinoids in *Capsicum* are predominantly capsaicin (C 69 percent), dihydrodcapsaicin (DHC 22 percent), nordihydrocapsaicin (NDHC 7 percent), homocapsaicin (HC 1 percent), and homodihydrocapsaicin (HDHC 1 percent). Several more analogues of these in trace amounts bring the number to ten (Masada et al., 1971; Treace and Evans, 1983). The primary heat contributors are C and DHC, but the delayed action of HDHC is the most irritating and difficult to quell. These compounds form a pungent group, of which capsaicin is the most important. Two of these five capsaicinoids cause the sensation of "rapid bite" at the back of the palate and the throat, while the others cause a long, low-intensity bite on the tongue and midpalate.

Most of the organs secreting these pungent alkaloids are localized in the fruit's placenta, to which the seeds are attached, along with the dissepiment (veins or crosswalls). The seeds contain only a low concentration

CHILI, CHILLI, CHILE, OR PIMENTO?

Columbus believed that he had arrived in the Orient when he landed on the islands of the Caribbean Sea. He was so convinced of this that he called the islands the Indies, the natives were labeled Indians, and to the confusion of all who came after him, the pungent spice they ate was named *pimiento* after the completely unrelated black pepper—*pimienta*—that he sought. The indigenous Arawaks, his Indians, called the fruit *axí* (pronounced "aah hee") that was transliterated in Spanish to *ají (ajé* or *agí*).

Today the pungent varieties are still called *ají* in the Dominican Republic (formerly Española) and a few other places in the Caribbean and much of South America. In the Andean area the ancient words *uchu* and *huayca* are used for capsicums by some Amerindian groups. In Spain American peppers are called *pimiento* or *pimientón* (depending on the size) after *pimienta* or black pepper from India. However, the Spanish names did not stay with the plant through Europe; it is called *peperone* in Italy, *piment* in France, and *paprika* by the Slavic peoples in the Balkans.

In 1519 when the Spaniards arrived in Mexico, the Nahuatl-speaking natives called their fiery fruit *chilli*. The main interest of the initial Iberian explorers was conquest, then gold and silver; chilies and other plants were of little concern to them. Fifty years later a different type of Spaniard arrived. Dr. Francisco Hernandez, physician to the King of Spain, was the first European to collect plants in the Americas. Hernandez lived in Mexico from 1570 to 1577, and when he returned to Spain, he produced four books on the natural history of the plants and animals he had found in New Spain. He heard the Nahuatl speakers pronouncing the name of their pungent native spice "chee yee." Consequently, when he wrote about that plant, he gave the Nahuatl word a Spanish spelling, using the double *ll* to reproduce the "y" sound he had heard the natives make. The Nahuatl stem *chil-* refers to the chili plant. It also means 'red.' To the generic word "chilli" the term that described the particular chili cultivar was added (e.g., *tonalchilli* for a chili of the sun or summer, *chiltecpin* for a flea chili, etc.). At some point the Spanish speakers in Mexico changed the original Hernandez spelling to *chile*. Today, that word refers to both pungent and sweet types of chilies and is used Nahuatl-style combined with a descriptive adjective, such as *chile*

colorado (for a red chili) or *chile poblano* (for a Pueblo chili). Confusingly, the same Mexican variety can have different names in different geographic regions, in various stages of maturity, or in the dried state.

In Portuguese *pimenta* is used for capsicums and qualifies the various types—*pimenta-da-caiena*, cayenne pepper; *pimenta-da-malagueta*, red pepper; *pimenta-do-reino*, black pepper; *pimenta-da-jamaica*, allspice; while *pimentão* is pimento, red pepper, or just pepper. *Ají* and *chile* are not found in a Portuguese dictionary, nor did Portuguese settlers or explorers carry these words with them in their travels.

The Dutch and English were probably responsible for introducing the current capsicum names to the eastern part of the Old World because in Australia, India, Indonesia, and Southeast Asia in general, *chilli* (spelled *chillies* or sometimes *chilly*) is used by English speakers for the pungent types, while the mild ones are called capsicums. Each Far Eastern language has its own word for chilies—*prik* in Thai and *mirch* in Hindi, to name but two.

The most confusion with regard to spelling exists in the United States, especially in California and the Southwest. Here, one finds both the anglicized spelling *chili* (*chilies*) and the Spanish spelling *chile* (*chiles*) used by some for the pungent fruits of the *Capsicum* plant, while "chili" is also used as a short form of *chili con carne*, a variously concocted mixture of meat and chilies. *The Oxford English Dictionary* offers *chilli* as the primary spelling, calling *chile* and *chili* variants. *Webster's New International Dictionary* prefers *chili*, followed by the Spanish *chile* and the Nahuatl *chilli*. *Chilli* remains the spelling most used by English-speaking people throughout the world.

For the sake of clarity and consistency, it would help if capsicums or peppers were used when speaking of the fruit of the *Capsicum* in general, both sweet and pungent; chilli or chilli pepper for the pungent types; chili for the spicy meat dish; and pimento for the sweet, thick-fleshed, heart-shaped red capsicum. *Chile* (in italics) should refer to a native Mexican cultivar or, in its not italicized form, it should refer to the long green or red variety from New Mexico or California. Whenever possible, the name of the specific fruit type, group, or cultivar name should be used.

of capsaicin resulting from this contact. The amount of capsaicin in a pepper is influenced by the growing conditions of the plant and the age of the fruit and is possibly variety-specific. The amount of capsaicin will increase under dry, stressful conditions. About the eleventh day after the fruit sets, the capsaicin content begins to increase, becoming detectable when the fruit is about four weeks old and peaking just before maturity, then dropping somewhat as it ripens (Govindarajan, 1985). Sun-drying generally reduces the capsaicin content, but when the fruits are air-dried with minimum exposure to sunlight, the highest retention occurs.

Capsaicin has virtually no odor or flavor, making it hard to detect by chemical tests, but a drop of a solution containing one part in 100,000 causes a persistent burning on the tongue. Although capsaicin is eight times more pungent than the piperine in black pepper, it only obstructs the perception of sour and bitter; it does not impair the discernment of other gustatory characteristics of food, as does black pepper. Eating capsaicin also causes gustatory sweating. The neck, face, and front of the chest sweat as a reflexive response to the burning in the mouth. Capsaicin activates the digestive systems by acting as an irritant to the oral and gastrointestinal membranes. That is a desirable irritation because it increases the flow of saliva and gastric acids. Very little capsaicin is absorbed as it passes through the digestive tract, an uncomfortable consequence of which is "jaloproctitis," or burning defecation.

Ingesting capsaicin by eating chilies not only increases the flow of saliva and gastric secretions but also stimulates the appetite. These functions work together to aid the digestion of food. The increased saliva helps ease the passage of food through the mouth to the stomach where it is mixed with the activated gastric juice. These functions play an important role in the lives of people whose daily diet is principally starch-based (Solanke, 1973).

Although capsaicin is not water-soluble, the addition of a small amount of chlorine or ammonia will ionize the capsaicin compound, changing it into a soluble salt. The same solution can be used to rinse capsaicin from the skin. When handling more than one or two chili pods, one should wear rubber or plastic gloves and/or keep a bowl of water with chlorine handy so that hands and skin can be rinsed immediately. Capsaicin can be quite painful if it comes into contact with the eyes, nose, or any other orifice. Capsaicin is soluble in alcohol, as are many organic compounds. Oral burning can be relieved by lipoproteins such as the casein found in milk and yogurt. The capsaicin is removed by casein in a manner similar to the action of a detergent, thereby breaking the bond it had formed with the pain receptors in the mouth (Henken, 1991). It is the casein, not the fat found in milk products, which relieves the burning; therefore, butter and cheese do not have the same effect as milk and yogurt.

Studies of the relationship of capsaicin to substance P, a neuropeptide that sends the message of pain to the brain, suggest that capsaicin can deplete nerves of their supply of substance P, thereby preventing the transmission of these pain signals (Rozin, 1990). Thus, capsaicin

Chili peppers are an icon food for the American Southwest. This bundle of pods is drying in the sun near Santa Fe, New Mexico. © Lois Ellen Frank/CORBIS.

is being used to treat the pain associated with shingles, rheumatoid arthritis, and phantom-limb pain. Importantly, capsaicin may prove to be a non-habit-forming alternative to the addictive drugs used to control pain. It does not act on other sensory receptors such as those for taste and smell, but is specific to pain receptors. Medical researchers are finding this specificity to be a valuable aid in their studies.

Aroma, Flavor, and Color

The carotenoid pigments responsible for the color in capsicums make peppers commercially important worldwide as natural dyes in food and drug products. Red capsanthin is the most important pigment. All capsicums will change color as they mature from green to other hues—red, brown, yellow, orange, purple, and ripe green.

The flavor compound of capsicums is located in the outer wall (pericarp): very little flavor is found in the placenta and crosswall, and essentially none in the seeds. Color and flavor go hand in hand because the flavoring principle appears to be associated with the carotenoid pigment: strong color and strong flavor are linked. Two Latin American species, *Capsicum pubescens* (rocoto) and *C. chinense* (habanero), are more aromatic and have a

One of the first European depictions of peppers appeared in Leonhard Fuchs's *New Kreüterbuch* [New Herbal] published at Basel, Switzerland, in 1543. This plate from Fuchs shows the pepper now commonly known as Cayenne. ROUGHWOOD COLLECTION.

decidedly different flavor than those of the more commonly consumed *C. annuum* var. *annuum*.

Smell and taste are separate perceptions. Several aroma compounds produce the fragrance. The taste buds on the tongue can discern certain flavors at dilutions up to one part in two million, but odors can be detected at a dilution of one part in one billion. The more delicate flavors of foods are recognized as aromas in the nasal cavity adjacent to the mouth. Sensory cells with this function are much more discerning than the tongue.

Origin

It is difficult to determine where *Capsicum* originated because the genus is still not fully understood (Eshbaugh, 1980, 1993). If the genus is defined as limited to taxa-producing pungent capsaicin, the center of diversity occurs in an area from present-day Bolivia to southwestern Brazil. However, if it is redescribed to include other non-pungent taxa, a second center of diversity would center

in Mesoamerica (Eshbaugh, 1993). It is certain, nevertheless, that the first ancestor of all domesticates originated in South America.

There are indications that the better-known *Capsicum annuum* originally was domesticated in Mesoamerica, and the next best well-known, *C. chinense*, originated in tropical northern Amazonia. The two less familiar species, *Capsicum pubescens* and *C. baccatum*, are more commonplace in the Andean and central regions of South America. The first two species were introduced to the Europeans after Columbus's voyages to the New World, while the other two species were not encountered until later, only recently becoming known outside their South American homeland.

The tropical perennial capsicum spread rapidly around the Old World tropics after 1492. Chili pepper has since become the dominant spice and condiment in the tropical and subtropical areas known as the "pepper belt," and in temperate regions sweet peppers are an important green vegetable and are grown as an annual. Concentrated breeding studies have produced *Capsicum* varieties that can be cultivated in environments quite different from their original tropical home and modern forms of transportation have made peppers of all fruit types available worldwide.

History

In his journal Columbus faithfully recorded his sighting of a new pungent, red-fruited plant that he called pepper, and he brought back specimens to Spain, marking the beginning of the history of capsicums for the people of the Old World (Anghiera, 1964; Morison, 1963). However, the pungent fruits were not originally discovered by Columbus. When nonagricultural Mongoloid peoples from northeastern Asia, who had begun migrating across the Bering Strait during the last Ice Age, reached the subtropical and tropical zones of their new homeland in the Western Hemisphere, they found capsicums widespread, having been carried by their natural dispersal agents, principally birds, from their nuclear area in southeastern Bolivia or southwestern Brazil to other regions (Pickersgill, 1984). Prehistoric plant remains and depictions of chilies on artifacts provide archaeological evidence of the use and probable cultivation of wild capsicums as early as 5000 B.C.E. It has also been shown that native Americans had domesticated (genetically altered) at least four species by the time of Columbus's discovery (Heiser, 1976; MacNeish, 1967). No other species have been domesticated since that time.

When Columbus arrived in the West Indies, he found at least two species of capsicums being cultivated by the Arawaks, agriculturists who had migrated north from their homeland in northeastern South America to the Caribbean Islands during a twelve-hundred-year period beginning about 1000 B.C.E. (Anghiera, 1964; Watts, 1987). Those migrants had traveled by way of present-day Trinidad and the lesser Antilles, bringing with them a tropical capsicum that had been domesticated in their homeland. They also brought the word "*ají*"—by which the plant was, and still is, known in the West Indies and throughout its native South American habitat (Heiser, 1969). Later a second species that had been domesticated in Mesoamerica probably came over different trade routes to the West Indies along with other Mesoamerican food plants—maize, beans, and squash (Sauer, 1966). However, *chilli*, the native Nahuatl name for the endemic Mesoamerican pepper plant, did not travel with it. It was that later arrival, a more climatically adaptable pepper than its earlier South American relative, which was introduced by Columbus to the Old World (Andrews 1993, 2000).

The new American plants from the tropical West Indies were not suited to the climate and day length of the Iberian Peninsula and other parts of Europe and the Mediterranean. Twenty-nine years later the conquest of Mexico, followed by that of Peru, revealed plants that were more climatically suitable to cultivation in temperate Europe and the Middle East. Within fifty years of the first arrival of capsicum peppers on the Iberian Peninsula and on islands such as Cape Verde, the Canaries, Madeira, and the Azores, American chili peppers were being grown on African coasts and in India, monsoon Asia, southwestern China, the Middle East, the Balkans, central Europe, and Italy. In 1542 Leonhart Fuchs, a German, was the first to describe and illustrate several types of peppers, which at the time were considered to be natives of India. It was not the Spaniards but the Portuguese who were responsible for the early diffusion of New World food plants to Africa, India, and the Far East, abetted by local shipping and traders following long-used trade routes. These mariners and merchants enabled the spread of the new American plants throughout the Old World with great rapidity (Boxer, 1969a).

The Route from the New World
The dispersal of capsicum is not as well documented as that of plants such as maize (corn), tobacco, sweet potatoes, manioc (cassava), beans, and tomatoes. However, it is highly probably that capsicums followed the same trade route as the "three sisters"—corn, beans, and squash. The four plants have been closely associated throughout history.

In 1494 the pope's Treaty of Tordesillas divided the world on a line extending around the globe at a point 370 leagues west of the Cape Verde Islands. The Spanish were granted everything discovered west of the line and the Portuguese everything to the east of it. This arrangement persisted until the Dutch, followed by other European nations, challenged this monopoly at the end of the sixteenth century. Although the Portuguese were not active in the Spanish Caribbean until after 1509, when they brought the first slaves from Africa, they had acquired American maize by some yet unexplained means—per-

PLANTING PEPPERS

Pepper seed should not be planted directly into the soil outdoors; they are best transplanted. Start the seed in a greenhouse, in flats, or in hotbeds at least six weeks before the first frost-free date. Sow them as thinly as possible on a sterile medium and cover no deeper than the thickness of the seed. Water carefully from the top so as not to dislodge the seed. From the time of sowing until transplanting and well started, never permit the seed or seedlings to dry or wilt. Germination will require twelve to twenty-one days at a constant temperature of 70°F (21°C) for *Capsicum annuum* var. *annuum,* but longer for the other species. When four or more true leaves are well formed, transplant the seedlings into containers or flats containing equal parts peat, sand, and loam. Grow them at 70°F (21°C). After the plants attain a height of 12 to 15 centimeters and all danger of frost is past, transplant them deeply in friable soil that is not below 55°F (13°C). Space the plants 12 inches apart in rows 15 inches apart. Add a cup of water to each transplant and cover with a hot cap; irrigate immediately. Full sun and a well-drained soil are necessities. Peppers are a warm-season crop that grows better in a moderate climate, one that is not so cold as to cause freezing or too hot to set fruit. If night temperatures rise above 80°F (27°C), the plant will not bloom. The optimum temperature for good yield is between 65°F (18.5°C) and 80°F (26.5°C) during fruit setting (Andrews, 1993).

haps in Galicia, Madeira, or the Canaries—before 1500, and were growing it on the west coast of Africa from where it was introduced to the Cape Verde Islands in 1502 (Jefferys, 1975). From early Portuguese "factories" in Africa and/or the eastern Atlantic Islands, the American food plants went to the east coast of Africa and India on the annual voyages of the *Nao da Goa* and other trading ships traveling between Lisbon and Goa on the Malabar Coast of western India (Boxer, 1984). As evidence of their coming from that African area, they were called "ginnie" (Guinea) peppers.

The natives of Africa and India, who were long-accustomed to pungent seasonings such as the African melegueta pepper (*Afromomum melegueta*), a member of the ginger tribe, Indian black pepper (*Piper nigrum*), and ginger (*Zingiber officinale*), readily accepted the fiery new spice. The Old World tropics provided an acceptable climate for the New World spice. The plants produced by the abundant, easily stored seed were much easier to

There are thousands of varieties of peppers. Shown here are several heirloom specimens, including Bull's Nose, Yellow Cayenne, and Chile Azul de Guinea. PHOTO BY L. WILBUR ZIMMERMAN. ROUGH-WOOD SEED COLLECTION.

cultivate than native spices, making capsicums an inexpensive addition to the daily diet. Along the Malabar Coast of India, three varieties of capsicums were being grown and exported within fifty years of Columbus's discovery of the New World (Purseglove, 1963).

Once established in India, chili pepper became part of spice shipments from the Far East along the new Portuguese route around Africa to Europe, over the ancient trade routes to Europe via the Middle East, and also on existing routes to monsoon Asia (Lobelius, 1576). The Portuguese also brought chilies to Southeast Asia and Japan. Once established in these areas, birds carried pepper seed from island to island and to humanly inaccessible inland areas.

In southwestern China, American foods were known by the middle of that century, having been transported over the ancient caravan routes from the Ganges River across Burma and across western China into India and the Middle East (Ho, 1995). This is evidenced by the fact that today the cuisines of southwestern Szechuan and Hunan use more chili peppers than any other area in China.

After the Spanish conquest of the West Indies, Mexico, Mesoamerica, and Peru, trade with the new colonies was very limited (Braudel, 1976). Once Mexico was subjugated and opened for colonization, the Spaniards virtually deserted the West Indies for the North American continent, leaving the islands inhabited primarily by African slaves brought there by the Portuguese. By that time, the indigenous peoples of those islands were essentially extinct. For the first fifty years following the New World's discovery, the Spanish rulers were more interested in problems within the Habsburg Empire than in their new acquisitions and, as a consequence, Spanish trade with the New World came to a standstill (Watts, 1987). During this period Portuguese and other European opportunists entered the Caribbean and established trading footholds.

In 1492, after ousting the Moors from Spain following their seven-hundred-year occupation, the Spaniards established dominance over the western Mediterranean while the Ottoman Turks succeeded in seizing control of northern Africa, Egypt, Arabia, the Balkans, the Middle East, and the eastern Mediterranean Sea. At that time, for all practical purposes, the Mediterranean was two separate trading spheres divided by Italy, Malta, and Sicily with little or no trade or contact between the western Mediterranean and the Ottoman Empire (Braudel, 1976). This is an important consideration in the history of the diffusion of American peppers and other economic plants.

Venice was the center of the spice and oriental trade for central Europe, and Venetian merchants depended on the Ottoman Turks to supply them with goods from the Asia. The Muslim Arab and Gujurati traders received supplies from Portuguese ports on the west coast of India and Hormuz at the mouth of the Persian Gulf. Goods introduced to central Europe were taken to Antwerp and from there to the rest of Europe. Antwerp, the major European shipping port, also received goods from the Far

East, and from the Portuguese sources via India, Africa, and Lisbon. From these trading routes chili peppers came to be known in Italy by 1535 (Fernández de Oviedo, 1535), Germany by 1542 (Fuchs, 1543), England before 1538 (Turner, 1965), the Balkans before 1569 (Halasz, 1963), and in Moravia by 1585 (L'escluse, 1611). It was only in the Balkans and Turkey that chili peppers were used to any extent until the Napoleonic blockade cut off the supply of spices to Western Europe. Without their usual supply of spices, Europeans turned to Balkan paprika (chili pepper) as a substitute.

Most Europeans had grown capsicums only as ornamentals and believed that peppers were native to India and the Far East until the mid-nineteenth century when botanist Alphonse de Candolle produced convincing linguistic evidence for the American origin of the genus *Capsicum* (Candolle, 1852).

It was only after capsicums had become established in Asia, the Middle East, and Europe that the Spaniards played any part in the movement of New World plants to places other than Spain, Italy, and perhaps Western Europe. The Pacific Ocean route of the Spanish Manila-Acapulco *galleon* was established in 1565 and operated for 250 years (Schurz, 1939). This ship was a major means for transferring plants as well as trade goods between Mexico and the Far East. At approximately the same time the Spanish colonies of Saint Augustine, Florida, and Santa Fe, New Mexico, were founded. Those first European settlements in the present-day United States initiated Caribbean and Mexican trade with Florida and the Southwest, respectively, forty years before other northern Europeans began colonizing the east coast of North America. The first peppers to enter an English colony were sent to Virginia in 1621 by the governor of the Bermuda Islands.

Condiment, Spice, and Vegetable

At the time of World War II, one-fourth of the world's population, primarily in the pantropical belt and Korea, ate capsicums daily. Since that time the consumption of peppers as a spice, condiment, and vegetable has grown annually and is no longer limited to the tropical and subtropical areas. Some of the more common food products made with chilies are curry powder, cayenne pepper, crushed red pepper, dried whole peppers, chili powder, paprika, pepper sauce, pickled and processed peppers, pimento, and *salsa picante*. In 1992 *salsa picante*, a bottled sauce of Mexican origin made with a base of chilies, onions, and tomatoes, overtook tomato catsup as the top selling condiment in the United States.

Throughout the world capsicums are used as a source of color/pigment not only for commercial products such as cheese, sausage, salad dressings, and meat products, but also for drugs and cosmetics. Dried red peppers are added to hen feed to ensure yellow egg yolks and in caged bird feed to enhance the natural color of plumage.

The use of capsicums goes beyond that of a comestible. The florist and landscape industries have found their ornamental qualities to be of considerable value. The multihued, variform fruits of the attractive podded plant have become popular decorative motifs, not only in the Southwest but throughout the country. They can be found on chinaware, glasses, fabrics, in flower arrangements, as Christmas tree lights and ornaments, on men's neckties, even as hummingbird feeders, to name but a few.

Ritual, Folklore, and Magic Uses

The medical profession has discovered that certain folk medical practices employing chilies, many of which are prehistoric in origin, have merit and are being used by modern physicians to treat arthritis, shingles, toothache, and other types of pain. Research in this area continues. Solanaceous plants, which include capsicums, potatoes, datura, belladona, tobacco, and tomatoes, have long been used in charms, rituals, magic, ceremonies, divination, therapeutical practices, and other customs. Pre-Columbian Indian medicine men used peppers mixed with other substances for such ailments as coughs, poor digestion, ear infection, sore throat, injuries to the tongue, and to expedite childbirth.

The shape of most chili pepper pods, and their pungency/heat and redness have led them to be associated with male sexuality. In some cultures, eating chili peppers is thought to arouse passions, while in others people abstain from eating them in particular places or under certain conditions. Ancients used them in warfare and as torture or punishment and, even today, they are used as a repellent to ward off human or animal aggressors.

Diagnostic Descriptions

The Solanaceae, which includes such plants as potatoes, tomatoes, eggplant, petunias, and tobacco, is the family of which the genus *Capsicum* is a member. Currently, the genus consists of at least twenty-five species, four of which have been domesticated, and two others are cultivated extensively. The flowers, not the fruits, are the definitive feature of the genus. Although many of these are consumed by humans, it is those six species belonging to three separate genetic lineages that are of concern to human nutrition:

- *Capsicum pubescens* (first mentioned by Ruiz and Pavon, 1797). This domesticated species is the most distinctive in the genus. The flowers have comparatively large purple corollas (sometimes white infused with purple), which are solitary and erect at each node. The wavy, dark brownish-black seeds in the fruit, and those blossoms are unique among the capsicums. This extremely pungent chili, called *rocoto*, was domesticated in the Andean region of South America and is yet virtually unknown in other parts of the world. Its cultural requirements are cool, free-growing conditions and a long growing season.

SELECTION, PREPARATION, AND SERVING

Capsicums are a fruit that is used like a vegetable. Any type of pepper can be gathered when it is green, but when fully mature it is red, orange, yellow, purple, or brown. The two compounds that produce the pungency and flavor do not develop immediately, but increase gradually with maturity. As a consequence, immature fruits are less pungent and less flavorful than mature ones. A *chipotle*, or fully dried ripe red jalapeño is much more pungent than the green jalapeño, and a mature red bell pepper is much sweeter and flavorful than a green one. Until recently, the consumer had to settle for green rather than ripe fruit because the latter did not ship or store well. Better, faster shipping and storage facilities are changing that so that one may savor the flavor of a fully ripe pepper. Except for green bell peppers, capsicums are a seasonal crop, and the best selection will be available in the summer and fall. The most desirable fruits are those with glossy, smooth skin that is firm to the touch.

Peppers are best stored in the refrigerator. They may be kept there for weeks only if the fresh pods are dried with a clean cloth, and placed in an airtight container or a tightly sealed heavy zip-lock plastic bag. It is important to remove as much of the oxygen as possible before placing the tightly closed container in the refrigerator. Each time the container is opened, the unused pods must be dried and air removed before resealing. Once a week the peppers should be removed from the refrigerator and allowed to return to room temperature, then wiped dry, returned to the container, and sealed. If they cannot be stored this way, it is best to freeze them and then use them for cooking. If they are to be kept out of the refrigerator or if there is no time to withdraw the air, they should be placed in a paper container. If they are put in an air-filled plastic bag, they will rapidly spoil.

Dried peppers will keep almost indefinitely if properly stored. They should be kept in tightly closed jars or heavy plastic bags in a dry, cool place, preferably the refrigerator or freezer. Freezing the dried peppers before storing will kill any insect larvae and eggs. The peppers should be monitored for insects or mildew.

Before peppers are used in a favorite recipe, they must be washed, stemmed, veined, and seeded. Some cooks prefer to remove the skin but this is only necessary when using tough skinned *poblanos* or the New Mexican chile and any of its varieties. The large bell types, ethnic peppers (*Cubanelle*, Italian), pimentos, and others of these types should be parboiled or blanched for 2 to 3 minutes before being used whole for stuffing or filling, if the filling is not to be cooked in the pepper shell. Remove them from the heat immediately and plunge them into iced water to stop the cooking process. Small chilies need only to be washed, stemmed, seeded, and veined without skinning. Usually, if a recipe calls for a pepper to be roasted or blistered, it is not only to remove the skin, but also because the charred flavor is desirable.

Frozen peppers can be used for seasoning and cooking or as stuffed peppers; they are too soft for salads. If the skins are left on before freezing, most of the nutritive values is retained. When freezing pungent chilies, parboiling before freezing will prevent capsaicin loss. Dry small chilies and spread on a pan before freezing. When frozen hard, remove from the pan and immediately place them in a dry plastic bag. Return to freezer. Open bag and pick out a few as needed, being careful to prevent the thawing of those remaining in the bag. Return to freezer.

Peppers can be sun-dried, oven-dried, smoked, or dehydrated, but none of these methods are very practical for the modern home cook who is pressed for time. Sun-drying is an ancient method best adapted to arid climates, but is not feasible in humid areas. It takes several days in a dry, sunny locale. Oven-drying is a tedious process requiring the peppers to remain in a 140°F oven for up to 24 hours. Smoking is another method of artificially drying peppers that is seldom used in the United States. It is the procedure by which jalapeños are slowly dried and imparted with a smoky flavor to become *chipotles*. Dehydration is drying with heat from a man-made source. This process is not only faster, but also produces a much better product than the other methods.

The dried product can be placed in a processor or blender and flaked or powdered. The ground product will keep better once refrigerated. Whole pods may be used in recipes that require a long cooking time and a large amount of water such as those for soups or stews.

Many widely available and popular cookbooks provide directions and recipes for preparing and serving capsicums.

There are no sweet varieties. The fruit deteriorates rapidly because of its fleshy nature; consequently, it does not store or travel well. The best-known cultivars are *rocoto*, *locoto*, *manzana*, and *chile caballo*.

- *Capsicum baccatum* var. *pendulum* (mentioned in the work of Willdenow, 1808; Eshbaugh, 1968). It has an easily recognized flower with a cream-colored corolla marked with greenish-gold blotches near the base of each petal and anthers that are whitish yellow to brownish and is solitary at each node. An elongate fruit with cream-colored seeds is most typical. It is indigenous to the lowlands and mid-elevations of Bolivia and neighboring areas. In much of South America, where all pungent peppers are called *ají*, *C. baccatum* is the "Andean *ají*" (Ruskin, 1989). Little known beyond South America until now, it is being discovered by pepper fans. Only this species and the common annual pepper have nonpungent cultivars. The best-known cultivars are Andean *ají*, *cusqueno*, *puca-uchu*, *ají limon*, and *datil*.

- *Capsicum annuum* var. *annuum* (first mentioned by Linnaeus, 1753). The flowers with white corollas and purple anthers are solitary at each node (occasionally two or more). The variform fruit usually has firm flesh and straw-colored seeds. A multitude of pungent and nonpungent cultivars of this Mesoamerican domesticate now dominate the worldwide commercial pepper market. A relationship between *C. annuum*, *C. chinense*, and *C. frutescens* has caused the three to be known as the *C. annuum* complex. This relationship creates a taxonomic predicament. Some authors still recognize the first two as distinct but tend to have difficulty determining where *C. frutescens* fits into the picture, if indeed it is a separate species. The best-known cultivars are bell, cayenne, jalapeño, serrano, pimento, *poblano*, New Mexican chile/Anaheim, and cherry.

- *Capsicum annum* var. *glabrisculm* (mentioned in the work of Dunal, 1852; Heiser and Pickersgill, 1975). It is a semiwild species known as bird pepper. Its distinct flavor and high pungency cause it to be avidly consumed throughout its natural range, which extends through the southernmost parts of the United States to Colombia. This highly variable, tiny, erect, usually red pepper is cultivated commercially in the area around Sonora, Mexico, and seems to be in the process of domestication. Birds also consume it avidly. These chilies, which have many vernacular names and almost as many synonyms (*C. aviculare* is the most common), sell for ten times the rate of cultivated green bell peppers. The best-known cultivars are *chiltepin*, *chilpequin*, *malaqueta*, and bird pepper.

- *Capsicum chinense* (first mentioned by Jacquin, 1776). Its flowers are always two or more small, white to greenish white corollas with purple anthers hanging at each node, often in clusters. The variform fruit has cream-colored seeds that tend to require a longer germination period than *C. annuum*. Its domestication occurred in the lowland jungle of the western Amazon River basin and had been carried to the islands of the Caribbean before 1492. It has diffused throughout the world but to a much lesser degree than *C. annuum*, probably because it does not store or dry well; however, it is becoming more widely appreciated by cooks and gardeners for its pungency,

aroma, and unique flavor. Although this distinctive pepper is considered to be a part of the *C. annuum* complex, some authors question its position there. The best-known cultivars are *habanero*, West Indian hot, Scotch bonnet, *ají flor*, *rocotillo*, and red savina.

- *Capsicum frutescens* (first mentioned by Linnaeus, 1753). Some authors no longer consider this semiwild species of *Capsicum* to be sustainable. It has two or more small white to greenish white flowers with purple anthers at each node and was once considered to be a member of the *C. annuum* complex, which includes three white-flowered species thought to have a mutual ancestor—*C. chinense*, *C. frutescens*, and *C. annuum*. The small fruit with cream-colored seed is always erect, never sweet, and often two or more may occur at each node. The tabasco pepper, limited to the Western Hemisphere, is the only variety of this species known to have been cultivated commercially. Easily transported by birds, the tiny varieties of wild *C. frutescens* can be found throughout the world's tropical pepper belt. The cultivated varieties are closely controlled by the McIlhenny Company of New Iberia, Louisiana. The cultivars are tabasco, greenleaf tabasco, and select.

See also **Central America; Columbian Exchange; Folklore, Food in; Iberian Peninsula; Herbs and Spices; Magic; Mexico; Mexico and Central America; South America; United States: Cajun Cooking.**

BIBLIOGRAPHY

Andrews, Jean. "Diffusion of Mesoamerican Food Complex to Southeastern Europe." *Geographical Review* 83, no. 2 (1993): 194–204.

Andrews, Jean. *Peppers: The Domesticated Capsicums*. Austin, Tex.: University of Texas Press, 1986. Revised 1995.

Andrews, Jean. *The Pepper Lady's Pocket Pepper Primer*. Austin, Tex.: University of Texas Press, 1998.

Andrews, Jean. *The Pepper Trail: History and Recipes from Around the World*. Denton, Tex.: University of North Texas Press, 2000.

Anghiera, P. M. D. *Decadas del Nuevo Mundo, por Pedro Martir de Angleria, primer cronista de Indias*. Mexico, D.F.: Jose Porrua y Hijos, Sucs, 1964.

Boxer, C. R. *Four Centuries of Portuguese Expansion: 1415–1825*. Berkeley, Calif.: University of California Press, 1969a.

Boxer, C. R. *The Portuguese Seaborne Empire, 1415–1825*. London: Hutchinson, 1969b.

Boxer, C. R. *From Lisbon to Goa 1500–1750: Studies in Portuguese Maritime Enterprise*. London: Variorum Reprints, 1984.

Boxer, C. R. *Portuguese Conquest and Commerce in Southern Asia, 1500–1750*. London: Variorum Reprints, 1985.

Braudel, F. *The Mediterranean and the World in the Age of Philip II*. Vols. 2 and 1. New York: Harper and Row, 1976.

Candolle, A. P. *De prodromous*. Paris: Masson, 1852.

Columbus, Christopher. *Journal of First Voyage to America by Christopher Columbus*. Freeport, Me.: Books for Libraries Press, 1971.

Diehl, A. K., and R. L. Bauer. "Jaloproctitis." *New England Journal of Medicine* 229, no. 20 (1978): 1137–1138.

Eshbaugh, W. H. "A Nomenclatural Note on the Genus *Capsicum*." *Taxonomy* 17 (1968): 51–52.

Eshbaugh, W. H. "The Taxonomy of the Genus *Capsicum* (Solanaceae)." *Phytologia* 47, no. 3 (1980): 153–166.

Eshbaugh, W. H. "The Genus *Capsicum* (Solanaceae)." In *Africa Bothalia* 14, nos. 3, 4 (1982): 845–848.

Eshbaugh, W. H. "Peppers: History and Exploitation of a Serendipitous New Crop." In *New Crops* by J. J. and J. E. Simon. New York: Wiley, 1993.

Eshbaugh, W. H., S. I. Guttman, and M. J. Mcleod. "The Origin and Evolution of Domesticated Capsicum Species." *Journal of Ethnobiology* 3, no. 1 (1983): 49–54.

Fernández de Oviedo, Gonzalo. *Historia general y natural de las Indias occidentales.* Seville, 1535.

Fuchs, L. *Neue Kreuterbuch (De historia stirpium in 1542).* Basel: Isingrin, 1543.

Govindarajan, V. S. "*Capsicum:* Production, Technology, Chemistry and Quality, Botany, Cultivation, and Primary Processing." *Critical Reviews in Food Science and Nutrition* 22, no. 2 (1985): 108–175.

Halasz, Z. *Hungarian Paprika through the Ages.* Budapest: Corvina Press, 1963.

Heiser, C. B., Jr. "Peppers: *Capsicum* (Solanaceae)." In *Evolution of Crop Plants,* edited by N. W. Simmonds, pp. 265–268. London: Longman, 1976.

Heiser, C. B., Jr., and B. Pickersgill. "Names for Bird Peppers (*Capsicum,* Solanaceae)." *Baileya* 19 (1975): 151–156.

Henkin, R. "Cooling the Burn from Hot Peppers." *Journal of American Medical Association* 266, no. 19 (1991): 2766.

Ho, P. T. "The Introduction of American Food Plants into China." *American Anthropologist* 55 (1995): 191–201.

Jacquin, N. J. *Hortus botanicus vindoboncensis.* 3 vols. Vienna: C. F. Wappler, 1776.

Jeffreys, M. D. W. "Pre-Columbian Maize in the Old World: An Examination of Portuguese Sources." In *Gastronomy: The Anthropology of Food and Food Habits,* edited by M. L. Arnott, pp. 23–66. The Hague: Mouton, 1975.

Laufer, B. "The American Plant Migration." *Scientific Monthly* 28 (1929): 235–251.

Lee, T. S. "Physiological Gustatory Sweating in a Warm Climate." *Journal of Physiology* 124 (1954): 528–542.

L'escluse, C. *Curae posteriores post mortem.* Antwerp: 1611.

Linnaeus, C. *Hortus cliffortianus.* Amsterdam: 1753a.

Linnaeus, C. *Species plantarum.* 1st ed. Stockholm: 1753b.

Lobelius, M. *Plantarum sev stirpium historia.* Antwerp: 1576.

Maga, J. A. "Capsicum." In *Critical Revisions in Food Science and Nutrition,* pp. 177–199. Cleveland, Ohio: CRC Press, 1975.

Masada, Y., K. Hashimoto, T. Imoue, and M. Suzui. "Analysis of the Pungent Principles of *Capsicum Annuum* by Combined Gas Chromatography." *Journal of Food Science* 36 (1971): 858.

Mathew, A. G., Y. S. Lewis, N. Kirishnamurthy, and E. S. Nambudiri. "Capsaicin." *The Flavor Industry* 2, no. 12 (1971): 691–695.

Mcleod, M. J. S., S. I. Guttman, and W. H. Eshbaugh. "Evolution of Chili Peppers (*Capsicum*)." *Economic Botany* 36, no. 4 (1982): 361–368.

Morison, S. E. *The Journals and Other Documents of the Life of Christopher Columbus.* New York: Heritage Press, 1963.

Nelson, E. K. "Capsaicin, the Pungent Principle of *Capsicum,* and the Detection of Capsaicin." *Journal of Industrial Engineering Chemistry* 2 (1910): 419–421.

Pickersgill, B. "Migrations of Chili Peppers, *Capsicum.* spp. in the Americas." In *Pre-Columbian Plant Migration,* edited by Doris Stone, pp. 106–123. 14th International Congress of Americanists. Cambridge, Mass.: Peabody Museum of Archaeology and Ethnology, Harvard University, 1984.

Proctor, V. W. "Long-Distance Dispersal of Seeds by Retention in Digestive Tract of Birds." *Science* 160, no. 3825 (1968): 321–322.

Purseglove, J. W. "Some Problems of the Origin and Distribution of Tropical Crops." *Genetics Agraria* 17 (1963): 105–122.

Ridley, H. N. *The Dispersal of Plants through the World.* Ashford, Kent, England: L. Reeve, 1930.

Rozin, P. "Getting to Like the Burn of Chili Pepper." In *Chemical Senses,* edited by B. G. Green, J. R. Mason, and M. R Morley, pp. 231–269. New York: Marcel Dekker, 1990.

Ruiz, H. and J. Pavon. *Flora peruviana et chilensis.* 4 vols. Lehrey, N.Y.: F. A. Staflen and J. Cramen. Reprint of 1797 Madrid ed.

Ruskin, F. R., ed. *Lost Crops of the Incas: Little-Known Plants of the Andes with Promise for Worldwide Cultivation.* Washington, D.C.: National Academy Press, 1989.

Sauer, C. O. *The Early Spanish Main.* Berkeley, Calif.: University of California Press, 1966.

Schurz, W. L. *The Manila Galleon.* New York: E. P. Dutton, 1939.

Smith, P. G., and C. B. Heiser. "Taxonomic and Genetic Studies on the Cultivated Peppers *C. annuum* L. and *C. frutescens* L." *American Journal of Botany* 38 (1951): 367–368.

Solanke, T. F. "The Effect of Red Pepper (*Capsicum frutescens*) on Gastric Acid Secretion." *Journal of Surgical Research* 15 (1973): 385–390.

Todd, P. H., Jr., M. C. Bensinger, and T. Biftu. "Determination of Pungency due to *Capsicum* by Gas-Liquid Chromatography." *Journal of Food Science* 42, no. 3 (1977): 660–665.

Trease, G. E., and P. W. C. Evans. "Drugs of Biological Origin." In *1983 Pharmacognosy,* 12th ed., edited by Bailliere Tindall. London, 1983.

Turner, W. *Libellus de re herbaria.* London: Ray Society, 1538. Reprinted 1965.

Watt, G. *A Dictionary of the Economic Products of India,* Vol. 2. Delhi, India: Cosmo, 1889. Reprinted 1972.

Watts, D. *The West Indies: Patterns of Development, Culture, and Environmental Change since 1492.* Cambridge, U.K.: Cambridge University Press, 1987.

Willdenow, C. L. *Enumeratio plantarum horti regii botanici Berolinensis.* 2 vols. Germany: 1808.

Jean Andrews

378

CHINA.

This entry includes six subentries:
Ancient and Dynastic China
Beijing (Peking) Cuisine
Fujian (Fukien) Cuisine
Guangzhou (Canton) Cuisine
Sichuan (Szechuan) Cuisine
Zhejiang (Chekiang) Cuisine

ANCIENT AND DYNASTIC CHINA

China's foodways began to take shape at the end of the last Ice Age. The glacial period was extremely cold and dry. As it broke, from 15,000 to 8000 B.C.E., conditions rapidly ameliorated. By 10,000 B.C.E., China was becoming warmer and wetter. Plant growth increased, making agricultural innovation more reasonable. As in the Near East at the same time, agriculture seems to have followed rapidly—stimulated, presumably, by increases in population, environmental productivity, trade, and communication.

Rice (*Oryza sativa*) was domesticated in the Yangzi Valley by 8000 B.C.E. By 5000–6000 B.C.E., it was abundant, and modern varieties had emerged: the long-grain "indica" types, the short-grain, tougher "japonicas," and probably the sticky rices. (These latter, miscalled "glutinous," are sticky because of a mutant form of the starch amylose.) Foxtail millet (*Setaria italica*) was domesticated farther north, by 6000 B.C.E. at the latest. It remained for millennia the staple of the areas too dry for rice agriculture. By 4000 B.C.E., it was joined by panic millet (*Panicum miliaceum*), which appeared about the same time in eastern Europe, having probably spread from China across central Asia. (The term "millet" refers to any small-seeded grain; several species of "millets" grow in China.) Foxtail millet is a more broadly

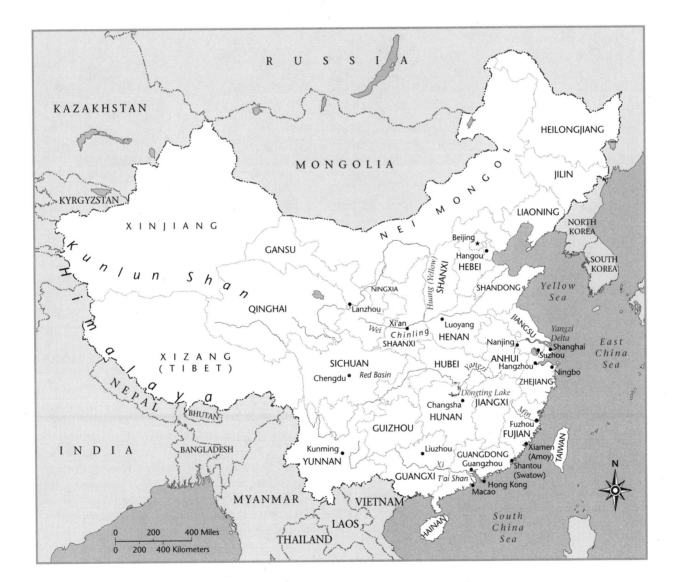

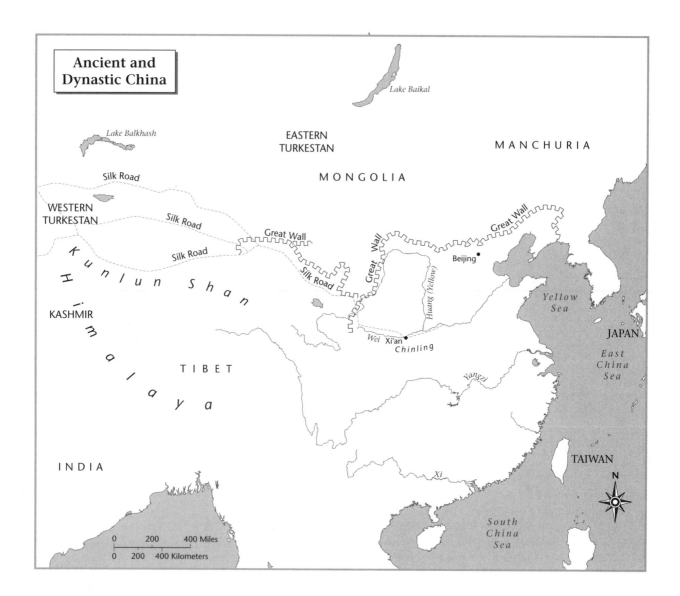

tolerant crop than rice, or indeed than almost any other grain staple. It grows best in hot summers (being a C4 plant) but is widely tolerant of different soils and water regimes. Rice, though less responsive to high heat (being a C3 plant), is an extremely efficient photosynthesizer, producing huge crops, even in cloudy conditions. C4 plants, as opposed to C3, have a metabolic pathway that allows more rapid growth in hot weather but less rapid growth in cool.

The earliest animal domestication reported so far is of pigs at Zengpiyan in Guangxi, a site dated to 7,600–9,000 years ago. The east Asian pig is the same species as, but a very different variety from, the Near Eastern one, and represents an independent domestication. Well before 6000 B.C.E., large villages with complex cultures and abundant domesticated rice occurred widely in the Yangzi Valley and elsewhere.

By 4000 B.C.E., chickens, pigs, sheep, dogs, and Chinese cabbages (*Brassica campestris*) were found widely. The chicken is native to southeast Asia and southern China. Its first archaeological occurrence, however, is in the north, near Xian; it may have once been native there (considerably older bones of wild chicken-like or pheasant-like birds have been found), or it could have been domesticated in the south and spread northward (Anderson, 1988). Sheep possibly were independently domesticated in China and in the Near East.

After this point, China's Neolithic cultures developed dramatically. Huge, rich, intensively agricultural sites are found throughout the modern eighteen provinces, as well as in neighboring areas. (China traditionally had eighteen provinces, today the eastern and southern parts of the country; China today has twenty-two provinces.) Agriculture spread rapidly into southeast Asia; Taiwan was settled by farmers, probably Austronesian-speakers ancestral to the modern "Taiwan aborigines," by 4000 B.C.E. The pig quickly became the dominant animal. By 3000 B.C.E., it was supplying 90 percent of the meat in the core areas, and it still supplies 90 percent of the meat in those areas today.

Meanwhile, wheat and barley spread across Asia from their domestication sites in the Fertile Crescent region of the Near East. By 5000 B.C.E. these grain crops were in Afghanistan. Their dates of arrival in China are obscure, but they were well established by 2000 B.C.E. Barley never became important, except in Tibet, but wheat was to revolutionize Chinese food in historic times, the period since 2000 B.C.E. Goats—a characteristic Near Eastern species, not found wild anywhere near China—appear about that time. Cattle, probably from the Near East, and water buffaloes, probably domesticated in or near the Yangzi Valley (and independently in India), may have been available by then, but their record is obscure. Finally, the horse, domesticated in the steppes of Ukraine and western Russia by 4500–4000 B.C.E., also reached China by about 2000 B.C.E. (the exact time being unclear).

All these introductions are related to the rise of civilization in China: the controversial "Xia dynasty" (c. 2200–1500 B.C.E.), whose existence is still sometimes debated, and the better-known Shang dynasty (c. 1500–1000 B.C.E.). These civilizations culminated a long-standing trend: the rich got richer, the poor poorer. The elite had great quantities of pork, grain, and wine, as well as other foods, while the ordinary people lived humbly on millet and coarse greens such as mallows (*Malva* spp.).

The origin of minor plant crops is poorly known. Sporadic finds of cultivated buckwheat are reported from

THE WOK

One characteristic Chinese cooking implement is the wok (a Cantonese word; the Putonghua is *guo*). This is a round-bottomed or parabolic pan, similar to the *kuali* of India and probably historically related to it. The wok was traditionally of cast iron, but is now usually aluminum. It first appears—so far as we know—in the Han Dynasty; pottery models of woks are found on the small pottery models of stoves that—along with other household-good models—accompanied the dead in tombs. The wok is made to fit into holes on the tops of the large clay stoves of traditional Chinese houses. Today it fits well over a gas ring. The wok is designed to heat rapidly to a very high temperature. Its rounded bottom allows heat to flow up rapidly along the sides. This allows stir-frying (*chao*), in which foods are cut into small, thin bits and stirred rapidly in smoking-hot oil. As items cook, the wok is shaken, often so violently that the contents fly up in the air—cooling them quickly so that they do not burn. The goal of stir-frying is to sear the outside of the food, while leaving the inside crisp or succulent. The wok, covered and set over lower heat, can also be used for slower cooking—steaming rice, even, though flat-bottomed cooking pots are usually used for that.

very early archaeological levels in Japan, but are questionable. Certainly, buckwheat was cultivated in the centuries before the Common Era in China and Japan; it probably was domesticated in northwest China's mountainous areas. A problem in interpreting China's food history is the massive disturbance to most sites. Millennia of agriculture, rodent burrowing, tomb digging, flooding, and the like have scrambled the record. Thus, peanuts—a New World crop known to have been introduced to China in the sixteenth to seventeenth centuries—turn up in Han dynasty sites, probably thanks to seed-burying rodents. By 1500 B.C.E., written records are available, but the earliest of these mention only staple grains and animals.

The history of plant domestication in China becomes brilliantly clear in the Zhou dynasty (ca. 1000 B.C.E.–221 B.C.E.). The *Book of Songs*, a collection of Zhou folk and court poetry, records dozens of plants. This work was edited in final form by Confucius himself, in the fifth century B.C.E.—according to historical records that we have no reason to doubt. Its 305 songs mention more plants than the whole of the Bible, as well as 88 animal species (some mythical). Coming from

CHINESE NOODLES

Chinese noodle technology is complex. Wheat, rice, bean starch, and coarse grains are all used; wheat is most common. Noodles can be cut from a flat sheet of dough (as in Europe), extruded through a colander into boiling water, or pulled and stretched by hand. A specialty of north-central China is the swung noodle. A lump of dough is stretched out and then swung in a circle like a jump-rope; the dough stretches and gets thinner and thinner. It is folded back on itself and swung again and again. This takes a very skilled hand; otherwise the dough necks down and breaks. With skill, however, it allows ordinary wheat flour to produce a texture similar to the *al dente* texture of durum wheat pasta. (Durum wheat, the usual Italian pasta material, is virtually unknown in China.)

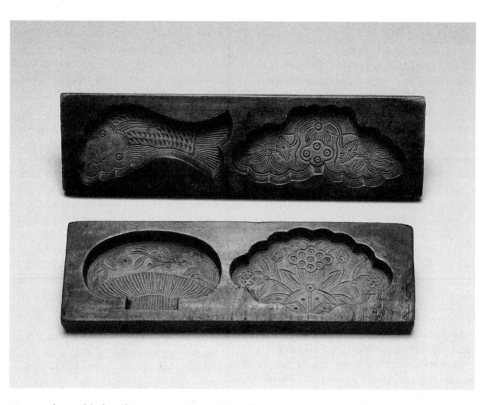

Moon cake molds for Chinese New Year cakes. China, Ch'ing Dynasty (1644–1912), ca. 1800. Plum wood. The bat, fish, and fan motifs are symbols of good luck and prosperity. ROUGHWOOD COLLECTION. PHOTO CHEW & COMPANY.

north China, the songs reflect a world dependent on millets. Wheat is mentioned in passing a few times. There were beans, cabbages, gourds, melons, and a huge host of vegetables and fruits. Pigs and chickens were the animals of daily use, but China was still rich in game and fish at the time.

CHOPSTICKS

Chopsticks are first mentioned in Zhou Dynasty texts. These small sticks, used to pick up pieces of food, probably go back to the very remote past. They have conditioned Chinese food preparation; foods are virtually always cut, or made, into pieces small enough to be easily manipulated with them. Routine use spread in early historic times to Korea, Japan, and Vietnam. The Chinese name is *kuaizi,* "little quick ones," whence the English name—"chop" being pidgin-English for "fast." See sidebar on page 386.

Soybeans enter the Chinese record in early Zhou, supplementing adzuki beans, which had been grown for centuries or millennia. Soybeans originated in far north China and Manchuria, and seem to have been domesticated by non-Han peoples there, possibly the bearers of the mysterious Hongshan civilization around 2000 B.C.E.

By this time, brewing was a major art form. Chinese *jiou,* translated "wine" but technically beer or ale, was invented long before the Shang dynasty. It was made from millet, and in the south (later, at least) it was made from rice. Shang wine vessels were of heroic proportions, and all sources agree that feasting went with heavy drinking. The histories allege that the last emperor of Xia was a debauchee who had a lake of wine and a forest of meat (i.e., a forest in which strips of meat were being wind-cured hanging from trees—a sight one could still see within living memory). This is generally taken as an exaggeration by Shang propagandists after Shang overthrew Xia. Be that as it may, heavy drinking was a part of Shang feasting, and is well documented for Zhou.

A major guide to foodways are the Zhou ritual books, the *Zhou Li* and *Li Ji.* These were compiled from damaged sources in the Han dynasty (206 B.C.E.–220 C.E.), but probably reflect Zhou reality as far as food is concerned. These sources confirm the importance of wine, mentioning many types, including herb-flavored ones. They also indicate that China, like other ancient civilizations, was deeply devoted to sacrificing animals and then eating them. Elites seem to have run through hecatombs of pigs, cattle, sheep, deer, and even horses. The trinity of pig, sheep, and cattle seems to have been dominant in sacrifice, indicating a possible indirect link with the Romans and their *suovetaurilia*. Chickens and ducks were not neglected. Old people were honored with rich, easily digestible, fatty cuts of meat, and the same favors were shown to the revered gods and ancestors. The *Li Ji* contains long passages on agriculture and on conservation.

In Han, new crops, notably grapes, came from West Asia. More important was the rise in food technology. Flour milling and oil production progressed dramatically. Bean curd and soy sauce production seem to have started about this time. (Fermented sauces were known in Zhou, but their exact nature is unclear.) Distilling of alcohol seems to have been invented in later Han. By Han, also, the idea of using food as medicine was established. The earliest surviving medical books from China are of Han date, and they have much to say about nutrition and diet therapy, always important in famine-torn China.

After Han, central Asian influences became very strong, and a flood of western foods entered China. The Silk Road, the great trade route across central Asia, linked East and West; its golden age stretched from Han through the Tang (621–960), Sung (960–1279), and Yuan (1279–1368). Persian bread, spinach, walnuts, broad beans, and even obscure herbs like fenugreek and cumin came to China, accompanied by Galenic medical concepts and Indian Buddhist foodways. Perhaps most important was the spectacular elaboration of wheat products. China, fed on millet mush and boiled rice until Han, became a land of noodles, breads, filled and unfilled dumplings, and countless other complex wheat preparations. Gradually, during this period, wheat replaced millet as the staple of the north.

The climax came in the Mongol Empire—China's Yuan Dynasty (1279–1368)—when the court in Beijing was serving dishes from Arabia, Persia, Turkistan, Kashmir, and indeed the whole Mongol-dominated world. Nomadic Mongol dishes, such as roast wolf, vied for place with Arabian delicacies such as rack of lamb marinated in saffron and rosewater (Buell and Anderson). Not until the twentieth century would the world again see such eclectic dining.

A nativistic reaction in the Ming dynasty (1368–1644) rehabilitated a Chinese food vastly more sophisticated and complex than that of Han or even Tang. The rise of an affluent middle class, especially in Sung, had led to the development of haute cuisine. Merchants and bureaucrats vied in feasting. Markets were well stocked; internal and external trade flourished. Broad regional

TOFU

Chinese food depends heavily on a wealth of soybean products. The soybean seems to have come from non-Chinese peoples in north China and to have been borrowed by the Chinese in the Zhou Dynasty. At first it was a low-class food, but soon cooks learned how to use it to advantage. Apparently the first gourmet use was in fermented thick sauces (*jiang*), ancestral to Japanese *miso*. At some early point, brewed liquid soy sauce (*dou yu*) was invented, as well as the black-fermented soybeans popular in south China. These basic products have spawned a spectacularly diverse array of local ferment products, often using wheat flour, other bean species, vegetables, chilies, spices, or other ingredients. Soy ferments were often the only source of Vitamin B12, a necessary nutrient, in the diets of the poor. Bean curd (tofu, *doufu*) has long been said to have been invented in the Han Dynasty; there are no unequivocal references until much later, but recent evidence supports the Han date. Tofu is made by grinding soybeans with water, boiling the resulting milk, and then coagulating the boiled milk with calcium phosphate, alum, or some similar coagulant substance. The result is highly nutritious, and, if made with a calcium substance (as it almost always is), a very important calcium source. The oil and certain nutrition inhibitors go out with the waste water, leaving a low-calorie, high-nutrient product. It has served as the protein source of the poor through much of history. The skin that forms on the boiling milk, the lees, and other related products are all used, especially in vegetarian cuisine. With rising affluence, tofu consumption has declined in China—but risen explosively in the health-conscious western world. H. T. Huang provides a definitive history of soybean products in China. (See also Anderson, 1988.)

styles had long been important—the meat-eating northwest contrasted with the fish-eating east and south, for instance—but now every city and many a town developed its own distinctive dishes and food specialties. Tea and distilled liquor had joined wine as common drinks, and gourmetship in tea and wine took extreme forms. Tea might be made, for instance, with water obtained from melting snow that fell on flowering-apricot blossoms; the carnation scent of the latter very delicately perfumed the tea. Nor were the less fortunate forgotten; a Ming prince, Zhu Xiao, compiled an excellent and thorough guide to famine foods in the early 1400s, and had it distributed to local governors throughout the country.

The most important food event of Ming, however, was the rise of sea trade, and especially the coming of contacts with the New World. Much of China, especially in the south, was not suitable for rice or wheat. Millet was at best a poor substitute. Suddenly, maize, white potatoes, and sweet potatoes appeared. Maize was common before 1600.

The great spread of New World crops came in the subsequent Qing dynasty (1644–1911). Sweet potatoes reached China by the late 1600s, and white potatoes by 1800. They continue to spread. Peanuts, tomatoes, chiles, guavas, and other New World crops revolutionized nutrition by introducing productive, easy-to-grow, nutrient-dense foods. Chilies, in particular, are extremely rich in vitamins and minerals; they, and the other New World crops, were critical in allowing the population explosion that has taken China from fifty million people in early Ming to today's 1.25 billion. Travelers in nineteenth-century China remarked on the availability and cheapness of a varied, nutritious diet.

Yet, China remained the "land of famine," in Walter Mallory's telling phrase. Deforestation and consequent flooding, overhunting, overfishing, and other environmental devastation led to disasters. Unfortunately, the pace of abuse greatly accelerated through the twentieth century (Brown; Edmonds).

See also **Japan; Korea; Noodle in Asia; Rice; Southeast Asia.**

BIBLIOGRAPHY

Anderson, E. N. *The Food of China*. New Haven: Yale University Press, 1988.

Bray, Francesca. "Agriculture." In *Science and Civilization in China*, edited by Joseph Needham, vol. VI, part 2. Cambridge, U.K.: Cambridge University Press, 1984.

Brown, Lester. *Who Will Feed China? Wake-up Call for a Small Planet*. New York: Norton, 1995.

Buell, Paul D., and Eugene N. Anderson. *A Soup for the Qan*. London: Kegan Paul, 2000.

Chang, Kwang-chih, ed. *Food in Chinese Culture: Anthropological and Historical Perspectives*. New Haven: Yale University Press, 1977.

Cohen, David J. "The Origins of Domesticated Cereals and the Pleistoce-Holocene Transition in East Asia." *Review of Archaeology* 19 (1998): 22–29.

Edmonds, Richard Louis, ed. *Managing the Chinese Environment*. Oxford: Oxford University Press, 1998.

Ho Ping-ti. *The Cradle of the East: An Inquiry into the Indigenous Origins of Techniques and Ideas of Neolithic and Early China, 5000–1000 B.C.* Chicago: University of Chicago Press, 1975.

Karlgren, Bernhard. *The Book of Odes*. Stockholm: Museum of Far Eastern Antiquities, 1950.

Loewe, Michael, and Edward L. Shaughnessy, eds. *The Cambridge History of Ancient China: From the Origins of Civilization to 221 B.C.* Cambridge, U.K.: Cambridge University Press, 1999.

Mallory, Walter H. *China, Land of Famine*. New York: American Geographic Society, 1926.

Mazumdar, Sucheta. "The Impact of New World Food Crops on the Diet and Economy of China and India, 1600–1900." In *Food in Global History*, edited by Raymond Grew. Boulder, Colo.: Westview Press, 1999.

Simoons, Frederick J. *Food in China: A Cultural and Historical Inquiry*. Boca Raton, Fla.: CRC Press, 1991.

E. N. Anderson

BEIJING (PEKING) CUISINE

The cuisine of the city of Beijing is rooted in the broader tradition of north Chinese food. As the capital of China for most of the last eight hundred years, Beijing has been the beneficiary of two additional forces. First was the development of an imperial court cuisine perhaps unrivaled in the world. Second, as political center of China, Beijing has been a magnet for people from all over the world. Inevitably, they bring their foodways with them. The Mongols who established their court there in the Yuan dynasty brought barbaric delicacies such as wolves and swans, and today MacDonald's hamburgers are familiar.

Beijing occupies a dry, dusty region, oppressively hot in summer, bitterly cold and windy in winter. Nearby hills give relief from the summer heat, but there is no escape from winter's chill. Today, and even to some extent in the historic past, smoke and soot densely cover

Nineteenth-century print of daily life in China. © ARCHIVO ICONOGRAFICO, S.A./CORBIS.

the city, adding to the discomfort. The familiar foods of China's warmer, wetter regions, such as rice, fish, and subtropical fruits and vegetables, were rare luxuries until very recently.

Beijing's basic foodways can stand as exemplar for the north Chinese style of cooking. This style is found throughout northern China, with outstanding substyles in Shandong and Hebei as well as Beijing. It is China's simplest, and in the northwest—Shaanxi and Shanxi especially—it can become very simple indeed. These areas were, and in some areas still are, hunger zones, hard hit by famine. Often, only two meals a day are eaten, and coarse grains (maize, sorghum, buckwheat) are often important foods. Even so, they have their specialties, including Shanxi's outstanding vinegar.

North China produced very little rice until recently. Wheat and soybeans are staples. In early times, millets, especially foxtail millet (*Setaria italica*), were staples. Millet has now been almost entirely replaced by maize. This New World crop came north from southern China in the Qing dynasty, but was rare and unpopular. People correctly saw that millet was much more nourishing. In the twentieth century, however, vast increases in the productivity of maize have tipped the balance; foxtail millet has not benefited significantly from Green Revolution research. However, maize is still unpopular as a human food, and is largely fed to animals. Today rice is also produced well north of its historic range, and has become more familiar in the area. At the same time, the traditional oilseed, oil cabbage (rape cabbage), has been supplemented by sunflower, maize, and soybean. Vegetables, until recently, were also rather limited. In winter there was little beyond the Beijing cabbage—the cylindrical-headed form of Chinese cabbage, with pale leaves and greatly enlarged, crisp leaf bases. A conscious effort has recently been made to diversify winter vegetable availability. Melons were major fruits, especially the watermelon, extremely popular in summer for its cooling and diuretic qualities as well as its sweet taste. Their seeds were a popular snack, to the point that some varieties of watermelon were bred only for seeds, having many large seeds and very little flesh. In season, peaches and jujubes ("Chinese dates," *Zizyphus Ziziphus chinensis*) were common. Walnuts, lotus nuts, and other fruits and nuts were luxury items.

As in most of inland China, the pig was the main meat source, but beef and even lamb (or mutton) were frequent—the latter especially in Hui (Chinese Muslim) neighborhoods, which are extensive and are famous for their food. Chicken and duck were common, but the ordinary citizen saw them only at very special events.

Standard northern flavorings are ginger, sliced scallions, garlic, sesame oil, Chinese "wine," and soy sauce. Spices were traditionally quite rare. Coriander leaves

LAMB WITH EGGPLANT

Adapted by the Mongol court for Beijing use.

1 medium-sized eggplant
8 oz. lamb stew meat, with some fat
1 small onion, chopped fine
Dried mandarin-orange peel, 1–2 pieces (available in Chinese groceries as "dried orange peel")
1–2 cloves garlic
4 oz. yogurt
2 tsp crushed mint

Cut eggplant in half and remove central seedy part. Chop this, mix with lamb, onion, orange-peel, and stuff the eggplant. Steam or bake. Make a sauce: mash garlic, mix with yogurt. Put this over the eggplant and then sprinkle with the dried mint.

This is a version of a dish still common in Turkey and neighboring areas.

—Buell and Anderson, pp. 313-314

CARP WITH GINGER AND CORIANDER

Here is a Chinese dish from the same source.

1 carp, about 2 lb.
Flour for dusting
Bean flour batter, enough to cover fish pieces
1 tsp ground coriander
Salt to taste
Vegetable oil
Fresh (sprouting) ginger
Cilantro (coriander leaves)
$\frac{1}{2}$ tsp turmeric (or safflower)
Radish slices

Scale the carp. Make a batter with the flour, bean flour, ground coriander, and salt. Batter the fish, let sit for an hour, and fry. Garnish with ginger (shaved), cilantro, turmeric (or safflower), and radish slices fried briefly. "Adjust flavors with onions" (apparently meaning: garnish with green scallions, slivered).

—Buell and Anderson, p. 308

HOW TO USE CHOPSTICKS

For Westerners accustomed to knives and forks, the proper handling of chopsticks is one of the most puzzling and awkward aspects of Chinese table etiquette. In the past, the way someone held chopsticks conveyed a great deal about his or her education and social class. Once mastered, chopsticks are much easier to use than knives and forks since the food is already cut up before it is served. These directions, illustrated by the accompanying drawings, describe the way to hold chopsticks in a manner generally acceptable throughout Asia.

Step 1. Place a chopstick in the right hand between the thumb and index finger and rest it on the ring finger. The narrow end of the chopstick, the end used to pick up food, should point down. Slide the chopstick so that when it is held between the thumb and index finger about two-thirds of it is below the fingers.

Step 2. Place the other chopstick between the index finger and thumb, with the narrow end resting on the third finger. Hold the chopsticks firmly.

Step 3. Use the second chopstick to grasp food by pinching it against the first chopstick (which remains stationary). The tops of both chopsticks should be kept even so that they can be used like large tweezers. Never stab food with a chopstick.

Practice before going to an Asian restaurant. If there is an Asian store in your community, visit it to see what types of chopsticks are being sold. There are many styles, and some shapes are easier to use than others (square chopsticks are less likely to slip while smooth plastic ones can be difficult to hold in place). A true connoisseur will own several sets of beautifully ornamented chopsticks, which are kept in their own cases.

William Woys Weaver

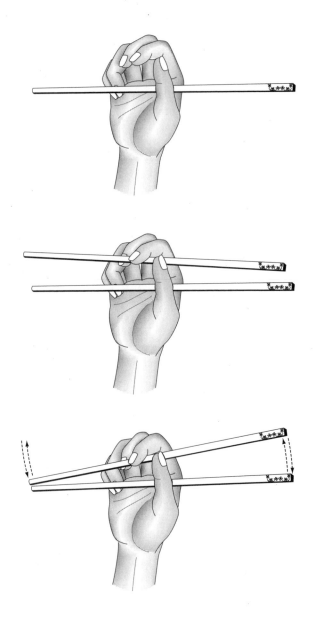

(cilantro), introduced from the Near East in early medieval times, are a frequent flavoring or garnish.

The long, harsh winters forced the development of a sophisticated pickling and preserving industry. Pickled vegetables, sausages, dried meat, salted foods, and preserved fruits are important.

The court, of course, had far different fare. Exotic delicacies were the rule. Perhaps only the Mongols actually ate wolves. According to a more authentically Chinese tradition, the "eight delicacies" were served—the list is variable, but includes such things as camels' humps, apes' lips, and bears' paws, as well as various mythological animal parts. At least the bears' paws were in fact eaten; they are cooked long, into a gelatinous state. The appeal of such items is their rarity rather than their taste, but bears' paws are relished also by actual bear hunters in Siberia and north Canada. More prosaic but presumably much more common were rare species of mushrooms, bamboo shoots, and other vegetable foods, as well as complex and detailed preparations of ordinary animals such as chicken, duck, and fish. Dishes from the remote reaches of the empire, such as central Asia and Tibet, often graced the table, especially when dignitaries from those areas were being entertained. From southeast Asia came preservable exotica such as birds' nests (edible nests of swifts of the genus *Collocalia*) and sea cucumbers. Thus the court showed its cosmopolitan, world-ruling power as well as its hospitality. Many imperial recipes are preserved, and restaurants occasionally arise that re-create them.

History records that many emperors ignored the elaborate dishes and preferred simple fare. This is a formula, meant to indicate the virtue of the emperor; simplicity, indifference to vain show, and empathy with the ordinary people are virtues in all Chinese religious and philosophical traditions. However, the story is told circumstantially enough of some emperors to be apparent literal truth. In these cases, it stands as a telling comment on the quality of the formal service. Kenneth Lo, in *Peking Cooking*, records some imperial menus and other lore, including cutting remarks on the quality of the pompous feast fare. The last emperor, Aisin Gyoro Puyi, commented: "One big tasteless spread. All show and no flavour!" (1971, p. 24).

More usual fare—the fare of the vast majority, including, perhaps, those emperors—was based on wheat products. Noodles in soup, large steamed breads, and filled dumplings were staples. The large breads, usually chemically leavened, were called *mantou*, which means "barbarian heads." Forms of this word are used from Korea to Greece; the word may actually be from an Altaic language, or it may be Chinese from the start. It used to refer to filled dumplings, and still does everywhere except in China, but at some obscure time the Chinese term came to refer to solid wheat loaves. Today, large filled dumplings (typically with leavened dough) are *paozi*. Smaller filled dumplings are *jiaozi*, a term limited to China, but denoting dumplings virtually identical to the *mantu* or *manti* of Korean, Turkic, and Greek kitchens. They are also clearly related to the *kreplachs*, *pelmeny*, and *vareniki* of eastern Europe, and to many other steamed or boiled dumplings of Eurasia. The complex history of these foods is still unclear.

The rich had rice congee: rice cooked in considerable water to make a thin porridge. The poor had an equivalent in porridge of millet, soybean meal, or wheat meal. Millet porridge, especially, was the most ancient foodstuff, having been prepared since earliest Neolithic times. It could be thick or thin. Often it was plain, but it could be flavored with sweet or savory ingredients. Cakes of coarse corn meal stood at the bottom of the prestige scale.

For centuries, Beijing has had countless eateries, from expensive and exclusive restaurants to food carts along the streets. Tea houses flourished everywhere, serving varying grades of tea along with snacks. These establishments varied from exclusive and refined, with the finest tea and foods, to rough stands for ordinary workers. They served as meeting houses, poor folks' offices, and centers of political and social activity. Also common are food stalls and small, inexpensive restaurants selling noodles and dumplings. The food at these is consistently fresh and good, but not notably diverse.

Once chopsticks are mastered, it is easy to remove slippery dumplings from a large common bowl, as this family is doing in a Hong Kong restaurant. © RANDY FARIS/CORBIS.

As elsewhere in China, freshness is an ideal. Fish and poultry are sold alive whenever possible, and even larger animals may be. A new load of vegetables or fruit commands a high price, which may drop by the hour if the sun wilts the produce.

Ingredients in Chinese food are cut or otherwise prepared in bite sizes for ease in handling with chopsticks. Since earliest recorded times, eating large hunks of food was considered barbaric.

More ambitious restaurants have far more varied offerings. Traditionally, restaurants specialize in one type of cuisine. Some offer the dishes of a particular province or ethnic group. Others may focus on only one dish. Several classic Beijing dishes are so elaborate, and so popular, that restaurants focus solely on them.

The most famous such dish was, and is, Beijing duck. Ducks were domesticated in north China, and the most successful variety worldwide remains the "white Pekin" (or, more recently, its improved descendents). A proper Beijing duck is carefully raised from hatching onward. It is specially fed to give it the right amount and flavor of fat and meat. Killed at some three months of age, it is hung for a while, then inflated to separate the skin from the flesh. Preparation is simple: it is seasoned and roasted. As is true with ducks and with marinated pork slabs in much of China, Beijing duck is hung on a hook to roast, so that all sides are evenly cooked. Then the flesh and skin, cut up, are eaten rolled in small wheat pancakes, with fermented sauce (several variants are allowable) and slivered scallions. Some gourmets would eat only the skin, leaving the meat for servants.

Other dishes indicate the strength of Muslim and central Asian influence. Most pervasive are *shaobing*. These are small raised sesame breads, traditionally cooked Iranian style in a small *tandoor* oven. They are miniaturizations of Iranian *nan*, and seem to have been introduced in the Tang dynasty, when the Iranian court took refuge in China from the Arab armies that conquered Iran for Islam. Iranians were to be found on street corners everywhere in Xian (then Chang'an) selling these breads (see Schafer, 1963), which were soon nativized as Chinese fare. In Beijing today, they are often stuffed with meat that is slivered and then grilled or stir-fried. One such dish, of presumptive "barbarian" origin, is "Mongolian barbecue." This dish is not necessarily Mongolian in origin; it seems more likely a modern evolution from traditional Muslim Chinese dishes. It involves meat sliced very thin, drenched in a selection of piquant sauces, and grilled on a metal brazier over a high flame.

Another famous Muslim dish that has its specialty restaurants is lamb hot-pot. Chinese diners love to do their own cooking. Most often, this is done by dipping very thinly sliced ingredients into boiling stock at the table. The slices cook quickly, and flavor the stock, which is eaten as soup at the meal's end. Every province has its own versions of this hot-pot meal; Beijing's is based on lamb. The lamb has to be sliced evenly and very thinly. Chinese cooks spend years learning how to slice properly, and this dish provides a rigorous test of their accomplishments.

From farther afield come such dishes as the sweet-sour fish of Hebei. Made from fresh-water fish (usually species of carp), this is said to be China's best version of the dish. Shandong restaurants provide that province's superior dumplings and fish dishes.

In recent years, Beijing has added American fast foods to its diverse scene. Yan Yunxiang (1997) reports that McDonald's was, in the 1990s, the place to be seen—at least, many young people thought so. Young men would spend hours over a cup of coffee—all they could afford—simply to show they were sophisticated and cosmopolitan enough to be there. McDonald's, the symbol of bottom-scale eating in its native land, thus took on the prestige that, in that land, is reserved for exclusive Con-

tinental-style restaurants. More recently, Starbucks and other chains have been added to the youth scene.

See also **Japan; Noodle in Asia; Rice; Southeast Asia.**

BIBLIOGRAPHY

Anderson, E. N. *The Food of China*. New Haven: Yale University Press, 1988.

Buell, P. D., and E. N. Anderson. *A Soup for the Qan*. London: Kegan Paul International, 2000.

Huang, H. T. *Science and Civilization in China*. Vol. 6, *Biology and Biological Technology. Part 5: Fermentations and Food Science*. Cambridge, U.K.: Cambridge University Press, 2000.

Lo, Kenneth. *Peking Cooking*. London: Faber & Faber, 1971.

Schafer, Edward H. *The Golden Peaches of Samarkand: A Study of Tang Exotics*. Berkeley, Calif.: University of California Press, 1963.

Simoons, Frederick J. *Food in China: A Cultural and Historical Inquiry*. Boca Raton, Fla.: CRC Press, 1991.

Yan, Yunxiang. "McDonald's in Beijing: The Localization of Americana." In *Golden Arches East: McDonald's in Asia*, edited by James Watson. Stanford: Stanford University Press, 1997.

E. N. Anderson

FUJIAN (FUKIEN) CUISINE

The foods of southeast China are exceptionally diverse. Fujian, moist and both semitropical and tropical, is in that region and sixty-eight nautical miles across the straits from Taiwan. For those who divide Chinese food by compass points, Fujian, also spelled Fukien or Fu Chien, is distinctly eastern and has culinary similarities with nearby regions. Its foods are influenced by rivers, long coastlines, and interior rugged mountains, some reaching to the sea. This region, its landscape and its foods, is called *shan shui*, meaning mountain and water. It is one of China's five outstanding traditional cuisines, the others originating from the Guangzhou (Canton), Honan, Shandong, and Sichuan provinces. Fujianese foods are easily recognized: their rich stocks and sauces are used in a plethora of thin and thick soups. Two or three soups are commonly consumed at main meals and five or six at banquets. Many main ingredients are marinated in wine or the leftover red wine sediment called *lees* or *hung jiu*.

With a population of almost thirty million people and an area of forty-eight thousand square miles, the foods of Fujian—also called Min—are common wherever the Min or Wu dialects are spoken. They can be found in Fujian and in the southern Guangdong province in Shantou or Swatow, where many descendants of a well-known statesman exiled during the eighth century fled. This variation of Teochiu, Chiuchow (also spelled Chaochow and Chaozhou), is considered the finest cuisine. Concentrating on foods of the sea, it uses many seasonings, fish sauces, citrus marmalades, and satay-type sauce pastes. Every Fujianese food is loved locally, by those living on Hainan Island and by peoples in nearby areas. It is missed by more than 2.5 million Fujianese living overseas. Although popular throughout China, this cuisine is little known outside of the country.

The foods of Fujian are closely related to Taiwanese cuisine as many Fujianese fled there during several disruptive historical periods. This ancient cuisine, its origins predating 135 B.C.E. when the state of Min Yue was established in the Fujian province, has food roots in ancient Hakka migrants from northern provinces, aboriginal groups, and local Han peoples. With only 10 percent of its land arable, the remaining extensively cultivated areas grow a reasonable amount of rice, wheat, and sweet potatoes. They also grow fruits, soybeans, peanuts, and other oil seeds; people eat these agricultural products year-round, fruits included, because the region specializes in drying and preserving them. Sweet potatoes were not an important dietary component until they helped alleviate famine during Sung times (960–1280 C.E.) and again in the late 1500s. A shortage of rice propelled interest in this tuber, shredded and dubbed "sweet potato rice." Wheat foods also substituted for rice, and currently both are major dietary components in the region.

The sweet potatoes are roasted, boiled, and dried, used as snacks and meal components, and made into flour. Along with wheat, they are eaten in amounts equal to rice and used to make noodles, pancakes, dumpling skins, and other foods. Wheat and sweet potatoes are used to produce noodles in every imaginable shape. More are eaten here than in any other Chinese province; they are frequently served in soups when their solid content is finished. Noodles are also served plain, in stir-fried dishes and soups and stews, and transformed into batters. The latter is called "swallowskin" and is made from thin poured noodle batter. The batter, or *kuopien*, is cooked in a wok, and soup is added to it when a soft crust is formed. Swallowskins may also be served plain, have dried powdered pork or wine lees as ingredients, and can be used as wrappers for dumplings and fried foods. Some batters are made only of egg whites. These are called *kao li* and often have foods buried underneath.

Chou, better known also as *juk* or *congee*, is a popular southeastern breakfast-type rice soup. Other beloved Fujianese foods are fish balls, turtle meat, and a large variety of fungi including black or silver (white) cloud ears called *mo-er* or *yin-er*, respectively. Dishes are made with coagulated pig or chicken blood, with foods from local waters, and with chicken, pork, duck, and some goose. It is not uncommon in this province to be served a bird's nest or shark's fins as a main course, served as a thick stewlike soup. Many foods are cooked more slowly, fried with lard, and seasoned more liberally than in neighboring provinces. Soy sauce, with famous varieties made from local water, is employed sparingly in dishes, but large amounts are used in dipping sauces.

Contrary to practice in other provinces but similar to that in Guangzhou, tea is commonplace at meals. Grown in the north, it is preferred black, but more accurately called red for the color of the brew. The most popular variety is local; it is called *tit guan yin* or "Iron Goddess of Mercy." Local dishes are sweetened with sugar cane grown in the south, vegetables harvested wherever they can be grown, and animals raised where crops do not prosper.

Fujianese foods are typically served in three daily meals; they are easily recognized. Mornings start with rice soup and other small dishes or seasonings for the *juk*, two to three soups accompany other dishes at main meals, and five or six and an equal number of other dishes make up a banquet. Other than the breakfast *chou* or *juk*, soups may be clear, with contents, or thick and stewlike. Dipping sauces accompany other dishes, such as garlic crushed in a vinegar base if the main protein is poultry, or maltose if it is fried fish. Dishes and soups are based on complex stocks, maybe a sweet and sour sauce. Some are highly colored, many red from the marinade of red wine lees.

Fuzhou, also transliterated as Foochou or Foo Chow, was founded in 202 B.C.E. Meaning "happy city," this provincial capital on the Min River is blessed with more than a hundred different kinds of freshwater fish. It enjoys Fujianese and Fuzhou dishes cooked with fermented red wine lees, dumplings wrapped in swallow skin, noodles made with powdered pork, and meat and fish in one dish—sometimes one ball as in fish balls stuffed with meat in soup. Fermented fish sauces are used, as are different types of soy sauce, an influence from other southeastern countries that, in turn, were influenced by Fujian.

Xiamen, once called Amoy, is the second largest city in Fujian. Both are important up-river port cities sheltered from typhoons; they helped the province become a major maritime trading center. Known for their *popia*, Xiamenese people love this pancake. It is commonly filled with cooked meat and vegetables such as bean sprouts, garlic shoots, carrots, and bamboo shoots. Seaweed may also be added and the mixture flavored with hot mustard and/or plum sauce. Other popular dishes with roots in this city are stir-fried Xiamen noodles and Xiamen spring roll. Both are made with carrots, bean sprouts, peanuts, and grilled seaweed strips.

Well-known Fujianese dishes include diced and fried wine-marinated pork, steamed chicken in preserved tofu, drunken spare ribs, sweet and pungent litchi pork, deep-fried eel in wine lees, oyster omelet, stir-fried razor clams with ginger, hot and sour squid soup, duck tongue with white and black fungus, fried peanuts, and dried longan soup with lotus seeds. Also well known is *chi ping*, a Hainanese chicken-rice dish. Peace noodles are served everywhere on the first day of the first lunar month and eaten during *Ao Jiu* festival that same month. Another special dish is "Buddha Jumping Wall," a multiboiled thick casserole with shark's fins and ten other ingredients. Herbal soups are popular, too, and made with peony or rheumannia root, angelica (*sinensis*), star anise, wolfberry (*Lycium chinense* miller), cassia bark (*Cinnamonum aromaticum*), or a member of the prickly ash/fagara family (*Zanthoxylum avicennae*). In addition, they and other herbs are used as tonics, concentrates, and pastes.

Current literature divides China into many culinary regions, regional or provincial. Almost all include Fujianese food, whose essence may be found in its plethora of soups, sauces, vegetables, seafood, fruits, mushrooms, herbs, preserved fruits, and a special treat called "Tribute Candy." This after-dinner or snack sweet is a blend of baked peanuts ground into maltose or ground peanuts wrapped in a paperlike layer made from glutinous rice. Served with fresh fruit at the meal's end, it is enjoyed by everyone who adores sweet and tasty foods.

See also **Buddhism**; **Japan**; **Korea**; **Noodle in Asia**; **Rice**; **Southeast Asia**.

BIBLIOGRAPHY

Anderson, E. N. *The Food of China.* New Haven: Yale University Press, 1988.

Buell, P. D., and E. N. Anderson. *A Soup for the Qan.* London: Kegan Paul International, 2000.

Chang, K. C., ed. *Food in Chinese Culture.* New Haven: Yale University Press, 1977.

Davidson, A. *The Oxford Companion to Food.* New York: Oxford University Press, 1999.

Facciola, S. *Cornucopia II, a Source Book of Edible Plants.* Vista, Calif.: Kampong Publications, 1998.

Gernet, J. *Daily Life in China on the Eve of the Mongol Invasion, 1250–1276.* Stanford, Calif.: Stanford University Press, 1962.

Goodrich, L. C. *A Short History of the Chinese People.* New York: Harper Torch Books, 1969.

Ho, P. T. "The Introduction of American Food Plants into China." *American Anthropologist* 57 (1955): 191–201.

Juang, Je Tsun. *The Regional Dishes of Fukien.* Hong Kong: Wan Li Book Company, 1998.

Kiple, K. F., and K. C. Ornelas. *The Cambridge World History of Food.* Cambridge, U.K.: Cambridge University Press, 2000.

Knightley, D. N. "A Literary Feast: Food in Early Chinese Literature." *Journal of the American Oriental Society* 106 (1983): 49–63.

Meskill, J. T. *An Introduction to Chinese Civilization.* Lexington, Mass.: D.C. Heath, 1973.

Newman, J. M. "Fujian: The Province and Its Foods." *Flavor and Fortune* 6, no. 2 (1999): 13, 20.

Newman, J. M. "China's Fujian Province: Cuisine and Culture." Paper presented at the Crossing Borders Meeting of Association for the Study of Food and Society, Ryerson Polytechnic University, Toronto, Canada, 1999.

Sabban, F. "Court Cuisine in 14th Century Imperial China." *Food and Foodways*, 3 and 4 (1986): 209–219.

Simmons, F. J. *Food in China: A Cultural and Historical Inquiry.* Boca Raton, Fla.: CRC Press, 1991.

Jacqueline M. Newman

GUANGZHOU (CANTON) CUISINE

Cantonese food has attracted a world following for its quality and variety. As to the former, a Chinese proverb says that one should "marry in Suzhou, live in Hangzhou, dine in Guangzhou, and die in Liuzhou," since these cities have, respectively, the prettiest girls, best views, best food, and best coffin woods. As to the variety, Chinese say that the Cantonese "eat everything with legs except a table, and everything with wings except an airplane."

Cantonese food is, broadly speaking, the food of Cantonese speakers. Cantonese is a separate language (though not dialect; there are, rather, several dialects of Cantonese) spoken throughout most of Guangdong province and well into Guangxi, and also by migrants who have radiated throughout the entire world. More narrowly, Cantonese food is the food that reaches its highest level of development in Guangzhou (the capital city of Guangdong) and in late-twentieth-century Hong Kong. The north parts of Guangdong are inhabited by Hakka and Teochiu people who speak other languages within the Chinese family; they have their own distinctive cuisines. Much of Guangxi, especially in the west and south, is inhabited by Zhuang and other Thai-speaking minority peoples, who also have their own cuisines. This leaves Cantonese food and language to some fifty million or more people.

This area is roughly coterminous with the part of China in which rice agriculture has always been most intensive. Lowland paddies produce up to three crops a year, and have since imperial times. Yields in the early twentieth century reached 2500 kg/ha. Today, with new varieties and intensive fertilizing, yields reach four or five times that figure. Nowhere else in China does rice so dominate the scene. Therefore, rice traditionally supplied some 90 percent of calories in the typical diet, and was the only true staple food. Other starchy foods—notably sweet potatoes and maize, since their seventeenth-century introduction from the New World—were mere famine backups.

In traditional times, a tightly integrated farming system developed, which combined this intensive rice agriculture with aquaculture, duck and pig rearing, and fruit and vegetable gardening. Every crop was fitted tightly into its place. For instance, ducks were taken by boat from field to field; they would be turned into a field when the crops were too old to be tempting food. Instead, they would eat the snails and insects, and leave fertilizer behind. Several species of fish were raised, each eating a different set of natural pond life-forms. Pigs and chickens were raised on leftovers and on items inedible to humans. Frogs and other wildlife were caught and eaten. What escaped the system and washed out to sea was cycled through shellfish and finfish. Nothing was lost and nothing was wasted. This system, along with related systems in southern Japan and central Java, was the most intensive and productive agriculture in the world before the rise of green revolution crops in the mid-twentieth century.

In coastal and delta areas, the most important animal protein is fish. Thousands of species of marine life occur and are utilized. Recently, overfishing has made aquaculture relatively more important. Away from the coast, pork is overwhelmingly the major meat, with poultry reserved for festive fare and other meats quite rare. Dogs, cats, and game animals are eaten, but not often. Soybean products, including bean curd, soy sauce, and fermented black beans (*tau si*), probably supplied more protein in the past than meat did. The most abundant vegetables are Chinese cabbages (many varieties) and the onion family (five species, in order of importance: onions, green onions, garlic, garlic chives, Chinese leeks). Also important are lettuce, tomatoes, potatoes (both white and sweet), taro, bamboo shoots, and dozens more. Condiments include vinegar, strong mustard (from *Brassica juncea)*, white pepper (not black), chili sauces, and, above all, soy sauce and its variants. Food is almost unthinkable without soy sauce. Rice by itself is not a meal, but rice with soy sauce is, and for the poor in earlier times it was, often the only meal of the day. Distinctively Cantonese, and a real marker of the cuisine, are *tau si*, soybeans boiled, salted, and fermented such that they turn black and acquire a strong meaty flavor.

Freshness, tenderness, and delicate subtle flavor are ideals. Relatively young animals and vegetables are preferred to old ones. Fresh items are always preferred. Not only are fish kept alive until wanted; they are preferred if kept alive in clean ocean water (rather than tanks), and they are sometimes taken at a dead run to the kitchen, so as not to lose a moment outside the water. Poultry was traditionally fed specially on high-quality foods. (Pigs, however, were fed on anything available.) The quality of the ingredients was once the most important dimension for evaluating food and restaurant quality. The goal of cooking was to preserve the essence of the fresh food item by cooking it quickly in a simple yet perfectly calculated way. Split-second timing was characteristic; a change in the sound of boiling or frying signified doneness, and the item was instantly whisked off the flame. Items are often briefly boiled before being stir-fried, so they would be tender in spite of quick frying.

Traditional food preparation includes salting and drying fish and vegetables. Small shrimps, salted and self-digested, produce a paste that is liked by some individuals. Pork sausages of various kinds are prepared; the most

A set of brown glazed soup pots reinforced with wire to prevent expansion and cracking. Pots of this kind are used all over China for making both stews and soups. Whole ducks or chickens can be placed inside the pots of larger size. ROUGHWOOD COLLECTION. PHOTO CHEW & COMPANY.

popular, *laap cheung*, traditionally includes rose-flavored alcohol. Unique to Cantonese cuisine is pork, roasted and marinated while hanging from forks in a tandoori-like clay oven. This dish is now usually baked in a more modern style, but retains the name *ch'a siu*, "fork-roasted."

The diet was based on rice eaten with a vast variety of vegetables and animals. The basic division in the diet was between *faan*, cooked rice, and *sung*, a word unique to Cantonese and referring to anything cooked to eat with or on the rice. Rice is regarded as the perfect food—indeed, a true "cultural superfood"; people feel they have not really eaten unless they have eaten it, and the standard Cantonese greeting around mealtime is "have you eaten rice yet?" (One always answers "yes," because if one says "no" the greeter is more or less duty bound to offer food. This custom harks back to the old days, when poverty was widespread and eating was by no means a regular thing.) Foods not eaten with rice are primarily mere snacks, sometimes called *siu sik*, "small eats." These include fruit, sweets, and the elaborate snacks called *tim sam*, "dot-the-hearts," which have evolved into the "dim sum" of global Chinese restaurants. The only substantial fare that does not involve rice are the noodle dishes, and even the noodles are sometimes made of rice—though wheat and wheat-and-egg noodles are commoner. Noodles are usually boiled in soup, or boiled and then stir-fried with vegetables and meat (the famous *ch'ao mien* or "chow mein").

The usual breakfast is tea with fried pastries and/or *juk* (congee), a small amount of rice boiled in a lot of water, producing a thin mush. It is eaten with peanuts, salt vegetables, soy sauce, or similar strong-flavored foods mixed in. Special occasions call for a long, lingering breakfast over tea and *tim sam*. This ritual, known as *yam ch'a* "drinking tea," has recently migrated to brunch or even lunch hour, and become a weekend fixture.

The main meal of the day can be at noon, midafternoon, or evening. It is based on a large amount of cooked rice. With this, typically, one finds a steamed dish and a stir-fried dish, and perhaps another steamed dish. Steamed fish and stir-fried vegetables would be a typical combination. It is common to prepare a four-dish meal in one pot by putting small saucers of raw foods on top of the rice, and simmering all in a closed pot; the other dishes steam while the rice boils. Almost invariably, there is soup, usually at the end of the meal. Water is known to be unsafe to drink unboiled; boiled water by itself is neither tasty nor nourishing. Tea is expensive. Soup, in contrast, is known to extract the nutrient values of foods, and can be made from tough vegetables and other economical items. It is thus the preferred way to take liquid.

The other meal (lunch or casual supper) will normally be noodles in soup, or a similar substantial but unassuming dish.

Banquets involve large amounts of meat and fish, and little or no rice. Whole fish and other impressive seafoods are usually the most expensive and prestigious items. Pork and duck are normally present. Special ritual foods abound, and include whole roast pigs and stews of great pieces of meat. Men are the cooks for these large sacrificial dishes. In general, women are the cooks in China, but men are the restaurant chefs, specialists, and preparers of large ritual meals.

Desserts are unimportant, simple fruit being generally preferred, but some sweets are prepared. Notable are small cream tarts called *taan t'a*, "egg tarts," probably English (via Hong Kong) but identical also to Portuguese *pastel de nata* and thus perhaps borrowed through Macao. Cookies and fruit are traditional gift items.

An important aspect of Cantonese food is eating for medicinal value. Dozens of foods are eaten largely for perceived healthy qualities: snake for warming during winter, watercress for cooling, wild ducks or pork liver for strength and energy (their high available iron content explains this), certain herbs for cleaning the system, and—of course—chicken soup for almost everything. In Chinese medicine, foods are heating, cooling, or neutral. Heating foods—high-calorie, fatty, reddish, or spicy—make the body hotter, or give rashes and sores. Cooling foods—very low-calorie, watery, sour, or cool-colored—make the body cooler, and in excess lead to loss of energy and strength. Neutral foods are balanced; cooked rice, noodles, and white fish are examples.

Chinese wolfthorn fruits (*kau kei ji*) and leaves (*kau kei ch'oi*) are the highest in vitamins and minerals of any common food, and are thus used as nutrition supplements. In Chinese medicine, all foods have significance for health. Food grades into medicine. Many foods, such as the wolfthorn, are eaten purely for their medicinal value. White fungus, dried scallops, and other items are on the borderline. Even medicinal herbs such as ginseng could be called foods. Food is the first recourse when an individual feels less than well. After childbirth, women eat foods perceived as strengthening and warming; modern analysis shows these foods to be high in iron, calcium, and other minerals, in vitamins, and/or in easily digestible protein. It is well known that such foods restore health and benefit milk production.

There are regional variants of Cantonese cuisine—often coterminous with dialects of the Cantonese language. The T'ai Shan area, for instance, is home to the Toisanese dialect, and to such dishes as *tsap seui* "miscellaneous leftovers." This became the infamous "chop suey" of third-string Chinese restaurants in the western world, but it began life as a good if humble dish among the specialist vegetable farmers of the area. At the end of the day, they would stir-fry the small shoots, thinnings, and unsold vegetables—up to ten species in a dish!

Changes in recent decades have been dramatic. Affluence has eliminated the famine and want that drove many within living memory to live on sweet potato vines, outer leaves of cabbages, and tiny shellfish gathered at low tide. A greater variety of food is available. Standardization has meant better and safer processed foods. Meat is relatively cheaper, and consequently more used. On the other hand, mass production in agriculture, and volume feeding in huge restaurants and chains, has spelled neardoom for the concern with quality ingredients. Much more oil, sugar, and salt is used now than forty years ago. Monosodium glutamate (isolated in Japan in the early twentieth century) spread into Cantonese cooking via overseas restaurants, and is now almost universal. Hamburgers, fried chicken, and other American fast foods abound in south China, and have inspired adaptations and hybrid descendents.

Cantonese cooking has spread throughout the world, and is the main ancestor of the simplified "Chinese cooking" found in small Chinese restaurants everywhere. Humbler variants on this theme include the "takeouts" of England, the "chop suey joints" of North America, and the "chifas" (from Putonghua *chi fan* "eat rice"[?]) of Peru. Much more sophisticated and elaborate Cantonese restaurants exist overseas, especially in major American and Australian cities; those in Vancouver, San Francisco, Sydney, and elsewhere now rival Hong Kong and Guangzhou in quality. These diaspora restaurants have affected the homeland; the fortune cookie, invented in California around the end of the nineteenth century, was only beginning to reach Hong Kong in the 1960s, but is now found worldwide.

In the future, as world population rises, the intensive, high-yielding, efficient food production and processing system of southeast China will become a more and more attractive model.

See also **Japan; Korea; Noodle in Asia; Rice; Southeast Asia.**

BIBLIOGRAPHY

Anderson, E. N. *The Food of China*. New Haven: Yale University Press, 1988.

Buck, John Lossing. *Land Utilization in China: A Study of 16,786 Farms in 168 Localities, and 38,256 Farm Families in Twenty-two Provinces in China, 1929–1933*. Chicago: University of Chicago Press, 1937.

Ruddle, Kenneth, and Gongfu Zhong. *Integrated Agriculture-Aquaculture in South China: The Dike-Pond System of the Zhujiang Delta*. New York and Cambridge, U.K.: Cambridge University Press, 1988.

Simoons, Frederick J. *Food in China: A Cultural and Historical Inquiry*. Boca Raton, Fla.: CRC Press, 1991.

E. N. Anderson

SICHUAN (SZECHUAN) CUISINE

What is widely called Sichuan cuisine is part of a broader suite of culinary traditions more properly regarded as the cuisine of west China. Traditionally, Chinese schematize the world in sets of five. In this scheme, the great cuisines of China are those of Beijing, Sichuan (or Hunan-Sichuan), Shandong, the Yangzi delta, and Guangdong. It is, however, more ecologically and geographically accurate to divide Chinese cuisine into north (including Beijing and Shandong), east, south, and west.

Included in the western group are the cuisines of Hunan, Sichuan, Yunnan, Gueizhou, and (marginally) Hubei. Boundaries of culinary regions do not correspond exactly with the boundaries of provinces. Yunnan and Gueizhou have large aboriginal populations with distinctive foodways. Parts of Hubei and other provinces shade off into other culinary regions.

West of Sichuan lies Tibet. This vast highland produces few foodstuffs. Barley and buckwheat, which grow at high elevations, are staples. Particularly important to nomadic herders and other travelers is *tsamba*: barley parched (roasted in the oven) and ground into meal. This can be mixed with tea, milk, or broth to provide an instant meal. Dairy products are extremely important and are often made from yak milk. Butter is not only a food but also serves as sunblock, sculpture medium, gift item, and more. Vegetables are few; wild herbs are used. Feast dishes include dumplings and meat dishes related to those of China and central Asia and—especially in the south—mixed dishes with Indian and Nepalese ancestry.

Several small ethnic groups related to the Tibetans live in mountainous parts of Sichuan. Many rely on thick cakes of buckwheat, maize, or other montane grains. Most share the Chinese avoidance of dairy products, but some—those near Tibet and dependent on herding—use dairy products heavily.

North of Sichuan is Shaansi, which has its own foodways. These are simpler than Sichuan's and are dominated by wheat products: noodles, dumplings, buns, and much more. Lamb is popular. Vegetables are rather few,

and spicing is simple; chilies are used, but not so much as in Sichuan. The leading city of Shaansi is Xian, which was the capital of China—under the name Chang'an—for many centuries; it finally lost out to Beijing in the Liao Dynasty. Xian has a wide range of dishes, many of them using wheat, lamb, onions, and vinegar. (Vinegar is even more a specialty of Shansi, Shaansi's eastern neighbor.) Tang Dynasty texts already reflect this relatively simple cuisine. Central Asian influences were strong in those days and are still apparent (especially in the importance of lamb), though the popularity of dairy products—well-attested in texts between 400 and 900 C.E. has waned considerably.

The specifically west Chinese culinary world is that of the densely settled urban and agricultural regions of the middle and upper Yangzi River drainage and the plateau country south of it in Yunnan and Gueizhou. Most densely populated and agriculturally rich are the Yangzi valley and Dongting Lake area of Hunan and Hubei and the Red Basin (named for its red sandstones) and Min River outwash plains of Sichuan. Culinary dynamos have been the cities of Changsha in Hunan; Zhongqing and Chengdu in the Red Basin of central Sichuan, named from its red sandstones; and, to a lesser extent, Kunming in Yunnan. These areas have long been united by trade and communication. In addition, they have long-established ties to the north; the passes from Sichuan to Shaanxi have been major communication corridors for thousands of years.

The core of Sichuan was, in ancient times, the independent state of Shu, and Hunan was part of the great state of Chu. Chu, whose population probably spoke largely Thai languages, was one of the most powerful of the Warring States. Under the Han dynasty it retained considerable local authority for a long time. Han tombs reveal foods much like those of later periods; rice, wheat products, vegetables, and a stunning variety of fruits and nuts were eaten. Yunnan entered history as the ancient state of Tian, probably a Tibeto-Burman polity, which had a culture tied to both China and southeast Asia. Later, much of what is now Yunnan was the independent kingdom of Nanzhao, a non-Chinese state with Thai and Tibeto-Burman inhabitants. Nanzhao reached a peak during the Tang dynasty. Today, Yunnan is China's most ethnically diverse province, with almost forty minority groups; their languages belong to at least four totally unrelated phyla. Most of these groups have simple cuisines, based on grain and local vegetables, but the Thai-speaking peoples of the far south have complex dishes very similar to those of north Thailand.

Sichuan's population was reduced by perhaps as much as 75 percent in the violent period between the Ming and Qing dynasties, and was repopulated largely from Hunan and neighboring areas, resulting in a great culinary similarity between Hunan and Sichuan. Yunnan in turn received many of its Chinese inhabitants from

Sichuan, but they adapted to local conditions and were influenced by non-Han nationalities, and Yunnan cuisine remains rather distinctive.

Agriculture is intensive throughout the region, especially in Hunan and Sichuan. Much of the Red Basin and nearby mountain land is terraced. Heavy use of fertilizer and compost has long been typical. Sophisticated irrigation works are typical. The Min River irrigation scheme, designed by the Li family of engineers in the third century B.C.E., is still in use, being one of the oldest (and most sophisticated) irrigation systems still in use.

Historically, this was millet and rice country, with wheat important in the northern fringes. Rice is intensively cultivated in the Yangzi drainage. Locally, in areas too high and rough for rice, buckwheat becomes important; it was traditionally the staple of the Yi nationality of the Liangshan Mountains in Sichuan.

The area has long been a recipient of new crops from outside. In medieval times, Near Eastern foods such as broad beans, sesame, and walnuts became important. Since New World food crops entered China, the extent of maize, white potatoes, and sweet potatoes has exploded in the region. Maize in particular proved ideal for the climate, and quickly replaced millet. (It is often called "Sichuan millet"—*Shu shu*, using the ancient name for Sichuan.) Unfortunately, maize is a heavy feeder and a poor protector of the soil, and its cultivation has led to considerable deforestation and erosion. White potatoes, introduced apparently by Catholic missionaries, do better at higher elevations, and are more important in this region than in most of China. Soybeans do only moderately well, and so were supplemented by broad beans, which entered from the Near East in early medieval times. Later, with the New World food crops, lima beans came to the region; they are locally very important in Yunnan. A variety of fermented bean products is prepared, as elsewhere in China, but this region is distinctive for the common use of broad beans in these, and for the enormous amounts of chili peppers in many fermented sauces. Distinctive, high-quality types of pickled and salted vegetables, particularly garlic, Chinese cabbages, and bamboo shoots, are typical of Sichuan, and are widely exported. The final characteristic flavor element of Sichuan cooking is dried tangerine peel, which is most often found in mixed stir-fried dishes with relatively rich, complex sauces.

The region is even more pig-dependent than other parts of China. Pork is overwhelmingly the major meat. Yunnan produces hams generally regarded as the finest in China, being quite similar to the mountain (*serrano*) hams of Spain; the quality of such hams owes much to their production in cool, dry montane regions. Some minority groups of Yunnan produce a cured pig product consisting of a whole fat hog with the flesh, bones, and intestines removed, leaving only the fat in the skin, which is then sewn up. The pig wind-cures in the high, cool mountain air.

Chickens and ducks abound. Fish are found only in rivers and lakes, being abundant in Hunan but relatively less so elsewhere. Sheep and goats are raised. Cows and buffaloes are traction animals, but rare as food. Yogurt is made and consumed by Han Chinese (and some minorities) in Yunnan—a rare case of traditional consumption of dairy products by Han people. The custom probably spread from India via Tibet in medieval times. Mixed herds of livestock are, of course, common on the Tibetan plateau (including all west Sichuan), and dairy products are standard fare there.

Salt is produced from salt springs and wells. Drilling very deep salt wells has been an important and profitable industry in Sichuan for two millennia. Unlike sea salt, this salt lacks iodine, as does most food in these mountainous regions; goiter was thus common in historic times, and was known to be associated with eating local salt as opposed to sea salt.

West Chinese food is shaped by geography as well as history and communication. In stereotype, and indeed in reality, the cuisine is distinguished by two things: its use of mountain products, and its hot spicing. China's wettest and most biologically diverse areas occur in this mountainous region. Dense forests, the most diverse outside the wet tropics, provide a variety of mushrooms and fungi. Many species can be seen at a typical street market. Also abundant are bamboo shoots, herbs, and other wild plant foods.

A variety of game was once abundant, but this is now sadly depleted because of overhunting and habitat destruction. One animal of note is the pangolin, a superficially anteater-like creature with hair matted into hard scales. It is believed to be powerfully nourishing and is eaten as medicine rather than as a delicacy. A recipe from Gueizhou involves cooking it with almost every strong-flavored ingredient in the Chinese repertoire, suggesting that there is a need to kill the flavor of the animal. The pangolin appears to have no scientifically verifiable healing qualities, and is probably regarded as medicinal because of its strange appearance, which suggests powerful *qi* (spirit or energy).

The piquant spicing is an old tradition. The chile pepper now dominates, making this by far the spiciest cuisine in China. Chile entered from the New World in fairly recent times, probably overland from India and/or upriver from Macau and east China in the seventeenth century. However, the area relished piquancy before this. The *Songs of the South*, a compilation of poetry from the old state of Chu, mentions the use of smartweed, southernwood, and other pungent herbs and spices. Ginger and garlic were always commonly used. Dried daylily buds, also peppery in the mouth, have also been used since time immemorial. Also ancient in importance is *huajiao*, known in English as "Sichuan pepper," "brown pepper," or "fagara," and scientifically as *Zanthoxylum* spp. This plant is a sprawling shrub or small tree. Being thorny, it is sometimes used as a living fence that has the side benefit of producing useful fruit. The latter is a small brown berry. The berries grow twinned on a short stem, and provided an ancient poetic euphemism for the male genitalia. They have a pungent, rich taste with overtones of citrus as well as pepperiness, and they produce a peculiar numb feeling in the mouth when chewed.

At some point in ancient historic time, true pepper began to be traded into China from southeast Asia. It was enthusiastically accepted in west China. As elsewhere in China, pepper is used almost exclusively in the white form, made from immature fruits with the dark coat rubbed off, as opposed to the black form (entire mature fruits) used in most of the world.

Thus, west Chinese cooking was spicy long before chilies came, and preadapted it to the latter. Today, Hunan-Sichuan cuisine is the only one in the world that makes heavy use of all three types of pepper—brown, white, and red—and routinely uses all three in the same dishes. Chinese, like English, classes all as "peppers" (*jiau* is the Chinese equivalent, and originally referred to brown pepper); they are botanically unrelated. Only black (and white) pepper is in the pepper family (Piperaceae); brown pepper is in the citrus family (Rutaceae), while chilies are in the Solanaceae along with tomatoes and white potatoes.

A full meal normally consists of a starch staple, usually rice, with steamed and/or stir-fried dishes as topping, and an accompanying soup. Minor meals (breakfasts, light lunches) or snacks involve dumplings or noodle soups. Chilies, brown pepper, and other hot spices are found primarily in the stir-fried dishes and the soups.

Several Sichuan dishes have become widely known. Duck smoked over smoldering tea leaves and camphor chips is the most elegant of these. It is smoked briefly in the cooking process, not smoke-cured for long storage. More common is hot and sour soup (*suan la tang*), which traditionally involves dried daylily buds, montane fungi, slivered bamboo shoots, coagulated chicken or duck blood and/or meat, sesame oil, white grain vinegar, chilies, white pepper, and sometimes other ingredients. It is a flexible recipe, varying greatly according to taste and circumstance.

Chicken is often cut into small cubes and stir-fried with chilies and various vegetables. A variant of this with peanuts (from the New World) and (usually) dried tangerine peel is Gung Bao chicken, named for a military officer said to have invented (or relished) it. A range of "fish flavored" dishes, especially eggplant, are named not because they taste like fish but because they are flavored as fish are: that is, with garlic, ginger, scallions, oil, and often Chinese "wine."

Particularly characteristic are stir-fried dishes of bean curd with garlic, brown pepper, and chilies. The

Woman selling steamed dumplings from a street stall in Sichuan province. © NIK WHEELER/CORBIS.

most famous of these today is *ma po dou fu*, literally "hemp woman's bean curd," which consists of small cubes of bean curd stir-fried in sesame oil with garlic, brown pepper, chilies, and fermented broad bean–chile paste; ground or finely chopped pork is often added, as is white pepper. As usual, countless variants of this dish exist, involving such items as mushrooms or fungi. Some are quite mild, but true Sichuan versions can be literally blistering. Also countless are the theories about the name; the most believable is that the dish was invented by women of the Ma ("hemp") family.

Hunan's cuisine has the same basic flavor mix as Sichuan's, but uses more fish and chicken. Finely chopped pork, flavored and then steamed in a bamboo tube, is a distinctive dish. Yunnan cuisine is simpler. The distinctive Yunnan ham enters into almost everything. Being expensive and strong-flavored, it is used more as a spice than as a main ingredient; small amounts of chopped ham are added to dishes. Most common, and spectacular, is a dish in which oil is heated in a pan until it actually catches fire; then cooked lima beans, garlic, chilies, and ham bits are thrown into the flaming oil and quickly seared. Noodle dishes are abundant. Often the noodles are only partially cooked, then at the table they are slid into soup that is served at the boiling point; the noodles finish cooking in the soup while the diner waits. This is known as "across-the-bridge noodles."

Drinks include some of China's best tea, raised in the mountains of the area. Yunnan in particular is famous for tea. The plant originated nearby, in the area where Tibet, Burma, and India come together. Spreading to metropolitan China at some uncertain point in early historic times, it became popular during the Tang dynasty, being seen as an exotic southwestern luxury at that time. Only during Sung did it become widely important as an everyday (if expensive) drink. Other herbal teas and drinks are common and are used for a range of ills.

Alcoholic drinks run the usual gamut of grain-based "wines" and distilled liquors. Gueizhou is famous for its *maotai*, powerful clear liquor traditionally distilled from millet. Most of the minority groups brew distinctive "wines" or beers from rice or other grains. Drinking these local products is important on festive occasions, including the widespread spring festivals at which groups of adolescent boys sing courting songs to groups of girls, who answer in kind.

Today, west China supports an enormous food industry. Yunnan hams and teas, Sichuan pickles, Gueizhou *maotai*, and Hunan hot bean pastes are world famous. Sichuan-style restaurants are found in major cities around the globe, and classic Sichuan dishes are found in virtually every eclectic Chinese restaurant.

See also **Japan; Korea, Noodle in Asia; Rice; Southeast Asia.**

BIBLIOGRAPHY

Anderson, E. N. *The Food of China.* New Haven: Yale University Press, 1988.

Hawkes, David. *The Songs of the South: An Ancient Chinese Anthology.* Oxford: Clarendon Press, 1959.

Hosie, Archibald. *Szechuan: Its Products, Industries and Resources.* Shanghai: Kelly and Walsh, 1922.

Huang, H. T. *Science and Civilization in China.* Vol. 6, *Biology and Biological Technology.* Part V, *Fermentations and Food Science.* Cambridge, U.K.: Cambridge University Press, 2000.

Simoons, Frederick. *Food in China: A Cultural and Historical Inquiry.* Boca Raton, Fla.: CRC Press, 1991.

E. N. Anderson

ZHEJIANG (CHEKIANG) CUISINE

Zhejiang Province includes the core of the vast Yangzi delta region, China's richest, most highly educated, and most progressive region throughout much of history. Its great cities of Shanghai (now a separate metropolitan area), Suzhou, Hangzhou, and Ningbo form an arc around the Yangzi mouth. Each of these cities has its own culinary specialties.

Shanghai has grown very recently to prominence as a city; it is basically a product of imperialism, having been developed as a port by the English in the nineteenth century. It has its own variant of Eastern foodways, based on local traditions but adding influences from all up and down the Yangzi valley.

Zhejiang is also the core of the ancient state of Wu, which may have been largely non-Chinese-speaking, and which certainly maintained a sophisticated and elaborate culture rather different from that of the Central Plain to the northwest. The name "Wu" is still used for the region, and for the language spoken there—a language usually miscalled a "dialect," but as separate from Putonghua as French is from Spanish.

Zhejiang cuisine is the most elaborate form of a culinary style more broadly called "eastern," and found throughout the old state of Wu and its bordering areas. Besides Zhejiang, the provinces involved are Jiangsu, Anhuei, and at least part of Jiangxi. Fujian province (ancient Min) is linguistically and culturally a very different entity, but its cuisines fall into a broadly eastern pattern, blending southward into more Cantonese-oriented foodways.

Agriculture in the region is as intensive as any in the world. Multiple cropping, heavy fertilizer use, systematic intercropping, and special production systems allow farms as small as an American suburban lot to produce a (bare) living. One common system, described by writers such as F. H. King, Fei Hsiao-Tung, and Philip Huang, involved producing rice and silk; mulberries grew along the dikes between the ricefields, holding the soil while producing leaves for silkworms. The mountains that ring the delta country are usually too steep for grain farming, but they are ideal for tea. This tea region, which includes much of Fujian and leaps the narrow strait to include northern Taiwan, produces what is generally regarded as the best in the world. Green (unfermented) and oolong (slightly fermented) teas dominate, as opposed to black (fermented) teas, which are notably less important. An extreme connoisseurship of tea exists in the area. Gourmets once not only discriminated teas from particular mountains and estates, but saved snow water for tea, or went to great lengths to obtain water from special wells and springs.

The markets of Zhejiang have always been famous for their size and the variety of offerings.

The staple foods in Zhejiang, and in most of the Yangzi region, are rice and wheat. The former can be grown in the summer, the latter in winter. Both were, and are, about equally important in the daily diet. Foxtail millet was once common, but has been recently replaced by maize. Soybeans can be produced, but flourish better in more northern climes. A vast range of vegetables and fruits is produced. Specialty fruits include giant pears, mentioned by many authors, including Marco Polo. These can weigh several pounds apiece. Among the vegetables are specialized gourmet varieties of Chinese cabbage and snowpeas. The tender tips of the peavines are preferred to the pods and seeds, and are, in fact, often the most expensive items in a market. They are considered the ultimate in refinement because of their delicate taste and their *cuei* texture. This quintessentially Chinese term is the highest praise for vegetables; it refers to foods that offer initial resistance to a bite, then suddenly give way and are succulent and moist. (Usually translated "crisp," it refers to the crispness of a ripe apple, not that of a potato crisp.) Peavines are now appearing in the United States, and one can obtain seeds of the varieties in question.

Pigs, chickens, and ducks abound; sheep and cattle are uncommon and rarely eaten. The most important source of animal protein, however, is the water. Zhejiang is as amphibious as the Netherlands, with fresh and salt water interpenetrating and interdigitating in complex patterns. No one is far from water.

When the state of Wu flourished, the river carried incredible quantities of nutrients. Currents and tides brought still more nutrient from the seaward side. The result was a high-energy, high-nutrient environment, one of the most biotically productive on earth. Vast schools of fishes migrated up the river or along the coast. Alligators, river dolphins, and turtles of many species abounded. Huge beds of shellfish existed. The land was rich in game of all sorts. Today, this bounty is virtually gone. The Yangzi flow is reduced and terribly polluted. Overhunting, overfishing, pollution, and land reclamation have destroyed almost all the game and large water animals, and most of the fish stocks.

Even now, however, the delta region is relatively rich in seafood. Fish, crabs, shrimps, and shellfish remain common. Overfishing of wild stocks has been compensated by a huge expansion of aquaculture. Practiced since ancient times, fish farming now supplies most of the fish in China, and is concentrated in the Yangzi basin.

Wu's dependence on water foods was a source of merriment in earlier times. Northern and especially northwestern Chinese, from drier and more grazing-oriented lands, laughed at the "southern" taste for frogs and snails much as English used to laugh at French for eating the same. The citizens of Wu replied in kind, ridiculing the rank mutton and "barbaric" yogurt of the northwest. Françoise Sabban notes that, as early as the third century, Zhang Hua could write: "The people of the South and the East eat seafoods while the people of the North and West delight in hares, rats and other game and are not aware of their gamey smell" (p. 2). Such comments were barbed because the north usually had the political power while the southeast usually had the wealth; mutual envy sharpened tongues.

The other distinctive qualities of Zhejiang food are a proclivity for sweet and unctious flavors; a rich quality, with much oil and thick sauces; and a devotion to extreme freshness. The sweet taste seems to be ancient; in the classic fivefold division of the cosmos, typical of Chinese thought since the early Han dynasty, the flavor associated with the east is sweetness. This obviously is not mere cosmological speculation, but a recognition of reality. (The west is associated with pungency, as is true of its cuisine to this day. The north is salt, south bitter, east sour, and center sweet.)

The freshness is also a result of landscape; preserving food is not easy in the hot, wet climate, and is unnecessary because of the twelve-month growing and fishing season. However, some interesting ferments are prepared, and China's best vinegar, the aged vinegar of

Chinese wolfberries or boxthorn (*Lycium chinense*) are known as *gau gei choi* in Chinese. They originate in the hot western regions of China and are used extensively in cookery and in botanical medicines. The leaves are used for herbal tea. PHOTO L. WILBUR ZIMMERMAN. ROUGHWOOD SEED COLLECTION.

Zhenjiang, comes from Jiangsu. This vinegar occupies the place in Chinese cuisine that balsamic does in Italian, and, in fact, it is vaguely reminiscent of balsamic in appearance. In Fujian, a brilliant purple-red fungal ferment is cultivated, and applied to almost anything and everything. Noteworthy is a dish of raw crab marinated in this ferment along with grain "wine," vinegar, and other flavorings. It is an acquired taste.

Those affluent enough ate three meals a day and snacks as well. The basic main-meal pattern is rice with one to three dishes for topping. Wheat appears as the basis of minor meals and snacks: filled dumplings, noodle soups, and various cakes. Sticky rice is made into cakes and noodles as well. The hot and amphibious landscape makes soup an attractive option. (China's—if not the world's—center of soup-eating is just southward, in Fujian, where it is perfectly routine to serve three or four different soups among the main courses in a twelve-course banquet, and Simoons reports a banquet at which "seven out of ten dishes were soups" [p. 50]). Ginger, green onions, garlic, local "wine," sugar, and vinegar are common flavorings. Less use is made of spices and bean pastes than in the west and south of China.

Among the major uses for the aquatic bounty are fish in sweet-sour or rich brown sauces, West Lake fish (from the West Lake at Hangzhou), braised eels, softshell crabs, crabs with roe in breeding season, countless shrimp dishes, stir-fried frogs' legs, and many snail and clam dishes. Even the tiniest shellfish are eaten. Among dishes drawing on the land, beggar's chicken is perhaps the most interesting; it is associated with the Shanghai area. A whole chicken is stuffed with fragrant leaves, buds, and spices, wrapped in still more leaves, encased in clay, and baked in a fire. The clay is broken (today, often, with an unromantic soft drink bottle) and the chicken served.

Men making nang bread at Hotan, Xinjiang Uygur Autonomous Region, China. © KEREN SU/CORBIS

Like similar preparations around the world, this dish is said to originate among thieves who had to hide their stolen fowl.

Zhejiang was once a center of Buddhism, including Zen, and thus a great vegetarian cuisine developed. Based largely on soybean and wheat gluten preparations, it sometimes extends to include oysters and similarly sedentary shellfish, which do not seem alive. Imitation meats are prepared from bean curd skin and wheat gluten; they are convincing to the degree that their flavors are disguised by thick sauces.

At the other end of the puritanism scale is a dish centered on northern Fujian, "Buddha Jumped over the Wall"; it consists of long-simmered innards and tough cuts of meat. It smells so wonderful as it cooks that it would make a meditating Buddha leap the wall of his temple compound to get to it.

Besides tea, major drinks include superb grain "wines" related to Japanese sake. Most famous is that of Shaoxing. Ningbo and other cities produce interesting and complex brews. These "wines" are technically beers or ales, being brewed from grain, but they are not carbonated, and they occupy the place in Chinese culture that wine does in Europe. They are brewed, however, in a very different way: with a complex mix of ferments, involving species of yeasts and of fungi in the genera *Rhizopus*, *Aspergillus*, and others, as well as bacteria such as *Lactobacillus* (see Huang). Each brewery has its own strains and preparations. The resulting brews differ greatly from place to place, and have rich, complex, subtle flavors. They have inspired a gourmetship equal to that of tea, or of French wine. Of course, such "wines" exist throughout China, but those of the Yangzi delta are generally considered the finest.

See also **Japan, Korea, Noodle in Asia; Rice; Southeast Asia.**

BIBLIOGRAPHY

Anderson, E. N. *The Food of China.* New Haven: Yale University Press, 1988.

Fei Hsiao-tung. *Peasant Life in China: A Field Study of Country Life in the Yangtze Valley.*. New York: Oxford University Press, 1946.

Huang, H. T. *Science and Civilization in China.* Vol. 6, *Biology and Biological Technology. Part 5: Fermentations and Food Science.* Cambridge, U.K.: Cambridge University Press, 2000.

Huang, Philip. *The Peasant Family and Rural Development in the Yangzi Delta, 1350–1988.* Stanford: Stanford University Press, 1990.

King, F. H. *Farmers of Forty Centuries*. New York: Mrs. F. H. King, 1911.

Sabban, Françoise. "Chinese Regional Cuisine: The Genesis of a Concept." Paper, Sixth Symposium on Chinese Dietary Culture, Fuzhou, 1999.

Simoons, Frederick. *Food in China: A Cultural and Historical Inquiry*. Boca Raton, Fla.: CRC Press, 1990.

E. N. Anderson

CHITLINS (CHITTERLINGS).

Chitlins or chitterlings, the small intestines harvested from a hog, are a frugal staple of myriad cuisines. After being soaked, thoroughly scraped, and cleaned, chitterlings have long been stuffed with forcemeats and spices and served as sausages. But chitterlings usage has never been limited to sausage making.

In England, cooks combine diced, sautéed chitterlings with mashed potatoes, form the mix into rounds, cap the resulting dumplings with grated cheese, and term the dish Down Derry. In and around Lyon, France, chitterlings, or *andouillettes*, are fried in lard or butter and served with vinegar and parsley.

No matter the cuisine or continent, chitterlings have long signaled linkage to the farm-based butchery of pigs. In rural districts worldwide, the cold weather killing of a pig and the removal of the chitterlings is a ritual of great import. In the American South, chitterlings, pulled hot from a cauldron of simmering water and eaten with a dose of vinegary or peppery condiment, are considered by many to be a reward for the hard work of farm-based butchery. This farm-to-table linkage has acquired special significance in the American South, where chitterlings (termed "chitlins" by most in an approximation of the prevailing pronunciation) have come to acquire a cultural importance that arguably exceeds traditional culinary usage.

In the book *Chitlin Strut and Other Madrigals*, the novelist and essayist William Price Fox of South Carolina asks the rhetorical question, "Who will eat a chitlin?" The answer: "You take a man and tie him to a stake and feed him bread and water and nothing else for seven days and seven nights, and then he will eat a chitlin. He won't like it, but he will eat it." Fox ascribes to the idea of chitlins as a marker of poverty. According to this often espoused rationale, chitlins and other pork offal products have long been a staple of the southern diet, and their presence was dictated not by preference but by a poverty-engendered creativity that could be claimed by all denizens of rural and impoverished southern districts.

White rural Southerners of the twentieth century, faced with the prospect of a rapidly industrializing and homogenizing region, doted on both boiled and deep-fried chitterlings. For these men and women, chitterlings served as both symbol and sustenance. By mid-century

there were active chitterling eating clubs, like the Royal Order of Chitlin Eaters of Nashville, Tennessee, and the Happy Chitlin Eaters of Raleigh, North Carolina. The traditional song "Chitlin Cookin' Time in Cheatham County" gives voice to the same:

> There's a quiet and peaceful county in the state of
> Tennessee
> You will find it in the book they call geography
> Not famous for its farming, its mines, or its stills
> But they know there's chitlin cookin' in them
> Cheatham County hills
> When it's chitlin cookin' time in Cheatham County
> I'll be courtin' in them Cheatham County hills
> And I'll pick a Cheatham County chitlin cooker
> I've a longin' that the chitlins will fill

African Americans with roots in the rural South also claimed a specific cultural meaning for chitlins. At an early date, forced reliance upon offal marked the foods of black southerners with a meaning different from those of whites. Until emancipation, African American food choice was restricted by the dictates of white society. Despite these restrictions, perhaps even as a retort of sorts, African Americans fashioned a cuisine of their own. Laws may have been enacted to regulate slave dress and codify slave mores, but in the kitchen freedom of expression was tolerated, even encouraged. As a result, African American cooks reinterpreted traditional foodways in an African-influenced manner and claimed chitterlings as distinctly African American.

Chitterling imagery pervades African American culture. The informal circuit of juke joints and clubs patronized by African Americans has long been called the "Chitlin Circuit." The bluesman Mel Brown, a veteran of the circuit, chose to title his early 1970s greatest hits album *Eighteen Pounds of Unclean Chitlins and Other Greasy Blues Specialties*.

When soul food came to the fore in the United States during the late 1960s and early 1970s, chitlins—along with watermelons and okra—were celebrated as a cultural sacrament. But not all African Americans embraced chitterlings as a preferred marker of identity. "You hear a lot of jazz about soul food," observed Eldridge Cleaver in 1968. "Take chitterlings: the ghetto blacks eat them from necessity while the black bourgeoisie has turned it into a mocking slogan . . . . Now that they have the price of a steak, here they come prattling about Soul Food."

The novelist Ralph Ellison understood how chitterlings functioned as both preferred cultural marker and liability. In the novel *Invisible Man* (1952), the protagonist imagines a scenario wherein he accuses Bledsoe, a pompous but influential educator, of a secret love of chitterlings:

> I saw myself advancing upon Bledsoe . . . and suddenly whipping out a foot or two of chitterlings, raw, uncleaned, and dripping sticky circles on the floor as I shake them in his face, shouting: "Bledsoe, you're a shameless chitterling

eater! I accuse you of relishing hog bowels! Ha! And not only do you eat them, you sneak and eat them in private when you think you're unobserved! You're a sneaking chitterling lover!"

See also **Pig; Sausage; United States,** subentries on **African American Foodways** and **The South.**

BIBLIOGRAPHY

Cleaver, Eldridge. *Soul on Ice.* New York: McGraw-Hill, 1967.

Ellison, Ralph. *Invisible Man.* New York: Random House, 1952.

Fox, William Price. *Chitlin Strut and Other Madrigals.* Atlanta: Peachtree Publishers, 1983.

Schwabe, Calvin W. *Unmentionable Cuisine.* Charlottesville: University Press of Virginia, 1979.

John T. Edge

CHOCOLATE.

Chocolate is the name applied to the variety of products manufactured from the seeds of the tropical tree *Theobroma cacao* L. The Swedish naturalist Carl Von Linné (1707–1778), known as Linnaeus, gave the tree the attribution *theobroma* or "food of the gods," taken from the Greek. When adjoined to *cacao*, the indigenous Mixe-Zoquean term for the plant, the name is symbolic of the social, religious, and economic importance of chocolate in both New and Old World cultures. Yet while it was revered, it was also reviled, an ambivalence that attends chocolate even in the twenty-first century. Among all the fruits of tropical and subtropical America, why would this one elicit so much passion?

The Plant and Its History

The geographic origin of *T. cacao* is obscure. While most texts place its origin in either the Amazon or Orinoco River basins of northern South America, it is equally likely that a separate variety originated in Mesoamerica, perhaps in the Lacandón rainforest of the Mexican state of Chiapas. It has been hypothesized that wild *T. cacao* was broadly distributed in Central and South America and that at some time trees in the isthmus died out, leaving a northern variety and a southern variety to develop independently. The fruit of *criollo*, the northern variety, is characterized by elongated, deeply ridged yellow to red pods containing ivory or pale purple seeds, while *forastero*, the southern variety, is characterized by more ovoid, smooth, melon-like green or yellow pods with pale to deep purple seeds. The pigmented substances and related compounds in the cacao seeds impart bitter and astringent qualities to the chocolate. Hence the *forastero* variety has a robust flavor, while the delicate, "fine" flavor of the *criollo* is generally considered of superior quality. In the early twenty-first century, greater than 80 percent of commercial cacao was *forastero*, since this variety is hardier and more productive.

The word "cacao" seems to have come to the Maya from the Olmec, who inhabited the lowlands of the coast of the Gulf of Mexico between about 1500 and 400 B.C.E. and who probably first domesticated the tree. The Izapan culture that bridged the Olmec and the Classic Maya (250–900 C.E.) likely planted the *criollo* plantations of Xoconochco (Soconusco) on the Pacific coastal plains of Chiapas, later a prize possession of the Aztec (Mexica) Empire. While this suggests that cacao was an important crop to the Olmec and the Izapan, it is not known to what extent chocolate was an icon food. The pre-Classic Quiché Maya of the Guatemala highlands apparently did not hold it in exceeding high regard for it is mentioned only in passing in the sacred *Popol Vuh* or "Book of Counsel." But sometime before 250 C.E. this changed. Chocolate appears in Classic Maya iconography, where the glyph symbolizing cacao adorns ritual burial vases. Classic Maya, particularly the wealthy, imbibed cacao in betrothal and marriage ceremonies, reminiscent of the modern use of expensive French champagne. However, the ritual use of cacao reached its height during the time of the Aztec (Mexica) Empire between 1300 and 1521 C.E.

Cacao was both an elite drink and coinage among the post-Classic Maya and the Aztecs. Chocolate was considered a drink for warriors and nobles and had ritual significance as a symbol of human blood. Since cacao could not be grown in the Valley of Mexico, the site of the Aztec capital of Tenochtitlán, it had to be imported from either the conquered lands in Xoconochco or obtained by trade from the Maya of the Yucatán, which gave chocolate an exotic quality. It has been oft repeated that Motecuhzoma Xocoyotzin (the familiar "Montezuma") drank fifty flagons of chocolate a day, most especially before entering his harem, but the account of the conquistador Bernal Díaz del Castillo says of those fifty large mugs, "he would drink a little" (Dillinger et al., 2000, p. 2058S). While cacao was an integral part of the beliefs and practices of the ruling Aztec elite, the image they held of it was not wholly positive. This warning is part of one Aztec tale: "You have become old, you have become tired because of the chocolate you drink and because of the foods you eat" (Coe and Coe, 1996, p. 80). The exuberance of the puritanical Aztecs for chocolate may have been tempered by its association with the luxury-loving Maya of the warm lands to the south. This north-south conflict was repeated in Europe.

In American English usage, "cacao" refers to the tree and its dried seeds prior to further processing; "cocoa" refers to the partially defatted, roasted, and ground cacao seeds; and "chocolate" refers to a food prepared from roasted cacao seeds. Although not leguminous, the cacao seeds are often referred to as "beans." The composition of the edible cotyledon or "nib" is by weight approximately 55 percent fat; 30 percent carbohydrates, half of which is dietary fiber; 10 percent protein; and a host of minor nutrients. This breakdown provides a key to the basis for chocolate's status as a luxury food.

Cacao seeds, numbering twenty to forty, develop within a thick-hulled pod surrounded by a white, sweet, mucilaginous pulp that, with the potential to be fermented into ethanol, could have been what first attracted *Homo sapiens.* Wild cacao is dispersed by primates, who consume the sweet pulp and discard the bitter seed. *Cupuaçu,* a product made from the pulp of the fruit of *Theobroma grandiflorum,* a relative of *T. cacao,* is consumed by peoples of the Amazon. The preparation of cacao seeds for chocolate making begins with a fermentation step that at one point generates ethanol, which may explain why chocolate has at times been described as intoxicating. A "wine" produced from the liquid expressed from the cacao pulp is consumed in the Yucatán. It is speculative but possible that consumption of the cacao seeds was an afterthought, as the bitter flavor of the seeds is an acquired taste.

Processing Cacao

Fermentation is required for the characteristic chocolate flavor to develop when the seeds are roasted. The mucilaginous pulp surrounding the seeds is fermented to ethanol, then progressively to acetic and lactic acids, which facilitates its removal. The acid and heat generated during fermentation kill the seed embryo, preventing germination and allowing enzymatic changes that generate flavor precursors and reduce bitterness and astringency. Following fermentation, the seeds are dried, preferably in the sun, to a final moisture content of about 7.5 percent. In this form, the seeds are transported from the country of origin to the major chocolate manufacturing regions.

For the Maya and the modern American alike, the conversion of the fermented and dried cacao to chocolate involves three major operations: roasting, winnowing, and grinding. Just as with meat, roasting cacao generates complex aromas appealing to the human sense of smell. Winnowing is the removal of the inedible shell surrounding the nib. Grinding, which the Maya accomplished by hand using a *metate* and for which later processors have used a variety of mechanical mills, liberates the cacao fat (cacao "butter") from within the plant cells, extracts the aroma, and permits easy suspension of the cacao in beverages.

The quantity of protein in cacao is significant, and the amino acid composition, while limited in lysine and methionine, can be considered good for a protein of plant origin. However, unlike the leguminous beans that complement maize nutritionally, the digestibility of cocoa proteins is only about 16 to 17 percent. Therefore the proteins of cacao have little practical nutritional value.

The nitrogenous compounds of cacao include both proteins (80 percent) and the methylxanthines theobromine and caffeine, which are present in chocolate liquor (ground cacao nibs) at levels of about 1.22 percent and 0.21 percent respectively. They are both central nervous system stimulants, diuretics, and smooth muscle relaxants, although theobromine tends to be less so than

Chocolate swizzle sticks (*molinillo*). Mexico and Nicaragua, ca. 1800. Instead of pouring chocolate from a high position to create foam (the best part), the Spaniards copied indigenous forms of whisks to create foam on chocolate by spinning a stick between the hands. Both types of whisk are shown here. ROUGHWOOD COLLECTION. PHOTO CHEW & COMPANY.

caffeine. It is certainly reasonable to assume that the physiological effects of the plant alkaloids are part of chocolate's appeal. Chocolate introduced Europe to these stimulants, though in a milder form than the coffee and tea that followed. The caffeine-containing kola nut, derived from an African tree of the same order as cacao (*Sterculiaceae*), became the basis of the American icon food Coca Cola. But it is likely that cacao butter is the soul of chocolate's appeal.

While wild game, including deer, peccaries, monkeys, tapir, birds, reptiles, and smaller mammals, were abundant in the New World, the only domesticated animals routinely used for meat were the dog and the ocellated turkey (*Meleagris ocellata*). Muscle foods were not ordinary fare for the indigenous inhabitants of Mesoamerica, and "when the meat-eating Europeans arrived, they described Maya life as perpetual Lent" (Coe, 1994, p. 153). Perhaps just as significant, this lack of large domesticated livestock meant the Maya had no source of butter, lard, or tallow. Fats and oils have been sought for cooking, lighting, and medicine since the earliest times. Hence some of the earliest domesticated plant species in the Old World were the almond (*Prunus amygdalus*) and the olive (*Oleo europea*). Perhaps the well-documented Maya distaste for the fat of European animals resulted from Maya familiarity with the preeminent fat, cacao butter.

Nutritional Value

Cacao butter is unique among natural fats. Its constituent fatty acids are principally the medium-chain saturated fatty palmitic acid and stearic acid and the monounsaturated oleic acid, so cacao butter exhibits a remarkable

Chocolate truffles are considered among the most luxurious of all chocolate confections. © C/B PRODUCTIONS/CORBIS.

stability against oxidative rancidity. Furthermore, the manner in which these fatty acids are distributed on the major molecule of natural fats, triacylglycerols, makes cacao butter solid at normal ambient temperatures, but it melts quickly just below body temperature. Bishop Diego de Landa reportedly said the Maya "get from cacao a grease which resembles butter, and from this and maize they make another beverage which is very savory and highly thought of" (Coe and Coe, 1996, p. 61). Fernández de Oviedo observed, "Cacao ground, and cooked with a bit of water, makes an excellent fat for cooking" (Coe, 1994, p. 54).

As in other fats, the caloric content of cocoa butter is high. Chocolate liquor contains approximately 520 kilocalories per 100 grams, 460 of which are from fat. The 1878 edition of *Encyclopedia Britannica* refers to "Cocoa, or more properly Cacao," as "a valuable dietary substance" and points out that, while only infusions are made from coffee and tea, leaving large portions of their total weights unconsumed, the entire substance of the cacao seed is utilized. Henry Stubbe, in *The Indian Nectar, or, a Discourse Concerning Chocolata* [*sic*] (1662), reported that both English soldiers and Indian women in Jamaica sustained themselves for long periods by eating only chocolate yet did not exhibit a decline in strength. The nutritional qualities of chocolate have been praised by numerous authors since the sixteenth century, and some people have called it a complete food, like bread or milk, containing as much nourishment as a pound of beef. While this helped the Hershey Chocolate Company earn the Army-Navy E award for the Ration D, it caused much consternation within the Catholic Church. Twice the residents of Chiapas consulted Pope Gregory XIII on the question of whether or not drinking chocolate broke the ecclesiastical fast, and both times he responded that it did not because it was a drink. So while coffee and tea can

only be regarded as stimulant in effect, a cup of cacao is nutritive in value.

In preconquest Mesoamerica, cacao was an ingredient of a wide variety of drinks, gruels, and porridges, to which were added a great diversity of other flavorings, notably vanilla *(Vanilla planifolia)*, chilli pepper *(Capsicum annum)*, and "ear flower" *(Cymbopetalum penduliflorum)*. It is likely that some of these concoctions were served hot and others cold. The simplest chocolate drink consisted of adding ground cacao and flavorings to water and agitating the mixture by beating or by pouring the liquid from one vessel to another to raise a foam, which was considered the best part of the drink and a sign of quality. During preparation the foam was reserved, then it was added back before serving. While the Maya added indigenous plants to augment the foam, modern consumers have replaced it altogether with whipped cream or marshmallow. The ground cacao was often ameliorated with ground maize or ceiba seed *(Ceiba pentandra)*, though not in the most elite drinks. The bitter taste of most chocolate drinks was not immediately appealing to the European palate. Notable among the ingredients Europeans added to their chocolate are sugar and milk.

From at least the time of the Aztecs, people have been ambivalent about chocolate. Wolfgang Schivelbusch portrayed this ambivalence as a contest between diametrically opposed cultures: capitalist, middle-class, Protestant northern Europe versus aristocratic, Catholic southern Europe. Chocolate was a status symbol of the ancien régime, while coffee appealed to the bourgeois intellect. That chocolate became a status symbol in Europe had much to do with its richness, rarity, and exotic origins. As a status symbol, drinking chocolate vanished with the ancien régime. Cocoa became a breakfast drink for women and children; what formerly symbolized power and glory was now in the hands of the disenfranchised in middle-class society. However, at the same time, solid eating chocolate gained new significance as a luxury in its own right. Once again prestige followed the fat.

While the calories provided by chocolate may have been advantageous to a solider on the march, the idle European nobility found it exceedingly fattening and disagreeable at times to the stomach. In search of a better beverage, Coenraad Van Houten in 1828 developed a means of partially defatting cacao using a mechanical press, an invention that had unanticipated consequences.

The development of solid eating chocolate was evolutionary. Chocolate liquor is solid below 85°F (30°C); formed into small pellets or wafers, it was issued to Aztec warriors on campaign. It was an obvious step to add spices and maize to the cacao during grinding and then form the mixture into cakes. These tablets could later be dispersed into water to prepare a beverage. Seventeenth-century texts mention "eating" as well as drinking chocolate, and recipes for solid confections containing cacao appeared in the eighteenth century. In the 1820s,

Goethe wrote of chocolate, "Enjoy this whenever it suits your mood, Not as a drink, but a much loved food" (Morton and Morton, 1986, p. 67). But it was the surplus cacao butter resulting from Van Houten's invention that accelerated the trend toward solid chocolate confections.

The addition of cacao butter to chocolate liquor made it possible to add more sugar to balance the bitterness of the cacao while still producing a thin paste that could be cast into a mold or used as a coating. Solid eating chocolate became an object of trade in the mid-1800s. However, these early products were coarse and gritty. Rudolph Lindt is credited with the 1879 invention of the conch that by grinding the sugar exceedingly fine and homogenizing the mixture creates a smooth and creamy textured chocolate with enhanced flavor and aroma. This "fondant" chocolate became a world standard.

Chocolate has been lauded for its purported medicinal value. Greater than one hundred medicinal uses for chocolate have been reported, and the majority fall into three main categories: 1) to aid emaciated patients in gaining weight; 2) to stimulate the nervous systems of apathetic, exhausted, or feeble individuals; and 3) to improve digestion, stimulate the kidneys (diuretic), and improve bowel function (Dillinger et al., 2000, p. 2057S). These uses can be explained either by cacao's caloric content or by the presence of methylxanthines. In the late twentieth century, attention focused on a class of compounds, phytonutrients, that tend to have antioxidant properties and are said to lower the risk of cancer and cardiovascular disease. Among these phytonutrients are the polyphenols, in particular the catechins, which have demonstrated physiological antioxident properties. Pigment cells in the cacao seed, especially in the *forastero* variety, are rich in these compounds, which may mean redemption for the lowly cousin of the *criollo*.

Chocolate has long been called an aphrodisiac, a quality that entered into the debate over whether or not it could be consumed by Catholics during Lent, and references to its stimulation of the sexual appetite are numerous. Like other luxury items, chocolate is a symbol of excess wealth, but the association of chocolate and eroticism may not be entirely iconographic in nature. While no specific chemical compounds have yet been identified that could account for either chocolate's supposed addictive or aphrodisiac properties, debate continues on its physiological and psychological effects. Chocolate has become an essential ingredient in the act of seduction. It could be that the melting of the cacao butter in chocolate is symbolic of the melting of the heart and the breakdown of sexual resistance.

BIBLIOGRAPHY

Bailleux, Nathalie, et al. *The Book of Chocolate*. Paris: Flammarion, 1995.

Beckett, S. T., ed. *Industrial Chocolate Manufacture and Use*. 3rd edition. Oxford: Blackwell Science, 1999.

Coe, Sophie D. *America's First Cuisines*. Austin: University of Texas Press, 1994.

Coe, Sophie D., and Michael D. Coe. *The True History of Chocolate*. New York: Thames and Hudson, 1996.

Dand, Robin. *The International Cocoa Trade*. 2nd edition. Cambridge, U.K.: Woodhead Publishing, 1999.

Dillinger, Teresa L., Patricia Barriga, Sylvia Escárcega, Martha Jimenez, Diana Salazar Lowe, and Louis E. Grivetti. "Food of the Gods: Cure for Humanity? A Cultural History of the Medicinal and Ritual Use of Chocolate." *Journal of Nutrition* 130 (2000): 2057S–2072S.

Drewnowski, Adam, and Carmen Gomez-Carneros. "Bitter Taste, Phytonutrients, and the Consumer: A Review." *American Journal of Clinical Nutrition* 72 (2000): 1424–1435.

Girard, Sylvie. "Les vertus aphrodisiaques du chocolat [The aphrodisiac qualities of chocolate]." *Cahiers Sexol. Clin.* 11 (1985): 60–62.

Knight, Ian, ed. *Chocolate and Cocoa, Health and Nutrition*. Oxford: Blackwell Science, 1999.

Morton, Marcia, and Frederic Morton. *Chocolate: An Illustrated History*. New York: Crown Publishers, 1986.

Schivelbusch, Wolfgang. *Tastes of Paradise: A Social History of Spices, Stimulants, and Intoxicants*. Translated from the German by David Jacobson. New York: Pantheon Books, 1992.

Gregory R. Ziegler

CHOLESTEROL. Cholesterol is one of the most widely disseminated organic compounds in the animal kingdom. Almost three hundred years ago, Antonio Vallisnieri observed that gallstones were soluble in turpentine or alcohol. Poulletier de la Salle, some thirty years later, demonstrated that the main constituent of gallstones could be crystallized from alcohol. This substance was thought to be a wax until 1815, when Michel Eugène Chevreul showed that it was not saponifiable and gave it the name "cholesterine" derived from the Greek *chole*, bile, and *steros*, solid. Soon thereafter, it was isolated from blood, brain, tumors, and egg yolk. The isolated compounds were shown to be identical. In 1843 Vogel found it in atherosclerotic arteries.

The chemical structure of cholesterol was elucidated over the years beginning in 1859. The compound was shown to contain a secondary hydroxyl group and a double bond. The exact empirical formula ($C_{27}H_{46}O$) was established in 1888 by Friedrich Reinitzer. Proof of structure was obtained chiefly through the brilliant work of Adolf Windaus and Heinrich Wieland. The structure of cholesterol suggested by Windaus and Wieland in the 1920s was incorrect, but that does not detract in any way from their contribution. The true structure was established in the 1930s based on X-ray diffraction data.

There were many suggestions regarding the biological synthesis of cholesterol. The biosynthetic pathway became accessible with the introduction of radioactive carbon in the 1940s. The biosynthetic scheme was generally elucidated by the work of Konrad Bloch, George Popjak, and John Cornforth. It was first shown that cholesterol could be synthesized in mammals and ergosterol in yeast from small organic molecules. Eventually it was shown that all twenty-seven carbon atoms of cholesterol were derived from the two carbon atoms of acetate. The methyl group of acetate contributed fifteen of the twenty-seven carbons of cholesterol and the carboxyl group contributed twelve. The pathway began with the condensation of two acetate residues to give acetoacetate and addition of one more two-carbon moiety to yield hydroxymethylglutaric acid (HMG). HMG lost a carbon atom and the resulting compound rearranged to provide an isoprene unit. Two five-carbon units combined to give a geranyl derivative that added another isoprene to give a farnesyl unit. Two farnesyl units united to provide squalene ($C_{30}H_{50}$), a hydrocarbon found in the livers of some species of shark that cyclyzed to yield lanosterol, a thirty-carbon atom sterol also found in sheep wool. In a series of rearrangements and demethylations, lanosterol yielded cholesterol. The key step in this complex synthetic pathway involves the reduction of HMG-CoA. Inhibition of HMG-CoA reductase is the basis of a number of potent new serum cholesterol-lowering drugs.

Cholesterol represents about 0.2 percent of the weight of the human body. As Table 1 shows, the bulk of the body's cholesterol is present in two tissues; one is the brain and nerve tissue, the other is muscle. In the brain, cholesterol is thought to act as an insulator, but there have been relatively few studies of the metabolism of brain cholesterol. The next large reservoir of cholesterol is muscle. Between them, nervous tissue and muscle carry 44 percent of the body's cholesterol. The cholesterol in these reservoirs turns over slowly.

Cholesterol is ubiquitous in the human body, where it plays structural and metabolic roles. Together with phospholipid, cholesterol is present in every cell membrane. In the adrenals, cholesterol is converted to adrenocortical hormones such as cortisone. In the gonads, cholesterol is converted to the appropriate sex hormone—estradiol in women, testosterone in men. The cholesterol in skin is the precursor of 7-dehydrocholesterol, which is ultimately converted to vitamin D. The major catabolic products of cholesterol are the bile acids—cholic and chenodeoxycholic. These are designated as the primary bile acids; they are metabolized in the liver to deoxycholic and lithocholic acids. It has been estimated that over 90 percent of biologically synthesized cholesterol is metabolized to bile acids. In general, the body synthesizes more cholesterol than it ingests.

In 1912 Nicolai Anitschkow showed that cholesterol-fed rabbits developed aortic deposits similar to early human atherosclerosis. His experiments presented a possible explanation of human atherosclerosis and that particular debate has not yet abated. Simultaneously with Anitschkow's studies, A. I. Ignatowski demonstrated the atherogenic potential of animal protein, but compared to work on cholesterol and fat there has only been a desultory interest in protein effects.

Since Anitschkow's results were obtained by dietary manipulation, the view that dietary cholesterol was implicated in atherogenesis was accepted generally. With development of simple, rapid methods of cholesterol analysis, it became possible to screen populations for blood cholesterol content. Large epidemiological studies were launched and their results helped to develop the concept of risk factors for heart disease. Currently, the major risk factors are hypercholesterolemia, hypertension, smoking, obesity, and maleness. However, emerging data suggest that homocysteinemia and inflammation (due to infection with cytomegalovirus or *chlamydia pneumoniae*) are also important factors.

When cholesterol is ingested, it is emulsified with phospholipid and absorbed. The absorbed lipid circulates in the blood as a water soluble lipid-protein complex called lipoprotein. Initially, absorbed cholesterol is part of a large, triglyceride-rich particle called the chylomicron. In the course of circulation, the triglyceride is removed by activity of cellular lipases and the particles become smaller and their cholesterol content increases. The cholesterol-containing, lipid-protein complex consists of several fractions that are separable by virtue of their hydrated densities. In general terms, the four major fractions are the triglyceride-rich chylomicrons and very low density (VLDL), the cholesterol-rich low density (LDL), and the protein-rich high density (HDL).

Due to development by John Gofman of methods for ultracentrifugal separation of lipoproteins, researchers have been able to isolate and study lipoproteins. The cholesterol-rich low density lipoproteins (LDL) are thought to be major risk factors for coronary disease. It was demonstrated that oxidized LDL is the real villain in coronary disease. It also was shown that LDL can be subfractionated into small, dense and large "fluffy" particles. The small particles appear to infiltrate the artery preferentially.

TABLE 1

Distribution of cholesterol in a 70-kg man

Tissue	Cholesterol content (g)	% of Total
Brain, nervous system	32.0	23
Connective tissue, body fluids	31.3	22
Muscle	30.0	21
Skin	12.6	9
Blood	10.8	8
Bone marrow	7.5	5
Liver	5.1	4
Heart, lungs, kidneys, spleen	5.0	4
Alimentary tract	3.8	3
Adrenals	1.2	1
Skeleton	0.7	—
Other glands	0.2	—

Researchers also know that the process of atherogenesis is not simple and is mediated by an array of small proteins. The high-density lipoproteins are about 50 percent protein. In the simplest terms, LDL facilitates entry of cholesterol into cells and HDL facilitates its removal. LDL receptors on the cell surface facilitate LDL uptake. The proteins of lipoproteins are very important because they provide recognition by cells, and it is now becoming evident that genetic differences in apolipoproteins may dictate susceptibility to disease as well as chances for the efficacy of medication.

The effects of dietary cholesterol became a concern shortly after Anitschkow's observation and warnings regarding excess levels of cholesterol intake, which constitute one of the foundations of dietary therapy. Since cholesterol occurs only in food of animal origin, it was a simple extension to seek an explanation of the role of cholesterol by examining the lipids of food from animal sources. Although no dietary fat is totally saturated or unsaturated, attention also turned to effects of fat saturation.

The amount of cholesterol in the average American diet is in the range of 300–350 mg/day. It used to be much higher. The levels of cholesterol in a number of common animal foods are given in Table 2. It is evident that most muscle contains about the same amount of cholesterol, 81 ± 7 mg/100g. Cholesterol content of butter (per 100 g) is high, but we rarely eat more than 5–10 g of butter per meal. Shrimp is high in cholesterol but very low in fat. Eggs are also high in cholesterol. Continuing research nevertheless indicates that the cholesterol level of a food per se has little effect on serum cholesterol levels. The cholesterolemic effect is a function of dietary fat saturation. It has been shown that the absorption of cholesterol is more a function of the accompanying dietary fat than of cholesterol itself. Saturated dietary fat leads to higher cholesterol levels than does unsaturated fat. This observation is true for most people who are called "non-responders" (to dietary cholesterol). A small number of people are "responders," meaning they absorb more cholesterol, regardless of accompanying fat. In the late 1960s, Keys and Hegsted developed formulas for estimating changes in serum cholesterol based upon changes in dietary fat. There have been a number of more complex formulas developed, but the originals are referred to most often today. Essentially, they found saturated fatty acids to be hypercholesterolemic and unsaturated fatty acids to lower cholesterol. Stearic acid was considered neutral. The polyunsaturated fats lower cholesterol across the board so that HDL cholesterol (the "good" cholesterol) falls as does LDL cholesterol. Oleic acid seems to affect only LDL cholesterol. The reduction in total cholesterol may not be as profound, but the LDL/HDL cholesterol ratio is improved. Recent findings show that the structure of individual triglycerides may also influence their atherogenicity.

In summary, cholesterol is a substance that appears in all cells and also has a number of metabolic functions.

TABLE 2

Cholesterol content (mg/100g) of selected foods

Food source	Cholesterol (mg/100g)
Egg	504
Butter	250
Shrimp	150
Mackerel	95
Herring	85
Chicken	81
Turkey	74
Lamb	71
Veal	71
Beef	68
Pork	62
Flounder	50
Milk	15

It is synthesized in the body and is part of every cell membrane. Cholesterol is metabolized to adrenocortical or sex hormones, bile acids, and vitamin D. Levels of serum cholesterol are related to risk of coronary disease, but it should be borne in mind that cardiovascular disease is a metabolic disease, not one of cholesterol deposition. Dietary cholesterol is absorbed, but its effects on serum cholesterol are slight. Generally, there is an increase of about 2 mg of serum cholesterol for every 100 mg ingested. Cholesterol should be viewed as a chemical necessary for life and not as a toxic substance. As with so many other aspects of life, moderation is the key.

See also **Fats; Health and Disease.**

BIBLIOGRAPHY

Gibbons, G. F., K. A. Mitropoulos, and Nick B. Myant. *Biochemistry of Cholesterol.* Amsterdam: Elsevier Biomedical Press, 1982.

Howell, Wanda H., et al. "Plasma Lipid and Lipoprotein Responses to Dietary Fat and Cholesterol: A Meta Analysis." *American Journal of Clinical Nutrition* 65 (1997): 1747–1764.

Keys, Ancel, Joseph T. Anderson, and Francisco Grande. "Serum Cholesterol Response to Changes in Diet, IV: Particular Fatty Acids in the Diet." *Metabolism* 14 (1965): 776–787.

Kritchevsky, David. *Cholesterol.* New York: Wiley, 1958.

Kritchevsky, David. "Food Lipids and Atherosclerosis." In *Food Lipids and Health,* edited by Richard E. McDonald and David B. Min. New York: M. Dekker, 1996.

Leinoneu, M. "*Chlamydia pneumoniae* and Other Risk Factors for Atherosclerosis." *Journal of Infectious Diseases* 181, Suppl. 3 (2000): S414–S416.

Myant, Nick B. *The Biology of Cholesterol and Related Steroids.* London: Heinemann Medical Books, 1981.

Myant, Nick B. *Cholesterol Metabolism, LDL, and the LDL Receptor.* San Diego, Calif.: Academic Press, Inc., 1990.

David Kritchevsky

CHOLINE, INOSITOL, AND RELATED NUTRIENTS.

Choline (2-hydroxy-*N,N,N*-trimethylethanaminium) and inositol (*cis*-1,2,3,5-trans-4,6-cyclohexanehexol) are water-soluble chemicals common in animal tissues and seeds of plants. Both compounds have been designated as water-soluble vitamins, and have also been referred to as "quasi-vitamins." Choline and inositol, while having distinctly different chemical structures, are often discussed together because they are integral components of phospholipids, some of the most important lipids in both plants and animals. Two of the most important functions of phospholipids are as structural components of cellular membranes and as second messengers, transmitting signals through cell surfaces into the cell.

Choline and the phospholipid phosphatidylcholine (PC) are typically high in foods containing relatively high amounts of fat and cholesterol such as beef liver, beef steak, and eggs. Plant-based foods follow the same generalization in that those containing relatively high levels of fat also contain relatively high levels of PC (peanuts, soybeans, and so on). All foods contain some choline or PC. "Lecithin" is a term describing the commercially available phospholipids, which can contain a variety of compounds including free fatty acids, triglycerides, and most of the phospholipids. Estimates of lecithin intake in the American population are approximately 6 g/day and an accompanying 0.6 to 1.0 g/day of choline. Adequate levels of intake are 0.125 to 0.15 g/day choline for infants, 0.2 to 0.375 g/day for children, 0.55 g/day for adult males, and 0.4 to 0.55 g/day for adult females. However, intake of choline and PC is probably decreasing in the United States because of our changing food habits. As Americans decrease intake of fats from animals, their intake of choline and PC will also decrease. Maximum daily recommended choline is 16 to 20 g/day. No maximum intake level has been identified for lecithin, but 40 g/day has been tolerated. Reactions to excessive intakes of choline include nausea, perspiring, anorexia, and cardiac arhythmias. Adults involved in strenuous exercise (such as participating in marathons) can experience significant decreases in plasma choline concentration (up to 40 percent), and there appears to be an enhancement of performance with supplemental choline intake. Commercially available sources of choline, lecithin, and PC are considered GRAS (generally recognized as safe) by the U.S. Food and Drug Administration.

Choline interacts with several drugs including anticancer drugs and nonsteroidal anti-inflammatory drugs (NSAIDs). Methotrexate is a relatively common drug in the fight against cancer and it leads to a decrease in liver choline concentrations and resulting increase in liver lipid concentrations. NSAIDs are known to facilitate changes in the gastrointestinal tract mucosal surface including perforations. Intake of PC improves such lesions.

Insufficient intake of choline can affect both acetylcholine and PC concentrations. Significant decreases in acetylcholine can result in a condition known as tardive dyskinesia (impaired movement and defective neural transmission), which can be corrected by increasing choline intake. There is also interest in choline as an aid in alleviating short-term memory loss (for example, Alzheimer's disease) and some concern that chronic inadequate intake of choline may facilitate the onset of Alzheimer's. Deficiencies of PC can result in increased lipid concentrations in liver (hepatic lipidosis), which is an analogous condition to cirrhosis of the liver caused by chronic alcoholism. If the deficiency persists, cirrhosis eventually leads to carcinoma. Choline deficiency also leads to infertility, bone abnormalities, hypertension, impaired kidney function, and decreased hematopoiesis. Similarly, deficiencies of inositol in laboratory animals leads to hepatic lipidosis and alopecia (hair loss). An inability to break down PI (Niemann-Pick disease) leads to enlarged spleen and liver, as well as mental development abnormalities.

Phospholipids are antioxidants commonly used in food products to inhibit oxidation and as emulsifying agents. Phosphatidylcholine can bind minerals such as iron and copper that are considered prooxidant minerals, or those that facilitate oxidation of lipids. Phosphatidylcholine can also help degrade hydroperoxides, or partial breakdown products of lipids and is commonly used for this purpose. The nitrogen-containing phospholipids phosphatidylethanolamine and phosphatidylserine (PI) are even more active than PC in protecting against oxidation of lipids. The two most common sources of phospholipids are soybeans and egg yolk. Lecithin from soybeans is more commonly used in commercial applications because of its lower cost. Soybean lecithin contains 50 to 70 percent phospholipid and is extracted with other prooxidants in vegetable oil processing. This process separates the oil from phospholipids, vitamin E, and other potentially beneficial nutrients. An older mechanism of lipid separation has been revived in the United States using simple pressing of soybean seeds to remove the oil instead of solvents. This results in oil with high levels of vitamin E and phospholipids. Lecithins containing higher concentrations of phospholipids and PC are also becoming available.

See also: **Antioxidants; Fats; Lipids; Minerals; Soy; Vitamins: Overview; Vitamins: Water-soluble and Fat-soluble Vitamins.**

BIBLIOGRAPHY

Berdanier, Carolyn D. *Advanced Nutrition: Micronutrients.* Boca Raton, Fla.: CRC Press, 1998.

Berdanier, Carolyn D. "Tables of Clinical Significance." In *Handbook of Nutrition and Food,* edited by Carolyn D. Berdanier. Boca Raton, Fla.: CRC Press, 2002.

Canty, David J. "Lecithin and Choline: New Roles for Old Nutrients." In *Handbook of Nutraceuticals and Functional Foods,* edited by Robert E. C. Wildman, pp. 423–443. Boca Raton, Fla.: CRC Press, 2001.

Combs, Gerald F., Jr. *The Vitamins*. New York: Academic Press, 1992.

Lampi, Anna-Maija, Afaf Kamal-Eldin, and Vieno Piironen. "Tocopherols and Tocotrienols from Oil and Cereal Grains." In *Functional Foods: Biochemical and Processing Aspects*, edited by J. Shi, G. Mazza, and M. Le Maguer. *Functional Foods: Biochemical and Processing Aspects*, vol. 2. Boca Raton, Fla.: CRC Press, 2002.

Pappas, Andreas M. "Diet and Antioxidant Status." In *Antioxidant Status, Diet, Nutrition, and Health*, edited by Andreas M. Pappas, pp. 89-106. Boca Raton, Fla.: CRC Press, 1999.

Pokorny, Jan, and Jozef Korczak. "Preparation of Natural Antioxidants." In *Antioxidants in Food: Practical Applications*, edited by Jan Pokorny, Nedyalka Yanishlieva, and Michael Gordon, pp. 311-330. Boca Raton, Fla.: CRC Press, 2001.

Rudra, Parveen K., S. D. Sudheera, James W. Nair, James W. Leitch, and Manohar L. Garg. "Omega-3 Polyunsaturated Fatty Acids and Cardiac Arrhythmias." In *Handbook of Nutraceuticals and Functional Foods*, edited by Robert E. C. Wildman. Boca Raton, Fla.: CRC Press, 2001.

Yanishlieva-Maslarova, Nedyalka V. "Inhibiting Oxidation." In *Antioxidants in Foods: Practical Applications*, edited by Jan Pokorny, Nedyalka Yanishlieva, and Michael Gordon. Boca Raton, Fla.: CRC Press, 2001.

Paul B. Brown

CHRISTIANITY.

This entry includes two subentries:
Eastern Orthodox Christianity
Western Christianity

EASTERN ORTHODOX CHRISTIANITY

Food plays an important role in the liturgical, ritual, canonical, and dogmatic life of the Eastern Orthodox Church. Throughout the ages, Orthodoxy—from the Greek *orthós* (correct) and *dóxa* (belief)—has come to encompass many nationalities throughout the world. Historically the early church was geographically separated into a Latin West (centered in Rome) and a Greek East in Constantinople (modern Istanbul). The Roman emperor Constantine, who sanctioned tolerance of Christians in 313, moved his capital to the Greek city of Byzantium (and renamed it Constantinople) in 330, and convened the first Ecumenical Council there. Although the Catholic Church and the Orthodox Church remained in communion through the Seventh Ecumenical Council, the Great Schism of 1054 is the generally accepted date for the division of the Christian churches.

The Russians, Ukrainians, and White Russians (also referred to as Belorussians or East Slavs) were proselytized by Orthodox missionaries beginning in the ninth century, and eventually adopted the liturgy, calendar, and many customs of the Greek Orthodox Church. (While the Slavic Orthodox and some "old calendarist" Greeks follow the older Julian calendar, non-Slavic Orthodox,

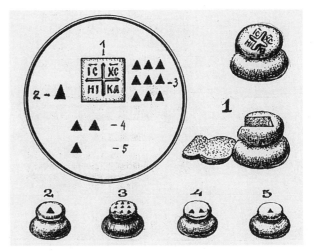

The five main *prosforo* which are consecrated during the *proscomidia* at the beginning of the Greek Orthodox communion. Shown here are the signs on the pieces that are taken from the communion loaf: 1) the *prosforo* for St. Charalambos, 2) the *prosforo* for the Virgin Mary, 3) the nine-part *prosforo* for the saints, 4) the prosfora for the living, and 5) the *prosforo* for the dead. Original drawing by Tatiana Voronina.

such as most Greeks, Syrians, Egyptians, and the Balkan nations, have followed the contemporary Gregorian calendar since the early part of the twentieth century. Dual dates are given throughout this entry.) Despite the multiethnic and multilingual composition of Orthodox Christians worldwide, Orthodoxy remains united in dogma, virtually unchanged for almost two thousand years. There is a similar unity in the role that food plays in the life of the church.

Holy Bread (*Prosforo, Antidora, Artos*)

Holy bread, or *prosforo* (from *prosfora* 'offering'), plays a central role during Communion, the most important rite of the Orthodox church. For Orthodox Christians, the *prosforo* (Russian *prosvira*) becomes the Body of Christ. Often prepared by a parishioner, the bread is is round and consists of two separate parts made from leavened wheat bread. The stamped design on the upper part of the loaf is that of a cross with the letters *IC, XC, NIKA*, which stands for "Jesus Christ Conquers," and is cut out by the priest during the preparation of the Eucharist ("thanksgiving"). The service of *artoklasia* (breaking of bread) represents a thanksgiving for God's blessings and commemorates Christ's miracle of multiplying five loaves to feed thousands. Other sacred breads include *antidora* (from *dōra*, 'gift'), which is distributed by the priest to the faithful following the Divine Liturgy, *artos, panagia*, and Easter cake (Greek, *tsoureki*).

The commandment to sacrifice bread is found in the Old Testament: "Besides the cakes, he shall offer for his offering leavened bread with the sacrifice of thanksgiving of his peace offerings" (Leviticus 7:13). In

accordance with ancient traditions, a least five *prosforo* are used during the first part of the liturgy (*proscomidia*). The wheat used to make the *prosforo* is symbolic of the human essence, which consists of the many elements of nature; the yeast represents the life-giving force of the Holy Ghost. The division of *prosforo* into two parts is symbolic of the distinction between human flesh (flour and water) and soul (yeast and Holy Water). Traditionally, the *prosforo* is prepared by pious women and widows.

It is customary for Orthodox who are named after a particular saint to celebrate their "name day." In Greece and Cyprus the celebrant provides the five *prosforo* to their church on the eve of the saint's day. The small round loaves of white bread, which are spiced with cloves and bitter orange-blossom water, are then blessed by the priest, and one of the loaves is sent to the *yortaris*, or feast giver, while the other loaves are cut into pieces and offered to the congregation and to the poor.

Antidoron (Greek) or *antidor* (Russian) is a small piece of *prosforo* that is distributed after a mass to those who did not receive communion. *Antidoron*, from the Greek *anti* (instead) and *dōron* (gift), dates to the seventh century in the Orthodox church.

Artos, the third type of sacred bread, includes an image of the cross with a crown of thorns, which is symbolic of Christ's Resurrection. A leavened bread that is consecrated by the priest on Easter, the *artos* remains on the lectern before the iconostasis during the week. Easter cake is a kind of *artos* that is consecrated on Saturday before Easter Sunday.

Bread appears in various customs of the Orthodox church. Orthodox monasteries celebrate a ceremony to the Panagia (the Virgin Mary) in which sacred bread—*prosforo* or *panagia*—is solemnly taken to a refectory after the liturgy, reminiscent of the apostolic tradition. Special breads also mark periods of Orthodox fasting. For Greek Orthodox, Lenten fasting begins on "Clean Monday," when a special flat bread called *lagana* is baked. Among Russians, Ukrainians, and White Russians there was a custom of baking an unleavened bread with the image of a cross during the fourth week of Lent.

Orthodox Feasts and Fasts

Various Orthodox feasts and fasts mark the life of Christ, the Virgin Mary, and the saints. The Orthodox Church recognizes twelve Great Feast Days, eight of which are events in the life of Christ, and four in the life of the Virgin Mary. Easter stands alone as the most important Orthodox holiday, and is celebrated on the first Sunday after the first full moon following the vernal equinox. (The date is calculated on the Julian calendar and therefore differs from that of Easter in the Western Church.) Feasts like Christmas are fixed, while others such as Easter are moveable.

Easter. Special Easter bread and boiled eggs that are dyed blood red (symbolic of Christ's crucifixion) are the most important food items for Orthodox during the Easter season. In Greece a large loaf of leavened bread is always present on the Easter table together with traditional sweet rolls (*koulouria*), sweetened bread (*tsoureki*), and little filled cheese envelopes (called *kaliitsounakia* on the island of Crete).

The tradition of presenting Easter eggs has its roots in the ancient notion of the cosmic Golden Egg. Early Christians regarded the egg as a symbol of life, and rebirth was made manifest through the Resurrection of Jesus Christ.

Following the midnight Easter service—held on Saturday night—the Greeks have the traditional *Anastasimo* meal, the first meal of the Resurrection, which consists of a special paschal soup (known in Greek as *mayeritsa*) made from the intestines and other organs of lamb. The soup is eaten in the early morning following the midnight service, along with the sweet bread called *tsorekia* (flavored with the spice *machlepi*, which is made from a ground seed from Syria), *koulourakia pascalina* (bread rolls), the *kalitsounia* (cheese pies), and a salad of greens. The red-dyed boiled eggs, which are prepared on Holy Thursday, are cracked by faithful Greek Orthodox accompanied with the words *Christos Anesti!* ("Christ is Risen!") and the reply *Alithos Anesti* ("He is truly Risen"). The Easter Sunday meals consists of spit-roasted lamb, salads, grilled offal, Easter rolls and bread, and red wine.

Greek Orthodox bread stamps, olive wood. From left to right, Bulgarian stamp for the funeral mass, eighteenth 18th century; Cypriot stamp for Holy Communion, Machairas Monastery, 2001; Greek stamp for Holy Communion, Mt. Athos, Greece, ca. 1890. ROUGHWOOD COLLECTION. PHOTO CHEW & COMPANY.

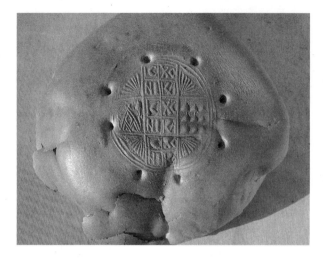

Holy bread stamped with religious symbols. Photo by Gian Berto Vanni. © Vanni Archive/CORBIS.

Russians, Ukrainians, and White Russians celebrate Easter by preparing sweet bread (Russian *kulich*; Ukrainian *paska*) and sweet curds with raisins or fruits (*pasha*) and by painting boiled eggs that have been consecrated. East Slavs dye eggs by boiling them with onion husk or fuchsine. Ukrainian Easter eggs are famous for their decorative art and symbolic designs.

Christmas and New Year. Christmas (25 December/ 7 January) is the second important festival in the Orthodox calendar. Roasted pig was an obligatory dish in the Orthodox tradition, but it has been superseded by stuffed roast turkey for Christmas Day, doubtless influenced by the customs of Western Europe. Turkeys are stuffed with a mixture of minced beef or lamb, rice, and pine nuts and served with a variety of salads and potatoes. During the Christmas season Greek cooks prepare *loukanika* (sausages) and *lountza* (smoked fillet), *hiromeri* (smoked ham), and *zalatina* (brawn). The Greeks also eat rose water–flavored shortbread and syrup-drenched honey cakes called *kourambiédes* and *melomakárona*, respectively.

A New Year tree is symbolic of the Tree of Life in Slavic Orthodox cultures, and is decorated with candles denoting the spiritual light and fruits implying the kingdom of paradise and its salutary fruits in Greece. The feast of St. Basil is celebrated on New Year's Day, and on New Year's Eve the head of the household cuts the *vasilopita* (literally "bread of the king"). The first slice is laid aside for Jesus Christ, and then everyone receives a slice; a lucky coin is traditionally hidden somewhere in the loaf. (The recipient of the coin is said to enjoy good fortune for the coming year.) This custom is repeated by town officials as an expression of the wish for good health and prosperity for the whole community. The story of the *vasilopita*, or the loaf of St. Basil (the Great; 330–379), dates to an incident in ancient Cappadocia (in central Anatolia), when the Archbishop Basil was said to have saved the church treasury from plunder by baking coins in small loaves that were then distributed to the whole congregation.

Other major feasts. The Holy Trinity (in Greek, *Aghia Triada*) is celebrated on the fiftieth day (the Pentecost) after Easter. Russians, Ukrainians, and White Russians historically decorated their houses with branches of birch tree, green grass, and flowers imitating an ancient harvest tradition. In Greece, on the Saturday before Pentecost, sweet cereal porridge, sweet bread, and other foods are consecrated in the church and then brought to cemeteries where they are distributed to the poor. There is a similar tradition among East Slavs.

Many Orthodox consecrate both grapes and wheat on the feast day of the Transfiguration (6 August/19 August) as an expression of thanksgiving. In Russia, where grapes are not cultivated everywhere, a related feast (of the "Apple Savior") sanctifies apples and other fruits and vegetables in the church.

Fasting

Fasting among Orthodox Christians has its basis in the Old Testament and has ancient roots in the Church. Orthodox insist that the body must be disciplined as well as the soul, and strict fasting in the Orthodox Church is demanding, especially when compared to the fasting known to some Western Christians. Extended and one-day fasts, which are linked to major Christian feasts, account for more than two hundred days of the year. There are four extended fasts in the Orthodox tradition, but their duration and the level of strictness vary. The Great Fast of Lent begins seven weeks before Easter; the Fast of the Apostles starts on the Monday eight days after Pentecost, and ends on 28 June (11 July), the eve of the Feast of Saints Peter and Paul; the Assumption Feast lasts from 1 to 14 August (14 to 27 August); and the Christmas Fast lasts forty days, from 15 November to 24 December (28 November to 6 January).

Each of the major fasts has associated foods and food traditions, but there is great variation in the duration, severity, and exceptions made (for example, monks and clerics versus the laity, the infirm versus the healthy, and so on.) In fact, there is great variation in the strictness of fasting among Orthodox worldwide, and dispensations, especially among the Orthodox diaspora, are common.

The last week before Lent is marked by carnival or Shrovetide, a celebration that dates from ancient times and has much in common with the cult of the deceased. In Greece the pre-Lenten period is called *Apokries* (literally "away from meat"). Devout Orthodox visit cemeteries with sweet wheat porridge (called *kolivo* in Greek) and other foods. In Russia the period before Lent is known as *Maslenitsa* (or "Cheese Week"), and during this time quantities of *bliny* (pancakes) and milk products, especially butter, are eaten in place of meat products. In Russia, on Saturdays before the feasts of St. Trinity and St.

Dimitry, as well as other days, a special sweet porridge (*kutja*), similar to the Greek *kolivo*, and made from cereals with honey, raisins, or fruits, is blessed during the liturgy. Such rituals are closely connected with the ancient beliefs of farmers that treat the souls of the deceased with grain, wine, oil, honey, and *panspermia*—a porridge made from cereals and leguminous plants.

During Lent, only vegetable-based foods are permitted: meat, fish (with backbone), dairy products, eggs, and sweets are specifically excluded from the diet. On Saturdays and Sundays dishes containing vegetable oil (except on Saturday of Holy Week) and wine are permitted. The greatest severity in fasting is reserved for Holy Week, when Orthodox around the world abstain from all animal products, oil, and wine. On Great Friday (Good Friday), in particular, devout Orthodox eat nothing in preparation for the church services.

Strict one-day fasts occur on Christmas Eve, when East Slavs consume nothing but bread and water until the conclusion of the evening mass (when they eat a special porridge called *sochivo* made with boiled wheat, barley, or rice with honey); on the eve of the Epiphany or the Twelfth-Day (5 January/18 January); on the Feast of the Beheading of St. John the Prophet (29 August/11 September); and on the Feast of the Exaltation of the Holy Cross (14 September/27 September). In addition, Orthodox faithful fast on Wednesdays and Fridays every week (with some days excepted).

Historically in Russia, peasants who grew their own crops and vegetables were better able to endure times of fasting than those in urban areas. "Black" or rye bread and pies made from the mixture of rye and wheat flour were a part of the everyday meal. A variety of cereals allowed the peasantry to prepare different kinds of nutritious porridges. Potatoes, cabbage, and carrots were cultivated in many provinces and were the main ingredients of traditional soup or *shchtee*.

In every family the customs of fasting were passed on from generation to generation, but there was notable differentiation even within one family. Elderly people were the authority in the practice of fasting and abstained more strictly. Children were trained to fast from the age of two or three years. The larger part of the population in Russia kept fasts.

During the Soviet period (1917–1991) the tradition of fasting was compromised in Russia by Communist Party doctrine that held organized religion a suspected enemy of the state. Adherents of the Orthodox faith nevertheless carried on these practices despite official intolerance.

See also **Christmas**; **Easter**; **Fasting and Abstinence**; **Feasts, Festivals, and Fasts**; **Greece and Crete**; **Religion and Food**; **Russia**.

BIBLIOGRAPHY

Alexandrov, V. A, I. V. Vlasova, and N. S. Polichshuk, eds. *Russkiye* [Russians]. Moscow: Science, 1997.

Chistov, Kyrill V., ed. *Ethnography of East Slavs*. Moscow: Science, 1987.

Kalinsky, J. A. "A Church-Folk Monthly Calendar in Russia." In *The Notes of the Imperial Russian Geographical Society*. St. Petersburg, 7 (1877).

Loucatos, D. *Religion Populaire a Cephalonie* [Popular religion in Cephalonia]. Athens, 1951.

Megas, G. *Greek Calendar Customs*. Athens, 1958.

Rouvelas, Marilyn. *A Guide to Greek Traditions and Customs in America*. Bethesda, Md.: Attica Press, 1993.

Sitas, Amaranth. *Kopiaste. The Cookbook of Traditional Cyprus Food*. Limassol, Cyprus: K.P. Kyriakou, 1995.

Tokarev, Sergej A., ed. *Kalendarnye Obychai i Obrjady v Stranah Zarubezhnoj Evropy: vesennjye prazdniki* [Calendar customs and rites in the countries of West Europe: Spring feasts]. Moscow: Science, 1977.

Tokarev, Sergej A., ed. *Kalendarnye Obychai i Obrjady v Stranah Zarubezhnoj Evropy: Istoricheskie Korni and Razvitie Obychaev* [Calendar customs and rites in the countries of West Europe: Historical roots and a development of customs]. Moscow: Science, 1983.

Voronina, Tatiana A. "Problemy Etnograficheskogo Izuchenija Russkogo Pravoslavnogo Posta" [The problems of ethnographical study of Russian Orthodox fasts]. In *Etnograficheskoye Obozrenie* (Moscow), 4 (1997): 85–95.

Voronina, Tatiana A. "Russian Orthodox Fasts and the Peculiarities of Their Practice at the End of the 19th Century." In *Studies in Folklore and Popular Religion. Papers Delivered at the Symposium Christian Folk Religion*. Edited by Ulo Valk. Tartu, Estonia, 1999. Vol. 3., pp. 73–86.

Ware, Timothy. *The Orthodox Church* (1963). Reprint. London: Penguin, 1987.

Tatiana Voronina

WESTERN CHRISTIANITY

Christianity traces its origins to the life and preaching of Jesus, a Jew living in Palestine in the first century of the Common Era (C.E.). He taught that all humans are children of God and need to repent of their sins. According to Christian sacred writings, recorded in the New Testament, he was put to death by the Roman colonial authorities but was brought back to life three days later. Christians believe that he was the son of God, and that his death and resurrection save them from sin and death.

Christianity began as a movement within Judaism but quickly spread outside the Jewish community; by the late fourth century it was the official religion of the Roman Empire. During the Middle Ages, there was theological and political conflict between the followers of the patriarch in Constantinople and the followers of the pope in Rome, leading to a split between the Western Church and the Eastern Church (also known as the Eastern Orthodox Church) in 1054. In the sixteenth century, the Western Church divided still further between Roman Catholics and a variety of Protestant groups. Although

Unlike Eastern Christianity, the Latin Church developed numerous powerful orders, each with its own dietary rules. The order known as the Teutonic Knights originated during the Crusades and became the most powerful military force in Christianity. The headquarters of the order, shown here at Malbork (former Marienburg), Poland, is one of the largest brick castles in Europe. The account books outlining the order's daily food expenses still exist and offer valuable insights into the complexities of the medieval kitchen. © PAUL ALMASY/CORBIS.

separated into hundreds of large and small groups, Christianity is now a global religion. As it has spread, it has encountered other cultures and belief systems. In the process, Western Christianity has assimilated its early practices, which were shaped by first-century Judaism, with those of its host cultures. This assimilation has influenced its food practices.

Ritual Food

One food ritual stands at the center of the religion. Christians believe that on the night before his death, Jesus gathered with a small group of followers for a meal, which, according to the Gospels of Matthew, Mark, and Luke, was a Jewish Passover dinner, but according to the Gospel of John was a *berakah* (blessing) before the Passover. Presiding over the meal, Jesus, in prayerful thanksgiving, proclaimed that the bread and wine were his body and blood; he enjoined his followers to repeat this repast in his memory.

Christians today still reenact that meal, under a variety of names. Catholics call this ritual of reenactment the Mass or Eucharist (from a Greek word meaning "thanksgiving"). Protestants call it the Eucharist, the Lord's Supper, the Last Supper, Holy Communion, or simply Communion. In early Christianity it was a real meal with a full menu, sometimes known as an *agape* (love feast). Now the ritual is celebrated as part of the worship service with only vestiges of the meal; worshipers generally eat only a small piece of bread and drink a small amount of wine or grape juice. Instead of emphasizing food, the ritual focuses on words; participants retell the story of Jesus' life and death and thank God for his salvation.

While sharing this general framework for the Eucharist, different groups of Christians carry out the ritual in different ways. In fact, many of the divisions between Christians are rooted in the different beliefs and practices regarding Communion. Throughout Christian history, believers have engaged in theological disputes as well as actual warfare over the proper celebration of the ritual.

Roman Catholics believe that the Eucharist is a sacrament, a ritual that connects them with God. For them, celebrating the Mass is a repetition of Jesus' self-sacrifice in his death; they believe that receiving Communion will help them reach salvation. In the course of the ritual, Catholics believe, the bread and wine become the body and blood of Jesus. The food attains a distinct and profound holiness. The Catholic Eucharist is very formal; the same words and gestures are used wherever it is celebrated. Specially trained and ordained priests must lead the ritual, using only wine from grapes and wheat bread. Catholic churches celebrate the Mass at every Sunday service; many congregations celebrate it daily. Episcopalians and Lutherans also believe that the Eucharist is a sacrament. Certain Episcopal churches—known as Anglo-Catholic or "High Church" parishes—are very close to the Roman Catholic Church in their beliefs and practices.

In contrast, some Protestant groups—Baptists, for instance—believe that Communion is simply a remembrance of Jesus, without any direct impact on an individual's salvation. The bread and wine remain bread and wine, serving as reminders of Jesus' death but not actually becoming his body and blood. The meal symbolizes the partakers' union with God and with each other. For these Protestants, Communion lacks the formality of the Catholic Mass, and their Communion practices can differ significantly from one place to another. In some cases, lay Protestants can lead the ritual, and it is not uncommon for some Protestant churches to administer grape juice instead of wine. Many of these groups celebrate Communion only three or four times a year. Other Protestant groups occupy a middle ground between the Catholics and the nonsacramental Protestants. They believe that Jesus is somehow present in the meal, but not that the bread and wine have become his body and blood. In their churches, Communion is a slightly more formal service, celebrated perhaps once a month; it is increasingly common in the Lutheran church for communion to be celebrated every Sunday.

Like observers of other religions, Christians also practice domestic food rituals. Many Christians, for instance, pray before meals, giving thanks to God for the food. Some churches also bless farmers' crops and animals. Particularly in the United States, many churches organize informal fellowship meals for their members, designed to strengthen the community within the church.

Taboos, Fasts, and Feasts

Since Christianity began as a movement within Judaism, many of its practices—including those involving food—are variations or adaptations of Jewish ones. Judaism has clear guidelines on proper eating behavior, including a taboo on certain "unclean" foods (pork and shellfish, for example) and rules for the preparation of other foods. In the first century C.E., Christians argued over whether they had to abide by Jewish law. There is little in Christian scripture that requires adherence to such food taboos; several texts explicitly free believers from previous laws. Nevertheless, some Christians retained the Jewish dietary laws, while others held that Jesus' teachings did away with these restrictions. Since the latter group became dominant, Western Christianity has no formal food taboos.

Some small groups do shun certain foodstuffs, based on their interpretation of Jesus' teachings. The Manicheans (members of an early Christian movement condemned as heretics by the Catholic Church), for instance, required vegetarianism. The Seventh-Day Adventists also discourage the eating of meat, while members of the Church of Jesus Christ of the Latter Day Saints (Mormons) avoid caffeine. These and several other groups also discourage the drinking of alcohol. Other than these semiofficial taboos, however, Christianity has little impact on believers' daily diets.

Christian fasting practices have changed over time. Like their Jewish brethren, early Christians fasted twice a week—but on different days. As Christianity grew, fasting became less common among most Christians; the practice was more frequent among religious elites, like monks and nuns. During the Middle Ages, particularly ascetic Christians would abstain from any food—except the Communion bread and wine—for months at a time. Most Christians, however, observed the penitential season of Lent—the forty days (not including the Sundays) before Easter, the spring festival commemorating Jesus' resurrection. Rather than fasting, most Christians would abstain from meat or some other luxury. The medieval Church also introduced a weekly fast, requiring all members to abstain from meat on Fridays, observing the day of the week on which Jesus was killed. After the sixteenth-century Reformation, newly formed Protestant groups abandoned many of the fasts, although some continued to fast during special times of prayer and penitence. Fasting is rare in modern Protestantism, although some Protestants fast as a spiritual-physical discipline. In recent decades, the Roman Catholic Church has loosened its fasting directives.

THE BOOK OF COMMON PRAYER (1979)

We celebrate the memorial of our redemption, O Father, in this sacrifice of praise and thanksgiving. Recalling his death, resurrection, and ascension, we offer you these gifts. Sanctify them by your Holy Spirit to be for your people the Body and Blood of your Son, the holy food and drink of new and unending life in him. Sanctify us also that we may faithfully receive this holy Sacrament, and serve you in unity, constancy, and peace; and at the last day bring us with all your saints into the joy of your eternal kingdom.

While early Christians adopted some of their practices from Judaism, they replaced Jewish feasts with their own set of holidays, tied to historical events in the life of Jesus. The most important ones are Christmas (December 25), marking his birth, and Easter Sunday (a movable feast that can fall from March 22 to April 25), observing his resurrection. These have become major celebrations both in the Church and in Christian societies; in many cultures, the holidays have become secularized as days for shopping and gift giving. Whether Christian or secular, food remains an important part of the holidays, often celebrated by large family meals. There are no common menus for these feasts, however; the meals are determined by the local culture rather than by the religion. In some parts of the United States, for instance, turkey is traditional fare for Christmas and ham for Easter, but other regions and other countries have their own menus.

CORINTHIANS 11:23–25

For I received from the Lord what I also handed on to you, that the Lord Jesus on the night when he was betrayed took a loaf of bread, and when he had given thanks, he broke it and said, "This is my body that is for you. Do this in remembrance of me." In the same way he took the cup also, after supper, saying, "This cup is the new covenant in my blood. Do this, as often as you drink it, in remembrance of me."

(Revised Standard Version)

Charitable Food

Like many other religions, Christianity puts a great deal of emphasis on the importance of charity. It inherited from Judaism the requirement to help feed the hungry. In the first few centuries, Christians would invite hungry strangers to join their shared meals. Certain church leaders, called deacons, were responsible for making sure that widows, orphans, and other poor people were fed. Later, monks and nuns established hospices where the hungry and travelers could stay and eat. In the middle of the twentieth century, Western Christians established agencies to help feed the hungry. They opened soup kitchens and food pantries to feed the urban poor. They also raised money to send to countries where natural disasters and poverty threatened starvation. The acquisition and distribution of food and food-related supplies for the needy continues to be among the most visible practices of modern Western Christian charity.

See also **Christianity**, *subentry on* **Eastern Orthodox Christianity**; **Fasting and Abstinence: Christianity**; **Feasts, Festivals, and Fasts**; **Fish**; **Judaism**; **Taboos**.

BIBLIOGRAPHY

Bynum, Caroline Walker. *Holy Feast and Holy Fast: The Religious Significance of Food to Medieval Women.* Berkeley: University of California Press, 1990.

Capon, Robert Farrar. *The Supper of the Lamb: A Culinary Reflection.* New York: Random House, 2002.

Juengst, Sara. *Breaking Bread: The Spiritual Significance of Food.* Louisville, Ky.: Westminster John Knox Press, 1992.

Sack, Daniel. *Whitebread Protestants: Food and Religion in American Culture.* New York: St. Martin's Press, 2000.

Tappert, Theodore G. *The Lord's Supper: Past and Present Practices.* Philadelphia: Muhlenberg Press, 1961.

Daniel Sack

CHRISTMAS. The word "Christmas" means the mass of Christ and is the name for the Christian observance of the nativity of Jesus on 25 December. In liturgical importance, Christmas was originally in fourth place, following Easter, Pentecost, and Epiphany, yet in terms of popular observance it has become the most important feast day of the year and the basis for a vast commercial retail industry derived from it, even in countries like Japan and Korea, where Christianity is not the predominant religion.

The early Christians were not initially concerned with the Nativity of Christ, and even in the fourth century C.E. it was not a universally fixed observance among Christians. The choice of 25 December is considered arbitrary and not based on evidence provided in the New Testament, the Christian text dealing with the life of Christ. Many theories have been put forward for the choice of the 25 December as Christ's Nativity, but that it fell during Roman Saturnalia is now largely dismissed. It appears to have been fixed in relation to Epiphany (6 January), counting backward twelve days (now the twelve days of Christmas) or thirteen nights by the lunar calendar. It also falls three days after the winter solstice, a date when a number of pagan gods underwent resurrection after the shortest day of the year. This includes Sol Invictus of the Roman state religion during pagan times, a cult associated with the deification of the emperor. Whatever the explanation, it is evident that the early Christian Fathers, in their struggle for political and psychological supremacy, turned the *interpretatio romana* (the process of romanizing foreign gods) on its ear by expropriating a number of pagan symbols and observances and providing them with new Christian meanings. For this reason, Christmas and especially the foods associated with it represent a fusion of diverse pagan strands varying widely in emphasis from one country to the next. The celebration of Yule in Scandinavia has become one of the most distinctive aspects of the holiday as observed in northern Europe. The tradition of St. Nicholas of Myra in the Netherlands and the Franciscan cult of the Bambino Gesu in Italy are examples of the many forms these fusions have taken. All are expressed symbolically in food.

The mass and the various mystery plays dealing with the Nativity and the ales, or community-wide feasts, were the core of the old observance. The mass was often preceded by abstinence, a period called the vigil, that was then broken at midnight with a large meal in which the entire village or community participated. Such midnight feasting was practiced in many predominantly Roman Catholic countries, such as Poland and Spain, into the twenty-first century.

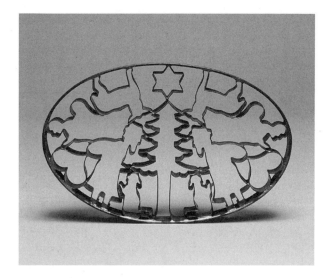

Tin cookie-cutter dating from about 1900 makes twelve cookies at once. The cookies are small and therefore could be used as Christmas tree decorations. ROUGHWOOD COLLECTION. PHOTO CHEW & COMPANY.

Outside of the church but parallel to its liturgies existed the folk customs carried over from pagan beliefs. Thus the ales exhibited a prevalence of mumming (playful imitations of old gods and their stories), antlered beings, pigs (associated with butchering, of course), and other oral traditions given the shape of festive breads and cakes or reflected in the choices of certain foods, such as roast goose, or dishes containing blood, such as blood soups, blood sausages, and black puddings, from which English plum pudding and mincemeats evolved. In the Orthodox tradition of the Eastern Church, which broke with Latin practice, Epiphany remained the official Nativity of Christ, and dishes containing blood are fully absent from the diet, festive or otherwise.

The late Middle Ages retained community feasting, although it became more centered on the manor house, a practice later continued on the plantations of the American South, while in towns it moved into the private homes of wealthy merchants and the nobility. The Protestant Reformation, with its emphasis on individual salvation, broke down the old community-wide feasts in favor of the family and home. This shift brought a widespread erasure of older village and folk customs (in England and northern Germany, for example) and the rise of the commercial Christmas. Gingerbreads, marzipans, and various festive foods hitherto made and sold by monks or by nunneries, moved into the general marketplace and become available to anyone with the financial means to purchase them. Dutch paintings from the seventeenth century often depict domestic feasts that present holiday foods in great abundance. In Protestant areas, the alms formerly associated with Christmas doles for the poor disappeared and did not return until the rise of urban missionaries in the nineteenth century.

The American Christmas, the primary theme of this article, inherited its major characteristics from England during the colonial period. Some religious groups, such as the Puritans of New England and the Quakers of Pennsylvania, abjured the observation of Christmas altogether on the theological basis that the day was fixed artificially by the early Church and therefore was not a real holiday. The Puritans originally created Thanksgiving as a substitute for Christmas. Thanksgiving subsequently became attached to the Christmas holiday, more or less marking the commercial beginning of the Christmas season.

Other American regionalisms gradually emerged into mainstream custom. The Christmas tree, with its huge array of food ornaments, first appeared among the Pennsylvania Dutch in the form of table-top branches of cherry trees (which were forced to bloom) or a large limb from an evergreen shrub, such as mountain laurel or cedar. These table-top trees were set into large flower pots and surrounded with plates of festive food. The shift to small table-top trees is well-documented by the 1790s, and their appearance in store windows is noted in a number of newspapers during the 1820s. Later, in the 1840s, the Christmas tree custom was further reinforced by Ger-

My parents dress for me,
The pretty Christmas tree.

This hand-tinted picture depicts on old type of Christmas tree set up on a table. The woman is decorating the tree with jumbles (ring cookies), gingerbread animals, marzipan cherries, and small baskets of candy. Her husband is holding a large package of toys under his arm. WOOD ENGRAVING FROM THE PICTORIAL SCRAP BOOK (PHILADELPHIA, 1860), ROUGHWOOD COLLECTION.

man immigrants, and it quickly became a symbol of status in Victorian households. While its origins are undoubtedly pagan, the tree was adopted by many churches during the Sunday School movement of the 1840s and 1850s as a means of teaching Christian values to children.

Likewise, during the revival of medieval themes led by the Oxford movement in England, St. Nicholas (called Santa Claus in America), the old gift bringer of the New York Dutch, underwent a complete rejuvenation, especially after his popularization in newspapers and magazines by the immigrant artist Thomas Nast. Thus by the beginning of the twentieth century the American Christmas had acquired a new and much less liturgical focal point, that is, Santa Claus and the exchange of gifts, including a tree under which the family displayed symbols of its economic well-being.

Throughout these evolutionary changes, the basic foods of the American Christmas remained the same, especially the format of the Christmas dinner. The dinner is based on eighteenth-century English models, and at its centerpiece is a roast, normally turkey. This centerpiece is surrounded by side dishes reflecting regional tastes and often ethnic backgrounds. Italian families may add a dish of pasta, although in households adhering to a more traditional Italian fare, the "five" fishes are served. African-American families may feature sweet potatoes and cowpeas, and Mexican-American families may incorporate a salsa and the custom of breaking a piñata, which culminates the festivities on Christmas Eve. The traditional explanation for the piñata custom is that the image symbolizes the devil, and, by breaking it, he is destroyed. The act is thus rewarded by a shower of good things to eat. However, the custom of creating a shower of plenty has numerous parallels with other pre-Christian fertility rites, most of which are associated in some manner with Christmas. The earliest recorded Christmas trees (in seventeenth-century German guildhalls) were left ornamented with food until Second Christmas (December 26) or New Year's Day, when they were shaken violently to shower the food on a mob of happy children. In other parts of Germany and central Europe, apple trees were shaken on Christmas Eve to ensure that the trees would bear a good crop of fruit.

The Christmas Day meal continues to evolve as newer immigrants add their own symbolism to the old theme or as older groups create new variations, as in the case of Kwanzaa of African Americans. Ethnic nuances aside, the basic meal focuses on roast turkey, repeats much the same meal format as Thanksgiving, and finishes with a variety of traditional desserts, including pumpkin pie, mincemeat pie, and fruit cake. It has been said that the unchanging quality of the Christmas dinner has endeared it to Americans, who find a sense of continuity in its year-to-year repetition.

See also **Christianity; Epiphany; Feasts, Festivals and Fasts; Kwanzaa; Thanksgiving.**

BIBLIOGRAPHY

Restad, Penne L. *Christmas in America.* New York: Oxford University Press, 1995.

Shoemaker, Alfred L. *Christmas in Pennsylvania.* Edited by Don Yoder. Mechanicsburg, Pa.: Stackpole, 1999.

Weaver, William Woys. *The Christmas Cook.* New York: HarperPerennial, 1990.

Weber-Kellermann, Ingeborg. *Das Weihnachtsfest* [The Feast of Christmas]. Lucerne: Bucher, 1978.

William Woys Weaver

CHRISTMAS DRINKS. Christmas is celebrated at the time of the winter solstice, and in the passage from one year to the next. The hopes and fears triggered by these two dates in the world's calendar have shaped the customs that cluster around Christmas itself, while the

joy of that festival has cast a glow over the entire season. In the course of centuries, many ingenious ways have been devised to defy the darkness, feast on the bounty of the year's harvest, and perform good-luck rituals, half in jest and half in earnest, to ensure health, happiness, and abundance in the next twelve months. Christmas calls for a tightening of social bonds, and an enlargement of social sympathies. Drink, with its power to raise spirits and relax constraints, plays an important part in the characteristic ceremonies of the holiday.

A touch of extravagance, indeed excess, matches the spirit of the season and marks many traditional Christmas drinks. France and Spain may be content with a fine champagne or the best wine available, but other countries favor more elaborate concoctions. Wassail and punch in Britain, heated mulled wine in cold northern countries, and their cooling equivalents in the warmer south have one characteristic in common. They are mixed

"Bringing in Christmas," depicts a romanticized Victorian recreation of medieval English Christmas festivities. Prominently featured is a huge bowl of wassail, itself a symbol of Christmas merriment. Wood engraving from Christmas Poems and Pictures (New York, 1866). ROUGHWOOD COLLECTION.

416

drinks, in which some combination of sugar, spice, and fruit juice has been added to the principal ingredient, whether that be ale, cider, or wine, while in certain cases the whole has been given an extra kick with a shot of brandy or bourbon, rum or gin. Eggnog, the old American favorite, starts life as a blend of eggs and cream, but this blameless nursery food is transformed into nourishment for grownups by a potent blend of sugar, spice, and spirit.

Whatever its components, the Christmas drink has ceremonial and symbolic functions. It is a pledge of goodwill to present company and absent friends. Indeed, the name of the oldest toast in Britain, "Wassail," is derived from the Middle English words for "be well." Sometimes the ritual takes the form of toast and response; sometimes the drink is shared as a loving cup passed from one person to the next so that each can share its contents in a companionable way. In local traditions throughout the Christian world, wine has been blessed at Christmas by the church, and cider has been poured on apple trees to encourage next year's harvest. The permitted breakdown of normal social barriers in this special season is played out in small, symbolic dramas. The master of a household will prepare eggnog with his own hands and offer it to his servants. Strangers may carry a wassail bowl to any door and assume the right of entry and reward.

There is nothing immutable about any Christmas tradition. At the core is always joyful celebration, but the ways in which that sentiment is expressed are infinitely variable, depending from age to age and place to place on ingredients locally at hand, and on the tastes and fashions of the time. Anything may be acceptable, as long as the message stays the same: "Merry Christmas!"

BIBLIOGRAPHY

Bickerdyke, John. *The Curiosities of Ale and Beer: An Entertaining History* (1889). London: Spring Books, 1965.

Chambers, Robert. *The Book of Days: A Miscellany of Popular Activities*. London and Edinburgh: W. & R. Chambers, 1864. See entries on "Punch" and "Wassail."

Edwards, Gillian. *Hogmanay and Tiffany: The Names of Feasts and Fasts*. London: Geoffrey Bles,1970.

Gayre, G. R. *Wassail! In Mazers of Mead: The Intriguing History of the Beverage of Kings*. London: Phillimore and Company, 1948.

Irving, Washington. *Old Christmas: From the Sketchbook of Washington Irving*. London: Macmillan, 1876.

Levy, Paul. *The Feast of Christmas*. London: Kyle Cathie,1992.

Miles, Clement A. *Christmas Customs and Tradition*. New York: Dover Publications, 1976. Originally published in 1912.

Nissenbaum, Stephen. *The Battle for Christmas*. New York: Vintage, 1997.

Pimlott, J. A. R. *The Englishman's Christmas: A Social History*. Hassocks, Sussex, UK: Harvester Press, 1978.

Bridget Ann Henisch

CHUTNEY. Chutney is a term applied to a variety of spicy relishes and condiments in Indian cookery. The term itself is an anglicized form of the Hindi word *chatni*. In India, there is an implied understanding that these preparations are also freshly made from fresh ingredients. For example, chutneys using nutmeg are prepared only when nutmeg is in season, although chutneys can be composed of a wide variety of ingredients and thus represent many types of flavors and textures. In general, chutneys fall into two distinct categories: freshly-made preparations for immediate consumption, and cooked preparations intended to keep as long as a year, which can be grouped further according to their saltiness, sweetness, sourness, or spiciness. Many recipes combine several elements of these basic flavors, and textures range from coarsely chopped preserves to smooth sauces. Conceptually, they blur the neat distinction made in Western cooking between preserves and pickles.

Some of the most common chutneys in India are those made with mangoes, coconut, sesame, peanuts, or the ground leaves of herbs, especially mint or coriander. Chutneys are served as condiments (side dishes) at Indian meals, and historically were only eaten on special occasions such as weddings or by the rich. Since Indian independence from Great Britain in 1947, the technology of canning in glass jars has now made commercial chutneys widely available throughout the country at affordable prices. Traditional cooked chutneys made for home consumption were generally infused or slowly cooked in the hot Indian sun over a period of several days until they attained the right flavor and consistency. This method is still employed in modern India in homes which do not own stoves. In fact, many cookbooks written for Indians make no mention of stoves. For example, in Aroona Reejhsinghani's *Indian Pickles and Chutneys* (1977), a Keralan region chutney made from jackfruit (a relative of the breadfruit) specifies solar cooking for one week.

Indian cookbooks devoted to chutneys generally arrange the recipes according to region, since chutney styles are strikingly different in various parts of the country and among different religious groups. The various flavors and textures are of special importance to Hindus. A few of these are worth mentioning: mango, plum, apple, and apricot chutneys, and various murabbas (fruit in thick syrup) from West Bengal; garlic, sweet and sour mango, and peanut chutney from Uttar Pradesh; dry fish, shrimp, and onion chutney from Kerala; pork sepotel and shrimp ballachong from Goa; kanji, tomato and jeera chutney from Punjab; tamarind chutney from Haryana; hot mango chutney, guramba, and panchamrit from Maharashtra; chundo and hot lime chutneys from Gujarat; guava and eggplant chutneys from Himachal Pradesh; Nagaland fish chutney; and the various Jain, Parsee, and Sindhi chutneys defined by religious dietary rules. In fact, the murabbas (also written morabbas) evolved out of the Unani system of medicine and owe their origin to Indian contact with the Arab world.

Made mostly from salted limes and garlic, Lucknow chutney (or Lucknow sauce) was a popular condiment in nineteenth-century England and America. It was commonly served at hotels and appears on many menus from the period. The chutney was sold in fancy ceramic jars like the one shown here dating from about 1876. COLLECTION OF THOMAS NEFF.

The first Indian chutneys to reach the West appeared as luxury imports in England and France during the late 1600s. They were mostly mango chutneys put up in sticky syrups and shipped in ceramic pots. These luxury goods soon served as models for Western copies which appeared in cookbooks as "mangoed" fruit or vegetables. The most popular substitutes were unripe peaches or melons. However, by the nineteenth century, many chutneys were manufactured in India specifically for export to Europe, among them Lucknow Chutney (a purée of salted limes), and various brand-name chutneys like Major Grey's or Bengal Club. All of these export products were created from recipes appealing to British rather than to Indian tastes, meaning that they were generally sweet and lacked the intense flavors, saltiness, or peppery heat preferred by Indians.

See also **Condiments; Herbs and Spices; India**.

BIBLIOGRAPHY

Achaya, K. T. *Indian Food: A Historical Companion.* Dehli: Oxford University Press, 1994.

Achaya, K. T. *A Historical Dictionary of Indian Food.* Dehli: Oxford University Press, 1998.

Brennan, Jennifer. *Curries and Bugles: A Memoir and a Cookbook of the British Raj.* New York: HarperCollins, 1990.

Cost, Bruce. *Ginger East to West.* Berkeley, Calif.: Aris, 1984.

Reejhsinghani, Aroona. *Indian Pickles and Chutneys.* Dehli: Orient, 1977.

Steel, F. A., and G. Gardiner. *The Complete Indian Housekeeper and Cook.* Bombay: Bombay Education Society Press, 1893.

Veerasawmy, E. P. *Indian Dishes for English Tables.* London: Chapman & Hall, 1902.

William Woys Weaver

CIVILIZATION AND FOOD. If by "civilization" we mean the culture of cities, assumed to have emerged with the Bronze Age, in about 3000 B.C.E., then food was the decisive factor in terms of both production and consumption. Before this time, in the farming revolution of the New Stone (Neolithic) Age, crops and animals that have continued until today to provide much of human food had been domesticated. This represented a shift from hunting and gathering, from the collection of wild plants and animals, to food raised under the control of humans, leading to a great increase in the population. The bulk of cultivated foods (cereals) came from the domestication of local grasses, hitherto gathered in their wild state; root crops and vegetables proved more of a problem to grow, and fruit cultivation appeared only later on.

The Bronze Age saw another formidable move forward. The strength of animals was harnessed to wheeled transport and to the plow. Complex irrigation systems were developed. A further great increase in food production thus became possible. The animal-drawn plow enabled an individual to cultivate considerably larger areas of land; wheeled transport meant that the surplus could be shifted more easily; and irrigation in the sun-drenched lands of the Near East, India, and China again brought about increased yields, especially of rice but also of the other main Neolithic cultigens, wheat and barley. A parallel change took place in Mexico, centering on maize (corn).

These various changes led to increased production and therefore to population expansion, but they also led to socioeconomic differentiation. With hoe (manual) agriculture and a plentiful supply of land, it had hardly been profitable or indeed possible to employ others to work, except under conditions of slavery.

Landholding before the Bronze Age had been relatively egalitarian, as had food production. Most households had a roughly similar supply of food, as indeed had been the case with earlier hunter-gatherer regimes, in which the sharing of food was institutionalized to a high degree. With the plow, that equality disappeared rapidly.

One man could cultivate a much larger area than another; the acquisition of additional land became a way of maintaining a higher standard of living, not only paying agriculturalists to perform work but also using the surplus to exchange with local specialists, or to obtain luxury goods from traders. Those luxuries included culinary delicacies imported from elsewhere, particularly those that could withstand travel, such as cheese from the Massif Central of France brought to Rome, or sugared foods carried from India to China, or wine and olive oil shipped throughout the Mediterranean.

What has been called the urban revolution of the Bronze Age, giving rise to civilization in the form of cities, enabled societies to use their food surpluses to support full-time specialists; this meant the development of activities that included trading, metalworking, and writing. Trade and transport opened up distant and different food supplies and resources; metalworking and the use of ovens made possible new modes of food preparation, such as the baking of bread; and writing led to the elaboration and transmission of more complex recipes, and eventually to the emergence of a differentiated—even a high—cuisine, the latter occurring in China, in India, in the Arab and Muslim world, and later, with the Renaissance, in Italy and France. But hierarchical differences in diet aside, greater agricultural productivity meant that a society could supply a larger number of people, a proportion of whom could be engaged in activities not connected with the production of essential foodstuffs. Among other things, town dwellers required the large-scale transport of food, to markets as well as restaurants and other eating places outside the house. It was China with its vast cities that first experienced the rise of a restaurant culture, as well as the emergence of prepared foods, such as tofu (bean curd), sold in the marketplace.

Food and Class

Initially such developments affected only the rich and high-status groups. For this change in food production meant an increase not only in population but also in differentiation between owners of large estates, peasants cultivating their own fields, and the newly emergent stratum of landless laborers. A similar degree of socioeconomic stratification emerged in urban areas. These "classes" were now marked not only by differences in amounts consumed, as had long existed in the under hoe cultures, but also by qualitative differences in styles of life, with largely in-marrying subcultures, conserving their particular practices. The rich had access to dishes and drinks unavailable to the poor, either because of their lack of economic power or because of sumptuary legislation (or indeed of internalized preference or "taste"). Such differences were elaborated on and conserved in cookbooks originally compiled for the households of nobles and rich merchants and taken up more widely only with the coming of the printing press and the flowering of the urban middle classes in the sixteenth and seventeenth centuries.

This process of democratization was the result of the industrialization of prepared foods that could be said to have effectively begun with the invention of bottling by Nicolas Appert in France (1806) and its subsequent expansion into canning, especially in America during and after the Civil War, which altered the whole economy of food, interposing the grocer and later the supermarket between the producer and the consumer. Not only the industrialization of food preparation was involved but advances in food production itself, with changes in farm practice. For example, the rotation of crops and the use of manure had been adopted early on in the medieval period. The nineteenth century saw not only mechanization but also the coming of artificial fertilizers and chemical sprays and the more rapid transformation of crops by seed selection and finally by manipulation of the genes of crops, and above all the shift from the use of animal energy (which began with the plow) to that derived from mineral (fossil fuel) sources. Water of course had long been significant for food production, especially in arid regions. Its early control gave rise to extensive irrigation schemes with their heightened productivity (and problems of distribution, dangers of salinization and soil exhaustion), and later on it could be harnessed to provide the power for mills to grind grain and, much more recently, for other manufacturing processes, including the generation of electricity as a new source of power. But the basic activities of cultivation, such as plowing, were not affected by the use of waterpower nor yet by that of coal, which transformed other forms of production, leading up to the First Industrial Revolution. Farming was radically changed only with the advent of the use of gasoline in the combustion engine, during the Second Industrial Revolution, and the introduction of tractors and then of combine harvesters, inventions that affected the whole use of manpower on the land, freeing labor (and sometimes creating unemployment) as well as transforming villages from productive communities to ones dominated numerically by commuters, pensioners, and holiday makers. If by "democratization" we refer not only to political arrangements but also to the diffusion of products to the mass of the people, the transformation of small luxury into larger consumer cultures, then these changes in the production of food were as important as the changes in manufacturing and employment with which they were associated.

The Modern World

Despite enormous recent increases in world population, levels of food consumption per capita have risen rather than fallen in most regions. Owing to the Green Revolution and the adoption of "improved" plant varieties, with improved water control and fertilizing, famine has become less frequent in India and China. That is not true, however, of Africa, where total food production has decreased in relation to population growth and to consumption, mainly because the production of food is still based on the hoe; the plow (together with animal traction and elaborate water control) crossed the Sahara only recently, and its use remains scattered. Regional food deficits are largely made up through trade and aid, allowing imports of food from the surpluses of the more productive regions of the world (especially North America). The overall increase in well-being has been substantial, at all levels of society, with better health for most inhabitants—albeit with obesity and other food-related ills for some. Such productivity increases have always depended on the deliberate modification of crops, but recently the capacity to increase production by chemical means (such as adding hormones to beef), and to manipulate genes directly, has given rise to fears about the effects on human health and on our relationship to the natural world. People have always been concerned about their intake of food, fearing poison, sorcery, adulteration, and other modes of interference that might compromise their physical or mental health. That is nothing new, but these fears have grown with our capacity to intervene—that is, with the growth of civilization.

See also **Agriculture, Origins of; Agriculture since the Industrial Revolution; American Indians; Anthropology and Food; Australian Aborigines; Horticulture; Hunting and Gathering; Inuit; Maize; Packaging and Canning; Paleonutrition, Methods of; Prehistoric Societies.**

BIBLIOGRAPHY

Chang, K. C., ed. *Food in Chinese Culture: Anthropological and Historical Perspectives.* New Haven, Conn.: Yale University Press, 1977.

Cohen, Mark Nathan. *The Food Crisis in Prehistory: Overpopulation and the Origins of Agriculture.* New Haven, Conn.: Yale University Press, 1977.

Flandrin, Jean-Louis, and Massimo Montanari, eds. *Histoire de l'alimentation.* Paris, 1996. In English as *Food: A Culinary History from Antiquity to the Present,* edited by Albert Sonnenfeld, translated by Clarissa Botsford. New York: Columbia University Press, 1999.

Goody, Jack. *Cooking, Cuisine, and Class: A Study in Comparative Sociology.* Cambridge: Cambridge University Press, 1982.

Mintz, Sidney W. *Sweetness and Power: The Place of Sugar in Modern History.* New York: Penguin, 1985.

Prakash, Om. *Food and Drinks in Ancient India.* Delhi: Munshi Ram Manohar Lal, 1961.

Renfrew, Jane M. *Paleoethnobotany: The Prehistoric Food Plants of the Near East and Europe.* New York: Columbia University Press, 1973.

Tannahill, Reay. *Food in History.* London: Eyre Methuen, 1973.

Jack Goody

CLASS, SOCIAL. Social class or social stratification is defined by unequal access to desirable resources (such as money, goods, and services) or personal gratification (such as prestige or respect). The sociologist Max Weber argued that social class was a function of differential wealth, political power, and status. The various dimensions of social class have different influences on food consumption and its consequences. Income and wealth provide access to food or constrain food purchases. Education provides knowledge, skills, and beliefs that shape food desires and place constraints on food choices by means of information acquisition and food preparation. Occupation not only represents prestige but also structures time and constrains the attention that can be given to food. Occupation-generated work hours and lifestyle choices affect what is eaten as well as where and with whom food is eaten.

Distinctions are made between classes. The lower class (often referred to as "working class" or blue-collar workers) is generally associated with people with low levels of education, unskilled or semiskilled occupations, and low income. Middle-class people (often seen as "white-collar" workers) generally have more education, usually having graduated from high school or college, hold technical or mid-level managerial positions, and earn average to above average incomes. Upper-class people tend to have high education, the highest salaries, and the most prestigious occupational positions.

The whole notion of taste, as refined food sensibilities, is class-based. Members of lower classes often strive to emulate the taste and taste practices of higher classes, who in turn attempt to change their notions of taste and eating behavior to maintain the distinction between themselves and those perceived as of lower status. Thus, what, where, and when food is eaten is shaped by social class in many societies. Historically, members of the lower class have found many of the foods of the wealthy to be strange if not disgusting. (Such stereotyping, however, applies equally to both groups: while the so-called lower classes might find raw oysters disgusting, the middle or upper classes might find roast goat equally unpalatable. These kinds of tastes—or distastes—evolve over time and cultures and are not fixed.) Members of higher classes have come to identify certain foods with impoverished status. For instance, after World War II, chicken became associated with low income and was eschewed by the wealthy because of this association. Currently whole-wheat or brown bread tends to be consumed more by people of middle- or upper-class background; by contrast, bread prepared with processed wheat (white bread), which is less expensive, is more often the choice of working-class consumers. The reason for this difference is a historical reversal of fortune. The white flour was once that of the elites, who would even color it with alum. The highly refined flour was reserved for those with great status, whereas the whole-grain flours were those of the poor. Beer is the alcoholic beverage of the working class—the exception being pricey imported beers, microbrews, and gourmet beers that are popular with "yuppies"—while wine, particularly wines with a lin-

An American postcard from circa 1900 taking a humorous aim at upper-class table manners. ROUGH-WOOD COLLECTION.

eage, tend to be the choice of individuals of upper-middle and upper-class backgrounds.

Restaurants were once a place where only the upper class would dine, while today persons of all classes eat in restaurants. However, the choice of type of restaurant and the frequency of eating meals out varies by social class. Part of this difference is a function of income. Those with higher salaries or greater wealth can afford to eat out more frequently and to visit more expensive restaurants. Use of restaurants, however, is also a function of attitudes, which themselves vary by social class. Those in blue-collar positions are more likely than those in white-collar jobs to perceive eating out—in restaurants, that is, not fast-food establishments—as something that is done for pleasure. Those with higher incomes, university degrees, and white-collar positions seek more variety in restaurant fare. Interest in eating a variety of ethnic foods, an indication of cultural cosmopolitanism, is also more frequent among those with greater education, income, and occupational prestige.

The desire to imitate those of higher social class background is practiced by some individuals, and restaurants play a role in this phenomenon. Restaurants with expensive dishes with a cosmopolitan atmosphere are sometimes the choice of people who wish to exhibit the consumption of the upper class. At the same time, differences in consumption represent a routine form of social dominance exercised by upper-middle and upper-class members. Thus, efforts of the lower-middle class to imitate upper-class behavior are met by changing behavior among the upper class. New, more exclusive restau-rants are often sought in attempts to maintain a class distinction in restaurant patronage.

Class background is also associated with the use of meals as a form of entertaining friends. As income and education rise, so does the likelihood of entertaining friends by feeding them a main meal. Those with white-collar positions are more likely to entertain friends by having them over for a main meal, though this generalization may apply more to urbanites; poor folk in the country often have big dinners, where everyone brings something potluck-style. Low-income families not only lack the money to provide such entertainment but may also inhabit housing that lacks the space to feed many people at one time. Among the very low-income, space may be so limited that the family itself cannot sit down to a meal together. Eating in the homes of kin is not a function of class, but eating with friends and coworkers is: professional and managerial classes are more likely to eat in the homes of friends than those in working-class occupations. When it comes to cooking, those with more education and income are more likely to be willing to experiment with new dishes or dishes of their own creation than are those with less income and education.

Social class background makes a difference in the food-related lifestyles practiced by many people. In addition, people's life chances are affected by their social class. The poor tend to devote high percentages of their household budgets, after paying rent, to food, yet generally have to settle for lower-quality food items and a more monotonous diet. Obesity is far more likely among persons of low income than persons in higher income groups. In more economically developed countries, the poor are more likely to experience food insecurity or food insufficiency, and in less economically developed countries, the poor are more likely to experience various nutrient deficiency diseases.

See also **Cost of Food; Fast Food; Food Pantries; Food Politics: United States; Food Stamps; Food Supply, Food Shortages; Hunger Strikes; Malnutrition; Obesity; Places of Consumption; Poverty; Restaurants; School Meals; Sociology; Soup Kitchens; WIC (Women, Infants, and Children's) Program.**

BIBLIOGRAPHY

Bourdieu, Pierre. *Distinction: A Social Critique of the Judgement of Taste.* Translated by Richard Nice. Cambridge, Mass.: Harvard University Press, 1984.

Calnan, M. "Food and Health: A Comparison of Beliefs and Practices in Middle-Class and Working Class Households." In *Readings in Medical Sociology*, edited by S. Cunningham-Barley and N. P. McKegany, pp. 9–36. New York: Tavistock/Routledge, 1990.

Charles, N., and N. Kerr. *Women, Food, and Families.* Manchester, U.K.: Manchester University Press, 1988.

DeVault, M. J. *Feeding the Family: The Social Organization of Caring as Gendered Work.* Chicago: University of Chicago Press, 1991.

Dubois, L., and M. Girard. "Social Position and Nutrition: A Gradient Relationship in Canada and the USA." *European Journal of Clinical Nutrition* 55 (2001): 366–373.

Erickson, Bonnie H. "What Is Good Taste For?" *Canadian Review of Sociology and Anthropology* 28 (1991): 255–278.

McIntosh, William A. *Sociologies of Food and Nutrition.* New York: Plenum, 1996.

Sobal, J. "Obesity and Socioeconomic Status: A Framework for Examining Relationships between Physical and Social Variables." *Medical Anthropology* 13, no. 3 (1991): 231–247.

Warde, A., and L. Martens. *Eating Out: Social Differentiation, Consumption, and Pleasure.* New York: Cambridge University Press, 2000.

Wm. Alex McIntosh
Jeffery Sobal

CLIMATE AND FOOD. Throughout most of prehistory, humans acquired food by hunting, fishing, gathering, foraging, or scavenging. The animals and plants they consumed were native to the local climate and environment and provided highly variable diets. Arctic and subarctic populations fished, gathered shellfish, and hunted land and sea mammals; temperate forest populations gathered seasonal plants and hunted wildlife; prairie and savanna dwellers hunted and trapped large mammals; and tropical forest dwellers fished, gathered a variety of plant foods, and hunted small mammals. Climatic influences on the flora and fauna included in the local diet were rainfall, temperature, seasonality, and longer-term

cooling and warming trends. The most extreme climate changes were the Pleistocene glacial advances and retreats in the northern hemisphere. Climatic variation in temperature and precipitation became central to food procurement when plants and animals were first domesticated about ten thousand years ago at the end of the Pleistocene epoch.

There are only a few small populations that subsist entirely on hunting and gathering of wild plants and animals, although many populations continue to supplement their diets with wild foods. An exception to this is the fish and shellfish that provide substantial amounts of food to people through commercial fishing. Nevertheless, most peoples around the globe consume domestic plants and animals that are grown or raised locally or are produced commercially.

Climate and World Biomes

Climate (general, longer-term) and weather (specific, short-term) tend to structure ecosystems around the world by regulating rates of plant photosynthesis and production and contributing to patterns of vegetation and animal life. The principal factors are temperature, which is largely a function of global latitude and elevation; precipitation, drainage, and stored fresh water resources; windflow, which can dry or chill; solar radiation; and seasonal patterns in all of these, particularly temperature and rainfall. Polar and subpolar ecosystems, which are unsuitable for agriculture, are characterized by cold winters, cool summers, and limited precipitation. Some livestock are kept in polar and mountain ecosystems: llama and alpaca in the Andes, yak in the Himalayas, reindeer in the Arctic. Temperate and subtropical zone ecosystems may have relatively high precipitation, marked seasonality in temperature, and agricultural growing seasons up to six months. Drier temperate continental ecosystems (prairies, steppes) are also highly seasonal in rainfall with cold winters. Relatively dry, temperate zones can be highly productive with the practice of irrigation. Mediterranean ecosystems (including California, Chile, and parts of the Near East) have cool, wet winters and hot, dry summers. Many of the major cereal crops of the world were domesticated in these seasonally dry, temperate, or Mediterranean ecosystems: maize or corn in Middle America, wheat and barley in the Near East, rice in Asia, and sorghum in Africa. Quinoa, a member of the goosefoot family, was domesticated in the cool, seasonally dry reaches of the Andes. Tropical ecosystems have warm temperatures throughout the year but often with seasonality of rainfall. Those ecosystems with limited and seasonal rainfall grade into tropical grazing lands or savanna, while increased rainfall yields forests from sparse woodlands up to densely wooded rainforests. Widespread rainforest agriculture today includes a form of shifting, swidden, or slash-and-burn cultivation. Within each of these broadly-defined ecosystems or biomes, there is consid-

422

erable variation: variation by season and by year, with inherent risks to livestock and agricultural production. For example, dramatic heat waves or cold periods, droughts, floods, hailstorms, and hurricanes can destroy crops and domestic livestock, producing a loss in food security and even famine. These extreme events have a major impact when they occur in heavily populated areas.

World Biomes and Food Production

Plants and animals were first domesticated in the seasonally dry Mediterranean climate of the Fertile Crescent in the Near East. These farming and livestock practices then spread along the Eurasian east-west axis zone of similar latitude and climate. Most domestic seed plants (e.g., cereals, goosefoots) and pulses (e.g., beans, lentils, grams, peas) were temperate-zone domesticates, whereas some tubers and root crops were domesticated in the tropics (e.g., manioc, yams, taro). With the discovery of the New World by Europeans, many native American foods spread to parts of the Old World: the potato became a staple in temperate zones of Europe and the Himalayas; maize became a staple in the drier African tropics; manioc became a staple in the wetter African tropics. Other New World temperate-zone domesticates, such as chocolate, peanuts, and tomatoes, became favored foods around the globe.

Today, temperate and subtropical agroclimatic zones of the United States, Argentina, Europe, and eastern Asia (China and Japan) still have the highest productivity of domestic grains and livestock that feed a substantial portion of the world. This results from a favorable combination of sophisticated agrotechnology and climate. Figure 1 illustrates how climatic inputs interact with the flows of information and resources in a Western industrialized system of agriculture.

Temperate and subarctic marine biomes are highly productive sources of fish and shellfish, although these food resources are in decline because of effective commercial exploitation by Western nations.

Food Intake and Climate

Some patterns of food intake are indirectly or directly linked to climate. For example, tropical populations are often limited in protein intake. Solomon Katz (1987) noted that this occurs in traditional agricultural populations dependent on grains (maize, rice, sorghum, millet) or tubers (potato, manioc) that are high in calories, but relatively lower in protein. Among tropical forest dwellers, as in the Amazon and the Congo basins, protein must come from fish, insects, some game animals, and plant foods. A direct effect of climate is the high metabolic need for calories in arctic or subarctic zones and temperate zone winters because of increased energy needs for temperature regulation in the cold. Derek Roberts (1978) documented that arctic dwellers have an elevated basal metabolic rate (BMR), which may be adaptive in the cold. Infants who are kept under cool condi-

tions have higher food calorie requirements for normal weight gain than infants kept under warmer conditions. In Western industrialized nations, reduced activity levels during the winter season lead to unhealthy increases in the accumulation of human body fat (and weight) or energy storage. On the other hand, the accumulation of body fat in Ama women who dive for edible seaweed throughout the year allows them to withstand the cold water off the shores of Korea and Japan.

Climate Change and Food Production

An alarming trend that is certain to influence human patterns of food intake is recent climate change. Some variation in weather and climate is normal. Yet within the past 250 years, however, increased atmospheric carbon dioxide (CO_2), resulting from fossil fuel combustion, deforestation, and agricultural activities, has led to a "greenhouse" effect and global warming. A major compilation of research by Houghton and other scientists from the Intergovernmental Panel on Climate Change (IPCC) in 2001 has demonstrated beyond any reasonable doubt that human activities have produced a 1.1°F (0.6°C) rise in average global temperature over the past 150 years (see Figure 2). And by the year 2100, this global temperature is expected to rise another 1.8 to 6.3°F (1.0 to 3.5°C), a change that is greater than any experienced on the globe within the past ten thousand years.

Global warming will have variable effects on local weather and climate that are dependent on latitude, elevation, and geographic location. For example, McCarthy and others (2001) have shown that sea level rise from melting glaciers during the twentieth century has been about 6 inches (15 cm), and a projected rise during the twenty-first century is an additional 18.9 inches (48 cm). This will contribute to a loss of coastal agricultural lands and an increased salinization of water and coastal lands. Influences on agricultural food production are likely to be pronounced. Higher temperatures will cause rises in rainfall and the likelihood of floods in some areas and declines in rainfall and consequent drought in other areas: extremes in weather events (floods, hurricanes, heat waves, droughts) will be more common. Both conditions will lead to crop losses and decreased plant productivity. There will be increased heat stress in livestock leading to lower milk and meat production. At the same time that coastal agricultural and grazing land will be lost to sea level rise and salinization, the human population will continue to increase, putting greater pressure on food resources.

It is estimated that the impacts of global warming will be greatest in those regions of the world such as Asia, Africa, Latin America, and the Pacific Islands, where the adaptive capacity is low and vulnerability is high because of the lack of economic resources. Africa is likely to be especially hard hit because such a large part of its land resources is arid or semi-arid savanna lands. Of the total desertification and degradation around the globe, nearly

30 percent is in Africa. Although the debate continues on whether overgrazing, overpopulation, or warming trends are the cause of desertification, nevertheless, global warming will certainly increase the expanse of dry lands on this continent and elsewhere.

Humans have a remarkable capacity to adapt to change, including climate change, through culture and technology. Global warming and its consequent negative effects on our capacity to produce food will be an unprecedented challenge to this adaptability.

See also **Agriculture, Origins of; Biodiversity; Food, Future of; Hunting and Gathering; Maize; Potato; Prehistoric Societies; Swidden.**

BIBLIOGRAPHY

Houghton, J. T., et al., eds. *Climate Change 2001: The Scientific Basis*. Contribution of Working Group I to the Third Assessment Report of the Intergovernmental Panel on Climate Change. Cambridge, U.K.: Cambridge University Press, 2001.

Katz, Solomon H. "Food and Biocultural Evolution: A Model for the Investigation of Modern Nutritional Problems." In *Nutritional Anthropology*, edited by Francis E. Johnston. New York: Alan R. Liss, 1987.

McCarthy, J. J., et al., eds. *Climate Change 2001: Impacts, Adaptation, and Vulnerability*. Contribution of Working Group II to the Third Assessment Report of the Intergovernmental Panel on Climate Change. Cambridge, U.K.: Cambridge University Press, 2001.

National Research Council. *Climate and Food: Climatic Fluctuation and U.S. Agricultural Production: A Report on Climate and Weather Fluctuations and Agricultural Production*. Board on Agriculture and Renewable Resources, Commission on Natural Resources, National Research Council. Washington, D.C., National Academy of Sciences, 1976.

Roberts, Derek F. *Climate and Human Variability*. 2nd ed. Menlo Park, Calif.: Cummings, 1978.

Michael A. Little

COCKTAIL PARTY. The cocktail party is a social gathering, held early in the evening, usually for a period of about two hours, typically from 5:00 to 7:00 P.M. or 6:00 to 8:00 P.M. It may take place in the home, in a food-service setting such as the private room of a restaurant or hotel, or in a business such as an art gallery or bookstore. Cocktails, wine, and soft drinks are served, though contemporary cocktail parties may in fact offer wine and soft drinks exclusively and skip the cocktails. In any case, beverages are accompanied by finger foods, which are meant to delight the palate, stave off hunger until dinnertime, and complement the cocktails.

Depending on variables such as the host's budget and degree of formality desired, the cocktail party may be catered or prepared at home, drinks may be mixed and served by a bartender, or the host may act as bartender.

Servers may be employed to pass around hors d'oeuvres or the host may simply pass them around or arrange them on a buffet.

Certain physical and social behaviors on the part of the guests characterize cocktail parties. Normally, guests are not seated, but remain standing. Drinks in hand, they mill about, socializing to the strains of music, typically an instrumental arrangement, solo piano, or vocal jazz, played at a volume that encourages conversation. Rather than allowing participants to engage in deep and lengthy discourse, the social aim of the cocktail party is for guests to participate in small talk. At purely social cocktail parties, friends catch up or become reacquainted; new friends are introduced. At business-related cocktail parties, new contacts are made, business cards exchanged, and connections renewed.

History of the Cocktail Party

The cocktail party is a modern invention, conceived in the 1920s. Before World War I, most home entertaining was quite formal: people hosted teas, dinners, and balls. After 1918 informal entertaining became much more accepted.

In 1920 when the Eighteenth Amendment put Prohibition into effect, public consumption of liquor was driven underground into the speakeasy, and brought for the first time into the home. Before that, Americans may have served wine at dinner, but the consumption of hard liquor was generally confined to the tavern; and women, for the most part, did not drink alcohol at all. Speakeasies, in an attempt to compete for business, created fanciful cocktails, heretofore unknown in the United States, and even welcomed women. Those Americans who made their own spirits at home ("bathtub gin") adapted these new cocktail recipes for home use. A boom in the manufacture and sales of bar accessories ensued, including cocktail glasses and shakers.

For the power players in the business world, the drinks are secondary to the networking and the sealing of deals. Even with lawyers present, everyone always smiles. © PAUL BURTON/CORBIS.

A simultaneous explosion in the importation of fancy canned foods, such as olives, anchovies, and smoked oysters, encouraged people to serve hors d'oeuvres incorporating these comestibles along with their cocktails. Friends came to call before dinner, as was the habit, and the cocktail party was born. When Prohibition was repealed in 1933, American zeal for the cocktail party only increased, encouraged by idealized depictions of cocktail parties in motion pictures.

With the post–World War II economic boom, cocktail parties became institutionalized as an appealing way to entertain friends at home. In addition, it became a form of business entertaining brought into the home. The man of the house (typically the sole wage-earner) would invite his employer and his wife, along with friends, coworkers, and other acquaintances; the woman of the house would act as hostess. Women wore "cocktail dresses," the knee-length sleeveless sheaths that are still in fashion.

The popularity of the cocktail party waned in the 1960s, with the rise of the counterculture. It began to see a renaissance in the mid-1980s, though at that time it was taken out of the home. Cocktail parties became popular forums for celebrating art gallery openings, book publications, product launches, and other commercial ventures. The 1990s saw a resurgence of cocktail parties given in the home, fueled partly by young adults who found the kitsch value of cocktail culture appealing.

Although the cocktail party is a purely American institution, it has been exported around the world, adopted by many other cultures. In France, for instance, the cocktail party is known as *le cocktail*.

Food and Drink

Hors d'oeuvres may be hot or cold, passed around, or placed on tables. Traditionally, cocktail party foods have tended toward the salty and fatty, encouraging the consumption of cocktails. At contemporary cocktail parties, traditional hors d'oeuvres from other cultures frequently appear—from Caribbean cod fritters to sushi. So do ingredients and techniques from other cultures used in new ways—for instance, tuna tartare canapés or mini-pizzas. Hors d'oeuvres tend to be more or less elaborate depending on whether the party is given at a business or a home, and whether they are prepared at home or catered.

Traditional cold hors d'oeuvres include boiled shrimp with cocktail sauce, smoked salmon, caviar, and olive canapés. Cold hors d'oeuvres incorporating vegetables, such as endive leaves filled with herbed goat cheese, have become popular.

Meatballs, *rumaki* (skewered chicken livers wrapped in bacon), shrimp toast, and hors d'oeuvres made with puff pastry are traditional hot cocktail party hors d'oeuvres, but today anything from Italian rice dumplings to mini "burgers" made of seared foie gras might be served. Skewered, grilled foods have become popular, including Thai satés.

The less powerful gather in the office over Chablis and potato chips to discuss résumés, rumors of downsizing, dysfunctional elevators, and the cost of MBAs. PHOTO BY RICHARD RADSTONE. © RNT PRODUCTIONS/CORBIS.

Classically, the beverages served were cocktails in the strict sense of the word, that is to say a spirit combined with bitters (or a bitter element such as vermouth), and perhaps sugar and/or water (sometimes in the form of ice). Examples of this would be martinis, Manhattans, Old-Fashioneds, Rob Roys, and champagne cocktails. Contemporary cocktail party beverages would be cocktails, especially cosmopolitans and martinis, liquor served straight-up or on the rocks, wine, champagne, and sparkling mineral water. Beer is generally avoided.

In the 1920s little single-subject recipe books began to appear, featuring recipes for cocktails and/or finger foods, many, but not all of them, published by liquor companies. These books grew in popularity with the cocktail party itself, culminating in a large number of titles published in the 1950s. Their publication died down until the mid-1980s, when a few titles appeared; by the mid-1990s they had reemerged as a significant subgenre of cookbooks.

See also **Cocktails; Fads in Food; Spirits; Symbol, Food as; Table Talk; Whiskey (Whisky).**

BIBLIOGRAPHY.

Brenner, Leslie. *The Art of the Cocktail Party*. New York: Plume, 1994.

Editors of Esquire. *Esquire's Handbook for Hosts*. New York: Grosset & Dunlap, 1949.

Grimes, William. *Straight Up or on the Rocks: A Cultural History of American Drink*. New York: Simon & Schuster, 1993.

Leslie Brenner

COCKTAILS. Ever since America invented the cocktail, at the beginning of the nineteenth century, it has evolved: from sweet to dry; hot to icy; stirred to

BLUE BLAZER.

Bartender making a Blue Blazer, a drink which has since given its name to a man's jacket. Wood engraving from Jerry Thomas, *Bartender's Guide* (New York, 1862). ROUGHWOOD COLLECTION.

shaken—a morning eye-opener to a conclusion to the day's activities.

Originally the name of a few specific drinks, the word "cocktail" soon became the generic name for almost any mixed drink. No one knows exactly why drinks came to be called cocktails, but there are many theories. In taverns, a cock is a tap; the dregs from the tap were called its tail, so some say the name signified the last dregs of a tavern tap. Others tell of a beautiful Revolutionary era barmaid who decorated drinks with cock's feathers and called them cocktails. The word might have originated with a medicinal chicken soup–like drink the English made from a cock boiled with ale, sack (wine from the Canary Islands), dates, and raisins. Thought to cure consumption, it was called cock-water or cock-ale. Another possibility is that since people generally started their day with a drink, the cocktail was named after the cock's wake-up call. Breakfast drinking was common, even among children, for centuries in Europe and continued in America from colonial times until the early mid-nineteenth century when the temperance movement gained strength. Beer soup was especially popular.

The most prosaic, and likely, theory is based on the fact that mixed, or nonthoroughbred, horses were called cocktails because their tails were clipped and stuck up like roosters' tails. Over time, the word "cocktail" came to stand for any mixture: mixed drinks, food mixtures such as fruit cocktails, and pharmaceutical combinations.

The first known definition of a cocktail appeared in an 1806 Hudson, New York, publication called the *Balance and Columbian Repository*. It defined a cocktail as "a stimulating liquor, composed of spirits of any kind, sugar, water, and bitters." By the late twentieth century, a typical dictionary definition changed the meaning of the word to "any of various short mixed drinks, consisting typically of gin, whiskey, rum, vodka or brandy, with different admixtures, as vermouth, fruit juices or flavorings, sometimes sweetened."

The definition changed because drinks changed. A late-nineteenth-century martini was made with equal parts gin and sweet vermouth, plus sugar syrup and orange bitters. A late-twentieth-century martini was made with vodka, not gin, and a few drops of dry, not sweet, vermouth, and no bitters and sugar syrup.

The First Mixed Drinks

Originally, spirits were taken for medicinal purposes. Called *aqua vitae*, or the water of life, they were thought to improve health and promote longevity. Monks and apothecaries made potions from spirits mixed with herbs, spices, and fruits. They prescribed them for the pox and the plague, and even rubbed them on stiff joints. By the seventeenth century, Europeans were drinking the concoctions for pleasure as well as for pain relief.

When settlers came to North America, they brought a taste for spirited drinks with them. They made punch with rum, tea, sugar, water, and lemon juice. They drank flips made with beer, rum, molasses or sugar, and eggs or cream, all mixed together and heated with a red-hot poker. Possets combined hot milk and spirits. Slings were made of gin or other spirits, water, sugar, and lemon and served either hot or cold.

In 1862 preeminent bartender Jerry Thomas published *How to Mix Drinks, or The Bon-Vivant's Companion*, America's first mixed drink primer. Thomas wrote, "The 'Cocktail' is a modern invention, and is generally used on fishing and other sporting parties, although some *patients* [author's italics] insist that it is good in the morning as a tonic." He called just nine of his two hundred–plus recipes "cocktails," but within a few years the term became ubiquitous.

The Party Begins

The Gilded Age was the golden era of the cocktail. At the turn of the twentieth century, affluent Americans frequented elegant hotels, bars, and restaurants; champagne cocktails were among their favorite drinks.

Talented bartenders knew how to make hundreds of cocktails—from the Adonis to the Zaza—and came up with new ones at will. They created and named drinks for regular patrons, news events, cities, and celebrities, and mixed them with great flair. Jerry Thomas was famous for his "Blue Blazer," a mixture of whiskey and boiling water, which he set ablaze and tossed back and forth between two silver-plated mugs. He said it looked like a "stream of liquid fire."

Cocktail shakers were invented in the late 1860s, and since ice was more available than it had been previously, the proper way to ice a drink became important. Drink manuals specified that some drinks be shaken, others mixed in a glass and stirred with a fork rather than a spoon.

In London, hotels and restaurants opened American bars and served American cocktails. They even hired American bartenders, especially after Prohibition went into effect in the United States in 1920.

America's party did not end with Prohibition—in fact, some might argue that drinking intensified during this era, with drunkenness becoming more commonplace—but it did go underground, and the cocktail

A DRINK BY ANY OTHER NAME

The names of cocktails are often as inventive as the recipes. Here are a few intriguing examples.

- Cocktails named for animals: Bird, Chanticleer, Goat's Delight, Hop Frog, Hop Toad, Grasshopper, Prairie Hen, Mississippi Mule, Rattlesnake, Sherry Chicken, Yellow Parrot.
- Cocktails named for people: Bobby Burns, Charlie Lindbergh, Gene Tunney, Jack Kearns, Mamie Taylor, Mary Pickford, Phoebe Snow, Rhett Butler Slush, Rob Roy, Rudolph Nureyev, Tom and Jerry, Tom Collins, Will Rogers.
- Cocktails named for places: Big Apple, Brazil, Bronx, Brooklyn, Champs Elysées, Chicago, Cuba Libre, Fifth Avenue, Havana, Hawaiian, Manhattan, Martha's Vineyard, Richmond, Ward Eight.
- Cocktails named for occupations: Bishop, Chorus Lady, Commodore, Crook, Diplomat, Doctor G., Grenadier, Huntsman, Judge, Journalist, Kentucky Colonel, Merry Widow, President, Presidente Seco.
- Old school cocktails: Annapolis Fizz, Columbia, Cornell, Eton Blazer, Harvard, Old Etonian, Oxford Grad, Princeton, Yale.
- Royal cocktails: Count Stroganoff, Duchess, Duke, King Cole, Prince Edward, Prince's Smile, Queen, Queen Charlotte, Queen Elizabeth.
- Cocktail contradictions: Church Parade, Presbyterian, Prohibition, Puritan, Reform.

changed. Bartenders disguised the harsh taste of bootleg liquor by adding cream to drinks. Gin became the spirit of choice because it was easy to make faux gin by mixing juniper oil into alcohol. It was more difficult to replicate the taste of whiskey. Many people opted to drink in the privacy of their own homes, and cocktail sets—tray, shaker, and glasses—became popular wedding presents.

After Prohibition, which was repealed in 1933, most of the creamy cocktails disappeared, and trendsetters began ordering their martinis dry. However, in the 1933 "Repeal Edition" of the *Cocktail Book*, a dry martini was two-thirds gin, one-third French vermouth, and two dashes of bitters.

Just the Basics

During World War II, the cocktail repertoire shrank. People turned to basic drinks such as highballs, martinis, and Manhattans. In the 1950s Americans frequented cocktail lounges, threw cocktail parties, and women wore cocktail dresses. They ate bite-sized cocktail snacks and carried on brief, snappy cocktail-party conversations. Bartenders were not expected to know how to make hundreds of drinks, but they were expected to make ever-drier martinis.

Vodka, so little known in America that it was once sold as "white whiskey," began its rise in popularity. Gradually, it took the place of gin in the standard martini and eventually became the best-selling spirit in America.

During the late 1960s and early 1970s, trendy young people drank white wine or smoked marijuana instead of drinking spirits. Cocktails were for old folks. Sales of brown liquors, such as whiskey, plummeted. However, cocktails began showing signs of life during the 1980s. The martini became hip again, and bartenders created dozens of variations on the theme. At the beginning of the twenty-first century, new cocktails—cosmopolitans, chocolate martinis, black icebergs—signal the beginning of yet another era in the evolution of the cocktail.

See also **Cocktail Party; Fads in Food; Spirits; Symbol, Food as; Table Talk; Whiskey (Whisky).**

BIBLIOGRAPHY

Barr, Andrew. *Drink: A Social History of America.* New York: Carroll and Graf, 1999.

Brown, John Hull. *Early American Beverages.* Rutland, Vt.: Tuttle, 1966.

Craddock, Harry. *The Savoy Cocktail Book.* London: Constable, 1933.

Crockett, Albert Stevens. *Old Waldorf Bar Days.* New York: Aventine Press, 1931.

Dias Blue, Anthony. *The Complete Book of Mixed Drinks.* New York: HarperCollins, 1993.

Edmunds, Lowell. *Martini Straight Up: The Classic American Cocktail.* Baltimore and London: The Johns Hopkins University Press, 1998.

Forbes, R. J. *Short History of the Art of Distillation: from the Beginnings Up to the Death of Cellier Blumenthal.* Leiden, Holland: Brill, 1948.

Glasse, Hannah. *The Art of Cookery Made Plain and Easy.* Connecticut: Archon Books, 1971. Reprint of 1796 edition.

Grimes, William. *Straight Up or on the Rocks: A Cultural History of American Drink.* New York: Simon and Schuster, 1993.

Lanza, Joseph. *The Cocktail: The Influence of Spirits on the American Psyche.* New York: St. Martin's Press, 1995.

Lender, Mark Edward, and James Kirby Martin. *Drinking in America: A History.* New York: Free Press; London: Macmillan, 1987.

Mariani, John F. *The Dictionary of American Food and Drink.* New York: Ticknor and Fields, 1983.

Markham, Gervase. *The English Housewife,* edited by Michael R. Best. Kingston and Montreal: McGill-Queen's University Press, 1986. Reprint of the 1615 edition.

Mr. Boston Official Bartender's Guide. New York: Warner Books, 1988.

Paget, R. L. *The Cocktail Book: A Sideboard Manual for Gentlemen.* Boston: Page, 1913.

Paget, R. L. *The Cocktail Book: A Sideboard Manual for Gentlemen.* Repeal edition. Boston: Page, 1933.

Quinzio, Jeri. "In Favor of Flavor." *The Massachusetts Beverage Price Journal* (August 1995): 4–8.

Quinzio, Jeri. "Toasting Vodka's Success." *The Massachusetts Beverage Price Journal* (August 1996): 7–8.

Thomas, Jerry. *How to Mix Drinks, or The Bon-Vivant's Companion.* New York: Dick and Fitzgerald, 1862.

Trader Vic. *Bartender's Guide.* New York: Halcyon House, 1948.

Wilson, C. Anne. *Food and Drink in Britain: From the Stone Age to the Nineteenth Century.* Chicago, Ill.: Academy Chicago, 1991.

Jeri Quinzio

CODEX ALIMENTARIUS. Codex Alimentarius is a small global agency that establishes international standards for substances potentially harmful to human health and the environment—that is, food additives, chemicals, pesticides, and contaminants. Created jointly in 1963 by the World Health Organization (WHO), responsible for food safety and public health, and the Food and Agriculture Organization (FAO), responsible for food production, Codex is located in FAO headquarters in Rome. FAO is the dominant partner, contributes more than two-thirds of the cost of the organization, supervises the staff, and generally sets an agenda favorable to concerns of industrial agriculture.

Some 170 developed and developing countries are members of Codex. Their representatives meet as the Codex Commission every two years, alternately in Rome and Geneva, Switzerland (where WHO is headquartered), to review the status of standards being developed in some three dozen Codex committees, and to adopt or return standards recommended by those committees. Each committee is chaired by a nation that agrees to pay the committee's administrative and operational costs, an arrangement that makes a virtue out of the necessity of a small Codex budget. Not surprisingly, all major committees are headed by developed nations, with some countries chairing more than one committee. Codex members may self-select membership in committees, the choices being determined by national interest in specific standard issues and limited by national budgets for travel and staff. All substantive work on standards is done in Codex committees. The commission elects an executive committee and a chairperson every two years to supervise the work of a secretariat staff and to coordinate the work of the committees. Codex operates under consensus rules (that is, votes are rarely taken), a practice that avoids the impression that standards are based on political maneuvering for votes rather than on scientific research. Codex has voted on standards only six times in its forty-year history, and only once prior to 1994. In each of those events, the tally was so close as to lead observers to conclude that no consensus exists on global standards. Codex has a small administrative staff of six people, does no research, and relies instead on the scientific capabilities of its member countries and on the advice of international scientific bodies.

Codex was established to provide a reliable standard-setting process to assist developing countries lacking the infrastructure to create domestic safeguards for food safety and health. Codex standards also offer developing countries the assurance of a floor for health and environmental standards on which to build export markets, primarily to developed countries. A recent study estimated that, on average, each developing country would need to spend $150 million to achieve the internal capability of providing food safety and environmental standards. However, less than a fifth of developing-country members of Codex allocate staff or financial resources to participate regularly in Codex committees or in the development of a strategic Codex plan to accelerate adoption of standards. The Codex Executive Committee proposed a $98 million fund to assist developing countries to comply with the accelerated adoption procedures, with the understanding that developed countries would pay for the fund, which would become available after 2003 if the Codex Commission were to approve the fast-tracking of standards and developed countries contribute the funds.

Until 1994, Codex provided standards that were global floors that countries could apply domestically to protect consumer health and the environment. Countries could set and enforce standards higher than those recommended by Codex. After 1994, with the creation of the World Trade Organization (WTO), Codex standards were transformed into global ceilings limiting the ability of individual nations to employ standards for health and environmental protection that exceed Codex levels. Countries may adopt higher domestic standards than those approved by Codex, but those standards are considered a trade violation when challenged in the WTO, where the measures for trade-rule violations are Codex standards. No country can be forced to drop more precautionary standards, but failure to do so will result in economic penalties being imposed by the WTO. However, neither the WTO nor other global agencies penalize countries that adopt standards less protective than those that Codex provides.

See also **Additives; FAO (Food and Agriculture Organization); Food Safety; Food Supply and the Global Food Market; Food Supply, Food Shortages; Food Trade Associations; International Agencies; Pesticides.**

Rodney E. Leonard

COFFEE.

Coffee refers to both a plant and to the hot and cold beverages made from the pit or "bean" of its fruit. Coffee contains significant amounts (between 0.8 percent and 2.5 percent) of the stimulant alkaloid caffeine (trimethylxanthine) as well as protein and carbohydrates. The coffee shrub or bush grows as two species, *Coffea arabica* and *C. canephora*, and is indigenous to Africa, specifically to the Kaffa region of Ethiopia. The word "coffee" is derived from the Turkish word *kahveh*, which is rooted in the Arabic word *kahwah*, meaning wine, this indicating the use of the beverage as a replacement for alcoholic beverages that are forbidden under strict Muslim religious law.

The coffee plant is an evergreen with elliptical, dark shiny green leaves that yields a red husked berry containing a seed pit or "bean." Coffee belongs to the Rubiaceae family and, depending on which of two species from which it is harvested, propagates differently. *Coffea arabica* is grown principally in Southeast Asia, Latin America, and the Caribbean. *Coffea canephora* (also known as *Coffea robusta*) is grown in Africa (mostly in the Congo), India, and Vietnam, which is its leading producer. The *arabica* is self-pollinating, while the *canephora* or *robusta* needs cross-pollination to fruit. After planting, the shrub requires four to five years of growth before it will fruit. When harvested, the ripe red husk is removed from the berry, and the fresh seed can be planted to generate seedlings or dried for planting at a later time. (It is this seed that is the coffee bean as it is commonly understood.)

Processing the beans requires two steps. In the first step, usually in the country of origin, the husk of the berry is left to ferment and soften, which facilitates the extraction of the seed or bean. The beans are then dried and shipped "green" or unroasted to a destination where they are roasted either for local consumption or for packaging and transshipping to other markets. The roasting process has a substantial effect on the color and flavor of the bean and the beverage it will produce. The darker the roast, the stronger the flavor. It is also the roasting process that eliminates water, making the bean more brittle and easier to grind.

Coffea arabica produces the "Arabica," also known as "Brazilian," varieties, which are often preferred for their balanced aroma and rich flavor. The best, rarest, and most sought after *arabica* types are harvested in Indonesia, Jamaica, Hawaii, and Colombia, where they are grown on small production farms at a relatively slow and steady growth rate, developing flavorful berries. (In this way they may be said to parallel wine production.) *Coffea canephora*, or *robusta*, tends to be strong and bitter. Because *Coffea canephora* can resist frost and disease and can sustain warmer climates and lower elevations, it experiences faster growth patterns and higher fruit yields. This generally results in beans that contain more caffeine than *arabica* types but that lack subtlety and flavor. The *canephora* bean is said by experts to be neutral by comparison to *arabica*.

TABLE 1

TOTAL COFFEE PRODUCTION By the top 15 producing countries Crop years 1999/00 to 2001/02 (in thousands of bags)					TOTAL EXPORTS OF ALL FORMS OF COFFEE The top 15 producing countries Calendar years 1999 to 2001 (in thousands of bags)			
Crop year commencing		1999	2000	2001	Calendar year	1999	2000	2001
Brazil	(A/R)	32,345	32,204	33,549	Brazil	23,139	18,016	23,172
Vietnam	(R)	11,648	14,775	12,600	Vietnam	7,742	11,619	13,946
Colombia	(A)	9,398	10,532	11,500	Colombia	9,996	9,175	9,944
Indonesia	(R/A)	5,432	6,733	6,446	Indonesia	5,065	5,194	4,992
Mexico	(A)	6,442	5,125	5,500	Cote d'Ivoire	2,406	6,110	4,174
India	(A/R)	5,457	4,611	5,293	Guatemala	4,681	4,852	4,110
Côte d'Ivoire	(R)	6,321	4,587	4,100	India	3,613	4,441	3,769
Ethiopia	(A)	3,505	2,768	3,917	Mexico	4,358	5,304	3,408
Guatemala	(A/R)	5,201	4,700	3,900	Uganda	3,841	2,513	3,060
Uganda	(R/A)	3,097	3,205	3,250	Peru	2,407	2,362	2,663
Peru	(A)	2,663	2,596	2,747	Honduras	1,987	2,879	2,392
Costa Rica	(A)	2,404	2,246	2,364	Costa Rica	2,195	1,964	2,018
Honduras	(A)	2,985	2,667	2,300	El Salvador	1,890	2,536	1,533
El Salvador	(A)	2,835	1,717	1,630	Ethiopia	1,818	1,982	1,376
Cameroon	(R/A)	1370	1,113	1,500	Nicaragua	984	1,345	1,365
All other producers	13,935	13,043	12,742		All other producers	9,302	8,708	8,313

(A) Arabica producer
(R) Robusta producer
(A/R) Produces both types. Predominantly Arabica
(R/A) Produces both types. Predominantly Robusta

SOURCE: International Coffee Organization

It is believed that the earliest producers of coffee, the Ethiopians, did not brew coffee as it is recognized in the twenty-first century from the roasted beans but made drinks from the bitter berries, combined the roasted beans with butter or animal fat (most likely that of mutton), or chewed roasted beans as a mild stimulant. Numerous tales on the subject of coffee and its discovery exist. One of the most persistent is of a ninth-century Ethiopian goat herder intrigued by his intoxicated, hyperactive flock. Having grown curious, he sampled berries his goats had been eating and felt similarly stimulated.

No extensive or significant use of the coffee crop has developed among Ethiopia's indigenous peoples, and it became an exotic crop for them, exported first to Yemen, then to other Arab nations. It is noteworthy that coffee production did not develop in Africa until the twentieth century and that consumption there is minor. (The berries are sometimes used to enhance teas, which are generally preferred as beverages there.)

A primitive approach to making the coffee beverage may have originated at the beginning of the eleventh century in Ethiopia, however, this was likely learned through Arab traders who ground roasted beans into a fine powder and stirred it into hot water. Most scholars believe the antecedents of modern brewed coffee drinks were developed in the late fourteenth or early fifteenth centuries in Yemen and accredit the processing of the beans—

roasting, grinding, and ultimately brewing the pungent hot drink—to a sheik of the Sufi order. Irrespective of the drink's origins, wild coffee plants may have been cultivated as early as the sixth century, but it was not until the fifteenth century that the coffee bush, *Coffea arabica*, is believed to have been domesticated, developed as an agricultural product, and spread throughout Muslim nations from Southwest Asia to Southeast Asia, including the Indonesian archipelago.

When first brought into widespread use, coffee was usually taken as a dark, bitter drink. Sugar was rarely used in the Arabian beverage, perhaps for fear that it would overstimulate the mind. The spice cardamom was often added to the brew for a naturally sweet flavor, and perhaps to counterbalance or mediate its bitter essence. Cardamom-flavored coffee is most commonly associated with the beverage known as Turkish coffee, as is the eleventh-century approach to boiling the grounds as a brewing technique. (Sugar is often added in this version as well.)

Historically coffee was the subject of frequent controversy and confusion, and its rise—much like tea—parallels the development of international trade and economic interdependencies. Coffee was perceived, for example, early in its development to have medicinal benefits, including as a curative for mange, sore eyes, dropsy, and gout. However, it was also feared that, when mixed with milk, coffee caused leprosy. Coffee was often at the center of political turmoil, especially through the development of coffeehouses in the Ottoman Empire and throughout Europe, where people could congregate and discuss ideas in an atmosphere conducive to (literally) stimulated conversation. Coffeehouses were associated with the plotting of insurrection in the Ottoman Empire and of both the American and French Revolutions, for example.

Coffee is one of the most common delivery systems for drugs in the world. Its caffeine stimulates the brain, improving one's focus. It is also a diuretic, washing out the kidneys. When taken in large quantities, the stimulant causes irregular heartbeat, uncontrollable shaking, and dehydration. Despite—or because of—these characteristics, by the beginning of the sixteenth century coffee drinking was widespread in the Middle East. Its powerful physical effects, however, were such that some Muslim scholars interpreted it as being contradictory to the spirit of the Koran and tried to forbid it. Others opposed its banishment and ironically included the beverage in religious worship. (Records of the period indicate that coffee was drunk inside the Sacred Mosque in Mecca, in present-day Saudi Arabia.) Early accounts exist of coffee drinking, ostensibly for the purpose of staying awake to pray and chant, during the evenings of the one-month fasting of Ramadan.

Coffee is also associated with superstitions and rituals. For example, not unlike tea leaf reading by Chinese fortune tellers, Turkish fortune tellers use the finished cup of coffee—which contains both liquid and grounds—turning it onto the saucer until cool. The cup is then turned back up, and any coffee grounds remaining in the cup are "read" as a basis for predicting the future.

From roughly the fifteenth century to the eighteenth century, coffee trade was monopolized by the Yemenis. The English and the Dutch traded with the Arabs at the major trading port of Mocha in Yemen for nearly half a century before they found a way to break the Arab monopoly. Ultimately Dutch smugglers stole beans from Mocha, carrying them to colonial Java in Indonesia for propagation. Through the Dutch act of pilferage, Indonesian coffee plantations came to produce an *arabica* bean popularly known as "Java." (Eventually this bean was described by connoisseurs as among the finest *arabica* available.) The Dutch also sent beans back to Amsterdam for propagation in greenhouses. In short order coffee propagation and drinking spread rapidly throughout the Western Hemisphere and the European colonies. In an act of repilferage, for example, the French king Louis XIV engineered the theft of plants from Amsterdam, and these plants eventually were responsible for the development of coffee plantations in French colonial Martinique. In 1723 the coffee business was born of a coffee bush originating in Martinique and eventually engendered a New World coffee industry that by the twentieth century was responsible for 90 percent of coffee production internationally.

The coffeehouse became a symbol of the Beat generation during the 1950s and early 1960s. The Gaslight Coffeehouse in New York's Greenwich Village was once a well-known setting for various bohemian movements. This 1959 photo shows poet Dick Woods sitting over coffee with Eddy Slaton. © BETTMANN/CORBIS.

The early to mid-seventeenth century saw the rapid spread of coffee consumption throughout Europe, especially northern Europe, resulting in a significant demand. The possibility of financial fortunes along with the possibilities of lucrative taxes and perceived medical benefits made for both free market and government-encouraged spread of cultivation in tropical and subtropical climes across the globe.

Cultivation spread throughout Southeast Asia, the Caribbean, Latin America, Africa, and Brazil. The first Brazilian coffee bush was planted in 1727, for example, and it was cultivated by slave labor. While the crop experienced a somewhat slow beginning there, by the end of the nineteenth century Brazil's coffee-growing industry was profitable. By the early twenty-first century Brazil was the world's largest coffee exporting nation with Vietnam running second.

Coffee and its patterns of consumption were historically linked to politics as well as perceived curative and stimulant benefits. Originally coffee was enjoyed almost exclusively in coffeehouses, which were founded as specialty shops for the purpose of selling coffee by enticing traders to try the new beverage. The first coffeehouse (or café) opened in Constantinople in 1555, and within a few years the city counted hundreds of such establishments. In rapid turn the coffeehouse became a place for socializing. Paralleling the social patterns of teahouses in China, coffeehouses became meeting places for casual conversation and business and political discussions, including revolutionary

In the Arab world, the coffee break is much more than a pause in the day's schedule; it is a period of intense conversation and male socialization. These men are talking business over their cup of coffee in the Gulf Hotel at Manama, Bahrain. © ADAM WOOLFITT/CORBIS.

strategies. The empire's rulers quickly became concerned with the popularity of such places, where discontented commoners and intellectuals alike could gather and political uprising could be discussed. (Restaurants either did not exist or were forbidden.) Ottoman coffeehouse proprietors were subject to harsh punishments, including being sewn in a bag and thrown in the Bosporus.

Political mechanisms proved inadequate to stem rising enthusiasm for coffee and coffeehouses, however. Great profit centers, coffeehouses were often built in extravagant styles, imparting a social caché to the beverage. Spread by war and commerce, coffeehouses opened in European capitals throughout the early to late seventeenth century, increasing the beverage's popularity and supporting demand.

While coffee was a sort of luxury beverage at first, by the eighteenth century even less-fortunate Europeans could enjoy it (or some adulterated version of it) through sales by street hawkers. Innkeepers also made it part of their family-style menus, and some food historians link the introduction of coffee to creating the sequencing of a meal. In the mid– to late eighteenth century North American colonials drank coffee increasingly as a sort of protest against high British taxes on tea. Free to trade after independence (1776), Americans imported coffee initially from Haiti and Martinique, then Portugal and Brazil. By the mid-nineteenth century Americans

consumed an average of over six pounds per capita annually. To a large extent the commercialization, mechanization, marketing, and democratization of coffee in North America evolved the beverage in modern times. The nineteenth century also saw the introduction of the drink in various styles, including Italian espresso (a concentrated one-ounce liquid), cappuccino (a "long" espresso with frothed milk), French *café au lait* or Spanish *café con leche* (strong coffee with plenty of hot milk), or iced coffee with or without milk. Other popular combinations are Irish coffee, which includes whiskey and Baileys Irish Cream, and Vietnamese or Thai coffees, in which sweet condensed milk is added.

Coffee can be "pure," using either the *arabica* or *robusta* bean, or it can be a blend of the two. One of the oldest blends simply combines various proportions of *robusta* and *arabica* beans, making the resulting item either more smooth or more bitter. Some of the more innovative blends include hazelnut and vanilla flavorings, these tied to the late twentieth-century, principally American interest in "gourmet" coffees. While for hundreds of years coffee consumers in Europe purchased a brewed cup of the beverage for quick consumption, in the United States green beans generally were sold in bulk for home roasting. This shift from public coffeehouse to domestic brewing had a profound effect on the industry and psychology of coffee consumption. The American development essentially stripped coffee of its political import, making it a modern commodity.

In other North American developments, at the end of the American Civil War, San Francisco's Folger's Coffee company gave customers a choice, offering both traditional green coffee beans and the more efficient and time-saving roasted beans. A new industry was born, and the tendency toward efficiency and rapid brewing was exacerbated. The Maxwell House company soon followed in Folger's footsteps, and in 1901 the first Maxwell House "instant" coffee came to market. This instant coffee was made by extracting water from brewed coffee and freeze-drying the remains. Other innovations followed. Decaffeinated coffee, which has significantly reduced amounts of caffeine, was made by steaming unroasted beans or by using a solvent, usually chlorine, to remove the caffeine. Because this process also removes some of the flavor from the beans, the stronger *robusta* variety is usually employed for decaffeinated coffees.

While coffee was added to a pot of water and boiled to produce the earliest versions of the beverage, Arab producers eventually filtered the brew through herbs to hold back the sediment. In eighteenth-century France, coffee was filtered through muslin bags, an innovative but ultimately inadequate process. The expatriate American inventor Benjamin Thompson—also known as Count Rumford—developed the broadly successful metal "drip pot," and a number of other inventors developed variations on coffee-brewing devices, many of which have remained in use in the twenty-first century. In 1819, for example, the percolator was invented in which hot water rises through a tube and into an upper container and infuses coffee. The early twentieth century saw the advent of true coffee filtering devices, particularly through the development of paper filters by the German Melitta Bentz Company in 1908.

The espresso machine (from Italian *caffè espresso*, literally, "pressed-out coffee") is usually associated with Italy, but it was pioneered in the early nineteenth century in German and French machines that used steam to push steam through coffee grounds. The modern espresso machine, patented in Italy in early-twentieth-century Italy, was developed by Desidero Pavoni (who bought the rights to the espresso machine patent in 1905), and was dramatically improved in Italy after World War II. The hiss of the espresso machine was a common sound in the Italian caffés of San Francisco's North Beach and in New York City's Greenwich Village decades before espresso and cappuccino became fashionable around the 1980s.

The difference in machines and grounds is important in the outcome of any coffee brew. For example, the espresso machine uses twice the amount of coffee as a percolator, a much finer ground of coffee, and much less water (actually steam), resulting in a dark, strong, bitter extraction. Different grinds exist for different styles of brewing. Coarse grounds are used to make filtered cof-

Like tea, coffee evolved its own distinctive implements in the form of differently shaped cups, serving pots, and table accoutrements. This "Dragon Coffee Service" manufactured by the Komilov Brothers factory in St. Petersburg, Russia, between 1840 and 1860, transforms the traditional Russian tea service into a porcelain fantasy. © THE STATE RUSSIAN MUSEUM/CORBIS.

fee, fine grounds are used to make Italian espresso, and even finer grounds resembling the consistency of flour are used to make boiled Turkish coffee.

Harvested, roasted, traded worldwide, and consumed by people from different walks of life, coffee has created significant social crossroads for centuries. Once a luxurious beverage, coffee is enjoyed internationally by a diverse populace. Most often a morning beverage, its popularity has soared as both an afternoon and an after-dinner beverage. Variations abound. Aside from flavored and decaffeinated coffees, bottled coffees, coffee sodas, and other drinks are available.

Embracing this trend, and operating over 5,500 stores internationally (over four thousand in the United States alone), Starbucks is the leading coffeehouse chain of the twenty-first century. It sells coffees with multiple options (would you like a slice of banana nut loaf with your iced, decaf mocha java?) at the elevated average price of $3.50 per cup in a lounge setting, and has pastries (and sometimes, sandwiches) available for purchase. This creates a comfortable atmosphere for conversation and reading, without any pressure to make a purchase and leave. Thus, since the early 1990s Starbucks has created a coffeehouse culture for the masses. With its appeal extending from corporate executives to students and housewives, it has brought the former aristocratic atmosphere into the mainstream. In this way it typifies the late-twentieth-, early-twenty-first-century "mass-class" and "leisure-time entertainment" marketing strategies. The success of Starbucks is also bolstered by its ability to extend the brand by selling T-shirts, travel mugs, and other coffee-related accessories in its stores. Starbucks also sells coffee beans and ice cream.

Coffee is not only a modern beverage but also an ingredient in desserts, including coffee ice creams, coffee gelati, and coffee-flavored cakes. Variations include the American "chimney sweep" recipe, in which vanilla ice cream is topped with powdered coffee and drizzled with a shot of whiskey. Italian tiramisu has lady fingers soaked in espresso coffee and set in a whipped mascarpone cream. In addition, an American classic dish called "Black-eyed steak" employs coffee to deglaze a cast-iron pan in which a slice of salt-cured Virginia Smithfield ham has been pan-fried; the bitter and salty *jus* is poured over the meat prior to serving.

See also **Advertising of Food; Marketing of Food; Stimulants; Tea: Tea as an Icon Food; Tea (Meal).**

BIBLIOGRAPHY

Bramah, Edward. *Tea and Coffee: A Modern View of 300 Years of Tradition.* 2d ed. London: Hutchinson, 1972.

Filho, Olavo B. *A fazenda de cafe em Sao Paulo.* Rio de Janiero: Ministerio da Agricultura, 1952.

Guyer-Stevens, Stephanie, et al. "Starbucks: To Drink or Not to Drink?" *Whole Earth,* Summer (2002): 15.

Hattox, Ralph S. *Coffee and Coffeehouses: The Origins of a Social Beverage in the Medieval Near East.* Seattle: University of Washington Press, 1988.

Heise, Ulla. *Kaffee und Kaffeehaus* [Coffee and the coffee house]. Hildeshiem, Germany: Olms Presse, 1987.

Kiple, Kenneth F., and Kriemhild Coneè Ornelas. *The Cambridge World History of Food.* Cambridge: Cambridge University Press, 2000.

McGee, Harold. *On Food and Cooking: The Science and Lore of the Kitchen.* New York: Scribners, 1984.

Poole, Buzz. "Café Culture." *Whole Earth* Summer (2002): 10.

Samrowski, Dietrich. *Geschichte der Kaffeemuehlen* [History of coffee grinders]. Munich, Self-published, 1983.

Schoenholt, Donald N. "The Economy of Coffee, Supply Glut, Crashing Prices, Desperate Farmers: What's the Solution?" *Whole Earth,* (Summer 2002): 12–14.

Tannahill, Reay. *Food in History.* New, fully revised, and updated edition. New York: Crown, 1989. Original edition 1973.

Thurber, Francis B. *Coffee: From Plantation to Cup.* New York: American Grocer Publishing, 1881.

Toussaint-Samat, Maguelonne. *History of Food.* Translated by Anthea Bell. Cambridge, Mass.: Blackwell, 1993.

Windridge, Charles. *The Fountain of Health: An A–Z of Traditional Chinese Medicine.* Consulted and edited by Wu Xiaochun. Edinburgh: Mainstream, 1994.

Corinne Trang

COLORING, FOOD. Humans have always used the color of a food to form judgments about its desirability. The act of eating (and deciding what to eat) is a multisensory experience, synthesizing perceptions of sight, taste, smell, and touch. Color provides visual information about a food's quality and condition, and influences the perception of its flavor.

In nature, color is determined by a food's inherent qualities, indicating types of flavor, and degrees of sweetness, ripeness, or decay. However, humans have contrived to add or change the natural color in foods from very early times and for a variety of reasons—for aesthetic purposes, to increase appetite appeal, for symbolic effect, to make a less desirable food seem more desirable, and to mask defects.

From ancient times, wide varieties of food colorants were derived from natural sources—plant, animal, or mineral. This changed in the middle of the nineteenth century with the discovery of synthetic dyes that soon found their way into food. These synthetics were, in general, less expensive as well as more stable, controllable, and intense in hue than natural color sources. Since that time, the safety and acceptable use of food colorants, both natural and synthetic, remain controversial topics, eliciting debate, continual scientific study, and periodic legislative action.

History of Coloring in Food

There is ample evidence that early civilizations introduced color into their food. Ancient Egyptians colored food yellow with saffron, and saffron is mentioned in Homer's *Iliad*, dating from 700 B.C.E. Pliny the Elder relates that wines were artificially colored in 400 B.C.E. Wealthy Romans ate white bread that had been whitened by adding alum to the flour.

In the great houses of medieval Europe, cooks employed plant extracts of many hues. Along with the period's painting and stained glass, the cuisine of the late Gothic period was informed by rich and ornate color. Parti-colored dishes, jewel-toned cordials, and shimmering jellies were colored red, purple, blue, green, and yellow. Saffron had migrated from Persia as far as England by the mid-fourteenth century, and indigo, turnsole, alkanet (borage root), red saunders (a powdered wood), marigold, turmeric, safflower, parsley, spinach, fruits, and flower petal extracts commonly colored the foods of the wealthy.

In the early Renaissance (1470–1530), a common belief in Europe, based on Arabic ideas, was that color in food not only indicated nutritional value, but also inherent medicinal power connected to spiritual, celestial substances. Eating sweet red grapes produced full rich blood, black food like pepper or fungi induced melancholy, and coloring foods golden promoted divine solar healing.

In the sixteenth century the New World food colorants annatto, paprika, brazilwood, and cochineal arrived in Europe. In Mexico in 1518 Hernando Cortés observed the Aztecs cultivating the tiny cochineal insects (*Dactylopus coccus costa*) that fed on red cactus berries. These insects were gathered by hand and ground into pigment, requiring 70,000 carcasses to make a pound. By

TABLE 1

Naturally occurring colorants

Substance	Colors	Sources	Used in
Anthocyanins	orange-red to red to blue	berries, grapes, apples, roses, hibiscus, red cabbage, sweet potato	candy, fruit beverages, ice cream, yogurt, jams
Betacyanins	red	red beets, red chard, cactus fruit, bougainvillea	candy, yogurt, ice cream, salad dressing, cake mixes
Caramel	beige to brown	heated sugars	baked goods, gravies, vinegars, syrups, colas, seasonings, sauces
Carmine	red	cochineal insects	candy, dairy products, drinks, fruit fillings, surimi
Carotenoids	yellow to orange to red	saffron, tomatoes, paprika, corn, butter, palm oil, red salmon, marigolds, marine algae, carrots, annatto	meat products, cheese, butter, spice mixes, salad dressings
Chlorophylls	green to olive green	green plant leaves	green pasta, dehydrated spinach
Riboflavin	yellow	vegetable leaves, milk, eggs, organ meats, malt	flour, bread, pastries, cereals, dietary products
Turmeric	yellow	*Curcuma longa* rhizome	pickles, mustard, spices, margarine, ice cream, cheese, baked goods, soups, cooking oil, salad dressings

1600 approximately 500,000 pounds of cochineal were shipped annually to Spain.

It was common during the eighteenth and nineteenth centuries to employ food colorants to disguise inferior products, and the colorants used were frequently harmful (although natural) substances. In 1820 Frederick Accum described flour whitened with alum, pickles colored green with copper sulphate, and cheeses tinted with red lead and red mercuric sulfide. By the mid-nineteenth century, black lead, Prussian blue, lead chromate, copper carbonate, vermillion, and copper arsenite were also used to color food.

The British chemist Sir William Henry Perkin created the first synthetic dye, mauveine, in 1856 by oxidizing aniline. By the end of the century, eighty synthetic dyes colored foods, and coal tar derivatives were the principle source of synthesized dyes. Americans and Europeans were consuming varieties of unregulated, artificially colored food, including jellies, butter, cheese, ice cream, sausage, pasta, and wine.

Food Coloring Regulation

Government attempts to regulate coloring agents in food have had a long history. There was a 1396 edict in Paris against coloring butter. In 1574 French authorities in Bourges prohibited the use of color to simulate eggs in pastries, and Amsterdam forbade annatto for coloring butter in 1641. Denmark listed colors permitted for food coloring in 1836, and Germany's Color Act of 1887 prohibited harmful colors in food. A report to the British Medical Association in Toronto in 1884 resulted in the Adulteration Act, the first list of prohibited food additives. Australia passed the Pure Food Act in 1905.

The United States Food and Drug Act of 1906 restricted synthetic food colors to those that could be tested as safe. Of the eighty colors in use, only seven were approved as certified colors. In 1938 the Food, Drug, and Cosmetics (FD&C) Act approved fifteen dyes for use in food, drugs, and cosmetics and assigned color numbers instead of their common names (thus, amaranth became Red No. 2).

Government and consumers' concerns regarding food additives intensified in the 1950s with new scientific findings. In 1960 the U.S. Congress passed the Color Additives Amendment to the FD&C Act, which placed the burden of establishing safety on the food manufacturing industry and created a new category, "color additives exempt from certification." This includes both "natural colors" and "nature-identical" colors (those synthetically made but chemically identical to natural colors, like beta-carotene and canthaxanthin). The Delaney Clause prohibited any color additive that could be shown to induce cancer in humans or animals.

Since the 1970s the inclusion of colorants in food has received considerable scrutiny based primarily on concerns regarding the carcinogenic properties of colorants. In 1992 a U.S. court decision interpreted the Delaney Clause to mean that zero levels of carcinogens are permissible. With further research findings, certified colors continue to be delisted.

In response to increased consumer perception that natural colorants are safer, manufacturers have moved toward more natural and less synthetic colorants in food. However, the term "natural," as it pertains to colors, has never been legally defined and has no universally accepted definition. In addition, a small percentage of the population demonstrates sensitivity or allergic reactions to some natural colorants such as cochineal. Currently, consumer groups advocate the minimized use of food colorants, as well as a detailed listing of specific colorants on food labels.

See also **Additives; Artificial Foods; Food Politics: U.S.; Food Safety; Natural Foods; Presentation of Food; Styling of Food**.

BIBLIOGRAPHY

Albala, Ken. *Eating Right in the Renaissance*. Berkeley: University of California Press, 2002.

Bober, Phyllis Pray. *Art, Culture, and Cuisine: Ancient and Medieval Gastronomy*. Chicago: University of Chicago Press, 1999.

"Colorants." In *Foods and Food Production Encyclopedia*, edited by Douglas M. Considine and Glenn D. Considine, pp. 471–474. New York: Van Nostrand Reinhold, 1982.

"Coloring of Food." In *Foods and Nutrition Encyclopedia*, edited by Audrey H. Ensminger, M. E. Ensminger, James E. Konlande, and John R. K. Robson, vol. 1, pp. 458–461. Boca Raton, Fla.: CRC Press, 1994.

Dalby, Andrew. *Dangerous Tastes: The Story of Spices*. Berkeley: University of California Press, 2000.

Farrer, K. T. H. "Food Additives." In *The Cambridge World History of Food*, edited by Kenneth F. Kiple and Kriemhild Coneè Ornelas, vol. 2. Cambridge, U.K.: Cambridge University Press, 2000.

Gullett, Elizabeth A. "Color and Food." In *Encyclopedia of Food Science and Technology*, edited by Y. H. Hui, vol. 1. New York: John Wiley & Sons, 1992.

Hunter, Beatrice Trum. "What Are Natural Colors?" *Consumers' Research* 82, issue 8 (August 1999): 20–25.

Marmion, Daniel M. *Handbook of U.S. Colorants for Foods, Drugs, and Cosmetics*. New York: Wiley, 1984.

Peterson, T. Sarah. *Acquired Taste: The French Origins of Modern Cooking*. Ithaca, N.Y.: Cornell University Press, 1994.

Watson, R. H. J. "The Importance of Colour in Food Psychology." In *Natural Colours for Food and Other Uses*, edited by J. N. Counsell, pp. 27–37. London: Applied Science Publishers, 1981.

MM Pack

COLUMBIAN EXCHANGE. The title of this article refers to the interchange of plants and food products that took place between America and Europe after Columbus's voyages to the New World. Although the exchange was carried out in both directions, the article places greater emphasis upon the transfer of American plants and food products to Europe than in the other direction. European products that brought about significant changes in New World diets include wheat; meat and meat products such as milk, cheese and eggs; sugar; citrus fruits; onions; garlic; and certain spices such as parsley, coriander, oregano, cinnamon, and cloves.

Among the products that arrived in Europe after the discovery of the Americas were many plants native to the New World and unknown to Europeans. Some plants were transported intentionally, perhaps by a returning Spaniard who had become accustomed to the exotic flavors of America; others traveled uninvited, hidden in the nooks and crannies of ships or mixed with the ballast that Spanish ships carried on their return trips to the Old World.

Over the years, the seeds and plants were scattered throughout the nearby hills of the Mediterranean Basin by the wind, water currents, or birds, or by humans themselves. Now, over 500 years after their introduction to the area, they form such an integral part of the landscape that this would be unrecognizable for any Roman citizens who came in search of their ancient environment.

New World Plants in the Old World

American plants were not well received when they arrived in Europe. Some were the object of suspicion because of their similarity to a group of hallucinogenic plants already known and used by Europeans. Others had to undergo a genetic transformation before they could produce in the new climate and latitudes. American plants eventually became incorporated into the Mediterranean diet and now serve to identify it as readily as wheat, olives, and wine, traditional food plants of the area.

Spain became the route of dispersion for the new plants in Europe, since most of them initially arrived in the port of Seville. They extended along two distinct routes: one group was diffused toward the north of the continent, while others were found to adapt and prosper better in the south. The southern group first arrived in Italy, which should not be surprising since Spain controlled parts of Italy during the sixteenth century, and this facilitated the introduction of American plants to the area. The well-established trade routes set up by the Aragonese long before the sixteenth century were important factors in the dispersion of American products. The mild climate and loose soil that predominate in the Mediterranean helped make the area a favorable ecological niche for the adaptation and development of the new plants.

Maize and beans, subsistence crops throughout much of the Americas, prospered well in the Mediterranean Basin. Tomatoes and chili peppers adapted easily to the new atmosphere. Other crops that had little trouble in establishing themselves were several varieties of squash, sweet potatoes, the nopal, or prickly pear cactus, and the agave, or century plant. The potato, a plant that generated important changes in European social life, adapted better in the cold climates and high altitudes of Northern Europe, because of a greater similarity to their original habitat in the Andes Mountains of Bolivia and Peru.

Some of the plants rejected upon their arrival in Europe were the tomato, potato, and chili pepper. All are members of the *Solanaceae* plant family and had to confront the famous "curse of the nightshades" before being accepted in European diets. Europeans were already familiar with some poisonous members of this group of

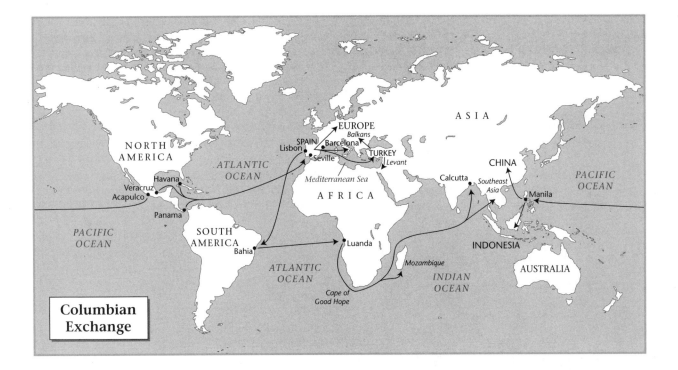

plants such as mandrake, henbane, and belladonna, hallucinogenic plants used by witches and sorcerers of the time. They recognized these three plants as members of the same plant family by their leaves and flowers and were suspicious of them. In addition to being hallucinogenic and poisonous, the plants were believed to cause leprosy and syphilis. Soon they acquired fame as aphrodisiacs, although it is doubtful that this contributed to their rejection.

It was in the Mediterranean area where New World plants had their earliest acceptance. The Mediterranean Sea served as a background for the struggle between the Ottoman Turks and the Spanish Hapsburgs in the sixteenth century. These two empires played a dominant role in the region and were probably the most important distributors of American plants in Mediterranean countries.

The role played by the Turks is evident in the nomenclature of American plants in the sixteenth century. Maize appeared in European herbals with the name of Turkish grain, *blé de Turquie*, or *turkisher korn*. The chili pepper was called Turkish red pepper and squash was known as Turkish cucumber; even the American turkey received its well-known name in English at this time, when it was called the turkie-bird.

A Historical Comparison of Plant Introductions

The arrival of American plants in the Mediterranean during the sixteenth century can be compared to a similar occurrence during Roman times. During the first years of the Empire, Romans followed a fairly simple diet. Their meals consisted mainly of boiled grains such as millet, rye, and wheat, and of vegetables grown in the area. With the expansion of the Empire, trade and commerce began to flourish, and some Roman merchants began to introduce new food products from far-reaching corners of the Roman Empire. The best of the ancient world arrived at the tables of upper-class Romans. The variety of available food products increased considerably, and the new foods soon became a necessity in the Roman diet, giving rise to an elaborate and sophisticated cuisine.

It was not until the sixteenth century and the arrival of New World plants that this phenomenon was repeated in history. Plant specialists calculate that seventy-eight new plants, including fruit trees, vegetables, and spices, arrived in Italy during the centuries of the Roman Empire, while 127 arrived from America during just the first century following the discovery of the New World.

Factors Determining the Acceptance of Plants

Some plants were easily accepted in the Mediterranean diet due to their similarity to other plants already known in the area. This was the case for the common bean (*Phaseolus vulgaris*) that showed a similarity with the fava bean (*Vicia faba*), known since Roman times and diffused throughout the area by Romans during their conquests.

The maize plant does not resemble other grains, although its preparation in the form of ground flour in breads and gruels gave it a certain similarity to them. Maize flour was combined with other ground cereals and used in the preparation of rustic breads, favored by the poor. It also came to substitute for millet in the preparation of Italian polenta, an ancient Roman dish that had been a mainstay of the poor for centuries.

While the foods of the New World radically changed the diet of the Old, so too did many Old World foods become staples of Native American diets. Here, a Kuna Indian woman is preparing to plant rice. She is holding the young seedlings in her hands. This picture was taken among the Kuna people at Comorcas de San Blas, Panama, in 1996. © DANNY LEHMAN/CORBIS.

The squash bore a resemblance to other cucurbits known to the Romans, although they belonged to other plant species. It received the name of *calabash* and a false identity as *zucco* from Syria. From this comes its present-day name, zucchini.

The chili pepper and the tomato arrived as new and strange plants, and people were suspicious of them. The fact that Europeans did not know how to prepare them and that they bore no resemblance to foods already in their diets made their acceptance more difficult. Chili peppers were too hot for the European palate, and they found the tomato difficult to prepare. It was too acrid to eat in its green stage, but when it ripened, it appeared to be spoiled, and when cooked, it disintegrated. Finally, they adopted the Aztec technique of grinding it into a purée. The tomato that arrived in the Mediterranean in the sixteenth century was not the bright red, smooth,

juicy fruit we know today, but rather a pale fruit with an acid flavor and unpleasant smell. The first illustrations in herbals show a small, ridged, hard fruit that does not look very appetizing. It was the caring hands of Italian gardeners that improved the American tomato and turned it into the vivid, plump, thin-skinned fruit we appreciate today. They also modified the chili pepper, turning it into a large fruit without the characteristic heat of the Mexican pepper. When transformed into a green pepper, it could be eaten as a vegetable, stuffed with meat or cheese, and it has found an important place in Mediterranean salads. Sweet potatoes and the prickly pear cactus adapted and grew wherever the climate and soil permitted them.

The Turks introduced American plants into the Balkans during their sixteenth century invasions of the region. Today the Hungarian chili pepper, called paprika, is one of the predominant flavors in Balkan cooking. Maize, squash, and tomatoes also play an important role in the cuisine.

American Plants Incorporated into the European Diet

American plants arrived in Europe during the sixteenth century, but did not play a significant role in the European diet for two-hundred years. They became incorporated into the eighteenth-century diet, not as exotic or innovative dishes, but rather as additional ingredients in traditional foods already known and eaten by the masses. Cooks began adding maize and potatoes to popular soups and stews. American beans became a substitute for Roman fava beans in Spanish *fabada* (a bean stew from Asturias); white beans came to be used in *cassoulet* (a dish of southern France, made with beans and pork), as well as in Tuscan bean dishes. Sicilians discovered that tomato sauces were a good complement to pasta and pizzas and provided more color and flavor than the traditional butter or olive oil dressings. *Peperonata*, made with sautéed red and green peppers, occupies a place in all Mediterranean cuisines. The tomato and the chili pepper became a common ingredient in Greek dishes such as *moussaka*, made with lamb and eggplant, and in Hungarian dishes like chicken paprika or goulash.

Andalusian *gazpacho*, an ancient bread soup, possibly of Roman origin, suddenly took on a new presentation with tomatoes and green peppers. Valencian *paella* (a dish of rice, chicken, and seafood) and *bacalao* (a codfish casserole) soon included foods from America in their preparation. Innovative cooks created new dishes such as the *tortilla española*, a Spanish omelet cooked with potatoes, and "*pa amb tomàquet*," thick Catalan bread slices smeared with tomatoes and olive oil. The Muslim tradition of filling vegetables with meat and sauce soon found new receptacles in American vegetables such as green peppers, tomatoes, and squash. Over the years, they learned to make Moroccan couscous with tomatoes, served with harissa sauce, made with mashed chili peppers, salt, and garlic.

The exchange of food plants from the New World to the Old moved in several directions. One was trans-Atlantic, the other was trans-Pacific. In these market baskets at Neiafu, Vava'U Island, Tonga Islands, New World manioc (center) is sold side by side with mangoes, fruits that came to the islands by way of Asia. © WOLFGANG KAEHLER/CORBIS.

Conclusion

After an uncertain beginning upon their arrival in Europe, American plants revolutionized European diets as they slowly began replacing traditional ingredients and became staples in the basic diets of the area. They provided a more nutritional diet and helped put an end to the chronic famines that had affected Europe since the Middle Ages. Two New World plants, maize and potatoes, are considered among the four most important subsistence plants of the world and are believed to have played a role in the population explosion that began in the middle of the eighteenth century.

Maize quickly became a mainstay in the Venetian and Roman diets. It was easy to grow and so productive that many country people began living on a diet made up almost exclusively of maize products. Maize contains an incomplete protein and lacks trytophan, a precursor of niacin, which helps the body synthesize vitamins. Without this amino acid, the body cannot absorb vitamins and thus produces a nutritional deficiency called pellagra, which affects the digestive and nervous systems as well as the skin. In extreme cases, it can be fatal. No Mediterranean country was saved from this terrible disease. It was not abolished completely in Italy until after the Second World War, when the diet and living conditions improved in that country. Potatoes were accepted in the diet in places like seventeenth-century Ireland, where the people were undergoing a severe food crisis; two centuries later, they were the cause of Ireland's "great

hunger" of the nineteenth century when the loss of the potato crop in consecutive years left people with nothing to eat.

See also **Caribbean**; **Central America**; **Diaspora**; **Iberian Peninsula**; **Inca Empire**; **Maize**; **Mexico and Central America, Pre-Columbian**; **South America.**

BIBLIOGRAPHY

Braudel, Fernand. *The Mediterranean and the Mediterranean World in the Age of Philip II.* 2 vols. Translated from the French by Siân Reynolds. New York: Harper and Row, 1972.

Casanova, Rosa, and Marcos Bellingeri. *Alimentos, remedios, vicios y placeres.* México: Instituto Nacional de Antropología e Historia, 1988.

Elliott, James H. *Spain and Its World, 1500–1700.* New Haven: Yale University Press, 1989.

Fernández Pérez, Joaquin, and Ignacio González Tascón, eds. *La agricultura viajera.* Barcelona, Spain: Lunwerg Editores, S. A., 1991.

Hobhouse, Henry. *Seeds of Change: Five Plants That Transformed Mankind.* New York: Harper and Row, 1987.

Viola, Herman J., and Carolyn Margolis, eds. *Seeds of Change: A Quincentennial Commemoration.* Washington and London: Smithsonian Institution Press, 1991.

Janet Long-Solís

COMBINATION OF PROTEINS.

A thousand years ago, the Chinese poet Wu Tzu-mu listed the "seven necessities" of life that are still memorized by every Chinese schoolchild: firewood, rice, soy sauce, sesame oil, salt, vinegar, and tea. The list does not include meat. Now as then, we place great value on animal flesh as a food source, but depend on plants. Protein complementarity—or combining certain vegetable foods to achieve complete protein—solves a singular problem with that dependence.

Plant protein is an incomplete source of protein. Protein is built of amino acids, and of the twenty-two found in nature, our bodies can synthesize all but eight. These are termed "essential," and must be found in the diet. Nearly all plants, however, are deficient in the essential amino acid methionine; only soybeans (*Glycine max*) and some seeds and nuts, especially the Mongongo (*Ricinodendron rautanenii*) and sesame seeds (*Sesamum indicum*), can provide over 50 percent of our daily need. Legumes and pulses, such as peanuts (*Arachis hypogoea*), lentils (*Lens esculenta*), chickpeas (*Cicer arietinum*), and lima beans (*Phaseolus lunatus*), typically contain about half as much protein by weight as meat, and are good sources of lysine, but lack methionine. Many vegetables such as the squashes (*Cucurbita maxima, pepo*), cauliflower (*Brassica oleracea*), and runner or green beans (*Phaseolus coccineus*) have small amounts of protein, typically 1 to 2 percent by weight, but reasonably balanced amino acids.

Many populations, however, must find their protein in the same starchy carbohydrates that provide their calories. Corn (*Zea mays*), about 3 to 4 percent protein by weight, lacks methionine, lysine, and tryptophan, and is overrich in leucine. Rice (*Orza sativa*, typ), also limited in methionine and lysine, has less total protein than corn by weight. However, its even amino acid profile gives rice greater bioavailability (how many of the amino acids our bodies can utilize). Whole wheat (*Triticum aestivum*) has four times more protein than corn or rice, but has low amounts of methionine, lysine, and tyrosine. Some tubers such as potatoes (*Solanum tuberosum*) have superior amino acid profiles to cereals, while others such as the yams (genus *Dioscorea*) and cassavas (genus *Manihot*) offer only about 1½ percent protein by wet weight.

Plants, moreover, contain tannins, phytates, and other indigestible fibers that bind with amino acids, reducing gut absorption and increasing fecal transit rates. Cereal protein digestibility, for instance, depends on whether one eats only the endosperm, source of most amino acids, or includes the fibrous pericarp.

Taking digestibility into account, we can calculate the utility of plant proteins relative to a benchmark—egg white. Soybeans, with a score of 99, are more bioavailable than beef, while peas and beans have scores between 60 and 75, nuts fall to the thirties, and most cereals are in the 20 to 30 range. Culturally important foods such as plantain (*Musa* spp), yams, and cassava (manioc) begin with modest total protein, contain high fiber, and thus end up with very low protein scores.

Mixing Plant Proteins

With ingenuity, such shortfalls can be met by mixing amino acids from different plant foods. This has become known as protein complementarity. The best-understood example comes from Latin America's menu. Squashes supply lysine, which corn lacks, and beans provide methionine. In sufficient quantity, the triad of squash, corn, and beans provides ample protein.

Moreover, as Solomon Katz has demonstrated, Latin American cultures typically soak their tortilla corn in lime. Besides enhancing availability of the B vitamin niacin, the alkali reaction reduces the amino acid availability of all amino acids except lysine, already deficient in corn. Paradoxically, this is useful. While total protein is reduced, amino acids are "leveled," making a higher percentage of protein (approximately 8 percent by weight) complete. Finally, one of the amino acids reduced is leucine, an overabundance of which relative to lysine may be involved in the etiology of the disease pellagra. Thus lime soaking is a deceptively simple cultural practice that solves complex nutritional dilemmas.

Language itself attests to protein complementarity's importance in East Asia. The Chinese *fan* literally translates as 'grain' (usually rice), but also signifies 'food'. *Ts'ai* literally translates as 'edible leaf and stem vegetable', but also signifies 'what goes over rice to complete the meal.' One is reminded of the phrase from the Lord's Prayer, "our daily bread," that signifies all necessary food. Complementarity here rests on the soybean. Rice or wheat is mixed with dozens of soybean products, including curds (tofu), soy milk, boiled or fermented soybeans, and soy sauce. Soy sauce, in turn, typically is made with wheat flour, whose methionine enhances an already strong amino acid profile. Digestion of soy protein, moreover, is enhanced by traditional fermentation, accomplished in water containing dissolved calcium or magnesium. These inactivate the antagonists to trypsin, a digestive enzyme, found in soybeans. Finally, sesame oil, a rich source of methionine, has been a preferred cooking oil in China since the Sung dynasty. Not surprisingly, even in times of famine, straightforward protein malnutrition has been rare in East Asia.

As one proceeds inland west or north, pulses and legumes such as the red bean (*Vigna angularis*), broad bean (*Vica fava*), the mung bean (*Vigna mungo*), the peanut, and the common pea (*Pisum sativum*) are mixed with cereals to aid complementarity. Fermented milk products such as yogurt become significant in Central Asia.

In the Middle East, South Asia, and Asia Minor, complementarity typically involves green vegetables, cheese, and lentils or peas with wheat. Wheat and pulses nicely complement each other's lysine and methionine ratios; amino acid scores attain at least 85 percent of egg white. Protein malnutrition is again rare.

Comparatively protein-poor Oceanic foods such as breadfruit (*Artocarpus communis*), bananas (*Musa*), taro

(*Colocasia esculenta*), and yams tend to be served together, often with green vegetables. Fish or pork is typically added in small amounts. Except in mountainous areas of New Guinea, protein malnutrition is rare.

Both Southeast Asia and coastal West Africa illustrate a dilemma stemming from substitution of meat for plants. The dominant carbohydrate, rice, typically is topped by small amounts of fish, as a fermented paste (Southeast Asia), or dried fragments (West Africa); peanuts and green vegetables may also contribute to the sauce. With much rice and little fish, protein can become quite diluted. In northern Thailand, for instance, small children may not eat enough rice with fish paste to meet caloric needs. However balanced, the protein is broken down for energy. In Senegal, among the Wolof, dried fish tends to fragment during cooking and be diluted throughout the rice gruel. Adults consider this less tasty, and following their example, children may resist eating sufficient rice.

Origins of Complementarity

The ingenuity and specificity of protein complementarity demands explanation. How did so many cultures independently discover protein mixing? Simple trial and error is unlikely, since protein undernutrition has ambiguous symptoms; even obvious malnutrition (kwashiorkor) has been variously attributed to supernatural intervention, inappropriate parental morals, or a failure of the child's will. On the other hand, dietary practices show good congruence with underlying biochemical advantages in growth and resistance to infection. Folk knowledge of these connections, however, remains poorly documented.

The origins of protein complementarity may be ecological. Optimization strategies must lead to a cost-benefit honing of the total menu available within any ecosystem. Nutritional benefits will be balanced against procurement costs. The !Kung San, for instance, select plant foods on the basis of abundance, ease of acquisition, and nutrient value. Elaborate taboos are reserved for meat, which costs more calories to obtain than it yields. Ultimately, any population whose long-term optimizations transgress nutritional requirements will suffer demographic collapse. We may, in other words, see close linkages between food choice and protein scores because cultures that ignored such an association are no longer extant.

Practices that enhance complementarity may operate through individual health-seeking behavior. Pairing introduced foods with familiar, liked components, such as mixing cereals with pulses, has been shown to facilitate acceptance in humans, but not in animals. The !Kung San typically equate nutrient value with tastiness, including texture, flavor, and smell. Such findings locate protein complementarity within what Pierre Bordieu terms "cultural habitas": a habitual, unremarked, individual practice that reflects group consensus about "how things are done." This habitas serves to internalize biologically adaptive food choices.

Over evolutionary time spans, finally, some behaviors may have become encephalized, or incorporated into neural functioning. Monoamine neurotransmitters such as serotonin, dopamine, and norepinephrine are synthesized from two amino acids, tryptophan and tyrosine. Neuronal levels of these amino acids in plant-eating monkeys, for instance, vary systematically with intake when dietary protein is scant, but are insensitive to intakes above 10 percent. Reductions in neuronal level limit neurotransmitter synthesis in the hypothalamus, which in turn regulates appetite. The brain, then, may receive constant information about the amino acid balance of our diet, and mediate appetite to achieve optimal rates of utilization when protein is scarce. Individuals would not be conscious of such nutrient-seeking appetites. Rather, diets that yielded appropriate mixes would become associated with elevated affect; they would taste richer, or better satisfy cravings, thus conditioning individuals to seek those foods. Protein complementarity consequently appears to follow multiple adaptive paths, individual and social, using both biology and culture.

See also **Legumes**; **Maize**; **Nuts**; **Proteins and Amino Acids**; **Rice**; **Soy**; **Squash and Gourds**; **Wheat**.

BIBLIOGRAPHY

Chang, K. C. *Food in Chinese Culture: Anthropological and Historical Perspectives.* New Haven: Yale University Press, 1971. Definitive source for historical development of Chinese diet.

Davidson, Stanley, R. Brock Passmore, and J. F. Truswell. *Human Nutrition and Dietetics.* 8th ed. Edinburgh, London, and New York: Churchill Livingston, 1986. Unusual for its detailed coverage of specific food groups.

Fernstrom, John, and Madelyn Fernstrom. "Monoamines and Protein Intake: Are Control Mechanisms Designed to Monitor a Threshold or a Set Point?" *Nutrition Reviews* 59, no. 8, part 2 (2001): 60–65. Review of recent psychobiology of food choice.

Guthrie, Helen. *Human Nutrition.* St. Louis: Mosby, 1995. Solid overview of human nutritional needs.

Harris, Marvin. *Good to Eat: Riddles of Food and Culture.* New York: Simon and Schuster, 1985. Chief advocate of ecologically adaptive food choice.

Katz, Solomon, Mary Heidiger, and L. Valleroy. "The Anthropological and Nutritional Significance of Traditional Maize Processing in the New World." In *Biosocial Interrelations in Population Adaptation*, edited by Elizabeth Watts, Francis Johnson, and Gabriel Lasker, pp. 195–234. The Hague: Mouton, 1975. Seminal exploration of a specific adaptive practice.

Katz, Solomon, and Sara Schall. "Fava Bean Consumption and Biocultural Evolution." *Medical Anthropology* 3 (1979): 459–476. First link of specific food choice to human genetic variation.

Lee, Richard Borshay. *The !Kung San: Men, Women, and Work in a Foraging Culture.* Cambridge: Cambridge University

Press, 1979. Includes detailed investigation of diet among hunter-gatherers.

Rozin, Paul. "Psychobiological Perspectives on Food Preferences and Avoidances." In *Food and Evolution: Toward a Theory of Human Food Habits*, edited by Marvin Harris and Eric Ross. Philadelphia: Temple University Press, 1987. Useful introduction to the psychology of food choice.

Stephen M. Bailey

COMFORT FOOD. Comfort food is an increasingly prominent concept in the twenty-first century. Indeed, as a consequence of the term's increased use in the English language (likely a response to increasingly stressful living conditions), the editors of the *Oxford English Dictionary* added "comfort food" to its list of 1997 entries, defining it as "food that comforts or affords solace; hence any food (frequently with a high sugar or carbohydrate content) that is associated with childhood or with home cooking." That same year *Merriam-Webster's Collegiate Dictionary* added "comfort food" to the tenth edition, defining it as "food prepared in a traditional style having a usually nostalgic or sentimental appeal." Comfort food may be best thought of as any food consumed by individuals, often during periods of stress, that evokes positive emotions and is associated with significant social relationships.

Throughout history and across cultures, food arguably has always been associated with the provision of comfort. Indeed, from the moments following birth, the crying infant is immediately soothed with mother's milk or, in more modern times, infant formula. Only in the last decade of the twentieth century, however, did the notion of comfort food as a unique concept become part of the vernacular of everyday life. Julie L. Locher and colleagues have observed that "daily life in the modern world, with its concomitant stress, psychological discomfort, and personal dislocation, has given rise to the need for comfort foods, and in a capitalist economy, of course, manufacturers have fully exploited such a need" (2002, p. 5). Restaurateurs and cookbook writers have taken advantage of individuals' needs for comfort as well. Contemporary societies have witnessed a proliferation of restaurants, including high-end restaurants, that feature comfort food on their daily menus. Additionally, growing numbers of cookbooks are dedicated exclusively to recipes for comfort foods, and whole cookbooks focus entirely on single comfort foods, such as macaroni and cheese (Schwartz, 2001). The notion of comfort food appears regularly in popular magazines (aimed primarily at women), television, and literature. Heralding the rise in the popularity of comfort food, *Bon Appetit* devoted most of its February 1998 issue to comfort food.

Several researchers have either demonstrated or speculated that links exist between physical or psychological aspects associated with mood and the consumption of particular foods, especially those foods high in carbohydrates (both sugar and starch) and fat. The most conclusive and widespread evidence arising from this investigation is that foods high in carbohydrates increase the availability of tryptophan, which increases the level of serotonin in the brain and results in a better mood state. Another plausible biological explanation for the link between food and mood maintains that foods that taste good may promote the release of endogenous opioids and thereby alter one's mood state. These physical and psychological observations may help explain some of the food objects individuals consume to provide comfort but certainly not all foods. Further, they do not explain the diversity of food choices among individuals and groups or why people choose some foods and not others for comfort.

Some researchers have emphasized the social dimensions of comfort food, noting that comfort foods are those familiar to the individual, are associated with feelings of nostalgia, are usually convenient to prepare and consume, are often indulgent, and typically provide a sense of physical as well as emotional comfort. According to Brian Wansink and Cynthia Sangerman, the most commonly reported comfort foods consumed in the United States are potato chips, followed by ice cream, cookies, and candy (2000, p. 1). All of these investigators found gender differences in what individuals perceive as comfort foods. Men are more likely to prefer entire meals, while women are more likely to prefer sweets (including chocolate) and snack foods. Age differences were identified also. Younger people prefer sweets and snacks, while older people prefer hot foods like soup and mashed potatoes.

Comfort foods are consumed under different circumstances in individuals' lives. Both social and psychological research indicates that when persons are feeling either sad or lonely, they may be more likely to consume particular foods. Additionally, researchers have found that persons consume comfort food when they are feeling "jubilant," when they need an incentive to get through something particularly stressful, or when they wish to be rewarded for something they have accomplished. The emphasis in most writings on comfort foods, in both the popular press and the academic press, is on personal sources of distress that encourage consumption of comfort foods.

Comfort foods are consumed during periods of societal uncertainty and crises. For example, immediately following the 11 September 2001 terrorist attack on the World Trade Center, restaurateurs across the United States reported increased sales of comfort food items, such as soup, mashed potatoes, puddings, and macaroni and cheese (Thorn, 2001). A Nielsen survey of grocery stores reported a significant increase in the sales of both snack foods and instant potatoes ("Nation Turning to Comfort Food," 2001). These reports may help explain why the notion of comfort foods became so important at that particular time in history. Conditions of postmodern societies present individuals with stressors that are often beyond their control. At the same time, societies have become consumer-oriented, and individuals have become more defined by the objects they consume. The consumption of particular food objects for comfort may be one of the primary ways individuals can maintain control. Thus, eating comfort foods may be a means of maintaining control over the self when all else seems out of control. In essence, comfort food provides individuals with a sense of security during troubling times by evoking emotions associated with safer and happier times.

See also **Slow Food; Snacks.**

BIBLIOGRAPHY

Christensen, Larry. "The Effect of Carbohydrates on Affect." *Nutrition* 13, no. 6 (June 1997): 503–514.

Drewnowski, Adam. "Why Do We Like Fat?" *Journal of the American Dietetic Association* 97 (1997): S58–S62.

Edgson, Vicki, and Ian Marber. *The Food Doctor: Healing Foods for Mind and Body.* London: Collins and Brown, 1999.

Fischler, Claude. "Food, Self, and Identity." *Social Science Information* 27 (1988): 275–292.

Locher, Julie L., William C. Yoels, and Jillian Van Ells. "Comfort Foods: An Exploration into the Social and Emotional Significance of Food." Unpublished manuscript, 2002.

Lupton, Deborah. *Food, the Body, and the Self.* London: Sage, 1996.

"Nation Turning to Comfort Food." Associated Press, 6 November 2001. Available at http://www.msnbc.com.

Schwartz, Joan. *Macaroni and Cheese: More Than Fifty Recipes, from Simple to Sublime.* New York: Villard, 2001.

Somer, Elizabeth. *Food and Mood.* 2nd ed. New York: Henry Holt, 1999.

Thorn, Bret. "Seeking Comfort, Diners Indulge in Feel-Good Fare." *Nation's Restaurant News*, 15 October 2001. Available http://www.findarticles.com.

Wansink, Brian, and Cynthia Sangerman. "The Taste of Comfort: Food for Thought on How Americans Eat to Feel Better." *American Demographics* 22, no. 7 (July 2000): 66–67.

Julie L. Locher

COMMODITY PRICE SUPPORTS.

Commodity price supports are statutory devices designed to enhance the net income of agricultural producers. These laws are called subsidies because they use the power and wealth of the state to "subsidize" producers by artificially supporting prices of agricultural commodities, reducing the cost of producing them, or, in some cases, providing direct cash payments to producers. In the United States, the core of statutory authority for price supports rests in Title 7 of the U.S. code and the Agricultural Act of 1949, as amended. These laws authorize loans that producers are not legally required to repay, open-market purchase of cranberries, and direct cash payments to dairy farmers under the Obey-Kohl Amendment to the 2001 Agri-

cultural Appropriations Bill. Most of these laws were enacted in the Depression era of the 1930s but have been modified and extended up to the present time. Price support programs started out with six "basic" commodities (four from the South: peanuts, cotton, tobacco, and rice, and two from the North: wheat and corn). There now are some two dozen commodities that receive price support benefits. Both the cost and the complexity of these laws have grown dramatically. Sometimes these programs have collided with each other (like in 1983 when a federal law to kill aging dairy cattle in a futile attempt to raise milk prices seriously depressed beef prices as an avalanche of dairy cow meat buried the beef market).

While price support laws are aimed at achieving income parity for farmers and ranchers, there are many other laws that affect agricultural prosperity. For example, the Conservation Reserve Program currently idles about 36 million acres of fragile cropland. While conservation and environmental concerns may be the prime objective of this program, a substantial side-effect is the income stability for crop producers that comes from idling that enormous acreage. This phenomenon is present in other USDA conservation programs such as wetlands and forestry.

Another important agricultural law that has a major impact on farm prices and income is P.L. 83-480, the "Food for Peace" program. Through the years this major trade law has funneled billions of agricultural commodities into developing foreign nations, thus boosting domestic prices.

Other laws that indirectly boost U.S. farm prices include: Farm Credit Programs by USDA such as FmHA (Farmers Home Administration) and crop insurance. Also helping farm prosperity are the banking services of the Farm Credit Administration.

At this point it should be noted that states use their "negative" pricing power to reduce farm prices and farm income. Examples range from price controls during World World II and Korea to embargoes by Presidents Nixon, Carter, and Bush. Even seemingly unrelated programs involving agricultural research, such as the use of genetically modified organisms (GMOs), affect farm prices. Tax policy by federal, state, and local governments can also play a major role in the economics of farm owners and operators.

One final thought: In ancient Athens, it is said that the people despaired over the high price of figs, so that Archon commissioned a bevy of "fig watchers" or sycophants to keep both fig exports and fig prices low. It was probably the first "cheap food policy," but governments have been struggling ever since to organize a price support system that will be fair to both producers and consumers.

See also **Agriculture since the Industrial Revolution; Food Politics: United States; Government Agencies, U.S.**

Hyde H. Murray

COMPOTE. The word "compote" comes from *compositum*, the past participle of the Latin verb *componere* used as a noun. The basic culinary meaning refers to any preparation assembled from a variety of ingredients, with the added inference that this was done in a predetermined or formulaic arrangement. The English word "composition" also derives from this same root, and in both terms the aspects of visual appearance and texture play a key role. Roman cooks seem to have recognized a *compositum* when they saw one, but so few culinary texts have survived from Roman times that we seem to have only one recipe from Apicius as a reference point: *Rapae ut Diu Servuntur*, or turnips preserved in honey and vinegar with or without myrtle berries, mustard seeds and salt (Lib. I, xxiv; Milham, 1969). Significantly, Apicius did not use the term *compositum* anywhere in his surviving text.

It is not until the Middle Ages that the term *compositum* appears with any regularity, and it is clear from the medieval texts themselves that several distinctly different preparations went by the name of *compositum*. One of the oldest references, from the 1300s, was called a *confectio compositi* (Moulon, 1971) and consisted of parsley and celery root, cabbage, vinegar, pork, and other ingredients. It was a layered dish evidently baked in a deep earthenware pot and the prototype of a common one-pot dish known throughout southwest Germany, Alsace, and Switzerland as *Gumbis* (or some variation of that spelling).

In his *Theatrum Botanicum* (Basel, 1696) Swiss physician Theodore Zwinger described a common *Gumbis* made from pared turnips laid down in tubs with layers of barberries and sloes, then covered with spring water and salt. This sweet-and-salty vegetable preserve was eaten as a dessert, while the liquid was used in home remedies. This is not a cooked dish, yet it does follow in the tradition of Apicius and thus must be a recipe of considerable age. It is echoed in an eighteenth-century American recipe for preserving stone fruit in honey and spring water.

Hans Wiswe (1970) published a number of medieval German recipes for *compositum* and noted that they fell into three groups: First, a type of preserve employing fruits or vegetables, or a mixture of both, together with honey. In Renaissance cookery this evolved into fruit stewed in honey or in a sugar syrup. Second, layered sauerkraut mixtures, such as the addition of root parsley (Hamburg parsley) and turnips or some other root vegetable, even, perhaps, horseradish. Third, food mixtures prepared in deep earthenware baking pans and arranged in layers, invariably with shredded cabbage, shredded turnips, sauerkraut, fruit, and quite often small pieces of meat. Thus a recipe made primarily with sliced apples becomes *poma composta* or *Gumbis äpfel* (apple Gumbis). The traditional *Gumbistöpfel* of Canton Aargau in Switzerland employs dried pears. Many of the recipes are highly regionalized and thus point to the great age of this concept.

Such medieval layered mixtures continued to be made in North America by German-speaking settlers from Switzerland, Alsace, and southwest Germany. These fruit-cabbage-and-meat mixtures are discussed by Weaver (1993), who pointed out that they represent a type of one-pot meal once common throughout the Pennsylvania Dutch settlement area. Published recipes have also emerged in a number of nineteenth century sources, such as George Girardey's *Höchst nützliches Handbuch über Kochkunst* (The Handbook of the Art of Cooking; Cincinnati, 1842). It is the sweet *compositum*, however, which has gained the most widespread acceptance in European cookery today. It is almost universally referred to by its French name: compote.

Sweet Compotes

The sweet *compositum* is doubtless itself of great age and probably draws upon antecedents in the eastern Mediterranean. A preparation known as *mahés* (pronounced mah-CHESS) made in rural Cyprus points toward the antiquity of this concept. Grapes are partially dried in the sun, then packed tightly into a *goumni* (a type of small earthenware jar holding 5 to 6 liters), closed tightly, and allowed to ferment for two to three months. The result is a thick, syrupy, alcoholic delicacy which is eaten for dessert with a spoon. Slight fermentation appears to be one of the defining elements in this type of preparation and thus would explain why "compost," the old English term for it, eventually migrated in meaning to the more narrow sense of fermenting garden debris, as in the term "compost heap."

Hieatt and Butler (1985) published a reference to *datys in compaste*, mentioned on a medieval English menu,

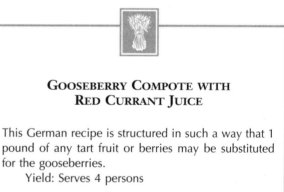

GOOSEBERRY COMPOTE WITH RED CURRANT JUICE

This German recipe is structured in such a way that 1 pound of any tart fruit or berries may be substituted for the gooseberries.

Yield: Serves 4 persons

1 pound (500g) ripe gooseberries
1/2 cup (125ml) red currant juice
3 tablespoons (45g) sugar or to taste

Pick the gooseberries of their stems and tails. Put them into a sieve and blanch in boiling water for a few seconds. Then place them in a stewpan with the currant juice and sugar and cook gently until they are soft. Serve warm or cold with vanilla ice cream or with crème fraîche.

SOURCE: Adapted and translated from Hedwig Heyl, *A B C der Küche* (Berlin, 1938), p. 317.

and suggested this might be preserved dates, describing it as something akin to chutney. It is difficult to know exactly what was meant, since there are a variety of ways the dates could have been preserved—even in simple syrup, but in all likelihood, the date mixture was probably more like *mahés*, since this was a common export item from the Latin kingdoms in the eastern Mediterranean. Whatever the case, two important points emerge: the use of the term "compote" in English and a direct association with something that is sweet and sticky.

A great deal has been written on the subject of the Arabic invention or perfection of this type of confectionery, especially where cane sugar was employed. Doubtless the technological trail can be traced to Persia or even India, where sugarcane was known and used for thousands of years. If there was a more westerly epicenter for sugar confectionery, then it was most certainly Syria, for the Syrians held a monopoly on sugar technology for a very long time during the Middle Ages. Even in the Latin kingdoms established in that region during the Crusades, Syrian Christians remained in charge of the sugar mills and confection shops. Let it be said, however, that before the arrival of sugar and its commercialization in the eastern Mediterranean, *epsima* (grape syrup), carob syrup, pomegranate syrup, date syrup, and, of course, honey played a significant role in the preparation of sweet fruit dishes. These preparations were primarily medical in nature but also pleasant-tasting.

The Move to the West
Wet, sticky fruits were exported to the West as luxury medicines, but as sugar became more available to Europeans, the art of making these medicines quickly spread as well, especially among druggists. These foods were often eaten at the end of the medieval meal to help rebalance the bodily humors, but in time became associated more and more with the banqueting course, as the dessert course was eventually called during the Renaissance. Cookbooks of that period generally lump the compotes together with cakes and other desserts, and that is where the preparation has remained on the menu down to the present day.

Culturally, fruits stewed in sugar play a far more significant role in the cuisine of Scandinavia, Russia, German-speaking Europe, and the Balkans than they do in modern American cookery. In those countries, the compote is a popular warm-weather food, almost a midsummer institution, whereas in the eastern Mediterranean, fruits prepared in sticky syrup are generally eaten as a delicacy served with very strong coffee.

See also **Apicius**; **Candy and Confections**; **Fruit**; **Middle East**; **Sugar and Sweeteners**; **Syrups**; **United States: Pennsylvania Dutch Food.**

BIBLIOGRAPHY

Dembinska, Maria. *Food and Drink in Medieval Poland*, William Woys Weaver, ed. Philadelphia: University of Pennsylvania Press, 1999.

Flandrin, Jean-Louis, and Massimo Montanari, eds., *Food: A Culinary History from Antiquity to the Present*. English edition by Albert Sonnenfeld. Translated by Clarissa Botsford. New York: Columbia University Press, 1999.

Hieatt, Constance B., and Sharon Butler. *Curye on Inglysch*. London, New York, and Toronto: Oxford University Press, 1985.

Kellar, Jane Carpenter, et al., eds. *On the Score of Hospitality: Selected Receipts of a Van Rensselaer Family, Albany, New York 1785–1835*. Albany, N.Y.: Historic Cherry Hill, 1986.

Milham, Mary Ella, ed. *Apicii Decem Libri qui Dicuntur De Re Coquinaria et Excerpta a Vinidario Conscripta*. Leipzig, 1969.

Moulon, Marianne. "Deux traités inédits d'art culinaire médiéval," *Bulletin philologique et historique* (Paris, 1971), 369–435.

Weaver, William Woys. *Pennsylvania Dutch Country Cooking*. New York: Abbeville, 1993.

Wiswe, Hans. *Kulturgeschichte der Kochkunst*. Munich: H. Moos, 1970.

Zwinger, Theodore. *Theatrum Botanicum*. Basel, 1696.

William Woys Weaver

CONDIMENTS. The term "condiment" originally meant seasoned, pickled, or preserved foods in Latin. Today, the word is broadly applied to a variety of foods, including spices, herbs, sauces, seasonings, flavorings, colorings, and even beverages, such as tea, coffee, and alcoholic drinks. A more narrow definition is that a condiment is a substance added to other foods for the purpose of giving a strong flavor or relish. Condiments usually appear on the table and are intended for individual use by the diner.

Condiments fall into five nonexclusive categories. The first is salt, the earliest and most important condiment employed by humans. In addition to its ubiquitous presence on tables around the world, salt is often a constituent ingredient in many other condiments. It is employed on a wide range of foods, including vegetables, meats, fish, and poultry. Salt is also occasionally shaken on beer and sprinkled on watermelons. Salt is a major preservative and today is commonly found in most processed foods.

The second most common condiment is sugar or other sweeteners, such as honey or maple syrup. Sugar and honey are used directly in everything from bitter beverages, such as tea, coffee, and chocolate, to a topping for breakfast cereals. Sugar and honey are also employed in making other condiments such as jams, jellies, preserves, and marmalades, and are used extensively on bread, rolls, scones, and in pastries. Maple syrup is commonly used on pancakes.

A third category of condiments is pickled foods, which date back to the ancient world in Europe as well as Asia. Common pickled foods used as condiments today include ginger (Japan), chutney (South Asia), and cucumbers (dill, butter, and gherkins). Almost all vegetables have been pickled and used as condiments in some form. They are served whole, in slices, or diced in a relish. Sliced and diced pickles are frequently used on sandwiches.

Spicy and Hot Condiments

A fourth condiment category are those spicy or hot foods, such as black pepper, chili pepper, mustard, garlic, horseradish, and onions. A product of Asia, black pepper (*Piper nigrum*) is commonly served from shakers throughout the Western world in a dried state and is usually ground into coarse or fine state before consumption. Like salt, pepper is used in savory dishes. It is also a base ingredient in some pepper sauces. Chili pepper (*Capsicum*), a product of the Americas, is employed in dried form on diverse foods.

Fresh chopped chili peppers are also the base ingredient in a number of other condiments, including salsa. In pre-Columbian times, the Aztecs employed a number of sauces based on chili peppers along with tomatoes and ground pumpkin seeds. After the Spanish Conquest in 1521, fusion foods developed including *salsa*s, which combined salt with ground tomatoes and chili peppers from the New World and vinegar from the Old World.

Tabasco sauce was an early American condiment based on chili pepper and vinegar. As Mexican cookery became an important food for mainstream Americans in the latter part of the twentieth century, salsas became an important part of cookery in the United States. The fresh salsa market exploded during the 1980s and continued to increase during the following decade. By the 1990s, salsa outsold ketchup.

Salsa is also used in making other condiments, such as guacamole, a combination of mashed avocados, salsa, onions, garlic, and other ingredients. Today, guacamole is served in Mexican restaurants and used as a dip for tortilla chips. Numerous other condiments serve as dips for potato and corn chips.

Mustard and Horseradish

In ancient Roman times, mustard was made from seeds of a variety of plants in the genus *Brassica*. The word originated in Latin and meant the "must" of new wine, which suggests that mustard seeds were combined with wine or vinegar. At an early date, mustard was disseminated throughout China, where it also became an important condiment in Chinese cookery.

The use of mustard survived the Middle Ages in Europe and was commonly employed in French and British cookery. Special dishes were developed for mustard's use as a table condiment. A major area of mustard production in France was the region around Dijon. Powdered mustard was commercialized in England and was produced in the United States by the mid-eighteenth century. The R. T. French Company began bottling a mild

mustard in the United States about 1900. It was soon served on hot dogs and later hamburgers.

Horseradish (*Armoracia rusticana*), a product of western Asia, is a relatively recent addition to Western cookery. Pickled and ground, it is a highly pungent condiment used particularly with roast beef in England and other meats throughout Europe. In Japan, wasabi (*Eutrema wasabi*) serves a similar function for sushi.

Other Compound Sauces

The fifth and final condiment category is compound sauces, including ketchup, Worcestershire sauce, fish sauces, soy sauce, salad dressings, curries, and barbecue sauces. The earliest known compound sauces were made of fish. In widely separated regions, such as in the ancient Mediterranean and Southeast Asia, preservation of fish in a liquid form evolved.

In the ancient Mediterranean world, fish sauce called *garum* was initially made in the Greek communities along the Black Sea coast. It was heartily adopted by the Romans, who employed fish sauces lavishly on many dishes to enhance flavor. It was used as a cooking ingredient as well as a dip for fish and other foods at the table.

Fermented condiments were also developed in ancient China and Southeast Asia, where fish and other fermented sauces played significant culinary roles. By the seventeenth century, diverse sauces were manufactured throughout East and Southeast Asia. Today, China, India, and Japan produce small quantities of fermented fish sauces, but Southeast Asia remains the center of production and consumption. Beginning in the early twentieth century, authorities set standards for fermented fish sauce in French Indochina. These and subsequent standards formed the basis for commercial production. Fermented fish sauces, such as *nam pla* in Thailand, *nuoc mam* in Vietnam, *tuk trey* in Cambodia, *ngan-pye-ye* in Myanmar, *budu* in Malaysia, *patis* in the Philippines, and *nam pa* in Laos, continue to be very popular. These sauces are more than just flavor enhancers: they contain high levels of protein and other nutrients.

Another important Asian condiment was soy sauce. Soybeans had been converted into a sauce at least since 200 B.C.E. in China. It spread quickly throughout East and Southeast Asia. Although soy sauce production is believed to have started in China, eventually Japan became a major producer. Its popularity was spread by Buddhists, who used it as an alternative to fish sauce.

Ketchup

Another fermented East Asian and Southeast Asian sauce was *kê-tsiap*, which in the Amoy dialect of Chinese meant "the brine of pickled fish." The British encountered these sauces in Indonesia in the late seventeenth century. In the late seventeenth and early eighteenth centuries, *ke-cap* simply meant sauce, and usually referred to fermented black soybeans with a roasted cassava flour. The English word "ketchup" derived from the Indonesian word *kecap*. Anchovies were an important ingredient in early English ketchups. Although anchovies are no longer an ingredient in ketchup, anchovies were incorporated into several commercial brand-name sauces and relishes that were created during the nineteenth century, including Harvey's Sauce, Gentleman's Relish, and Lea & Perrins Worcestershire Sauce, which still feature anchovies as ingredients today.

Like fish sauces, ketchups were used in cooking to produce particular colors, consistencies, or tastes and were used as condiments on fish, fowl, and meats. Many types of ketchup were based on other products. Among the more important were walnut, mushroom, and later tomato ketchup, which became particularly popular in the United States. As the price for tomato ketchup decreased and became accessible to all Americans at the end of the nineteenth century, tomato ketchup became America's national condiment and other types of ketchup almost disappeared. Tomato ketchup has expanded beyond the English-speaking countries and today is manufactured in more than seventy countries and is consumed to some degree in nearly every country.

Tomato ketchup has also inspired other condiments. In the Philippines, banana ketchup, a takeoff on *jufran* and *mafran*, traditional Philippine hot and spicy banana-based condiments, is produced. Tomato ketchup was also used to make other condiments. For instance, many recipes for barbecue sauce contain ketchup. While barbecue has a long history, the first actual use of the term barbecue sauce does not appear until the mid-twentieth century.

Mayonnaise and Other Condiments

Mayonnaise was based on *aioli*, a Spanish sauce that combined olive oil and egg that probably dated back to Roman times. In the seventeenth century, the French took this basic notion, refined it, and gave the world a unique sauce that they called *mayonnaise*. It could stand alone or could be employed to make other sauces. Mayonnaise, one of the French "mother sauces," was exported to England and to America, where it was used as a sandwich spread in the nineteenth century. Around the turn of the century, it was first manufactured as a commercial product in America.

Mayonnaise was initially used on salads or to make salad dressings and other condiments. For instance, commercial tartar sauce is composed of mayonnaise, relish, and spices. Salad dressings have been consumed since ancient Roman times. Commercial dressings today include ranch, italian, blue cheese, thousand island, french, and caesar.

The rapid success of many condiments can be attributed directly to the globalization of American fast food establishments. For instance, ketchup, mustard, pickles, pickle relish, and mayonnaise are spread on hot dogs, hamburgers, and french fries.

See also **Chili Peppers; Mustard.**

BIBLIOGRAPHY

Costenbader, Carol W. *The Well-Stocked Pantry; Mustards, Ketchups & Vinegars; Dips & Dressing, Sauces & Oils.* Pownal, Vt.: Storey Communications, 1996.

Smith, Andrew F. *Pure Ketchup: A History of America's National Condiment, with Recipes.* Columbia: The University of South Carolina Press, 1996.

Solomon, Jay. *Condiments! Chutneys, Relishes and Table Sauces!* Freedom, Calif.: Crossing Press, 1990.

Thudichum, J. L. W. *The Spirit of Cookery: A Popular Treatise on the History, Science, Practice and Ethical and Medical Import of Culinary Art.* London and New York: Frederick Warne, 1895.

Andrew F. Smith

CONFECTIONS. *See* **Candy and Confections.**

CONSUMER PROTESTS. When enough consumers become dissatisfied with their conditions, such as the lack of nutritional food, the cost of food, and the way food is produced, they have a tendency to organize with other like-minded people. They are then likely to take part in some forms of social action. Compared to a spontaneous riot, protests tend to be relatively organized and are often catalyzed by special-interest groups—sometimes referred to as the "protest industry." That term is appropriate since some such groups are very well established and influential. They use a variety of techniques to draw attention to their cause and to obtain support.

Food riots and food protests are ongoing phenomena. Historically, food riots, common in the eighteenth and early nineteenth centuries, have generally occurred when food is in short supply, whether this is due to weather, insect infestation, or weak economic conditions and increased food prices. For example, as a result of poor harvests in late eighteenth-century France, the price of bread soared, and riots were common in all areas of the country. French farmers have become famous for protesting government policies by driving tractors to Paris. The Great Irish Potato Famine of the mid-nineteenth century was the launching point for bloody riots. It eventually led to the great Irish emigration and to technological advances in agriculture. The food riots of this period led to more organized food protests as basic needs for nutrition gave way to demands for food safety and security.

Increased food prices, along with insufficient and unequal distribution of food rations during both World Wars led women to protest all over Europe. More recently, economic mismanagement and rising food prices in Argentina led to riots despite the abundance of food on supermarket shelves. Likewise, riots in some African countries are commonplace as disreputable governments

Protesters dressed as cows protest outside the Ministry of Agriculture in England over the handling of Mad Cow Disease. COURTESY OF AP/WIDE WORLD PHOTOS.

hoard food shipments from other nations for themselves while starvation is rampant in the poorer, more rural parts of the country.

Protests also occur when food is plentiful, but these protests and boycotts can be more political in nature. For instance, the 1965 grape boycott in California began as a result of wage disputes between domestic union workers, migrant workers, and grape growers. When negotiations between growers and workers stalled, union leader César Chavez called for a national boycott of table grapes. The four-year dispute led to more equitable contracts for workers and was the most successful boycott in American history.

Fears over food quality and safety are also catalysts for protest. In the 1980s, a national protest group used a public relations agency to launch a protest against the chemical Alar, which was used to keep apples on the tree longer and produce redder colors. However, the U.S. government did little to limit use of the chemical, and sales of the product continued, as did the spraying of apples, under consumer protest that children's lives were at stake. By 1989, apple sales had fallen by half, and the manufacturer was forced to take Alar off the market. The event led to some lawsuits by apple farmers against the network that broke the story that led to the consumer boycott.

More contemporary food issues attracting global attention include food safety, such as "mad cow disease" in Europe and the possible spread of this disease to humans. Mad cow disease, or bovine spongiform encephalopathy (BSE), is a neurodegenerative disease that eventually destroys a cow's brain. It has been responsible for the slaughter of millions of cattle and other food animals. Its human form (Creutzfeldt-Jakob Disease) has killed 111 people in the United Kingdom alone (*New Scientist*, 20 July 2002). The death toll could rise because the incu-

bation period is long (the "second wave") and because the disease could spread to other animals or countries. Protests over BSE have arisen on several fronts. Farmers protest that they are not being compensated for their losses by insurance companies or the government. Consumers protest both the marketing of the suspected meat and the slaughter of affected animals.

Another issue that is prompting protests involves the genetic modification of food. That is, genes have been inserted or removed to provide specific benefits. Foods have been genetically modified to resist disease, adverse weather conditions, and insects, and are modified to contain beneficial human nutrients. Proponents of biotechnology report that the seeds are environmentally safe, reduce the need for pesticides, and can be modified to include useful nutrients. Opponents are concerned that genetically modified foods may have hidden health hazards, may be detrimental to the development of the poorest countries, and may be environmentally unsafe.

Protests against genetically modified food have occurred more often in Europe than in the United States. This reflects different cultural views on science, technology, and agriculture. There are also differences in the government's credibility. Europe is regulating the process of genetic modification based on a variety of political and economic interests.

One of the main things to note about consumer protests is that they are often well-funded and centrally coordinated by groups who have a vested interest in the outcome of the protests. Most average consumers have little interest in or even awareness of some of the protests. For example, a coalition including various players in the organic industry and some environmental groups has worked together to raise public fears about the safety of modern food production technologies (including pesticides and genetic modification). The ultimate goal is to increase the sales of the more profitable organic foods. Through their campaigns they have been quite successful.

Overall, it is interesting to note how the focus of food protests shifts as a country goes through the economic development process. In poor countries, the main concern involves getting enough food to eat. It is only in the richer countries that consumers are able to spend time and money to make sure that their foods are of high quality and safety. What is certain is that the future will see more protests over both sets of issues.

See also **Biotechnology; Food Riots; Food Supply, Food Shortages; Genetic Engineering; Meat.**

BIBLIOGRAPHY

Beardsworth, Alan, and Terresa Keil. *Sociology on the Menu*. New York: Routledge, 1997.

McIntosh, Alex. *Sociologies of Food and Nutrition*. New York: Plenum, 1996.

Taylor, Lynne. "Food Riots Revisited." *Journal of Social History* 30, no. 2 (1996): 483–497.

Thomas Jefferson Hoban IV

CONSUMPTION OF FOOD. Did humans once have some instinctive knowledge about which foods to eat for good health? No one knows, but whatever inherent wisdom about nutrition humans might once have had has been wiped out in most parts of the world by a persistent background "noise": from infancy, people are bombarded by the selective, but constant, advertising of certain foods and drinks. Advancing globalization has sent products such as cola drinks to remote parts of the world, and advertisements for them have been so pervasive that some people believe that water cannot satisfy their thirst. Social aspects of eating have also changed in some countries, from regularly scheduled family meals to a pattern of random snacking. Is this the way humans were programmed to eat, or is it the result of marketing? Scientific aspects of nutrition also influence food consumption in many countries as consumers decide whether to eat nutritional foods or those that have no nutritional value.

Why Humans Eat What They Eat

What, when, how, and why people eat and drink is linked not only with biological needs and the availability of various foods, but also with the customs, aspirations, and expectations of their societies. The quantity and quality of food consumed, whether people "graze" or eat discrete meals, the emphasis given to different foods (or to desirable body shapes related to diet), and the customs surrounding eating have varied throughout history and within cultures. Nevertheless, the major influence on the daily diet has been the availability of food. Humans can survive only a few days without water and, while the average healthy person can stay alive for weeks or even months without food, this will have adverse effects and sometimes cause permanent health problems.

As well as being a biological necessity, eating and drinking are enjoyable activities, and the more varied the foods available, the more most people will eat. Nutritionists generally recommend eating a large variety of foods as this increases the chances of achieving nutritional adequacy and lowers the risk of a high toxin load. Against this, however, the problem of overconsumption now affects the wealthiest countries in the world, coexisting with malnutrition in many areas. Cultural factors—taboos about eating certain items, appropriate times for meals and snacks, and the way food is distributed among members of a social group—have also played a role historically.

When debate involves morality, scientific considerations may be beside the point. Some people think that food choices have a moral dimension, for example, regarding it as wrong to kill animals for food. Scientists, however, who study the ideal proportion of fatty acids in

cell membranes maintain that, once our ancestors diverged from the apes, they adopted a diet that consisted primarily of marine creatures and plant-based foods. In *The Heretic's Feast: A History of Vegetarianism,* Colin Spencer, himself a vegetarian, traces the history of our ancestors' diets to show that human survival depended on being omnivorous, and notes that our close relatives, the chimpanzees, ate meat, although not in great quantities. Gastroenterologists support this, arguing that the human intestine is designed to digest both animal and plant foods. About 500,000 years ago, the discovery of fire almost certainly encouraged meat consumption because the heat softened connective tissue and produced enticing aromas and flavors. Having the physiological ability to eat any kind of food, however, does not mean that humans must be omnivores. Many people adopt a vegetarian lifestyle because of their religious or philosophical convictions without sacrificing a nutritionally balanced diet.

Until the twentieth century, the environmental consequences of the foods people consumed were largely ignored. With an increasing world population, however, the sustainability of the world's food supply has forced itself onto the agenda. Equity issues also arose because some countries were using up scarce energy and water resources to produce an ever-expanding range of foods for an overfed population while others starved because they did not have access to basic resources. The United States, for example, had approximately 5 percent of the world's population but consumed 26 percent of the world's energy resources as the twenty-first century began.

Growing grains or legumes to feed animals, rather than letting animals graze on lands not used for human crops, is particularly wasteful as lot-feeding requires approximately 100 times more water to provide about 1 kg of animal protein than is needed to produce the same amount of plant protein (Pimmental, Houser, and Preiss, 1997). There are also nutritional implications. Researchers found that the meat from grain-fed animals had fewer essential fatty acids than meat from grass-grazing animals, and there are also concerns about the effects on humans of the use of growth hormones to increase the size of cattle or their milk yield.

Myths, Customs, and Manners

Myths and superstitions associated with food exist in all cultures. Few people believe that cucumbers must be scored "to let the poisons out," tomatoes are no longer believed to be "toxic," and the belief that eating the brains of heroes will lead to bravery has almost disappeared, but myths abound, even when science has proven them wrong. As the twenty-first century began, for example, many people still believed that eating meat, especially beef, causes aggression. Others maintained that the body is unable to digest protein and carbohydrate at the same meal, which would make it impossible to digest foods containing both, such as human milk, nuts, seeds, grains, and legumes. Forty percent of the population in the United States is taking vitamin and herbal supplements because they believe advertising claims that vegetables and fruits no longer contains vitamins.

Some enduring customs relate to religious beliefs about food. These include feasts and fasts, kosher foods, foods regarded as "unclean," forbidden foods, "holy" foods, or the supernatural doctrine of the Roman Catholic and Eastern Orthodox Churches asserting the eucharistic transubstantiation of bread and wine into the body of Christ.

Wealth or social status also determines which foods people can afford to eat, although this can change over time. When peasants ate coarse whole-grain breads, for example, white bread was preferred by the upper classes. Because scientists determined that whole-grain breads are more nutritious than breads made of bleached white flour, highly educated people began to eat the more expensive whole-grain breads.

Etiquette also varies around the world. Where food is consumed with the hands and toilet paper is not used, it is customary for only one hand to be used for eating. Touching food or shaking hands with the hand used to wipe oneself in such countries is regarded as bad manners because it is unhygienic. Many people once considered it bad manners to eat while walking along the street, although the ubiquitous habit of snacking has led to greater tolerance of this practice.

In the West, many books have been written on table manners, but context is everything when it comes to etiquette. Much depends on the culture and social class, the context of the meal (a formal dinner demands adherence to complex social rules whereas a casual snack requires few or none), and the social group involved. In some cultures resting one's elbows on the table or making loud slurping noises is considered bad manners, whereas other societies have no objection to such habits. The polite way to put down cutlery at the end of a meal varies around the world, and sometimes even within a country. Some cultures regard burping at the end of a meal as a sign of satisfaction, even as a compliment to the cook; others think it is rude. Passing gas also has varying acceptance. In Western societies, some believe passing wind (flatus), even in private, indicates some medical problem. In fact, the quantity of gas produced is related to what has been eaten. As helpful bacteria break down dietary fiber and some types of starch, they produce beneficial acids with gas as a by-product.

Convenience

Over the past one hundred years or so, anything that reduced the need for domestic labor was popular, including kitchen appliances and convenience foods. Scholars such as Lebergott (1993) estimated that the average American housewife spent thirty-two fewer hours a week on meals and housecleaning in 1975 than she did in 1910. The noted nutritionist and ecologist Joan Gussow found that much of the time people once spent in the kitchen

is spent watching television, and watching television is how they learn about the latest convenience foods, which saves them more time, which allows them to spend more time watching television so they can be persuaded to buy more convenience foods, and so it goes.

By the end of the twentieth century, marketing of fast foods had shown how easy it is to change eating habits. Starting from scratch almost fifty years earlier, by 1997 McDonalds had 23,132 outlets in more than one hundred countries, with annual sales of $34 billion. The standardized foods offered by fast-food chains had come to appeal to all socioeconomic groups and changed food culture for many people in the West, encouraging eating-on-the-run rather than sit-down family meals. Somewhat ironically, the only time some families eat together is at a fast-food restaurant. Research done in the 1990s (Stanton) found that children liked fast-food restaurants because they felt welcome, the family was relaxed and happy (because no one had to cook), and there were playgrounds and gifts. The food was relatively unimportant, but they liked the standard menu and the fact that there were no vegetables except for French fries. One McNair survey in Australia (1999) found that the "golden arches" had become, in just twenty years, more recognizable as a symbol than the crucifix. As one commentator put it, "Hamburgers are now outselling heaven."

When fast-food hamburgers appeared in Rome in 1989, Carlo Petrini was so horrified that he began the Slow Food Movement, intended to counter what he considered the degrading effects of industrialized food and fast foods. In 2002, the movement operated Convivia in forty-five countries and was spreading but had not yet reached sufficient critical mass to alter the average consumer's eating habits.

Nutritional Science

Nutritionally, fast foods are a disaster: they have high levels of added saturated fat, salt, and sugar. An average fast-food hamburger contains twice as much fat as one that was served by individual outlets in the 1970s. Few fast foods feature vegetables, apart from fat-soaked potatoes, and the replacement of regular meals with fast foods partly accounts for the fact that most people in Western countries eat fewer vegetables than nutritionists recommend for good health.

Despite the increase in convenience foods, however, nutrition was gradually becoming more important in influencing consumers' decisions about which foods to buy. This is nothing new. Hippocrates said 2,400 years ago, "Let food be thy medicine." But it was not until the twentieth century that vitamins, amino acids, fats, and fiber were isolated and identified, and researchers have since been trying to unravel the role of hundreds of protective phytochemicals in plant foods.

Nutritional science can encourage change if it gets enough airtime to compete with the time purchased for "informing" consumers about the latest unhealthy con-

450

venience foods. Olive oil, for example, was vital to Mediterranean cuisines for thousands of years, but was shunned as food in other countries, although it was used as a skin moisturizer. Once studies showed its healthfulness, olive oil became popular in cooking beyond its original homelands and was outselling all other oils in Australian supermarkets by the close of the 1990s.

Nutrition may not, however, always overcome social custom. For example, among preschool children in Australia, boys are given more meat than girls, although there is no difference in their need for meat's nutrients. The assumption that men should receive more meat than women ("feeding the man meat") then continues into adulthood, with Australian men consuming more than one and a half times as much meat as women, even though women have greater requirements for meat's most important nutrient—iron.

There are also fashions in dietary recommendations and changes as new data becomes available. Consumer confusion is also fed by self-styled "experts" whose book sales depend on new diets that have little or no scientific support. Basic governmental advice to consume more vegetables, fruits, and whole-grain cereal products and less saturated fat, sugar, and salt has not changed, but governments are not immune to influence from powerful lobby groups that want more positive spin for their products.

Meals and Snacks

Studies with adults have shown that eating "small and often" can produce benefits for metabolism, reduce blood fats, and lower blood glucose levels. Babies who feed spontaneously on their mother's milk have fewer problems with health and weight than those who are given regulated formula feeds of known quantity.

Does this research mean that snacks are preferable to meals, and would a grazing pattern of eating fit our genetic background better than restricting food to three major meals a day? While nothing is true for everyone all of the time, in countries where snacking is common, so is obesity; where snacking is less common, as in France, obesity rates are lower. The grazing pattern suits makers of processed snack foods (who fund some of the positive snacking studies), but most studies favoring snacks have provided the snacks calculated to fit each individual's daily requirements. In practice, self-selected snack foods are less nutritious, and, for those who overeat every time they eat, snacking may not be ideal.

From the Past to the Future

Three prominent milestones in the changing human diet can be identified:

- hunter-gatherer diets consisting mainly of meat, birds, insects, and fresh or saltwater creatures plus fruits, seeds (including wild grasses), nuts, various green vegetables, yams, and other edible plant materials;

- the agricultural, farm-based period that began about 10,000 years ago when animals were domesticated to produce meat and milk, and crops of grains, fruits, vegetables, and nuts were planted, first for individual families and then also for urban dwellers;

- the technological age, which extended basic farm-produced foods using processing and additives to increase shelf life and provided a broader range of foods padded with extra sugars, fat, salt, flavorings, and colorings. This period decreased the role of home cooking in favor of mass-produced, ready-to-eat foods. At the beginning of the twenty-first century, 46 percent of the food dollar in the United States was spent on foods prepared outside the home.

Genetically modified (GM) foods began to extend the role of technology at the end of the twentieth century. Initially, such foods benefited only those who owned seed stocks, but this technology can also produce foods capable of filling particular nutritional or social needs. GM technology created unrest in Europe and many other parts of the world, especially because of concerns about the integrity of local foods and the plight of poorer nations forced to exchange subsistence family farming for GM crops whose seeds are owned by large agribusiness companies.

Each of the major dietary changes throughout human history has had social and environmental implications. Hunters (usually men) were given greater status in many communities than gatherers (usually women and children). Farming also divided society into owners and workers. That distinction was transformed in developed countries by mechanization and takeovers of small family farms by large commercial companies. Rural communities were impoverished and turned into ghost towns as people left, agribusiness took over what had been family farms, and farming the resulting large farms was done by machine. Whatever tasks remained that required manual labor were left to migrant workers.

The technological age of highly processed foods encouraged people of all ages and socioeconomic groups to purchase foods prepared outside the family kitchen. Increased use of such foods caused cooking skills to degenerate and even changed the physical layout of some dwellings, where there is no longer a dedicated kitchen.

The environmental effects of dietary changes were not taken into account until the end of the twentieth century. Hunting, for example, contributed to some animal species being wiped out. Farming based on technology and driven by the bottom line, with its inhumane methods of raising animals, lot-feeding, and monocultural crops, required increased use of fertilizers, herbicides, and pesticides, which caused environmental problems such as increased salinity, poor soil fertility, poisoned or polluted groundwater, loss of many plant cultivars, and climate change due to massive land clearing. As the twenty-first century began, the conflict regarding the full environmental costs of GM crops was just getting started.

See also **Biotechnology; Fast Food; Feasts, Festivals, and Fasts; Food Supply and the Global Food Market; Food Supply, Food Shortages; Genetic Engineering; Hunting and Gathering; Religion and Food; Slow Food; Sociology; Taboos.**

BIBLIOGRAPHY

Australian Bureau of Statistics. *National Nutrition Survey: Foods Eaten, Australia.* ABS Catalogue No. 4804.0. 1999.

Australian Institute of Health and Welfare. *Australia's Health 1996: The Fifth Biennial Health Report of the Australian Institute of Health and Welfare.* Canberra, Australia: Australian Government Publishing Service, 1996.

Coveney, John. *Food, Morals, and Meaning: The Pleasure and Anxiety of Eating.* 2nd ed. London & New York: Routledge, 2000.

Crotty, Patricia. *Good Nutrition? Fact & Fashion in Dietary Advice.* Australia: Allen & Unwin, 1995.

Germov, John, and Lauren Williams, eds. *A Sociology of Food and Nutrition: The Social Appetite.* South Melbourne, Victoria: Oxford University Press, 1999.

Larsen, Egon. *Food: Past, Present, and Future.* London: F. Muller, 1977.

Lebergott, Stanley. *Pursuing Happiness: American Consumers in the Twentieth Century.* Princeton, N.J.: Princeton University Press, 1993.

Pimmental, D., J. Houser, and E. Preiss. "Water Resources, Agriculture, the Environment, and Society." *Bioscience* 47 (1997): 97–106.

Price, C. "Sales of Meals and Snacks Away from Home Continue to Increase." *Food Review* 21 (1999).

Spencer, Colin. *The Heretic's Feast: A History of Vegetarianism.* London: Fourth Estate, 1993.

Rosemary Stanton

COOKBOOKS. Though essentially manuals of instruction for the preparation of food, cookbooks are now coming into their own as a genre. They are rich sources of information not only about the foods of a given period but about the people who cooked and consumed those foods. Scholars are turning to cookbooks for evidence of cultural values, and are showing a new appreciation for knowledgeable writers who write well about food and its context. Cookbooks have been moving away from their origins as humble recipe books to glamorous books with lavish photographs, more likely to be found on living-room coffee tables than kitchen counters. As a result of these enhancements, cookbook collectors are not only cooks and food scholars, but people who enjoy reading recipes with beautiful photographs of dishes they may never cook.

The history of cookbooks within a culture reflects its food traditions, so that while France has produced a rich cookbook literature, other countries have not. The evolution of restaurants in France, especially since the early nineteenth century, generated books written by chefs who have codified their recipes. But in a country such as Ireland, which has no restaurant tradition, historic recipes are to be found in the handed-down oral tradition of home cooks.

In America, early settlers brought with them books written in England, and later plagiarized recipes from British books for an American audience. Not until 1796 did an authentic American cookbook appear when Amelia Simmons published *American Cookery*, a collection of recipes that included such New World ingredients as corn meal and cranberries. Other decidedly American landmark cookbooks were published by Mary Randolph, Eliza Leslie, and Lydia Maria Child, whose *Frugal Houswife*, published in 1829, was later published in England and retitled *American Frugal Housewife*.

Nineteenth-Century Cookbooks

Because the mission of a cookbook is to instruct, the voice present in the text is authoritative and often didactic. In nineteenth-century America, the division of labor within most families required women to be responsible for the smooth running of the home and the proper feeding of husbands and children. Apart from offering recipes, cookbook writers of the period who saw themselves as guardians of the public morality took on the added responsibility of advising housewives on how to manage their duties.

Catherine Beecher, who carved out a career for herself by promoting the concept that housewives were professionals, believed that American women had control over the well-being of the country's democratic system and its future as a Christian nation. Beecher dedicates *The New Housekeeper's Manual* (1873) "to the women of America, in whose hands rest the real destinies of the republic, as moulded by the early training and preserved amid the maturer influences of home." To her mind, cooking well was the patriotic duty of homemakers. Beecher, who came from a family of preachers, was given to florid pronouncements such as these comments on the results of bad cooking: "Green biscuits with acrid spots of alkali; sour yeastbread; meat slowly simmered in fat till it seemed like grease itself, and slowly congealing in cold grease; and above all, that unpardonable enormity, strong butter!" She introduces her recipes declaring, "How one longs to show people what might have been done with the raw material out of which all these monstrosities were concocted!"

Another influential nineteenth-century voice was that of author Marion Harland, pen name of Mary Virginia Hawes Terhune, a woman whose privileged circumstances never prevented her from commanding the practical details of housekeeping. She published successful novels and advice manuals that gained her the confidence of readers. Her extraordinarily popular *Common Sense in the Household* (1871) holds that "it is a mistake of Christian civilization to educate girls into a love of science and literature, and then condemn them to the routine of a domestic drudge." Her task, as she saw it, was to encourage and reassure her readers by calling a kitchen disaster "a stepping-stone to success," for, as she puts it, "not to do it right is the next thing to success." Her book is a thick collection of typical American dishes that probably would have been cooked and served to Harland by the servants she employed in her affluent home. On the other hand, the assured Catherine Beecher, who had developed a system of scientific housekeeping, never had a home, husband, or children.

While the writings of Marion Harland and Catherine Beecher may project images that were different from the real women, there is consistency in their belief that a moral society depended on the skills of women working within the domestic sphere. Another writer of this period, Hetty Morrison, was, however, an out-and-out opponent of this view as her book, *My Summer in the Kitchen* (1878), makes abundantly clear. Morrison rails against the social forces that put women into the kitchen as though it were their natural habitat, and like Harland, deplores the quandary facing girls who were given no training in the domestic arts, yet were expected to be highly skilled homemakers when they married. But, unlike Harland, Morrison confronts the injustice of it all:

> The cunning of the serpent was nothing to that of man when he founded the institution of the kitchen and then placed woman there to tend it for him. Woman left to her natural instinct, would satisfy her appetite with a few chocolate caramels and an occasional cup of tea. But when her 'lord and master' appears upon the scene, then and there is hurrying to and fro, and fires and faces blaze, and terror, and death, and destruction go forth among the feathered, and furred, and fanny tribes.

Wartime Cookbooks

The authoritative voices in cookbooks can support the status quo by reinforcing current social values or they can dissent from conventional thinking. Another important function of cookbooks has been to help families in times of war when customary foods are scarce and often rationed. But even in times of national crisis, cookbook authors have varied in their approaches to how this challenge should be met.

During World War II, home economists and dietitians threw themselves into the war effort by educating the public about nutrition, and by trying to persuade all citizens to eat their fair share of what was allotted. Often wives would turn over their portion of the ration to husbands and sons, a sacrifice food writers hoped to correct. For instance, it was suggested that, instead of boiling eggs, they could be stretched further by scrambling them with breadcrumbs.

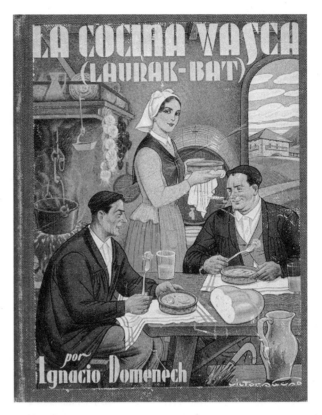

Cookbooks often serve as vehicles for ethnic identity. While *La cocina vasca* (The Basque Kitchen) is written in Spanish, the recipes also feature their names in the Basque language. Perhaps most important is the cover image, which emphasizes the point that the Basque kitchen is also the dining room. Shown here is the Barcelona edition of 1936. ROUGHWOOD COLLECTION.

British wartime cookbooks. This theme of making-do was found in British cookbooks (cookery books) with titles such as *Cookery under Rations* (1941), *Health for All Ration-Time Recipe Book* (1948), and *Feeding the Family in War-Time* (1942). Their authors tended to be domestic scientists or dietitians whose task was to suggest cooking tips to keep families eating as well as possible within the limitations imposed by wartime rations. Their books make clear that monotony of diet was a big challenge. While such old-shoe crops as cabbages, Brussels sprouts, and oats grew comfortably in the British climate, such favorites as peaches, tomatoes, and wheat had to be imported and were therefore scarce. Most British wartime cookbooks are fairly somber in their instructions for plain and healthy recipes, often substituting ingredients at hand for more desirable ones.

One writer, Margaret Brady, saw fit to use the crisis of war as an opportunity to promote her prewar commitment to vegetarianism, seeing virtue in brown rather than white bread, less meat and more vegetables, and sugar-free desserts. *Health for All Ration-Time Recipe Book* (1948) has directions for such concoctions as nut and carrot rissoles, nut meat stew, and oatmeal soup, and puts emphasis on the healthful properties of raw foods, a reminder that cooking fuel also had to be conserved.

Wartime exigencies turned cookbook writers into virtuous citizens. For example, Doris Grant, who was not a food or health expert before the war, was motivated to learn more about these subjects. *Feeding the Family in War-Time* (1942) has advice on healthy living followed by recipes for such fare as wartime ice cream (made with soy flour), potato sausages (made with oatmeal), and salads made with grated carrots, a vegetable that grows abundantly in the British Isles.

Marguerite Patten sums up wartime conditions in England in *We'll Eat Again: A Collection of Recipes from the War Years* (1985), a backward glance at how the country managed on the available food supply. She offers the surprising information that there was an improvement in overall health as measured by a decline in infant mortality and an increase in the average age of death from natural causes. The recipes and advice collected in this book make clear that poor people who subsisted mainly on bread and other starches were urged to eat more meat, eggs, and fresh produce than ever before, resulting in improved health statistics. The diet of the upper classes was also improved because people were obliged to ease up on the traditional prewar English breakfast of fatty meats and eggs, and the customary rich cakes and pastries served at afternoon tea.

Not all wartime cookbook writers addressed the needs of the body alone. In her *Come into the Garden Cookbook* (1942), Constance Spry explains, "I write this book for the people who see nothing unseemly in being enthusiastic about food, and who are willing to turn attention and energy into procuring and preparing it." Not for her are sausages extended with breadcrumbs or cabbage stuffed with oatmeal. She aims to grow good food in her garden, cook it skillfully, and pass on to others directions and encouragement for doing the same. All too aware that British cooks did not prepare vegetables with the respect they deserved, she offers excellent recipes to get people through wartime eating not just well, but deliciously so. As for gardening, she sees such activity as "a cure for frayed nerves and restless minds [that] can ease unhappiness and lighten apprehension." Spry's wartime cookbook is written as much for the spirit as for the body. Unlike other books of the time, hers does not reduce food to its nutritional components but instead describes it as a way to bring comfort and joy as well as sustenance to a population under stress.

American wartime cookbooks. In America, abundant advice about wartime cooking routinely appeared in articles and books, most of them offering practical information about gardening and canning as well as thrifty tips for dishes not requiring too much of what was rationed. A recurring theme in this material is that American housewives were performing their patriotic duty by following the advice offered by this assemblage of experts.

Alice Bradley, the principal of Miss Farmer's School of Cookery in Boston and an influential food writer of the time, published books that explained how to plan meals, shop for ingredients, and cook well despite shortages. Her dedication in *The Wartime Cook Book* (1943) is to "Women who are cooperating in winning the war by using those foods of which we have an abundance in such combinations as to make themselves and their families strong." The moral message was not dissimilar to what nineteenth-century women had been told by cookbook writers who believed that the health of the nation relied upon the smooth running of the home and the proper cooking of family meals. Bradley's wartime tips include substituting soybean flour for wheat in thickening sauces and soups, using a pressure cooker to conserve heat and retain vitamins in vegetables, replacing sugar with honey or syrup in fruit desserts, and making use of such animal parts as the liver, heart, kidney, sweetbreads, tripe, and tongue. She has a recipe for "heart ragout" that calls for "leftover heart" as its first ingredient, causing one to wonder what else Miss Bradley kept in her refrigerator. Always in the role of a teacher who dispatched cooking information with clarity and economy, Miss Bradley was never given to moments of speculation about living through difficult times.

Such thoughts were more in the mind of M. F. K. Fisher, who in 1942 brought out *How to Cook a Wolf*, a book about eating well during wartime. She states: "I believe that one of the most dignified ways we are capable of, to assert and then reassert our dignity in the face of poverty and war's fears and pains, is to nourish ourselves with all possible skill, delicacy, and ever-increasing enjoyment." Fisher was speaking to the human heart and not just to its stomach, and in so doing was taking on the food-writing establishment, who never looked beyond the mundane issue of the well-balanced meal, a concept Fisher loathed. Convinced that human requirements vary, Fisher reserved the right to eat just toast for breakfast if she felt like it, while others might feel better dining on protein alone. This is not to say that Fisher is never practical, for she does provide seventy-three wartime recipes for favorite foods using cheap and available ingredients, and it is a measure of her acclaim as a food writer that those recipes continue to have wide appeal. She talks about the comfort of such simple dishes as polenta, spaghetti, and kasha. But she is careful to say that the polenta must be made with coarsely ground cornmeal from Italian grocery stores, the spaghetti must not be overcooked, and the kasha can be made heavenly by the addition of butter and sauteed mushrooms. *How to Cook a Wolf*, a book about food that should have lost its audience when the war was over, is still read with curiosity and pleasure. For M. F. K. Fisher, writing about food was a way to share experiences and feelings, with her most memorable writing coming out of the exigencies of war. At a time when most other food writers were watering down butter or extending meat loaves and

Cookbooks by famous restaurant chefs have been an important genre since the eighteenth century. Chef Karl Sroubek's *Wie kocht man bei Sroubek* [The way we cook at Sroubek's], published in 1911, showcases dishes from this once famous temple of Central European cookery in Prague. ROUGHWOOD COLLECTION.

hashes with still more breadcrumbs, Fisher was advising her readers that "since we must eat to live we might as well do it with both grace and gusto." It was an inspiring message for a frightened world.

Modern Trends

Cookbooks have continued to reflect changes in American life in every decade following World War II. Some cookbooks of the 1950s reflect the prevalence of short-cut cooking and the use of technology. In *The Can-Opener Cookbook* (1951), Poppy Cannon tells us that "The use of a can opener may not be news, but the gourmet approach definitely is." The home freezer, an appliance that was increasingly popular after the war, inspired such books as Anne Seranne's *Your Home Freezer* (1953), which taught how "gourmet" dishes could be prepared in batches and frozen for a rainy day. Postwar inflation also prompted books that emphasized thrift. For example, Ida Bailey Allen's *Solving the High Cost of Eating* (1952) and James Beard's *How to Eat Better for Less Money* (1954) taught

Americans how to best manage their food budgets. By 1961, Lila Perl had published *What Cooks in Suburbia*, with a table of contents that refers to "Pot-luck from the deep freeze" and special recipes for dinner parties that were in vogue during this period. In the same year, Julia Child published *Mastering the Art of French Cooking*, the book that inspired many adventurous American cooks to take on the challenges of French cuisine.

By the late 1960s and the 1970s, the country was seeing a radicalized youth culture developing in response to antiwar protests and the movements for civil rights and women's rights. A group called the Friends of the United Farmworkers produced a cookbook in 1976 to raise money in support of grape pickers seeking fair wages. This book is a reminder of the successful grape boycott that was observed by many American families. A short time later, the Bloodroot Collective, a feminist commune that runs a Connecticut restaurant, produced *The Political Palate, a Feminist Vegetarian Cookbook* (1980). Their political convictions included the use of vegetarian, organically grown foods and excluded the celebration of traditional holidays that were seen as endorsing "a theology and value system which continues opposition to abortion and the Equal Rights Amendment [and] believes homosexuality to be a sin or disease." The collective's political approach to food is inclusive in that their recipes take in Native-American sources as well as a range of other ethnic influences.

American cookbook publishing has become noticeably ambitious in that it covers international cuisines of all kinds. Cookbooks are often lavishly illustrated, many of them authored by well-known chefs. Another trend has been in books with a nutritional slant, most frequently on weight loss, a clear indication that the American book-buying public is not suffering from deprivation or the need to economize. An affluent, increasingly overweight society has become a ready audience for a continuing supply of books that promise painless solutions to the vexing problem of weight control.

Cookbooks have value as historical documents that can provide us with insights into people or groups by examining their relationship to food. Any culture that has a tradition of cookbook writing can be similarly approached. Until recently, researchers have overlooked or trivialized cookbooks. Now these books are beginning to be recognized as valuable records of our past, full of information waiting to be interpreted.

See also **Beard, James; Child, Julia; Community Cookbooks; Fisher, M. F. K.; Food Studies; Leslie, Eliza.**

BIBLIOGRAPHY

Bower, Anne L., ed. *Recipes for Reading: Community Cookbooks, Stories, Histories.* Amherst: University of Massachusetts Press, 1997.

Brears, Peter, et al. *A Taste of History: 10,000 Years of Food in Britain.* London: English Heritage, in association with British Museum Press, 1993.

DuSablon, Mary Anna. *America's Collectible Cookbooks: The History, the Politics, the Recipes.* Athens: Ohio University Press, 1994.

Grover, Kathryn, ed. *Dining in America, 1850–1900.* Amherst: University of Massachusetts Press, 1987.

Inness, Sherrie A. *Dinner Roles: American Women and Culinary Culture.* Iowa City: University of Iowa Press, 2001.

Mendelson, Anne. *Stand Facing the Stove: The Story of the Women Who Gave America the Joy of Cooking.* New York: Holt, 1996.

Toomre, Joyce Stetson. *Classic Russian Cooking: Elena Molokhovets' 'A Gift to Young Housewives'.* Bloomington: Indiana University Press, 1992.

Trubek, Amy B. *Haute Cuisine: How the French Invented the Culinary Profession.* Philadelphia: University of Pennsylvania Press, 2000.

Wheaton, Barbara. *Savoring the Past: The French Kitchen and Table from 1300 to 1789.* Philadelphia: University of Pennsylvania Press, 1983.

Williams, Susan. *Savory Suppers and Fashionable Feasts: Dining in Victorian America.* New York: Pantheon, 1985.

Wilson, C. Anne. *Food and Drink in Britain: From the Stone Age to the Nineteenth Century.* Chicago: Academy Chicago, 1991.

Barbara Haber

COOKBOOKS, COMMUNITY. Community cookbooks (also known as compiled, regional, charitable, and fund-raising cookbooks) are a unique genre of culinary literature. These volumes are produced collaboratively by volunteer women from charitable organizations, churches, synagogues, heritage associations, clubs, schools, and museums, among others. They represent the group's members and cuisine. The practice of producing these volumes to raise money began shortly after the end of the Civil War (1860–1865) when they were compiled by Northern Protestant churchwomen to raise money for the Union Army wounded and their families.

Research Tool for Culinary Historians

Community cookbooks are a rich source for the culinary historian and foodways researcher. They can be read like texts, accurate and reasonably complete reflections of the food habits of the communities that produce them. Unfortunately, community cookbooks have only recently been taken seriously, and the greatest challenge for the researcher may be in locating the books (see the bibliography below). In defining "community," these books include certain people and traditions, and exclude others. For example, a cookbook prepared by a religious group that shuns alcohol will not include a drinks section or use liquor in its recipes. These volumes provide records of regional culinary cultures, and the historical, philosophical, and religious background of their compilers.

Community cookbooks focus on home cooking, often documenting regional, ethnic, family, and societal traditions, as well as local history. Some of the earlier ones served to preserve the cooking of the homeland, those countries in Europe and Russia that produced the great wave of immigration between the 1880s and the outbreak of World War I. The cookbooks often distinguish between common, everyday foods and special occasion foods; for example, two Midwestern cookbooks, *What Albion Congregationalists Eat* and *Our Favorite Recipes* mention that meat loaf or baked beans are served only to family, whereas festive dishes were reserved for holidays. Although not submitted to the rigors of professional recipe testing, the formulas have the weight of years of experience in the home kitchen. Indeed, many of the cookbooks advertise their recipes as "tried and true," providing access to the collective culinary skills and expertise of many women.

The volumes provide insight into food preferences as well as those dishes that are disliked or taboo and simply not included. For instance, the *Swedish American Cook Book*, published in 1941 by the West Hartford [Connecticut] Ladies Aid Society, includes a wealth of recipes using canned crushed pineapple, such as Pineapple Meringue Pie, Pudding, Frosting, Icebox Dessert, Pineapple Loaf, and Skillet Sponge. This book, as well as others that focus on a particular ethnicity, offers clues to the degree of assimilation of the community. Clearly, the extensive use of canned pineapple reflects the embracing of American processed foods rather than Swedish heritage and tradition. Similarly, *The Johnstown Area Heritage Association Cookbook*, published in Johnstown, Pennsylvania, in 1989, includes Mexican recipes based on the migration of laborers into the area looking for work in the mines and mills. It documents the celebration of the Feast of Our Lady of Guadalupe, the patron saint of Mexico, every December by this community, a tradition that was abandoned toward the end of the twentieth century.

A Few Best-Sellers

Community cookbooks have proved an extremely effective means of quickly raising funds. Some, in fact, have earned millions of dollars, and transcend popularity in their original communities to take on a life of their own. One of the best known, although it was actually prepared by only two women, is *The Settlement Cook Book*, subtitled *The Way to a Man's Heart*, first published by the Milwaukee Jewish Mission and The Settlement in 1901 to benefit newly arrived Jewish immigrants. It has gone through more than forty editions, and a hundred years after its first publication it had sold over 1,500,000 copies. It was one of the first ethnic cookbooks published in English, and one of the earliest to include German-Jewish recipes. Another big seller has been *Forum Feasts: Favorite Recipes of the Forum School*, first published in 1968 to raise funds for a school for emotionally disturbed children in northern New Jersey. The fact that *Forum Feasts* went through twenty printings and sold more than 300,000 copies before it went out of print shows that it was bought by great numbers of people who had no interest or involvement in the Forum School. Part of the widespread appeal of community cookbooks may well be the strong stand they make for home cooking.

Today, some community cookbooks are expensively and professionally produced. *The High Museum of Art Recipe Collection*, published by an art museum in Atlanta, Georgia, in 1981, contains four-color plates of museum paintings and features chapter headings such as "Dinner at Eight: Recipes for Seated Dinners at Home," which reveal a cosmopolitan community where gracious living and entertaining is the norm. Another chapter is entitled "Before the Game and After the Show: Prized Recipes for Brunches and Late-Night Suppers"; the "Picnic" chapter includes "elegant picnics."

Community Cookbooks as Women's History and Literature

Community cookbooks are uniquely women's literature, created by and for women, one of the earliest ways in which women could relate their stories and history. Like quilts and needlework that have also been perceived as trivial, domestic crafts, community cookbooks have often provided the prime, perhaps only, vehicle for women to express themselves. Since they fall under the rubric of "good works," the cookbooks evolved as permissible and appropriate activities for women for whom professional careers might not be acceptable in their own eyes or those of their communities. Some of the books go well beyond these goals to provide a platform for a political or social agenda. *Our Sisters' Recipes* (Pittsburgh, 1909), a Jewish community cookbook, uses a frontispiece of an African-American woman with a head scarf, apron and spoon to symbolize that the sponsors had achieved American middle-class status and could afford to employ cooks. the National Council of Negro Women's *The Black Family Dinner Quilt Cookbook* (1993) pays tribute to a civil rights leader and discusses food traditions.

By soliciting and contributing recipes for the cookbooks, women participate in a women's network, similar to quilting. As Anne Bower points out in *Recipes for Reading*, these are women "bound together by recipes" (p. 14). Community cookbooks institutionalize the informal practice of recipe exchange among women. This dynamic process has involved and defined a vast community of middle-class women, telling stories that are both personal/autobiographical and relational. By writing their cultures into the cookbooks, these women establish their identities and reveal their history, a major aspect of female cultural heritage.

See also **Cookbooks; Recipe.**

BIBLIOGRAPHY

Bower, Anne L. "Our Sisters' Recipes: Exploring 'Community' in a Community Cookbook." *Journal of Popular Culture* 31 (Winter 1997): 137–151.

Bower, Anne L., ed. *Recipes for Reading: Community Cookbooks, Stories, Histories.* Amherst: University of Massachusetts Press, 1997.

Cook, Margaret. *America's Charitable Cooks: A Bibliography of Fund-raising Cook Books Published in the United States (1861-1915).* Kent, Ohio: Privately printed, 1971. Single best source for investigating beginnings of fund-raising cookbooks from Civil War to First World War. Lists more than 3,000 community cookbooks published before 1916.

Ireland, Lynne. "The Compiled Cookbook as Foodways Autobiography." *Western Folklore* 40 (1981): 108–109.

Kirshenblatt-Gimblett, Barbara. "Jewish Charity Cookbooks in the United States and Canada: A Bibliography of 201 Recent Publications." *Jewish Folklore and Ethnology* 9 (1987): 13–18. Begins about 1970.

Kirshenblatt-Gimblett, Barbara. "Kitchen Judaism." In *Getting Comfortable In New York: The American Jewish Home, 1880–1950.* Bloomington: Indiana University Press, 1991.

Kirshenblatt-Gimblett, Barbara. "Recipes for Creating Community: The Jewish Charity Cookbook in America." *Jewish Folklore and Ethnology* 9 (1987): 8–11.

Leonardi, Susan J. "Recipes for Reading: Pasta Salad, Lobster à la Riseholme, and Key Lime Pie." *PMLA* 104 (1989): 340–347.

Longone, Janice B. and Daniel T. *American Cookbooks and Wine Books, 1797–1950.* Ann Arbor, Mich.: Clements Library and the Wine and Food Library, 1984.

Linda Murray Berzok

COOKIES. *See* Baking; Biscuit; Pastry.

COOKING. Cooking often means the transformation of raw food by the use of heat. Conceived this way, cooking's contribution to human pleasure, culture, and survival could hardly be overstated. When interpreted more widely to include everything involved in the preparation of meals, cooking is even more extraordinarily time-consuming and far-reaching.

Cooking is so universal that it has even been proposed as the distinguishing trait of *Homo sapiens*. In a journal entry for 15 August 1773, social observer James Boswell noted that other species possessed the abilities of toolmaking and rationality, but "no beast is a cook," and his definition of humans as the "cooking animal" was the subject of much discussion and amusement at dinner tables. The paradigmatic cultural transformation of "raw" into "cooked" was brought into a more recent scholarly context by the anthropologist Claude Lévi-Strauss, who wrote in *The Raw and the Cooked*, "Not only does cooking mark the transition from nature to culture, but through it and by means of it, the human state can be defined with all its attributes" (p. 164).

Modern recipe books demonstrate cooking's great array of visual, olfactory, and gustatory effects. Increasing the attractiveness of food and altering its nutritional properties, cooking has served fundamental social and cultural purposes. Cooking made possible the agrarian mode of production, based on food storage. Even earlier, cooking widened the range of available food species and therefore of habitats, its origins traceable to the use of the first stone cook's knife.

Cooking has often been depicted as part of women's housework, which supports "real" (male or public) production. It has belonged, as stated by Simone de Beauvoir in *The Second Sex*, to women's dreary sphere of "immanence" rather than men's artistic, intellectual world of "transcendence." This split helps explain why cooking has been little studied in any systematic way. Authorities are far from agreed on the basic cooking techniques, and words are used carelessly, such as "roasting" when "baking" is, in fact, meant. The central purpose of cooking has hardly been discussed, let alone settled.

Here cooking will be examined in the context of its narrow definition as heating. Then other techniques, which include cutting, grinding, mixing, drying, fermenting, and attractive presentation, will be discussed. These techniques are grouped according to their broad outcomes, thus helping to identify cooking's cultural significance and social location. For further information on cooking's technical aspects, see particularly Harold McGee's *On Food and Cooking;* for information on its cultural and social aspects, see Michael Symons's *A History of Cooks and Cooking.*

The Use of Heat

When Jean-Anthelme Brillat-Savarin assumed in *The Physiology of Taste* that the savory results of roasting derived from a juice in meat called "osmazome," his thinking was not all that unusual in the early nineteenth century. Later work has found instead that the pleasing taste results from a complicated set of changes produced through caramelization and the so-called Maillard browning reactions. Nonetheless, as Harold McGee argues in *The Curious Cook*, "Whatever it is about a roast that inspires such devotion deserves a name, and in the absence of a better one, osmazome serves admirably" (p. 296).

Roasting, baking, broiling, grilling, and frying reach the relatively high temperatures necessary for browning to be achieved sufficiently quickly. The relatively plain-looking and bland effects of boiling and steaming follow from their temperatures being limited to the boiling point of water, 212°F (100°C). Nevertheless, all heating methods alter the aroma, appearance, and texture of foods. Furthermore, heat can turn some otherwise poisonous or inedible substances into food, and change other nutritional properties, not always for the better.

The basic techniques of cooking (in the narrow sense) rely on the physicists' three modes of heat transfer—radiation, conduction, and convection. The glowing coals radiate at relatively high temperatures to roast a joint on the spit. When food is placed on a gridiron immediately over the radiant source, this is grilling. Broiling is similarly intense but from above. Energy is transferred to the food through conduction in the separate techniques of boiling, steaming, and frying. Gentle boiling (poaching or simmering) also relies on the circulation of heat through convection.

Practical methods combine all modes of energy transfer. In baking, the walls of the oven radiate heat, hot air moves through convection, and energy transfers through conduction. Nothing could seem more direct than roasting, until processes internal to the cooked article are considered, such as conduction of heat from the surface inward and steaming within the cavity of a fowl.

Cooking methods employ different mediums, most basically water, oil, or air. Food is boiled, poached, and steamed with water. Food is either deep-fried immersed in hot oil or shallow-fried on a layer of oil in a pan. Baking employs heated air. Again, practical methods combine mediums. An obvious example is braising, which expressly relies on frying and then, after adding liquid and closing the lid, poaching and steaming in the same container.

The promotion of the "economy" stove by British Count Rumford (Benjamin Thompson) added to the confusion at the beginning of the nineteenth century, because he claimed to roast a joint in a "closed" oven, which both improved efficiency and kept flue gases separate. However, since oven temperatures were much lower than those emanating from open coals, his "roast dinner" was a misnomer. An equivalent twentieth-century misconception resulted with the microwave oven, which employs an entirely different science—the stimulated vibration of water molecules so that food heats up internally—so that the device is not really an "oven."

According to the massive *Mrs. Beeton's Book of Household Management*, published in England in 1909, the six cooking methods "commonly spoken of" are roasting, boiling, broiling, frying, stewing, and baking. These are the same methods listed in the general prologue of the *Canterbury Tales* more than five centuries earlier, when Geoffrey Chaucer claimed the cook was able to "rooste, and sethe [boil], and broille, and frye, / Maken mortreux [stews], and wel bake a pye." Although ten basic methods have already been discussed above—roasting, broiling, grilling, baking, boiling, steaming, shallow frying, deep frying, and microwaving—Chaucer reasonably distinguishes stewing from boiling, and many modern-day cooks would also regard poaching as distinct.

Claude Lévi-Strauss's much-reprinted but, for many people, puzzling "culinary triangle" had three cooking methods placed at each corner (boiled, roasted, and smoked). By then finding places for another three (broiled, fried, and braised), he again assumed a total of six methods. He omitted baking, however, and added smoking, although this sort of drying and light tarring might be better listed under preservation methods. Stir-frying deserves its own place of recognition, and so do infusion (as in preparing tea), steam extraction (as in espresso coffee), and pressure-cooking. And yet another complication in this attempt at categorization is the fact that rice largely "cooks" by absorption. In the end, any list of cooking methods remains merely indicative and conveys only broad principles.

The Cooking Fire

Basic cooking (by heating) relies on various heat sources. Any list of principal cultural variants would have to include the spit, gridiron, grill (or salamander), boiling and stewing pot, enclosed braising pot, steamer, frying pan, stir-fry wok, deepfryer, vertical oven (*tannūr*), horizontal oven (baker's oven), range, and microwave oven. Some basic features can be demonstrated by discussing just four: the open fire, the stewing pot, the oven, and the brazier.

Although not necessarily the oldest method, the open roasting fire is primordially simple, with meat and

The most ancient images of cookery invariably depict women, since management of the hearth was one of the traditional domestic spheres assigned to females. This ancient Greek terracotta statuette from the third century B.C.E. depicts a woman cooking. © GIANNI DAGLI ORTI/CORBIS.

other foods skewered on vertical sticks or rotated horizontally on a spit. Roasting was first used by hunters, has often been called the *Homeric method* since its use is cited frequently in the ancient stories of Homer, and has held a particular appeal for the British in recent centuries.

Historically even more important than the spit is the stewing pot. In this vessel various ingredients are combined for long, slow heating; sometimes, the pot's contents are just continuously replenished over days and weeks. Pots have typically been made of clay but variations have included rock depressions (heated by hot stones), leather pouches, and, increasingly, metal containers. The pot was associated with the emergence of a settled society where it was used for both storage and the slow cooking generally required by storable crops.

Dedicated clay ovens are nearly as old as pots, dating from at least seven thousand years ago. These "vertical" ovens are most familiar to English speakers as tandoor ovens (from the Hindustani). Many similar words used in and around the Middle East derive from the ancient Persian, Arabic, and Hebrew *tannūr*. The classic version is a clay barrel containing the fire, entered from the top; it is characteristically used for flatbread placed briefly on the wall inside, so that one side browns through conduction and the other through radiation. Throughout Europe, the more familiar variation of this kind of oven has been the horizontal (or "baker's") oven often used to make leavened bread and sharing the floor with its fire in the simplest versions.

The brazier is another simple pot of burning dung or charcoal, on which appropriate containers are placed so that food is broiled, fried, stewed, or baked. Relatively efficient, it has been used when fuel is scarce and so has remained extraordinarily widespread—as common in ancient Athens as it has remained throughout Asia. An enlarged brazier with two or more apertures for heat is the range, fueled by wood, coal, gas, or electricity.

Most major English language dictionaries agree on the definition of the verb "cook" as "to prepare (food) by heating it," and the basic techniques and devices decribed here are commonly accepted. However, cooking plainly employs many other techniques. The development of artificial refrigeration in the nineteenth century only increased the importance of the removal of heat in certain preparations, such as freezing ice cream. Preparing mayonnaise, for instance, also involves combining oil and eggs entirely without heat.

Other important techniques will now be discussed under their broad outcomes, mainly shared by heating. For example, heat enhances pleasures, not merely taste but also texture by, among other methods, obtaining various concentrations of sugar syrup for soft fudges, firmer caramels, toffee, and spun sugar. Heating also supports two of cooking's other broad purposes, improved nutritional qualities and storage. Heating contributes less noticeably to an additional, presumably underlying task, food distribution.

Making Food Attractive

Cooks have become immensely skilled at enhancing the sensory appeal of food. Adding sugar, salt, and acid (such as vinegar) has a marked effect on flavor, although this might often be a side effect of some other desired outcome, such as preservation. Nonetheless, improved attractiveness has been the basic reason for many other simple additions, such as pepper, ginger, caraway seeds, mint, mustard, nutmeg, and vanilla. Spices typically modify aroma and taste, and sometimes they also impart a charming color, as with saffron. The English concept of "curry" does not do justice to the full range of spices ground and blended into much Indian cooking.

Subtly flavored sauces—the peak of grand French cooking—are classically based on stocks, made by simmering bones to extract gelatin (especially veal because younger bones are rich in gelatin-producing collagen). A brown stock flavored with red wine and shallots then becomes a bordelaise sauce, and so on. Other sauces are prepared by emulsification, in which oil is so finely dispersed in another liquid that it remains suspended. For instance, mayonnaise is oil dispersed in egg yolks. Flavored with garlic, mayonnaise becomes *aioli*. Other emulsions are made from butter and cooked egg, notably hollandaise and its derivatives, such as béarnaise with tarragon. McGee suggests that the "fragrant sauce" for asparagus in La Varenne's cookbook of 1651 may be the first recorded recipe for an egg-based emulsified sauce.

The improvement in the organoleptic appeal of food—and sophisticated cooking involves much tasting and visual adjustment—has been viewed as the essential purpose of cooking by ascetics and hedonists alike. Vegetarians have historically said that good cooking is necessary to disguise meat so that eaters might overcome their disgust. Likewise, the ancient philosopher Plato condemned cooking as the seduction of palates away from higher pursuits. In response, hedonists, whether on a par with Brillat-Savarin or not, have viewed cooking as not the devil's but God's gift.

A modern interpretation of this subject recognizes that food's attractiveness is for the most part socially conditioned, as proved by the wide variety of cultural taboos and preferences. Some groups, for instance, even embrace the poisonous reaction of chili. Thus, cooking does not enhance food's intrinsic attractiveness so much as transform it into a cultural or social symbol. Food has been "good to think" as much as "good to eat" (to borrow again from Lévi-Strauss in *Totemism*). Elaborate French sauces are the unspoken language of opulence and "good taste," haggis indicates Scottishness, red meat exhibits maleness, and the avoidance of pork suggests religious commitment.

Along these lines, cookbook writer Elisabeth Rozin has talked of cooking being responsible for distinct "flavor principles," so that flavoring with soy sauce, garlic, brown sugar, sesame seeds, and chili, for example, identifies food as Korean. The Hungarian flavor principle is paprika, lard, and onions. In this way, cooking adds little national flags, so to speak. Such a system might even have a sound nutritional basis in that, as omnivores, humans rely on cultural markers for safe, balanced, or otherwise appropriate foods.

Predigestion

Nutritionally, cooking is a kind of predigestion. Although cooking can reduce the nutritional value of raw foods, it may also make otherwise inedible foods accessible by releasing the nutritive parts of some foods and rendering others safe. Techniques include removing protective shells from seeds and nuts, physically softening or chemically tenderizing what would otherwise be unchewable, making certain nutrients more readily digestible, leaching out harmful compounds or inactivating them, and destroying troublesome bacteria.

Traditional cooks have gained impressively precise and presumably hard-won knowledge of how to handle local species, such as the detoxification of older strains of manioc (or cassava). Even in the industrialized world, cooks know to peel potatoes that are turning green. Through nutritional improvements, cooking has widened the spectrum of available foods, thereby increasing human adaptability to habitats.

Just as significantly, cooking has enabled different modes of production. In his *Geist der Kochkunst*, Karl Friedrich von Rumohr recognized nearly two centuries ago that the development of human settlements and agriculture approximately ten thousand years earlier had relied on cereals not readily eaten in their original state. The same qualities that keep staples through the year tend to demand that they be processed, as when wheat is laboriously milled and then parched, boiled, or baked.

This ensured the necessity of another nutritional achievement of cooking, the provision of balanced meals. The typical cuisine of agrarian societies has two building blocks: the staple and its accompaniment, a relish or sauce. The main stored agricultural product, such as wheat, corn, and potatoes, is bland, starchy and nutritionally incomplete. The staple is enlivened and supplemented by an appropriate sauce made from a little meat (fished, hunted, or taken from the herd), an animal by-product (such as cheese), or a legume or vegetable.

The ancient Athenians, for example, based their meals on the *sitos* of barleycake and wheaten bread or perhaps lentil soup. The *opson* then provided extra proteins, vitamins, and interest, in the form of a salad of bitter herbs, cheese, eggs, fish (fresh, salted, or dried), or, less frequently, meat. Eventually, the desirable *opson* was fish. A gourmand was called an *opsophagos*, a topping- or sauce-eater.

As another example, Chinese cuisine divides a meal into *fan* and *ts'ai*. In a narrow sense, *fan* means "rice" or "cooked rice," and *ts'ai* means "greens" or "vegetables." In a broader sense, *fan* includes all cereal and starchy dishes, among them porridge, steamed bread, dumplings, pancakes, and noodles. And, *ts'ai* refers to the accompaniments, whether made of vegetables, meat, or fish. As explained by anthropologist Eugene Anderson and others, *fan* is "grain foods" and *ts'ai* "dishes to go on rice." The two types of food have to be in balance, although more *fan* might be consumed at home and *ts'ai* dishes would be more numerous and prominent at feasts or on special occasions.

Although anthropologist Sidney Mintz has wanted to further divide agrarian cuisines into "core/fringe/legume," nutritionist Daniela Schlettwein-Gsell finds enough nutritional wisdom in the typical combinations of "core" and "fringe," as when wheat is complemented by leafy green vegetables. *Polenta con funghi* (cornmeal with mushrooms) exhibits a remarkably balanced nutrient density, as do the combinations involved in southern Italian pizza, Swiss raclette, Anglo-Indian kedgeree, North African couscous, Chilean empanadas, and so on.

Storage

Settled society was made possible by stored food, which typically was not just cooked to be made edible, but often was also preserved in the first place. Preservation methods include drying, chilling, sugaring, salting, pickling, fermenting, and storing in sealed containers (often under fats and oils). They slow down deterioration by such means as removing moisture, altering acidity, and closing off oxygen. Cooking by heat has also played a role, killing microorganisms—bacteria, yeasts, and molds—that compete for the food, a process exploited in pasteurization.

Fermentation actually uses microorganisms in a controlled way to help convert raw materials into more stable forms, such as wine, beer, cheese, leavened bread, fish sauce, sauerkraut, and soy sauce. For example, in making wine, yeasts transform the sugars in grape juice into alcohol and carbon dioxide, until the yeasts have nothing to survive on. Cheese-making converts excess spring milk through lactic acid fermentation, during which the protein coagulates, and the solid mass can be retained because of its reduced moisture, together with extra saltiness and acidity.

Since the earliest division of labor between the sexes, women have generally been more intimately involved in cooking than men. However, baking, brewing, vinification, sauce-making, and the like have become important spin-offs of cooking performed by specialists, often (but not always) men. While the cooking of women has had a domestic focus (home and hearth), that of men is generally more public, or market-oriented. In recent centuries, food production has been rapidly industrialized, so that now much cooking, whatever its form, has been taken over by factories.

Distributing

Meals are essentially sharing occasions and, in serving them, cooking should be seen as distributive at heart. Cooking employs a range of food-dividing techniques, including counting, weighing, and other forms of portion control. As Michael Symons has argued in *A History of Cooks and Cooking*, the most characteristic distributive activity has to be cutting, and the most obligatory distinctive culinary tool is the knife.

The classic American cookbook, *Joy of Cooking*, includes in its listing of essential kitchen equipment: two paring knives, one bread knife, one meat knife and grapefruit knife, along with such possible variants as spatula, two graters, wooden chopping bowl and chopper, meat grinder, doughnut cutter, biscuit cutter, pancake turner, apple corer, vegetable slicer or parer, can opener, and kitchen shears. These are used in peeling, coring, and chopping food into suitable pieces for cooking; they are also used to carve meat, slice bread, and cut out biscuits for all to share.

In Chinese cooking, the *tou* (cleaver) is employed to chop meat and vegetables. The quick stir-frying characteristic of this cuisine requires that the ingredients be cut up into same-size, relatively small pieces. Nonetheless, the chopping and slicing also make the food highly distributive. The cleaver allows diners to put aside their knives and rely on chopsticks and spoons. Chinese observers have a point when they view the Western use of table knives as dangerous and barbaric, and cutting up as best left to preparation in the kitchen. The first sharp cutters, made specially from pebbles, date back to approximately two million years ago, which makes the cook's knife about twice as old as the cook's fire. The stone cutters used in scrounging and dividing up flesh heralded the "cooking animal," and innovations in knife-making technology contributed to the names of the Stone, Bronze, and Iron Ages.

The importance of sharing sustenance through meals gives the cutting or carving of foodstuffs and therefore kitchen knives a central place in human life. They are essentially generous instruments. However, the very success of cooks' knives has led to their being overlooked, because the division of food goes hand in hand with the division of labor. Meals are the mechanism by which people share not merely food, but also the associated tasks; everyone brings their contribution to the table.

Unfortunately, while the value and importance of cooking have not always been recognized, specialists have aggrandized their in many ways subsidiary trades and tools, as when men distributed meat through such rituals as temple sacrifice and courtly carving. The fundamental instruments of humankind's social interaction with nature, knives, have thus cut people off from each other and their world.

See also **Beeton, Isabella Mary; Boiling; Brillat-Savarin, Anthelme; Broasting; Couscous; Dinner; Frying; Grilling; Lunch; Pizza; Preparation of Food; Presentation of Food; Roasting; Serving of Food.**

BIBLIOGRAPHY

Anderson, E. N. *The Food of China.* New Haven, Conn.: Yale University Press, 1988.

Brillat-Savarin, Jean-Anthelme. *The Physiology of Taste.* Translated by M. F. K. Fisher. New York: Knopf, 1971. Originally *La Physiologie du gout,* Paris, 1826.

Goody, Jack. *Cooking, Cuisine and Class: A Study in Comparative Sociology.* Cambridge, U.K.: Cambridge University Press, 1982.

Lévi-Strauss, Claude. *Introduction to a Science of Mythology, Vol. 1: The Raw and the Cooked.* Translated by John and Doreen Weightman. London: Jonathan Cape, 1970.

Lévi-Strauss, Claude. *Introduction to a Science of Mythology, Vol. 3: The Origin of Table Manners.* Translated by John and Doreen Weightman. London: Jonathan Cape, 1978. One of many sources for the "culinary triangle."

McGee, Harold. *Science and Lore in the Kitchen.* New York: Scribners, 1984.

McGee, Harold. *The Curious Cook: More Kitchen Science and Lore.* San Francisco: North Point, 1990.

Mintz, Sidney W., and Daniela Schlettwein-Gsell. "Food Patterns in Agrarian Societies: The 'Core-Fringe-Legume Hypothesis'." *Gastronomica* 3 (Summer 2001): 40–52.

Mrs. Beeton's Book of Household Management. London: Ward, Lock, 1909. The authors are unaknowledged. Isabella Beeton only lived to supervise the original *Book of Household Management,* 1861.

Rombauer, Irma S., and Marion Rombauer Becker. *The Joy of Cooking.* Indianapolis, Ind.: Bobbs-Merrill, 1953.

Rozin, Elisabeth. *Ethnic Cuisine: The Flavor-principle Cookbook.* Brattleboro, Vt.: Stephen Greene, 1983. Revised edition of *The Flavor-principle Cookbook* (New York: Hawthorn Books, 1973).

Rumohr, Baron von. *The Essence of Cookery: Geist der Kochkunst.* Translated by Barbara Yeomans. London: Prospect Books, 1993. Originally attributed to his cook, Joseph König, 1822.

Symons, Michael. *A History of Cooks and Cooking.* Champaign: University of Illinois Press, 2000. Also Blackawton, Totnes, Devon (U.K.): Prospect Books, 2001. Original title was *The Pudding That Took a Thousand Cooks: The Story of Cooking in Civilisation and Daily Life,* 1998.

Symons, Michael. "What's Cooking?" *Petits Propos Culinaires* 67 (June 2001): 76–86.

Michael Symons

COOKING APPLIANCES. *See* **Kitchen Gadgets; Preparation of Food; Utensils, Cooking.**

CORN. *See* **Maize.**

COST OF FOOD. The cost of food is viewed from two perspectives. One is the cost to households, the other is the cost of production and marketing. Since food is a basic necessity in every society, a falling portion of household income needed to purchase food is an indicator of growing households' incomes and a measure of improved national economic development. In high-income countries the percentage of income needed for food is smaller than in low-income countries. This phenomenon reflects an economic principle known as Engels' Law. As income rises, the percentage of the additional income spent on food declines.

Consumers' Food Costs

In the United States the percentage of personal disposable income (PDI) spent for food fell precipitously during the second half of the twentieth century from 20 percent in 1960 to 11 percent in 2000 (see Figure 1). At the beginning of the twenty-first century the United States had the lowest ratio of food expenditures to PDI in the world. Expenditures for food ingredients to cook at home fell in tandem with the decline in the percentage of income spent on all food. Expenditures on food

FIGURE 1

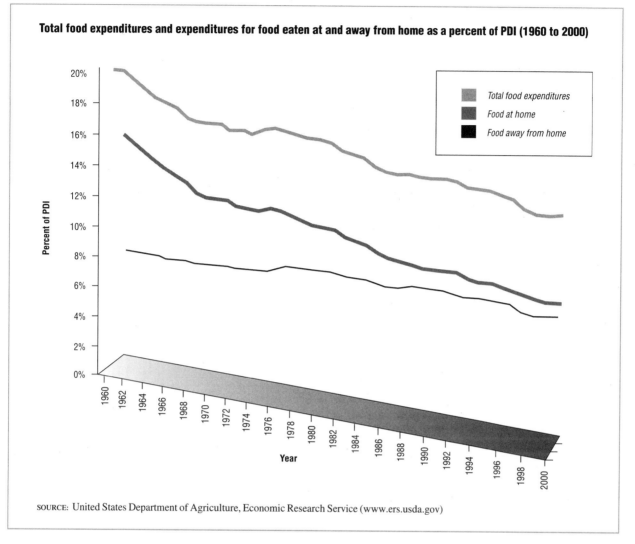

Total food expenditures and expenditures for food eaten at and away from home as a percent of PDI (1960 to 2000)

SOURCE: United States Department of Agriculture, Economic Research Service (www.ers.usda.gov)

from restaurants and other food service places remained steady at around 4 to 5 percent of PDI in the late twentieth century. Consequently the percentage of households' total food budget spent for food service increased from 27 percent in 1960 to 47 percent in 2000.

Expenditures on food rise with income and the number of people in the household. The absolute amount spent on food rises with income as consumers shift to more expensive brands, higher-quality food, and more convenient forms of food, including more food eaten away from home. Households with only one person spend 16 percent more per person on food than households with two people and 62 percent more per person than households with four people. Per capita expenditures for food are greater for single people because of the economies of scale involved in feeding more people in the same household. With more people to feed, less waste occurs from preparing full recipes, and people are more inclined to

cook food at home. Single persons tend to eat more food away from home, increasing their food costs (Blisard, 2000, pp. 23–26).

Lower-income households spend about two-thirds the number of dollars per person on food compared with higher-income households and about 85 percent as much compared with middle-income households. Even though households in the lowest income group spend fewer dollars on food, these expenditures account for almost half of their incomes. Those in the highest-income group spend only 8 percent of their incomes on food. The average food expenditure, 11 percent of PDI, represents middle-income households and hides the fact that great disparity persists.

Production and Marketing Costs
Production and marketing costs determine the minimum price of food in the retail marketplace. Production costs

are typically called the "farm value" of food, and they comprise about 20 percent of the final food cost. This percentage varies by type of food, depending on how highly processed or perishable the food is. The farm value for meats and dairy products is around 28 percent, for poultry around 41 percent, for cereals around 5 percent, for fresh fruits 16 percent, and for fresh vegetables 19 percent. As consumers demand more highly processed foods, fresh foods from distant places, and foods ready to eat, the farm value falls as a percentage of the retail price.

Marketing costs have risen as a percentage of retail food prices. The "marketing bill" as defined by the U.S. Department of Agriculture is the difference between the farm value of domestically produced foods and the final cost to the consumer (see Figure 2). Marketing costs rose 3.5 times faster than the farm value between 1990 and 1999. At 39 percent, labor is the largest portion of the cost of food, rising 56 percent during the 1990s. Over half of the 14 million food industry workers in 1999 were in food service. Retail food stores employed 3.5 million or about one-fourth of all food industry workers. About 12 percent of food industry employees worked in food processing, and about 7 percent worked in food wholesaling. The escalating demand for labor increased wages and the benefit costs for food workers. Food store employees' wages rose 27 percent during the last decade of the twentieth century. As consumers delegate more of the basic cooking and preparation of food to others in the food chain, labor costs can be expected to rise as a portion of the total food cost.

Packaging costs comprise about 8 percent of total food costs, and they increased almost 40 percent in the 1990s. This increase is a function of the cost of paper and plastics and the demand for more conveniently packaged foods. Package design changes and packages that can be used directly for cooking and for eating or drinking increase the cost of packaging relative to the basic food.

Raw commodities (farm value), labor, and packaging comprise 67 percent of the cost of food. The rest of the costs are in transportation, advertising, rent, profits, energy, business taxes, depreciation, interest payments, miscellaneous costs, and repairs. These last types of costs have increased at about the rate of inflation and have not changed their share of the food dollar much over time.

Since considerable price competition exists at the retail end of the food chain, the marketing chain tends to absorb increases in the cost of raw commodities. Also the cost of the raw commodity is a relatively small percentage of the total cost. In the case of cereals, cyclical fluctuations in grain prices barely affect the final food price. One way for manufacturers to decrease their risks of price fluctuations in raw materials is to contract with farmers for a set amount of commodity at a set price that does not change at the whims of the market.

Retail food costs are a function of the production and marketing costs and the intersection of supply and demand. Since most foods have a limited shelf life, retailers want to sell products as soon as possible, keeping prices competitive. On the other hand, total food

FIGURE 2

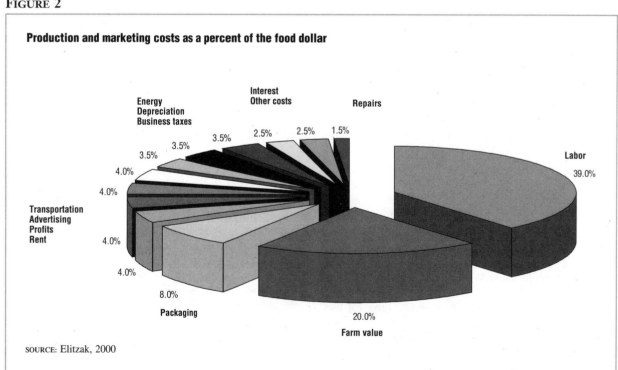

Production and marketing costs as a percent of the food dollar

SOURCE: Elitzak, 2000

expenditures are a relatively small part of most consumers' budgets, and an increase in the price of one food type does not change spending patterns much in the face of numerous substitutes. Taken together these two impacts are called the price and income effects on the quantity of food purchased. The other effect is the limited capacity of human beings to consume food. Once humans are physically satiated, food expenditures rise due to consumers' demands for more quality, variety, convenience, and service but not for more food to eat.

See also **Advertising of Food; Consumption of Food; Distribution of Food; Food Politics: United States; Food Supply and the Global Food Market; Food Supply, Food Shortages; Marketing of Food; Places of Consumption; Political Economy; Restaurants.**

BIBLIOGRAPHY

Blisard, Noel. "Food Spending by U.S. Households Grew Steadily in the 1990's." *Food Review* 23, no. 3 (September–December 2000): 23–26.

Elitzak, Howard. "Food Marketing Costs: A 1900's Retrospective." *Food Review* 23, no. 3 (September–December 2000): 27–30.

U.S. Department of Agriculture, Economic Research Service. Available at http://www.ers.usda.gov.

Jean D. Kinsey

COUSCOUS. Couscous (from the Berber word *k'seksu*) is the staple product of North Africa and the national dish of the countries of Maghrib, that is, Algeria, Morocco, and Tunisia. Couscous spread from this area, where it originated, to Libya, Mauritania, Egypt, and sub-Saharan countries. Couscous is also consumed in the Middle East, where it is called *mughrabiyya*.

Couscous is an icon food in northern Africa for dietary and cultural reasons. Similar to rice, pasta, or bread, couscous is an inexpensive and highly nutritive product made from wheat or other cereals (barley, sorghum, corn, millet, or minor grains) with the capacity for long-term preservation. With a basic cooking system, it is possible to prepare an everyday meal or a luxury feast, a main course or a dessert. A versatile dish, couscous can be mixed with vegetables, legumes, meat, or fish, or it can be eaten with butter or fresh fruit.

Couscous is an icon also because it permits the expression of national identities and ways of life, and it has religious and symbolic meanings. Women usually prepare the grain known as couscous during a family celebration, and the dish named couscous is eaten during a family feast, thereby associating both the product and the dish with solidarity. Couscous accompanies Friday and end of Ramadan celebrations and birth and wedding feasts. The association of couscous with these festivities also attaches it to the concepts of abundance, fertility, fi-

delity, and Barakah (God's blessing). For example, while preparing couscous, women have to make an invocation and converse about religious facts, prosperity, and positive feelings.

Preparation

The grain. Although the use of precooked couscous has spread widely, making couscous is traditionally a female activity that involves much work. On a big flat plate, the woman in charge puts a handful of freshly ground hard wheat, sprinkles on salted water and a bit of flour, and with her palms treats the grain with rolling movements until the couscous granules appear. Later she sifts the grain with sieves of different diameters to obtain granules of similar size. Finally, couscous is sun-dried and stored or cooked.

The dish. Couscous is cooked in a special pot (a couscous steamer), usually earthen, which has two components: a bottom-perforated pan, which contains the grain, and a globular pot that stands underneath it and contains water or a boiling stew whose steam cooks the granules.

Moroccan waiter with a large platter of couscous in Marrakesh. © ROBERT HOLMES/CORBIS.

Couscous is moistened with water and oil before cooking and then it is placed in the pan. Every ten or fifteen minutes, the couscous is taken out of the pan; oil or butter is added, and it is worked by hand to avoid the formation of curds. Couscous is ready when the granules are cooked, separated, soft, and moist.

The basic ingredients of the couscous stew are seasonal vegetables and legumes (usually chickpeas), fish or meat (chicken, lamb, beef, rabbit, hare, and even camel), and spices. There are regional preferences regarding couscous. Algerian couscous includes tomatoes and a great variety of legumes and vegetables, and Moroccan couscous uses saffron. Tunisian couscous includes fish and dried fruit recipes and always contains chickpeas and a hot salsa (*harissa*). Saharan couscous is served without legumes and without broth.

After the grain is cooked, a pile of couscous is placed in a big platter topped with the meat or fish and vegetables. The couscous broth is put in a side bowl and optionally mixed with hot sauce.

The History of Couscous

Origins. The origin of couscous is uncertain. Lucie Bolens affirms that Berbers were preparing couscous as early as 238 to 149 B.C.E. (Bolens, 1989, p. 61). Nevertheless, Charles Perry states that couscous originated between the end of the Zirid dynasty and the rise of the Almohadian dynasty between the eleventh and the thirteenth centuries (Perry, 1990, p. 177).

Iberian Peninsula. Bolens dates the introduction of couscous into the Iberian Peninsula to the period of the Berber dynasties in the thirteenth century (Bolens, 1989, p. 62). The popularity of couscous spread quickly among the Moors, and the two Arab cookbooks available from that time, the anonymous *Kitâb al Tabij* and *Fadalat al Jiwan* by Ibn Razîn al Tujibî, include couscous recipes. Sephardim incorporated couscous into their cuisine because of the Moorish influence and carried it to their asylum countries after their expulsion from Iberian lands (1492). It is still popularly consumed in Israel.

Couscous also was a staple for the Moriscos, who ate it during secular and religious celebrations. Consequently, the Inquisition prosecuted its consumption. The hostility toward Morisco culture and foodways led to the disappearance of *alcuzcuz* from Spain and to the development of a derivative, *migas.* In Portugal the gentry and nobility still consumed couscous during the sixteenth and seventeenth centuries; however, the *cozido à Madeirense* (a couscous dish) has its origin in African influences. According to Francisco Abad, the couscous recipes included in the Spanish court cookbook by Martínez de Montiño (seventeenth century) are related to the author's Portuguese origin (Abad, 2000, pp. 23–24).

Italy. *Cùscusu* is a typical dish of western Sicily, especially of Trapani, where it is eaten with a fish stew or in a sweet recipe. There is no agreement about the date of the introduction of couscous into Sicily. Some writers claim that couscous was introduced during the Muslim period (827–1063), while others state that it was introduced after the settlement of Sephardim in the island, at the end of the fifteenth century.

Brazil. The introduction of couscous into Brazil in the sixteenth century, according to Luis da Cámara Cascudo, was a result of the culinary influences of both Portugal and African slaves cultures (Cascudo, 1983, pp. 207–211). There are two varieties. Southern couscous (*Cuscuz paulista*) is a steamed cake made from corn flour, vegetables, spices, chicken, or fish (prawns and sardines). The northern variety (*cuscuz nordestino*) is a steamed pudding made from tapioca flour and sugar and moistened with coconut milk. This is a popular Brazilian breakfast.

Couscous in the Western World

Couscous has developed worldwide popularity. Among the explanations for its success are the increasing importance of vegetarianism, the preference for healthy foods that are aesthetically attractive, the trendy fascination with the Mediterranean cuisine, and the culinary influence of Maghribian immigrants in the Western world.

See also **Africa: North Africa; Brazil; Iberian Peninsula; Italy; Legumes; Mediterranean Diet; Middle East.**

BIBLIOGRAPHY

Abad, Francisco. *Cuscús: Recetas e Historias del Alzcuzcuz Magrebí-Andalusí* [Couscous: Recipes and stories about the Maghribian and Andalusian couscous]. Zaragoza: Libros Certeza, 2000.

Bolens, Lucie. "L'étonnante apparition du couscous en Andalousie médiévale (XIIIe siècle): Essai d'interprétation historique" [The surprising apparition of couscous in Medieval Andalusie, thirteenth century: An attempt of historical interpretation]. In *Mélanges en l'Honneur du Professeur Anne-Marie Piuz*, 61–70. Genève: Université de Genève, 1989.

Cascudo, Luís da Cámara. *História da Alimentação no Brasil* [History of food in Brazil]. 2 vols. São Paulo: Editora da Universidade de São Paulo, 1983.

Perry, Charles. "Couscous and Its Cousins." In *Staple Foods: Oxford Symposium on Food and Cookery 1989*, pp. 176–178. London: Prospect Books, 1990.

Teresa de Castro

CREOLE CUISINE. *See* **United States.**

CROP IMPROVEMENT. Crop improvement refers to the genetic alteration of plants to satisfy human needs. In prehistory, human forebears in various parts of the world brought into cultivation a few hundred species from the hundreds of thousands available. In the process they transformed elements of these species into crops though genetic alterations that involved conscious and unconscious selection, the differential reproduction of variants. Through a long history of trial and error, a relatively few plant species have become the mainstay of agriculture and thus the world's food supply. This process of domestication involved the identification of certain useful wild species combined with a process of selection that brought about changes in appearance, quality, and productivity. The exact details of the process that altered the major crops is not fully understood, but it is clear that the genetic changes were enormous in many cases. In fact some crop plants have been so changed that for many of them, maize, for example, their origins are obscure, with no extant close wild relatives.

The selection process was unconscious in many cases. For example, in wild wheats, the grains scatter by disarticulation, separation of the seed from the seed head. When these grains were harvested by cutting the heads with a sickle, an unconscious selection occurred for "nonshattering" types that would then be continually replanted. For some crops a clear conscious selection occurred, especially when the variant was obvious and would be maintained by vegetative propagation. Something so clearly useful as a seedless banana must have been immediately seized upon and maintained ("fixed") by planting offshoots of the plant. The changes wrought in domestication included alteration in organ size and shape; loss of many survival characters, such as bitter or toxic substances; disarticulation of seeds in grains; protective structures, such as spines and thorns; seed dormancy; and change in life span—increased in crops grown for roots or tubers and decreased in crops grown for seed or fruit. Selection by bulking desirable types (mass selection) is a powerful technique for making rapid changes easily while maintaining genetic diversity in the population.

The selection of naturally occurring variants is the basis of crop improvement. Over thousands of years this technique resulted in the development of modern basic crops. The discovery of techniques for asexual (vegetative) propagation, such as by using natural offshoots, rooting stem cuttings, or various grafting techniques, made it possible to "fix" genetic variants. This was the technique used for many tree fruits, enabling identical plants to be cultivated in orchards. Naturally produced seedlings derived from intercrosses of these selected plants were then available for selection again. Many present-day fruit crops are similar to those cultivated in antiquity, and some ancient selections are still cultivated—dates, for example. As humans carried improved crops to new locations, opportunities opened to increase genetic variation from natural intercrosses with new wild populations.

The changes that occur can be dramatic over time, as seen in the proliferation of breeds of animals and especially the wide range of changes brought about by fanciers of dogs, chickens, and pigeons. The observation of these changes influenced the thinking of Charles Darwin to suggest that natural selection, the survival of the fittest, could lead to enormous genetic changes if carried out over a long enough time, and could lead to the origin of new species.

In the eighteenth and nineteenth centuries a conscious attempt was made to predict the performance of plants that could be expected from one seed generation to the next. The concept that ancestry was important in crop improvement led to refinement in the selection process, brought about by keeping records and the assessment of lineage. Furthermore it became obvious that variation could be managed by controlling the mating process, an extension of what had long been known in animal breeding. This new type of selection, termed pedigree selection, was found to increase the efficiency of the process. Progeny testing (evaluating the genetic worth by progeny performance) increased efficiency of this process. The origins of commercial plant breeding began in the second half of the nineteenth century among seed producers. It involved controlled crosses (hybridization) between selections to control genetic recombination, followed by selection of improved types. This is still the basis of traditional plant breeding. Interestingly much of this early type of plant breeding was carried out without a clear understanding of the genetic mechanism involved in inheritance.

Until the famous experiments with the garden pea by Gregor Mendel (1822–1884), a Catholic priest in Brünn, a Moravian town then in the Austro-Hungarian Empire, the basic theory of inheritance involved the concept of blending. Mendel unraveled the basic concept of inheritance and clearly showed that characters in the pea were due to elements, later called genes, that remained unaltered as they were inherited. Many characters in peas, such as tallness and dwarfness, were shown to be controlled by a pair of genes, of which one member was not always expressed (the concept of dominance and recessiveness). Mendel demonstrated that the gametes of the pea contained one member of the gene pairs that controlled characters and that recombined randomly at fertilization. Mendel's paper was published in 1866, but it had no impact until the paper was "rediscovered" in 1900, when it created a sensation. It was soon obvious that the differences in appearance among plants (phenotypes) could be explained by the interaction of various genes (genotypes) as well as interaction with the environment.

Twentieth-Century Developments

In the twentieth century plant breeding developed a scientific basis, and crop improvement was understood to be brought about by achieving favorable accumulations and combinations of genes. Taking advantage of known genetic diversity could facilitate this, and appropriate combinations were achieved through recombinations brought about by the sexual process (hybridization). Furthermore it was possible to move useful genes by special breeding strategies. Thus a gene discovered in a wild plant could be transferred to a suitable adapted type by a technique known as the backcross method. A sexual hybrid was made, followed by a series of backcrosses to the desirable (recurrent) parent, while selecting for the new gene in each generation. After about five or six backcrosses, the offspring resembled the recurrent parent but contained the selected gene.

In the early twentieth century it was demonstrated that the extra vigor long associated with wide crosses (called hybrid vigor or heterosis), particularly in naturally cross-pollinated crops, could be exploited in plant breeding. For maize, a new system of hybrid breeding was developed, using a combination of inbreeding and outbreeding. Inbreeding was accomplished by crossing the plant with itself. This led to a decline in vigor as the step was repeated over several generations. Outbreeding was achieved by intercrossing the inbred lines to restore vigor. The hybrid between inbreds derived from divergent inbreds (called a single cross or F_1 hybrid) was uniform (homogeneous), and some were superior to the original populations before inbreeding. During the process of inbreeding, the inbreds became weak, but vigor was restored in the F_1. To increase seed set from weak inbreds, two hybrids were crossed; this was known as the double cross method.

Hybrid breeding technique in a sense is similar to arranging a Rubic's cube, where contradictory steps need to be taken to achieve the appropriate reformulation. In hybrid breeding, the first step produces a series of weak inbreds, followed by a series of specific combination, to produce a series of new hybrids. Hybrid maize breeding led to enormous increases in productivity, which were soon exploited in a wide variety of seed-propagated crops, including naturally self-pollinated ones, such as tomato and rice.

A number of genetic techniques were developed and refined in twentieth-century breeding, such as improved techniques to search for and store increased genetic variability, different techniques to develop variable populations for selection, and improved methods of testing to separate genetic from environmental effects. The exact details of the process for crops necessarily differed among naturally cross-pollinated plants (such as maize) and naturally self-pollinated plants (such as soybean or tomato) as well as those plants in which vegetative propagation (usually cross-pollinated) permitted the fixing of improved types directly.

Conventional plant breeding can be defined as systems for selection of superior genotypes from genetically variable populations derived from sexual recombination. The system is powerful because it is evolutionary; progress can be cumulative, with improved individuals continually serving as parents for subsequent cycles of breeding. Genetic improvement by conventional breeding has made substantial changes when the efforts have

been long-term. Characters improved include productivity, quality, and resistance to diseases, insects, and stress. There are, however, limits to the progress of conventional breeding. These are due to limitations of the sexual system, because it is usually not possible to incorporate genes from nonrelated species or to incorporate small changes without disturbing the particular combination of genes that make a particular type unique. Thus a useful gene in cabbage cannot be transferred to wheat. Limitations of conventional breeding are particularly apparent when a needed character (such as disease or insect resistance) is unavailable in populations that can be incorporated by sexual crosses. Mutations may be induced, but they are often deleterious or connected with undesirable effects.

With conventional breeding, it is also not possible to improve a unique genotype, such as "Bartlett" pear, by adding a single character, since the recombination that results from hybridization makes it impossible to reconfigure this cultivar exactly. Finally, conventional breeding has technical or economic limitations to detect infrequent or rare recombinants, the lack of sufficient time to generate cycles of recombination, space to grow necessary populations to recover superior recombinants, or resources to be able to select, identify, evaluate, and fix desired recombinants.

Developments Using DNA

It has been suggested that many of the limitations of conventional breeding can be overcome with advances in molecular biology that rely on DNA, the genetic material.

Recombinant DNA technology, called transgene technology or genetic engineering, is the most powerful and revolutionary of the new genetics developed in the last half of the twentieth century. It is possible to isolate stretches of DNA from one organism, store it in a bacterial host, select unique combinations, and then incorporate them into the DNA of another species, where it can be expressed. This technique, which relies on cell and tissue culture, is truly a marvelous process. Refinements in the technique make it possible to concentrate mutations in desired genes, further increasing variability. Other uses of molecular biology known as genomics involve the detailed mapping of the DNA and the identification of useful stretches of the molecule. This makes it possible to improve the efficiency of selection, because it is based directly on the genes rather than the organism, where the effects may be confounded by environment and genetic interactions.

The limitations of the new breeding methods include technical problems, such as the difficulty of transformation, problems of gene expression, or the lack of knowledge concerning suitable genes to transfer. There are also nontechnical issues, such as legal problems, since the techniques and the genes are usually patented. However, in the short run the greatest impediment has been problems of consumer acceptability and fear of the unknown.

The term "Frankenfood" has been coined to refer to food altered by the process of using exotic genes incorporated by transgene technology. No convincing evidence shows that genetic engineering has produced harmful products, and an abundance of evidence shows that many foods derived from traditional systems have inherent problems (consider the allergic reactions of many people to peanuts). Nevertheless, molecular techniques have incited fear of this new technology in many people. Moreover, the surplus of food in the West has reduced the imperative to make the case for the need for new technology to consumers.

The biotechnology industry has sold the technology to farmers (who have accepted it) and ignored consumers. They have not been sophisticated in exploiting the environmental virtues inherent in the new technology, such as reducing pesticides, or in making the case that increased yield could free up the agricultural use of fragile environments. Because of the benefits that could accrue from this new technology, especially in the problem areas of the world, it seems certain that future progress in plant breeding will involve both conventional and unconventional techniques, but the immediate course of events is fraught with uncertainty.

See also **Agronomy; Genetic Engineering; Green Revolution; High-Technology Farming; Horticulture.**

BIBLIOGRAPHY

Bassett, Mark J., ed. *Breeding Vegetable Crops.* Westport, Conn.: AVI Publishing, 1986.

Janick, Jules, and James N. Moore, eds. *Fruit Breeding.* 3 vols. New York: John Wiley, 1996.

Poehlman, John Milton. *Breeding Field Crops.* 3d ed. Westport, Conn.: AVI Publishing, 1986.

Jules Janick

CRUCIFER PLANTS. *See* **Cabbage and Crucifer Plants.**

CRUSHING. Crushing refers to the pressing, grinding, or pounding of an item into smaller particles, a powder, or a paste. The largest of the human teeth, the molars, are designed for crushing food into small particles that can be swallowed and digested. Digestion is enhanced by the breaking of food into small particles that expose more food surface to the action of digestive enzymes; the more food surface exposed, the more efficient the process of digestion.

The crushing of cereal grains (wheat, corn, rye, buckwheat, rice) into flour is a good example of the use of tools to reduce particle size. The flour can then be eaten raw, cooked with water into porridge, or moistened, formed into a loaf, and baked as bread. Another nutritional advantage of flour over the whole grain is that the flour can be sifted to remove the bran fraction, which is largely cellulose and indigestible. The germ fraction of the kernel is typically removed with the bran and hence considerably reduces the nutritional values of the flour in terms of protein, vitamins, and minerals. Flours, rather then whole grains, also have the advantage of cooking faster and can be used to make gruels that are useful for feeding infants and the elderly, who have a limited ability to chew foods into small particles.

A number of devices have been used to crush grains into flours. The Australian Aborigines used a simple wooden mortar and stone pestle to roughly crush grass seed, which they used a make bread, or *damper*. The ancient Egyptians developed a mill made of two circular stones to crush wheat into flour; modern mills operate on the same principle. Traditional peoples in Mesoamerica used a stone mortar and pestle to crush presoaked corn kernels into a wet mash to make tortillas. Foods with hard, inedible shells are crushed to facilitate removal of the shell and extraction of the edible component. Examples are hard-shelled nuts like walnuts and shellfish like lobsters. The devices used are tools like hammer-stones and metal pliers.

Other foods are crushed to extract a component of the food from the more fibrous matrix of the whole food. Seeds and palm fruits are crushed to extract the oil. Grapes and other soft fruits, as well as sugarcane, a tall grass, are crushed to extract the juice. Oils and juice tend to be more readily digested than the whole food. Also, the liquid can be added to other foods to improve their energy content and hence the energy content of the diet. This is especially important in rootcrop- and tuber-based diets, which are typically low in energy density.

Many foods are prepared or processed by crushing. This first-century C.E. Roman bas-relief depicts men crushing grapes for wine. © ARCHIVO ICONOGRAFICO, S.A./CORBIS.

The tools used in crushing foods vary with the foods themselves and level of technology. Grapes are crushed gently to avoid damaging the seed that can release bitterness into the wine. They were traditionally crushed by workers' treading on them or with wooden paddles. Olives are crushed to separate the pit from the pulp and the latter then pressed to extract the liquids. For the initial step the Romans used a roller-mill (*trapeta*), designed to ensure that the olive pit itself would not be damaged. Sugarcane was crushed historically in South America by squeezing the cane through a set of rollers (*trapiche*). The juice was then boiled to evaporate the water and the concentrated sugar allowed to crystallize.

Still other foods are crushed to achieve a particular texture in the preparation of certain dishes. In Hawaii, cooked taro corms (enlarged portion of the plant stem) are crushed to a smooth paste and then pounded in a mortar and pestle to make the famous *poi*. In Africa, cassava roots are left to soak and ferment in water and then crushed into dough that is molded into loaves and sun dried. Cooked yams are crushed with water to form soft dough called *fufu* in Ghana. In the highlands of Peru cooked potatoes are crushed on a grinding stone and then added to water or broth to make a thick soup or *masamora*. In Europe and North America, cooked potatoes are crushed to a soft uniform mass to make mashed potatoes. Nuts and meat are crushed into pastes to make sandwich spreads like peanut butter and potted meats or pâté.

In a number of different cuisines, spices are crushed to stimulate the release of flavor. In India, spices are ground in a mortar and pestle. In Mexico, spices were traditionally crushed to a paste with chili peppers using the same grinding stone (*mano* and *metate*) used for grinding maize, or in a stone bowl made from lava stone. Garlic, a flavoring agent, is also often crushed before being added to food. In all cases flavor enhancement and flavor release are the goals of the cook, but the crushing should also facilitate digestion.

Crushing is also used to meld two or more foods together. A classic example is the pemmican traditionally made by North American Indians. Pemmican is dried meat and animal fat pounded into a paste and preserved in the form of pressed cakes. A less well-known example is "desert fruitcake," a cake made of crickets pounded together with berries. Another example is *kibbeh*, a Lebanese dish made by pounding lamb and cracked wheat together in a stone mortar until they form a paste and seasoning the mix with mint and pine nuts. The resulting mix is rolled into sausage-like forms and cooked in oil or eaten raw.

See also **Combination of Proteins; Dietary Assessment; Preparation of Food; Rice; Wheat**.

BIBLIOGRAPHY

Davidson, Alan. *The Oxford Companion to Food.* Oxford: Oxford University Press, 1999.

Kimball, Yeffe, and Jean Anderson. *The Art of American Indian Cooking.* New York: Doubleday, 1965.

Kuper, Jessica, ed. *The Anthropologists' Cookbook.* New York: Universe Books, 1977.

Nickles, Harry G. *Middle Eastern Cooking.* New York: Time-Life Books, 1969.

Toussaint-Samat, Maguelonne. *History of Food.* Translated by Anthea Bell. Cambridge, Mass.: Blackwell, 1992. Original edition: *Histoire naturelle et morale de la nourriture.* Paris: Bordas, 1987.

Whitney, Eleanor N., and Sharon R. Rolfes. *Understanding Nutrition.* 8th ed. Belmont, Calif.: Wadsworth, 1999.

Darna L. Dufour

CRUSTACEANS AND SHELLFISH.

The crustaceans are not, strictly speaking, shellfish, although they are often described as such. They are members of the animal phylum Arthropoda, which also includes spiders, scorpions, and insects. Like these other creatures they are covered with hard, horny carapaces which are jointed for movement and sloughed from time to time as their owners grow. Many have a characteristic change of color when cooked, for example the blue-black lobster turns scarlet and the semitransparent shrimp turns pink and white.

The two principal orders are Decapoda Natantia and Decapoda Reptantia, that is to say, "ten-legged swimmers" and "ten-legged crawlers." In the first category are prawns, shrimp, lobster, and so on. The second consists of the crabs.

Prawns and Shrimp

The terms "prawn" and "shrimp" require a little explanation since the two terms are used in different ways in British and American English. The FAO (Food and Agriculture Organization of the United Nations) in their comprehensive *Catalogue of Shrimps and Prawns of the World* (1980), describes the differences in useage as follows:

> we may say that in Britain the term 'shrimp' is the more general of the two, and is the only term used for *Crangonidae* and most smaller species. 'Prawn' is the more special of the two names, being used solely for *Palaemonidae* and larger forms, never for the very small ones. In North America the name 'prawn' is practically obsolete and is almost entirely replaced by the word 'shrimp' (used for even the largest species, which may be called 'jumbo shrimp'). If the word 'prawn' is used at all in America it is attached to small species.

The smallest shrimp are of considerable interest in regions such as Southeast Asia where they are eagerly collected to be fermented and made into shrimp paste, most notably in the Philippines, where it is known as *patis*, and also Malaysia and Indonesia, where it is *blachan*. Use of these products is less widespread than the ubiquitous

Southeast Asian fish sauces, but they too make a significant contribution to the diet in the countries where they are made. In Europe, especially Britain, small shrimp may also be made into a paste, but without fermentation and packed in small jars as a delicacy for the tea table. Delicate shrimp paste sandwiches are considered a real treat. It is also possible in England to buy potted (cooked and packed in butter) shrimps from Morecambe Bay, a traditional preparation which has cultural overtones, being perceived as part of the British culinary heritage and identity. In North America the very smallest shrimps attract little interest, and it is the larger species such as the brown shrimp (*Penaeus aztecus aztecus*) and the white shrimp (*Penaeus setiferus*) which are most prominent in the markets. In Europe , the counterpart of these species is the so-called deep water prawn (also known as northern prawn, *Pandalus borealis*; but this is not exclusive to Europe, being found also in the North Atlantic from Greenland down to Martha's Vineyard).

Large shrimp, especially species of the genus *Macrobranchium* which thrive in brackish or fresh water, are now the subject of aquaculture in Southeast Asia, and the large quantities exported from there go a long way to meeting demand in Europe. Large shrimp are often presented on their own (for example boiled and then served cold with mayonnaise, or broiled), while smaller ones may be used to make the shrimp croquettes which are a particularly successful dish in the Netherlands and Belgium, or a shrimp sauce or shrimp soup.

Large shrimp in the Mediterranean belong to various species which resemble each other so closely that sometimes it is only an expert who can distinguish between them. One of the best is *Penaeus kerathurus*, the Italian *mazzancolla*. It may reach a length of 22 cm/9 inches, which is large for the Mediterranean but well short of 33 cm/13 inches, the maximum length of the Giant Tiger prawn of the Indo-Pacific, *Penaeus monodon*.

Lobsters
Lobsters are larger creatures, although the smallest of the the so-called Norway lobsters (often referred to by the Italian name scampi), are no bigger than the largest prawns. The archetypal lobster, that of the North Atlantic, is not one but two species, having developed in slightly different forms on the two sides of the ocean. The American lobster, *Homarus americanus*, attains a somewhat greater size than its European counterpart, *H. gammarus*. However, the whole question of maximum sizes has become one where precision is difficult to attain. The fishery for lobsters is now so intensive that few or none approach the maximum size recorded in the past. It is generally accepted that a specimen taken off the coast of Virginia in the 1930s holds the record; it measured more than a meter (3' 3") in length and weighed about 20 kg/45 lb. No lobster of comparable size has been taken since World War II. In any case, there is no special merit, for consumers, in great size.

FIG. 552. CRAYFISH SERVED EN BUISSON.

Lithograph showing crayfish *en buisson* arranged to resemble a cascade. From Theodore Garrett's *Encyclopedia of Practical Cookery* (London, ca. 1890). ROUGHWOOD COLLECTION.

The value of lobsters in the market is considerable, but the supply of adult lobsters from the wild is limited. One reason is that only certain types of seabed are suited to tiny postlarval lobsters. If they don't make it to a suitable place, they perish. Also, competition among lobster fishermen is intense. So, as long ago as the beginning of the twentieth century experimental lobster "farming" was being conducted in a number of countries.

Where lobsters are "farmed," one procedure is to raise them from fertilized eggs, keeping each tiny creature in its own compartment to prevent it from being eaten, and then releasing them into the wild when they are large enough to have a good chance of survival before they reach the minimum weight at which it becomes legal to catch them. This is generally around 450 to 500 grams (just over a pound). The alternative procedure involves keeping the lobsters in captivity until ready for sale. One advantage of this is that the fully "farmed" lobster may be sent to market at a weight of only about 250 g (half a pound) and will have attained that weight relatively quickly (further growth being slower). There is a large and growing literature on all this, whether conducted by institutions to increase stocks in the wild for the general benefit or by private "farmers" for their own profit.

The red color of a cooked lobster is intense and dramatic; it has been compared to that of a cardinal's hat. However, this cannot rival the amazingly bright and com-

Silver stand (*buisson*) for serving crayfish *en buisson*. France, ca. 1845. Poached crayfish were hung by their tails from the teeth around the rim of each tier, thus creating a cascade of crayfish, truffles, and parsley. ROUGHWOOD COLLECTION. PHOTO CHEW & COMPANY.

plex colorations of the "spiny lobsters," also known as crawfish, which belong to warmer and tropical waters. Lobsters in this other category are, some would say, not true lobsters. They lack the large claws of the Atlantic species, and hence have less meat, but they grow to a good size and are greatly appreciated as food. They too are "farmed," on an increasing scale. *Palinurus elephas* is one of several species that are present in the Mediterranean, while *Panulirus argus* is the most prominent in American waters. (The designations are confusing. The genus *Palinurus* has been recognized since the late eighteenth century, but it seems not to have occurred to the naturalist who created *Panulirus* halfway through the nineteenth century that he was sowing seeds of confusion by his choice of name.) The spiny lobsters of Asian waters include the remarkably beautiful *Panulirus ornatus* and *P. versicolor* (see illustration).

There are other "lobsters," of different shape, classified in the family Scyllaridae and going by names such as "flat lobster" and "slipper lobster." One, *Thenus orientalis*, has achieved fame and a certain cultural status in

Australia, where it is the "Moreton Bay bug," a name which combines an Australian geographical identifier with an indication of Australian plebeian insouciance.

Crabs

Most Europeans, invited to think of a crab, would have a mental picture of *Cancer pagurus*, the common crab of European temperate waters. North Americans would picture the famed blue crab of Chesapeake Bay and other parts of the eastern seaboard; or, if belonging to the western coast, the Dungeness crab. These three important species all share the familiar, compact, wide-bodied and big-clawed shape, and all are excellent tasting. The blue crab is, at least for east coast Americans, a cultural as well as a gastronomic phenomenon. The annual crab-picking "derby" at Crisfield, Maryland, is a symptom of its status. However, its reputation rests more on the fact that it is the crab which, when it has moulted and before the new hard carapace is grown, provides the basis for the soft-shell crab industry.

In waters that are either much colder or much warmer, crabs take on a different aspect. In the icy waters of the Arctic there is a vigorous fishery for two kinds of crab with extraordinarily long and thin legs, the snow crabs of the genus *Chionocoetes* and the king (or red) crab *Paralithodes camtschatica*. Their meat, which is of excellent quality, is usually frozen or canned, since the fishing grounds are so remote that it would be impracticable to do otherwise.

In tropical waters, on the other hand, there is a great diversity of swimming crabs and others, often brightly colored. Some spend some time on land, for example the large land crabs that are appreciated in the francophone West Indies and, in the Indo-Pacific region, the red crabs of Christmas Island and the robber crabs, which climb coconut trees and steal the nuts.

Crayfish

Although most edible crustaceans come from the sea, there are two important freshwater families, those of the crayfish (the family *Astacidae* in the northern hemisphere, and *Parastacidae* in the southern hemisphere). One interesting feature of the whole group of crayfish is that their distribution in the world is surprisingly, one might almost say inexplicably, patchy. Except for Papua New Guinea, there are none in the tropics. They are absent from most of Asia and are only found in two habitats in South America, yet there are over 250 species in North America. Europe has seven species and East Asia has four. Of the 120 species in the Southern Hemisphere, 110 are Australasian. They all resemble each other quite closely, but vary considerably in size and edibility. The largest is the giant Tasmanian crayfish, which may be 60 cm (two feet) from head to tail and may weigh as much as 4.5 kg (10 lb). Others are so small (2 cm / ¾ inch) in length that they are of no interest except perhaps as bait.

A chowder party on Fire Island. From *Harper's Weekly*, 23 August 1873. ROUGHWOOD COLLECTION.

Habitats vary. There are aquatic crayfish living in rivers or streams; semiaquatic species that live out of water in burrows connected by shafts to a body of water; and the tiny land crayfish, which live on land but only on land that has water underneath it.

Enthusiasm for crayfish is greatest in Scandinavia, France, and Australia, but nonexistent in many places where they can be found. In North America crayfish used to be a delicacy exclusive to Louisiana (where they are called "crawfish"), but appreciation of it has for some time been spreading.

The European crayfish *Astacus fluviatilis* was wiped out in many European countries early in the twentieth century. A species from North America was introduced to important crayfish regions, notably Sweden, as a replacement. Crayfish have considerable importance in the culture of Scandinavian countries, and there are many rules of procedure involved in a crayfish feast, for example, wearing huge napkins round the neck, sucking at the carapace, etc. This applies generally in countries such as Finland and Sweden, where enthusiasm is at its peak. This enthusiasm is sometimes puzzling to people from other regions, given the small amount of nourishment to be had from one small crayfish and the considerable effort and skill required to extract it. However, there are two kinds of crayfish in Australia, besides the Tasmanian one

already mentioned, which are large enough to be eaten with less difficulty: the yabby (not a single species but several in the genus *Cherax*) and the marron (another *Cherax* species), which belongs to western Australia and is the third largest crayfish in the world.

To avoid confusion, it is well to note that the word crayfish is properly applied to the species described above, while the word crawfish is normally used to refer to spiny lobsters.

An Oddball

One of the most delicious crustaceans has an appearance that resembles no other crustacean and does not suggest edibility. Moreover it is immobile and has a limited distribution centred on the Iberian Peninsula, to the cultural identity of which it makes a contribution. This strange creature is the goose-necked barnacle, *Mitella cornucopia*, best known under its Spanish name, *percebe*. It looks something like a rubbery, scaly tube with a hoof on the end. To eat it, one must prise off the outer tube, exposing a stalklike protuberance which may be bitten off entire. It is usual to boil the creatures briefly before serving them, but they can be eaten raw. It is in Spain and Portugal that *percebes* are most appreciated. They are costly, since gathering them from the rocks, at the foot of cliffs, to which they are typically attached, is often difficult and sometimes dangerous. A larger relation, *Megabalanus psittacus*, is found on the west coast of South America and is eaten with enthusiasm in Chile.

See also **Arthropods; Fish; Fishing; Iberian Peninsula; Southeast Asia; United States,** *subentries on* **Cajun Cooking** *and* **Middle Atlantic States.**

BIBLIOGRAPHY

Heron-Allen, Edward. *Barnacles in Nature and Myth.* London: Oxford University Press, 1928.

Holthuis, L. B. *Shrimps and Prawns of the World.* Rome: Food and Agriculture Organization, 1980.

Holthuis, L. B. *Marine Lobsters of the World.* FAO Species Catalogue, vol. 13. Rome: Food and Agriculture Organization, 1991.

Olszewski, Peter. *Salute to the Humble Yabby.* Melbourne: Angus & Robertson, 1980.

Warner, G. F. *The Biology of Crabs.* London: Elek Science, 1977.

Warner, William B. *Beautiful Swimmers: Watermen, Crabs and the Chesapeake Bay.* Boston: Little, Brown, 1983.

Alan Davidson

CUCUMBERS, MELONS, AND OTHER CUCURBITS.

Watermelon (*Citrullus lanatus*), cucumber (*Cucumis sativus*), and melon (*Cucumis melo*) are major crop species in the cucurbit or vine-crop family (the Cucurbitaceae), an important family of flowering plants (the angiosperms). The family also includes squash, pumpkin, and gourds.

Cucumber, melon, and watermelon are originally from the Old World (primarily Africa and Asia). Although they are in the same family (Cucurbitaceae) with the squashes, pumpkins, and gourds (mostly of the genus *Cucurbita*), they are only distantly related. The *Cucurbita* species are from the New World (primarily Central and South America).

Watermelon, cucumber, and melon plants are trailing or vining, tendril-bearing, frost-sensitive annuals. They are mostly monoecious (separate staminate and pistillate flowers, sometimes referred to as male and female flowers) and require various insects, especially bees, to effect pollination. The fruits are variously shaped, multiseeded, specialized berries called pepos. Together, plants in this family are called cucurbits.

Watermelon (*Citrullus lanatus*)

Watermelon is originally from central and southern Africa. The citron (*Citrullus lanatus* var. *citroides*) grows wild there, and is thought to be related to the wild ancestor of watermelon. The related species known as Egusi melon (*Citrullus colocynthis*) is found wild in west Africa and is also thought to be related to the wild ancestor of watermelon.

Watermelon is consumed for its fresh fruit, pickled rind, glacé candy, and for its dry seeds (harvested from confectionary type cultivars). The watermelon fruit contains 93 percent water, with small amounts of protein, fat, minerals, and vitamins (Table 1). In some arid regions, watermelon is used as a valuable source of water. The major nutritional components of the fruit are carbohydrates (6.4 g/100 g), vitamin A (590 IU), and lycopene (4,100

TABLE 1

Nutritional composition of cucumber, melon, and watermelon (amounts per 100 g edible portion)

Nutrient	Cucumber (slicing)	Cucumber (pickling)	West Indies gherkin	Casaba melon	Honeydew melon	Musk-melon	Watermelon (fruit)	Watermelon (seeds)
Water (percent)	96	96	93	92	90	90	93	5.7
Energy (kcal)	13	12	17	26	35	35	26	567
Protein (g)	0.5	0.7	1.4	0.9	0.5	0.9	0.5	25.8
Fat (g)	0.1	0.1	0.3	0.1	0.1	0.3	0.2	49.7
Carbohydrate (g)	2.9	2.4	2.0	6.2	9.2	8.4	6.4	15.1
Fiber (g)	0.6	0.6	0.6	0.5	0.6	0.4	—	4.0
Ca (mg)	14	13	26	5	6	11	7	53
P (mg)	17	24	38	7	10	17	10	—
Fe (mg)	0.3	0.6	0.6	0.4	0.1	0.2	0.5	—
Na (mg)	2	6	6	12	10	9	1	—
K (mg)	149	190	290	210	271	309	100	—
Vitamin A (IU)	45	270	270	30	40	3,224	590	—
Thiamine (mg)	0.03	0.04	0.1	0.06	0.08	0.04	0.03	0.1
Riboflavin (mg)	0.02	0.2	0.04	0.02	0.02	0.02	0.03	0.12
Niacin (mg)	0.30	0.4	0.4	0.40	0.60	0.57	0.20	1.4
Ascorbic Acid (mg)	4.7	19.0	51.0	16.0	24.8	42.2	7.0	—
Vitamin B6 (mg)	0.05	0.4	0.4	—	0.06	0.12	—	1.4

SOURCE: Gebhardt, Cutrufelli, and Matthews, 1982; Haytowitz and Matthews, 1984; Rubatzky and Yamaguchi, 1997.

μg/100g, range 2,300–7,200), an anticarcinogenic compound found in red flesh watermelon. Lycopene may help reduce the risk of certain cancers, such as prostate, pancreas, and stomach. The lycopene content of the new dark red watermelon cultivars is higher than in tomato, pink grapefruit, or guava. Orange flesh types do not contain lycopene, but have a high carotene (vitamin A) content. Citron and Egusi type watermelons are used to feed cattle in Africa. Watermelon seeds are rich in fat and protein.

Wild watermelons have hard, non-sweet, sometimes bitter, white flesh. Through plant breeding, the domesticated watermelon now being grown has fruit with a protective rind, sweet edible flesh, and bright red color. Specialty cultivars are available with orange, yellow, or white flesh.

Through history, watermelon was distributed throughout the world as trade and knowledge of central Africa developed. The crop was grown in India by at least 800 C.E., and in China by 1100 C.E. The Moorish conquerors of Spain introduced watermelon into Europe, where it was noted in Cordoba in 961 C.E. and Seville in 1158 C.E. Watermelon's spread into northern Europe was relatively slow, since it was not noted in the British Isles until late in the sixteenth century, perhaps because of the generally unfavorable climate for watermelon culture in much of Europe. About this time, watermelons were introduced into the New World, with culture of the plants noted in the Massachusetts colony in 1629. The introduction of watermelon into other parts of the world has followed established trade routes.

In the United States, Thomas Jefferson, as indicated in his garden record, was a watermelon gardener at Monticello, as was Henry David Thoreau in Concord, Massachusetts. Mark Twain wrote in *Puddn'head Wilson* that "The true southern watermelon is a boon apart and not to be mentioned with common things. It is chief of the world's luxuries, king by the grace of God over all the fruits of the earth. When one has tasted it, he knows what the angels eat." Even today, watermelon exerts an influence over popular culture in festivals throughout the rural South.

Watermelon is grown commercially in areas with long frost-free warm periods. Plants are widely spaced because of the long, trailing vines. They may be established in the field by planting seeds or by transplanting containerized plants. Management of plant pests (weeds, insects, and diseases, including nematodes) is essential during the production period. Three-fourths of the world production is grown in Asia (Table 2), with China the leading country in production.

Watermelons are grown in most states of the United States, but the major producers are in the South and West (Florida, Georgia, California, and Texas). The fruits are harvested by hand, with the most experienced workers doing the cutting (removal of the fruit from the vine) and

TABLE 2

World production of cantaloupe and melon, cucumber and gherkins, and watermelon (1997)

Continent or area	Production (mg x 1000)		
	Cantaloupe (melon)	Cucumber (gherkin)	Watermelon
Africa	1,045	390	2,679
North & Central America	1,966	1,589	2,539
South America	427	76	1,497
Asia	12,071	20,245	35,730
Europe	2,421	3,504	3,601
Oceania	78	22	90
World	18,009	25,827	46,135

SOURCE: *FAO Production Yearbook* 51 (1997).

the others loading the bins or trucks. The fruits are shipped to markets throughout the country, with some exported to Canada.

Watermelon fruit will keep for two to three weeks after harvest if it is stored properly at 10 to 15°C and 90 percent RH. Besides whole watermelons, it is becoming popular to sell watermelon in pre-cut halves, quarters, slices, and chunks. Whole fruit are usually cut in the store under cold, aseptic conditions since the cut product does not ship or store well. Seedless watermelons are especially popular for pre-cut sales, since that shows their seedless quality.

In the 1800s, most watermelon was grown for local sales. Development in the last few decades of rapid shipping in refrigerated railroad cars and trucks has led to distribution of watermelon throughout the United States from major production areas. Southern production areas begin shipping early in the year, and the harvest continues throughout the summer in more northern areas.

Depending on the cultivar, watermelon fruit are produced in different sizes: ice box, small, medium, large, or giant; different shapes: round, oval, blocky, or elongate; different rind patterns: gray, narrow stripe, medium stripe, wide stripe, light solid, or dark solid; different flesh colors: white, yellow, orange, or red; and different types: seeded or seedless. Commercially, the most popular seeded cultivars are red flesh, blocky shape, and large sized (8–11 kg), like the cultivar Allsweet. For seedless watermelons, the popular cultivars are red flesh, oval shape, and medium sized (5–8 kg), like the cultivar Tri-X-313. Per capita consumption of watermelons in the United States is 7.2 kg (Table 3). Watermelon seeds can be harvested and roasted for eating as well.

Watermelon is served fresh as slices, as chunks (often in fruit salad), as juice, and as edible seeds for the confectionary types. In the United States, watermelon has typically been part of the summer picnic, where the

TABLE 3

Per capita consumption of cucumber, melon, and watermelon in the United States, 2000	
Vegetable crop or group	Consumption (kg/person)
Cucumber (fresh)	3.13
Cucumber (processed)	2.18
Honeydew melon	1.27
Muskmelon	5.44
Watermelon	7.21
All vegetables (fresh)	104.33
All vegetables (processed)	102.06

SOURCE: USDA (2000), VGS-281.

giant (15 kg) fruit is popular. Picnic events that feature watermelon include eating contests (who can eat the most), seed spitting (who can spit the seeds the farthest), or greased watermelon games (which team can move a greased watermelon—which floats but is hard to hold onto—over to its side of the lake). However, watermelon is no longer just a summer fruit and is becoming an everyday fruit like apples, bananas, and oranges.

Cucumber (*Cucumis sativus*)

The cucumber is thought to have originated in India, where it is found wild and is cultivated in many diverse

WEST INDIAN GHERKIN (*CUCUMIS ANGURIA*)

The West Indian gherkin (*Cucumis anguria* var. *anguria*), also known as the bur gherkin, was thought to have originated in the Caribbean, but now is considered to be of African origin. The African progenitor is *Cucumis anguria* var. *longaculeatus*, formerly called *Cucumis longipes*. It was probably brought to Brazil and the West Indies (where it got its name) by Africans in the slave trade. The term gherkin is also used for the pickling type of cucumber, especially the small sizes.

Fruit of the bur gherkin are smaller (5 cm) than those of the cucumber, but the defining characteristic of this species is the long peduncle or fruit stem (up to 20 cm in length). The fruit are light yellow to pale green, and are covered with short, fleshy spines. The fruit are eaten fresh or pickled.

forms. Accessions of *Cucumis sativus* L. var. *hardwickii* may be related to the original ancestors of the cucumber, and have been collected in the foothills of the Himalaya Mountains. These forms are not directly useable in agriculture because of their bitter fruit, dormant seeds, and late maturity. However, they have some traits that have been transferred to elite cultivars by plant breeders.

Secondary centers of diversity for the cucumber exist in China and the Near East. Related species are *Cucumis hystrix* from China and the African *Cucumis*, such as melon (*Cucumis melo*), gherkin (*Cucumis anguria*), and their wild relatives.

Cucumbers were probably domesticated in Asia and then introduced into Europe, where the first cultivars were selected in the 1700s. The first cucumbers were brought to the Americas by Christopher Columbus, and Native Americans were growing cucumbers from Florida to Canada by the early 1500s. Formal plant breeding began in the United States in the 1880s, when cultivars diverged into fresh-market (slicing) and processing (pickling) types.

The cucumber is grown for its fruits, which are eaten fresh or pickled in most countries, but which are also eaten fried (usually when fruit have been harvested at a more mature stage). Slicing and pickling cucumber fruit are mostly water, but they provide some vitamin A and C, especially when pickled with dill and other spices (Table 1). Cucumber is the ideal food for people having trouble with body weight, because it is mostly water, with some fiber, and few calories. Cucumber causes burping and mild stomach upset in some people when eaten raw, but not when soaked in vinegar or pickled before eating. Cucumber is also among 35 fruits, vegetables, and herbs identified by the National Cancer Institute as having cancer-protective properties.

Cucumbers are served and eaten at home and in restaurants (especially fast food establishments) where pickle chips or relish are served on hamburgers and hot dogs. Pickles are also served as appetizers. Fresh cucumbers are sliced and served in salads or as garnishes to add color to the meal. Per capita annual consumption of fresh cucumber is 3.1 kg and processed cucumber 2.2 kg in the United States (Table 3).

Cucumber is used in most countries in the world, where particular types have been developed to fit local requirements. The common types are American pickling, American slicing, European greenhouse, Middle Eastern (Beit Alpha), Dutch pickling (parthenocarpic), oriental trellis, and specialty (such as the round or "lemon" cucumber). Some types referred to as cucumber, such as Armenian cucumber, are actually melon (*Cucumis melo*).

Fresh-market cucumbers are grown primarily in the southern and western states of the United States, especially Florida, Georgia, North Carolina, Texas, and California. Processing cucumbers are grown from Mexico to Canada so they are available year around for processors, often at a considerable distance from the production site. About 80 percent of the world's cucumber production is in Asia (Table 2), with China being the leading producer (Table 4).

Cucumbers are harvested by hand for fresh-market use, and by hand or machine for processing use. Michigan and Wisconsin have an estimated 50 to 75 percent and 25 to 50 percent machine harvest, respectively. Once-over harvest machines destroy the vines as they harvest the fruit (pickling type only). After harvest, the fruit are cooled, graded, packed, and shipped. The cucumbers will have fewer post-harvest rots and a longer storage life if they are cooled soon after harvest.

Fresh-market cucumbers are transported to market and displayed for a few days for sale to consumers. The fruit may be shrink wrapped in polyethylene or coated with vegetable wax to extend shelf life, or they may be sold with no protection. For fresh-market cucumbers, storage at 50°F (10°C) and 95 percent relative humidity (RH) will permit the produce to hold for approximately two weeks after harvest. The American slicing type cucumber has a thick tough skin to reduce shipping damage and increase storage life. Pickling cucumbers are graded and then loaded into tanks of brine (salt water) for fermentation and storage.

The pickling industry originally used brine tank storage to provide brine stock (pickles) to the factory during the off-season. Currently, however, more than half of the crop is processed without brining. Pasteurization is used to produce fresh pack pickles, and refrigeration is used to produce overnight pickles. Fermentation in brine tanks is used less for storage now, and more to produce particular types and flavors (for example, by using acetic acid or lactic acid fermentation).

Storage of pickling cucumber is usually in barrels, pails, jars, or plastic pouches. Preservation is by fermentation, pasteurizing, or refrigeration. For pickling cucumber, it is common and economical for growers to supply markets around the world. For example, growers in India and Sri Lanka supply small pickles in barrels of vinegar or salt brine to processors in Europe and North America.

In the 1700s, cucumber production in the United States probably was small scale; individuals and families would grow a few plants in their garden for the home, probably using the fruit fresh during the summer harvest season and pickled (using a favorite recipe to preserve the fruit) during the off-season. In the 1800s, family farmers grew small areas of cucumbers to supply the fresh market and pickle companies. Even when growers became specialized in cucumber production in the 1900s, family farmers continued to supply small size (grade 1, under 26 mm diameter) fruit to pickle companies. Large field crews generally do not harvest each field every day and usually do not search the vines for small fruit as required to produce a high percentage of grade 1 fruit from the field.

TABLE 4

Leading countries in production of cantaloupe and melon, cucumber and gherkin, and watermelon (MT x 1000) in 1997

Cantaloupe (melon)	Cucumber (gherkin)	Watermelon
China	China	China
Turkey	Turkey	Turkey
Iran	Iran	United States
United States	United States	Iran
Spain	Japan	Republic of Korea

SOURCE: *FAO Production Yearbook* 51 (1997).

Cucumber production is now being done by growers with large farms, specialized equipment, and excellent marketing skills. The small-scale production of cucumber has also increased, as home gardening in the United States has become very popular.

The major modification made to the cucumber in the 1930s was to begin breeding for disease resistance. In the 1960s, gynoecious cucumbers (pistillate or female flowers at every node) were developed, and are now used to make gynoecious hybrids using bee pollination (rather than the more expensive hand pollination). The gynoecious hybrid cucumber, usually with 15 percent monoecious hybrid pollenizer seeds blended into the seed packet, is a major success story. Current cultivars are resistant to anthracnose, downy mildew, powdery mildew, angular leafspot, scab, fusarium wilt, cucumber mosaic virus, and other major diseases found throughout the United States.

Plant breeders have developed a new type of cucumber capable of being grown in the greenhouse. The modifications include making the plant gynoecious (all pistillate or female flowers) and parthenocarpic (fruit set without pollination to eliminate the need for bees or hand pollination, and making the fruit seedless), and of high quality (genetically bitter-free plant for mild-flavored fruit).

Other modifications made by plant breeders include the development of cultivars having large diameter fruit for use in chipping. Thus, a sandwich or hamburger can be made using one large-diameter pickle chip rather than three of the standard size. However, that development was negated by the use of large pickling cucumbers (grade 3) sliced longitudinally to make a rectangular chip. Two of those can be used on a sandwich or hamburger instead of the single large chip, and the quality is often superior.

Melon (*Cucumis melo*)

Melon originated in southern Africa and has many wild relatives there. Related species include cucumber (*Cucumis sativus*), the West Indian gherkin (*Cucumis anguria*), and the

A cucumber melon in the Kalahari Desert of southern Africa. This region is also the genetic homeland of the watermelon. © ANTHONY BANNISTER: GALLO IMAGES/CORBIS.

horned cucumber (*Cucumis metuliferus*). Cucurbits, including melons, have complex symbolic associations with sex and sexuality, fertility, abundance, and gluttony. They may denote wealth in areas where melons do not normally grow.

Melon fruit have a high water content (about 90 percent), and contain sugars and fiber. Nutrients found in melon include vitamin C, and in the case of muskmelon (and other orange-fleshed types), carotenes. Nutritional compositions of casaba, honeydew, and muskmelon (cantaloupe) are shown in Table 1.

The major changes made by plant breeders to the domesticated melon compared with wild relatives have been to add disease resistance, remove seed dormancy, increase fruit size, increase the size of the mesocarp (the edible portion of the fruit), improve the quality, reduce the frequency of defects, and increase the sugar content.

Melon was brought from Africa to Europe and Asia, and from Europe to the Americas. It is now cultivated throughout the world, where specific types have been bred for local use. A useful horticultural classification of melons follows:

- The *Cantalupensis* group includes cantaloupe, muskmelon, and Persian melon. The fruits are oval or round; sutured or smooth; mostly netted, some slightly netted or nonnetted; and abscise from the peduncle when mature. The flesh is aromatic and is usually salmon or orange in color, but may be green. In the United States, the term "muskmelon" and "cantaloupe" are used interchangeably, but some horticultural scientists suggest that they be used to distinguish between types of the *C. melo Cantalupensis* group. This group includes the *Reticulatus* group used in some older classifications.

- The *Inodorus* group includes winter melon, casaba, Crenshaw, honeydew, Juan Canary, and Santa Claus. The fruits are round or irregular, smooth or wrin-

kled, but not netted; nor do they abscise from the peduncle at maturity. The flesh is mostly green or white, occasionally orange, and not aromatic.

- The *Flexuosus* group includes the snake or serpent melon and the Armenian cucumber. The fruits are quite long, thin, ribbed, and often curled irregularly.

- The *Conomon* group includes the oriental pickling melon. The fruits are smooth, cylindrical, and may be green, white, or striped. The flesh is white and can taste either sweet or bland.

- The *Dudaim* group includes mango melon, pomegranate melon, and Queen Anne's melon. The fruits are small, round to oval, and light green, yellow, or striped. The flesh is firm and yellowish-white in color.

- The *Momordica* group includes the phoot and snap melon. The fruits are oval or cylindrical with smooth skin that cracks as the fruit matures.

Melons require a long growing season with warm, sunny days and cool nights to achieve maximum quality. Plants are established by seeds or containerized plants after danger of frost is past. Stringent management of plant pests is necessary for high yield and quality. As with other cucurbits, it is necessary to have a large honeybee population to facilitate pollination. Asia produces about two-thirds of the world supply, with China being the largest producer (Tables 2 and 4). Several countries in Central America are major melon producers for export to the United States in late winter and early spring. In the United States, most melons are produced in California, Arizona, Texas, and Georgia. In Japan, melons are grown in greenhouses to produce high quality fruit commonly used as gifts.

Melons are harvested by hand from the vine. Maturity in the *Cantalupenis* group is by separation of the fruit from the peduncle (fruit stem) with minimal force. Maturity in the *Inodorus* group melons is not as easily determined, and they may be treated with ethylene after harvest to enhance the ripening process during transit to the market. Cantaloupes are best stored at 3°C and 95 percent RH, whereas other melons are best stored at 7°C and 95 percent RH. The effective postharvest life is about two weeks for both types.

Melon is served fresh as slices, chunks, or juice. Chunks are often used in fruit salad, made into melon balls and frozen, or prepared and sold in grocery stores to be eaten as is. Total per capita melon consumption in the United States is about 7 kg (Table 3). The vitamin A and C content make melon a nutritious food (Table 1).

See also **Fruit**; **Squash and Gourds**; **Vegetables**.

BIBLIOGRAPHY

Bates, David M., Richard W. Robinson, and Charles Jeffrey, eds. *Biology and Utilization of the Cucurbitaceae*. Ithaca: Cornell University Press, 1990.

Maynard, David, and Donald N. Maynard. "Cucumber, Melons, and Watermelon." In *The Cambridge World History of Food*, edited by Kenneth F. Kiple and Kriemhild Coneè Ornelas. Volume 2. Cambridge, U.K.: Cambridge University Press, 2000.

Maynard, Donald N., ed. *Watermelons. Characteristics, Production, and Marketing.* Alexandria, Va.: ASHS Press, 2001.

Robinson, R. W., and D. S. Decker-Walters. *Cucurbits.* New York: CAB International, 1997.

Whitaker, Thomas W., and Glen N. Davis. *Cucurbits, Botany, Cultivation, and Utilization.* New York: Interscience, 1962.

Todd C. Wehner
Donald N. Maynard

CUISINE, EVOLUTION OF.

Throughout evolutionary history humans have prepared or transformed foods to make them edible. The preparation of food before consumption, which is the foundation of cuisine, has always been a part of the human behavioral repertoire and helps define the species. Unlike most related mammals and primates that begin their digestion in the process of chewing their food, humans often begin digestive processes outside of the body, using tools for this purpose. In other words, what humans do to food before eating it often transforms the food in ways that make it more digestible.

Abundant archeological evidence shows all kinds of tools used for food preparation throughout human evolutionary history. For example, ancestors from the genus *Homo* perfected tools that could cut a piece of meat more effectively than their canine and incisor teeth. They found they could crush a nut or other hard seed pod more efficiently with a stone pestle than with their molar teeth. Human ancestors added controlled use of fire several hundred thousand years ago, so apparently the potential for predigesting food outside the body was well developed by the time *Homo sapiens* emerged. From a biological evolutionary perspective, the continued use of tools and fire and the broad effects of the domestication of plants and animals has altered important aspects of the human food chain and has significantly affected the evolutionary dynamics that underlie the species.

The effect of these important developments in the processing of foods is most evident in human digestive tracts and some of the metabolic pathways associated with the foods humans eat. Evolutionary biologists refer to the changes in the human digestive tract as a result of a relaxation in evolutionary selection. This is evident in the variability of structures that no longer have importance for survival, such as in the structural reduction in size and formation of human teeth or the function of the appendix.

Much of this biological evolution occurred prior to the origin of agriculture that was marked by the domestication of plants and animals. The enormous success of agriculture and horticulture (beginning approximately ten thousand and five thousand years ago respectively), provided the practicing societies with the ability to feed an excess number of their members and thus served as the basic economic subsistence engine for the broad emergence of human civilizations and the overall growth of humanity to its megapopulation size.

Influences of Agriculture

Since the Neolithic era, agricultural practices have continuously improved the productivity of certain plants over others. This intensification has led to an increased dependence on fewer and fewer plants to provide the bulk of most human diets. However, no single plant or any small group of plants, when consumed as raw products from the field, can satisfy all of the nutrient needs of the species. Hence, dependence on fewer plants could have produced nutritional problems (and to some extent this did happen) if humans had continued to eat them more or less raw, as more ancient ancestors did over the thousands of years before the Neolithic era. Thus the Neolithic agricultural diet, characterized by a narrow range of cereal grains and legumes, represented a substantial change from the Paleolithic diet, characterized by a great diversity of hunted and gathered foods. However, this substantial change in diet raises important questions about how and if the species continues to evolve biologically in response to the decrease in the diversity and contents of diets brought about by agriculture.

The relatively rapid shift to an agricultural diet represented a significant nutritional challenge because the diets were largely dependent on relatively few cereal grains and legumes that had serious nutritional limitations. These new limitations included specific nutrient deficiencies, antinutritional properties (such as antitrypsin factors, high levels of phytates, and lectins), and various toxic constituents (such as cyanates and tannins). This shift to agriculture could and did result in strong new sources of natural selection and the rapid evolution of biological traits that tended to compensate for these limitations. However, the vast majority of the adaptations to this new agriculturally based diet came from the increased use of cuisine-based technologies that went far beyond the use of tools and fire, already well established in Paleolithic times. In essence the emergence of a wide variety of cuisine technologies counterbalanced the more limited but important potential of the genetic changes required to adjust to the nature and rate of these new dietary constituents.

It is clear that significant biological adaptations underlie the success of the evolution of some agricultural practices. Many experts accept the evidence that it is the continued secretion of lactase enzyme that makes milk sugars digestible by most northern European adults in contrast to most other adults of the world, who stop secreting the enzyme at the time of weaning. This evolved trait for adult lactase enzyme sufficiency underlies the high and continued dependence of these populations upon dairy foods following the domestication of cattle over eight thousand years ago. Although the specific cultures of northern Europe have undergone many cultural and historic changes in diet over that long period, all of those cultures continue to consume dairy foods in unbroken traditions, such as making yogurts and cheeses that partly lower the milk sugar content. Likewise, good evidence indicates a genetic cline (or gradual geographical change in the gene frequency) of adaptations to the gluten protein in wheat (to which some people have serious intolerance) tracked with increasing frequencies from the Levant, where wheat was first domesticated, all the way across Europe, where it was introduced at later times.

Other genetic adaptations involving nutrition and food also work pharmacologically to influence disease problems. For example, the disease called favism, which results in a profound life-threatening, hemolytic anemia, is due to another enzyme deficiency that helps protect the affected populations from malarial infection. However, the gene Glucose-6 dehydrogenase deficiency (G6PD), a sex-linked gene associated with males, makes afflicted males particularly sensitive to the profound hemolytic affects of the oxidant compounds in the beans. Although the G6PD gene is widespread in all of the regions where fava beans are consumed and causes many deaths every year among sensitive individuals, the pharmacological effects of the beans help prevent malaria. Not surprisingly, more myths and stories promote and prohibit the consumption of these beans than any other food in Indo-European history. Thus foods may have pharmacological properties in addition to nutritional properties, which makes interaction between their consumption and the continued evolution of the populations that eat them complicated.

While genetic adaptations to diet did evolve over the last ten thousand years, most adaptations to agricultural diets evolved at the cultural realm in the form of cuisine technologies. While becoming more dependent on fewer plants in the diet, human forebears produced a classic evolutionary bottleneck in which the increased dependence on fewer plant crops increased the nutritional liabilities each plant retained. Consequently, a continuous complementary evolutionary process related the increased agricultural productivity with the evolution of new cuisine technologies that enhanced the nutrient composition and often simultaneously rid the plants of their toxic and antinutritional effects.

Nutriculture

The term "nutriculture" refers to the reciprocity of these preparatory technologies with the overall advantages that agricultural practices have provided for the enormous success in increasing the productivity of plants. In other words, every advance in the agricultural productivity of plants was accompanied by the evolution of cultural strategies to offset the nutritional disadvantages of de-

pending on so few nutritionally unbalanced and potentially toxic foods. Hence "nutriculture" represents the evolved cultural strategies that turn these disadvantages into advantages and the complementarity of these preparative technologies with agriculture. Treating foods before they are consumed can and often does have nutritional and pharmacological consequences for the finished consumable. For example, many different physical, chemical, biochemical, and microbiotic steps "prepare" the plant-based staples in the human diet. These transformations from the "raw to the cooked" become the culturally recognized foods humans eat, and with which they celebrate, remain nutritionally healthy, and ultimately survive and prosper around the world. Thus the evolution of food nutriculture has been just as important as the success of agriculture in producing enough food to continue to feed the world.

In fact many of these technologies become parts of long-standing recipes that fill this encyclopedia and the cookbooks and cooking traditions of the world. These technologies are so important in defining the foods consumed that they become part of the cultural worldview of every society that has ever lived. Every society celebrates with food and incorporates foods as symbols, and many of these traditions provide the cultural memory for how foods should be prepared for healthful consumption.

Although evolutionary anthropologists and biologists have not looked at what humans do to food as part of an evolutionary process equal in importance to agricultural practices, the evidence for such a process underlying basic cuisine practice is strong. Of course this does not mean that every aspect of cuisine practice involving innovations, presentation, and the like has some kind of evolutionary basis. However, it does suggest that many of the fundamental aspects of the transformation of raw materials into foods often has a long and highly evolved natural history that is not always readily recognized as optimizing their nutrient and other qualities. Hence transforming the raw foods for consumption can and does make a difference in health and survival. In some respects this knowledge about preparation and consumption of foods is so much a part of the existence and identity of a society that its members often are more conscious of making food "palatable" to culturally conditioned tastes and expectations than of the nutritional and pharmacological significance of the steps taken.

Importance of Preparation

Other major sources of nutrition follow the nutricultural principle. A classic example of the evolution of cuisine practices involves maize or "corn." While maize is the most productive crop in the world, and virtually all of the great Mesoamerican civilizations depended upon it as a staple, it is not nutritionally the best balanced of staples. Maize has low lysine and tryptophan levels, and its niacin levels, when stored as a staple, are nutritionally indigestible. Specifically the B vitamin niacin becomes bound in a complex called niacytin, and this bound form is indigestible to the effects of stomach acid and gastrointestinal enzymes. However, it is known that the chemical bond that makes niacytin resistant to digestive acid is broken in the presence of an alkali that frees the bound niacin. Although humans can make a small amount of niacin from the essential amino acid tryptophan, corn is deficient in tryptophan. Fortunately beans have relatively high levels of tryptophan, and as long as beans are consumed with corn (maize), the diet is balanced. However, if beans and other regular sources of tryptophan or niacin are not available in the diet, the disease pellagra makes people sick with diarrhea, dermatitis, dementia, and ultimately result in death.

While alkali treatment also enhances the solubility of lysine, it is not universally used, even in the Americas where the crop evolved. However, the Native American societies that were high consumers and growers of maize always used alkali in their cuisine technology. It was a one-to-one relationship between high consumers and growers and their subsequent use of this critical step in the preparation of their food staple. In terms of their recipes, the added alkali was prepared in several different ways, including crushed limestone, roasted mollusk shells, and wood ashes. The net effect of this step was always the same. The food was heated and "cooked" in the lime, and then most of the alkali was removed prior to consumption. Even though the recipes varied among different cultures and traditions, these basic cooking steps did not vary.

In this regard it is interesting to note that Christopher Columbus, who first introduced maize to the Old World, only introduced the food and not the critically important recipe. Pellagra became widespread, resulting in a gradual decrease in the use of maize as a human food. Not until the discovery of vitamins beginning in the 1920s, over four hundred years later, was pellagra defined as a nutritional deficiency associated with the consumption of maize.

However, considering the history of every major civilization, it becomes clear that all depended upon the solutions to similar problems to survive and prosper. Thus, while it is possible to innovate new food technologies that may not have many or any negative consequences in times of nutritional abundance, the same practices may produce serious deficiencies during times of nutritional stress. Thus food preparation has substantial survival advantages, and undoubtedly significant wisdom resides in the related food practices that maintain food preparation traditions.

The use of fermentation to enhance the nutrients of wheat and barley in the production of beer and bread is a classic example of how foods become staples of the diet. Fermentation of wheat and barley with yeast not only produces the alcohol in beer and, to a lesser extent, in bread; it also synthesizes nutritionally essential amino acids from nonessential ones, reduces the toxicity of the tannins in the wheat, and lowers the phytate levels that interfere with calcium absorption. Squeezing, crushing, and heating the manioc (a good source of nutrition known throughout the world for yielding the tapioca starch of dessert puddings) reduces the plant's cyanide content, which can be so high that even breathing the cooking fumes can be deadly. With the notable and important exception of fruits, which evolved to attract mammals to eat the seeds and thus to disperse them, the raw produce is not a viable source of nutrients without the culturally evolved capacity for transforming it into an appropriately edible food.

Biology and Culture

Over time, a trial-and-error process results in the nutritive success or failure of new cuisine strategies. Those strategies that satisfy basic nutritional needs become incorporated into food traditions and provide subtle and not so subtle advantages to the people who practice them. When the cause-and-effect relationship between the cuisine practice and the outcome are readily evident, as in changing the appearance, taste, or aroma of a food and then noting a benefit, it is relatively simple to understand the functional significance of the cuisine practice. However, when considering subtle cause-and-effect relationships not readily evident and expressed some time long after the prepared food is consumed, it is difficult to detect the relationship and consciously to behave in the appropriate way. For example, the time it takes to develop a nutritional disorder for a vitamin like niacin is so long that the appropriate cuisine practice may not ever evolve, as was the case for extracting the niacin from maize in Europe. Epidemiological studies of long-term disease outcomes that may extend over a substantial portion of a lifetime, such as cardiovascular disease and some forms of cancer, demonstrate how subtle some of these effects are.

On the face of it, the degree to which a culturally based diet satisfies basic nutritional needs is a matter related to the biology of humans as omnivores. Humans uniquely depend on cultural adaptations concerning diet to solve the nutrient problems that biology is incapable of solving on its own. Instead, humans have discovered and encoded in cultural traditions wisdom about diet that provides a culinary prescription for survival and good health. What people eat is largely dictated by cultural traditions, but the degree to which a diet satisfies basic nutritional needs largely depends on human biology. This obvious interface between biology and culture has encouraged the development of a new approach or paradigm that analyzes and interprets biological and cultural adaptability as continuously interacting phenomena throughout human evolution.

No doubt the evolution of agriculture would not have occurred without these counterbalancing nutricultural evolutionary steps. In fact this basic theme of nutriculture is repeated with other aspects of cuisine and thus forms the basis of a broad trend throughout history in the consumption of every major plant food.

The remarkable growth of knowledge about what people eat arises from an understanding of both the prehistory of diets and the recorded history of foods. Also a substantial and growing ethnographic and cross-cultural literature concerning folk cooking practices allows tests of specific hypotheses about food processing. The available data in food science and technology, the nutritional sciences, biochemistry, ethnobotany, pharmacology, and the neurosciences is extensive. Using this knowledge to extend the understanding of the biological and biocultural evolutionary processes produces the potential for providing important insights about this nascent study of nutriculture. The varied contents of this *Encyclopedia of Food and Culture* suggest avenues and examples of nutriculture for exploration.

See also **Agriculture, Origins of; Anthropology; Eating: Anatomy and Physiology of Eating; Evolution; Food Archaeology; Maize; Nutrition Transition: Worldwide Diet Change; Paleonutrition, Methods of; Prehistoric Societies; Preparation of Food; Vitamins.**

BIBLIOGRAPHY

Cavalli-Sforza, L. Luca, Paolo Menozzi, and Alberto Piazza. *The History and Geography of Human Genes.* Princeton, N.J.: Princeton University Press, 1994.

Katz, Solomon H. "The Biocultural Evolution of Cuisine." In *Handbook of the Psychophysiology of Human Eating,* edited by R. Shepard, pp. 115–140. Wiley Psychophysiology Handbooks. New York: John Wiley, 1989.

Katz, Solomon H. "An Evolutionary Theory of Cuisine." *Human Nature* 1 (1990): 233–259.

Katz, Solomon H. "Food and Biocultural Evolution: A Model for the Investigation of Modern Nutritional Problems." In *Nutritional Anthropology,* edited by Francis E. Johnston, pp. 41–66. New York: Allen Liss, 1987.

Katz, Solomon H., M. Hediger, and L. Valleroy. "Traditional Maize Processing Techniques in the New World: Anthropological and Nutritional Significance." *Science* 184 (1974): 765–773.

Katz, Solomon H., and M. Voigt. "Bread and Beer: The Early Use of Cereals in the Human Diet." *Expedition* 28, no. 2 (1987): 23–34. Also published in various forms in a number of textbooks, trade magazines, and the popular press.

Katz, Solomon H., and Fritz Maytag. "Brewing an Ancient Beer." *Archaeology* 44, no. 4 (1991): 24–27.

Katz, Solomon H., and Fritz Maytag. "Secrets of the Stanzas." *Archaeology* 44, no. 4 (1991): 28–31.

Katz, Solomon H., and Fritz Maytag. "A Thrilling Link with the Past." *Archaeology* 44, no. 4 (1991): 32–33.

Simoons, F. J. "The Determinants of Dairying and Milk Use in the Old World: Ecological, Physiological, and Cultural." In *Food, Ecology, and Culture: Readings in the Anthropology of Dietary Practices,* edited by J. R. K. Robson, 83–91. New York: Gordon and Breach, 1980.

Solomon H. Katz

CURDS. Curds are a by-product of milk, and in the traditional agrarian societies of Europe and America, indeed in most parts of the world, the processing of milk belonged to the woman's sphere. In many farmhouses, there was a cold room or a freestanding springhouse nearby known as the dairy, and like the kitchen, this was the domain of the wife and her daughters. For this reason, much information about curds and curd-making can be found in cookery books and in books on household management.

Curds may be best described as condensed milk fat that has not yet aged into cheese, although it is also fairly common to refer to unpressed curds as "fresh" cheese—fresh in the sense of raw or unprocessed. The most popular form of curds consumed in the United States is cottage cheese, which is fresh curds combined with cream, sour cream, or milk. Low-fat cottage cheese is generally considered a health food and therefore plays an important role in many types of weight-loss diets. Greek feta cheese is essentially fresh salted curds preserved in whey, the watery liquid that comes with every jar or package of feta.

The word "curd" evolved from Middle English *crouden,* a verb meaning 'to press or push hard in a downward direction'. This association may derive from the fact that curds were normally poured into a cloth bag and pressed dry of the whey, or hung from a hook and allowed to drip over a basin, hence the old term "hung cheese." In the eighteenth and nineteenth centuries,

GOAT CURDS

Goats lactate seasonally and while they produce less milk than cows, their milk is richer in vitamins and minerals. The ancient Greeks always recommended goat milk for babies because they observed that it was easier to digest. This is due to the fact that a high proportion of small- and medium-chain fatty acids are more easily absorbed into the body. Likewise, goat curds are much easier to digest than curds from cow milk. Goat milk is naturally homogenized because it lacks a protein called agglutinin; thus the fats in the milk remain dispersed. This, plus the lower casein proteins in goat milk, results in smaller curds, which is why fresh goat cheese has such a dense paste-like texture. The halloumi cheese of Cyprus is so dense that it can be grilled without melting or falling apart. It is made from goat curds that are pressed together with mint, then heated in salted whey.

curds were also pressed into molds made of ceramic or tin and sold in farm markets in a wide variety of shapes, usually hearts of various sizes.

From *crouden* also comes the Southern term "crowder," any sort of cowpea that was cracked (pounded) and cooked for porridge. A crowder pea was a porridge pea, and in the Scotch-Irish cookery of Appalachia, this porridge might also contain whey or curds, or even both. In rural Scotland, curdy-butter or cruddy-butter was a spread for oat cake made by mashing together fresh curds and salted butter. In Appalachia, it was eaten on johnny cake. It goes without saying that curds and whey have been dietary staples for thousands of years in every household where milk was readily available.

In composition, curds are the fatty part of milk that has become solid. When milk undergoes acidification, it sours. This souring process is induced by lactic acid bacteria streptococci and lactobacilli. They feed on milk sugars (lactose) and change it to acid. When this happens slowly at room temperature, the result is clabber or "thick milk," as it was often called in Colonial America. Clabber is milk that has attained a consistency resembling junket, and in this form, it was an important ingredient in traditional cookery. It was also eaten by itself as a breakfast and supper food, often mixed with fresh fruit (during the summer). German *Quark* is very similar to clabber in composition and is eaten like yogurt in many parts of Central Europe. Clabber is no longer eaten in the United States because of regulations requiring the pasteurization of milk. Pasteurized milk will not clabber because the bacteria have been killed during the heating process.

However, when the souring process of raw milk is speeded up, the acid causes the fatty solids in milk to migrate and stick together, thus forming curds (called protein clump among cheesemakers) and watery whey. In traditional cookery, whey was considered a useful food in its own right, mainly because it was easy to digest. It was therefore employed in foods prepared for children, the elderly, or the sick. In regions where dairy culture predominated, whey was available in such abundance that it was often fed to livestock, especially pigs. Whey was also used in hearth cookery for making griddle cakes, muffins, and cornbread, since the acid would react with such old-time leavening agents as Hirschhorn salts, saleratus, and pearlash. Cow's milk yields the largest amount of whey since it is about 85 percent water.

Renneting

Curd formation could also be hastened by a process known as renneting. This was based on an enzyme called rennin, which is found in the stomach lining of ruminant animals. The rennet preferred by most cheesemakers generally came from the stomach of a young animal, such as a calf for cow's cheese, kid for goat cheese, or lamb for sheep's cheese. The use of animal rennets in cheesemaking is the reason many vegetarians will not eat

Traditional tin curd molds. Left top and bottom: Pennsylvania, circa 1900; right: France, circa 1890. ROUGHWOOD COLLECTION. PHOTO CHEW & COMPANY.

cheese—the young animal of course must be killed in order to obtain the rennet. Tofu, a curd made from soybeans, has been eaten in Asia as a milk curd substitute for over a thousand years. However, there is also a long history of rennets obtained from plants, and cheeses made with them are acceptable to those vegetarians who consume dairy products.

One of the earliest known plants employed as a renneting agent was the wild artichoke of the eastern Mediterranean and North Africa. It is believed that the Phoenicians discovered this process and disseminated the technology, since the earliest cultivation of artichokes (and cardoons) is associated with Phoenician colonies. These plants may have been first brought under cultivation expressly for their renneting qualities, only later employed in cookery. In any case, it was the "choke" or flower head that was heated in the milk in order to make it curdle. These plants flower in late spring when milk production is at its peak, especially among goats.

Other renneting plants from this same region were milk thistle (*Silybum marianum*) and blessed thistle (*Cnicus benedictus*), which were also eaten as spring greens (the leaves were tied up and blanched under mounds of soil). In northern Europe, the flower heads of several species of native thistles were used in the same manner, as well as the old Celtic rennet plant, Lady's Bedstraw (*Galium verum*). In the case of Lady's Bedstraw, it is the golden yellow root that is used to curdle milk. In the Celtic areas of Spain and Gaul, this plant, like milk thistle and blessed thistle, was under the protection of the fertility goddess Brigantia, who presided over matters dealing with the dairy and whose name survives in many place names where her cult was celebrated annually at Imbolc (February 1).

Brigantia's offices were subsumed by the early Church and assigned, in Ireland at least, to St. Bridget (a goddess transformed into a saint) as well as to Maria Lactans, the Virgin Mary depicted with streams of milk flowing from her breasts. It was Maria Lactans to whom village women prayed not only to ensure their own lactation after childbirth, but also to ensure the proper curdling of milk during cheesemaking.

See also **Cattle**; **Cheese**; **Dairy Products**; **Goat, Lactation**; **Vegetarianism**.

BIBLIOGRAPHY

Berolzheimer, Ruth. *The Dairy Cook Book*. Chicago: Culinary Arts Institute, 1941.

Bray, D. A. "The Image of Saint Brigit in the Early Irish Church." *Études celtiques* 24 (1987): 209–215.

Crumbine, Samuel J., and James A. Tobey. *The Most Nearly Perfect Food: The Story of Milk*. Baltimore: Williams and Wilkins, 1930.

Green, Miranda J. *Dictionary of Celtic Myth and Legend*. London: Thames & Hudson, 1997.

Hole, Christina. *The English Housewife in the Seventeenth Century*. London: Chatto and Windus, 1953.

Morelli, L. *Manuale del Casaro* [*Handbook of cheese making*]. Milan, 1926.

New York State Agricultural Experiment Station. *Investigation Relating to the Manufacture of Cheese*. Part V, Fat in Milk. Geneva, N.Y.: New York Agricultural Experiment Station, 1894.

Ottenjann, Helmut, and Karl-Heinz Ziessow. *Die Milch: Geschichte und Zukunft eines Lebensmittels* [*Milk: the history and future of a food*]. Cloppenburg, Germany: Museumsdorf Cloppenburg, 1996.

Ränk, Gustav. *Från Mjölk till Ost* [*From milk to cheese*]. Stockholm: Nordiska Museet, 1966.

Vendryes, J. "Imbolc." *Revue celtique* 41 (1924): 241–244.

William Woys Weaver

CURRY. The term "curry" is an Anglicized spelling of Tamil *kari*, a general term for any spiced sauce, or in some south Indian dialects, an old word for black pepper. There is no fixed recipe for curry, and the Indians themselves generally refer to this broad range of spice preparations as *masala*, such as the powdered *garam masala* of the north, *chat masala* (tart and salty), *kala masala* (black curry), and *dhansak masala* (hot Parsi curry). These can be blends of powdered or whole spices and seasonings, wet or dry mixtures, mild or hot, depending on preference and regional style of cooking. As a rule, northern Indians favor dry powders, while in the South, pastes are more common. Most Indians prefer to make their spice mixtures fresh from raw or green ingredients, and this is one reason why recipes prepared in India taste so differently when made abroad.

However, curry, not *masala*, is now used the world over as a symbol for the spicy food of India, and especially for flavorings made for export, with powders based on such key ingredients as ground mustard seed, turmeric, coriander, cumin, and fenugreek. Cinnamon, cardamom, and chili peppers may also be added, as well as a variety of other flavorings. Most commercial curry powders are yellow, due to turmeric, a spice often connected with magic and ritual in traditional India. In spite of their universal appeal, spicy foods were condemned by most of India's ancient religions and forbidden to those seeking an austere and virtuous life. Curried foods were, therefore, equated with luxurious living.

Judging from the poems extolling them, the concept of serving a spicy sauce over rice is extremely old in India—there are references to crab and vegetable curries from ancient Jaffna in the south, but the term "curry" was not used to describe them. The Portuguese may have been the first Europeans to mention this type of cookery as early as 1502, but it was the Greek and Roman traders who first encountered it many centuries earlier. The traders are mentioned in Tamil accounts, which make it clear that they were quite fond of south Indian cookery, at least along the coast where they had established trading ports. The use of spice mixtures to flavor sauces, however, was not strange to either the Greeks or Romans, and such common curry herbs as cumin and fenugreek were actually introduced to India from the Mediterranean at a very early date.

The earliest reference to curry in English appeared in a 1598 Dutch travel account, but it was English cookbook author Hannah Glasse who first published a curry recipe in 1747, transforming it from a true sauce to a stew. This began the gradual yet steady evolution of curry into a dish quite at odds with its original Indian forms. Both the Dutch and English, through East India trade, spread the popularity of curry far beyond its original borders, but in doing so, they also changed it. The Dutch created the *rijstafel* and its numerous curried dishes out of their culinary experience in Indonesia. The English did the same with Indian *masala*.

True Indian-style curried sauce and rice are mentioned in numerous English accounts of life in India, even during the eighteenth century, and this remained a feature of the typical colonial meal; yet when it traveled back to England, it changed into a meat stew with rice added, or into something else altogether—such as the main flavoring for mulligatawny soup. Eliza Acton listed several curry dishes in her *Modern Cookery* (1847), including a rather telling discussion of curry, along with potted meats—telling because of its positioning among hashes as a supper dish or something for high tea, not a main course. She not only supplied a recipe for curry very similar to the powdered sorts sold in tins during that period, but she also detailed directions for making curried eggs (deviled eggs flavored with curry), curried sweetbreads, and curried oysters.

American cookery books do not trace as avid a taste for curries as their English counterparts, but Eliza Leslie did tackle curry in her *New Cook Book* (1857), and complained about the common adulterations and the widespread overuse of turmeric and hot chili. She made an interesting remark: "The best curry powder imported from India is of a dark green color, and not yellow or red. It has among its ingredients, tamarinds, not preserved, as we always get them—but raw in the shell. These tamarinds impart a pleasant acid to the mixture. For want of them, use lemon." Leslie was describing a true *masala*, and she stands out for taking a stance on authenticity mostly lacking in European cookery books of her period. However, her words were to no avail.

Tinned curry powder, imported or imitation, became a standard household spice, because it was an ideal ingredient for dressing up processed foods and the sort of bland preparations championed by the home economics movement of the late nineteenth and early twentieth centuries. Suddenly, curry was everywhere, "Beetonized" by the publishers of Isabella Beeton's *Book of Household Management*, the culinary bible of the British Empire. Curry met its ultimate apotheosis in the empress of India, the aging Victoria, presided over by Indian manservants and an Indian groom.

On the commercial side, marketing genius E. P. Veerasawmy promoted this lifestyle of the imperial raj as Edwardian chic. His food specialty company (established 1896) and famous restaurant on Regent Street in London (established 1926) became English institutions and synonymous with the "other English cuisine." Veerasawmy was also a champion of authenticity in his culinary writings. In *Indian Cookery* (1957), he said about curry: "Curries should always be served in separate dishes and never with rice as a border. The accompaniments of rice with curry are usually Bombay ducks, puppadums, chutneys (various kinds), Indian pickles, and sambals. It is best to eat curry and rice with a dessert spoon and fork. A knife should never be used. A well-cooked curry will not need one."

If curry has undergone a change since then, it has taken its cue from the large numbers of Indians and Pakistanis who have settled in Britain, Africa, South America, and the United States during the second half of the twentieth century. No longer do non-Indians imagine that curry is a flavor peculiar to one rare fragrant spice. The proliferation of Indian-style restaurants, especially the inexpensive ones with highly varied menus, has at least driven home the idea that curried sauces come in many styles and forms. Most importantly, however, is the printed menu itself. All over the world, anywhere English is spoken, Indians prefer to use the term curry, regardless of what they may call their sauces in the homeland.

See also **Beeton, Isabella Mary; British Isles; Herbs and Spices; India; Leslie, Eliza**.

BIBLIOGRAPHY
Achaya, K. T. *Indian Food: A Historical Companion*. Delhi and New York: Oxford University Press, 1994.

Brennan, Jennifer. *Curries and Bugles: A Memoir and Cookbook of the British Raj*. New York: HarperCollins, 1990.

"Indian Cookery." In *Mrs. Beeton's Book of Household Management*, pp. 1267–1280. London: Ward, Lock, 1920.

Veerasawmy, E. P. [*alias* Ketab]. *Indian Cookery*. Bombay: Jaico, 1957.

Veerasawmy, E. P. *Indian Dishes for English Tables*. London: Arco, 1964.

Yule, Col. H., and A. C. Burnell. *Hobson-Jobson: A Glossary of Colloquial Anglo-Indian Words and Phrases*. London: Curzon Press, 1985.

William Woys Weaver

CUSTARD AND PUDDINGS.

Custard and puddings are words that describe several important sweet foods. The strict culinary definition of custard is eggs and milk mixed and baked, or stirred over gentle heat until thickened. Used in desserts, pies, pastries, and as sauces, it is well known in European countries and in cultures influenced by them.

After this, there are significant differences between custards and puddings in North America and the United Kingdom. Currently, in North America, pudding, and often egg custard, is made up from a flavored cornstarch mix to give creamy-textured desserts, and is eaten alone or used as pie filling. Mixes are also known elsewhere, for instance, in Germany, Central Europe, and Southeast Asia. In Britain, pudding mix is unknown, but a similar product, custard powder, is found in most kitchens. It is vanilla flavored and used mostly to make a sauce for puddings. Puddings are a complex subject in English cookery. The word "pudding" is used for numerous sweet dishes—some crisp, some cake-like, some soft and smooth, some like plum pudding. They have no convenient overall definition, but sweetness and the presence of flour or other cereal is important, and they are essential to a proper dinner. Pudding is also used as a collective name for the dessert itself, and applied to special groups of savory foods, not discussed here.

In scientific terms, cornstarch puddings are starch gels, and egg-and-milk custards are protein gels. To achieve their creamy texture, old-fashioned cornstarch pudding mixes and British custard powder must be brought to the boil. This gelatinizes the starch: the granules of which it is composed swell and some long-chain starch molecules migrate out, making the liquid thick and viscous. When this cools, it becomes gel in which the starch molecules form a network, enmeshing the water. Instant pudding mixtures rely on chemically modified starches that

CUSTARD PIES

The appearance of early custards is unknown. In seventeenth-century England, the author Robert May (1685) gave patterns for baked custard tarts. Pastry for the base was cut to make fancy leaflike shapes. Vertical strips were added to the edges to make walls to retain the mixture. The shapes were baked blind, then filled with flavored egg and milk, and baked again to set the custard, which was finally decorated with a sprinkle of little colored candies. These custards were probably eaten by spooning the filling out of the pastry, which recipes suggest was tough and essentially for structural and decorative purposes.

Such elaborate dishes are unknown today, and custard pies are plain in appearance, their only decoration being a scatter of grated nutmeg, but individual custard tarts are made in deep pastry shells, recalling a little "flowerpot" shape, originally known as a dariole. The large French apricot tarts with custard baked around the fruit are not found in English cookery. A short pastry is always used for the crust in England, unlike Portuguese *pasteis de nata*, rich custard tartlets in flaky pastry.

Several distinctive North American variants of custard pie have appeared. These would not necessarily be considered custard pies by their makers, but a certain basic reliance on eggs and milk can be seen in the recipes. They include pumpkin pie, key lime pie, chess pies as made in the southern States, lemon meringue, and various "cream" pies. These products represent a distillation of centuries of ideas about custard and puddings from various European cultures, with some distinctively American twists added. Finally, custard pies also became important in early movies, but as ammunition, rather than as food. They were specially constructed with pastry sturdy enough to hold in the hand and included a satisfyingly messy filling.

gelatinize without heating. Flavors of pudding mixes are limited only by technology and the tastes of consumers; almond, vanilla, chocolate, coconut, caramel, butterscotch, and lemon are considered old favorites.

Egg-based custards require gentle cooking. A standard recipe is one cup milk, scalded, mixed with two eggs and two tablespoons sugar, poured into a dish or a pie shell and baked at an oven temperature of about 350°F (180°C). During baking, the egg proteins coagulate to become a firm but tender gel (milk contains naturally occurring salts that aid this process). Alternatively, the mixture is cooked in a double boiler on the stove top to make a boiled custard. This is a confusing name, as the temperature of the custard must not rise above 189–193°F (87–90°C) or it curdles and the texture is spoiled. Richer custards require cream or high proportions of egg yolk.

Custard or pudding recipes that involve both cornstarch (or flour) and eggs are also known; *crème pâtissière* (pastry cream) is based on this principle. These are heated to boiling, but do not curdle because the starch stabilizes the egg proteins. Other special types of custard dessert, such as the decoratively molded *bavaroise* (Bavarian cream) rely on gelatin to hold a firm shape. In the tropics, cow's milk is replaced with that of water buffaloes, or by coconut milk. Some Chinese custards have a sugar syrup base, and the Japanese make savory *chawan mushi* using *dashi* stock as the liquid. Vanilla is the classic haute cuisine flavoring for custards, but the English use nutmeg on baked custards, the Spanish and Portuguese flavor with lemon and cinnamon, and the Chinese with fresh ginger.

In the complex history of custards and puddings, mixes are a relatively recent invention. Convenience was a factor in their development over time, but they must also have resonated with ideas about soft milky desserts from previous centuries. To disentangle these, one has to look at the European history of such dishes.

Baked egg and milk custards are of ancient origin; a Roman recipe of this type survives. The combination was also liked in the Middle Ages, when pastry was used to contain the mixture. The word "custard" comes from *crustade*, meaning a single-crust pie. Sugar, spices, vine fruit, almonds, and ground meat were added to custards. Little distinction was made between sweet and savory foods until the seventeenth century (the idea of a savory custard containing meat has survived into the twenty-first century as quiche Lorraine.) Possets, warm drinks of eggs, cream, wine or ale, sweetened and spiced, were also made. They were popular in the seventeenth century, and may have influenced ideas about custard as a dessert sauce, as well as being ancestors of eggnogs.

With or without pastry, custards were popular in eighteenth-century Europe. In England, rich ones flavored with almonds, pistachios, or orange flower water were called creams. Lemon cheese, a mixture of lemon juice and rind, butter, sugar and eggs—almost a milkless custard—was popular for tartlets, as was egg custard. Custards also acquired a new role as a base for ice creams, which later became important in North America.

Elsewhere, elegant custard desserts developed, such as the egg yolk and cream *crème brûlée*, with a crust of caramel sugar, and *petits pots de crème*, cooked in little cups or *ramekins* (itself a Flemish word which originally meant 'little cream'). Custards cooked in molds lined with caramel sugar—*crème caramel*, Spanish *leche flan*—later became cliches of restaurant cookery in the twentieth century.

The history of English puddings is obscure, but sixteenth century versions seem to have been sausage-like, with meat and cereal fillings, ancestors of suet and plum puddings. Early eighteenth-century recipes included boiled custard puddings and quaking puddings of egg, cream, and flour. Both types were wrapped in cloths and boiled. These were all staple foods, as was hasty pudding, hot milk with flour stirred in to thicken it. Sweet baked puddings in pastry-lined dishes became fashionable, too; a custard done this way was sometimes called a custard pudding. Other recipes used fruit, nuts, vegetables such as carrots, or sweetened rice, barley, or sago with milk, cream, and eggs. Similar cereal mixtures with milk, sugar, and eggs were known elsewhere in Europe.

In early nineteenth-century America, ideas about custard and puddings were probably little different than those of the English. One influence at this time was the availability of easy-to-use starches such as arrowroot, tapioca, and potato flour, which gave a pleasing transparent appearance, and were used for invalid food. The critical development was the extraction of cornstarch in 1842 in New Jersey; by 1850, food-grade starch was being produced. Secondly, in Birmingham, England, in 1844 a pharmacist named Alfred Bird devised custard powder, a flavored starch mix, for his wife who was fond of custard but allergic to eggs. It is unclear if he used cornstarch (at that point, mostly used in laundries) or another type such as arrowroot or sago. Custard powder soon became popular in Britain.

American housewives continued to make puddings with cornstarch, milk, and eggs, using chocolate, vanilla, or fruit as flavors. Cooks also found that cornstarch "stretched" an inadequate egg supply and, added to custard, made it more stable. Recipes increased in number, and flavors increased—caramel, lemon, almond—recalling custards and puddings of other traditions and centuries.

Convenience puddings appeared in the mid-1920s, when the Jell-O Company introduced a chocolate mix for use in institutions. Surprisingly, in view of the move toward convenience foods, ordinary consumers had to wait until 1934 until they could buy a similar product, sold as Walter Baker's dessert. Although the British used starch mixes for cold-molded blancmanges, they never took to pudding mixes. In contrast, in North America, other flavors soon appeared and the mixes were also marketed as pie fillings. Instant mixes came onto the market in the 1950s.

By this time, the defining characteristics of pudding seem to have emerged as softness and sweetness, echoing custards, batter, and milk puddings. Speed was also important, perhaps influenced, by the idea of hasty pudding, to which cornstarch puddings bear some resemblance when reduced to basic principles. Puddings and custards also converged as cornstarch mixes were increasingly uses in pies. "Cream" pies have picked up elements of the sweetness and softness of custard and acquired a name associated with it, while maintaining a link, through cornstarch, with the cereal element so important in puddings.

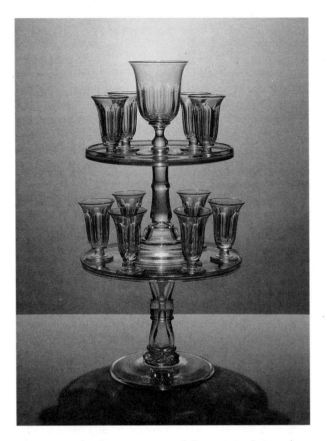

Glass pyramid with cream or custard glasses. Mixed pieces from England and America, circa 1790–1800. The custards were cooked in a double boiler, then poured hot into the glasses, which were then stored away in a cool place until the custard set. The custards were brought to the table and served from the pyramid. The large glass on top is intended for a fruit or floral centerpiece. ROUGHWOOD COLLECTION. PHOTO CHEW & COMPANY.

Nutritionally, a standard egg custard provides about 380 calories, a little under 20 g protein and 17 g fat, plus about 170 mg calcium. The composition of richer custards or English puddings is infinitely variable, depending on the whim of the maker: more cream, more sugar, higher calories. Standard mixes and custard powder made up with whole milk provide about 90 calories per 100 g when mixed; most of the calories are from sugar and starch. The high-protein or low-sugar pudding mixes marketed in the United States as snacks and for dieters are a notion that would amuse the English originators of puddings, for whom it was, by definition, a high-calorie, filling food and an essential part of a proper dinner.

See also **British Isles: England; Gelatin; Pastry; Starch.**

BIBLIOGRAPHY

Davidson, Alan. "Custard." In *The Oxford Companion to Food*, edited by Alan Davidson, pp. 237–238. New York: Oxford University Press, 1999.

Davidson, Alan. "Pudding." In *The Oxford Companion to Food*, edited by Alan Davidson, pp. 637–638. New York: Oxford University Press, 1999.

Leslie, Miss. *Miss Leslie's Lady's New Receipt Book*. Philadelphia: A Hart, 1851.

McGee, Harold. *On Food and Cooking*. New York: Scribners, 1984.

May, Robert. *The Accomplished Cook*. Facsimile of the 1685 edition. Foreword and introduction by Alan Davidson, Marcus Bell, and Tom Jaine. Totnes, Devon, U.K.: Prospect Books, 1994.

Laura Mason

CUTLERY. For a very long time humans used their fingers to convey food to their mouths, tearing pieces off with their teeth, which had evolved for this purpose. Then they found that, by using small flakes of sharp-edged flint as cutting tools, they could skin and cut up the carcass of a heavy animal and remove the small pieces to a safer place to eat. Similarly, natural objects, such as shells, could be used to hold and carry water.

With the discovery and use of copper, humans moved into the age of metal. The early Egyptians, who already had very beautiful and skillfully executed flint knives, made copper knives that were small and leaf-shaped in design and may have been used for domestic or ceremonial purposes. These copper knives did not have as hard and sharp an edge as flint and probably did not replace the flint knives entirely until it was discovered that combining the soft copper with tin produced the much harder alloy of bronze. This extended the use of metal into everyday objects and gave bronze knives a hard and sharp edge; the distinct advantage of these blades was that they could be resharpened.

Further specialization of knives occurred throughout the Middle East and spread among the Celts of central and northern Europe in the Bronze Age. There are some extant small knives with considerable decorative style that were probably personal eating implements, perhaps carried on a type of chatelaine. Additionally, other larger and decorative knives, capable of being used for eating or defense purposes, were possibly carried in a sheath on a belt.

The next important advancement was the slow introduction of the use of iron, which started with meteoric iron in Egypt in the third millennium B.C.E. with very small improvement in the technology and was probably in the beginning not a great improvement on bronze.

During the Roman period, divisions of society appeared with their own rituals for eating and drinking. Some Roman illustrations show diners in a reclining position, which must have made cutting food with a knife quite difficult. Perhaps the food was cut into bite-sized pieces before serving, similar to the custom in most Asian countries today. The reclining style of eating was not for everyday, but for banquets and entertaining. Iron knives, some with decorative bronze handles, were now common, and the Romans had a large range of knives to meet their various requirements, including specialized knives for eating and food preparation.

The Romans also developed folding knives with blades of iron, some with spoons attached, with decorative bronze handles showing hunting scenes of hounds chasing hares; another version of the folding type is a figure of a lion with an iron knife blade, folding spoon and sometimes a "spike," perhaps for eating snails. It is not inconceivable that these utensils were used and lost by legionaries moving around the country; they are among the more common Roman objects excavated in Britain.

There is evidence from Saxon grave sites of women and children having small personal knives of iron interred with them during the early centuries following the withdrawal of the Romans. Some of these knives reflect the style that was developed by Northumbrian monks. The larger knife, called a "scramasax," was a general-purpose iron knife having a very distinct shape and point, with a thick back and a blade that was sometimes inlaid with silver and brass in a wooden "bobbin" handle. Some of the better examples show great skill in the patterned inlay work on the blade. The scramasax became quite famous and popular throughout Europe; a well-recorded knife owned by Charlemagne is an example of its status. Some of the excavated medieval knives from the foreshore of the Thames still show this influence.

Illustrations from medieval manuscripts show rich tables set with ewers and bowls, a knife or two, and occasionally a fork. The number of knives on the table does not match the number of diners present, so, according to the custom of the time, the diner would carry and use his own knife and spoon, or perhaps share a knife provided on the table. The ewers and bowls were for cleansing the fingers before taking food from the communal dishes. A small fork was most likely provided for picking up preserved and sticky food. The fork was shared and, like the spoon, did not become an eating companion with the knife until after the second half of the seventeenth century. Most of these early forks are bronze and silver, with two tines, and have been excavated in Europe, particularly Italy. They did not change very much in style until the late sixteenth and early seventeenth centuries, when the number of tines varied from two to four. However, the two-tined fork, also in steel, lasted in common usage in western Europe, including Britain, until the twentieth century.

The personal carrying of knives is well illustrated by Bosch and later by Breughel, both of whom show knives worn in the belt ready for eating or, if need be, self-defense. Spoons were usually tucked into hats and clothing and were perhaps easily lost. This might explain the many spoons that have been excavated at the apparent crossing point of one of London's ditches where we can assume people dropped the spoons when they jumped and then failed to retrieve them.

Medieval travelers were expected to supply their own eating utensils at any lodging house or inn in which they stayed overnight. Most men carried a knife of some sort in their belts as a matter of course, but a rich traveler might have a more elaborate sheath, perhaps containing a large knife and an extra sheath containing a small eating knife and spoon. Later medieval knives were subjected to considerable innovation in both design and construction. The reason for this is not entirely clear, but one suspects that location, novelty, desirability, and profit were factors.

National styles were also appearing, although with so much trade and importation plus the movement of people, it is not always easy to determine where a particular excavated knife was made. The style and cutler's mark or other inscription might help to identify country or origin. Knives from the Thames foreshore would suggest that knives were frequently dropped overboard from visiting foreign ships and that local inhabitants were using the river as a highway and rubbish dump, thus increasing the difficulty of identification many years later.

Eating knives of the seventeenth century became thin and elegant and, toward the end of the century, were more decorative, with carved ivory figures and composite handles of jet, ebony, amber, colored bone, hardstone, agate, cut steel, and precious metal. Such knives were accepted as a decorative part of dress and were suitable as impressive gifts. Very few of the common knives have survived except in an excavated condition, whereas many of the fine-quality knives that were often given as gifts have survived and been handed down through the centuries.

A pair of knives given by the groom to his bride as a wedding gift was an indication of wealth. The bride then wore the knives as a token of her position as mistress of the house. This custom lasted until the early seventeenth century. Many other crafts were involved in the making of these quality knives. Although a cutler was required by his guild to make a complete knife, the handles were made by specialized craftsmen and even imported from abroad. The sheaths were made by experts in the field of leather, wood, fabric, and beadwork.

Parallel with the decorative knives was a type of knife that was very long and elegant; it was made of one piece of iron, and the handle was decorated with balusters and turning. These knives, with handles showing traces of black enamel, may have been given as "memento mori" presents.

The first half of the seventeenth century saw a change in the size and style of the knife. It was getting shorter, the point was removed (since it was no longer required as a spike to transfer food to the mouth), the blade was sometimes wider at the tip than at the bolster, and there was a short handle of a round tapering section in ivory, bone, or wood, sometimes decorated with inlaid wire. The result was a strong, very purposeful "prime" knife that matches the basic simple Puritan spoon of this

Plush-lined knife box with cutlery, showing a typical "scimitar" knife blade and fork with pistol handle. It was this distinctive knife that gave its name to the eighteenth-century "caseknife" bean, due to the similar shape of its pod. WILLIAM H. BROWN COLLECTION.

period, which has a plain, flattish oval bowl with a simple parallel-sided bar stem.

The early seventeenth century also saw the general introduction of a fork at all social levels, usually as a matching companion to the knife. Forks had been used in Europe from early times, perhaps among the Romans—after all, a trident is only a large-sized fork—and large iron forks had been used for many years as cooking implements. This is well illustrated in the Bayeux Tapestry, which shows a cook removing a piece of meat from a cauldron with a long wooden-handled "fleshing" fork. Travelers from abroad brought back from Italy the habit of eating with a fork—they were probably impressed with the novelty, not least the hygiene—and after some resistance, the custom was accepted in England. At first the style, construction, and material of the fork

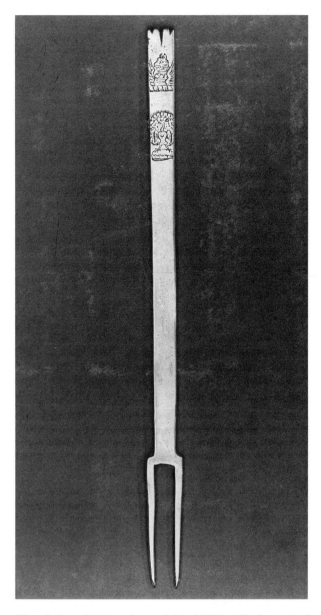

Silver fork made in London and dated 1632, with the crest of John Manners of Haddon Hall. COURTESY OF THE VICTORIA & ALBERT MUSEUM.

However, another introduction of the fork emerged at the same time; this was in silver and was hallmarked in London, dated 1632, and engraved with the crest of John Manners of Haddon Hall. This simple one-piece silver fork was in the style that was current in Paris at that time and matched the very plain Puritan spoon used in Paris and London. This set the custom of a spoon and fork matching, with the knife following suit and later in the eighteenth century all three pieces came together in large services of various patterns.

During the latter part of the seventeenth century, traveling sets containing knives, forks, and spoons were still necessary and continued throughout this and the next century. Most of these sets consisted of a knife and fork in a slip case, some with spoons. Others were more elaborate, containing a folding or dismantling knife, fork, and spoons with a beaker, corkscrew, and perhaps other items. The sets were likely to be made to special order, making the container very compact.

With the restoration of the monarchy in 1660, the design of knives slowly changed from the rather severe Puritan knife. The blade became longer, very curved, and spatulate at the tip, and the handle had a distinct pistol-shape, By the first quarter of the eighteenth century, it finally evolved into a prime example of a Baroque knife. The popular term for this type of knife is "scimitar," and it can be found in all its stages, from its rudimentary beginnings to another "prime" knife of 1720. The silver-handled scimitar knife is very satisfying and comfortable to use and is a favored antique for the table even today.

Contemporary with this change of style and the practice of laying the table with matching knife, fork, and spoon was the introduction of the separate dining room with dining table and chairs and other furniture. Some of the wealthier middle-class merchants began to supply their guests at the table with cutlery from fishskin-covered boxes on the dining room sideboard that contained knives, forks, and spoons in quantity, thus making the carrying of cutlery by guests unnecessary.

One of the most prolific suppliers of this style of cutlery, and probably an early entrepreneur of the factory system using local labor, was the Master Cutler Ephraim How. He and his son John made cutlery first at Chingford, then at the Southend Mill, Lewisham, and sold it from their shop at Saffron Hill, London.

From 1720 the scimitar became debased with the straightening of the blade and a hump on the back, but it still retained the round spatulated end; the handle lost its pistol shape. All of this disappeared after the middle of the century when a change occurred in the evolutionary chain of the eighteenth-century knife with the introduction of the "French" style. This was consistent with all the other similar fashions in the second half of the eighteenth century.

Knife blades became long and spear-shaped with the point on the central axis and the widest section halfway

matched that of the knife with the handle being slightly smaller in size and the tines of the fork made of steel. This continued to the middle of the seventeenth century when the spoon finally joined the knife and fork, giving us a typical Puritan knife, fork, and spoon.

The evolutionary design of knife blades goes through a line of many peaks and troughs throughout the centuries. The "peaks" throw up a perfect "prime" knife, highly suitable for its purpose; this depends on all the components' being sympathetic to each other whether they were made by one or by many craftsmen.

along the length of the blade. Handles were tapered with a round to oval section and sometimes capped with silver. Others were made of stamped silver with a raised foliate design, soldered together and filled with resin; they later became straight-sided and square using green-stained ivory, bone, or ebony.

Knife boxes continued to be used as pieces of quality furniture, holding a dozen or more knives and forks and sometimes silver spoons. Spoons in a larger variety of sizes, including servers, could be found in a separate box, that is, the middle box of a set of three. Most early- and late-eighteenth-century boxes had locks with keys and were kept in the dining room; the contents were washed *in situ* after each meal by the servants and locked away until required again.

It is about this time—1800—that dessert sets appeared; they were popular as gifts right through the nineteenth century. This was exploited by the cutlery trade, as knives have always been acceptable gifts.

There was no return to the evolutionary course of the design of the knife until 1820, when British style, after making weak attempts at bringing back the scimitar blade, settled for a large, parallel-sided blade with a rounded tip and a straight, simple handle made of ivory, stained green or plain, or of figured silver in many styles. This continued to the end of the nineteenth century with only small interruptions from the influence of various art movements and fashions that affected the decoration rather than the construction or size. Examples would be the influence of art nouveau and of gardening implements, such as serving utensils shaped like spades; the term "butter spade" is still in use.

Industrial exhibitions in this period were popular and fashionable and would have provided ample scope for displaying high-quality skills and innovations. During the early part of the twentieth century came a slow reduction in the size of the knife, along with corresponding changes in other pieces of tableware. The days of having to carry personal eating equipment were long gone, but with modern traveling by train and motor car, small folding fruit knives, cutlery for picnic hampers, and military and camping canteens were developed.

In 1914 there was an important change in the construction of the knife: stainless steel was commercially produced. Its application to knife blades was enormous. It meant that blades would no longer rust readily and would resist staining from acids and foods, both being the bane of most carbon steel blades.

There was one style of knife that appeared at the end of the nineteenth century and evolved slowly, both in England and in Germany. This was the all-metal one-piece knife in both iron and steel that had appeared at various times in the past and reappeared with the introduction of stainless steel. This knife is an obvious candidate for a "prime" knife of the first half of the twentieth century and, with the partnership of stainless steel spoons and forks, must have seemed the ultimate in cutlery. Such knives were produced in large quantities.

However, in recent times, industrial and silversmith designers have been involved in producing a proliferation of styles and novelties, perhaps to cause comment as well as to eat with.

See also **Etiquette and Eating Habits; Kitchen Gadgets; Utensils, Cooking.**

BIBLIOGRAPHY

Bailey, Major C. T. P. *Knives and Forks.* London: Medici Society, 1927.

Beard, C. R. "Wedding Knives." *The Connoisseur* 85 (1930): 91–97.

Brown, Bill. "Eating Implements." *Antique Collecting* 29, 9 (1995): pp. 21–23.

Brown, Peter, ed. *British Cutlery: An Illustrated History of Design, Evolution, and Use.* London: Philip Wilson, 2001.

Hayward, J. F. *English Cutlery: Sixteenth to Eighteenth Century.* London: Victoria and Albert Museum, 1957.

Himsworth, Joseph Beeston. *The Story of Cutlery: From Flint to Stainless Steel.* London: Ernest Benn, 1953.

Hughes, G. B. "Old English Wedding Knives." *Country Life* 105 (1949): 666–667.

London South Kensington Museum. *Masterpieces of Cutlery and the Art of Eating.* Exhibition catalogue. London: Victoria and Albert Museum, 1979.

Moore, Simon J. *Cutlery for the Table: A History of British Table and Pocket Cutlery.* Sheffield: Hallamshire Press, 1999.

Pickford, Ian. *Silver Flatware: English, Irish, and Scottish, 1660–1980.* Woodbridge, England: Antique Collectors' Club, 1983.

Singleton, Howard Raymond. *A Chronology of Cutlery.* Sheffield: Sheffield City Museum, 1973.

Bill Brown

CZECH REPUBLIC AND SLOVAKIA. *See* Central Europe.

D

DAIRY PRODUCTS. Dairy products are derived from milk, the secretion of the mammary glands of mammals, usually cows (bovine), sheep, goats, buffalo, mare, camel, or yak. Most dairy products originate from bovine milk and, to a lesser extent, sheep and goat milk. As milk contains approximately 80 to 90 percent water, it is prone to undesirable microbial growth with concomitant product deterioration. To prevent this problem from occurring, and to ensure a longer shelf life, milk is processed to form different products such as ice cream, cheese, milk powders, yogurt, butter, lactose, and anhydrous milk fat (also known as butteroil). Milk can be separated into a cream fraction and a skim milk fraction by a centrifugation technique called separation. This process concentrates the fat present in the milk into the cream phase, leaving a skim or partially skimmed phase with much lower fat content. Typical fat and water contents of selected dairy products are shown in Table 1. The speed of centrifugation can be adjusted to yield different fat content in cream. Milk processing applies different preservation techniques to allow for longer storage of dairy products. Milk powders are produced by concentration to remove some of the water, followed by atomization into a fine mist and drying at high temperatures. Heat and dehydration (water removal) are employed to give a long shelf life for milk powders. Ice cream is a dairy product preserved by the action of freezing. Yogurt and cheese are both fermented products. A bacterial culture is used to inoculate milk, for which the primary function is to lower the pH from 6.7 (typical for fresh bovine milk) to 4.2 for yogurt and in the range 4.6 to 6.0 for most cheese varieties. The bacterial cultures also assist in breaking down proteins and fats in the milk product to develop some of the flavor. The preserving function of added bacterial culture is to compete with unwanted pathogens for nutrients. Thus cheese and yogurt are preserved by dehydration, acidification, and competition with pathogens for survival in the product.

Heat Treatment of Milk

For food safety reasons, milk is often heat-treated prior to consumption or further processing. The most common heat treatments are holding at 162°F (72°C) for 15 seconds, called pasteurization, or at 145°F (63°C) for 30 minutes, called batch pasteurization. Both of these treatments have similar effects on killing undesirable microorganisms in milk. The treatment is sufficient to destroy two indicator organisms, *Mycobacterium tuberculosis* and *Coxiella burnetti.*

Another common heat treatment is to hold milk at 284°F (140°C) under pressure for 2 to 3 seconds, producing ultra high temperature (UHT) milk. This milk is essentially sterile and can be packaged in cardboard containers and stored at room temperature for up to six months with little microbial-induced deterioration. UHT milk is more commonly consumed in Europe than in Australia, New Zealand, or North America.

An alternative to preserving milk by heat pasteurization is high-pressure processing, where pressures of around 300–600 MPa are employed to rupture the membranes of pathogens and denature enzymes that cause de-

TABLE 1

Average composition of selected dairy products (grams per 100 grams of milk)						
	Water	Fat	Protein	Lactose	Sodium chloride	Calcium
Cheddar cheese	37	32	24	0	1.6	0.8
Ice cream	61	10-14	3.6	22	0.2	0.15
Full-fat yogurt	89	3	3.5	7	0.15	0.1
Butter	16	81	0.9	0.06	0-1.2	—
Skim milk powder	3–4	1	35	52	1.3	1.3
Whole milk powder	2	27	26	38	1	0.9
Whey powder	4	0.6–6	80–93	1–7	3	0.8–2.2
Cream	55–80	12–40	1.8–2.6	2.5–4.5	0.01	0.1

terioration in milk quality. This process has not been adopted to any significant commercial extent as the milk must be processed in batch quantities rather than in a continuous fashion as in a pasteurizer. Gamma irradiation of milk for the purpose of preservation is not practiced as it tends to produce off-flavors. Ultraviolet light can be used to pasteurize milk, and has the additional benefit of increasing the amount of available vitamin D. Bactofugation is sometimes employed to remove bacteria in milk by a process of centrifugation. Hydrogen peroxide can also be used to improve poor-quality milk. This preservative can be removed by heating milk to 122–131°F (50–55°C), whereupon the enzyme catalase present in milk destroys the added hydrogen peroxide.

Milk Composition

Milk contains proteins, fat, water, lactose, inorganic salts, and other minor organic material such as phospholipids, organic acids, enzymes, hormones, vitamins, nucleotides, amines, amino acids, alcohols, aldehydes, ketones, and esters. (A complete set of detailed compositional tables can be found in Noble P. Wong et al., *Fundamentals of Dairy Chemistry*, pp. 1–38.) An understanding of how the major constituents are structurally arranged in milk is necessary to predict how milk processing conditions affect flavor, texture, and the keeping qualities of dairy products.

The gross composition of milk varies according to the species of mammal, the breed of the cow (especially for bovine milk), and the stage of lactation. Note the relatively low amount of casein in human milk, rendering it difficult to make cheese. The breed of cow will affect the level of fat and protein. Holstein cows are common in dairies in North America, Australia, and New Zealand.

An important advancement in milk compositional study was the development of a rapid test for milk fat by Stephen M. Babcock of the University of Wisconsin in 1890. This procedure allowed for accurate marketing of milk, resulted in a more consistent quality of dairy products, and facilitated the development of better farming practices to optimize fat content in milk.

Milk composition and volume are affected by the season, particularly in milder climates such as Australia and New Zealand where cows are pasture-fed all year round. Milk production drops during the winter months of May to August in the Southern Hemisphere, to a level such that there is little excess milk available for dairy processing beyond that of market consumer milk. In the colder climates found in Canada and the north of the United States and Europe, cows are fed on silage during the winter months. This produces a more uniform supply of milk and often results in paler and less yellow-colored dairy products, especially butter and cheese, due to the lower levels of beta-carotene in silage feed. Fat and total milk solids (fat, protein, and minerals) are lower in summer months compared to winter in both hemispheres. The effect of pasture quality and quantity on milk composition is a complex issue. Feed quality is affected by the level of roughage, fat, protein, energy level, and the fatty acid profile.

One important factor in milk quality that has important consequences in dairy processing is the health of the cow. Mastitis is an infection of the udder that results in high somatic cell counts in the milk. Immunoglobulin levels are higher in mastitic milk, whereas fat, lactose, casein, and whey protein levels are lower. Treatment for mastitis requires antibiotics; however, this has the undesirable effect of killing introduced bacterial cultures in the manufacture of cheese and yogurt. Milk processing factories rigorously and routinely check milk samples from individual farms for antibiotics, as well as for levels of fat, whey proteins, caseins, urea, and lactose. Milk containing antibiotics is discarded and a penalty fine may be imposed on the farmer. Routine testing also allows correct payment to be made to the farmer, usually based on the amount of casein plus fat. In addition, due to the variable composition of milk, testing allows batches of milk to be standardized to a particular casein or fat content depending upon the type of dairy product to be made.

Milk Fat Globules

The fat in milk is emulsified with a membrane material consisting primarily of proteins, phospholipids, and enzymes. Other minor components of the membrane include glycoproteins, phospholipids, carotenoids (including beta-carotene), and sterols (including cholesterol). There are approximately 15 trillion fat globules in one liter of milk, with a size in the range of 0.1 to 20 micrometers. The membrane surface serves to protect the fat from undesirable oxidation. Fat globules will still cream given sufficient time. The creaming effect is accentuated by the agglutinin reaction, which results in fat globules clustering and rising rapidly to the surface to form a cream layer.

Approximately 98 percent of the fat in milk exists in the form of a triacylglyceride, where three fatty acids are attached to a glycerol molecule. The fatty acids comprise CH_2 methylene groups linked together to form a chain of varying carbon lengths. Milk fat has a significant proportion of fatty acids with a length of four carbon atoms (C4), known as butyric acid, which causes the sharp, acidic taste in some cheese varieties. This flavor is often described as rancid. Other major fatty acid components of the triacylglyceride include myristic acid (C14), palmitic acid (C16), stearic acid (C18), and oleic acid, which also contains 18 carbon atoms but differs from stearic acid in that it contains one unsaturated C=C bond.

Due to the many possible arrangements of different length fatty acids, the melting point of milk fat is not as sharply defined as for pure compounds, but rather extends over a wide range of temperatures. Milk fat is entirely solidified at −40°F (−40°C), and has melted completely at 104°F (40°C). At refrigeration temperature milk fat is between 40 and 50 percent solid, despite the apparent solid appearance at this temperature.

Milk fat, when solidified, crystallizes into three main forms (alpha, beta, and beta' polymorphs) depending upon the rate of cooling. Tempering of a food product containing milk fat is a process of careful adjustment of the temperature at different heating and cooling rates. This process promotes the formation of a particular polymorphic structure with desirable texture. Tempering is used in butter manufacture.

Unsaturated Milk Fat

Butters, spreads, and margarines that are high in unsaturated fatty acid content are believed to protect against heart disease. Margarines usually contain a higher level than butter. The unsaturated C=C bond in oleic acid (and other unsaturated acids) can exist in two forms, the cis form where hydrogen atoms are on the same side as the C=C bond, and the trans form where the hydrogen atoms are on either side. The cis form is more common in nature and believed to offer better protection against heart disease.

Conversion of a polyunsaturated liquid oil to a higher melting point mono-unsaturated solid fat (such as in margarine manufacture) can take place by the process of partial chemical hydrogenation, where hydrogen atoms are added to some of the C=C bonds to form saturated C=C bonds. The process of hydrogenation requires the initial removal of polar lipids such as phospholipids, and heating the oil at 320°–428°F (160°–220°C) under a pressure of 2–10 atmospheres with a 0.01–0.2 percent nickel catalyst. Consumption of trans mono-unsaturated fatty acids has been associated with heart disease (see Beardsley, p. 34).

The degree of unsaturation is measured by the iodine test, where the number of grams of iodine reacting with the C=C bonds in 100 grams of oil or fat is determined. Generally, the higher the number of unsaturated bonds and the lower the carbon chain length, the lower the melting point of the fatty acid.

Milk Fat Deterioration

Deterioration of milk fat can occur by two main mechanisms: fatty acid release and oxidation of C=C bonds. Release of fatty acids occurs by cleavage (hydrolysis) of a fatty acid from a triacylglyceride molecule. The presence and release of butyric acid will give the typical rancid flavor found in blue and Italian-style cheeses. Oxidation of C=C bonds results in formation of hydroperoxide radicals that form high molecular weight compounds over time with increased viscosity and propensity for foaming. This is more of a problem with vegetable oils used for frying where extreme temperature fluctuations take place. Oxidation is promoted by the presence of oxygen at high temperatures and high water activity.

Fatty acid hydrolysis is catalyzed by an enzyme called a lipase. Milk contains 1–2 milligrams per liter of a native lipase called milk lipoprotein lipase. This enzyme is 90 percent inactivated under pasteurization conditions.

Hydrolysis (more specifically lipolysis, in the case of oils) is exacerbated at higher pH, a temperature of around 37°C, by light, and by the degree of agitation of milk. Exposure of milk fat as a result of agitation will provide access by the milk lipoprotein lipase, and lipolysis will occur. Sufficient agitation of milk can occur during homogenization. If milk is not pasteurized prior to homogenization, enough lipolysis can take place, with release of fatty acids, to burn the throat of someone unfortunate enough to consume this milk. Needless to say, milk is always pasteurized before homogenization.

Milk obtained fresh from the cow is partially protected against lipolysis by the milk fat globule membrane, and also by the separation of milk lipoprotein lipase (largely bound to the casein micelles) from the milk fat substrate. As already stated, agitation of milk promotes lipolysis. Heating fresh unpasteurized milk to 86°F (30°C) then cooling back to refrigeration temperatures will cause rancidity to occur within twenty-four hours. This problem will occur if warm fresh morning milk is added to cooled evening milk from the previous day, then cooled back down again. In addition, spontaneous lipolysis occurs in one out of five cows after cooling milk to 59–68°F (15°–20°C). This problem is circumvented by mixing with four to five times the volume of normal milk. Freezing and thawing of milk can also promote lipolysis. A slower rate of freezing will increase the rate of lipolysis.

In the United States, whole milk powder from lipase-treated milk is used in the manufacture of milk chocolate to impart a slight rancid flavor note. This flavor is what the U.S. consumer has come to expect in milk chocolate flavor, presumably for historical reasons when low-quality and less expensive milk may have been used in the manufacturing process. This flavor is absent in milk chocolate produced in Europe, Australia, and New Zealand.

Milk Proteins

Proteins in milk are broadly classified as either caseins or whey proteins. Caseins are mostly insoluble in water and exist in an aggregated form called a casein micelle of average size 0.2 micrometers. This is sufficiently small to scatter light and render to milk its white appearance. Whey proteins are soluble over a wide pH range and have high nutritional value.

Whey comprise the class of proteins that are soluble in milk. They are globular proteins of size 2–4 nanometers. The major subcomponents of bovine whey are a-lactalbumin and β-lactoglobulin. Human milk does not contain β-lactoglobulin, and a-lactalbumin is highly valued when extracted from bovine whey for use in powdered infant formula. Consumption of bovine milk or formula containing β-lactoglobulin may elicit an allergic response when consumed by very young infants. The main utility of β-lactoglobulin is as a gelling agent in food products such as comminuted meats. The presence of a-lactalbumin will impair the gel structure formed from

HOMOGENIZATION

Food products that contain fat and water phases must be emulsified to prevent creaming or sedimentation. In most biphasic dairy-based food products (with the exception of butter), water is the predominant phase, and the fat phase is emulsified. Emulsions are energetically unstable systems, and given enough time, will separate out into the two phases. This process is greatly hindered by covering the surface of the emulsion globules with some kind of surface-active component, commonly a protein, polysaccharide, and/or monoacylglyceride. Slowing down the rate of destabilization of an emulsion enables a food product to be stable over a period of weeks or months. Milk and cream are naturally occurring oil-in-water emulsions. Others include mayonnaise, spreads and dips, cheese, yogurt, sauces, ice cream, and salad dressing.

For fat to be broken up into small micrometer-size globules, energy must be supplied to the food product. This process is called homogenization. The types of homogenizers range from simple rapid and turbulent stirring devices, to more complex valve equipment that forms emulsions under high pressure, turbulence, and cavitation. A detailed overview of the different types of homogenizers is given by Mulder and Walstra in *The Milk Fat Globule* (pp. 163–194) and by McClements in *Food Emulsions: Principles, Practice, and Techniques* (pp. 161–184).

As a general rule, the more energy supplied by a homogenizer, the smaller the fat globules formed, with a greater stability against creaming. Typical pressures for homogenization of milk in a dairy factory are 17 MPa first stage and 3.5 MPa second stage, the latter of which is used to break up aggregates of fat globules that may form in the first stage. This process produces globules of size 2–3 micrometers in bovine milk.

Other types of homogenizers that are not commonly used in dairy processing include ultrasonic and membrane units. Some of the effects of milk homogenization on dairy products include smaller fat globules as pressure increases, whiter colored cheese with higher moisture, increased viscosity of yogurt, increased lipolysis of milk, less oxidized off-flavors in milk, faster clotting of milk in cheese manufacture, and inactivation of the agglutinin properties (the agglutinin reaction causes clustering of fat globules).

β-lactoglobulin, hence the requirement to separate these two components from whey.

Other components of bovine whey include bovine serum albumin, immunoglobulins, lactoferrin, and lactoperoxidase. Lysozyme is an enzyme found in milk that also has antimicrobial activity. This enzyme is found in higher concentrations in milk colostrum, protecting the gut of a newborn calf against invasion by pathogenic bacteria.

Colostrum is the initial secretion of the mammary gland after birth and contains a much higher casein and whey protein concentration than milk at later stages of lactation. The level of lactose is less than in milk, and the amount of fat is slightly higher. Colostrum confers immunity to a newborn calf through the high levels of immunoglobulins, and also provides a high-quality nutritional diet.

Whey is the main by-product of cheesemaking. It has historically been considered to be of low value, and used as pig food, fertilizer for agricultural fields, or simply disposed of into the ocean. Now, whey is spray-dried to produce a powdered protein ingredient, highly valued by the food processing industry for its excellent nutritional and textural modifying properties. Whey can be further fractionated into components that are spray-

dried, and these command a premium price for food and pharmaceutical applications.

Functional Properties of Whey Proteins

Functional properties of whey proteins include its water solubility, viscosity modification ability, gelation, texturization, high nutritional value, flavor-binding, foaming, emulsification, fat and water retention, and control over shrinkage in products such as yogurt and gelled foods. The high solubility and excellent nutritional properties allow whey proteins to be used to fortify high-energy sports beverages. Increasing the viscosity of fluid food products by whey protein addition will affect the sensory properties, and reduce the tendency for particulate matter (if present) to sediment. Different types of gels can be created by heating β-lactoglobulin. The pH, concentration and types of mineral salts present, and the rate of heating will affect the properties of the gel, such as opacity, elasticity, and the propensity for shrinkage with expulsion of liquid during storage (syneresis). Gels that are formed far from the isoelectric point (around pH 5.5, where there is no average net charge on the whey proteins) will tend to be less opaque, more fine stranded, and more elastic.

Texturization of whey proteins is achieved by heating to form a coagulum followed by extrusion though small diameter holes under high pressure to align the protein fibers. These can be further processed between heated rollers to remove more moisture, promote adhesion, and increase the toughness and chewiness. Textured dairy proteins have an application in forming vegetarian meat-like products.

Food products that contain oil require stabilizers to emulsify the oil and prevent excessive separation from the water phase. Both whey proteins and caseins can perform this function by homogenization to create small oil globules coated with proteins. Generally, the smaller the globules, the more stable the food product will be against creaming or oil separation. Examples of this type of food product include salad dressing and mayonnaise. Most oil and water food products are emulsified such that the oil globules are suspended in the water phase. If the oil or fat content is too high, a phase inversion takes place where water droplets are then suspended in the oil phase. In this case, whey proteins have little efficacy to act as emulsifiers. An example of a water-in-oil emulsified food product is butter.

Foam formation and stability are important attributes in food products such as ice cream, cappuccino coffee foam, meringue, marshmallow, mousse, and bread. Air bubbles are induced by rapid whipping and are lined with stabilizers to prevent rapid collapse of the foam. Whey proteins are excellent foaming agents, and their ability to unfold (denature) and cross-link at the air-water interface provides for good foam stability. Strong protein-protein interactions, such as that which occurs near the isoelectric pH of around 5.5, will promote foam stability. Free oil will cause a decrease in foam stability, which is the reason egg yolks (containing oil) are separated from egg white (containing proteins capable of stabilizing the foam) prior to whipping of the egg white. Emulsified oil, such as in milk or cream, will not affect foam stability to the same degree, as the oil is coated by the native milk fat globule membrane and does not come into direct contact with the protein foaming agents in dairy foams. However, if the native membrane is ruptured, perhaps due to enzymatic action or excessive turbulence when pumping milk during processing, the foaming ability is impaired. This is often a seasonal occurrence in some countries, creating cappuccinos with poor foams at certain times of the year when enzymatic activity is more pronounced. Special cappuccino milk is sometimes sold containing a higher proportion of added spray-dried foaming whey proteins to alleviate this problem. Further details about functional properties and emulsions are provided by Walstra in *Food Chemistry* (pp. 95–155).

Calcium Phosphate in Milk

The major mineral component in milk (and most dairy products) is calcium phosphate, an inorganic salt of low solubility in water. A high intake of calcium in the diet is believed to promote strong bone development, hence the recommendation of calcium in the diet of young children. The low solubility of calcium phosphate in water (and also in milk) would result in calcification, or boiler-scale, in the mammary gland if it were not for the unique properties of the casein micelle in solubilizing this mineral.

Each of the four main casein molecules (α-s1-casein, α-s2-casein, β-casein, and κ-casein) contain at least one phosphate group that is capable of binding to the calcium phosphate mineral complex in milk. Some twenty-five thousand of these casein molecules, with bound calcium phosphate, aggregate to form the heavily hydrated casein micelle of molecular weight 108–109 Daltons. Thus calcium phosphate is rendered soluble in milk (as the casein micelle itself can exist in milk as a stable suspension) and can be considered to be the binding agent that holds the micelle together. There is some controversy over the nature of the substructure of the casein micelle. The two main competing models are described by Pieter Walstra (1999) and Carl Holt and David S. Horne (1996).

Formation of Milk Curds

Cheese and yogurt making has been in existence for thousands of years. Milk would have been carried around in the warm Middle Eastern climate in sacks made from animal skins, such as the stomachs of ruminant animals. Milk stored in a sack made from the fourth stomach of a young calf and carried around at temperatures in excess of 68°F (20°C) would eventually coagulate and separate into curds and whey given sufficient mechanical disturbance. The curds would have provided a nourishing meal and the whey a refreshing and nutritious beverage. This process has evolved into the highly scientific and mechanized approach used today in modern cheese-making plants.

The casein micelle will undergo extensive aggregation as the pH approaches the isoelectric point. For caseins in milk, this occurs at pH 4.6. This is the basis for the coagulation of milk and separation of the curds from the whey to make cheese. A comprehensive treatment on the physical chemistry of curd formation and subsequent reactions is given by Dalgleish (pp. 69–100), Green and Grandison (pp. 101–140), and Walstra (pp. 141–191) in Patrick F. Fox, ed., *Cheese: Chemistry, Physics and Microbiology*.

Curds are composed of aggregated casein micelles and trapped fat globules within the protein matrix. The whey phase contains mostly water with soluble minerals, whey proteins, and lactose. Casein micelle clotting (with consequent curd formation) can also occur by addition of coagulating enzymes or 20 percent alcohol. Most cheese varieties are manufactured by enzymatic coagulation, with some formed by acid precipitation to pH 4.6. Acidification can also take place by the addition of bacterial culture, directly by addition of acids such as hydrochloric, sulfuric, or lactic acids, or a combination of bacterial culture and direct acidification. Most bacterial cultures used in fermented dairy products are classified as lactic acid bacteria, as they are capable of metabolizing lactose present in milk into lactic acid. This will lower the pH of milk and aid in the formation of a milk clot.

Casein micelles are prevented from forming a rapid milk clot in fresh milk by the presence of a hairy layer of adsorbed κ-casein molecules on the surface of the micelle. The κ-casein prevents the close approach of micelles at the natural pH of milk (6.7) by a mechanism known as steric stabilization. Both acid and alcohol addition cause a partial flattening of the κ-casein hairy layer, allowing coagulation to occur. Acid coagulation occurs via an electrostatic attraction mechanism, and alcohol coagulation by hydrophobic interaction. Casein micelles have sufficient inherent hydrophobicity to cause aggregation to occur in much the same way as hydrophobic oil droplets will coalesce, once the κ-casein layer has been flattened or removed.

Milk Clotting Enzymes

The enzyme present in the fourth stomach of a calf, chymosin, is extracted by maceration of the stomach lining in a salt solution. The purified salt solution containing chymosin is called rennet. Chymosin will cleave the κ-casein hairy layer on the casein micelle at a very specific location, between the phenylalanine and methionine amino acids at positions 105 and 106 in the primary sequence of the protein. This cleavage point is fortuitously located at the point where the κ-casein molecule extends away from the micelle surface to form the hairy layer. Chymosin is therefore capable of removing the k-casein steric stabilizing layer, allowing micelles to coagulate and form a curd, such as found in yogurt and cheese.

As the demand for chymosin is greater than the supply of calf stomachs, other enzymatic methods to coagulate milk have been investigated. An enzyme called pepsin, extracted from the stomach lining of pigs, calves, and chickens, has some efficacy; however, cheese made from this enzyme is often too soft due to excessive protein degradation. Often, rennet extracts contain a proportion of bovine or porcine (from pigs) pepsin in addition to bovine chymosin.

Enzymes extracted from fungi, bacteria, and plants can also be used to coagulate milk. Plant coagulants can be extracted from papaya, figs, pineapple, kiwi fruit, and *Cynara cardunaculus* (cardoons and artichokes), a thistle which in Portugal is used to make Serra cheese. Most enzymes derived from plant sources are highly proteolytic (capable of extensive degradation of proteins) and nonspecific in their action on proteins. The resultant small peptides, which are the degradation products of enzymes acting on proteins, produce a soft and pasty cheese with bitter flavor unless other steps are taken to circumvent these problems. Bitterness in cheese is correlated with higher amounts of hydrophobic peptides.

An increasingly common method to produce milk coagulant for cheese and yogurt manufacture is by recombinant DNA technology. The gene for expressing chymosin is spliced into the DNA sequence of bacteria, such as *Escherichia coli*, which is then grown in a reaction vessel to levels that permit the extraction and subsequent purification of chymosin.

Endogenous Milk Enzymes

The main native milk enzyme that hydrolyzes proteins is plasmin. This enzyme is located in the casein micelle, and therefore concentrated in cheese during the manufacturing process. Plasmin will hydrolyze proteins during cheese ripening and contribute to texture and flavor development. It has an optimum activity at pH 7.5, hence the term alkaline protease, and at 99°F (37°C). Pasteurization has an effect of increasing the total plasmin activity, as the otherwise inactive precursor, plasminogen, is activated. Plasmin itself can be inactivated by heating at 176°F (80°C) for ten minutes.

Alkaline phosphatase is another enzyme present in milk, and is inactivated by pasteurization. A test for alkaline phosphatase activity is used to determine if milk has been pasteurized, as the conditions of inactivation mirror those of pasteurization. This enzyme is preferentially adsorbed onto the surface of fat globules.

It is interesting to note that enzymes in milk are often segregated away from their respective substrates, thus preventing rapid deterioration of milk. Alkaline phosphatase reacts with the phosphate ester groups in the casein micelle, and would result in micelle disintegration if the enzyme were located there. In the same fashion, lipases are often found adsorbed into casein micelles away from the milk fat substrate.

Lactose, the Milk Sugar

Lactose, also known as milk sugar, is a disaccharide molecule comprising two simple sugars (glucose and galactose) linked together. This sugar is rarely found outside of dairy products, unless specifically added. Lactose crystals present in dairy products, particularly ice cream, can cause a sandy texture if the crystals are too large.

Lactose must first be hydrolyzed by the enzyme lactase into glucose and galactose before it can be further metabolized in the human body. If lactase is absent from the body, a common occurrence among adult Asians and Africans, digestion problems may arise after consuming milk. These problems are referred to as lactose intolerance, and for this reason, milk is not usually consumed by adults from these two racial groups. Lactose is water-soluble, therefore largely absent in high-fat dairy products such as butter, butteroil, and ghee. In aged, fermented dairy products such as cheese, all of the lactose is metabolized by lactic acid bacteria into lactic acid within the first three to four weeks, so consumption of this product will not cause lactose intolerance. Even freshly consumed cheeses such as cottage and cream cheese are low in lactose. Lactose intolerance is discussed in Wong et al., *Fundamentals of Dairy Chemistry* (pp. 328–330).

LACTOSE INTOLERANCE

Lactose intolerance is a disease characterized by symptoms such as abdominal cramps, bloating, and diarrhea, brought about by the inability to metabolize lactose. This condition is more prevalent among Asians and Africans. It is not a normal occurrence among young children, and the incidence rises as age increases.

Lactose, often called the milk sugar, is primarily found in milk. The level in bovine milk is around 5 percent. This relatively high concentration means that digestion of milk can be a problem for people who suffer from this disease. Lactose is a disaccharide consisting of a glucose and a galactose molecule joined by a glycosidic covalent bond. In normal digestion, an enzyme called lactase will hydrolyze lactose, producing glucose and galactose, which are subsequently further metabolized in the body. People who suffer from lactose intolerance lack this enzyme. The onset of symptoms is related to the level of lactose ingested. Small amounts of milk may not be a problem for some people who would otherwise suffer from lactose intolerance.

Lactose is found in relatively large quantities in milk, ice cream, and other nonfermented milk products. It is not usually found in matured cheese. Very small amounts may be found in yogurt and fresh cheeses, such as cottage or cream cheese, but probably not sufficient to cause lactose intolerance symptoms. Digestive complaints after consumption of pizza is most likely due to the high amount of fat in this food, rather than the presence of lactose, which is barely present at all.

A remedy to aid digestion is to consume lactase in liquid form or as a tablet. An alternative solution is to manufacture low-lactose milk by the addition of lactase during processing. This step will produce a much sweeter milk, as both glucose and galactose are sweeter than lactose. To prevent the problem of excessive sweetness in milk, lactose levels must be reduced before the hydrolysis step takes place. Other more novel techniques involve adding lactic acid bacteria to cold milk; the bacteria remain dormant until the milk is consumed and warmed up in the body. They then metabolize lactose in the human gut. Another processing technique utilizes encapsulated lactase added to milk. The microcapsules remain intact at the low temperature and pH of milk during storage. After consumption, the higher temperature and lower pH rupture the lactase microcapsules, allowing lactose hydrolysis to take place.

Browning Reactions in Milk

Two types of browning reactions occur in food products, enzymatic browning and the non-enzymatic Maillard reaction. The Maillard reaction is the more relevant of the two in dairy products, and is initiated by reactions between the amine part of a protein with sugars such as lactose. This reaction is inhibited at lower moisture content, pH below 6, and lower temperature. Besides the color change in some processed dairy products, there is also a nutritional consequence to the Maillard reaction. An important amino acid in milk proteins, lysine, contains an amine group that can participate in the Maillard reaction, resulting in a loss of bioavailability of this amino acid.

Goat and Sheep Milk

It is of interest to note that the average size of fat globules in goat milk is slightly smaller (2 micrometers) than bovine milk (2.5–3.5 micrometers), and that the agglutinin reaction does not occur in goat milk. This latter effect is the primary reason for the scarcity of goat cream and butter on the market today, as the fat globules will not rise to the surface to the same extent as in bovine milk. Before the advent of centrifugal separators, it would not have been possible to obtain large amounts of cream from goat milk. Most goat milk is processed into cheese, rather than into yogurt or consumed fresh. A component of goat milk fat, 4-methyloctanoic acid, is responsible for the "billy-goat" flavor of goat milk cheese.

Sheep milk has almost twice as much fat and protein, and slightly more minerals (ash), than bovine milk, and contains a higher proportion of immunoglobulins so is more resistant to unwanted microbial growth. The fat in goat and sheep milk is whiter than in bovine milk due to a lower amount of b-carotene, and contains a higher proportion of the medium chain length fatty acids C_6-C_{12} that provide a better and more rapidly utilized energy source than the more common longer chain fatty acids. The suckling period for young kids and lambs is three to six weeks, and the milking period extends for a six-month period in spring and summer.

The volume of goat and sheep milk obtained in traditional sized family-owned farms or nomadic flocks is 40–100 liters per year. In contrast, commercial goat and sheep milk farms produce about 400–600 liters of milk per year. By comparison, 4,000–7,500 liters per year are obtained from bovine cows in commercial dairies.

The milk fat globule membrane is more fragile in goat milk compared to bovine milk, therefore there is a

MILK NUTRITION

It is not always true that altering the dietary intake of fat, containing cholesterol, will alter the blood cholesterol level. Other factors such as the total diet, genetics, and exercise play an important role. The level of cholesterol in milk fat is 0.35 percent, whereas the level in milk is about 0.014 percent. Cholesterol levels in human blood average around 200 milligrams per 100 milliliters. Milk fat contains as much as 25 percent cis 18:1 fatty acid, one of the healthy fatty acids thought to help prevent heart disease.

Vitamins

All of the essential vitamins are found in milk, although in some cases the amount is not sufficient to meet the recommended daily allowance. Vitamin C levels are reduced by approximately one half under pasteurization conditions; however, this is of limited concern, as milk is such a poor source of this vitamin. Folacin and thiamin (vitamin B_1) are reduced by around 10 percent during pasteurization. The water-soluble vitamins (B and C) are largely lost into the whey during cheesemaking, whereas the fat-soluble vitamins are concentrated, although some molds are capable of synthesizing vitamin B in mold-ripened cheeses. Riboflavin has an orange color that is more evident in skim milk than whole milk, and can be seen very clearly if fat and protein are removed from milk by membrane filtration. A vitamin A precursor, beta-carotene, gives milk fat its characteristic yellow color.

Milk is an important source of vitamins A and D, the latter due largely to fortification, which is common in the United States. Vitamin D fortification came about as a result of research performed by Harry Steenbock at the University of Wisconsin in 1924, and is largely responsible for the virtual elimination of the bone disease rickets, caused by a vitamin D deficiency. Milk is otherwise a poor source of vitamin D; however, it assists in the absorption of dietary calcium. Vitamins A and B were first discovered by Elmer V. McCollum of the University of Wisconsin; vitamin A was identified in butter fat in 1913, followed later by the discovery of vitamin B in cheese whey.

Minerals in Milk

Dairy products are a good source of many minerals, particularly calcium (see Table 1) where it furnishes about 75 percent of the dietary need in the United States. The bioavailability of calcium from milk products is around 85 percent, compared to 20–75 percent from vegetable sources. Low calcium dietary intake is generally recognized to contribute to osteoporosis and to predispose people to hypertension when consuming large amounts of salt. Bone mineralization requires a ratio of calcium to phosphorous of between 1.3 and 1.5 to 1, such as found in dairy products. Other nondairy sources of calcium have a much lower ratio.

Other trace elements of nutritional importance found in milk include iodine, which is required for thyroid hormone production, magnesium for energy-requiring biological functions, and zinc for the function of some enzymes in the human body. Bovine milk is a poor source of dietary iron; infants can develop anemia if not breast-fed with human milk (which contains a higher bioavailability of iron compared to bovine milk) or if other dietary sources are not found.

---

greater propensity for development of off-flavors. Goat milk is also more liable to undergo spontaneous lipolysis at 39°F (4°C). Further information on the processing of goat and sheep milk is provided by Frank Kosikowski and Vikram V. Mistry in volume 1 of *Cheese and Fermented Milk Foods* (pp. 297–313).

Liquid Milk

Consumer milk is often sold in the United States according to the percentage of fat: 1 percent, 2 percent, whole milk (about 3 percent), and skim (less than 0.5 percent fat). The shelf life is usually around two weeks. The milk can be fortified with vitamins A and D. Full fat milk is often simply referred to as Vitamin D milk in the United States. Frozen milk may be stored for several months before use; however, it is prone to fat separation, lipolysis, and curd formation.

Flavored milks are becoming increasingly popular as a nutritious beverage, particularly among young people. These drinks are often low in fat with added stabilizers (such as guar and carrageenan) to compensate for the loss in creaminess. An unfortunate problem with gums and stabilizers is that drinks can frequently take on a viscous and elastic texture if too much is added. A wide range of flavors are added to milk, particularly in Australia, where chocolate, coffee, caramel, strawberry, banana, and vanilla are very popular. These have never reached the same level of popularity in North America.

Yogurt

Yogurt probably originated in the Middle East, where goat and sheep milk was soured by the presence of naturally occurring bacteria. It is a favorite food in India, where it is unflavored and made from the milk of buffalo. Its consumption in India signifies the end of the meal. Plain yogurt is often used as a garnish in Middle Eastern meals. A discussion on yogurt manufacture is given by Kosikowski and Mistry in volume 1 of *Cheese and Fermented Milk Foods* (pp. 87–108).

Lactic acid bacteria (a 1:1 ratio of *Lactobacillus delbrueckii* ssp. *bulgaricus* and *Streptococcus thermophilus*) convert lactose to lactic acid in milk, lowering the pH from 6.7 to around 4.2 and giving yogurt its characteristic clean, acid taste. Often fruit and fruit flavorings are added to make yogurt into a dessert or snack product. The reduction in pH by added bacterial culture, along with refrigerated storage, contribute to the preservation of yogurt. The most common form of yogurt is a smooth viscous liquid; however, it can be frozen and served as a nutritious and refreshing yogurt-based beverage. The trend in the United States is for reduced fat (or nonfat) yogurt, more so than in Europe. The fat content in North American yogurt is typically around one percent.

To enhance the creaminess sensation of reduced or nonfat yogurt, polysaccharide stabilizers such as gelatin, pectin, or locust bean gum are often added, although they are not entirely successful at mimicking fat. These stabilizers have the additional function of reducing syneresis, the clear yellow liquid (whey) that appears on the surface of yogurt due to partial shrinkage of the casein protein network. Probiotic cultures, such as *Lactobacillus* species (*casei* and *acidophilus*) and *Bifidobacterium* species can be added to yogurt and also to milk protein-based beverages. The combination of bacterial cultures, including probiotic cultures, found in yogurt has long been believed to provide good health. This may explain the relatively large number of centenarian inhabitants of the Caucasus region in southwest Asia, who consume large amounts of yogurt.

Milk for yogurt manufacture is firstly standardized to the appropriate fat and protein level (commonly 12–15 percent total solids and 1–2 percent fat) using skim milk powder. The milk is heated at 185°F (85°C) for thirty minutes, or alternatively, 194°F (90°C) for forty to sixty seconds. The stabilizers are next added, followed by homogenization at 7 MPa and cooling to 86–113°F (30°–45°C). Bacterial cultures are added, fruit puree is mixed in if desired, and the milk is allowed to set for sixteen hours to form a coagulum before refrigerating to 39°F (4°C) and packaged for consumption.

Homogenization of milk prior to yogurt manufacture increases the viscosity of yogurt and inhibits the formation of syneresis during refrigerated storage. The shelf-life of yogurt at 39°F (4°C) is from thirty to sixty days. The two main types of yogurt are stirred and set. In set yogurt, milk is allowed to coagulate to form the yogurt network structure without mechanical disturbance. In stirred yogurt, the coagulated milk is stirred while cooling down, then the fruit puree is added if required.

Yogurt cheese is prepared as for other types of yogurt in the initial stages of manufacture, except that *Lactococcus lactis* bacterial culture and rennet are mixed with the milk one hour into the setting period, and a cheese similar to cream cheese is manufactured.

Cream and Sour Cream

Cream is produced by separating milk into a skim phase (with less than 0.5 percent fat) and a cream phase. The fat content of the cream increases with the speed of the separator. A separator consists of concentric stainless steel cones rotating at high speed. Fat in cream can vary from as little as 10–12 percent in half-and-half, popular in the United States, to 30–40 percent in table cream and whipping cream. Plastic cream can contain up to 80 percent fat. Off-flavors can be removed from milk and cream by the process of vacreation, where steam is injected into the product and removed, along with the unwanted flavors, under a partial vacuum.

Sour cream is produced by lactose acid bacteria fermentation or direct addition of mineral acids to cream. Fresh cream is first standardized to 20 percent fat, homogenized at 20 MPa and 160°F (71°C), pasteurized at 165°F (74°C) for thirty minutes, cooled, and then inoculated with bacterial culture. Rennet can be added to produce a firmer product. The fermenting cream is incubated for sixteen hours at 72°F (22°C) until a pH of 4.5 is reached, then cooled and packaged. The shelf life is three to four weeks. Condiments such as blue cheese, seafood, and onion can be added to sour cream to produce a dip.

Ultra High Temperature Milk

Ultra high temperature (UHT) milk is produced by heat-treating milk at 284°F (140°C) for two to three seconds, essentially sterilizing the milk. It is packaged aseptically and stored at room temperature for up to six months. The two main methods of producing UHT milk are direct steam injection, and indirect heating by passing milk over a stainless steel surface that is heated by high pressure steam. UHT milk is characterized by a cooked flavor that dissipates over time and which is then replaced by a stale oxidized flavor that develops during storage. Another potential problem with UHT milk is that it is susceptible to gelation and sedimentation. The chemical and physical mechanisms for this are unclear.

Some work has been done using a spinning cone column to eliminate undesirable flavors from UHT milk. This technology utilizes a series of rapidly rotating concentric cones through which milk or cream can be passed down. Low temperature steam under a partial vacuum is passed up in the counter-current direction, which strips flavor components from the dairy product. The steam can be condensed and the flavor compounds distilled and kept for later use. This process can be used to remove feed-related off-flavors from milk, the oxidized flavor from UHT milk, or to strip desirable buttery flavors from cream for subsequent addition into low-fat dairy products.

Buttermilk, Butteroil, and Ghee

Buttermilk is a by-product of churning in butter manufacture. It is low in fat (about 1 percent), and rich in the phospholipid and protein components at the milk fat globule membrane layer. Milk fermented with lactic acid bacteria and subsequently separated into cream can be used in the manufacture of cultured or ripened butter. Cultured buttermilk is derived from cultured butter.

Butteroil is produced by centrifuging liquid butter to a fat content in excess of 99 percent, the remainder being mostly water. This product is solidified at room temperature. A higher grade, at more than 99.8 percent fat, is called anhydrous milk fat.

Ghee is a product similar in composition to butteroil and used for confectionery manufacture and for cooking in India, and in Egypt where it is called *samma*, or *samn*. Buffalo milk is boiled for one hour, the curd skimmed off, and churned for thirty minutes to form a butter. This is heated and strained to yield ghee, a clear oil with a characteristic cooked odor and flavor.

Other Milk Products

Kefir is an alcoholic, carbonated milk-based beverage popular in eastern and central Europe. Yeast and bacteria convert lactose into lactic acid, carbon dioxide gas, and alcohol (ethanol) overnight at ambient temperature. The levels of lactic acid and alcohol are around 1 percent each. Koumiss from central Asia is similar to Kefir but made from mare's milk, and has a higher alcohol content of 2.5 percent. Other nonalcoholic fermented milk beverages include acidophilus milk, and Bulgarian buttermilk with a comparatively high lactic acid content of 2–4 percent.

Evaporated and Condensed Milk

Concentrated milk can be produced by partial evaporation of water to yield either evaporated or condensed milk. The removal of water is done by heating under reduced pressure to avoid excessive heat damage to proteins. Evaporated milk is sterilized and aseptically packaged, whereas condensed milk does not have this extra heat treatment step. Variations of condensed milk include sweetened, where 18 percent sugar is added to milk before evaporation, and condensed skim milk.

Whey

Liquid whey is an orange-colored liquid comprising about 5 percent lactose, 0.7 percent whey proteins, and 1 percent minerals. The disposal of whey has always been an issue in the manufacture of cheese due to the large volumes produced. Approximately 90 percent of the volume of milk is removed as whey when making cheese. The high biological oxygen demand of whey prevents disposal into lakes and streams, where it can deprive fish of oxygen.

Whey proteins are very nutritious and have a high protein efficiency ratio (ratio of weight gained to weight of protein consumed). Fruit juices can be fortified with around 6 percent acid whey powder to increase the nutritional value without adversely affecting flavor and color. Whey powder is highly water-soluble and adds vitamins, minerals, and high-quality nutritional proteins to other food products.

Liquid whey can be manufactured into cheese by adding milk or cream and then concentrating by evaporation. Cheese made by this method includes Brunost, Mysost, Gjetost, and Primost, which are popular in Scandinavian countries. The last two of these cheeses are made from goat whey. Ricotta is a whey-based cheese made by heating acidified bovine milk.

Whey Protein Powder

The two main types of whey are acid and sweet whey. Acid whey is obtained by addition of acids such as lactic, phosphoric, hydrochloric, sulfuric, and acetic to skim milk, reducing the pH from 6.7 to 4.6 and causing the casein to precipitate (which is then removed). Milk has a very high buffering capacity, requiring large quantities of acid to reduce the pH to this level. Acid whey contains very little lactic acid, as curds and whey are separated without the fermentation step.

Sweet whey originates from the cheese manufacturing process. Curds and whey are separated at a pH of approximately 6.2 in cheddar cheese manufacture, therefore sweet whey from this cheese is less acidic than acid whey. Sweet whey from cheesemaking contains around 0.5 percent fat. Whey from cottage cheese contains little fat, and around 0.4 percent lactic acid as a greater amount of fermentation of lactose to lactic acid takes place before the curds and whey are separated.

Sweet whey contains an additional protein fragment, the glycomacropeptide (GMP), which originates from the surface of the casein micelle as a consequence of enzymatic hydrolysis during the milk clotting reaction. The presence of GMP affects the textural functionality of whey powder when used as a food ingredient. GMP does not contain the amino acid phenylalanine, which can cause brain damage in children suffering from the disease phenylketonuria, an inability to metabolize this amino acid. There has been some research done on the extraction of GMP from sweet whey for use as a protein source for phenylketonuriacs.

Fractionation of whey into components with very specific nutritional, textural (functional), and pharmaceutical properties is a burgeoning field of research with the potential of large profit margins for the dairy industry. Components of whey that inhibit microbial growth include lactoferrin, lactoperoxidase, lysozyme, and various immunoglobulins. Lactoferrin binds iron necessary for microbial growth. These antimicrobial agents have the potential for use as "natural" preservatives in food products.

Sweet whey from cheesemaking is first clarified to remove casein particulate matter, then separated to re-

WORLD DAIRY MARKET

The three largest export regions of dairy products, with the percentage of the total world dairy market in 2000, were the European Union (36 percent), New Zealand (31 percent) and Australia (16 percent). Australia and New Zealand each account for around 2 percent of the world's production of milk. Due to their relatively low populations, most of the milk in these two countries is processed and exported, hence the apparent over-representation in the export market.

The major export products on the international market are milk powders, cheese, and butter. There is no economic gain in exporting fluid milk as most of this product consists of inexpensive and readily available water, hence the development of the dairy processing industry to create products with lower water contents.

According to the United Nations Food and Agriculture Organization, the total volume of milk produced in the world in 1996 was around 550 billion liters, of which about 12 percent comes from buffalo, sheep, and goats. The two largest milk producing regions in 1996 were the European Union, with 24 percent of the world's production, and the United States with 15 percent. The United States accounts for only 4 percent of the export market.

Milk production per cow per year is around 4,500 liters in Australia, where cows are pasture-fed, and increases to 5,000–7,500 liters in Europe and North America where supplemental feed is given. The volume of milk per cow can be increased by administering a hormone, bovine somatotropin, a practice allowed in the United States, but not in Australia or New Zealand.

Dairy product commodities are subject to large price fluctuations on the international market. To even out the price instability, and to support the local dairy industry, governments (particularly in the European Union) heavily subsidize milk prices. This has resulted in a surplus of some dairy products.

According to the Australian Dairy Corporation (1996), consumption of milk is highest in Ireland and the Scandinavian countries at about 150 kg per person per year. Butter consumption is highest in France, Germany, and New Zealand at around 7–8 kg per person per year. Cheese is most popular in Germany, France, Italy, and Greece, the inhabitants of which consume around 20 kg per person per year. Consumption of yogurt is highest, at around 20 kg per person per year, in France and the Netherlands.

---

move most of the fat. The whey is initially concentrated to around 40–60 percent solids in a vacuum evaporator before homogenization and drying. Most drying is done using a spray-dryer where the concentrated viscous whey is passed through an atomizer and allowed to fall through a chamber with countercurrent heated air to produce a dispersible and nonhygroscopic powder of around 10 percent moisture. Spray-dryers can produce as much as twenty metric tons per hour of powder. Further processing can take place on a fluidized bed dryer where heated air is passed up through a vibrating layer of powder to further reduce the moisture to around 4 percent. A lecithin mixture can also be sprayed onto the powder to promote dissolution in water, a procedure known as instantization. Other types of dryers that are less commonly used include drum and roller dryers and freeze dryers. Roller dryers result in a much more irregularly shaped powder particle than spray-dryers.

Typical composition of whey powder is shown in Table 1. These powders are called whey protein concentrates (WPC), and suffixed with a number to indicate the percentage of protein, for example, WPC 80 contains 80 percent protein. Generally, the higher the protein content, the higher the price that the powder commands in the market. The solubility of powders can be enhanced by collecting the smallest particles in a spray-dryer cyclone and mixing back with the partially dried powder at the top of the dryer. This creates an agglomerated particle with a surface containing many crevices, thus increasing the total surface area of a particle and increasing the solubility.

Higher protein levels in excess of 90 percent can be achieved by a combination of ion-exchange chromatography, electrodialysis to remove minerals, evaporation, ultrafiltration, lactose crystallization, and filtration. Whey protein isolates (WPI) are produced by ion-exchange and have a typical protein content of 93 percent. These isolates command a higher market price than WPC powders. The amount of fat in WPI is much lower than WPC, at around 0.5 percent. Ingredient applications for WPC and WPI include fortifying beverages such as high energy sports drinks, infant formulas, salad dressings, ice cream, custards, reformed meats, yogurt, surimi, bakery, and dessert products (as an egg replacement).

Lactose in milk powder is in the form of a concentrated amorphous (non-crystalline) glass that is very hygroscopic (high propensity for absorbing water). Milk powders that are high in lactose can potentially aggregate and lose the ability to flow freely. To avoid this problem, concentrated liquid whey is held at refrigeration temperatures for twenty-four hours prior to drying to ensure that lactose crystallizes into the stable and non-hygroscopic α-hydrate polymorph to reduce the propensity for powder caking. The concentrated whey is injected into the spray-dryer at less than 126°F (52°C) to prevent solubilization of the α-hydrate crystals.

Lactose can be converted to galactose and glucose by the enzyme lactase. This procedure can be utilized to manufacture a low-lactose whey powder, which is sweeter, but more likely to undergo Maillard browning reactions than regular whey powder. Lactase can also be encapsulated and added to milk. Once the milk is consumed, the capsules break open, releasing the lactase, thus preventing the occurrence of lactose-intolerance symptoms.

The degree of heat-treatment of milk powders is quantified by the whey protein nitrogen index (WPNI), a measure of the quantity of whey proteins that are not denatured. Excessive heat during spray-drying causes a large degree of protein denaturation with subsequent loss of solubility of the powder. Low heat powder has a WPNI greater than 6 milligrams of nitrogen per gram, medium heat between 1.5 and 6 milligrams of nitrogen per gram, and high heat less than 1.5 milligrams of nitrogen per gram of powder. The degree of heating of powder during manufacture has implications for solubility, heat stability, viscosity, and flavor of the dairy product containing whey powder. High-heat powder will give high viscosity when added to yogurt, good heat stability in reconstituted evaporated milk, and intense flavor when used in milk chocolate, but poor clotting properties for recombined milk used in cheese manufacture.

Buttermilk Powder

Buttermilk contains many surface-active components that function as emulsifiers. By making changes to the butter manufacturing process, different kinds of buttermilk powder (BMP) can be produced with various functional properties when used as a food ingredient. There is some scientific evidence that the components of the milk fat globule membrane layer are essential for development of cheese flavor during the ripening period. If this is so, BMP could find a use in fortifying low fat cheese to improve the flavor. Other applications for BMP include emulsifying fat in salad dressing, bakery products, ice cream, dips, and spreads.

The composition of BMP is not as tightly controlled as for other milk powders, as it is often thought of as a secondary product coming out of the primary process of butter manufacture. Volumes produced of this powder are generally much lower than for other powders, so their full potential has not yet been fully explored. BMP comprises mostly lactose with around 10 percent fat. About one-fifth of the fat comprises phospholipids, the highly surface-active components that are used as emulsifiers.

Casein and Caseinate Powders

Casein powder is produced by isoelectric precipitation of milk using mineral acids, lactic acid bacteria fermentation, or enzymatic coagulation by chymosin (rennet). New Zealand is the world's largest producer of casein powder. A combination of acid and chymosin is used to prepare a low-viscosity casein for use in the paper industry to bind pigments. Precipitated casein curds are washed in water to remove residual lactose, whey proteins, and minerals, then pressed with rollers, dried (using a fluid bed dryer), and ground into a powder. Attrition drying occurs when casein curd is ground and dried by exposure to hot air concurrently. These particles are highly irregular in shape and more soluble in water.

Applications of casein powder include paper coating, adhesives, water-based paints, food ingredients, and animal feed. Food ingredient applications include beer and wine clarification, protein fortification of food, and texturized simulated meat products. Casein hydrolyzates are formed by partial acid hydrolysis of casein to improve the flavor of soups, dried meat products, crackers, and snack foods.

Caseinate is produced from acid casein by increasing the pH toward neutrality to dissolve the precipitated casein. Most commonly, sodium and calcium hydroxides are used to prepare sodium and calcium caseinate, respectively. Caseinates can be spray-dried after reconstituting in water to around 20–25 percent total solid material. The ingredient application for dried caseinates includes sausages, coffee whitener, ice cream and dairy-based desserts, soups, crackers, and sauces.

Other Milk Powders

Other types of milk powder include skim milk powder (SMP), whole milk powder (WMP), cream powder, lactalbumin, colostrum, cheese powder, and milk protein concentrate. WMP contains around 30 percent fat, whereas SMP contains less than 1.5 percent. Lactalbumin powder is formed by heat-induced precipitation of cheese whey followed by drying. This powder is insoluble in water.

Cheese powder is produced from highly flavored cheeses such as cheddar and parmesan, by grinding, adding water and emulsifying salts to form a viscous suspension, followed by pasteurization, homogenization, and spray drying. This product quickly deteriorates after several months. The major ingredient application is for use as a cheese flavoring in food products.

Cream can also be spray dried to form a high fat (40-75 percent) powder. The amount of free fat in milk powders is of importance and affects dispersibility in water. This free fat is usually located on the surface and within crevices on the powder particle.

Co-precipitates are produced by heating skim milk to 185°F (85°C), whereupon the whey proteins denature and bind to the casein micelles. This complex is precipitated by acid and processed to a powder using the same procedure as casein powder production.

Milk is an important food from a nutritional perspective, largely due to the presence of proteins and calcium. The high water content and only slightly acidic pH render this food susceptible to microbiological spoilage. The dairy processing industry has developed to circumvent the spoilage issue through production of products with low moisture and higher acidity. This allows the development of a dairy products export market, as milk products can now be shipped to distant lands without compromising quality and safety. The huge variety of dairy products, most notably illustrated by the seemingly unending array of cheeses, is a testimony to the potential of milk for continued development of nutritious and tasty milk-based foods.

See also **Butter; Cheese; Curds; Ice Cream; Lactation; Milk, Human; Pasteur, Louis.**

BIBLIOGRAPHY

Andrews, Anthony T., and Jennifer Varley, eds. *Biochemistry of Milk Products*. Cambridge, U.K.: Royal Society of Chemistry, 1994.

Beardsley, Tim. "Trans Fat. Does Margarine Really Lower Cholesterol?" *Scientific American* 264 (1991): 34.

Cogan, Timothy, and Jean-Pierre Accolas, eds. *Dairy Starter Cultures*. New York: Wiley, 1995.

Early, Ralph. *The Technology of Dairy Products*: New York: Aspen, 1997.

Fennema, Owen R., ed. *Food Chemistry*. New York: M. Dekker, 1996.

Fox, Patrick F., ed. *Developments in Dairy Chemistry: Proteins*. Vol. 1. New York:, 1982.

Fox, Patrick F., ed. *Developments in Dairy Chemistry: Lipids*. Vol. 2. New York: Elsevier, 1983.

Fox, Patrick F., ed. *Developments in Dairy Chemistry: Lactose and Minor Constituents*. Vol. 3. New York: Elsevier, 1985.

Fox, Patrick F., ed. *Developments in Dairy Chemistry: Functional Milk Proteins*. Vol. 4. New York: Elsevier, 1989.

Fox, Patrick F., ed. *Advanced Dairy Chemistry: Proteins*. Vol. 1. New York: Elsevier Applied Science, 1992.

Fox, Patrick F., ed. *Cheese: Chemistry, Physics and Microbiology. General Aspects*. Vol. 1. London: Chapman & Hall, 1993.

Fox, Patrick F., and Paul L. H. McSweeney, eds. *Dairy Chemistry and Biochemistry*. New York: Blackie Academic & Professional, 1998.

Friberg, Stig. E., and Kåre Larsson, eds. *Food Emulsions*. New York: M. Dekker, 1997.

Grandison, Alistair S., and Michael J. Lewis, eds. *Separation Processes in the Food and Biotechnology Industries*. Cambridge, U.K.: Woodhead, 1996.

Hasenhuettl, Gerard L., and Richard W. Hartel, eds. *Food Emulsifiers and Their Applications*. New York: Chapman & Hall, 1997.

Holt, Carl, and David S. Horne. "The Hairy Casein Micelle: Evolution of the Concept and Its Implications for Dairy Technology." *Netherlands Milk and Dairy Journal* 50 (1996): 85–111.

Hui, Yiu H., ed. *Dairy Science and Technology Handbook*. New York: Wiley, 1993.

Jenness, Robert, and Stuart Patton. *Principles of Dairy Chemistry*. Huntington, N.Y.: Krieger, 1976.

Jensen, Robert G., ed. *Handbook of Milk Composition*. San Diego: Academic Press, 1995.

Kosikowski, Frank, and Vikram V. Mistry. *Cheese and Fermented Milk Foods*. Great Falls, Va.: Kosikowski, 1997.

Law, Barry A., ed. *Microbiology and Biochemistry of Cheese and Fermented Milk*. London: Blackie Academic & Professional, 1997.

Marth, Elmer H., and James L. Steele, eds. *Applied Dairy Microbiology*. New York: M. Dekker, 1998.

McClements, David J. *Food Emulsions: Principles, Practice, and Techniques*. Boca Raton, Fla.: CRC Press, 1999.

Miller, Gregory D., Judith K. Jarvis, and Lois D. McBean. *Handbook of Dairy Foods and Nutrition*. Boca Raton, Fla.: CRC Press, 1999.

Mulder, Hendrik, and Pieter Walstra. *The Milk Fat Globule*. Farnham Royal, Bucks., U.K.: Commonwealth Agricultural Bureaux, 1974.

Robinson, Richard K., ed. *A Colour Guide to Cheese and Fermented Milks*. London: Chapman and Hall, 1995.

Robinson, Richard K., ed. *Dairy Microbiology*. New York: Elsevier Applied Science, 1990.

Singh, R. Paul, and Dennis R. Heldman. *Introduction to Food Engineering*. San Diego: Academic Press, 2001.

Singh, Rakesh K., and Syed S. H. Rizvi, eds. *Bioseparation Processes in Foods*. New York: M. Dekker, 1995.

Spreer, Edgar. *Milk and Dairy Product Technology*. Translated by Axel Mixa. New York: M. Dekker, 1998.

Tamime, Adnan Y., and Richard K. Robinson. *Yogurt: Science and Technology*. Boca Raton, Fla.: CRC Press, 1999.

Walstra, Pieter, and Robert Jenness. *Dairy Chemistry and Physics*. New York: Wiley, 1984.

Walstra, Pieter. "Casein Sub-micelles: Do They Exist?" *International Dairy Journal* 9 (1999): 189–192.

Walstra, Pieter, T. J. Geurts, A. Noomen, A. Jellema, and M. A. J. S. van Boekel. *Dairy Technology: Principles of Milk Properties and Processes*. New York: M. Dekker, 1999.

Wlech, R. A. S., D. J. W. Burns, and S. R. Davis. *Milk Composition, Production, and Biotechnology*. Wallingford, Oxon, U.K.: CABI Publishing, 1997.

Wong, Noble P., Robert Jenness, Mark Keeney, and Elmer H. Marth, eds. *Fundamentals of Dairy Chemistry*. New York: Van Nostrand Reinhold, 1988.

David W. Everett

DAY OF THE DEAD. In Mexico, the festival of Día de los Muertos embodies the greatest expression of both popular Catholicism and the national cuisine. People construct altars in homes and graveyards throughout the country in order to feed the souls of the dead. Church

The Mexican Day of the Dead combines customs from both the ancient Aztecs and the Spanish who settled in Mexico. These women are holding a vigil in Michoacán, Mexico. © CHARLES AND JOSETTE LENARS/CORBIS.

officials recognize two holy days, November 1 (All Saints' Day), in commemoration of saints and martyrs, and November 2 (All Souls' Day), in memory of the faithful departed. According to popular belief, the *angelitos* (deceased children) return on the evening of October 31 and the adults on the following night, although the dates in local celebrations vary all the way from October 28 to November 4. The feast for the dead originated as a form of ancestor worship, and the clergy were long reluctant to incorporate such pagan practices into the liturgical calendar. The festival held particularly strong associations with pre-Hispanic agrarian cults because it coincided with the maize harvest.

Celebrations begin with the cleaning of the graves and the construction of the *ofrenda*, or altar. At home this consists of a table or platform hung from the ceiling, covered with a white cloth and supporting an arch of palm fronds. The *ofrenda* are decorated with flowers, particularly the *cempasúchil* (marigold), the "flower of the dead," as well as the magenta-colored cockscomb, a white gypsophila, gladioli, and carnations. The same flowers are also used to decorate tombs, and the sweet smell of copal, the Native American incense, is ubiquitous. Other altar decorations include images of the deceased as well as *papeles picados*, colored paper with cutout designs.

The foods offered to the dead vary according to age and taste, but bread, water, and salt are always included. The bread is made from a special egg dough in a round shape, with crisscrossed strips of dough forming bones, and a skull in the center. Sugar candies with similar skull and *calavera* (skeleton) designs are also popular. In some areas of Oaxaca and Michoacán, bakers shape the bread to resemble humans or animals. Offerings for children are miniature in size and relatively simple: breads, candies, fruits, and milk or soft drinks. The adult dead receive the finest foods, grown-up breads and sugar figures, as well as candied pumpkin and other sweets. More elab-

orate preparations include mole (turkey in a rich chili sauce) and tamales (corn dumplings stuffed with meat and chili and steamed in husks or banana leaves). The spirits also drink their favorite beverages, whether soft drinks, coffee, chocolate, beer, or tequila. Some people maintain that the level of the liquid decreases overnight, showing that the dead do indeed return to share in the feast.

The Day of the Dead has recently become an important tourist attraction for towns such as Mixquic, near Mexico City, and in the state of Oaxaca. Yet despite this increasing commercialization, the festival exemplifies the distinctiveness of the Mexican mentality; rather than a time of trick or treat, it celebrates the intimate connections between the living and the dead.

See also **Christianity; Death and Burial; Feasts, Festivals, and Fasts; Halloween; Holidays; Mexico; Religion and Food.**

BIBLIOGRAPHY

Barnés de Castro, Francisco, et al. *Ofrenda de muertos.* Mexico, D.F.: Universidad Nacional Autónoma de México, 1998.

Carmichael, Elizabeth, and Chloë Sayer. *The Skeleton at the Feast: The Day of the Dead in Mexico.* London: British Museum Press, 1991.

Garcíagodoy, Juanita. *Digging the Days of the Dead: A Reading of Mexico's Días de muertos.* Niwot: University Press of Colorado, 1998.

Nutini, Hugo. *Todos Santos in Rural Tlaxcala: A Syncretic, Espressive, and Symbolic Analysis of the Cult of the Dead.* Princeton: Princeton University Press, 1988.

Ríos, Guadalupe, et al. *Día de muertos: La Celebración de la fiesta del 2 de noviembre en la segunda mitad del siglo XIX.* Mexico, D.F.: Universidad Autónoma Metropolitana, 1995.

Verti, Sebastián. *Tradiciones mexicanas.* Mexico: Editorial Diana, 1991.

Jeffrey M. Pilcher

DEATH AND BURIAL. As far back as records go, we have evidence of the dead being laid to rest with care and ritual. Burial gifts, including food vessels and household utensils from different eras, have been discovered in archaeological remains in various parts of the world. These gifts are thought to have been intended for the use of the deceased on his or her journey to paradise or the land of the dead and to secure entry and acceptance in the new abode. Even those who suffered violent death were buried in specific ways, and it is of interest to note that two young men who appear to have been ritually sacrificed during the European Iron Age had consumed a meal before being killed. The so-called "Tollund Man," buried in a Danish bog about 500 B.C.E., had eaten a meal of porridge of some kind, and the "Lindow Man," buried in a peat bog at Lindow Moss, Cheshire, England, sometime during the fourth century B.C.E., had consumed "a kind of wholemeal bread consisting of different kinds of grains," just prior to his violent death (Green, 1992, pp. 132 and 210–111).

Although the Christian churches have, for centuries, regulated the liturgy and ceremonies for the dying and the dead, people everywhere have created their own death rites and have often retained them in addition to those of the official Church. Food and drink are often important elements of these rites, and they are sometimes associated with the dying state. In Ireland, for example, as Patricia Lysaght has shown, the dying were thought to suffer from hunger and thirst at death, and thus a dying person's request for food and drink always had to be granted. This food, served in anticipation of death, was termed *lón báis* (death sustenance); it was thought to be necessary to enable the person to die and thus to enter upon the journey to the land of the dead (Lysaght, 1995, p. 32). In many cultures this journey was said to be long and hazardous, and sustenance, provided by the living, was considered necessary. Food and drink were, therefore, served at various junctures during the wake and funeral, so that, as Greek tradition expresses it, "the dead may eat" (Danforth, 1982, Plate 22).

These foodstuffs were often left specifically in the presence of the deceased or placed in the coffin, or put into or placed on the grave. Formerly, in parts of Britain, bread and beer, or salt and bread, were consumed by a so-called "sin-eater" in the presence of the deceased; this person was thought to take on the sins of the deceased and thus enable him or her to be incorporated into the Christian otherworld (Hole, 1953, pp. 224–225; Kvideland, 1993).

Food and drink consumed by the living during the wake and at the post-funeral meal were evidently also thought to provide necessary nourishment for the deceased, and thus to facilitate the transfer to the other world. Such food and drink have also been looked upon as a means of strengthening family and community in the face of death.

Food and drink also featured in ceremonies for the dead held at intervals varying from thirty or forty days after death in some societies, to three years among the Skolt Lapps of northern Europe when the dead person's final incorporation among the confraternity of the dead was thought to take place (Storå, 1971, p. 272), to several years in cultures where secondary burial was customary. At Christmas, Easter, and Whitsuntide (or Pentecost), the family dead were remembered by, among other things, gifts of food and drink. On November 2, the Feast of All Souls, prayers were recited throughout much of Catholic Europe for the souls of the dead. In addition, food and drink were placed on graves or left ready in the family home for deceased members, particularly the suffering souls in purgatory, who, according to an ancient and widespread popular belief, were thought to congregate there from midnight until cockcrow.

FOOD AND THE SIN-EATER

Sin-eating as a funeral custom was once common in parts of England, Scotland, and Wales. It is mentioned in records from the seventeenth to the nineteenth century. For a trifling payment, a man or woman of the locality known as a sin-eater was believed to take upon him or herself, by eating and drinking, the sins of the deceased. According to John Aubrey, writing in 1686–1687 (Aubrey, 1972, p. 179) and referring to the County of Hereford in England, the rite was performed when the deceased was being removed from the house for burial. The corpse was placed on a bier before the door, and a loaf of bread and a bowl of beer were passed over the deceased to the sin-eater, who consumed them and was given a sixpence as payment. The sin-eater was thus thought to assume the sins of the deceased and thereby bring ease and rest to the departed soul.

What is probably an older form of the custom is mentioned for western Scotland in 1879. Here the sin-eater was taken into the corpse-room where he was said to have consumed a plate of salt and a plate of bread placed on the breast of the corpse, and thus to have eaten his sins (Napier, 1879, 60–61).

The custom of sin-eating is apparently older than the seventeenth century and is said to derive from the scapegoat in Leviticus 16: 21, 22. What might be regarded as a symbolic survival of the custom in parts of Europe was the passing of drink and a funeral biscuit over the corpse, or the placing of a funeral cake on the breast of the deceased for consumption by the nearest relative, or, indeed, the placing of salt on the breast of the deceased as was common, for example, in Ireland. The "death cakes" introduced into America from Europe in the seventeenth century and served to guests at a funeral and the "burial cakes" still made in parts of rural England in the early twentieth century might well reflect the custom of sin-eating.

Kinds of Drink and Food

Alcoholic beverages were a feature of wake and funeral hospitality throughout much of Europe until relatively recent times (Ó Súilleabháin, 1967, pp. 154–157). In Latvia, for example, the expression *dzert bīres*, 'to drink a funeral', is testimony to this (Dumpe, 2002, p. 125). The apparently liberal provision of alcohol at wakes and funerals in Ireland was repeatedly condemned by secular and ecclesiastical commentators from the seventeenth to the twentieth century. Occasional references to elaborate funeral meals that included beer, wine, beef, and wheaten

Philadelphia funeral biscuit mold from about 1785 depicting the plumes that decorated the corners of the hearse and were also worn by the horses pulling it. There were bakers in most East Coast cities who specialized in funeral biscuits and in catering funerals. ROUGHWOOD COLLECTION.

bread occur in seventeenth- and eighteenth-century literature, but by the late nineteenth century, the wake-foods commonly mentioned include shop-bought goods, especially white bread, fruit cake, jam, and tea, and alcoholic beverages in modest quantities. Today, where wakes survive, food (sandwiches, cake, tea, coffee), and alcoholic beverages (wine, beer, Guinness, spirits) are served, but the most significant funeral repast in rural and urban Ireland today is generally the postburial meal in the mourning home or in a restaurant (Lysaght, 2002).

In eighteenth-century Scotland, England, and the Isle of Man, food and alcohol were liberally provided at wakes and funerals by people of rank (Bennett, pp. 207–211; Hole, pp. 228–229 and 233; Moore, p. 160). More typical, at least for Scotland, in recent times, was the provision of cheese and oatcakes, sometimes shortbread, served with ale or tea, and spirits, to which could be added wine and biscuits. The corpse-watchers received whisky (and pipes and tobacco), and often tea, or bread and cheese with ale, about midnight. Funeral guests were similarly treated. If the cemetery was some distance away, whisky was sometimes served at a particular spot en route, and again in the cemetery after burial. In parts of northern Scotland a meal called a *dredgy* was served in the deceased's home after the burial (Fenton, 2002, pp. 212–213).

In Portugal, as shown by Mouette Barboff, grain, bread, and wine have played significant roles in death customs. Lamenting women were paid in rye and wheat, while water, millet-bread soaked in wine, and a coin were placed in the deceased's coffin, for the journey to the otherworld. In the north, where death customs remain particularly strong, funeral bread is distributed at the church and cemetery. In the Beira region, two cornbread loaves, divided into eight pieces, are given to the poor on removal of the coffin from the house, while in the Barroso,

rye loaves (*o carolo*) are distributed on leaving the church. In the Minho, a slice of cornbread with a piece of fish (sardine or cod), or wheaten bread (*molete*), is distributed to all funeral guests. The priest is given bread, wine, or grain, and perhaps fish or meat. Nowadays, the tendency is to pay the priest in cash. On the first anniversary of the death, thirty or forty loaves of bread called *pão da caridade* (charity bread) or *pão das almas* (soul bread), baked by the family, are distributed to the poor of the parish in return for prayers for the deceased. On the Feast of All Souls (November 2), children call to houses asking for the *pão por Deus* (God's bread) for the holy souls (Barboff, 2002, pp. 204–206).

Elsewhere in Europe, the provision of food and drink on the occasion of death has also been highly structured. In Westphalia in northern Germany, it is still customary to provide *Beerdigungskaffee* (funeral coffee), with plain or sugar biscuits (*Zwieback/Zuckerzwieback*), pastries, and open sandwiches (*belegtes Brötchen*) for the funeral participants in a local hostelry after the burial. As late as the 1960s, a very elaborate meal (*Leichenmahl*) consisting of, for example, *bouillon*, a large meat platter with roast sausage, pork, and fowl, served with potatoes, red cabbage, and applesauce, followed by a pudding dessert, cigars for the menfolk, and afternoon coffee with pastries and sandwiches, might still be provided in well-to-do farmhouses for the relatives and near neighbors of the deceased.

In parts of Lower Austria in the 1970s, food and drink were served at certain junctures during the wake for the dead. On completion of the rosary, bread, wine, and fruit such as apples, dried prunes, and pears were provided. After the singing of funeral songs, more food and drink, which could include coffee and the much-

A funeral biscuit made from the circa 1785 mold. Reconstructed recipe and icing technique by William Woys Weaver. ROUGHWOOD COLLECTION.

An Irish wake, complete with wailing relatives and a spread of whisky on the table to the far right. An engraving from Mr. and Mrs. Samuel Carter Hall's *Ireland. Its Scenery, Character &c.* (London, 1841). PUBLISHED WITH PERMISSION OF THE FOLKLORE SOCIETY, LONDON.

appreciated crumbled bread soaked in coffee and eaten with a spoon, were served. Schnapps was provided in most areas, followed sometimes by black bread but mostly by white *Totenbrot* (funeral bread), with wine or beer. Much alcohol was drunk. Meat was only seldom offered.

Early on the morning of the funeral, relatives, friends, neighbors, and the coffin bearers were invited to the funeral breakfast, consisting mostly of coffee and white bread, although a nutritious meal with a substantial fat content was sometimes served to the coffin bearers. Schnapps and wine were also provided.

The funeral meal (*Leichenmahl*), to which relatives, neighbors, helpers, the priest, and mass servers were invited, was held either at an inn or in the mourning house. It could be very elaborate, consisting of several courses and including various kinds of bread and cheese, and, in certain areas, wine or beer (Huber, 1981, pp. 74–147).

In eastern Europe, festive food and drink were also associated with death in Slovakia. A slice of bread and a small glass of brandy were placed in the room for the soul of the deceased. Bread was placed in the coffin or grave or given to beggars or gravediggers in payment for prayers for the deceased. In the mountain regions, bread, salt, curds or cheese, and brandy were served. A cock was killed for the death of a farmer and a hen for that of his wife. A weddinglike feast was held for an unmarried deceased, especially a young man or woman (Stoličná, p. 118). A similar practice formerly took place in Hungary (Viski, pp. 181–182) and elsewhere in Europe (cf. Fielhauer, 1970).

In parts of southern Europe, for example in Greece, food plays a very substantial role in the elaborate and extended funeral customs of Greek Orthodox tradition. (Danforth). At the burial, prior to the closing of the coffin in the grave, the priest pours a bottle of red wine in the form of a cross over the shrouded body of the deceased. *Koliva* (boiled wheat mixed with sugar and cinnamon and decorated with nuts and raisins) and bread are shared in the church courtyard by the funeral participants, who pray for the forgiveness of the deceased. None of this food is brought into the deceased's house, where the guests are offered water, cognac, cigarettes, and candy as they convey their condolences to the relatives. After coffee and biscuits have been served, the priest blesses *koliva*, wine, and bread (i.e., *makario*, "that which is blessed") and distributes them to the close relatives of the deceased (Danforth, 1982, pp. 42–43).

On the eve of the third day after death, *koliva*, bread, candy, and pastries are again distributed in the church courtyard after the memorial service at the grave, and guests again receive coffee, cognac, biscuits, and candy in the house of the deceased. These ceremonies may be repeated on the ninth day and six months after the death. Forty days after death, another memorial service is performed in the cemetery, after which a sweet wheaten pudding called *panhidha* is blessed by the priest and served to the guests in the church courtyard together with special funeral bread, pastries, honey, candy, and vermouth. Finally, guests are invited to the deceased's house for a very elaborate meal that includes meat, indicating that the relatives—who have abstained from meat for forty days—are being reincorporated into the normal life of the community (Danforth, 1982, pp. 43–44).

On occasions of collective commemoration of the dead, called *Psihosavato* (Soul Saturdays or All Souls' Days), offerings of *koliva*, bread, cheese, olives, and fruit are brought by women in rural Greece to the village church. There they are blessed by the priest, who also recites the names of the village dead. The food offerings brought by the women individually in honor of their own dead are then distributed to the others present in honor of all the dead (Danforth, 1982, p. 56).

The rite of exhumation, in which food and drink also feature, is normally performed after five years, at which stage the deceased is thought to have reached his or her final resting place. The priest pours a bottle of red wine over the bones, making the sign of the cross three times with the liquid. Those present are offered "a small glass of sweet red wine," *koliva*, "a slice of bread, a spoonful of honey, and several pastries, sweets, and other candies," by distant relatives and friends of the family. On returning to the family's house, they are "offered water, cognac, and candy" and later "coffee, small biscuits, and pastries," after which they compliment the family in a traditional manner for the reception provided (Danforth, 1982, p. 21).

Many Old World death customs, including the provision of refreshments at wakes and funerals, traveled to the New World with emigrant groups. William Woys Weaver shows that in colonial America, the provision of lavish funeral hospitality, either in the deceased's home or in a local hostelry, was well established by the late eighteenth century. Among the foods served by the Pennsylvania Dutch was a rich fruit cake, but funeral biscuits were also common. Some varieties, like the Dutch *doodkoecks* (death cakes), bore the initials of the deceased and were given to mourners in old New York. Others featured highly symbolic motifs such as a rooster, a heart, "a cherub or winged head . . . an hourglass, or even a skull" (Weaver, pp. 107–108). As in the Yorkshire Dales and Lincolnshire in England, the biscuits were flavored with caraway or tansy seeds (Weaver, p. 108). In Montgomery County, Pennsylvania, "funeral bread" (bread "sweetened with sugar or honey and containing caraway seeds or dried fruit"), funeral biscuits, and wine were served to the guests as they left the church on their way to the cemetery (Weaver, 1989, p. 110).

Commemoration of the dead during the feasts of All Saints and All Souls (November 1 and 2) is an especially exuberant affair in Mexican Catholic tradition. During the festival of *Todos Santos* (All Saints), or *Dia* or *Dias de Muertos* (Day or Days of the Dead), extending from the eve of October 30 to the evening of November 2, offerings of food and drink are made to the dead by being placed on the "dressed" graves and on the very elaborate altars for the dead that are prepared in the family home (Carmichael and Sayer, 1991, pp. 14–21).

In the New World, therefore, as in the Old, the provision of food and drink at wakes and funerals was an important act of *pietas* and effectively a social obligation. Thus, their provision was highly regulated and a matter of strict observance in many different societies.

See also **Christianity; Day of the Dead; Religion and Food; Sin and Food.**

BIBLIOGRAPHY

Aubrey, J. *Remains of Gentilisme and Judaisme*. In *John Aubrey, Three Prose Works*, edited by J. Buchanan-Brown. London: Centaur Classics, 1972.

Barboff, Mouette. "Bread and the Life Cycle in Portugal," In *Food and Celebration: From Fasting to Feasting*, edited by Patricia Lysaght, pp. 204–206. Ljubljana, Slovenia: Založba, ZRC, 2002.

Bennett, Margaret. *Scottish Customs from the Cradle to the Grave*. Edinburgh: Polygon, 1992.

Brears, P. *The Gentlewoman's Kitchen: Great Food in Yorkshire, 1650–1750*. Wakefield, U.K.: Wakefield Historical Publications, 1984.

Carmichael, E., and C. Sayer. *The Skeleton at the Feast: The Day of the Dead in Mexico*. London: British Museum Press, 1991.

Danforth, Loring M. *The Death Rituals of Rural Greece*. Princeton: Princeton University Press, 1982.

Dumpe, L. "On the Early History of Festive Beverages in Latvia: Beer" In *Food and Celebration: From Fasting to Feasting*, edited by Patricia Lysaght, pp. 125–134. Ljubljana, Slovenia: Založba, ZRC, 2002.

Feglová, Viera, and Kornélia Jakubíková. "Family Customs." In *Slovakia: European Contexts of the Folk Culture*, edited by Rastislava Stoličná, pp. 232–236. Bratislava: Veda. Publishing House of the Slovak Academy of Sciences, 1997.

Fenton, A. "The Teminology of Food for Personal Occasions in Lowland Scotland." In *Food and Celebration: From Fasting to Feasting*, edited by Patricia Lysaght, pp. 207–214. Ljubljana, Slovenia: Založba, ZRC, 2002.

Fielhauer, Helmut Paul. "Die 'Schwartze' und die 'Weisse Braut' beim Begräbnis Lediger." *Das Waldviertel* 19, 30 (1970): 72–79.

Green, Miranda J. *Dictionary of Celtic Myth and Legend*. London: Thames and Hudson, 1992.

Gregor, Rev. Walter. *An Echo of the Olden Time from the North of Scotland*. Edinburgh and Glasgow: John Menzies, 1874.

Hole, C. *The English Housewife in the Seventeenth Century*. London: Chatto & Windus, 1953.

Huber, H. *Totenbrauchtum in Niederösterreich: Häusliche Leichenwache in der alpinen Zone; Erscheinungsformen des 20. Jahrhunderts*. Wien: VWGÖ, 1981.

Kvideland, Karin. "Boundaries and the Sin-Eater." In *Boundaries and Thresholds: Papers from a Colloquium of the Katherine Briggs Club*, edited by Hilda Ellis Davidson, pp. 84–90. Woodchester, U.K.: Thimble Press, 1993.

Lysaght, Patricia. "Visible Death: Attitudes to the Dying in Ireland." *Marvels and Tales* 9, 1 (May 1995): 27–60, 85–100.

Lysaght, Patricia "Wake and Funeral Hospitality in Ireland in the Nineteenth and Twentieth Centuries: Continuity and Change." In *Food and Celebration: From Fasting to Feasting,* edited by Patricia Lysaght, pp. 197–296. Ljubljana, Slovenia: Založba, ZRC, 2002.

Moore, A. W. *The Folk-Lore of the Isle of Man.* Douglas, Isle of Man: Brown & Son; London: D. Nutt, 1891.

Napier, James. *Folklore: or Superstitious Beliefs in the West of Scotland within this Century.* Paisley: A. Gardner, 1879. Facsimile reprint: Wakefield: EP Publishing, 1976.

Ó Súilleabháin, S. *Irish Wake Amusements.* Cork and Dublin: Mercier Press, 1967.

Stoličná, Rastislava. "Food and Eating." In *Slovakia: European Contexts of the Folk Culture,* edited by Rastislava Stoličná, p. 118. Bratislava: Veda. Publishing House of the Slovak Academy of Sciences, 1997.

Storå, Nils. *Burial Customs of the Skolt Lapps.* FF Communications No. 210. Helsinki: Academia Scientiarum Fennica, 1971.

Viski, Károly. *Hungarian Peasant Customs.* Budapest: G. Vajna & Co, 1932.

Weaver, William Woys. *America Eats: Forms of Edible Folk Art.* New York: Harper & Row, 1989.

Patricia Lysaght

DELICATESSEN. *See* **Retailing of Food.**

DELMONICO FAMILY. The Delmonicos are a family dynasty of restaurateurs of Italian Swiss origin who created some of the most legendary and opulent restaurants in the United States.

The principal founders of the American clan were the brothers Pietro Antonio (1783–1861) and Giovanni (1788–1842) Del Monico, who established themselves under the names Peter and John Delmonico at 23 William Street in New York in 1827. Shrewdly advertising their business as a European-style café in New York's business district, the brothers quickly amassed a fortune based on excellent service and a menu that became a magnet for New York's European expatriates and American nouveaux riches.

As the business grew and thrived, other members of the family emigrated from Switzerland and joined Peter and John, including a nephew Lorenzo (1813–1881) who eventually became the genius behind the success of the family's restaurant empire. Lorenzo joined the firm in 1831 when it expanded from a café into a true *restaurant française.* This first restaurant, at 25 William Street, was only the first of several locations that eventually opened and operated under the Delmonico name. As businesses moved uptown, Delmonico's followed. In 1876, Lorenzo moved the main restaurant to Fifth Avenue and Twenty-sixth Street, facing Madison Square. This new address, complete with a ballroom that quickly became the centerpiece of New York society, launched Delmonico's into

A private dinner at Delmonico's Forty-fourth Street restaurant in 1898. © BETTMAN/CORBIS.

New York's Gilded Age and perhaps the restaurant's greatest period of fame.

Under the oversight of European-trained chef Charles Ranhofer, Delmonicos became synonymous with ostentatious banquets and gastronomic sensations. Ranhofer's encyclopedic cookbook called *The Epicurean* (1894) records many of the recipes and menus that made Delmonico's famous during his culinary reign. *The Delmonico Cookbook* (1880), a less opulent cookbook by former Delmonico chef Alessandro Filippini, also records many of the foods served in the restaurant. Throughout much of the history of the various restaurants owned by the family, the majority of customers were businessmen; women were not served in the public dining rooms unless escorted, although this rule was relaxed somewhat during the 1880s. The famous dinners at which women were present were held in ornately furnished private rooms designed for this purpose.

The restaurant's last move occurred in 1897 when it took up a new location on Fifth Avenue at Forty-fourth Street. The Delmonico restaurant empire eventually became overextended and difficult to manage. The business closed its doors in 1923, a victim of income tax, Prohibition, and changing lifestyles of New York's rich and famous. Today the name Delmonico survives in a pudding, a melon, and a cut of steak taken from a rib of beef, the American equivalent of entrecôte.

See also **Restaurants**.

BIBLIOGRAPHY

Filippini, Alessandro. *The Delmonico Cookbook*. New York, 1880.

Rimmer, Leopold. *History of Old New York and the House of Delmonicos*. New York, 1898.

Stephenson, Byron C. "Delmonico's." *The Illustrated American* (16 May 1891).

Thomas, Lately. *Delmonico's: A Century of Splendor*. Boston: Houghton Mifflin, 1967.

Ward, Samuel. *Lyrical Recreations*. London: Macmillan, 1883.

William Woys Weaver

DENTISTRY.

Food and dental health interact, with each having effects on the other. Patterns of eating affect the health of the teeth and other tissues in the mouth, while the ability to chew a variety of foods without discomfort influences a person's nutritional state as well his or her enjoyment of eating.

Sugar and Dental Caries

The clearest link between food and dental health is between sugar consumption and caries (cavities). A study in the 1940s compared the dental health of children in an area of northern India, where food was scarce and malnutrition common, to that of better-nourished children in Lahore and in Rochester, New York. The poorly nourished children had the fewest cavities. Subsequent research confirmed that populations who enjoyed a good nutritional status had more caries than less well-nourished populations.

Researchers then looked at the mechanism of caries development to discern the role of diet. Cavities are the end result of a process that involves bacteria and sugars in the mouth over time. *Streptococcus mutans*, bacteria that are normally present in plaque, a very fine film which covers the surfaces of the teeth, metabolize sugar and form acid. When a person consumes sugar in foods or beverages, acid is formed that can dissolve minute amounts of minerals from the enamel surface of the tooth. When this happens repeatedly over time, enough minerals are lost for a cavity to form.

This relationship between sugar consumption and caries was tested in a classic study conducted at Vipeholm, a mental institution in Sweden, and reported in 1954. Although modern ethical standards would preclude a study in which subjects were unable to give informed consent, it remains a landmark piece of research. Residents were assigned to several groups. All ate the standard diet of the institution, but some were given additional sweets in varying quantities and frequency, up to twenty-four sticky toffee candies per day. After five years of observation, the researchers concluded that the stickiness of the sweets and the frequency with which they were consumed, both increasing the amount of time that the bacteria in plaque could produce acid, were more important than the total amount of sugar.

Streptococcus mutans can feed on any carbohydrate, not just sugars. The bacteria make no distinction between "natural" carbohydrates, such as the sugars in fruit, and refined sugars; they make acid from any of them.

Oral bacteria also make acid from sugar in liquids. This can lead to a particular pattern of caries called "baby-bottle caries," which develops when a baby is put to bed with a bottle filled with sugar-containing liquid, including milk. When the baby falls asleep, the liquid pools in the mouth, leading to decay, most often of the front upper teeth.

Since sugar has been shown to play such a significant role in the development of tooth decay, a basic preventive measure is to limit the frequency of sugar consumption. Because it is the action of bacteria on the sugar that is of concern, minimizing the bacteria by careful attention to oral hygiene is equally important. Fluoride, a mineral that is naturally present in water in some areas, has a strong protective effect as well. It binds to the other minerals to become part of the enamel, making the enamel harder and more resistant to decay. It also slows acid formation and promotes repair of places on the teeth where acid has dissolved some of the minerals.

In areas where the naturally occurring level of fluoride in water is low, it is often added during water treatment. Although there have been controversies about water fluoridation, public health authorities, including the American Dental Association, the United States Public Health Service, and the World Health Organization, all support it as a safe and effective preventive measure. One can see its effectiveness in the fact that, although sugar consumption in the United States has been increasing, children have fewer cavities than they had in the years before fluoridation became widespread.

Sugar substitutes are used to produce candies, chewing gum, and beverages that taste sweet without harming the teeth. Chewing gum containing xylitol, one of these alternative sweeteners, has been shown to be protective.

Diet and Periodontal Disease

Gingivitis, or periodontal disease, is the other common dental disorder. The bacteria in dental plaque cause an infection of the gums and structures that hold the teeth in place. The gums become red, swollen, and tender. Food does not play an important role in the development of gum disease, as it does in the formation of caries. Good oral hygiene is the most important preventive measure. A nutritious diet, which supplies generous amounts of vitamins and minerals, can offer some benefit by helping to maintain the immune system's ability to fight the infection.

Dental Status and Eating

The other side of the food and dental health interaction is the importance of healthy dentition in enabling people to eat and enjoy a wide variety of foods. The absence of a significant number of teeth or a condition such as periodontal disease or poorly fitting dentures, which makes chewing uncomfortable, may limit a person's food choices and compromise his or her nutritional status. This problem occurs most frequently in elderly and low-income populations, who are more likely to be at risk for nutritional problems.

Some researchers do not find this effect, possibly because the subjects with poor dentition have chosen nutritious foods that are easy to chew, or because the comparison population ate no better in spite of good dental status. In general, however, poor dental health increases the risk of poor nutritional health. Good dental care can correct most of these problems and enable individuals to enjoy eating a nutritious diet.

See also **Digestion**; **Fluoride**.

BIBLIOGRAPHY

American Dental Association web site. Available at www.ada .org.

Burt, B. A., and S. Pai. "Sugar Consumption and Caries Risk: A Systematic Review." Paper presented at the Consensus Development Conference on Diagnosis and Management of Dental Caries throughout Life, Bethesda, Md., March 2001.

FDI Working Group. "Nutrition, Diet, and Oral Health: Report of and FDI Working Group." *International Dental Journal* 44 (1994): 599–612.

Gustaffson, B. E., C. E. Quensel, L. S. Lanke, et al. "The Vipeholm Dental Caries Study: The Effect of Different Levels of Carbohydrate Intake on Caries Activity in 436 Individuals Observed for Five Years." *Acta Odontologica Scandinavica* 11 (1954): 232–364.

Mona R. Sutnick

DESSERT. *See* **Cake and Pancake; Chocolate; Ice Cream; Pastry; Sherbet and Sorbet.**

DIASPORA. The term "diaspora" was first used to describe the shared experience of the Jewish peoples—experience of exile and displacement, but also of continuing (some would say strengthening) connection and identification. Etymologically, "diaspora" derives from Greek *dia* ('through') and *speirein* ('to sow, scatter'). The word is used more broadly to refer to the cultural connections maintained by a group of people who have been dispersed or who have migrated around the globe. Each distinct "diasporic group" or "community" is a composite of many journeys to different parts of the world, occurring over very different timescales. The experiences of particular subgroups can therefore vary considerably—to the extent that some writers argue it is meaningless to talk of shared identities and experiences of, for example, "the South Asian diaspora," at the global level. Avtar Brah's book *Cartographies of Diaspora* provides a detailed discussion of the complex history and uses of the concept.

A key characteristic of diasporas is that a strong sense of connection to a homeland is maintained through cultural practices and ways of life. As Brah reminds us, this "homeland" might be imaginary rather than real, and its existence need not be tied to any desire to "return" home. The maintenance of these kinds of cultural connections can in some cases provoke both nostalgic and separatist tendencies. The focus here is on the place of cooking and eating among the enduring habits, rituals, and everyday practices that are collectively used to sustain a shared sense of diasporic cultural identity, in recognition that culinary culture has an important part to play in diasporic identifications.

Diasporic Foodscapes

Among the everyday cultural practices routinely used to maintain (and in some cases enhance or even reinvent) diasporic identities, food is commonly of central importance. There are a number of reasons for this. First, food traditions and habits are comparatively portable: groups that migrate around the world often carry with them elements of the diet and eating habits of the "homeland." Indeed, the migrations of foods can be used to track the past movements of people, a cornerstone of research into foodways and foodscapes. Every nation's diet therefore bears the imprint of countless past immigrations. Second, foodways are adaptable: While migrations can map the movements of ingredients, foodstuffs, or methods of preparation into new habitats unchanged, they also tell tales of adaptation, substitution, and indigenization. As people and their cuisines move, they also change to suit local conditions. Ghassan Hage's research with Lebanese migrants in Australia provides a simple illustration. In his essay "At Home in the Entrails of the West," based on interviews with Lebanese migrants to the Parramatta area of Sydney, Hage reports on this process of adaptation and substitution. One of his respondents talks about using peanut butter in Lebanese dishes in place of tahini, which was not at the time available in Australia. (In fact, when tahini later became available, the respondent admits to craving peanut butter.) Over time, this reshaping of ingredients and cooking methods often leads to a reshaping of diasporic culinary cultures, such that the dishes sometimes bear little resemblance to the original version. Comparing the same dishes among diasporic groups in different countries (say, the Chinese in the United States and in the United Kingdom) makes this clear, as does comparing diasporic versions of dishes with those served "back home."

This mobility and adaptability assures that food habits are usually maintained (even while they are transformed) among diasporic groups. Occasionally entire culinary cultures may be preserved. More often, "traditional" foods are maintained only in particular symbolic meals or dishes. For example, the small community of Russian Molokans in the United States perpetuates the rituals of preparing and sharing formal community dinners, or *obedy* (as reported by Willard B. Moore in "Metaphor and Changing Reality"). Alternatively, a particular dish can be singled out as embodying and preserving diasporic identity, as in the case of the *ghormeh-sabzi*, a stew eaten by Iranian immigrants in central England. This dish has particular significance as a way to reconnect with Iranian culture, tradition, and beliefs. A detailed discussion of the place of *ghormeh-sabzi* can be found in Lynn Harbottle's essay, "'Bastard' Chicken or *Ghormeh-sabzi?*" Harbottle's respondents report that they had to make compromises in their families' diets, allowing some Western dishes onto the table, even though they were generally wary of losing their cultural identity through Westernization. However, they expressed health concerns about the inferiority of the food in England compared with their diet back in Iran, and were keen to maintain the cultural and religious significance of food habits and pass them on to future generations. (These habits were mainly connected with their Shi'ite faith and the consumption of *halal* ingredients in accordance with Islamic dietary law.) In some cases, this led to the transformation of some staples of contemporary English cuisine, such as pizza or burgers, to realign them with Shi'ite

custom. The diasporic transformation of diet is, therefore, a two-way process.

In fact, the arrival of diasporic foodways can more broadly transform the "host culture" into which migrants move. In Britain, for example, the migration of South Asian peoples has brought with it a variety of "immigrant" cuisines. While these were maintained initially for the migrant communities as a reminder of "home," their popularity among non-Asian Britons is longstanding and has continued to grow. Certain indigenized dishes, such as chicken *tikka massala*, are among the most enthusiastically and widely eaten meals in Britain today. (This, of course, need not signal comfortable race relations away from the table; see Uma Narayan's essay on Indian food in the West, "Eating Cultures.")

Diasporic Dilemmas
It would be wrong to simply equate the popularity of chicken *tikka massala* in Britain with the comfortable accommodation of South Asian migrants into a commonly shared and widely adopted multicultural identity. This is one of Hage's main points: the adoption of diasporic cuisines by host cultures often does little to encourage other forms of productive encounter between different ethnic groups. In fact, for Hage, the availability of diasporic foodstuffs permits a lazy "cosmo-multiculturalism," in which eating foreign dishes substitutes for other forms of engagement. Moreover, the necessity of maintaining "exotic" foodways can produce a distinct diasporic burden, fixing migrant culinary cultures rather than allowing them to change. There is, therefore, a set of ethical questions attached to the existence of diasporic foodscapes: For whom are they produced? What are their outcomes and effects? What alternatives might be suggested?

Two discussions can serve as illustrations of this dilemma. The first focuses on the role of the *döner kebap* among Turkish "economic migrants" in Germany. In his essay "*McDöner*," Ayse Caglar traces the ways in which the symbolic meaning of the *döner* has shifted over time. He notes its immense popularity in Germany, and reminds us that the dish was invented for non-Turkish Germans and does not exist in Turkey in the form it is now served—as a fast food consisting of meat slices in *pide* (Turkish flatbread), garnished with salad and sauces, bought on the street from an *Imbiss* (mobile stand). Moreover, the vast majority of *döners* are eaten by non-Turkish Germans. Back in the 1960s, *döner* vendors traded heavily on the ethnic exoticness or Turkishness of the *döner*, but since the early 1990s the food has been increasingly deracialized, shedding its ethnic signifiers and in many cases being rebranded using American symbols—hence the "*McDöner*" of Caglar's title. This shift, Caglar explains, mirrored the mounting social marginalization of Turks in Germany.

In the case of the *döner kebap*, then, we can witness the "invention" of a food symbolic of ethnic identity, though in this case (unlike the Iranian *ghormeh-sabzi*) the food is largely consumed by the "host culture" rather than by the immigrants. The "ethnic" markers attached to the *döner* have subsequently been shed, reflecting the shifting social position of the migrant group. As a final irony, Caglar notes that successful Turkish caterers in Germany have switched to serving Italian food to a more up-market clientele.

A second example is provided by David Parker, in an essay called "The Chinese Takeaway and the Diasporic Habitus." Like the indigenized Indian curry house (a key provider of chicken *tikka massala*), the Chinese takeaway (takeout shop or restaurant) has come to occupy a particular symbolic location on the British culinary landscape. However, foods from the South and East Asian subcontinents are available through all kinds of other food outlets, from supermarkets to trendy eateries. Moreover, food is only one cultural product used in diasporic identifications; the development of distinct "ethnic quarters" such as Chinatowns in many cities testifies to a broader-based cultural infrastructure. For critics, the existence of such "ethnic quarters" merely furthers the economic exploitation of diaspora, while for other commentators it suggests the success of multiculturalism. Food outlets are commonly center stage in these kinds of urban areas, testifying to the significance of the food distribution as a site for diasporic cultural production.

Parker reads the Chinese takeaway as a key site for the negotiation of British Chineseness in relation to the global Chinese diaspora. By focusing on the encounters between workers and customers, Parker reveals a mode of interaction that he names the "diasporic habitus," defined as "the embodied subjectivities poised between the legacies of the past, the imperatives of the present, and the possibilities of the future" (p. 75). This habitus shapes ways of "being Chinese" in diasporic contexts, and is the result of the uneven distribution of "imperial capital" between Chinese and non-Chinese Britons: what occurs in the takeaway bears the enduring imprint of colonial contact between Western and non-Western peoples. Parker shows not only how these encounters are overlaid by orientalist racialization, but also how this "contact zone" offers critical possibilities. Parker argues (like Hage) for a contested (instead of celebratory) multiculturalism that explores the complex interplay of identities in everyday locations. The takeaway, therefore, is an emblem of British Chineseness rather than Chineseness—a situational outcome of one particular diasporic foodscape.

Of course, the notion of British Chineseness still retains an emphasis on being (at least in part) Chinese, rather than simply British. This is part of the diasporic burden mentioned earlier: the necessity of retaining some degree of ethnic difference. In some cases, of course, migrant groups may wish to reject, either partially or wholly, their ethnic identity, and adopt the identity of their new "home." They may, however, be denied that possibility by the "host culture," which wants to preserve their ethnic identity for a variety of reasons. The deracializing of *döner kebap* illustrates an attempt by German Turks to integrate more fully into German society at the same time that the ethnic marker of Turkishness was becoming increasingly problematic there.

The existence of diasporic cuisine marks a complex negotiation between cultural identities. For both German Turks and British Chinese, elements of their cuisines (or "invented" versions of them) have become institutionalized on the foodscape. While this may provide some level of economic security—the "success" of Chinese takeaways in Britain is often reported as evidence for multiculturalism, at least in terms of business culture—there are many compromises and dilemmas involved as well. As the *döner Imbiss* and the Chinese takeaway both illustrate, mundane yet intensely symbolic items such as food are woven in complex and shifting ways into discourses of tradition and transformation, identity, and community. Diasporic diets, like all aspects of diasporic identity and culture, are constantly remade, even while some key elements endure over time.

See also **Judaism**; **Travel**; **United States: Ethnic Cuisines**.

BIBLIOGRAPHY.

Brah, Avtar. *Cartographies of Diaspora: Contesting Identities*. London: Routledge, 1996.

Caglar, Ayse S. "*McDöner: Döner Kebap* and the Social Positioning Struggle of German Turks." In *Marketing in a Multicultural World: Ethnicity, Nationalism, and Cultural Identity*, edited by Janeen Costa and Gary Bamoosy. London: Sage, 1995.

Hage, Ghassan. "At Home in the Entrails of the West: Multiculturalism, Ethnic Food, and Migrant Home-Building." In *Home/World: Space, Community, and Marginality in Sydney's West*, edited by Helen Grace, Ghassan Hage, Lesley Johnson, Julie Langsworth, and Michael Symonds. Annandale: Pluto, 1997.

Harbottle, Lynn. "'Bastard' Chicken or Ghormeh-sabzi? Iranian Women Guarding the Health of the Migrant Family." In *Consumption Matters*, edited by Stephen Edgell, Hetherington, Kevin, and Alan Warde. Oxford: Blackwell, 1996.

Moore, Willard B. "Metaphor and Changing Reality: The Foodways and Beliefs of the Russian Molokans in the United States." In *Ethnic and Regional Foodways in the United States: The Performance of Group Identity*, edited by Linda Keller Brown and Kay Mussell. Knoxville: University of Tennessee Press, 1984.

Narayan, Uma. "Eating Cultures: Incorporation, Identity, and Indian Food." *Social Identities* 1 (1995).

Parker, David. "The Chinese Takeaway and the Diasporic Habitus: Space, Time, and Power Geometries." In *Un/Settled Multiculturalisms: Diasporas, Entanglements, 'Transruptions'*, edited by Barnor Hesse. London: Zed, 2000

David John Bell

DIETARY ASSESSMENT. Dietary assessment is the process of evaluating what people eat by using one or several intake indicators. It is the best approach for identifying nutrients that are likely to either be under- or overconsumed by the individual or groups of interest. It also can be used to identify food patterns and preferences.

Dietary Status versus Nutritional Status

Dietary status is related to but not necessarily reflective of nutritional status. Nutritional status is a more comprehensive term, referring to health status as it is affected by nutrition. It is measured not only by assessing dietary status, but also by anthropometric, biochemical, and clinical measures. Because dietary methods are less invasive, somewhat easier to obtain than other physiological measures, and do not require medical training, they often are used initially for assessing nutritional inadequacy or excess. Physiological measurements are then used to confirm and corroborate dietary intake evaluation and to arrive at definitive assessments of nutritional status.

Tools and Standards for Assessment

To assess dietary intake, food composition tables for translating foods consumed into nutrients, and a reference against which dietary intakes may be compared, are needed. These tools have been updated and refined periodically and appropriate ways for applying them to assessment tasks are steadily clarified.

Overcoming Imperfections in Assessing Dietary Intake

All dietary assessment methods are imperfect, regardless of how well they are designed. Their major shortcomings and measures for dealing with the imperfections are described briefly below.

Capture Actual Intakes

The various methods for assessing dietary intake are summarized in Table 1 and elsewhere in detail (Dwyer, 1999). All assessment methods fail to capture actual energy intakes precisely and probably intakes of nutrients as well. Some of the errors are inevitable because human beings tend to misreport their food intakes, but the method used also influences assessment outcomes.

Dietary intake is sometimes assessed by an objective observer rather than by the eaters themselves. For example, the intake of a hospitalized patient often is assessed from measured differences of the food served to a patient less any unconsumed amounts. Such objective methods have the advantage of being less subject to reporting biases than those that rely solely on recall. However, more objective methods are time-consuming, costly, cannot usually be employed to assess typical intake, and fail to record all intake. Moreover, they may not reflect what people really eat, since people may eat differently when they know that they are being observed.

For these reasons, most commonly used dietary assessment methods rely on eaters' self-reported intakes.

Most methods such as twenty-four-hour recalls, food records, and diaries underreport actual energy intake by at least 20 percent. Underreporting errors are even higher (30 percent or more) in certain groups, such as the obese, women, and the elderly. However, they also vary among individuals in ways that are not always easily identified by demographic or other distinguishing characteristics. The causes of underreporting include forgetting, unconscious alterations in recalling foods eaten (for example, when the individual knows that he or she is being watched), attempts to please the questioner, and occasionally lack of cooperation by the subject. Nonrandom biases are difficult to deal with statistically.

Intakes obtained using semiquantitative food frequency questionnaires have other shortcomings. This method presents the respondent with a food list. These prompts may decrease forgetting, but insertions and "false memories" of foods consumed or of the consumption of socially desirable foods may be reported rather than true intakes. Semiquantitative food frequency questionnaires are too imprecise to estimate individual intakes quantitatively. Nutrient intakes from semiquantitative food frequency questionnaires usually are overestimated. They usually are adjusted statistically to obtain more accurate estimates of usual intakes. Measures of usual energy intakes for accurate groups specified by sex and age obtained by other methods or from estimates of energy outputs are used to adjust them. They are often derived by "food frequency" approaches and may be accurate enough to provide reasonable group estimates, although such measures are not sufficiently accurate for individuals. Also, precise quantification of absolute amounts (as opposed to levels of intake ranked into quartiles or quintiles) is not possible. The biases involved in food frequency questionnaires are complex, and statistical methods for obtaining valid estimates of intakes are unavailable.

Understandably, retrospective methods that rely on memory are subject to "forgetting bias." Prospective methods, which rely on reporting food intake immediately or shortly after eating, are more subject to alterations in intake due to the individual's awareness that his or her intake is being recorded. The extent to which social desirability and reporting biases intrude in the various methods is unknown, but is probably considerable.

Not all of the problems associated with misreporting can be overcome by the method of choice, but some can be minimized by selecting the appropriate tool for the task at hand.

Obtain Representative Intakes

Dietary assessments must be done frequently and randomly to reflect usual intake faithfully. This is an important shortcoming because only usual intake is

TABLE 1

Dietary assessment methods

Method	Description, advantages, and limitations of method
Retrospective Methods	
24-hour recall	Respondent recalls all foods and beverages consumed in a given 24-hour period and reports them to a trained interviewer, who probes to get additional details on portion sizes, frequency, and forgotten items. Positive aspects include low respondent burden, ease in administration, and minimization of biases associated with altering food intake because of knowledge that one is being observed. Negative aspects of the method include forgetting, deliberate misreporting, need for a trained observer to administer, need for several days of intakes to obtain estimate of usual diet, and costs associated with computerized analysis of records
Telephone recall	The respondent is contacted or instructed in advance and given instructions about estimating portion sizes and other details. Then the respondent is called by telephone and asked to report dietary intake over the past 24 hours. Probes and techniques are usually standardized to minimize reporting error. Positive aspects of the method include those listed above plus ability to obtain representative random days of intake, and decreased cost of administration. Negative aspects include inability to obtain interviews from those without telephones, and for those who find telephones difficult to use, and errors in reporting portion sizes.
Food frequency and semiquantitative food frequency questionnaire	Respondent chooses from a list of different foods or food groups usually eaten over the past month or year. The number and type of foods, and whether portion sizes are specified, varies from one questionnaire to another. Positive aspects of the method include ease of administration, low expense, less forgetting because of prompts furnished by food lists, somewhat more of an estimate of usual intake (perhaps equivalent to 2–3 days), and low costs of data analysis. Negative aspects of method include incomplete reporting of items not included in food lists, overreporting, incomplete or inaccurate response, inaccurate translation of food and food groups to nutrients, and imprecise estimates of nutrient intake
Dietary history	Respondent reports all foods and beverages consumed on a usual day to a trained interviewer. The interviewer then probes further on the frequency amount and portion size consumed. Diet diaries are sometimes used to assist respondents in recalling their intakes. Positive aspects of the method are that respondent burden is low and complete intakes are provided. Negatives include high cost, need for trained interviewers, and lack of standardization
Prospective Methods	
Weighed food record	After being instructed, respondent weighs all food and drink consumed on a small weighing scale and reports it on a record that is kept as close to the time of consumption as possible. If observers are available, they can carry out the weighing themselves. Positive aspects of the method are lack of forgetting bias, and ability to obtain random days of intake. Negatives include high respondent burden, refusal to record intakes, need for an expert observer to review and clarify intakes reported, tendency of respondents to alter food intake when they know they are under observation, and costs of data analysis.
Food diary	The respondent records all foods consumed in household measures, usually without measuring them, or only measuring foods that are particularly difficult to estimate. Positive aspects are same as food records but respondent burden is less. Negative aspects are that more errors in estimation of portion size may occur
Duplicate portion analysis	An observer takes duplicate portions of all foods consumed by the individual and weighs or measures them; in some cases, these may also be chemically analyzed. Positive aspects are similar to food records. Negative aspects are lack of respondent cooperation, need for trained observers, cost of food analysis, and inability to obtain estimate of usual intake.
Other: Direct observation by trained observers or by videotaping subjects	Observer records or watches food intake in a controlled or highly supervised environment in which it is possible to videotape or directly observe food intakes. Positive aspects of the methods are that they do not rely on respondent burden. Negative aspects are that the methods are usually too imprecise for obtaining valid estimates of individual intakes.

correlated with nutritional status. A representative sample of randomly chosen days that includes both weekdays and weekends is best for obtaining accurate twenty-four-hour recalls or records. Semiquantitative or other food frequency questionnaires also may assist in providing information on usual food intake patterns.

Obtain Total Intakes

Many foods and beverages are fortified with nutrients, and a substantial proportion of the population takes nutrient supplements on a regular basis. For some individ-

uals, these nutrient sources contribute a substantial amount of vitamins and minerals. Nutrient intakes from all sources, including foods and beverages, fortified foods, and nutrient supplements must be included in all dietary assessments. If only food sources are queried, this fact should be noted.

Use Complete Food Composition Tables

Once food intakes are obtained, these must be translated into nutrients using food, beverage, and supplement composition tables. Accurate nutrient intakes can be obtained if up-to-date and complete food composition tables are available; that is, the composition of fortified foods, nutrient supplements, and beverages must be included and tables must be complete for all nutrients and other bioactive substances of interest.

Appropriate References

Estimated nutrient intakes must be compared with appropriate references; in the United States and Canada, these are the Dietary Reference Intakes, or DRIs. Their use in dietary assessments is the subject of a recent report (*Dietary Reference Intakes*, 2000).

Inadequacies, Excesses, and Imbalances May Coexist

In the past, dietary assessments focused on dietary inadequacies. Although these are still relevant, nutrient excesses and imbalances of nutrients also are of concern in most Western countries, and therefore also must be considered. Several of the DRIs are helpful in these respects. DRIs for macronutrients will be published in the near future.

Appropriate Interpretation of Assessment Results

The estimated average requirement, or EAR, is the nutrient intake estimated to meet the requirement of half the healthy individuals in a particular life stage or gender group. The recommended dietary allowance, or RDA, is the average daily dietary intake that suffices to meet the nutrient requirement of nearly all (97–98 percent) healthy individuals in a particular life stage and gender group. The adequate intake, or AI, is a recommended intake based on observed or experimentally determined approximations or estimates of nutrient intake by a group (or groups) of healthy people whose intakes are assumed to be adequate. The AI is used when an RDA cannot be determined. When the AI's are not based on mean intakes of healthy populations, these values are likely to be less accurate. The tolerable upper intake level (UL) is the highest usual daily nutrient intake likely to pose no risk of adverse health effects to almost all individuals in the general population. As intakes increase above the UL, the risks of adverse effects also increase. The assessment of dietary adequacy is imprecise. A specific individual's actual requirement for a specific nutrient generally is never known. Second, often the number of days that intakes are measured are likely to be insufficient to overcome errors in measuring intake and normal day-to-day variation. Although dietary data alone are not sufficient to assess nutritional status, intakes of individuals can be compared to certain of the DRIs. A usual intake based on a large number of days that is at or above the RDA or AI has a low probability of inadequacy. An intake above the UL places an individual at risk of adverse effects from excessive nutrient intakes. When observed intakes are habitually below the EAR, increased intakes usually are needed because the probability of adequacy is 50 percent or less. Habitual intakes between the EAR and the RDA also

probably need to be improved because the probability of adequacy is less than 97 to 98 percent. Quantitative estimates of risk of inadequacy are more difficult to obtain. However, they can be calculated using methods described in a recent report (*Dietary Reference Intakes*, 2000).

The DRIs also are used to assess the dietary intake of groups. These assessments determine the percentage of individuals whose intakes are estimated to be inadequate. The EAR is used to estimate the prevalence of inadequate intakes within a group. A mean usual group intake at or above the AI implies a low prevalence of inadequate intakes. The UL is used to estimate the percentage of the population at risk of adverse effects from excessive intakes consumed on a chronic basis. Thus, the RDA is not used to assess nutrient intakes of groups.

Conclusions

Dietary assessment is a necessary component of nutritional status assessment of individuals, and also is useful for other purposes. It can be done using a variety of methods, each of which has advantages and limitations. However, regardless of which method is chosen, it is important that certain criteria be met. Intake from all sources (food, fortified food, beverages, and nutrient supplements) must be included. Sufficient numbers of days to represent usual intakes must be obtained. Complete food and supplement composition tables must be employed. Appropriate reference standards and statistical procedures for assessing intakes must be used. Dietary assessment methods work best in combination with other methods for the assessment of nutritional status.

See also **Dietary Guidelines; Nutrition.**

BIBLIOGRAPHY

Dwyer, J. T. (1997). "Assessment of Dietary Intake." In *Modern Nutrition in Health and Disease*, edited by M. Shils, J. A. Olson, M. Shike and A. C. Ross, 8th ed., pp. 887–904. Baltimore: Williams and Wilkins, 1997.

Dwyer, J. T. "Dietary Assessment." In *Modern Nutrition in Health and Disease*, edited by M. Shils, J. A. Olson, M. Shike, and A. C. Ross, 9th ed., pp. 937–962. Baltimore: Williams and Wilkins, 1999.

Nusser, S., A. L. Carriquiry, K. W. Dodd, and W. A. Fuller. "A Semiparametric Transformation Approach to Estimating Usual Daily Intake Distributions." *Journal of the American Statistical Association* 91 (1996): 1440–1449.

Poehlman, E. T. "Energy Needs: Assessment and Requirements in Humans." In *Modern Nutrition in Health and Disease*, edited by M. Shils, J. A. Olson, M. Shike, and A. C. Ross, 9th ed., pp. 95–104. Philadelphia: Williams and Wilkins, 1999.

Subcommittee on Interpretation and Uses of Dietary Reference Intakes and Upper Reference Levels of Nuturients, Food and Nutrition Board, Institute of Medicine. *Dietary Reference Intakes: Applications in Dietary Assessment*. Washington, D.C.: National Academy Press, 2000.

Johanna Dwyer

DIETARY GUIDELINES.

The 1969 White House Conference on Food, Nutrition, and Health was instrumental in the development of the first set of U.S. dietary guidelines. Specific recommendations emerged out of this conference, which advocated that the government examine more closely the links between diet and chronic disease. The 1969 conference was followed in 1977 by the release of the U.S. Senate Dietary Goals, which summarized specific recommendations for the American diet.

The dietary guidelines are the cornerstone of the federal nutrition policy for the U.S. nutrition programs; thus programs such as food stamps, school lunch/school breakfast, and WIC use the dietary guidelines in developing program services. In addition, all nutrition education programs at the federal level must have messages that are consistent with the dietary guidelines. Thus the impact of the dietary guidelines is wide-ranging. It is estimated that one of every five Americans participates in at least one federal nutrition program.

History of the Dietary Guidelines for Americans

The Dietary Guidelines attempt to answer the question, "What should Americans eat to stay healthy?" Specifically, the dietary guidelines provide advice for healthy Americans aged two years and older about food choices that promote health and reduce the risk of disease.

The Dietary Guidelines were first developed in 1980 and have been updated every five years since then—1985, 1990, 1995, and 2000. The National Nutrition Monitoring and Related Research Act of 1990 requires the Secretary of Agriculture and Secretary of Health and Human Services (HHS) to publish jointly every five years a report entitled *Dietary Guidelines for Americans*. The report must contain nutrition and dietary information and guidelines for the general public; be based on the preponderance of scientific and medical knowledge current at the time of publication; and be prompted by each federal agency in carrying out federal food, nutrition, or health programs. The 1995 Dietary Guidelines were the first to be statutorily mandated by the U.S. Congress.

Since 1985, USDA and the Department of Health and Human Services have used essentially the same process to prepare the dietary guidelines. An external Dietary Guidelines Advisory Committee (DGAC) has been appointed by the two secretaries to review and revise as necessary the guidelines. The members of the DGAC are widely recognized nutrition and medical experts. A series of public meetings are held to review and discuss the guidelines. Upon completion of the DGAC process, a technical report is sent to the two secretaries and reviewed within the two departments. In addition, in both 1995 and 2000, consumer research was conducted to test consumer reaction to specific design and content elements of the technical report. The consumer research is also used as one element in promoting the dietary guidelines.

Elements of the Dietary Guidelines

Between 1980 and 1995, the dietary guidelines were relatively stable (Table 1), maintaining seven guidelines. However, the 1995 guidelines reflected some exciting and important changes. More so than ever before, they put an emphasis on total diet; the wording in the 1995 guidelines moved away from individual foods in the direction of a total diet based on variety, moderation, and proportionality. The concept of total diet is reflected symbolically through the graphic of the 1995 Dietary Guidelines bulletin that links all seven guidelines together, anchored around the admonition to "Eat a variety of foods."

In the 1995 guideline on variety, the bulletin stresses a total diet rather than an individual food approach to healthy eating. The recommendation is to choose foods from each of the five major food groups in the Food Guide Pyramid. Also an emphasis is placed on foods from the base of the pyramid (grains) to form the center of the plate accompanied by food from other food groups.

For the first time, the dietary guidelines in 1995 recognized that with careful planning, a vegetarian diet can be consistent with the dietary guidelines and the Recommended Dietary Allowances. The guidelines also present a clear message that food sources of nutrients are preferred to supplements. This "food first" strategy is reinforced by a discussion of other healthful substances present in food, but not in dietary supplements. However, the 1995 guidelines do provide specific examples of situations where dietary supplements may be needed.

The 1995 guidelines also moved more forcefully in the direction of providing a discussion of the direct link between diet and health. Weight gain with age was discouraged for adults. Weight maintenance is encouraged as a first step to achieving a healthy weight. The benefits of physical activity are emphasized. And for the first time, a statement was included on the benefits of moderate alcohol in reducing the risk of heart disease. On this later point, both HHS and USDA were clear that the alcohol guideline was not intended to recommend that people start drinking.

In the 1995 guidelines there was also direct reference to the nutrition education tools that could be used to promote the dietary guidelines. The guidelines explain how consumers can use the three "crown jewels" to build a healthy diet: the Dietary Guidelines, the Food Guide Pyramid, and the Nutrition Facts Label.

The Dietary Guidelines 2000, released by President Bill Clinton in May 2000, break with the tradition of seven guidelines and now include ten separate guidelines. Not only do the Dietary Guidelines 2000 continue to emphasize a total diet approach, they also emphasize a healthy lifestyle. This is reflected clearly in three new concepts that are used as organizing principles for the 2000 Guidelines: "Aim for fitness," "Build a healthy base," "Choose sensibly."

TABLE 1

Dietary guidelines for Americans, 1980 to 2000				
1980 **7 Guidelines**	**1985** **7 Guidelines**	**1990** **7 Guidelines**	**1995** **7 Guidelines**	**2000** **10 Guidelines**
Eat a variety of foods	Eat a variety of foods	Eat a variety of foods	Eat a variety of foods	Let the Pyramid guide your food choices
Maintain ideal weight	Maintain desirable weight	Maintain healthy weight	Balance the food you eat with physical activity—maintain or improve your weight	Aim for a healthy weight
Avoid too much fat, saturated fat, and cholesterol	Avoid too much fat, saturated fat, and cholesterol	Choose a diet low in fat, saturated fat, and cholesterol	Choose a diet low in fat, saturated fat, and cholesterol	Choose a diet that is low in saturated fat and cholesterol and moderate in total fat
Eat foods with adequate starch and fiber and fruits and vegetables	Eat foods with adequate starch and fiber and fruits and vegetables	Choose a diet with plenty of grain, fruit, and vegetable products	Choose a diet with plenty of grain, fruit, and vegetable products	Eat a variety of grains daily, including whole grains Eat a variety of fruits and vegetables daily
Avoid too much sugar	Avoid too much sugar	Use sugars only in moderation	Choose a diet moderate in sugars	Choose beverages and foods to moderate your intake of sugars
Avoid too much sodium	Avoid too much sodium	Use salt and sodium only in moderation	Choose a diet moderate in salt and sodium	Choose and prepare foods with less salt
If you drink alcohol, do so in moderation	If you drink alcoholic beverages, do so in moderation	If you drink alcoholic beverages, do so in moderation	If you drink alcoholic beverages, do so in moderation	If you drink alcoholic beverages, do so in moderation
				Keep food safe to eat
				Be physically active each day

There is now a separate guideline for physical activity that states, "Be physically active every day." In addition to helping to maintain a healthy weight, this guideline also discusses the other health benefits of physical activity. Specific quantitative recommendations are given for amount of physical activity for adults (30 minutes or more) and children (60 minutes or more) per day. For the first time ever there is now a guideline on food safety. Again, this reinforces components of a healthy diet and healthy lifesyle.

The consumer research that was conducted as part of the Dietary Guidelines 2000 process influenced the development of the guidelines. One clear message is that consumers preferred simple, action-oriented guidelines. Thus the guidelines themselves are much more direct and action-oriented as evidenced by: "Aim for a healthy weight!" or "Keep foods safe to eat."

The guidelines are more consumer-friendly and emphasize practical ways in which consumers can put the concepts into practice. To that end, sections entitled "Advice for Today" are included at the end of each individual guideline and include suggestions on key ways to operationalize the guidelines. The consumer research on the 2000 Dietary Guidelines indicated that consumers particularly liked the Advice for Today section.

Comparison with Other Dietary Guidelines

A large number of countries—both industrialized and developing countries—have authoritative sets of dietary guidelines. Despite the vastly different geographical and sociocultural contexts of the countries, there are six elements that are common to the sets of dietary guidelines that are in place. Those elements are: (1) Aim for a healthy weight; (2) Let the Food Pyramid guide your choices; (3) Eat a variety of grains daily, especially whole grains; (4) Choose a diet that is low in saturated fat and cholesterol and moderate in total fat; (5) Choose and prepare foods with less salt; (6) If you drink alcoholic beverages, do so in moderation.

A guideline on variety is common, and is often the core element used to reflect the concepts of dietary diversity. The variety ranges from general statements such as, "Eat a variety of foods," to a very specific quantification, as found in the Japanese guideline, which states that, to obtain well-balanced nutrition with a variety of foods, one should eat thirty foodstuffs a day.

Many of the country-specific dietary guidelines emphasize limiting or moderating total fat and saturated fat intake. Where there is a quantification of limits, this is most commonly a diet containing no more than 30 percent of total energy from fat and less than 10 percent of energy from saturated fat.

Countries typically also include a weight guideline, which emphasizes very clearly the maintenance or achievement of a healthy weight; in the French guideline, there is more specificity indicating individuals should weigh themselves monthly. Most of the dietary guidelines worldwide promote a plant-based diet as the building block of healthful eating. To that end, many countries emphasize grains as the basis of good diet. Reduction of salt and/or sodium is emphasized in a number of the sets of dietary guidelines.

Finally, the issue of alcohol consumption is addressed in many sets of dietary guidelines. There is always a level of caution related to the role of alcohol as part of a healthy diet. The 2000 dietary guidelines for Americans, as an example, indicate that benefits of alcohol in reducing the risk of heart disease can be achieved in other ways, such as maintaining a healthy weight, cessation of smoking, increasing physical activity, and reducing the level of fat and saturated fat in the diet. Indeed, countries like Venezuela go even further and specify: "Alcoholic beverages are not part of a healthy diet" (14).

Comparison with Disease-Specific Guidelines

A number of professional associations such as the American Heart Association (AHA) and American Cancer Society (ACA) have developed sets of dietary guidelines. Clearly the AHA and ACS have somewhat different objectives in developing their specific sets of guidelines; the American Heart Association guidelines put forward recommendations for a healthful diet, which if followed, reduces the risk of heart disease. Similarly, recommendations from the American Cancer Association are for dietary guidelines which, if followed, reduce the risk of cancer. Given the somewhat different objectives, there is a remarkable degree of similarity in the three sets of guidelines. Here again, the USDA/HHS, the AHA, and the ACA each recommend dietary guidelines related to weight, total saturated fat, salt, and alcohol in moderation as the basis of a healthful diet.

Guidelines for Children under Age Two

A limited number of countries have some parts of their food-based guidelines devoted to children less than two years of age. In most cases, the advice relates to a discussion of breast-feeding. Australia, for example, states: "Encourage and support breast-feeding." There is similar wording in guidelines from the Philippines and Singapore.

Most industrialized countries rely on national pediatric associations to guide the broad policy recommendations for infant feeding and/or feeding practices for the first two years of life. In almost all cases advice from pediatric associations stresses that human milk is the preferred form of infant feeding.

In devising food-based dietary guidelines for children under two, there is a clear need to segment this group of children by age groups: birth to 6 months, 6 to 12 months, and 13 to 24 months.

Future Directions

Worldwide major improvements in public health will be accomplished by an improvement in dietary patterns. Food-based dietary guidelines have been developed in a broad range of countries. A move toward consensus on food-based dietary guidelines is a practical way to develop core elements of global dietary guidelines that can be effectively promoted by individual countries as well as international health organizations.

See also **Body Composition; Eating: Anatomy and Physiology of Eating; Food Stamps; Government Agencies, U.S.; Nutrients; Nutrition; Nutrition Transition: Worldwide Diet Change; School Meals; WIC (Women, Infants, and Children's Program).**

BIBLIOGRAPHY

American Academy of Pediatrics. "Breastfeeding, and the Use of Human Milk." *Pediatrics* 100 (1997): 1035–1039.

American Cancer Society Advisory Committee on Diet, Nutrition, and Cancer Prevention. "Guidelines on Diet, Nutrition, and Cancer Prevention: Reducing the Risk of Cancer with Healthy Food Choices and Physical Activity." *CA Cancer Journal for Clinicians* 46 (1996): 325–341.

Krauss M., et al. "Dietary Guidelines for Healthy American Adults: A Statement for Health Professionals from the Nutrition Committee, American Heart Association." *Circulation* 94 (1996): 1795–1800.

National Research Council, Academy of Sciences. *Recommended Dietary Allowances*. Washington, D.C.: National Academy Press, 1989.

Peng, M., and V. Molina. *Food Dietary Guidelines and Health-Based Promotion in Latin America*. Washington, D.C.: Pan American Health Organization, 1999.

Shils, Maurice E., et al., eds. *Modern Nutrition in Health and Disease*. 9th ed. Baltimore, Md.: Williams and Wilkins, 1999.

U.S. Department of Agriculture and U.S. Department of Health and Human Services. *Nutrition and Your Health: Dietary Guidelines for Americans*. Home and Garden Bulletin 232. Washington, D.C.: U.S. Government Printing Office, 1980.

U.S. Department of Agriculture and U.S. Department of Health and Human Services. *Nutrition and Your Health: Dietary Guidelines for Americans*. Home and Garden Bulletin 232. Washington, D.C.: U.S. Government Printing Office, 1985.

U.S. Department of Agriculture and U.S. Department of Health and Human Services. *Nutrition and Your Health: Dietary Guidelines for Americans*. Home and Garden Bulletin 232. Washington, D.C.: U.S. Government Printing Office, 1990.

U.S. Department of Agriculture and U.S. Department of Health and Human Services. *Nutrition and Your Health: Dietary Guidelines for Americans*. Home and Garden Bulletin 232. Washington, D.C.: U.S. Government Printing Office, 1995.

U.S. Department of Agriculture and U.S. Department of Health and Human Services. *Nutrition and Your Health: Dietary Guidelines for Americans*. Home and Garden Bulletin 232. Washington, D.C.: U.S. Government Printing Office, 2000.

U.S. Department of Agriculture. *The Food Guide Pyramid*. Home and Garden Bulletin 252. Washington, D.C.: U.S. Government Printing Office, 1992.

U.S. Senate Select Committee on Nutrition and Human Needs. *Dietary Goals for the United States*. 2d ed. Washington, D.C.: Government Printing Office, 1977.

Eileen Kennedy

DIETARY SYSTEMS: A HISTORICAL PERSPECTIVE.

The urge to classify foods and frame complex dietary laws is as old as civilization itself, if not older. Most dietary systems around the world are explicitly religious. But some dietary systems that arose were more secular in nature; their ultimate goal was to maintain or restore physical health. The most influential of these were produced in Greece, India, China, and the modern West.

The superficial similarity of the ancient systems may have arisen from a common prehistoric root, or they may have influenced each other across trade routes. Separate civilizations also may have arrived at similar ways of describing physiologic functions because some human experiences are universal. The fact that most of these systems assess food qualitatively, using descriptive terms such as hot, cold, moist, and dry, appears to be coincidental. They do not understand or apply these terms in the same way.

Greece

The Greek dietary tradition stems ultimately from the body of writings attributed to Hippocrates of Cos. Dietary regimen in all these works was considered the most important way to prevent and cure disease, but the concept of diet encompassed much more than food intake. It also considered air quality, exercise, sexual activity, emotions, and the elimination of waste products. Although a fully elaborated theory of the four humors was not yet in place among the Hippocratic writers, in later years and especially in the writings of Galen of Pergamum it came to be the cornerstone of this system. Just as four elements were considered the building blocks of all physical matter, so four basic regulatory fluids were believed to control the human body. These are blood, phlegm, choler, and black bile or melancholy. Each in turn was described as hot and moist, cold and moist, hot and dry, or cold and dry, respectively. Every individual is born with a tendency for one humor to predominate, sometimes excessively so. This was called the complexion, which also was considered affected by age, gender, and a variety of external factors.

The Greeks also classified foods according to their propensity to increase particular humors in the body. Thus cucumbers were considered cold and moist, spices hot and dry. In a body with an abundance or plethora of any given humor, a food or medicine of the opposite quality would act as a corrective. This therefore was an allopathic system that corrected with opposites. The Greeks also were intensely conscious of the texture and consistency of food and how easily it might be broken down and passed through the body.

The Greek system was elaborated upon in several succeeding civilizations, the most important of which were the Byzantine Empire; the Muslim world, which stretched from northern India to Spain; and medieval and Renaissance Europe. Although folk beliefs in Central and South America were influenced by Hippocratic ideas introduced by the Spanish, it appears that an older native system forms the foundation of ideas there.

India

Ayurvedic medicine is rooted in medical texts known as the *Carakha Samhita*, which may have originated before the first millennium B.C.E. but were written down much later. They include a dietary system still practiced in the twenty-first century. This system bears some similarities to the Greek system, but in practical application it is quite different. Ayurvedic physiology also begins with elements, but it recognizes five: air, fire, water, earth, and space. Each in combination with another creates what is called a *dosha*, a basic life force that governs physiologic functions but not exactly a humor. For example, space and air combine to create the *vata dosha*, which controls movements within the body, such as respiration, circulation, nerve impulses, and even ideas. Fire and water combine to form the *pitta dosha*, which is the principle of digestion and metabolism. Water and earth create the *kapha dosha*, which is the structural principle, giving solidity to the body. Too much or too little of each of these forces causes illness. The key here is a balance. As in the West, individuals are presumed to be born with a certain predilection toward an excess of one *dosha*. This is the *prakriti*, comparable to the concept of complexion in the West.

Just as in the Western system, foods and medicines can increase or decrease the power of any one of the *doshas*. For example, a weak digestion (*pitta*) is improved by heating the body with spicy foods, while an excess of *pitta* causes inflammation and dehydration and is corrected with foods that moisten the body. A weak *kapha dosha* leads to brittle bones and joints, so solid foods that strengthen the body are required.

Another concept in this system is that of the *ojas*, a form of vital energy that supports the immune system. *Ojas* can be increased by meditation and moderate eating but also with special substances like ghee or saffron. Foods also are classified according to their specific virtues or *gunas*, twenty in total, which assign foods values, such as cold or hot, soft or hard, oily or dry, heavy or light, dull or sharp, solid or liquid. All these terms reflect how food behaves in the body. With an excess of hot *pitta* (digestion), a cold food would be prescribed. With an excess of *vata* (transport), something heavy or dry would be corrective. Like the Greek system, this one is allopathic.

China

Another major system arose in ancient China, and it too was based on a revered text, in this case *The Yellow Emperor's Classic of Internal Medicine*, composed by one of the so-called celestial emperors, Huang-ti. Probably it was written during the Han dynasty and thus is roughly contemporaneous with the other systems. The first important concept in this system is *qi*, translated as energy, life force, or spirit. *Qi* supports life and helps fight off malign external influences. It also flows through the entire universe, so the individual microcosm is linked to the macrocosm. Health results when the two are in harmony, as do prosperity, peace, and good crops.

The central governing principle in the Chinese system is the opposition of two basic universal forces, yin and yang. Yin is female, dark, cold, soft, empty, night. Yang is male, light, warm, firm, full, day. Universal as well as physical harmony depends on a balance of these two forces. In addition, phases or processes of transformation in nature, not exactly elements as building blocks of nature, exist. Here too are five: earth, fire, wood, metal, and water. As processes of change, they govern, for example, generation. Water makes trees grow, wood burned creates fire, fire creates ash. Earth is the source of metals, and metals flow like water when heated.

All physiological functions can be described in terms of these transformations, like breaking down and processing foods. Specific foods or drugs aid a particular process, build up good *qi*, or promote the flow of *qi* through the body, as does acupuncture. Just as in the other systems, this is a holistic medicine that takes into account exercise, air quality, sleep patterns, sexual activity, and of course diet to keep the yin and yang forces in balance, the *qi* flowing, and physiological transformations in good order. The idea that certain foods are heating, cooling, drying, or moistening appears to have been imported from India around the sixth century C.E.

The Modern West

The modern concept of diet is much narrower than in the ancient systems, for it is concerned merely with food intake, calories, vitamins, and the like. Little consideration is given to the holistic aspect of living in harmony with external influences. Diet is not carefully prescribed according to the individual's unique complexion and habits. Calorie needs are defined by the rate at which energy is expended. All bodies are assumed to require the same nutrients of a specified range to allow for genetic and other sources of variation. This line of reasoning stems from envisioning the body as an engine fueled by food, a concept that arose in the nineteenth century fol-

lowing the research of the chemist Antoine-Laurent Lavoisier and later of Justus von Liebig. Only with the discovery of vitamins in the early twentieth century was this transformation complete. The concept of diet also was defined more narrowly as food intake or as a strict regimen intended to promote weight loss.

See also **Calorie; China: Ancient and Dynastic China; Dietetics; Greece, Ancient; Indus Valley; Nutrition Transition: Worldwide Diet Change.**

BIBLIOGRAPHY

Anderson, E. N. "Traditional Medical Values of Food." In *Food and Culture: A Reader*, edited by Carole Counihan and Penny Van Esterik. New York: Routledge, 1997.

Fieldhouse, Paul. *Food and Nutrition: Customs and Culture*. 2d ed. London: Stanley Thornes, 1998.

Galen. *Galen on Food and Diet*, translated by Mark Grant. New York and London: Routledge, 2000.

Veith, Ilza, ed. and trans. *The Yellow Emperor's Classic of Internal Medicine*. Berkeley: University of California Press, 1972.

Ken Albala

DIETETICS. Dietetics is the integration and application of principles derived from several disciplines—including nutrition, biochemistry, physiology, food science and composition, management, food service, and the behavioral and social sciences—to achieve and optimize human health. Dietetic professionals translate the scientific evidence regarding human nutrition and use that information to help shape the food intake or choices of the public (ADA, 2002).

Dietetic professionals work with individuals and groups of all ages to assess nutritional health and provide recommendations and therapies to assist individuals, groups, and populations in achieving a diet based on scientific evidence. The diet is generally a variety of foods but may include supplements and tube or parenteral feedings. Nutrient needs vary based on age, genetics, body composition, health status, and lifestyle. Dietetic professionals specialize in different aspects of care: They serve as translators of nutrition science to the public, as specialists in business and industry, as advocates to change food policy, as managers of food operations, as educators and researchers, and as clinicians in many different settings.

Education of Dietetic Practitioners

The majority of dietetics professionals are registered dietitians (R.D.s) and members of the American Dietetic Association. These individuals have various job titles including but not limited to dietitian, nutritionist, medical nutrition therapist, food service director, and public health or community nutritionist. The R.D. signifies that the individual has completed an academic education leading to at least a B.S. in dietetics, with coursework in

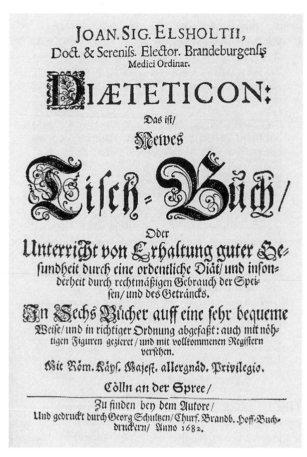

The 1682 *Diaeteticon* of Prussian physician Johann Sigismund Elsholtz (1623–1688) was one of the first medico-culinary works to treat the subject of dietary regulation and health, thus foreshadowing modern dietetics. ROUGHWOOD COLLECTION.

nutrition, social sciences, biological sciences, and food science, along with a planned clinical experience conducted under supervision for at least six months, and has passed a national credentialing examination. The credentialing examination for the R.D. was introduced in 1969. The education and clinical experience components were first established in 1927. In 2002, about 41 percent of R.D.s had master's degrees and about 4 percent had doctorates (Bryk and Soto).

Established in the early 1980s, a two-year credential as a dietetic technician registered (D.T.R.) involves the same three-prong approach of education, experience, and examination. The D.T.R. functions clinically under the supervision of an R.D., and often manages a food-service operation. The D.T.R. has a more limited scientific education, but has similar management skills. The accreditation of entry-level dietetics programs is done by the Commission on Accreditation for Dietetic Education, and the credentialing is under the Commission on Dietetic Registration. In 2002 there were about 75,000 R.D.s or D.T.R.s in the United States.

The Evolution of Dietetic Professionals

The American Dietetic Association was founded in 1917. Its immediate goal was to assist in the feeding of World War I soldiers and to "benefit as many as possible." At that time, preventing deficiencies and providing enough food to support health were key goals. The feeding of institutionalized patients in hospitals and sanitariums quickly followed, as well as the provision of diet therapy for conditions such as diabetes mellitus and nephritis. In the 1940s, recommended dietary allowances (RDAs) were introduced, setting a standard in gauging what to feed groups; the RDAs were established to feed populations, not individuals. At the same time, the role of diet therapy was expanding. By the 1960s, understanding of the role of nutrition in the treatment of chronic diseases such as cardiovascular disease was emerging. Dietetic professionals were designing formulas for feeding patients via tubes and evaluating the composition and consistency of commercial tube-feedings that were beginning to be introduced.

In the 1970s the role of dietetic professionals expanded to include assessing the nutritional health of hospitalized patients and recommending feeding based on this assessment. Dietetic professionals began to educate the public on the use of food labeling to encourage eating properly, and to place emphasis on the use of nutrition to prevent chronic disease. Programs such as WIC (the federal Women, Infants, and Children nutrition program) expanded the dietetic practitioners' role in women's and children's health. During the 1970s roles for dietetic practitioners diversified, with dietitians working in dialysis centers, in rehabilitation, in marketing and public relations firms, and for food companies. Within the American Dietetic Association, practice groups formed to meet needs in specialty areas, for example, taking consulting roles in long-term care facilities and nutrition support roles in hospitals. During the 1980s roles continued to expand, and specialty credentials in diabetes, nutrition support, renal care, and pediatrics were introduced. The 1990s saw an expansion into outpatient care, expanding private-practice opportunities, and a movement to cross-train and become multiskilled.

Medicare part B reimbursement for nutrition counseling of nondialysis renal patients and individuals with diabetes mellitus was introduced in January 2002. It is anticipated that reimbursement would expand to cover counseling for other conditions. Private insurance coverage for medical nutrition therapy is also increasing as proper diet and lifestyle are recognized as key elements in maintaining or enhancing the health of the American public. The role of the dietetic professional continues in managing disease, has expanded in prevention, and will expand to include forecasting disease as the impact of genetics research reaches health care. As Americans eat out more and purchase more prepared foods, the role of the dietitian in dining establishments and supermarkets should expand.

The early twenty-first century is witnessing a focus on enhancing well-being and physical strength and stamina through nutrition. The dietetics profession promotes a total-diet approach to nutrition, with balance, variety, and moderation key to successful nutrition health. The newest aspects of dietetic and nutrition counseling include functional foods (that is, foods that are modified to provide a health benefit beyond the food's traditional nutrients) to enhance health, the use of dietary supplements, and the integration of alternative products such as botanicals. Dietetic practitioners assist individuals in determining if products are beneficial, whether research has been too limited to be determinative, or if the products may in fact be detrimental. Opportunities for research on the value of these products in promoting health abound. With technological advances in data collection and storage, better analysis of dietary intakes should contribute to a better understanding of the role of nutrition in health and disease.

Summary

Dietetic practitioners translate the science of nutrition into practical applications for individuals, groups, and communities. This requires a solid foundation in cultural competency, including knowledge of food composition, preparation methods and cultural values associated with particular foods, and skills in the culinary arts as well as in nutrition, science, social sciences, management, and communications. Dietetic practitioners will continue to provide nutrition therapy to individuals and groups, manage the feeding of individuals and groups, provide public education, and contribute to research about the links between food, nutrition, and health. Dietetic practitioners have a major contribution to make in the public-policy debate on issues such as obesity and its prevention and management, hunger and its prevention, and genetic modification of foods. The role of dietetic professionals will expand as nutrition becomes a major focus in addressing health issues in the nation and the world.

See also **Dietary Assessment; Dietary Systems; Nutrition Transition: Worldwide Diet Change; WIC (Women, Infants, and Children's) Program.**

BIBLIOGRAPHY

American Dietetic Association (ADA). *Commission on Accreditation for Dietetics Education Accreditation Handbook.* Chicago: The American Dietetic Association, 2002.

American Dietetic Association (ADA). *Definition of Dietetics.* January 2002.

Bryk, J., and T. Soto. "Report on the 1999 Membership Database of the American Dietetic Association." *Journal of the American Dietetic Association* 101(8): 947, 2001.

Julie O'Sullivan Maillet

DIGESTION. Digestion can occur at many levels in the body; generally, it refers to the breakdown of macro-molecules or a matrix of cells, or tissues, into smaller molecules and component parts. This particular section will focus on digestion of food in the gastrointestinal tract: the process that is required to obtain essential nutrients from the food we eat. The gastrointestinal tract (GIT) is a highly specialized organ system that allows humans to consume food in discrete meals as well as in a very diverse array of foodstuffs to meet nutrient needs. Figure 1 contains a schematic of the GIT and illustrates the organs of the body with which food comes into contact during its digestion. These organs include the mouth, esophagus, stomach, small intestine, and large intestine; in addition, the pancreas and liver secrete into the intestine. The system is connected to the vascular, lymphatic, and nervous systems; however, the function of these systems in gastrointestinal physiology is beyond the scope of this article, which focuses primarily on the process of breaking down macromolecules and the matrix of food.

Mechanical Aspects of Digestion

Food is masticated in the mouth. Chewing breaks food into smaller particles that can mix more readily with the GIT secretions. In the mouth, saliva lubricates the food bolus so that it passes readily through the esophagus to the stomach. The sensory aspects of food stimulate the flow of saliva, which not only lubricates the bolus of food but is protective and contains digestive enzymes. Swallowing is regulated by sphincter actions to move the bolus of food into the stomach. The motility of the stomach continues the process of mixing food with the digestive secretions, now including gastric juice, which contains acid and some digestive enzymes. The action of the stomach continues to break down food into smaller particles prior to passage to the intestine. The mixture of food and digestive juices is referred to as digesta, or chyme. The stomach, which after a meal may contain more than a liter of material, regulates the rate of digestion by metering chyme into the small intestine over several hours. Several factors can slow the rate of gastric emptying; for example, solids take longer to empty than liquids, mixtures relatively high in lipid take longer to empty, and viscous, or thick, mixtures take longer to empty than watery, liquid contents.

In the upper part of the small intestine, the duodenum, receptors appear to influence the rate of gastric emptying either through hormonal or neural signals. Peristaltic motor activity in the small intestine propels chyme along the length of the intestine, and segmentation allows mixing with digestive juices in the intestine, which include pancreatic enzymes, bile acids, and sloughed intestinal cells. Digestion of macronutrients, which began in the mouth, continues in the small intestine, where the intestinal surface provides an immense absorptive surface to allow absorption of digested molecules into circulation. While the intestine from the outside appears to be a tube, the lining of the inner surface contains tissue folds and villi that are lined with intestinal cells, each with microvilli, or a brush border, which greatly amplify the absorptive surface. The intestinal cells can absorb compounds by several cell membrane–mediated transport mechanisms and then transform them into compounds, or complexes, that can enter circulation through the blood, or lymphatic, system.

What is not digested and absorbed passes into the large intestine. In this organ, water and electrolytes are reabsorbed, and the movements of the large intestine allow mixing of the contents with the microflora of bacteria and other microbes that are naturally present in the large intestine. These microbes continue the process of digesting the chyme. Eventually the residue enters the rectum and the anal canal, and stool is formed, which is defecated. Transit time of a non-digestible marker from mouth to elimination in the stool varies considerably: normal transit time is typically twenty-four to thirty-six hours, but can be as long as seventy-two hours in otherwise healthy individuals.

Breakdown of Macromolecules in Foods

Foods are derived from the tissues of plants and animals as well as from various microorganisms. For absorption of nutrients from the gut to occur, the cellular and molecular structure of these tissues must be broken down. The mechanical actions of the GIT help disrupt the matrix of foods, and the macromolecules, including proteins, carbohydrates and lipids, are digested through the action of digestive enzymes. This digestion produces smaller, lower molecular weight molecules that can be transported into the intestinal cells to be processed for transport in blood, or lymph.

Proteins are polymers of amino acids that in their native structure are three-dimensional. Many cooking or processing methods denature proteins, disrupting their tertiary structure. Denaturation, which makes the peptide linkages more available to digestive enzymes, is continued in the stomach with exposure to gastric acid. In addition, digestion of the peptide chain begins in the stomach with the enzyme pepsin. Once food enters the small intestine, enzymes secreted by the pancreas continue the process of hydrolyzing the peptide chain either by cleaving amino acids from the C-terminal end, or by hydrolyzing certain peptide bonds along the protein molecule. The active forms of the pancreatic enzymes include trypsin, chymotrypsin, elastase, and carboxypeptidase A and B. This process of protein digestion produces small peptide fragments and free amino acids. The brush border surface of the small intestine contains peptidases, which continue the digestion of peptides, either to smaller peptide fragments or free amino acids, and these products are absorbed by the intestinal cells.

Carbohydrates are categorized as digestible or non-digestible. Digestible carbohydrates are the various sugar-containing molecules that can be digested by amylase or the saccharidases of the small intestine to sugars that can be absorbed from the intestine. The predominant digestible carbohydrates in foods are starch, sucrose, lactose (milk sugar), and maltose. Glycogen is a glucose polymer found in some animal tissue; its structure is similar to some forms of starch. Foods may also contain simple sugars such as glucose or fructose that do not need to be digested before absorption by the gut. Alpha amylase, which hydrolyzes the alpha one to four linkages in starch, is secreted in the mouth from salivary glands and from the pancreas into the small intestine. The action of amylase produces smaller carbohydrate segments that can be further hydrolyzed to sugars by enzymes at the brush border of the intestinal cells. This hydrolysis step is closely linked with absorption of sugars into the intestinal cells.

Non-digestible carbohydrates cannot be digested by the enzymes in the small intestine and are the primary component of dietary fiber. The most abundant polysaccharide in plant tissue is cellulose, which is a glucose polymer with beta one to four links between the sugars. Amylase, the starch-digesting enzyme of the small intestine, can only hydrolyze alpha links. The non-digestible carbohydrates also include hemicelluloses, pectins, gums, oligofructose, and inulin. While non-digestible, they do affect the digestive process because they provide bulk in the intestinal contents, hold water, can become viscous, or thick, in the intestinal contents, and delay gastric emptying. In addition, non-starch polysaccharides are the primary substrate for growth of the microorganisms in the large intestine and contribute to stool formation and laxation. Products of microbial action include ammonia, gas, and short-chain fatty acids (SCFA). SCFA are used by cells in the large intestine for energy and some appear in the circulation and can be used by other cells in the body for energy as well. Thus, while dietary fiber is classified as non-digestible carbohydrate, the eventual digestion of these polysaccharides by microbes does provide energy to the body. Current research is focused on the potential effect of SCFA on the health of the intestine and their possible role in prevention of gastrointestinal diseases.

For dietary lipids to be digested and absorbed, they must be emulsified in the aqueous environment of the intestinal contents; thus bile salts are as important as lipolytic enzymes for fat digestion and absorption. Dietary lipids include fatty acids esterified to a glycerol backbone (mono-, di- or triglycerides); phospholipids; sterols, which may be esterified; waxes; and the fat-soluble vitamins, A, D, E, and K. Digestion of triglycerides (TG), phospholipids (PL), and sterols illustrate the key factors in digestion of lipids. Lipases hydrolyze ester bonds and release fatty acids. In TG and PL, the fatty acids are esterified to a glycerol backbone, and in sterols, to a sterol nucleus such as cholesterol. Lipases that digest lipids are found in food, and are secreted in the mouth and stomach and from the pancreas into the small intestine. Lipases in food are not essential for normal fat digestion; however, lipase associated with breast milk is especially important for newborn infants. In adults

526

the pancreatic lipase system is the most important for lipid digestion. This system involves an interaction between lipase, colipase, and bile salts that leads to rapid hydrolysis of fatty acids from TG. An important step in the process is formation of micelles, which allows the lipid aggregates to be miscible in the aqueous environment of the intestine. In mixed micelles, bile salts and PL function as emulsifying agents and are located on the surface of these spherical particles. Lipophilic compounds such as MG, DG, free sterols, and fatty acids, as well as fat-soluble vitamins, are in the core of the particle. Micelles can move lipids to the intestinal cell surface, where the lipids can be transported through the cell membrane and eventually packaged by the intestinal cells for transport in blood or lymph. Most absorbed lipid is carried in chylomicrons, large lipoproteins that appear in the blood after a meal and which are cleared rapidly in healthy individuals. Bile salts are absorbed from the lower part of the small intestine, returned to the liver, and resecreted into the intestine, a process referred to as enterohepatic circulation. It is important to note that bile salts are made from cholesterol, and drugs such as cholestyramine or diet components such as fiber that decrease the amount of bile salt reabsorbed from the intestine help to lower plasma cholesterol concentrations.

Regulation of Gastrointestinal Function

Regulation of the gastrointestinal response to a meal involves a complex set of hormone and neural interactions. The complexity of this system derives from the fact that part of the response is directed at preparing the GIT to digest and absorb the meal that has been consumed in an efficient manner and also at signaling short-term satiety so that feeding is terminated at an appropriate point. Traditionally, physiologists have viewed the regulation in three phases: cephalic, gastric, and intestinal. In the cephalic phase, the sight, smell, and taste of foods stimulates the secretion of digestive juices into the mouth, stomach, and intestine, essentially preparing these organs to digest the foods to be consumed. Experiments in which animals are sham fed so that food consumed does not actually enter the stomach or intestine demonstrate that the cephalic phase accounts for a significant portion of the secretion into the gut. The gastric and intestinal phases occur when food and its components are in direct contact with the stomach or intestine, respectively. During these phases, the distension of the organs with food as well as the specific composition of the food can stimulate a GIT response.

The GIT, the richest endocrine organ in the body, contains a vast array of peptides; however, the exact physiological function of each of these compounds has not been established. Five peptides, gastrin, cholecystokinin (CCK), secretin, gastric inhibitory peptide (GIP), and motilin are established as regulatory hormones in the GIT. Multiple aspects have been investigated to under-

stand their release and action. For example, CCK is located in the upper small intestine; protein and fat stimulate its release from the intestine, while acid inhibits its secretion. Once released, it can inhibit gastric emptying and stimulate secretion of acid and pancreatic juice and contraction of the gall bladder. In addition, it stimulates motility and growth in the GIT and regulates food intake and insulin release. Among the other established gastrointestinal peptides, secretin stimulates secretion of fluid and bicarbonate from the pancreas, gastrin stimulates secretion in the stomach, GIP inhibits gastric acid secretion, and motilin stimulates the motility of the upper GIT. In addition to investigating the various factors causing release of these hormones and the response to them, physiologists are also interested in the interactions among hormones as well as those with the nervous system, since the response to a meal involves release of many factors.

Obtaining food and digesting it efficiently are paramount to survival. The human GIT system most likely evolved during the period when the species acquired its food primarily through hunting and gathering. The overlapping regulatory systems, combined with an elevated capacity to digest food and absorb nutrients, insured that humans used food efficiently during periods in which scarcity might occur.

See also **Eating; Intestinal Flora; Microbiology.**

BIBLIOGRAPHY

Cordian, L. "Cereal Grains: Humanity's Double-edged Sword." *World Review of Nutrition and Dietetics* 84 (1999): 19–73.

Johnson, Leonard R., ed. *Gastrointestinal Physiology*. St. Louis, Mo.: Mosby, 1997.

Barbara O. Schneeman

DINNER. Dinner is the important meal in the daily or another cycle of meals, typically requiring more formal culinary arrangements, table trappings, and etiquette, and probably more abundant foods and drinks. While rural households have tended to share the main daily meal during daylight hours, industrial societies have pushed dinner into the evening, thereby making this meal more important than breakfast, lunch, tea, subsequent supper, or any intervening or alternative snack. Major meals within weekly, monthly, and annual cycles are often identified as "dinner" (Sunday meals, Christmas, and Thanksgiving). However, with rites of passage, dinner's importance may be transcended by something grander: a banquet, feast, wake, or wedding breakfast.

In the West, all family members attend the conventional dinner. In religious homes, the meal may be offered with grace. In some patriarchal versions of the family dinner, the head of the family sits in a carver (chair with arms) at one end of the table while a woman (generally the wife)

A large dinner given by the Third Army Corps Union for former commander Major General D. E. Sicles at Delmonico's in New York, February 22, 1873. It was not customary in this period for women to be present at such "public" meals. FROM *FRANK LESLIE'S ILLUSTRATED NEWSPAPER*, MARCH 2, 1873. © CORBIS.

serves the meal. The household might bring out a special set of matching crockery or "dinner service," especially when guests are in attendance. A succession of courses is served that often centers on a meat dish—most impressively, turkey, prime rib, or spring lamb—and some occasions conclude with a dessert course.

Beyond immediate family gatherings, a dinner can be elaborate, involving written invitations, keen anticipation (or dread) on the part of the guests, and requiring toasts and speeches. On such formal occasions, diners wear special clothing, such as a dinner jacket or tuxedo for men. As it is maintained by dedicated food-and-wine societies, dinner extends through many courses of exquisite foods and matching drinks. Courting couples become acquainted over restaurant dinners and cook together for newly shared friends. Homecomings, departures, graduations, new jobs, business deals, and the like are ready excuses for a dinner date, often outside the home.

In the language of anthropologist Mary Douglas in her essay "Deciphering a Meal," dinner is a "stressed" event. She found her everyday, culinary pattern to be "one element stressed accompanied by two or more unstressed elements" (p. 67), that is, she cooked one main meal (dinner) and two minor meals (breakfast and lunch). Further, dinner tended to comprise one main and two minor dishes, and each dish had one centerpiece food and two accompaniments. This approach to dinner was no more than the pattern within a "certain segment of the middle classes of London" when Douglas wrote in 1972.

Meals are highly culturally variable, with one, two, three, four, or more meals per day being quite common. Meals vary considerably in timing and format, with fixed hours being a modern obsession. The daily meal routine differs among town and country settings, social classes, and between the sexes. In ancient times, monarchs dined behind screens as the gods had done; then they came to sit in full view or "in state." Women and men have dined apart in many cultures, perhaps in separate rooms or with the men going "out," leaving women and children at home. Women and men have also alternated flirtatiously around tables as "roses and thorns." The patterns of dining of present-day diners and their immediate forebears have remained constantly in flux.

Given the difficulty of establishing general principles of dinner, let alone transferring the concept to other cultures, this entry concentrates on a recognizable Western tradition that took shape in the nineteenth century. During that time, wealthy families agreed on smaller evening dinner parties, while working-class families gathered in their homes for dinner after a hard day at work or school. Much gastronomic attention has been devoted to this central social occasion, yet as meals are always evolving, questions arise regarding dinner's survival.

The Invention of Dinner

Throughout history, city dwellers tended to dine later and longer. Also, many travelers made the evening meal their main meal, as this was the time when they and their horses generally settled into an inn. In agrarian communities, however, where work began at daybreak, the first and principal meal occurred in the middle of the day. In medieval Europe, this midday meal was ideally eaten at the ninth hour after sunrise or "none," from which the word "noon" derives its meaning. This meal might have been taken in the fields and, especially in hotter climates such as the Mediterranean, been followed by a siesta.

President Thomas Jefferson illustrated the typical routine of an eighteenth-century rural gentleman. During his retirement at his home Monticello, he had two main meals per day: breakfast at around 9:00 A.M. and dinner at around 4:00 P.M. In a letter to Thaddeus Kosciusko on 26 February 1810, Jefferson described this routine: "My mornings are devoted to correspondence. From breakfast to dinner I am in my shops, my garden, or on horseback among my farms; from dinner to dark, I give to society and recreation with my neighbors and friends; and from candle-light to early bed-time I read."

Consuming two substantial meals—a late breakfast and a dinner (around 3:00 or 4:00 P.M. in the country and as late as 6:00 P.M. in town)—was also the pattern in England. During the nineteenth century, however, Arnold Palmer indicates that mealtimes became very uncertain. Eventually 8:00 P.M. became fashionable for dinner, a move that was in response to the longer business day and later parliamentary and court sittings. Workplaces were increasingly located at a greater distance from households, making it harder to return home for a main meal before work ended. This change was not a problem, as the evening meal was more easily lit with gas and electricity rather than the candles of the previous centuries. A more substantial luncheon occurring around 12:30 or 1:00 P.M. eventually filled the emerging hole in the middle of the day.

Confirming a similar pattern in the United States, Harvey A. Levenstein claims in *Revolution at the Table* that a new fascination with sophisticated food helped move dinner well into the evening. Before the 1870s, dinnertime was usually in the early or mid-afternoon, followed by tea and supper. In the last quarter of the nineteenth century, however, "upper-class males liked at least to appear to be engaging in productive activities during the day" and wanted their main meal afterward (p. 17).

Meanwhile, the emerging working class settled into their principal meal immediately after work, which was generally around 6:00 P.M. In the new world of highly differentiated production and consumption, social reformers and others, often with religious motivations, depicted the ideal family around their humble but sufficient table—the husband having put food there through his honest labors and the good woman through her thrifty shopping.

A similar movement occurred in France and was detailed in "Food Allocation of Time and Social Rhythms" in the journal *Food and Foodways*. The social elite used the same words for meals for several centuries, but they fluctuated in times, content, and relative importance. Most strikingly, each meal gradually moved later in the day until it replaced the next one. In particular, dinner (*dîner*) shifted from around 10 A.M. in 1550 until it reached late afternoon around the time of the Revolution, finally replacing supper (*souper*), which had previously been shifted from late afternoon to evening (p. 268). As a further complication, the schedule differed between social classes so that, according to a mid-nineteenth-century account, "the people déjeune, the bourgeoisie dines, the nobility sups. A man's stomach gets up earlier or later depending on his distinction" (p. 210). The French word *déjeuner* has been left untranslated rather than choosing between "breakfast" and "lunch."

A second major change in the wealthy European table contributed to the emergence of a recognizably modern dinner. This was the replacement of a series of grand tableaux of dishes, which servants would offer around, called *service à la française* (French service), with the succession of individually plated dishes, often served at smaller tables. This type of service was termed *service à la russe* (Russian service).

"Dinner, being the grand solid meal of the day, is a matter of considerable importance; and a well-served table is a striking index of human ingenuity and resource," extolled Isabella Beeton in 1861 in the long-lasting English "bible," the *Book of Household Management in London* (p. 905). In her sample "Bills of Fare," breakfasts warrant a mere half-page, although this is twice as much as luncheons. Three pages are devoted to "Ball Suppers" for sixty persons. In comparison, dinners occupy forty-seven pages. This section lists each month's menus, which are divided into five successive sets of dishes: "First Course" (soups and fishes); "Entrees" (various "made" meat dishes, such as pork chops and lobster ragout); "Second Course" (impressive meats such as roasts, hams, and pies); "Third Course" (game "removed" or replaced by sweet dishes); and "Dessert" (fruits and ices). Diagrams show

how each course is to be arrayed on the table around the central vase of flowers.

In deference to the direction in which dinner was heading, Beeton's book has a few concluding suggestions on *service à la russe*. The menus run through a simplified version of the *service à la française* progression that would become the standard dinner, namely, soup, fish, meat, and dessert. (Evocatively, the four courses make an evolutionary ascent from the primordial stew to the ethereal.) Yet confusion rules because, to cite one small complication, the British and Australian "entrée" precedes the main dish, which is the "entrée" for Americans. Cheese is a common additional course, before dessert in the French system and after dessert in the English.

In addition, Beeton's monthly suggestions conclude with "Plain Family Dinners," where she gives two menus for each day of the week. These comprise either two dishes (a meat dish plus sweet pudding) or, more often, three (with the addition of preliminary soup or fish dish). In the early twenty-first century, three-course dinners remain standard. For example, in the American classic *Joy of Cooking*, the successors to Irma S. Rombauer suggest lunch and dinner menus, both possibly with only two courses, whereas dinner usually has three (pp. 22–23). Lunch is lighter and more likely to include something obviously ethnic, particularly Italian (for example, minestrone). Dinner perhaps opens with soup (Greek lemon soup), salad, or fish, followed by a meat dish (lamb chops with roast garlic and cognac) accompanied by perhaps two vegetable dishes (pommes Anna, turnip purée) or rice or sometimes bread. Both lunch and dinner conclude with a tart, cake, or other dessert (such as apple spice cake).

The gastronomic literature that blossomed in the early nineteenth century promoted the intimate bourgeois supper that became the modern dinner. Writers of this period stressed the dependence on a good cook, the host's responsibility for the well-being of guests, the guests' responsibility to be punctual, and the optimum number at table in order to preserve "general" (that is, shared) conversation. Instead of large, aristocratic gatherings, the ideal number of guests became "not fewer than the graces [three] nor more than the muses [nine]."

Jean Anthelme Brillat-Savarin, who published *The Physiology of Taste* in 1825, assumed that a dinner (*dîner*) could be the "last affair of the day" and should conclude between 11:00 P.M. and midnight. Brillat-Savarin's "Meditation 14" includes twelve rules to optimize the "pleasure of the table," such as a room temperature between 13–16 degrees Réaumur (around 60–68°F), a progression from the most substantial foods to the lightest, and from the simplest wines to the most heady, and so on. Guests had to number "no more than twelve, so that conversation may always remain general," although he plainly enjoyed even smaller dinners that met just four conditions: "food at least passable, good wine, agreeable companions, and enough time" (1949, pp. 192–193).

A decade later, in London, Thomas Walker wrote about "aristology," or the art of dining, in his weekly newspaper *The Original*. In urging that dinner invitations make clear who is attending and what will be served, Walker included: "we shall sit down to table at half-past seven," yet he preferred the old system of an afternoon dinner (with male colleagues) and a separate supper as an opportunity for "wit, brilliancy and ease." As for guests, he stated: "Eight I hold to be the golden number, never to be exceeded without weakening the efficacy of concentration."

Walker's enthusiasm was not restricted to simplifying the dinner of the wealthy. As a police magistrate, he believed that the cure for poverty was self-dependence, which required the cultivation of domestic economy. In the "cheerless home," he wrote, the wife was absent or intoxicated, and possessions were often taken to the pawnbrokers. Coming home to angry words, then blows, the husband fled to the public house, where the wife came to collect him but also tended to stay herself. Meanwhile, in the "well-ordered" home, the returning husband found a "kindly woman, a cheerful fire, quiet children, as good a meal as his means will allow, ready prepared, every want anticipated."

The ideal of the modern dinner—ranging in style from the elegant dinner party to the virtuous, homely repast—was in place before the twentieth century. The advocates of this ideal helped set the stage for the "proper meal," to which British diners became committed, as evidenced in surveys such as *Women, Food, and Families* by Nickie Charles and Marion Kerr. People expected a hot course of "meat and two veg," which would be cooked by the mother or wife. However, dinner's relatively stable form was already breaking up again.

Disintegration

In the early twenty-first century, Sunday dinner has been giving way to more casual alternatives, notably brunch. Except for the exceptional "dinner party," the evening meal has become less rigid in expected fare, manners, and even attendance. Where morning newspapers had once intruded upon breakfast, prime-time television now interrupts dinner conversation. With both parents having to work, children often turn into individualistic snackers.

The conventional dinner has been perhaps an unnecessarily private refuge of the nuclear family or a showplace for privilege, with items such as fabulously expensive wines. The expansion of the food-service industry with street outlets, informal cafés, and restaurants has opened up an often more pluralistic, democratic marketplace that has restored the street life of the past. Yet many studies have demonstrated that family dinners assist in the socialization of children; psychological research has found that children who share meals are better adjusted and do better at school. At the same time, epidemiological studies (some of which are summarized in the article by James S. House and colleagues) have suggested that people who share meals with others live longer than solitary eaters. Treating late twentieth-century meal trends as alienating, Australian gastronomic author Michael Symons argues in *The Shared Table* for more "authenticity," in the sense of meals that bring people closer to each other and their physical world; that is, dinner makes us human.

These are not trifling particulars, as Thomas Walker, in *The Original* on Wednesday, 9 September 1835, maintained:

> Dining is an occurrence of every day of our lives, or nearly so, and as our health and spirits depend in great measure upon our vivid enjoyment of this our chief meal, it seems to me a more worthy object of study than those unreal occupations about which so many busy themselves in vain.

See also **Breakfast**; **Etiquette and Eating Habits**; **Lunch**; **Meal**; **Table Talk**; **Tea (Meal)**.

BIBLIOGRAPHY

Brillat-Savarin, Jean Anthelme. *The Physiology of Taste: Or, Meditations in Transcendental Gastronomy.* Translated by M. F. K. Fisher. New York: The Heritage Press, 1949. Originally *La Physiologie du gout*, Paris, 1826, although appearing in 1825.

Charles, Nickie, and Marion Kerr. *Women, Food and Families.* Manchester, U.K.: Manchester University Press, 1988.

Douglas, Mary. "Deciphering a Meal." *Daedalus* 101 (1972): 61–81.

"Food Allocation of Time and Social Rhythms." Special double issue. *Food & Foodways* 6, no. 3–4 (1996).

House, James S., Karl R. Landis, and Debra Umberson. "Social Relationships and Health." *Science* 214 (July 1988): 540–545.

Levenstein, Harvey A. *Revolution at the Table: The Transformation of the American Diet.* New York: Oxford University Press, 1988.

Palmer, Arnold. *Movable Feasts: A Reconnaissance of the Origins and Consequences of Fluctuations in Meal-times with Special Attention to the Introduction of Luncheon and Afternoon Tea.* London: Oxford University Press, 1952. Second edition, 1984.

Rombauer, Irma S., Marion Rombauer Becker, and Ethan Becker. *Joy of Cooking.* Revised edition. New York: Scribners, 1998. Original edition, 1931.

Symons, Michael. *The Shared Table: Ideas for Australian Cuisine.* Canberra: AGPS Press, 1993.

Wilson, C. Anne. *Luncheon, Nuncheon, and Other Meals.* Stroud, U.K.: Alan Sutton, 1994.

Michael Symons

DISEASE: METABOLIC DISEASES.

Metabolism may be defined as those changes in liver cells that provide energy for vital processes. "Metabolic diseases" is a term that includes a vast array of genetic disorders whose effects may be exacerbated or ameliorated by diet. Several groups of these are recognizable and treatable.

One group of metabolic diseases is concerned with errors in the body that fail to preserve equilibrium of the water and salts. Dehydration results from excess water loss compared to intake. Normally, this is compensated for by thirst and the subsequent ingestion of water. Diseases result from loss of the thirst mechanism; excessive water is lost with diseases of the kidney or of the pituitary gland (diabetes insipidus). Diseases of the sweat glands may result in excessive loss of salt. Shock due to low salt in the circulation may occur as a normal blood pressure is not maintained.

Cystic fibrosis of the pancreas is a severe metabolic disease caused by an abnormality of a gene on chromosome 7. Infants may be born with obstruction of the intestine, develop severe diarrhea and/or chronic lung disease, or fail to grow properly. At present, treatment includes special easily absorbable formulas, large doses of vitamins, supplements of enzymes that are made in the pancreas, and frequent administration of specific antibiotics to treat or prevent lung infection.

Salt is lost in patients with the genetic disease cystic fibrosis, an error in one aspect of the function of the pancreas. Loss of function or destruction of pancreatic islet cells, another part of the pancreas, causes type 1 diabetes mellitus, one of the severe common metabolic diseases. The islets of the pancreas are the source of insulin, a hormone responsible for the metabolism of sugar. Without insulin, sugar (glucose) rises in the blood and is excreted in the urine together with excessive water and salt (sodium and chloride). Dehydration results in loss of excess sodium (a base or alkali) and results in the tissues becoming acidotic and the body is in "acidosis." Treatment requires administration of fluids and an excess of sodium compared to chloride (chloride functions as an acid in the body). Because insulin functions in fat metabolism, patients with diabetes may develop atherosclerosis, heart disease, and other complications due to abnormal deposition of fat. The amount of carbohydrate, protein, and fat in the diet must be regulated even in those receiving regular amounts of insulin.

In addition to the pancreas, disturbed function of any of the endocrine glands may result in metabolic disease. For example, the pituitary gland secretes growth hormone. Excessive growth hormone results in gigantism and acromegaly (i.e., overgrowth of parts of the body or the whole body, e.g., progressive enlargement of hands, feet, and face). Deficiency of growth hormone results in dwarfism. The thyroid gland secretes thyroxine, a hormone that controls metabolic rate. Excessive thyroxine results in excessive burning of calories, and affected children fail to thrive (Graves's disease). Insufficiency results in hypothyroidism. In the baby, this may be called cretinism (physical shortness and mental deficiency), and in the older child, myxedema (form of inelastic swelling of the connective tissue). If not treated, these children may be mentally retarded and fail to grow properly. The adrenal glands secrete hormones for maintaining blood pressure. Lack of adrenal function may result in shock. The adrenal glands also are important in sugar metabolism and lack of function may result in low blood sugar (hypoglycemia). Abnormalities of the fetal adrenal glands result in abnormalities of the development of the sexual characteristics and in hypotension or low blood pressure. The parathyroid glands are essential for normal bone function and metabolism. Abnormalities may result in a ricketslike syndrome, or in low blood calcium that may cause seizures. Abnormalities of the ovaries or testes result in abnormalities in sexual development. Abnormalities due to endocrine deficiencies may be corrected by replacement hormones. For those with excessive hormone secretion, surgery or treatment with drugs to inhibit the secretion of the hormone may be effective.

Vitamins

Inappropriate vitamin intake also causes metabolic disease. Vitamin A deficiency results in blindness; night blindness is due to lack of a specific metabolic product, rhodopsin, of vitamin A. Excessive vitamin A may result in increased intracranial pressure due to abnormalities of metabolism of cerebral spinal fluid. Thiamine is necessary for carbohydrate metabolism, and lack of thiamine results in beriberi, a very severe disease involving edema and heart failure. Some people with thiamine deficiency develop central nervous system abnormalities. Niacin is necessary for carbohydrate metabolism. Deficiency results in pellagra, a condition marked by diarrhea, abnormal coloration of the skin, central nervous system abnormalities, and death. Pyridoxine, vitamin B_6, is necessary for nerve and other functions. Deficiency results in seizures, abnormal sensation in the hands and feet, and anemia. Biotin is necessary for protein and fatty acid metabolism. Deficiency of biotin results in abnormalities of the hair and skin. Deficiency may occur in those who eat significant amounts of raw eggs. Deficiency of folic acid results in anemia. Deficiency in a pregnant woman results in a fetus with abnormalities of the spinal cord (e.g., spina bifida, myelomeningocele). Vitamin B_{12} deficiency results in abnormalities of nucleotides that are essential for gene replication and transcription. Clinically, vitamin B_{12} deficiency manifests as pernicious anemia, which, in addition to anemia, includes abnormalities of the central nervous system. Vitamin C (ascorbic acid) is necessary for the metabolism of interstitial (collagen) support substance. Deficiency results in bleeding, bone pain, and scurvy. Vitamin D is necessary for calcium metabolism. Deficiency results in abnormal bone formation and rickets. Deficiency also may result in secondary hypoparathyroidism, low serum calcium, and seizures. Excess may result in abnormal deposition of calcium in the kidneys and brain resulting in kidney failure and brain abnormalities. Vitamin E participates as an antioxidant. Vitamin K functions in clotting mechanism and bone

metabolism. Treatment of any of the vitamin deficiencies or excesses requires control of intake, unless due to primary metabolic diseases that may inhibit absorption of the vitamin or its proper metabolism.

Minerals

Of the sixteen minerals said to be essential to humans, several are of special importance. Sodium, already discussed, is essential for acid-base homeostasis (maintenance of a steady state). Potassium is essential for nerve transmission and its importance is noted in maintaining heart rate regularity. Chloride is essential for water homeostasis and acid-base balance. Low sodium and chloride may result in hypotension, and elevated sodium chloride, in hypertension. Calcium and phosphorus participate in bone metabolism and in nerve transmission. Low serum calcium may result in seizures. Iron and copper are necessary for hemoglobin formation. Copper is also important in protein formation. Iodine is essential for thyroid metabolism. Zinc participates as a cofactor for many of the liver enzymes. Other trace minerals have been suggested as essential elements. Deficiency or excess of any of the minerals may be prevented by appropriate dietary intake unless, like the vitamins, metabolic errors due to genetic abnormalities may relate significantly to ranges of intake needed to avoid deficiency or excess.

Organs

Any of the organs may participate in metabolic disease. Two are especially prominent, liver and kidney. The liver enzymes participate in protein, carbohydrate, and fat metabolism. Low protein intake may result in edema due to lack of serum albumin. Liver enzymes help maintain glucose homeostasis, and levels of vitamin and fat metabolism. Common metabolic diseases seen with liver failure include albumin deficiency, hematologic disease, hypoglycemia, abnormalities of vitamin D metabolism, abnormalities of fat metabolism, and metabolism of some of the minerals. The liver also is essential for acid-base homeostasis. The liver enzymes are most responsible for detoxification of various chemicals. Liver failure may manifest itself by high serum ammonia levels and ammonia intoxication. Liver scarring (cirrhosis) may be the end result of several insults. Dietary treatment usually includes a low-protein diet that helps avoid ammonia toxicity and may help hepatic healing. Dietary supply of those substances that cannot be produced because of deficient liver metabolism may mitigate deficiencies partially.

The kidney is important in excreting and conserving water. If the body is alkaline, the kidney secretes base; if the body is acidotic, the kidney secretes acid. The kidney regulates secretion of small proteins, amino acids, and glucose. Kidney disease (nephrosis, where body swelling is related to the loss of serum protein, or nephritis, due to inflammation of the kidney) may result in loss of protein. The kidney is active in the metabolism of vitamin D, and deficiency results in abnormalities of bone and parathyroid metabolism. Kidney disease may result in retention or excess of normal products such as ammonia and urea, or excretion of essential substances such as water. Lack of control of water excretion is renal diabetes insipidus (excessive urine due to kidney abnormality), in contrast to pituitary diabetes insipidus (excessive urine due to pituitary abnormality, resulting in a deficiency of the antidiuretic hormone).

"Inborn errors of metabolism" was a term first used by Sir Archibald Garrod in his Croonian lectures published in 1908. He defined these inborn errors as blocks in metabolic pathways causing genetically determined diseases. He developed the concept that certain diseases of lifelong duration occur because an enzyme governing a single metabolic step is reduced in activity or missing completely, based on his observations of patients with alkaptonuria (urine that turns black upon exposure to light due to the presence of an amino acid breakdown product), albinism (lack of pigment in body tissues, such as hair, due to a lack of enzymes associated with melanin), cystinuria (excessive amounts of the amino acid cystine in urine resembling a form of kidney stone), and pentosuria (abnormal excretion in the urine of pentose, a form of sugar not utilized by humans).

When Garrod diagnosed these patients, most were adults who had been asymptomatic in infancy and childhood. Moreover, he noted that these conditions occurred in families and in many of the families more than one sibling was affected. Parents and other relatives usually were normal. A high incidence of intermarriage was common among affected families.

Following Garrod's work, others began to look for distinguishing characteristics in related families. For example, in 1934, Folling was working in an institution for the mentally delayed. He tested urine with a chemical, ferric chloride, and found a number of severely retarded children and adults whose urine turned purple upon that reagent's addition. The cause of the color change was found to be due to phenyl ketone. He and others determined that the phenyl ketone resulted from an error in the metabolism of phenylalanine, an amino acid found in nearly all proteins (Jervis). Many patients were identified with phenylketonuria (PKU) over the next twenty years, but little could be done to prevent mental delays that accompanied this condition.

Though chromatography was invented in Russia at the end of the nineteenth century, it was a technique used mainly for identification of complex substances. In the early 1950s, a number of investigators, particularly Armstrong and co-workers (Armstrong et al.), developed a technique to remove phenylalanine from milk proteins and the ability to diagnose this condition in growing infants became available. A formula with low phenylalanine content was developed at about this time. This formula was prescribed for those diagnosed with PKU and is very similar to the formula that is fed infants with phenylke-

tonuria today. Though the infants with phenylketonuria progressed better than previously and indeed some progressed normally, a large number continued to experience delays in mental development. It was not until the Guthrie test was developed in the mid-1960s (Guthrie) that the diagnosis of phenylketonuria could be made almost at birth. This permitted the diet to be started at a much younger age. Many patients treated from birth progress normally.

Phenylketonuria is due to a disorder of the phenylalanine hydroxylating system. The gene for phenylalanine hydroxylase has been localized. Phenylalanine hydroxylase converts phenylalanine to tyrosine. Excess phenylalanine may be toxic or may convert to other toxic substances, or lack of the product tyrosine may be detrimental. Attempts to treat PKU only with added tyrosine did not completely correct the condition.

Newer instrumentation, gene analysis, and dietary control permit screening of the newborn for a large number of amino acid and other abnormalities; thus, many inborn errors of metabolism can be identified in the newborn and for some of these effective or palliative treatment is instituted. The studies of PKU are a model for many of the errors of amino acid metabolism (Barness and Barness). Each of these inborn errors of metabolism may present as a medical emergency, particularly in the newborn. One group of amino acids, termed branch-chain amino acids because of their chemical structure, improperly may form substances that smell like maple syrup. The disease is called maple syrup urine disease. Its treatment requires adjusting the intake of the branched-chain amino acids. Another group of branched-chain amino acids results in severe acidosis and depression of the bone marrow when inadequately metabolized. Two disorders are relatively common, methylmalonic acidemia and propionic acidemia. Some of these individuals respond to diet manipulation and large doses of vitamin B_{12}. Some patients present with an odor of sweaty feet due to a defect in the metabolism of leucine, one branched-chain amino acid. Decreasing dietary protein may ameliorate some of the worst signs of this disease.

One group of infants with amino acid and metabolic error may present with the odor of ammonia. They may become comatose rapidly. They have errors related to the breakdown into urea of one of the five amino acids. They cannot make urea from ammonia. Urea is a benign substance easily excreted in the urine. Affected infants are treated with a low-protein diet and frequently must also be treated with dialysis and ammonia-binding drugs to prevent catastrophic effects to the nervous system (Brusilow et al.).

Fatty acid metabolic disorders are causes of several muscle weakness diseases. Some patients affected by these conditions present with high blood ammonia, heart abnormalities, and coma. Liver disease may be a complication (DeVivo). These are divided according to the size (length) of the implicated fat. Many of the affected fats normally are excreted conjugated to the amino acid carnitine. Some of the worst effects of these disorders respond to the administration of carnitine and to limited intakes of the implicated fatty acid. Symptoms are aggravated by fasting, and intravenous glucose may be required.

Mason and Turner in 1935 reported a reducing substance identified as galactose in the urine of a number of children who were delayed markedly in development. The substance was found to be galactose and its source was human or cow's milk. Very young infants with the abnormal urinary substance were identified by this test. If allowed to drink milk, these infants frequently had seizures, became jaundiced, and vomited perniciously. They did not grow well. When milk was removed from the diet, they seemed to thrive. They experienced improved growth when they were fed with a soybean-based formula that contained no lactose, the principal sugar found in milks, human and other. Lactose is normally digested to galactose and glucose. The condition is called galactosemia because of the abnormally elevated galactose concentration in the blood.

Since the discovery and treatment of galactosemia, other errors in the metabolism of carbohydrates have been recognized. Some children cannot utilize fructose and develop symptoms similar to those experienced by untreated galactosemics. Children with hereditary fructose intolerance are interesting in that they consume breast milk and infant formulas made with lactose without difficulty. However, when given any food with table sugar, their symptoms become frightening. They quickly learn to avoid sugar or any food containing the fruit sugar, fructose. They grow normally and have wonderfully noncarious teeth. Other diseases of carbohydrate metabolism result in liver, heart, and kidney abnormalities. Some are accompanied by physical abnormalities.

Pauling and colleagues (1949) studied hemoglobin structure and found a specific mutation causing an alteration in the structure of hemoglobin. This led to the discovery of the errors in sickle cell disease. Subsequently, other genetic abnormalities have been identified as responsible for many hereditary anemias.

A common disease in adults is arteriosclerotic heart disease. Genetic abnormalities in cholesterol metabolism are believed to be responsible for atherosclerotic heart disease in some who suffer from this condition. Dietary manipulations and exercise beneficially affect a large percentage of these individuals. Others require drugs. Another group of patients with heart disease demonstrates a defect in metabolism of the amino acid homocystine. Treatment of the elevated homocystine with the same agents used for the treatment of the inborn error homocystinuria may reverse the condition.

Over four hundred inborn errors of metabolism have been diagnosed. Future genetic studies may reveal many more. Many carbohydrate, amino acid, and fatty acid abnormalities have yielded to effective treatment that must be maintained lifelong—a form of treatment is available for approximately forty to fifty of these conditions, with a similar number having experimental approaches. Some complex abnormalities, particularly those related to body structures and muscle diseases, await gene modification for effective therapy. Although each of the inborn errors, excluding the more common hematologic ones, may occur in only 1 in 4,000 to 1 in 100,000 live births, cumulatively they account for more than 1 in 1,000 of live births. Early diagnosis may prevent severe disabilities in progeny.

See also **Health and Disease; Microbiology; Proteins and Amino Acids.**

BIBLIOGRAPHY

Armstrong, M. D., K. N. F. Shaw, and K. S. Robinson. "Studies on Phenylketonuria." *K. Bop. Cje.* 213 (1955): 797–799.

Barness, E. G., and L. Barness. *Metabolic Diseases. Foundations of Clinical Management, Genetics, and Pathology.* Natick, Mass.: Eaton Publishers, 2000.

Brusilow, S. W., M. L. Batshaw, and L. Waber. "Neonatal Hyperammonemic Coma." *Advances in Pediatrics* 29 (1982): 69–86.

DeVivo, D. C. "Reye Syndrome." *Neurologic Clinics* 3 (1985): 95–114.

Garrod, A. E. "Inborn Errors of Metabolism (Croonian Lectures)." *Lancet* 2 (1908): 1–4.

Guthrie, R. "Blood Screening for Phenylketonuria." *Journal of the American Medical Association* 178 (1961): 863–866.

Jervis, G. A. "Studies of Phenylpypyruvic Oligophremia: The Position of the Metabolic Error." *Journal of Biological Chemistry* 169 (1947): 651–654.

Mason, H. H., and M. E. Turner. "Chronic Galactosemia." *American Journal of Diseases of Childhood* 50 (1935): 359–364.

Pauling, I., H. A. Itano, S. J. Singer, and I. C. Wells. "Sickle Cell Anemia: A Molecular Disease." *Science* 110 (1949): 543–545.

Lewis A. Barness

DISGUST. Some philosophers doubt that there is such an emotion as disgust, yet in spite of the concept's overlap and fuzzy edges, there is a learned discourse about disgust defined as a feeling of revulsion. The prime example is in the context of food. Disgust may cause shock, faintness, even vomiting, or at the least it may dull the appetite. Not only to taste, but also to smell putrefying flesh, to touch excreta or slime, or even to set eyes on an open wound may provoke disgust. As a form of strong rejection, disgust is not the antithesis of desire; its effects are too immediate, even unexpected and uncontrollable, like an instinctive reaction. Why should humans be equipped by nature with this capability?

Training

A social explanation of disgust focuses on nutrition and the need to train children to avoid known poisons. Babies are taught by their parents' expressions of disgust not to eat noxious things. From the classifying of foods as edible or disgusting, the idea is extended to reprehensible behavior and despised classes of people. The ascription of filthy doings to outsiders accords with theories about the construction of ethnic identity. This approach allows for local differences due to training: some people reject snakes, worms, live grubs, or mud as food, but others relish them. Cannibalism evokes widespread disgust except among cannibals.

The limitation of the social training explanation is that the things commonly regarded as disgusting are not especially harmful. The people who habitually eat what others call disgusting would seem to enjoy as much good health as their critics. Furthermore, if early training in discriminating nutritious food explains disgust, the training is inefficient: it lets pass a lot of poisonous plants, roots, and living organisms.

Hygiene

The work of Louis Pasteur (1822–1895) and Joseph Lister (1827–1912) on microbial infection gained new relevance to disgust through the revival of Darwinism. An approach via hygiene starts from finding a strong convergence of evidence across the world to show that disgust is a direct response to waste products of the human body, including feces, slime, spittle, pus, mucus, and phlegm, which may carry infection. The same feeling of revulsion is extended to eating similar products of other living organisms and to anything that suggests these body wastes, like snails, slugs, and bugs. Evolutionary biology suggests a genetically inherited disgust mechanism that protects from infectious diseases.

Both the social training argument and the biological argument are open to the objection that the risks of disease from eating sick animals are only probabilities. House flies, mosquitoes, rats, and lice are dangerous to the same degree of probability, but they provoke more annoyance than disgust in those they afflict. Many deadly poisons are not slimy and are quite unlike body wastes, and comparative evidence is missing.

The evolutionary approach invites interesting comparisons. Animals may feel disgust, but the theory of genetic inheritance needs to take account of the exceptions. Many female mammals habitually dispose of afterbirth, smelly, sticky, and slimy as it is, by eating it. Hares and other coprophagous ruminants eat their own feces as part of the normal process of digestion. Sows are known to eat their young. Carnivorous animals do not discriminate between the best cuts and the messy-looking entrails, and some species subsist mainly on carrion.

These two approaches to human disgust conflict, and each side can reproach the other for using selected evidence. The social theory focuses on what the biological theory regards as exceptional, and the biologists focus on the common behavior, discounting the exceptions. Obviously, inherited feelings of revulsion can be overcome by training. Cannibals are trained to surmount disgust at eating human flesh, as are those who enjoy mucus-like turtle soup, slimy innards, snails, live grubs, and sticky buns. If no evidence against the thesis is allowed to count, the argument must come to a standstill.

Both arguments are causal and teleological. Both downgrade the importance of this emotion, taking it to be designed (inefficiently) to achieve a limited objective. Neither explains why the onset of disgust should be so sudden or so violent, liable to rack the whole body. Apart from causal thinking, there is analogy.

Analogy

A new direction in brain sciences challenges the separation between mind and body (Damasio). In continuous interaction, physical and intellectual energies sift through a succession of images and order them by creating analogies. Instead of looking for specific functions, analogists look for interactions between a system and its parts. Instead of starting with nutrition, analogists start with the body-mind relation and ask how disgust responds to pressures from the cognitive system.

Analogy maps similarities, checks similar patterns for structural consistency. It is a precarious process of reasoning, like trying to hold a pattern steady in a shifting kaleidoscope. The number of possible analogies for any one pattern is infinite, and the pattern always threatens to dissolve. Only repeated enactment entrenches an idea. Entrenchment needs to be fortified by a mechanism of rejection that protects the established pathways from slippage. The digestive organs are the root for making sensations of disgust analogous to other contexts of rejection and for extending disgust to moral or social contexts. Disgust churns the stomach and produces nausea and a cold sweat. Interacting with the cognitive system, its various vivid analogies are a team of watchdogs protesting against changes that, if adopted, would tumble the edifice laboriously constructed by experience.

One of the side effects of disgust may be to reduce the risk of infectious food. Its main function is in the body-mind system, where it limits conceptual slippage. Disgust warns against concepts threatening dangerously to slide between categories.

See also **Acceptance and Rejection; Aversion to Food; Pasteur, Louis; Sensation and the Senses; Taboos.**

BIBLIOGRAPHY

Curtis, Valerie, and Adam Biran. "Dirt, Disgust, and Disease: Is Hygiene in Our Veins?" *Perspectives in Biology and Medicine* 44 (2001): 17–31.

Damasio, Antonio R. *Descartes' Error: Emotion, Reason, and the Human Brain.* New York: Putnam, 1994.

Goodman, Nelson. "Seven Strictures against Similarity." In *Problems and Projects*, pp. 437–447. Indianapolis: Bobbs-Merrill, 1972. Reprinted in *How Classification Works*, edited by Mary Douglas and David Hull. Edinburgh: Edinburgh University Press, 1992.

Mitchell, Melanie. *Analogy-Making as Perception: A Computer Model*. Cambridge, Mass.: MIT Press, 1993.

Mary Douglas

DISTRIBUTION OF FOOD.

The distribution of food in the United States can be as short as the distance from a farmer's or a consumer's garden to his or her kitchen table or as long as the journey from vineyards in South Africa to homes in South Dakota. Typically, the distribution of food moves along a complex supply chain that starts with chemical, seed, and feed companies in the agricultural input or agribusiness sector and ends on the consumer's plate at home or in a restaurant. This discussion, using corn as an example, follows food along a few relatively simple food distribution channels to reveal the many paths it takes as it travels from farm to fork.

Corn (maize) is one of the most widely produced grains in the world. In the United States, corn represents more than 40 percent of all grains produced. Four times more bushels of corn than bushels of wheat or soybeans were produced in the year 2000 (U.S. Department of Agriculture, 2001). For decades, university researchers and seed company scientists designed hybrid corn varieties that increase yields and improve quality. In tandem, chemists in public and private laboratories formulated fertilizers and pesticides to further enhance crop yields. In the late twentieth century, many seed and chemical companies merged and redefined themselves as life science companies to reflect advances in biotechnology. The application of genetic science to create new types of seed for corn, soybeans, and other crops touched off a controversy around the world about the safety and efficacy of the new seed supply and the food it produced. The link between the life science companies and consumers leapfrogged over the entire food distribution network as consumers protested this new and relatively untested technology that they perceived as a threat to their health and environment. While the controversy continued, food safety agencies in developed countries struggled with safety and labeling issues surrounding foods made from genetically modified ingredients. Life science companies and other agribusiness firms meanwhile continued to supply farmers with the seed, chemicals, and equipment needed to produce their chosen agricultural commodity, in this case, corn.

Once a farmer harvests the corn crop for the year, distribution of the raw commodity begins. At least two basic types of corn are produced, sweet corn for direct food consumption and field corn for food ingredients and animal feed. Each type has numerous varieties, brands, colors, and end uses. A small portion of fresh sweet corn might be sold at a roadside stand or in a farmers' market. In smaller communities, a farmer may deliver some sweet corn directly to a local grocery store or restaurant. Most of the new sweet corn crop is sold to commercial food processors, where it is canned or frozen.

Corn designed to be used as seed, animal feed, ingredients for food, or industrial products is sold to a local grain elevator. The choice for the farmer is to store the field corn on the farm and wait for the best market price over the course of the next year or to sell it to a grain elevator immediately. Some grain elevators are independent businesses, and some are owned by large food or feed companies that collect grain from across the land. At the elevator, corn is usually mixed and matched to achieve the quality demanded by the next buyer. Occasionally an elevator may handle only one type of corn grown by a few farmers who have contracted with a large food or feed company to supply a particular quality and quantity of grain. In this case, the identity of each type of corn is preserved. With bioengineered corn and other new varieties, the issue of identity preservation became a major issue. Traditional farming methods and grain elevator operations were incapable of keeping all varieties of corn separated and identified throughout the food distribution chain.

At the beginning of the twenty-first century, however, the development of technology and methods to preserve the identity and origins of all types of food was under great pressure to succeed quickly. Tagging and following foods from their origins to the point of retail sale was considered important for consumer choice and as a way for superior foods to capture higher market prices. It would also permit foods proven unsafe or undesirable to be traced back to their sources.

After leaving the grain elevator, about 20 percent of the corn was exported to a foreign country in 2000 (U.S. Department of Agriculture, 2001). The rest was sent to a feed mill or to a food processing or manufacturing plant. Some went to industrial plants that produce products like ethanol or plastics. At a feed mill, corn is further mixed with other grains and additives on its way to being fed to animals, such as hogs or chickens, many of which are later slaughtered for food. In fact, the bulk of the corn produced is used as animal feed. Corn used for human food usually goes directly to a food processing plant that specializes in producing basic ingredients, such as corn oil, starch, or flour. These ingredients are sold to food manufacturers, who use them in manufactured foods for consumers to eat. More complex food products, like taco shells, corn flakes, or corn bread, generally use ingredients purchased from food processors.

At the food manufacturer, major research and development departments create and test the safety and efficacy of food ingredients, flavors, and additives. They also experiment with new recipes, new packaging, and new ways to use corn in foods. Much attention is paid to the image of the food, its safety, its shelf life, its nutrition, and labeling. Several hundred new corn products are introduced to grocery shelves each year in an attempt to meet consumers' preferences and to capture part of their food dollars. This is also true for foods from other raw commodities, like rice, milk, eggs, and wheat. The average annual number of new food products introduced during the 1990s was 12,700, peaking in 1995 at 16,863 (Food Industry Institute, 1999; Food Industry Institute, 2000). Less than 5 percent of these new products were still on the grocery store shelves two years later.

Food products designed for the food service distribution channel also undergo extensive development and market research before going to market. These foods need less elaborate packaging and labeling and less advertising. They are designed to solve problems in a restaurant kitchen, problems of consistency and fail-safe cooking. Food service firms, such as quick service chains, purchase large and predictable quantities of food, often tailored to their specific needs. The distribution channel to food service firms was growing while the grocery channel was stable to declining at the end of the twentieth century. In any case, by the time the food product containing corn leaves the food manufacturer's warehouse, corn represents less than 20 percent of the value of the product. By the time a consumer purchases that product, corn represents less than 5 percent of the value (Elitzak, 2000).

The Grocery Channel

When a consumer food product leaves the manufacturer's plant for a grocery store, it has three channels through which it may travel. One is through a wholesaler's warehouse, where it is stored until a grocery store orders it. A traditional way of doing business is for the manufacturer to discount large quantities of freshly made food products to entice a wholesaler to "forward buy" the product. The wholesaler then stores it, marks it up, and sells it to a grocery store, making a profit on the difference in price. The costs of holding large inventories of food drove the industry to find more efficient ways to distribute food. With low inflation and fierce price competition at retail stores, wholesalers could not mark up their products enough to make reasonable profits. The quest to decrease distribution costs led to a consolidation of wholesale and retail firms and to the adoption of new information technologies.

Trade associations of retail food companies and manufacturers, such as the Food Marketing Institute (FMI) and Grocery Manufacturers of America (GMA), have long led the industry in adopting information technology. In the early 1970s, with the high cost of labor amplified by price inflation, the grocery store industry saw great potential in automating pricing activities. The Ad Hoc Committee on Universal Product Codes was established with representatives from major retailer and product manufacturing associations to develop a set of standards for identifying products that both the retailers

FOOD DISTRIBUTION SYSTEMS IN COUNTRIES OTHER THAN UNITED STATES

The food distribution system used in the United States is similar to that used in most of the westernized world (Europe, Australia, New Zealand, Japan). It requires good transportation and telecommunication systems and a modern food processing/manufacturing sector. In the United Kingdom there are few broad-line wholesalers, since the retail sector is more consolidated and handles its own distribution through tighter relationships with food manufacturers and producers. In other countries, large supermarket chains and chain restaurants receive food in much the same way as those in the United States, but there are a larger number of small retailers that procure their food directly from farmers or through third-party specialty wholesalers. In lower-income and emerging economies, the distribution of food is developing along the lines of the system used in the United States. Some level of household income and urbanization must emerge before supermarkets will become part of the retail food scene, and roads and communications need to be in place before a third-party distribution system can develop. For example, in China in 2002, Western-owned food manufacturers provided their own delivery to large supermarkets like Wal-Mart in the absence of a wholesale sector in the supply chain.

Globally, a few very large retailers are appearing around the world; their buying power tends to drive the delivery system and the types of food being purchased for retail sale. As these large retailers become more prevalent, the delivery system gets more consolidated, more responsive to consumers, and less open to small producers and farmers.

and manufacturers could agree upon. Two years later the committee decided to adopt a ten-digit Universal Product Code (UPC) as its standard (Kinsey, 2000). The ubiquitous bar codes were born, and in 1974 a supermarket in Troy, Ohio, became the first to implement scanning. The first grocery store chain to implement scanning chainwide (Giant Foods) did not do so until 1980 (Walsh, 1993). By 2000 virtually every supermarket used scanners, though they were not widely adopted in convenience stores. At the time, scanners were still not widely used in the food service sector due in part to a lack of standardized products and packages for food service buyers.

Using the information in banks of scanner data can give retailers valuable information with which to forecast sales, design customer loyalty programs, and con-

The Red Cross distributes food during a food shortage in Zaire.
© SABA PRESS PHOTOS.

trol inventory. When Wal-Mart appeared as a major competitor with the most sophisticated information and distribution system yet known to retailers, it became obvious that those in the retail food industry would have to learn how to do business in the same fashion. In 1992 an industrywide program called Efficient Consumer Response (ECR) was developed to solicit conversion to electronic technologies and sharing of retail data with suppliers. By 1999 this program was declared dead by industry leaders partly because it had outlived its usefulness, partly because only the largest chains were able to invest in the technology and talent that would make it work, and partly because many ECR activities had already been adopted under separate names, such as category management and activity-based costing. By the end of the twentieth century, however, developing systems that would allow business-to-business, electronic-commerce methods of sharing information about final sales at retail stores with wholesalers and manufacturers became an industry goal. With real time sales data, manufacturers could adjust production and shipment of new products to match the flow of sales and accomplish continuous replenishment and lower distribution costs.

Wholesalers were vulnerable in this new distribution system since retailers could bypass them by using their own distribution centers. To keep their retail customers, wholesalers developed new services, like helping stores with their billing, merchandising, inventory management, and a number of other tasks. Wholesalers make it possible for small stores to carry a large number of items even though they may sell only a few of some specialty items each year. Some wholesalers specialize in particular types of foods, such as organic food, imported food, or fresh produce. Those who handle the whole line of groceries are called broad line wholesalers. Shipping food from manufacturers to wholesalers and from wholesalers to retail stores involves a large number of trucks, many of which need to be refrigerated to keep cold and frozen foods at a consistent and safe temperature. One of the difficulties in transporting food is the attention that must be given to temperature and the time the product will last before its quality or safety deteriorates.

The third party, broad-line wholesaler channel declined in size with the rise of large grocery chains like Wal-Mart and Kroger. Large chains have their own distribution centers in which to aggregate, store, and ship foods to their own stores. In this case, manufacturers sell food products directly to supermarket chain's distribution centers. In 2000, forty-five of the largest fifty supermarket chains in the United States were self-distributing chains.

A third channel by which food reaches grocery stores is called "direct store delivery." In this case, manufacturers have their own delivery trucks and sales representatives who deliver products to individual stores, stock the shelves, remove out-of-date products, and promote their products in stores. Most beverages and salty snacks are delivered directly to stores by manufacturers' trucks and personnel. At the beginning of the twenty-first century, each of the three distribution channels carried roughly one-third of the volume of food to grocery stores.

In 1999 about 127,000 grocery stores operated in the United States, of which 25 percent were supermarkets and 45 percent were convenience stores. At that time a supermarket was defined as a retail store that carries a full line of groceries, meat, milk, and produce and has over $2 million in sales per year. Supermarkets captured 77 percent of all retail food sales, while convenience stores had only 6 percent. About 70 percent of the food eaten was purchased at some type of grocery store, where consumers spent about 53 percent of their food dollars in the late 1990s (Carlson et al., 1998).

With the advent of large and efficient supermarket chains, the propensity for grocery chains to build long-term relationships directly with manufacturers increased. The sharing of sales forecasts based on large volumes of computerized sales data facilitated these relationships. Knowledge about customers' preferences and shopping habits gained through analysis of sales data made it possible for large retail chains to negotiate for bargain prices as they placed orders that matched what they needed, when they needed it. In some cases this eliminated the need for "slotting fees," the price retailers charge manufacturers to place new products on their shelves. Computerized scanner data and Internet communications made it possible to integrate the supply chain between manufacturers and food retailers and to streamline the inventory in distribution centers. Sharing sales data and mutual tracking and analysis made it possible to substitute information for inventory, cutting costs in the distribution channel. It became possible to match deliveries more closely to the time of sales, converting the food distribution channels into a semblance of just-in-time delivery. The adoption of business-to-business e-commerce, a new way to do business for retail food stores and their suppliers, focused mostly on ways to save labor costs and to speed up ordering, delivery, and invoicing. The goal was to move products through the system as freshly and as quickly as possible.

Food Service Channel

The food that goes to food service establishments (restaurants, fast-food places, cafeterias) goes through a separate distribution channel. Here again are broad-line wholesalers, specialty wholesalers, and some distribution companies dedicated to a large retail chain like McDonald's or Burger King. This complex distribution channel links over 740,000 food service locations with more than 2,600 distributors. Consolidation among broad-line wholesalers was rapid around the beginning of the twenty-first century. They distributed about half of the food to various food service places (Friddle et al., 2001). Over 30 percent of the food eaten in the United States went through the food service channel. Consumers spent almost half of their food dollars in food service places.

Food service is divided into commercial and noncommercial enterprises. The noncommercial segment comprises about 10 percent of the food service sector and includes schools, hospitals, prisons, and the military. The commercial food service sector includes bars and restaurants, travel and leisure, vending machines, and take-out (ready-to-eat) food from grocery stores and various types of restaurants. Restaurants and bars comprise about 62 percent of all food service sales and are further defined by the type of service they provide. Quick service (fast food) restaurants captured thirty-three percent of consumer expenditures at food service places, while full-service restaurants captured 28 percent. Full-service restaurants are further classified by whether the average size of the check is over or under $10. The lower-priced full-service restaurants were growing in importance as a proportion of food service sales in the late 1990s. These restaurants also represented the largest consolidation of individual units into national and international chains.

Summary

Food is distributed from retailers to consumers primarily through grocery stores or take-out food places. For the most part, consumers shop and take home their own food. Home delivered food experienced a resurgence with the rise of Internet food companies in the 1990s and beyond. Online shopping and home delivery made up less than 1 percent of all food purchased for home consumption but was a persistent phenomenon in some neighborhoods. Food distributed through food service became ubiquitous by the end of the twentieth century. Food and beverages could be purchased from vending machines, street-side stands, drive-through eateries, office cafeterias, shopping mall food courts, and home delivery.

When consumers finally eat the food that has traveled all the way down a long supply chain, few think about the corn delivered to a grain elevator or the canning plant months earlier. Corn oil is in their salad dressing, their soft drink sweetener, and their taco shell, but it is largely taken for granted. It is assumed that it is fit to eat, nutritious, and safe. Few think about the hundreds of people involved in producing and transporting the final food product or the plethora of food regulatory agencies that license, monitor, and inspect the process. Food distribution is a long and complicated journey, but somehow an army of scientists, truck drivers, forklift operators, computer specialists, government scientists and inspectors, and many others make the system work.

See also **Biotechnology; Consumption of Food; Food Supply and the Global Food Market; Green Revolution; Marketing of Food; Political Economy.**

BIBLIOGRAPHY

Carlson, Andrea, Jean Kinsey, and Carmel Nadav. "Who Eats What, Where, and When?" Working Paper 98-05. St. Paul: The Retail Food Industry Center, University of Minnesota, 1998.

Elitzak, Howard. "Food Marketing Costs: A 1990's Retrospective." *Food Review* 23, no. 3 (September–December 2000): 27–30.

Food Industry Institute. *Food Industry Review 2000.* Elmwood Park, N.J.: Food Institute, 2000.

Friddle, Charlotte G., Sandeep Mangaraj, and Jean Kinsey. "The Food Service Industry: Trends and Changing Structure in the New Millennium." Working Paper 01-02. St. Paul: The Retail Food Industry Center, University of Minnesota, 2001.

Kinsey, Jean. "A Faster, Leaner Supply Chain: New Uses of Information Technology." *American Journal of Agricultural Economics* 82, no. 5 (December 2000): 1123–1129.

U.S. Department of Agriculture, Economic Research Service. *Agricultural Outlook.* (October 2001), Table 17, p. 39.

Walsh, John P. *Supermarkets Transformed: Understanding Organizational Technological Innovations.* New Brunswick, N.J.: Rutgers University Press, 1993.

Jean D. Kinsey

DIVISION OF LABOR. Division of labor, the parceling out of work based on various categories of identity, is understood commonly as a division made on the basis of gender. Indeed, food production, preparation, and even consumption are often differentiated on the basis of gender: men do some tasks and women do others. For example, cooking is widely recognized as an essentially female task (Murdock and Provost, p. 208). However, division of labor can apply to class, ethnicity, and age as well, and these categories also intersect with how people produce, prepare, and consume food.

Food Production

The division of labor begins when food production begins, which is a pattern rooted in the history of humanity.

The earliest humans tended to divide their work by category, where men hunted and fished and women gathered vegetable foods (fruits, vegetables, grains, and nuts). Among foraging societies, women still take on the greater portion of food-preparation tasks, such as grinding, pounding, boiling, and otherwise processing gathered and hunted foods into edible meals. For the few societies that still procure their food in the hunting-and-gathering strategy, a large percentage of the diet is made up of non-meat foods, with meat functioning as a much-desired and prized treat (Lee, pp. 256–258).

As societies adopted farming as a means of food production, dividing food production by gender persisted, yet much of this division was based on cultural understandings of gender rather than a physical advantage on the part of men or women. For example, among the Maring of New Guinea, numerous agricultural tasks are divided on the basis of gender: men and women together clear gardens, but only men fell trees. Both men and women plant crops, but weeding is a primary female occupation. At harvest time, men harvest above-ground crops and women harvest below-ground crops (Rappaport, pp. 38–40, 43). These are categories based on cultural understandings, similar to how grilling and barbecuing are identified as male tasks in many Western societies.

An extreme case of agricultural specialization is found in much of sub-Saharan Africa, where subsistence agriculture is a predominantly, sometimes exclusively, female task. Agricultural economist Ester Boserup notes that in sub-Saharan cultures, the shift to a more urbanized society often reduces women's status, for although rural farm women may not be socially equal to their husbands, their work on farms is recognized and valued. A shift into a more "Westernized" work pattern can eliminate what power such women do have (pp. 53–63). However, agricultural work patterns vary widely. In societies where plow agriculture is common, women are often likely to process food in the home, while the actual farm labor falls to men; yet even in those societies, women may weed and harvest or keep kitchen gardens. In the United States, women's farm participation varies from negligible to great. The publication *Marketing to Women* notes that although the number of women farmers in the United States is on the rise, women tend to own the smallest farms. At the same time, women are far more likely to own their farms: fully 80 percent of women farmers are farm owners, in contrast to the 58 percent of male farmers who own their farms.

Preparing Foods

Food preparation, particularly that which occurs in the home and family, is most strongly associated with women and women's work. This is a pattern that has been documented widely. Journalist Laura Shapiro and food writer Ruth Reichl outline the history of this development in the United States in *Perfection Salad*, their account of the

"domestic science" movement. As a result of this movement, women's work came to be viewed as professional, and cooking and other domestic activities were elevated to a woman's highest calling. (See also Cowan. Numerous works from a range of disciplines document this pattern. Among them are works by Sherrie A. Inness and the U.S. sociologist Arlie Hochschild.)

Similar patterns have emerged in other societies, although the underlying cultural ideals may differ. Anne Allison describes the great attention that Japanese mothers give to the preparation of their preschool children's boxed lunches. Young children attend preschool from three to six years of age, where they bring elaborately prepared lunches with them. Mothers organize other family meals around lunch preparation and spend as much as forty-five minutes each morning preparing lunch for their preschoolers. Men never prepare such lunches, and no adult that Allison interviewed could ever recall their father preparing a lunch. Indeed, the elaborate and beautifully presented lunch reflects well on the mother and signals her devotion to her children in the eyes of other mothers and of the preschool staff.

The association of women and domestic food preparation is sufficiently strong that men's cooking requires explanation. In some societies, men prepare special or ritual meals. The ethnographic film *The Feast*, by Timothy Asch, shows Yanomamo men preparing and eating a ritual meal, which is unusual in this strongly patriarchal Amazonian society.

Other Types of Divisions

However, gender is not the only way that labor is divided. This is true for food preparation, as it is for many other types of labor. Class or rank is a major category of division. For example, among the affluent in society, in modern times as well as in the past, servants often prepare food for the household. Also, certain kinds of foods might only be prepared or consumed by people of specific social classes. Archaeologist Christine Hastorf's work in Peru traced the preparation and consumption of corn, in the form of corn beer, through the pre-Incan and Incan periods. Using a sophisticated array of techniques, Hastorf compared the presence of corn pollens among different house sites and throughout neighborhoods. Over time, the presence of pollen, generally found in the patios and yards where women prepared food, was concentrated in the house sites of elite classes. The preparation of corn slowly shifted from most women to elite women. Further comparisons of this type showed that over the same period of time, women's consumption of corn decreased overall, while men's consumption increased in elite neighborhoods. Hastorf hypothesized that with the rise of the Incan Empire, elite women became increasingly specialized corn-beer producers and elite men became the beer's main consumers.

Perhaps the most striking change in U.S. food preparation is that most people do not prepare their own food.

An increasing number of people pay to eat food that is prepared elsewhere, whether they pick up burgers at a drive-through restaurant, order pizza, or buy prepared meals in markets. This pattern has been noted for much of the past twenty years (see Gonzales) and continues to intensify.

See also **Gender and Food; Preparation of Food; Time.**

BIBLIOGRAPHY

Allison, Anne. "Japanese Mothers and 'Obentos': The Lunch Box as Ideological State Apparatus." *Anthropological Quarterly* 64 (1991): 195–209.

Asch, Timothy. *The Feast*. Watertown, Mass.: Documentary Educational Resources, 1969. Film.

Boserup, Ester. *Woman's Role in Economic Development*. New York: St. Martin's Press, 1970.

Cowan, Ruth Schwartz. *More Work for Mother: The Ironies of Household Technology from the Open Hearth to the Microwave*. Reissue. Boston: Basic Books, 1985.

Gonzales, Monica. "Faster's Better." *American Demographics* 10, no. 7 (July 1988): 22.

Hastorf, Christine A. "Gender, Space and Food in Prehistory." In *Engendering Archaeology: Women and Prehistory*, edited by Joan Gero and Margaret Conkey. London: Blackwell, 1991.

Hochschild, Arlie. *Second Shift: Working Parents and the Revolution at Home*. Reissue. New York: Avon, 1997.

Inness, Sherrie A. *Dinner Roles: American Women and Culinary Culture*. Ames: University of Iowa Press, 2001.

Inness, Sherrie A., ed. *Kitchen Culture in America: Popular Representations of Food, Gender, and Race*. Philadelphia: University of Pennsylvania Press, 2001.

Lee, Richard B. *The !Kung San: Men, Women, and Work in a Foraging Society*. Cambridge: Cambridge University Press, 1979.

Murdock, G. P., and Catarina Provost. "Factors in the Division of Labor by Sex: A Cross-Cultural Analysis." *Ethnology* 9 (1973): 122–225.

"The Number of Women Farmers Is on the Rise." *Marketing to Women: Addressing Women and Women's Sensibilities* 14, no. 2: (February 2001): 7.

Rappaport, Roy. *Pigs for the Ancestors: Ritual in the Ecology of a New Guinea People*. 2d ed. Prospect Heights: Waveland, 2000.

Shapiro, Laura, and Ruth Reichl. *Perfection Salad: Women and Cooking at the Turn of the Century*. Reissue. New York: Modern Library, 2001.

Robin O'Brian

DURIAN. The durian is a tropical fruit encased in a spherical or ovoid spiny hard shell, which can be quite large—a single unhusked durian can be the size of a football. Within the shell are five or six segments of golden or cream-colored custardy pulp, the flavor of which is reputed to be so delectable that it is commonly known in

ORIGIN OF THE DURIAN

In Africa, on the Indian Ocean island of Zanzibar, there grows a stand of durian trees near the site of the former slave market. Two stories account for its origin. One is that Arabs had brought back the durian from Indonesian explorations in the eighteenth century. Another story is that the British colonial governor of the 1850s decided to plant every tropical fruit in this garden, but it was the durian that took root and predominated. The durian is beloved by the Zanzibari (although mainland Tanzanians find it repulsive).

Southeast Asia as the "king of fruits." But perhaps even more notable about the durian than its taste is its remarkably foul odor.

Nasal Nightmare or Palate Pleasure?
Sir Stanford Raffles, doughty founder of modern Singapore, proudly told friends in 1819 that whenever he caught a whiff of the fruit, he would "hold his nose and run in the opposite direction." The distinguished nineteenth-century naturalist Henri Mouhot found it relatively easy to trudge boldly through the Cambodian jungles when he discovered Angkor Wat, but give him a durian, and his delicate French olfactory senses would be offended to a point of desperation. "On first tasting it," he reported in his diaries, "I thought it like the flesh of some animal in a state of putrefaction."

What makes the durian both hostile and iconic is the thick rind of the fruit. As cleavers chop through it, an aroma propels upward, inspiring unsavory images: old unwashed socks, subway bathrooms, carrion in custard, fetid cheese. How nearly unimaginable that the taste of this source of nasal distress could evoke such imaginative and savory descriptions as "a bouquet of wild honey with a hint of smoked oak" or "bittersweet butterscotch." But such is indeed its reputation. The flavors of durian varieties range from nutty (the common Thai *chunee*, or "gibbon" durian) to butter-almond (the *maung thong*, or "golden pillow" durian) to crème brûlée (the newly crowned king of flavors, *daan yao*, or "long-stem" durian).

A Cultural Identity
While no festival is devoted to the durian, its Thai devotees crowd the ten-cent ferries from Bangkok to the province of Nonthaburi, where the finest durian grow, from April through July. There, along the port, the laughter of appreciation, the sounds of thick spiky rinds being chopped open, and a pervasively acrid aroma float and mingle together over the Chao Phrya River.

Defending the Durian

It has been said that Asians enjoy pricking the somewhat constrained food preferences of foreigners by offering them durian and watching the knee-jerk negative reactions. Usually the results are harmless and amusing, but sometimes when the untrained nose meets the noisome fruit, the culture clash can be more antagonistic than amicable. Some years ago in Thailand, where durian is a matter of national pride, a Thai lady from Bangkok's red-light district was accused of slashing an American's face with the sharp spines of the durian. Her excuse was that she had been innocently dining on the durian in the back of a bar, when the American stormed in to castigate the revolting smell coming from the fruit. What choice did this woman have but to claim durian rights and defend the fruit? The Thai magistrate, a patriotic durian eater himself, found the assault was, alas, criminal. But in deference to the noble durian, he penalized the woman the equivalent of a mere five dollars and, as if to underscore the virtue of her actions, paid the fine himself.

In 2000, Hong Kong filmmaker Fruit Chan wrote and directed *Durian Durian*, a movie that explores the lower classes of Hong Kong's steamy tenement district of Mongkok. The two durian in the title represent the story's two vulgar, ambitious women, who, like durian the fruit, are repulsive to outsiders but charming to their own society. And, like the Malays (who say "when the durian falls, the sarong falls"), the Chinese consider durian an aphrodisiac.

Botanical Profile

The durian (which the French dub "cheese-vending tree") is a member of the bombax family (Bombacaceae), a diverse family of trees that includes the thick-trunked baobabs of Africa and Australia, the fast-growing balsas of tropical America, and the kapok-yielding ceibas of Africa and tropical America. The durian (specifically *Durio zibenthus*) probably originated in Borneo, and today its numerous varieties are cultivated primarily in Malaysia, Thailand, Indonesia, and the Philippines. The durian tree, resembling the American elm, is of majestic height, reaching up to 120 feet. For its first five years, the trees are delicate, requiring humid climate and protection from fruit borers and leaf-cutters. From its fifth year, it begins to bear approximately forty fruit; by the tenth year, up to 200 fruits. Each of the spiky green fruits can weigh up to eight pounds, so during the harvesting season, it is most inadvisable to walk under a tree, since,

upon beginning to ripen, the fruits fall from their lofty branches.

Humans are by no means the only eager consumers of the durian. According to a Thai maxim, "the first to note the malodor is the elephant, which shakes the tree to bring down the fruit. After the elephant noses open the fruit with its tusks, the tiger fights the elephant for the fruit. Rhinoceros, wild pig, deer, tapir, monkey, beetle, and ant follow the tiger. The human must be very quick to get the durian."

The Marketplace

Assuming no frugivorous animals have broken the husks, durians are trucked to market, where the durian buyers make their selections. As an iconic fruit, social status is important here, and only the most desperately poor will be satisfied with the lowly *chunee*. Others will look for the more desirable—and more costly—*maung thong* pile.

Which are the best in the pile? Some Western writers claim that the odor is the hallmark of a good durian, but in fact the husk is so tough that only a scintilla of the smell can pierce through the young fruit, which takes two or three days to ripen fully after falling. Those experienced in the durian trade know that it is sound, not scent, that identifies an acceptable specimen. The durian merchant will hold the durian by the stem, while the buyer lightly taps on the top of the fruit with a hand or (preferably) a carved teakwood stick. The other hand is held behind the buyer's ear to catch the resonance of the tap, much as a conductor will catch the timbre of violins in an empty auditorium. If the sound from the durian is a thud, the fruit is touching the husk and not ripe enough. If the sound is hollow, then it is overripe and mushy. Something between a thud and hollow, therefore, is ideal.

The export market for durian is limited, since no airline allows the transport of fresh durian (even in the luggage compartment, the aroma can seep up to within sniffing range of the passengers). Nonetheless, the de-

TABLE 1

Durian: Nutritional Information

Components	Per 100-gram portion
Calories	153.0
Moisture	64.1 g
Protein	2.6 g
Fat	3.4 g
Carbohydrate	27.9 g
Minerals	103.9 g
Beta-Carotene	140.0 mg
Vitamin B_1	0.1 mg
Vitamin B_2	0.13 mg
Vitamin C	23.2 mg

SOURCE: Ministry of Agriculture Malaysia at www.agrolink.moa.my/comoditi/durian/durian.html

mand for this "king of fruits" among Western consumers is on an increase. To be sure, canned durian brought some 30 million dollars in exports in the year 2000, with the United States comprising one-third of this market.

Preparation and Consumption of the Durian

Slicing the durian open with a sharp cleaver offers a dissonance of reactions. The smell is indeed fetid, but the compartments within contain generous servings of pulp that is solid (but not dry) and creamy (but not milky). The fruit can be consumed by hand or spoon, extracting the chestnut-sized seeds embedded in the pulp. Fresh durian pulp can be wrapped in foil and stored in a freezer but inevitably loses its delicate taste.

Different cultures use the durian in a variety of ways. In Borneo, the indigenous Iban boil or salt unripe durian, using it as chutney on their sticky rice. In mainland Malaysia, the seeds are roasted or fried and eaten like popcorn. In Sri Lanka, where durian grows wild, farmers will take durian pulp and mix it with curdled buffalo milk, sugar, and sometimes cinnamon or cloves.

Other variations, like durian jam and candy, are made for those who want a taste of durian without the effort of the aroma. Among the most popular recipes is durian ice cream: chunks of the fresh fruit are blended into a puree, mixed with pineapple or orange syrup, and poured onto the ice cream. Fresh durian is also used for a durian "cake." This Malaysian treat is made with durian pulp and sugar, slowly boiled together and wrapped in palm leaves. These cakes keep up to one year in the freezer. Incidentally, consuming durian, in any form, with liquor is strictly avoided. It is a long-standing belief that fermenting the fruit in the stomach with alcohol can be lethal.

See also **China; Southeast Asia.**

BIBLIOGRAPHY

Genthe, Henry. "Durian." *Smithsonian Magazine* (September 1999): pp. 99–104.

Harris, Marilyn Rittenhouse. *Tropical Fruit Cookbook.* Honolulu: University of Hawaii Press, 1993.

Rolnick, Harry. "The Durian." *Kris: Malaysian Airline Magazine*, 1982.

Rolnick, Harry. "The Fruit They Love To Hate." *Asian Wall Street Journal*, 1981.

Root, Waverley Lewis. *Food: An Authoritative and Visual History and Dictionary of the Foods of the World.* New York: Simon and Schuster, 1980.

Stobart, Tom. *The Cook's Encyclopedia.* New York: Harper and Row, 1981.

Harry Rolnick

E

EASTER. Easter, the Christian festival commemorating the resurrection of Christ, was the earliest feast day decided upon by the ancient Christian Church. Like its Jewish predecessor Passover, it is a movable feast, based on the lunar calendar rather than falling on the same Sunday every year.

The complicated dating for Easter was set in 325 at the Council of Nicaea, which scheduled the festival to be celebrated on the first Sunday following the full moon occurring next after the vernal equinox (about March 21); however, if the full moon occurs on a Sunday, Easter will be celebrated the following Sunday. Hence, the date of Easter can fluctuate between March 22 and April 25. Because the Western churches (Catholic and Protestant) now follow the Gregorian calendar, the Eastern churches, which follow the unrevised Julian calendar, celebrate Easter (and other Church holidays) on different dates. In the Orthodox Churches, Easter marks the beginning of the ecclesiastical year.

Like many other Christian feasts, the celebration of Easter contains a number of originally pagan or folk-religious elements tolerated by the Church. Among these are customs associated with the Easter egg, Easter breads and other special holiday foods, and the European concept of the Easter hare, or, in America, of the Easter rabbit, which brings baskets of candies and colored eggs during the night.

The pagan roots of Easter involve the spring festivals of pre-Christian Europe and the Near East, which celebrate the rebirth of vegetation, welcoming the growing light as the sun becomes more powerful in its course toward summer. It is significant that in England and Germany the Church accepted the name of the pagan goddess "Easter" (Anglo-Saxon *Eostra*—her name has several spellings) for this new Christian holiday. In Mediterranean Europe (Italy, Spain, and France), Christianity adopted *pascha*, a word derivative of Passover, from which comes the adjective "paschal" for things pertaining to Easter, such as the Paschal Lamb.

Aside from the fact that Easter Sunday officially ended the long fast of Lent, one of the most distinctive food elements of the Easter celebration is the Easter egg. In earlier times, Easter eggs were much more a part of the formal culture than they are in America today, where individual families determine the range of the custom. In the European village context, Easter eggs were once used as part of one's tithe to the landlord, or given as festive (and expected) gifts to the village pastor, the schoolmaster, the sexton and bell-ringer, the parish gravedigger, and even the village shepherd. Of course, they were hospitably presented to visitors, bestowed as favors upon servants, and, above all, given to children. Courting couples exchanged them as tokens of love, and godparents usually regaled their godchildren with gifts of decorated eggs.

The Easter rabbit (Easter hare in Europe) is not documented before the seventeenth century. While the Easter hare is the major egg supplier in European Easter celebration, there were other runners-up in the form of egg birds, Easter hens, cranes, storks, even foxes and other creatures. With its late origin, scholars are still debating the reasons for the association of the rabbit with Easter custom and lore. It is generally thought that, like the Christmas tree—and the recent development of Easter egg trees—the custom first emerged in the cities, then filtered down into the country villages. Among the theories of the origin of the Easter rabbit belief, the most plausible (although still not without difficulties) is that it may be connected in some way with the so-called March Hare of folktale. The Easter rabbit was believed to actually lay the eggs; hence, children went to elaborate lengths to build attractive "nests" for the elusive egg layer, who was summoned by whistling or by saying a charm.

The elaborate decoration of Easter eggs became a major form of home-produced folk art both in Europe and America. Among the Pennsylvania Dutch, who produced an elaborate Easter culture, eggs are dyed with onion skins, producing a rich reddish-brown color, or with other natural dyes. These eggs are then scratch-carved with designs, dates, names, or even religious verses, or elaborately decorated by winding the pith of a reed around the egg to create patterns. The Pennsylvania Dutch also make Easter birds out of large goose or duck eggs, furnishing them with wings, beaks, and tails. These are hung from the ceilings of farmhouse kitchens as festive seasonal decoration.

French ceramic mold for baking Easter bread in the shape of a Paschal lamb, circa 1850. ROUGHWOOD COLLECTION. PHOTO CHEW & COMPANY.

In areas of Canada and the United States where Russian and Ukrainian Orthodox Christians as well as Poles and other Eastern Europeans settled, unusual methods of egg decoration are found. Such Easter eggs are generally referred to as *pysanka* (plural *pysanky*). In Eastern Europe, egg decoration is an ancient folk craft treasured in families and passed down from generation to generation. In Czarist Russia, this craft was elevated to such a degree that it was even imitated by such famous jewelers as Fabergé. Whether created with gold leaf and sapphires or just homemade dyes, the designs involve a variety of standard motifs—geometrical, animal, and floral. The geometrical motifs are probably the oldest, and range from simple horizontal and vertical lines to sectionalize the egg to sun symbols like the tripod, or to the "endless line" forms. Some of the most complex patterns incorporate stars and rosettes. Animal and bird designs are the rarest; the reindeer is said to symbolize wealth and prosperity, while the hen, or the feet of a hen, symbolizes fertility and fulfillment of wishes. Butterflies, fish, and horses are also occasionally included in the design repertoire. From the plant world, pine trees are drawn to symbolize eternal youth and health. Many of the Slavic methods of decoration are similar to those used by the Pennsylvania Dutch, but the range of motifs is different, the colors more striking, and the designs richly elaborate. Background colors are often red or black, although green and yellow are also popular, but multicolored designs seem to be the most popular.

In the family and community of all the various Christian denominations, Easter Sunday has always been a day of joyous celebration. In the Middle Ages it was often chosen as the day to crown kings since Easter feasting was, and remains, quite elaborate, especially in the Orthodox tradition. Since the day marked the official end to forty days of the Lenten fast, many special foods were prepared to mark the occasion. Easter breads have been researched widely and form a huge genre of ornamental foods made especially for this feast. Among the Greeks, lung soup is very much associated with Easter cookery, while in America baked ham seems to be one of the most common features of the Easter dinner. Many games were played with Easter eggs prior to or following Easter dinner, such as egg picking, where the player forfeits his or her egg if it cracks during the picking, egg eating contests, and egg rolling contests. In Europe and in parts of colonial America, Easter was often extended into a two-day celebration, with feasting, gaming, and other secular entertainments continued into Easter Monday.

Easter has undergone further evolution in more modern times, especially since the latter half of the nineteenth century. The confectionery trade began to commercialize Easter during the 1870s, with the introduction of an entirely new line of sweets employing Easter themes. Chocolatiers in particular discovered that candies once only sold as luxury foods for Christmas could become just as lucrative when transformed into rabbits and similar gift items. Today Easter is one of the most important seasons for selling confectionery, from chocolate bunnies, marshmallow chicks, and jelly beans, to music box coconut eggs, spun sugar tulips, and edible crucifixes filled with brandied fruit.

The most concise reporting of Easter customs in Europe occurred at a symposium on Easter organized by Robert Wildhaber of Switzerland. Wildhaber edited the papers and published them in 1957 in the *Schweizerisches Archiv für Volkskunde*. The papers cover Eastertide as cel-

The blessing of food at Easter is an important rite in the Orthodox Church. A priest of the Donskoi Monastery in Moscow is shown blessing food during Easter 1998. AP/WIDE WORLD PHOTOS.

ebrated in Switzerland, Germany, Austria, France (especially Alsace), Slovenia, the Czech Republic, Slovakia, Poland, Hungary, Rumania, Bulgaria, and Greece. The majority of the contributions deal with Easter eggs, their history, function, decoration, role in folk medicine, and in riddles. Several contributions treat Easter foods, especially Easter breads and other baked goods. Venetia Newall's *An Egg at Easter* (1971) is the most expert introduction in English to the history of the Easter egg and its place in ecclesiastical and folk culture.

See also **Bread; Christianity; Folklore, Food in; Judaism; Lent; Passover; United States: Pennsylvania Dutch Food; Shrove Tuesday.**

BIBLIOGRAPHY

Bradshaw, Paul F., and Lawrence A. Hoffman, eds. *Passover and Easter: Origin and History in Modern Times.* Notre Dame, Ind.: University of Notre Dame Press, 1999.

Gulevich, Tanya. *Encyclopedia of Easter, Carnival, and Lent.* Detroit: Omnigraphics, 2002.

Newall, Venetia. *An Egg at Easter: A Folklore Study.* Bloomington: Indiana University Press, 1971.

Rodrigue, Denise. *Cycle de Pâques au Québec et dans l'Ouest de la France.* Québec: Les Presses de l'Université Laval, 1983.

Santino, Jack. *All Around the Year: Holidays and Celebrations in American Life.* Urbana: University of Illinois Press, 1994.

Shoemaker, Alfred L. *Eastertide in Pennsylvania: A Folk-Cultural Study.* Mechanicsburg, Pa.: Stackpole, 2000.

Watts, Alan W. *Easter: Its Story and Meaning.* New York: Abelard-Schuman, 1959.

Wildhaber, Robert, ed. "Osterbrauchtum in Europa." *Schweizerisches Archiv für Volkskunde* 53, nos. 2, 3 (1957): 61–204.

Don Yoder

EASTERN EUROPE. *See* **Balkan Countries; Central Europe; Russia.**

EATING: ANATOMY AND PHYSIOLOGY OF EATING.

"Eating is the action of taking solid foods in the mouth in order to nourish oneself: this action is carried out by insertion [of the foodstuff] in the mouth, followed by mastication, swallowing, and digestion." This is the definition of "eating" proposed by Diderot in his famous Encyclopedia. He goes on to say that eating is specifically not the ingestion of non-food substances such as clay, chalk, stones, and charcoal, but only the ingestion of materials that can be conceived of as foods proper for nourishment. As a result, they also exclude such potential foodstuffs as blood and urine. In the present article, we follow the lead of our predecessor in adopting this definition.

Taking in nourishment is necessary for survival, and this usually involves eating. The following chapter provides an overview of the anatomy and physiology of eating, including the major nutritional processes that take place during digestion.

Eating can be divided into the following processes: eating proper, or ingestion, whereby food enters into the body; and digestion, the process through which nutrients from food are extracted in the gastrointestinal tract. Digestion is followed by absorption, the process through which nutrients are passed through into the blood stream; and by excretion, through which indigestible and unabsorbable products from food are eliminated.

Anatomy

The ability to eat and digest food hinges on an intricate, complex, and coordinated system known as the digestive system, all under control both of the central nervous system (brain and spinal cord) and of digestive system's own intrinsic nervous system, which is sometimes called the body's "second brain." The digestive system comprises two main groups of organs: the organs of the alimentary canal, also known as the gastrointestinal (GI) tract, and the accessory digestive organs.

The GI tract is a continuous tube that runs from the mouth to the anus. The organs of the gastrointestinal tract include the mouth, pharynx, esophagus, stomach, small intestine (consisting of duodenum, jejunum, and ileum), and large intestine. It is within the GI tract that food is chewed or masticated, then broken down into still smaller fragments, and absorbed into the blood.

The accessory organs of the digestive system are the teeth, tongue, salivary glands, liver, gallbladder, and pancreas. The teeth and tongue allow for chewing, tasting, and rasping of food. The other accessory organs of the digestive system produce secretions that aid in digestion. In embryonic life, these organs develop as outpouchings from the primitive GI tract, and their secretions travel into the GI tract via ducts.

In order to understand eating and digestion, it is important to imagine what the body needs to do when you think about food, eat food, swallow food, when food lands in your stomach, and when food makes it way through the small and large intestines. The digestive system is designed to prepare the body for eating and digestion before the first piece of food passes our lips. Once food is ingested, this system is designed to efficiently extract and absorb nutrients while it rids the body of waste products.

Preparation for Eating

In order to understand how the body prepares for eating, it is important to realize that eating and digestion require that our body maximizes blood flow to the digestive organs, in order to both supply oxygen and energy to these organs, and to carry away the nutrients that have been absorbed.

Blood flow to the digestive system is controlled primarily by the autonomic nervous system (ANS). The

ANS has two anatomically and functionally different subdivisions, the sympathetic nervous system and the parasympathetic nervous system. The sympathetic nervous system is designed to stimulate the body to prepare for and engage in activities and behaviors that are highly arousing, for example, "fight or flight reactions," while the parasympathetic nervous system is designed to prepare the body to engage in activities and behaviors that are relaxing.

Eating and digestion require the body to be relaxed, to allow for blood to be shunted away from the muscles to the digestive system. In fact, from an evolutionary point of view, the process of eating requires us to stand still or (preferably) to sit or lie down, and concentrate on taking apart the food item and ingesting it, rather than running around. Thus the processes involved in eating are antithetical to moving about, either to get somewhere or to escape danger.

As a consequence of this organization, the body cannot appropriately engage in relaxing behaviors if the sympathetic nervous system is activated, and it cannot engage in arousing behaviors if the parasympathetic nervous system is activated. In other words, if you feel stressed, or you are engaged in physical activity, or you must flee from danger, you will not be able to eat and digest food, and vice versa.

Both mental stress and aerobic exercise involve activation of the sympathetic nervous system. You may have noticed that if you try to eat while you have been highly stressed, or while you are "on the go," or after you have exercised aerobically, your mouth may have been dry, making it difficult to moisten, taste, and swallow food. You may have also experienced stomach cramping and pain upon ingesting food. These responses occur because your sympathetic nervous system is stimulated. Your body is worried about maximizing its ability to fight or run; it is not ready to eat a meal.

If, however, you are in a relaxed state, the thought of food, the sight of food, or simply making a mental association with food, sets into motion a series of events that prepares the GI tract for incoming food. Upon sensing that eating is imminent, the parasympathetic nervous system prepares the GI tract via signals sent though three cranial nerves that exit from the brainstem: the vagus nerve (cranial nerve X), the trigeminal nerve (cranial nerve V), and the glossopharyngeal nerve (cranial nerve IX).

Preparation in the mouth. In the mouth, food must be wetted by saliva, so you can taste it, chew it, begin to break it down into smaller particles, and swallow it. When your parasympathetic nervous system is stimulated, cranial nerves V and IX stimulate the salivary glands to release saliva into the mouth. The average person produces about 1500 ml of saliva each day.

Once food is wet, it can be tasted. Tasting food is critical for identifying it, receiving pleasure if it tastes good, rejecting it if it tastes bad, and for signaling to the

body that food is indeed about to be ingested. There are five primary tastants: sweet, sour, salt, bitter, and umami, which is the taste of the amino acid glutamate, a major ingredient of monosodium glutamate (MSG). Tasting is accomplished by taste receptors, which are located in structures called taste buds. Taste buds are housed in small bumps on the tongue and the roof of the palate called papillae. Fungiform papillae house the taste buds located on the anterior surface of the tongue, foliate papillae house taste buds that are located toward the back and side of the tongue. Circumvallate papillae, which form the chevron-like pattern in the back of the tongue, house very large numbers of taste buds. In addition, there are a scattering of taste buds in the palate, the posterior oropharynx, and the esophagus. It is interesting to note that the ideas that only sweet can be tasted at the tip of the tongue, only sour and salt can be tasted on the sides of the tongue, and only bitter can be tasted at the back of the tongue are myths. In fact, all taste buds are capable of tasting all tastants; however, they do so at varying levels of sensitivity.

Another reason for wetting food in the mouth is that it makes food easier to masticate and swallow. Furthermore, once food is chewed, it can be acted upon by salivary enzymes, which are compounds that work to chemically break down food into its molecular components. For example, saliva contains the enzyme salivary amylase, which begins the breakdown of carbohydrates, and lingual lipase, which begins the digestion of fat.

Preparation in the stomach. Food needs to be mixed with fluid in the stomach as well. Therefore, upon the initial cue that the arrival of food is imminent, cranial nerve X (the vagus nerve) stimulates the stomach to release the gastric juices that will be necessary for digestion. Contained in the gastric juices are water, hydrochloric acid (HCl), and pepsin, an enzyme that breaks down proteins in the stomach's acid environment. Water is necessary to keep food liquified. Hydrochloric acid serves several purposes: it signals further digestive events to occur; it dissolves food into smaller particles; it kills many microorganisms that may have been ingested; and it denatures proteins, causing the proteins to lose their structure so that they can be further digested.

In response to parasympathetic activation, the stomach also produces a protective coat of mucus. There are two types of mucus, visible mucus and soluble mucus, consisting of highly glycosylated proteins, called mucins. Mucous neck cells that surround the openings of the stomach's acid-producing glands (called gastric or oxyntic glands) produce visible mucus, which continuously forms a protective coat on the surface of the stomach. As the gastric gland sends out hydrochloric acid and enzymes, soluble mucus, formed by the cells that line the upper part of the gastric pits, is secreted ahead of it, and also covers the surface of the stomach. Together, the two types of mucus form a protective coat, called the glycocalyx. This coat is soluble in alcohol, while aspirin prevents the formation and secretion of mucin. Therefore, alcohol abuse, or excessive use of aspirin, can permit hydrochloric acid to attack the stomach lining, which leads to bleeding. In addition, individuals who are highly anxious do not experience proper parasympathetic activation when eating, and consequently do not produce sufficient mucus. Therefore, given the presence of other triggers for ulcer formation (and specifically infection with bacteria of the *Helicobacter* species), anxious individuals are often susceptible to peptic ulcers.

Preparation by the pancreas. Cranial nerve X stimulates the pancreas to release insulin from its beta cells. Insulin is the hormone responsible for moving glucose and amino acids out of the blood and into cells so that they can be used for fuel and for forming new or renewed tissue. Insulin is needed once food is digested and absorbed, because the concentration of glucose and amino acids in the blood then increases. Cranial nerve X also stimulates the pancreas to release bicarbonate into the small intestine, which will be used to neutralize the acid coming from the stomach. This process will be discussed in more detail in a later section.

Ingestion: The Mouth and Esophagus

Once the digestive system has properly prepared itself for its incoming meal, food is ingested. Food is wetted by saliva, tasted by the tongue and palate, and chewed or masticated by the teeth. Once the food is mechanically broken down into small enough pieces, it is ready for swallowing, or deglutition. Swallowing is actually a complicated process that requires coordinated activity of the tongue, palate, pharynx, and esophagus, over twenty-two muscle groups in all, controlled by separate regions of the brain. This activity requires strict control to guarantee that the food makes its way into the esophagus and not the trachea. If food is swallowed into the trachea, breathing is blocked and choking ensues. Once food enters the esophagus, the tongue blocks the mouth, the palate rises to close off the nasopharynx, and the larynx rises so that the epiglottis, a muscular flap, covers its opening into the respiratory passageways. Food is subsequently squeezed through the pharynx and into the esophagus by wavelike peristaltic contractions.

At the bottom of the esophagus is the cardiac or lower esophageal sphincter. The esophageal sphincter acts like a valve controlling the entry of food into the stomach. With each peristaltic contraction, the esophageal sphincter opens and a bolus of food lands in the stomach. The esophageal sphincter is also designed to stay closed while the stomach contracts, so that the acid from the stomach cannot reflux into the esophagus. The burning a person feels when acid refluxes into the esophagus is commonly known as heartburn.

Breakdown and Digestion: The Stomach

The stomach is responsible for a large proportion of both the mechanical and chemical breakdown of food. Once

The act of eating, and some of the psychological pleasures connected with it, are captured in this photograph of a teenage girl nibbling her way through a cupcake. © LARRY WILLIAMS/ CORBIS.

it accomplishes its goal, it delivers the resulting material (called chyme at this point) into the small intestine, at a rate that is dependent upon the mixture it digests.

The stomach is anatomically designed to stretch to accommodate the entry of food, and to churn and mix food thoroughly so it may be acted upon by stomach secretions and enzymes. At the top of the stomach is the fundus, a dome shaped section where the majority of hydrochloric acid is secreted. Below the fundus is the body of the stomach. The body of the stomach and the antrum of the stomach are separated by the incisura. Below the incisura is the antrum, which narrows and terminates at the pylorus. The pylorus opens into the duodenum through the pyloric sphincter, a muscular valve that controls the emptying of chyme into the duodenum.

When food arrives in the stomach. When food arrives in the stomach, the esophageal sphincter closes; the stomach muscles relax, with the result that the pressure inside the stomach decreases. These two actions prevent food

CHINA AND EATING: TAOIST FIVE ELEMENTS

The Chinese healing tradition is centered on a fundamental concept—balance—and three fundamental ways of delineating the elements involved in this balance: yin and yang, or the principle of opposites that are complementary and mutually dependent; the Taoist concept of the five elements or five evolutions; and the concept of *qi*, or "intrinsic energy." Daily eating should promote a harmonious balance among these systems, while eating in times of disease should be managed in order to restore balance.

Traditional Chinese knowledge of the anatomy of the digestive organs is reasonably accurate. However, the physiological concepts based on the ideas outlined above differ considerably from their Western counterparts. All parts of the body, and actions of the body, have either a yin or a yang quality. Eating is yin, while bodily activity is yang. Thus overeating causes an excess of yin, and can only be compensated for by increasing yang, for example, by exercise. Foods themselves have yin or yang qualities, so that a properly balanced meal is one where foods are chosen in order to balance their yin and yang qualities.

The organs of digestion are each either yin (liver) or yang (stomach, small and large intestine, gallbladder). Emotions affect the balance of function of these organs, so that, for example, anger affects both the liver, the organ corresponding to yin, and the gallbladder, corresponding to yang, leading to dysfunction of both.

The Taoist five elements (wood, fire, earth, metal, and water) can be used to classify the organs of the digestive system, as well as tastes and smells, the orifices and tissues of the body, the emotions, and natural phenomena such as the seasons. The order of the elements also provides directionality, in the sense that the Elements follow each other in the order of their corresponding seasons, and the function of one organ is dependent on the good function of the organ preceding it in the sequence. Furthermore, this scheme functions in parallel with the yin/yang system, so that, for example, both the liver, a yin organ, and the gallbladder, a yang organ, correspond to wood, and anger, being associated with both of these organs, corresponds to wood as well.

As the "intrinsic energy" of the body, *qi* is critical to the processes and transformations that move food to its appropriate location in the body, and transform it into nourishment. Each food provides its quota of *qi* or activation of *qi*, or, if toxic, depletes or stagnates *qi*. In health, foods can help *qi* move downward through the "triple burner," consisting of the three divisions of the torso: the upper burner, devoted to respiration and containing the lungs and the heart; the middle burner, devoted to digestion and containing the spleen, stomach, liver, and gallbladder; and the lower burner, devoted to elimination, and containing the kidneys, bladder, and lower intestines. For example, radishes are thought to help *qi* move downward and thereby promote digestion and good health.

Thus these three interlocking systems serve to organize and direct eating behavior by providing a scheme for balancing the perceived characteristics of each food eaten and each health condition experienced.

---

from refluxing back into the esophagus. The stomach's relaxation reflex is also designed to accommodate the increased volume and develops in response to the stretching of the stomach's walls. Note that this relaxation reflex can be "trained." When a person regularly eats large meals, relaxation is greater, and when a person eats small meals, the relaxation reflex is less vigorous. This less vigorous reflex is why people feel their stomach "shrinks" when they go on a diet.

Hydrochloric acid is secreted by parietal cells in glands of the fundus of the stomach. As a result, the pH in the fundus can be on the order of 1–2. With this low pH, pepsinogen, secreted by chief cells, also located in these glands, is converted to pepsin. Pepsin breaks down protein-containing foods in the fundus into peptides and amino acids, and calcium and vitamin B_{12} are released. These food components arrive in the antrum, where they induce the production of the hormone gastrin. Gastrin travels via the blood to the fundus to increase hydrochloric acid secretion. Incidentally, due to this signaling function of protein in the stomach, it is nutritionally important to consume some protein with each meal. Gastrin also enhances closure of the pylorus and esophageal sphincter. Local histamine secretion sensitizes parietal cells to the effects of activation the vagus nerve and of gastrin. These three processes form a carefully coordinated system that is designed to maximize hydrochloric acid secretion and retention of material in the stomach so that it is properly mixed with each wave of contraction.

To prevent dumping of the stomach's contents into the duodenum, the pylorus closes, so that only about one-tenth of the amount of food that entered the stomach actually reaches the duodenum immediately after ingestion. As the pylorus closes, the area around the incisura contracts; this provides a narrow round opening separating the antrum from the body and fundus of the stomach. The antrum then contracts, shooting the food back through this narrow opening into the fundus, a process known as retropulsion. As mentioned above, the fundus secretes hydrochloric acid, so the food, the hydrochloric acid, and the enzymes become thoroughly mixed. At the same time, fats are broken down into small globules through this churning process. The incisura then relaxes, and the food mixture is propelled forward into the antrum. This process repeats itself time and time again.

Digestion in the stomach. As noted earlier, proteins are first digested in the stomach by an enzyme called pepsin. Pepsin breaks down protein into smaller molecules called peptides or polypeptides, which make their way into the small intestine for further digestion and absorption.

The digestion of fat begins in the stomach as well, through emulsification by churning and retropulsion. Fats that we consume are mostly in the form of triglycerides. A triglyceride is a molecule that has a glycerol backbone and 3 fatty acid chains attached to it. Fats are not water soluble ("oil and water do not mix") and therefore need to be packaged for absorption into the blood. One process that aids in the digestion and packaging of fat is emulsification. Emulsification increases the surface area of the fat that is available for enzymatic action in the duodenum.

Finally, the stomach secretes intrinsic factor, which is required for vitamin B_{12} absorption in the intestine. Vitamin B_{12} is a large molecule, and requires intrinsic factor to protect it from destruction by the stomach, and to enable its absorption through a specific receptor in the ileum.

Reflexes designed to clear out the lower GI tract. Before chyme can adequately make its way into the small intestine, there is a series of reflexes that are designed to prepare the lower gut (small and large intestine) for digestion. The result of these reflexes is that the lower gut gets cleared of old material so that there will be room for the new material coming down.

One reflex is known as the gastrocolic reflex and is due to stretching of the stomach after food lands in it. This reflex moves fecal material into the rectum, so you have a desire to defecate. This is why you may need to go to the bathroom after eating, especially after breakfast.

Gastrin is involved in the gastro-ileal reflex. This reflex clears chyme from the ileum, the furthest point of the small intestine, moving the chyme into the colon. Finally there is a duodenocolic reflex that is brought about when chyme enters the duodenum. This reflex also brings fecal material into the rectum in preparation for defecation.

Digestion and Absorption: The Small Intestine

After the chyme is thoroughly mixed in the stomach, it moves into the small intestine. The small intestine is the primary site for the chemical digestion and the absorption of food. The small intestine has three subdivisions: the duodenum, the jejunum, and the ileum. The duodenum, which connects to the stomach, is the point of entry for the secretions from the pancreas and from the liver via the gall bladder. The jejunum is the longest section of the small intestine and is the site where the majority of nutrients are absorbed. The ileum is the third division and connects to the beginning of the large intestine.

The small intestine is anatomically designed for efficient nutrient absorption. Not only is it very long, but it also has three structural modifications which further amplify its absorptive area: plicae circulares, villi, and microvilli.

The plicae circulares are deep folds of the intestinal mucosa which force the chyme to spiral through the lumen of the intestine. This effect slows the movement and increases the mixing of the chyme, thereby creating time for maximal nutrient absorption.

Villi are fingerlike projections that lie on the surface of the plicae. These projections increase the amount of contact between the surface of the intestine and the chyme, and they make absorption more efficient because they each contain a dense capillary bed and a lymphatic capillary called a lacteal, which act to transport nutrients into circulation. Lacteals are essential for fat absorption.

Finally, at the end of each villus cell are tiny microscopic projections called microvilli, which form the intestine's brush border. The microvilli dramatically increase the absorptive surface area of the small intestine. Moreover, there are enzymes that reside on the brush border that complete the final stages of chemical digestion of carbohydrates and proteins.

When chyme arrives in the duodenum. Chyme must enter into the duodenum at a rate the duodenum can handle. Furthermore, the acidic mixture must be neutralized so that it does not damage the duodenum. Finally, the digestion of the chyme must continue, and the process of nutrient absorption must begin.

It is important to note that the hormones and nerve activities discussed below are usually responsible for more than one of these above processes, and that more than one hormone or nerve activity is involved with each of these processes. In other words, the digestive system has in place a number of checks and balances to ensure that each responsibility is met during intestinal digestion and absorption.

Gastric inhibitory peptide (GIP), released by the small intestine, is one such hormone. As its name suggests, GIP inhibits gastric motility, thereby slowing down the delivery of chyme to the duodenum. In addition, GIP is responsible for helping tissues prepare for an influx of glucose, by causing release of insulin from the beta cells of the endocrine pancreas.

Other ways in which the flow of chyme is slowed enough to accommodate digestion and absorption are through intrinsic nerve signals from the gut, through a decrease in the activity of the vagus nerve or an increase in sympathetic activity, through the hormones secretin and cholecystokinin-pancreozymin (CCK-PZ), which are secreted by the duodenum in the presence of chyme. Not surprisingly, these hormones also have several other functions, discussed below.

In order for the digestive enzymes of the small intestine to be activated, they have to be in an alkaline environment. Neutralization of stomach acid is accomplished by secretions from the pancreas and from Brunner's glands, which line the duodenum. Both secretions are rich in bicarbonate, a basic compound that neutralizes stomach acid. The process of secretion for both of these systems begins with activation of the vagus nerve, which itself begins with the thought of food, as noted earlier. Secretion is further enhanced by secretin and CCK-PZ release from the duodenal wall in response to fat and amino acids in chyme. Vitamins and minerals do not require digestion for absorption.

Fat digestion and absorption. In the small intestine, fat is further emulsified by bile, a fluid that is produced in the liver and stored in the gallbladder. The release of bile into the duodenum is induced by contraction of the gallbladder, which propels the bile into the common bile duct, and from there into the pancreatic duct. The sphincter of Oddi relaxes, letting the bile and pancreatic juices flow into the duodenum. Contraction of the gallbladder, relaxation of the sphincter of Oddi, and release of pancreatic juices are all induced by cholcystokinin-pancreozymin (CCK-PZ), produced, as noted above, by the duodenal wall in response to the presence of fat and amino acids.

Once fat is emulsified by bile, it can be acted upon by enzymes called lipases, which break down fat. Pancreatic lipase requires a high pH for activation, which is accomplished through secretion of pancreatic bicarbonate. Pancreatic lipase breaks off fatty acids from the triglyceride's glycerol backbone, leaving a monoglyceride and two fatty acids. Bile acids then join up with the monoglycerides and fatty acids to form mixed micelles. Bile salts need to be present at or above the proper concentration—the critical micellar concentration, or CMC—in order for micelles to form.

Mixed micelles are shaped like hockey pucks, with bile salts forming the outer ring of the micelles, and the hydrophilic (water-soluble) ends of the fatty acids and monoglycerides forming the circular surfaces. Because of this packaging, the micelles can cross the water layer at the surface of the cells of the small intestine. It should be noted that long-chain triglycerides (>12 carbons) require both breakdown by lipase and incorporation into mixed micelles in order to be absorbed, while medium-chain triglycerides (with 8–12 carbons in each fatty acid chain) only require breakdown by lipase, and not micelle formation, because they are more hydrophilic.

Bile acids are recovered from the chyme in the terminal ileum, and returned to the liver for re-use. Note that the terminal ileum is also where vitamin B^{12} is absorbed. No other part of the intestine can compensate for these functions should the terminal ileum be diseased or lost, although absorption of other nutrients can occur successfully with loss of a considerable length of jejunum.

Carbohydrate digestion and absorption. Carbohydrates are also digested and absorbed in the small intestine. They are hydrophilic compounds, and therefore do not require complex packaging to be absorbed. Carbohydrates in our diet exist as monosaccharides, which are one sugar unit long (simple sugars: e.g., glucose, fructose, and galactose); disaccharides, which are two sugar units long (e.g., sucrose, lactose, and maltose); and polysaccharides, which are long complex strings of sugar units (e.g., glycogen and starch).

The majority of carbohydrates are consumed as polysaccharides, either as starch or glycogen. It should be noted that fibers, either soluble or insoluble, are types of polysaccharides that cannot be digested because we lack enzymes capable of chemically breaking them down.

Carbohydrates that can be digested begin to be broken down into small sugars in the mouth by the enzyme salivary amylase (noted earlier). You may have noticed that a piece of bread that you keep in your mouth for some time begins to taste sweet because the amylase in your saliva breaks down complex sugars into sweeter-tasting simple sugars.

The majority of carbohydrate digestion takes place in the small intestine via enzymes that are secreted by the pancreas. Pancreatic enzymes break polysaccharides down into oligosaccharides (2–8 sugars long), which are then acted upon by enzymes of the intestinal brush border. Within the brush border, oligosaccharides are further broken down into glucose, fructose, or galactose, depending on their initial composition. Glucose is the primary source of fuel used by cells in the body, and fructose and galactose can be converted into glucose via biochemical mechanisms.

Protein digestion and absorption. Protein digestion in the small intestine is accomplished by pancreatic enzymes as well. The large polypeptides created by the action of pepsin in the stomach are broken down into small peptides and amino acids by the pancreatic enzymes trypsin, chymotrypsin, and carboxypeptidase, as well as by peptidases in the brush border. Amino acids, the smallest functional unit of proteins, and small peptides are then absorbed into the blood, where they can be transported to cells for protein synthesis or for fuel.

The Large Intestine: The End of the Journey

The undigested portion of food that does not get absorbed by the small intestine passes on into the large intestine. The large intestine is responsible for reabsorbing the water added by the stomach and the small intestine to keep the chyme fluid, for fermentation of undigested products by bacteria, and for packing waste products into feces for excretion. The subdivisions of the large intestine are the cecum, appendix, colon (ascending colon, transverse colon, and descending colon), rectum, and anal canal.

Bacteria normally live in the large intestine. These bacteria either make their way into the large intestine by surviving the journey through the stomach and small intestine, or via the anus. These bacteria break down the fiber that is consumed, releasing gases, as well as the very smelly short-chain fatty acids that provide the major source of fuel for the wall of the large intestine. In addition, these bacteria are capable of synthesizing some B vitamins and vitamin K.

Once the contents of the colon are moved along via contractions, they reach the rectum, which otherwise is usually empty. Stretching of the rectal wall initiates a defecation reflex. This reflex is mediated by the parasympathetic nervous system and causes the walls of the sigmoid colon and the rectum to contract and the anal sphincter to relax. Once feces are forced into the anal canal, the stretch sends a signal to the brain informing us of the need to defecate. Under normal circumstances, the defecation response is under voluntary control.

Such a complex process as eating, in which each step is predicated on the preceding one, is prone to large variations in normal function. Specifically, the timing and efficiency of each of the steps described here show wide variability both from person to person, and for different food choices and consumption patterns. Some people have rapid intestinal transit time, and some slow nutrients are more easily digested and absorbed from some diets than from others. However, the basic scheme outlined here holds true for all healthy people.

See also **Appetite; Sensation and the Senses.**

BIBLIOGRAPHY

Encyclopédie, ou Dictionnaire Raisonné des Sciences, des Arts et des Métiers, par une Société de Gens de Lettres. 3d ed. Geneva and Neuchâtel, 1778.

Gershon, Michael D. *The Second Brain: A Groundbreaking New Understanding of Nervous Disorders of the Stomach and Intestine.* New York: HarperCollins, 1999.

Guyton, Arthur C., and John E. Hall. *Textbook of Medical Physiology.* 10th ed. Philadelphia: Saunders, 2000.

David R. Bauer
Virginia Utermohlen

EATING DISORDERS. *See* **Anorexia, Bulimia; Eating: Anatomy and Physiology of Eating; Obesity.**

ECOLOGY AND FOOD. Naturalists and geographers have commented on human, food, and natural-resource relationships throughout history. Religion and politics have influenced their ideas. Once, many societies strongly valued community and balance between nature and humans. With industrial modernization, the philosophy changed to conquering or controlling nature via education, "objective" science, new technology, and new ideology emphasizing individualism. Education in the fields of agriculture, soil science, genetics, and food science greatly expanded to explore and promote new methods for increased food production, processing, storage, and distribution. While tractors, machinery, chemical fertilizers, and pesticides sharply increased food production for a growing population (hailed in the 1960s as the "Green Revolution"), some pointed to the limits of natural-resource use and "progress."

Ecology, Science, and Modernization in Food Production and Distribution

Ecology—or *Ökologie*, as coined by German biologist Ernst Heinrich Haeckel in 1911—was largely a twentieth-century development. In this perspective studied in the natural sciences, the world is an interrelated system where changes in one part of the system affect everything else. The sun's energy and the earth's minerals nourish a cycle of plant "producers," herbivore "consumers," carnivore and omnivore "consumers," and bacteria, fungi, and parasite "degraders" that return the organic waste of the producers and consumers back into the system. The plant producers, animal consumers, and microorganisms are all food to each other, with humans generally being among the omnivores. Overall population of plants and animals is limited by the resources available to consume, as well as the ability to adapt to environmental stressors such as extreme weather, disease, or toxic waste. Ecological systems are more stable, or in balance, when a large number or diversity of plant and animal species is present, rather than few species in any location. Hence, forests or prairies are more diverse and stable than hog farms or cornfields, whose single species are highly susceptible to environmental stressors. Intercropping and crop rotation allow some diversity, even though the plant varieties are nevertheless limited.

Human systems studied through anthropology or geography gave rise to cultural ecology, human ecology, and political ecology, as understanding of ecological complexity grew. Cultural ecologists studied human cultures around the world as a product of desert, grassland, temperate forest, rain forest, mountain, or tundra environments in which people live. Each human culture was characterized by its particular foods and processes for daily living that were particular to the environmental qualities and limitations of these different habitats. Viewed within the industrial modernization paradigm emphasizing specialized technology, cultural evolution was measured by how much energy was harnessed from the environment per unit of human caloric input for hunter-gatherers, early small-scale cultivation and animal

FOOD PRODUCTION COSTS AND BENEFITS

The tremendous nonhuman energy fuel inputs in the more technological modern societies demonstrate ecological imbalance. The United States, for example, has one-twentieth of the world's population, but uses one-third of the world's fuel resources. Growing one calorie of food requires three calories of fossil fuel input for machinery, electricity, and fertilizer, and at least nine calories of fuel when processing and market transportation are included. This still excludes building the transportation vehicles, roads, and factories.

Genetic breeding of high-yield seeds and animals has led to more monocropping and less genetic diversity in the globalized cash-crop agriculture. Often the seeds are hybrids that do not reproduce new seeds to grow crops, so farmers must purchase each year's seeds from the agricultural industry. Nor are the high-yield seeds adapted to environmental stressors in diverse habitats without purchased chemical fertilizer and pesticide inputs. While new chemical pesticides are less immediately toxic than old arsenicals, cyanide, or nicotine, DDT (dichloro-diphenyl-trichloroethane) fatally weakens birds' eggs nearby, and there have been strong sugges-

tions of a link between pesticides (particularly DDT) and the tumors, reproductive problems, and cancer that occur among farmhands who have direct and repeated contact with the chemicals. Thus pesticides' long-term safety to consumers and the environment is questioned by those such as biologist Rachel Carson, who in 1962 exposed the dangers of pesticides in her seminal book, *Silent Spring*.

Also, farmers receive much less income for their food-production efforts compared to others in the overall marketing system. The twentieth-century Green Revolution that was to produce volumes of food for global markets also produced environmental and cultural degradation as traditional food-production practices, decision-making, and locally adapted seed and animal varieties were replaced. Since Neolithic times, increased crop volume has not necessarily produced better nutrition, since food distribution, access, and nutrient quality of the ensuing diet are frequently inadequate. High food volume allows high population density, increasing the risk of infectious disease because of waste management problems and peoples' proximity to each other.

---

husbandry, more advanced agriculture of state societies, and then global industrial society. Animal, mechanical, transportation, and fossil-fuel inputs were often overlooked so that technological modernization was perceived to produce great volumes of food and caloric energy for the exponentially growing population.

Human ecologists further examined ecological interrelations of humans, food production, and consequent health status in different habitats. Calculating detailed energy flow of food and fuel calories in particular groups' ecological systems illuminated the limits of the natural environment, and the adaptiveness of people's physiology and behavior to particular environments, foods, and climate. Human ecologists, like Michael Watts, defined the causes of severe droughts and food shortage in sub-Saharan Africa in the mid-1970s and 1980s. Since drought is cyclical, human ecologists investigated how traditional populations avoided famine via many traditional strategies to modify, buffer, distribute, resist, avoid, or conform to the perturbation. Food storage techniques, crop diversity, and irrigation are prime examples of buffering, distributing, or modifying environmental stressors. Continued use of such indigenous knowledge was recommended. Researchers also began to understand how the limits of natural-resource accessibility have been controlled by local, regional, and global politics and eco-

nomic market forces throughout history. Political and economic decisions made by new groups resulted in short-term gains, which often disrupted the longer-term environmental sense of traditional practices that had permitted people to survive over time. Hence, political ecology became the study of these combined factors, to improve food production further.

Environmentalism and Scientific Ecology

Some argue that the conservation movement arose through scientific application of ecological concepts so as to rationally plan economic development, thus replacing the public's or business's inefficient, shortsighted use of natural resources. Others believe that conservation occurred in reaction to modern industrialization's political grip over nature and people. Nevertheless, the environment has been known through an emotional, spiritual relationship of people who identify with their natural surroundings. Academic ecology initially had the premise that, by understanding ecological relationships, one could better control the parts of the process. "Objective" science and technology was the tool of industrial modernization's goal: controlling nature and other humans. Many public environmental movements identified with earlier religious and political philosophies oriented to the beauty and balance in nature, whereby taking too much from the system sends it into imbalance and ecological disaster.

Environmentalism has various forms that consequently advocate different philosophies and strategies for maintaining a balance among humans and the natural environment. Radical environmentalism includes deep ecology, social ecology, and ecofeminism. Radical environmentalism suggests eliminating the current political economic system to reach a more environmentally sound existence, whereas "surface" ecology advocates tinkering within the current system to direct it toward more sustainable or lower-impact options. Contrasts in environmental approaches have long existed, as reflected in John Muir's transcendental philosophy and Sierra Club in the early 1900s, versus Chief U.S. Forester Gifford Pinchot's scientific resource management of agriculture, forestry, livestock, and mining lands during Theodore Roosevelt's administration (1901–1909). Other environmentalists would emulate Aldo Leopold, who in the 1930s departed from scientific resource management to more spiritual approaches. Many scientific ecologists also gain insight from philosophical teachings and select career objectives that will serve the needs of humans and nature.

Sustainable Agriculture and Globalization

The counterculture of the 1960s and 1970s heightened interest in "health food" and food co-ops. This, and returning to organic farming, bioregional marketing, and sustainably "living off the grid" were reactions to capitalist globalization, vertical integration, and concentration in the food industry. Vertical integration involves ownership of the entire process of food production, processing, shipping, and marketing by a corporation or set of related corporations. The corporation may subcontract the riskier lower-profit aspects of the process to a separate small business that coordinates the farmers to meet the corporation's demand for specific qualities and timing of crop or livestock production. Concentration involves controlling entire food types (for example, pork, chicken, or flour) by only a few corporations. Contrastingly, community-supported agriculture and local farmers' markets feature direct marketing between the farmer and consumer.

The U.S. Food and Drug Administration (FDA) began as the "Division of Chemistry," created in 1862 as an agency of the Department of Agriculture and charged with the responsibility of regulating toxic food additives, preservatives, quack drugs, and insecticides. However, the FDA (so named in 1930) has become associated with industrial pharmaceutical business, authoritative curative medicine, and health-insurance interests by those preferring self-directed disease prevention with "health" foods and herbal and vitamin supplements. Vegetarian and organic products are often selected for reasons philosophical (to protect animals) or environmental (to eat chemical-free or low on the food chain). Europeans react strongly against genetically modified food because of

RADICAL ENVIRONMENTALISM: DEEP ECOLOGY, SOCIAL ECOLOGY, ECOFEMINISM

The term "deep ecology" was coined in the late 1960s by its leading proponent, Arne Naess, Norwegian mountaineer and teacher of Eastern and Western philosophy. Bill Devall and George Sessions, as well as David Foreman (founder of the radical group Earth First!) are more recent promoters. According to deep ecologists, the natural world is understandable through deductive subjectivity and consciousness raising. Examples of nature's value are gleaned from many religious philosophies. Population control and the biocentric valuing of plants and animals are deep ecology's hallmarks, rather than an anthropocentric orientation based on human needs. This has disturbing political implications when applied by elite classes or countries to the global system, since wildlife preservation is promoted over human needs in poverty-stricken areas. Neglect of these human needs becomes, therefore, population control.

Murray Bookchin pioneered the idea of "social ecology" in the 1960s as a means to address social inequity and sustainability by arguing for a more equitable decentralized political economic system using more alternative technology. But social ecology's Marxist and German Greens influences are often contrary to the philosophy and practices of the modern global market system. According to Bookchin, the natural and human ecological system develops through an educative, mediated, cumulative approach, versus the deductive understanding of nature, or the mechanistic evolutionary continuum of modernization found in deep ecology.

"Ecofeminism," promoted especially by female social scientists, notably Carolyn Merchant, explains environmental degradation and means for balance based on historical inequity of male and female social relations and decision-making. However, numerous evolutionary, structural, and political economic paradigms are confounded in selection of examples, much as deep ecology muddles religious philosophy from stratified and egalitarian social systems. According to ecofeminists, ritual, myth, and intuition are among methods of women's knowing, versus authoritative knowledge of male-centered "objective" science, business, and politics.

possible harm to others in the food chain, and against large-scale animal-husbandry practices that increase infectious disease, such as animal foot-and-mouth disease or "mad cow" disease—also feared for suspected neurological problems in humans. Yet the health-food market is subsumed by the corporate vitamin and supplement industry; the industrialization and mass marketing of "organic," "natural," or "health" food (a world market worth more than twenty-two billion dollars annually); more chain stores; and the U.S. Department of Agriculture's national organic standards of December 2000. Previous standards varied among regional organic farming associations, some being so strict that industrial organic farming would be prohibitive.

Interestingly, industrial and alternative agriculture claim overlapping goals, although careful examination reveals very different ideals behind those goals. Industrial corporations see a sustainable food system as ecologically sound, economically viable, and socially acceptable. When asked to identify their visions of a food system, supporters of alternative agriculture use such terms as ecologically sustainable, knowledgeable and communicative, proximate, economically sustaining, participatory, just and ethical, sustainably regulated, sacred, healthful, diverse, culturally nourishing, seasonal and temporal, economically value-oriented, relational. Conventional, industrial agriculture—centralized, dependent, competitive, specialized, and exploitative—attempts to dominate nature and the enterprise. Alternative agriculture is decentralized, independent, community-oriented, and restrained, with an emphasis on diversity and harmony with nature. The former maintains company profits; the latter attempts to maintain broader sociocultural and biological integrity of the local community and ecosystem.

See also **Additives; Environment; Food Politics: United States; Food Safety; Food Waste; Green Revolution; Herbicides; Organic Agriculture; Organic Food; Pesticides; Political Economy; Toxins, Unnatural, and Food Safety; Water: Safety of Water.**

BIBLIOGRAPHY

Bookchin, Murray. *The Philosophy of Social Ecology.* Second Edition. Montreal: Black Rose Books, 1995.

Carson, Rachel. *Silent Spring.* Cambridge, Mass.: The Riverside Press, 1962.

Devall, Bill, and George Sessions. *Deep Ecology: Living as if Nature Mattered.* Layton, Utah: Peregrine Smith, 1985.

Ellen, Roy. *Environment, Subsistence and System: The Ecology of Small-Scale Social Formations.* New York: Cambridge University Press, 1982.

Grey, Mark A. "The Industrial Food Stream and its Alternatives in the United States: An Introduction." *Human Organization* 59(2000): 143–150.

Hays, Samuel P. *Conservation and the Gospel of Efficiency: The Progressive Conservation Movement 1890–1920.* Cambridge, Mass.: Harvard University Press, 1959.

Leopold, Aldo. *A Sand County Almanac.* New York: Ballantine Books, reprint in arrangement with Oxford University Press, 1949.

Merchant, Carolyn. *Radical Ecology.* New York: Routledge, 1992.

Odum, Eugene P. *Fundamentals of Ecology.* 2d edition, in collaboration with Howard T. Odum. Philadelphia: W. B. Saunders, 1959.

Simmons, I. G. *Earth, Air and Water: Resources and Environment in the Late 20th Century.* London: Edward Arnold, 1991.

Thomas, R. Brooke, Sabrina H.B.H. Paine, and Barrett P. Brenton. "Perspectives on Socioeconomic Consequences and Responses to Food Deprivation." *Food and Nutrition Bulletin* 11 (1989): 41–54.

Thomas, R. Brooke, Bruce Winterhalder, and S. D. McRae. "An Anthropological Approach to Human Ecology and Adaptive Dynamics." *Yearbook of Physical Anthropology* 22 (1979):1–46.

Watts, Michael. *Silent Violence: Food, Famine and Peasantry in Northern Nigeria.* Berkeley: University of California Press, 1983.

Sabrina H. B. Hardenbergh

EDUCATION ABOUT FOOD.

EDUCATION ABOUT FOOD. Traditionally, chefs' proprietary interest in their culinary knowledge has hindered their efforts to educate successors. Before the late eighteenth century, culinary education meant apprenticeship in private—or royal—kitchens. To some extent, it still does mean that, although modern kitchens are more commonly commercial. Today, culinary education other than apprenticeship occurs in two primary forms: formal and independent, each subdivided into professional and domestic training.

Formal Study

In the late eighteenth century, chefs began to seek the respect accorded to other professionals. Recognizing that formal education is required for professional status, E. Kidder opened the first school for chefs in England in 1781. It was not until 1874, however, that the prestigious London Cookery School emerged. The pioneer French culinary school, École Professionnelle de Cuisine et des Sciences Alimentaires, debuted seventeen years later, but was short-lived (1891–1892). Le Cordon Bleu (1895), the first truly successful professional cooking school, became the prototype for most subsequent culinary programs.

Outside the United States, culinary schools generally issue certificates, not degrees. Since the end of World War II, many American chefs have been educated in collegiate culinary programs, receiving degrees from Cornell's School of Hotel Administration (1922), The Culinary Institute of America (1946), Johnson & Wales University (1973), or dozens of other colleges.

Cooking schools for domestic (primarily female) cooks began earlier than those for professionals. The first American cooking school, Mrs. Goodfellow's, opened in Philadelphia around 1820. Its anonymous textbook *Cookery As It Should Be* (1853) was reprinted in 1865 as *Mrs. Goodfellow's Cookery As It Should Be.*

The learning experience of a cooking school for young ladies is the subject of this John Leech caricature in 1851. The student in the center is curtsying although holding her ground: "I think I know my plum pudding!" On the right, another student bemoans that she will never learn how to make a proper omelet. From John Leech's *Follies of the Year* (London, 1864). ROUGHWOOD COLLECTION.

The Boston Cooking School (1878) was the most influential of the early cooking schools, resulting in the publication of *Mrs. Lincoln's Boston Cook Book: What To Do and What Not To Do in Cooking* in 1884. Fanny Farmer's *The Original Boston Cooking-School Kitchen Cook Book* (1896) applied scientific structure and principles in the home kitchen—foreshadowing Auguste Escoffier's *Le Guide Culinaire* (1903), which attempted to do the same for the professional kitchen.

Independent Study

Early professional cookbooks—written by and for men—such as Apicius's *De Re Coquinaria* (first century) or the *Viandier of Taillevent* (fourteenth century) were simply collections of recipes. They did not attempt to teach technique because they were intended for professional cooks who—presumably—understood their vague, missing, or abbreviated instructions. Charles Carter's cookbook, *The Complete Practical Cook: Or, A New System of the Whole Art and Mystery of Cookery* (1730), was typical of early cookbooks in that it was written for the management of wealthy households, but it consciously strove to educate the reader in the "most useful and noble Mysteries of their Art."

Most early home cookbooks, such as Torquatto Tasso's *The Householders Philosophie* (1588), were intended for women. They featured cooking instruction as just one of the duties comprising home economics or "domestic science." Home economics was envisioned—especially in the late nineteenth and early twentieth centuries—as a way to modernize—and professionalize—women's household work with "scientific" respectability. The Boston Cooking-School's textbook (1887) was such a treatise on "domestic science."

The earliest professional magazines for chefs and bakers—*L'Art Culinaire* (not the *L'Art Culinaire* available today), *Le Progrès des Cuisiniers*, *L'Étoile* and *Le Progrès Gastronomique*—first appeared in the 1880s. Today, there are hundreds of trade magazines for food professionals in almost every imaginable language. Even more food magazines are targeted at home cooks, and almost every major newspaper carries at least a column—and, more often, an entire section—devoted to food preparation.

Televised cooking lessons have grown in popularity and sophistication since Julia Child's *The French Chef* (1963). An entire network is now devoted to food programming—although it is intended largely for amateur cooks. The Culinary Institute of America and the California Culinary Academy (1977), however, produce series for public television that teach professional techniques for home use.

The Internet is a major supplier of culinary information for both home and professional cooks, offering recipes, reviews (of books and restaurants), nutritional data, links with TV cooking shows, and dozens of specialized culinary discussion groups.

Food Studies

Aside from cooking instruction, "Food Studies" is beginning to be recognized as a legitimate scholarly subject in its own right. Today, one can earn a master's degree in gastronomy at Boston University or the University of Adelaide, or a doctorate in Food Studies and Management from New York University.

Professionals in food science and nutrition have long had academic societies, but more recently scholars working in food studies have formed such groups. The Oxford Symposia on Food and Cookery (1981) provide opportunities for scholars from diverse backgrounds to share their research. The Association for the Study of Food and Society (1986) and the Agriculture, Food and Human Values Society (1987) promote research and scholarship on food-related issues, drawing on disciplines as diverse as anthropology, sociology, geography, literature, nutrition, and history.

Excellent culinary libraries—including the Arthur and Elizabeth Schlesinger Library on the History of Women in America (Radcliffe College); the James Beard Foundation Archive and Library (New York); the Conrad N. Hilton Library (Culinary Institute of America); Culinary Archives & Museum (Johnson & Wales University); Foundation of Chinese Dietary Culture (Taipei); Foundation B. IN. G. (Bibliothèque Internationale de Gastronomie, Italy); and Bibliothèque Municipale de Beziers, Bibliothèque Municipale de Dijon, and G. Sender (France)—inform food scholars.

The American Institute of Food & Wine (1981) and the James Beard Foundation (1985) spread awareness of gastronomic excellence through education, publications, scholarships, and events. Oldways Preservation & Exchange Trust (1988) and Italy's Arcigola Slowfood (1986) are preserving the knowledge and practice of traditional foodways.

Several societies of professional culinary educators have been organized to enhance respect for chefs. The American Culinary Federation (1929) awards the culinary equivalent of a doctoral degree—Certified Master Chef (CMC)—and accredits over one hundred American culinary education programs. Similar groups include the Council on Hotel, Restaurant, and Institutional Education (1946) and the International Association of Culinary Professionals (1990).

Les Dames d'Escoffier (1976) and Women Chefs and Restaurateurs (1993) were formed specifically to advance the professional status of women in the food service industry, successfully doing for professional female culinarians what the domestic science movement attempted to do for home cooks.

See also **Beard, James; Child, Julia; Cookbooks; Escoffier, Georges-Auguste; Food Studies; Gastronomy; Goodfellow, Elizabeth; Taillevent.**

BIBLIOGRAPHY

Allen, Gary. *The Resource Guide for Food Writers.* New York and London: Routledge, 1999.

Carter, Charles. *The Complete Practical Cook: Or, a New System of the Whole Art and Mystery of Cookery.* London: Prospect Books, 1984 (facsimile of the 1730 edition).

Davidson, Alan. *The Oxford Companion to Food.* Oxford and New York: Oxford University Press, 1999.

Escoffier, Auguste. *Le Guide Culinaire.* Translated by H. L. Cracknell and R. J. Kaufmann. New York: Wiley, 1997.

Farmer, Fannie Merritt. *The Original Boston Cooking-School Cook Book.* New York: H. L. Levin Associates, 1896 (facsimile: New York: Crown, 1973).

Goodfellow, Mrs. *Cookery As It Should Be.* Philadelphia: T. B. Peterson, 1865.

Lincoln, Mary J. *Mrs. Lincoln's Boston Cook Book: What to Do and What Not to Do in Cooking.* Revised edition. Boston: Little, Brown, 1918.

Mennell, Stephen. *All Manners of Food: Eating and Taste in England and France from the Middle Ages to the Present.* Oxford: Basil Blackwell, 1985.

Ruhlman, Michael. *The Making of a Chef: Mastering Heat at the Culinary Institute of America.* New York: Henry Holt, 1997.

Sculley, D. Eleanor, and Terence Sculley. *Early French Cookery: Sources, History, Original Recipes and Modern Adaptations.* Ann Arbor: University of Michigan Press, 1995.

Shapiro, Laura. *Perfection Salad: Women and Cooking at the Turn of the Century.* New York: Farrar, Straus and Giroux, 1995.

Trubek, Amy B. *Haute Cuisine: How the French Invented the Culinary Profession.* Philadelphia: University of Pennsylvania Press, 2000.

Gary Allen

EGGS. Eggs have been known to, and enjoyed by, humans for many centuries. Jungle fowl were domesticated in India by 3200 B.C.E. Records from China and Egypt show that fowl were domesticated and laying eggs for human consumption around 1400 B.C.E., and there is archaeological evidence for egg consumption dating back to the Neolithic age. The Romans found egg-laying hens in England, Gaul, and among the Germans. The first domesticated fowl reached North America with the second voyage of Columbus in 1493.

Eggs are a staple of the diet in most of the world. They are used as main dishes or served as garnish with other parts of the meal. Barer-Stein points out that Austrian and Croatian cuisines are rich in eggs. In Africa eggs are regarded as a symbol of fertility and accompany yams in many festive dishes.

While most discussions of eggs and egg nutrition refer to bird's eggs, it should be borne in mind that many other animal species also lay eggs. Among mammals the echidna and the duck-billed platypus lay eggs. Reptiles, among them lizards, chameleons, and the tuatara of New Zealand, lay eggs, as do toads and frogs. Mollusks and

TABLE 1

Proximate composition of a large raw egg

(59 g shell, 33.4 g white, 16.6 g yolk)

Nutrient	Whole egg (g)	% in yolk
Water	37.665	21.5
Protein	6.245	44.5
Carbohydrate	0.61	48.4
Fat	5.01	100.0
Ash	0.47	57.9

crustaceans lay eggs that appear in a variety of forms. The eggs of fish offer a wide range of number and form; for instance, salmon eggs are deposited in a trough prepared by the parent, while eggs of perch are adhesive and stick to water plants.

The number of eggs laid by fish varies widely but increases with age and weight. The salmon may produce 1,000 eggs for every pound of weight. The sturgeon lays about 7,000,000 eggs, whereas the herring and sole produce 50,000 and 134,000 eggs, respectively. The number of eggs laid is proportional to the risk of destruction or loss.

The greatest knowledge of eggs, their physiology and chemistry, comes from observing hens. The hen's reproductive system consists of the ovary, where the yolk develops, and the oviduct where the egg is completed. At birth the female chick has a fully formed ovary containing several thousand tiny ova, or future yolks. The ova begin to develop, one at a time, when the chick reaches sexual maturity. Each yolk is enclosed in its own sac or follicle. The follicle contains a system of blood vessels that supply nourishment to the developing yolk. At ovulation the follicle ruptures, thus releasing the yolk into the oviduct. The yolk passes into the infundibulum (funnel), where fertilization could occur. After about fifteen minutes the yolk passes into the magnum, where, in a period of three hours, albumen is deposited around the yolk. The yolk next passes into the isthmus where two shell membranes are formed in about seventy-five minutes. The egg has now achieved its full size and shape. It now passes into the uterus, where, over a period of nineteen to twenty hours, it acquires its shell, shell color, and outer shell coating. After a few minutes the egg is released via the vagina, cloaca, and vent. During formation the egg moves through the oviduct small end first, but just before laying, it is rotated and laid large end first. It takes the hen twenty-four to twenty-six hours to produce an egg. Within fifteen to thirty minutes after laying, the hen starts the process all over again.

The egg is designed to support life (to bring a chicken into the world) and has been called nature's ideal food. The yolk comprises about one-third of the weight of the egg. The albumen or white of the egg is primarily protein and water. The yolk of a large egg contains fifty-nine calories and the albumen carries about seventeen calories. See Table 1 for the proximate composition of a large raw egg.

Protein is required for synthesis and maintenance of muscles, body organs, nerves, bones, and blood. Protein quality is measured by how efficiently it is used for growth. Only mother's milk has higher quality protein.

Egg protein contains different amino acids, including all the essential amino acids (essentiality of a nutrient means that it cannot be synthesized by humans and must be obtained from the diet).

Fat (lipid) comprises about 10 percent of the total weight of a large egg. The lipid composition of the egg is presented in Table 2.

Saturated, monounsaturated, and polyunsaturated fatty acids comprise 37.5, 46.0, and 16.5 percent of the total, respectively. Oleic acid (18:1) represents 40 percent of egg yolk fatty acids. There is a nutritional ambivalence with regard to eggs. Although the superior quality of egg protein is acknowledged, there is concern regarding the cholesterol content, this despite evidence that moderate intake of egg yolk is generally not harmful. Since polyunsaturated fats reduce plasma cholesterol levels, efforts have been made to increase their presence in the yolk. Feeding laying hens high levels of polyunsaturated fats such as corn or soybean oil will raise the level of their component yolk fatty acids to a slight degree. "Polyunsaturated" eggs are commercially available, but there is little evidence regarding any sustained hypocholesterolemic effect. There are also efforts to increase levels of antioxidant vitamins and fish oil

TABLE 2

Yolk lipids of a large raw egg

(59 g shell, 33.4 g white, 16.6 g yolk)

Fatty acids	G
Total	4.43
Saturated	1.59
Myristic (14:0)	0.02
Palmitic (16:0)	1.14
Stearic (18:0)	0.40
Monounsaturated	1.95
Palmitoleic (16:1)	0.15
Oleic (18:1)	1.78
Eicosenoic (20:1)	0.01
Polyunsaturated	0.70
Linoleic (18:2)	0.59
Linolenic (18:3)	0.02
Arachidonic (20:4)	0.07
Docosahexaenoic (22:6)	0.02
Cholesterol	0.21
Lecithin	1.11

Floating island was one of the most popular meringue desserts in eighteenth-century English and American cookery. It is still popular in England today. Egg whites whipped with wine are shown here floating in a creamy Madeira sauce. The "island" is garnished with crystallized violet petals and toasted almonds. © MICHAEL BOYS/CORBIS.

fatty acids in egg yolk and those products, too, are available to the public.

Hen's eggs are the most common source of egg nutrition. In 1989 the three largest egg-producing countries were China (140,900 × 10⁶ eggs), Russia (84,600 × 10⁶ eggs), and the United States (67,042 × 10⁶ eggs). However, eggs of other avian species are eaten around the world. Hen's eggs contain less fat and less cholesterol than those of the duck, goose, quail, or turkey. The amount of fat in a yolk is partly a function of the size of the embryo and its future requirements. Caviar, for instance, contains almost 18 g of fat per 100 g of edible portion, but its cholesterol content is only 38 percent greater than that of the hen's egg. The major fatty acids of all the yolks are palmitic and oleic.

The egg is an easily available, inexpensive source of high-quality nutrition. It is an especially important source of nutrition for young people, old people, and sick people. Starting about forty years ago, as the relation between blood cholesterol and the risk of coronary heart disease was unfolding, the egg came under fire because of its cholesterol content. The assumption was that eating cholesterol-rich foods led directly to elevations in blood cholesterol and hence in risk of disease. That elevated blood cholesterol presents a risk for heart disease is fairly well established, but a direct link between dietary cholesterol and levels of blood cholesterol is not. Many other aspects of the diet influence blood cholesterol to a greater extent than does dietary cholesterol; principal among them are the amount of saturated fat in the diet and the type and amount of fiber in the diet. There are dietary prescriptions limiting the permissible amount of cholesterol in the diet. These are easy to follow, but are based on relatively little hard data. The emphasis on cholesterol has overshadowed the greater impact of saturated fat. The fat of the egg is relatively unsaturated, or the raw yolk would be solid. A calculated iodine value (measure of unsaturation) of egg yolk is about 72, which is not much below that of olive oil.

The relation of dietary cholesterol to blood cholesterol levels has been studied for many years. In the early 1950s it was demonstrated that while cholesterol levels of subjects with coronary disease were significantly higher than those of control subjects there was no relation to the level of cholesterol in the diet. In 1970 the subjects in the Framingham Study, both men and women, were segregated by serum cholesterol level under 180 mg/dl, over 300 mg/dl, and 181–300 mg/dl. The study found no correlation of serum cholesterol with any dietary component. The Framingham Study also showed that ingestion of one or nine eggs per week had the same influence on serum cholesterol. A study conducted by the NIH over twenty years ago attempted to correlate dietary factors with actual heart attacks in three large studies—Framingham, Puerto Rico, and Hawaii. At no location were there differences in cholesterol intake between those subjects who had suffered a heart attack and those who had not.

Epidemiological studies of dietary cholesterol have to be aware of possible confounding by other dietary factors. Many foods high in cholesterol are also high in saturated fat. High-fat diets are often poor in fiber. Since saturated fat intake has been linked to coronary disease and fiber appears to be protective, both must be considered when evaluating the role of dietary cholesterol.

Data relating dietary cholesterol to heart disease are available. A study of middle–aged men in the Netherlands showed no significant relationship between cholesterol intake and coronary death after ten years. A positive relationship appeared after twenty years of follow-up but was not significant after adjustment was made for standard risk factors, occupation, and energy intake.

More pertinent to the discussion is the relationship, if any, between egg consumption and coronary disease. A study of women in Italy found no association between egg consumption and nonfatal myocardial infarction. A study among Seventh Day Adventists in California found no association between egg consumption and risk of cardiovascular disease, whereas a study of vegetarians in Oxford, England, found a significantly greater risk in those consuming six or more eggs a week than in those eating less than one egg per week.

One study, conducted at Harvard University, was aimed at investigating an explicit relationship between egg consumption and risk of cardiovascular disease. The authors addressed data derived from ongoing studies of more than eighty thousand female nurses and more than forty-three thousand male health professionals. After adjustment for age, body mass index, cigarette smoking, parental history of heart disease, vitamin intake, alcohol use, hypertension, physical activity, energy intake, bacon consumption, and in the women, menopausal status and postmenopausal hormone use, there was no association between egg consumption and coronary heart disease in either group.

The diet-heart hypothesis holds that a diet high in saturated fat and cholesterol and low in polyunsaturated fat leads to hypercholesterolemia and subsequent development of atherosclerosis. Addition of eggs to the usual diet of free living subjects does not affect cholesterolemia. Addition or deletion of eggs in the diet leads to other changes in diet that must be evaluated and corrected for. The Framingham data suggest that addition of eggs to the diet does not affect serum cholesterol levels. The egg is a source of a number of essential nutrients; that, plus its high-grade protein and low price, make the egg a desirable food, especially for the very young, old, and infirm. The presence of a high level of cholesterol in the egg has led to suggestions that it not be included in healthful diets since elevated blood cholesterol is a risk factor for cardiovascular disease. Data are accumulating which show that dietary cholesterol has a minimal effect on blood cholesterol levels. Epidemiological data also show little association between eggs and risk of cardiovascular disease. Eggs can be an important part of the diets of healthy persons.

See also **Cholesterol; Combination of Proteins; Lipids; Poultry; Proteins and Amino Acids; Sea Birds and Their Eggs.**

BIBLIOGRAPHY

American Egg Board, The. *The Incredible Edible Egg Eggcyclopedia*. Park Ridge, Ill.: American Egg Board, 1999.

Ascherio, Alberto, Eric B. Rimm, Edward L. Giovanucci, Donna Spiegelman, Meir Stampfer, and Walter C. Willett. "Dietary Fat and Risk of Coronary Heart Disease in Men: Cohort Follow-up Study in the United States." *British Medical Journal* 313 (1996): 84–90.

Barer-Stein, Thelma. *You Eat What You Are: People, Culture, and Food Traditions.* 2d ed. Willowdale, Ontario: Firefly Books, 1999.

Published in 1940 by Ruth Berolzheimer, director of the Culinary Arts Institute in Chicago, *300 Ways to Serve Eggs* was both a booster for the egg industry and a novel attempt to make egg dishes the focal point of the menu. The rustic country basket on the cover is intended to imply farm-raised and down-home goodness, although no egg grower would pile eggs that high—they would crush one another. ROUGHWOOD COLLECTION.

Dawber, Thomas R., Rita J. Nickerson, Frederick N. Brand, and Jeremy Pool. "Eggs, Serum Cholesterol and Coronary Heart Disease." *American Journal of Clinical Nutrition* 36 (1982): 617–625.

Hu, Frank B., Meir J. Stampfer, JoAnn E. Mason, Eric Rimm, Graham A. Colditz, Bernard A. Rosner, Charles H. Hennekens, and Walter C. Willett. "Dietary Fat Intake and the Risk of Coronary Heart Disease in Women." *New England Journal of Medicine* 337 (1997): 1491–1499.

Hu, Frank B., Meir J. Stampfer, Eric B. Rimm, JoAnn E. Manson, Alberto Ascherio, Graham A. Colditz, Bernard A. Rosner, Donna Spiegelman, Frank E. Speizer, Frank M. Sacks, Charles H. Hennekens, and Walter C. Willett. "A Prospective Study of Egg Consumption and Risk of Cardiovascular Disease in Men and Women." *Journal of the American Medical Association* 281 (1999): 1387–1394.

Kannel, William B., and Tavia Gordon. "Section 24: The Framingham Study: Diet and the Regulation of Serum Cholesterol." In *The Framingham Study: An Epidemiological*

Investigation of Cardiovascular Disease. Vol. 24. Bethesda, Md.: U.S. Dept. of Health, Education, and Welfare, 1970.

Kiple, Kenneth F., and Kriemhild Coneè Ornelas. *The Cambridge World History of Food.* Vol. 2. Cambridge, U.K.: Cambridge University Press, 2000.

Kritchevsky, Stephen B., and David Kritchevsky. "Egg Consumption and Coronary Heart Disease: An Epidemiological Overview." *Journal of the American College of Nutrition* 19 (2000): 549S–555S.

Kromhout, Daan, and C. deLezenne Coulander. "Diet, Prevalence and 10-year Mortality from Coronary Heart Disease in 871 Middle Aged Men: The Zutphen Study." *American Journal of Epidemiology* 119 (1984): 733–741.

McNamara, Donald J. "Dietary Cholesterol and Atherosclerosis." *Biochimica et Biophysica Acta* 1529 (2000): 310–320.

David Kritchevsky

EGYPT. *See* **Middle East; North Africa.**

ELECTROLYTES. Electrolytes are molecules that, in solution, dissociate into positively charged ions (cations) and negatively charged ions (anions). Principal ions in body fluids are sodium, potassium, and chloride. A 70 kg adult has a body content of approximately 100 g sodium, 140 g potassium, and 95 g chloride. To maintain a stable body content, the amount of principal ions lost must equal the amount consumed. During growth and during pregnancy, the amount accreted for tissue formation also must be considered.

Physiological Functions

Sodium is the predominant cation in fluids outside the cells (extracellular fluid), whereas potassium is the predominant cation in the intracellular fluid. Chloride is the major anion of the extracellular fluid. Sodium plays a central role in regulating body fluid balance and distribution of fluid between the extracellular and intracellular compartments. As sodium is the major osmotically active particle in the extracellular fluid, sodium and its accompanying anion determines the osmolar concentration, or osmolarity, of this compartment. An increase in sodium concentration will increase the osmolarity of the extracellular fluid, thus causing water to move out of the cells into the extracellular compartment. It will also cause water retention by stimulating the thirst mechanism and by decreasing urine flow. The opposite occurs when sodium concentration is decreased. Thus, sodium plays a central role in regulating body fluid balance and the distribution of fluid between the extracellular and intracellular compartments.

Potassium is necessary for normal growth and plays an important function in cell metabolism, enzyme reactions, and synthesis of muscle protein. Both sodium and potassium are involved in maintaining proper acidity (pH) of the blood and in maintaining nerve and muscle functions. Normal resting membrane potentials of nerve and muscle cells range between -50 and 100 mV, with the inside of the cells negative with respect to the outside. These resting membrane potentials are maintained by the chemical gradient of potassium across cell membranes. Activation of excitable cells alters their membrane permeabilities to sodium and potassium, leading to changes in their membrane potentials. A weak stimulus causes a small depolarization (the inside of the cell is made less negative) as a result of sodium influx along its electrochemical gradient via the voltage-gated sodium channels in cell membranes. This is followed by repolarization, which is a manifestation of potassium efflux. If the stimulus is sufficiently strong, large changes in the membrane potential occur, during which the membrane potential may change from -70 mV to $+30$ mV, and then repolarize back to its resting membrane potential. This action potential, cause by alternation of potassium steady-state potentials with pulsed sodium potentials, gives rise to a traveling wave of depolarization that is conducted along the nerve fiber to exert an effect on the effector cells it innervates (supplies with nerves). In muscles, action potential leads to muscle contraction.

Dietary sodium chloride in foods and beverages is absorbed mostly in the small intestine. Active transport of sodium out of the small intestinal epithelial cells across their basolateral membrane provides an electrochemical gradient for the absorption of sodium across the luminal membrane. Entry of sodium through carrier proteins can either transport other solutes against their concentration gradient in the same direction (co-transport) or in an opposite direction (counter-transport). A number of transporters have receptor sites for binding sodium and glucose, galactose, or amino acids. Therefore, entry of sodium across the luminal membrane also brings in a solute. Counter-transport mechanisms operating in the kidneys allow excess hydrogen and potassium to be excreted in the urine.

Consumption of Sodium, Chloride, and Potassium

Consumption usually exceeds the needs of an individual, although the amount consumed varies widely with dietary habits. Most natural foods contain high potassium content but are lower in sodium content (Table 1). American adults consume an average of 2.5 to 3.5 g of potassium daily. Individuals consuming large amounts of fruits and vegetables may have a daily intake of as high as 11 g. Sodium is consumed mainly as sodium chloride (table salt). A small amount is consumed as sodium carbonate, sodium citrate, and sodium glutamate. Intakes of sodium vary, averaging 2 to 5 g/day of sodium or 5 to 13 g/day of sodium chloride. Only about 10 percent of sodium intake is from natural foods, the rest from sodium salts added during cooking and at the table, and from salts added during processing of foods. In regions where consumption of salt-preserved foods is customary, intake of sodium can be as high as 14 to 20 g/day.

Under normal circumstances, about 99 percent of dietary sodium, chloride, and potassium is absorbed. Absorption occurs along the entire length of the intestine, the largest fraction being absorbed in the small intestine and the remaining 5 to 10 percent in the colon. Potassium is also secreted in the colon. Various homeostatic regulatory mechanisms, the most important of which is aldosterone, modulate the absorption of sodium and secretion of potassium.

Loss of Sodium, Chloride, and Potassium
Obligatory loss of fluids through skin, urine, and feces invariably causes loss of these ions. Minimal obligatory loss for an adult consuming average intakes has been estimated to be 115 mg/day for sodium and 800 mg/day for potassium. Over 95 percent of loss is in the urine. Under most circumstances, loss of chloride parallels that of sodium. Loss of these ions can increase greatly in diuresis, vomiting, and diarrhea. Loss of sodium chloride can also increase greatly from profuse sweating.

Recommended Intake. Daily minimum needs can be estimated from the amount required to replace obligatory

TABLE 1

Food sources of sodium, chloride, and potassium (mg/100 g)

	Sodium	Chloride	Potassium
Natural Foods			
Beef, lean (ribs, loin)	65	59	355
Pork, lean (ribs, loin)	70	—	285
Chicken fryers (with skin)	83	85	359
Salmon, fresh	48	59	391
Milk (pasteurized, whole cow's)	55	100	139
Wheat flour (whole)	2	38	290
Rice (polished, raw)	6	27	110
Potatoes	3	79	410
Carrots	50	69	311
Beans (string, fresh)	1.7	33	256
Apricots	0.6	—	440
Dates (dried)	1	290	790
Oranges	1	3	170
Almonds	4	2	773
Processed Foods			
Bacon (medium fat)	1770	—	225
Beef sausages	810	1100	150
Smoked salmon	1880	2850	420
Cheese (Cheddar)	700	—	82
Butter (unsalted)	7	10	23
Bread (whole meal)	540	860	220
Potato chips	550	890	1190
Carrots (canned, drained solids)	236	450	110
Beans (string, canned, drained solids)	236	300	95

SOURCE: Lentner, Cornelius, ed. *Geigy Scientific Tables,* 8th ed., vol. 1.

TABLE 2

Estimated minimum requirement across the life cycle

	Sodium mg/day	Chloride mg/day	Potassium mg/day
Infants			
0–0.5 y	120	180	500
0.5–1.0 y	200	300	700
Children			
1 y	225	350	1000
2–5 y	300	500	1400
6–9 y	400	600	1600
10–18 y	500	750	2000
Adults			
>18 y	500	750	2000

SOURCE: National Research Council. *Recommended Dietary Allowances,* 10th ed.

losses (Table 2). The need is increased in infants and children, and during pregnancy and lactation. Estimated safe minimum intake levels are higher than the minimum requirements to account for the various degrees of physical activity of individuals and environmental conditions. Average intakes in the United States are higher than the estimated safe minimum levels of sodium chloride (1.3 g/day) and potassium (2 g/day).

The association of high salt intake with hypertension and the beneficial effects of potassium in hypertension has led to recommendations that daily intake of salt should not exceed 6 g and that of potassium should be increased to 3.5 g. This can be achieved by increasing intake of dietary fruits and vegetables.

Regulation of Sodium, Chloride, and Potassium Balance
Various mechanisms regulate excretion of these ions by the kidneys to maintain homeostatic equilibrium of body fluids. Urinary sodium excretion is controlled by varying the rate of sodium reabsorption from the glomerular filtrate by tubular cells, whereas potassium excretion is controlled by varying the rate of tubular secretion of potassium.

Abnormally low blood volume (hypovolemia) in sodium deficit increases renal sodium chloride reabsorption by increasing sympathetic discharge to the kidneys, and by stimulation of two hormonal systems, the renin-angiotensin-aldosterone and the antidiuretic systems. This results in the production of low urine volume with low sodium and chloride contents. Hypovolemia also initiates the thirst mechanism and increases an appetite for salt (or salt cravings). The presence of salt appetite in animals is to ensure an adequate intake of salt to protect the extracellular fluid volume from excessive loss of sodium due to sweating, diarrhea, pregnancy, or lactation. The development of salt appetite is of signif-

DIARRHEA

Daily, about 8 to 10 l of water and large amounts of ions enter the gastrointestinal tract; about 1 to 2 l are from the diet, the rest from secretions of the alimentary tract. The greater part of this fluid is absorbed by the intestinal cells so that only about 150 ml of fluid are lost daily in the stool of an adult. Stools contain a low content of sodium and chloride but a high content of potassium so that the daily losses averages 6 mmol for sodium, 12 mmol for potassium, 3 mmol for chloride, and 5 mmol for bicarbonate. Loss of this water and ions can increase greatly in diarrhea, and if extreme, several liters of fluid can be lost, leading to dehydration and electrolyte and acid-base disturbances.

Diarrhea is defined as an increase in stool liquidity and a fecal volume of more than 200 ml/day in adults. Clinically, the most common and important causes of diarrhea are osmotic and secretory. Ingestion of a poorly absorbable solute, such as magnesium sulfate, or malabsorption or maldigestion of a specific solute because of enzyme deficiencies, as seen in lactase deficiency, can cause osmotic diarrhea. The presence of these solutes increases the intestinal luminal osmolarity, causing water to be retained in the lumen.

Various viral and bacterial infections can cause secretory diarrhea. Enteroinvasive bacteria such as *Shigella* and *Salmonella* invade intestinal mucosa to produce ulceroinflammatory lesions resulting in a failure of normal absorption. On the other hand, bacteria such as *Vibrio cholerae* release toxins that increase secretion of sodium chloride and water. If the cholera is severe, up to 18 l of watery stools can be passed in a day. These stools contain ionic concentrations similar to that of plasma, so that large amounts of sodium, chloride, and potassium can be lost.

Dehydration caused by diarrhea ranges from mild to severe. The severity of dehydration can be assessed clinically by examining the patient for sunken eyeballs, skin turgor, mental status, blood pressure, and urine output. Fluid replacement is of utmost importance, especially in severe dehydration, to prevent circulatory collapse. Although diarrhea causes losses of sodium as well as potassium and bicarbonate, the immediate concern in treating severe diarrhea is to replace sodium and water to restore the circulatory volume. Dehydration in diarrhea can be reversed by oral or, in emergency, intravenous rehydration therapy.

The World Health Organization has recommended the use of oral rehydration therapy for treatment of mild to moderate cases of diarrhea. This program has been very successful in reducing mortality from diarrheal diseases, particularly in infants in developing countries. Oral rehydration fluid contains 3.5 g of sodium chloride, 2.5 g of sodium bicarbonate, 1.5 g of potassium chloride, and 20 g of glucose in 1 l of water. An alternative household remedy is to make a solution containing three "finger pinches" of salt, a "fistful of sugar" and one quart of water. Addition of sugar to the oral rehydration fluid helps to increase the absorption of sodium chloride through the sodium-glucose transporter system in the small intestine.

---

icance in the successful adaptation to a terrestrial life, especially in herbivorous animals. The need for salt can be satisfied by providing cattle and sheep with salt licks. Humans and other carnivores are less dependent on separate supplies of salt because dietary salt can be obtained from meat. However, they may develop a craving for salt when they are sodium deficient. This deficit-induced salt craving may be mediated by hormones acting on the brain and by changes in gustatory response. Abnormally high blood volume (hypervolemia) in sodium excess increases renal excretion of sodium chloride by suppression of sympathetic discharge to the kidneys, suppression of the renin-angiotensin-aldosterone and antidiuretic systems, and stimulation of the secretion of atrial natriuretic peptides.

Aldosterone is the most important hormone regulating secretion of potassium. Aldosterone secretion is triggered by angiotensin II, by high plasma potassium concentration, or by low plasma sodium concentration.

Plasma concentrations of potassium and hydrogen also affect directly the secretion of potassium by the distal nephrons. The rate of potassium secretion parallels the plasma potassium concentration. Secretion of potassium in response to changes in acid-base balance (which affects plasma pH) is complex. In general, acute acidosis decreases secretion of potassium, whereas acute alkalosis increases secretion and loss of potassium from the body. Response to chronic acid-base disorders is varied.

Sodium, Chloride, and Potassium Imbalance

Acute excessive intakes do not normally result in retention of sodium, chloride, and potassium because of the capacity of the kidneys to excrete these ions. Retention occurs when kidney function is compromised. Dietary deficiency does not normally occur because normal consumption usually exceeds body needs.

THERMOREGULATION THROUGH PERSPIRATION

Heat is produced continuously by the body during metabolism, and it is also taken up by the body from the environment by radiation and conduction. Heat is lost from the body by radiation, conduction and convection, and evaporation. Even in the absence of perspiration, water is lost continuously from the body by evaporation from the upper respiratory tract and by passive evaporation from the skin. These insensible water losses amount to a total of about 0.6 l/day, of which slightly more than 50 percent is from the skin. For every liter of water that evaporates from the body, 580 kcal (2428 kJ) of heat is dissipated. During intense physical exertion or at a high ambient temperature, loss of heat from radiation, conduction, and insensible water loss are insufficient to prevent a rise in body temperature. Under these circumstances, heat loss is enhanced by the production and evaporation of sweat. Loss of heat by evaporation of sweat is an effective means of removing excess heat from the body, and it can be controlled by regulating the rate of sweating. When the body temperature rises above 98.6°F (37°C), stimulation of the temperature-regulating center in the hypothalamus causes sweating.

Sweat is produced by sweat glands by actively secreting into ducts a fluid similar in composition to that of plasma. As this primary secretion passes along the ducts of the sweat glands to the surface of the skin, sodium and chloride are absorbed in excess of water, resulting in the production of a dilute fluid that has a lower content of sodium and chloride. Sodium chloride content in sweat varies; it depends on the rate of flow. For a young adult, the average value is about 50 mmol/l for sodium and 30 mmol/l for chloride. The transport mechanisms for sodium and chloride are affected in patients suffering from cystic fibrosis so that their concentrations in the sweat are increased. For the purpose of diagnosis, the upper limit of the normal values for children and young adults are set at 70–80 mmol/l for sodium and 60–70 mmol/l for chloride (Lentner, ed.).

Rate of sweat production depends on the ambient temperature and humidity, and the degree of activity of the individual. For a 70 kg man doing light work at an ambient temperature of 84°F (29°C), daily loss is about 2 to 3 l. An unacclimatized individual who is performing hard physical activity in a hot, humid environment may lose, for a short time, up to 2 to 4 l/hour of sweat. As the duration of perspiration increases, the rate of production decreases to about 0.5 l/hour. Therefore, even at maximal sweating, the rate of heat loss may not be rapid enough to dissipate the excess heat from the body. Dehydration from excessive loss of water and sodium chloride stimulates the thirst mechanism, and if water intake is not increased, it can cause weakness and, if severe, circulatory collapse.

Adaptation to heat leads to physiological changes that include an increase in sweat production, an increase in plasma volume, and a decrease in concentration of sodium and chloride in the sweat and urine. These latter two effects are caused by an increase in aldosterone secretion as a result of dehydration and loss of sodium from the body. The decrease in the concentration of sodium and chloride in sweat and urine allows for better conservation of these ions in the body. An unacclimatized person who sweats profusely often loses as much as 13 to 30 g of salt per day for the first few days, but after four to six weeks of acclimatization the loss can be as low as 3 to 5 g a day.

There is a limit at which the body can lose heat even when perspiring maximally. The progressive rise in body temperature will affect the heat-regulating ability of the hypothalamus, resulting in a decrease in sweating. Therefore, a high body temperature tends to perpetuate itself unless measures are taken specifically to decrease the body temperature. When the body temperature rises beyond a critical temperature of 106°F (41°C), the person is likely to develop heat stroke. Symptoms include dizziness, abdominal distress, delirium, and eventually loss of consciousness. Some of these symptoms are exacerbated by a mild degree of circulatory shock as a result of sodium loss and dehydration.

Since the extracellular fluid volume changes in parallel with its sodium concentration, sodium retention in renal failure or congestive heart failure results in edema and possibly hypertension (Table 3). Excessive loss of sodium resulting in hypovolemia and hypotension can occur through diuresis, Addison's disease, severe vomiting, or diarrhea.

Changes in plasma concentration of potassium affects the excitability of nerves and muscle cells (Table 3). Re-

tention of potassium causes hyperkalemia (plasma potassium concentration exceeding 5.0 mmol/l), and depletion causes hypokalemia (plasma potassium concentration less than 3.5 mmol/l). Retention of potassium occurs when there is a lack of aldosterone secretion, or a lack of responsiveness of the kidney to aldosterone. An important clinical manifestation of hyperkalemia is cardiac arrhythmia, which can lead to cardiac arrest. Depletion of potassium can occur through hyperaldosteronism, diuresis,

TABLE 3

Imbalance of sodium and potassium

Primary defect	Pathological causes	Clinical manifestation
sodium retention	congestive heart failure renal failure Conn's syndrome	edema, hypertension
sodium depletion	excessive perspiration Addison's disease diuretic therapy renal diseases prolonged vomiting diarrhea	orthostatic hypotension, muscular weakness and cramps, dizziness and syncope, circulatory shock
potassium retention	aldosterone deficiency	cardiac arrhythmias leading to cardiac arrest
potassium depletion	wasting diseases and starvation hyperaldosteronism metabolic alkalosis diuretic therapy renal diseases prolonged vomiting diarrhea	muscle weakness, impairment of neuromuscular function, cardiac arrhythmias

SOURCE: Palmer, Alpern, and Seldin; Rodriguez-Soriano; Toto and Seldin.

vomiting, or diarrhea. Manifestations of hypokalemia include depressed neuromuscular functions and, in more severe hypokalemia, cardiac arrhythmias.

Nutritional Considerations

Epidemiological and experimental evidence has implicated habitual high dietary salt consumption in the development of hypertension, but controversy remains regarding the importance of sodium salts in the regulation of blood pressure and the mechanisms by which salt influences blood pressure (Stamler, 1977). Intervention studies of dietary salt restrictions to lower blood pressure have produced mixed results. Nevertheless, various clinical trials indicate some beneficial effects of dietary restriction of sodium on blood pressure, and it may also decrease the incidence of stroke and ischemic heart disease.

High consumption of potassium, found in foods like oranges, apricots, and dates, on the other hand, appears to have a protective action against cardiovascular diseases, although the mechanism of action is not known. Epidemiological studies have demonstrated an inverse relationship of potassium intake with blood pressure, incidence of stroke, and other cardiovascular diseases (Young, Huabao, and McCabe). A direct relationship between blood pressure and the ratio of sodium to potassium in the urine has also been found (Stamler).

Repeated intake over a long period of salt from salted and smoked products is associated with atrophic gastritis and gastric cancer. However, experimental evidence indicates that salt alone is not carcinogenic; the high dietary salt content may enhance the initiation of cancer by facilitating the action of any carcinogen, such as polycyclic aromatic hydrocarbons, present in the diet (Cohen and Roe, 1977), or potentiating Helicobacter pylori–associated carcinogenesis (Fox et al., 1999).

See also **Minerals; Nutrient Requirements; Nutrition; Salt; Sodium; Thirst.**

BIBLIOGRAPHY

Cohen, A. J., and F. J. Roe. "Evaluation of the Aetiological Role of Dietary Salt Exposure in Gastric and Other Cancers in Humans." *Food and Chemical Toxicology* 35 (1997): 271–293.

Fox, James G., et al. "High Salt Diet Induces Gastric Epithelial Hyperplasia and Parietal Cell Loss, and Enhances Helicobacter pylori Colonization in C57BL/6 Mice." *Cancer Research* 59 (1999): 4823–4828.

Lentner, Cornelius, ed. *Geigy Scientific Tables*. 8th ed., vol. 1. Basel: Ciba-Geigy Limited, 1981.

National Research Council. *Recommended Dietary Allowances*. 10th ed. Washington, D. C.: National Academy Press, 1989.

Palmer, Biff F., Robert J. Alpern, and Donald W. Seldin. "Physiology and Pathophysiology of Sodium Retention." In *The Kidney: Physiology and Pathophysiology*, edited by Donald W. Seldin and Gerhard Giebisch. 3d ed., Philadelphia: Lippincott Williams and Wilkins, 2000. Vol II, Chapter 54, pp. 1473–1517.

Rodriguez-Soriano, Juan. "Potassium Homeostasis and Its Disturbance in Children." *Pediatric Nephrology* 9 (1995): 364–374.

Stamler, Jeremiah. "The INTERSALT Study: Background, Methods, Findings, and Implications." *American Journal of Clinical Nutrition* 65 (1997): 626S–642S.

Toto, Robert D., and Donald W. Seldin. "Salt Wastage." In *The Kidney: Physiology and Pathophysiology*, edited by Donald W. Seldin and Gerhard Giebisch. vol. 2, 3d ed., pp. 1519–1536. Philadelphia: Lippincott Williams and Wilkins, 2000.

Young, David B., Huabao Lin, and Richard D. McCabe. "Potassium's Cardiovascular Protective Mechanisms." *American Journal of Physiology* 268 (1995): R825–R837.

Hwai-Ping Sheng

ENERGY. Sufficient dietary energy is essential to the survival and health of all animals. For understanding the biology and health of humans, energy is particularly important for a number of reasons. First, food and energy represent critical points of interaction between humans and their environment. The environments in which humans live determine the range of food resources that are available and how much energy and effort are necessary to procure those resources. Indeed, the dynamic between energy intake and energy expenditure is quite different for a subsistence farmer of Latin America than it is for

566

an urban executive living in the United States. Beyond differences in the physical environment, social, cultural, and economic variation also shape aspects of energy balance. Social and cultural norms are important for shaping food preferences, whereas differences in subsistence behavior and socioeconomic status strongly influence food availability and the effort required to obtain food.

Additionally, the balance between energy expenditure and energy acquired has important adaptive consequences for both survival and reproduction. Obtaining sufficient food energy has been an important stressor throughout human evolutionary history, and it continues to strongly shape the biology of traditional human populations today.

This article examines aspects of energy expenditure and energy intake in humans. How energy is measured is first considered, with a look at how both the energy content of foods and the energy requirements for humans are determined. Next, aspects of energy consumption and the chemical sources of energy in different food items are examined. Third, the physiological basis of variation in human energy requirements is explored, specifically a consideration of the different factors that determine how much energy a person must consume to sustain him- or herself. Finally, patterns of variation in energy intake and expenditure among modern human populations are examined, with the different strategies that humans use to fulfill their dietary energy needs highlighted.

Calorimetry: Measuring Energy

The study of energy relies on the principle of calorimetry, the measurement of heat transfer. In food and nutrition, energy is most often measured in kilocalories (kcal). One kilocalorie is the amount of heat required to raise the temperature of 1 kilogram (or 1 liter) of water 1°C. Thus, a food item containing 150 kilocalories (two pieces of bread, for example) contains enough stored chemical energy to increase the temperature of 150 liters of water by 1°C. Another common unit for measuring energy is the joule or the kilojoule (1 kilojoule [kJ] = 1,000 joules). The conversion between calories and joules is as follows: 1 kilocalorie equals 4.184 kilojoules.

To directly measure the energy content of foods, scientists use an instrument known as a bomb calorimeter. This instrument burns a sample of food in the presence of oxygen and measures the amount of heat released (that is, kilocalories or kilojoules). This heat of combustion represents the total energetic value of the food.

Basic principles of calorimetry are also used to measure energy expenditure (or requirements) in humans and other animals. Techniques for measuring energy expenditure involve either measuring heat loss directly (direct calorimetry) or measuring a proxy of heat loss such as oxygen consumption (O_2) or carbon dioxide (CO_2) production (indirect calorimetry). Direct calorimetry is done under controlled laboratory conditions in insulated chambers that measure changes in air temperature associated with the heat being released by a subject. Although quite accurate, direct calorimetry is not widely used because of its expense and technical difficulty.

Thus, methods of indirect calorimetry are more commonly used to quantify human energy expenditure. The most widely used of these techniques involve measuring oxygen consumption. Because the body's energy production is dependent on oxygen (aerobic respiration), O_2 consumption provides a very accurate indirect way of measuring a person's energy expenditure. Every liter of O_2 consumed by the body is equivalent to an energy cost of approximately 5 kilocalories. Consequently, by measuring O_2 use while a person is performing a particular task (for example, standing, walking, or running on a treadmill), the energy cost of the task can be determined.

With the Douglas bag method for measuring O_2 uptake, subjects breathe through a valve that allows them to inhale room air and exhale into a large collection bag. The volume and the O_2 and CO_2 contents of the collected air sample are then measured to determine the total amount of oxygen consumed by the subject. Recent advances in computer technology allow for the determination of O_2 consumption more quickly without having to collect expired air samples. One computerized system for measuring oxygen consumption, like the Douglas bag method, determines energy costs by measuring the volume and the O_2 and CO_2 concentrations of expired air samples.

Sources of Food Energy

The main chemical sources of energy in our foods are carbohydrates, protein, and fats. Collectively, these three energy sources are known as macronutrients. Vitamins and minerals (micronutrients) are required in much smaller amounts and are important for regulating many aspects of biological function.

Carbohydrates and proteins have similar energy contents; each provides 4 kilocalories of metabolic energy per gram. In contrast, fat is more calorically dense; each gram provides about 9 to 10 kilocalories. Alcohol, although not a required nutrient, also can be used as an energy source, contributing 7 kcal/g. Regardless of the source, excess dietary energy can be stored by the body as glycogen (a carbohydrate) or as fat. Humans have relatively limited glycogen stores (about 375–475 grams) in the liver and muscles. Fat, however, represents a much larger source of stored energy, accounting for approximately 13 to 20 percent of body weight in men and 25 to 28 percent in women.

The largest source of dietary energy for most humans is carbohydrates (45–50 percent of calories in the typical American diet). The three types of carbohydrates are monosaccharides, disaccharides, and polysaccharides. Monosaccharides, or simple sugars, include glucose, the body's primary metabolic fuel; fructose (fruit sugar); and galactose. Disaccharides, as the name implies, are sugars formed by a combination of two monosaccharides. Sucrose (glucose and fructose), the most common disaccharide, is found in sugar, honey, and maple syrup. Lactose, the sugar found in milk, is composed of glucose and galactose. Maltose (glucose and glucose), the least common of the disaccharides, is found in malt products and germinating cereals. Polysaccharides, or complex carbohydrates, are composed of three or more simple sugar molecules. Glycogen is the polysaccharide used for storing carbohydrates in animal tissues. In plants, the two most common polysaccharides are starch and cellulose. Starch is found in a wide variety of foods, such as grains, cereals, and breads, and provides an important source of dietary energy. In contrast, cellulose—the fibrous, structural parts of plant material—is not digestible by humans and passes through the gastrointestinal tract as fiber.

Fats provide the largest store of potential energy for biological work in the body. They are divided into three main groups: simple, compound, and derived. The simple or "neutral fats" consist primarily of triglycerides. A triglyceride consists of two component molecules: glycerol and fatty acid. Fatty acid molecules, in turn, are divided into two broad groups: saturated and unsaturated. These categories reflect the chemical bonding pattern between the carbon atoms of the fatty acid molecule. Saturated fatty acids have no double bonds between carbons, thus allowing for the maximum number of hydrogen atoms to be bound to the carbon (that is, the carbons are "saturated" with hydrogen atoms). In contrast, unsaturated fatty acids have one (monounsaturated) or more (polyunsaturated) double bonds. Saturated fats are abundant in animal products, whereas unsaturated fats predominate in vegetable oils.

Compound fats consist of a neutral fat in combination with some other chemical substance (for example, a sugar or a protein). Examples of compound fats include phospholipids and lipoproteins. Phospholipids are important in blood clotting and insulating nerve fibers, whereas lipoproteins are the main form of transport for fat in the bloodstream.

Derived fats are substances synthesized from simple and compound fats. The best known derived fat is cholesterol. Cholesterol is present in all human cells and may be derived from foods (exogenous) or synthesized by the body (endogenous). Cholesterol is necessary for normal development and function because it is critical for the synthesis of such hormones as estradiol, progesterone, and testosterone.

Proteins, in addition to providing an energy source, are also critical for the growth and replacement of living tissues. They are composed of nitrogen-containing compounds known as amino acids. Of the twenty different amino acids required by the body, nine (leucine, isoleucine, valine, lysine, threonine, methionine, phenylalanine, tryptophan, and histidine) are known as "essential" because they cannot be synthesized by the body and thus must be derived from food. Two others, cystine and tyrosine, are synthesized in the body from methionine and phenylalanine, respectively. The remaining amino acids are called "nonessential" because they can be produced by the body and need not be derived from the diet.

Determinants of Daily Energy Needs

A person's daily energy requirements are determined by several different factors. The major components of an individual's energy budget are associated with resting or basal metabolism, activity, growth, and reproduction. Basal metabolic rate (BMR) represents the minimum amount of energy necessary to keep a person alive. Basal metabolism is measured under controlled conditions while a subject is lying in a relaxed and fasted state.

In addition to basal requirements, energy is expended to perform various types of work, such as daily activities and exercise, digestion and transport of food, and regulating body temperature. The energy costs associated with food handling (i.e., the thermic effect of food) make up a relatively small proportion of daily energy expenditure and are influenced by amount consumed and the composition of the diet (e.g., high-protein meals elevate dietary thermogenesis). In addition, at extreme temperatures, energy must be spent to heat or cool the body. Humans (unclothed) have a thermoneutral range of 25 to 27°C (77–81°F). Within this temperature range, the minimum amount of metabolic energy is spent to maintain body temperature. Finally, during one's lifetime, additional energy is required for physical growth and for reproduction (e.g., pregnancy, lactation).

In 1985 the World Health Organization (WHO) presented its most recent recommendations for assessing human energy requirements. The procedure used for determining energy needs involves first estimating BMR from body weight on the basis of predictive equations developed by the WHO. These equations are presented in Table 1. After estimating BMR, the total daily energy expenditure (TDEE) for adults (18 years old and above) is determined as a multiple of BMR, based on the individual's activity level. This multiplier, known as the physical activity level (PAL) index, reflects the proportion of energy above basal requirements that an individual spends over the course of a normal day. The PALs associated with different occupational work levels for adult men and women are presented in Table 2. The WHO recommends that minimal daily activities such as dressing, washing, and eating are commensurate with a PAL of 1.4 for both men and women. Sedentary lifestyles (e.g., office work) require PALs of 1.55 for men and 1.56 for women. At higher work levels, however, the sex differences are greater. Moderate work is associated with a PAL of 1.78 in men and 1.64 in women, whereas heavy work levels (for example, manual labor, traditional agriculture) necessitate PALs of 2.10 and 1.82 for men and women, respectively.

TABLE 1

Equations for predicting basal metabolic rate (BMR) based on body weight (Wt in kilograms)

Age (years)	BMR (kcal/day)	
	Males	Females
0–2.9	60.9 (Wt) − 54	61.0 (Wt) − 51
3.0–9.9	27.7 (Wt) + 495	22.5 (Wt) + 499
10.0–17.9	17.5 (Wt) + 651	12.2 (Wt) + 746
18.0–29.9	15.3 (Wt) + 679	14.7 (Wt) + 496
30.0–59.9	11.6 (Wt) + 879	8.7 (Wt) + 829
60+	13.5 (Wt) + 487	10.5 (Wt) + 596

SOURCE: FAO/WHO/UNU, 1985

In addition to the costs of daily activity and work, energy costs for reproduction also must be considered. The WHO recommends an additional 285 kcal/day for women who are pregnant and an additional 500 kcal/day for those who are lactating.

Energy requirements for children and adolescents are estimated differently because extra energy is necessary for growth and because relatively less is known about variation in their activity patterns. For children and adolescents between 10 and 18 years old, the WHO recommends the use of age- and sex-specific PALs. In contrast, energy requirements for children under 10 years old are determined by multiplying the child's weight by an age- and sex-specific constant. The reference values for boys and girls under 18 years old are presented in Table 3.

Human Variation in Sources of Food Energy

Compared to most other mammals, humans are able to survive and flourish eating a remarkably wide range of foods. Human diets range from completely vegetarian (as observed in many populations of South Asia) to those based almost entirely on meat and animal foods (for example, traditional Eskimo/Inuit populations of the Arctic). Thus, over the course of evolutionary history, humans have developed a high degree of dietary plastic-

TABLE 2

Physical activity levels (PALs) associated with different types of occupational work among adults (18 years and older)

Sex	PAL			
	Minimal	Light	Moderate	Heavy
Male	1.40	1.55	1.78	2.10
Female	1.40	1.56	1.64	1.82

SOURCE: FAO/WHO/UNU, 1985

TABLE 3

Energy constants and PALs recommended for estimating daily energy requirements for individuals under the age of 18

Age (years)	Males	Females
	Energy constant (kcal/kg body weight)	
<1.0	103	103
1.0–1.9	104	108
2.0–2.9	104	102
3.0–3.9	99	95
4.0–4.9	95	92
5.0–5.9	92	88
6.0–6.9	88	83
7.0–7.9	83	76
8.0–8.9	77	69
9.0–9.9	72	62
	PAL	
10.0–10.9	1.76	1.65
11.0–11.9	1.72	1.62
12.0–12.9	1.69	1.60
13.0–13.9	1.67	1.58
14.0–14.9	1.65	1.57
15.0–15.9	1.62	1.54
16.0–16.9	1.60	1.52
17.0–17.9	1.60	1.52

SOURCE: FAO/WHO/UNU, 1985; James and Schofield, 1990

ity. This ability to utilize a diverse array of plant and animal resources for food is one of the features that allowed humans to spread and colonize ecosystems all over the world.

Table 4 presents information on per capita energy intakes and the percentage of energy derived from plant and animal foods for subsistence-level (i.e., food-producing) and industrial human societies. The relative contribution of animal foods varies considerably, ranging from less than 10 percent of dietary energy in traditional farming communities of tropical South America, to more than 95 percent among traditionally living Inuit hunters of the Canadian Arctic.

Subsistence-level agricultural populations, as a group, have the lowest consumption of animal foods. Among hunting and gathering populations, the contribution of animal foods to the diet is variable, partly reflecting the environments in which these populations reside. For example, the !Kung San, who live in arid desert environments of southern Africa, have among the lowest levels of animal food consumption among hunter-gatherers. In contrast, hunters of the Arctic rely almost entirely on animal foods for their daily energy. Foragers living in forest and grassland regions of the tropics (for example, the Ache and the Hiwi) have intermediate levels of animal consumption.

Regardless of whether they are from plant or animals, the staple foods in most human societies are calorically dense. Indeed, one of the hallmarks of human

TABLE 4

Per capita energy intake (kcal/day) and percentage of dietary energy derived from animal and plant foods in selected human populations

Population	Energy intake (kcal/day)	Energy from animal foods	Energy from plant foods
Hunter-gatherers			
!Kung San (Botswana)	2,100	33	67
Ache (Paraguay)	3,827	56	44
Hiwi (Venezuela)	2,043	68	32
Inuit (Canada)	2,179	96	4
Pastoralists			
Turkana (Kenya)	1,411	80	20
Evenki (Russia)	2,617	31	69
Agriculturalists			
Quechua (highland Peru)	2,002	5	95
Coastal Ecuador	1,851	7	93
Yapú (lowland Colombia)	1,968	11	89
Industrial societies			
United States	2,095	27	73

evolutionary history has been humankind's success at developing subsistence strategies that maximize the energy returns from available food resources. The initial evolution of human "hunting and gathering" economies some 2 million years ago is an example of this. By incorporating more meat into their diet, man's hominid ancestors were able to increase the energy contents of their diets.

With the evolution of agriculture, human populations began to manipulate relatively marginal plant species so as to increase their productivity, digestibility, and energy content. Today, staple agricultural crops such as rice, wheat, and other cereal grains are calorically dense (more than 300 kilocalories per 100 grams), and are much richer sources of energy than the wild plants from which they evolved.

Novel methods of food processing also allow humans to increase the energy content and digestibility of their foods. The most fundamental of these techniques is the use of fire for cooking, a strategy adopted by man's hominid ancestors at least 400,000 years ago. Cooking makes plant foods more digestible by helping to break down complex carbohydrates. Recent work has shown that cooking can increase the energy content of starchy tubers (potatoes, cassava) by more than 70 percent.

Another interesting example of processing food to raise its energy content is seen among populations living in the high Andes of South America. Here, small potatoes are left outside for several days to be repeatedly frozen during the cold nights and then dried under the intense daytime sun. The resulting product, called *chuño*, can be stored for many months and has an energy content more than three times that of a fresh potato (330 kilocalories per 100 grams versus 90 kilocalories per 100 grams).

Human Variation in Energy Expenditure

Humans also show considerable variation in levels of energy expenditure. Recent work by Allison E. Black and colleagues indicates that daily energy expenditure in human groups typically ranges from 1.2 to 5.0 times BMR (i.e., PAL = 1.2–5.0). The lowest levels of physical activity, PALs of 1.20 to 1.25, are observed among hospitalized and nonambulatory populations. In contrast, the highest levels of physical activity (PALs of 2.5–5.0) have been observed among elite athletes and soldiers in combat training. Within this group, Tour de France cyclists have the highest recorded daily energy demands of 8,050 kcal/day (a PAL = 4.68)!

Table 5 presents data on body weight, total daily energy expenditure, and PALs of adult men and women from selected human groups. Men of the subsistence-level populations (that is, foragers, pastoralists, and agriculturalists) are, on average, 20 kilograms (45 pounds) lighter than their counterparts from the industrialized world, and yet have similar levels of daily energy expenditure (2,897 versus 2,859 kcal/day). The same pattern is true for women; those from subsistence-level populations are 12.5 kilograms (28 pounds) lighter than women of industrialized societies, but have higher levels of daily energy expenditure (2,227 versus 2,146 kcal/day).

Thus, daily energy needs are expressed relative to BMR; it is found that adults living a "modern" lifestyle in the industrialized world have significantly lower physical activity levels than those living more "traditional" lives. Among men, PALs in the industrialized societies average 1.67 (range = 1.53 to 1.84), as compared to 1.90 (range = 1.58 to 2.38) among the subsistence-level groups. Physical activity levels among women average 1.63 in the industrialized world (range = 1.48 to 1.69) and 1.78 (range = 1.56 to 2.03) among the subsistence-level societies.

The differences in daily energy demands between subsistence-level and industrialized populations are further highlighted in Figure 1, which shows daily energy expenditure (kilocalories/day) plotted relative to body weight (in kilograms). The two lines denote the best-fit regressions for both groups. These regressions show that at the same body weight, adults of the industrialized world have daily energy needs that are 600 to 1,000 kilocalories lower than those of people living in subsistence-level societies.

It is these declines in physical activity and daily energy expenditure associated with "modern" lifestyles that are largely responsible for the growing problem of obesity throughout the world. In the United States, rates of obesity have increased dramatically over the last twenty years, such that now over half of the adult American population is either overweight or obese. Equally disturbing has been the emergence of obesity as a problem in part of the developing world where it was virtually unknown less than a generation ago. In some sense, obesity and other chronic diseases of the modern world (diabetes and

TABLE 5

Weight (kg), total daily energy expenditure (TDEE in kcal/day), basal metabolic rate (BMR in kcal/day), and physical activity level (PAL) of selected human groups

Group	Sex	Weight (kg)	TDEE (kcal/day)	BMR (kcal/day)	PAL (TDEE/BMR)
Industrialized populations:					
18–29 years	M	75.6	3,298	1,793	1.84
	F	69.2	2,486	1,480	1.68
30–39 years	M	86.1	3,418	1,960	1.74
	F	67.9	2,390	1,434	1.67
40–64 years	M	77.0	2,749	1,673	1.64
	F	70.0	2,342	1,386	1.69
65–74 years	M	76.4	2,629	1,650	1.59
	F	60.2	2,055	1,267	1.62
75 and older	M	72.6	2,199	1,434	1.53
	F	48.3	1,458	980	1.48
Average	M	77.5	2,859	1,702	1.67
	F	63.1	2,146	1,309	1.63
Subsistence-level populations:					
!Kung San foragers	M	46.0	2,319	1,383	1.68
	F	41.0	1,712	1,099	1.56
Ache foragers	M	59.6	3,327	1,531	2.17
	F	51.8	2,626	1,394	1.88
Inuit hunters	M	65.0	3,010	1,673	1.80
	F	55.0	2,350	1,305	1.80
Evenki pastoralists	M	58.4	2,681	1,558	1.75
	F	52.7	2,067	1,288	1.63
Aymara agriculturalists	M	54.6	2,713	1,355	2.00
	F	50.5	2,376	1,166	2.03
Highland Ecuador, agriculturalists	M	61.3	3,810	1,601	2.38
	F	55.7	2,460	1,252	1.96
Coastal Ecuador, agriculturalists	M	55.6	2,416	1,529	1.58
	F	47.8	1,993	1,226	1.63
Average	M	57.2	2,897	1,519	1.90
	F	50.6	2,227	1,247	1.78

FIGURE 1

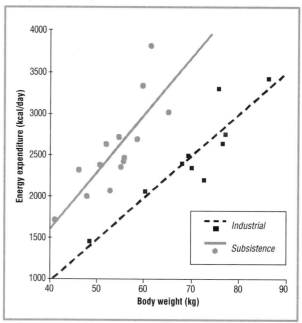

cardiovascular disease, for example) represent a continuation of trends that started early in man's evolutionary history. Humans have developed a diet that is extremely rich in calories while at the same time minimizing the amount of energy necessary for physical work and activity. Ongoing work in nutritional science is attempting to better understand the biological and environmental factors that influence patterns of energy consumption and expenditure to promote human health and well-being.

See also **Assessment of Nutritional Status; Body Composition; Hunting and Gathering; Inuit; Nutrition Transition: Worldwide Diet Change; Physical Activity and Nutrition.**

BIBLIOGRAPHY

Black, Allison E., W. Andrew Coward, Tim J. Cole, and Andrew M. Prentice. "Human Energy Expenditure in Affluent Societies: An Analysis of 574 Double-Labelled Water Measurements." *European Journal of Clinical Nutrition* 50 (1996): 72–92.

Consolazio, C. Frank, Robert E. Johnson, and Louis J. Pecora. *Physiological Measurements of Metabolic Functions in Man.* New York: McGraw-Hill, 1963.

Durnin, John V. G. A., and Reginald Passmore. *Energy, Work and Leisure.* London: Heineman, 1967.

Food and Agriculture Organization, World Health Organization, and United Nations University (FAO/WHO/UNU). *Energy and Protein Requirements. Report of Joint FAO/WHO/UNU Expert Consultation.* WHO Technical Report Series No. 724. Geneva: World Health Organization, 1985.

Gibson, Rosalind S. *Principles of Nutritional Assessment.* Oxford: Oxford University Press, 1990.

James, William P. T., and E. Claire Schofield. *Human Energy Requirements: A Manual for Planners and Nutritionists.* Oxford: Oxford University Press, 1990.

Kleiber, Max. *The Fire of Life: An Introduction to Animal Energetics*, 2d ed. Huntington, N.Y.: Krieger, 1975.

Leonard, William R. "Human Nutritional Evolution." In *Human Biology: A Biocultural and Evolutionary Approach*, edited by Sara Stinson, Barry Bogin, Rebecca Huss-Ashmore, and Dennis O'Rourke, pp. 295–343. New York: Wiley-Liss, 2000.

Leonard, William R., and Marcia L. Robertson. "Comparative Primate Energetics and Hominid Evolution." *American Journal of Physical Anthropology* 102 (1997): 265–281.

McArdle, William D., Frank I. Katch, and Victor L. Katch. *Exercise Physiology: Energy, Nutrition and Human Performance*, 5th ed. Philadelphia: Lippincott Williams and Wilkins, 2001.

McLean, Jennifer A., and G. Tobin. *Animal and Human Calorimetry.* Cambridge: Cambridge University Press, 1987.

Ulijaszek, Stanley J. *Human Energetics in Biological Anthropology.* Cambridge: Cambridge University Press, 1995.

William R. Leonard

ENGLAND. *See* **British Isles.**

ENRICHMENT. *See* **Additives; Vitamins.**

ENTERAL AND PARENTERAL NUTRITION. The ascent of enteral and parenteral nutrition into a major therapeutic advance in the clinical care of critically ill patients as well as those with temporary or permanent loss of gastrointestinal function only occurred during the last thirty years of the twentieth century. Enteral tube feeding was first employed in the 1600s and was made popular in the medical profession by the famous English surgeon John Hunter at the end of the eighteenth century.

Three important developments accelerated the widespread acceptance of invasive feeding by tubes in the gastrointestinal tract (enteral nutrition) or in veins (parenteral nutrition). Milton Winitz and his colleagues developed chemically defined diets that provided all the essential nutrients in their predigested form. Protein and carbohydrates were provided as their basic building blocks, amino acids and glucose, with minimal amounts of fat sufficient only to meet basic requirements along with all the essential vitamins and minerals. Originally intended as low-residue diets for the American space program, they were made available, particularly by Henry Randall, via a feeding tube to surgical patients who could not be nourished with regular food by mouth. Later formulas were made more complex with protein present as peptides, which contain a number of linked amino acids, more complex carbohydrates, and larger amounts of fat. Subsequently Stanley Dudrick, Douglas Wilmore, Harry Vars, and Jonathan Rhoads administered similar predigested nutrients in concentrated form into large veins of six beagle puppies, who tolerated them well and experienced normal growth and development. Similar successes in a human infant and in malnourished surgical patients with gastrointestinal dysfunction led to widespread adoption of this life-saving and sustaining technique. Parenteral fat became available for intravenous administration as a component of parenteral formulas several years later. Finally, scientists recognized that protein calorie malnutrition (PCM) affected from one-quarter to one-half of all hospitalized adults and children (Bistrian et al., 1974; Bistrian et al., 1976), that PCM had a major impact on morbidity and mortality from an underlying disease, and that nutritional support by enteral or parenteral means could improve outcomes in malnourished or stressed individuals.

Initially a few interested individuals employed these techniques mainly in academic centers. However, enteral and parenteral nutrition have become essential components of care in critical care units, important adjuncts for many patients recovering from major abdominal surgery, and lifesaving methods for tens of thousands of individuals with permanent impairments of intestinal functions.

During the late twentieth century investigators developed a greater understanding of why PCM occurs, better methods and formulas for providing enteral and parenteral nutrition, and improved techniques for identifying the patients most likely to benefit. Whereas primary PCM develops as a consequence of inadequate intake of protein, energy, and often other essential nutrients, the PCM seen in hospitalized patients is largely due to the underlying primary disease. A process named the systemic inflammatory response develops following any major tissue injury, infection, or inflammatory disorder, such as inflammatory bowel disease or rheumatoid arthritis, and is a part of the body's innate defense system that supports the immune system and fosters healing. However, the response has potentially harmful side effects, including muscle wasting and severe PCM, if it is prolonged or severe, as when anorexia and gastrointestinal dysfunction limit the spontaneous dietary intake of food and increase the protein breakdown that are parts of the systemic inflammatory response.

The well-nourished individual can tolerate up to one week of illness without requiring invasive nutrition to avoid complications, usually infections or poor wound healing, from PCM. When malnutrition is a problem at the outset, feeding is helpful within three to five days. In the severely malnourished patient, defined by an unintentional weight loss of 20 percent or more, or the severely ill patient, especially one with a closed head injury, a major skeletal trauma, severe body burns, or a severe infection, feeding begun early can improve the outcome. The American Society for Parenteral and Enteral Nutrition developed specific guidelines for the roles of enteral and parenteral feeding that incorporate these principles (Klein et al.).

An important recognition that feeding critically ill patients, particularly if done incorrectly, could be harmful soon followed its broader application. The primary complications of parenteral nutrition include lung collapse, vein clots, infections related to the tube or as a consequence of poorer blood sugar control, or metabolic complications related to introducing all essential nutrients directly into a vein without modification by the gastrointestinal tract and the liver. With enteral nutrition the primary complication is intestinal intolerance as reflected in vomiting, diarrhea, or aspiration pneumonia. Although some have asserted that enteral feeding is more efficacious than parenteral feeding, a close look at the evidence suggests that they are probably equally effective but that enteral feeding would be preferred whenever possible. The potential complications of both modes of feeding can be minimized by assuring that trained, skilled individuals and teams use them only when indicated.

Subsequent developments included immune-enhancing diets with oils, such as fish oil and certain vegetable oils like flaxseed, containing omega-3 fatty acids; the amino acids arginine and glutamine; and nucleotides. Usually provided in combination, these nutrients, when added to a standard enteral formula, seem to improve outcomes by reducing infection rates and shortening hospital stays after major abdominal surgery for malnourished patients, patients with major traumas or burns, and patients in critical care units (Beale et al.). In addition the placement of feeding tubes by endoscope dramatically increased the number of patients who can receive enteral feeding. Placement into the upper small bowel improves tolerance to enteral feeding among critically ill patients, and placement into the stomach or small bowel with exit of the tube through the abdominal wall avoids surgical placement in less severely ill patients who need chronic feeding. The development and wide application of enteral and parenteral feeding was one of the major medical advances of the twentieth century.

See also **Health and Disease; Medicine; Nutrients; Nutrition.**

BIBLIOGRAPHY

Beale R., D. Bryg, and D. Bihari. "Immunonutrition in the Critically Ill: A Systematic Review of Clinical Outcome." *Critical Care Medicine* 27 (1999): 2799–2805.

Bistrian B., G. Blackburn, E. Hallowell, and R. Heddle. "Protein Nutritional Status of General Surgical Patients." *Journal of the American Medical Association* 230 (1974): 838–860.

Bistrian B., G. Blackburn, J. Vitale, D. Cochran, and J. Naylor. "Prevalence of Malnutrition in General Medical Patients." *Journal of the American Medical Association* 235 (1976): 1567–1570.

Dudrick S., D. Wilmore, H. Vars, and J. Rhoads. "Long-term Parenteral Nutrition with Growth, Development, and Positive Nitrogen Balance." *Surgery* 64 (1968): 134–142.

Klein S., J. Kinney, K. Jeejeebhoy, D. Alpers, M. Hellerstein, M. Murray, and P. Twomey. "Nutrition Support in Clinical Practice: Review of Published Data and Recommendations for Research Directions." *American Journal of Clinical Nutrition* 66 (1997): 683–706. Summary of a conference sponsored by the National Institutes of Health, the American Society for Parenteral and Enteral Nutrition, and the American Society for Clinical Nutrition.

Stephens R., and Henry Randall. "Use of a Concentrated, Balanced, Liquid Elemental Diet for Nutritional Management of Catabolic States." *Annals of Surgery* 170 (1969): 642–667.

Winitz M., J. Graff, N. Gallagher, A. Narkin, and D. Seedman. "Evaluation of Chemical Diets as Nutrition for Man-in-Space." *Nature* 205 (1965): 741–793.

Bruce Ryan Bistrian

ENVIRONMENT. People farm Earth's biosphere to produce food for the sustenance of the human species. Thus, human food systems are part of Earth's complex ecological systems. All of these systems begin with interactions with the sun, which is the ultimate energy source. Sunlight enables plants to manufacture carbohydrates through the process of photosynthesis, in which chlorophyll converts sunlight into chemical energy, synthesizing organic compounds from inorganic compounds. Plants take carbon dioxide, water, and inorganic elements for this conversion process from the air and soil. Humans obtain their nourishment directly from plants, or from animals nourished directly or indirectly by plants. Thus humans ultimately rely on air, soil, water, and sunlight for sustenance.

Humankind has a strong interest in not fouling the environment, as contaminants in the air, water, or soil can end up in the plants that people or their food animals eat. An extreme example of such contamination was the 1986 Chernobyl nuclear power plant explosion in the Ukraine. Although hundreds of thousands of people fled the area that was immediately affected by the explosion, as many as three million people still live in contaminated areas in this farming region. As a result of the ecological devastation from this disaster, enormous amounts of money have been and continue to be spent in an effort to relocate communities and decontaminate the rich farmland.

Environmental Progress and Challenges for Agriculture

Agriculture and food systems play a major role in the ecological health of Earth, including the number and

URBANIZATION AND DEVELOPMENT: THE GREATEST THREAT TO AGRICULTURAL LAND IN THE UNITED STATES

Between 1992 and 1997 more than 3.2 million acres of prime farmland were converted to developed land, at an average rate of 645,000 acres of prime farmland per year. From 1982 to 1997 approximately 30 percent of newly developed lands were converted prime farmland. Conversion of farms and farmland to the scattered and fragmented development of "urban sprawl" also causes the loss and fragmentation of other farm, pasture, and rangelands, as well as forests, wetlands, and other important habitats.

In *Farming on the Edge*, A. Ann Sorenson and others reported that 21 percent of prime or unique farmland conversions occurred in twenty major land resource areas that make up 7 percent of the U.S. land base. These most threatened land resource areas are part of or adjacent to expanding population centers and produce some of the highest value agricultural crops and products.

Shorelands and wetlands lose the buffering provided by farm- and forestlands, and non-point-source pollution from storm water runoff increases. Wetlands are a vital natural resource that provide flood protection and enhance water quality, wildlife habitat, and air quality. According to the 1997 National Resources Inventory, nearly 59 percent of wetland acreage is on forestland and 16.5 percent is on agricultural cropland, pasture, and land in the Conservation Reserve Program.

diversity of life forms that inhabit it. Half of the land mass of the United States, excluding Alaska, is privately owned crop, pasture, and range land. As noted in *America's Private Lands: A Geography of Hope,* the farmers and ranchers who manage these 907 million acres play a key role in maintaining the abundance of these natural resources for present and future generations.

Driven by changing economic and demographic trends, agriculture has become more consolidated, intensified, and specialized. At the same time, there has been increased scientific and public awareness of the detrimental environmental impacts of some agricultural activities, such as the problem of soil erosion. However, by adopting new practices and working with government conservation cost-share and technical-assistance programs, farmers are significantly reducing many of those detrimental impacts. Although soil erosion threatens the future productivity of 29 percent of cultivated acres in

the United States, farmers reduced soil erosion on U.S. farmland by 38 percent from 1982 to 1997. Much of this reduction was accomplished by changing from traditional plowing to no-till or minimum-tillage systems that disturb the soil less and leave a protective layer of crop residue. The United States Department of Agriculture (USDA) programs, such as the Conservation Reserve Program and Wetland Reserve Program, take marginal or fragile croplands out of production and assist landowners with plantings or practices to buffer stream banks and enhance wildlife habitat. Wetlands, including productive yet fragile ecosystems like prairie potholes, have been restored, and the nesting success of ducks has increased.

Many livestock farmers and ranchers have improved grazing management to benefit livestock productivity as well as soil, water, and wildlife resources. For example, the United States and several western European nations are addressing the problem of excess manure in areas with high concentrations of livestock. Farmers are developing nutrient-management plans to make the best use of fertility-building resources in manure and to prevent excessive field applications or run-off into waterways.

Problems with water quality and water supply due to agricultural practices persist in some areas and have recently emerged in others, such as in the northeastern United States, where the water supply has not been a problem historically. Water quality also affects both freshwater and saltwater fisheries (discussed in more detail below). Careful management of agricultural production is critical in maintaining the ecological health of many estuaries (nurseries for fish and shellfish stocks and food webs). Efforts to improve nutrient management and agricultural conservation practices in the extensive watershed of the U.S. Chesapeake Bay are evidence of the growing awareness of the ecological links between farming and fishing.

Developed countries in North America and western Europe use a combination of technical assistance, incentives, and regulatory approaches to address environmental problems associated with agriculture. However, a lack of human and economic resources limits the ability of developing countries to address environmental problems associated with agriculture or other human activities. The clearing of forests in Brazil continues to accelerate in an effort to develop agricultural production for export. Land is cleared for crops and cultivated pasture, much of it to expand livestock and crop production for export markets. The USDA's *Agricultural Baseline Projections* February 2002 report (Westcott) predicted that the conversion of undeveloped land into arable land in Brazil's interior will gain momentum over the next decade. Brazil's share of the world soybean market is projected to grow from 28 to 35 percent by 2011.

In his 2000 Nobel anniversary lecture, agricultural researcher Norman Borlaug noted that irrigated agriculture uses 70 percent of global water withdrawals, covers

17 percent of cultivated land (about 679 million acres), and accounts for 40 percent of world food production.

Loss of genetic diversity in crop plants and livestock—driven by market rewards for high yield, cost-efficiency, and product uniformity—is increasingly recognized as an environmental concern for agriculture. Other concerns include agriculture's effects on biodiversity and health of critical habitats. Working agriculture can be a positive or negative factor in all these areas of environmental concern, depending on local site conditions and management practices.

World Fisheries and Food Security

Fisheries contribute to world food security, especially since fish are a major source of protein for some of the world's poorest populations. Per capita fish consumption varies among countries, depending on economic wealth, cultural traditions, and fisheries resource base. According to the United Nations Food and Agriculture Organization (FAO), world per capita fish consumption has been increasing since the 1960s, a trend that has been accompanied by increasing incomes. Global trade in fish and shellfish continues to grow and gain importance in developing countries. However, a practice of overfishing now threatens fisheries around the world. Consumption of fish has been increasing quite dramatically for at least half a century, and stocks have been severely depleted. Too many fish have been harvested with too little thought or provision for protecting the resource base so that it can continue to produce sustainably. U.S. efforts to protect fisheries from over-fishing are showing some results. For example, some long-threatened resources, such as cod and haddock stocks in New England, have begun to recover after decades of decline. However, achieving international cooperation to protect coastal and estuarine environments and to manage and sustain world fisheries remains a challenge.

Toward a More Sustainable Aquaculture

Aquaculture, often promoted as a solution to over-fishing, has expanded dramatically in Asia for domestic and export markets. As with agriculture, the environmental impacts of aquaculture can vary greatly over the range of management systems and practices. The article "Effect of Aquaculture on World Fish Supplies," by Naylor et al., describes the paradox of aquaculture as both a possible solution and a contributing factor to the collapse of fisheries stocks worldwide.

In the late twentieth and early twenty-first centuries, capture fisheries provided a decreasing share of world food fish, while the share that aquaculture provided surged—nearly tripling from 10 million metric tons in 1987 to 29 million metric tons in 1997. World capture fish harvests leveled off at around 85–95 million metric tons per year, with the catch shifting from larger, higher value carnivorous species of fish to smaller, lower value

THE AQUACULTURE RUSH IN CHINA

Asia produces 90 percent of the world's aquaculture output, with China alone producing more than two-thirds of the total. Europe, North America, and Japan combined produce just over 10 percent of the total, but these areas consume most of the internationally traded farmed seafood. Excluding mainland China, world fish supplies from aquaculture grew from 3.5 pounds per capita per year in 1991 to 4.7 pounds in 1998. During the same period, according to the United Nations Food and Agriculture Organization (FAO), the per capita supply of aquaculture products in mainland China nearly tripled, growing from 13.2 to 37.4 pounds. Fish consumption in China is strongly correlated with economic growth, and freshwater aquaculture is responding rapidly to market stimulus. Many Chinese aquaculture enterprises are family and cooperative farms, often using integrated multiple-species systems to produce lower value, herbivorous species for household subsistence and local markets. As competition increases for land and water resources, more operations are intensifying, and some are producing higher value carnivorous or omnivorous species such as shrimp for export.

The FAO expects aquaculture to continue to grow in Asia, but it also expects the rate of growth to slow when China becomes a member of the World Trade Organization and thus more open to food imports. China may become a market for cultured fish produced in other Asian countries.

fish used to make feed for farmed fish. Four of the top five capture fish species were used in feed production for the aquaculture and livestock industries.

Alteration of habitat—especially the large-scale transformation of mangroves and coastal wetlands in Asia into fish- and shrimp-farming ponds—also harms wild fish nurseries and the ecological health of coastal wetlands, coral reefs, and related marine habitat. Other factors that diminish wild fisheries are the collection of wild seed stock, food-web interactions (e.g., over-fishing of small fish species that form the food supply for marine predators, including valuable fish species consumed by humans), introduction of exotic species and pathogens, and nutrient pollution from fish farms.

Aquaculturists farm more than 220 species of finfish, shellfish, and crustaceans. Raising carnivorous species such as salmon, which consume wild fish for feed (producing one pound of farm-raised salmon takes eight pounds of wild fish), can create problems such as interbreeding of wild fish with escaped farmed fish. But some aquaculture benefits estuarine and marine ecosystems, such as filter-feeding oysters, mussels, clams, and some carp, all of which help purify water. A range of fish and shellfish farming systems are being developed for different species, locations, and conditions. Naylor et al. (pp. 1021–1023) offered four primary goals for the sustainability and continued growth of the aquaculture industry: (1) expand farming of smaller, lower feeding-level fish; (2) reduce use of fish meal and fish oils in feed; (3) develop integrated farming systems; (4) promote environmentally sound aquaculture practices and resource management.

Food and Ecosystems: Linked since the Rise of Civilization

Humans have always interacted with their environment in order to obtain food. Local ecosystem characteristics, such as the types and quantities of edible plants and plants eaten by food-producing animals, have significantly affected the evolution and development of human societies and cultures. In his Pulitzer-Prize-winning book *Guns, Germs, and Steel: The Fates of Human Societies,* Jared Diamond traced many of the outcomes of human history, including the comparative advantages of different societies and the availability and relative abundance of different types of plants and animals. For example, a hospitable growing environment with deep, fertile soil, adequate rainfall, and moderate temperatures provides people with a food-producing advantage. (Examples are the traditional "breadbasket" regions of the world: the midwestern United States, the pampas of South America, the plains of central Europe and the Ukraine, and China's river valleys.) However, through ingenuity, skill, and careful stewardship of resources, humans have produced ample food supplies in challenging environments such as the mountains of Switzerland, the Nile Valley, and arid parts of Australia.

In his book, Diamond also links the development of civilizations to people's ability to produce abundant food supplies in an environment. For example, settlements could become permanent only when people no longer had to wander in search of food, and when they learned to protect and replenish the soil so that they did not have to abandon exhausted farming sites. A sustained and ample food supply enabled societies to develop technology, writing, and political systems, all of which advanced agriculture even further. Highly developed farming systems were the cornerstone of the rise of the Roman Empire and the unification of China. The ancient Romans understood, and wrote extensively about, the practice of sustainable agriculture. They improved plants and animals through selective breeding, and they emphasized the use of manure and composts to replenish and enrich the life-giving capacity of farmed soils.

Lessons from Famines and Ecological Disasters of the Middle Ages

Cycles of disaster and famine in medieval Europe offer an instructive study in the interplay of agriculture and the environment. A series of extreme natural disasters including floods, crop failures, and epidemics among humans and livestock culminated in the Great European Famine of the early 1300s. In the mid-fourteenth century, another wave of natural disasters, which included the spread of bubonic plague, resulted in the loss of about one-third of the population of Europe, with death rates as high as 60 percent in some communities. These famines and ecological disasters most likely resulted from a complex combination of causes. Bruce M. S. Campbell discussed several theories about the famines in "Ecology Versus Economics in Late Thirteenth- and Early Fourteenth-Century English Agriculture," in *Agriculture in the Middle Ages* (pp. 76–97). The floods were most likely part of a period of climate change to cooler, wetter weather, accompanied by storm surges in the North Sea.

Medieval agriculture lacked the dynamism to keep pace with the demands of growing urban populations. In response to food shortages, marginal lands that had been used for livestock, hay, and pasture were now used to raise crops for human consumption. However, reducing livestock numbers not only reduced the quantity of foods produced from animals, but also the supply and use of manure on cropland, which ultimately lessened crop yields.

Lack of technical progress in agriculture, nearly continuous wars, and the extractive feudal economic system made the bad situation worse. Campbell explained (p. 94) that warfare wreaked ecological havoc on the food and agriculture system through physical destruction of crops, livestock, stock, equipment, and physical structures. Burdensome taxes levied to finance warring armies and the expropriation of stock, crops, equipment, and marketing and transportation systems also weakened the existing agricultural systems.

This pattern of famine during and after periods of war or civil strife, often coinciding with epidemics and disastrous droughts or floods, recurs in most modern famines, such as those afflicting Africa since the 1970s. Modern famines show how the ecological, economic, and social destruction of war disrupts the production and distribution of food and, subsequently, a society's ability to feed itself.

From Renaissance to Agricultural Revolution

Significant changes in farming systems that began in parts of Europe during the later medieval period brought about major changes in the ecological health and productivity of the land. Farmers began to combine and integrate crops and livestock in ways that promoted soil quality and fertility and that boosted production. They adopted more intensive and flexible crop rotations, as well as new crops such as oats, turnips grown for animal feed, and nitrogen-fixing legumes. These innovations eliminated the need for fallowing (idling) of land, adding further to sustainable production gains. Campbell found (p. 92) that farmers adopted these systems most readily in areas with natural resource advantages, access to markets, or fewer institutional constraints such as feudal servile tenure or common property rights.

The enclosure of common lands across England in the 1700s and early 1800s transformed agriculture and the English landscape. Well over six million acres, or one-fourth of the cultivated acres in England, were converted from communally held and farmed lands to lands that were privately owned and managed. This conversion enabled farmers to integrate livestock and crops, using manure and crop rotations to restore and improve depleted lands that were formerly pastured or cultivated continuously. The dramatic gains in productivity and prosperity reflect the key role of private property and free enterprise in resource management.

The large amount of available land in the midwestern and western United States lured families to seek new land when the soil became depleted. As a result of this, President Theodore Roosevelt called for a national sense of duty to the land during a 1908 White House Conservation Conference. However, it was not until the dust bowl disaster of the 1930s that major efforts to protect soil and water finally emerged.

The Agricultural Revolution of 1750–1880 improved yields and adaptation of crops and livestock to local conditions around the world. This period of innovation also set the stage for unprecedented scientific and technical progress in the latter half of the twentieth century. In his Nobel address, Borlaug also noted that in 1940 U.S. farmers produced 56 million tons of corn on 77 million acres of land. In 1999 U.S. farmers produced 240 million tons of corn on 71.7 million acres—a greater than fourfold increase in yield per acre, reaped from hybrid seed, fertilizer, and weed control. The Green Revolution of the 1960s and 1970s applied these techniques to rice, wheat, and other crops in the developing world.

Biotechnology and Questions for the Future

In a response to critics who questioned the environmental effects of advances in agricultural science and technology, Borlaug noted that without the dramatic gains in yields brought about by those advances, three times as much land of equal quality would have been required to match food production in the world at that time. Much of that additional 4.4 billion acres of land would have to come from more marginal and environmentally fragile lands.

By the late twentieth century, biotechnology was yielding new adaptations of crops and animals for food and medicine. U.S. farmers quickly adopted new genetically modified crops. According to the USDA National Agricultural Statistics Service 2002 report *Crop Production—Prospective Plantings*, U.S. farmers intended to plant genetically modified seed on 74 percent of soybean acreage, 71 percent of cotton, and 32 percent of corn

grown for grain in 2002. Most first-generation genetically engineered varieties were designed to reduce pesticide use or to allow use of more benign chemicals.

Proponents maintain that through biotechnology people will find new ways to increase yields, nutritional and health values, and environmental sustainability of food production. Still, controversy persists about environmental impacts, consumer concerns, and access to the new technology for impoverished people and nations. Some people question the new methods of genetic manipulation on philosophical grounds. Despite his strong support of biotechnology, Borlaug said that national, regional, and world policymakers must resolve serious issues raised by the dominant role of proprietary companies in biotechnology investment and research. He questioned how resource-poor farmers in developing countries could obtain products of biotechnology research and what amount of time product patents should last. Thus, in policymaking processes, societies, governments, and international agencies need to make policy decisions based on credible information about how best to meet human food needs from the land and water while safeguarding valuable resources, ecological integrity, and future productivity.

See also **Agriculture since the Industrial Revolution; Aquaculture; Biodiversity; Biotechnology; Crop Improvement; Ecology and Food; Genetic Engineering; Green Revolution; High-Technology Farming; Pesticides; Population and Demographics; Sustainable Agriculture; Toxins, Unnatural, and Food Safety.**

BIBLIOGRAPHY

Borlaug, Norman. "The Green Revolution Revisited and the Road Ahead." Anniversary lecture. Oslo: Norwegian Nobel Institute, 2000. Available at http://www.nobel.se/peace/articles/index.html.

Campbell, Bruce M. S. "Ecology Versus Economics in Late Thirteenth- and Early Fourteenth-Century English Agriculture." In *Agriculture in the Middle Ages: Technology, Practice, and Representation*, edited by Del Sweeney. Philadelphia: University of Pennsylvania Press, 1995.

Chambers, J. D., and G. E. Mingay. *The Agricultural Revolution 1750–1880*. New York: Schocken Books, 1966.

Diamond, Jared. *Guns, Germs, and Steel: The Fates of Human Societies*. New York and London: Norton, 1997.

Food and Agriculture Organization of the United Nations. *The State of World Fisheries and Aquaculture 2000*. Rome: 2000.

Gebauer, Anne Birgitte, and T. Douglas Price, eds. *Transitions to Agriculture in Prehistory*. Madison, Wis.: Prehistory Press, 1992.

Hardin, Garrett. "The Tragedy of the Commons." *Science* 162 (1968): 1243–1248.

Horne, James E., and Maura McDermott. *The Next Green Revolution: Essential Steps to a Healthy, Sustainable Agriculture*. Binghamton, N.Y.: Haworth Press, 2001.

Naylor, Rosamond L., et al. "Effect of Aquaculture on World Fish Supplies." *Nature* 405 (June 2000): 1017–1024.

Pollack, Andrew. "The Green Revolution Yields to the Bottom Line." *The New York Times*, 15 May 2001.

Russell, Howard S. *A Long, Deep Furrow: Three Centuries of Farming in New England.* Hanover, N.H.: University Press of New England, 1976.

Sorenson, A. Ann, Richard P. Green, and Karen Russ. *Farming on the Edge.* DeKalb, Ill.: American Farmland Trust and Center for Agriculture in the Environment, Northern Illinois University, 1997.

Steinfeld, Henning, Cees de Haan, and Harvey Blackburn. *Livestock-Environment Interactions—Issues and Options.* Rome: Food and Agriculture Organization of the United Nations, 1997.

U.S. Department of Agriculture National Agricultural Statistics Service. *Crop Production—Prospective Plantings.* March 2002.

U.S. Department of Agriculture Natural Resources Conservation Service. *America's Private Lands: A Geography of Hope.* 1996.

U.S. Department of Agriculture Natural Resources Conservation Service. *National Resources Inventory 1997: Highlights.* Revised December 2000.

U.S. Environmental Protection Agency. *Managing Nonpoint Source Pollution from Agriculture.* 1997.

Westcott, Paul. *Agricultural Baseline Projections.* U.S. Department of Agriculture Economic Research Service. February 2002.

Lorraine Stuart Merrill

EPICURUS. Epicurus, a Greek philosopher (341–270 B.C.E.), has involuntarily given his name to the fastidious pursuit of pleasure. Born on the Greek island of Samos, Epicurus lived and taught mainly in Athens, where he was a precise contemporary of the playwright Menander. The Epicurean school of philosophy, which he founded, centered on his house and garden in Athens. He and his pupils, who included slaves and women, followed a secluded and austere lifestyle there.

Epicurus taught that the gods have no effect on human affairs, that the universe was created by the random swerve of an atom, and that pleasure is the goal of a happy life. His definition of pleasure is, however, a rather negative one, the removal of disturbance and pain. Since pain is caused by unsatisfied desire, one must reduce one's desires to the minimum. The unavoidable demands of instinct must be satisfied; philosophical study is the best way to conquer all desires beyond that point.

Epicurus is not an ideal choice as a spiritual patron of gastronomes or hedonists. Yet he invited this view of his philosophy with such pronouncements as, "The beginning and root of all good is to make the stomach happy: wisdom and learning are founded on that" (Athenaeus, *Deipnosophists* [Professors at dinner], 546 ff.). The belief that Epicurus favored sensual pleasures can be traced to his contemporaries, and to their understandable misinterpretation of his own words.

See also **Greece, Ancient**.

BIBLIOGRAPHY

A few short writings by Epicurus survive. See Eugene Michael O'Connor, trans., *The Essential Epicurus: Letters, Principal Doctrines, Vatican Sayings, and Fragments* (Amherst, N.Y.: Prometheus Books, 1993), and Brad Inwood and L. P. Gerson, trans., *The Epicurus Reader: Selected Writings and Testimonia* (Indianapolis, Ind.: Hackett, 1994). His beliefs are eloquently explained in a Latin poem by Lucretius, *Lucretius on the Nature of the Universe*, translated by Ronald Latham, with an introduction by John Godwin (London: Penguin, 1994; first published 1951). The papyrus rolls found at Herculaneum in the eighteenth century had come from the working library of an Epicurean teacher of the first century B.C.E. and include some of Epicurus's works. For the *Deipnosophists* of Athenaeus, quoted above, see vol. 5, pp. 477–481, of C. B. Gulick's translation (London: Heinemann, 1933; New York: Putnam, 1933).

Andrew Dalby

EPIPHANY. Epiphany (from the Greek word for 'manifestation') is the Christian festival that commemorates the revealing of Jesus Christ to the Gentile world,

Epiphany Parade at Tarpon Springs, Florida, 1990. Epiphany parades are popular among Greek Orthodox Christians, and the event serves as a community focal point among immigrants. © NIK WHEELER/CORBIS.

Detail of the *Triptych of the Epiphany* by Hieronymus Bosch, showing the Adoration of the Magi. Collection of the Museo del Prado. © FRANCIS G. MAYER/CORBIS.

as personified by those "wise men from the east" who came "to worship him" (Matthew 2:1–2). In Britain it has another, more prosaic, name, Twelfth Day, because it falls on 6 January, twelve days after Christmas. Over time, the plain gospel account of this momentous encounter became richly embroidered with learned commentary and loving speculation. The "wise men" stepped from the shadows and were deemed to be three in number, each one a mighty king who knelt in turn to pay homage and present his gift to the greatest king of all. The festival formed the end and climax of the Christmas season, marked by a joyful and elaborate church service and much cheerful celebration, with parties and presents, fine feasting, and a favorite game. In this game, played in many parts of medieval Europe, a mock-king was selected to reign over the party, be toasted by loyal subjects, and, sometimes, enjoy the doubtful privilege of paying for the wine downed in his honor. He was chosen not on merit but by the chance that was hinted at in his official title, "King of the Bean." A bean had been hidden in a cake, and the lucky man who found it became king of the company. The woman who pulled out the corresponding pea was hailed as his queen.

This traditional game remained popular, but in Britain a variation was developed during the late seventeenth century. Guests still enjoyed their cake, which was dark, dense, packed with dried fruit, and often crowned with almond paste and white icing. However, instead of choosing their king and queen by bean and pea, they drew paper lots. The new custom became a craze, and was elaborated until every slip or card bore the name of some character. Each person present thus had a part to play, and the monarchs mingled with such farcical figures as Sir Tunbelly Clumsy and Miss Flirt, Captain Tearaway, and Lady Racket. The character cards might be homemade or bought at any bakery or toy shop during the Christmas season.

In the eighteenth and early nineteenth centuries, the Twelfth Night cake and characters were enormously enjoyed, so much so that the custom found its way to those parts of America, such as Virginia, that were strongly influenced by British taste.

But the fashion that flared so brightly for a while had burned itself out by the end of the nineteenth century. Twelfth Day became just an ordinary date in the British calendar, and its cake was absorbed into the Christmas Day festivities. In France, however, and, incidentally, in Louisiana, where French traditions are strong, the Bean King still reigns. Bakery windows display tempting versions of the "Galette des Rois," made of sweet brioche or puff pastry, and in each a bean or, alternatively, a tiny porcelain baby Jesus, is concealed, a guarantee of instant pleasure for children.

See also **Christianity**; **Christmas**; **Christmas Drinks**; **Easter**; **Feasts, Festivals, and Fasts**; **Lent**; **Shrove Tuesday**.

BIBLIOGRAPHY

Bauman, James. "Les Galettes des Rois: The Eating of Fine Art." *Petits Propos Culinaires* 27 (October 1987): 7–16.

Belden, Louise Conway. *The Festive Tradition: Table Decoration and Desserts in America, 1650-1900.* New York: W. W. Norton, 1983.

Chambers, Robert, ed. *The Book of Days.* Detroit: Omnigraphics, 1990. Entry on 6 January, Twelfth Day.

Edwards, Gillian. *Hogmanay and Tiffany: The Names of Feasts and Fasts.* London: Geoffrey Bles, Ltd., 1970.

Hadfield, Miles and John Hadfield. *The Twelve Days of Christmas.* London: Cassell, 1961; Boston: Little, Brown, 1962.

Henisch, Bridget Ann. *Cakes and Characters: An English Christmas Tradition.* London: Prospect Books, 1984.

Hone, William. *The World of William Hone: A New Look at the Romantic Age in Words and Pictures of the Day.* Compiled, introduced, and annotated by John Wardroper. London: Shelfmark Books, 1997.

Miles, Clement A. *Christmas Customs and Traditions: Their History and Significance* (1912), reissued New York: Dover, 1976.

Saint-Ange, Mme. E. *Le Livre de Cuisine.* Paris: Larousse, 1927.

Bridget Ann Henisch

Photogravure portrait of Escoffier dated 1907. ROUGHWOOD COLLECTION.

ESCOFFIER, GEORGES-AUGUSTE.

Georges-Auguste Escoffier (1846–1935) was born in Villeneuve-Loubet in France, a village located between Nice and Cannes. During his lifetime he was proclaimed "the finest cook I ever met" by César Ritz of the world-famous Ritz Hotels. Kaiser Wilhelm of Germany praised Escoffier's exceptional culinary talent, telling him "I am the emperor of Germany, but you are the emperor of chefs." Escoffier was more than just a great chef. He is credited with simplifying the complex French haute cuisine of the day— he favored less elaborate dishes, prepared lighter sauces, and used more seasonal ingredients. His reorganization of the professional kitchen eliminated duplication of efforts and resulted in more efficient operation.

Growing up, Escoffier's chief interest was art; he loved to draw and yearned to be a sculptor. However, his grandfather and his father, who was a blacksmith and also grew tobacco, decided otherwise; they said he needed a trade, and they arranged his apprenticeship at age thirteen in his uncle's Restaurant Français in Nice.

At age eighteen, Escoffier was cooking at the Hotel Bellevue in Nice and making an impression on those who ate his food. At nineteen, he became *commis rôtisseur* and then *saucier* at the Petit Moulin Rouge in Paris. At the outbreak of the Franco-Prussian War, Escoffier was drafted into the military and became *chef de cuisine*, first at the headquarters of the general of the Army of the Rhine in Metz, and then for a variety of other regimental commanders. Five years later, he was appointed head chef at the Petit Moulin Rouge, where he fed such dignitaries as the Prince of Wales and Sarah Bernhardt. At the age of thirty, he opened Le Faisan Doré in Cannes.

Escoffier's experience in the military taught him the importance of preserving food, and he began working on methods of canning meats, vegetables, and sauces, and developed a way to preserve tomato sauce in champagne bottles. In his restaurant cooking, he experimented with techniques for simplifying meals and sauces and encouraged the use of seasonal foods. Other accomplishments included helping to found the successful review *L'Art Culinaire* (Culinary art). In this publication, he reflected on problems of feeding the military, published an item about portable stew for soldiers, and wrote about other artistic and practical matters.

In 1884, César Ritz invited Escoffier to become *chef de cuisine* at the Grand Hotel in Monte Carlo in the winter and at the Grand National in Lucerne in the summer. While at these hotels, he designed many things including serving-dishes, some of which bear his name. In 1885 he published *Le Traité sur l'Art de Travaille les Fleurs en Cire* (Treatise on the art of creating wax flowers). In time, Ritz moved on and managed hotels in Cannes and Baden-Baden, while Escoffier stayed behind and thought more about large, complex kitchens. At this time, he also started collecting, recording, and making available his recipes for cooks and headwaiters to use.

In 1890, César Ritz took over the management of Richard d'Oyly Carte's Savoy Hotel in London and invited Escoffier to develop an elegant restaurant there. The Savoy's restaurant quickly became the delight of its clientele, including the Duke of Orleans, one of the hotel's first royal residents, and the Prince of Wales, a frequent guest. Escoffier and the Savoy became known worldwide, and it was there that Escoffier perfected the codification of French haute cuisine. One of the dishes he invented was *pêche Melba*, created in 1894 for Australian opera diva Nellie Melba, who lived at the hotel while singing at Covent Garden. Another was cherries jubilee, invented three years later to celebrate Queen Victoria's Diamond Jubilee.

Escoffier also wrote many books that became bibles in their field, including *Le Guide Culinaire* (1903), a compendium of about five thousand recipes, *Le Carnet d'Epicure* (1911), and *Le Livre des Menus* (1912). In 1920, Escoffier retired to his family home in Monte Carlo where he continued to write many books, including *Le Riz* (1927), *La Morue* (1929), and *Ma Cuisine* (1934). That same year, he was awarded France's Legion of Honor.

See also **Cookbooks; Kitchens, Restaurant; Places of Consumption; Restaurants.**

BIBLIOGRAPHY

Escoffier, Georges-Auguste. *The Complete Guide to the Art of Modern Cookery.* Translated by H. K. Cracknell and R. J. Kaufman. London: Heinemann, 1979.

Flandrin, Jean-Louis, and Massimo Montanari. *Food: A Culinary History.* New York: Columbia University Press, 1999.

Herbodeau, Eugène, and Paul Thomas. *Georges Auguste Escoffier.* London: Practical Press, 1955.

Trager, James. *The Food Chronology: A Food Lover's Compendium of Events and Anecdotes from Prehistory to the Present.* New York: Henry Holt, 1995.

Jacqueline M. Newman

ESKIMOS. *See* **Inuit.**

ETHNICITY. *See* **National Cuisines, Idea of; United States: Ethnic Cuisines.**

ETHNOBOTANY. Ethnobotany is the study of the relationship between people and plants. This interdisciplinary field includes studying plants as wild foods and as agricultural crops; as constructs for houses and modes of transportation; as baskets, pottery, and art; as clothing and types of weaving; as medicines and alternative methods for healing; and in the context of cultural myths and religious ceremonies. Research topics address more complex issues, including the cultural consequences of the extinction of a particular plant species on the diet of a culture, impacts of acculturation on a culture's uses of plants, and the transmission of ethnobotanical knowledge from one generation to the next.

Ethnobotanists study all types of cultures, from the past to the present, from indigenous communities in the Amazon Basin to complex plant usage by immigrants in New York City. This field incorporates techniques and research from many fields, especially anthropology, archaeology, biology, botany, chemistry, entomology, geography, history, linguistics, medicine, and zoology.

How Does Ethnobotany Study Culture?

Ethnobotanists study culture by examining how plants were used in the past as well as the present. By studying farming practices of the past or examining fossilized plant or human remains, researchers are able to determine what plants were used by ancient civilizations.

Anatomically speaking, modern human beings (*Homo sapiens*) have existed for approximately 150,000 to 200,000 years, but have practiced widespread cultivation for only a fraction of that time. Evidence that agriculture was practiced includes abundant fossilized remains of plants known to have been cultivated or of tools used for preparing soil, cultivating, or harvesting food.

Human skeletons can provide information about the kinds of plants eaten and the ways in which food was pre-

Bora man is shown cooking coca leaves to prepare a paste that he and other members of his tribe will use to enable them to hunt for days without rest and food. © JAY DICKMAN/CORBIS.

PLANTS THAT STAND BETWEEN SURVIVAL AND STARVATION

There are at least twelve plant species that have had an enormous impact on cultures throughout history. Without them, humankind could not have developed past single a hunting-and-gathering lifestyle.

In the grass family [Poaceae], four plants have been instrumental in the survival of human culture. These plants include wheat (*Triticum aestivum*), which was cultivated more than eleven thousand years ago in the Middle East as a staple grain and today has more than seventeen thousand varieties. Wheat is one of the staple crops of the United States since it is the primary ingredient in bread. Corn (*Zea mays*) was domesticated five thousand years ago in Mexico and Central America and ultimately became dependent on people for its reproduction. Corn has thrived with the assistance of humankind for so long that it can no longer effectively reproduce itself in the wild. Rice (*Oryza sativa*) was cultivated in Southeast Asia by many different cultures as long as five thousand years ago and is a staple in much of Asia and Latin America. Finally, sugar cane (*Saccharum officinarum*) was the staple crop of the indigenous peoples of New Guinea undergoing domestication about five thousand years ago. Nowadays, sugar cane is highly prized as a sweetener.

Two types of potatoes were also considered staples throughout history: the common potato (*Solanum tuberosum*) [Solanaceae] and the sweet potato (*Ipomoea batatas*) [Convolvulaceae]. These tubers actually come from different plant families and are unrelated to each other despite the fact that both are cultivated in South America and both are called potatoes. The common potato was cultivated before 5000 B.C.E. primarily by the multitude of cultures living in the Andean highlands. Hundreds of varieties now exist worldwide. The sweet potato also grows in the mountains, but was more commonly found in the tropical regions of South America and cultivated by Amazonian cultures.

The common bean (*Phaseolus vulgaris*) and the soybean (*Glycine max*)—both members of the Fabaceae bean family—have also been instrumental in the survival of cultures in Latin America and Asia, respectively. Beans were cultivated at least five thousand years ago in Mex-

ico and Peru and often used in combination with corn, providing essential proteins. Soybeans originated in northeast China around the same time and eventually spread worldwide. Soybean production has now shifted from China to the United States, where more than 52 percent of world production occurs.

Coconuts (*Cocos nucifera*) [Araceae] and bananas (*Musa sapientum*) [Musaceae] are often touted as the world's most perfect foods. Although the origins of coconuts are unclear since their fibrous seeds can float in salt water for more than eighty days, researchers believe this important food plant originated in the Indo-Pacific region or possibly Southeast Asia. Bananas also originated in the tropical regions of the Pacific Islands and Southeast Asia more than five thousand years ago and are rich in potassium. The fruits from both of these plants provide high levels of carbohydrates. Sap from banana plants is used as medicine, while their leaves are used in wrapping food for cooking. The husks from coconuts provide strong fibers for weaving, while the fronds of the trees are used as thatching for homes.

Cassava, also known as yucca or manioc (*Manihot esculenta*) [Euphorbiaceae] is a tuber similar in consistency to the common potato and is very starchy. This plant originated in South America and its cultivation began around 5000 B.C.E. Hundreds of varieties now exist of two different types: bitter cassava that contains poisonous cyanogenetic glycosides and sweet cassava that is sold today in marketplaces around the world. Generally, cultures that were more sedentary raised bitter cassava because they were reliant on one garden and therefore would suffer more if herbivorous predators destroyed their gardens. Seminomadic hunter-gardeners would often plant two or three gardens that they could visit throughout the year so damage to one garden was not felt as sharply.

Perhaps the most recent example of a cultivated and important food plant is the sugar beet (*Beta vulgaris*) [Chenopodiaceae]. Beets were cultivated in the eighteenth and nineteenth centuries in Europe. These tubers contain large amounts of sugar and have long been highly prized in Europe, the Mediterranean, and Russia.

---

pared. Grasses have a ratio of two stable carbon isotopes (C12 and C13) different from that of most other plants eaten by people. Changes in the ratio of these isotopes in human skeletons over time from grass ratios to that found in grains can indicate a shift to grains as a primary source of food. Similarly, the consumption of large

amounts of grains can be documented by examining patterns of wear on the teeth of archeological skeletons.

Do Plants Have Cultural Roles?

It is easy to think about plants as being used for food or medicine, or even as a source of technology, for example, in the making of spears or blowguns by Amazonian peoples or the furniture in your own house. But, how many people associate a particular plant with a particular culture? Plants had cultural roles in ancient civilizations, are tied to historical events, and can be important identifiers in modern-day cultures.

South and Central American cultures such as the Aztecs, Maya, and the Inca were often associated with particular types of food. For instance, the Aztecs were well known to have cultivated *Amaranth* sp. [Amaranthaceae], a high-protein grain that was considered sacred by its cultivators. The Maya people were linked to the production of corn, as were many other smaller tribes scattered across South and Central America, and Mexico. The Inca were known to cultivate potatoes and quinoa, a high-protein grain that is still grown by the Quechua and Aymara Indians, descendants of the Inca. North American natives used various dye plants to produce unique colors for weavings that symbolized their particular tribe, family, and sometimes their ethnolinguistic identity.

Plants That Made History

Historically, plants have been known to make or break a culture (see sidebar, Plants That Stand between Survival and Starvation). In addition to plants being food staples in societies, many plants are integrally linked to a culture because they improved or adversely affected its history. The tea tree (*Camelia sinensis*) [Theaceae] has huge cultural significance in many Asian cultures. Elaborate methods to cultivate and prepare tea began in China and later spread to Japan, where the tea ceremony became linked with Zen Buddhist beliefs. Egyptians are credited with inventing paper by pressing together strips of papyrus (*Cyperus papyrus*) [Cyperaceae], but real paper, made by separating plant fibers and matting them together in a thin sheet, was invented by the Chinese using paper mulberry (*Broussonetia papyrifera*) [Moraceae].

A darker side of history includes two plants integrally linked to slavery: cotton (*Gossypium* sp.) [Malvaceae] and sugar cane (*Saccharum officinarum*) [Poaceae]. Both plants were big money crops in the Americas and required significant labor, resulting in the enslavement of many African cultures and their transport to the United States and Central America.

Some may argue that the apple tree (*Malus domestica*) [Rosaceae] also had a hand in shaping world history from the moment Eve took that first bite. Few people realize that the intoxicating drug derived from the opium poppy (*Papaver somniferum*) [Papaveraceae] was one of the main reasons China shut down its borders to all outside trade after the establishment of the People's Republic of China in 1949. Production of the opium poppy has increased in present-day Afghanistan in an effort by terrorist groups to raise money in combatting U.S. military presence. Finally, spice plants in general led Christopher

IMPORTANT SPICE PLANTS

Common Name	Scientific Name
Anise	*Pimpinella anisum*
Basil	*Ocimum basilicum*
Bay leaves	*Laurus nobilis*
Caraway	*Carum carvi*
Cardamom	*Elettaria cardamomum*
Celantro	*Coriandrum sativum*
Celery	*Apium graveolens*
Chervil	*Anthriscus cereifolium*
Chives	*Allium schoenoprasum*
Coriander	*Coriandrum sativum*
Cumin	*Cuminum cyminum*
Dill	*Anethum graveolens*
Fennel	*Foeniculum vulgare*
Fenugreek	*Trigonella foenumgraecum*
Garlic	*Allium sativum*
Horseradish	*Amoricana rusticana*
Leek	*Allium porrum*
Marjoram	*Origanum majorana*
Mustard	*Brassica alba, B. nigra*
Onion	*Allium cepa*
Oregano	*Origanum vulgare*
Parsley	*Petroselinum crispum*
Peppermint	*Mentha piperita*
Rosemary	*Rosmarinus officinalis*
Sage	*Salvia officinalis*
Savory	*Satureja hortensis*
Shallot	*Allium ascalonicum*
Spearmint	*Mentha spicata*
Star anise	*Illicium verum*
Tarragon	*Artemesia dracunculus*
Thyme	*Thymus vulgaris*

Columbus to search for a new trade route to India, but resulted in his discovery of the Americas in 1492.

The Future of Ethnobotany

The future of ethnobotany lies squarely in conservation of both plant species and the cultures that know how to use them. As scientists who work directly with cultures and their natural resources, ethnobotanists are in a unique position to promote strategies for conservation. Ethnobotanists of the future need to develop methods that empower the people with whom they work.

For much of the last century, ethnobotanists have spent their time documenting uses of plants and in finding ways to apply the knowledge of one culture for the benefit of another. They must look beyond this and find ways to safeguard the rights and knowledge of the people with whom they study as well as analyze more complex issues relating to interdisciplinary applications of cultural knowledge and uses of plants.

Ethnobotanists must develop methods to convey important information to the communities with which they work, treating indigenous collaborators as coauthors and establishing contracts with communities or tribal groups to ensure that a percentage of any future profits are returned to those cultures which originally held such knowledge.

See also **Agriculture, Origins of; Biodiversity; Botanicals; Herbs and Spices; Horticulture; Paleonutrition, Methods of; Prehistoric Societies.**

BIBLIOGRAPHY

Balick, M. J., and P. Cox. *Plants, People, and Culture: The Science of Ethnobotany.* New York: Scientific American Library, 1996.

Gibbons, E. *Stalking the Wild Asparagus.* New York: David McKay, 1962.

Reis, S. V. R., and F. J. Lipp, Jr. *New Plant Sources for Drugs and Foods from the New York Botanical Garden Herbarium.* Cambridge, Mass.: Harvard University Press, 1982.

Schultes, Richard Evans, and Siri von Reis, eds. *Ethnobotany: Evolution of a Discipline.* Portland, Ore.: Dioscorides Press, 1995.

Simpson, B. B., and M. C. Ogorzaly. *Economic Botany Plants in Our World*, 3d ed. Boston: McGraw Hill, 2001.

Camille Tipton-Allaband

ETHNOPHARMACOLOGY. Although the medicinal uses of plants can be traced to earliest human history and many modern pharmaceuticals are based in botanicals (about 30 percent), Western scientists have been reluctant to extend credibility to the therapeutic potential of plants from other cultures. During the last quarter of the twentieth century, however, attitudes about botanical sources of pharmaceuticals and other medicines shifted dramatically in the West. Renewed interest in plant medicines is substantiated in ethnopharmacology, the study of the chemistry and physiologic actions of (primarily plant) medicines used by native populations. *Ethno* denotes cultural group, and *pharmacology* refers to the science of drug sources, activities, and uses (Etkin, 1996; Rivier and Bruhn, 1979; Rivier and Anton, 1991). Scholarly journals that publish research and reviews on the topic include the *Journal of Ethnopharmacology, Pharmaceutical Biology, Economic Botany, Planta Medica, Phytotherapy Research,* and *Fitoterapia.*

Ethnopharmacologists represent diverse academic traditions, most prominently anthropology, pharmacology, and botany, and some commercial domains, including the pharmaceutical industry and the rapidly expanding market for "herbal" (botanical) medicines and medicinal foods. Given the diversity of contributors to ethnopharmacology, the field has considerable breadth in objectives and approaches. At one end of a continuum, anthropologists and a small percentage of ethnobotanists link the ethnography of health and illness to the chemistry and physiologic action of plant medicines. This extends traditional ethnomedical research that addressed the cultural basis of therapeutics and the social relations of healing and that treated plants largely as cultural objects. Anthropological ethnopharmacology has come to include the biodynamic qualities of plants, to acknowledge that tangible attributes may be as important as symbols in the selection of particular species and the interpretation of their physiologic actions.

This biocultural perspective on ethnopharmacology takes into account that native peoples, like Western scientists, are keen observers of their natural environments who embellish the cultural meaning of plants by marking and managing bitter, wound healing, symptom mediating, and other physical attributes. Yucatec Maya populations, for example, distinguish medicinal from nonmedicinal species (including foods) by smell and taste, noting especially astringent, aromatic, and sweet characteristics. These culturally defined clues not only encode information about which symptoms a particular plant treats best but also juxtapose cultural salience to bioactivity. For example, constituents (polyphenols) present in the plants used by Yucatec Maya for digestive complaints are responsible for both astringent taste and efficacy in the treatment of intestinal disorders (Ankli et al., 1999; Brett and Heinrich, 1999). Anthropologists discern these subtleties through extensive field studies (ethnography) of indigenous peoples to understand the complex cultural and environmental circumstances that shape plant selection and use. They have observed that many medicinal species are used for other purposes as well, thus extending human exposure to pharmacologically active constituents.

Medicines overlap especially with foods, and some cultural groups, for example, the Hausa in Nigeria, acquire knowledge of some wild food plants through their experiences with those species as medicines (Etkin and Ross, 1994). In other circumstances the incorporation into cuisines of "novel" plants, such as unusually bitter, astringent, or otherwise unpalatable plants, takes advantage of the healthful effects of bioreactive species, some of which may later be used as medicine proper (Johns, 1994). The point is not to judge whether or not some indigenous group "got it right," that is, used pharmacologically active plants in a way consistent with the principles of biomedicine, but to apply the techniques of bioscience as one aspect of comprehensive research based in extensive field study.

At the other end of the continuum are ethnopharmacologists whose primary objective is drug development. Logically this is the perspective of researchers who do want to know whether or not some indigenous group "got it right" and if so how that lead can be pursued to discover new pharmaceuticals. Bioprospecting pharmacologists have begun to collaborate with botanists, who offer chemo-taxonomic insights to guide the search for new sources of known drugs (on the principle that closely related plants have similar chemical profiles) and new plant compounds. For example, the potential to develop medicines for diabetes is suggested in plants that have insulin-stimulating effects, inhibit carbohydrate-digesting enzymes in the intestine, or increase glucose utilization (Raman and Skett, 1998). This research is primarily entrepreneurial (discovering products rather than indigenous knowledge) and necessarily involves only short-term field study with greater emphasis on laboratory and clinical phases. As such this version of ethnopharmacology is not as likely to uncover overlapping uses and the potential pharmacologic significance of certain indigenous food plants.

In the West the bioscientific perspective of ethnopharmacology is applied also to the study of foods. For example, researchers have found that the antioxidant lycopene, which gives tomatoes their red color, diminishes the risk of cardiovascular disease and cancers of the digestive tract and prostate (Rao and Agarwal, 1999). Similarly sulforaphane in broccoli has anticancer activity; hesperidin in grapefruit inhibits poliomyelitis, herpes, and influenza viruses; capsaicin in chili pepper lowers the risk of stomach cancer; sulfides in garlic and onion inhibit blood clotting; and glucaric acid in orange lowers serum cholesterol (Debrovner, 1993; Montanari et al., 1997).

These examples of healthful constituents in everyday (nonexotic) foods overlap the rapidly expanding public and scientific interest in complementary and alternative medicines (CAM), many of which are variably promoted as functional foods, medical foods, supplements, nutraceuticals, health foods, pharmafoods, phytofoods, and phytochemicals ("phyto-" denotes plant). Although the popularity of CAM has been primarily commercially driven, these products increasingly are subjected to scientific scrutiny. For example, studies suggest that constituents of saw palmetto protect against prostrate cancers and that dandelion extracts are diuretic. Pharmacologic studies of previously uncharacterized medicinal foods also reveal potential risks. For example, the blood-thinning and insulin-promoting actions of ginseng may act synergistically with drugs prescribed for the same effects; Saint-John's-wort decreases the effectiveness of some pharmaceuticals, including Indinavir (used to treat HIV/AIDS); and licorice may increase the side effects of oral contraceptives (Newall et al., 1996).

Ethnopharmacologists of all persuasions want to move beyond catalogs of plant use and action to address issues of context. How are the activities of plant components affected by preparation according to real instructions for use? What is the outcome when foods, medicinal foods, medicines, and other biodynamic substances are combined? These are complex questions. They are also the most interesting questions, and their answers will have the broadest implications for people who interact with biodynamic foods and medicines in their daily lives.

See also **Botanicals; Health and Disease; Health Foods; Medicine; Neutraceuticals.**

BIBLIOGRAPHY

Ankli, Anita, Otto Sticher, and Michael Heinrich. "Yucatec Maya Medicinal Plants versus Nonmedicinal Plants: Indigenous Characterization and Selection." *Human Ecology* 27 (1999): 557–580.

Brett, John, and Michael Heinrich. "Culture, Perception, and the Environment." *Journal of Applied Botany* 72 (1999): 67–69.

Cotton, C. M. *Ethnobotany: Principles and Applications*. Chichester, U.K.: Wiley, 1996.

Debrovner, Diane. "Edible Remedies." *American Druggist* 205 (1993): 36–40.

Etkin, Nina L. "Ethnopharmacology: The Conjunction of Medical Ethnography and the Biology of Therapeutic Action." In *Medical Anthropology: Contemporary Theory and Method*, rev. ed., edited by Carolyn F. Sargent and Thomas M. Johnson. Westport, Conn.: Praeger, 1996.

Etkin, Nina L., ed. *Plants in Indigenous Medicine and Diet: Biobehavioral Approaches*. Bedford Hills, N.Y.: Redgrave, 1986.

Etkin, Nina L., and Paul J. Ross. "Malaria, Medicine, and Meals: A Biobehavioral Perspective." In *The Anthropology of Medicine*, 3d ed., edited by Lola Romanucci-Ross, Daniel E. Moerman, and Laurence R. Tancredi. Westport, Conn.: Bergin and Garvey, 1997.

Etkin, Nina L., and Paul J. Ross. "Pharmacologic Implications of 'Wild' Plants in Hausa Diet." In *Eating on the Wild Side: The Pharmacologic, Ecologic, and Social Implications of Using Noncultigens*, edited by Nina L. Etkin. Tucson: University of Arizona Press, 1994.

Etkin, Nina L., and Paul J. Ross. "Should We Set a Place for Diet in Ethnopharmacology?" *Journal of Ethnopharmacology* 32 (1991): 25–36.

Johns, Timothy. "Ambivalence to the Palatability Factors in Wild Food Plants." In *Eating on the Wild Side: The Pharmacologic, Ecologic, and Social Implications of Using Noncultigens*, edited by Nina L. Etkin. Tucson: University of Arizona Press, 1994.

Johns, Timothy. "The Chemical Ecology of Human Ingestive Behaviors." *Annual Review of Anthropology* 28 (1999): 27–50.

Johns, Timothy. *The Origins of Human Diet and Medicine*. Tucson: University of Arizona Press, 1996.

Montanari, Antonio, Wilbur Widmer, and Steven Nagy. "Health-Promoting Phytochemicals in Citrus Fruit and Juice Products." In *Functionality of Food Phytochemicals*, edited by Timothy Johns and John T. Romeo. New York: Plenum, 1997.

Newall, Carol A., Linda A. Anderson, and J. David Phillipson. *Herbal Medicines: A Guide for Health-Care Professionals*. London: Pharmaceutical Press, 1996.

Prendergast, Hew D.V., Nina L. Etkin, David R. Harris, and Peter J. Houghton, eds. *Plants for Food and Medicine*. Kew, U.K.: Royal Botanic Gardens Press, 1998.

Raman, Amala, and Paul Skett. "Traditional Remedies and Diabetes Treatment." In *Plants for Food and Medicine*, edited by Hew D.V. Prendergast, Nina L. Etkin, David R. Harris, and Peter J. Houghton. Kew, U.K.: Royal Botanic Gardens Press, 1998.

Rao, A. V., and S. Agarwal. "Role of Lycopene as Antioxidant Carotenoid in the Prevention of Chronic Diseases: A Review." *Nutrition Research* 19 (1999): 305–323.

Rivier, Laurent, and Robert Anton, eds. "Ethnopharmacology 1990: Proceedings of the First International Congress on Ethnopharmacology." *Journal of Ethnopharmacology* 32 (1991): 1–239.

Rivier, Laurent, and Jan Bruhn. "Editorial." *Journal of Ethnopharmacology* 1 (1979): 1.

Nina L. Etkin

Portrait of Emily Post, the American doyenne of good manners. PHOTO COURTESY OF THE LIBRARY OF CONGRESS.

ETIQUETTE AND EATING HABITS.

No society can survive or flourish unless its members accept rules governing food sharing and consumption. Mealtime manners, which govern the way food is eaten in the company of others, provide for giving and receiving small, vital, and constantly reiterated signs that these rules are in working order. Without them food would be hogged by the physically powerful, violence would frequently erupt during meals, civility in general would decline, and eventually society would break down altogether. Furthermore, the specific fashion in which a culture manages eating helps to express, identify, and dramatize that society's ideals and aesthetic style.

Civilized and considerate people the world over demand that meals shall be eaten with respect, not only for the food and the effort and good fortune it represents but also for the people in whose company it is eaten. Human beings normally eat in the company of others. The word "company" is derived from Latin, meaning "bread with," and therefore "those who share food." The act of sharing a meal becomes a symbol of every kind of relationship and of the acceptance of cultural values that may seem to have little to do with consuming nutrients. Since eating normally happens more than once a day, human beings turn meals into opportunities to learn and to practice "culture." Politeness at meals provides daily exercise in making socially desirable norms "second nature."

However, mealtime etiquette is not morality. It is convention, an agreement to behave, in the particular circumstances of mealtimes, as if one were virtuous. Like any convention it is liable to degenerate into a facade, which can be used as a barrier to protect power and class distinction.

Taboo

Eating rules exist mainly to ensure that meals shall be shared peacefully, the reason being that such an outcome is far from inevitable. People have killed, chopped, and submitted to fire what they are eating together; they are often armed with knives and certainly with teeth, primary human weapons. They are hungry, each looking out for his or her own interests, and they are sitting at close quarters. They might also be consuming alcohol, which lowers inhibitions. Mealtime rules provide not only the safety but also the predictability that allows eaters to relax.

Different societies have different ways of keeping violence out of the sacred eating space. In European and American cultures knives are on the table. Their blades are given rounded ends unless they are exceptionally competent "steak" knives. Rules insist on no pointing with knives, forks, or spoons. Diners should not impale their food on their knives to carry it to their mouths, or hold their knives in their fists (that is, too competently and therefore aggressively). They should direct their knives toward their plates with their forefingers, and they should lay down their knives with blades facing inward, not toward neighbors. Attempting to reduce the actual use of the knife, diners, when in doubt and if possible, use a fork or a spoon instead. North Americans traditionally cut their food then put aside their knives, blades facing in, and eat with their forks. Carving up a whole joint or a bird in front of the assembled company would be, in many societies, an unthinkably barbarous act. The Chinese and Japanese, for example, have banned knives from the table altogether. They cut up everything in advance, far away and out of sight. The eating implements provided are blunt wooden sticks.

Mealtime manners usually work by keeping any thought of violence from occurring. Many myths, however, reveal the roots of the conventions by including a murder that is especially appalling because of its mealtime setting. The drama resides in the horror of that which good behavior while eating so successfully prevents. (An example is Homer's *Odyssey* 11: 409–420.) And because mealtime manners are a mild form of taboo, hearing about infractions, such as people flinging food about, wiping their mouths on the tablecloth, or grabbing food with their hands (especially where knives, forks, and spoons or chopsticks are the rule), causes shock or laughter.

During meals all mammals are extrasensitive to the possibility of enemies stealing their food or otherwise taking advantage of their concentration on eating. They are alert to tiny signs and abnormalities in the environment that otherwise they might let pass. For human beings, who normally eat in a previously prepared and protected area, this heightened attention is applied to the behavior of their eating companions. Strange table manners or an affront to a visitor's culturally formed expectations are often the subject of dramatic travelers' tales. Westerners, for example, might note with surprise and then find unforgettable the Arab custom of pouring tea into a glass until it overflows into the saucer beneath it. This is a sign in Arab cultures of magnanimity, but foreigners can misinterpret it as sloppy and incompetent behavior. On the continent of Europe, propriety enjoins diners to sit with both hands in full view of the company; most correctly, unused hands should rest on the table's edge, being visible only from the wrists. The Anglo-Saxon custom of permitting guests to sit with one hand hidden seems, to Continentals, at best a sad sign of naivete. Since mealtime etiquette is drummed into people so early and so thoroughly, its obedient practitioners rarely find it a matter for comment; they take it for granted. It is outsiders usually who report on the idiosyncrasies of a society's manners at meals.

Consideration for the Company

Other themes expressed by systems of mealtime manners worldwide include who dines with whom and when, and the solidarity of the dining group; consideration for the needs, fears, and sensitivities of the other people present; and cleanliness, which may have as much to do with purity and all its connotations as with health. These themes may be articulated in mealtime rituals that are common to many cultures, or behavior may be highly idiosyncratic yet witness to widely held meanings. Mealtime rules simultaneously express preferences that are culture specific.

VIOLENCE

To attack corn on the cob with as little ferocity as possible is perhaps the only direction to be given, since from the point of view of grace a series of ferociously snatching, teeth-bared bites that can be heard as well as seen, to say nothing of butter and corn fragments sprinkled on chin and cheeks, while delectable to the palate, is a horrible sight. (Post, 1937, p. 758)

The neighing sound that some people make when they laugh is … unseemly. And the person who opens his mouth wide in a rictus, with wrinkled cheeks and exposed teeth, is also impolite.… If something so funny should occur that it produces uncontrolled laughter … the face should be covered with a napkin or with the hand. (Erasmus, 1530)

HOST AND GUEST

The diner who lets his *fan* (rice) bowl stay on the table and eats by picking up lumps of *fan* from the bowl is expressing disinterest [sic] in or dissatisfaction with the food. If he or she is a guest in someone's house, that is seen as an open insult to the host. (F. L. K. Hsü and V. Y. N. Hsü, "Modern China: North," in *Food in Chinese Culture*, edited by K. C. Chang, 1977, p. 305)

If you are fortunate enough, as a guest, to be given a piece of fruit by the ruler, you should suck the kernel clean and put it down the front of your robe, to show that you are not throwing any of his gift away. (*Li Chi*, compiled in the early first century B.C.E., translated by James Legge, 1967)

NOISE AND TALKING

When eating refrain from speaking, lest the windpipe open before the gullet, and life be in danger. (Babylonian Talmud, c. 450 C.E.)

Certain hot foods are best when very hot. The technique for eating them is to draw in air over a narrow opening so as to hasten evaporation and diffuse the flavor. This is most effective when the air roughens the surface of the liquid. That is why hot soup, hot soup-noodles, hot congee etc. are best when sucked in with as loud a noise as possible. (Chao, 1956, p. 34)

[Do not mention at table] a rope in the house of a man who has been hanged. (Lord Chesterfield's letters to his son, no. 259, 1777)

For example, in modern Europe and America meals are eaten around a table, which expresses the oneness of the group. Solidarity established, the separateness and

SNOBBERY

[Etiquette is] the barrier which society draws around itself, a shield against the intrusion of the impertinent, the improper, and the vulgar. (*Manners and Tone of Good Society; or, Solecisms to Be Avoided*, 1879)

Nothing indicates a well-bred man more than a proper mode of eating his dinner. A man may pass muster by *dressing well,* and may sustain himself tolerably in conversation; but if he is not perfectly "au fait," *dinner* will betray him. (Agogos, *Hints on Etiquette and the Usages of Society,* 1834)

DELICATESSE

Turn away when spitting to avoid spitting on or spraying someone. If any disgusting matter is spat onto the ground, it should ... be ground under foot lest it nauseate someone. (Erasmus, 1530)

Withdraw when you are going to vomit; vomiting is not shameful, but to have vomited through gluttony is disgusting. (Erasmus, 1530)

If you happen to have eaten something that cannot be swallowed, you should discreetly turn away and toss it somewhere. (Erasmus, 1530)

Drinking much and long leads to unavoidable consequences. Will it be credited that, in the corner of the very dining room, there is a certain convenient piece of furniture, to be used by anybody who wants it. The operation is performed very deliberately and undisguisedly, as a matter of course, and occasions no interruption of the conversation. (Louis Simond, *Journal of a Tour and Residence in Great Britain during the Years 1810 and 1811,* 1815, vol. 1, p. 49)

self-sufficiency of each individual is stressed. The cutlery is laid out like a fence surrounding every "place." Everyone sits on his or her own upright chair. Portions are divided out before people begin eating and are served on separate dishes. Any crossing of the boundaries represented by the enclosed "place" is either a transgression (a "transgression," derived from Latin, means a "stepping over") or demonstrates great intimacy between people allowed to break this rule and transfer "tastes" from one plate to another. In this same culture it used to be thought polite and benevolent, therefore "good manners," repeatedly to pass food to one's companions. People are exhorted not to lean into someone else's space; not to reach across the table, let alone across a neighbor's plate; not to share the cutlery. Such insistence on the boundaries between the diners is different from the etiquette of people who eat from a common spread, taking from it with their hands, often sitting on the ground to do so.

Equality, Hierarchy, and Reciprocity

When equality is the overriding theme of a meal, meat is likely to be prechopped or minced and perhaps formed into cakes of equal sizes, or all the ingredients might be mixed in one dish so everybody eats the same thing (Watson, 1988). But hierarchy frequently cuts across commensal equality. It matters, for example, who gets served first. Where a whole bird, representing the oneness of the group, is carved up before the diners, the proceeding ensures that differences are expressed. No portion is exactly like any other, and differing values might be assigned to each piece. Carving, in the Western tradition, was once called "doing the honors."

The allocation of sitting spaces at a banquet is exceedingly important in many cultures and subject to specific rules. Often women, who usually have prepared the food, are not allowed to join the men in eating it. Written records of feasts in the European past frequently describe the seating of the guests while not bothering to say what it was they actually ate.

Hospitality, or accepting nonfamily members into one's house, has always been thought a difficult or dangerous proceeding, and for this reason is often the subject of rules and constraints. Hosts have to make guests "feel at home," yet guests must refrain from demanding different food, ordering the host's children about, or otherwise overstepping their essentially passive role. Hosts are at home, giving, while guests are away, receiving, and these roles are underlined in different ways, for instance, in some of the rules for seating.

Meals eaten with friends and acquaintances are widely thought of as helping to bind a society's members together, especially in cultures where familial solidarity is strong enough to create the potential isolation of people into family groups (Ortner, 1978). Such meals normally demand a repetition of the exercise at a later date, when the present guest will become the host. The imbalance created between hosts and guests demands to be righted and produces the highly desirable social virtue of peaceful reciprocity (Lévi-Strauss, 1969; Pitt-Rivers, 1977).

Teaching Children to Behave

In all cultures children have to be taught mealtime manners, which deliberately complicate the actions of taking and eating. They learn gradually not to grab, splash, or shout at meals. They practice giving and receiving in the manner acceptable to the culture, and they find they must ask for rather than demand what they want. Children may also become familiar with social hierarchies or elaborate kinship patterns in their rule-bound expressions at meals, that is, how and when to keep quiet, how to hear and apply admonitions, how to wait and to share (Raum, 1940; Read, 1959; Richards, 1932, 1939). Mealtimes, with clear needs, swift rewards, and adult examples on view, are perfect occasions for children to learn to talk. It is understood that little children, if they are allowed to join the commensal group, have not yet learned to "behave." They may be permitted to run around, beg for tidbits from adults, and otherwise break the rules. Their eventual admission to adult status at meals is a kind of initiation and a proof that they now are capable of self-control.

Noise

Different attitudes toward food are expressed by two types of mealtime manners as they relate to sound. For some groups the polite response to a meal is gratitude to the cook or the host for providing it and pleasure, which should be clearly dramatized. People are expected to express their delight verbally or to provide physical signs of it, like slurping their noodles and sighing with satisfaction. Contentedly burping after the meal may show a kindly abandon to the generosity of the host, who might be hurt if guests remain cool, detached, and apparently either unsatisfied or unimpressed by what has been offered them.

In other cultures people feel they should not be unduly interested in the food; they should at least appear to revel mainly in the company of the other people present. They refrain from exclaiming about the food, although a polite murmur of appreciation might be permitted. They must not look too enthusiastic for fear of seeming greedy. People are expected instead to concentrate on the conversation.

In some cultures talking during meals may be strictly undesirable. In others only certain people present are allowed to talk, or it may be deemed essential that everybody contribute to the conversation. The etiquette of eating from a common spread versus that of eating previously apportioned food interlocks with these preferences for either talking or keeping silent. The system in which each person eats from a separate plate divides the companions, and talk provides the needed interchange among them. People who take their food from a central dish or set of dishes necessarily interact in the process, so they concentrate on eating with fairness and consideration and tend to talk little. People who use chopsticks eat quickly because cut-up food, sizzling hot, could get cold if too much time is taken in chatting rather than eating. Talking for these last two groups tends to be done before the meal or afterward.

Complication

Politeness, which overlays "nature," is usually a complication of behavior deemed by other people to be "fitting" and "proper." In the modern West, for example, where conversation is a necessary part of the formal proceedings at dinner, well-behaved people must nevertheless eat with their mouths closed. To eat and talk but never to be seen opening your mouth with food in it is far from simple. Dining "properly" and remaining relaxed while doing so (showing uneasiness at mealtimes is always distracting and annoying for the other diners) has to be learned and then honed by constant practice.

Silver punch strainer, London, England, 1757. According to proper eighteenth-century etiquette, punch was strained of fruit pulp as it was poured into cups. ROUGHWOOD COLLECTION. PHOTO CHEW & COMPANY.

Not being mannerly, and effortlessly mannerly, can arouse irritation, unease, disgust, contempt, and finally rejection by other people. Manners, which are supposed to ease relationships, can be turned into a series of tests to sift out people who have not learned the niceties and therefore are kept outside the privileged circles of the "well bred." Here manners are no longer "for the sake of other people" but only for the complacency of some and the exclusion of others. Mealtime manners make a more draconian demand than most aspects of "proper" behavior because ignoring them can violate largely unexamined or unconscious taboos. People often use the differences between their own systems of manners and those of others to make derogatory judgments about those others. In the modern West people frequently shudder at or mock the behavior of their own ancestors, who, for example, ate with their hands.

Yet people who eat with their hands have just as many rules and elaborations as do the wielders of chopsticks or knives, forks, and spoons. People might, for example, always have to eat with their right hands (Needham, 1973) and might even have to restrict the number of fingers used on that hand. They must never reach for more food while still chewing and must never fill both cheeks or even fill one too full, which shows uncontrolled appetite. Hand washing is demanded before and after meals and sometimes during meals as well. No spilling or grabbing and no fiddling with the food is allowed, such actions being all too easy when eating with the hands. Eating gracefully, or the reverse, is defined, and rules establish how to take up a morsel and just how and how much to dip it into sauce. Restrictions govern general physical postures at meals, and the pressure is to offer delicacies to others. Rules such as these regulated eating

CLOSING THE MOUTH

Item, that he fil not his mouth so ful of meat as he cannot hold his lips together while he is chawing: for otherwise, men shal look into his mouth, and see the meat rowle by and downe while he is eating: which is a foule sight and loathsome: and for that cause, a man must forbear to speake with meat in his mouth, except he have so litle as hee bee sure to hide it in his mouth while he is speaking. (*The Court of Civill Courtesie,* translated from the Italian, 1591)

COMPLICATION

American manners [regarding the use of knife and fork] are, if anything, a more advanced form of civilized behavior than the European, because they are more complicated and further removed from the practical result, always a sign of refinement. (Martin, 1983, p. 124)

The expert removes the bones from his mouth with his chopsticks. (Chao, 1956)

behavior before the imposition of the set of cutlery now common in the West.

The History of Table Manners

Mealtime etiquette is a conservative force in all societies. Since it expresses culture, it resists deconstruction and alteration. Manners do change over time. But no matter how trivial it may seem, any modification in a traditional mealtime convention is likely to be a sign of a momentous shift in socially determined sensibilities.

Forks have become in the West part of every diner's eating equipment. Eating with the hands is permissible only in a restricted number of cases, such as eating artichokes, asparagus, or radishes, or on informal occasions. The difficult, unnatural, skill-demanding fork has replaced fingers at nearly all tables most of the time. It took eight centuries to accomplish this.

Before forks achieved general usage as eating implements, people had to devise flat, hard surfaces on which each individual diner could impale portions with forks and cut them with knives. Those surfaces then had to be accepted and made available to everybody. The new plates ("plate," derived from the French, means "flat") were first metal, then ceramic, making them more affordable. They gradually replaced the traditional bowls and hollows carved into the dining table and the "trenchers" or bread bases for supporting morsels of food eaten with the hands. Even after the general acceptance

of the fork, polite people continued until the early twentieth century to feel free to carry their food to their mouths with their knives.

The provision of special implements for moving food from serving dish to plate also came about slowly. European manners gradually and unevenly changed from several people taking it in turns to dip the one shared spoon into the pot and to eat from it, to wiping the communal spoon carefully on a napkin before passing it on, to provision of a spoon for each person for dipping and eating, to wiping that individual spoon on a napkin after sipping from it before dipping it into the common dish again, to using a special spoon for serving and nothing else. A person must never forget and use his or her own spoon by mistake. All this purity required more and more cutlery.

The slow developments just outlined together with a growing restriction on bodily relaxation at table reflected an increasing desire for self-sufficiency and separateness in the culture. Ideally others should neither impinge nor need assistance. Such changes can be tracked in European and American history by studying surviving writings describing etiquette. These writings include pamphlets and lists of rules published from the medieval period down to the twenty-first century for people wanting to "polish" their manners, including their table manners, in order to become upwardly mobile. The sociologist Norbert Elias (1939) used these texts, especially those concerned with table manners, to show the development of Western inhibitions following the Renaissance, when Erasmus (1530) published the most accomplished and famous example and included in it a chapter on manners at meals.

The printing press helped disseminate books of etiquette, and learning mannerly behavior began to spread outside the narrow but innovative circles of the court first to the bourgeoisie, who became stricter than the nobility was about certain kinds of correct behavior, and then to everybody else. Elias chronicled not only the growth of separating "walls of restraint," underwritten by embarrassment, in Western culture but the gradual imposition of an insistence that people control and hide bodily functions, where once people were far more tolerant about such matters. In all cultures manners must have changed in analogous ways, even if the changes have not been recorded.

Formality and Informality

Mealtime etiquette governs settings for meals, the seating of hosts and guests, dishes, decorations, lights, napkins and washing facilities, eating implements and their placement in the eating area, the sequence in which food is eaten, how food is served, the correct ways of issuing invitations to dinner, what people wear when eating, and much else besides. Each of these customs and artifacts has a specific meaning and a history. When all these things are enumerated, however, the reference is to full, formal meals, the ones with the widest range and intri-

590

cacy, where hospitality is offered to guests. Such meals are likely to be "feasts" on the occasion of events important for the community. People come together to eat when they wish to celebrate, especially when they are eager to express what is held in common (Douglas and Gross, 1981).

Feasts by definition are out of the ordinary, extravagant, complicated, often pointedly traditional, highly organized, and therefore commonly formal. The food itself is typically shaped or molded and prepared in elaborate, time-consuming ways, often requiring the efforts of many people. Preparing becomes part of the sharing. Ordinary eating is simpler, less copious, and takes less time; it is informal.

This does not mean that manners are less important at everyday family meals, but it does mean that decorum at these daily events is usually and deliberately lowered. Mealtime taboos are fiercely maintained (no one at a European or American meal puts his or her feet on the table, no one spits, or causes an uproar without disapproval), but formal flourishes are dispensed with. People might feel comfortable eating in silence, handle their food casually, or not clear the entire table before laying it for a meal. Membership in a high social class frequently entails relatively high decorum at ordinary meals. A deliberate lowering of decorum gives the strongest messages when the "full," formal model is previously understood.

Formality by design increases social distance; informality brings people closer. In the modern Western world being "casual" has come to be seen as nearly always de rigueur because of modern egalitarian ideals and because modern society has more than enough devices for keeping people apart. The insistence that people shall behave casually but in the prescribed manner is in itself a mannerly social convention.

Some Factors Informing Table Etiquette in Modern Europe and North America

Formality is a lot of work—work that has traditionally been performed with regard to meals mostly by women and by servants. In the course of the first half of the twentieth century, even upper-middle-class households learned to manage without live-in servants. The immediate result was the lowering of decorum, including that at the dinner table. Being served meals by people not part of the commensal group became part of the relatively unusual experience of dining in restaurants.

With the ongoing feminist revolution, women are no longer automatically expected to remain dedicated to the house and devoted to the maintenance of "polish." Once again formality at the family dining table has diminished, even where once it ruled. However, one of the principles of manners has always been "Do not improperly impose upon others." It is possible to accept a certain lowering of decorum at the dinner table as even more mannerly than formality once was. The rules of propri-

Comic valentine from circa 1930 spoofing the bad table manners of the newly rich. Roughwood Collection.

ety are negotiated rules. Whatever is no longer thought proper is rude or at best ridiculous. Politeness at table as elsewhere has everything to do with the accepted conventions.

Formality is among other things the taking of time; elaboration takes time. In the "developed" world time has become part of the system of social constraints. People feel they have "no time." The immediate effect upon manners of this culturally induced perception is almost invariably, again, to simplify them. Eating meals can become not a pleasure but something done purely out of necessity and as quickly as possible to get it out of the way in favor of other activities. Preparing food is often foregone entirely, and prepared food is substituted. Eating "fast food," however, still conforms to the limits set by table manners. Predictability, equality, and cleanliness, all of them the concern of mealtime manners, are also assured by the fact that the food is always exactly the same, is served in similar surroundings, and is hedged about by a lot of paper wrappings and other signs that convey "cleanliness" and "control."

Manners, including mealtime manners, are at present undergoing change and renegotiation in many human cultures worldwide; this is a sign of important transformations underway. Such modifications must take time and occur neither smoothly nor evenly. People increasingly come into contact with systems of manners different from their own. They often have to endure unpredictable and annoying behavior from others and relatively weak social mechanisms for preventing or punishing transgressions. Many complain that others have "no manners." But as long as human society continues to function, manners will exist. And among the most fundamental of these are manners governing and involving eating.

See also **Meal**; **Table Talk**; **Taboo**.

BIBLIOGRAPHY

Athenaeus of Naucratis. *The Deipnosophists.* Translated by Charles Burton Gulick. 7 vols. London: Heinemann, 1927–1941. Table talk, much of it about food and eating habits in ancient Greece and Rome.

Befu, Harumi. "An Ethnography of Dinner Entertainment in Japan." *Arctic Anthropology* 11, Supplement (1974): 196–203. Acute explication by an insider of the meanings expressed by the way the Japanese serve and drink sake.

Belden, Louise Conway. *The Festive Tradition: Table Decoration and Desserts in America, 1650–1900.* New York: Norton, 1983.

Chao, Pu-wei Yang. *How to Cook and Eat in Chinese.* London: Faber and Faber, 1956. Includes some unusually revealing remarks about Chinese manners.

Douglas, Mary. *Purity and Danger: An Analysis of Concepts of Pollution and Taboo.* London: ARK, 1984. First published 1966.

Douglas, M., and J. Gross "Food and Culture: Measuring the Intricacy of Rule Systems." *Social Science Information* 20 (1981): 1–35.

Elias, Norbert. *The Civilizing Process.* Translated by Edmund Jephcott. 2 vols. New York: Pantheon Books, 1982. First published 1939.

Erasmus, Desiderius. "De Civilitate Morum Puerilium Libellus." Translated by B. McGregor. In *Literary and Educational Writings.* Volume 25 of *Collected Works of Erasmus,* ed. by J. K. Sowards. Toronto: University of Toronto Press, 1985.

Furnivall, Frederick James, ed. *The Babee's Book.* London: Chatto and Windus, 1908.

Furnivall, Frederick James, ed. *Early English Meals and Manners.* London: N. Trübner, 1868. Reprint Detroit: Singing Tree, 1969.

Grover, Kathryn, ed. *Dining in America, 1850–1900.* Amherst, Mass.: University of Massachusetts Press, 1987.

Kanafani, Aida S. *Aesthetics and Ritual in the United Arab Emirates.* Beirut: American University of Beirut, 1983. An eloquent insider's view, including remarks on social behavior at meals.

Lévi-Strauss, Claude. "The Principle of Reciprocity." In *Sociological Theory.* Edited by Lewis A. Coser and Bernard Rosenberg. New York: Macmillan, 1969.

Martin, Judith. *Miss Manners' Guide to Excruciatingly Correct Behavior.* New York: Warner Books, 1983.

Needham, Rodney, ed. *Right and Left.* Chicago: University of Chicago Press, 1973. Includes explanations for the common, culturally induced preference for the right hand, especially at meals.

Okere, L. C. *The Anthropology of Food in Rural Igboland, Nigeria.* Lanham, Md.: University Press of America, 1983. Perceptive insights into how these people feel about their mealtime rituals.

Ortner, Sherry B. *Sherpas through Their Rituals.* New York: Cambridge University Press, 1978. First-rate anthropology, including an important commentary on the uses and the management of feasts.

Pitt-Rivers, Julian. "The Law of Hospitality." In *The Fate of Shechem.* Cambridge, U.K.: Cambridge University Press, 1977.

Plutarch. *Symposiacs.* Vols. 8, 9 of *Moralia.* Translated by P. A. Clement and H. B. Hoffleit. Cambridge, Mass.: Harvard University Press, 1936. Questions and answers, often about food rituals in Ancient Greece and Rome.

Post, Emily. *Etiquette.* New York: Funk and Wagnall, 1922, 1931, 1937.

Raum, O. F. *Chaga Childhood.* London: Oxford University Press, 1940.

Read, Margaret. *Children of Their Fathers: Growing Up among the Ngoni of Nyasaland.* London: Methuen, 1959.

Richards, Audrey I. *Hunger and Work in a Savage Tribe.* London: Routledge, 1932.

Richards, Audrey I. *Land, Labour, and Diet in Northern Rhodesia.* London: Oxford University Press, 1939. This book and the two preceding ones give vivid descriptions of children in Africa being taught good behavior through food and during meals.

Schlesinger, Arthur M. *Learning How to Behave: A Historical Study of American Etiquette Books.* New York: Cooper Square, 1968. First published in 1946.

Visser, Margaret. *The Rituals of Dinner: The Origins, Evolution, Eccentricities, and Meaning of Table Manners.* Toronto: HarperCollins, 1991. The bibliography suggests further reading.

Watson, J. L. "From the Common Pot: Feasting with Equals in Chinese Society." *Anthropos* 82 (1988): 389–401.

Margaret Visser

ETYMOLOGY OF FOOD. The words of a language can be traced to two sources. Some have been a part of that same language as far back as its history is known, although, since no language remains fixed, they will have gradually changed in form and sound. Others are loanwords, borrowed from another language with which the speakers of the first have been in contact.

Food words fall into both categories. Food and drink are necessities of life, basic elements of which are likely to remain fixed (and to retain the same vocabulary) through the centuries. Yet innumerable details will change (and demand new names) in response to taste, fashion, and the love of variety; also in response to the migration of peoples, the development of trade, and the transplanting of food species. Thus in English the names of foods and drinks mirror the cultural history of English speakers. Some names remain unexplained: no one knows the origin of "raspberry," "syllabub," or "toffee."

Some basic foods have had the same name in English and in its ancestral languages all the way back to Proto-Indo-European, an unrecorded, reconstructed language that might have been spoken some time between 5000 and 3000 B.C.E. in the southern Russian steppes. Such words include *water* (compare modern Russian *voda* [water] and *vodka*), *mead* (Sanskrit *madhu* [honey]), *barley* (Latin *far* [emmer wheat]), *milk* (Latin *mulgere* [to milk an animal]). Also from Proto-Indo-European come the names of certain basic preparation methods, *bake* (compare Greek *phogein*), *brew*, and *broth* (Greek *broutos* [a kind of beer]).

The names of some foods go back to the unrecorded Proto-Germanic language of the first millennium B.C.E. (the immediate ancestor of English, German, and others) but cannot be traced to any earlier stage. This applies to *meat*, *bread* (German *Brot*), *honey*, *eel* (German *Aal*), *egg* (German *Ei*). Some of these words may have been borrowed into Proto-Germanic from other unrecorded prehistoric languages of Europe.

Moving forward in time, some Mediterranean foods and luxuries were introduced to northern Europe by the Romans. Thus English uses words of Latin origin for important products such as *cheese* (from Latin *caseus*) and *wine* (from Latin *vinum*) and also for a few fruits and vegetables that were first planted in northern Europe by the Romans, such as *plum* (from Latin *prunum*) and *fennel* (from Latin *feniculum*).

Certain new foods came to England with the Norman conquest in 1066. During the period of English-French bilingual culture that followed, English cuisine changed and developed rapidly. Thus many terms relevant to food were borrowed into English from Anglo-Norman, the dialect of Old French that was spoken in Medieval England. Examples include *pear* (French *poire*), *chestnut* (French *châtaigne*; originally from ancient Greek *kastanea*), *salmon* (French *saumon*), *sausage* (French *saucisse*). Anglo-Norman was also the source of names for cooking methods, *fry* (French *frire*) and *boil* (French *bouillir*).

English has continued to borrow food concepts from other cultures and food words from other languages. *Steak* comes from Old Norse, the language of the Vikings; *lozenge* from Arabic by way of Old French; *pickle* from Dutch; *tomato*, *chocolate*, and *chili* from Nahuatl, the language of the Aztecs. In modern times, with the globalization of tastes, this kind of borrowing has become even more frequent. So we have *curry* from Tamil or Kannada of southern India, *toddy* and *chutney* from Hindi, *pasta* and *pizza* from Italian, *marzipan* from German (the word originated in Italian), *blini* from Russian, *tofu* from Japanese (the word originated in Chinese). Cooks and restaurateurs like to make the names of dishes evoke their origins by retaining an authentically foreign form, such as the French *coq au vin* and *tripes à la mode de Caen* (cockerel cooked in wine, tripe in the Caen fashion). They also like to use foreign names for methods of preparation, as in *chicken chasseur* (French *chasseur* [huntsman]).

Local specialities in food and wine mean that place-names often have a special food meaning. *Cheddar* is a village in Somerset, England (but cheeses with this name are now made in many countries). *Cognac* and *Armagnac* are towns in southwestern France. *Parmesan* is an English form of the Italian adjective *Parmigiano*, meaning 'from Parma', a town in northern Italy. *Sherry* is an English form of the Spanish place-name *Jérez* (*de la Frontera*); *Port* is an English form of the Portuguese place name *Porto*.

Since English is spoken so widely across the world, its vocabulary is astonishingly varied. Many foods have different names, and many food names have different meanings in Britain and the United States. *Cider* is apple juice in the United States; it is an alcoholic drink in Britain. *Corn* is maize in the United States, wheat in Britain. The spice called *turmeric* in Britain and the United States is known in South Africa as *borrie* (a loan from Malay by way of Afrikaans). The European spice known in Britain as *coriander* is called in Indian English *dhania* or *dhunia*; in the United States the fruit is called *coriander* but the leaves are called *cilantro*, a word borrowed from Spanish. The Afghan spice known as *hing* in Indian English is *asafoetida* in Britain and the United States, while it is *duivelsdrek* in South African English: this is a loanword from Afrikaans meaning literally 'devil's dung' (because that is what asafoetida smells like). The spice called *jeera* in Indian English is *cumin* or *cummin* in British and U.S. English. Indian English *methi* is British English *fenugreek*. Indian English *sitaphul* is known elsewhere as *custard-apple*. Indian English *alu* is U.S. and British English *potato* (also British *spud*). The fruit *okra* (this name is borrowed from the Akan language of Ghana) is also known regionally as *gumbo* (borrowed from Mbundu of Angola), *bhindi* (borrowed from Marathi of India), and *ladies' fingers*. The *chickpea* is also known as *chana* (borrowed from Hindi) and *garbanzo bean* (borrowed from Spanish). Even where the English names derive ultimately from a single foreign word, they may have different forms and connotations in different regions, like U.S. English *kabob* for British English *kebab* (a word that is Turkish in origin).

Corn

The English words *corn* and *grain* are linguistic doublets: both of them originate in a Proto-Indo-European word (of about 4000 B.C.E.) that may be reconstructed as *grnom*. This word meant 'cereal grain'. As the Indo-European languages grew apart, it took a different form in Proto-Germanic, in Latin, and in other early languages. In Proto-Germanic (about 500 B.C.E.) the form was *kurnam*: this became *korn* in Old High German and Old Norse and *corn* in Old English (Anglo-Saxon), and that is the immediate origin of the modern English word *corn*. In classical Latin, meanwhile, the form was *granum*. This became *grano* in Spanish and Italian and *grain* in French, meaning 'cereal grain', and the French word was borrowed into English. The French words *graine* (seed) and *grange* (barn) derive from the same Latin word.

What does *corn* mean? In British English it means 'cereal'—and usually it means 'wheat', the favorite cereal of Europe. When English speakers in the New World (the "Indies") encountered a cereal that was new to them, they invented a new name for it: *Indian corn*. In the United States, this name was eventually shortened to *corn*, which is why, in the United States, *corn* now means 'Indian corn'. Meanwhile, back in Europe, where Indian corn was soon transplanted, people came to know it under the name *maize* (a Carib word, transmitted by way of Spanish *maíz*). In South Africa it has a different name again, *mealie* or *mielie* (a word borrowed from Afrikaans and said to derive originally from Portuguese *milho* [millet]).

So what are *Corn Flakes* made from? Indian corn, of course, because they were invented and named in the United States; but British people often assume that they are made from wheat, because that is what *corn* means in Britain.

Sugar

Sugar, in ancient and medieval Europe, was a rare and costly spice. India was the nearest source of supply; sugar was shipped across the wide Indian Ocean, the Red Sea, and the Mediterranean to reach its European purchasers.

Sugar was originally traded as solid cakes. It was in India that granulated sugar was invented, perhaps about 200 B.C.E.; its ancient Indic (Pali and Prakrit) name, *sakkhara*, reflects this fact, because literally *sakkhara* (also *sakkara*) means 'gravel, grit'. This word reached the ancient West along with the sacks of sugar; it was adopted into classical Greek (*sakkhar*, later *sakhar*), Latin (*saccharum*), and early Arabic (*sukkar*). Medieval Russians got their sugar from the Greeks of Byzantium, so they called it *sakhar*. Medieval western Europe bought sugar from Arab traders, and therefore gave it names that resemble the Arabic: medieval Latin *succarum*, Italian *zucchero*, Old French *sukere*, modern French *sucre*.

Sugar must have been almost unknown in Britain until Norman times. The English name for it is borrowed from Norman French: the form is *suker* or *zuker* in thirteenth-century manuscripts, then *suger*, and finally *sugar*.

Cooking for William the Conquerer

The most familiar examples of food words borrowed into English from the Anglo-Norman form of French are names for the meat of the pig, sheep, and ox, the three major farm animals of medieval Europe. In the Anglo-Saxon (Old English) language, just one basic word existed for each of these three animals, alive or dead. So also in Old French; so also in modern French, in which the basic words are *porc* (pig), *mouton* (sheep), and *boeuf* (ox).

In Norman times, English borrowed those three French words, *pork, mutton, beef*. So, unusually, ever since then, English has had six basic words in this semantic field, three for the living animals and three for the meats. Why were the extra three words borrowed at all? Why were the borrowed words used in the special sense of ready-to-eat meats?

The likely answer is that because the English nobles of that period spoke French and ordered their food in French, others eventually thought it fashionable and classy to use French for the names of fine foods. In just the same way, after a successful hunt, the huntsmen demanded in French to be served with *la veneson*, meaning literally 'the game we just hunted', and that is why *venison* has its modern English meaning of 'deer meat'.

See also **Language about Food; Metaphor, Food as; Naming of Food; Symbol, Food as.**

BIBLIOGRAPHY

The history of English words can be traced in: Clarence L. Barnhart, editor, *The Barnhart Dictionary of Etymology* (New York: H. W. Wilson, 1988). For food words see also: John Ayto, *The Glutton's Glossary* (London: Routledge, 1990). For English words of Asian origin see: Henry Yule, A. C. Burnell, *Hobson-Jobson*. London: Murray, 1903.

Words in Proto-Indo-European and in later Indo-European languages can be tracked down in: Carl Darling Buck, *A Dictionary of Selected Synonyms in the Principal Indo-European Languages: A Contribution to the History of Ideas*. Chicago: University of Chicago Press, 1949. *The Encyclopedia of Indo-European Culture*, ed. J. P. Mallory, D. Q. Adams. Chicago, London: Fitzroy Dearborn, 1997. Joseph T. Shipley, *The Origins of English Words: A Discursive Dictionary of Indo-European Roots*. Baltimore: Johns Hopkins University Press, 1984.

The books listed above are fairly easy to use. To go further, one needs to use etymological dictionaries of foreign languages, most of which are written for historical linguists. For guidance in finding and using such works see: Andrew Dalby, *A Guide to World Language Dictionaries*. London: Library Association Publishing; Chicago: Fitzroy Dearborn, 1998. Yakov Malkiel, *Etymological Dictionaries: A Tentative Typology*. Chicago: University of Chicago Press, 1976.

Andrew Dalby

EVOLUTION. Jean-Louis Flandrin, in his introduction to *Food: A Culinary History*, sets out many of the crucial questions basic to our understanding of the evolution of human diet:

When and how did the eating behavior of human beings diverge from that of other animal species? Did humans distinguish themselves by the type of variety of foods they ate? By the fact that they prepared their food before eating it? By the ceremonial forms with which they surrounded the act of eating? Or by the conviviality of dining and its characteristic social forms? (p. 14)

These questions, as they relate to the evolution of human foodways, remain unanswerable. A major reason is the vast gulf that separates the living from earlier ancestors. Today, virtually all humans subsist on the products of agricultural activities, which include the raising of domestic animals for food. However, this way of life developed very late in the course of human evolution, with the domestication of plants appearing in several locations around the world at some point after 12,000 years ago; the domestication of food animals followed somewhat later. The vast earlier time, during which humans evolved from more primitive beings, was marked by other forms of subsistence. This time span, more than six million years in duration, witnessed dramatic changes in human biology, behavior, and adaptation. Although we have a treasure trove of fossil bones and archaeological materials that document much of this development, there is little in the record that can inform us of the precise dietary items consumed by these remote ancestors of ours, or enable us to answer the questions posed by Flandrin. There are, however, tantalizing hints of the ways of life followed by these earliest members of the human family, and in this essay, this record will be described, and the available evidence for the evolution of human foodways evaluated.

The data at our disposal for this investigation include the fossil bones and teeth of our ancestors, testaments to their evolving biological structures. There are also the residues of their activities, in the very earliest deposits often preserved as parts of natural accumulations of organic and inorganic remains, jumbled in with the fossil bones of very early human ancestors. Later in time, we find the archaeological remains of the actual living areas, where our ancestors slept, made tools, prepared and ate their food, and often buried or left their dead. All this varied information provides important insights about our evolutionary past, but it is very incomplete data for reconstructing dietary patterns. For example, very little in the way of actual food remains is found during archaeological excavations, and only relatively durable items like animal bones are preserved. This may provide some indication of the presence of meat in the diet, but it is not clear just how much it represents the total subsistence pattern and how much was composed of other foods, like vegetables and insects, which leave no archaeological traces. Similarly, the bones and teeth of our ancestors may preserve chemical and other traces of the sorts of foods that were emphasized in their diets, but these signs are often complex and must be carefully evaluated.

Given the difficulties in deciphering the actual residues, other, more indirect, sources of information have come to play an important role in reconstructing the foodways of our ancestors. These data come from the study of our closest living primate relatives, the chimpanzees, and observations recorded from the anthropological studies of those few modern human groups, called gatherers and hunters, who did not practice agriculture, but subsisted on an assortment of gathered vegetable foods, the collection of small animals, such as insects and small vertebrates, and the occasional successful hunting of larger animals. Comparisons with these living examples are often used to furnish clues to what sorts of foods our ancestors consumed. However, correlations of this sort have numerous limitations, and they must be used with caution. Chimpanzees and humans have had separate evolutionary pathways for at least six million years, and it is possible that during this time, chimpanzees have changed as much as humans in their biology and adaptation, making comparisons of living chimpanzees with our earliest ancestors tenuous at best (we have no fossil record of the specific evolutionary history of chimpanzees). Further, those few living gatherers and hunters who have been studied exist in environments that may be dramatically different from the locales of our ancestors. Finally, and perhaps most importantly, our early ancestors were neither bipedal apes nor humans in fur suits, but a series of biologically and behaviorally unique species whose way of life and biology are now wholly extinct.

Both modern chimpanzees and those gatherers and hunters who have been studied, and do not live in very specialized environments (like the Arctic, for example), have somewhat similar diets. The field research by Jane Goodall and her associates on chimpanzees living in the Gombe National Park in western Tanzania, as well as observations from other chimpanzee living-sites in Africa, indicate that these animals are overwhelmingly vegetarians, with a broadly based diet composed, at the Gombe, of the fruits, leaves, stems, blossoms, and gums of more than eighty different plants. Chimpanzees, however, emphasize a variety of fruits as the major part of their diet. Chimpanzees have also been observed consuming insects, sometimes using twigs, specially broken off and trimmed as tools, to obtain termites. Chimpanzees (often males), behaving together in a cooperative fashion, also deliberately hunt, kill, and eat a variety of small vertebrates, including bush pigs, monkeys, and antelopes. Meat, however, makes up a very small percentage of their total diet.

Human gatherers and hunters in tropical or subtropical areas also subsist on a diet that emphasizes a broad array of vegetable food sources, with smaller amounts of insects and vertebrate animals. The exact percentage of each of these elements differs seasonally or yearly, as well as varying between specific groups.

Like living gatherers and hunters, until the advent of agriculture, our ancestors probably lived an unsettled existence, regularly shifting their encampments to new locales in search of resources. Food storage would have been very difficult, and consumption of collected and hunted foods was probably immediate. Groups would have been small, with the social organization flexible enough to allow group size to fluctuate with the seasonal availability of food and other resources.

These comparisons provide only a very limited insight, and for more information, it is necessary to examine the direct evidence from the archaeological and fossil records.

Diet and Human Evolution

A variety of comparative genetic studies document that chimpanzees are our closest living relative. It has been estimated, for example, that humans and chimpanzees share about 98.5 percent of their genetic material. Calculations of the rate of genetic change over time indicate that humans last shared a common ancestor with this African ape between five and eight million years ago. This is the period when the evolutionary line that eventually led to living humans split from the line that led to chimpanzees, representing the beginnings of human evolution. The living and extinct members of this human evolutionary lineage are traditionally grouped into a biological family, the Hominidae, members of which are known as hominids.

We have no fossil or other evidence of the earliest members of the hominid family, just after they split off from the lineage leading to chimpanzees. We do not know what sorts of environments they lived in or what sorts of foods they ate. Because chimpanzees are native to Africa, and the earliest known hominid fossils are limited to Africa, it seems reasonable to place the homeland of the human family on that continent.

The Earliest Hominids

The recognition of Africa as the human homeland first came in 1924, with the discovery of the fossilized skull and jaw of a young child at T'aung, in the Cape Province of South Africa. Named *Australopithecus africanus* by its discoverer, Raymond Dart, hundreds of additional fossil specimens of this group, known collectively as the australopithecines, have subsequently been uncovered in south, east, and central Africa. There are now at least eight species of australopithecines, sometimes placed in other genera, like *Paranthropus* or *Kenyanthropus*. The australopithecines lived in Africa from about four million to perhaps as late as one million years ago. Like all members of the hominid family, they walked upright, allowing them to efficiently carry objects and food. Chimpanzees habitually walk on all four legs. However, the australopithecines were apelike in many of their biological features, possessing small, chimpanzee-sized brains in an apelike skull with a large, projecting face positioned out in front of the braincase. Their teeth were humanlike in form, but they possessed massive back chewing teeth, the premolars and molars, that were much larger

than those of living humans. The australopithecines, like all hominids, possessed nonprojecting canine teeth. This is in marked contrast to the large, tusklike canines of the apes. Like gorillas, australopithecines also seem to have been sexually dimorphic in body size, with the males considerably larger than the females.

There are fossil bones found in East Africa of still earlier-in-time creatures, for example, *Orrorin tugenensis*, at six million years, possibly the earliest hominid yet discovered, and *Ardipithecus ramidus*, who lived about four and a half million years ago, but little is currently known about these creatures and their biology.

The fossil bones of the australopithecines are most often discovered in natural accumulations that are the result of various sorts of geological activities. These fossil bones may have been transported by water over long distances before they were deposited in their final location. They are only infrequently discovered in a context that represents the locale where they actually lived. Thus, little is known about the kinds of environments in which the australopithecines lived, or how the various australopithecine species may have differed in habitat usage or in food choice and general diet.

For many years after the initial discoveries of the australopithecines, there was a prevalent idea that these creatures lived on the open grasslands or savannas of eastern Africa. According to this theory, their habitat would have provided only a limited selection of foods, and was the selective factor responsible for the development of hunting and meat eating. More recent reconstructions, however, have revealed a much more complex environmental context for these early hominids, with evidence for the use of forests and woodlands. Just how important hunting and meat eating has been in human evolution continues to be debated, and its importance in the ultimate appearance of modern humans remains unclear.

Australopithecine fossil bones have been carefully examined in a number of ingenious ways, in order to learn more about their dietary patterns, but thus far with only limited success.

For example, on the basis of comparisons with the teeth of other mammals, it is clear that these early hominids were not specifically adapted to meat eating. As in modern humans, the chewing surfaces of the teeth are covered with thick layers of enamel. Some australopithecine species, known as the "robust" australopithecines, possessed truly massive back teeth, along with very large jawbones to house them, and large chewing muscles, sometimes so large that they formed a crest on the top of the skull. These general biological features of australopithecine jaws and teeth suggest that they emphasized the chewing of coarse vegetable food sources, but not the consumption of grasses, whose high cellulose content would have been very difficult for these creatures to digest.

596

Other studies of the dentition have attempted to determine more specific aspects of the dietary patterns of the australopithecines. One series of studies utilized scanning electron microscopy to examine the minute scratches and pits left by food particles on the chewing surface of the teeth. The results of these observations suggest that some of the australopithecines ate a diet rich in fruits, while others were consuming a more varied, but basically vegetarian, diet. One problem with these sorts of studies is that they tend to focus on the final meals the creatures ate before they died, providing a somewhat limited view of their overall diet, especially if they were seasonally exploiting a variety of different habitats and foods.

Other studies have examined the chemical composition of australopithecine fossil bones. One study employed the ratio of calcium and strontium in the fossil bones to determine whether the australopithecines were generally herbivorous, carnivorous, or omnivorous.

Another chemical analysis, based on staple isotopes including ^{13}C and ^{12}C, has reached a conclusion similar to that from the calcium-strontium analyses: some australopithecines, at least, were consuming animal foods, though the identity of these animals, and whether they were vertebrates or invertebrates, has not been determined.

These studies continue to support a variety of opinions about the dietary patterns of these early hominids, with some anthropologists suggesting a diet based primarily on fleshy fruits, nuts, and seeds, while others advocate a more broadly based diet, including some animal foods.

There is no direct evidence that the australopithecines collected foods to be brought back to some central camp to be consumed as part of a group activity. Rather, like chimpanzees, it appears likely that they consumed food continuously as they foraged in their environment.

The Evolution of the Genus *Homo*

Good evidence of the evolution of members of our genus, *Homo*, begins to appear around two million years ago at sites in East Africa. There was a dramatic increase in brain size, from the 500 ml common in the australopithecines to brains as large as 800 ml in these early humans (though still about half the size of those of living people). They also possessed smaller back chewing teeth. Chipped stone tools, first used about two-and-a-half million years ago, now became more common. These durable tools, made from water-rounded pebbles, are known as Oldowan tools. They were made by striking two stones together, knocking off chips to produce a cutting edge or point. Though crudely made, their development represented a major advance in the ability of the early hominids to exploit a wider variety of food sources. Hominids lacked sharp and hardened claws, as well as projecting and pointed canine piercing teeth, making them inefficient in dealing with many potential food sources. For example,

without a digging tool or claws, many subterranean foods like insects, small burrowing mammals, tubers, and rhizomes, would have been impossible to obtain. The australopithecines are only rarely found in association with these chipped pebble tools, and most anthropologists believe the first stone tool makers were early members of the human genus *Homo*.

Also found at this time are animal bones, mainly from antelopes, with butchery marks made by a sharp stone edge. Although isotopic studies have indicated that the earlier australopithecines may have consumed animal foods, these cut marks represent definitive evidence of early meat eating. What is still being debated is the origin of these bones. They may have been the result of hunting activities, which is entirely reasonable given our knowledge of the cooperative hunting patterns of chimpanzees, but some scientists have suggested that they may also have been the result of scavenging activities. A safe way, it is said, to obtain bones with scraps of meat still adhering to them would be to claim animal bones from a predator kill after primary scavengers, such as hyenas and jackals, have finished with them. Thus, the initial meat eating in human evolution, according to this view, was to utilize stone tools to scrape off bits of rotting tissue from the bones of predator kills. One major flaw with this notion is that no primate is equipped with digestive mechanisms to protect them from the serious consequences of eating spoiled meat.

By about 1.8 million years ago, there are a number of different species of early *Homo* coexisting in eastern Africa. In addition, several species of robust australopithecines were also living at this time. What the possible dietary differences, if any, between all these hominids is unknown.

Expansion Out of Africa

At some point after 1.8 million years ago, in one of the most momentous events in human evolution, the hominids begin to move out of Africa. One site along the Jordan River Valley in Israel, dated at about one and a half million years old, is located along what must have been a major route into Eurasia. Along with stone tools similar to those from Africa were found numerous bones of African mammals, suggesting that the hominids were not the only creatures moving out of that continent.

Hominid sites in the Republic of Georgia and on the island of Java also testify to this dramatic increase in range. Although the reasons the hominids left Africa at this moment are unclear, one reasonable explanation is that stone tools enabled hominids to expand the range of dietary items open for exploitation, allowing them to move into new habitats.

During the course of the next million years, hominid brain size increased, so that by about 300,000 to 400,000 years ago, the volume of the braincase reached 1,200 ml, within the range of living humans. It may be that there was an associated increase in body size during this period as well. Increasing brain size would have required greater intakes of oxygen, as well as nutrients. It has been suggested that this brain size expansion relied on increased amounts of dietary fats. Hunted animals could have supplied these fats, but gathered insects, many of which are richly endowed with this nutrient (especially the essential fatty acid, linoleic acid), are equally likely sources. Larger body size also necessitated a greater number of calories.

The occupation of the European subcontinent appears to have taken place later than human expansion into more hospitable habitats in Asia. This is no doubt related to the presence of glaciers, which, beginning about two million years ago, periodically covered major parts of Europe. The earliest occupation site in Europe, dating to about 800,000 years ago, is located in northern Spain, near the present city of Burgos. From that time onwards, hominid presence in Europe was closely tied to the advance and retreat of the glaciers, with the continent relatively uninhabited during times of maximal glacial activity.

By 500,000 years ago, hominids, placed in the category *Homo erectus*, were intermittently occupying a large cave on the outskirts of what is now the village of Zhoukoudian, about twenty-five miles from Beijing, in northern China. Although there was no glacial activity in this part of Asia, winter would have been severe (Zhoukoudian is about as far north as Philadelphia). While it remains unclear if hominids actually wintered this far north, the earliest well-documented evidence of fire has been found here. Fire allowed hominids to use food sources that would be uneatable, or actually toxic, without cooking. Burned deer bones, as well as those with cut marks, testify to the use of meat by the inhabitants of the cave, but whether the meat was obtained by hunting or scavenging remains unknown.

From about the same time, a hominid skull was found in Ethiopia with cut marks on its frontal bone, suggesting skinning or scalping. Cannibalism has been documented at a number of other, later-in-time hominid sites; was the flesh a part of the diet, or was eating a dead friend or relative part of a ritual?

Modern Human Origins

The last 200,000 years of human evolution are much richer in data because actual living places have been located and excavated. Prior to this time, only a very few sites, like Zhoukoudian, represented the remains of an encampment, where the evidence of hominid activities are directly preserved. By about 115,000 years ago, our ancestors had begun the practice of the deliberate burial of their dead, thereby reducing the risk that the body would be destroyed by scavengers. Burying the dead re-

sulted in a vast increase of ancient skeletons that have been preserved for study.

There continues to be debate about the precise way by which living humans emerged from our earlier ancestry. Some anthropologists suggest that modern humans evolved from these earlier hominids and, thus, are the culmination of a very long evolutionary history in various geographic areas. For example, living Asians are the descendants of ancestors who reached Asia more than a million years ago.

Most anthropologists support another theory, that all modern humans originated in Africa some 100,000 to 300,000 years ago and, subsequently, spread out from there to populate the rest of the planet, replacing the earlier hominids who were already living in these areas, descendants of the much earlier initial expansion.

One extinct fossil group that has figured prominently in these theories is the Neanderthals, a group of hominids who lived in Europe and the Middle East from about 130,000 to about 30,000 years ago, when they disappeared from the scene. Because they lived in Europe, where the most intensive archaeological investigations have taken place over the last 150 years, we have much more evidence about these creatures than about any other fossil hominids. This has provided a rich data source, but it also has a number of serious limitations. The most important is that emphasizing the Neanderthals gives a very Eurocentric view of human origins. The final glaciation occurred during much of the time Neanderthals were in Europe; this made major portions of the continent uninhabitable. Those parts that could be occupied by humans represented marginal environments that would have limited population density to extremely low levels.

Given the harsh environments of Europe in which the Neanderthals were living, vegetable foods were probably relatively scarce through much of the year, and meat was almost certainly a major dietary resource. This is confirmed by chemical analyses of their bones, which indicate that for some Neanderthals, fully 80 percent of their diet came from meat. The bones of numerous large animals, such as deer, aurochs, wild boar, and horses are preserved at Neanderthal sites, along with smaller animals. At sites along the Mediterranean, shells testify to the consumption of seafoods. Our evidence for the diet of peoples contemporary with the Neanderthals, but living in Africa and southern Asia, remains limited. At one site, located on the very southern coast of Africa, Klasies River Mouth Cave, there is abundant evidence of the use of a variety of food resources, including land and sea animals and shellfish. Because much of our current evidence comes from humans, like the Neanderthals, who lived in a harsh environment, the emphasis on hunting and meat eating that has come to characterize the diets of earlier hominids may represent a very biased picture.

Although the precise evolutionary relationships of the Neanderthals to living humans remain shadowy, excavation of their sites has revealed a complex picture. Often, living areas with hearths and signs of social areas around them have been uncovered. The bones of selected parts of animals, often with butchery marks on them, are scattered about. Clearly, Neanderthals, like living human gatherers and hunters, were carrying back to a central camp chosen pieces of animals. They may also have brought back other dietary items from their foraging and hunting activities, but the relative absence of small animal bones suggests that they may have been consumed immediately where they were found. It is quite possible that they sat around a fire sharing and consuming food, perhaps engaging in the uniquely human dinnertime interactions of storytelling and discussions of the day's activities. It is unclear, however, if the Neanderthals were actually able to use language, so this reconstruction remains a tentative one.

Sometime after 40,000 years ago, modern human-like peoples appeared in Europe, perhaps migrating there from their origins in Africa, or developing from ancestors already living in Europe. These modern humans brought with them new sorts of tool-making technologies, based on a broader array of raw materials, such as ivory, bone, and wood, with a wider assortment of beautifully made stone tools that show far greater sophistication than those made by the Neanderthals. The first artistic expressions also made their appearance at this time, with plastic art in the form of ivory and bone carvings of animals and people. Deep inside caves, they produced engravings and painted images of animals, and occasionally humans, some of them of great genius.

The sites occupied by these modern humans are littered with the bones of the same sort of animals, the earlier Neanderthals hunted, but the concentrations of bones indicate greater skills in hunting and a corresponding larger number of captured animals. This is also the case with much larger accumulations of shellfish along the coast.

These early modern humans continued this sort of hunting activity to the end of the last glacial period, about 12,000 years ago. In Europe, the retreat of the glaciers resulted in the spread of forests and a major change in dietary habits, with peoples hunting forest animals, like deer and rabbit, and utilizing to a much greater extent the riches of the sea. By this time, however, peoples in the Middle East and along the Yangtze River Valley in southern China were beginning to experiment with the cultivation of plants, which represented the beginnings of the agricultural revolution, and formed the foundations of settled urban life and the origins of civilization.

Although this sketch brings together much of our current knowledge of the evolution of human foodways, much clearly remains to be learned. For one thing, it tells us little about how human diet changed from eating what was necessary for nutritional needs to consuming what was enjoyable and pleasant to eat. Perhaps our ancestors always selected those foods that were enjoyable to eat,

bringing about the basis of the consumption of food as a central focus in the social life of humans.

See also **Agriculture, History of; Cannibalism; Hunting and Gathering.**

BIBLIOGRAPHY

Eaton, S. Boyd, and Melvin Konner. "Paleolithic Nutrition." *The New England Journal of Medicine* (1985) 312:283–289.

Flandrin, Jean-Louis, and Massimo Montanari, eds. *Food: A Culinary History from Antiquity to the Present.* New York: Columbia University Press, 1999. (English edition edited by Albert Sonnenfeld; first published as *Histoire de l'alimentation*; Rome, 1996.)

Goodall, Jane. *The Chimpanzees of Gombe: Patterns of Behavior.* Cambridge, Mass.: Harvard University Press, 1986.

Hayden, Brian. "Cultural Capacities of Neandertals: A Review and a Re-evaluation." *Journal of Human Evolution* (1993) 24:113–146.

Kelly, Robert L. *The Foraging Spectrum: Diversity in Hunter-Gatherer Lifeways.* Washington, D.C.: Smithsonian Institution Press, 1994.

Klein, Richard. *The Human Career.* 2d ed. Chicago: University of Chicago Press, 2002.

Mann, Alan. "Diet and Human Evolution." In *Omnivorous Primates: Gathering and Hunting in Human Evolution.* Edited by R. Harding and G. Teleki. New York: Columbia University Press, 1981.

Somer, Elizabeth. *The Origin Diet.* New York: Henry Holt, 2001.

Stiner, Mary C. *Honor Among Thieves: A Zooarchaeological Study of Neandertal Ecology.* Princeton, N.J.: Princeton University Press, 1994.

Stringer, Chris, and Clive Gamble. *In Search of Neanderthals.* New York: Thames and Hudson, 1993.

Wolpoff, Milford H. *Paleoanthropology.* 2d. ed. New York: McGraw Hill, 1999.

Alan Mann

EXTENSION SERVICES. Extension services extend information to users—farmers, growers, and homeowners. The Cooperative Extension Service (CES) is a publicly funded research and education network linking the resources of federal (U.S. Department of Agriculture), state (land-grant universities), and local (county) governments. The common mission—helping people to solve the problems that affect residents in U.S. communities—remains unchanged since its beginnings in the late 1800s.

Early in our government's development, George Washington and Thomas Jefferson advocated a national agency for teaching the agricultural sciences. Many years later, CES evolved from the needs of rural people for local education in agriculture, business, and home economics. In the 1800s, farmers needed help solving problems such as controlling insects or soil erosion or applying the right amount of manure to crops. Nonfarmers needed an education in business and trade. Housewives needed information on family nutrition and food preservation. In response, the Morrill Act of 1862 provided for the establishment of at least one college in each state. Under this act, many states established colleges of agriculture whose objective was to teach agriculture and the mechanical arts without excluding the classical studies.

In 1887, the Hatch Act established an agricultural experiment station at each land-grant college as well as a system of cooperative funding between the USDA and land-grant institutions. As a result, scientists and educators at experiment stations conducted research, published the results, and disseminated information to farmers. Several years later, in 1890, the second Morrill Act extended the land-grant provisions to the sixteen southern states and ultimately led to the establishment of land-grant universities for black students.

Seaman A. Knapp (1833–1911), a former professor of agriculture in Iowa, is credited with starting the agricultural demonstration method around the turn of the century. He conducted farm demonstration work in Louisiana and then served in the Department of Agriculture as a special agent to promote better methods of farming in the South. His work led to the development of the Farmers Cooperative Demonstration Work division, which he headed. The demonstration method proved effective and was copied by CES personnel throughout the country; it remains an important CES tool today.

The Smith-Lever Act of 1914 established the CES as we know it today—a partnership among federal, state, and local governments. Land-grant colleges and the USDA were directed "to work together to provide for the practical and liberal higher education of all Americans," reaching out to teach agriculture and home economics both in and outside of colleges. In 1925, the Purnell Act added agricultural economics, rural sociology, and home economics to the experiment stations' mission. The Extension Indian Reservation Program (EIRP) was authorized by the 1990 Farm Bill, and provided for the establishment of extension education programs on Indian reservations and in tribal jurisdictions.

Some states were early in recognizing the need for agricultural education. In 1857, the Agricultural College of the State of Michigan was founded. The Michigan Agricultural Experiment Station at Michigan State University, founded in 1888, was among the first stations created. The first county agricultural agent in New York State was hired in 1911 with funds provided by a Chamber of Commerce, a railroad, and the U.S. Department of Agriculture. New York was one of several states that went one step further, and by state legislation, created a partnership between the State Extension Service and the state itself. Alaska established its first experiment station in 1900.

The Cooperative Extension Service has kept pace with the farmer's search for ways to remain economically and environmentally viable. The Sustainable Agriculture Research and Education (SARE) program works to increase knowledge about—and help farmers and ranchers adopt—sustainable agriculture. To advance such knowledge nationwide, SARE administers competitive grants for research, education, and professional development. In other areas, CES offers programs to help children and their families cope with disasters and develop an emergency preparedness plan.

To contact a Cooperative Extension Service locally, check the government listing in your telephone directory for Cooperative Extension Service, or look under "Agriculture." Information about national programs can be obtained from the following address:

The Cooperative State Research, Education, and Extension Service
U.S. Department of Agriculture
1400 Independence Avenue S.W., Stop 2201
Washington, DC 20250-2201
Telephone: 202-720-7441
http://www.reeusda.gov/

BIBLIOGRAPHY

Buswell, Arthur S. *Evolution of the Cooperative Extension Service in Alaska*. University of Alaska. Available at http://www.uaf.edu/coop-ext/esp/history.html

A History of American Agriculture 1776–1990. Agricultural Education and Extension. USDA Economic Research Service. Available at http://www.usda.gov/history2/text10.htm

Graham, Donna L. "Cooperative Extension System." *Encyclopedia of Agricultural Science* 1 (1994): 415-430. Available at http://www.cals.ncsu.edu/agexed/aee501/extension.html

St. Clair, Charles. "The History and Philosophy of Extension." Impact. A Council Development Project. Leaflet No. 9. Outreach & Extension. University of Missouri Lincoln University. Available at http://outreach.missouri.edu/extcouncil/Impacts/9.htm

Patricia S. Michalak

F

FADS IN FOOD. Food fads are interwoven with people's lifestyles, trends, and class aspirations. In all forms, fads are usually ideas that enjoy a quick popularity and soon disappear. Some fads, however, may actually become trends that develop into accepted style, indicating where society is moving. Fads in food are not a new occurrence. Ancient Roman recipes document demand for fattened snails and dormice as popular appetizers. During the 1700s, Americans craved ice cream, newly introduced from France, and lobster Newburg became fashionable in the 1800s. Lollipops were the rage in the 1920s. Current nostalgia for "retro" 1960s foods, such as fondue, accompanies a renewed interest in retrospective house and automotive design.

Health Food Surges in Popularity

Nutrition is often a rationale for food fads. In the late 1800s, Kellogg, General Mills, and other manufacturers created cereals from grains, in the interest of promoting a cleansing diet. Turning fad into substance, the interest in health food became entrenched in American diets over the succeeding decades, with foods like smoothies, meatless burgers, and whole wheat baked goods emerging in the marketplace. Fears of irradiated foods, the drive for organic, calorie-reduced foods, brand name diets, and multivitamins all contributed to the faddish style of healthy living. Vegan and macrobiotic diets, brown rice, tofu, and "live foods," now readily available, once were fads. Vegetarianism, seen as a fringe diet, has become mainstream, and organic ingredients are now basic supermarket fare.

The Orient and Other Ethnic Influences

America's fascination with the "exotic Orient" is an example of the pervasive influence of ethnic food fads. In the 1930s Chinese mah-jongg parties were popular among the socially style conscious. Accompanying food included *egg foo yung* and fried rice. Oriental themes characterized popular restaurants like Trader Vics, where diners could surround themselves with a sanitized Western version of exotic travel. Bars served unusually named Polynesian drinks with paper parasols. A Hawaiian craze followed, and backyard luau parties paralleled the emergence of Polynesian restaurants. Processed Spam with a sweet and sour sauce was a popular dish. Rumaki, a chicken liver, bacon, and water chestnut hors d'oeuvre, wowed guests. Japanese steak houses cooked sukiyaki and tempura before admiring diners.

Many other ethnic groups have contributed to fads in American cuisine. In the late 1960s the growth of the civil rights and Black Power movements led to the rediscovery of African-American roots, including southern soul food. Grits, collard greens, and ham hocks were served side by side with other American traditional foods. Interest grew in Zen Buddhism, Hinduism, transcendental meditation, and other beliefs of India and Asia, which emphasized the spiritual aspect of foods. The immigration of Latinos, Vietnamese, and Middle Easterners have added to foreign food interests. Immigrant grocers have introduced new foods to Americans, increasing demand for exotic imports. In the late twentieth century, fusion cooking, combining several cultural food styles, created a second wave of interest in Oriental "style" foods, popularizing sushi bars and sushi kits.

Travel and Tourism Contribute

Since the 1880s, immigrants and overseas tourism have influenced American cuisine. While some believe that GIs returning from World War II initiated the discovery of foreign food in postwar America, there is no strong substantive evidence to this effect. Sociologists theorize instead that, with an improved lifestyle, Americans had time and resources for travels abroad, from which they brought home cookware and ingredients. Hibachis enabled the suburbanite to barbecue Japanese style; fondue pots evoked trips to Zurich; copper pots decorated the French gourmet kitchen. Italian pizzerias and spaghetti houses sprang up to meet the demand for Neapolitan food. Chains of Italian restaurants and take-out pizza counters are their descendants.

Similarly, the popularity of Scandinavian design in the 1950s included appreciation of the smorgasbord, deli plates, and unusual drinks, such as Aquavit. European simplicity was not inexpensive. Stores featuring the high-end styling of Dansk, Braun, and later Crate and Barrel kitchenware changed the appearance of home kitchens and tables.

Haute Cuisine

Fashionable in the last century, haute cuisine restaurants featured haughty waiters and showy decor. Servers cooked flambéed dishes, such as crêpes suzette, tableside. At home, any recipe that evoked the Parisian food scene had style. Chiffon pies with meringue toppings suggested restaurant desserts. In her kitchen, the trendsetting housewife would use readily available preprocessed sauces for dishes, such as lobster Thermidor, beef stroganoff, and chicken divan, served in chafing dishes to recreate the fine dining of four-star restaurants.

Media Influence

Food magazines, epitomized after 1941 by *Gourmet* magazine, promoted food as fashion. *Sunset* magazine depicted the Western California scene, a sophisticated style of casual living, including football weekend tailgating, backyard cocktail parties, and barbecues. *Playboy* appealed to the urban bon vivant with a monthly column for the male chef, contributing to the craze for shish kebabs.

The chef as personality. The cult of personality chefs created through television programming resulted in the notion of the chef as star and creator of fancy cookbooks based on image, as well as in the exploding growth of fancy foods. One of the most significant personalities was *The French Chef*, Julia Child. She led the way for other television personality chefs to teach home viewers about good cuisine. James Beard, a food writer and chef, popularized classic American cooking. Paul Prudhomme, a Cajun New Orleans chef, demonstrated the "blackened fish" style of cooking. He used fiery spice rubs on fish, then seared them over high heat. There were many other food celebrities in the 1960s. In the 1990s, television's Food Network catapulted interest in the celebrity chef, professional techniques, and personalized ingredients. The growth in cooking stores and vocational cooking schools is a direct response to the cult of the personality chef. Through these chefs, recipes that made use of goat cheese, aioli, beurre blanc, and green peppercorns became trendy pantry staples.

Among the fads connected to food are political movements targeting agricultural practices. In the 1960s César Chávez led a boycott of grape harvests in California to advertise the plight of farmworkers. Bans on large tuna nets in order to save dolphins were an early precursor to contemporary concerns about overfishing.

Time Savers

As early as the 1900s, the goal of saving time created fashionable food fads. Refrigerators allowed homemakers to create quick, chilled desserts, epitomized by heavily sweetened marshmallow salads, fruit cocktails, and gelatin parfaits. The crock-pot, blender, and electric wok all promised to save time. One notable example that has faded is the 1980s "Impossible Bisquick Pie," in which preblended ingredients sink to the bottom of an egg custard to form the "crust."

Space-Age Influence

Fascination with the National Aeronautics and Space Administration (NASA) and the space race in the 1960s produced many fads. Even before the emergence of health foods and healthy planet foods, space technology influenced trends, especially snacks. TV dinners and other aluminum-clad, quickly prepared foods surged in popularity. After the astronauts appeared on American television, anything freeze-dried or dehydrated, previously associated only with military rations or camping, became food for the modern age. Space sticks, chewy rolls of power food flavored with vanilla or chocolate, predated today's energy bars. Tang, the sugar-powdered orange drink, was advertised as "drunk by astronauts."

A fad develops as a result of a social aim, interest in other cultures, and advances in technology that promise that the home cook can become a chef like Escoffier—or at least cook like a pro. Some, like space sticks, fade with time, while others, such as organic foods, have helped to change dietary and farming practices. Within an evolving lifestyle, food fads both reflect and change contemporary society.

See also **Beard, James; Child, Julia; Comfort Food; Escoffier, Georges-Auguste; Fast Food; Food, Future of; Food Politics: United States; Health Foods; Ice Cream; Kellogg, John Harvey; Kitchen Gadgets; Macrobiotic Food; Marketing of Food; Nostalgia; Organic Food; Take-out Food; Vegetarianism.**

BIBLIOGRAPHY

Lovegren, Sylvia. *Fashionable Food: Seven Decades of Food Fads.* New York: Macmillan, 1995.

Stern, Jane, and Michael Stern. *American Gourmet, Classic Recipes, Deluxe Delights, Flamboyant Favorites, and Swank "Company" Food From the '50s and '60s.* New York: HarperCollins, 1991.

Terrie Wright Chrones

FAO (FOOD AND AGRICULTURE ORGANIZATION OF THE UNITED NATIONS).

The Food and Agriculture Organization of the United Nations traces its origin to the foundation of the International Agriculture Institute in 1905 under the pioneering work of David Lubin. This institute, which preceded FAO, consisted of forty member nations and sponsored the first World Agriculture Census in 1930, a census which has been undertaken every ten years since that time and which has become one of the responsibilities of FAO since 1950.

The Food and Agriculture Organization was born out of the Hot Springs Conference held by forty-four nations at the Homestead Hotel, Hot Springs, Virginia, in May and June of 1943. It was established as an agency of the United Nations on 16 October 1945 to assume the work of the International Agriculture Institute and is presently governed by the U.N. Conference of Member Nations. The Conference convenes every two years to review the work carried out by the organization and to approve its programs and budget for the next biennium. The director-general of FAO serves a six-year term. In addition to its headquarters in Rome, FAO maintains five regional offices (Africa, Latin America, Asia and the Pacific, the Near East, and Europe), five sub-regional offices, five liaison offices, and over seventy-eight country offices. The purpose of the organization is to serve as a neutral forum for all members of the United Nations through numerous international programs and initiatives. Due to this political neutrality, FAO has been able to act as a conduit for the completion of hundreds of international agreements covering food and agricultural matters.

One of FAO's activities involves the development of international codes and norms, such as the standards established for food processing in connection with Codex Alimentarius and the related conventions negotiated by the FAO/WHO Codex Alimentarius Commission and the Joint Expert Committee on Food Additives (JECFA). In a similar manner, FAO's Emergency Prevention System for Transboundary Animal and Plant Pests and Diseases (EMPRES) has provided the international framework for dealing with such agricultural plagues as the desert locust.

Another area of FAO activity is the gathering and dissemination of information on food and agriculture by means of databases organized under the umbrella of the World Agriculture Information Centre (WAICENT) in Rome. The center provides information to governments, research institutes, and universities, as well as to private individuals, using a wide range of media. This includes databases on soils and terrain (SOTER), information on soil and climate requirements for more than 1,700 plant species, domestic animal diversity information, lists of mutant plant varieties, a seed information system (SIS), a feed and forage database, a fertilizer yearbook, nutritional profiles of U.N. member countries, and vast amounts of material on food crops and crop shortages. FAO is also the world center for information on fisheries, aquaculture, and forestry.

The Food and Agriculture Organization has also become deeply involved in fighting world hunger and poverty by developing special programs for food security. This has involved a commitment to sustainable agriculture and rural development, the establishment of food cooperatives, seed saving programs at the small-farm level, land conservation, and an environmental agenda designed to better manage natural resources. FAO has taken this campaign to the public through its World Food Day programs in mid-October of each year. In 1997, FAO launched Telefood, a series of concerts and broadcasts designed to raise money for specific programs dealing with hunger and poverty. Money from these events, which are held in different places throughout the world each year, have funded over eight hundred small community-based projects in rural areas of such countries as Bangladesh, Somalia, Nepal, and Uganda.

See also **Aquaculture; Codex Alimentarius; Food Supply, Food Shortages; Government Agencies; International Agencies; Political Economy; Sustainable Agriculture.**

BIBLIOGRAPHY

Food and Agriculture Organization. *Dimensions of Need: An Atlas of Food and Agriculture.* Rome: FAO, 1995.

Food and Agriculture Organization. *Constitution of the Food and Agriculture Organization of the United Nations.* Washington, D.C.: 1945.

Food and Agriculture Organization. *FAO: The First 40 Years.* Rome: FAO, 1985.

Food and Agriculture Organization. *The State of World Fisheries and Aquaculture.* Rome: FAO, 2000.

Food and Agriculture Organization. *The State of the World's Forests.* Rome: FAO, 2001.

Loftas, Tony, ed. *Reforming FAO into the New Millennium.* Rome: FAO, 2000.

Phillips, Ralph. *FAO: Its Origins, Formation and Evolution, 1945–1981.* Rome: FAO, 1981.

William Woys Weaver

FARMERS' MARKETS. Farmers' markets are common facilities or areas where several producers gather on a regular basis to sell various fresh meat, fruit, vegetables, and other food products directly to consumers. They circumvent the middleman and provide small- and medium-sized producers with an immediate, convenient, and economical sales outlet for their agricultural products. They are also established for the benefit of the urban consumer who values quality, variety, and freshness in food.

Farmers' markets vary greatly in terms of their physical shapes and configurations. The simplest form is the open-air market, where shelter is provided by the producers themselves or by structures already in place, such as bridges, arcades, and elevated highways. A more complex form is the market shed, which provides minimal protection from the elements yet allows easy access from all sides. The fully enclosed market house offers still greater shelter and facilitates year-round selling. Market districts, the most complex form, combine elements of the open-air market, the market shed, and the market house with other facilities, services, and related businesses.

Farmers' markets are an urban phenomenon worldwide and they assume characteristics determined by the social, political, and economic factors particular to their locales. The environment, natural features of the landscape, cultural norms, and the historic relationship between the countryside and the town also contribute to a wide range of market types. For example, the Tsukiji

Some markets open short-term retail space to local farmers in an effort to bring the producer and customer face to face. Amish farmers in Philadelphia's Reading Terminal Market often rent tables on Saturdays to sell their produce during harvest season. PHOTO COURTESY OF DAVID K. O'NEIL.

Market in Tokyo specializes in the wholesale and retail fish trade, with nearly 1,700 stalls covering a huge (54-acre/22-hectare) site. The market at Otovalo, Ecuador, one of many open-air markets in South America, functions as a principal trading point for Indian farmers selling local produce and handicrafts. And the daily market at Campo de'Fiori continues the long tradition of food marketing in one of the oldest public squares in Rome. Regardless of types or locations, farmers' markets around the world create a vibrant environment where consumers and producers are brought together for the benefit of the local community.

Although farmers' markets vary in terms of ownership and facilities, most operate by standard criteria in accordance with traditional trading ethics and standards. Vendors are subject to environmental, health, licensing, and other market ordinances and legislation. They must also adhere to the market's own rules and guidelines, which typically establish days and hours of operation, the payment of rents, and other business matters. A market

manager is usually engaged to oversee the daily activities of the market and to ensure that rules and guidelines are met.

The most important criteria for farmers' markets are that goods be locally produced and that vendors sell their own products. These criteria change over time and differ from place to place. "Locally produced" may be defined strictly in terms of the radius from the market, for example, thirty miles, but the actual distance depends on a number of circumstances. Farmers' markets near coastal areas may encompass a large radius that includes the source of locally caught fish. For markets in major urban areas, farms are of necessity some distance away, so the radius may be larger than that for smaller communities. Available transportation from farm to market as well as consumers' own perception of "local" may also influence definitions.

The other important criterion, that goods be the direct product of the merchant's labor, is again subject to different interpretations. In general it holds that fresh

Curbside farmers market in Dubuque, Iowa, circa 1900. Courtesy of the National Archives.

meat and produce have been grown or finished on the producers' land. Cheese, honey, and processed meat products, such as sausage, are also produced on the vendor's land or at least within the defined radius of the market and with local ingredients. In general crafts and processed products using materials from outside the area of the farmers' market are excluded in favor of food products that have an entirely local origin. This restriction, however, is often lifted during winter months or when local products are not in season.

Farmers' markets belong to an ancient tradition of urban food retailing, in which the governing authority designated specific places for the exchange of life's necessities. Known as public markets, these places were intended to attract local and regional producers to the city to ensure citizens an adequate supply of healthful food at fair prices. They were critical to the survival of the town, because without them unbridled competition and unfair dealings in the sale of perishable food could jeopardize the public welfare. The local authority also maintained public markets to ensure a healthy population of workers, to prevent emigration, and to encourage agriculture near the city.

One of the most famous farmers' markets in nineteenth-century America was the city-owned High Street Market in Philadelphia. By midcentury this market con-

sisted of a series of sheds in the middle of High Street extending from the foot of the Delaware River to Eighth Street and again from Fifteenth to Seventeenth streets, with breaks only at the intersections. Space in the market was divided by types of goods, including meat, fish, garden seeds, produce, roots, herbs, vegetables, meal, locally produced earthenware, and New Jersey produce. The market was demolished in 1859, when it was replaced by a series of large, off-street market houses owned by private companies.

The majority of farmers' markets in the United States were municipally owned and operated until the mid-nineteenth century, when the movement for privatization generated alternative food-marketing establishments, including private shops and market companies. As a result, farmers' markets may be owned and managed by a municipality, but more often they convene on public property and are sponsored by nongovernmental entities, which may be farmers' associations, chambers of commerce, cooperatives, or other community organizations.

A quasi-public corporation, the Pike Place Market Preservation and Development Authority, oversees Pike Place Market in Seattle, Washington, one of the most successful markets in the United States. Established in 1907, the market encompassed a nine-acre historic district by the year 2000, with more than 100 farmers, 150 craftspeople, nearly 300 commercial businesspeople, 50 performers, and various services for low-income residents. During the 1990s the historic district hosted approximately 9 million visitors per year, and annual gross sales were estimated at $9 million.

The number of farmers' markets has been growing steadily in recent years. Cities throughout the world are taking an interest in developing farmers' markets to add vitality to their public spaces, to redevelop their historic marketplaces, to revitalize neighborhoods, and to make fresh food available in areas underserved by supermarkets. In the United States, for example, the number of farmers' markets grew 63 percent in the last decade of the twentieth century, from 1,755 in 1994, when the U.S. Department of Agriculture began collecting data, to 2,863 in 2000. Other factors have contributed to their popularity. Most significantly, small farmers cannot afford to invest in the costly marketing systems required for mass food retailing and distribution. Direct access to the consumer therefore offers an alternative source of revenue and immediate cash flow.

Consumer demand for farmers' markets has also increased worldwide, primarily in response to the growing organic food movement and to public health disasters resulting from mass food marketing and production practices. Sophisticated consumers take a great interest in nutrition and wholesome eating habits, and they seek the sources of the foods they eat. As a result they view farmers' markets as healthy alternatives or supplements to supermarkets and other outlets of mass-marketed food. Farmers' markets devoted exclusively to the sale of organic food are abundant in France, one of the world's leading consumers of organic food. The demand for organic food markets, coupled with the larger international movement to resist the globalization of food marketing and production, will continue to foster farmers' markets as critical sources of fresh, healthful, and affordable food for the urban consumer.

See also **Food Cooperatives; Marketing of Food; Marketing of Food: Alternative (Direct) Strategies; Retailing of Food.**

BIBLIOGRAPHY

Balkin, Steve, Alfonso Morales, John C. Cross, and the Open Air-Market Net Board of Adivsers. "OpenAir-Market Net: The World Wide Guide to Farmers' Markets, Street Markets, Flea Markets, and Street Vendors." Available at http://www.openair.org.

Burns, Arthur F. *Farmers' Market Survey Report.* Washington, D.C.: U.S. Department of Agriculture, 1996.

Goodwin, Arthur E. *Markets: Public and Private: Their Establishment and Administration.* Seattle: Montgomery Printing, 1929.

Sheffer, Nelli, and Mimi Sheraton. *Food Markets of the World.* New York: Harry N. Abrams, 1997.

Shorett, Alice, and Murray Morgan. *The Pike Place Market: People, Politics, and Produce.* Seattle: Pacific Search Press, 1982.

Spitzer, Theodore, and Hilary Baum. *Public Markets and Community Revitalization.* Washington, D.C.: Urban Land Institute and Project for Public Spaces, 1995.

Tangires, Helen. *Public Markets and Civic Culture in Nineteenth-Century America.* Baltimore: Johns Hopkins University Press, 2003.

United States Department of Agriculture. Agricultural Marketing Service. "Farmers' Markets." Available at http://www.ams.usda.gov/farmersmarkets.

Helen Tangires

FAST FOOD. What is termed "fast food" in the United States today most commonly consists of hot, freshly prepared, and wrapped food items, served to customers across a counter or through a drive-up window. Known as both "fast food" and "quick-service food" in the restaurant industry, these items are routinely sold and delivered in an amount of time ranging from a few seconds to several minutes; they now vary widely in food type, encompassing virtually all kinds of meats, preparation methods, and ethnic cuisines. Inexpensive hamburgers and french fried potatoes are still the products most readily identified as fast food, but the list of items sold in the format continually increases. Fried fish and shellfish, hot dogs, chicken, pizza, roast beef, and pasta are commonly sold at quick-service outlets. In addition to these staples, many quick-service restaurants sell a broad menu of Americanized Mexican, Greek, and Chinese foods. Some fast-food outlets offer specialty items, such as sushi, clams, or ribs, and others even sell complete "home-cooked" meals over their counters. Though menus and delivery formats vary greatly, fast food's chief common denominators include immediate customer service, packaging "to go," and inexpensive pricing.

The precise origins of fast food are vague, probably predating written history. Hungry people are as old as civilization itself, as are entrepreneurs eager to satisfy their hunger. Food vendors in ancient cities sold prepared items to passersby on the street. The actual foods varied greatly, depending on period and culture, but they generally comprised simple, inexpensive fare sold to people of modest means.

Immigrants brought a variety of food styles to America, often preserving these for decades as a comforting connection with their ethnic past. Though many immigrant foodways were elaborate and ritualistic, most groups had one or two simple items that they consumed on a daily basis. As a rule, immigrant groups preferred their indigenous grains: corn from the Americas, rice from Asia, and wheat from Europe. Often these served as the basis for the "peasant" foods of their homelands. Pasta and flat breads came over with Italians; tortillas, beans, and tamales arrived with northbound Mexicans; and Germans brought dark breads, along with a variety of fatty sausages (which later mutated into the hot dog).

Asian immigrants continued to eat rice as the basis of their diet.

In the early twentieth century fast food remained primarily the fare of the masses. Vendors wheeled their pushcarts daily to factory gates, selling their wares to hungry workers. Often catering to the tastes of the particular factory's dominant ethnic group, they charged customers pennies for basic items such as sausages, meatballs, or stew. Though popular among male industrial workers, this pushcart version of fast food never became mainstream cuisine.

The urban diner was the transitional phase between the vendor's pushcart and modern fast food. Most early diners were small restaurants, with limited seating, sometimes constructed out of converted railway carriages or streetcars. They served simple foods to working-class customers on a "short-order" basis, usually cooking each meal individually when ordered. Menus varied, but fried foods were common. Though diners often emphasized speed in delivering food, customers routinely lingered before and after eating.

The hamburger still stands out as the single most important American fast food, though the precise origin of this meat sandwich is the subject of historical disagreement. People have eaten chopped beef throughout the ages, and it was long a fixture in many world cultures. The lineage of the American hamburger seems to point directly, as its name indicates, back to the German city of Hamburg. First appearing on American restaurant menus in the mid-nineteenth century, ground beef patties bore the title "hamburg steak." By the century's close, vendors regularly sold meatballs wrapped in slices of bread at county fairs and summer festivals. Regional legends attribute the invention of this snack to several different individuals, but its true originator remains a mystery.

The Rise of Modern Fast Food

Our modern image of the fast-food restaurant dates back to 1916, when Walt Anderson began selling "hamburger sandwiches" from an outdoor stand on a Wichita street corner. Anderson simply flattened a meatball and placed it between two halves of a bun. His sandwich quickly became popular, attracting long lines of hungry buyers. By 1921, Anderson had joined local insurance broker Edgar "Billy" Ingram to form the White Castle System. After opening several identical restaurants in Wichita during their first year, the partners quickly spread their business to neighboring cities, then to nine major urban areas throughout the Midwest and on the East Coast. What separated the White Castle System from earlier short-order restaurants was its very streamlined menu, comprising only hamburgers, coffee, Coca-Cola, and pie; a uniform architectural style; and strict standardization of food quality, preparation methods, and employee performance. By the close of the 1920s, White Castle's ag-

Fast foods have generated their own type of architecture. To attract attention and customers, some buildings were quite whimsical, like this 1930s hot dog stand. © CORBIS-BETTMANN.

gressive marketing and rapid spread had made the hamburger one of the most popular foods in America.

Other entrepreneurs soon noticed White Castle's success in the hamburger business. Very closely copying White Castle's products, architecture, and company name, competing new chains also thrived, carrying the hamburger craze across the nation to smaller cities and towns. The White Tower chain appeared in 1925, eventually challenging White Castle's dominance in several northern cities. Krystal's, opened in 1929 in Chattanooga, soon became the hamburger powerhouse of the southeastern states. White Castle's hamburger sandwich, along with its many imitators, became a daily staple for many working-class Americans. It proved so successful, in fact, that by 1930 the president of the American Restaurant Association identified the fast-food hamburger as the most important food item in the nation.

Hamburgers became even more a mainstream food during the 1930s. The larger restaurant chains began marketing their products to middle-class buyers, and even more Americans became burger lovers. Despite the harsh economy of the Great Depression, most fast-food chains continued to thrive, and in many cases grew considerably. Most continued selling the White Castle–style hamburger, but late in the decade the Big Boy chain spread east from California, introducing its new double-decker hamburger sandwich along the way. By the end of the Depression, America was a solidly hamburger-eating culture.

After prospering in the Depression, however, the fast-food industry suffered a serious setback during World War II. Shortages of necessary foodstuffs, such as meat, sugar, tomatoes, and coffee, meant limited menu offerings and often a significant loss of business. Attempting to continue providing meals to their customers, fast-food restaurants experimented with different items that were still in abundance, including soy patties, chili, and french fried potatoes. Even more damaging than commodity shortages was the very low unemployment rate, which meant that most workers bypassed the restaurant industry in favor of higher-paying work. Adjusting to this labor shortage, chains soon replaced their all-male workforce with women and teenagers, two groups who would become their most common employees. Despite attempts to find palatable alternative foods, and despite the shifts in workforce, much of the fast-food industry was a casualty of the war; by 1945, more than half of America's restaurants had closed down, including several of the major fast-food chains.

Rebuilding the fast-food industry after the war proved a slow process. No single chain emerged to claim dominance, and little innovation occurred. Individual companies struggled to restore their prewar prosperity, and new regional chains tried to gain a foothold. Suffering the effects of escalating costs and still under the threat of continued shortages due to unstable food supplies in war-torn countries, fast-food restaurants often had to double prices to remain in business.

As population shifted from America's cities to suburbia during the 1950s, the fast-food industry quickly followed. Early chains such as White Castle and White Tower, resisting moving to the suburbs, were quickly eclipsed by upstart franchised chains. Burger King and McDonald's outlets became common fixtures at suburban crossroads, selling burgers, fries, and shakes to hungry families. Burger King's Jim McLamore and McDonald's Ray Kroc each sought to build one of his restaurants in every American town, and they opened hundreds of new Burger Kings and McDonald's each year in the 1960s. To accomplish this rapid expansion, they relied heavily on franchise investors, enforced strict product uniformity throughout their chains, and aggressively advertised in every newly opened territory. With McDonald's and Burger King's success, Burger Chef outlets soon appeared nearby. Arby's, Kentucky Fried Chicken, and Taco Bell were not far behind. By the late 1960s, fast food no longer meant just hamburger restaurants, but had diversified to include quick-service pizza, roast beef, chicken, and tacos. To give an idea of the dimensions to which the fast-food industry has grown, in 1999 Americans consumed over 26 billion pounds of beef, much of it as hamburgers. In that year McDonald's alone had more than ten thousand restaurants in the United States, from which it grossed in excess of $13 billion in revenue.

Criticism of Fast Food

Despite the widespread popularity of fast food in modern American culture, critics abound. Since the 1930s, articles and books have condemned the industry, exposing allegedly poor sanitary conditions, unhealthy food products, related environmental problems, and unfair working conditions. Whether it warrants the attention or not, the fast-food industry is still regularly cited for exploiting young workers, polluting, and contributing to obesity and other serious health problems among American consumers. American beef consumption, and more specifically the fast-food hamburger industry, is often blamed for the burning of the Amazon rain forests to make way for more grazing lands for beef cattle. Early foes of fast food cited the deplorable filth of many hamburger stands, in addition to claiming that the beef ground for their sandwiches was either spoiled, diseased, or simply of low quality. In fact, many critics maintained that much of the meat used in fast-food hamburgers came from horse carcasses. The high fat content of fast food was also controversial. Despite deceptive industry claims about the high quality and the health benefits of their products, in the 1920s and 1930s concerned nutritionists warned the public about the medical dangers of regular burger consumption. This distrust and criticism of fast food continue today, extending even further to include dire warnings about the industry's use of genetically modified and antibiotic-laden beef products. Most major chains have responded to recent attacks by prominently posting calorie and nutritional charts in their restaurants, advertising fresh ingredients, and offering alternatives to their fried foods. Despite a few more health-conscious items on the menu, fast-food chains now aggressively advertise the concept that bigger is better, offering large "super-size" or "biggie" portions of french fries, soft drinks, and milkshakes. Critics point to this marketing emphasis as a reason for an excessive and greatly increasing per-capita caloric intake among fast-food consumers, resulting in fast-growing rates of obesity in the United States.

Increased litter is another problem that critics have blamed on the fast-food industry. Selling their products in paper wrappings and paper bags, early outlets created a source of litter that had not previously existed. Wrappers strewn about city streets, especially those close to fast-food restaurants, brought harsh criticism, and often inspired new local ordinances to address the problem. Some municipalities actually forced chains to clean up litter that was imprinted with their logos, but such sanctions were rare. Fast-food wrappers became part of the urban, and later suburban, landscape. Since bags and wrappers were crucial in the delivery of fast food, the industry as a whole continued to use disposable packaging, superficially assuaging public criticism by providing outside trash receptacles for the discarded paper. Years later, environmentalists again attacked the industry for excessive packaging litter, criticizing both the volume and the content of the refuse. By the early 1970s, the harshest criticisms focused more on the synthetic materials used in packaging, and less on the carelessly discarded paper. Critics derided the industry's use of styrofoam sandwich containers and soda cups, claiming that these products were not sufficiently biodegradable and were clogging landfills. Facing mounting opposition from a growing environmental movement, most of the major chains returned to packaging food in paper wrappings or small cardboard boxes.

Labor activists have criticized fast-food chains' tendency to employ inexpensive teenage workers. Usually offering the lowest possible wages, with no health or retirement benefits, these restaurants often find it difficult hiring adults for stressful, fast-paced jobs. Many critics claim that the industry preys on teenagers, who will work for less pay and are less likely to organize. Though these accusations may have merit, the industry's reliance on teenage labor also has inherent liabilities, such as a high employee turnover rate, which result in substantial recruiting and training costs. Companies have countered criticism about their use of teenage workers with the rationale that they offer young people entry-level work experience, teaching them both skills and responsibility.

Despite the relentless attacks, hundreds of millions of hungry customers eat fast food daily. The media constantly remind American consumers about its supposed evils. Most are conscious of the health risks from fatty, greasy meals; most realize that they are being served by a poorly paid young worker; and if they choose to ponder it, most are aware that the excessive packaging causes millions of tons of trash each year. But they continue to purchase and eat fast food on a regular basis. Fast food remains central to the American diet because it is inexpensive, quick, convenient, and predictable, and because it tastes good. Even more important, Americans eat fast food because it is now a cultural norm. As American culture homogenized and became distinctively "American" in the second half of the twentieth century, fast food, and especially the hamburger, emerged as the primary American ethnic food. Just as the Chinese eat rice and Mexicans eat tamales, Americans eat burgers.

And fast food has grown even beyond being just a distinctive ethnic food. Since the 1960s, the concept has extended far beyond the food itself, with the term becoming a common descriptor for other quick-service operations, even a metaphor for many of the negative aspects of mainstream American life. Theorists and pundits sometimes use the term "fast food" to denigrate American habits, institutions, and values, referring to them as elements of a "fast-food society." In fact, "fast-food" has become a frequently used adjective, implying not only ready availability but also superficiality, mass-produced standardization, lack of authenticity, or just poor quality.

In the last two decades of the twentieth century, fast food gained additional economic and cultural significance, becoming a popular American export to nations around the world. Some detractors claim that it is even deliberately used by the United States, as a tool of cultural imperialism. The appearance of a McDonald's or Kentucky Fried Chicken restaurant on the streets of a foreign city signals to many the demise of indigenous culture, replacing another country's traditional practices and values with American materialism. In fact, the rapid spread of American fast food is probably not an organized conspiracy, rather more the result of aggressive corporate marketing strategies. Consumers in other countries are willing and able to buy fast-food products, so chains are quick to accommodate demand. Thought of around the world as "American food," fast food continues its rapid international growth.

See also **Cattle; Fish and Chips; Food Politics: United States; French Fries; Hamburger; Meat; Obesity; Packaging and Canning; Potato; Sandwich; Slow Food; Take-Out Food.**

BIBLIOGRAPHY

Boas, Max, and Steve Chain. *Big Mac: The Unauthorized Story of McDonald's.* New York: Dutton, 1976.

Emerson, Robert, L. *Fast Food: The Endless Shakeout.* New York: Lebhar-Friedman, 1979.

Halberstam, David. *The Fifties.* New York: Villard Books, 1993. Chapter 11 discusses the origins of the McDonald's empire.

Hogan, David Gerard. *Selling 'em by the Sack: White Castle and the Creation of American Food.* New York: New York University Press, 1997.

Jakle, John A., and Keith A. Sculle. *Fast Food: Roadside Restaurants in the Automobile Age.* Baltimore: Johns Hopkins University Press, 1999.

Langdon, Philip. *Orange Roofs, Golden Arches: The Architecture of American Chain Restaurants.* New York: Knopf, 1986.

McLamore, James, W. *The Burger King: Jim McLamore and the Building of an Empire.* New York: McGraw-Hill, 1998.

Mariani, John. *America Eats Out.* New York: William Morrow, 1991.

Schlosser, Eric. *Fast Food Nation: The Dark Side of the All-American Meal.* Boston and New York: Houghton Mifflin, 2001.

Tennyson, Jeffrey. *Hamburger Heaven: The Illustrated History of the Hamburger.* New York: Hyperion, 1993.

Witzel, Michael Karl. *The American Drive-In: History and Folklore of the Drive-In Restaurant in the Car Culture.* Osceola, Wisc.: Motorbooks International, 1994.

David Gerard Hogan

FASTING AND ABSTINENCE.

This entry includes four subentries:
Christianity
Hinduism and Buddhism
Islam
Judaism

CHRISTIANITY

Fasting or abstaining for a period from food and drink is common to various religions and is often an expression

Fasting was an integral part of Christian diet during the Middle Ages, but clever cooks devised numerous ways to create tasteful foods without meat or animal fats. These Polish fast-day dumplings are stuffed with mushrooms, a popular meat alternative. PHOTO BY ANDRÉ BARANOWSKI.

of penitence or mourning. Christian fasting and abstinence can be a purely personal matter or a social event at a special occasion, but it should be distinguished from the regular fasting that is prescribed by ecclesiastical authority and fixed on the Church calendar. The institution of fasting is a commandment for all Christians, and the Church's acceptance of it is thought to go back to Pope Calixtus I (217–222).

Fasting can be abstinence not only from food or drink, but also from sexual intercourse or other activities. This article focuses on food and looks at when Christians fast. Early monastic communities enforced abstinence from meat and wine, following in part the classical argument of Hippocrates and Galenus that warned against such "warm and humid" foods, which were thought to stimulate luxury. These strictures proved too severe—the religious lacked the energy to complete their daily tasks, and the laymen who worked outside the walls could not be expected to observe such stringent restrictions on food and drink.

By the tenth and eleventh centuries, the Roman Catholic Church had modified its rules for fasting, distinguishing between monastics and ordinary people, and regulating the severity of fasts on the Church calendar.

The Church never prescribed total fasts (without food and drink) or even those allowing just water and bread during a whole day or longer. Instead, several forms of the discipline were practiced, the more severe of which is called "fasting" and the milder "abstinence."

During fasting periods, Christians were forbidden to eat the meat (and other products, such as milk and eggs) of quadrupeds and birds. Christians did not consider these animals and their products "unclean," as did the Jews (Acts 10–16), but eating them was proscribed by the Church during certain times of the year. At such times, Christians fed on seafood, fish (including hard and soft fish roe), grains, and other field produce. The prohibition on dairy produce and eggs, in particular, and the resulting lack of protein nourishment, placed an enormous strain on medieval people. Chicken eggs were replaced by hard roe and butter, lard, and bacon by vegetable oil. For the European countries north of the Alps, where olives and almonds could not be grown, there was a substantial rise in the cost of living. Those who could afford them obtained expensive olive oil or almonds from the Mediterranean, which were mashed into a binding agent for sauces and chowders. Dried fruits, including dates, figs, raisins, and currants, from the Mediterranean were highly sought in northern Europe, as were the indigenous walnut and hazelnut.

During the milder periods of abstinence, milk could be consumed. It was not clear whether the meat from birds could be consumed during these times, but their eggs were permitted. Late medieval household accounts (fourteenth to fifteenth centuries) show that Christians lived according to these rules, especially during the longest fasting period in the church calendar, the forty weekdays of Lent or the so-called *quadragesima* (Latin *quadraginta* = 40, hence *quadragesima*), which precedes Easter, when the faithful switched over to a fish-and-oil kitchen.

In addition to Lent, the Catholic Church had four fasting periods called Ember days during the year (Latin *quatuor tempora* = four times, corrupted to *quatember*, then to "ember"). These days, prescribed by Pope Gregory VII (1073–1085), correspond to the turn of the seasons: the Wednesday, Friday, and Saturday of the week after St. Lucia (13 December) at the beginning of winter; then the Wednesday, Friday, and Saturday after Ash Wednesday (therefore, part of Lent) at the beginning of spring; next, the Wednesday, Friday, and Saturday of the week after Whitsuntide (Pentecost) at the beginning of summer; last, the same days of the week after Holy Cross Day (14 September) at the beginning of fall. Because the Christian calendar, unlike that of the Muslims, has a solar year with twelve months of more than the twenty-eight days of the orbit of the moon, these so-called Ember days always occur in the same season. Unlike the Muslim Ramadan, which shifts through the year, the Christian *quadragesima* always occurs during the turn from winter to spring.

In contrast to the *quadragesima* and the Ember days in which the severe abstinence that we call "fasting" was observed, a milder abstinence was obligatory all other weeks of the year on Wednesday and Friday, or Friday and Saturday, depending on the diocese in which one lived. On those days fish, which might be served with butter, was consumed. Fishermen strove to bring fresh fish to the market on those days, knowing that they would find ready consumers. Long after the fasting prescriptions in Catholic Europe had been mitigated by the Protestant Reformation of the sixteenth century, the habit of eating fish on Friday or Saturday remained common.

Religious generally did not observe a more severe fasting regimen than lay people, but the duration of the fast was greater. Monks and nuns started the *quadragesima* ten days prior to Ash Wednesday, thereby making a *quinquagesima* of fifty days, and they also fasted on the Monday, Tuesday, and Wednesday before Ascension Day, the so-called Rogation Days. Advent, the four weeks before Christmas, formed a fasting period for them, not just the Ember days of St. Lucia that fall during this period.

The Rule of St. Benedict forbade the consumption of the meat of quadrupeds unless the religious was ill. The eating of birds was allowed, as was the consumption of eggs and dairy produce, except, of course, on fasting days. In this Rule it was stated that on fasting days, but not before Vespers, only one meal should be served that would be finished before dark. On other days, two meals were eaten, earlier or later depending on the season but always with daylight.

Mindful of the heresy of the Manichees and the Cathars, who taught that the body and the material world were the work of Satan and only the immaterial spirit was the work of God, Christians of the Western Church attempted to strike a balance between gluttony on the one hand and too rigorous an asceticism on the other.

The forty days of Lent referred to the forty years during which the Jews, under the guidance of Moses, had wandered through the desert before reaching the Holy Land (Deuteronomy 1:1–3), as well as to the forty days of Christ's temptation by Satan in the desert (Matthew 4:1–11, Mark 1:12–13, Luke 4:1–13). But this does little to explain the timing of the Lenten fast, which commences at the turn of winter into spring. There is no text in the Bible prescribing this particular fast period. Also, the other Ember days coincide with the turn of the seasons.

Perhaps a key can be found in the reference to the humoral system of Hippocrates and Galenus, which was used to condemn the consumption of meat and wine as a stimulus of luxury. In this system of thought, every season has its own qualities—dry or humid, hot or cold—and the human body, which also has humoral qualities, needs a little digestive pause to switch over to another season. So fasting might have served such a function. This reasoning was seldom explicit, but in one example, a Latin schoolbook of chronology from 1436 (*Computus Magistri Jacobi*), the comparison was made between the qualities of the seasons and the capital sins, from which the human mind should be cleansed by fasting.

However, not all questions concerning the Christian traditions for fasting and abstinence can be answered. Why was the longest fasting period the one from late winter to early spring? And why did the church not forbid the consumption of fish and seafood? Were there economic motives at stake—should eggs be allowed to hatch instead of being eaten by humans? Should the milk of animals be reserved for their newborn? Since Church authorities never clearly explained the reasons behind fasting and abstinence, we may never know the answers to these questions.

See also **Christianity**; **Lent**; **Middle Ages, European**; **Shrove Tuesday**.

BIBLIOGRAPHY

Bazell, Dianne M. "Strife among the Table-Fellows: Conflicting Attitudes of Early and Medieval Christians Toward the Eating of Meat." *Journal of the American Academy of Religion* 65 (1997): 73–99.

Dembinska, Maria. "Fasting and Working Monks: Regulations of the Fifth to Eleventh Centuries." In *Food in Change: Eating Habits from the Middle Ages to the Present Day*, edited by Alexander Fenton and Eszter Kisban, pp. 152–160. Edinburgh: John Donald Publishers/National Museums of Scotland, 1986.

Gumbert-Hepp, Marijke. *Computus Magistri Jacobi: Een schoolboek voor tijdrekenkunde uit 1436*. Hilversum: Uitgeverij Verloren, 1987. See pp. 108–111.

Hanslik, Rudolphus, ed. *Benedicti Regula: Corpus Scriptorum Ecclesiasticorum Latinorum*. Vol. 75. Vienna: Hoelder-Pichler-Tempsky, 1960. See capita 36, 41, 49.

Henish, Bridget Ann. *Fast and Feast: Food in Medieval Society*. University Park, Pa., and London: Pennsylvania State University Press, 1976.

van Winter, Johanna Maria. "Obligatory Fasts and Voluntary Asceticism in the Middle Ages." In *Food in Change: Eating Habits from the Middle Ages to the Present Day*, edited by Alexander Fenton and Eszter Kisban, pp. 161–166. Edinburgh: John Donald Publishers/National Museums of Scotland, 1986.

Johanna Maria van Winter

HINDUISM AND BUDDHISM

Hinduism

Food (in Sanskrit, *anna*) plays a very important role in the social and ritual life of the Hindus. Its importance is illustrated in a regular greeting at the Indian subcontinent: "Have you eaten?" is asked in the same way as people elsewhere might ask, "How are you?" Food is

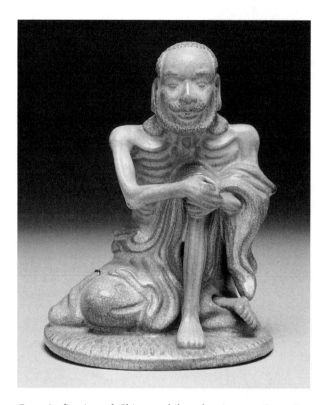

Ceramic figurine of Chinese philosopher Lao-tse. Sung Dynasty, 960–1126 C.E. The bony, wasted body of Lao-tse, who flourished in the sixth century B.C.E., was a perennial symbol of abstinence and asceticism in Chinese culture. ROUGHWOOD COLLECTION. PHOTO CHEW & COMPANY.

Fasting in the sense of not eating for a specific time (*upavāsa*), or abstaining from specific substances during certain periods, is a well-established part of all Hindu spiritual practices. In the early times it was related to *tapas*, ascetic practices, and it is still a major aspect of the religious practices of many of the *sādhus* or "holy men" in India. Also, many ordinary Indians fast on specific days during the year, either by taking no food at all or by restricting their diet. For instance, Vaisnavas fast on the eleventh day of each half of the lunar month (*ekādaśī*), when they are only allowed to eat what has grown below the ground, along with dairy products. Before and during rituals, like sacrifices, but also before going on a pilgrimage, fasting and abstinence from certain food items are part of the practice of Hindus.

It is all part of the concept of *vrata* or religious vow. A *vrata* can be taken during a religious festival, or a pilgrimage, and also in conjunction with pursuing some goal in life, which may include material or spiritual wellbeing or success in business, love, or a good job. *Vratas* are applied following ritually significant and meaningful patterns, depending on which deity is addressed or which goal is pursued, or on a person's station in life. Fasting and abstinence lead to the attainment of religious merit, which is then "used" to achieve the desired goal.

There is, however, also a spiritual aim: the control of the physical body as well as of emotions and the mind, which may lead eventually to the ultimate goal of unconditioned consciousness or liberation from the cycle of rebirth, in union with the transcendent (either considered personal or impersonal).

Complete fasting, in its most radical form, can be pursued until death, in which case it is called *prāyopavista* ("one who sits down and quietly awaits the approach of death" by not eating). Suicide through starvation has been well documented in Jainism, a religion that originated in the sixth century B.C.E., but Jain customs regarding this kind of suicide may be based on Hindu practices from around the fourth century B.C.E. Elderly people, who feel they are of no use any more to the community or feel they are a burden to the family, can choose this way of ending their lives. Suicide by ending the cycle of rebirth (*samsāra*) through not eating is beyond mainstream Hinduism, which sees it as another attachment that will even bring a worse rebirth unless the person has already been detached of all worldly concerns. A person can fast for a specific period to attain some goal, thereby pressuring family or community members, as exemplified by the fasting of Mahātma Gandhi for political and humanitarian ends.

In the general practice of Hinduism, fasting and abstinence are not clearly distinguishable and are performed under the general concept of *vrata* or vow. The most common form of abstinence practiced by communities as a whole is vegetarianism. The consumption of substances that entail the killing of a living animal—in principle this

mentioned in the early Hindu sacred writings known as the Vedas (Sanskrit, "knowledge"). In the Taittiriya Upanishad it is written, "Food is life, therefore one should give food; eating is the supreme sacrifice." Hindus have hundreds of traditional health rules, most of them regarding food and the preparation of meals. A traditional Hindu housewife spends a large amount of time cooking. Also religious books—such as the Dharmaśātras, the ancient "law books"—treat food and all that is related to eating extensively. Caste borders were sharpened by the many rules on eating, or rather not eating, together. In Vedic times (1500–500 B.C.E.), people ate everything, including beef, but in later times, probably under the influence of Buddhism, meat eating became a taboo, as was the killing of animals, either for food or for a sacrifice. One could argue that many of these food taboos were instigated by climatic conditions and by ideas about hygiene. Different groups and castes developed their own food rules, although there were regional differences. The Vaisnava community classifies food according to the three qualities (*guna*) of the Sāmkhya philosophy: *sattva* food, which is pure; *rajas* food, which is energetic or exciting; and *tamas* food, which is impure. Only *sattva* food is allowed, which means no meat and fish, onions, garlic, specific fruits, and sharp spices.

also includes eggs—is considered to create demerit, which has to be avoided at all cost by people belonging to those communities. Many others also practice vegetarianism as a spiritual practice by personal choice, either all the time, or even just one day a week.

Certain other substances are also avoided when a person performs a vow, because they are known to stimulate the senses, and therefore are contrary to the goal of control over the body and the senses. In particular, onions and garlic are avoided. For some groups or individuals this restriction is followed all the time. For others these foods are only avoided on certain occasions that call for a stricter diet. Especially on days that are set aside for rituals for ancestors, onions and garlic are forbidden.

Vrata or spiritual vow has three main branches. The first one is called *nitya*, which means permanent or always. Persons undertaking this type of vow are usually seeking the grace and blessing of a particular divinity toward a particular wish or desire (such as a good job, success at exams or business, or a good marriage). Hindus sometimes abstain from certain foods permanently. Or, they fast completely during one day of the week or month.

The second form of *vrata* is called *naimittika*, which means occasioned by some particular cause. It pertains to people who experience remorse or repentance in connection with a sin they have committed. They practice a vow in order to be relieved from the karmic consequences of their sin. The third type of vow is called *kāmya vrata*, which means a vow for what one desires. This form of vow is performed in order to achieve property, popularity, wealth, or health. An example of this kind of vow is called *somavrata*, which involves complete abstention from food on Mondays.

Vows follow many diverse patterns, depending on which deity is beseeched for blessing, the nature of the objective, or the wish that the devotee wants to see fulfilled. Such vows can require not eating, eating less, eating only certain substances, or avoiding certain substances altogether. The choice of the days on which or the periods during which the vow is performed is regulated by the ritual calendar.

The days of the week are ruled by the planetary deities and are also indirectly related to the main deities of Hinduism. People may choose to fast, or abstain from certain substances like meat or fish, or also from onions and garlic, on the day dedicated to the deity they are addressing with their vow. Sunday, Ravivāra, is ruled by Sūrya, the sun, and is dedicated to the achievement of victory, as in the case of disputes and court cases, but also when starting Vedic studies or a journey. Monday, Somavāra, is dedicated to Candra, the moon, and to Śiva. Fasting on Monday is directed to all general spiritual purposes. Tuesday, Mangalavāra, is dedicated to Mars, and Kārttikeya, Śiva's son and the god of war. Fasting on Tuesday is directed toward victory, childbirth, and good

health. Wednesday, Budhavāra, belongs to Mercury. It is said that fasting on this day has twice the value of other days. It is mostly dedicated toward education and success in business. Thursday, Brhaspativāra, is dedicated to Jupiter, ruler over education and scholarship. Friday, Śiukravāra, is ruled by Venus. Fasting on this day is dedicated to prosperity, marriage, and a harmonious family life. Saturday, Śianivāra, is ruled by Śiani or Saturn. Fasting on Saturday will give the blessing of Saturn and longevity.

Another aspect that is important to the ritual calendar is the phases of the moon. One pattern of fasting and abstinence, which relates to the phases of the moon, starts on new moon day, when the practitioner eats fourteen hands full of food. Then every next day one eats one handful less, until on the day of the full moon one eats nothing at all. During the waning moon one eats again one handful more each day, until the vow is completed on the next new moon day, when again fourteen hands full of food are eaten.

Generally, all kinds of vows of fasting and abstinence are practiced on the occasion of the many religious festivals celebrated during the course of the year, and also on the occasion of the Hindu rites, which are related to specific stages in life, such as birth, name-giving, first eating of solid food, puberty, the beginning of Vedic studies, marriage, and cremation.

On the other hand, certain foods are especially dedicated to certain deities. Such foods are regularly prepared at home and offered to the deity as part of certain festivals or during home worship, after which they are enjoyed by those present, and often also sent to relatives and friends. These special foods are also prepared and offered as part of the daily temple worship. After being offered to the deity, they are distrbuted as *prasāda* or sanctified food among the worshipers and visitors. Examples of such special food are rice prepared with black pepper and cumin fried in clarified butter or ghee, which is dedicated to Śiva; *laddu* or sweet balls for Krishna and Ganeśa; or rice prepared with tamarind, which is specially offered to Visnu. A person can also make a vow in connection with a certain deity to eat only the deity's special food for a period of time.

Some examples of this kind of *vrata* include twenty-one days of drinking only milk, or eating only the leaves of the bilva and banyan trees, after dipping them in water, a vow dedicated to Śiva. A fasting vow that is dedicated to Ganeśa is practiced from the day after the new moon in the month of Kārttika (October–November), through the sixth day of the waxing moon in the month of Mārgaśīrsa (November–December), which means complete fasting for three weeks. Those who follow this vow are given a yellow thread bound around their wrist, a *raksabandha*, worn on the right wrist for men and on the left for women. On the concluding day they give a donation of money to a priest as well as food, and then

613

they eat again. A vow for the goddess Devī involves complete fasting on the Friday in the month of Caitra (March–April). During the day the practitioner meditates on the goddess. The person concludes by offering *jagari*, which is raw sugar from sugarcane. After this worship one eats again. A vow dedicated to Visnu is called Vaikuntha *caturdasī* and involves complete fasting on the fourteenth day of the waxing and waning moon.

One other place where fasting is given great importance within the many traditions and practices of Hinduism is in Ayurveda and Siddha medicine. According to these traditional healing methods, fasting is considered one of the great medicines. Both apply fasting for the cleansing and balancing of the physical body, as well as for the emotions and the mind. Here three kinds of fasting are distinguished: purification fasts to clean the system; healing fasts to overcome a specific disorder; and austerity fasts, which are undertaken to deny the bodily urges on the way toward liberation from the cycle of rebirth.

Buddhism

According to the Buddhist tradition, Siddhārtha Gautama, the Buddha, lived between 560 and 480 B.C.E., although recent research indicates that he may have lived about a hundred years later. In that period northeast India was being transformed from a agricultural society to a more complex urban society. The ancient religious traditions of early Brahmanism no longer fitted the needs of society and of individuals. Therefore, many left society to find new religious ways, mostly by practicing asceticism. The Buddha was one of them. The Buddha used traditional ascetic practices including a very strict fast, reducing his intake of food to a few drops of bean soup a day. This starvation almost killed him, and he became aware of the fact that the body should not be ignored to arrive at man's spiritual core, but should be supported in a healthy and moderate way: no consciousness without a body; no experience of liberation or *nirvāna* without a body. After his "awakening" (*bodhi*) he formulated his "middle path," holding the middle between extreme asceticism and indulgence. This is the reason why fasting and abstinence in Buddhism are always placed within the context of the middle path.

In Asian as well as in Western Buddhist communities, certain traditions regarding food are followed in which there is a difference between the customs of laypeople and the stricter rules for monks and nuns. In general, Buddhists prefer to abstain from eating meat, since this involves the killing of living beings, although, even for the monks and nuns, there is no rule forbidding the eating of meat, unless the monk or nun, who is provided with a meal by a layperson, knows that the animal has been specially killed for the occasion. According to the monastic rules, the Vinaya, monks and nuns should have only two meals a day, in the early morning and before noon, and abstain from food for the rest of the day. One

of the reasons is that meditation practice is considered to be difficult if the stomach is full. On festive days, especially at full and new moon, and during meditation retreats, laypeople regularly follow those rules too. In lay Buddhist practice, the Hindu custom of sharing "sanctified" food or *prasāda*, food that is pure (no meat or sharp spices) and has been offered to monks and nuns or to statues of the Buddha or Buddhist deities, is also followed.

In the Buddhist practices of the Newars in the Kathmandu Valley, one finds observances, *vrata*, similar to those of the Hindus, in which fasting takes a prominent role, for example, in the observances connected with full and new moon, but also in those directed to a specific deity; for example, on the eighth day after full moon the fasting is held to honor the bodhisattva Avalokitesvara-Lokesvara, the embodiment of compassion. During public or private ritual performances fasting is observed to maintain purity. And, similar to the Hindu custom, an observance is also a way to achieve a specific spiritual or material goal. Some examples include the fasting for Lokesvara, which is supposed to cause the birth of a son; a fast for Tārā, which frees one from illness, dangers, pain, and untimely death; a fast for Hārītī protects against smallpox; and other deities are invoked by following rules of purity, including abstaining from sex, and fasting for good jobs, before an exam, or before going on a journey.

See also **Buddhism; China; Hinduism; India; Religion and Food; Southeast Asia.**

BIBLIOGRAPHY

Gellner, David N. *Newar Buddhism and Its Hierarchy of Ritual.* Cambridge: Cambridge University Press, 1992.

Harvey, Peter. *An Introduction to Buddhist Ethics.* Cambridge: Cambridge University Press, 2000.

Johari, Harish. *Dhanwantari.* Calcutta: Rupa, 1992.

Klostermaier, Klaus K. *A Survey of Hinduism.* New York: State University of New York Press, 1989.

Stevenson, Mrs. Sinclair. *The Rites of the Twice-Born.* New Delhi: Oriental Books Reprint Corporation, 1971.

Raja Deekshitar
Ria Kloppenborg

ISLAM

The fast of the month of Ramadan is one of the five major obligations of individual Muslims (the other four being the pronunciation of the confession of God's Unity, the five daily prayers, the religious tax, and the pilgrimage to Mecca). The Qur'an, the holy book of Islam, charts a middle position—"Thus we have made you a community of the middle path" (2:143)—between the ascetic ideal of Christian monastic practices and the more materialistic style of Jewish religion. Islamic fasting during Ramadan is quite harsh by Western standards and includes a full month of total abstinence from food and drink during the hours between dawn and sunset, although the evenings are a time of joy and celebration. The period of fasting during Ramadan is not an individual religious exercise, but part of a great social event that binds individual Muslims collectively.

The Qur'an explains the significance of this time of prayer and abstinence. During the Medina period, which marked the last ten years of the life of the prophet Muhammad (570–632 C.E.), Muslims were instructed to join the Jews in prayer in the direction of Jerusalem, to the north. After the Jews of Medina refused to recognize Muhammad as a prophet and obstructed his ideal of an Islamic state, the Prophet received a revelation that his followers should turn to the Ka'aba of Mecca (to the south of Medina). The Qur'an (2:183–187) prescribes fasting during the month of Ramadan, but prior to Muhammad's revelation, followers observed the fast of the day of Atonement or Ashura, as did the Jews. The institution of the Ramadan fast marked a return to an older Arab tradition that included abstaining from warfare and blood feuds. (In the same chapter of the Qur'an a third Arab institution was restored and reinterpreted: the pilgrimage to Mecca [2:196–203].)

The fast of Ramadan was reinterpreted as an instrument for the forgiveness of sins. It was instituted in commemoration of the Prophet's first revelation, which occurred during that month (on the twenty-first, twenty-third, twenty-fifth, and twenty-seventh of Ramadan) and in awareness of God's decision about man's fate for the coming year. From dawn—in fact, from the moment when a black thread can be distinguished from a white one—until sunset nothing may enter the body through any of its parts. Therefore, not only are eating and drinking forbidden, but also the use of fragrant perfume and even sexual intercourse. Women who menstruate during this period are not allowed to observe fasting but must make up for the days they miss by fasting later on.

In the first generations after Muhammad the basis was laid for what is known as the *shari'a* or Islamic law. Scholars during the first century after Muhammad developed the rules for determining the beginning and end of the month of Ramadan. It is commonly accepted that some part of the new moon must be "seen" (physically or intellectually, i.e., directly observed or by calculation), although there is a divergence of opinion among Muslim communities concerning the correct method for defining the start and finish of the month of Ramadan. Travelers and those who are sick are excused from the fast, but even these exceptions are disputed, as are the various compensations for some days of fasting or the alms given to the poor.

In addition to the month of Ramadan, there are voluntary days of fasting for Muslims, such as the tenth day of Muharam (Ashura, a continuation of the Jewish day of atonement, although the Islamic lunar calendar does not

Bakers in the Old City of Jerusalem are selling holiday bread for Ramadan. PHOTO COURTESY OF AP/WORLD WIDE PHOTOS.

coincide with the solar calendar of Jews and Christians). For the very pious there is a voluntary fast on all Mondays and Thursdays.

Fasting not only constitutes abstinence from food. Pious Muslim preachers stress that fasting is more an exercise of the mind than of the body. The prophet Muhammad said, "He is not a good Muslim who eats his fill and leaves his neighbor hungry" (Glassé, p. 112). The mystical theologian al-Ghazali (d. 1111) proposed a category of fasting that included "other parts of the body" (besides the mouth and the sexual organs): The eyes and the hands should be kept under control and prevented from evil. Attention must be given to the poor during the month of Ramadan, and the special "alms tax" (*zakat fitra*) or "gift of breaking the fast" consists of 2.5 kilograms of rice or the equivalent in money given to the poor. Slander and gossip in particular are forbidden during Ramadan, and a saying from Muhammad supports this admonition: "If one does not give up saying false words and doing false deeds in Ramadan, giving up eating and drinking means nothing to Allah" (Buitelaar, p. 22).

Some preachers suggest that the daily fast should be followed by a light meal only and by many prayers. A folk custom ends a day of fasting in the manner of Muhammad: Commonly, a Muslim eats a date first, following the example of the Prophet. In countries where fresh dates are not available, they are imported from abroad to facilitate this custom of the believers. It is also quite common for Muslims to invite friends and relatives to their homes on certain days so that they might experience this rewarding moment together after a full day of fasting: breaking the fast together with a first light meal (*iftar*, literally meaning the breaking snack), accompanied by the pious words of a preacher.

Local kitchens serve a great variety of dishes during the evenings of Ramadan. In the Indonesian province of

Aceh, known for its devout Islam, believers eat *beras tape*, a porridge of fermented sweet rice, as their first snack after a day of fasting. Because of the process of fermentation, this snack contains a significant amount of alcohol, but it is considered a traditional food, not a drink, and is therefore acceptable to pious Muslims. Fish is not considered a good choice for Ramadan meals because it is too light and does not provide a good base for the next day of fasting. A tomato soup (*harira*) that is prepared with a variety of vegetables and beef, buffalo, or lamb is much more substantial and provides longer-lasting nutrition. In countries of the Middle East it is closely identified with the celebration of Ramadan. Sometimes before dawn a heavy "breakfast" (*sahur*) is consumed in preparation for a full day of fasting. Buitelaar mentions (p. 47) a daily meal of rabbit that is eaten at 3:00 A.M. in Morocco.

After Ramadan, on the first day of the month of Shawwal, the so-called small festival is celebrated. A major festival also occurs on the tenth day of the month of the *hajj*, when the sacrifice of Abraham is recalled, but the end of Ramadan brings the greatest joy to Muslims: Relatives are visited and many types of sweets are consumed. In Turkey, this celebration is known as the sugar festival, a celebration also marked in recent decades in parts of Europe where Turkish migrants have settled.

Some mystical or local groups have developed special kinds of fasting, which are either not generally accepted or even denounced by other Muslims. In order to obtain special favors from God, Muslims in Indonesia, especially on the island of Java, practice the *mutihan*, or "white fasting." Muslims there only eat white rice and boiled eggs, and they drink plain ("white") water during a certain period, often to implement a vow. Members of the Khalidiyah branch of the Naqshbandiyah brotherhood practice *suluk* (spiritual travel) or *khalwat* (loneliness), a forty-day period of abstinence from meat and some other dishes; believers also refrain, as much as possible, from talking. Their opponents blame them for introducing a Christian habit (forty days of fasting, and abstinence from meat) into a well-defined Muslim regulation.

The Islamic rules on *haram* (forbidden) foods and drink, such as pork and wine, are not considered akin to the pious acts of fasting or abstinence, but rather are part of the regular observance of taboos and are therefore beyond the scope of this entry.

In many regions and during different periods of Muslim culture, ascetic and mystical movements have introduced elements of abstinence, some from sexual intercourse, others from various luxuries such as perfumes during certain periods. For the especially pious and for those who make special vows, milk and meat are avoided, and there are even vows of abstinence from sleep.

In modern Muslim communities, both in countries with Muslim majorities and also in the new Muslim diaspora in Western countries, the fast of Ramadan is one of the most carefully observed aspects of Islamic custom.

Even among secularized Muslims, who do not say their prayers five times each day or who only very seldom join the Friday prayers, there is an attempt to keep the fast for part of the month of Ramadan, as a way of keeping in touch with their spiritual and cultural roots. As with those who are more devout, the festive moment in which the fast is broken is a central element. In 1963 Ahmad Hasan al-Zayyat, the editor of the journal of the Al-Azhar mosque and university in Cairo, commented bitterly on the way of fasting: "We do not have any more thirty days of fasting, but thirty days of breaking the fast" (Goitein, p. 108). This comment may reflect the general practice of fasting and abstinence found in Islamic culture, where a middle path has been found: between strict religious and cultural interpretation, between individual piety and communal belief. The middle path of Islamic fasting and abstinence lies between asceticism and pure materialism.

See also **Christianity**; **Feasts, Festivals, and Fasts**; **Islam**; **Judaism**; **Middle East**; **Ramadan**.

BIBLIOGRAPHY

Buitelaar, Marjo. "Fasting and Feasting in Morocco. An Ethnographic Study of the Month of Ramadan." Ph.D. diss., Nijmegen University, 1991.

Glassé, Cyril. *The Concise Encyclopaedia of Islam.* London: Stacey International, 1989.

Goitein, S. D. *Studies in Islamic History and Institutions.* Leiden: Brill, 1968.

Parshall, Phil. *Inside the Community. Understanding Muslims through Their Traditions.* Grand Rapids, Mich.: Baker Books, 1994, pp. 196–201.

Qardawi, Yusuf. *The Lawful and the Prohibited in Islam.* Indianapolis, Ind.: American Trust Publications, 1990.

Wagtendonk, Kees. *Fasting in the Qur'an.* Leiden: Brill, 1969.

Karel Steenbrink

JUDAISM

The phenomenon of fasting in the variegated history of Judaism has its roots in the biblical text. Though it is not entirely clear why and when this practice arose, it is certain that in ancient Israel, abstaining from food and drink on both the individual and communal level was considered an act of piety that one would (in most cases spontaneously) undertake as a means of entreating God's compassion or in the hope of averting divine punishment (Judges 20:26; 1 Kings 21:9, 27; 1 Sam. 7:6; 2 Sam. 12:16, 22; Jer. 14:12, 36:6, 9; Joel 1:14, 2:12, 15; Jonah 3:5; Ps. 35:13, 69:11–12; Esther 4:16; Dan. 9:3; Ezra 8:21, 23; Neh. 1:4; 2 Chron. 20:3) or as a sign of mourning and lament (1 Sam. 31:13; 2 Sam. 1:12; 12; Zech. 7:5; Esther 4:3; Ezra 10:6; Dan. 10:2–3; 1 Chron. 10:12).

Fixed Fasts

The four fixed fast days mentioned by the post-exilic prophet Zechariah relate to calamities centered about the destruction of Jerusalem and the Temple (Zech. 8:19): the fast of the fourth month corresponds to what is celebrated as the seventeenth of Tammuz, which marks the breaching of the walls of the city (in 2 Kings 25:4 and Jer. 39:2 the date is the ninth); the fast of the fifth month, the ninth of Av when the Temple was destroyed (in 2 Kings 25:8 and Jer. 52:12–13 the date is the tenth); the fast of the seventh month, the third of Tishrei when Gedaliah, the Babylonian-appointed governor of Judah, was murdered (2 Kings 25:25, Jer. 41:1–2); and the fast of the tenth month, the tenth of Tevet, which marks the beginning of the siege of Jerusalem by Nebuchadnezzar, king of Babylon (2 Kings 25:1–2, Jer. 52:4). The custom to fast on the thirteenth of Adar, the day before the holiday of Purim, which celebrates the downfall of Haman and the redemption of the Jewish people, does not commemorate a tragedy in Jewish history but rather stands as a reminder of a precarious moment when disaster was averted (Esther 4:16).

By contrast, the Day of Atonement, Yom Kippur (celebrated on the tenth day of the seventh month, which is enumerated as the first month of the new year), the one fast specified in the Pentateuch, is part of the afflicting of the body—according to later rabbinic law this comprises five forms of self-denial: abstention from eating, washing, anointing, wearing shoes, and cohabitation; Mishnah Yoma 8:1—that is a means of purification from transgression (Lev. 16:29–34, 23:27–32; Num. 29:7–11). From other verses we can deduce that refraining from eating and drinking was considered one of various methods of abstinence by which one could afflict the body, acts that were often accompanied by oaths and vows (Num. 30:2–16; Dan. 10:12). There is evidence to suggest that fasting was also practiced as preparation for communing with the spirits of the dead (1 Sam. 28:20). The narrative about Moses being with God for the forty days in which he wrote the tablets of law specifies that during that time he neither ate bread nor drank water, indicating that he was in a transformed state wherein the normal physical needs could be discarded (Exod. 34:28; Deut. 9:9, 18), a theme that is applied as well to Elijah when he had the theophany on Horeb, the mountain of God (1 Kings 19:8–12). In the case of Daniel as well, acts of prayer, which included fasting, were answered with a vision of the divine (Dan. 9:20–27, 10:7–21).

Abstention from food was considered one of the several typical acts of humbling oneself, which may have included renting one's clothes, lying in sackcloth, walking about in a subdued posture, sleeping on the floor, and not washing, anointing, or changing one's clothes (2 Sam. 1:11–12, 12:16–20; 1 Kings 21:27; Jonah 3:5; Ps. 35:13, 69:12; Esther 4:3; Dan. 9:3; Neh. 9:1). Fasting could also accompany weeping and the offering of sacrifices (Judges 20:26; Joel 2:12) or the confession of one's iniquities (1 Sam. 7:6; Neh. 9:2; Dan. 9:4), but on occasion it takes the place of the sacrificial cult (Joel 1:13–14). The purpose of fasting as a ceremonial expression of remorse and supplication is underscored in the prophetic pronouncements against those who would fast without the proper intent as if God demanded of the Israelites external forms of self-affliction without commitment to act justly (Isa. 58:3–7; Jer. 14:12). Indeed, according to the messianic declaration of Zechariah, the fast days in Israel commemorating past suffering centered around the destruction of Jerusalem and the Temple would be transformed into occasions for joy provided there would be love of honesty and integrity (Zech. 8:19).

Fasting without repentance is of no value. In the Second Temple period, abstaining from eating and drinking continued to serve as a primary means of atonement, but in addition we have evidence that on occasion it functioned as an ascetic regimen that served to purify the heart and bring one closer to God, and even in some cases to induce an ecstatic state wherein a supernatural vision was granted (2 Bar. 12:5, 20:5–6, 43:3; 4 Ezra 5:13–20, 6:35–36). There is evidence from the rabbinic corpus that select individuals similarly fasted excessively in order to have visionary experiences (Palestinian Talmud, Kil'ayim 9:4, 32b), a phenomenon attested as well in the Heikhalot literature, the magical and mystical texts that began to take shape roughly during the time that Judaism and Christianity began to emerge as distinct liturgical communities. We know little about the social background of the individuals responsible for these texts, but we can conclude with some degree of certainty that they adopted ascetic practices, primarily fasting and sexual renunciation, as preparation for dream-vision, angelic adjuration, or heavenly ascent. In the tenth century, a leading rabbinic figure, Hai Gaon, summarized these older practices by saying that anyone who wished to gaze at the chariot must "sit fasting for a specified number of days, place his head between his knees, and whisper to the earth many prescribed songs and hymns." It is likely that fasting or even a restricted diet (together with sexual abstinence) was viewed as means by which the human could be transformed into an angelic being, a prerequisite for the attainment of the visionary encounter with an angel or the glory.

Perhaps some of the rabbis developed a critical stance vis-à-vis fasting as an appropriate form of piety to combat such individuals and their anomian customs. Thus, a dictum is transmitted in the name of R. Yose: "An individual is not permitted to torment himself in fasting lest he fall upon the community and they will need to support him" (Tosefta, Ta'anit 2:12). According to another statement attributed to Samuel, "Whoever sits in a fast is called a sinner" (Babylonian Talmud, Ta'anit 11a). In the words of a maxim ascribed to Reish Laqish, "the scholar is not permitted to sit and fast for it diminishes the work of heaven" (Babylonian Talmud, Ta'anit 11b). Finally, Rav reportedly declared that "in the future a man will have to give an account for everything that his eye saw but he did not eat" (Palestinian Talmud, Qiddushin 4:12, 66b).

An especially interesting concern for the rabbis was the abstinent woman whose constant fasting "causes her to lose virginity" (Palestinian Talmud, Sotah 3:4, 19a). Indeed, on account of the reduced intake of food she is called the "fasting virgin," a term that suggests that the challenge such a woman posed was that she disrupted the societal expectations by abdicating the domestic responsibility of child bearing. In contrast to early Christianity where virginity and fasting were considered virtuous acts of piety, the rabbinic sages castigated the woman who adopted an ascetic lifestyle with regard to sexuality and eating. According to one rabbinic ruling, the ascetic woman is enumerated among those who bring destruction to the world (Mishnah, Sotah 3:4), an expression meant to convey that female celibacy results in the breakdown of marital life and the bearing of progeny.

Additional Fasts

The basic approach to fasting was continued by the rabbis who, in their characteristic fashion, codified specific regulations to fashion the biblical references into binding rituals. In addition, the rabbis decreed additional fasts in the course of the calendar, generally associated with the fixed fasts and other calamitous events in biblical and postbiblical history. Yet, the rabbinic authorities were opposed to extreme forms of abstinence, including fasting, as we find, for instance, in the Therapeutaue community described by Philo, early Christian communities, and the individuals whose experiences are preserved in the Heikhalot texts. It must be pointed out, however, that the rabbinic sources themselves yield proof that some members of the academies were more positively disposed toward voluntary abstinence as a way to cultivate the highest form of piety. Thus, there is substantial textual evidence to indicate that sages (many from the third and fourth centuries) undertook excessive fasts as part of an ascetic lifestyle, to attain an extraordinary experience (usually of a visual nature), or for penance (Palestinian Talmud, Kil'ayim 9:3, 32b, Ta'anit 2:13, 66a, Nedarim 9:2, 40d; Babylonian Talmud, Pesahim 68b, Hagigah 22b, Qiddushin 80b, Baba Metsi'a 85a, Nazir 52b).

Additionally, there is verification that some rabbis preserved an ancient custom, apparently initiated in the land of Israel, to fast every week on Monday and Thursday (Palestinian Talmud, Ta'anit 1:6, 64c; Babylonian Talmud, Shabbat 24a, Ta'anit 12a), and there is as well confirmation of the fact that some considered fasting appropriate for Sabbath (Babylonian Talmud, Pesahim 68b, Beitsah 15b) even though others clearly thought the opposite and prohibited fasting on Sabbath (Palestinian Talmud, Ta'anit 3:13, 67a, Nedarim 8:10, 40d), maintaining that Sabbath is a day of joy and rest, the sanctification of which involves physical pleasure, encompassing eating and drinking (Palestinian Talmud, Shabbat 15:3, 15a; Babylonian Talmud, Berakhot 32b). A residue of the former orientation is found in the ruling that fasting because of a troubling dream (ta'anit halom) is allowed even on Sabbath (Genesis Rabbah 44:12; Babylonian Talmud, Berakhot 31b, Ta'anit 12b). Interestingly, the routine of fasting on Sabbath was revived in the twelfth and thirteenth centuries by figures like Judah he-Hasid, the leader of the Rhineland German Pietists (Hasidei Ashkenaz), who adopted an ascetic form of devotion, and we even have a report by Avigdor ben Elijah ha-Kohen that Judah fasted on Rosh Hashanah, the Jewish New Year, a practice followed by other rabbis connected to this group, such as Abraham Haldiq of Bohemia, though by no means accepted by everyone. Finally, there are rhetorical flourishes in rabbinic literature that assign supreme theurgical significance to fasting as a means of atonement. Perhaps the best illustration of this approach is the prayer offered by Rav Sheshet before God, which is predicated on the symbolic equation of fasting and sacrifices: "May it be your will to account my fat and blood, which have been diminished, as if I sacrificed them before you on the altar, and you should find favor with me" (Babylonian Talmud, Berakhot 17a).

In spite of the admonitions against excessive fasting, it must be said that an ascetic tendency is well entrenched in the classical rabbinic corpus, an orientation that served as the foundation for pietists and mystics at later stages of Jewish history. In particular, the Rhineland Pietists and the Provençal and Spanish kabbalists of the twelfth and thirteenth centuries cultivated ascetic practices to attain a state of holiness and removal from the bondage of the corporeal world, in part based on earlier mystical tracts. An especially important part of the pietistic regimen was fasting, which, together with sexual abstention, was viewed as the mechanism by which the mortal being could be transmuted into an angel. For example, Eleazar of Worms, another leading member of the Hasidei Ashkenaz, chronicles an elaborate ceremony for the transmission of the divine name, which involved ritual immersion, being clad in white clothes, and fasting. Acts of self-denial and self-affliction were considered to be the way of fulfilling the hidden will of God.

Kabbalistic Piety

In kabbalistic literature as well we find a central concern with fostering an ascetic piety predicated on acts of behavior that transform the human into an angel. Moreover, kabbalists articulated a contemplative goal of union with God, which is often described as the merging of the finite and infinite will, as we find in Azriel of Gerona, Jacob ben Sheshet, and the authors of the Zohar. The rabbinic analogy comparing fasting to sacrifice played a crucial role in shaping the mystical sensibility of offering one's heart fully to God and subjugating desire (Zohar 2:20b, 119b, 153a). From the symbolic vantage point endorsed by kabbalists, fasting is the instrument by which one becomes a sacrifice and is submerged thereby in the Godhead. In somewhat different terminology, but expounding a similar ascetic ideal, in zoharic literature the members of the mystical fraternity engaged in Torah study are said to partake of the spiritual food that angels eat, the "bread of the mighty" (*lehem 'abirim*) (Ps. 78:25), the overflow of divine wisdom, rather than the coarse food of this world (Zohar 2:61b). With this idea we reach the paradoxical reversal characteristic of mystical insight: abstention is genuine consumption.

Utilizing an older midrashic gloss (Leviticus Rabbah 20:10) on the verse "And they saw the God of Israel, and they ate and drank" (Exod. 24:11), the kabbalists affirm that this refers to an "actual eating," which does not entail physical ingestion, but deriving sustenance from basking in the visual presence of God, a state applied to the righteous and angels in the world to come (Zohar 1:104a, 2:126a). By fasting the kabbalist anticipates that condition in this world and thus has a foretaste of the food that is perpetually fulfilling.

See also **Buddhism; Christianity; Feasts, Festivals, and Fasts; Hinduism; Islam; Jewish Food; Judaism; Middle East; Religion and Food; Sin and Food.**

BIBLIOGRAPHY

Fraade, Steven. "Ascetical Aspects of Ancient Judaism." In *Jewish Spirituality from the Bible to the Middle Ages*, edited by Arthur Green, pp. 253–288. New York: Crossroad, 1986.

Hecker, Joel. "Eating Gestures and the Ritualized Body in Medieval Jewish Mysticism." *History of Religions* 40 (2000): 125–152.

Kanarfogel, Ephraim. *Peering through the Lattices: Mystical, Magical, and Pietistic Dimensions in the Tosafist Period.* Detroit: Wayne State University Press, 2000.

Swartz, Michael D. *Scholastic Magic: Ritual and Revelation in Early Jewish Mysticism.* Princeton: Princeton University Press, 1996.

Weinstein, Sara E. *Piety and Fanaticism: Rabbinic Criticism of Religious Stringency.* Northvale, N.J.: Jason Aronson, 1997.

Wolfson, Elliot R. "Eunuchs Who Keep the Sabbath: Becoming Male and the Ascetic Ideal in Thirteenth-Century Jewish Mysticism." In *Becoming Male in the Middle Ages*, edited by Jeffrey J. Cohen and Bonnie Wheeler, pp. 151–185. New York: Garland, 1997.

Elliot R. Wolfson

FATS. Fat is a generic term for triacylglycerols, which are a class of structurally similar chemical compounds that contain three fatty acid molecules that are linked or chemically esterified to one glycerol molecule (Figure 1). Mammals store triacylglycerol as lipid droplets in specialized cells referred to as adipocytes, which compose the white or yellow tissue known as adipose or neutral fat tissue. White fat has several functions in mammals. It is a reservoir for storing excess energy obtained from the diet. Fatty acids are a dense storage form of chemical energy in mammals. Adipose tissue also has an important role in padding and thereby protecting various organs throughout the body from temperature extremes and physical impact or trauma. Triacylglycerol, when converted to phospholipid, is a primary constituent of cell membranes and therefore is critical for all forms of life. Mammals also contain brown fat in various locations throughout the body including the neck, thorax, and abdomen. Brown fat functions to generate body heat and therefore it is an important tissue for energy expenditure, otherwise referred to as "burning calories." Brown fat can generate heat because it contains mitochondria with a unique and specialized function. In most other cells, mitochondria are the energy-producing compartments in the cell that generate adenosine triphosphate (ATP), which is a chemical form of cellular energy that is required for numerous cellular chemical reactions. In brown fat, the energy generated by mitochondria is used to generate heat. Brown fat cells contain an "uncoupling" protein that diverts energy away from ATP synthesis and toward heat production. Energy utilization by brown fat is tightly regulated by signals it receives from the sympathetic nervous system. Animals that are adapted to cold temperatures display increased heat production from brown fat, and brown fat is proportionally more abundant in infants than in adults.

Classes of Fatty Acids

Fatty acids are a diverse family of structurally similar carbon chains that contain a single carboxylic acid group (see Figure 1). Fatty acids differ from one another by their carbon chain length, which is usually an even number of carbons that can exceed twenty carbon atoms. Fatty acids are often categorized as short-chain, medium-chain, or long-chain fatty acids because each of these groups displays distinct physical properties. Short-chain fatty acids contain up to seven carbon molecules and are liquids even at cold temperatures. Medium-chain fatty acids, which contain between eight and twelve carbons, are liquids at room temperature but solidify when refrigerated. Long-chain fatty acids contain greater than twelve carbons and are solids at room temperature, but liquefy at elevated temperatures. Long-chain fatty acids are the most abundant fatty acids in plant and animal foods. Short-chain fatty acids are found in whole cow's milk, and medium-chain fatty acids are abundant in coconut milk.

Fatty acids also differ by the number and location of carbon–carbon double bonds, otherwise called the degree of saturation. Saturated fatty acids do not contain any carbon–carbon double bonds because all carbon molecules are "saturated" with hydrogen molecules. The most abundant saturated dietary fatty acids are palmitic and stearic acids, which are long-chain fatty acids found in foods derived from animals and are abundant in meat and dairy products (Table 1; see Figure 1). Monounsaturated fatty acids contain a single carbon–carbon double bond (see Figure 1). Oleic acid is a monounsaturated fatty acid and a common dietary component found in canola and olive oil. Polyunsaturated fatty acids contain up to six carbon–carbon double bonds that are always separated by

FIGURE 1

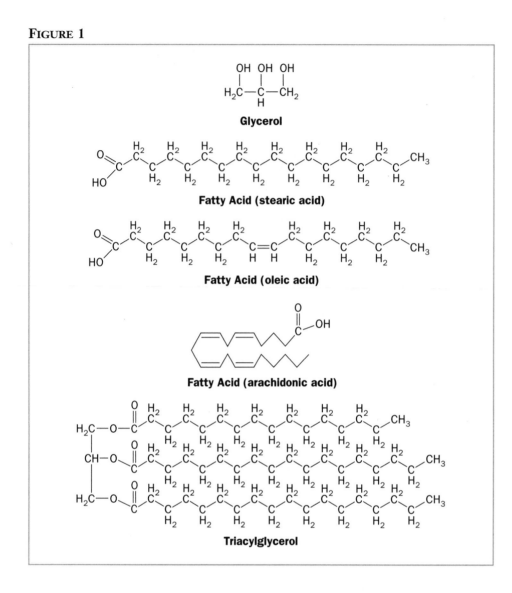

Glycerol

Fatty Acid (stearic acid)

Fatty Acid (oleic acid)

Fatty Acid (arachidonic acid)

Triacylglycerol

a methylene group (—CH₂—) (Figure 1). Polyunsaturated fatty acids that contain a series of double bonds that begins between the third and fourth carbon from the methyl or omega end of the molecule (see nomenclature system below) are referred to as omega-3 fatty acids. Linolenic, eicosapentaenoic (EPA), and docosahexaenoic (DHA) are omega-3 fatty acids and flaxseed oil, walnut oil, and fatty fish are good sources of omega-3 fatty acids. Omega-6 fatty acids are another class of polyunsaturated fatty acids that includes linoleic acid and arachidonic acid. They contain a series of carbon–carbon double bonds that begin between the sixth and seventh carbon from the omega end of the fatty acid. Linoleic acid is the most common omega-6 fatty acid in Western-style diets and is found in corn, safflower, and soy oils.

The fatty acid composition of triglycerols found in mammals is usually complex and is influenced by the fatty acid consumed in the diet and by the tissue where it re-

sides. The most common fatty acids in humans are 16, 18, and 20 carbons in length, but longer-chain fatty acids are found in the central nervous system. Most diets contain mixtures of all types of fatty acids, but saturated and monounsaturated fatty acids constitute the vast majority of fatty acids that are consumed in a typical Western diet. A single triacylglycerol molecule rarely contains three identical fatty acids.

Essential Fatty Acids

Rodents placed on a fat-restricted diet are growth impaired, infertile, and develop lesions in the skin and kidney. These pathologies are not observed if the diet is supplemented with linolenic (omega-3) and linoleic acid (omega-6). The results of these studies indicated that mammals cannot synthesize these fatty acids and therefore that these fatty acids are essential components of a healthy diet. Human deficiencies of these essential fatty acids are rare but can occur in infants and children or as a result of intestinal absorption disorders. Human essential fatty acid deficiency compromises liver function, results in unhealthy skin, and impairs growth and development in infants including impaired cognitive function, visual acuity, and hearing.

Essential fatty acids are necessary to maintain the architecture of cell membranes and the integrity of the skin. They are also precursors for the synthesis of eicosanoids ("eicosa" meaning twenty carbons in length), which are bioactive, hormone-like compounds derived from linoleic and linolenic acid. The eicosanoids include prostaglandins, which elicit numerous and varied biological responses including induction of labor, regulation of the female reproductive cycle, and modification of pituitary function. Thromboxane is an eicosanoid that functions in platelet aggregation and blood clotting; leukotrienes function in the inflammation and allergic responses. The omega-3 fatty acid alpha-linolenic acid is also a precursor for eicosapentaenoic acid (EPA) and docohexaenoic acid (DHA) synthesis. Both DHA and arachidonic acid are important for nervous system and retina development. DHA may be an essential dietary fatty acid for preterm infants because studies indicate that it is not synthesized in sufficient quantities to meet the infant's needs.

There is no Recommended Dietary Allowance (RDA) for essential fatty acids. The minimal adequate adult intake of omega-6 fatty acids is estimated to be 2 to 4 g/day of linoleic acid. Americans normally consume about 10 to 15 g/day. The minimal adequate adult intake of omega-3 fatty acids is estimated to be 0.2 to 0.4 g/day, but intakes as high as 3 g/day may have added benefit. Omega-3 fatty acid intakes should be increased during pregnancy and lactation. The World Health Organization recommends an omega-6/omega-3 ratio of 4:1 to 10:1.

Fatty Acids Derived from Food Processing
Synthetic or unnatural types of fatty acids are also common components of Western diets and result from food processing. Fats are processed to increase their shelf life and to alter their physical properties. Monounsaturated and unsaturated fatty acids are chemically inert, whereas polyunsaturated fats are susceptible to oxidation. Polyunsaturated fatty acids degrade by oxidation and become rancid, thereby spoiling foods that contain these compounds. Therefore, products containing polyunsaturated fatty acids tend to have a reduced shelf life, but can be stabilized by converting the polyunsaturated fatty acids contained within these products to more stable monounsaturated and saturated fatty acids through the process of chemical hydrogenation. This processes converts carbon–carbon double bonds to single bonds (Reaction 1):

—HC=CH— → —2HCNCH$_2$
(Reaction 1; Chemical Hydrogenation)

FAT AND HEART DISEASE

Risk for heart disease results from excess fat consumption and the type of fat that is present in the diet. Diets high in saturated fatty acids, especially those found in animal fat, increase the concentration of low-density lipoprotein (LDL) cholesterol or "bad" cholesterol. Elevations in serum LDL concentrations increase risk for arteriosclerosis. Consumption of *trans*-fatty acids, although only representing between 2 and 4 percent of calories in Western diets, also increases risk for heart disease, but the pathogenic mechanisms are not certain. *Trans*-fatty acids may be as efficient as natural saturated fat in increasing serum LDL concentrations, and their consumption replaces foods that contain beneficial unsaturated fatty acids. Consumption of omega-3 and omega-6 fatty acids, especially when they replace consumption of saturated fat, decreases risk for heart disease, in part by lowering LDL cholesterol levels. Omega-3 fatty acids are more protective than omega-6 fatty acids. Omega-6 fatty acids may lower serum HDL cholesterol, which is harmful because HDL protects the heart from disease. Omega-3 fatty acids may prevent heart disease by improving immune function, lowering blood pressure, and inhibiting the growth of plaques on blood vessel walls. Omega-3 fatty acids obtained from whole food sources such as fatty fish seems to be more beneficial than dietary supplements.

This process not only stabilizes food, but also changes its physical properties. For example, margarine is produced by the chemical hydrogenation of vegetable oils. This process produces a product that is more stable and solid than vegetable oil and mimics the consistency of natural butter. However, chemical hydrogenation of polyunsaturated fatty acids also results in the formation of "unnatural" *trans*-fatty acids, which are normally found only in trace quantities in foods from natural sources. *Trans*-fatty acids do not differ from natural fatty acids in their carbon chain length or degree of saturation, but differ in the orientation or stereochemistry of the carbon–carbon double bonds. Carbon–carbon double bonds can exist in both a *cis* (the hydrogen atoms that are attached to the carbon atoms that flank the double bond reside on a common plane) or *trans* (hydrogen atoms reside on different planes) conformation; this is a fundamental principle of organic stereochemistry. The double bonds present in fatty acids from natural, unprocessed food sources usually exist in the *cis* conformation (see Figure 1). *Trans*-fatty acids are abundant in foods that undergo chemical hydrogenation and their consumption may increase risk for disease.

Nomenclature of Fatty Acids

All fatty acids can be identified by their "trivial" names, such as oleic or linoleic acid, but these names do not contain information that is necessary to infer their structure or physical properties, that is, the length of their carbon chains or the number and location of carbon–carbon double bonds. Therefore, a nomenclature system has been devised that describes the precise chemical structure of the molecule (see Table 1). The carbon atom that constitutes the carboxylic acid of the fatty acid is referred to as the *alpha carbon* and is designated as carbon number one; the methyl carbon that constitutes the other end of the molecule is referred to as the *omega carbon*. Fatty acids are named by the number of carbons in the chain and the number and location of carbon–carbon double bonds. For example, oleic acid is referred to as *cis*-9-octadecenoic acid, or 18:1(9); the 18 refers to the number of carbons in the fatty acid carbon chain, the 1 refers to the number of carbon–carbon double bonds, and the 9 in parentheses refers to the position of the double bond counting from the carboxylate carbon that is in the *cis* conformation.

Fatty acids as membrane components and emulsifiers.
Fatty acids and triglycerols are lipid soluble and there-

fore are hydrophobic molecules that do not dissolve readily in water (as evidenced by the appearance of distinct oil and water layers in many oil-based salad dressings). In aqueous environments, fatty acids aggregate and form ordered structures. All life forms have taken advantage of the hydrophobic properties of fatty acids to make cell membranes, which are semipermeable barriers that separate cells from their environment. Membranes delineate the boundaries of the cell, enable cells to retain water, and form specialized internal structures called subcellular organelles that include mitochondria, Golgi apparatus, and lysosomes. Cell membranes are lipid bilayers that are primarily composed of lipid and membrane-bound proteins. Fatty acids present in cell membranes are components of phospholipids, and phosphoglycerides are the most abundant phospholipids in membranes. Phosphoglycerides are similar in structure to triglycerols. They contain two fatty acid molecules and one phosphate molecule esterified to a glycerol molecule. The phosphate molecule has a hydrophilic amino acid or sugar molecule attached to it. Phospholipids are amphipathic molecules because one end of the molecule contains a water-soluble phosphate molecule, and the other end contains a lipid-soluble carbon chain of the fatty acids. Therefore, phospholipids are ideal components of cell membranes because the phosphate end can dissolve in water while the fatty acid end interacts with other lipid molecules to form a barrier that restricts the efflux of water.

The amphipathic properties of phospholipids make them effective *emulsifiers*, which are chemicals that interact with both water and oils and prevent them from separating and forming two layers. Lecithin is a phospholipid that is synthesized by mammals and is found in high concentrations in eggs. It is also an effective emulsifier and a common food additive in margarine, salad dressings, chocolate, and a variety of baked items. Fatty acids are components of many household products including lubricants, cooking oils, soaps, and detergents.

Dietary and Biosynthetic Sources of Fat

Fatty acids found in mammals are derived from both dietary sources and intracellular biosynthesis. Humans can synthesize all of the necessary fatty acids with the exception of the essential fatty acids. Fatty acids are synthesized in most cells from excess dietary carbohydrate, amino acids, and from other fatty acids. Palmitic acid (16:0) is synthesized by mammals and is a precursor for the synthesis of all other nonessential fatty acids. The carbon chain of palmitic acid is extended by the sequential addition of two carbons to the carboxy terminal end of the molecule. This is an enzyme catalyzed reaction that uses acetyl coenzyme A (CoA) as a source of the two carbon atoms. Mono- and polyunsaturated fatty acids are synthesized by the desaturation of saturated fatty acids. The first double bond is formed between the C–9 and C–10 of palmitate or stearate to form palmitoleic or oleic acid. This is the first step in the synthesis of polyunsat-

TABLE 1

Classes of fatty acids

Trivial name	Systematic name	Numerical symbol
Saturated fatty acids		
Lauric acid	Dodecanoic	12:0
Myristic acid	Tetradecanoic	14:0
Palmitic acid	Hexadecanoic	16:0
Stearic acid	Octadecanoic	18:0
Monounsaturated fatty acids		
Palmitoleic acid	*cis*-9-hexadecenoic	16:1(9)
Oleic acid	*cis*-9-octadecenoic	18:1(9)
Polyunsaturated fatty acids (omega-6)		
Linoleic acid	*cis*,*cis*-9, 12-octadecadienoic	18:2 (9,12)
Arachidonic acid	All *cis*-5,8,11, 14-eicosatetraenoic	20:4 (5,8,11,14)
Polyunsaturated fatty acids (omega-3)		
Linolenic acid	All *cis*-9-12- 15-octadecatrienoic	18:3 (9,12,15)
EPA	All *cis*-5,8,11,14, 17-Eicosapentaenoic	20:5 (5,8,11,14,17)
DHA	All *cis*-4,7,10,13,16, 19-Docosahexaenoic	22:6 (4,7,10,13,16,19)

urated fatty acids. This reaction is inhibited by dietary polyunsaturated fatty acids but activated by insulin and thyroid hormone.

Triglycerols are synthesized by most tissues from glycerol 3-phosphate, an intermediate in carbohydrate metabolism, and chemically activated fatty acids known as fatty acyl CoAs. This reaction occurs most frequently in the liver and white adipose tissue. In the liver, triacylglycerol synthesis is necessary for the assembly of lipoproteins, whereas triacylglycerol synthesis in adipose tissue functions to create long-term energy stores for mammals. Although a storage form of energy, fat is a dynamic tissue. Triacylglycerols constantly undergo hydrolysis and resynthesis in adipocytes. Newly synthesized triacylglycerol molecules remain intact for only a few days.

Digestion and Transport
About 90 percent of dietary lipid is in the form of triacylglycerols, and typical adults consume about 60 to 150 g/day. During digestion, dietary lipids aggregate and form water-insoluble particles in the gut that must be disrupted before absorption. Specific enzymes in the stomach, called gastric lipases, and in the intestine, called pancreatic lipases, bind to the lipid droplets and catalyze the hydrolysis or removal of fatty acids from triacylglycerols resulting in the liberation of free fatty acids, diacylglycerols, and monoacylglycerols. Fatty acids are also liberated from phospholipids by pancreatic phospholipases. The products of triglycerol hydrolysis are made soluble by bile acids, which are negatively charged detergents that are synthesized from cholesterol in the liver and secreted into the duodenum. Bile acids form micelles, which are disc-shaped particles with a negatively charged exterior that is water soluble and a hydrophobic center that sequesters fatty acids. During digestion, liberated fatty acids are continuously transferred from lipid droplets to micelles. Virtually all free fatty acids are transported from the micelles into intestinal epithelial cells by passive diffusion. Lipids that cannot be made soluble are not absorbed and are excreted.

Once absorbed into the intestinal cells, short- and medium-chain fatty acids are released directly into blood and taken up by the liver. Long-chain fatty acids are resynthesized into triacylglycerols and complex with apolipoproteins to form lipid globules known as chylomicrons. Chylomicrons travel through the lymphatic system and then through the venous plasma. Most triacylglycerol in chylomicrons is metabolized by lipoprotein lipase that is bound to the surface of adipose and muscle cells.

Metabolism of Fat
Most fat cells are derived in infancy and adolescence except in instances of severe childhood obesity. As fat stores accumulate, adipocytes increase in size but generally not in number. Normal fat stores provide sufficient energy to sustain humans for several weeks during total starvation. During fasting, fatty acids are catabolized or broken down to acetyl-CoA, which is an intermediate in the citric acid cycle. This reaction requires carnitine, a derivative of the amino acid lysine. The oxidative breakdown of fatty acids occurs in mitochondria through a series of reactions known as beta-oxidation. Fatty acids are rich sources of energy; 44 moles of ATP are generated by the complete oxidation of 1 mole of a six-carbon fatty acid, whereas only 38 moles of ATP are generated from 1 mole of glucose, a six-carbon sugar. During starvation, acetyl-CoA can be converted to ketone bodies, which include acetone, acetoacetate and alpha-hydroxybutyrate. These compounds are produced exclusively in the liver but readily enter the circulatory system by passive diffusion. The odor associated with the generation of these ketones becomes apparent in the breath and urine of individuals. Ketone bodies are an alternative energy source for glucose during starvation, and are utilized by the brain and other tissues. Normally, ketones are rapidly metabolized by the peripheral tissues and do not accumulate in blood. However, if the citric acid cycle is depressed by low glucose due to starvation, diabetes mellitus, or a high-fat, low-carbohydrate diet, ketones accumulate in serum and a state of ketosis can result. High concentrations of ketones in blood can lower its pH and result in metabolic acidosis, which can be fatal during diabetic ketosis.

Fatty Acid Regulation of Gene Expression
Polyunsaturated fatty acids and eicosanoids are informational or signaling molecules that can influence the expression of certain genes involved in lipid synthesis, breakdown, and transport. Omega-3 and omega-6 polyunsaturated fatty acids lower the accumulation of triacylglycerol in muscle by inhibiting triacylglycerol synthesis in the liver and accelerating the breakdown of fatty acids in the liver and skeletal muscle. Linoleic and linolenic acid, as well as certain pharmaceuticals, bind to and activate the transcriptional activity of a family of related nuclear receptors known as the peroxisome proliferator–activator receptors (PPARs). These receptors are transcription factors that can directly bind DNA and elevate the transcription of genes. The target genes are involved in the metabolism, storage, and transport of lipids, triacylglycerol, and fatty acids. These receptors also regulate the differentiation of immature adipocytes into mature fat cells.

Individual members of the PPAR family have different functions. In the fasting liver, PPAR-alpha activates genes that encode enzymes that metabolize lipids to ketone bodies and decreases expression of genes involved in fatty acid synthesis. As fatty acids are hydrolyzed from triacyglyceride, PPAR-alpha is further activated. PPAR-alpha activates the expression of genes in fat cells that are necessary for fatty acid uptake, triacylglycerol synthesis, and fat storage.

PHARMACEUTICALS THAT TARGET FAT METABOLISM

Many of the most prevalent diseases in Western cultures are related to excessive caloric intake and sedentary lifestyles, diseases that include obesity, hyperlipidemia, diabetes, and arteriosclerosis. These states often occur in combination, and are diagnosed as syndrome x. Pharmaceutical have been developed to manage these disorders. These agents either inhibit intestinal fat absorption or affect fat metabolism by manipulating the activity of PPARs.

Fibrates (gemfibrozil, bezafibrate, fenofibrate) are pharmaceuticals that target and inhibit the function of PPAR-alpha. Thiazolidinediones target PPAR-alpha. Fibrates are effective in the treatment of cardiovascular disease. They function to elevate HDL levels by increasing the expression of proteins necessary for its structure, and decreasing plasma triglyceride by accelerating fatty acid oxidation in the liver. TZDs are effective in the treatment of Type 2 diabetes because they have a hypolipidemic and hypoglycemic effect.

Nondigestible commercial lipids have also been developed to limit total fat intake. One product, Olestra, contains fatty acids linked to the sugar sucrose. These products replace natural fat in foods, and were designed to taste like natural fat. However, they cannot be hydrolyzed in the gut and therefore are not absorbed. Other pharmaceuticals target and inhibit pancreatic lipase, such that natural dietary lipids are not broken down to fatty acids and therefore are not absorbed.

Determinants of Total Body Fat

Fat is a storage form of energy, and as such only accumulates when energy intake exceeds energy output. Total body fat accumulation is determined by complex interactions among genes, environment, and behavior. The human body can adjust to a wide range of fat intake, but both deficiency and excess are associated with disease. In a normal, healthy individual, fat stores constitute 12 to 18 percent of total body weight in males and 18 to 24 percent in females. Excessive consumption of high-calorie foods and/or a lack of exercise elevate fat stores. In some cases, the genetic background alone can determine total body fat in the absence of strict dietary control. Children with obese parents are at higher risk of becoming obese, and studies of identical twins also indicate that risk for obesity has a strong hereditary component. Furthermore, more than 75 percent of the Pima Indians are obese, again indicating a strong influence of genetics on fat accumulation. Many genes have been identified that control weight gain. The products of these genes regulate energy balance and expenditure and are signaling hormones that regulate appetite and fat metabolism. Some studies indicate that genetic factors, and the metabolic signals they generate, balance energy expenditure and appetite to form an individual's "set point" that specifies body weight. These signals include the satiety hormones such as serotonin and leptin. The neurotransmitter serotonin is responsible for "cravings" that can increase consumption of particular food types. Leptin is a peptide hormone that is secreted by fat cells and signals the hypothalamus. Leptin secretion is proportional to fat cell size, and increased leptin concentrations in blood signal the brain to increase energy expenditure and decrease food intake. Mice lacking the leptin gene or the leptin receptor become obese. Human mutations in the leptin gene are rare but result in obesity.

Dietary Fat and Disease Risk

Lipids constitute about 33 percent of total energy intake in the typical North American diet, whereas Japanese diets have a lower fat intake (11 percent of energy from fat). Western-style diets are deficient in omega-3 fatty acids and contain excess omega-6 fatty acids. Some evidence indicates that prehistoric diets that were consumed through much of human evolution contained an omega-6/omega-3 fatty acid ratio that was near 1.0, whereas this ratio is about 20 in the typical Western diet. Vegetarian diets also tend to contain excess omega-6 fatty acids. Diets deficient in omega-3 fatty acids or diets that contain an elevated omega-6/omega-3 ratio may increase risk for cardiovascular disease and cancer.

Research over the past few decades has indicated that excess consumption of saturated fat increases risk for disease including heart disease (arteriosclerosis), obesity, diabetes, and certain cancers (see "Fat and Heart Disease"). Obesity is a clinical condition defined as having a body weight that is greater than 20 percent above a desirable body weight standard or a body mass index that exceeds 30 kg/m². Obesity occurs in epidemic proportions in the United States and other Western societies, especially in individuals from lower socioeconomic level. Its prevalence is rapidly increasing in developing societies that are adapting Western lifestyles. The combination of increased fat intake and sedentary lifestyle (otherwise referred to as excess energy intake) increases risk for overweight and obesity. Increased body fat, in turn, is an independent risk for heart disease, diabetes, and high blood pressure. Elevated fat intake can also increase risk for cancers of the colon, prostate, and breast. The incidence of cancers of the breast is high in populations with high intakes of either natural saturated fat or *trans*-fatty acids, but not diets rich in olive oil, which contains high levels of monounsaturated fatty acids. High polyunsaturated fat intake in the form of linoleic acid (omega-6) increases risk for breast cancer incidence in mice, compared to diets high in omega-3 fatty acids.

Cultures in which traditional foods have high concentrations of monounsaturated fats, products that include olive oil and fish, have lower incidence of heart disease compared to the United States. The prevalence of heart disease in Mediterranean countries is only 50 percent of that found in the United States, even when fat represents almost 40 percent of total energy intake. However, the decreased rates of heart diseases in these countries also reflects other dietary patterns including a high consumption of fresh fruits and vegetables and other lifestyle differences.

See also **Assessment of Nutritional Status; Body Composition; Cholesterol; Gene Expression, Nutrient Regulation of; Mediterranean Diet; Nutrition.**

BIBLIOGRAPHY

Berdanier, Carolyn D., and James L. Hargrove. "Nutrient Receptors and Gene Expression." In *Nutrition and Gene Expression*, edited by Carolyn D. Berdanier and James L. Hargrove, pp. 207–226. Boca Raton, Fla.: CRC Press, 1993.

Devlin, Thomas M. *Biochemistry*, 5th ed. New York: Wiley-Liss, 2002.

Kersten, Sander, Beatrice Desvergne, and Walter Wahli. "Roles of PPARs in Health and Disease." *Nature* 405 (2000): 421–424.

Simopoulos, Artemis P. "The Mediterranean Diets: What Is So Special About the Diet of Greece?" *Journal of Nutrition* 131 (2001): 3065S–3073S.

Smolin, Lori A., and Mary B. Grosvenor. *Nutrition, Science and Application*. Philadelphia: Saunders College Publishing, 2000.

Stipanuk, Martha H. *Biochemical and Physiological Aspects of Human Nutrition*. Philadelphia: W. B. Saunders, 2000.

Patrick J. Stover

FAUCHON, AUGUSTE FÉLIX.

Auguste Félix Fauchon (1856–1939) was a Parisian grocer who founded Fauchon, the luxury food store in the Place de la Madeleine in the 8th Arrondissement in Paris. Fauchon, who was born in Calvados, left school and moved to Paris, where he bought a wagon to peddle fruit and vegetables outside La Madeleine. In 1886, he bought a small shop across from the church, where he began to specialize in high-quality foods including charcuterie, cheeses, poultry, confectionery, and wines, as well as produce.

Fauchon became more and more popular among the rich and fashionable of Paris along with its reputation for quality, luxury, and exclusivity. During Fauchon's lifetime, his shop sold only French products; importing exotic items from outside France remained the domain of the neighboring grocery owned by Fauchon's friend Ferdinand Hédiard.

Between the two world wars, Fauchon expanded his operation to include a catering service, a tea and pastry salon, and a food laboratory to prepare products such as confits and bottled fruit. After his death, the company added specialty items from around the world and continued to develop its own luxury products, including teas, honeys, jams, spices, pâtés, chocolates, and pastries.

Today, Fauchon includes several departments, including the tea salon, wine cellar, patisserie, charcuterie, produce shop, and épicerie for Fauchon-brand products, including teas, coffees, and spices.

See also **Hédiard, Ferdinand.**

BIBLIOGRAPHY

Cranford, Helen. "Sold in the Best Possible Taste." *Daily Telegraph* (London, 1 April 1998).

"Fauchon, Auguste Félix." In *Larousse gastronomique*, edited by Prosper Montagné. New York: Clarkson Potter, 2001.

Gardner-Loew. "Madame President." *Bon Appétit*, 36, Issue 5 (May 1991): 28.

Johnson, Margaret M. "World's Fare/Visit to Paris." Minneapolis *Star Tribune* (June 21, 1998): 7G.

MM Pack

FAVRE, JOSEPH.

For the first half of his career, Joseph Favre (1849–1903) followed the traditional path of a chef. He was apprenticed as a teenager in his native Swiss canton of Valais, and thereafter moved around Europe serving in aristocratic households, grand hotels, and restaurants in Switzerland, Germany, England, Italy, and France. In Paris he was also employed by the fashionable caterer Chevet, whose shop was located in the Palais Royal.

Once he had received recognition as a chef, Favre turned his attention to promoting the welfare and status of cooks, founding a professional society and a trade journal. He also wanted to bring the best of French cuisine to the masses, a view which put him at odds with some of his fellow chefs.

Favre wrote prolifically on all sorts of culinary topics, and in 1894 his articles were gathered together into the four-volume *Dictionnaire universel de cuisine: Encyclopédie illustrée d'hygiène alimentaire* (The universal dictionary of cuisine: illustrated encyclopedia of food health). The *Dictionnaire* contained thousands of recipes, menus, profiles of well-known people in the field (including Favre himself), and a history of cooking that was pronounced "very interesting" in Prosper Montagné's *Larousse gastronomique*. Today, manufacturers of traditional foods included in the *Dictionnaire* continue to use the mention by Favre as an endorsement for their products.

See also **Chef; France; *Larousse gastronomique*.**

BIBLIOGRAPHY

Favre, Joseph. *Dictionnaire universel de cuisine: Encyclopédie illustrée d'hygiène alimentaire* [The universal dictionary of cuisine: illustrated encyclopedia of food health]. Paris: Librairie-Imprimerie des Halles et de la Bourse de Commerce, 1894.

Montagné, Prosper. *Larousse gastronomique*. New York: Crown, 1961.

Alice Arndt

FEASTS, FESTIVALS, AND FASTS. A feast is commonly thought of as a lavish meal; in a religious sense, it is also a day of commemoration set aside for an important personage, such as a saint. The word "feast" also connotes sensual delight, often excessive, as in the expression "a feast for the eyes."

A festival is a period of celebration, often centered around a religious feast day or a holiday, such as Christmas, a period of holidays celebrating an event (such as the completion of harvest), or a season (e.g., a winter carnival). Also, a festival can mean an unusually intensive or exaggerated series of presentations, such as a film festival. Finally, a fast (when used as a noun) marks a period of abstinence, such as the Lenten fast for Christians or the Ramadan fast for Muslims.

The concepts of feast, festival, and fast are closely interconnected. A feast day, such as St. Patrick's Day, for instance, is often the center of prolonged festivities. In such cases, the religious rituals such as attending church and, perhaps, fasting, are components of a larger festival event that frequently includes feasting, in the sense of excessive eating or drinking.

Food and Festival

Food is a major component of festival. Often it is part of a ritualized exchange, as when Halloween trick-or-treaters are given candy or are invited in for doughnuts and cider, or when Christmas carolers are rewarded with cookies. Food is often present in a formal, sacred meal. For instance, the Roman Catholic mass centers around the sacrament of the Eucharist, the transubstantiation and eating of bread and wine as the body and blood of Christ. While individual communicants each partake of only small amounts of the host, the Eucharist is invariably described by Catholics and Orthodox Christians as a (sacred) meal. The ritual most probably derives from the celebration of the Jewish Passover, which is celebrated with the sacred meal known as the Seder. The Seder is generally celebrated in the home, but is no less sacred or ritualized for that fact. Traditionally, during the meal four questions are asked by the youngest male child present, and certain foods are present on the table, each with specific symbolic value. Wine is consumed on four occasions during the meal, and the proceedings can take on a very festive demeanor, but the Passover Seder is a religious, historical, and sacred feast. Conversely, Jews fast from sundown to sundown on the high holy day of Yom Kippur.

The American Thanksgiving holiday is also centered on a meal, a feast that is likewise symbolic, ceremonial, and formalized, but not specifically belonging to any particular religion or denomination. However, the occasion is frequently used to express religious sentiments. The Thanksgiving feast commemorates an early harvest celebration held among English Puritan settlers in Massachusetts and their Native American benefactors. The tradition became an officially proclaimed national holiday under President Abraham Lincoln, in 1863, during the Civil War. As such, Thanksgiving has always had a strong element of patriotism and nationalism associated with it. While not a religious celebration in any strict sense, Thanksgiving can still be said to be a sacred event, in the sense of a secular ritual, one with strong political overtones (Moore and Myerhoff, 1977).

The events above are all more than simply meals. They are highly elaborated performances done with reference to religious and political worldviews, and are usually carried out by a group. One can examine the role of food in other celebratory events along these axes of formal-informal, and sacred-secular, such as Emancipation Day picnics or house-warming potlucks. For instance, in the United States people frequently gather at a home to watch the Super Bowl, the championship game of the National Football League. This televised sporting event has been promoted as an unofficial American holiday, and it is said to be played on "Super Bowl Sunday." Since people gather together, food is served on these occasions, but generally there is no formal, sit-down meal. Frequently, it is a potluck, with the hosts providing a large and plentiful central dish such as chili or spaghetti. Very often, the food consists of store-bought goods such as submarine sandwiches, or pizza, and beer. Thus, the food served at the Super Bowl Sunday party is itself mediated—it is bought in supermarkets or ordered by telephone—as the game itself is mediated.

Michael Dietler (2001) defines "feast" as any meal marked as different from everyday domestic meals, or from the exchange of food without consumption. He emphasizes that it is a kind of ritual activity. Likewise, the concept of "fast" depends on a ritual context in order to distinguish the abstinence from food from a diet or an eating disorder. Idiosyncratic fasting is often done to signify devotion to a saint or deity, for instance, or to a cause, as when individuals go on hunger strikes to protest certain situations. Idiosyncratic fasting often becomes a badge of marginality. In this latter regard, Caroline Walker Bynum points out that in Europe in the Middle Ages it was far more common for religious Christian women to use the denial of food as a sign of sacrifice and devotion than it was for men, and she suggests that many of what are regarded as eating disorders in the present time are also overwhelmingly a female problem. That is, many aspects of feasts and fasts are gendered, including food preparation, consumption, cleanup, and disposal.

For the denial of food to be considered a "fast," both the faster and the scholar consider the denial of food and/or drink as occurring in response to a sacred calendar that proscribes the consumption of certain foods during certain ritual periods or holy days; or the individual decides to fast in order to fulfill a vow of some sort, to purify oneself, or to show intense devotion to a deity. Feast and fast represent the overrating and underrating of food, respectively—food as plenty and food as denial.

Feast and fast meet in the Islamic holy month of Ramadan. Muslims do not eat between sunrise and sunset, but break the fast every evening with a festive meal. Neighbors and friends routinely visit during these evening events, which feature special desserts to mark the occasion. The end of Ramadan is celebrated with the festival of Eid. With Ramadan a ritualized relationship, a rhythm, of feast, fast, and festival may be observed—periods of fast interspersed with periods of feasts. Each takes increased meaning from its juxtaposition to the other. Eid, as a celebration, is especially meaningful coming at the end of a holy month of fast and reflection, much as Mardi Gras and carnival precede the forty days of Lent in Christendom. Very generally, it is often thought that feasts usually occur during periods of plenty, particularly after a harvest is completed. Surplus is consumed in celebration, as well as stored against the winter, famine, or other periods of want. Indeed, many celebratory feasting events mark both the pastoral and the agricultural cycles: ox slaughterings, grape harvests, apple butter festivals. However, as cultural events, both feasts and fasts are more complicated than this.

How, for instance, might the various proscriptions against the eating of certain foods in various religions be explained? Mary Douglas has produced the best analysis of the Jewish dietary laws in her book *Purity and Danger* (1970). She argues against the standard interpretations of the taboos involved in keeping kosher, that the foods involved such as pork were likely to be unhealthy due to poor means of preservation available in the biblical period. Such an explanation, she points out, does not explain the continued existence of these laws. In her analysis, she demonstrates that each of the animals listed as "abominations" in the biblical Book of Leviticus are creatures that possess characteristics of other species, who therefore blur the boundaries and cultural categories, and that are therefore considered taboo. "The unclear is the unclean," she concludes. While this interpretation may or may not be universally valid, it does show the complexities of culture that are inherent in food, eating, and ideas of the edible (Long, 2000).

Holiday eating is a ubiquitous form of feasting, often with foods that are themselves symbolic. Many religious feast days are also secular holidays, such as Christmas; or, at least, many popular holidays have religious underpin-

The *Ngusaba* or Volcano Festival celebrated by twenty-eight Hindu villages near the Gunung Agung Volcano at Duda, Bali (Indonesia). © ROGER RESSMEYER/CORBIS.

nings to them. Some, such as St. Patrick's Day or Valentine's Day, are not governmentally recognized holidays. No days off from work or school are granted. Still, they are celebrated traditionally by large numbers of people. Likewise, Halloween is the Eve of All Hallows, or All Saints' Day, in the Roman Catholic Church. Most traditional holiday and celebratory occasions, including religious and ethnic events such as Hanukkah, or Passover, are marked with special foods. The American Thanksgiving typifies the feast as experienced by many people today. The celebration of Thanksgiving is traced to a harvest feast in Plymouth, Massachusetts, in 1621, even though there were many other religious services of thanksgiving, usually involving fasts rather than feasts, that preceded the Plymouth event in the New World. Many Native Americans today regard the occasion as a national day of mourning, since the indigenous peoples were thanked for their assistance to the early colonists by later policies of betrayal and genocide.

Nevertheless, Thanksgiving is thought by many to be an inclusive celebration. For the occasion, the foods are prepared not only to be consumed, but also to be displayed. They are appreciated for their appearance and for their abundance. The table setting is important—special china and silverware, rich in family history, may be brought out. The dishes and the foods are arranged aesthetically, with the turkey being the centerpiece (Long, 2000).

Many aspects of personal and social identity are displayed along with the foods. For instance, family relationships are indexed by the favorite dished prepared by members of the extended family—a cousin's stuffing or a grown sibling's apple nut cake. Ethnicity, too, may be present in the form of additional dishes such as lasagna. There are even vegetarian organizations that have a meatless Thanksgiving with a live turkey present. Likewise, regional background is manifested in the foods and the ways they are prepared (Long, 2000).

First Communion procession in the Duomo Square of Positano, Italy. The communion service is followed by large family meals. © JONATHAN BLAIR/CORBIS.

Ritual Feasts and Ritual Fasts

Feasting done in ritual contexts or as rituals themselves (again, the Passover Seder, e.g., or even the Sunday dinner) is usually in some way festive. Even foods served during mortuary rituals (the eating and drinking during the Irish wake; the cold cuts served after a funeral) serve this socially integrative, generally light-hearted function. Fasts are thought to be "fasts," rather than "diets" or "eating disorders," precisely because they are carried out in reference to a sacred overarching symbolic system, usually religious, but sometimes political.

Ritual, festival, and celebration have in one form or another long been a source of great interest to folklorists and anthropologists. In fact, anthropology had its beginning in (the now largely repudiated) theories of Sir James George Frazer (originally published in 1911) concerning religion, belief, magic, and ritual, as well as the related work on belief by Edward Tyler from 1873. In 1925 Bronislaw Malinowski revolutionized the practice of anthropology in the twentieth century with his field studies of ritual, along with religious and magical beliefs and customs. The list can go on, but any such list will include the work of the French folklorist and sociologist Arnold van Gennep who, in the first decades of the twentieth century, provided systematic analysis of life cycle and calendrical rites of passage, and the later work of Victor Turner in the 1960s through 1980s. Both these scholars produced analyses and vocabularies that have become paradigmatic, not only in anthropology but in other disciplines as well. Scholars are widely familiar with Tur-

ner's ideas concerning communitas and liminality that, along with his phrase "betwixt and between," are regularly used to this day not only by anthropologists but also folklorists, ethnomusicologists, historians, and indeed anyone working with ritual materials. Van Gennep's term "rites of passage" has become part of everyday speech. Along with Mary Douglas, Turner put the study of symbols and symbolic action at the top of the research agenda for the second half of the twentieth century.

With the rise of cultural studies critiques that have engaged questions of politics, race, social class, gender, and power, newer approaches to the study of ritual have arisen that complement rather than entirely supplant the symbolic analyses inspired by Turner. After Stanley Tambiah's article "A Performative Approach to Ritual" was published in 1985, along with Turner's own growing interest in performance, a great many important recent studies of what folklorist Beverly Stoeltje (1993) calls "the ritual genres" came out of performance studies—a field influenced by Turner's work but also by more recent perspectives on feminism, postmodernism, and cultural studies, as well as earlier movements in rhetoric and theater.

At the same time, the emphasis on performance and performativity has led to an expansion of the materials of ritual studies. Felicia Hughes-Freeland says, "The focus on performance allows us to understand situations interactively, not in terms of communication models, but in terms of participatory ones" (p. 15). Parades, protests, and street theater generally are increasingly being referred to and studied as ritual or at the least as ritualized behavior, with the work of folklorist Susan G. Davis being particularly influential. Further, such events are compared and contrasted in other works to performances such as Jacobean theater or the mass media. National ceremonies, nationalizing events, and beauty pageants all take their place in the literature on ritual. In fact, people find the kinds of meanings scholars refer to under the rubric of "ritual" in a wide range of events and activities; that is, people invest certain actions with symbolic meaning or transformative power. That is ritualization, and it is up to the researcher to determine how people create this kind of dynamic. Likewise, feasting is emerging as a critical site for investigation within archeology, anthropology, and folklore. Foodways or food studies is a growing subfield within these disciplines, and is an important component of the study of ritual, festival, and celebration, as seen in works by Caroline Walker Bynum (1987), and Michael Dietler and Brian Hayden (2001).

The present author argues that ritual is not necessarily in opposition to festival (i.e., one confirms; the other subverts) but simply that ritual is a discrete form, distinctive from festival and celebration but frequently a component of these, much as game, sport, music, dance, food, story, and so on, are each discrete genres but also available as constitutive components of festival. Because festival and ritual are closely intertwined, because both often mark transitional points in the life cycle or recurrent, transitional, or important points in the year, festival is thought of as ritualistic. As has been seen, marking, commemorating, or celebrating something is not the same as causing it. However, these two features—celebration and performativity—are both capable of being potentiated in ritual, as well as in other genres such as festival and demonstration. It is not the scope of an event that makes it ritual. One may light a candle simply because one likes candlelight, or to ward off insects in the summer, and not think of these activities as special. However, lighting a candle at Christmas, even decoratively, is done because of the sense that it is a special time (another frame) and therefore may be felt to be ritualistic, despite the informality and secularity of the act. These continua—formal-informal, religious-secular—are self-evident. One may light Advent candles in the home before Christmas, a more formal and more religiously oriented activity, but not as formal or religious as the lighting of candles in church for Sunday or Christmas services.

Ritual, festival, celebration, holidays, public display events—what links these terms analytically is the combination of their performative and celebratory aspects, and the fact that rites of public display, like ritual, are performative. Food presentation and consumption—and the lack of it—are used to mark social time and establish social identity. Feasts precede and follow days or weeks of fast; they mark and celebrate periods of plenty after seasonal harvests or animal slaughterings. Fasts also indicate special days of the week, month, or year; may be used as part of life-cycle rituals such as coming-of-age; and are used by individuals to communicate being in a special state—denial as devotion to a deity or a cause (e.g., the Irish hunger strikers) or penance and suffering as a means to purification.

See also **Christmas; Fasting and Abstinence; Festivals of Food; Folklore, Food in; Kwanzaa; Lent; Metaphor, Food as; Passover; Ramadan; Religion and Food; Shrove Tuesday; Thanksgiving.**

BIBLIOGRAPHY

Bynum, Caroline Walker. *Holy Feast and Holy Fast: The Religious Significance of Food to Medieval Women.* Berkeley, Calif.: University of California Press, 1987.

Davis, Susan G. *Parades and Power: Street Theatre in Nineteenth-Century Philadelphia.* Berkeley, Calif.: University of California Press, 1986.

Dietler, Michael. "Theorizing the Feast: Rituals of Consumption, Commensal Politics, and Power in African Contexts." In *Feasts: Archeological and Ethnographic Perspectives on Food, Politics, and Power,* edited by Michael Dietler, and Brian Hayden, pp. 65–113. Washington, D.C.: Smithsonian Institution, 2001.

Dietler, Michael, and Brian Hayden. *Feasts: Archeological and Ethnographic Perspectives on Food, Politics, and Power.* Washington, D.C.: Smithsonian Institution, 2001.

Douglas, Mary. *Purity and Danger.* Reprint. Baltimore, Md.: Penguin, 1970.

Frazer, Sir James George. *The Golden Bough: A Study in Magic and Religion.* 3d ed. 10 vols. London: Macmillan, 1955. Originally published in 1911.

Hughes-Freeland, Felicia, ed. *Ritual, Performance, Media.* London and New York: Routledge, 1998.

Long, Lucy M. "Holiday Meals: Rituals of Family Tradition." In *Dimensions of the Meal: The Science, Culture, Business, and Art of Eating,* edited by Herbert L. Meiselman. Gaithersburg, Md.: Apsen, 2000.

Malinowski, Bronislaw. *Magic, Science and Religion, and Other Essays.* Reprint. Glencoe, Ill.: Free Press, 1974. Originally published in 1925.

Moore, Sally F., and Barbara G. Myerhoff, eds. *Secular Ritual.* Amsterdam: Van Gorcum, 1977.

Roach, Joseph. *Cities of the Dead: Circum-Atlantic Performance.* New York: Columbia University Press, 1996.

Santino, Jack. *New Old-Fashioned Ways: Holidays and Popular Culture.* Knoxville, Tenn.: University of Tennessee Press, 1996.

Stoeltje, Beverly J. "Power and the Ritual Genres: American Rodeo." *Western Folklore* 52 (1993): 135–156.

Tambiah, Stanley J. "A Performative Approach to Ritual." In *Culture, Thought, and Social Action: An Anthropological Perspective,* edited by Stanley J. Tambiah. Cambridge, Mass.: Harvard University Press, 1985.

Turner, Victor. *The Forest of Symbols: Aspects of Ndembu Ritual.* Ithaca, N.Y.: Cornell University Press, 1967.

Turner, Victor. *The Ritual Process: Structure and Anti-Structure.* Ithaca, N.Y.: Cornell University Press, 1969.

Tyler, Edward B. *Primitive Culture.* 2d ed. 2 vols. London: John Murray, 1873.

Van Gennep, Arnold. *The Rites of Passage.* Chicago: University of Chicago Press, 1960. Originally published in 1909.

Jack Santino

FERMENTATION. Fermentation is one of the oldest known food preservation techniques. Along with drying and salting, fermentation was a key method of extending the life of foods, allowing them to be available, and eaten safely, in times of scarcity or seasonal non-availability. These methods helped allow the transition from hunting and gathering to organized food cultivation and storage, which took place some ten to fifteen thousand years ago in the Middle East.

Fermentation involves the action of desirable microorganisms, or their enzymes, on food ingredients to make biochemical changes, which cause significant modification to the food. Often lactic-acid bacteria convert the carbohydrate energy source of food, such as lactose in milk, to lactic acid; examples are yogurt and cheeses from milk, and pickles from fruits and vegetables. Alternatively, yeasts, often of the *Saccharomyces* species, may convert the glucose to ethanol and carbon dioxide in leavened breads, or the sugars in grain or fruit beverages to beers and wines. Molds also can be active in certain fermentations, such as Stilton cheese and soy sauce. It is estimated that about one-third of all the food we consume is fermented. World estimates for beer consumption are about 22 million gallons, and a total of 15 million tons of some one thousand varieties of cheese are eaten annually.

Fermented Beverages and Foods

Fermentation is often the key to the safe, enjoyable consumption of perishable food materials, as it changes their composition, flavor, and texture. For example, milk is a nutritious but highly perishable beverage. Originally, in the Middle East, milk carried in animal-skin containers, often on horseback, would sour naturally, to produce acidic fermented milk. The combined action of the two lactic-acid bacteria, *Streptococcus lactis*, producing lactic acid, and *Lactobacillus bulgaricus*, producing lactic acid and acetaldehyde, a major contributor to flavor, are involved in yogurt production. The Tartars of Central Asia used the milk of horses, donkeys, or camels to produce a fizzy, gray acidic and alcoholic drink, *kumiss*, in which yeasts were active.

In acid conditions, the milk protein, casein, denatures and is precipitated to form a curd, producing cot-

Sugar products are shown fermenting in an open tank at a rum distillery in Guadeloupe. © REINHARD EISELE/CORBIS.

tage and soft cheese. By stirring and pressing, whey is removed and a more solid curd is produced, which by ripening or maturation produces semi-hard or hard cheeses. Surface-active bacteria of *Brevibacterium linens* are active in producing the aroma of Limburger type cheeses, while the blue molds of the genus *Penicillium* give Stilton and Gorgonzola cheeses their character.

The use of *Saccharomyces* yeasts has allowed the production of a range of fermented beverages, enabling safe consumption of liquid when fresh water supplies are not available. Lagers, the light golden, gassy beverage made by "bottom" yeast fermentation of cereal extracts, were first made in the regions of Germany and Czechoslovakia, but are now produced and consumed throughout the world. In Africa, a thick, sour alcoholic beverage is made from sorghum or millet, or sometimes maize or banana. These sorghum beers are important sources of nutrients, particularly B vitamins, to people on marginal diets in these regions. The Romans planted extensive vineyards in North Africa to harvest and ferment their grapes into wine, thereby producing a fermented beverage that could be readily stored, transported, and consumed when and where required.

Distillation of these alcoholic beverages, such as whiskey from beers, brandies from grape wines, or arrack from palm or rice wine, further extend our range of drinks and play important cultural roles in festivities.

Fermentation Vessels and Starter Cultures

Art meets science in the production of fermented foods. Traditional practices are passed down through generations of producers, often small in scale, and consumption patterns often have great cultural importance. In Scandinavia, traditionally the brides and mothers jealously guard their own supplies of sourdough starters, so that they can always make the desired bread for their partners and families. In West Africa, a homeowner keeps a supply of *dawadawa*, a dried fermented African locust bean paste (*Parkia* species); it is used to give everyday soups and stews the desired "meaty" flavor, while also providing important nutrients, such as riboflavin, the B vitamin that protects against blindness, which is endemic to the region due to nutritional deficiency.

In Korea, few meals are complete without *kimchi*, a pickled fermented cabbage, which may also contain fish and other components. The practice of every home having their own *kimchi* jars, often on their verandahs, originated as a way of preserving vegetables through the cold winter season, providing year-round vitamin C. *Kimchi* together with *kochujang*, the fermented red pepper paste, give Korean preparations a unique and characteristic attractive color and flavor.

Where food fermentation occurred naturally as conditions favored particular organisms, an important art arose to encourage the desired fermentation organisms, while preventing undesirable microorganisms from developing, for successful fermented food production.

Food storage often took place in earthenware vessels, whose semipermeable inner walls were difficult to clean completely. This allowed a biofilm of desirable microorganisms to remain, to initiate a successful fermentation of the next batch of food. Because of their significance, the vessels themselves were artistically designed and treasured. Interesting examples can be seen in museum collections, such as the Nezu Museum in Tokyo, Japan, and a museum dedicated to *kimchi* in Seoul, South Korea.

In Europe, the fermented meat producers, while using ceramic or metallic vats with smoother, more easily cleaned surfaces, developed the technique of "backslopping" to introduce a small quantity of the fermenting liquor from the previous batch of meat to initiate successful fermentation.

In many cases, dried grains or balls of the derived fermenting microorganisms on cereal or other substrates would be used to start fermentation. Baker's yeast may be used in this work. Kefir grains are used in North Africa, the Middle East, and Russia for production of kefir, *laban*, or *leben* fermented milks. *Ragi* is used in Indonesia and throughout East and Southeast Asia as *inoculum* for *lao-chao* and other fermented foods.

Cultural Diversity

The production, consumption, and enjoyment of different fermented foods reflects the diversity of cultures and cuisines that make up our varied world. In Chinese and Japanese cuisines, *shoyu*, or soy sauce, is added almost universally to dishes, while the Indian vegetarian diet depends on fermented cereals and legumes, often in combinations, as in *dosas* and *vadas*. The art and science of fermenting meat to a wide range of salamis are vital to the enjoyment

of Eastern and Central Europeans, while Italian food market stall holders proudly display their mold-covered fermented sausages and traditional cheeses.

As people migrate, they normally carry their traditional fermented food practices with them. The range of fermented cheeses and meats in Latin America reflects the European origins of these populations, and the wineries of Chile were originally established by French families. Consumers of imported wine, chocolate, coffee, or tea are all beneficiaries of the internationalism and significance of fermented foods.

See also **Beer; Bread; Cheese; Meat; Microorganisms; Preserving; Spirits; Wine.**

BIBLIOGRAPHY

Campbell-Platt, Geoffrey. *Fermented Foods of the World: A Dictionary and Guide.* London: Butterworth, 1987

Steinkraus, Keith, ed. *Handbook of Indigenous Fermented Foods.* 2nd ed. New York: Marcel Dekker, 1995.

Wood, Brian J. B., ed. *Microbiology of Fermented Foods.* 2nd ed. London: Blackie, 1998.

Geoffrey Campbell-Platt

FERMENTED BEVERAGES OTHER THAN WINE AND BEER.

Fermented beverages have been produced and consumed all over the world and over a very long time span. Man discovered that sugar solutions of different origins, if left standing rather warm, will start fermenting spontaneously into an alcoholic beverage that also often contains lactic acid. The requisite microorganisms, *Saccaromyces* yeasts and *Lactobacillus* bacteria, are abundant almost everywhere and will do their duty, producing alcohol and lactic acid. A similar fermentation process of animal and vegetable foods is the lactic-acid fermentation that yields, for instance, sour herring in Sweden, and sauerkraut.

Fermented beverages can be divided into two groups, wines and beers, broadly defined. Wines are fermented from various fruit juices containing fermentable sugars. Beers come from starch-containing products, which undergo enzymatic splitting by diastase, malting, and mashing, before the fermentable sugars become available for the yeasts and bacteria. The enzymatic splitting of the starch can also be performed either by human saliva, containing amylases, or by molds. Narrowly defined, beer is barley beer and wine is grape wine.

Detailed information on fermented beverages all over the world can be found in Hardwick and colleagues (1995, 63–68), Steinkraus (1979), Arnold (1911), and Campbell-Platt (1987).

Beer from Cereals

Bouza is produced in Egypt and is probably the forerunner of beer in Ancient Egypt. It is prepared from malt of

Old cider press at Happy Land near Ashton Keynes, England, 1934. Two hundred sacks of apples were pressed daily to make cider during the harvest season. English cider is fermented while Americans generally drink the unfermented juice, either raw or pasteurized. © HULTON-DEUTSCH COLLECTION/CORBIS.

milo (a grain sorghum that resembles millet) and crushed baked loaves of bread. Residue from an earlier fermentation is used as a starter and both lactic-acid bacteria and *Saccaromyces* are involved in the fermentation process to get this sour alcoholic beverage. *Talla* from Ethiopia is a very similar to *bouza* and can be produced from barley and wheat. The bread loaves are heated to give a roasted character, and the pots are fueled by olive wood to give a smoky taste. *Talla* can also be spiced with hop leaves and stems, and spices.

Wheat beer. Wheat beer—and rye and oat beer as well—are frequently made from mixtures of malt and the crushed grains of these cereals with barley. Often the beer is bottled with the yeasts for continued fermentation in the bottle. Wheat beer—which is top-fermented and thus, technically, an ale—is particularly popular in Bavaria and in Belgium and northern Germany, in varieties such as *lambic*, *Gueuze*, Wit beer, Trappist beer, and *Berliner Weisse*.

Rye beer. Rye beers such as *kalja* and *sahti* in Finland, similar beverages in the Baltic area, and *kvas* ("kvass" in English) in Russia are produced in northern and eastern Europe, where cultivation of rye is widespread. *Kvas* has been the basic beverage for the Russian people for centuries. Its importance is indicated by many proverbs such as "Eat cabbage soup with meat, but if you don't have it, eat bread and *kvas*." The use of *kvas* is documented from about the year 800. Traditionally it is spontaneously fermented. In a broad sense, *kvas* is any sour and alcoholic fluid made from honey, bread, cereals, birch sap, fruits, beets, or cabbage. Red-beet *kvas* should always be used to produce *borshch* ("borscht," in English—red-beet

soup). In a narrow sense, *kvas* (that is, bread-*kvas*) is produced from rye malt with or without other cereals or sour-fermented rye bread as adjuncts, and the beverage is spiced with peppermint. Most of the consumed *kvas* is of low alcohol content, only some few percent.

Oat beer. Oat beer is today mostly used as an adjunct in certain stouts called oat stouts. A stout is a dark ale, made of roasted malt, which occurs in several varieties such as sweet and dry (Guiness). Oats have also been used in traditional Norwegian beer production.

Rice beer. Another type of cereal beers is made from rice, and these have been produced in all the rice-growing areas of the world. The best-known example is sake from Japan, which has a documented history of more than two thousand years. The principal difference from the malting of barley lies in the *koji*-process of rice. *Koji* is a culture of *Aspergillus oryzae*, which grows on steamed rice, and saccharifies the rice starch (that is, converts it to sugar) and decomposes the rice proteins. The sugar produced in the sake mash is later fermented by the already-present *Saccaromyces cerevisiae*. The mash is acidified either by adding lactic acid to it or by facilitating the growth of lactic bacteria to form the seed mash, *moto*. Sake is a clear, pale-yellow liquid with an alcoholic content of about 15 percent and a characteristic estery (artificially fruity) aroma. It is slightly sweet and slightly acidic and has a high amino-acid content compared to wine and beer. Other similar beverages from rice are known from other eastern and southern Asian countries such as China, Thailand, India, Malaysia, and the Philippines.

Another similar fermentation process is performed by the inoculum *ragi*, present in Southeast Asia. *Ragi* contains the mold *Amylomyces rouxii*, the yeast *Endomycopsis burtonii*, and sometimes *Hansenula* yeasts; it produces a pleasant alcoholic and acid beverage from rice or cassava, called *tape ketan* in Malaysia.

Sorghum and millet beer. Sorghum beers, known as kafir beers in Africa, are made from malt from sorghum (*Sorghum bicolor*) or from the related grain, millet (*Pennisetum typhoides* and *Eleusine coracana*). Often-used adjuncts are maize (corn), malted or unmalted sorghum or millet, and malt amylase. Lactic acid is used as a flavoring and preserving agent, and the alcoholic fermentation is performed by *Saccharomyces*. Nowadays, these traditional African beers are not only produced in tribal areas; they are also available in home-brewed urban and industrially produced versions. They are opaque, rather thick pinkish-brown liquids with an estery (artificially fruity) or fruity odor, and a sweet and sour taste.

Maize beer. *Tesquino* and *zendecho* from Mexico and Latin America are made from malted maize and spontaneously fermented by *Saccaromyces cerevisiae*. These beverages might be as ancient as the oldest beers of the Old World, dating back about eight thousand years. Another beer is *chicha*, made by Andean and Central American Indians. The starchy material is chewed into dough, which is dried and later placed into warm water where the amylase action is finished. Then a starter (a small amount taken from a prior fermentation) is added, and the lactic-acid and alcoholic fermentation begins. Today much of the chicha is made using a maize malt rather than saliva.

Beer from Starch Products

All kinds of starchy items, such as manioc (cassava), potatoes, beets, and various roots, are included in this group. To get fermentable sugars, the starch has to be split either by diastase in malt, by saliva, or by molds, as with rice. In South and Central America, almost all of the traditional beers were originally produced by chewing either the cereal maize or other starchy vegetables. One of the most popular has been the manioc, both the sweet and the bitter; sweet potatoes, mangabeira (*Hancornia speciosa*), cashew, Jaboticaba (*Myrciaria cauliflora*), pineapples, bananas, and algarroba pods have also been used. In the tropical forest tribes, the favorite manioc beer was prepared as follows:

> The roots, cut into think slices, were first boiled, then squeezed and partly chewed by young girls. The mass, impregnated with saliva, was mixed with water and heated again over the fire. The liquid was afterward poured into huge jars, half buried in the ground, covered with leaves, and left two to three days to ferment. A fire was built around the jars to warm the beverage before serving it. Each extended family manufactured its own liquor. When a bout was organized, drinkers went successively to each hut, exhausting the available supply. The women served the liquors in huge calabashes (Steward, vol. 3, 1948, p. 127).

An earlier popular American low-alcoholic beverage is root beer, which consists of an infusion of sarsaparilla, sassafras, spruce, wild cherry, spikenard, wintergreen, and ginger, with sugar and yeast. Today, it is a soft drink containing some of these ingredients at its best; otherwise, it is artificially spiced.

Wine from Fruit and Vegetable Juices

Fruit wine. Fruit wines are produced with almost the same technique as grape wines. Specifically-named fruit wines such as cider (from apples) and perry (from pears) are produced, as well as wines from other fruits. The technical difference between these two groups is the alcohol content—5 to 7 percent in the first group and up to 18 percent in the second group—which depends on sugar addition.

Tree-sap wine. Saps from various trees have been used to produce alcoholic beverages; examples include maple sap (from *Acer saccharum*, the sugar maple) in North America, and birch sap (from *Betula pubescens*, the downy birch) in northern Europe. The manifestation of the symbiosis of yeast and bacteria cultures, which looks like a jellyfish, on the wounds of spring birches has been used in Europe as a folk medicine and is called "*Volga-swamp.*"

Sugarcane wine. Wine made from the sugarcane, *Saccharum officinarum*, together with molasses, is distilled into rum.

Cactus-plant wines. The tall perennial plants of the genus *Agave*, which grow in Mexico and nearby areas, give a sweet, slightly bitter sap, called *agua miel* (literally, honey water), which is fermented into pulque, either spontaneously or through the use of an inoculum from a previous fermentation. The Aztecs were familiar with the product. Pulque is an important food beverage for the poor in the semiarid areas of Mexico. If pulque made from *Agave tequilana* is distilled, the resultant liquor is called tequila; if pulque made from another agave is distilled, it is called mescal. Before the contacts with the European settlers, only a few American Indian tribes north of Mexico made alcoholic beverages. They were the Akimel O'odham (Pima), Tohono O'odham (Papago), and the River Yuman peoples in southern Arizona and northern Mexico, and they produced wine from the saguaro cactus as well as from the agave and the mesquite. In the East, the Cherokees made wine from persimmons. During an important ceremony in July, the Papagos and the Pimas drank enormous quantities of the wine to induce rainfall in their desert areas.

Sugar-palm wine. Some examples of wines made from palm sap are *surra* from *Borassus flabillifer*, *toddy* and *temba* from the coconut palm *Cocus nucifera* (from which arrack is obtained by distillation), *malovu* from *Elaeis guineensis*, a kind of undistilled "rum" from *Hyphaene coriaca* and *Hyphaene critina*, *Phonix reclinata*, *Raphia pedunculata*, and *Raohia vinifera*.

"Wine" from Animal Sources

Mead. Honey is probably among the first foods gathered by *Homo sapiens* and its predecessors, and mead, the wine fermented from honey, may well be one of the oldest alcoholic beverages. Honey has also been much used as an adjunct to sweeten many kinds of beers over the centuries. Mead was the drink of the Nordic gods, whereas the people drank beer. The modern methods of production of mead are described by Andrej Jarczyk and W. Wzorek (1977).

Fermented milk. Only milk from human beings and horses has a relatively high concentration of milk sugar (lactose)—6.9 percent, in comparison with the 4.9 percent in cow's milk—which makes it easier to ferment milk from mares than that from cows. People from central Asia (Tajikistan, Uzbekistan, and Kazakhstan) and Mongolia have fermented mare's milk, making the alcoholic beverage *kumiss*, and it appears that milk from camels, sheep, yaks, and reindeer has been used similarly.

See also **Beer**; **Fermentation**; **Fruit**; **Spirits**; **Wine**.

BIBLIOGRAPHY

Arnold, J. P. *Origin and History of Beer and Brewing*. Chicago: Wahl-Henius Institute of Fermentology, 1911.

Beech, F. W., and J. G. Carr. "Cider and Perry." In *Alcoholic Beverages: Economic Microbiology*, edited by A. H. Rose. Volume 1. London: Academic Press, 1977.

Booth, Peter MacMillan. "Tohono O'odham (Papago)." In *Encyclopedia of North American Indians*, edited by Frederick E. Hoxie, pp. 635–637. Boston: Houghton Mifflin, 1966.

Campbell-Platt, Geoffrey. *Fermented Foods of the World: A Dictionary and Guide*. London: Butterworths, 1987.

Davidson, Alan. *The Oxford Companion to Food*. Oxford: Oxford University Press, 1999.

Eidlitz, Kerstin. "Food and Emergency Food in the Circumpolar Area." *Studia Ethnographica Upsaliensia* XXXII. Uppsala, Sweden, 1969.

Hardwick, William A., Dirk E. J. van Oevelen, Lawrence Novellie, and Kiyoshi Yoshizawa. "Kinds of Beer and Beerlike Beverages." In *Handbook of Brewing*, edited by William A. Hardwick. New York: M. Dekker, 1995.

Jarczyk, Andrej, and W. Wzorek "Fruit and Honey Wines." In *Alcoholic Beverages: Economic Microbiology*, edited by A. H. Rose. Volume 1, 387–421. London: Academic Press 1977.

Kobert, R. "Ueber den Kwass. Zur Einführung desselben in Westeuropa. Historische Studien aus dem Pharmakologischen Institute der Kaiserlichen Universität Dorpat" (About Kvass: On its Introduction into Western Europe. Historical Studies from the Pharmacological Institute of the Imperial University of Dorpat). Volume V, 100–131. Halle, Germany 1889–1896. In *Historische Studien zur Russischen Volksmedizin* (Historical Studies of Traditional Russian Medicine). Leipzig: Zentralantiquariat der Deutschen Demokratischen Republik, 1968.

Kodama, K., and K. Yoshizawa. "Saké." In *Alcoholic Beverages: Economic Microbiology*, edited by A. H. Rose. Volume 1. London: Academic Press, 1977.

Levy, Jerrold E. "Alcoholism, Indian." In *Encyclopedia of North American Indians*, edited by Frederick E. Hoxie, p. 17. Boston: Houghton Mifflin, 1996.

Nordland, Odd. *Brewing and Beer Traditions in Norway: The Social Anthropological Background of the Brewing Industry*. Oslo: Universitetsforlaget, 1969.

Olsson, Sven-Olle R. "Kvass." *Gastronomisk Kalender 1978*, Stockholm, 1977.

Sapeika, N. *Food Pharmacology*. Springfield, Ill.: Charles C. Thomas Publisher, 1969.

Steinkraus, K. H. "Nutritionally Significant Indigenous Foods Involving an Alcoholic Fermentation." In *Fermented Food Beverages in Nutrition*, edited by W. J. Darby, C. F. Gastineau, and T. T. Turner. New York: Academic Press, 1979.

Steward, Julian H., ed. *Handbook of South American Indians*. Bulletin 143, Bureau of American Ethnology. Volumes 1, 3, 4. Washington, D.C.: U.S. Government Printing Office, 1946 and 1948.

Sven-Olle R. Olsson

FERTILE CRESCENT. *See* **Mesopotamia, Ancient.**

FESTIVALS OF FOOD. Food festivals can celebrate one particular ingredient, single dishes, or entire culinary cultures. Their public display, orgiastic consumption, or their playful way of dealing with food provide us with illustrations of the fundamental importance of such festivals for the development of culture.

Prehistoric Roots

Alternating periods of malnutrition with certain occasions of extraordinary food consumption is typical for economies of penury. In the early phases of cultural development, therefore, the simple abundance of food was already reason enough for the celebration of a feast. Greenland's Eskimo communities, for instance, had spontaneous feasts whenever a large animal like a whale was captured. In order to hunt game and gather fruits in a world perceived as filled with spirits (animism), hunting and gathering societies depended on the help of shamanic rites. These rites were intended to persuade faunal and floral spirits to release animals and plants for human consumption. Game was always divided among the hunters and their community according to a customary ratio of distribution. This ancient practice gave rise to a variety of ideas and rituals. Sacrifice was one of the most prominent. There have been attempts to deduce the principle of gift giving and the exchange of gifts

Pig roast at Atuona, Hiva Oa, French Polynesia, in 1998. Pig roasts are popular adjuncts to all sorts of public feasting in the islands. © Nik Wheeler/CORBIS.

from this primordial partitioning of food. Even though various disciplines have theorized and discussed the subject extensively, its original character has not developed clearly. The attempted explanations ranged from the sacrifice as an act of reciprocity to the sacrifice as a community at table, where gods and humans take part. Essential, however, was the fact that the food offered was consumed during the festive ceremony and only the inedible parts (bones, gall bladder) or minor pieces (fat) were offered to the higher beings. Bulk slaughtering, like that on the occasion of the "hekatomb" sacrifices in Greek antiquity, originally limited to the offering of one hundred head of cattle, became popular festivals with plenty of food for everyone.

Mass feeding in ancient societies certainly was an effective instrument for the manipulation of public opinion. In the case of Julius Caesar, it helped to create a dictatorship. He celebrated his victory over Gaul, Egypt, Pontus, and Africa in September 46 B.C.E. In order to outdo the triumphs of his predecessors, Caesar not only rewarded his soldiers, but almost the entire Roman citizenry. Approximately 320,000 people received a present of 100 denars and a special allocation of oil and grain. Meat also was distributed gratuitously and the Roman masses were entertained at 22,000 tables before viewing the games. The obligatory social mechanism behind this phenomenon was first described by Marcel Mauss as "potlatch" in his fundamental study on the "gift." Individuals who are offered a gift are obliged to reciprocate. This system, widely operating in traditional societies, could be seen in two different forms: the potlatch of gifts and the potlatch of destruction. Only the wealthy were capable of leadership because they could oblige others, upon whom they bestowed gifts. Even the deliberate destruction of goods or gluttony was a strong signal of the social segregation of the elite. So it is not surprising that feeding the poor became a customary social act among the European elites of the Middle Ages.

Charitable and Social Traditions

Byzantine emperors, for instance, invited the poor to their annual banquets on "vow day" (2 January). When an imperial prince was born, the event was celebrated by the distribution of *lochozema*, a "childbed soup," in Constantinople's main street. The ingredients, consisting of wheat flour, honey, butter, and sesame suggest the high prestige attached to this soup.

In many cultures, the birth of children or other rites of passage provide occasions for the public dispensation of food. Besides the wish to celebrate the happy event, elements of reciprocity also add to these customs. So, for instance, in eighteenth-century France it became customary for godfathers to throw "dragées" (sugar-coated sweetmeats), hazelnuts, almonds or aniseed among the children standing in front of the church. Yet these presents were eventually interpreted as the obligatory gift of the newcomer to those whose company they would share.

Some food festivals are of a religious nature. Every year the people of Morave, Slovenia, bring baskets of food into church to have them blessed for Easter. © CORBIS.

In the nineteenth century the custom was also integrated into wedding ceremonies. Another example of this reciprocal exchange is the *sihk puhn* feast (eating from the common pot) of the Cantonese ethnic groups in the rural suburbs of Hong Kong. For this feast, nine separately cooked ingredients, mostly luxury foods, are mixed in a big pot from which each guest, rich or poor, is invited to eat. Representatives of every single household and the village's elders are invited to the feast. Hence. the hosts symbolically feed the entire community. *Sihk puhn* banquets are the only way to legitimize social transitions, since any marriage or birth that is not celebrated with a *sikh puhn* is not considered legitimate. The annual appointment of the village guardsmen also depends on the *sihk puhn*. If a significant number of lineage elders refuse the food, the selection procedures must be repeated.

Some existing festivals are rooted in the pious traditions of the medieval period, for instance, the feast of the Holy Spirit in the Portuguese-speaking world, especially in the Azores. There, the entire local community shares in an enormous banquet, which includes the distribution of food and money to the indigent. During the festivities a child is crowned as the "Emperor of the Holy Spirit." The festival, now nearly extinct in Portugal, first appeared on the Azores during the fifteenth century. Its origins are closely connected to the ideas of the Calabrian monk Joachim of Flore (c. 1135–1202/5), who professed the arrival of the age of the Holy Spirit, an era of peace and prosperity.

Cockaigne and Carnival

In addition to these social and charitable aspects, the themes of utopia and carnival became important elements of medieval and early modern festival culture. Of course, the idea of a utopian terrestrial paradise in which the lazy

The Guelaguetza festival is held annually in Oaxaca, Mexico. Shown here are young girls in native dress holding pineapples. © ROSE HARTMAN/CORBIS.

are rewarded and the diligent punished was already known to Greek and Roman authors like Lucian, Herodotus, and Strabo and was projected either onto foreign countries or the island of the blessed. But in the medieval and early modern period, the idea of a gastronomic utopia, the land of Cockaigne (Cuccagna, Schlaraffenland, Lubberland), developed in times of famine. This made an ideal theme for feasts of feeding. The "Cuccagna Napoletana" of the eighteenth century is a famous example. It was originally celebrated as the culmination of carnival in Naples with a procession of food carriages sponsored by the guilds of bakers and butchers. In 1746 the king ordered the food to be heaped up in front of the royal palace. For obvious reasons, the *cuccagna* had to be protected by guards until the king gave the sign from the balcony of his palace and the crowds were allowed to plunder the mountain of food. The *cuccagna* was conceived as a work of art, and all the victuals were displayed in the form of landscapes, gardens, or architectures. From 1759 a firm construction was used to drape the foodstuffs. The term *cuccagana* was also applied to more traditional forms of food distribution. So the disposal of food hanging from a wheel placed on the top of a post was called a *cuccagna* just as was the famous Carnival *degli gnocchi* of Verona. The latter is believed to date back to the year 1531, when the rich Veronese citizen Tommaso da Vico handed out flour, butter, and cheese to the starving masses of his hometown. Even though there is no documentary evidence for this festival prior to the eighteenth century, the event today is advertised as the "oldest carnival of Italy." Once the "gnocchi" were cooked and distributed, the sponsors of the festival, pompously dressed, took part in the procession of the "macaroni."

Numerous European festivals originate from charitable foundations or social obligations. An example of the latter is the Sindelfingen cake-ride in southern Germany, reflecting the millers' duty to deliver cakes and bread to the local authorities as well as to the pupils of the town. First mentioned in 1535, the annual delivery developed into a traditional horse race, until in 1837 "enlightened" officials abolished this custom. Nevertheless, the millers were obliged to continue the payment of a fee to the graduating pupils up until 1961. Only five years afterward, the cake-ride was reactivated as a tourist attraction and has been celebrated ever since.

Aspects of Economy and Amusement

Modern food festivals are generally characterized by the predominance of economic interests. There are few wine, beer, fruit, or vegetable festivals that originated prior to World War I. One of them is the Circleville Pumpkin Show (1903), in Circleville, Ohio. Despite its humble origins, this agricultural street fair soon developed into one of the largest festivals of the United States, attracting hundreds of thousands of visitors each year.

Countless agricultural festivals arose during the Depression of the 1930s. The intention was to promote consumption and to advertise products from certain areas. In the United States, such festivals were mainly founded by local voluntary associations like the Lion's Clubs, whereas in Europe the government played a more decisive role in their creation. For example, in 1930 the Italian ministry for agriculture ordered an annual countrywide celebration of a grape festival on 28 September. Nevertheless, the virtual mushrooming of food festivals is a recent phenomenon. The redefinition of ethnic and communal relations in a post-colonial and post-totalitarian world, as well as the revival of interest in regional foods since the 1970s, has contributed to this growth. Marketing also recognized the importance of festivals in providing firsthand experience with foods that would later be recognized by the potential consumer in the store. Yet, sheer human creativity still can lead to spontaneous festivities. The most spectacular food events of the present, the "tomatina" of Buñol, Spain, and the "battle of the oranges" at the carnival of Ivrea, Italy, are examples. Their key element is an orgiastic row, in which 55 tons of tomatoes and 350 tons of oranges are consumed, respectively, each year—and the numbers are rising. Food is used as a projectile and to soil others. The event of Buñol came into being in 1944/45, when a carnival parade got out of hand. In Ivrea the "battle of the oranges" dates back to around 1850 when upper-middle-class children practiced throwing oranges from the balconies of their houses. Today the contracting parties are organized in eight teams, each consisting of 100 to 300 members, who have to contribute to the festival's costs. Their main targets are the people on the thirty-two horse-driven floats moving through the masses. Here adults turn into children for a few hours. Georges Bataille explains this behavior as the most archaic element in festival culture and world economy. Since enjoyment of waste engenders the will for surplus production, excess is the essence of a festival, as Sigmund Freud writes in his essay "Totem and Taboo."

See also **British Isles; Christianity; Day of the Dead; Fasting and Abstinence; Feasts, Festivals, and Fasts; Halloween; Holidays; Metaphor, Food as; Shrove Tuesday; Symbol, Food as.**

BIBLIOGRAPHY

Argentero, Rolando. *Storico carnevale di Ivrea.* Ivrea, Italy: Priuli and Verlucca, 1998.

Bataille, Georges. *La Part Maudite, Précédé de la Notion de Dépense.* Paris: Editions de Minuit, 1967.

Bringmann, Klaus. "Der Triumph des Imperators und die Saturnalien der Sklaven in Rom." In *Das Fest: Eine Kulturgeschichte von der Antike bis zur Gegenwart,* edited by Uwe Schultz, pp. 50–58. Munich: C. H. Beck, 1988.

Burkert, Walter. *Kulte des Altertums: Biologische Grundlagen der Religion.* Munich: C. H. Beck, 1998.

Decroisette, Françoise. "Carnavals urbains en Italie: La bacchanale ou cocagne des gnocchi à Vérone." In *Les Fêtes Urbaines en Italie a l'Époque de la Renaissance,* edited by Françoise Decroisette and Michel Plaisance, pp. 31–63. Paris: Klincksieck, 1993.

Mauss, Marcel. *The Gift: Forms and Functions of Exchange in Archaic Societies.* Translated by Ian Cunnison. With an introduction by E. E. Evans Pritchard. London: Cohen and West, 1954.

Metken, Sigrid. "Dragées als Souvenir-Gabe zu Taufe: Hochzeit und Erstkommunion in Frankreich." *Volkskunst* 9 (1986): 44–51.

Petzoldt, Leander. *Volkstümliche Feste: Ein Führer zu Volksfesten, Märkten und Messen in Deutschland.* Munich: C.H. Beck, 1983.

Quadros, António. "Do Imperio do Espirito Santo ao Imperio da Filosofia." In *Memória das Origens, Saudades do Futuro: Valores, Mitos, Arquétipos, Ideias,* edited by António Quadras, pp. 326–339. Mem Martins: Publicaçoes Europa-América, 1992.

Richter, Dieter. *Schlaraffenland: Geschichte einer populäre Phantasie.* Cologne: E. Diederichs, 1984.

Solinas, Pier Giorgio. "Cibo, Festa, Fame: Spartire e Dividere." In *Festa: Antropologia e Semiotica,* edited by Carla Bianco and Maurizio Del Ninno. Firenze: Nuova Guaraldi, 1981.

Tinnefeld, Franz. "Die Rolle der Armen bei Festfeiern im byzantinischen Hofzeremoniell." In *Feste und Feiern im Mittelalter,* edited by Detlef Altenburg, Jörg Jarnut, and Hans-Hugo Steinhoff, pp. 109–113. Sigmaringen: Jan Thorbecke, 1991.

Watson, James L. "From the Common Pot: Feasting with Equals in Chinese Society." *Anthropos* 82 (1987): 389–401.

Oliver M. Haid

FIBER, DIETARY. In 1972 British physician Hugh Trowell defined dietary fiber as "that portion of the food which is derived from cellular walls of plants which is digested very poorly by human beings" (*Revue Européenne d'Etudes Cliniques et Biologiques*). Most of the current interest in dietary fiber stems from the efforts of Trowell and other researchers in the 1960s and 1970s to examine the differences in disease patterns between populations consuming diets high in refined foods (typical of developed countries) and populations consuming diets high in unrefined foods (typical of less developed or undeveloped countries). Populations with a higher intake of unrefined food, and thus a higher intake of dietary fiber, had lower risk of chronic diseases, such as heart disease, intestinal cancers, and gastrointestinal disorders, as compared to populations consuming highly refined, low-fiber diets. These observations stimulated a large number of research studies and, while the ability of fiber to prevent chronic disease is difficult to prove, the data gathered since the 1960s strongly supports the importance of dietary fiber for the health of the gastrointestinal tract and thus its importance in the general diet.

Definition of Dietary Fiber

In 2001 the U.S. National Academy of Sciences Institute of Medicine (IOM) recommended that "dietary fiber" be defined as the nondigestible carbohydrates and lignin that are intrinsic and intact in plants and that the term "added fiber" be used to characterize isolated, nondigestible carbohydrates that are added to foods or supplements. Defined as such, dietary fiber includes nonstarch polysaccharides (NSP) and oligosaccharides that cannot be digested in the small intestine by alpha amylase or any of the sugar-hydrolyzing enzymes in the gut. The most commonly consumed NSPs include cellulose, pectins, glucans, hemicelluloses, and gums. Inulin, a nondigestible carbohydrate of lower molecular weight than NSP, also is included in this definition of dietary fiber. The only noncarbohydrate component of dietary fiber is lignin; however, this is probably a minor component of most edible portions of plant foods since it is associated with tough or woody tissues. An important distinction of the IOM definition is that dietary fiber is the term applied to plant foods in which the nondigestible carbohydrates remain intact and part of the structure of the plant cells. Because of inconsistencies in the precise definition of dietary fiber within the research community, the methods to analyze the fiber fraction of foods have been controversial. Earlier food composition tables provided crude-fiber values; however, this value does not include most of the dietary fiber in foods and should not be used to estimate fiber intake. Food tables that contain data using the enzymatic total dietary fiber (TDF) method or that include analysis of NSP provide more accurate estimates of fiber intake.

Dietary fiber is characterized as soluble or insoluble depending on its extraction by one of the steps in the TDF analytical method. Originally it was believed that this characterization might predict physiological effects of different fibers; however, this has not been the case, and more detailed descriptions of chemical-physical properties are needed to understand the metabolic response to diverse sources of fiber. Some fibers that are categorized as soluble fibers, such as hydrolyzed gums or oligosaccharides, are not very effective in lowering cholesterol. On the other hand, fibers vary in their physical properties, which appears to be important in understanding how fiber can affect metabolism. Certain polysaccharides can become viscous or thick when mixed with water. Viscosity is associated with slowing gastric emptying, lowering plasma cholesterol, and reducing the increase in blood glucose due to consumption of digestible carbohydrates. NSPs that can become viscous include glucans, pectins, and gums. Nondigestible carbohydrates can be fermented by the microflora in the large intestine, and these carbohydrates are the primary substrates for their growth and metabolism. To be fermented by microorganisms, polysaccharides must have water-holding capacity (WHC) so that microbes can penetrate the fiber matrix. Those polysaccharides with relatively high WHC are degraded to a larger extent than those with low WHC. In addition to viscosity, fermentability, and WHC, dietary fiber provides bulk in the intestines, and some fibers may bind bile acids and increase their excretion. Most foods contain a mixture of different types of polysaccharides; however, certain foods are good sources of particular types of fiber. For example, oats and barley contain mixed beta-glucans, fruits provide pectins, wheat

bran is high in cellulose and hemicelluloses, and dry beans are a source of viscous polysaccharides. Cellulose is the most abundant NSP in foods.

Fiber Content of Food

The table that follows provides values for some foods that are sources of fiber, including fruits, vegetables, cereals and grains, and dry beans and nuts. Based on the proposed definition from IOM, animal products contain no dietary fiber; it is derived only from plant foods. Some food products that are formulated with animal products could be a source of fiber if plant foods with dietary fiber or isolated polysaccharides are added in the preparation. The values in the table are reported as grams per 100 grams of edible portion so that it is easy to compare foods. Information is given in the conversion column so that the value can be converted to the foods as normally eaten. The table helps to illustrate how the handling and preparation of foods influence fiber content. As the data show,

TABLE 1

Fiber content of some foods

Food description	Dietary fiber	Water	Conversion information
			g/100 g of edible portion
Fruits			
Bananas	2.4	74.3	1 medium = 118 g
Apples	2.7	83.9	1 medium = 138 g
Oranges	2.4	86.8	1 medium = 140 g
Orange juice	—	88.4	8 ounces = 248 g
Grapes	1.0	80.6	1 grape = 5 g
Plums, dried	7.1	32.4	1 dried plum = 8.4 g
Vegetables			
Tomatoes	1.1	93.8	1 medium = 123 g
Broccoli, cooked	2.9	90.7	1 spear = 37 g
Corn, cooked	2.4	76.7	½ cup = 82 g
Snap beans, cooked	2.8	89.9	1 cup = 124 g
Lettuce, romaine	1.7	94.9	½ cup = 28 g
Potatoes, baked without skin	1.5	75.4	½ cup = 61 g
Potatoes, French-fried, oven-baked	3.2	57.1	10 pieces = 50 g
Peas, cooked	5.5	77.9	1 cup = 160 g
Cereals and Grains			
Bread, whole wheat	4.3	37.1	1 slice = 25 g
Bread, white	2.3	36.7	1 slice = 25 g
Bread, rye	5.8	37.3	1 slice = 32 g
Rice, white, cooked	0.4	68.4	1 cup = 158 g
Rice, brown, cooked	1.8	73.1	1 cup = 195 g
Oatmeal, cooked	2.3	77.0	
Bran flakes	14.1	2.5	1 cup = 49 g
Corn flakes	2.8	3.2	1 cup = 28 g
Dry Beans and Nuts			
Kidney beans, canned	3.5	77.9	
Garbanzo beans, canned	4.4	69.7	1 cup = 240 g
Almonds, dry-roasted	11.8	2.6	1 cup = 138 g
Walnuts, English	6.7	4.1	1 cup chopped = 120 g
Peanuts, dry-roasted	8.0	1.5	1 cup = 146 g

SOURCE: Data obtained from the USDA Nutrient Database, release 13 at www.nal.usda.gov/fnic/foodcomp/

changing the water content of a food will change its fiber content. Dried plums have the highest fiber content for the fruits listed but also the lowest water content, due of course to the drying process. Likewise, the fiber content of potatoes is higher when the water content is lower. Cooking per se does not generally alter the fiber content of foods unless the water content is changed in the process. The cooking of vegetables will break down the cell wall structure and hence soften tissues; however, this does not remove the polysaccharides associated with the cell wall.

Food preparation methods that remove or separate parts of the food also can alter fiber content. Raw oranges and orange juice have similar water content, but no fiber is present in the juice because the process of squeezing the fruit extracts the watery fraction and leaves behind the fiber associated with the pulp. The milling of whole grains removes fiber, which is concentrated in the outer bran layers of the cereal grain. White rice has a lower fiber content than brown rice due to milling. Likewise, breads made with whole grains that have the bran layer intact will have higher fiber content than breads made with refined grains such as white wheat flour. In some starchy products the presence of resistant starch can contribute to the amount of fiber measured by the TDF method. Starch is digested normally by alpha-amylase in the intestine; however, some starch, because of retrogradation or the structure of the starch polymers, cannot be digested and passes into the large intestine as does NSP. Bran fractions are used in food product formulations to increase the fiber content of cereal products. A breakfast cereal made with wheat bran has a much higher fiber content than one made with a whole grain or a refined grain. Consumers can make quick assessments of such differences, as most food products are labeled with nutrition facts that give the per-serving fiber content.

Fiber Intake and Health

Because fiber is nondigestible by enzymes in the mammalian small intestine, it mediates its effects on metabolism by its impact on the functioning of the gastrointestinal tract. Although fiber has not been considered a nutrient from a traditional perspective, it appears to be essential for the normal function of the small and large intestines. Fiber-containing foods take longer to masticate and involve more chewing than do highly refined foods. Because of the WHC of certain polysaccharides, their presence will increase the amount of water in, and therefore the volume of, the gut contents. The presence of viscous polysaccharides, as well as an increased volume of contents, will slow the rate of gastric emptying. The rate of gastric emptying determines the rate at which nutrients are exposed to the digestive enzymes and absorptive surface in the small intestine and hence the rate of nutrient absorption. Within the contents of the small intestine, the presence of nondigested carbohydrates will expand the bulk phase of the contents;

this type of dilution affects the mixing of gut contents and the process of digestion and absorption.

The net effect of these factors is that a diet high in fiber-rich foods is likely to slow the rate at which nutrients are digested and absorbed and cause digestion and absorption to occur along a greater length of the small intestine. Extending the period in which nutrients are available for absorption might result in a prolonged feeling of fullness and improve the satiety effects of meals. Because fiber is not digested in the small intestine, it passes into the large bowel, where it can remain undigested or serve as a substrate for the microflora that are normally present. Fiber is the only dietary component that increases stool weight. Its ability to improve laxation in this manner is either direct, by providing bulk as nonfermented carbohydrates, or indirect, by allowing growth of the microflora, which contribute to stool bulk. Scientific reviews have estimated that at least eighteen to twenty grams of NSP per 2,000 kilocalories should be consumed daily for adequate stool formation. Thus the properties of fiber result in a slower transit of food through the stomach and small intestine; however, transit through the large intestine may be shorter due to a high fiber intake. The net effect of fiber is to shorten total transit time through the gastrointestinal tract since residence time in the large bowel accounts for more than 90 percent of the total transit time.

Epidemiological or population-based studies have demonstrated that diets rich in plant foods are associated with a lower risk of chronic diseases such as cardiovascular disease, certain cancers, obesity, and Type 2 diabetes. The clinical and experimental studies to examine this relationship indicate that dietary fiber is one of the components of plant foods associated with reducing this risk. The ability of fiber to be protective relates to its functions within the gastrointestinal tract. Sources of viscous polysaccharides such as glucans, pectins, and gums reduce plasma cholesterol (and specifically LDL-cholesterol) levels by reducing absorption of cholesterol and bile acids, which are made from cholesterol. Viscosity helps to blunt the increase in blood glucose after a meal, which reduces the amount of insulin needed to clear glucose from the blood. Diets high in fiber-containing foods such as whole grains, fruits, vegetables, and dry beans tend to be lower in total fat and saturated fatty acids, which is a dietary pattern associated with a lower risk of cardiovascular disease and cancer. These foods also appear to be more filling and may help to regulate short-term appetite. Although fiber has not been proven to facilitate weight loss, its potential effects on appetite may help with weight maintenance. Because of fiber's importance to the microflora in the large bowel, there is considerable interest in its ability to protect against colon cancer. However, the primary evidence for this role of fiber is from epidemiology or experimental animal studies rather than from clinical studies. When microbes metabolize fiber, short chain fatty acids (SCFA) are produced. These SCFA are used by cells in the colon and have been associated with maintaining a healthy mucosal layer in the gut. Advancing our understanding of the role that these compounds play in the health of the gut and in prevention of bowel diseases continues to be an active area of research.

In summary, dietary fiber has specific attributes that promote the normal functioning of the gastrointestinal tract. In addition, actions of fiber contribute to the ability of plant foods to lower the risk of chronic disease; however, it is difficult to isolate the effects of fiber from the overall response to a diet rich in plant foods, which provides many compounds that contribute to a lower risk of disease. As a consequence most recommendations of dietary fiber emphasize the importance of consuming foods high in fiber rather than relying on isolated fiber supplements.

BIBLIOGRAPHY

Food and Nutrition Board, Institute of Medicine. *Dietary Reference Intakes: Proposed Definition of Dietary Fiber.* Washington D.C.: National Academies Press, 2001.

Gallaher, Daniel D., and Barbara O. Schneeman. "Dietary Fiber." In *Present Knowledge in Nutrition.* 8th ed., edited by Barbara A. Bowman and Robert Russell. Washington, D.C.: ILSI Press, 2001.

Schneeman, Barbara O. "Fiber, Inulin and Oligofructose: Similarities and Differences." *Journal of Nutrition* 129 (1999): 1424S–1427S.

Trowell, Hugh. "Dietary Fibre and Coronary Heart Disease." *Revue Européenne d'Etudes Cliniques et Biologiques* 17 (1972): 345–349.

United States Department of Agriculture and Department of Health and Human Services. *Dietary Guidelines for Americans.* Washington, D.C.: U.S. Government Printing Office, 2000.

Barbara O. Schneeman

FISH.

This entry includes three subentries:
Overview
Freshwater Fish
Sea Fish

OVERVIEW

When did human beings begin to eat fish? This question is an endless source of speculation. What can be said with confidence is that our very distant ancestors, if they lived near sea, lake, or river, would have picked up the idea quickly enough; watching the activity of diving birds, and finding fish trapped in rockpools or in naturally formed barriers in rivers, would have been sufficient prompts.

In prehistoric times, the availability of fish as food was distinctly limited. Of the marine species, only inshore ones ran any risk of being caught; deep-sea species, save for the occasional stranding on a beach, were not seen, much less caught and eaten. Even the most accessible of inshore species were relatively safe. So many fish, so few humans. And, to judge by archaeological evidence, humans found it easier to prize mollusks off rocks than to chase darting fish; witness the huge deposits of bivalve shells found in coastal Stone Age communities. Some of these deposits, for example those at Skara Brae in Shetland, are well known; but they are found in many parts of the world.

Freshwater fish enjoyed less immunity. Even before the arrival of nets and harpoons and fishing rods, they could be caught in fish traps made from simple, natural materials such as beavers used for making their dams.

Moving forward in time, it is clear that, at the dawn of recorded history, fishing and eating fish were well established practices. William Radcliffe's highly readable and wide-ranging *Fishing from the Earliest Times* (1926) shows that in most regions of the Old World—China, the civilizations of India and the Middle East, classical Greece and Rome—fish were a significant feature of the diet.

It is also abundantly clear that in early historic times the art of fishing and the scale of consumption developed rapidly. The works of early Chinese writers and of classical Greek authors, although some survive in mere fragments, exhibit a sophisticated range of specific fishing techniques and considerable discrimination among the species. Radcliffe observes that fishing techniques, at least for freshwater fish, have changed less over the centuries than corresponding techniques in, say, hunting (changed by the introduction of the gun); and that the spear, the line and hook, and the net remained preeminent fishing implements.

Special Attributes of Fish as Food
Early humans may have known instinctively that fish constituted a beneficial food. There are many reasons for this. One reason, which no one would have been likely to articulate until recent times, is that fish need a less elaborate skeleton than land animals, since their weight is supported by the water in which they live, providing them more flesh in relation to body weight. They are therefore an excellent source of low-fat protein. (Incidentally, not all species of fish have true, bony skeletons. The category of certain important groups, notably sharks and rays, as "non-bony" indicate they have a skeleton of cartilaginous substance, not bone.)

There are other ways in which fish are unique among the categories of food. First, they constitute by far the largest resource of wild food in the world. Second, the huge number of species of edible fish distinguishes them from other foods. Not even the citizens of Norway or

640

Fisherman hanging fish to dry in the sun at Sunderbans, Bangladesh, 1996. © Tiziana and Gianni Baldizzone/CORBIS.

Singapore (the top two countries worldwide in per-capita consumption) could hope to sample them all.

In addition, humanitarian considerations have been applied only rarely and selectively to fish and other marine or freshwater creatures, in contrast to the land animals (especially mammals) and birds. True, it has recently become unseemly for anyone except the Inuit (Eskimos) to eat marine mammals, and concern is sometimes shown over how to kill lobsters and crabs painlessly; but compassion rarely extends to fish. Nonetheless there may be a gradual change of attitude on this matter; indeed the first signs have already emerged of campaigns to include fish in "animal rights."

This last point would fit in with the reverence that in many cultures has been accorded to fish, and with the symbolic importance they have enjoyed. It is common knowledge that a fish was the first symbol of Christianity, that several disciples of Jesus were fishermen, and that some of his best-known miracles involved fish as well as bread and wine.

In other religions and cultures too fish have had a special place. In ancient Egypt and elsewhere, fish were sacrificed for the gods. They could also take on the role of "scapegoats" or sin bearers. Thus in ancient Assyria people gathered on New Year's Day by a lake or stream and, if they found numerous fish, took this as an omen for the expiation of human sins, and cast their clothes into the water for the fish to bear away, and their sins with them.

Fish could also be used, in Babylon and classical Rome, for auguries and oracular responses, based on a study of their movements. However, it was in Christian cultures that the religious role of fish led to practical consequences. In medieval times the demand for fish, stimulated by the Christian Church's insistence on meatless days, combined with realization that abundant stocks of fish such as cod existed in northerly waters, stimulated voyages of exploration and the development of techniques for fishing in distant waters.

So, at least in Europe, fishing and trade in fish took a new turn as the medieval period began. Northerly peoples such as the Scandinavians emerged from relative obscurity. The powerful Hanseatic League, centered on the Baltic Sea, was based to a considerable extent on its near monopoly of the trade in salted and dried fish; these fish came from the huge stocks of the North Atlantic. Indeed, the subsequent colonization of North America was certainly stimulated—some would say largely caused—by the search for ever more effective ways of exploiting these stocks and by the competition between the maritime powers for them.

The effects of all this activity are still with us. The salted and dried cod of medieval times survives today as an important article of commerce, under Scandinavian names such as *klippfisk*. In many parts of the world people who now have better means of preserving fish, notably freezing, continue to eat these products because they have acquired a taste for them. The same applies to the famous lutefisk which Swedes, for example, devotedly eat at Christmas despite all the bother involved in preparing it. Indeed it applies to many kinds of cured fish, including the hundred and one forms of cured herring such as kippers and bloaters, red herring and rollmops.

All this activity implies a recognition of fish as a valuable food resource. Indeed in the Orient, the Chinese have a consistent record, stretching back for more than four thousand years, of recognizing the nutritional (and often the medical) value of most seafoods, and of honoring fish. Bernard Read in his invaluable "Chinese Materia Medica" comments that:

> Owing to its reproductive powers, in China the fish is a symbol of regeneration. As fish are reputed to swim in pairs, so a pair of fish is emblematic of connubial bliss. As in water fish move easily in any direction they signify freedom from all restraints, so in the Buddha-state the fully emancipated know no restraints or obstructions. Their scaly armour makes them a symbol of martial attributes, bringing strength and courage; and swimming against the current provides an emblem of perseverance. The fish is a symbol of abundance or wealth and prosperity, because they are so plentiful in the seas and rivers.

In the Western world, however, attitudes have been more ambivalent. Although the fish was a symbol of Christianity and prescribed as Lenten fare, opinions were divided on its merits, even on its suitability, as food. In Britain, for example, the evidence of eighteenth-century cookbooks indicates increased consumption of fresh fish from the sea, but the literature of dietetics shows a countervailing current among some medical authorities. As recently as 1835 the respected author of a manual on "modern domestic medicine" declared that fish "affords, upon the whole, but little nourishment, and is, for the most part, of difficult digestion, and this appears to be the general sentiment of intelligent medical men." One author even devoted a lengthy book to arguing that the fundamental cause of leprosy was "the eating of fish in a state of commencing decomposition." These examples remind us that it is only in the present century that seafood has been fully accepted in the West as an admirable source of nourishment. More specifically, it is only in recent decades that the importance of fish oils for health has been fully recognized. The recognition of fish as a valuable article in the diet has led to a flowering of books devoted to fish cookery. The prominence given by authors and by the media generally to fish as food, especially in the English-speaking world, is a new phenomenon which has its effect on demand.

The question arises: what are the future prospects for supplies of fish, and will they be adequate for the growing world population? There are many considerations involved here. Perhaps the most important is the development of aquaculture. Colin E. Nash has shown that there is a wealth of evidence from early sources in Egypt, China, and the Mediterranean region to show how the primitive origins of the industry led long ago to relatively sophisticated practices.

In classical Rome, for example, there were numerous *vivaria* (fish tanks), which served in part as status symbols for the wealthy but were essentially devoted to the production of food. Later, from the early Middle Ages onwards, fishponds became almost ubiquitous in Europe, particularly in association with religious institutions such as monasteries. It does not need a genius to perceive the benefits, and it is not surprising that there is an ancient and strong tradition of constructing and stocking fishponds in Asia also. These, of course, are for freshwater fish, especially carp and (more recently) tilapia. However, even in classical Rome there were *vivaria* for marine species and progress was already being made in taking advantage of saltwater lagoons and suitable parts of estuaries to create enclosures in which seafish could be raised to maturity. Carol Déry has demonstrated that the Romans had progressed amazingly far in this sort of activity, perhaps further than modern people until the last quarter of the twentieth century. Now, however, the pace is quickening. Techniques for raising salmon in sea lochs or similar environments and for dealing with the attendant risks (pollution, infections, etc) are constantly improved. The number of species involved is growing as trials show that more and more can be successfully brought to marketable size in protected surroundings. Atlantic cod are being raised in Norwegian fjords, catfish are brought up in "farms" in the southern states of the United States, and so on. The future looks promising.

As for the sea fisheries, it is difficult to be equally optimistic, since so many fishing grounds are now being exploited up to and beyond the sustainable limits, and some stocks, for example cod in the northwest Atlantic, have already been overfished to the point of extinction. Politics enter into the matter in a big way. To put it very mildly, not everyone in the fishing industry is willing to sacrifice short-term gains for long-term benefits. The same applies to consumers, and it is significant that at the beginning of the present century a new international organization, the Marine Stewardship Council, set about establishing a broad set of Principles and Criteria for Sustainable Fisheries. A system of "eco-labeling" is advocated, whereby special labels will indicate to people buying fish whether these are from an endangered source or not.

Progress may be slow but it is being made, and there is one comforting thought. Humans are now better equipped than ever before to harvest the waters, and also better informed about the ways in which harvests can safely be maximized.

See also **Aquaculture**; **Christianity**; **Crustaceans and Shellfish**; **Fishing**; **Mammals, Sea**; **Mollusks**.

BIBLIOGRAPHY

Déry, Carol A. "Fish as Food and Symbol in Ancient Rome." In *Fish: Food from the Waters*, edited by Harlan Walker, Proceedings of the Oxford Symposium on Food and Cookery. 1997 Totnes, Devon, U.K.: Prospect Books, 1998.

FAO Fisheries Department. *The State of World Fisheries and Aquaculture 2000*. Rome: Food and Agriculture Organization, 2000.

Heen, Eirik, and Rudolf Kreuzer, eds. *Fish in Nutrition*. London: Fishing News, 1962.

Lee, Mercédès. *Seafood Lover's Almanac*. Islip, N.Y.: National Audubon Society, 2000.

Nash, Colin E. "Aquatic Animals." In *The Cambridge World History of Food*, edited by Kenneth F. Kiple and Kriemhild Coneè Ornelas, vol. 1. Cambridge, U.K.: Cambridge University Press, 2000.

Radcliffe, William. *Fishing from the Earliest Times*, 2d ed. London: John Murray, 1926.

Read, Bernard E. "Chinese Materia Medica: Fish Drugs." *Peking Natural History Bulletin* (1939).

Alan Davidson

FRESHWATER FISH

Fish have been a major source of human food and of oil, fertilizer, and feed for domestic animals since the dawn of history. Efforts to propagate fish as a source of high-grade protein for human consumption have been more recent but still date to ancient China and the Roman Empire. In the twenty-first century, fish provide about 25 percent of the animal protein consumed by people in developing countries and as much as 75 percent in countries such as Bangladesh and the Philippines.

One reason for the long-standing popularity of fish as food is sheer numbers. More than 70 percent of the Earth's surface is covered with water, and well over twenty thousand different species of fish live in marine, fresh, and brackish waters, making them the most diverse of all the animals. Fish can live at temperatures ranging from below freezing in Antarctic waters to over 100°F (40°C) in hot springs. They range in size from the .5-inch (1.3-centimeter) dwarf goby of the Philippine Islands to the 45-foot (14-meter), 25-ton whale shark of the tropical oceans. The nutritional profile of fish is also outstanding. Rich in the essential omega-3 unsaturated fatty acids so lacking in other foods, fish are also high in protein yet low in calories, sodium, sugars, saturated fats, and cholesterol.

Biology

Scientifically speaking, fish are aquatic vertebrates with gills instead of lungs and fins instead of external limbs. In contrast to the higher animals, fish are also cold-blooded, that is, their body temperatures remain the same as that of the water. A few species, such as tuna, are able to maintain their body temperatures a degree or two higher than the water.

The chain of life leading to fish production begins with the microscopic diatoms and algae in lakes, rivers, and the ocean. These aquatic plants, collectively termed phytoplankton, use the energy in sunlight to convert carbon dioxide dissolved in the water into the organic matter that eventually becomes food for fish. Fish were the earliest animals with backbones to appear in the fossil record, evolving from more primitive forms over 500 million years ago. In turn, the terrestrial animals evolved from the fishes.

Biologists class the more than twenty thousand known species of fish into three main groups, the Agnatha (primitive jawless fishes, such as the blood-sucking lamprey), the Chondrichthyes (sharks, skates, and rays that have skeletons of cartilage instead of bone), and the Osteichthyes (fishes with a bony skeleton, such as salmon and trout). All of the fish important as food are members of this latter group.

A typical bony fish is torpedo-shaped with a head containing a brain and eyes, a trunk with a muscular wall, and a postanal tail. Fish generally propel themselves through the water by undulating movements of the muscular trunk, using their fins to control direction. All have skins covered with a layer of mucus that decreases friction with the water, and nearly all are covered with an external layer of scales (catfish are one exception). Fishes also have a system of sensory organs along their sides, called the lateral line, that can detect pressure changes in the water caused by sounds. Fish obtain oxygen and eliminate carbon dioxide (breathe) by sucking water into the mouth and pumping it out over the gills. Oxygen dissolved in the water thus diffuses into the bloodstream, and carbon dioxide diffuses out. A few species (such as the African lungfish) also have air-breathing lungs as an additional means of respiration.

Most fish live in either saltwater or freshwater, but some important food fish are physiologically capable of migrating from one to the other. For example, Pacific and Atlantic salmon are hatched and reared in freshwater but then migrate to the ocean to grow and mature, returning to their natal streams and lakes to spawn. The eel has the opposite life history pattern. Thus eel and salmon may be thought of as either freshwater or saltwater fishes depending on age and season.

Over the years, a number of other aquatic animals have been given common names that include the term "fish," such as shellfish, but these do not resemble and are not related to true fish. Furthermore, some animals that have adopted an aquatic way of life, such as whales, seals, and sea snakes, superficially resemble fish and may even be called fish. But they are air breathers, and their anatomical structure is that of land animals.

Preparation and Food Safety

Fish are a highly perishable food product, and historically they had to be marketed live or preserved (cured) by smoking, salting, pickling, or a combination of these methods. Fish to be cured by any method are first cleaned, scaled, and eviscerated. They are salted by packing them between layers of salt or by immersion in brine. Smoking preserves fish both by permeation of smoke ingredients and by partial drying due to heat penetration. Fish can also be dried per se by carefully controlling temperature, humidity, and air velocity.

Freshwater fishing is idealized in this nineteenth-century engraving of a brook trout fisherman by James Merritt Ives. © FRANCIS G. MAYER/CORBIS.

However, dried fish are relatively unappetizing, and rehydration is slow. With the exception of smoked fish, the ready availability of ice and modern freezing and canning facilities has largely supplanted curing as a method of fish preservation. Fish are routinely shipped around the world either fresh or frozen. Fresh fish are shipped on ice and have an acceptable shelf life of about ten days. Frozen fish packaged in oxygen-impermeable plastic wrap, such as Saran, may be stored frozen at –20°F (–29°C) for up to six months with no appreciable loss in quality.

Fresh fish are almost always marketed as either whole fish on ice (viscera removed), dressed fish (head, fins, and viscera removed), fillets (sides cut lengthwise away from the backbone), or steaks (cut longitudinally into sections). Due to consumer demand, boneless cuts are increasingly available in the United States and Europe.

Fish is a naturally tender protein food, free of tough fibers that need to be softened by prolonged cooking. Thus fish products are best cooked using high-temperature, short-time methods. They may be deep-fat fried (325–350°F; 163–177°C), pan fried (sautéed) in a small amount of butter, broiled, poached (simmered, never boiled), or baked (400–450°F; 204–232°C). Pan frying or sautéing is one of the most widely used methods of cooking thin fillets in general. Microwaving is especially well suited to the high-temperature, short-time method of cooking fish. The advent of individually quick-frozen fish fillets has enabled timesaving cooking techniques, such as brushing marinades directly on the frozen

product and grilling or oven roasting without the necessity of defrosting. Fish is generally ready to eat when cooked to a temperature of 140°F (60°C) and the flesh has turned opaque and flakes easily. Fish is eaten raw by some ethnic groups (such as Asians). Other ethnic specialty preparations, such as blackened fish (Cajun) or gefilte fish (Yiddish), are also popular.

To ensure food safety, fresh fish should be clean smelling, and the flesh should be firm and resilient when pressed. Fish should be kept wrapped and refrigerated at 40°F (4°C) or less and eaten within two days. Frozen fish should be rock hard, free of ice crystals, and have no white spots, visible drying, or browning around the edges. In the home, fish should be stored frozen at 0°F (–18°C) or below and for no more than three months. It should be thawed in a refrigerator, never at room temperature.

Freshwater Fish Commonly Used as Food

Historically, the human race has used literally thousands of different species of fish in its continuing search for sustainable sources of food. In the twenty-first century, the most popular in North America and Europe include carp, catfish, crappie, eel, lake herring, mullet, muskellunge, yellow perch, yellow pike, pickerel, salmon, suckers, sunfish, tilapia, trout, lake trout, and whitefish. In Indonesia, the Philippines, and Taiwan, milkfish have been used for food for centuries. In Asia, carp, ayu, and eel are important freshwater food fish. Some of the most interesting of these freshwater fish are discussed in more detail below.

Ayu. The ayu *(Plecoglossus altivelis)*, also known as sweet fish in Japan and aroma fish in China, is an extremely popular and economically important freshwater food fish in many Asian countries. Historically, it was caught by Japanese fishermen using trained cormorants with rings around their necks to prevent them from swallowing. In the twenty-first century, it is wild-caught in rivers by sport and commercial fishermen or raised commercially for both restaurant consumption and home use. Ayu are usually sold live, on ice in the round, or frozen. The food quality of wild-caught ayu is especially desirable, characterized by a sweet, delicate taste and an odor reminiscent of cucumber or watermelon.

Carp. Carp *(Cyprinus carpio)* are the largest members of the minnow family and can easily reach a weight of ten kilograms or more. Although greatly underutilized in North America, the common carp has always been a widely popular freshwater food fish in the rest of the world. History records that carp were grown in ponds for food in ancient China in the fifth century B.C.E. In Europe, carp were grown in monastery ponds as early as the sixth century C.E. so the monks would have something to eat during the many meatless fasting days prescribed by the church. By the late Middle Ages, carp had become a well-established food item for the general populace. In the twenty-first century, carp are wild-caught or grown for food in Russia, Ukraine, Hungary, Poland, India, China, Japan, Latin America, Egypt, Iran, Indonesia, and Israel, to name only the major consumer nations. The world's leading producer is China, where carp are often grown in rice paddies in rotation or even simultaneously.

The most common market forms of carp are fresh whole fish, dressed fish, or fillets. Gefilte fish, fish balls blended with egg and matzo meal and simmered in a vegetable broth, is an ethnic specialty item (Yiddish) traditionally made from carp.

Catfish. The channel catfish *(Ictalurus punctatus)*, native to warm water lakes and rivers in North America, is a traditional food fish in the southern United States. Consumer demand has moved from regional to national and even international. In the United States, the per capita consumption of catfish is exceeded only by that of tuna, shrimp, pollack, and salmon. To satisfy American consumer demand, several hundred thousand metric tons of channel catfish are produced by aquaculture each year in the southern United States.

Imported catfish from Vietnam has been marketed aggressively to restaurant chains and food service companies with considerable success. Advertised as delta-raised catfish, it is actually a catfish relative raised in the delta of the Mekong River. Another catfish species, the walking catfish, is a popular food fish in tropical regions and even in some European countries, especially the Netherlands.

Catfish is firm textured and has a mild, slightly nutty taste that complements a variety of flavors. It is a lean fish, and modern processing methods have eliminated bones. That, together with its lack of a fishy odor, gives it wide consumer appeal. Catfish were traditionally wild-caught and marketed as iced whole dressed fish. Modern farm-raised catfish are processed within minutes and shipped either on ice or as individually quick-frozen fillets, making it one of the freshest fish available. In addition to fresh or frozen fillets, steaks and nuggets (pieces) breaded or marinated with flavors and spices, such as Cajun spices or mesquite, are also common in seafood markets and restaurants and have even been introduced into school lunch programs. As Mark Twain once said, "The Catfish is a plenty good enough fish for anybody."

Eel. Although appreciated before the Civil War in North America, freshwater eels (primarily *Anguilla anguilla* and *A. japonica*) are a widely popular food item in Asian countries, particularly Japan, Korea, China, and Taiwan. Eels are also an important delicacy in Europe, particularly Italy, where they must be produced commercially by aquaculture to satisfy consumer demand. Overall, however, China produces more than 70 percent of the eels sold in the world, and many rice paddies have been converted to eel production. Japan is the world's largest eel consumer, where *kabayaki*, eel fillets grilled with a sweet basting sauce, is practically a national dish.

As mentioned, eel consumption in North America is minor. However, freshwater eel *unagi* is common in Japanese restaurants in the United States, where it may be served grilled with teriyaki sauce or used in sushi or *unadon* (eel over rice). In addition, each year many tons of market-sized eels are wild-caught by U.S. fishermen and exported to Europe, where it is eaten roasted or even jellied and baked into pies.

Eels have an interesting life history in that they live in freshwater rivers and lakes, where they grow to adult size, then they migrate into the ocean, where they swim long distances to the Sargasso Sea to spawn and die. The newly hatched young eels may then ride the ocean currents for several years until they reach coastal waters and swim back to freshwater rivers. There they grow to adult size and can be harvested for food.

Eels under a kilogram in size are the most tender. The rich, sweet, firm flesh of eel must be refrigerated and eaten immediately, so the best restaurants keep live eels in aquarium tanks. The skin and outer layer of fat are removed by the chef, and the fillets are either grilled or roasted. Eel is also available frozen, smoked, or jellied in cans.

Asian folklore holds that eel consumption confers strength and vitality, particularly in hot summer weather. Eels are amazingly rich in vitamin E and in the omega-3 fatty acids (DHA) that are essential to brain functions involving mood.

Milkfish. Milkfish *(Chanos chanos)* have been an important food fish for people in Southeast Asia for many

Traditional fish cage made of split bamboo and reeds (China, twentieth century). Fish were placed inside the cage, which was then submerged in water to keep them alive for market. ROUGHWOOD COLLECTION. PHOTO CHEW & COMPANY.

centuries. Although they are an oceanic fish, milkfish spawn in shallow coastal areas, where fry and fingerlings are collected in nets and carried to freshwater or brackish water ponds for rearing to market size. Milkfish have been raised in this fashion for at least seven hundred years in the Philippines and Indonesia. Taiwan is also a major producer. Milkfish (*bangus*) is sold in Asian markets and restaurants either fresh, smoked, marinated, as fish balls, as fish sausages, or as fish nuggets. It is also exported frozen to North America, where *sinigang na bangus* (milkfish in sour broth) is a popular dish among ethnic Indonesians and Filipinos.

Tilapia. Although relatively new to North American fish markets, tilapia are actually a group of fish (cichlid) that traces its origins to North Africa and the Middle East. These mild, white, sweetly flavored fish have been wild-caught or pond-raised around the world for centuries. Called St. Peter's fish in many parts of the world, legend has it that the fish Jesus multiplied to feed the multitudes in the story of the seven loaves and fishes was tilapia (Matt. 17:24–27).

Because of their versatility, tilapia have been nicknamed "the aquatic chicken" and can be baked, broiled, fried, blackened, grilled, poached, or sautéed. Sautéing is one of the most popular methods of preparing thin fillets in general, and in most recipes tilapia can easily substitute for catfish or even sole and flounder.

Tilapia are grown in floating cages, ponds, or rice fields in temperate and tropical regions around the world. Only Chinese carp and salmon or trout exceed tilapia in total worldwide fish production. Although they are less popular in the United States, tilapia consumption has grown to rival trout among the commercially raised fish species. Since relatively modest numbers of tilapia are produced by U.S. aquaculture, large quantities of frozen fillets are imported from Indonesia, Taiwan, and Mexico to satisfy consumer demand. Many large U.S. cities report a significant demand for live tilapia delivered to ethnic Asian markets.

Trout. Many trout species have historically been used for food, but rainbow trout (*Oncorhynchus mykiss*) have been by far the most popular. Originally native to cold water environments in the north temperate zone, this prized food fish has been transplanted around the world and is well established in North and South America, Japan, China, Europe, Australia, New Zealand, and parts of Africa. Top trout-producing countries include Chile, Denmark, France, Italy, and the United States.

Most rainbow trout is marketed as head-on dressed fish, as fresh or frozen boneless fillets, or as smoked fish. Farmed trout are typically rich in the omega-3 fatty acids so essential to normal brain and eye function, while they are less expensive than most other fish products.

Walleye pike. Walleye (*Stizostedion vitreum*), a member of the perch family with an excellent reputation for its food quality, is a widely sought cool-water fish mostly caught by anglers for home use but also available in fish markets and restaurants in much of the northern United States and Canada. In the United States, a limited commercial harvest comes from the Great Lakes. However, most of the commercial harvest is from Canadian fishing on Lake Erie and the inland waters of Ontario and Saskatchewan. The walleye is Canada's most economically valuable freshwater fish. Only a few commercial growers produce food-size walleye, but because of its reputation for excellent food quality (aroma, flavor, and texture), its name recognition, and its high retail price, walleye has considerable aquaculture potential. Traditionally, walleye are sold as scaled, skin-on fillets. A two-pound fish yields about two eight-ounce dinner-size fillets.

Whitefish. Lake whitefish (*Coregonus clupeaformis*) native to the deep cold lakes of North America are popular food fish in the United States and Canada. They are widely sold in restaurants, and some believe their flaky, non-oily white meat is the best tasting of all the freshwater fish. Early settlers claimed they could eat nothing but whitefish for days at a time and never tire of it. A large commercial fishery for whitefish exists in Lake

Superior and the other Great Lakes of the midwestern United States. In Canada, close to 600,000 kilograms of whitefish a year is caught and sold by tribal fishermen of the Great Slave Lake alone. Most whitefish is marketed frozen and sold in restaurants or supermarkets, but limited amounts are also available smoked or fresh. Whitefish eggs, termed freshwater or golden caviar, are sometimes sold as a less-expensive substitute for sturgeon caviar.

See also **Aquaculture; Fishing; Fish, Salted; Fish, Smoked.**

BIBLIOGRAPHY

American Tilapia Association. Available at http://www.ag.arizona .edu. Hosted by the University of Arizona as a service to the industry.

Catfish Institute. Available at http://www.catfishinstitute.com.

Costa-Pierce, Barry A., and James E. Rakocy, eds. *Tilapia Aquaculture in the Americas.* Baton Rouge, La.: World Aquaculture Society, 1997–2000.

Lagler, Karl F., John E. Bardach, Robert R. Miller, and Dora R. Miller Passino. *Ichthyology.* 2d ed. New York: John Wiley, 1981.

National Fisheries Institute. Available at http://www.nfi.org.

Nelson, Joseph S. *Fishes of the World.* 3d ed. New York: John Wiley, 1994.

Restaurants USA. 1992–1996. National Restaurant Association. Washington D.C., various issues.

Schweid, Richard. *Consider the Eel.* Chapel Hill: University of North Carolina Press, 2002.

Stickney, Robert E., ed. *Encyclopedia of Aquaculture.* New York: Wiley, 2000.

Tucker, Craig S., and Edwin H. Robinson. *Channel Catfish Farming Handbook.* New York: Van Nostrand Reinhold, 1990.

U.S. Trout Farmers Association. Available at http://www.ustfa .org.

Gary A. Wedemeyer

SEA FISH

In all the oceans of the world, fish have abounded for countless millennia, most of them doomed to spend their whole lives swimming until they are eaten by bigger fish. Shakespeare put it well when he had the Third Fisherman in *Pericles* ask how the fishes live in the sea, to which the First Fisherman replies: "Why, as men do on land; the great ones eat up the little ones." Only a tiny minority of fish are sufficiently large or well protected to escape predators. Even they may fall prey to the latest predators to arrive on the scene—to wit, ourselves.

Until human populations began to increase at an exponential rate, and until methods of preserving and transporting foods approached their present level of sophistication, mankind's need for food had little impact on the vast resources of the oceans and seas.

Radical change in this situation began in medieval times, when European fishing boats reached the rich cod-fishing grounds in the northwest Atlantic. Salting techniques, as well as wind-drying, meant that huge quantities of fish could be processed in, for example, Newfoundland and then brought back on the long voyage to Europe. Meanwhile the ascendancy of the Roman Catholic church, with its numerous fast days, in an increasingly populous Europe caused a sharp increase in demand. Salt cod became, and remains to this day, a staple food in the Iberian Peninsula, the south of France, and Italy.

In more recent times fishery techniques evolved swiftly, culminating in the modern fishing industry. This has such deadly accuracy in finding shoals of fish and in catching them, and such advanced means of freezing, that overfishing occurs wherever effective controls have not been instituted. These controls are hard to establish and maintain. The initial impact on fishermen is adverse. Boats have to be laid up; an appreciable number of fishermen lose their livelihood; fishing ports where many people earned a living by servicing the fleets risk falling into a slump. However, if supplies are to be maintained, fish stocks must be allowed to survive in viable number and every ancillary means, notably more and better fish "farming," must be developed.

Considering the merits of fish as a food, nutritionists give it high marks. Sea fish, like freshwater fish, are an excellent source of protein, but have additional health benefits to offer, for example in the form of vitamins, iodine, and phosphorus. Joyce Nettleton (1987) gives a comprehensive survey of the vitamins in which seafoods are rich, including pyridoxine, niacin, and vitamin B_{12}.

So far as fat and oils are concerned, there is a major distinction between what are sometimes called "white fish" (for example, the cod family and flatfish) and what the Spaniards refer to as *pescado azul*, meaning blue fish. The latter category includes the powerful surface swimmers such as tuna and mackerel, which roam at speed over deep waters and whose coloration is usually dark blue with a pale underside, to make them inconspicuous to predators from above or below. Their lifestyle calls for very strong muscles, creating a need for more oil in their bodies. As a group they may be categorized, less romantically than in Spain, as "oily" fish.

There is, as one would expect, no sharp dividing line between oily and nonoily, but a spectrum with "white fish" clustering at one end and "blue fish" at the other. The oil content may be as high as 15 percent (sardines at certain times of year) or as low as 1 percent or even less (flatfish); in general, a content of over 5 percent would be enough to rate a fish as oily. The oily fish contribute more fat to the diet, which makes dieters wary of them, but the fish oils are in fact highly beneficial from several points of view, so much so that people who do not include oily fish in their diet may be advised to take fish oil supplements. Joyce Nettleton provides a clear and full exposition of the merits of the omega-3 fatty acids (present in seafood because it is made in the first place by the phytoplankton in the oceans) and their special virtues.

Summarizing the health benefits of eating sea fish, Nettleton points out that they are low in calories, that most of them are very low in fat, while all are low in saturated fat. The long-chain omega-3 oils have been shown to protect against heart disease and some other afflictions, and are definitely low in cholesterol and in sodium. She refers also to the vitamins and minerals mentioned above, explaining that dark-fleshed fish have especially abundant amounts of iron, and that seafood is the best source of many trace minerals such as zinc, selenium, fluoride, and copper.

Sea fish in general, and "white fish" in particular, are usually easy to digest, partly because they have very little connective tissue. Indeed certain white fish with delicate flesh (for example, whiting) are traditionally recommended as invalid food. Moreover, they can be eaten cold as well as hot.

Fish bought from a fishmonger or in a supermarket are usually from a limited number of familiar species, and bear labels saying what they are. But for some people, for example, travelers and expatriates, choosing and identifying fish can be a problem; and of course a sure means of identification is a necessity for all who are involved in the international fish trade. In these other situations there is potential for confusion, arising mainly from the sheer multiplicity of edible species. There are not many sorts of meat in common consumption, and the number of species of bird which are widely eaten is limited. But the number of edible fish is very large, and even in one market there may be scores available.

The number of species is quite enough by itself to cause perplexity, but there are aggravating circumstances of two kinds, which compound confusion. One source of confusion may be regarded as natural and viewed with tolerance. This is the confusion caused by the fact that even within one language, indeed sometimes within one dialect, the same fish will have a range of different names. These reflect local practice in small coastal communities, which were often isolated from each other in the past by poor overland communications. In Italy, for example, the common grey mullet, *Mugil cephalus*, has more than forty different names.

The other sort of confusion applies to European languages, especially English, and is a by-product of colonization. Its effect is quite the contrary—to make it seem that there are fewer families or species of fish in the world than there really are. What happened was that early English colonists, to take the main culprits as an example, applied familiar but inappropriate names to the species that they encountered in the New World, Australasia, and elsewhere. Understandably, they called the fish they found overseas by names they already knew, on the ba-

sis of a real or fancied resemblance. This could sometimes work satisfactorily. English settlers in North America, familiar with salmon at home, found salmon there too, not always of the same species, but at least of the same family (Salmonidae). But sometimes the results were less happy. The fish that settlers in Australia called salmon are not akin to the salmon of the Northern Hemisphere, while the so-called "Murray cod" of Australia is not a cod and is not even a sea fish.

In a situation affected by so many causes of confusion, it is only the scientific names of the species that can provide certainty. Fortunately, international and national authorities have been working for some time to rationalize commercial names for the species, and more and more authors are adopting the practice of identifying the species they mean, if there is any room for doubt, by its scientific name as well as by popular ones. The work of the Fisheries Division of the Food and Agriculture Organization (FAO) of the United Nations has made, since the 1950s, an outstanding contribution to clarification and precision.

In any case, and in practical terms for consumers, the sort of confusion described above is not the norm; nor does it necessarily cause bad results. A number of species occur around the world, for example, *Xiphias gladius*, the swordfish, and *Mugil cephalus*, one of the grey mullets. Nearly all the families of fish have representatives in both the great ocean areas, and these representatives differ little from the cook's point of view (although the scientists properly distinguish between them by counting their fin-rays or examining their air-bladders). Thus the famous red mullet of the Mediterranean have close relations in the Indo-Pacific; but the latter are known as goatfish, and treated by Asian cooks in a different way, and for this reason people often fail to see the connection.

There are certainly wide variations in the manner of fish consumption. In many European countries it would be normal to serve a small fish whole and a larger fish in full portions (say, 5 oz [150 g]) either separately (to be followed by a vegetable, as often in France) or with vegetables. In Britain, for example, the tradition is that fish is either what you have with chips or something to be served, like meat, with "two veg." But these traditions, although spread around the world to some extent by the influence of France and of the British Empire, are not widely shared. In most parts of the world, especially Asia and Africa, fish is more likely to be one constituent of a combination of different foods, or an element in a one-pot dish, or something that accompanies pasta, or rice, or goes into fish balls, fish puddings, or pies, or is part of a soup-plus-fish-stew dish. Many such modes of presentation produce delicious results, and make a relatively small quantity of fish "go further."

This last point has an even wider application. In most countries of Southeast Asia a product known as fish sauce

Herring barrels stacked along the docks of Aberdeen, Scotland, circa 1900. The barrels await shipment to Europe and North America. ROUGHWOOD COLLECTION.

(*nuoc mam* in Vietnam) plays an important part in the diet as a source of protein. These sauces are prepared by fermenting large quantities of small fish, usually such as would serve no other purpose, and straining the liquor which this process generates. This liquid resembles soy sauce, both in appearance and in its composition. Added to rice or other savory dishes, it enhances both flavor and nutritional qualities.

The preparation of fish sauce is one example of how fresh fish can be turned into a product that will keep for a long time. The various sorts of fish paste are others. The fish used for these purposes lose their identity, whereas those that are dried or salted or smoked (or undergo all three processes) can still usually be seen for what they are. They may also become better to eat, or anyway come to be preferred, as in the case of the kipper (salted, dried, and smoked herring) or the salt cod mentioned above, which has for centuries been a staple food in the Mediterranean region, or the smoked salmon that is now an almost inevitable feature of restaurant menus. That freshwater fish are less often subject to preservation

processes may simply reflect their greater availability—trout can be found in the river (or, nowadays, fish farm) at any time and marketed on the same day, whereas many marine fish can only be harvested by distant fishing boats.

Some species of fish are purely freshwater, others are entirely marine. But the division is not clean-cut, for there are species, and important ones, of sea fish that can, and in some instances must, move from one environment to another. In many instances species that live most of their lives in the sea have to go up rivers to spawn. They are called anadromous. Some famous examples are salmon, shad, and eel. However, the eel differs from the other two in that its stay in freshwater covers the greater part of its life. It is a marine fish only in Act One of its life, when it drifts in larval form across the Atlantic from the Sargasso Sea to the river mouths of Europe, and in Act Five, when it goes back into the sea years later and sets off on its arduous journey back to the Sargasso Sea, there to spawn and die. Indeed, although the sea thus provides both its birthplace and its grave, the eel counts for many purposes as a freshwater species.

If only because of this sort of anomaly, there is little point in asking which are better, freshwater or marine species. It is true, however, that there is some division of opinion, misguided or not, about their respective merits. In inland countries and regions the former may be preferred because they have been accessible for much longer and are established as traditional dishes. Where sea fisheries are established, the reverse is usually the case. However, there are exceptions. To take two examples, people in Bangladesh and Burma prefer freshwater fish and use spices, notably ginger, to mask the marine flavor of sea fish, the very flavor that people in many other countries prize.

Even within the category of sea fish it is interesting to note that some people believe that fish from cold waters are better, the idea being that they lead a particularly active and healthy existence, whereas fish from semitropical or tropical waters laze about and have a less firm consistency. If this belief were to be investigated, it would probably turn out to have little or no foundation.

There is one respect, however, in which sea fish from colder and warmer waters do differ significantly. In cold waters it is usual to find a relatively small number of species, normally existing in huge populations. In tropical or near-tropical waters, on the other hand, there is a very great diversity of species, but few of them are anything like as numerous as those of cold waters.

However, as usual when trying to make generalizations about sea fish, one finds that this contrast is not entirely valid. Some species of tuna are among those which pass, apparently without any problem, from cold to warmer zones and back again. The whole great family of tuna is extraordinary in other ways too. One is the degree of ceremony, drama, and cultural significance with which the fishery for them in the Mediterranean is invested. The tuna traps, of which about a hundred were still operating in the 1960s, were certainly in use in classical times, and some authorities believe that they date even further back. Essentially the trap consists of a long net stretching out to sea, across the expected path of the migrating bluefin tuna. This net diverts the fish into a series of pounds, each of which leads into the next, and finally into the death chamber. There, a net stretched across the bottom can be hoisted up periodically, when there are enough tuna present, bringing them up to a position where they can be taken with gaffs. The fishermen jump in to deliver the death blows. The scene is bloody and to spectators horrifying. The Greek tragedian Aeschylus likened it to the slaughter of the Persians at the battle of Salamis. In Sicily, where the event is called the *mattanza*, and in other places around the Mediterranean the capture and slaughter of the tuna is an event that has more significance than a mere fishery episode; it has served to reaffirm, annually, the cultural identity of the whole community.

In contrast, in most communities in the Western world, the catching and killing of sea fish take place completely offstage; indeed, many of them finish up as neatly trimmed fillets whose identity would be a mystery unless revealed by the label. This distancing of the scene in a dining room from that on the deck of a trawler has left people without the feeling for fish so eloquently expressed by classical writers. This was still evident in nineteenth-century writings such as the Reverend Badham's *Prose Halieutica: Ancient and Modern Fish Tattle*. However, the Greek word in the title is a direct echo of the Greek poet Oppian's *Halieutica*; Badham wishes his readers to know that his own picture of the fishy world, in which the personalities and habits of so many of the fish are described, stems from classical times. If modern writers allude at all to these aspects of the fish, it is only in terms of the struggle fishermen are perceived as waging against the fish, so that the attributes of the fish are generally restricted to terms such as "wily," "valiant," "predatory," etc.

It was in classical Greece that the earliest known guide to finding good food was composed. The author was Archestratus. Enough of the work survives (and has recently been published in translation) to demonstrate the point that is relevant here: that more attention was paid to good sources for fish of the highest quality than to any other category of food. The recommendations were not just of the "Syracuse is the best place to buy fish" variety, but were completely specific. Thus connoisseurs were directed to the straits of Rhegium for sea-caught eels and to Ephesus for a fat gilthead bream. This argues a greater public awareness of quality in fish, and of the various species, than is common nowadays. It is of course relatively easy to have this commendable awareness in a small city-state with an economy based on slave labor and ready access to freshly caught fish. In the modern world, with much of the population inhabiting huge conurbations, far from the fishing ports, and relying in the main on what supermarkets find it economic to provide (there are far fewer fishmongers nowadays), it would be fruitless to expect to find many connoisseurs of fish. Nevertheless, there is one favorable trend, noticeable in the last decades of the twentieth century and the first of the twenty-first. This is the gradual recognition of fish that qualify for an "organic" label as desirable, leading to greater appreciation of quality in fish. This is accompanied by a growing proliferation of cookery books whose recipes frequently call for a particular species of sea fish, and not necessarily one which is in common supply. To take one example, what has happened to the anglerfish (often called monkfish and, in America, goosefish) is instructive. It used to be spurned on both sides of the North Atlantic and was appreciated only in the Mediterranean. Now it has become a valuable and relatively expensive kind of fish, and recipes for it abound. The ability to make greater use of species that had been underexploited in the past is one necessary element in maximizing the harvest of the seas, to the benefit of all.

See also **Crustaceans and Shellfish; FAO (Food and Agriculture Organization); Fish, Salted; Fish, Smoked;**

Fish and Chips; Fishing; Mammals, Sea; Sea Birds
and Their Eggs.

BIBLIOGRAPHY

Archestratus. *The Life of Luxury*. Translated with introduction
and commentary by John Wilkins and Shaun Hill, Totnes,
Devon, U.K.: Prospect Books, 1994.

Badham, Rev C. David. *Ancient and Modern Fish Tattle*. London, 1854.

Davidson, Alan. *Mediterranean Seafood*. Berkeley, Calif.:
Ten Speed Press, 2002.

Davidson, Alan. *North Atlantic Seafood*. Berkeley, Calif.:
Ten Speed Press, 2002.

Food and Agriculture Organization of the United Nations.
Species Identification Sheets. Rome: FAO. Published as a continuing series since the 1970s and now covering most families and most fishing regions.

McClane, A. J. *Saltwater Fishes of North America*. New York:
Holt, 1978.

Nettleton, Joyce A. *Seafood and Health*. Huntington, N.Y.: Os-
prey Books, 1987.

Wheeler, Alwyne. *Fishes of the World*. London: Ferndale, 1975.

Alan Davidson

Fishmonger cutting dried codfish at a fish market in Rome,
Italy. The counter on which he is cutting the fish is covered
with salt. © Owen Franken/CORBIS.

FISH, SALTED.

Sodium chloride (NaCl), also called
salt, common salt, and table salt, is generally recognized
as a safe (a status sometimes abbreviated by the acronym
GRAS) antimicrobial and incidental food additive
(Klaassen). Salt has been used for centuries as a seasoning and flavor enhancer as well as a preservative or curing agent. Salt has played a major role in many aspects
of human life: nutritional, economic, political, and military. Egyptians preserved food by salting or sun-drying;
Roman soldiers were paid in salt; Napoleon's campaign
in Russia suffered a setback because of lack of salt; and
salt was used in trade and exchanged for slaves in ancient
Greece (Pszczola; Salt Institute). The Greeks also salted
fish and used them as a part of their diet. Later, they
passed this practice on to the Romans (Jay).

Fish Preservation

Fish are highly perishable, and they will spoil rapidly if
improperly handled. Fresh iced fish generally are spoiled
by bacteria, but dried fish are usually spoiled by fungi
(Jay). Salting as a method of preserving fish has been used
for centuries and in many places around the world such
as Asia, Europe, and Latin America. The simplicity of the
salting process, the low cost of production and the ease
with which it combines with other preservation methods,
such as drying or smoking, has led to its popularity and
extensive use (Berhimpon et al.).

In the usual process of dry-salting, whole fish are
eviscerated, cleaned, washed, dry-salted, stacked in containers with more NaCl in between the pieces, stored for
a salting or curing period, and then dried (using sunlight
or artificial indoor drying chambers). The salting period
depends on several factors including the desired ripened
characteristics in fish, the fish species, the amount of salt
used, and the storage temperature. For example, increasing the amount of NaCl reduces the required time
of storage.

Use of salt in fish preservation is not limited to dry
application. Salt is an important additive in the preparation of fermented, pickled, or processed fish or fish
products. In the making of fermented fish, known concentrations of salt are added to promote degradation of
proteins and retard the growth of undesirable, putrefac-
tive microorganisms. Also, this allows desirable, NaCl-
tolerant (halotolerant), fermentative species such as lactic
acid bacteria to grow. Pickled fish are marinated in salt
brine or brine containing vinegar. Curing salt (containing sodium nitrate, NO_3) can be added to the pickle to
delay spoilage and control microbial activity during storage (Pederson and Meyland). Other ingredients—spices,
sugar, herbs, or vinegar—are incorporated during the
process to impart a particular flavor, texture, or color.
Herring, haddock, and anchovies are fish species often
available in the market in pickled form.

In manufacturing processed fish products, adding
certain amounts of NaCl assists in the extraction of salt-
soluble proteins and the formation of a sticky paste of
fish meat. The development of the gelled paste might be
due to the formation of a protein network structure or
polymerization of myosin-heavy chains (Kumazawa,
Numazawa, Seguro, and Motoki). In breaded processed
fish products, NaCl is used in the predusting step to enhance adhesion of the batter to the fish (Claus, Jhung-
Won, and Flick). Processing fish has created a niche
market for products that otherwise would have been

wasted because of overharvesting of species, low consumer appeal, high processing costs, or limited shelf life.

Salt, Spoilage, and Preservation

Over the years, a number of spoilage and pathogenic microorganisms, including lactic acid bacteria, *Pseudomonas* spp., *Staphylococcus* spp., *Salmonella* spp., *Clostridium perfringens, Clostridium botulinum, Escherichia coli* O157:H7, and *Listeria monocytogenes,* have been associated with fish and fish products. At certain concentrations, salt was found to prevent growth of many microorganisms by exerting a drying effect on microbial cells and tissue, which concentrates solutes in them, creating an environment unsuitable for microbial proliferation. Because some halotolerant or halophilic (salt-loving) microorganisms are not affected by salt, additional treatments such as drying, heating, curing, or smoking are helpful in controlling them. Dry-salted fish (that is, dried by the salting method), for example, are dried and/or smoked to extend their shelf life.

In addition to microbial spoilage, fish that contains high levels of lipids—salmon, herrings, and mackerel—are prone to oxidation and become rancid as microbial spoilage occurs (Jay). Because of their unsaturated nature, fish body oils are susceptible to oxidation and also easily develop rancid and unacceptable odors and flavors during storage (Waterman). Once fatty compounds are oxidized, the breakdown products of lipid oxidation potentially can react with proteins and vitamins, leading to a loss of nutritional value and quality of the fish (Pokorny). Salted sun-dried fish are more prone to oxidation than fish preserved by other methods because of their exposure to light and oxygen (Smith and Hole). Use of crude NaCl (which contains impurities such as chlorides, sulfates, calcium, and heavy metals) accelerates lipid oxidation during fish processing and will adversely affect the overall quality of the finished product (Yankah et al.).

In order to reduce the adverse effects of NaCl on lipid oxidation, color, and flavor of fish, fish and fish products are handled, prepared, and processed under refrigerated temperatures. Low temperatures reduce the rates of oxidative reactions and retard microbial growth. Products also can be vacuum packaged after drying and/or cold or hot smoking. Vacuum packaging creates an environment that virtually lacks oxygen, a promoter of oxidative rancidity. Chelating agents, bio-preservatives, antioxidants, and other compounds also can be added to maintain color, flavor, and integrity of the products.

Throughout history NaCl has been a popular and important food additive. The many advantageous properties that NaCl possesses led to its incorporation in several unprocessed and processed foods. Its functionality as a preservative, catalyst in extraction of NaCl-soluble proteins (binder), flavor enhancer, and color developer has played a major role in food processing and preparation. Improvements and advancements in technology worldwide have allowed even better use of NaCl by the food industry, such as production of processed fish products. Because salt does have its limitations and disadvantages, its utilization conditions must be optimized to provide safe food for consumers, at the same time addressing their needs and concerns.

See also **Fish; Fishing; Iodine; Meat, Salted; Military Rations; Preserving; Salt; Sodium.**

BIBLIOGRAPHY

Berhimpon, S., R. A. Souness, R. H. Driscoll, K. A. Buckle, and R. A. Edwards. "Salting Behavior of Yellowtail (*Trachurus mccullochi Nichols*)." *Journal of Food Processing and Preservation* 15 (1991): 101–114.

Claus, J. R., C. Jhung-Won, and G. J. Flick. "Processed Meats/Poultry/Seafood." In *Muscle Foods: Meat, Poultry, and Seafood Technology*, edited by D. M. Kinsman, A. W. Kotula, and B. C. Breidenstein. New York: Chapman and Hall, 1994.

Jay, J. M. *Modern Food Microbiology.* 4th ed. New York: Van Nostrand Reinhold, 1992.

Klaassen, C. D. "Principles of Toxicology." In *Casarett and Doull's Toxicology: The Basic Science of Poisons*, edited by C. D. Klaassen, M. O. Amdur, and J. A. Doull. New York: Macmillan, 1986.

Kumazawa, Y., T. Numazawa, K. Seguro, and M. Motoki. "Suppression of Surimi Gel Setting by Transglutaminase Inhibitors." *Journal of Food Science* 60 (1995): 715–717, 726.

Pederson, E., and I. Meyland. "Nitrate, Nitrite, and Volatile Nitrosamines in Pickled Fish Prepared with Addition of Nitrate." *Zeitschrift für Lebensmitteluntersuchung und forschung A* [European food research and technology] 173 (1981): 359–361.

Pokorny, J. "Browning from Lipid-Protein Interactions." *Progress in Food and Nutrition Science* 5 (1981): 421–428.

Pszczola, D. E. "Salty Developments in Food." *Food Technology* 51 (1997): 79–90.

Salt Institute. *Facts about Salt.* Alexandria, Va.: Salt Institute, 2000.

Smith, G., and M. Hole. "Browning of Salted Sun-Dried Fish." *Journal of the Science of Food and Agriculture* 51 (1991): 193–205.

Waterman, J. J. "The Production of Dried Fish." *FAO* [Food and Agriculture Organization] *Fish Technical Paper*, 160 (1976): 1–52.

Yankah, V. V., T. Ohshima, H. Ushio, T. Fujii, and C. Koizumi. "Study of the Differences between Two Salt Qualities on Microbiology, Lipid, and Water-Extractable Components of Momoni, a Ghanaian Fermented Fish Product." *Journal of the Science of Food and Agriculture* 71 (1996): 33–40.

James L. Marsden
Maha N. Hajmeer

FISH, SMOKED. Wind-drying is the most ancient and basic way of preserving fish. Add the discovery of fire, and early humans might have found that fish hung up over a fire dried more quickly, and that, if the fire was

Worker preparing smoked bonito at a fish smoking establishment in Miyazaki, Kyushu, Japan. © MICHAEL S. YAMASHITA/CORBIS.

smoky, fish would acquire a different flavor and keep better. Indeed Cutting (1955) suggests that people might have begun to smoke fish deliberately in the Neolithic. However, it seems to be uncertain whether such smoking of fish was carried out later on, in ancient Egypt or classical Greece and Rome.

As Sue Shephard (2000) points out, archaeologists have uncovered the remains of what was evidently a substantial fish-smoking "factory" in Poland, dating back to the seventh century. And it is clear that European use of the technique was greatly expanded, perhaps mainly in order to deal with gluts of herring, in the medieval period. Dedicated smoke houses used for this purpose were in common use in England, and no doubt elsewhere in the fourteenth century.

Smoke is highly complex, having a couple of hundred or more constituents. So what it does to fish is also complex, but can be summarized by saying that it deposits on the fish various phenols, aldehydes, tars, etc. and that the combined effect of some of these, which have bactericidal properties, is to make the fish keep noticeably better.

In modern times progress has been made in the construction of special ovens for smoking fish; in analyzing the constituents of smoke which are responsible for changes of flavor; in the choice of wood shavings or chips whose smoke produces the best results; and in elaborating the techniques of both hot and cold smoking.

Hot smoking was developed in northern Europe in medieval times. In this process the smoke temperature is very high and the fish is wholly or partly cooked by being smoked. Herring which were hot smoked on the northern coast of Germany were known as *Bücklinge*, which became "buckling" in English, but the process was also used for many other species of fish. The hot smoking of fish is also common in Africa. For example, a kind of shad is hot smoked in Ghana in primitive kilns made from oil drums. Hot smoked fish is succulent and tasty but in general does not travel or keep as well as cold smoked. Cold smoking, on the other hand, is not a cooking process; it consists simply in hanging fish in smoke (which may of course be slightly warm, but that is irrelevant), and the result keeps well.

As for the choice of combustible, the traditional preference in Britain was for oak, with ash as second choice and peat being used until recently in Scotland, especially for domestic smoking in their kitchen chimneys by fishermen's wives. In Russia, the woods used have included

HADDOCK

Since haddock does not take salt as well as cod, the traditional ways of curing haddock were by drying and smoking. In the category of smoked haddock the most famous have been what was originally a product of the fishing village of Findon, near Aberdeen in Scotland. Peat was used as the source of heat and smoke, and the haddocks, when sold, proudly bore the name Finnan haddocks or Finnan haddies. The taste spread to France where the product became so popular that in French the term "haddock" means 'smoked haddock', one significant instance of an English word invading the French language (which does of course possess its own word for fresh haddock, *églefin*). The taste also spread to the United States in the nineteenth century, witness the statement by G. Brown Goode and his associates (see bibliography) that smoked haddock were even then being manufactured in large quantities in Portland and Boston. It is interesting that Goode called them Finland haddocks, perhaps reflecting a misunderstanding of the true name by the American manufacturers.

The production of Finnan haddocks or the like no longer involves the use of peat and is carried out in many places. However, the essential process still involves the traditional stages. The fish, cleaned and split open, are left in brine for a while and then hung up to drain. As the surface dries, it develops an attractive gloss. Smoking comes next and is normally continued until the fish have taken on a straw color (which will darken further after the fish have been taken out of the smoking plant). Small haddock which have been treated in this way but withdrawn from the smoking process while their color is a very pale straw are known as Glasgow pales. This light coloration is at the opposite extreme from the lurid yellow hue often imparted artificially to the fish by large-scale commercial smokers.

Hot smoking is used for what are called Arbroath smokies. Arbroath is the Scottish town where their production became a local industry.

alder, oak, poplar, and lime. Wood from coniferous trees has also been used, but imparts a resinous flavor.

Nowadays there are numerous books on home smoking, explaining how various small contraptions can be used to produce smoked fish; and a few books which treat the subject in a general and historical manner, while not neglecting technical aspects. In this last category falls the book by Cutting and that by Burgess and others (including Cutting, 1965). Zaitsev and others (1969), in their 700-page manual *Fish Curing and Processing*, are also helpful on the technical aspects. Sea fish smoked in Russia include sturgeon, cod, herring, whitefish and grey mullet. Freshwater fish include carp, bream, and pike-perch.

In modern times, the best known smoked fish is smoked salmon, now prepared in many countries and figuring on innumerable restaurant menus around the world. Many of the salmon which are smoked are farmed salmon, but the proportion of farmed to wild varies greatly. In North America more than half of the smoked salmon are farmed, most coming from British Columbia, but even so smoked wild salmon is much easier to obtain there than in Europe. Traditions of smoking salmon in the Pacific Northwest go back a long way, and Shephard has an interesting passage about the cultural significance which American Indians attached to these fish, believing them to be "undersea people who put on salmon skins to swim ashore and offer themselves as food."

Smoked eel, of which the best comes from the Netherlands, is now being produced in the United States, in Scotland, and elsewhere; and smoked mackerel has become a success internationally. These are all fish with a relatively high oil content, a feature which works well with smoking. However, less oily fish such as cod and haddock are also smoked successfully. In Britain there is a long tradition of smoking haddock.

Despite the ubiquity of smoked salmon and the importance of smoked haddock, many people in Britain regard the kipper, a form of smoked herring, as their top favorite. It dates back only to the 1840s, the period when railways began to facilitate rapid transport of cured fish from the ports to other areas, and soon achieved prominence because it was so useful in helping to conserve the huge catches of herring which used to be made off British coasts.

In North America, smoking has been used for more and more species, both freshwater (e.g., trout, also a highly popular smoked fish in Europe) and marine. Whitefish, marlin and tuna are examples of larger fish which have to be smoked in fillets. Swordfish is another large fish of global distribution that is smoked in many of the countries where it is caught. Halibut may be smoked, indeed this treatment seems to be the best way of dealing with Greenland halibut, a delicacy in Denmark.

In Asia, much of the smoking of fish is carried out on an artisanal small-scale basis, and the number of species involved is large. Smoked snapper (for example *pla kaphong* in Thailand) is excellent. In China, especially in the south, smoked pomfret is an important delicacy.

It is not only whole fish or fillets of fish which are smoked. Smoked cod roe is a prominent example of other parts being so treated. In Greece, imported smoked cod roe has largely replaced the dried roe of grey mullet as the basis for the delicious fish roe paste known internationally as *taramosaláta*.

The indications are that the list of smoked fish and smoked fish products will be progressively extended, since most fish are susceptible to smoking and smoked fish, with smoked salmon in the vanguard, has been winning greater and greater consumer acceptance. In times gone by, smoking fish was done to preserve it. Nowadays there is a further, gastronomic, reason. The flavor of smoked fish has come to be appreciated in its own right. If the proportion of the global catch of sea fish which is smoked goes up, that should be viewed as a favorable development. It should lead to less waste, greater flexibility in the use of fish, and often more pleasure for the consumer.

BIBLIOGRAPHY

Burgess, G. H. O., et al. *Fish Handling and Processing*. London: Her Majesty's Stationery Office, 1965.

Cutting, C. L. *Fish Saving*. London: Leonard Hill, 1955.

Goode, G. Brown, and Associates. *The Fisheries and Fishery Industries of the United States*. Washington D.C.: Government Printing Office, 1884-1887.

Shephard, Sue. *Pickled, Potted and Canned: The History of Food Preservation*. London: Headline, 2000.

Zaitsev, V., et al. *Fish Curing and Processing*. Translated by A. de Merendol. Moscow: Mir Publishers, 1969.

Alan Davidson

FISH AND CHIPS. Fish and chips has a strong historic claim to the status of the national dish of industrial Britain. Perhaps fittingly, in postindustrial and postcolonial times it has been hit hard by competition from a proliferating variety of ethnic restaurants and takeout restaurants, especially Indian and Chinese, and by the rising cost of the traditional fish species to which its loyal adherents are firmly attached. Its origins coincided with the sustained rise in working-class purchasing power that was ushered in by falling prices in the last quarter of the nineteenth century. Although the identity of the first fish and chip shop cannot be confirmed, it was either in London's East End or in the textile factory districts of northern England, and it opened in about 1870, combining two commodities, fish fried in batter and chipped potatoes, which had previously been hawked through the streets as separate entities. It was a cheap and filling dish, enlivened with salt and vinegar, and it began as a late-night snack for revellers on the way home after the pubs had closed. By the turn of the century, however, the fish and chip shop had become a general feature of the urban industrial landscape, selling to women and families as well as to men, and to factory workers (and housewives) in the midday break as well as in the early evening and at night.

By 1910 there were about 25,000 fish and chip businesses in Britain, almost all of them single-family oper-

Fish and chips are a great favorite in Britain, although the health implications from eating this kind of fried food are much debated by nutritionists and physicians. This queue is eagerly awaiting lunch in Derbyshire, England. © ROBERT HOLMES/CORBIS.

ations (the success of the Harry Ramsden chain in the late twentieth century was novel and anomalous). By 1927, as the industry reached its peak, there were perhaps 35,000. Fish and chips provided the dominant market for the catches of the steam trawler fleets that were rapidly expanding at the turn of the century. The business also consumed huge quantities of potatoes and generated a major specialized engineering industry to supply frying ranges and related products. It was both mocked and celebrated in music-hall song, and different British regions took pride in their own preferred species and specialities, especially "jumbo haddock" fried in beef dripping in the coal-mining and woollen-manufacturing districts of West Yorkshire.

As a labor-saving foodstuff, prepared outside the home and often defying the "civilising process" by being sold in newspaper wrapping and eaten in the street with the fingers, fish and chips attracted a lot of snobbish and pseudo-scientific criticism. Social reformers associated it with slovenly domestic habits and claimed that it was expensive, while local government medical officers alleged that it spread illnesses, and in many towns it was regulated as an "offensive trade" alongside soap boiling and rag picking. In Scotland, where many of the fish friers were Italian immigrants, authority was particularly suspicious. But the balance of the evidence suggests that it provided a valuable and palatable boost to working-class diets, while taking some of the strain off hard-working domestic labor and providing an outlet for aspiring petty capitalists in working-class communities. It was even claimed that fish and chips played an important part in winning World War I by sustaining morale and stamina on the home front, and by the 1930s it was becoming increasingly acceptable to middle-class consumers, although by that time it was beginning a long, slow decline that still continues at the turn of the millennium.

See also **England; Fast Food; Fish; Fishing; French Fries; Potato.**

BIBLIOGRAPHY

Priestland, Gerald. *Frying Tonight: The Saga of Fish and Chips.* London, Gentry: 1972.

Walton, John K. *Fish and Chips and the British Working Class, 1870–1940.* Leicester: Leicester University Press, 1992; reprint, New York: Continuum, 2000.

John K. Walton

FISHER, M. F. K. Mary Frances Kennedy Fisher (1908–1992) wrote twenty-three books and hundreds of articles in which cuisine was virtually always her metaphor of choice. Many of her works included recipes, and she is often characterized as a food writer; this description, however, underestimates her powers as a highly creative author and a keen observer. She wrote of human hungers in the deepest sense. Fisher recognized the rich psychological, social, and cultural meaning of cuisine, identifying food, security, and love as fundamental and intertwined needs. Memorable meals eaten, rich wines and liqueurs imbibed, and the company she kept are equally important in her often highly personalized writing.

Mary Frances Kennedy Fisher at home in Sonoma, California, 1971. © AP/WIDE WORLD PHOTOS.

Born in Albion, Michigan, but raised in Whittier, California, from the age of four, Mary Frances Kennedy was the eldest of four children. At the age of nine she began experimenting in the kitchen and preparing meals. She wrote that food preparation brought recognition from her family, as well as proof of her own ontological being. Her father, Rex Kennedy, owned and published the local newspaper. Whittier was a conservative Quaker town, and the Kennedys, Episcopalian. Their religion prevented their complete assimilation into the community; thus, Mary Frances grew up with a perspective akin to an ethnographer: never fully part of the local culture, but with a defined role to play in it. She developed a discerning eye and used it to interpret others' lives while remaining removed from them.

At age twenty-one, the author married Alfred Young Fisher, the first of her three husbands. He received a graduate fellowship to study in France, and Mary Frances accompanied him, choosing to study art at the University of Dijon. The next three years proved formative as she became fluent in French and was introduced to regional cuisines. Although she was not to consider herself a writer for some years, she was a passionate correspondent throughout her life. Her expertise as a wordsmith was already apparent in her letters home from France (Barr et al., 1997).

Fisher's permanent home was California, but she passed numerous extended periods in France. Her writing reflects these distinct parts of the world. She also owned a home and a vineyard in Switzerland with her second husband, Dillwyn Parrish. She frequently wrote of her trans-Atlantic journeys by ocean liner and train travels within Europe. These accounts included descriptions of dining rooms and dining cars, the cuisine, its preparation, and its service. The journeys became symbolic of transitions in her life, as in one of her most compelling works, *The Gastronomical Me* (1943).

Fisher wrote in a broad range of genres including fiction, nonfiction, journalism, screenplay, poetry, and children's literature. Although her writing includes two novels, she excelled at essays. While many of her writings were based on events in her own life, she fictionalized these first-person narratives, transcending the boundaries of autobiography.

Fisher had a bold character; she was strikingly independent and she spun a worldly mystique around her tales. After divorcing Donald Friede, her third husband, she raised two daughters as a single parent. Her worldly panache convinced many readers that she was wealthy. In reality, her commitment to writing meant that she often struggled to make ends meet, earning less from her books than her published essays, which included a two-year series for the *New Yorker*, compiled afterward in *With Bold Knife and Fork*.

Among Fisher's greatest contributions was the translation of Jean Anthelme Brillat-Savarin's *The Physiology of*

Taste. The early-nineteenth-century book of French manners is a masterpiece of droll commentary. Fisher's achievement lies not only in a masterful translation, but in her witty notations, equal to Brillat-Savarin's original, self-effacing, humorous style.

Fisher generously mentored young writers and had significant impact on Jeannette Ferrary and Anne Lamott. She was a close friend of both James Beard and Julia Child; the three visited, corresponded, and influenced one another. She advised and befriended restaurateurs including Alice Waters of Chez Panisse in Berkeley, California. Fisher favored fresh and local foods; she called them honest. Her approach had a significant impact on the evolution of California cuisine in the last quarter of the twentieth century. She passed her last years in the California wine country, and the region became the subject of some of her work.

W. H. Auden stated that had M. F. K. Fisher's subject been anything other than food, she would have been appreciated as the United States's finest twentieth-century author. Her books were widely translated and repeatedly republished. She made French cuisine and culture accessible, opening the doors of western European gastronomy to North Americans and other readers worldwide; her work reflects the sense of place she felt on two continents. Fisher received numerous literary prizes, including a lifetime achievement award from the James Beard Foundation. She was elected to the American Academy of Arts and Sciences in 1991.

See also **Beard, James; Brillat-Savarin, Anthelme; Gastronomy; Metaphor, Food as; United States: California and the Far West.**

BIBLIOGRAPHY

Barr, Nora K., Marsha Moran, and Patrick Moran, eds. *M. F. K. Fisher: A Life in Letters: Correspondence 1929–1991.* Washington, D.C.: Counterpoint, 1997.

Brillat-Savarin, Jean Anthelme. *The Physiology of Taste, or, Meditations on Transcendental Gastronomy.* Translated by M. F. K. Fisher. Washington, D.C.: Counterpoint, 1997.

Fisher, M. F. K. *The Art of Eating.* Contains *Serve It Forth, Consider the Oyster, How to Cook a Wolf, The Gastronomical Me, An Alphabet for Gourmets.* New York: 1990 [1954].

Fisher, M. F. K. *Two Towns in Provence.* Contains *Map of Another Town* and *A Considerable Town.* New York: Vintage, 1983.

Fisher, M. F. K. *With Bold Knife and Fork.* New York: Putnam, 1969.

Susan L. F. Isaacs

FISHING. Fishing is the art and science of catching animals that live in water. This pursuit can be for fun or profit. Recreational angling is often practiced as an art, with little to no expectation of actually catching and keeping a fish for personal use. In commercial fishing, there

This rare manual on fishing called "The Excellent Little Fish Book" was published anonymously in Nürnberg about 1660. Parts of the text are based on Georg Mangolt's *Fischbuoch* [Fish Book] printed in Zurich in 1557, one of the first books to deal with fishing as an art and as a sport. ROUGHWOOD COLLECTION.

is an expectation of catching and keeping fish or invertebrates and an expectation of selling those animals for profit. This article will focus on commercial fishing.

Hunting and gathering animals that live in water is an ancient form of food gathering. Today, aquatic animals caught from wild populations are one of, if not the last, major food category we still predominantly hunt and gather. Virtually all of the other foods we consume are grown in agricultural operations. However, we are in the early phases of a major transition from hunting and gathering fish and shellfish to agricultural production (aquaculture) of aquatic animals.

We live on a wet planet. Water comprises greater than 70 percent of Earth, and that habitat is home to far more vertebrates than the dry portion of the planet. Given the size and scope of aquatic habitats and the diversity of species present, it is not surprising that it took until 1989 to reach maximum sustainable yield from the world's oceans. Maximum sustainable yield is the tonnage of aquatic animals that can be harvested annually while maintaining healthy populations. It is important to note that there are two distinct groupings when discussing fish: individual species and the sum of all species. Further subdivisions are possible, but the important point is that individual populations or species can be in poor condition (for example, low numbers) while overall, fishes in that body of water are generally healthy.

Since 1989, global commercial harvest has been close to 90 million metric tons, and that figure is not expected to increase. The largest commercial harvest industries are for species used for making fish meal (anchovy, herring, and menhaden) and those used for food (pollack, mackerel, and capelin). The largest species-oriented industries are listed in Table 1.

There are over 22,000 species of fish, and the United Nations Food and Agriculture Organization monitors commercial harvest of slightly over 1,100 species. Further, a thorough understanding of fish taxonomy (the science of fish identification) is not commonplace among many commercial fishermen. Thus, many species simply are grouped into a nonspecific category such as marine fishes. From the data above, it seems clear that the commercial fishing fleets from the western coast of South America (Chile and Peru) and Southeast Asia (China, Thailand, Vietnam, Myanmar, and Japan) harvest more fish than other parts of the planet. Not shown in Table 1 are the most productive fishing grounds, which are the Pacific Northwest, Pacific Southeast, and the northeastern portion of the Atlantic Ocean.

There are several reasons postulated for the plateauing of commercial harvests. Pollution and other environmental stressors on fish populations are common speculations, as well as overharvest by commercial fishing fleets. From the industrial revolution to current times, pollutant levels in the oceans increased and certainly had some negative impact on populations of animals in aquatic habitats. Over the same time period, commercial harvesting equipment improved significantly and also contributed to declines in populations and leveling of harvest volumes. Regardless of the cause, wild populations of many fish and shellfish declined in the latter half of the twentieth century. However, it is important to grasp the scope of the situation before assigning blame to any particular cause.

The average depth of oceans is over 13,000 feet (4,000 meters). Over 84 percent of the oceans are deeper than 6,500 feet (2,000 meters). The Marianas Trench in the western Pacific Ocean is the deepest place at 36,000 feet (11,000 meters), deeper by a mile than the altitude of Mount Everest (29,000 feet, or 8,845 meters high). As stated earlier, the vast majority of our planet is under water. Many species of fish either travel long distances in their normal habits or the populations inhabit large areas. Given these facts, establishing accurate population estimates is virtually impossible. Fishing gears and efficiency of commercial harvest have increased significantly and also contribute to attaining maximum sustainable yield.

Fishing gears are largely unchanged from ancient times. Nets of various types are the most commonly used commercial fishing gear. The basic concept of a net, regardless of the configuration, is the same today as it was when ancient man first wove fibers together to make nets. Impaling devices such as spears and harpoons are also unchanged from ancient times. There are numerous types of traps in use, mainly for trapping crustaceans (lobsters, crabs, crayfish), and those have ancient origins. Fishing gears have become more efficient, but in subtle ways. Prior to about 1980, trawls (nets pulled behind a boat) could attain only a limited depth and were nonspecific in their catch. Significant research efforts resulted in trawls that could be fished deeper (up to 8,200 feet, or 2,500 meters) and had devices that would tend to exclude mammals or turtles. Harpoons are not routinely used in the twenty-first century, and spears have evolved to spear guns for individual fishermen. Trap materials have changed with the advent of polymers, but the basic configurations have not changed for hundreds of years. The major change that occurred is not in gears, but in the boats.

Commercial fishing boats are capable of staying at sea for months at a time, giving fishermen the ability to fish anywhere in the world. Technological advances in

TABLE 1

Commercial harvest of fish and shellfish in 1999 and the country of landing

Species	Harvest (million metric tons)
Anchovy, Peru	6,740,225
Marine fishes, China*	3,853,814
Anchovy, Chile	1,983,040
Pollack, Russian Federation	1,500,450
Marine mollusks, China*	1,445,303
Freshwater fishes, China*	1,394,610
Largehead hairtail, China	1,222,454
Jack mackerel, Chile	1,219,689
Marine crustaceans, China*	1,131,643
Anchovy, Japan	1,096,916
Pollack, United States	1,055,016
Herring, Norway	821,435
Araucanian herring, Chile	782,142
Marine fishes, Vietnam*	770,000
Marine fishes, Thailand*	750,000
Capelin, Iceland	703,694
Marine fishes, Myanmar*	695,904
Gulf menhaden, United States	694,242

*Many species are listed under a general heading.

SOURCE: United Nations Food and Agriculture Organization

Caboclo fishermen fishing in the Amazon River of Brazil. © WOLFGANG KAEHLER/CORBIS.

engines, fuels, and boat designs, coupled with international treaties that allow foreign fishing fleets safe harbor, increased the efficiency of commercial operations. Harvested animals can be cleaned on board and frozen at −76°F (−60°C) for extended storage. Large companies evolved to more efficiently harvest fish, and those companies developed the concept of multiple fishing boats and a mother ship for processing and storing fish. It is not uncommon to find Japanese fishermen in the North Atlantic Ocean harvesting giant bluefin tuna. Fishermen also take advantage of the other forms of commercial transport, taking some of their harvest to nearby ports and consigning them to air freight companies for transport back to home bases. Frozen giant bluefin tuna are flown from New York to Tokyo regularly.

Restrictions on commercial harvest have been common since the early 1980s. As populations declined, state or federal regulatory agencies restricted harvest by establishing quotas (limited number of fishing licenses), restricting harvest volume (limitation on volume, which can be expressed per day, week, or season), or restricting gears (numbers of traps, length of nets, number of nets). There is at least one example on every coast of the United States in which commercial harvest has been significantly cur-

tailed, even to the point of declaring the species rare and endangered. However, as mentioned above, the size and scope of fishing demands that many countries contribute toward management of populations.

International agreements are in place that define who can fish where, seasons for fishing, and gear acceptance. Most countries claim some distance from their shores as available only to local fishermen. The Fisheries Conservation and Management Act (or the Magnuson Act) was adopted in 1976 and declared the first two hundred miles (322 kilometers) from U.S. shores as open only to U.S. fishermen. The International Whaling Commission was established in 1946 to regulate the global harvest of whales, but has only slowly gained momentum and has no real authority to enforce agreements. Native Americans retained many of their rights to traditional fisheries and harvest those populations in the twenty-first century. Many times, these harvests are contrary to recommendations from regulatory agencies and are controversial with other fishermen.

Fishing communities in New England, the Gulf Coast, and the West Coast have been seriously impacted by the decline in commercial fishing. Whole communities are in significant economic crisis. New industries are not readily apparent for a labor force trained in commercial fishing, processing, and distribution of fish and shellfish. Since the 1980s the fisheries have been in sharp decline, and with it a way of life. Some fishermen, with modified gears, are able to switch species. For example, in 1970, the harvest of the Argentine shortfin squid was 1,300 metric tons. However, harvest of anchovy became erratic and new species were sought, including the shortfin squid. Between 1970 and 1999, total harvest of the Peruvian anchovy by all countries varied from 93,000 metric tons to over 13 million metric tons. Over this same time period, harvest of the shortfin squid increased to just over 1 million metric tons. Harvest of the Atlantic cod, the species used in most fish sandwiches in the United States, has declined from over 3 million metric tons to around 1 million metric tons. A replacement has not been identified in the North Atlantic ocean. Creative marketing techniques also opened opportunities for commercial fishermen. A deep-water species around Australia, New Zealand, and Tasmania was once unmarketable. The local name for this fish was the slime head. However, under its new name, orange roughy has found a ready market in the United States.

The newest of the commercial harvest industries developed in the past forty or fifty years and focused on species inhabiting coral reefs. The pet or hobby aquarium trade increased significantly as technology made it possible to maintain saltwater fish tanks in any temperature-controlled room. Harvest was often by hand, using small dip nets, but more recently other forms of harvest have been used, including poisons (cyanide) and explosives. These collection methods are indiscriminate and have been banned in most countries. The demand for ornamental fishes coupled with the gradual bans on many harvest techniques led to development of aquaculture industries focused on tropical fishes for home aquaria. The same scenario is occurring with fishes destined for food. However, culture of fishes for making fish meal is not occurring and appears unlikely. Fish harvested for fish meal do not command high prices and need large areas. The economics of that form of aquaculture are not favorable.

See also **Crustaceans and Shellfish; Fish and Chips; Fish; Mollusks; Fish, Salted; Fish, Smoked.**

BIBLIOGRAPHY

Levinton, Jeffrey S. *Marine Biology: Function, Biodiversity, Ecology*, 2d ed. New York: Oxford University Press, 2001.

Moyle, Peter B., and Joseph J. Cech, Jr. *Fishes: An Introduction to Ichthyology*, 3d ed. Upper Saddle River, N.J.: Prentice Hall, 1996.

Von Brandt, Andres. *Fish Catching Methods of the World*. 3d ed. Surrey, Great Britain: Fishing News Books, 1984.

Paul B. Brown

FLATWARE. *See* **Cutlery.**

FLOWERS. Throughout history, flowers, like seeds, leaves, and stems, have contributed to human cookery. But edible flowers, when added to food, provide more than sustenance and flavoring. They add form and color. They are an exception to the rule, a spark of interest, and a spectacle that cannot last. Whole fresh flowers connect people to food in a way that nothing else does. Just as beauty is associated with good in children's fairy tales, so too with food: flowers add to the pleasure of eating. Flowers have long been an essential link in the human food chain. The joining of flower pollen with flower ovules is a starting point in the cycle of life. More than we imagine, life depends on a sequence that starts with flowers and progresses to pollination, seeds, and plants. Without the rebirth of plants, without continuous replacement, life would cease to exist. To sustain life, there must be birth and growth.

Flower Biology

Flowers are the blossoms of plants and the reproductive organs of angiosperms. Edible and nonedible flowers alike have a common concentric structure of distinct parts that, beginning at the base of the flower and proceeding up to the center, include the stem, ovary, sepal, petal, stamen (filament and anther), and pistil (style and stigma).

Flowers have been used in cookery for centuries. Here, flowers offer a touch of exotic color and texture to a salad garnished with pansies and nasturtiums. PHOTO BY ANDRÉ BARANOWSKI.

Ah tar.

Flowers also figure as a flavoring in cookery, from violet syrup to rosewater, which was popular in both Byzantine and Arabic cookery. Rosewater still plays an important role in the cookery of many Eastern Mediterranean countries. In this 1838 engraving, a vendor is shown selling rose-water in Istanbul. His still is on the left. Roughwood Collection.

Flower petals are showy, fragrant, and often fully flavored. Sepals, on the other hand, are leaflike structures that enclose the flower before it blooms and, unlike petals, are not valued as a source of food, flavor, or color. Stamens are the male parts, and they produce pollen. Anther sacs hold pollen, and in the case of pine trees, so much pollen is produced in the early spring that it accumulates in masses on lake shorelines and can be scooped up, dried, and used as an ingredient in bread and soups. Pollen is a complete food, rich in proteins, carbohydrates, vitamins, minerals, and enzymes. It can tone, detoxify, and balance the human organism.

Pistils are the female flower part. When pollen grains light on pistils, they absorb moisture, grow tubes, penetrate ovaries, and, finally, connect to ovules to fertilize seeds. Flower nectaries, or nectar glands, secrete nectar, which is used by bees to form honey. Nectar glands are located at the base of the ovary and above the anther.

History

In Roman times rose petals were used to flavor cooked brains, sweet marjoram flowers were baked in hash, and safflower petals were used for a boiled sauce. Roses and violets were added to wine to enhance flavor.

Later, in the Middle Ages, rose petals were used to flavor cakes, creams, and confectionery. Both orange blossom and rose petal water are flavorings made from flowers. Since the third and fourth centuries C.E., rose water has been made by steeping petals and then distilling the water. Middle Eastern and Indian sweets such as

shola, baklava, firni, and halvah are flavored with rose water. It is also used to flavor Middle Eastern beverages such as lassi and sherbet. Flower use varies from culture to culture and age to age. While in America today roses are used more as a decoration than a flavoring, dried rosebuds are used as a condiment in Asian cookery.

Symbolism and Healing

Flowers are a symbol of life and a source of birth and healing. For example, when placed on a wedding cake flowers signify new life, and at times of sickness and death they comfort the grieving. During the Easter season the passionflower is a symbol of the holy passion, the suffering of Jesus Christ. In ancient Greece the rose symbolized love, beauty, and happiness, and during the Roman era, roses were associated with Venus, the goddess of love.

Edible flowers are used with various foods to mark events such as graduation, marriage, and retirement. Christians associate flowers with Christmas, Easter, Ascension, and Epiphany. States and nations have adopted flowers as emblems. For example, the emblem of the Netherlands is the edible tulip, and Illinois, New Jersey, Rhode Island, and Wisconsin have adopted the violet as their state flower. Four states—Georgia, Iowa, New York, and North Dakota—have adopted roses. Florida adopted the orange blossom, and Hawaii the hibiscus.

But in addition to their symbolic and spiritual uses, flowers are consumed for their healing properties. Flowers from the great scarlet poppy contain alkaloids such as thebaine, which is a source of codeine. The unripe pods

POPULAR GARDEN FLOWERS AND THEIR FLAVORS

ANISE HYSSOP: sweet, anise, or licorice; used to flavor red meats and as an herb

CARNATION: mild to sweet; use petals only in salads

CHIVE: onion smell, peppery, savory; use as garnish, flavoring for meats, salads, sauces

CHRYSANTHEMUM: savory, mild to strong, and bitter (some are poisonous)

DAISY: sweet and savory; flower buds are pickled, flowers used on salads, used to make wine

DANDELION: savory; a bitter herb mentioned in the Old Testament: used in salads and wine, the greens are eaten as a vegetable and sold canned

DAY LILY: savory (can be toxic)

FUCHSIA: mild flavor; use whole as garnish on salads and cooked fish

GRAPE HYACINTH: grape flavor, slightly sour, bitter aftertaste (can be toxic)

HOLLYHOCK: mild; use as garnish or container (can be toxic)

HIBISCUS: slightly acidic, sweet; used in tropical fruit salads

HONEYSUCKLE: sweet; use in salads and with fish

LILAC: strong smell; sweet and savory; crystallize the flowers to use on cakes or confectionary; used in tea blends

MARIGOLD: savory; small four- and five-petal varieties best; use in soups

NASTURTIUM: savory, peppery, piquant, like watercress; used in salads and used fresh as a garnish for hot vegetables

PANSY: sweet and savory; crystallized to use on cakes; used fresh on salads

POPPY, EUROPEAN AND CALIFORNIA: mild; use in salads for color

RED CLOVER: mild, like hay; used with wild herb salads; add florets to salads

ROSE: sweet to bitter; herbal teas; use old varieties; also used to decorate cold platters of meat and fish

ROSE PETALS: sweet to bitter, crystallize; add to salads; garnish plates

SCENTED GERANIUM: tastes like variety, either lemon or rose used to make tea and an herb in pastry

SQUASH: savory; batter and fry into fritters; serve as vegetable; also served stuffed

SUNFLOWER: member of daisy family; use unopened flowers like artichokes or use the bitter petals; garnish for granola made with sunflower seeds; use with pasta salads

TULIP: mild, sweet to bitter; use with asparagus or rhubarb

VIOLET: sweet; use in salad, as a garnish for poke sallet, an egg dish that includes cooked poke; use crystallized on cakes

---

of opium poppies are used to make many alkaloids including morphine, thebaine, narcotine, and codeine. The list of flowers used as medicine is extensive, and it includes arnica used as an anti-inflammatory analgesic and hawthorn used as an antispasmodic, cardiac, and vasodilator. The marsh mallow is a diuretic, antitussive, and demulcent. Passionflowers are a sedative. Rosemary is used as a tonic, diaphoretic, antiseptic, and astringent. And finally, due to their astringent qualities, some flowers, including nasturtiums, roses, and yarrow, are used as bath oils.

Preparation and Consumption

While flowers are often used fresh, they are also preserved for later use when they are stored dried, freeze-dried, candied, crystallized, or even frozen in ice cubes.

Flowers or flower parts are eaten as sweeteners, vegetables, flavorings, beverages, and garnishes. In terms of quantity, the most widely used flower today is the hop, a conelike flower or strobilus that is dried and used to flavor beer and ale and is also an antimicrobial

agent. Squash blossoms are served stuffed, fried, or deep-fried. The great variety of flower foods is typified in honey, a sweetener made by bees from flower nectar. Cauliflower, broccoli, and pickled capers are flower buds. Pansy and lilac flowers are crystallized and then used for cake, cookie, and pastry decorations. Lavender, chamomile, lilac, and jasmine flowers are used to make herbal teas. Hibiscus flowers are boiled and sweetened to become *agua de jamaica* or jamaica water, a Mexican beverage made like tea, but served like iced tea or fruit juice. Violets, mimosa, and forget-me-nots are used to flavor confectionery.

Today, out-of-season blossoms, as well as dried flowers and flowers made of marzipan and frosting, are common on wedding and birthday cakes. Flowers are stored and shipped fresh, pressed, dried, and crystallized. Some institutions even use flowers of plastic, silk, paper, wood shavings, and wire to decorate food. This pursuit of flowers is epitomized by upscale restaurant chefs who order a box of mixed fresh flowers, and then use them indiscriminately, either whole or in parts, as the finishing touch to elegantly served dishes from medallions of venison to creamy custards with Grand Marnier.

The stigmata of the fall-blooming saffron crocus provide an essential spice for the bouillabaisse of southern France, the paella of Spain, the risotto of Italy, and the pilaf and biriani of India. Saffron, which is native to Asia Minor, adds an orange-yellow color to these dishes and gives them a spicy, pungent, and bitter flavor. Today, some of the finest saffron is produced in Spain. Saffron is costly because it must be handpicked; it takes four thousand stigmata to yield one ounce of powdered saffron.

Issues

The use of edible flowers as food also raises a number of concerns. First, culinary flowers must be free from insecticides and herbicides. In one sense, assuring toxin-free flowers is easy because fresh flower buds and flowers grow quickly. On some plants it takes only a few days for new buds and flowers to form. On the other hand, commercial flowers are often sprayed to keep them pest-free and visually attractive.

But of even greater concern than pesticides is the loss of historical species. As a result of evolution and environmental degradation, there has been a loss of species and genetic diversity. This, however, is somewhat offset by natural evolution and, in the case of flowers, the constant breeding of new and more beautiful varieties. A third problem is the use of personal or regional nomenclature that makes it difficult to trace the use of flowers in history. Cultures from Native Americans to tribal Africans have celebrated food with flowers, but these traditions are largely lost.

See also **Herbs and Spices; Presentation of Food; Weddings.**

BIBLIOGRAPHY

Kowalchik, Claire, and William H. Hylton. *Rodale's Illustrated Encyclopedia of Herbs.* Emmaus, Pa.: Rodale Press, 1987.

Morse, Kitty. *Edible Flowers: A Kitchen Companion with Recipes.* Berkeley, Calif.: Ten Speed Press, 1995.

Sohn, Mark F. "From Anise Hyssop to Zucchini: Edible Flowers From Home Gardens." *Appalachian News-Express,* July 23, 1997.

Sohn, Mark F. *Southern Country Cooking.* Iowa City: Penfield Press, 1992.

Sohn, Mark F. *Mountain Country Cooking: A Gathering of the Best Recipes from the Smokies to the Blue Ridge.* New York: St. Martin's, 1996.

Weaver, William Woys. *Heirloom Vegetable Gardening.* New York: Henry Holt, 1997.

Mark F. Sohn

FLUORIDE. Fluoride is an important trace element in human nutrition. Daily exposure to small quantities is widely considered to be vital for maintenance of sound tooth structure. Ingested or systemic fluoride has long been known to offer significant benefit when supplied during tooth formation in childhood. More recently, topical exposure (that is, making fluoride available at the tooth surface) has been shown to provide benefits throughout life, even for older adults.

Sources of Fluoride

Water, rocks, soil, and living tissue all have naturally occurring fluoride as a constituent. Crystalline and carbonate minerals containing fluoride are common throughout the earth's near-surface crust. As water flows through the environment, fluoride and many other ions dissolve from sedimentary rock layers and soil into aquifers, streams, rivers, and oceans. Dissolved ions are essential for humans and all living things. Fluoride ions are absorbed directly from the water we drink.

Fluoride in Bone and Tooth Tissue

Fluoride ions taken systemically can become incorporated within bone and tooth tissue. Although bones and teeth have an organic matrix, it is their inorganic or crystalline hydroxyapatite composition that gives them their strength and hardness. Living human cells use available calcium and other minerals to form strong hydroxyapatite matrices. When fluoride ions are also available to the cells, an additional material called fluorapatite is formed. Integration of a small amount of fluorapatite within a hydroxyapatite matrix may produce a more durable substance than is found with hydroxyapatite alone.

Topical Mechanism

Fluoride ions can also provide a very strong surface or topical effect for teeth when available on a regular basis. One such effect is that topical fluoride inhibits the ability of some bacteria to produce dental plaque by blocking the function of important intracellular bacterial enzymes. Much more significantly, topical fluoride also leads to reduced demineralization and increased remineralization of enamel surfaces.

Bacterial Acid and Chemical Balance

Demineralization of a tooth occurs when bacteria create an acidic or low pH environment at the tooth surface. The acidity dissolves hydroxyapatite, releasing positively charged calcium ions and negatively charged carbonate and phosphate ions into saliva. When normal saliva flow dilutes the acidity, the positive and negative ions recombine and remineralize the surface.

This cycle represents a balance. Diets rich in fermentable carbohydrates such as mono- and disaccharides, which are relatively simply sugars, disrupt the balance. They stimulate some oral bacteria to produce dental plaque and acid. Dental plaque is a substance that attaches to tooth enamel and is colonized by the bacteria that form it. Once such a colony is established, each ingestion of fermentable carbohydrate causes approximately one half-hour of intense acid production by the bacteria. This burst of acid production lowers the pH near the tooth surface, demineralizing large amounts of hydroxyapatite. The balance is disrupted and, as the cycle is repeated, it damages the tooth's surface.

Topical Fluoride and Stronger Enamel

When sufficient amounts of negatively charged fluoride ions are routinely present topically at the tooth surface, a different pattern emerges for this cycle. The balance of demineralization and remineralization actually builds fluoride into the tooth's surface structure. Over long exposure to fluoride in saliva, more and more fluoride is incorporated, and the enamel surface becomes stronger. A much greater increase in acidity is then necessary before a destructive imbalance in the cycle will be initiated. This surface or topical effect is thought to be the primary means by which fluoride prevents dental caries.

Benefits of Community Water Fluoridation

In studies of many communities over several decades, it has become clear that there is great benefit to maintaining proper fluoride levels in the public water supply. A concerted public health effort throughout the decades since the 1950s has led to the maintenance of fluoride at these levels in many public water supplies.

Community water fluoridation is intended to provide fluoride at concentrations ranging from 0.7 to 1.2 ppm. Coincidentally, this is about the same concentration of fluoride that is found in ocean water. Levels are adjusted within this range regionally and throughout the year. This provides lower concentrations of fluoride when people are likely to drink more water and higher concentrations when less water consumption is expected.

Without other significant sources of fluoride during the 1950s and 1960s, community water fluoridation produced reductions of 40 to 50 percent in the number of cavities or dental caries among children. Their teeth had enamel that was more resistant to caries both when it was formed and throughout life.

Other countries have assessed a variety of alternative means for delivering protective levels of fluoride. These have included supplementation with tablets or drops, salt fluoridation, and milk fluoridation. However, in the United States, fluoridation of public water as part of purification treatment remains the most effective and economical means for providing this benefit to communities. Currently about 60 percent of the U.S. population has fluoride maintained at these levels in their drinking water.

In the 1980s, it became clear that the positive effects of water fluoridation were not limited to developing teeth. Studies of people age sixty-five and older showed that it was beneficial even when all of the fluoride exposure took place after tooth eruption. Those who lived in communities with fluoridated water as adults had significantly lower rates of dental caries on exposed tooth root surfaces than comparable older adults without fluoridated water.

Fluoride and Osteoporosis

There has been interest in potential positive effects of fluoride supplementation on increased bone density. When ingested, fluoride is absorbed primarily from the upper gastrointestinal tract and is excreted in urine. Fluoride that is not excreted is deposited in calcified tissues—bones and teeth.

Osteoporosis, loss of bone density, is an increasingly prevalent problem in the U.S. population among both men and women. Unfortunately, research to date does not suggest a useful effect of fluoride on bone strength, even when it is supplemented at concentrations twenty times greater than that found in fluoridated water.

Early Research on Fluoride

It was research on the effects of prolonged intake of excessive amounts of naturally occurring fluoride that led scientists to understand the protection afforded by healthy fluoride levels. In the 1930s, a dentist in Colorado, Dr. Frederick McKay, became curious about a brown surface stain seen on some of his patients' teeth. These teeth often had a rough and porous surface texture, yet they were also far less prone to develop dental caries.

McKay's early observations led to a long series of investigations. It became clear that this problem, a severe form of fluorosis, resulted from very high levels of naturally occurring fluoride in drinking water. McKay's water samples had fluoride concentrations as much as fourteen times greater than that recommended today for community water systems. These investigations led to the discovery that when fluoride was present at the low levels that are now widely used, it offered powerful protection from dental caries without any adverse effects.

Reevaluation of Fluoride Use

By the 1990s, the wide availability of fluoridated water led scientists to reevaluate fluoride use practices. Particular attention was paid to the potential for a diffuse exposure to fluoride throughout the population. Many packaged foods are processed in communities with fluoridated water, becoming sources of small amounts of fluoride to those who consume them. Far more important, however, is the use of toothpaste and other products containing fluoride. It was concluded that community water fluoridation levels remain appropriate, but that greater care must be taken in the use of fluoride toothpaste.

Levels of fluoride in treated drinking water are extremely low when compared to concentrations in common therapeutic products. For example, fluoride concentration in over-the-counter fluoride mouth rinses is generally about 230 parts per million (ppm); toothpastes contain about 1,000 ppm; prescription home-use mouth rinses and home-use gels range from 1,000 to 5,000 ppm; professionally applied fluoride gels contain 10,000 to 12,300 ppm; and professionally applied fluoride varnishes contain about 22,000 ppm.

The additional sources of fluoride, primarily toothpaste, have led to lower rates of dental caries in U.S. communities not provided with fluoridated water. However, even with these lower background rates of dental caries in the population, it is estimated that community water fluoridation alone still provides an additional reduction of 20 to 40 percent in dental caries when comparison is made to caries rates for Americans who do not have fluoridated water but who use fluoride toothpaste.

Fluoride Issues for the Future

During the reevaluation of fluoride in the 1990s, concerns were raised regarding the potential for fluorosis. In contemporary studies of fluorosis in the U.S. population, nearly all observed cases have been classified as "very mild" or "mild." These are categories of "white-spot" discoloration that are usually only apparent to a dentist conducting an intraoral examination. Ingestion of fluoride toothpaste is considered the primary explanation for these white-spot discolorations.

Children are likely to swallow toothpaste while brushing, ingesting an unintended and excessive amount of fluoride. The most effective strategy for avoiding mild fluorosis is to limit children to a pea-sized quantity of toothpaste at each brushing. This quantity is adequate for caries prevention and oral hygiene, but it should not lead to development of fluorosis.

Use of infant formula and some baby foods has also raised a degree of concern. Because of infants' very small body mass, the proper intake of systemic fluoride is lower than that for slightly older children. Some studies have identified varying levels of fluoride in these products, some approaching levels that are associated with increased risk for very mild or mild fluorosis in infants. Physicians and dentists are urged to use caution in prescribing fluoride supplements for infants and very young children living in communities without fluoridated water because they might be consuming these fluoride-containing products.

The U.S. Environmental Protection Agency has set a standard of 4.0 ppm as the maximum allowable fluoride level in drinking water. Within the United States, fluoride levels in drinking water are actually maintained at about one-fourth of this level. However, in some developing countries, particularly in southern Asia and northern Africa, natural fluoride is present at extremely high levels. In India, for example, a study sponsored by the World Health Organization found natural fluoride levels exceeding 1.5 ppm in about 8 percent of samples, with some concentrations as high as 22.0 ppm. In such areas, public health workers actively engage in efforts to reduce fluoride exposure and eliminate fluorosis.

Conclusion

Nearly one hundred organizations with related expertise, including the World Health Organization, the U.S. Public Health Service, the American Medical Association, the American Public Health Association, the American Society for Clinical Nutrition, the American Society for Nutritional Sciences, the International Association for Dental Research, the FDI World Dental Federation, and the American Cancer Society have recognized the importance of daily fluoride intake for dental health. Particularly when supplied through community water fluoridation, ensuring adequate dietary fluoride exposure has been an extremely safe and cost-effective public health measure. Fluoride is a trace element that has extremely important personal and public health benefits for promotion and maintenance of optimal oral health.

See also **Dentistry**; **Digestion**.

BIBLIOGRAPHY

American Dental Association. "Statement on Water Fluoridation Efficacy and Safety." Available at http://www.ada.org/prof/prac/issues/statements/fluoride2.html.

American Dental Association. "Fluoride and Fluoridation." Available at http://www.ada.org/public/topics/fluoride/facts-intro.html.

American Dietetic Association. "Position of the American Dietetic Association: The Impact of Fluoride on Health." *Journal of the American Dietetic Association* 100 (2000): 1208–1213.

Burt, Brian A., and Stephen A. Eklund. *Dentistry, Dental Practice, and the Community* 5th ed. Philadelphia: W.B. Saunders, 1999.

Clarkson, John J., and Jacinta McLoughlin. "Role of Fluoride in Oral Health Promotion." *International Dental Journal* 50 (2000): 119–128.

Ekstrand, J., and A. Oliveby. "Fluoride in the Oral Environment." *Acta Odontologica Scandinavica* 57 (1999): 330–333.

Gillcrist, James A., David E. Brumley, and Jennifer U. Blackford. "Community Fluoridation Status and Caries Experience in Children." *Journal of Public Health Dentistry* 61 (2001): 168–171.

Griffin, S. O., K. Jones, and S. L. Tomar. "An Economic Evaluation of Community Water Fluoridation." *Journal of Public Health Dentistry* 61 (2001): 78–86.

International Collaborative Research on Fluorides: Research Needs Workshop, sponsored by the National Institute of Dental and Craniofacial Research, May 1999. "International Collaborative Research on Fluoride." *Journal of Dental Research* 79 (2000): 893–904.

National Institutes of Health (NIH). "Diagnosis and Management of Dental Caries Throughout Life." Consensus Statement 2001, March 26–28, Vol. 18, No. 1.

Office of the Surgeon General. *Oral Health in America: A Report of the Surgeon General.* Rockville, Md.: U.S. Department of Health and Human Services, 2000.

Stephen, K. W. "Fluoride Prospects for the New Millennium: Community and Individual Patient Aspects." *Acta Odontologica Scandinavica* 57 (1999): 352–355.

ten Cate, J. M., and Cor van Loveren. "Fluoride Mechanisms." *Dental Clinics of North America* 43 (1999): 713–742.

Warren, John J., and Steven M. Levy. "Systemic Fluoride: Sources, Amounts, and Effects of Ingestion." *Dental Clinics of North America* 43 (1999): 695–711.

Rob Berg

FOLIC ACID. Folic acid is a water-soluble B-vitamin first identified in 1930 by Wills and Mehta as "Wills factor." Wills factor cured the anemias of pregnant women in India, a clinical condition that commonly results from undernutrition. This vitamin was later isolated from spinach leaves and named folic acid (Latin *folium*, leaf). Unlike most bacteria and yeast, mammals cannot synthesize folate and, therefore, require folate in the diet. This vitamin is present in the body as a family of at least nine structurally related chemical compounds that are collectively referred to as folate. The term *folic acid* refers to a synthetic form of the vitamin. Folic acid, which is biologically inactive, is found in foods that have been fortified with it. Folic acid is also the form that is present in nutritional supplements. Folic acid can be converted by living cells to a biologically active form called tetrahydrofolate. This active form serves the same biological function as natural folates. The terms "folic acid" and "folate" are therefore often used interchangeably.

Chemical Forms of Folate

The different forms of folate found in the body exist primarily as modified forms of tetrahydrofolate. Each tetrahydrofolate form differs by modification of the selected positions in the molecule that involve the placement of a single carbon unit. Additionally, folate derivatives found in cells contain a glutamate polypeptide tail that consists of two to eight glutamate residues in length. This polyglutamate chain is required for folates to perform their biochemical functions and also to retain folate in the cell. The glutamate chain prevents the molecule from crossing cell membranes.

Dietary Folate

Vegetables are good dietary sources of naturally occurring folate, especially dark green leafy vegetables. Citrus fruits and fresh juices, berries, legumes, liver, and whole grains are other good sources. Most naturally occurring folates are sensitive to degradation by air and heat but are stabilized when bound to proteins present in foods. For this reason, fresh fruits and vegetables are the best sources of dietary folates since many food folates are destroyed during food preparation. Dietary folates contain a polyglutamate chain that must be removed by digestive enzymes in the intestine. These enzymes leave a single glutamate residue on the folate, and the folate is then absorbed by the intestinal cell. Most folates are taken up by the liver, which is the primary storage site for folate. Folates can then be redistributed to other tissues from the liver. Glutamate chains are re-elongated by the body after the absorption of folates with single glutamates.

Overview of Folate Metabolism

Folate serves as a cofactor that delivers single carbon units to particular enzymes that catalyze biochemical reactions. These folate-dependent biochemical reactions are referred to collectively as one-carbon metabolism. Folate functions in both the cytoplasm and mitochondria, the energy-producing units, of mammalian cells. Folate metabolism in mitochondria is responsible for the generation of formate, a source of one-carbon unit. Formate escapes the mitochondria and is a primary source of the single carbon units for one-carbon metabolism in the cytoplasm. One-carbon metabolism in the cytoplasm is required for the synthesis of DNA precursors, and the amino acid methionine from its precursor, homocysteine. Methionine, in turn, is converted to the cofactor S-adenosylmethionine or SAM. SAM serves as an additional source of single carbon units in the form of methyl groups that are required for other metabolic reactions including the methylation of DNA, RNA, and proteins. SAM also is required for the synthesis of phospholipids, neurotransmitters, and many small metabolites.

Folate as a Therapeutic Target

Folate-dependent reactions are fundamental for DNA synthesis and maintenance of DNA integrity. Therefore, folate is required for cell growth and replication. It is not surprising that folate-dependent enzymes have proven to be effective targets for antitumor and antimicrobial drug therapies. These pharmaceutical agents are structurally similar to folate and are referred to as antifolates. Agents including 5-fluorouracil and methotrexate (and related antifolates) bind to folate-dependent enzymes by mimicking the structure of folate but do not serve the same biological function. These agents enter the cell and inhibit folate-dependent reactions associated with DNA synthesis and result in cell death. Antifolates are used in the treatment of many cancers, Crohn's disease, rheumatoid arthritis, lupus, and other autoimmune disorders.

Folate Deficiency and Disease

The most common impairments of folate metabolism result from inadequate folate intake, certain drug therapies, smoking, malabsorption disorders, alcoholism, genetic mutations, and subtle individual genetic variations that occur normally in populations. Additionally, certain dietary factors can interfere with folate absorption in the gut and result in malabsorption of the vitamin. Inadequate folate status has been reported in many population groups including pregnant and lactating women, women twenty to forty-four years of age, adolescents, and the elderly. Folate requirements are greatly increased during pregnancy due to the high demand for folate by the growing fetus and placenta. Folate deficiency can present itself clinically as megaloblastic anemia, a clinical condition associated with enlarged red blood cells due to decreased DNA synthesis. Other clinical symptoms include an inflamed, red-looking tongue, nausea, vomiting, diarrhea, anorexia, hyperpigmentation, and fever. Folate deficiency during pregnancy is highly associated with several congenital defects including spina bifida. Population studies implicate impaired folate metabolism in other pathologies including cardiovascular disease, colon cancer, cervical dysplasia, and pre-eclampsia.

Folate and Homocysteine

One of the first biochemical indicators associated with impaired folate metabolism is increased serum homocysteine (resulting from decreased methionine synthesis). Both folate and vitamin B_{12} are required for converting homocysteine to methionine. Plasma homocysteine level is a sensitive marker of folate status, but homocysteine can be influenced by other vitamins, including vitamin B_6 and B_{12} status, as well as age. The relationship between folic acid and homocysteine levels in the body is important because of the association between homocysteine and vascular disease. Elevated plasma homocysteine is now considered an independent risk factor for atherosclerotic vascular disease. The risk of cardiovascular disease rises in proportion to an individual's serum homocysteine concentrations. Some studies also suggest an independent role of folate deficiency in cardiovascular disease. The relationship between homocysteine and disease is not understood, but two mechanisms are the focus of current research. Homocysteine contains a reactive thiol group that can modify proteins and affect their function. Alternatively, homocysteine can also be converted to S-adenosylhomocysteine, which is a potent inhibitor of many methylation reactions that modify DNA proteins and influences gene expression. Either or both of these mechanisms may account for pathologies that are associated with elevated homocysteine in humans.

Dietary Recommendations

In 1998, the National Academy of Sciences released the Dietary Reference Intake (DRI) values for folate that include a recommended dietary allowance (RDA) of 400 micrograms for males and females aged fourteen years and younger. For these individuals, the source of folate is not important. However, it is recommended that women of childbearing age consume an additional 400 micrograms of folic acid per day from fortified foods and/or supplements in addition to the intake of food folate from a varied diet. It is critical that women be folate-sufficient prior to pregnancy, since most birth defects that result from folate deficiency occur before the twenty-ninth day of pregnancy, often before the woman realizes she is pregnant. Maintaining adequate folate status is especially critical for women with a history of bearing children with neural tube defects, to prevent future incidence of birth defects. Pregnant women should consume an additional 600 micrograms of synthetic folate per day in addition to a naturally folate-rich diet. It is not normally recommended that anyone consume more than 1 milligram of folate per day.

The RDA is expressed as dietary folate equivalents (DFEs) because synthetic folic acid is more easily absorbed in the intestine than naturally occurring folate. One microgram of naturally occurring food folate is equivalent to 0.6 microgram of folic acid from fortified foods or supplements consumed with meals and to 0.5 microgram of supplements not consumed with meals. Because of recent federal regulations for food fortification, synthetic folic acid can now be found not only in dietary supplements, but also in enriched grain products (0.43 to 1.4 micrograms of folic acid per pound grain product) such as flour and pasta. Initial results from the fortification program indicate that plasma folate levels have more than doubled among adults who do not use folic acid supplements. The effect of this program on reducing spina bifida and other folate-associated birth defects and pathologies is yet to be determined.

See also **Fiber, Dietary**; **Vegetables**.

BIBLIOGRAPHY

Centers for Disease Control and Prevention. "Knowledge and Use of Folic Acid by Women of Childbearing Age—United States, 1997." *Morbidity and Mortality Weekly Report* 46, no. 31 (8 August 1997): 721–723.

Centers for Disease Control and Prevention. "Recommendations for the Use of Folic Acid to Reduce the Number of Cases of Spina Bifida and Other Neural Tube Defects." *Morbidity and Mortality Weekly Report*, 41 no RR–14 (11 September 1992).

Gregory, Jesse F. "The Bioavailability of Folate" In *Folate in Health and Disease*. Edited by Lynn B. Bailey. New York: M. Dekker, 1995.

Lindenbaum, John, and Robert H. Allen. "Clinical Spectrum and Diagnosis of Folate Deficiency" In *Folate in Health and Disease*. Edited by Lynn B. Bailey. New York: Marcel Dekker, 1995.

Shane, Barry. "Folate Chemistry and Metabolism." In *Folate in Health and Disease*. Edited by Lynn B. Bailey. New York: Marcel Dekker, 1995.

Standing Committee on the Scientific Evaluation of Dietary Reference Intakes, Food and Nutrition Board, Institute of Medicine. "Dietary Reference Intakes: Folate, Other B Vitamins, and Choline." Washington, D.C., National Academy Press (7 April 1998).

Wagner, Conrad. "Biochemical Role of Folate in Cellular Metabolism" In *Folate in Health and Disease*. Edited by Lynn B. Bailey. New York: M. Dekker, 1995.

Patrick J. Stover

FOLKLORE, FOOD IN. While doing folklore fieldwork with the Singing and Praying Bands of tidewater Maryland and Delaware, the present author observed a minor event that made a major impression on him. The Singing and Praying Bands are groups within some African-American Methodist churches in the Chesapeake Bay area of the East Coast of the United States that hold services in which they sing and pray with escalating fervor to invoke the Holy Spirit and to convert the unsaved. That day in particular, they were having no success: the Spirit simply was not stirring. Finally, one senior member slipped into the center of the singing group and called out the following verse to be added to the hymn:

Old man Moses must be dead;
Children in the wilderness crying for bread.

This couplet combines two episodes from the book of Exodus. The first line refers to the episode when Moses ascended Mount Sinai and disappeared from the camp of the Israelites, causing them to wonder about his continued survival (Exodus 32:1). The second line refers to the Israelites' muttering against Moses for leading them out of Egypt, only to face starvation in the wilderness (Exodus 16:2–3). In response to the murmuring of the Israelites, God caused bread, or manna, to rain from the heaven. This couplet, drawn from a large repertoire of folk poetry distinct to the band, summarizes the attitude of desperation of the Israelites, and applies their condition to that of the band members on that particular summer Sunday afternoon.

The moment the singing group heard this verse, they increased the energy of their singing, their clapping, and their foot stomping in a way that finally was successful in invoking the Holy Spirit. After receiving this blessing from the Spirit, people in the bands seemed to decide that the service could begin to wind down.

This use of "bread" as a metaphor for the Holy Spirit among the bands is not uncommon. On other occasions, the same groups append the line "Bread of heaven, bread of heaven, feed me till I want no more"—a line drawn form the hymn "Guide Me, O Thou Great Jehovah" by William Williams (1717–1791)—to the end of long, lined out hymns. They sing this line repeatedly as a meditation to focus the minds of the members of the group so that they can all come together in religious solidarity, as the disciples did on the day of the Pentecost (Acts 2:1-2), and the Spirit may become manifest among them.

In the liturgical language of the Judeo-Christian tradition, the word "bread" is often used as a metonym for food in general. Used as a symbol of all bodily nourishment, it may also become a symbol of the Holy Spirit, which provides band members with what they refer to as their "spiritual food." This story and the interpretation of its larger implications can be usefully employed to introduce the rich subject of food—in this case, bread—in folklore.

In actuality, references to food are made in all genres of folklore, and presumably in all cultures around the world. References occur in folktales (such as the story Hansel and Gretel, in which the witch's house is made of gingerbread and sugar candy, and Hansel almost becomes dinner himself), in folksongs (the hobo anthem, "The Big Rock Candy Mountain"), in folk dance (the Cake Walk, the Mashed Potato), in festival pranks (trick or treat during Halloween), in costume (a couple dressed as "a night at the movies" for Halloween, one attired as a theater ticket, the other as a bag of popcorn), and even in vernacular architecture (American roadside vernacular architecture includes buildings such as a duck-shaped drive-in restaurant selling roast duck as well as fast-food stands topped with sculptures of hot dogs amply slathered with condiments, as documented in the influential book on postmodern architecture *Learning from Las Vegas*).

While it would be impossible to develop a unifying theory or classification scheme that accounts for all such references to food in folklore, a loose framework of analysis can provide a prism through which the subject of food in folklore can be viewed. In order to establish such a framework about food in folklore, however, we should first examine the subject of folk cuisine itself, and folk eating habits. Together, these constitute the domain that scholars in the field of folklore and folklife have come to call "foodways." The food traditions of any one community include not just recipes, but the methods by which foods are gathered, stored, prepared, displayed, served, and disposed of. Such traditions include also culturally transmitted rules that govern ideas of health and cleanliness as related to food. Further, the academic analysis of foodways includes the study of foods that are especially esteemed or shunned by any particular identity group, and the study of culturally specific rules governing the contexts in which particular foods may or may not be eaten.

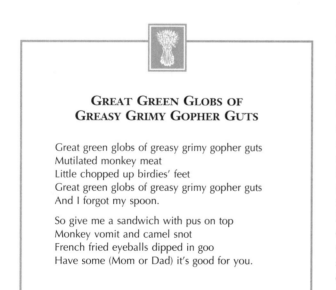

GREAT GREEN GLOBS OF GREASY GRIMY GOPHER GUTS

Great green globs of greasy grimy gopher guts
Mutilated monkey meat
Little chopped up birdies' feet
Great green globs of greasy grimy gopher guts
And I forgot my spoon.

So give me a sandwich with pus on top
Monkey vomit and camel snot
French fried eyeballs dipped in goo
Have some (Mom or Dad) it's good for you.

Like the North American cowboy, the Argentine gaucho plays a large role in South American food-lore. Here a trio of gauchos is depicted preparing *churrasco* on the pampas. Detail from a 1951 menu for La Cabaña Restaurant y Grill in Buenos Aires. Roughwood Collection.

In events that involve the serving of food—from ordinary meals to holiday feasts—ties of reciprocity between networks of preparers, as well as relationships between those preparing and those being served, become articulated. Differing customs pertaining to food also signal boundaries between differing groups of identification. Food events, therefore, tend to provide a rich subject for folk commentary about any one group's culture and social organization.

It is axiomatic in the field of folklore that folklore genres—whether food, story, art, or song—are expressive culture. Such expressive culture is not passively received and mechanically reproduced. Instead, when engaged in folk expression, individual tradition bearers in any cultural setting consciously build on the past to create the emerging culture. A corollary to this axiom is the idea that any such folk expression is rhetorical in intent: That is, it is designed to persuade its audience of the validity of its point of view about a subject. From this axiom and corollary, it follows that folklore about food in particular—that is, food in folklore, the subject of this essay—can be viewed first as expressive culture that offers a commentary on the foodways of the people from whom

the commentary arises, and second as commentary designed to persuade its hearer or viewer of its point of view.

Folkloric commentary about food can be glowingly positive, even sentimental, or intensely negative. These extremes manifest themselves positively in festive, holiday cooking on the one hand, and negatively in food taboos on the other. Americans still listen longingly to songs or poems about chestnuts, wassail, and sugar plums long after these foods have disappeared as a regular feature of their diet. Americans do not just bake gingerbread men and cookies shaped like stars during this time of year. These foods are also turned into folk art when they are used as decorations on Christmas trees, thereby offering a commentary about our reverence for them as holiday foods.

Nontraditional food choices, conversely, may elicit disgust. In the United States, children's folklore, for example, abounds with songs or sayings about foods thought to be inedible. Children may enjoy the playing with the images of such foods to elicit disgust in others. In doing so, they demonstrate that they have internalized many of their culture's food taboos. In general, it is dif-

GOOD, THOUGH!

Chorus: Oh, the Wild River crew is a rough old
             crew,
   And I'll tell you the reason why:
   We live on brew and cat-liver stew,
   And a daily piece of moose-turd pie.

1. Old Jigger Jones kicked the knots off logs
With his bar feet, so they say,
But he hung around Wild River too long,
And it drove him nuts one day.

2. Now old Jigger Jones he got pretty tired
Of doin' all of our cookin',
So he says, "If I hear one more guy bitch,
For a new cook you'll be lookin'."

3. Jones was out in the woods next day
Chasin' a big deer herd;
Coming back to camp without any luck,
He slipped upon some fresh moose turds.

4. He scooped 'em up in his old game bag,
The grin on his face was sly;
He thought the boys would surely bitch
If they tried a piece of his moose-turd pie.

5. The boys come in for supper that night—
Their appetites were high;
They chawed their way through a ten-course
   meal,
Then they started in on the moose-turd pie.

6. One by one the boys turned green,
Their eyeballs rolled to and fro;
Then one guy hollered as he sank to the floor,
"My God, that's a moose-turd pie!
[Shouted] Good, though!" [cheerfully, with eye-
   brows and one finger raised]

In Barre Toelken, *Dynamics of Folklore,* Boston: Houghton
Mifflin, 1979, pp. 179–180.

---

ficult to say a great deal about an item of folk expression without knowing the author, the author's motivation, the context, or the audience response. But in a society in which many children spend their formative years eating often nondescript cafeteria foods, they may also be offering a commentary on institutional food when they sing a song such as "Great green globs of greasy grimy gopher guts, mutilated monkey meat, little chopped up birdies' feet. . . ." Similarly, young people who refer to certain cafeteria offerings as "mystery meat" can be thought of as authoring a rather negative commentary on the food they are being served.

Other folk commentary about mass-produced foods is not so humorous. One urban legend tells of a couple who buy a fast-food dinner of fried chicken. When the woman bites into her meal, she finds that she has been served breaded, fried rat. The story can be viewed as a commentary on the anxiety of many Americans about potential contamination of industrially processed food. The folklorist Gary Alan Fine, who examined a large number of variations of this legend, suggests that the story also seems to chastise contemporary American women. Since the victim is always the woman of the couple, the legend seems to be contending that the whole episode might be her fault: if she had remained in the home and provided her partner with home cooking, the event would never have happened.

In African-American folklore, similar worries about the adulteration of the food supply have on occasion become transformed into rumors that blacks are vulnerable to being specifically targeted with toxic substances. In the late 1980s, folklorist Patricia Turner documented a rumor circulating among some African Americans to the effect that Church's Fried Chicken was owned by the Ku Klux Klan, and that their food contained a substance that would sterilize black men. The rumor seems to have been exacerbated by the fact that Church's located its franchises primarily in inner-city neighborhoods and did little advertising as compared with other fast-food companies. Furthermore, by offering food commonly identified with the African-American home kitchen, Church's had transgressed into somewhat sacred territory. Those who reported hearing the rumor had no problem believing that the Klan was capable of carrying out such a widespread secret plan, as the rumor claimed.

Another cycle of recent urban legends focusing on the disgust elicited by the eating of tabooed foods developed when Southeast Asian refugees began immigrating to the United States after the war in Vietnam. When several thousand refugees settled in Stockton, California, a rumor arose in adjacent communities that an expensive pet dog had disappeared; a neighbor's boy claims he saw a Vietnamese family eating the dog, and remains of the dog were later discovered by a garbage collector. While appearing to focus on racial stereotypes about the divergent eating habits of the new immigrants, according to researcher Florence Baer, this legend actually comments quite articulately on the white community's fear that new immigrants were swarming into the country and consuming so many resources and social services that none would be left for longer-term citizens.

Yet folk commentary on food taboos is not exhausted by urban legends about contamination of the food supply or diversity of eating habits. The most severely tabooed substances, according to esteemed folklore scholar Roger Abrahams, are human flesh, feces, and carrion. Nevertheless, items of folklore that speak of violating these taboos abound. In several predominantly male societies, for example, such as the logging camps of Maine, and railway construction camps in the West, a story known to folklorists as "Moose Turd Pie" has circulated as a song, a legend, and a joke. As the story is told by folksinger Utah Phillips, a new worker comes to work without knowing the workplace custom that whoever complains about the food will have to do the cooking until the next person complains. When the new man inevitably complains, he is forced to cook. To rid himself of the job, he sets about making a pie out of moose feces. On taking a bite of the pie, one of the more experienced coworkers calls out his disgust, "Moose turd! . . . Good though!"

This story comments on foodways in several ways. First, it humorously remarks on the horror of eating a grossly tabooed substance. Second, it seems to comment on gender roles in food preparation by taking for granted the idea that the men involved would rather do physically demanding manual labor than cook, which is often perceived as women's work. Third, the version told in concert by Phillips hints at traditional hazing practices to which new workers in male societies are sometimes subjected. During such hazing practices, the rookie worker is inducted into full-fledged membership in a group only after being ritually feminized—in this case by being assigned a "woman's" job. It also hints that the appropriate way for the new worker to endure such an initiation with his sense of masculinity intact is to develop a prank in retaliation that is as humiliating to the hazers as the hazing to the low man on the totem pole.

Folklore about food can reveal a great deal about gender identity. That life on the western frontier of the United States necessarily required pioneers to enlarge their repertoire of foods is incontrovertible, as folklorist Charles Camp has discussed in his review of the foodways data gathered by the Federal Writers Project during the New Deal years. Ranchers and cowboys who, like Native Americans, believed that no part of the animal on which their livelihood depended should be wasted on slaughter, developed the habit of eating bull testicles, which they often have referred to as "rocky mountain oysters." In Montana, where this specialized food may also be referred to as "Montana tendergroin" or "cowboy caviar," several festivals have come to be held every year in which all festival goers combined eat several tons of rocky mountain oysters. While there are a number of such events around the state, the first and largest, called "the Testicle Festival," takes place in Clinton, Montana, just east of Missoula.

Proverbial expressions in American English seem to imply that American males admire the virility of bulls. One speaks of being "strong as a bull." Manual labor that requires heavy lifting is called "bull work." A robust stock market is a "bull market." The eating of bull testicles can be interpreted as the human male's appropriating the bull's virility for himself. A festival that features this as its raison d'être, becomes in turn a celebration of human masculinity.

But the eating of such identifiable body parts of the bull also demands of many people who attend a suspension of some of their usual food inhibitions. Eating of such animal organs as eyeballs, brains, or sexual organs would under normal circumstances elicit displeasure from many Americans, old cowboy traditions notwithstanding. At the Testicle Festival in Clinton, Montana, this relaxation of eating habits—combined with the celebratory drinking of intoxicating beverages—seems to cause a lowering of other inhibitions as well. Human body parts that are usually covered are publicly displayed. Behaviors usually undertaken in private may be acted out or simulated in public. The result is a carnival-like folk festival the rationale of which celebrates masculinity in a way that inverts usual cultural inhibitions and exposes—as good festivals do, as good folklore does, and as some folklore about food does—human passions in their most naked form.

See also **Art, Food in: Literature; Bible, Food in the; Bread, Symbolism of; Taboos**.

BIBLIOGRAPHY

Abrahams, Roger. "Equal Opportunity Eating: a Structural Excursus on Things of the Mouth." In *Ethnic and Regional Foodways in the United States: The Performance of Group Identity*, edited by Linda Kelly Brown and Kay Mussell, pp. 19–36. Knoxville: University of Tennessee Press, 1984.

Abrahams, Roger D. "Introductory Remarks to a Rhetorical Theory of Folklore." *Journal of American Folklore* 81 (1968): 143–158.

Baer, Florence E. "Give Me . . . Your Huddled Masses: Anti-Vietnamese Refugee Lore and the Image of the Limited Good." *Western Folklore* 41 (1982): 275–291.

Broudy, Saul Frederick. "The Effect of Performer-Audience Interaction on Performer Strategies: 'Moose-Turd Pie' in Context." Ph.D. diss., University of Pennsylvania, 1982.

Brunvand, Jan Harold. *The Vanishing Hitchhiker: American Urban Legends and Their Meanings.* New York: W. W. Norton, 1981.

Camp, Charles. *American Foodways: What, When, Why, and How We Eat in America.* Little Rock, Ark.: August House, 1989.

Douglas, Mary. *Purity and Danger.* London: Routledge and Kegan Paul, 1966.

Fine, Gary Allen. "Cokelore and Coke Law: Urban Belief Tales and the Problem of Multiple Origins." *Journal of American Folklore* 92 (1979): 477-482.

Fine, Gary Allen. "The Kentucky Fried Rat: Legends and Modern Society." *Journal of the Folklore Institute* 17 (1980): 222-243

Kalcik, Susan. "Ethnic Foodways in America: Symbol and Performance of Identity." In *Ethnic and Regional Foodways in the United States: the Performance of Group Identity*, edited by Linda Kelly Brown and Kay Mussell, pp. 37–65. Knoxville: University of Tennessee Press, 1984.

Morse, Kendall. "Good Though! Seagulls and Summer People." Folk Legacy Records C-79 1980.

Phillips, Utah. "Good Though!" *Good Though!* Philo Records #PH1004, 1973.

Theophano, Janet. "It's Really Tomato Sauce but We Call It Gravy." Ph.D. diss., University of Pennsylvania, 1982.

Toelken, Barre. *The Dynamics of Folklore*. Boston: Houghton Mifflin, 1979.

Turner, Patricia. "Church's Fried Chicken and The Klan: A Rhetorical Analysis of Rumor in the Black Community," *Western Folklore* 46 (1987): 294–306.

Venturi, Robert, Denise Scott Brown, and Steven Izenour. *Learning from Las Vegas: The Forgotten Symbolism of Architectural Form*. Cambridge, Mass.: M.I.T. Press, 1972.

Yoder, Don. "Folk Cookery." In *Folklore and Folklife: An Introduction*, edited by Richard M. Dorson, pp. 325–350. Chicago: The University of Chicago Press, 1972.

Jonathan C. David

FOOD, COMPOSITION OF.

Food composition activities include data generation in an analytical laboratory, data compilation in a database management system, data dissemination through print and electronic media, and data use by various professional and lay users.

Historically, food composition activities were limited to data on nutrients. Increasingly, food composition work deals with data for any component found in food: nutrients, bioactive nonnutrients, antinutrients, pesticide residues, other contaminants, additives, and more. A single food composition database, with proper documentation, can accommodate data on all these types of components.

Sectoral Elements

Food composition data are useful to many professions and sectors. Health, agriculture, environment, and trade are the sectors most fundamentally involved in food composition activities. Over time, agriculture has been the dominant sector involved in food composition research and service. This is demonstrated most clearly in international organizations such as the Food and Agriculture Organization of the United Nations (FAO), with a history of food composition work dating back to its inception in the 1940s; and in countries having the longest history of formal food composition activities such as the United Kingdom, where the Ministry of Agriculture, Fisheries and Food has had most of the responsibility, and the United States, where responsibility lies with the United States Department of Agriculture (USDA), and has since the late 1800s. Nevertheless, more than half of the participants in food composition conferences, and the researchers publishing food composition papers and books, are health sector professionals. In many countries it is the health sector that provides a high percentage of the funding for the work, and constitutes the highest percentage of the users of the information. Involvement of the environment sector is becoming increasingly important as it relates to the composition of indigenous or protected plant and animal species used as foods, and the content of environmental chemicals in the food supply. Trade has also gained more dominance in recent years.

Nutrient information panels on processed foods have become regulatory requirements in many countries. And analytical data on both nutrient and contaminant content are necessary documentation for global food trade.

Organizational Elements

The international level. INFOODS, the International Network of Food Data Systems, was established in 1983 by United Nations University (UNU), with an organizational framework and international management structure that includes a global secretariat and regional data centers. Its mandate is "to improve data on the nutrient composition of foods from all parts of the world, with the goal of ensuring that eventually adequate and reliable data can be obtained and interpreted properly worldwide." In the mid-1990s, the Food and Agriculture Organization joined UNU in partnership for INFOODS. The main activities of INFOODS at the international level include development of technical food composition standards, assistance to Regional Data Centers and individual countries in developing their food composition activities, and publication of the *Journal of Food Composition and Analysis*.

The regional level. There are seventeen Regional Data Centers in operation. Some were created in the mid to late 1980s and have well-established and effective coordination (for example, LATINFOODS, ASEAN-FOODS, OCEANIAFOODS, and EUROFOODS); some are relatively new, yet making progress; and a few have been newly created and are trying to establish their regional or national priorities and capabilities. Regional food composition tables have been prepared, both electronically and in printed form (for example, Pacific Islands, ASEANFOODS, LATINFOODS), and many regions have regular food composition coordination activities and technical task forces involving all the individual countries in the region.

The national level. Most countries have food composition activities of one form or another. A national food composition program is usually the result of the combination and coordination of activities, within some defined administrative framework, related to food composition data generation, compilation, dissemination, and use. A steering committee is a useful structure, functioning well in many countries. This steering, or advisory, committee is ideally composed of individuals directly involved in food composition work, that is, the data generators, data compilers, and data disseminators. Crucial to the effectiveness of a steering committee is the involvement of data users. The users can be selected among dietitians, nutritionists, food industry personnel, and consumer group representatives.

Often a single organization holds the overall responsibility for managing a national food composition program, yet it is rare that a single organization accomplishes all the activities itself. Regardless of their affiliations, the laboratory-based data generators must interact closely with the data compilers, and the compilers must interact closely with the data users. In most countries there are other agencies with activities that have direct or indirect relationships with food composition data, but operate in concert with the national program. In addition to the desirability of a coordinated national approach for accomplishing essential activities, it is productive and important for a national food composition program to operate in conjunction with its Regional Data Center, and with ongoing international activities.

Technical Elements

Data generation is the process whereby foods are sampled, prepared for analysis, and analyzed in the laboratory. Data compilation is the process whereby the data from the laboratory are examined, manipulated, and incorporated into a food composition database. Data dissemination refers to the preparation and publication of books and electronic data products, which are made available to users in the various sectors. Data use also includes the application of these data to tasks, projects, and programs in the various professional sectors.

Data generation. Sampling, the process and procedures for obtaining foods that are representative of those available and consumed, is fundamental to any food composition activity. Preparation of a sampling plan often requires involvement of all the major contributors to a food composition program. Data generators must be involved in the sample collection, or at least the scheduling of sample collections, so that samples may be immediately and properly prepared for analysis. Data compilers must be involved because information on the sampling plan and details such as when and where sampling took place are important parts of a food composition database's metadata. Data users must be involved because they have the best appreciation of the foods that need to be analyzed, and often the location from which the samples should be collected. The services of a statistician are useful for developing a sampling plan, because representativeness is dictated by the number of food units collected—and analyzed—to achieve the goal. The goal might be to compare compositional differences between cultivars, or to achieve year-round, nationwide mean values for a food composition database. The overall quality of food composition data is determined largely by the sampling plan.

The collected samples must be properly handled so that they arrive at the laboratory without changes that might affect their composition. The key component, crucial to the correct determination of almost all other food components and most easily affected by improper handling and storage, is water (moisture). Once samples are delivered and documented, they are prepared for analysis. Preparation may involve separation of edible from inedible portion (for example, removal of bones from fish, or skins and seeds from pumpkins); kitchen-type preparation (for example, boiling rice); or combining of many samples into fewer samples (for example, combining five brands of similar biscuits into one representative composite sample). After this type of preparation, samples will be stored, or immediately analyzed. As with sample collection and sample handling, proper documentation of all aspects of sample preparation is essential.

Analyses. Most laboratories undertake a limited range of analyses for food composition purposes. This includes a set of core components and then additional components of interest, for example, laboratory research dealing with diet-related health problems. Core nutrients usually include the complete range of proximate components (water, nitrogen for the protein calculation, fat, glycemic carbohydrate, dietary fiber, ash, alcohol where relevant, and an energy value using factors applied to the energy-yielding proximates), some vitamins, and some nutrient elements. Additional components of interest often include cholesterol, individual fatty acids and aggregations of fatty acids (for example, total saturated fatty acids), carotenoids (both provitamin A carotenoids and antioxidant carotenoids with no provitamin A activity), other bioactive nonnutrients, heavy metals, and some so-called antinutrients (for example, phytates). Proper laboratory practices must be strictly adhered to, as well as laboratory quality assurance and quality control procedures, and details of analytical methodologies must be properly documented.

Data compilation. Data compilation requires a relational database management system, and adherence to international food composition standards where they exist. The database should accommodate numeric data, text, and graphics. Ideally, all the raw analytical data, and their attendant documentation, should be captured. The system should then be able to manipulate these data in many different ways. The same data system should provide an exhaustive reference database and any number of abridged user databases to satisfy the broad range of user requirements for food composition data. Many compilers only capture mean values, a practice that will satisfy many users. Other compilers provide more information, and therefore higher-quality databases, by including the number of samples and some expression of their variability. Other compilers are able to capture all the analytical data and prepare user databases with ranges (that is, high and low values), medians, and many different statistical expressions of the data, satisfying a broader spectrum of users and ensuring the highest quality database.

Some compilers prepare their databases with aggregations, excluding the baseline data (for example, a calculated value for vitamin A in retinol equivalents [RE] without individual values for retinol and each provitamin A carotenoid), whereas other compilers provide the analytical data for the individual components, in addition to the aggregations. This latter practice should be encouraged, since conventions for calculating aggregates based on biological activity change, and many of these individual components have other functions in addition to their roles as provitamins.

In data compilation, all food composition data can be included in the database. Complete information for all components in all foods is not necessary. Ideally, a database with one thousand foods should have complete information for core nutrients, but should also be able to accommodate sporadic data for other components in the foods included.

The early work of INFOODS included the development of standards and guidelines for compiling food composition databases for national and regional use (Rand et al., 1991), standards for unambiguously identifying food components (Klensin et al., 1989), and standards for ensuring international comparability and interchange of food composition data (Klensin, 1992). These standards are being maintained and further developed by INFOODS expert committees and consultative groups.

Data dissemination. With appropriate data compilation, food composition data can be disseminated in many different forms to satisfy all user requirements. Table 1 shows examples of some of the common forms in which food composition data are disseminated. Data disseminated as a set of relational files offers users with very specific needs, or those with customized software, the opportunity to use the data as they wish. Other common dissemination formats provide the types of information most often required by users.

Different countries have different approaches for charging, or not charging, for their data and data prod-

ucts. The United States Department of Agriculture prepares the largest single body of food composition data in the world and disseminates it freely via the World Wide Web, as both a downloadable set of relation files and a searchable reference volume.

Data Use

Food composition data are the basic, most fundamental information resource for most nutrition activities. Some of the specific uses of food composition data, along with examples of their uses, are listed below by sector.

Health sector. Food composition data are used in health protection activities in most countries in the world. "Food control" laboratories monitor mostly harmful components of foods. Other health protection activities include food composition activities involving total diet surveys or "market basket surveys" designed to determine the risk to populations from intakes of selected nutrients, antinutrients, and contaminants. The sampling, sample preparation, sample handling, analyses, and reporting requirements are virtually identical to the requirements of other food composition activities.

Health promotion. Health promotion activities include campaigns aimed at reducing or increasing the intake of certain nutrients in certain populations. Examples include healthy heart campaigns, typically using energy, fat, fatty acid, and cholesterol compositional data to educate the public about diet-related cardiac morbidity and mortality. In many developing countries, health promotion focuses on micronutrient data, including the necessity for including iodine in salt and provitamin A carotenoids in fruits and vegetables.

TABLE 1

Data dissemination forms

Output form	Foods	Components	Basis	Numeric data	Metadata
Set of relational files	All	All	Per 100 g e.p.; amino acids in mg/gN, fatty acids in g/100 gTFA; others as available	Mean, standard deviation, standard error, number of samples; raw analytical data as requested	Various; often as requested per sample, or per nutrient per record
Diet analysis software product	All	Subset of core nutrients with no missing values	Per 100 g or any serving size as user selection	Mean	Not provided
Tables, large reference volume, or Web format	All; portrait format; one food over 1–2 pages	All	Per 100 g e.p.; amino acids in mg/gN, fatty acids in g/100 gTFA	Mean, standard deviation, standard error, number of samples	Abridged and general; provided in introductory pages
Tables, concise	Subset of 200–800; landscape format; 15–25 foods over 1–2 pages	Subset of 12–28	Per 100 g and up to two common serves	Mean	Very general

e.p.=edible portion; N=nitrogen; TFA=total fatty acids.

Clinical research. Food composition data are central to many clinical research trials. Examples include studies focusing on amino acid digestibility in ileostomy patients, vitamin A intake in breast-fed infants, and serum cholesterol levels in vegetarians. Knowledge of the composition of the test and control food(s) and/or diet(s) is fundamental to these studies.

Clinical care. Clinical dietitians must know the composition of foods in order to provide effective and therapeutic meals in a clinical setting. Special diets for patients are often based on individual nutrients in the foods: low-sodium diets for hypertensive patients, diets low in saturated fats for heart disease patients, diets containing proper ratios of protein and fat, and those containing the proper amount of carbohydrate for diabetics, high-protein diets for burn patients, diets containing low phenylalanine for phenylketonuric patients, and so forth.

Epidemiological research and diet studies. Epidemiological and diet studies take many forms. Some studies address food intakes and relate them to nutrient content of the diet and the incidence of diseases. Interpretations of the findings of these studies often focus on individual nutrients. Recent examples include Dutch and Finnish studies of dietary antioxidants and lung cancer, and studies of vitamin E and colon cancer among Iowa women.

Public health policies. Many public health policies relating to noncommunicable disease focus on food composition. Such policies set forth nutrition goals and guidelines and include recommended dietary intakes (RDIs). An example of such goals and guidelines is "choose a diet low in fat, saturated fat, and cholesterol"; and an example of an RDI is "females between the ages of fourteen and eighteen should get 15 mg of iron daily." In order for such recommendations to be useful, both health professionals and the public must have access to data on the nutrient composition of foods.

Nutrition intervention policies. Nutrition supplementation typically takes the form of fortification of the food supply or supplementation of the population. Examples of food fortification include the addition of iodine to salt (most countries), of vitamin A to sugar (for example, in Guatemala), and of minerals and B vitamins to refined cereal products (United States, United Kingdom). Such interventions are only carried out after the nutrients in the food and water supply of a country have been studied, and a baseline position has been established and carefully monitored over a period of time.

Household food security. Although food security is an issue that spans the health, agriculture, environment, and trade sectors, household food security is usually considered to be a health sector issue. Knowledge of the nutrient content of the foods consumed by household members is a precondition for assessing household food security.

Agriculture sector. The intensive livestock industries require accurate nutrient composition data on the feeds used. These data are generally far more extensive than those required for human foods, and include many micronutrients and individual amino acids. "Performance" in these animals usually refers to weight at time of slaughter; muscle tissue to fat tissue ratios; and in the case of milk-producing animals, an accurate profile of the proximate composition (protein, fat, lactose, water, and ash).

Food security. National and global food security is generally considered an agriculture sector issue related to food production, rural development, irrigation, fertilizer and pesticide use, crop yields, and so on. A common tool used to assess national and global food security is the FAO food balance sheets that examine, at the commodity level, the amount of food available to a country. The amount of food is then converted into individual components and reported as the amount of protein, fat, and energy available per person per day from the domestic food supply. Food composition data assigned to the commodity data are the basis for many food security assessments, including FAO's yearly report on the number of undernourished people in the world.

Export food industries. The agriculture sector is responsible for ensuring that food exports meet the regulatory requirements of the intended market. Food composition data are important, as product specifications (for example, the fat content of butter) and as nutrition label panels.

Domestic food production. Agriculturalists have long professed that malnutrition is not just a health problem, but also an agriculture problem. Increased consumption of imported food commodities has brought about changes in food patterns and diets that have contributed to the increase in diet-related health problems previously unheard of in certain parts of the world. Agricultural extension workers are combating the incidences of diet-related diseases in some developing Pacific Island countries by using nutrient composition data in family food production, helping families in designing home garden projects to supply nutrients that would otherwise be consumed in insufficient quantities.

Molecular and traditional food plant and animal breeding. Breeding has been done to modify certain nutrients in foods. Familiar examples include corn bred for higher lysine and cattle bred for lower fat content of the carcass.

Environment sector. Knowledge of the nutrient composition of the native diet of endangered animal species is an important requirement for protecting them. In New Zealand, scientists have undertaken studies to determine the nutrient composition of the original diets of birds in their native habitat, to ensure that the same nutrients in the same quantities and proportions were being supplied in their human-made offshore island sanctuaries and other protected, artificial habitats.

Climate change also affects food composition. Ozone depletion affects both food production and the composition of crops and agricultural products. Like ozone depletion, global warming affects agriculture in terms of production implications. Its other major effect, now and in the future, is the creation of conditions that will permit certain food products to be cultivated where temperature conditions did not permit their cultivation previously. This will alter the food supply, and along with it the nutrient composition of certain foods, in certain countries. Food composition data have been used as markers in modeling and predicting environmental change, for example, monitoring the changes in fatty acid composition of fish to chart the climatic phenomenon of El Niño.

Trade sector. Trade has emerged in recent years as one of the more important and demanding of the sectors involved in food composition activities. Food composition in various forms features in the World Trade Organization agreements, the Codex Alimentarius Commission and several of its committees, multilateral and bilateral trade agreements, and national food regulations and standards. More than other sectors, trade has illustrated most poignantly the need for standards and harmonization in technical food composition activities. Many trade-related court cases have involved food composition data, both in the charges filed and in evidence presented, and many of the food product detentions and rejections at U.S. borders are due to the absence of the Nutrition Facts panel of nutrient content data.

See also **Agricultural Research; Climate and Food; Codex Alimentarius; Ecology and Food; FAO (Food and Agriculture Organization); Food Consumption Surveys; Food Safety; Food Security; Food Trade Associations; Government Agencies; Green Revolution; International Agencies; Nutrition Transition: Worldwide Diet Change; Toxins, Unnatural, and Food Safety; Water: Safety of Water.**

BIBLIOGRAPHY

AOAC. *Official Methods of Analysis for AOAC International*, 17th ed. Arlington, Va.: AOAC International, 2002.

Burlingame, B., ed. "Special Issue: 3rd International Food Data Conference." *Journal of Food Composition and Analysis*. Volume 13, 4. London: Academic Press, 2000.

FAO. Available at http://www.fao.org/. Provides links to Codex Alimentarius, FAO Statistical Databases (includes food balance sheets).

Finglas, P. M., ed. "Special Issue: The 2nd International Food Data Base Conference." *Food Chemistry*. Volume 57, 1. New York: Elsevier, 1996.

Greenfield, H., ed. *Proceedings of the 1st International Food Data Conference. Quality and Accessibility of Food Related Data* (1st ed., vol. 1). Arlington, Va.: AOAC International, 1995.

Greenfield, H., and D. A. T. Southgate. *Food Composition Data: Production, Management, and Use*, 2nd ed. Rome: FAO, 2002.

INFOODS. Available at http://www.fao.org/infoods. Provides comprehensive information and links to all food composition resources, including databases, printed food composition tables, standards and expert committees, regional data centers, reference and textbooks, software products, conferences, training courses, and so on.

Klensin, J. C. *INFOODS Food Composition Data Interchange Handbook*. Tokyo: United Nations University Press, 1992.

Klensin, J. C., D. Feskanich, V. Lin, A. S. Truswell, and D. A. T. Southgate., *Identification of Food Components for INFOODS Data Interchange*. Tokyo: United Nations University Press, 1989.

Rand, W. M., J. A. T. Pennington, S. P. Murphy, and J. C. Klensin. *Compiling Data for Food Composition Databases*. Tokyo: United Nations University Press, 1991.

Barbara A. Burlingame

FOOD, FUTURE OF: A HISTORY.

Food is the first of the essentials of life, the world's largest industry, and our most frequently indulged pleasure. Food means creativity and diversity. Food is also the object of considerable concern and dread. Probably nothing is more frightening than the prospect of running out of food. Reflecting humanity's deep-rooted heritage of food insecurity, there have always been prophets warning us against complacency. And given mounting environmental concerns about population growth, global warming, soil erosion, water scarcity, agrochemical pollution, energy shortages, diminishing returns from fertilizers, and so on, it seems justified to wonder whether the banquet is over. Will our grandchildren's grandchildren enjoy the dietary abundance that most of us take for granted? And how will we feed a rapidly growing, urbanized population in the developing world?

As policy analysts debate scenarios, starkly different forecasts and proposals emerge. Some futurists predict unprecedented affluence, while others worry about global shortages and famine. Some are confident that the conventional industrial agriculture can take care of the future, while others see the status quo as a sure route to disaster. While many in government, academia, and industry look to new technologies—especially genetic engineering—to feed the world tomorrow without any modification of modern high-consumption values, others propose "low-tech" alternatives organized around smaller-scale, localized food systems dependent on a return to a more traditional appreciation of limits.

The Policy Debate

The European-American policy debate dates back at least as far as the late eighteenth century. When the economist and clergyman Thomas Malthus (1766–1834) published his *Essay on the Principle of Population* (1798) in response to "the speculations" of the French mathematician and philosopher the Marquis de Condorcet (1743–1794) and the English radical philosopher William Godwin (1756–1836), he crystallized a three-way argument about the future of the food system. As the demographer Joel Cohen writes in *How Many People Can* the *Earth Support?* (1995)—an analysis of the carrying-capacity debate—there are three enduring positions on the question of how we might feed everyone adequately in the future: 1) bake a bigger pie; 2) put fewer forks on the table; or 3) teach everyone better table manners. Condorcet offered the "bigger pie," or techno-cornucopian position: since there are no limits on human ingenuity, science and industry can always devise ways to bake bigger and better pies for everyone. Doubting the cornucopians' faith in technology, Malthus took the "fewer forks" position: humanity's capacity for reproduction outruns the farmers' capacity for production, or the scientists' capacity for miracles, so prudence dictates a more conservative, less expansive approach to the future. Profoundly pessimistic about human nature, Malthus also voiced severe doubts about Godwin's romantic-utopian "better manners" position, which held that in an egalitarian society with altruistic values, people would figure out ways to share nature's bounty and overcome scarcity. Godwin's democratic optimism was inherited and elaborated by both socialists and liberals who promoted a more equitable redistribution of resources as the solution to hunger.

In the two centuries following Malthus's *Essay*, the debates went through several cycles, becoming more pressing in particular periods such as the 1890s, the 1920s, the late 1940s, the 1970s, and the 1990s. These scares were precipitated by certain conditions and events, such as food price inflation, spikes in birthrates, exceptional environmental stresses, and acute cultural anxieties about migration and rapid demographic change. The discussion also had a self-reinforcing synergy as the three debating partners fed off each other: Doubting that science could keep performing miracles, Malthusians predicted still more hunger. Defying Malthus, cornucopians took steps to produce more food. Pointing to mounting surpluses, egalitarians critiqued an economic and political system that fattened the rich with cheap meat while depriving the poor of basic grains and depleting the soil. The debate continues today. Citing two hundred years of unexpected, indeed miraculous, productivity gains, cornucopians at the World Bank, the U.S. Department of Agriculture, and the leading agribusiness corporations hope for still more yield improvements through biotechnology. Citing two hundred years of environmental disaster and resource depletion, neo-Malthusians like Paul Ehrlich and Lester Brown worry about the limits to growth. And as over a billion people remain hungry amid mounting agricultural surpluses, neo-socialists like Frances Moore Lappé and Vandana Shiva argue that only with a more equitable economic system can the poor feed themselves.

Popular Visions of the Future

It is important to note that discussion of these issues has not been confined to the professionalized realm of academic demography, agricultural economics, and agronomy.

Rather, it can be found in a diverse array of expressive, prescriptive, and material forms. Thus, speculative fiction has been a primary forum for the expression of serious doubt about the ability of modern technology to keep up with population growth. Indeed, Godwin's daughter, Mary Shelley, wrote one of the first cautionary tales about technological hubris in *Frankenstein* (1818), while her husband, the poet Percy Bysshe Shelley, promoted vegetarianism as a more just and sustainable food system in *Vindication of Natural Diet* (1813). Having been conditioned by popular novels like Aldous Huxley's *Brave New World* (1932) and films like *Soylent Green* (1973) to equate cornucopian ingenuity with distasteful synthetic foods, many modern consumers remain understandably skeptical about the latest claims of genetic engineers. Similarly, utopian novels have long offered a lively medium for the presentation of egalitarian alternatives. Thus, during the Progressive Era of the late nineteenth and early twentieth centuries, many utopian writers followed Edward Bellamy (*Looking Backward*, 1888), Mary E. Bradley Lane (*Mizora: A World of Women*, 1890), and Charlotte Perkins (*What Diantha Did*, 1910) in proposing scenarios that harnessed highly industrialized means of food production to socialistic distribution goals. In the 1970s, countercultural utopians Ernest Callenbach (*Ecotopia*, 1975) and Marge Piercy (*Woman on the Edge of Time*, 1976) inspired a generation of food radicals with their scenarios coupling localized, ecologically sensitive agriculture with communal, neotribal distribution and postmodern consumption—the outlines of what Kloppenburg, Hendrickson, and Stevenson have called sustainable "foodsheds."

Three Cornucopian Positions

Given the hegemony of techno-optimism in modern culture, however, the cornucopian position has probably had the widest dissemination, with promises of abundance available in many arenas and formats: supermarkets, restaurants, World's Fairs, Disney theme parks (especially Tomorrowland and Epcot), food advertising, mainstream editorial opinion, and the space program. Popular cornucopian thought tends to divide into three very different views of the future: classical, modernist, and postmodernist. The classical future is a smooth continuation and elaboration of past progress, a future of ever bigger and better things made available largely through the materialistic, quantitative expansion of frontiers—overseas and under the seas, in deserts and in tropical forests, under the ground and in outer space. The classical view of the future is the most traditional and often employs the most imperialistic methods of expanding the food supply (and wealth), appropriating other lands, peoples, and resources.

The modernist future represents a distinct break with the past, a radically new vision based on the very latest technologies and scientific breakthroughs, often producing a simpler, more "streamlined" and consolidated result. If the classical future eyes the visible riches of untapped frontiers, the modernist looks for wealth in the invisible—nitrogen from air, protein from microbes, energy from atoms, better yields through better genes. Suspicious of nature and tradition, the modernist vision is comfortable with the synthetic, artificial, and chemically fortified. Ultramodernistic solutions to the food-population dilemma include meal pills (a Victorian fantasy), meat analogues synthesized from soy, cellulose, and algae, and the space program's menu of tubed and "rehydratable" analogues.

While culinary modernism has been favored most by pure scientists, it may also tend to scare off consumers wary of extreme discontinuities. The postmodernist future is thus perhaps the most palatable and marketable because it blends the classical and the modern, envisioning, for example, a world of neo-traditional foods mass-produced by modernist means such as microwavable stir-fries, aseptically packaged chai, and "fifties-style hamburgers" cooked on automated grills. Recognizing the human need for "authentic" tastes, NASA's dieticians have abandoned tubed food in planning interplanetary meals that now include fajitas, pad Thai noodles, barbecued tofu, and curried lentils. Less confident in the new than modernism, more eclectic and multicultural than classicism, the postmodernist menu may reflect how most people actually approach and experience the future: one foot forward with the other planted in an imagined past.

See also **Agriculture since the Industrial Revolution; High-Technology Farming.**

BIBLIOGRAPHY

Brown, Lester R. *Tough Choices: Facing the Challenge of Food Security.* New York: Norton, 1996.

Cohen, Joel E. *How Many People Can the Earth Support?* New York: Norton, 1995.

Ehrlich, Paul R. *The Population Bomb.* New York: Ballantine Books, 1968.

Kloppenburg, Jack, Jr., John Hendrickson, and G. W. Stevenson. "Coming into the Foodshed," *Agriculture and Human Values* 13 (1996): 33–42.

Lappé, Frances Moore, and Joseph Collins. *World Hunger: Twelve Myths.* 2nd ed. New York: Grove Press, 1998.

Malthus, Thomas. *An Essay on the Principle of Population.* Edited by Anthony Flew. London: Penguin Books, 1970.

Piercy, Marge. *Woman on the Edge of Time.* New York: Knopf, 1976.

Shiva, Vandana. *Stolen Harvest: The Hijacking of the Global Food Supply.* Cambridge, Mass.: South End Press, 2000.

Warren Belasco

FOOD ARCHAEOLOGY. As part of their general research, archaeologists have long been interested in food remains under the rubric of diet and subsistence. This work contributes to understanding the long-term historical development of food, and its impact on cultures. Recently, there has been increased interest in food archaeology (although it is not yet identified as a separate discipline), fueled by new technologies and curiosity about implications that go well beyond diet to the role food played in social organization, and ultimately, in the development of civilization itself.

As in all archaeology, there are essentially two broad periods that are of interest to researchers. The first is prehistory, before written records were kept. For that time, scholars are wholly dependent on the interpretation of archaeological finds. The second period is historical archaeology, during which literary and written sources, including poetry, frescoes, and government record-keeping, have been retrieved. Comparisons of excavated food remains with records is particularly valuable because the finds may either contradict or augment the historical record. For example, at the site of a former Roman villa on the Greek island of Lesbos, 7,300 animal bones from a wide variety of species, including goat, deer, hare, pheasant, capon, boar, suckling pig, sheep, lamb, starling, and woodcock, confirm contemporary reports of lavish banquets.

The Evidence

Direct evidence of diet consists of preserved food remains, both plant (paleoethnobotany) and animal (zooarchaeology); analysis of human bone and teeth; undigested stomach contents; and coprolites (fossilized feces). Collection and analysis of plant remains is often futile because most decay. If, however, they have been charred (burned), perhaps during a cooking accident, the material is preserved indefinitely. To collect and isolate tiny floral fragments, samples of excavated sediment may be placed in a flotation tank through which water is forced electronically, forcing the buoyant seeds, pollen, and grains to the surface. Once salvaged, these items can be dated by the system known as radiocarbon dating, based on carbon's known rate of very slow decay. Tiny grains of manioc, yams, and arrowroot from an ancient settlement in Panama, Central America, have been carbon-dated to five thousand to seven thousand years ago, providing the earliest evidence of cultivation of root crops in the Americas.

Microscopic examination of charred plant remains can also determine whether they were cultivated or wild, indicating whether the society was agrarian or hunter-gathering. Charring leaves silica ghosts of the epidermal cells that when examined under the electron scanning microscope reveal telltale markers that distinguish between domesticated and wild crops. Such investigation of grains, husks, and plant remains in China helped push back the date for earliest domestication of rice from 8,000 to 11,500 years ago, and pinpointed the location to the middle Yangtze River.

The more recent technique of DNA "fingerprinting" offers an alternative for establishing domestication. When applied to einkorn wheat, one of eight "founder crops" that launched agriculture in the fertile crescent of the Middle East around 9000 B.C.E., the method pinpointed earliest domestication to the Karacadaq mountains of southeast Turkey.

Skeletal Remains

Human bones provide a wealth of clues about diet. Isotopic analysis of collagen can distinguish chemical signatures of foods. It becomes possible to determine proportions of land to marine foods in the diet, for example, and even to demonstrate the relationship of nutrition to social class. Excavation of skeletons at the former Mayan city-state Caracol in Mexico established that the upper classes, living in the city center, consumed the best diets. The worst were documented in the surrounding inner-city slums while diet improved in the outlying "suburbs," proof that socioeconomic class and nutrition were related even this early.

Learning from Context

Diet may also be inferred indirectly by examining the context of food remains, the environment in which they were found: pottery with grain impressions; eating, drinking, and storage utensils with food residues; hearths where charred grain is found; and gravesites where cut or charred bone indicates funeral feasting. Chemical analysis of food residues from eating and drinking vessels, a technological advance, has provided detailed information about the ingredients used to make a dish. University of Pennsylvania archaeologists pioneered the use of infrared spectroscopy, gas liquid chromatography, and gas chromatography mass spectrometry to examine remains on cups and plates from the 2,700-year-old tomb of the legendary King Midas located in Turkey. Analysis of the protein and lipids allowed scientists to conclude that the menu for this royal funerary feast included barbecued goat or lamb; lentils in olive oil; honey and wine spiced with fennel and anise; and an alcoholic drink composed of grape wine, barley beer, and mead.

Gravesites typically yield a wealth of information. Since Neolithic times, people have been buried with food for the afterlife. Less often, people are buried in food. In a prehistoric Iron Age (500 B.C.E. to 500 C.E.) cemetery at Noen U-Loke in northeast Thailand, archaeologists found a huge sample of carbonized rice, much used in burials, "rice beds" in which some citizens were laid to rest on layers of rice, and then covered over with more. Finally, the "bed" was set on fire to purify the grave. Rice burials have been found nowhere else in the world. Since these graves also contain lavish jewelry and bronze goods, they indicate that the burial practice was reserved for those of special rank. It can be also deduced that the community produced a tremendous rice surplus under the distribution control of a chieftain, who wielded power over the rice farmers or producers.

Also of interest are containers in which food was stored and shipped. Often these were clay jars known as amphoras, ubiquitous throughout the ancient world for

The recovery of food from archeological sites is one of the most challenging of all tasks due to the fragile nature of the remains. The stakes are raised when the food is buried in jars under the sea, as in the case of these Phoenician amphorae that sank with a ship during a storm about 750 B.C.E. off the coast of what is now Israel. Vestiges of the contents proved that the amphorae once held wine. They are shown here in an underwater photo released by *National Geographic* in 1999. © AFP/CORBIS

carrying olive oil, fish sauce, olives, fruit, and wine. Excavation at the fortress Masada in Israel has turned up Roman amphoras with wine residues bearing the inscription "For Herod of Judea" (73–4, r. 37–4, B.C.E.), indicating that this potentate favored Italian vineyards.

Another aspect of food archaeology is culinary archaeology, the study of food preparation and utensils. Rice steamers have been recovered from Noen-U Loke in Thailand and other locations. Sophisticated techniques even make it possible to identify the temperature at which an ancient meal was cooked. When Lindow Man, a body discovered in a British bog, was retrieved, the charred bran-and-chaff stomach contents were subjected to electron spin resonance, capable of measuring the highest temperature to which a material has been subjected and for what length of time. The conclusion: the meal was probably a griddle cake, cooked on a flat, heated surface for about half an hour at 392°F (200°C).

Preserved Meals

Occasionally, archaeologists unearth actual charred meals, most notably at Pompeii and Herculaneum, covered by ash when Mt. Vesuvius erupted in 79 C.E. There, inhabitants left complete meals on tables, food in shops, and loaves of bread in bakery ovens. The Egyptian priests at the Temple of Isis in Pompeii were eating a meal of fish and eggs when the eruption occurred. Researchers at Pompeii have taken their work a step further to investigate how the Romans, master urban planners, incorporated growing, processing, distribution, and storage of food and drink into the city layout. By measuring distances from dwellings to restaurants and bakeries, they can determine how far a citizen had to travel to quench his thirst or get something to eat.

After excavating artifacts (manmade objects) and subjecting them to laboratory analysis, the broader task is to document processes of cultural change such as the beginning of agriculture in a particular area. Food plays a critical role in the development of civilization and culture. The problem of subsistence must always be solved first before a food surplus can be generated, the population expands, and there are the beginnings of a ranked society with some elite members engaging in ruling, military activities, directing religion, and craft making. It is food that propels the development of ever more complex societies.

See also **Anthropology and Food**; **Greece, Ancient**; **Mesopotamia, Ancient**; **Mexico and Central America, Pre-Columbian**.

BIBLIOGRAPHY

Brothwell, Patricia, and Don R. Brothwell. *Food in Antiquity: A Survey of the Diet of Early Peoples.* Baltimore: Johns Hopkins University Press, 1998.

Curtis, Robert. *Ancient Food Technology.* Vol. 5, *Technology and Change in History.* Leiden: Brill, 2001.

Heun, Manfred, et al. "Site of Einkorn Wheat Domestication Identified by DNA Fingerprinting." *Science* 278 (1997): 1312–1313.

McGovern, Patrick, Stuart J. Fleming, and Solomon H. Katz. *The Origins and Ancient History of Wine.* Luxembourg: Gordon and Breach, 1995.

McGovern, Patrick, et al. "A Funerary Feast Fit for King Midas." *Nature* 402 (1999): 863–864.

Normile, Dennis. "Yangtze Seen as Earliest Rice Site." *Science* 275 (1997): 309.

Renfrew, Colin, and Paul Bahn. "What Did They Eat?" In *Archaeology: Theories, Methods and Practice.* 2d ed. New York: Thames and Hudson, 1996.

Ruscillo, Deborah. "When Gluttony Ruled!" *Archaeology* (November–December 2001): 20–25.

Linda Murray Berzok

FOOD AS A WEAPON OF WAR.

Providing or withholding food during times of conflict can be just as potent a weapon as the guns, bombs, and explosives of opposing armies. Control of food supplies during war is important because wars disrupt the seasonal pattern of growing crops, displace farming populations, and prevent the transport of food within the area of conflict. The economic costs of war may so impoverish citizens and local governments that they are unable to purchase or distribute needed food, even if it is available. A major focus of the Marshall Plan for Europe after the Second World War was to prevent the kind of starvation and social upheaval that had followed World War I. More recent relief efforts have focused on distributing food to refugees of many regional conflicts, where imposed famine was part of the combatants' military strategy in countries like Liberia, Mozambique, Somalia, and Sudan.

Withholding Food

Food can be withheld by preventing it from being grown and harvested, by destroying it after harvest, by preventing it from being shipped to where it is needed, or by contaminating it and rendering it unfit for consumption. Indigenous farming populations have been scattered or exiled from their native lands by conquering armies to make room for their own colonists who would subjugate and establish their hegemony over the local inhabitants, and provide food and warriors for future campaigns. Ancient armies have "salted the earth" and destroyed irrigation systems to make an area unsuitable for growing crops. In the culmination of the Punic Wars with Carthage in the third and second centuries B.C.E., Rome defeated the armies of Hannibal, destroyed his empire, and ploughed the land with salt to make it infertile. The Roman practice of contaminating water supplies by dumping dead animals into wells has continued into recent history as demonstrated by an instance during the American Civil War when Confederate soldiers fouled the water supplies of Union forces with dead animals. There are no instances of widespread contamination of food during war in the modern era, perhaps because of the universal condemnation of such practices by all civilized nations. Sieges of fortified positions have been used since time immemorial to starve, demoralize, and physically weaken the ensconced combatants. Pictorial representations in Egypt depict sieges over 4,000 years ago, while the *Iliad* of Homer describes the siege of Troy by the Greeks over 3,000 years ago. It, like many of the numerous sieges that followed, ended not through force of arms, but through deception and treachery. The Spartan siege of Athens that ended the Peloponnesian Wars (431–404 B.C.E.) was ineffective as long as Athens could obtain food by sea. Only by allying themselves with Persia and destroying the Athenian navy were the Spartans able to starve them into submission. A similar maritime strategy was employed, but in reverse, by Emperor Leo III of the Eastern Roman Empire, whose forces destroyed the Arab navy, maintained food imports, and broke their siege of Constantinople in 717. Sieges often do not work because the besieged forces have stored or can obtain enough food for the duration, or because the invading forces cannot obtain enough food or maintain their supply lines because of the surrounding hostile population.

A continuing problem with siege warfare was that the attackers could run out of food or succumb to disease in their unhealthy encampments. For this reason, the parties of siege warfare in the medieval West often agreed on a time limit, after which the besieged forces could leave without penalty. Such civility was rare even then, and certainly has not persisted to modern times of total war. Parisians were reduced to eating rats during the siege that ended the 1870 Franco-Prussian War, and over a million Russians starved to death during the 500-day siege of Leningrad in World War II; more civilians died in Leningrad than in the bombings of Hamburg, Dresden, Tokyo, Hiroshima, and Nagasaki combined.

In modern times, sieges have expanded and evolved into embargos of critical war materials (for example, food, medicine, oil, strategic metals, technology, etc.) by nation-states. England imposed an embargo by sea for that area of Europe occupied by Napoleon, and Germany tried to embargo food and war materials to England and Russia by the United States in the Second World War. While food is now usually not embargoed for humanitarian reasons by the major powers, economic sanctions remain an implement of international policy and genocidal starvation as accepted strategy in some regional conflicts.

Scorched Earth

Many countries have adopted a "scorched earth" policy (destroying anything that might be of use to an invading enemy) to prevent an invading army from living off the land. Both attackers and defenders in conventional wars and guerrilla struggles have used this strategy. During the U.S. Civil War, General William T. Sherman brought "total war" to the heart of the Confederacy by his infamous "March to the Sea" across Georgia and South Carolina, a scorched earth policy that is still debated as being barbarous or sound military strategy. The British used a scorched earth policy during their war with the Boers in South Africa, and the French conquest of Algeria (1830 to 1844) used it to starve the natives into submission. Unless ruthlessly enforced, it is often difficult to convince people to destroy all they have in advance of an invading force. The conquest of Gaul by Julius Caesar was almost prevented by this tactic, but Vercingetorix's guerrilla campaigns were ineffective because he could not persuade his countrymen to adopt this painful policy wholeheartedly.

Russia very effectively used a scorched earth policy during its invasion by Swedish armies in 1709, Napoleon's armies in 1812, and Hitler's armies in 1941. Because the Russians removed most of the food and crops in advance, Napoleon's half-a-million-man army could not live off the land as they had in previous campaigns. Despite being able to capture Moscow, they were too emaciated to hold it and had to retreat. The inability to find food locally also created severe problems for the German military in World War II, which was trying to feed three million soldiers. Forests, stores and transports were set afire; all grain and millions of cattle were shipped from the Ukraine to Russia, leaving nothing for the advancing German armies. However, nothing was left for the peasants who were equally bereft of food and shelter. As the Germans retreated towards Berlin, they too implemented a scorched earth policy to slow the pursuing Russian army.

Providing Food

Since, as Napoleon is quoted as saying, "An army marches on its stomach," procuring enough food to support an army in the field is a paramount concern for all commanders. Although weapons, clothing, and shelter are of the greatest immediate importance to soldiers, logistical support to provide food and material is often the decisive element in winning wars. Soldiers often had to truly "live off the land" even when in permanent garrisons or semipermanent encampments during lengthy sieges. Improvements in food preservation, packaging, and transportation have made modern armies immune to local vagaries in the availability of food.

The technologies of canning, freezing, dehydrating, and irradiating food were greatly advanced by the necessities of war. In 1795 Nicholas Appert, a French chef, won a prize offered by Napoleon for a way to prevent military food supplies from spoiling. By 1806, Appert's principles for canning meats and vegetables in jars had been successfully applied to the canning of meat, vegetables, fruit, and even milk for the French Navy. The English adopted the process to use with metal containers in 1810, and when Napoleon faced Wellington at Waterloo in 1815, both of their troops ate canned rations.

Frozen foods had been around since the 1920s, but did not become important until they were used to feed U.S. troops overseas during the Second World War. At home, frozen foods caught on with American consumers because canned foods required precious metal and were rationed, while frozen foods were not. Dehydration has been practiced for millennia by peoples who dried grasses, herbs, roots, berries, and meats by setting them out in the sun. Dehydrated foods are important for the military because of their light weight and minimal volume. During World War II, the U.S. Army tested irradiation on fruits, vegetables, dairy products, and meat. Irradiated food has been pioneered and extensively used since the 1960s by the military and NASA. The responsibility to feed large numbers of people on military bases and on the battlefield, and its enforced administrated structure provides an excellent opportunity for large-scale testing of new food-handling and preparation technologies by the military. Coupled with the mandated desires of the U.S. Congress for the military to eat domestically grown food, even in distant military operations, and the realities of combat, many food-handling technologies have been first implemented by the military before they gained widespread acceptance by civilians.

See also **Military Rations; Preserving.**

BIBLIOGRAPHY

Catton, William B. *Bruce Catton's Civil War: Mr. Lincoln's Army; Glory Road; A Stillness at Appomattox.* New York: Fairfax Press, 1984.

Dunnigan, James F. *How to Make War.* 3rd ed. New York: William Morrow, 1993.

Keegan, John. *A History of Warfare.* New York: Vintage Books, 1994.

Leckie, Robert. *Delivered From Evil: The Saga of World War II.* New York: Harper and Row, 1987.

Marshall, Samuel L.A. *World War I.* New York: American Heritage, 1985.

Walzer, Michael. *Just and Unjust Wars.* New York: Harper Torchbook, 1977.

Mikal E. Saltveit

FOOD BANKS. Warehouses that collect and store donations of surplus foods, food banks distribute the foodstuffs to authorized nonprofit organizations that provide assistance to the needy. The food comes from many sources, including individual contributions, local food drives, regional grocery stores, farmers, food service companies, and national food corporations. The surpluses arise from mislabeling, mispackaging, mishandling, and other factors that contribute to loss of commercial value—however, all the foods are safe and edible.

Food banks began in the late 1960s when the retired Arizona businessman John Van Hengel volunteered in a soup kitchen and began to solicit donations of food products that would otherwise be wasted. When the soup kitchen received more food than it could handle, Van Hengel set up a warehouse to store and distribute these food products. As other cities learned of the food bank concept, they began to duplicate it in their areas. A grant from the federal government in 1976 assisted the development of food banks throughout the nation. Although food banks developed as temporary emergency food relief organizations, they have become permanent fixtures

A volunteer moves boxes of groceries inside a Contra Costa food bank warehouse in Concord, California. © BOB ROWAN; PROGRESSIVE IMAGE/CORBIS.

in America because of economic recessions, job insecurity, erosion of public assistance benefits, and sharp increases in housing and other costs. Food banks multiplied from a few dozen in the 1980s to over 250 in 2002.

Today, approximately 80 percent of all food banks in the United States are networked through an organization called America's Second Harvest, which is the largest domestic hunger relief organization. Food banks have the capacity to receive large volumes of food and distribute it efficiently and quickly. America's Second Harvest serves as a link between food banks in its network, and can assist with moving food out of one bank and into another (thus helping to control inventory), move product quickly, and minimize waste. The banks are typically operated by a small staff of employees who direct the program, manage the warehouse operation, and oversee a large corps of volunteers. Financial records are kept and the banks are audited annually. Food banks must comply with local health codes regarding sanitation and safe food handling. Because of the Tax Reform Act of 1976, corporate donors can take advantage of tax deductions for their contributions—not only for 100 percent of production costs, but also for 50 percent of the difference between the product cost and the normal sale price. As a result of the Good Samaritan Act passed by Congress in 1981, donors are absolved from liability for the food's safety as long as they make an effort to determine that the food is edible and fit for human consumption when donated.

The funding for food banks comes from private contributions, foundations, some government sources, and fund-raising. The organizations that receive the food are also charged what is called a shared maintenance fee. This is a small amount (18 cents per pound in 2002) to help cover the cost of handling the product, and is not based on the value of the food. Grant monies are often available to those organizations that cannot afford even this small fee. Very perishable food items are sometimes given away at no cost as they cannot be stored for long periods of time.

Large food bank operations have developed innovative ways to distribute even more food. The food banks in Delaware and Washington, D.C., operate onsite community kitchens where donated foods are prepared into meals that can be distributed to programs such as the Kids Café, which is an after-school feeding program for low-income children.

Food banks collectively distribute nearly a billion pounds of food annually, feeding more than 23 million needy Americans, including 8 million children and 4 million senior citizens. As the problem of hunger in America continues to grow, low-income families will continue to rely on food banks to provide a source of low-cost food assistance and a means of decreasing their food insecurity.

Hunger and poverty go hand-in-hand, and the poor will always exist in every society. While food banks cannot eliminate poverty, their mission is to abolish hunger;

they do an admirable job of it, providing assistance to nearly a tenth of the population. They augment the many federal food assistance programs that play the larger role in the food-security safety net for limited-income families. Unfortunately, it does not look as if food banks will disappear from America as their founders had once hoped. The United States produces enough food to adequately feed all of its citizens. The problem is often getting the food to those who need it; food banks are one solution.

See also **Food Pantries; Government Agencies; Homelessness; Poverty; Soup Kitchens; WIC (Women, Infants, and Children's) Program**.

BIBLIOGRAPHY

History of America's Second Harvest, The. Available at http://www.secondharvest.org/.

Kantor, Linda, Kathryn Lipton, Alden Manchester, and Victor Oliveira. "Estimating and Addressing America's Food Losses." *Food Review* 17 (1997): 1–11.

Kim, Myoung, Jim Ohls, and Rhonda Cohen. *Hunger in America 2001 National Report*. Princeton, N.J.: Mathematica Policy Research, 2001.

Poppendieck, Janet. *Sweet Charity? Emergency Food and the End of Entitlement*. New York: Viking, 1998.

Riches, Graham, ed. *First World Hunger: Food Security and Welfare Politics*. New York: St. Martin's Press, 1997.

Nancy Cotugna

FOOD CONSUMPTION SURVEYS. Food consumption surveys—sometimes referred to as food intake surveys or dietary surveys—monitor food use by data collection at three different levels. On the national level, food availability may be described by supply data such as food balance sheets. These results express food availability rather than food consumption in a nation and are not further discussed here. The second type of food consumption survey measures food use within a household, and the third type assesses individual intake of foods and beverages. These latter two survey types collect information on kinds, amounts, and frequencies of food consumption and occasionally on expenditure for food purchases. Furthermore, these surveys include information on factors influencing food intake patterns such as socioeconomic criteria, food perceptions, and beliefs.

At the beginning of the twentieth century, the investigation of food consumption patterns became necessary in order to identify inadequate and insufficient diets in parts of the population. This was especially important among urban industrial workers for whom mass production of food was needed because they no longer had ready access to farm produce. The first small-scale studies were carried out in different countries. As the number of participants in such surveys increased, the scope widened to include health issues related to food consumption. To

FOOD CONSUMPTION SURVEYS IN THE UNITED STATES

Since the 1930s, food consumption surveys have been carried out by the U.S. Department of Agriculture (USDA). After small-scale studies, nationwide monitoring began in the 1950s. In 1955 the Household Food Consumption Survey, which was first based on a representative sample of households, was initiated. The survey investigated food use on the household level. Beginning in 1965, a component of individual dietary assessment has been included in the National Food Surveys. Since 1985, household consumption has been replaced by the Continuing Survey of Food Intakes by Individuals, which is based on dietary assessment through twenty-four-hour dietary recalls. Since the late 1980s, food surveys have been combined with the Diet and Health Knowledge Behavior Survey (DHKS). Knowledge and attitudes toward diet as well as dietary behavior are assessed to improve understanding of individual dietary patterns.

gain up-to-date information, these surveys were repeated on a regular basis. Advanced sampling techniques enabled researchers to design representative surveys.

Methods and materials of data collection are selected in accordance with the objectives of the survey. If the household is the focus, food inventories and household accounts are used to collect data on present food use, while food-list recalls monitor food use in the past. Food consumed outside of the home and the food distribution among household members are not assessed. Results are expressed in quantities of food consumed, expenditures for food purchases, and energy or nutrient availability per household. Comparisons of food availability in households among different communities or socioeconomic groups can be made. Dietary changes in a total population or subgroups of a population can be investigated.

The method for assessing individuals' dietary intake is the food record. Quantities are either accurately weighed or estimated by household measures. The twenty-four-hour recall assesses food intake during the previous day while diet histories focus on usual dietary patterns in the past. Food Frequencies Questionnaires (FFQ) ask how often food items are usually consumed within a defined period. The questionnaires and the diet histories focus on long-term subjective perception while food records and twenty-four-hour recalls are suitable for investigating absolute or relative nutrient intakes of groups and individuals.

TABLE 1

Dietary assessment methods

Method	Period	Features
Food record	Present diet	Quantities and kinds of foods Time and location of consumption Presence of fellow eaters
Twenty-four-hour recall	Last 24 hours	Quantities and kinds of foods Time and location of consumption Presence of fellow eaters
Diet history	Last month(s)	Meals usually consumed Dishes and foods usually consumed
Food frequency questionnaire	Last weeks or months	Food list provided Frequency of consumption of food items Quantities, e.g., portion sizes

---

With assistance from food composition tables or data banks, energy and nutrient intakes are estimated. Thus quantities and qualities of diets as well as nutrient intakes of groups or individuals are monitored. Some surveys focus on specific target groups—for example, age groups (such as infants or elderly persons) or individuals with particular diets, conditions, or diseases such as pregnancy or diabetes, or on selected food groups (for example, fruits and vegetables).

Food and nutritional planning on the national or international level is based on these data sources, as are estimates of the adequacy of dietary intakes of population groups. The development and evaluation of educational programs is based on these results. The relationship of diet and health status as well as estimates of average intakes of additives and contaminants are other important issues.

The main limitation of food consumption surveys is that they depend on accurate report or recall of food quantity and type by the participants in the study. The quality of nutrient and energy values depends on the quality and accuracy of food consumption tables.

See also **Dietary Assessment; Intake.**

BIBLIOGRAPHY

Bingham, Sheila A. "Limitations of the Various Methods for Collecting Dietary Intake Data." *Annals of Nutrition and Metabolism* 35 (1991): 117–127.

Cameron, Margaret E., and Wija A. van Staveren, eds. *Manual of Methodology for Food Consumption Studies.* Oxford: Oxford University Press, 1988.

FAO/WHO. *Preparation and Use of Food-Based Dietary Guidelines: Report of a Joint FAO/WHO Consultation.* WHO Technical Series 880. Geneva: World Health Organization, Food and Agriculture Organization of the United Nations, 1998. Chapter 3 gives a general description of methodological aspects of food surveys.

Gibson, Rosalind S. *Principles of Nutritional Assessment.* Oxford: Oxford University Press, 1990.

den Hartog, Adel P., Wija A. van Staveren, and Inge D. Brouwer. *Manual for Social Surveys on Food Habits and Consumption in Developing Countries.* Weikersheim, Germany: Margraf Verlag, 1995.

Macdiarmid, Jennie, and John Blundell. "Assessing Dietary Intake: Who, What and Why of Under-reporting." *Nutrition Research Review* 11 (1998): 231–253.

Mark, Steven D., Donald G. Thomas, and Adriano Decarli. "Measurement of Exposure to Nutrients: An Approach to the Selection of Informative Foods." *American Journal of Epidemiology* 143, no. 5 (1996): 514–521.

Thompson, Frances E., and Tim Byers. "Dietary Assessment Resource Manual." *Journal of Nutrition* 124 (1994): 2245S–2317S.

Tippett, Katherine S., Cecilia Wilkinson Enns, and Alanna J. Moshfegh. "Food Consumption Surveys in the US Department of Agriculture." *Nutrition Today* 34, no. 1 (January/February 1999): 33–46.

U.S. Department of Health and Human Services, Public Health Service. *The Surgeon General's Report on Nutrition and Health: Summary and Recommendations.* Washington, D.C.: U.S. Government Printing Office, 1988.

Welten, Desiree C., Ruth A. Carpenter, R. Sue McPherson, Suzanne Brodney, Deirdre Douglass, James B. Kampert, and Steven N. Blair. "Comparison of a Dietary Record Using Reported Portion Size versus Standard Portion Size for Assessing Nutrient Intake." *Public Health Nutrition* 3 (2000): 151–158.

Winkler, Gertrud. *Validierung einer Food-Frequency Erhebung.* Ph.D. diss., Technical University of Munich, 1992. In German.

Simone Meyer

FOOD COOPERATIVES. Food cooperatives represent a particular subset of a larger environment of cooperative businesses. Cooperative business enterprises are primarily distinguished from other forms of business organization by the fact that their members consider other goals to be more important than return on invested capital. In its Statement of Identity, the International Cooperative Alliance defines a cooperative as "an autonomous association of persons united voluntarily to meet their common economic, social and cultural needs and aspirations through a jointly-owned and democratically-controlled enterprise."

Several characteristics commonly typify a cooperative enterprise. These characteristics, based on values that are made explicit to (and by) their members, include:

Autonomy: the cooperative is as independent of government and private enterprise as possible;

Association of persons: the definition deliberately does not read an "association of individuals";

Voluntary: members are free to join and leave at will, within the purposes and resources of the cooperative;

Meet needs: the central purpose of the cooperative is to meet member needs, which can be purely economic or social and cultural;

Joint ownership and democratic control: the members own the cooperative on a mutual basis. Decisions are made democratically by the members and are not controlled by capital or by government;

Enterprise: the cooperative is an organized entity that typically functions in the marketplace and engages in the exchange of goods and services.

There are over three hundred food cooperatives in the United States today. Through food cooperatives, consumers have sought to improve the quality and nutrition of available foods, to become better educated about food and environmental issues as they pertain to food choice, and to create a marketplace for organically grown foods. Food cooperatives often have mission statements that support such goals. For example, Puget Consumers Cooperative, based in Seattle, Washington (the largest food cooperative in the United States) has as its mission statement, "to provide the highest quality natural foods and products. We create and cultivate the marketplace for locally grown and organic products and are a vital community resource on food, nutrition and environmental issues."

History

The concept of cooperation germinated in the middle 1800s during the early period of industrialization. A small group of weavers in Rochdale Village, England, is considered to be the first practical application of the concept. There, in 1844, twenty-eight weavers combined their skills and ambitions, agreeing to share the burdens and rewards of a self-supporting economic colony. Other examples of co-ops appeared in the late 1800s throughout England and Europe, particularly in Finland.

It is not clear which consumer co-op in the United States was the first. According to one source, it was a buying club for household supplies created in 1844. Another source claims that the first consumer cooperative in the United States was established in Philadelphia in 1862. Whichever was actually the "first," the popularity of consumer cooperatives has tended to increase in waves coincident with periods of economic decline (the Great Depression) and political and consumer unrest (the 1960s). What is now referred to as the "old wave" of growth in the number of cooperatives in the 1930s was inspired largely by economic depression. The cooperative was viewed by the Hoover and Roosevelt administrations as an "American concept" and as a solution to the suffering farming industry. But with the improved

war-oriented economy of the 1940s, support waned for co-ops and the philosophies that went with them. The impetus for the most recent expansion (the "new wave") of American cooperatives in the relatively prosperous 1960s lay in a desire to harness and enhance social capital, build community, and achieve local autonomy from an increasingly global food system. In the 1960s and 1970s in the United States, food cooperatives were viewed as a political as well as economic alternative to conventional supermarkets.

Co-Op Values and Principles

From the earliest days of the Rochdale Pioneers, food cooperatives have emphasized the importance of honest dealings in the marketplace: accurate measurements, reliable quality, and fair prices. Members have insisted that their co-op have honest dealings with them. Ideally, this has led to honest dealings with nonmembers and a unique level of openness throughout the organization.

Since its creation in 1895, the International Cooperative Alliance (ICA) has been recognized as the authority for defining cooperatives and for determining the underlying principles that provide motivation for such enterprises. One of the major purposes of the ICA is to "promote and protect cooperative values and principles."

Three formal statements of the cooperative principles have been made by the ICA—in 1937, 1966, and 1995. Each statement was carefully crafted to adopt and explain principles that were both relevant to and of value for the contemporary world. The latest statement of principles reflects substantial changes in the global economy, in international political alignments, in the economic development of Asia, Africa and Latin America, and in the worldwide human condition. These changes brought new challenges and opportunities to cooperatives worldwide. Some traditional cooperative assumptions were challenged, giving rise to new interpretations of cooperative values and inspiring a reconsideration of the role of cooperative enterprise in the twenty-first century and in societies undergoing rapid change.

Cooperative values. Cooperative values reflect convictions that these enterprises hold about how to achieve a better society and what form that society should take. Common values among food co-ops include: *Self-help:* People have the will and the capability to improve their destiny peacefully through joint action, which can be more powerful than individual effort, particularly through collective action in the market. *Democracy:* Members have the right to participate, to be informed, to be heard and to be involved in making decisions. Members are the source of all authority in the cooperative. *Equality:* Equal rights and opportunities for people to participate democratically will improve the use of society's resources and foster mutuality, understanding, and solidarity. *Equity:* Fair distribution of income and power in society and its economic life should be based on labor, not ownership of capital. *Solidarity:* Cooperatives are based on the assumption that there is strength in mutual self-help and that the cooperative has a collective responsibility for the well-being of its members.

The 1995 cooperative principles. Principles are guidelines for putting ideals and values into practice. If successful, principles are incorporated into the organizational culture of the cooperative; they are the broad vision statement for cooperatives and cooperators individually and collectively.

Seven ICA principles (revised from the 1966 statement and adopted in 1995) in abbreviated form are:

1. Voluntary and Open Membership: Cooperatives are voluntary organizations, open to all persons able to use their services and willing to accept the responsibilities of membership, without gender, social, racial, political or religious discrimination.

    Participation as active and responsible members should be based on a clear understanding of the values for which cooperatives stand and on support for those values.

2. Democratic Member Control: Cooperatives are democratic organizations controlled by their members, who actively participate in setting policies and decision-making. Members of these societies should enjoy equal voting rights (one member, one vote) and participation in decisions affecting their societies.

3. Member Economic Participation: The economic benefits arising out of the operations of a society belong to the members of that society and should be distributed in such a manner as to avoid one member gaining at the expense of others. This may be accomplished by the following means: (a) by provision for development of the cooperative's business; (b) by provision of common services; or (c) by distribution among members in proportion to their transactions with the society.

4. Autonomy and Independence: This principle emphasizes that cooperatives must be free of intervention from governments or other sources so that ultimately the members are able to control their own destiny.

5. Education, Training, and Information: Education is a priority in cooperative enterprises. Education here is meant to be more than advertising products or distributing information. Rather, it means engaging the minds of members, elected leaders, managers, and employees of food co-ops in critical thinking regarding food, nutrition, health, and the food system.

6. Cooperation among Cooperatives: All cooperative enterprises, in order to best serve the interests of their members and their communities, should actively cooperate in every practical way with other cooperatives at local, national, and international levels.

7. Concern for Community: Grounded in the values of social responsibility and caring for others, this principle (added in the 1995 revision of ICA principles) articulates an interest in making contributions to a better society at large. By taking ownership over portions of the economy, cooperative members are saying, in effect, we can meet our needs and the needs of others better than they are currently being met. Because the effort is a mutual one, cooperative members understand that to provide for any member is to provide for all members.

The Food Co-Op Shopper

Consumer research conducted in the 1970s, 1980s, and 1990s indicated important differences between food cooperative shoppers and their supermarket counterparts. Areas of difference included food-related behaviors; attitudes toward food and food safety, health, nutrition, and the food system; and political views. Food-related behaviors studied included dietary patterns and cooking habits. Food co-op shoppers were shown to buy items such as tofu, brown rice, alfalfa sprouts, honey, dried beans, yogurt, granola, and spinach with greater frequency than supermarket shoppers. Supermarket shoppers, on the other hand, tended to consume franks, beef, poultry, pork, white bread, white rice, candy bars, and potatoes with more frequency than co-op shoppers. Food co-op shoppers tended to have a greater enjoyment of cooking and to cook "from scratch" more often than the general population. This is consistent with a strong skepticism toward heavily processed foods associated with food co-op shoppers, particularly in the 1970s and early 1980s.

Environmental concern and concern over food system issues such as globalization, genetic engineering, and corporatization are more meaningful to food co-op members than nonmembers. Co-op shoppers also tend to put relatively less importance on year-round availability of produce items.

Over the years, consumers have been motivated by several factors to join and shop at food co-ops. Research from the 1970s suggests that lower prices, availability of natural foods, and product quality were dominant motivating factors for joining a food cooperative. Support for co-op values, economic and ecological interests, freshness of the food, the availability of locally grown food, social atmosphere, variety of products, and the availability of bulk items are additional motivators for co-op shoppers.

The growth of food cooperative membership observed in the 1970s and 1980s is thought to stem in part from concerns about food safety and the impacts processed foods may have on health as well as an increasing awareness of the diet and health relationship. The use of whole and organic foods among coop shoppers may be related more to the desire to decrease control of large companies and food processors and a sense

Women making pasta at a women's cooperative in Walata, Mauritania. © JUAN ECHEVERRIA/CORBIS.

of increased personal responsibility than to the nutritional value of such products. Access to bulk items, herbs and spices, organic foods, farm-fresh eggs and preservative-free bread were incentives for shopping at the cooperative. Co-op shoppers believed that organically grown foods possess beneficial nutritional attributes, and they were willing to pay a higher price for them. This preference was largely motivated by a belief that pesticide residues in foods posed a health risk. They also felt that there are environmental factors other than food processing that are harmful to health and to the environment.

Establishing a Niche
From their beginning, consumer food co-ops have distinguished themselves from traditional food retailing by establishing active consumer education programs designed to increase awareness and understanding not only of food composition, but of the source of food and the production methods used. Co-op policies often reflect the values related to food and the marketplace that members consider to be important, such as a diverse product line that emphasizes quality, nutrition, and organic growing methods, health and nutrition awareness through education of members and staff, and shared participation by the staff in co-op decision-making.

Goals common to most food cooperatives include democracy, member education and participation, and a dedication to "pure" or "natural" foods. The latter goal in particular created the expectation that food cooperatives were places where natural foods could be found, and further defined the niche of these retail outlets. However, the demand for natural and organically grown foods is increasing dramatically, and shoppers are able to find these foods in a wide range of retail and wholesale food outlets.

Modern Trends
Food cooperatives continue to constitute a very small proportion of the food-retailing segment. As the availability of organic produce and multi-ingredient processed products has expanded throughout the food-retailing industry, and as supermarket chains have initiated active consumer education programs, the characteristics that distinguish food cooperatives as unique alternatives have become less clear. Expanded availability of "whole foods" and certified organic foods means that food cooperatives are no longer exclusive sources for these choices. However, these food-retailing enterprises may still provide important alternatives to supermarket chains. For example, food cooperatives still provide a space for debating agriculture and food system trends that is difficult to find in other institutions. Decisions about inventory are based less on market demand than on established goals, values, politics, and principles. Also, cooperatives still provide an atmosphere of community that is not found in more conventional supermarkets and megastores. In the past, food cooperatives have been innovators in the marketplace in the areas of unit pricing, consumer protection, and nutritional labeling. They may offer innovations in the future that are adopted throughout the retail industry. Finally, recent trends in food retailing in the United States and elsewhere may serve to renew interest and participation in food cooperatives. Food retailing, like agricultural production before it, is increasingly concentrated. Warehouse food stores and mass retailers with

grocery sections are gaining market share in some of the most profitable categories of food products and capturing the food expenditure of families with children, who comprise the most lucrative segment of the shopping public. This threat to the traditional grocery store may provide an opportunity for food cooperatives to offer an alternative food store that, by their very nature, are resistant to such trends.

See also **Distribution of Food; Food Marketing: Alternative (or Direct) Strategies; Natural Foods; Retailing of Food**.

BIBLIOGRAPHY

Fjeld, C. R., R. Sommer, F. D. Becker, and J. Warholic. "Nutrition Knowledge and Preferences of Food Cooperative Shoppers. *Journal of the American Dietetic Association*, 82, 4 (1983): 389–393.

Fjeld, C. R., J. Storer, J. Warholic, R. Sommer, and F. D. Becker. "Food Intake Frequencies of Food Co-op Shoppers." *Journal of Nutrition Education*, 16, 3 (1984): 142–144.

Ehlers, K. M., and H. Fox. "Food Cooperative Shoppers: Nutrition Knowledge, Attitudes, and Concerns." *Journal of the American Dietetic Association* 80 (1982): 160–162.

Hennessy, T. "Fresh Ideas." *Progressive Grocer*. March 2000: 85–91.

Kahn, Barbara E., and Leigh McAlister. *Grocery Revolution: The New Focus on the Consumer*. New York: Addison-Wesley, 1997.

Kreitner, P. "Research: Who Shops Co-op, and Why?" *The New Harbinger* 3 (1973): 1–17.

Jennifer L. Wilkins

FOOD PANTRIES. What are known as emergency feeding organizations in the United States include food banks, food pantries, soup kitchens, and shelters operated by nonprofit organizations and faith-based agencies. The emergency food assistance network provides food to people who lack the resources to obtain adequate amounts of food through conventional means. Food banks solicit donations of surplus or salvage food that they distribute to food pantries (which provide emergency grocery packages), soup kitchens and shelters (which provide on-site meals), and other feeding programs. Although religious organizations and nonprofit agencies have historically distributed food and meals to people in need, the sharp increases in such requests beginning in the 1980s associated with high unemployment, cuts in the social safety net, decline in the value of public assistance benefits, and increases in housing and other costs led to a proliferation of food pantries, soup kitchens, and government programs that defined hunger and homelessness as temporary "emergency" problems.

In 2001 the America's Second Harvest provider network included approximately 26,300 food pantries in the United States, three-quarters of which are run by faith-based agencies affiliated with churches, mosques, synagogues, and other religious organizations. These food pantries received more than half (59 percent) of the food they distributed from food banks, with religious organizations, direct purchases, and federal government commodity programs supplying the remainder. More than 90 percent of these food pantries use volunteer staff, and many rely entirely on volunteers. Only 33 percent of the pantry programs have any paid staff.

Food pantries, also known as food closets, food shelves, or grocery programs, distribute nonprepared foods and other grocery items to needy clients, who then prepare and use these items where they live. In the United States, food pantries are primarily operated through referral systems, in which trained staff at nonprofit organizations screen clients and refer them to pantries operated by volunteers. The majority of food pantries prebag the food distributed to clients, while others allow clients to select their own food "grocery-store style." To the extent possible, pantries use several different factors, including household size, household composition (number of children, adults, elderly), and health status of household members, to determine the contents of a food order. Some follow nutritional guidelines in selecting prebagged items. On average, food pantries distribute food items to provide three meals per day per household member for three to five days. A sample list of items distributed to a single adult by a Pittsburgh, Pennsylvania, food pantry includes cereal, canned vegetables, Jell-o, juice, bread, canned beef stew, ground turkey, canned fruit, pasta, spaghetti sauce, and paper products. Some food pantries provide additional services. In 2001, 18.2 percent of the food pantries in the America's Second Harvest food provider network also provided nutrition counseling, 15 percent provided eligibility counseling for food stamps, 20.3 percent provided utility bill assistance, and 42.9 percent provided clothing assistance.

Many food pantries require that recipients run out of food prior to requesting assistance and categorize this condition as a food emergency. They also focus on serving clients compatible with their service mission and have much less need for documentation and much more trust in recipients' testimonies than government agencies. Only recently have U.S. food pantries begun to enforce explicit eligibility standards, such as income or residency, or require documentation of eligibility.

In the late twentieth century, the U.S. Conference of Mayors Task Force on Hunger and Homelessness surveyed the twenty largest American cities, revealing steady increases in demand for emergency food assistance, a rising proportion of those requesting food assistance who are families with children, more requests from working families and individuals, unmet demand for emergency food assistance, and numerous cities where food assistance facilities must turn people away. In 2001 more than half (59.8 percent) of the food pantries in America's Second Harvest food provider network served more clients than they had in 1998. More than two-thirds (67.9 percent) of these pantries experienced problems related to funding, and about two-fifths (39 percent) had problems related to food supplies.

Government data indicate that at least 9.2 million households in the United States were food insecure in 1999 and that approximately 3 million households had experienced hunger at some point in that year. The food insecure households contained an estimated 27 million people, of whom 11 million were children (Andrews et al., 2000). The existence of large numbers of people without secure access to adequate nutritious food represents a serious national concern. An important response to this problem has been the growth of private sector institutions created to provide food for the needy.

Throughout the United States, food pantries, soup kitchens, and homeless shelters play a critical role in meeting the nutritional needs of America's low-income population. These organizations help meet the needs of people and households that otherwise would lack sufficient food. However, emergency feeding organizations are ultimately limited by the depth of the hunger problem, their reliance on volunteers, the availability of government and food industry surpluses, lack of legally enforceable rights for food recipients, and the discrepancies between where food providers are located and where those who need food live. Seeing these organizations as the primary solution to the problem of hunger diverts attention from the societal relationships that produce hunger, including economic restructuring, erosion of public assistance benefits, major cuts in social welfare programs, and high housing, medical, and other costs.

See also **Class, Social; Food Banks; Meals on Wheels; Poverty; School Meals; Soup Kitchens; WIC (Women, Infants, and Children's) Program.**

BIBLIOGRAPHY

Andrews, Margaret, Mark Nord, Gary Bickel, and Steven Carlsen. *Household Food Security in the United States, 1999.* Washington, D.C.: U.S. Department of Agriculture, Food and Nutrition Service, 2000.

Daponte, Beth Osborne, Gordon Lewis, Seth Sanders, and Lowell Taylor. *Food Pantries and Food Pantry Use in Allegheny County.* Pittsburgh, Pa.: H. John Heinz III School of Public Policy and Management, Carnegie Mellon University, 1994.

Kim, Myoung, Jim Ohls, and Rhonda Cohen. *Hunger in America 2001: National Report.* Princeton, N.J.: Mathematica Policy Research, 2001.

Poppendieck, Janet. *Sweet Charity?* New York: Viking, 1998.

U.S. Conference of Mayors. *A Status Report on Hunger and Homelessness in America's Cities: 2001.* Washington, D.C.: U.S. Conference of Mayors, 2001.

Karen A. Curtis

FOOD POLITICS: UNITED STATES. Food, the fuel of life and a source of lifelong pleasure, might seem to be the antithesis of politics, a term redolent of power, manipulation, and commerce, but the two are tightly linked. Commercial interests affect nearly every aspect of the systems of food production, distribution, and consumption, from farm to fork. The extraordinary size of the food enterprise and the vast sums at stake readily explain the ferocity of debates about dietary advice to the public, health claims on food package labels, regulations for meat safety, nutritional requirements for school meals, and labeling of genetically modified foods, to cite just a few examples. Debates over such issues derive from the disparate interests of the principal stakeholders in the food system, including the food industry and the consuming public of course but also government regulators, public health officials, and nutrition researchers and educators. Because all stakeholders should benefit from a food supply that is adequate, healthful, safe, environmentally sound, culturally appropriate, affordable, and delicious, the interests of these groups might appear to be congruent. The food industry, however, has an additional and compelling interest—to sell products. The conflict between the commercial interests of food companies and the widely varying concerns of other stakeholders is a principal reason why food issues are so controversial.

In this context the term "food industry" encompasses the full range of companies in the United States that produce, process, manufacture, sell, and serve foods, beverages, and dietary supplements (see the sidebar "The U.S. Food Industry"). Taken together the various sectors of this industry provide a food supply so plentiful, varied, relatively inexpensive, and devoid of dependence on geography or season that all but the poorest of Americans can obtain enough energy and nutrients to meet their biological needs. Indeed the U.S. food system as a whole—food produced in this country, plus imports, less exports—provides enough energy to meet the needs of every man, woman, and child in the country nearly twice over: 3,800 calories per capita per day. This amount is one-third higher than the caloric needs of most men, is twice the level needed by most women, and exceeds the requirements of babies, young children, and the sedentary elderly by even greater amounts. Even if, as the U.S. Department of Agriculture (USDA) estimates, 1,100 of those calories might be wasted (for example, in spoiled fruit or discarded oil for frying potatoes), the overabundance of food poses a major problem for the industry. It forces competition.

Because people, even those who overindulge, are limited in the number of calories they can consume, a choice of any one food means rejection of others. Thus food companies must convince people either to select their products over competitors' products or to consume more food overall, no matter how consumption or overconsumption might affect nutritional status or body weight. Food, beverage, supplement, and food service companies spend more

THE U.S. FOOD INDUSTRY

The huge U.S. food industry is best understood in sectors. The agribusiness sector raises food crops and animals and makes and sells fertilizer, pesticides, seeds, and feed. Other sectors sell machinery, labor, real estate, and financial services to farmers or transport, store, distribute, export, process, and market foods after they leave the farm. The food service sector includes restaurants, fast food outlets, and bars but also service by institutions, such as schools, hospitals, prisons, and workplaces, and by food carts and courts. The retail sector includes supermarkets, convenience stores, and vending machines. This vast food system generates nearly $1 trillion in annual sales, accounts for nearly 15 percent of the U.S. gross national product, and employs 17 percent of the country's labor force. Of the more than $800 billion or so that the public spent directly on food and drink in 2000, alcoholic beverages accounted for about $100 billion. The rest was distributed among retail food enterprises (54 percent) and food service (46 percent).

Within this industry huge national and multinational corporations vie for control of production or sales of specific food commodities. In 1997, for example, just three companies, Philip Morris (Kraft General Foods and Miller Brewing), ConAgra, and RJR–Nabisco, accounted for nearly 20 percent of all food expenditures in the United States. In 2000 seven U.S. companies (Philip Morris, ConAgra, Mars, IBP, Sara Lee, Heinz, and Tyson Foods)

ranked among the ten largest food companies in the world and generated up to $50 billion in sales annually. Others, such as Coca-Cola, McDonald's, PepsiCo, Procter and Gamble, and Roche (vitamins), ranked among the top one hundred worldwide. The nearly thirteen thousand outlets of McDonald's, the leading U.S. food service company, brought in about $20 billion in sales in 2000, more than twice as much as its nearest competitor.

These companies and others introduce 10,000 to 15,000 new food and beverage products annually into a marketplace that already contains about 320,000 such items. These items must compete for supermarket shelf space; even the largest supermarkets have room for just 50,000 products. Of the 11,000 new products introduced in 1998, for example, more than two-thirds were condiments, candies and snacks, baked goods, soft drinks, and dairy products (cheese products and ice cream novelties), foods largely allocated to the top ("eat occasionally") section of the U.S. Department of Agriculture's 1992 Food Guide Pyramid. Slightly more than one-fourth of the products were "nutritionally enhanced" so they could be marketed as low in fat, cholesterol, salt, or sugar or as higher in fiber, calcium, or vitamins. Some enhanced products, among them no-fat cookies, vitamin-enriched cereals, and calcium-fortified juice drinks, contain so much sugar that they belong at the top of the pyramid even though they are marketed as "healthy."

than $30 billion annually to promote their products to the public, and nearly 70 percent of this amount is applied to convenience foods, candy and snacks, alcoholic beverages, soft drinks, and desserts. In contrast, just over 2 percent is used to advertise foods considered more healthful, such as fruits, vegetables, grains, or beans. Furthermore the annual advertising expenditures for any single, nationally distributed food product are tenfold to fiftyfold higher than the total expenditures by government agencies to educate the public about food and nutrition.

The inequality of funding for dietary advice is only one aspect of U.S. food politics. Food companies also use the political system to convince Congress, government agency officials, food and nutrition experts, the media, and the public that their products promote health (or at least do no harm) and should not be subject to restrictive regulations. To protect their marketing environment, they contribute to congressional campaigns, lobby members of Congress and federal agencies, and when all else fails, engage in lawsuits. Nearly every food company is represented by a trade association or public relations

firm whose job is to promote a positive image of the company's product among consumers, professionals, and the media. The companies form partnerships and alliances with professional nutrition organizations, fund research on food and nutrition, sponsor professional journals and conferences, and make sure that influential groups, including federal officials, researchers, doctors, nurses, schoolteachers, and the media, will favor and not criticize their products. To distract attention from health, safety, or environmental concerns, they may argue that restrictive regulations overly involve the government in personal dietary choices and threaten constitutional guarantees of free speech.

Such actions are routine, legal, and thoroughly analogous to the political activities of any other major industry—tobacco, for example—in influencing health experts, federal agencies, and Congress. Promoting sales of food raises more complicated issues than promoting use of tobacco, however, in that food is required for life and causes health problems only when consumed inappropriately. Nevertheless the primary mission of food

690

FOOD POLITICS IN ACTION

Two examples, dietary recommendations and trade disputes, illustrate the breadth of ways politics connect to food. Food guides and dietary guidelines sometimes advise restriction in one or another food or component. When they do, industries affected by the advice raise objections. In 1991, for example, the U.S. Department of Agriculture (USDA) cancelled publication of its Food Guide Pyramid. Producers of meat and dairy foods protested that the placement of their products in the triangular design of the pyramid conveyed an "eat less" message. In turn nutrition and health experts protested the cancellation, arguing that the pyramid design was fully supported by research. The USDA released the guide one year later, after investing nearly a million dollars in face-saving research and agreeing to several design changes favored by meat and dairy producers. In another incident in 2000 the committee developing national dietary guidelines suggested Americans "limit" sugar consumption, but federal agencies changed that word to "moderate" in response to pressures from sugar trade associations. Although sugar contributes calories but no nutrients to diets, the trade groups maintained that existing science did not justify recommendations to restrict sugar intake. Sugar producers famously contribute large sums of money to both political parties, and the agencies did not want to do battle over so seemingly trivial a change in wording.

Trade disputes constitute an example of food politics on a global scale. The United States participates in a treaty with the World Trade Organization (WTO), an international body that sets standards for food safety and domestic farm subsidies. WTO rules are designed to prevent nations from instituting farm policies that might unfairly favor their ability to compete in world markets. In 2001 U.S. participation in the WTO came into conflict with long-standing policies that subsidize agricultural producers to protect them against price fluctuations. The most visible subsidies are price supports for sugar and milk, but taxpayers also support production and market quotas, import restrictions, and marketing and promotion programs for major food commodities. The total cost of such subsidies, most of which go to large agricultural corporations, exceeded $32 billion in 2000. In 2001 at least eight members of Congress, five of whom held positions on committees that consider agricultural policies, personally received farm subsidies ranging from nearly $40,000 to $650,000 annually. In this situation the interests of agricultural producers and their congressional supporters directly conflict with U.S. foreign policy and raise political dilemmas that cannot easily be resolved.

companies, like that of tobacco companies, is to sell products. For this reason alone basic dietary advice to prevent disease by restricting consumption of saturated fat, sugar, salt, or alcohol or to prevent obesity by eating less food in general directly conflicts with the commercial interests of food companies. Similarly, concerns about pollution of air, water, and soil conflict with the economic interests of agricultural producers and giant chicken and hog operations.

Food and politics are connected in ways both great and small, as illustrated in the sidebar "Food Politics in Action." As those examples demonstrate, food is a political issue. Overabundant food and its consequences occur in the context of increasing centralization and globalization of the food industry. Because food affects lives as well as livelihoods, almost any aspect of its production or consumption stimulates attention from interest groups and the public at large. Food issues inevitably involve struggles over the way the government balances corporate against public interests. Although all stakeholders have the same right to use the political system as do food companies, most others are motivated by health, safety, or environmental concerns rather than by profit, and they rarely have equivalent resources. Nevertheless they sometimes achieve political objectives. In this manner struggles over food issues reflect and contribute to essential functions of the American political system.

See also **Advertising of Food**; **Marketing of Food**.

BIBLIOGRAPHY

Environmental Working Group. Frazão, Elizabeth, ed. *America's Eating Habits: Changes and Consequences.* Washington, D.C.: U.S. Department of Agriculture, 1999.

Kluger, Richard. *Ashes to Ashes: America's Hundred-Year Cigarette War, the Public Health, and the Unabashed Triumph of Philip Morris.* New York: Knopf, 1996.

Nestle, Marion. *Food Politics: How the Food Industry Influences Nutrition and Health.* Berkeley: University of California Press, 2002.

Nestle, Marion, and Michael F. Jacobson. "Halting the Obesity Epidemic: A Public Health Policy Approach." *Public Health Reports* 115 (2000): 12–24.

U.S. Department of Agriculture. *The Food Guide Pyramid.* Washington, D.C.: U.S. Department of Agriculture, 1992.

Marion Nestle